GunDigest
2024
78th EDITION

EDITED BY

PHILIP P. MASSARO

Published by

Gun Digest® Books, an imprint of Caribou Media Group, LLC
5583 W. Waterford Ln., Suite D, Appleton, WI, 54913
gundigest.com

To order books or other products call 920.471.4522 ext.104
or visit us online at gundigeststore.com

CAUTION: Technical data presented here, particularly technical data on handloading and on firearms adjustment and alteration, inevitably reflects individual experience with particular equipment and components under specific circumstances the reader cannot duplicate exactly. Such data presentations therefore should be used for guidance only and with caution. Caribou Media accepts no responsibility for results obtained using these data.

ISBN-13: 978-1-951115-88-3

Edited by Phil Massaro and Corey Graff
Cover Design by Gene Coo
Interior Design by Jon Stein

Printed in the United States of America

10 9 8 7 6 5 4 3 2 1

42nd ANNUAL
John T. Amber
LITERARY AWARD

The John T. Amber Literary Award is named for the editor of *Gun Digest* from 1950 to 1979, a period that could be called the heyday of gun and outdoor writing. Amber worked with many of the legends in the business during his almost 30 years with the book, including the great shooting and hunting writer Townsend Whelen. In 1967, Amber instituted an annual award, which he named for Whelen, to honor an outstanding author from the previous year's *Gun Digest* edition. In 1982, three years after Amber's retirement, the award was renamed in his honor.

Pierre van der Walt

Each year, an author of a feature article in the *Gun Digest* is chosen to be recognized for his or her efforts and presented with the John T. Amber Literary Award. This year, it is my honor to present the award to Pierre van der Walt, who penned "Chronology of Czech Bolt-Action Rifles" in the 77th Edition of the *Gun Digest*. A native South African, van der Walt is no stranger to writing, having authored numerous magazine articles as well as the books *African Dangerous Game Cartridges* and *African Medium Game Cartridges* (Safari Press), both of which are very valuable to anyone planning to hunt the Dark Continent.

Born in Boksburg, South Africa, in 1958, van der Walt would graduate college with two degrees, and ultimately pass the bar exam in 1984, establishing a law practice and championing the gun rights of South Africans after serving as an officer in the South African Armoured Corps in the late 1970s. As is so common with those of us who choose to write about our passions, Pierre was a sponge as a child, soaking up any and all information about hunting, firearms, and cartridges. Perhaps he may tell his own story best.

"We farmed and lions wreaked havoc on the cattle in what today is the Umbabat Private Nature. In 1967, at the age of 10, I had to back up during a lion hunt. The lioness came at us and paid the price. I chased one of her cubs down and caught myself a cub as a pet, and I still bear the scars of that encounter.

"When I was at school, rural South Africa was still quite wild. Telephones worked through a manual exchange and most roads were gravel. Bar a license purchased at the local Court; hunting was for free as nobody owned wildlife. Hunters lobbied for legal changes that gave landowners ownership of game on their land. That succeeded, and game ranches exploded from six back then to more than 10,000 game ranches today. South Africa has more game today than since the rinderpest of 1896.

"When you grow up farming, with a rifle as important as a tractor, and when you deal with wildlife and predators every day, you have to get to know your tools and your adversaries if you want to come out on top. The more I learned about wildlife and wildlife managing tools, the more fascinated I became with nature, wildlife, and firearms.

"Apart from having to pull my weight on the farm, the hunting side was my responsibility as a 5th grader; I also had to look after the Lee-Enfields, Mausers, Winchesters, and Mannlichers I used, and learned to load ammunition for them by trial and mostly error. In high school, I lived in the nearby town school hostel and had access to the town library.

"After 'lights-out' I used a torch *(editor's note: "flashlight")* under a blanket and devoured every book I could find on wildlife, firearms, and cartridges. I also spent every minute I was permitted and not doing sport, at the town gunshop," van der Walt relates.

For an author, there is nothing like personal experience, and in the opinion of your humble editor-in-chief, the best writing comes from the yearning for both experience and knowledge.

Pierre has spent a lifetime gathering both. His writing shows that, being a wonderful balance of detailed statistics and first-hand, applicable knowledge. I'm proud to have him as a part of the *Gun Digest* stable of writers, and even more proud to present the John T. Amber Literary Award to him. Congratulations Pierre, and I look forward to reading many more of your books and articles. Though my Afrikaans is assuredly lacking, *goeie werk, en baie dankie.*

Phil Massaro, Editor-in-Chief

Gun Digest 2024

Photo: Weatherby

INTRODUCING THE
Gun Digest 2024
78th Edition

PHILIP P. MASSARO
EDITOR-IN-CHIEF

Hello all. Welcome to the 78th Edition of the *Gun Digest* — the World's Greatest Gun Book. This 2024 Edition is packed full of great articles, from firearm, ammunition, and optic reviews, to a look back at inspiring firearms and ammunition that remind us of some of the reasons we became gun owners in the first place.

Within the covers of this esteemed tome, you'll find coverage of everything from modern muzzleloaders, rimfire handguns, shotguns for turkey hunting, and falling block single-shot rifles. In the history department, Joe Coogan walks us through the timeline of the prestigious British firm of Holland &

Holland, Terry Wieland covers the inner workings of the Connecticut Shotgun Manufacturing Company, and George Layman unlocks a decades-old mystery regarding the Indonesian Jungle Carbine.

In the cartridge world, Kristin Alberts gives some love to the venerable .45-70 Government, Dick Williams heralds the resurgence of the 10mm Auto, Wayne van Zwoll asks you whether or not you're giving enough attention to the .30-06 Springfield, and Stan Trzoniec covers those cartridges with the Remington surname.

Yours truly has the pleasure of introducing you to Hornady's new 7mm PRC, as I took it not only to a prestigious shooting instruction school but on hunts in Wyoming and British Columbia. Remington has proudly introduced its .360 Buckhammer, a straight-wall, rimmed cartridge that will give lever-gun fans a reason to smile, as it's partnered with Henry Rifles to offer a brand new rifle/cartridge combination.

Winchester brought its .400 Legend to the table in the spring of 2023; both this and Remington's Buckhammer were designed to meet the combined rules and regulations of several Midwestern states.

Bill Vanderpool shares the history of exhibition shooters, Rick Hacker gets nostalgic about the guns of the revered Hollywood Western movies and television shows, and Brad Johnson walks us through 10 essential firearms that everyone should own, at least at one point in their life. On the hunting side of things, Professional Hunter Jay Leyendecker opines on five rifle cartridges to hunt the wide world, and elk guide Colton Heward helps you turn your deer rifle into a suitable elk rifle. My squirrel hunting buddy Will

Brantley covers the guns best suited to drop those bushytails out of the treetops, and Mike Dickerson weighs in on his choice of the ideal cartridge for pursuing black bears.

Ron Spomer revisits the New Ultra Light Arms rifle in the far-too-often-overlooked .284 Winchester, and Jim House shows off his Ruger Model 77 in .257 Roberts. Larry Weishuhn and Bob Campbell both spend some time with a Taurus revolver in hand, and famed Alaskan guide Phil Shoemaker brings up three 'palindrome' cartridges, which have a special place in history.

Josh Wayner relates the tale of the development of the AR-18/AR-180 rifle, while my pal L.P. Brezny takes a candid look at the pleasures and pitfalls of long-range shotgunning. And as always, Tom Turpin brings us some serious eye candy in his Custom & Engraved Guns section. Handgun aficionados will be happy to read Corey Graff's report on the Glock 48, with its slim-line frame, and Robert Sadowski's review of the Springfield Armory Prodigy 1911. For those devotees of the uber-American M1 Garand, Pat Sweeney gives some insight into shrinking your groups and getting the most out of the time-honored platform.

All in all, there's going to be something in here to make almost everyone happy.

The availability of ammunition has certainly improved over the last year, to the point that some of the resources have been diverted to reloading components. Yes, primers, powder, and projectiles are more expensive than they've ever been, but at least the press handles are swinging again. There are some new powders — which will fill a couple of holes in the current market — and some ammunition that blends popular brands;

Remington is now loading a Speer bullet in its centerfire rifle ammunition, and Federal Premium is now offering Hornady's ELD-X bullet in its loaded ammunition.

Sadly, since last year's edition, there have been some losses within the firearms community, including handgun cartridge pioneer John Linebaugh, father of the .500 and .475 Linebaugh cartridges, as well as Bart Skelton — firearms author and son of famed handgunner 'Skeeter Skelton — and Gun Digest author and founder of the Shootrite Firearms Academy, Tiger McKee. We mourn their loss and offer condolences to their families.

In happier news, our Reports From the Field section covers a huge amount of new shooting products, including firearms — handguns, rifles, shotguns, and muzzleloaders — as well as airguns, optics, ammunition, and reloading tools and components. There are plenty of new and exciting products for shooters from all walks of life, from the long-range competition shooter to the avid waterfowler to the big game hunter to the handgunner focused on self-defense.

Our famed Catalog section will give you the highlights of available firearms; while some folks have misunderstood this section to be a sort of price guide for used/vintage firearms, it is a fairly comprehensive listing of currently available firearms. Nonetheless, our catalog of firearms represents the majority of the firearms available on the market, complete with pricing.

So sit back with a glass of whatever your drink of choice may be, and dig into the World's Greatest Gun Book; may you enjoy the 78th Edition as much as you have the previous editions. **GD**

GUN DIGEST STAFF

JIM SCHLENDER	Group Publisher
PHILIP P. MASSARO	Editor-In-Chief
COREY GRAFF	Features Editor

DEPARTMENT CONTRIBUTORS

Wayne van Zwoll | Rifles
Todd Woodard | AR Rifles
Robert Sadowski | Semi-Auto Pistols
Shane Jahn | Revolvers & Others
Kristin Alberts | Shotguns

Brad Fenson | Muzzleloaders
Joe Arterburn | Optics
Jim House | Airguns
Philip P. Massaro | Ammo, Reloading & Ballistics
Tom Turpin | Custom & Engraved Guns

Springfield Armory
DS Prodigy

This high-capacity 1911 9mm has the features to meet any demand — from competition to self-defense.

Firearm technology is constantly evolving, with some leaps being radical, and others a subtle twist on a design that was done right the first time around. Adding to that concept is the relatively inarguable fact that John Moses Browning — born in the 19th century, with minimal education — gave us some of the most iconic designs ever to be brought to market. Among those, his M1911 handgun — put to the U.S. Army's tests in 1906 — remains an American staple. Browning's .45 ACP cartridge is still as effective as it was over a century ago, but that's not to say that the progress of the cartridge/pistol combination ends there, especially according to Springfield Armory.

Having embraced a good number of traditional models of military arms, Springfield Armory offers its Prodigy line of double-stacked 1911 handguns. Using a polymer grip module textured with the same Adaptive Grip Texture treatment made popular on the Springfield Hellcat series, the Prodigy offers a vastly increased magazine capacity when compared to a traditional 1911-style handgun. Chambered in 9mm Luger, the double-stack Prodigy gives the shooter the capability of 17+1 in a standard

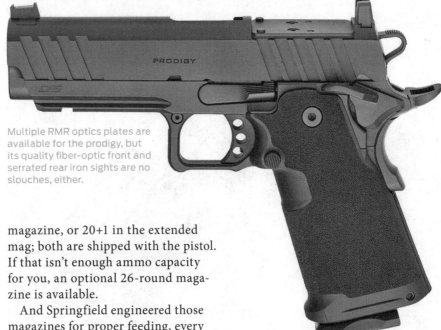

Multiple RMR optics plates are available for the prodigy, but its quality fiber-optic front and serrated rear iron sights are no slouches, either.

magazine, or 20+1 in the extended mag; both are shipped with the pistol. If that isn't enough ammo capacity for you, an optional 26-round magazine is available.

And Springfield engineered those magazines for proper feeding, every time; the Prodigy's tapered magazine well allows for smooth and efficient magazine changes. That's not my untested opinion. Our very own Robert Sadowski extensively field tested both Prodigy versions (Commander and full-size) for this edition of the *Gun Digest*, and you can find his TEST-FIRE report on page 305.

Designed to easily handle optics and accessories (there's a Picatinny rail under the forward area of the frame, and the Agency Optics System designed especially for this model fa-

cilitates the use of a red-dot sight) the Prodigy offers enhanced performance from a familiar-feeling package. An optics-mounting plate is shipped with every gun. The fiber-optic front sight and rear U-notch rear sight are indexed to be visible through the red dot, should you choose to use one.

"Even though nearly every new striker fire pistol is cut for an optic, it's still unusual to see older platforms like the 1911 come optics-ready," author Robert Sadowski told us. "In my opinion, Springfield Armory did it right, integrating the optic to the slide. They were also smart to equip these pistols with tall iron sights. Having a backup is a good thing."

Springfield Armory has equipped the Prodigy with an ambidextrous safety — an option I feel is imperative for everyday carry — and serrations on the slide both fore and aft to give a positive grip, even with gloves. The steel frame is coated in a black Cerakote finish, giving good resistance to the rigors of daily use and a non-reflective surface.

"At first glance, the Prodigy looks like a 1911 slide was Frankensteined to a fat polymer grip, and in a sense that's true," Sadowski says. "The thing is, it works. Having run these pistols for a few months now I'm

Leupold's Mark 3HD has an elevation turret boldly marked in 1/10 th mil graduations.

running low on 9mm ammo. The Prodigy is fun to shoot and it's easy to shoot well."

Springfield offers both 4 1/4- and 5-inch match-grade, bushing-less forged-steel bull barrels in the 1911 DS Prodigy line; both are equipped with 11-degree target crowns. Like all the 1911s to come before, the Prodigy is hammer-fired; that's a vital part of the classic feel. Both hammer and trigger are skeletonized to keep weight to a minimum, and that classic 1911 single-action trigger gives the feel that millions of shooters have come to appreciate over the decades.

"2011 platforms are typically finicky completion guns when it comes to the magazine," says Sadowski. "The Prodigy isn't. The trigger is good and it could always be better, but most users will find the single-action trigger of the Prodigy easier to shoot."

Weighing in at 33 ounces, Sadowski reports the Prodigy has enough heft to mitigate recoil, yet remains light enough to be your carry gun.

The Hex Dragonfly red-dot sight offers a crisp 3.5-MOA, a 6061 T6 Hardcoat anodized aluminum housing, and scratch-resistant, anti-glare glass lenses. The battery has an automatic shutoff after 16 hours to preserve battery life. At 1.9 inches long, and weighing a mere 1.2 ounces, the Hex Dragonfly is an excellent means of single focal plane target acquisition. The Dragonfly's MSRP is $249.00.

The Springfield Armory 1911 DS Prodigy has an MSRP of $1499 — add $200 if you want the Hex Dragonfly red-dot sight — and is a lot of pistol for the price, providing a modern, flexible twist on a user-friendly design. *springfield-armory.com* **GD**

Prodigy DS 1911 Survives 10,000-Round Torture Test

Springfield Armory announced that its 1911 DS Prodigy 9mm pistol has recently proven its mettle in a demanding 10,000-round torture test, with every round documented on video. Administered by Paul Carlson, owner of Safety Solutions Academy, the test — hosted on TheArmoryLife.com — saw the 5-inch pistol run thousands of rounds of PMC Bronze, 115-gr. 9mm ammunition, provided by True Shot for the test.

"The Prodigy just ate up all the ammunition I fed it," said Carlson. "I never tired of firing 9mm in this full-size pistol — all 10,000 rounds. I cannot recommend the Prodigy enough for anyone looking for a 1911 that adds the benefit of cutting-edge performance features and increased magazine capacity. This one is a proven performer!"

The 1911 DS Prodigy from Springfield Armory takes the proven 1911 platform and enhances it with double-stack capacity and a performance-driven feature set.

Optics-ready, the Prodigy employs AOS (Agency Optic System) plates designed in concert with Agency Arms exclusively for the 1911 DS. Machined from billet steel, each plate is designed specifically to deliver proper optic height for intuitive sight picture and instant target acquisition and features an integral rear sight.

"Paul did an amazing job managing this grueling test of the 1911 DS Prodigy," said Mike Humphries, editor of *The Armory Life*. "With every round fired documented on video, Carlson has shown us that the 1911 DS Prodigy has what it takes to burn through 10K rounds and stand ready for more."

The Guns of Hollywood Westerns!

A six-gun salute to the iconic cowboy guns of motion-picture fame.

❯RICK HACKER

The wild and woolly days of the American West have always lent themselves to hyperbole and exaggeration, creating, in the process, larger-than-life legends. Showmen like Pawnee Bill and William F. Cody, along with dime novelists such as Edward Zane Carroll Judson (aka Ned Buntline) and books by authors like Zane Grey, started the trend back when parts of the West were still untamed.

But around the turn of the 20th century, as things began calming down and the dust literally began to settle, we kept looking behind us to try and hang on to what was slowly fading away. That, in turn, became a ready-made tableau for the newly formed Hollywood motion picture industry and, later, television; both of which eagerly embraced those "thrilling days of yesteryear" (to quote from announcer Fred Foy's opening monologue of *The Lone Ranger*). In the process, the entertainment world found readymade and real tall-in-the-saddle heroes, along with admiration and appreciation for the rifles and revolvers they packed to dispense law and order, along with action and adventure.

At first, the revolvers and rifles used were based in reality because it was primarily Colt Single Action Armys and Winchester lever actions – mostly models 1873 and 1892 – which you saw on the silver screen. And the calibers were almost always .45 Colt, .44-40, or .38-40, for these were ready-made for the industry's standard 5-in-1 blank cartridges, which came in full-, half-, and quarter-load blackpowder, smokeless, and "flash" charges. Something like Smith & Wesson Schofields or Spencers would require specially-loaded blanks with original or prefabricated cases.

Cap and ball revolvers and muzzleloaders, of course, were loaded with blackpowder but no ball, but often there was no historical accuracy or distinction between guns that were proper for the period. One of the most egregious examples was the 1950 motion picture *Colt .45*, starring Randolph Scott, in which he plays a gun salesman showing off a pair of .44-caliber First Model Colt Dragoons — nothing to do with an actual Colt .45 Single Action Army, as intimated in the movie's title.

Cimarron produced a credible copy of the Buntline Special used in *Tombstone* and popularized by Stuart Lake in his semi-fictional biography *Wyatt Earp, Frontier Marshal.*

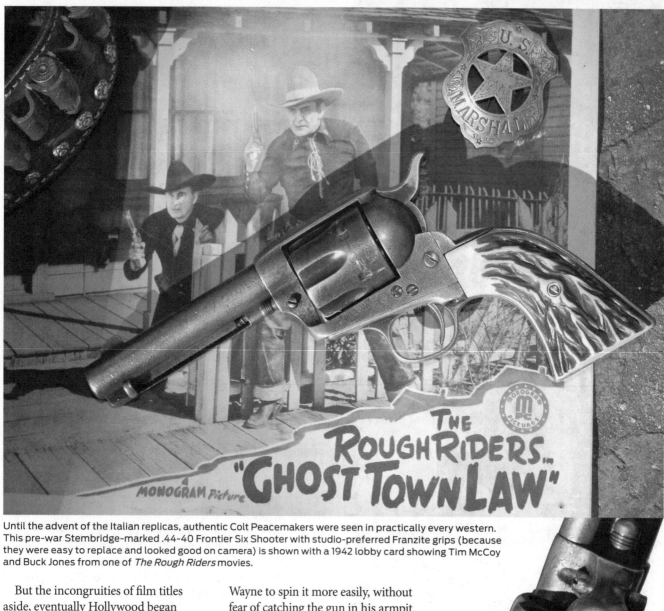

THE ROUGH RIDERS... "GHOST TOWN LAW"

a MONOGRAM *Picture*

Until the advent of the Italian replicas, authentic Colt Peacemakers were seen in practically every western. This pre-war Stembridge-marked .44-40 Frontier Six Shooter with studio-preferred Franzite grips (because they were easy to replace and looked good on camera) is shown with a 1942 lobby card showing Tim McCoy and Buck Jones from one of *The Rough Riders* movies.

But the incongruities of film titles aside, eventually Hollywood began to take liberties with the gun designs themselves to squeeze some extra drama out of them. And this, in turn, offers the question of just how practical – and useful – such movie-altered guns would have been in the real West, as opposed to the "reel West?"

THE DUKE

One of the first Hollywood-altered guns to appear in film was the loop-levered Winchester 92 carbine used by John Wayne as the Ringo Kid in the 1939 motion picture, *Stagecoach*. Actually, it was a 15 1/2-inch-barreled Model 92 Trapper, as the shorter barrel (possibly altered by the studio's prop department) made it easier for even the long-armed

Wayne to spin it more easily, without fear of catching the gun in his armpit. The gun itself was conceived by Wayne and stuntman Yakima Canutt after their director, the irascible John Ford, told Wayne, "When the camera zooms in on you for your opening shot, I want you to spin that rifle like a pistol." Of course, the only way for Wayne to do that would be with an enlarged and rounded lever.

However, such a gun never existed in the real West, as it would have made cocking it more awkward and time-consuming than the original Winchester design, which encompassed the shooter's hand more closely. Plus, in real life on the set, Wayne soon discovered that the wide three-quarter-circle lever was prone to becoming bent during action scenes. Consequently, sometime during the

Colt Peacemakers supplied by Stembridge Gun Rentals were marked with a stamped "S" on the underside of their frames.

The original loop lever John Wayne and Yakima Canutt designed for the movie *Stagecoach*.

Chuck Connors, with one of the three rifles he used in the TV series *The Rifleman*.

1950s, Stembridge Gun Rentals at Paramount Studios modified the lever into a pinched oval shape.

Affixed to a standard Winchester 1892 carbine, albeit with a 15-1/2-inch shortened barrel, this distinctive lever became one of Wayne's movie trademarks and appeared with him in westerns from *Rio Bravo* in 1959 to *The Shootist* in 1976. However, even though this smaller-contoured lever was not particularly suitable for spinning, the Duke does manage to give it a creditable twirl – after much off-screen practice - in one scene near the end of *El Dorado* and again, in *True Grit* (1969) when galloping on horseback, he spin-cocks it with aplomb. He again used that Stembridge-modified Winchester at Universal Studio's request in the 1975 sequel, *Rooster Cogburn*. Today, that basic egg-shaped lever design appears on several current-production lever actions, with the marketing rationale being that it is easier to use with gloves on.

I personally doubt the validity of that statement (I rarely shoot with gloves on, as it makes it difficult to get the "feel" of the trigger), and I certainly don't recommend spinning any rifle with live ammunition. But that egg-shaped lever lives on, kept alive by Hollywood's lore and lure.

THE RIFLEMAN

But an even more exaggerated loop-levered carbine that seemed even more impractical at first glance was the large D-shaped lever of the Model 92 saddle gun that was rapid-fired and spun so deftly by Chuck Connors as Lucas McCain in TV's *The Rifleman*, which aired on ABC from 1958 until 1963. At 6 feet, 5 inches, and a former athlete who played professional basketball and baseball in the Major and Minor Leagues before turning to acting, Connors had no trouble spinning his 20-inch carbine without hitting any part of his body. Connors was actually that fast and agile with the Model 92.

The only mystery to thousands of his fans was how he managed to crank off 12

Versions of this John Wayne-styled modified oval-shaped lever are found on several lever-action rifles today.

shots in slightly less than six seconds during the show's opening sequence, seeing as how the carbine only held ten rounds. The mystery is compounded by the fact that, if you watch and listen closely and play the scene in slow motion, you hear 13 staccato bursts of gunfire from The Rifleman's carbine.

The answer can be found in the fact that the actual shots were dubbed in during post-production to keep in cadence with the theme music. In fact, during the last flash and smoke from the carbine's muzzle, you can hear *two* shots, not one.

But Hollywood "magic" aside, the reality is that Connors did work the carbine's lever with amazing speed and dexterity in real-time and without accidentally plunging the trigger through his index finger. That's because his trigger finger never touched the trigger. Instead, the trigger is automatically tripped by a set screw in the triggerguard each time he slammed the lever home. The screw could be backed out during those scenes in which Connors fires his carbine in a conventional manner.

Still, I and countless other fans have often wondered how effective such a rapid-fire carbine setup would have been had it existed in the real West. Fortunately, I was able to find out. That's because during the latter years of his life, up until his death in 1992 from lung cancer at age 71, I had the pleasure of knowing Chuck. During my many trips to visit him at his Medicine Hat ranch in Tehachapi, California, he taught me the techniques of spin cocking and swing cocking his carbine, one of which he still had displayed among his other memorabilia on a ranch house wall.

Of course, during that time, the original carbines used in *The Rifleman* were long gone. Actually, there were three carbines used in the series, two Winchester Model 92s in .44-40 and an El Tigre in .44 Largo (the Spanish equivalent of the .44-40) that was reserved for distant camera shots, kept in Chuck's saddle scabbard, or occasionally used for scenes in which it was subjected to rough treatment. Of the two Winchesters, there were two slightly different lever designs during the show's 1958-1963 lifespan, the original large rounded loop and later a

Rapid firing *The Rifleman's* rifle, the author managed to get two shells in the air at once and scored nine hits out of 10 in just 11 seconds, but he could not beat Connors' time of 6 seconds during the opening sequence of the TV series.

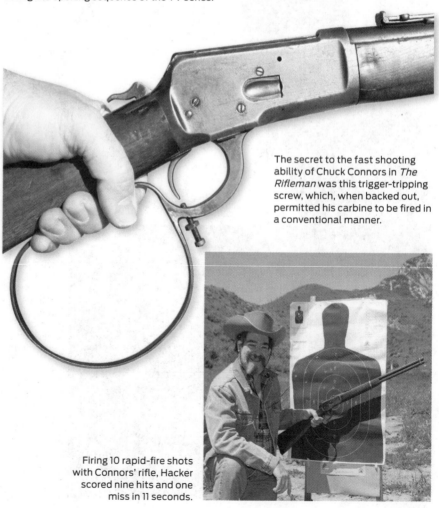

The secret to the fast shooting ability of Chuck Connors in *The Rifleman* was this trigger-tripping screw, which, when backed out, permitted his carbine to be fired in a conventional manner.

Firing 10 rapid-fire shots with Connors' rifle, Hacker scored nine hits and one miss in 11 seconds.

more squared-off version.

The identical loop lever carbines that Chuck owned afterward were used in many of his personal appearances long after the show was canceled and were made for him by the late Moe Hunt, a Canadian gunsmith and a dedicated fan. After Chuck's death, I purchased one of those carbines, which I still have, from his estate. Consequently, I decided to find out just how practical Connor's rapid-fire rifle would have been in an actual western shootout, using factory Remington High-Velocity 200-grain ammunition (rather than low-velocity cowboy loads, which wouldn't have existed in the 1880s) instead of 5-in-1 blanks and firing at a man-sized silhouette target set

Steve McQueen, as bounty hunter Josh Randall, with the original Mare's Leg he used in the *Wanted Dead Or Alive* TV series. Although the Model 92 he carried is a .44-40, he had .45-70 cartridges in his gunbelt because the program's producer thought they looked better on camera.

One of two later Mare's Leg versions used in the *Wanted Dead or Alive* series — made from octagon-barreled rifles — is on display at the Autry Museum of the American West (theautry.org), Los Angeles, California.

The author purchased this Winchester 92 carbine from a Universal Studios auction years ago and, because it was a movie gun, had it authentically transformed into a non-functional Mare's Leg, swapping out the real barrel for a solid aluminum 9-inch lookalike barrel.

Aiming the Mare's Leg, without a full-length stock to steady the carbine, was like holding it in mid-air.

up at a realistic Old West gunfighting distance of seven yards. But because rapid firing is not allowed at most public shooting ranges, I conducted my test at a private gun club in Los Angeles County.

Before loading the tubular magazine with 10 rounds of .44-40, I took five aimed shots offhand to make sure my carbine was zeroed in. It was and produced a nice one-inch cluster in the center of the target. Now for the test. With the stock pressed next to my side with my right arm (as Chuck had done during his opening sequence) and with the set screw properly adjusted to hit the trigger whenever the lever

was slammed home, I hip-pointed the carbine at the silhouette target and proceeded to crank off 10 timed shots as fast as I could. I managed to empty the magazine in 11 seconds. Needless to say, my rapid-fire sequence was not nearly as fast as Chuck's. But then — his superior reflexes notwithstanding — he did not have to contend with

Henry Repeating Arms is one of only two companies producing Mare's Leg-type pistols today. Its hardened brass-framed Big Boy Mare's Leg Pistol is available in .45 Colt, .44 Magnum, and .357 Magnum.

the recoil from live ammo, as he always fired blanks.

Of the 10 shots I fired, four hit in the right shoulder, one in the upper shoulder, two surprisingly close together in the upper torso, two more landed in the center of the chest area, and one shot was a complete miss. Interestingly, all of my hits generally veered to the left, which I assume was caused by how I held the carbine. But the final tabulation showed that five of my shots would have disabled my opponent, while the other four would have completely taken him out. So, while *The Rifleman's* rifle didn't exist in the Old West, if it had, it would have been a formidable weapon. But I did find myself wondering, had I been in an actual gunfight with this rifle 125 years ago,

would my one missed shot have been the first one I fired? If it had, I might not have gotten off the other nine.

WANTED DEAD OR ALIVE

So while the Duke's lever actions were "iffy" as far as practicality goes, and Connor's carbine would have been much more effective, the sawed-off, chopped-up Winchester Model 92 that Steve McQueen brandished as bounty hunter Josh Randal in TV's *Wanted Dead Or Alive*, which aired on CBS from 1958 to 1961, was totally impractical — as we shall soon see. Yet it was one of the most unforgettable firearms ever

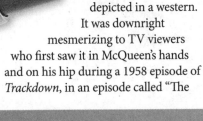

depicted in a western. It was downright mesmerizing to TV viewers who first saw it in McQueen's hands and on his hip during a 1958 episode of *Trackdown*, in an episode called "The

Bounty Hunter," which served as a pilot for the *Wanted Dead Or Alive* series. And that was precisely what producer John Robinson was striving for when he first devised McQueen's sidearm as something so unique it would set his series apart from every other western airing.

Starting with a standard Winchester 92 carbine (with two Winchester 92 octagon barreled rifles similarly altered later in the series but sporting teardrop-shaped loops for easier handling in action scenes), the barrel was cut to 9 inches (instantly making the carbine illegal and reducing the magazine capacity to five rounds in the process), the sights were removed, a wide "Rifleman-styled" D-loop lever was installed, and the stock was cut off just behind the comb. Moreover, because Robinson felt they

The author had a gunsmith slick the action on his Mare's Leg to make ejecting easier.

Hacker got some decent "gun fighting distance" groups at 7 yards with his Chiappa Mare's Leg. But beyond that, with no stock to anchor the gun, the shots became erratic.

looked better on camera, the cartridges in McQueen's gunbelt were .45-70s, even though he was packing a .44-40.

Ever the consummate Method Actor, and even though only blanks are used on Hollywood sets, McQueen decided to see what his sawed-off co-star would shoot like with real ammunition, so he took it out to the desert to find out. With a 9-inch barrel and no stock to anchor the gun when fired one-handed, the muzzle blast was notable. "It kicked like a mule," the actor said, "like a mare, at both ends, only harder." And thus, the Mare's Leg moniker was born.

For many TV viewers and gun fanciers, deciding whether the Mare's Leg was a handgun or a rifle was difficult. The U.S. Treasury's Alcohol and Tobacco Tax Division had that same problem when it first saw it on TV. It finally concluded it was a machine gun and saddled Robinson with $11,000 in fines and registration fees, making the Mare's Leg the most expensive and unique gun on any TV western.

Of course, due to the National Firearms Act of 1934 (NFA), unless anyone wants to fill out an ATF Form 4

Hacker proved the long-range validity of the Quigley movie rifle claims with his 1874 Sharps from C. Sharps Arms, firing at 1,000 yards.

to register what is classified as a Class 3 firearm and pay a $200 registration tax, any rifle with a barrel length less than 16 inches is illegal. Discontinued guns, such as the Puma Bounty Hunter and the Rossi Ranch Hand, were built on Model 92-styled actions but sported legal 12-inch barrels, as they were factory-designated as pistols rather than rifles. Thus, they helped fulfill some wishlists for *Wanted Dead Or Alive* fans.

I am aware of only two Mare's Leg-styled lever actions that are currently in production. One is from Henry Repeating Arms and is built using Henry's proprietary lever-action design rather than a Model 92 action. On the other hand, Chiappa produces an almost-exact replica of McQueen's Model 92 Mare's Leg, with either a 9- or 12-inch barrel, but only chambered in .45 Colt and .357 Magnum, and "… built from the ground up as a lever-action handgun with a pistol grip-length stock and pistol length barrel," to quote from its website. A takedown version in .44 Remington Magnum is also available. With any of these Mare's Legs, check with your local laws to be sure of their legality of ownership in your area.

All well and good, but like so many others, I wondered how effective McQueen's Mare's Leg would have been in an actual Old West gunfight. To find out (in a shootout against paper targets, of course), I selected a 12-inch Chiappa Mare's Leg in .45 Colt, which was the only version available to me. But even with those 3 extra inches of barrel, it was sufficient for my test, which was conducted on a private range, this time in the interest of privacy. Otherwise — and speaking from experi-

Although the original three 1874 Hartford Sharps rifles used in *Quigley Down Under* were made by Shiloh Rifle Manufacturing Company of Big Timber, Montana, this replica of the Quigley rifle was made by Pedersoli for Dixie Gun Works.

ence — any time you take one of these babies to a public range, you will attract a gathering of onlookers.

First, you can forget about any thoughts of rapid-firing the Mare's Leg, as without a standard-length stock, there is nothing against which to brace the gun while working the lever. Instead, I found the Mare's Leg much more adaptable to one- and two-handed point shooting when held at chest level and obviously at a close gunfighting range of approximately 7 yards. Surprisingly, I got some decent 2 1/2-inch groups at that distance, but beyond that, the shots began to spread to the point of my being lucky to get even a few hits on paper. And in the interest of safety and practicality, fanning was out of the question, although McQueen did have two hammer spurs widened for that purpose, which looked cool when he did it on TV. After all, this was showmanship.

But as McQueen demonstrates in numerous episodes, it's practically impos-

sible to sit down in a chair while wearing the Mare's Leg strapped to your hip in its special spring-held holster. Each time, he had to take the gun out of the holster and lay it across his lap while seated. That isn't a bad thing, as he always had it at the ready for close-range self-defense (with an emphasis on "close") under a poker table … just in case.

OTHER POPULAR GUNS OF THE WESTERN

As evidenced by the guns discussed thus far, the Winchester Model 92 carbine was the long gun of choice for Hollywood's westerns (the James Stewart movie *Winchester '73* being one of the few exceptions), whether the prop department tricked it out or, more often, making its as-issued on-camera appearance just as Winchester had cataloged it, with a 20-inch barrel and saddle ring. That makes sense, as in .44-40 or .38-40, the Model 92 could cycle

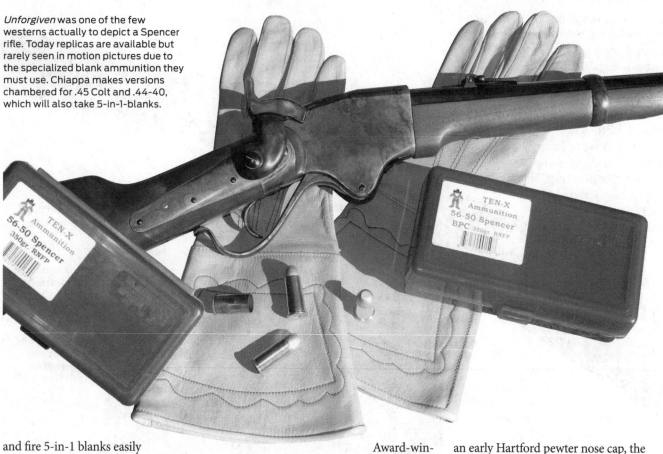

Unforgiven was one of the few westerns actually to depict a Spencer rifle. Today replicas are available but rarely seen in motion pictures due to the specialized blank ammunition they must use. Chiappa makes versions chambered for .45 Colt and .44-40, which will also take 5-in-1-blanks.

and fire 5-in-1 blanks easily and was much more readily available — with a smoother action — than the Winchester 73. Besides, during the heyday of B western movies, the Model 92 was still in production and remained so until 1941. Thus, replacement parts and the guns were readily available, while the Winchester '73 had been discontinued in 1921.

Of course, other rifles were used in western movies, including the trapdoor Springfield (think John Ford's classics like *She Wore A Yellow Ribbon* and the 1860 Spencer Carbine cast by director-actor Clint Eastwood in his Academy

Award-winning *Unforgiven*).

But these were standard configuration rifles, not Hollywood-tweaked versions, such as the 13 1/2-pound long-range 1874 Sharps rifle that co-starred with Tom Selleck (a gun fancier in real life) in his 1990 motion picture *Quigley Down Under*. Although the Quigley Sharps was an 1874 Hartford-stocked No. 3 Sporting Rifle with

an early Hartford pewter nose cap, the stock was inletted with an 1863 patch box for the movie and had no provision for a saddle ring. The Shiloh Rifle Manufacturing Company of Big Timber, Montana, produced all three guns used in the movie, including an aluminum-barreled version for easier carrying by Selleck when no shooting was involved. This is how Selleck, as Matthew Quigley, described his Sharps in the film:

"It's a lever-action breechloader. Usual barrel length's 30 inches. This one has

The popularity of the TV show, *The Life and Legend of Wyatt Earp*, which ran on ABC from 1955 to 1961, prompted Colt to bring out a 12-inch Buntline Special in 1957, which remained in the line until 1975. This second-generation SAA was one of the first made and remains in the author's collection today.

The author's authentic 10-inch-barreled *Tombstone* Buntline Special, made for him by the no-longer-existing United States Fire Arms Manufacturing Company, complete with grip medallion engraved by John Ennis, who did the originals for the movie.

an extra four. It's converted to use a special .45-caliber 110-grain metal cartridge with a 540-grain paper patch bullet. Fitted with double set triggers and a vernier sight. Marked up to 1,200 yards. This one shoots a might farther."

But could it in real life? Or was Selleck's long-range on-screen marksmanship just more Hollywood special effects? In this case, the movie's claims were true. First, there is the verified account of buffalo hunter Billy Dixon, pinned down with others by a war party of Comanche, Kiowa, Cheyenne, and Arapaho during the Battle of Adobe Walls in 1874, grabbing a friend's .50-90 Sharps, taking careful aim, and killing a warrior at a range of 1,538 yards — 7/8 of a mile, as subsequently verified by the U.S. Army.

Although Dixon later admitted it was a lucky shot, I proved the long-range reputation of the 1874 Sharps in an article I wrote back in the 1990s for the *Guns & Ammo* Annual, entitled, "I Believe You, Billy Dixon," in which John Schoffstall of C. Sharps Arms witnessed some 1,000-yard shots I made with one of my 1874 C. Sharps rifles. Not quite as far as Dixon's shot, but close enough to validate the on-screen reputation of "Old Reliable," as the 1874 Sharps was nicknamed.

Of course, when it comes to handguns used by good guys and bad in Hollywood westerns, the Colt Single Action Army reigns supreme. Just as they were ubiquitous in the real West, they are omnipresent on screens big and small. But unlike Winchester lever actions, there is not much you can do to a Colt Peacemaker other than solder a web underneath its barrel and try to pass it off as an 1858 Remington New Model Army (as was done in the 1952 movie *Springfield Rifle*) or an 1875 Remington, before replicas of those guns

The late Hugh O'Brian, with one of the last Buntline Specials made by Colt.

were available.

However, one of the more notable exceptions was the 12-inch Buntline Special that made its first on-screen appearance in *The Life and Legend of Wyatt Earp*, which ran on ABC from 1955 to 1961 and starred Hugh O'Brian in the

This replica of the .38 Special 1851 Navy used by Clint Eastwood as The Man With No Name in *Fistful of Dollars* is cataloged by Cimarron Fire Arms.

Uberti single actions with their 7 1/2-inch barrels swapped out for actual 10-inch custom-made Colt barrels. Today Cimarron Fire Arms catalogs a creditable copy of the Tombstone Buntline.

The reality of the Buntline Special is that, although approximately 19 Peacemakers with longer-than-standard-length barrels — ranging from 9 to 18 inches — were made between 1876 and 1884, none were ever presented by dime novelist Ned Buntline to Earp or any other lawman. And rather than be called Buntline Specials (a name conjured up by Earp's real-life biographer Stuart Lake), they were referred to by the factory as "buggy rifles" and sometimes included detachable shoulder stocks.

The fact that so few authentic "buggy rifles" existed in the Old West shows how unwieldy and impractical they were. I have both a 10-inch .45-caliber "Tombstone" Buntline Special made for me by the no-longer-existing United States Fire Arms Manufacturing Company (authentic right down to the engraved grip medallion by John Ennis, who did the originals for the movie) and a 12-inch second-generation .45 Colt Buntline

Special, and I shoot them both. Yes, they are accurate, but a bit awkward to draw from a suitably-lengthened holster, and the barrel on the 12-incher tends to "whip" a bit with recoil. Frankly, I'd rather be shooting a Peacemaker with a 7 1/2-inch barrel and packing a 4 3/4-inch version of the Model P, which is quicker, in scriptwriter parlance, "to fill my hand and clear leather."

Another TV western sidearm that was awkward to carry but was quite deadly in real life at close range was the French LeMat carried by Don Durant as Johnny Ringo in the TV series of that same name, which aired on CBS from October 1, 1959, until June 30, 1960. Although it only lasted one season, Durant's gun in a special spring-clip holster that gave him an edge in fast draw is a rare and highly collectible firearm. Original LeMats were nine-shot percussion revolvers that sported a single-shot 20-gauge shotgun barrel underneath the main barrel. However, in the TV series, an original (there were no replicas back then) was converted to a six-shot cartridge revolver and the single smoothbore barrel was altered to fire .45 caliber or 5-in-1 blanks; in the show, it was referred to as a "seven shooter."

Ironically, because of the LeMat's rarity, only one gun was used in the series (as previously noted, typically, there are three guns used on most western sets in case of breakage or other mishaps). Invented by Jean Alexandre LeMat and patented in 1856, fewer than 3,000 were produced, with many ending up in the hands of the

title role. The gun's appearance in an early episode was the catalyst that prompted Colt to bring out a 12-inch Buntline Special in 1957, which remained in the line until 1975, long after the series was off the air. Subsequent runs of Buntline Specials were made, although Colt no longer produces the gun. However, it was re-imagined as a 10-inch-barreled version in the 1993 film *Tombstone*, where it was wielded with a vengeance by Kurt Russell, who still has one of the three guns used in the film. Interestingly, those three consecutively numbered guns were

Confederacy during the Civil War. A later centerfire variant in the 1870s was not very successful, as it was competing against the emergence of double-action revolvers. Although weighing slightly more than 4 pounds, exceedingly bulky, and not very accurate, the LeMat did offer spectacular firepower at close range. As scarce as they were — even back then — I often wondered how Johnny Ringo got his hands on one in Arizona Territory.

SPAGHETTI WESTERNS

Of course, no discussion of the guns of Hollywood westerns would be complete without a six-gun salute to the late Italian film director Sergio Leone, whose "westerns" weren't filmed in Hollywood

at all but in various locations in Spain and Italy. It was Leone's classic trilogy of "spaghetti westerns," as they are called — *A Fistful of Dollars* (1964), *For a Few Dollars More* (1965), and *The Good, the Bad and the Ugly* (1966) — that reacquainted Americans to their cinematic creation and made them see the western movie in a whole new European way: extreme close-ups of the actors and their guns and even, as in *The Good, the Bad and the Ugly*, gunshots dubbed in as part of Ennio Morricone's theme music.

Leone was a lifelong fan of the Hollywood West and the guns used in western movies, but he always put his personal touch on their depiction. That is why Eli Wallach as Tuco in *The Good, the Bad and the Ugly* wears his Colt 1851 Navy cartridge conversion on a lanyard hung around his neck (mainly because Wallach told Leone he could not holster his gun without looking at the holster), while Clint Eastwood, as Blondie, demonstrates

his spinning and shooting dexterity with an Uberti 1851 Navy cartridge version outfitted with a silver coiled rattlesnake on the grip. The Uberti single action he used in *For A Few Dollars More* had the same silver rattlesnake grips. Fans of the 1959 TV series *Rawhide* may also recall episodes in which Eastwood has that same silver snake inlaid on the grips of his Colt Single Action Army, which he, as Rowdy Yates, took off of a gunslinger he had "killed" in the series. And Lee Van Cleef, as Angel Eyes in *The Good, the Bad and the Ugly*, uses a percussion 1858 Remington for non-shooting scenes and a cartridge conversion of the same gun when he fires it on screen. Yet throughout the movie, even when depicted as a percussion revolver, Van Cleef wears it cross-draw on a cartridge belt.

Such is the magic and the reality of the guns used in Hollywood's westerns. Like the actors who used them, they don't have to be based on reality — they just have to look good on screen. **GD**

These Colt double-action Police Positives were re-nickeled and outfitted by Stembridge Gun Rentals with non-functional Colt SAA-style ejector rods and used by Gail Davis in her starring role in the TV series *Annie Oakley*, which aired from 1954 until 1957.

THE .45-70 GOVERNMENT: Still Getting It Done

America's grandest cartridge turns 150 years young!

›KRISTIN ALBERTS

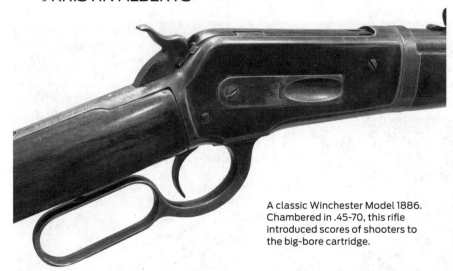

A classic Winchester Model 1886. Chambered in .45-70, this rifle introduced scores of shooters to the big-bore cartridge.

The massive frame of the Cape buffalo came into view as the beast stepped clear of the makeshift blind on the veld. Loaded with five rounds of heavy lead, I inched the hammer rearward on the .45-70. In an instant, days of stalking, months of preparation, and years of daydreaming culminated. The old round thundered, and the hard-bossed buff was mine, forever linked by America's grandest cartridge offering, half a world away in Africa.

My weapon of choice for this safari was neither rifle nor carbine, trapdoor nor lever, but rather, a revolver. That point proves the uniquely red-white-and-blue round's incredible versatility, reliability, and staying power. From military service to civilian arms, big game hunts to long-range competitions, dangerous game to cowboy action, and everything in between, the .45-70 Government celebrates its birthday as we revel in its rich, storied history — one that continues to this very day.

Kristin Alberts with her fallow deer, taken in South Africa using Henry's All-Weather .45-70 and Federal Premium Hammer Down ammo. The range? Just inside 200 yards.

BIRTH OF A LEGEND

The year was 1873. Remington built the first typewriter. The Indian Wars raged. Jesse James' gang robbed their first train, and Levi Strauss patented the first riveted blue jeans. President Ulysses S. Grant began his second term. And America's longstanding romance with a hulky, straight-walled cartridge began. The .45-70 Government round was born to a battle-stricken country on the verge of the long Depression, yet ingenuity and invention reigned supreme.

After extensive development and rigorous testing, the United States military adopted the .45-70 Government chambering, an improvement over the previous .50-70. The .45-70 cut its teeth with the U.S. Army, seeing use as late as the Spanish-American Wars. The given name of the initial round was .45-70-405, so named for its .45-diameter bullet, 70-grain blackpowder charge, and 405-grain projectile weight. Early days saw it listed simply as .45 Government before .45-70 US Government, with our currently abbreviated .45-70 Gov't tag. Though loads have changed dramatically, the round's specifications are quite straightforward. The .45-caliber round has a neck O.D. of .480 inches for .458-inch diameter projectiles. The brass casing measures 2.105 inches and is charged with large rifle primers. Bullet weights range from 250 to over 500 grains of lead, lending the overall capability.

The round's popularity as a useful breech-loading metallic centerfire cartridge allowed it to bridge the gap from black to smokeless powder. Unbeknownst to its forward-thinking designers and engineers, to this day, it lends itself to modern advancements in casings, powder, load pressures, and, ultimately, adaptability. Over the last 150 years, the round has found a home in single shots, over/unders, side-by-side doubles, rolling blocks, falling blocks, Gatling guns, bolt actions, Mausers, lever guns, carbines and even handguns. As I learned, even the smallest stature guns chambered for .45-70 Gov't produce the most intense excitement on big game. Yet we owe it all to one of the longest launchers, the 32.5-inch barreled Trapdoor rifle.

SPRINGFIELD 1873 "TRAPDOOR"

The roots of the .45-70 trace directly back to the Springfield Armory in Massachusetts. The U.S. Model of 1873, affectionately known as the Trapdoor due to its hinged breechblock design, goes down in history as one of the most successful breech-loading blackpowder centerfire cartridge arms, leading the way for countless advancements in both battle and civilian arms. Though it was far from the first such action, adopting the .45-70 Gov't chambering brought success and infamy. Rifle and carbine models led the way for a similar albeit improved Model 1884.

That quality steel and walnut aged gracefully, with a sideplate engraved with the Eagle, a U.S.-marked buttplate, and fitted with a bayonet and U.S.-emblazoned leather frog. Owning, firing, or simply holding one lends a genuine appreciation for our country's history. Many of those early specimens survive in perfectly shootable condition, a testament to the firearm's quality and the chambering. I count myself lucky to have found one years ago — worn and well-used but no less a prize — a constant reminder of how firearms and classic chamberings teach, inspire, and amaze us.

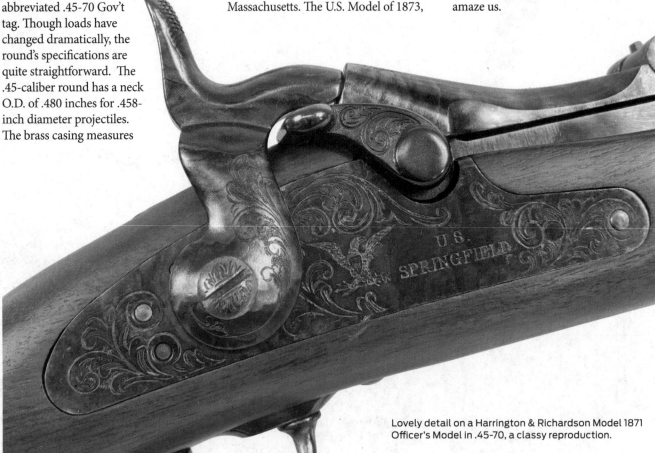

Lovely detail on a Harrington & Richardson Model 1871 Officer's Model in .45-70, a classy reproduction.

A happy .45-70 Gov't family from 1878 to the present.

Remington ammunition offers both ends of the power spectrum, as shown here with low-velocity, lower pressure on the left and high-velocity full pressure on the right.

The now iconic long gun saw service through multiple wars, leading to westward expansion. Brave souls toted it across the Great Plains. Early snipers mastered ladder sights at great distances. Short-barreled Trapdoor carbines played a now infamous role at the Battle of Little Big Horn. Though the .45-70 was phased out of military service with the widespread acceptance of repeating rifles in .30-40 Krag, the round's dominance was far from over.

AN UNLIKELY SUCCESS?

Writing an ode to the .45-70 celebrates its role in settling the American West, protecting American soldiers, stocking the freezers of big game hunters, and

The author harvested this old Nyala bull with her BFR handgun in .45-70 Gov't.

Sideplate detail on an original Springfield Trapdoor rifle in .45-70 Gov't.

growing recipes on loading benches worldwide. It defies ballistic logic to survive among modern designs. The .45-70 Gov't is the antithesis of fast and flat; two characteristics modern shooters have adopted as a near — albeit faux — necessity for success. Yet the cartridge, which according to Editor Phil Massaro "throws a D-cell battery for a projectile," continues to win shooters' hearts.

Its ballistics aren't impressive, as the trajectory resembles a leaded rainbow arc more closely than a straight-line speeding bullet. Yet the potency, the knockdown power, and the understated simplicity keep it succeeding.

Advancements in firearms and ammunition design, aided by state-of-the-art materials, have allowed for guns capable of handling higher pressures and better-built casings housing far zippier loads. With modern loads and the ample handloading recipes available in loading books galore, I've taken game on multiple continents. No braggadocio intended, but rather a testament to the trust I place in an aged chambering to harvest two Cape buffalos, a Nile crocodile, an African lion, whitetail deer, and plenty of plains game. Are there more ideal chamberings? Sure. But more romantic and nostalgic? Never.

Old and new: A Springfield Trapdoor and Henry X.

A healthy mix of modern .45-70 ammunition, including low-pressure and high-velocity choices.

THE POWER LEVELS

A look at .45-70 ammunition and load data through time reveal the power shift in the round, both in firearms and ammunition design. This room for growth means that the .45-70 stands alone in American cartridge longevity, versatility, and richness of history.

Older loads were built first with blackpowder at low pressures, symptomatic of the metallurgy of the era. For many early firearm designs, that's the correct and only safe type of ammo and load data to use. Though anemic by today's standards, those rounds still perform. Measuring the original's 405-grain projectile load

shows a muzzle velocity of roughly 1,350 fps. In comparison, hot rod loads for today's rifles can exceed 2,350 fps and 3,600 ft-lbs of energy. The bottom line, though, is not velocity but rather pressure.

The action that started it all — Springfield Armory's Trapdoor — is not a strong action for high-pressure loads. The first level of loading data uses either blackpowder loads or significantly weakened smokeless powder conversions, held to a Maximum Average Pressure (MAP) of 18,000 Copper Units of Pressure (CUP). This data applies to most early rifles, including Trapdoors, Remington Rolling Blocks, Sharps, and related accurate replicas. Like the eldest rifles, vintage casings should be avoided or used with extreme caution due to thinning brass, weak head construction, and mercuric primers.

Stepping up to level two encompasses the most common modern firearms and loads. Improvements in firearms design, materials, and action lockup lend themselves to considerably higher-performance ammunition. Practical lever actions fill this category, with models

Early Firearms of Note

Winchester's 1886 design ultimately bridged the gap between the single-shot Trapdoors and stout Model 1885s, allowing the .45-70 to boom rather than bust.

Winchester 1886. No discussion of the .45-70 Gov't is complete without a hat-tip to Winchester's Model 1886 lever action. While previous rifle designs were built for — and limited to — lower-pressure loads, the beefy 1886 was then, and is still now, one of the most substantial actions ever contrived. Yet another brainchild of the illustrious John M. Browning, the 1886 was engineered in the era of blackpowder yet ideal for the smokeless revolution.

There's good reason the 1886 is still reproduced, modified, and otherwise used as the basis for most every powerful round. Bighorn Armory leans heavily on the old '86 for its tank-tough lever guns in the highest SAAMI pressure chamberings — .460 S&W and .500 S&W. Thus, Winchester's 1886 design ultimately bridged the gap between the single-shot Trapdoors and stout Model 1885s, allowing the .45-70 to boom rather than bust. That tubular magazine, broad receiver, and blued steel against classic walnut define generations of lever guns.

Original production spanned 1886–1935, though not all were created equal. Dates are fuzzy, even to collectors, but 1905 is the major switch to smokeless powder. With any older rifles, caution in using higher-pressure loads is paramount. However, Buffalo Bore advertises that those Winchesters 1886s built since 1915 can handle its hottest + P loads. Browning put out a dandy pair of .45-70-chambered remakes in the mid-1980s. Luckily for us lovers of rifle and round, Winchester re-entered the fray with several slightly modified, even more practical 1886s. Still today, it catalogs multiple options, including a Saddle Ring Carbine, Short Rifle, and a Deluxe Case Hardened, sure to elicit drool.

Winchester 1885 High Wall. Yet another of J.M. Browning's pearls, the sturdy 1885 High Wall Falling Block chambered the snappiest blackpowder rounds of its day, including .45-90, .50-90, and of course, .45-70. With the High Wall's receiver frame sides covering most all the hammer and with engineering prowess, the design was then — and continues to be — one of the strongest actions ever contrived. The 1885s were built from the year of its name 'til 1920, with many specimens being its partner Low Wall for the smaller calibers. With a range of barrels, including some longer target types, the High Walls sold well as target guns and more affordable hunters. Browning debuted its version of the 1886 in 1985 and continued until 1997 when production switched to the "Traditional Model." Winchester picked up where Browning left off, bringing back the 1885s with High Wall Traditional Hunters in .45-70 in the mid-2000s.

Winchester 1895. We could go on for days about the many Winchester gems chambering the .45-70, but one more must be mentioned. Though not as revered as the previous two, the Model 1895 holds a place in history. The basis of Theodore Roosevelt's "Big Medicine," the 1895 lever gun was built for smokeless rounds and rose to fame in .405 Win. and .45-70 Gov't with its box magazine. An honest original rifle in the latter would be my dream companion on Safari.

Gatling Guns. In addition to the stalwarts above, our beloved .45-70 has eked out a home on numerous other firearms. Its timeline creates a veritable history of American weaponry. The rotating, multiple-barreled buzz saw known as the Gatling Gun predates the advent of the .45-70 Gov't chambering. As years passed and the touchy paper rounds gave way to brass casings, the .45-70 entered. When operated by a well-trained four-person team, the Model 1881 Gatling marked a noteworthy switch to the Bruce feed system, with a chow rate near 400 rounds per minute. Though the .45-70's useful American run in Gatling Guns was relatively short-lived, they saw service as mounted weapons on U.S. warships.

Relatively recent reproduction Colt 1877 Gatlings have found homes with deep-pocket buyers because, let's face it, few among us wouldn't want that five-barreled brass, steel, and hardwood tripod-mounted blender firing 800 rounds per minute. What more could one want besides an unlimited supply of .45-70 ammunition? Sign me up.

Winchester Hotchkiss. Born of a partnership between Benjamin Hotchkiss and Winchester Repeating Arms, the Winchester Hotchkiss bolt-action design vied for U.S. military acceptance before branching out to many other countries. Among several other chamberings, including .577-450 Martini-Henry and .43 Spanish, is the .45-70. The magazine rifles underwent numerous model improvements, seeing muskets, carbines, and sporting rifles culminating in the Model 1883, ideal for blackpowder .45-70 loads. The W-H put .45-70 arms out to areas as far-flung as Imperial China.

Remington Rolling Block. Yet another of the classic single shots chambering the round was Remington's Rolling Block. Debuted in the mid-1860s to 1888, these actions saw numerous chamberings. The rig drew international sales from Mexico through much of Europe, carrying the .45-70 Gov't and other rounds to a worldwide market.

Bolt actions. For no logical reason, bolt-action .45-70s are relative oddities. The round was so popular and, with its relatively short stature, adaptable to short actions. Thus, many Japanese-built Siamese Mausers were converted to .45-70, as were many Lee Enfield rifles and Mauser 98s. With robust actions and capable chambering, it's a surprise these turn bolts never garnered more significant fanfare.

Another little-known bolt gun is the Model 1878 Remington-Keene. Feeding from a nine-shot tubular magazine and with an unusual external hammer, the John W. Keene design struggled in U.S. trials yet was adopted by the Navy, seeing service aboard several ships. Though limited to roughly 5,000 production pieces, the Remington-Keene in .45-70 is recognized by collectors (who'll pay a premium for a Navy-marked specimen) as Remington's first foray into the bolt-action market, and with a .45-70 nonetheless.

Henry's All Weather .45-70 partnered with Leupold's CDS ZL scope turret system makes compensating for bullet drop simple. The author took this Kalahari Springbok at nearly 250 yards. Range the target, dial the custom turret, and send it.

like the Winchester 1886, Marlin 1895, the lengthy Henry Repeating Arms family, H&R Handi Rifles, and Shiloh and Pedersoli Sharps. Without delving into great detail (which any handloader must), mainstream loading manuals list MAP ratings anywhere from 28,000 to 34,000 CUP. Grab a box of ammunition from a gun store shelf tomorrow, and unless expressly stated as a low-pressure alternative, the odds are high it is the power rating you'll be buying. Likewise, most handloaders charging any common current firearms will work from recipes in this range.

Some loading manuals end there, while others take data one step further.

The final upgrade in highest octane handloads centers around Ruger's No. 1 and No. 3 falling block single shots. That accepted data lists a stunning MAP of 40,000+ CUP. These often heavily compressed loads require crimping, and extreme care must be taken not to fire them in lesser platforms. Some debate exists over whether bolt-gun conversions of Siamese Mausers or those built around Model 98 actions fall into power levels two or three, but prudence lies in safety over sorrow.

Just because an action may safely handle the pressures does not mean it need be loaded that hot to perform exceptionally well.

The author's much-anticipated hunt for a hard-bossed Cape buffalo with a handgun in none other than .45-70 Gov't, culminating with the dramatic downing of this big buff.

ADVANCEMENTS IN AMMUNITION

Luckily, ammunition in both major power levels is available today, including Federal Premium Hammer Down, Hornady LEVERevolution, Winchester, and Remington. Specialty factory loads amp up the bone-crushing power of the round to magnum +P style. Among several, Remington caters to both power ranges, with a "Reduced Pressure" Core-Lokt load sending a 405-grain pill at 1,330 fps. In contrast, its High Performance Rifle lineup packs what Remington calls a "Full Pressure" load for modern arms.

Based in Texas, Garrett Cartridge rolls some of the finest hardcast hunting rounds. Its Hammerheads show a broad, dinner-plate meplat with a track record of stellar penetration on dangerous game. Likewise, some of the most commercially available custom-level loads

come from Tim Sundles at Buffalo Bore in Idaho. Not only does Sundles offer several loads zipping more than 2,000 fps, but his MonoMetal non-expanding selection is a serious contender in dangerous game food.

Hornady even launched .45-70 Gov't as part of its SUB-X Subsonic line of ammunition, catering to the rise in suppressor use, including cans built for big bores like this one. Heck, companies like Henry and Marlin have even taken to blacking out .45-70 lever guns with synthetic stocks, muzzle brakes and adding features more closely affiliated with modern sporting rifles. Love 'em or hate 'em, few chamberings and firearms designs have crossed that great a divide.

SHOOTING SUPPRESSED

It's by no mistake that many of the .45-70 firearms coming off factory production

lines today have threaded muzzles. Note the Henry X, now discontinued Marlin Dark, new Marlin 1895s, and several Davide Pedersoli Model 86/71 Boar Busters. Even single-shot CVA Scout V2 models are available with a threaded barrel, some with an included muzzle brake. One might think the rise in suppressors would bypass an old clunker like the .45-70, but not so fast. Not only do cans control ear-splitting reports but tame recoil, though, at some performance sacrifice. Still, who among us with a threaded barrel big bopper hasn't pined for a matched suppressor?

To that end, manufacturers are on board. Suppressors rated to handle .45-caliber rifle rounds — such as the .45-70, .458 Socom, and .450 Bushmaster — abound from manufacturers like Coastal, SilencerCo, Dead Air, and Silencer Central's Banish 46. What good is such a device without subsonic factory ammunition? Recently, Hornady debuted its Sub-X line of ammunition, including, you guessed it, .45-70 Gov't. That load quietly drives a 410-grain Sub-X bullet with a 1,075 fps muzzle velocity. While effective range in terms of energy is more of a 100-yard wonder, pulling the trigger on a properly suppressed .45-70 with Sub-X ammo can't help but bring smiles on the range. That such a historic round can demonstrate such versatility today is remarkable.

NEVER TOO LATE TO JOIN THE .45-70 CLUB

Whether you're an aficionado of .45-70 firearms or a relative beginner building an adoration for the historical round, such firearms are readily available. While some of our favored firearms chambering the cartridge can be pretty pricey — think high-condition original 1873 Trapdoors or early '86s — a neat facet is that the market is reasonably accessible to even new hunters or budget shooters. Though discontinued,

Harrington & Richardson's single-shot Handi Rifle is perhaps the most cost-effective entry. H&R's related Model 1871 Buffalo Classic, with its lengthier barrel, bright case-color finish, and engraving, trends higher with increased collector interest but makes a darn sweet shooter.

Other pocketbook-friendly choices abound. Snagging a barrel is an option for those with Thompson-Center Encore and Contender platforms. The CVA Scout single shot in blued or stainless makes a solid entry into the chambering. Though any lighter-weight single shot will wake you up, CVA's triggers are quite nice. Henry's polished brass or blued steel single shots round out newer one-shooters.

The .45-70 butters its bread, though, in lever actions, and has since Winchester's 1886. By no mistake, Ruger's takeover of Marlin led not with the .30-30 Win., but

rather, the .45-70 Gov't. Henry Repeating Arms catalogs one dozen — yes, 12 — different models of lever-action rifles and carbines for the round. That's not even counting the many remakes. Given a chance to pursue my dream hunt for brown bears with my choice of weapon, you'd be safe taking the money line that it's the best kind of Government.

THE REPRODUCTIONS

You know things are going well when the reproductions come en masse, and the .45-70 cartridge finds itself the basis of many repro' builds. Though they may not be cheap, per se, the many reproductions of old classics are usually much more affordable than a high-condition original. Models like the Trapdoor, Winchester 1886, Sharps, Rolling Blocks, and High Walls have been copied many times.

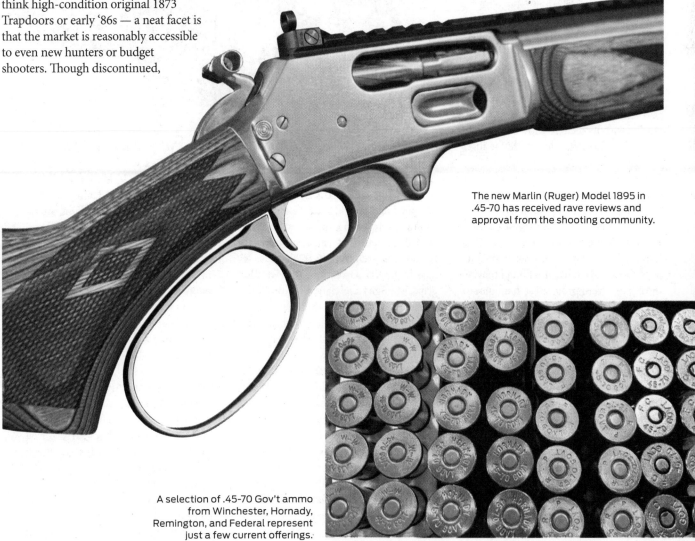

The new Marlin (Ruger) Model 1895 in .45-70 has received rave reviews and approval from the shooting community.

A selection of .45-70 Gov't ammo from Winchester, Hornady, Remington, and Federal represent just a few current offerings.

Companies such as Pedersoli, Chiappa, Uberti, Cimarron, Taylor's & Co., and Shiloh are building numerous classics chambering the .45-70 Gov't. Heck, even Browning built a sweet run of the '86 for the model's centennial. Winchester continues to turn out a slightly updated version of its original 1886. Though more of a stretch in this category, one of the .45-70 arms on my wish list is the repro-meets-custom Skinner Bush Pilot-- a takedown thumper riff on Chiappa's 1886, the brainchild of Andy Larsson of Skinner Sights fame. While some reproductions are more faithful to the original than others, these guns keep the large cartridge and the designs alive and accessible.

HEAVY-DUTY HANDGUNS

The .45-70 was born and thrives as a rifle round, but it's not limited to long guns. Old western days saw cowboys pairing handgun chamberings like the .44-40 or .45 Colt with a wheelgun and a lever action. It's rare, however, to build such a tandem in reverse. Not only in traditional rifle chamberings like the .45-70 but to partner big bores in a long gun and a handgun. Yet the nature of the .45-70, with its relatively low-pressure but serious performance, lends itself to just that.

Yes, Virginia, there is a current .45-70 Gov't handgun. And it's the perfect, American-made companion from Magnum Research. The Biggest Finest Revolver (BFR) is built for hunters. These long-cylinder single actions put the power of the .45-70 in hand. Though they're the only current production handgun for the round, they are neither the first nor the only to have done it. Single-shot icon Thompson-Center built handgun barrels for its break-action Contender series. The now out-of-production T/C family remains a favorite among hardcore handgun hunters, with its switch-barrel platform.

Hunting aside, believe it or not, .45-70 handguns have been built for self-defense-meets-Tyrannosaurus-backup. Magnum Research has produced at least one BFR custom dubbed "Thunder Snub" with a 3-inch barrel and metrics for CCW. The Bisley grip frame is undoubt-

Magnum Research BFR loaded with Federal Premium .45-70 Gov't ammunition.

edly a welcome addition when controlling this beast.

Those wanting to make a statement or live on the edge with an orthopedist on speed dial should squeeze off a few rounds from American Derringer's Model M-4 Alaskan Survival. That stainless steel double weighs only 16.5 ounces with its 4-inch O/U barrels and Rosewood grips. Though of a relatively short run in the mid-1980s, few .45-70 fans have forgotten the niche design, and I've yet to conjure the moxie to pull the trigger.

PRACTICAL HUNTING VERSATILITY

Though many folks write off the .45-70 as a big bore for only close-range, larger-sized, non-threatening game, in actuality, the round is much more flexible. The cartridge's characteristics (lacking super speed) assure that with the proper projectile selection, a .45-70 on even smaller-sized deer can and has damaged less meat than much faster, flatter shooters. On more than one whitetail

hunt, I've witnessed a weighty buck swept off its feet with one shot through the wheelhouse. Modern rounds like the Federal Premium Hammer Down, a bonded 300-grain soft point, are pure terror on deer and even much larger-sized game.

Others still are quick to claim the big ol' .45-caliber flying pumpkin lacks the ballistics to be a practical shooter at anything farther than a football field. To them, I call foul. While it's true that these heavy projectiles drop rapidly, getting the most from a .45-70 is not only possible but part of the joy. Think back to 1880 when Springfield Armory was conducting extreme long-range accuracy testing. Marksmen repeatedly hit a six-foot target at 2,500 yards. Yes, that's correct, well over one-mile shots with a Trapdoor rifle, iron sights, and genuine know-how. Much of that early work was done with variations from then earlier Springfield Master Armorer Erskine Allin and his masterminded muzzle-to-breech loading

Allin-Springfield conversions. Not only did such handiwork pave the way for decades of .45-70 Gov't military service, but it also put the round at the forefront of military and civilian dalliance.

While I'm in no way advocating taking anywhere near those types of shots on game, the fact remains that in both sniper marksmanship and civilian target competitions, the .45-70 has a history of use at ranges far beyond what we consider practical today. For ethical hunting,

however, defining effective longer-range parameters is more limited. The hefty point-four-five clunker requires an intimate knowledge of firearm, sighting device, load, and ballistics. Big chunks of lead fall like a rock thrown off a cliff. Yet compensating for the drop, along with the ability we have today to soup up handloads and shoot higher power factory rounds, opens up a brave new world for those romantics among us still out hunting, plinking — or plunking — and

Henry X Model .45-70 with Hornady Subsonic ammo and a suppressor.

arcing those bullets into distant targets.

I took a good amount of flak for taking a .45-70 on safari not once but twice. As part of my practice regimen before the first venture with Henry's All Weather lever gun and Leupold CDS-ZL optic, learning the intricacies of rifle and scope was paramount to setting my effective ranges for different shooting positions and projectile types. I was confident on smaller plains game out to nearly 300 yards from a solid rest. From the sticks, my comfort range halved. Fill me with adrenaline offhand — or while pursuing the Big Five — and I prefer to be eye-to-eye.

All that said, compensating for a hefty bullet drop is no joke. Modern technology makes the .45-70 more appealing than ever. I opted to top my rifle with Leupold's CDS-ZL scope turret system to take the guesswork out of bullet drop. For those unfamiliar, that's short for Custom Dial System-Zero Lock. It works with precision because Leupold builds you a complimentary dial tailored to your exact load, making mastering the drop effortless. Thus, my Henry got a turret customized for Federal Premium Hammer Down 300-grainers, including bullet details, muzzle velocity, and zero

African PH Stephen Bann takes his turn on the Henry .45-70 All Weather.

Today's .45-70 Choices

A century-and-a-half later, rifles, carbines, and revolvers are cranked out in the .45-70 Gov't chambering. Here are a few of our current crushes.

Henry lever actions: The company renowned for the slogan "Made in America or Not Made at All" is the ideal home for the ultimate USA-chambering .45-70 Gov't. Henry built not one or two but 11 big-bore lever guns, so chambered. The Side Gate Lever Action is lovely — embellished walnut stocks and polished brass — and practical with a 20-inch barrel. There's a color-casehardened beauty, a blacked-out X-Model, traditional steel and walnut, special editions, and more. Our favorite, having proven itself on hunts, is the All Weather Picatinny Rail Side Gate with its 18.5-inch barrel, industrial hard chrome finish, large loop, and full-length Picatinny rail. Even if levers aren't your *forte*, Henry builds a pair of single-shot, break-action .45-70s. I can attest firsthand that one shot is all that's needed on whitetails, and I've seen more than one hunter grinning after hunting with these singles.

Magnum Research BFR: And the cheese stands alone. In a veritable arsenal of long guns, Magnum Research's Biggest, Finest Revolver (BFR) — also known by other more, ahem, creative monikers — is the lone .45-70 handgun in current production. There's little doubt it requires a stout build to stand up to a traditional rifle round. Call it a single-action whopper wheelgun or hand cannon, but no matter the semantics, these solid stainless, five-shot long cylinders make the ideal home for what has always been a rifle round. Buyers can choose 7.5- or 10-inch barrels, two grip frames, and numerous finishes via the Custom Shop.

From whitetails in Wisconsin to Cape buffalo in Africa, I've put the BFR to the test and my well-being on the line based on trust in the firearm and chambering. Each time I gaze at my taxidermy on the wall, I relive those memories.

Heym Double: Though on the lower power spectrum of what has come to be termed "big bores" in terms of dangerous game, the .45-70 has accounted for all of the Big Five and Dangerous Seven animals. Unsurprisingly, the round has found its way into many double rifle configurations, including the Pedersoli, Rizzini, Beretta, Fausti, and Remington/Baikal. I'd gladly accept any, yet the one I've been admiring recently is Heym's Model 26B. That over/under is one of few stacked-barrel choices in .45-70, with 22-inch barrels, high-grade Walnut, a single trigger, and sleek lines. Sadly, the company's bread and butter finery — the 88 and 89B side-by-side doubles — do not catalog the round.

Ruger No. 1: Just when you thought single shots couldn't be sexy, a one-shooter makes our short list of the finest production guns, bar none. Ruger's venerable No. 1 series of rifles has been in continuous production for more than 55 years. The compact, Farquharson-style falling block action is incredibly strong and immaculately lovely. Ruger has built the No. 1 in .45-70 on several variants, including blued/walnut, stainless/walnut, and the eye-catching pepper laminate/stainless. Ruger's related No. 3 falling blocks were also built for the .45-70. Firing any of Bill Ruger's single-shot marvels never ceases to inspire a renewed appreciation for one-shot rifles, especially with a round like this.

Marlin 1895: Just when we thought the old horse-and-rider brand Marlin was defunct, Ruger's takeover has the lever-gun Marlin back and better than ever. And the first gun Marlin rolled off the factory line? The Model 1895 SBL dressed in gray laminate, polished stainless and chambered in .45-70 Gov't. Since the 2022 debut, Marlin has added a short-barreled Trapper and blued Guide Gun. The proof is in the sales of all three young Marlins, with demand far outstripping production. Currently, the trio is commanding prices far above MSRP based solely on demand, which is a testament to the .45-70's bright future.

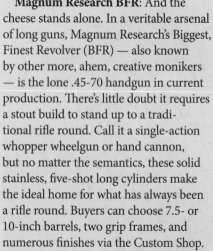

The old and the new .45-70s, Henry X and Springfield Trapdoor.

The author with her first Cape buffalo, taken with one shot from Henry's All Weather .45-70 at 55 yards.

distance. Placing shots then is as straightforward as dialing the turret to the necessary range and holding dead on for elevation. There was no question about maintaining the necessary energy at my practice distances for plains game, a feat proven more than once in the field with clean, one-shot harvests.

Give me my choice, though, in most any hunt, and I'd rather get inside 100 yards. And for the most part, that's where the .45-70 earns its keep. A brush buster, a heavy woods bear gun, a stiffer recoiling but even harder hitting choice for hunters seeking a do-all round. Likewise, the .45-70 makes a most viable option for hunting seasons in states with straight-walled cartridge restrictions. Though not legal in every limited area due to nitpicky case length limits, the .45-70 is a prime choice in Ohio and Iowa.

When turning the focus to much larger and more menacing game, even I'll admit there are more ideal dangerous game rounds; however, for practiced hunters with wise load selection, there are few more quixotic chamberings. Do you still need more reasons for the Gov't? In addition to delivering a wallop, its lever-driven carbines, akin to single shots, are compact and wieldy firearms, easily packed into timber, tucked into a horseback scabbard, or worked in close-quarters blinds. Its practical factor wins my heart time and again.

A WORTHY RENAISSANCE

Whether brush-busting, shooting longer-range silhouettes, thumping dangerous game, studying military history, or collecting uniquely American firearms, the .45-70 powers one heckuva heartbeat. By now, you've undoubtedly gathered my adoration for these practical antiquities continuing to influence our rich outdoor industry. How many of us can recount memories of parents, grandparents, or even great-grandparents hunting and passing down .45-70s?

No firearms collection is complete without at least one; no shooter or hunter has lived until pulling the trigger on a century and a half of rich, storied American history. Whether shooting a tricked-out, scoped, full-power new specimen or one of the earliest military long guns with reduced loads, the allure of America's Government cartridge remains the same: magically nostalgic, historically relevant, surprisingly potent, and purely ours. This fascinating round has not simply been surviving all these decades, but now more than ever, it is thriving. Happy Birthday, .45-70 Gov't. You've earned it; I'll raise a glass to many more. 𝄞

On Turkeys and Turkey Guns

Choice tactics, firearms, and loads for America's favorite big game bird.

› DAVE FULSON

If you hunt long enough in different areas, states, countries or even continents, you will no doubt experience a wide variety of big game animals. And you will also find out what you most enjoy hunting. My travels have taken me around much of the world, firearm in tow, and indeed I have found many species that inspired me, excited me, and sometimes even terrified me. All, to varying degrees, have been enjoyable.

But the one hunt I count the days to, I mean *really* look forward to, is calling and hunting the feathered 'King of Spring.' I have been hard after him every spring since my teenage years. Of course, I'm talking about the wild turkey of North America.

With a career where I am most generally recognized for hunting and filming dangerous and exotic game worldwide, it baffles clients and friends alike when they see me getting so worked up before the spring turkey season. A buddy told me not long ago, "Fulson, I think you would rather shoot a bull turkey than a bull elephant." And he was not off target by much — if at all!

Sunrise and multiple gobblers sounding off on the roost signal the start of the magical allure that is springtime turkey hunting.

And I'm not alone. Wild turkeys are one of America's most successful sportsmen-driven conservation stories. In the 1930s, wild turkey population estimates in the U.S. were as low as 30,000 total, a shocking number when you consider how decades of wise management and reintroduction efforts skyrocketed turkey numbers to seven million birds in 2022.

The United States is home to four subspecies of the wild turkey, with huntable populations found in every state except Alaska. The subspecies are classified as the Eastern, Rio Grande, Merriam's, and Osceola. If you head south of the border, you'll also encounter the Gould's and Ocellated varieties. Wherever you hunt him, and regardless of the subspecies, pursuing the spring gobbler is a passion that will get into your blood like few other sporting pursuits. This mighty bird, one Ben Franklin is said to have supported for our national symbol over the bald eagle, has an entire industry strictly dedicated to helping you and me enjoy and bag him.

Call makers, firearms companies, camo brands, decoy designers, ammunition manufacturers and more are constantly inventing, improving, and re-imagining gear that their customers will look at and say, "Now *that's* going to be the *difference maker* this spring!" And Lord knows armies of turkey hunters don't mind shelling out for a piece of gear that will allow them to accomplish the turkey hunter's primary quest: to outwit a bird with a brain the size of a marble!

TURKEY TACTICS

This past October, I was in southern Oklahoma filming some whitetail footage on a large ranch when, up the hill, came six mature Rio gobblers straight toward me. I was wearing a new Kryptek camo pattern called Obskura Transitional and saw the incoming bunch of gobblers - as they say in marketing, a perfect '*focus group.*' I sat still and watched the veteran

If Fulson were limited to just one call, he would choose a slate and striker due to the wide variety of turkey sounds it can mimic.

The author has always considered wild turkeys 'big game' despite the feathers. He looks justifiably happy with his morning efforts.

There are few feelings better than walking out of the springtime woods with a big gobbler over your shoulder.

The author took these longbeards on the same morning, but with different loads, including his first tom using TSS shot.

toms parade by at about 10 yards. Two long beards eventually pecked acorns at no more than 5 yards! Not a single bird spotted me nestled into a cedar clump before they eventually wandered off to their bachelor party. I was damned excited by the effectiveness of the new camo pattern, but, after all, it was just six *fall* turkeys puttering around.

Let me see those same six birds in the spring, and, well, it's a different Davey-boy altogether. Ho-hum will be replaced with adrenalin jolts as I fish the right call out of my turkey vest for the distance and situation. And so begins my favorite time of year and the most classic back-and-forth conversation in the natural world — hunter versus gobbler.

I've always been fascinated with the challenge of the calling game. It started with waterfowl, then came a lifetime passion for predator calling. Rattling giant whitetails certainly qualifies as calling, and then there were my years elk hunting and guiding, where Septembers in the Rockies were spent trying to lure rutting

Rifles for Turkey?

A small-caliber centerfire rifle, like this .17 Hornet, is suitable for cleanly taking turkeys.
PC: Massaro Media Group

If you read "The Good Book," you are undoubtedly familiar with heaven and hell. It is built on a foundation that 'not all folks will get to heaven,' and your sins, independent of how egregious they are, could land you in hell. *Gun Digest* editor Phil Massaro asked me to hold open the door to his eternal damnation by asking this humble writer, a turkey purist at heart, to address quickly — and forgive me, Lord, for even discussing it — *rifles for turkey hunting*!

I believe that turkey *calling* should precede turkey *killing* and that close-range encounters with gobblers are the top prize. And for the vast majority of turkey hunters, that means your weapon of choice is a shotgun. Those folks will one day wear wings. However, turkeys are taken with rifles from time to time, where legal. States such as Colorado, Montana, Florida, Texas, Virginia and more allow the use of a rifle for turkeys. And some folks prefer rifles exclusively. (Not only is this the fast track to damnation, but the devil might just give you a job in upper management!)

Most of these birds will be taken by a hunter guarding a feeder or watching a field. If a gobbler strolls by, he might catch a bullet intended for a whitetail. An explosion of feathers and pulverized breast meat will generally be your reward unless your wife has a great turkey leg recipe.

But if choosing a rifle for turkey, dial down to a .222 or .223 caliber, and opt for a full metal jacket bullet to reduce meat destruction. Turkeys are hardy birds, and I believe .22 magnum to be on the light side.

OK, boss, I actually said *turkey* and *rifle* in the same sentence. If I now begin a decade-long drought on killing a single gobbler, you can be assured where I will place all blame. "Forgive Phil, Lord; he knows not what he just made me do! Amen."

bulls into bow range, the very definition of excitement. I have called in some big bulls over the years, and exciting as that is, working an excited gobbler into range, especially a vocal one, is Calling Thrill #1!

I enjoy hunting with buddies, but I also like hunting turkeys alone. I tend to slow down when hunting on my own, as opposed to speeding up when trying to get a friend or a client on a gobbler. I call softer, stay in place longer, and let the day come to me. And I usually come away with a bird over my shoulder when I follow this strategy.

Successful calling is a never-ending challenge. You will never master it; if you did, you would never fail in your attempts. And fail you will, often and for endless reasons. But the veteran hunter understands that each unsuccessful calling session is a learning experience that might be used to your advantage on another day.

The successful turkey hunter learns to adapt to the hunting conditions they are presented with. These can include the early vs. late season breeding cycles, the weather, the number of turkeys present, and the competition from other hunters. All affect the birds' behavior, and more important than any other factor, you must learn to pay attention and adjust your calling techniques to the mood of the birds.

Certainly, learning to make realistic turkey sounds, especially hen sounds, is a requirement to be a successful spring hunter. Turkey calls come in various styles, such as box calls, mouth calls, tube calls, slates, push button, etc. I've used and killed gobblers around the country with all of these, but I have also learned, like the lures in the tackle box, each has a situation where it will be more effective than the others.

For the beginner, learn two or three calling styles. Buy a good slate and striker call, a quality two-reed mouth call, and a box call. The longer I hunt, the more I rely on a slate call. It makes the best variety of sounds, from the gentlest of purrs and soft clucks to the aggressive fly-down cackles that drive early-morning gobblers crazy. If you call a gobbler experienced and wise to hunting pressure, the soft sounds of a slate are far better than blasting overly loud yelps through the morning with a mouth call. On windy days, a mouth call will carry better, but a gobbler's sense of hearing is beyond belief, so start softly, then increase the volume as you try to get a distant tom to respond.

Study turkey hunting videos to see the techniques good callers use. Watch when the caller gets aggressive, and notice when they call sparingly. You will learn a great deal. Also, consider some of the many DVD offerings that show how to make the appropriate sounds and, equally importantly, when not to use specific calls. Online video offers endless workshops from different call manufacturers on using their products, including actual hunt footage with pro-staffers. You'll also see gobblers approaching and observing their behavior when hearing different calls. I wish I had had access to these tools when I started this game.

Nothing is better than calling a big tom in early, gobbling all the way, but it is generally not how it goes. He moves away; you move after him. He hangs up; you adopt a new plan. Maybe a decoy comes out. And we should spend some time here talking about that option.

Turkey decoys can make all the difference at the right time and with the right bird. But they can backfire on you, too. I use Deception brand hen decoys, and under the right circumstances, there is nothing better. They are as realistic as it gets without feathers. But in real life, a hot hen goes *to the gobbler*, not the other way around, which is a crucial fact to remember. If a boss bird comes to your call and sees the cute hen he thinks is calling,

he will often stop in his tracks, go into a full strut, and parade around in one spot, often well out of range. Soft, seductive calls (not *aggressive* calling indicating a red-hot hen) may get him moving in your direction. And then again, it may not. He is used to hens coming to him to breed and will often take your decoy not moving in his direction as an indication of an uninterested hen. This is the last thing he wants to waste prime breeding

The author considers the Remington V3 Turkey Pro the finest combination of design and functionality he has yet to find in a lifetime of serious turkey hunting.

Two nice gobblers from southern Oklahoma, the author called in for his clients.

time on, so a mature gobbler will often fold his wings and head to greener pastures in search of more willing wives.

I also have had memorable kills using the oversized MOJO Strutting Tom decoy. This is a large, intimidating decoy, to be sure. I have crawled into vast, open fields holding the decoy in front of me when no other option was available to approach a dominant strutting bird. It is a slow and generally sticker-filled process, so while resting and sticker picking, I turn the decoy and adjust the fan just as a real gobbler will do when trying to

intimidate another gobbler. Be warned; this is a clear *risk* vs. *reward* decoy tactic. Two-year-old gobblers often shy away or flat-out *run away* from old 'Mega Tom' headed in their direction. But a three-year-old or older tom will often charge your handheld rival. I've had them cover over one hundred yards at shocking speeds. This behavior becomes more predictable if two veteran longbeard buddies are running together. Feeling strength in numbers, a two-bird team generally heads straight toward the intruder, creating as intense a turkey encounter as the

sport offers!

Growing up as a turkey hunter in Texas generally found me hunting more ground than might be available to a hunter in the East. And much of the country I hunt is vast and relatively open, meaning I can see a long way. It was funny in my early guiding days when my clients — often Eastern hunters — would see me strapping on my pair of 10x40 binoculars over my turkey vest.

"Why do you carry binos on a hunt where you kill the bird at shotgun range?"

Remington's semi-auto V3 Turkey Pro is now offered by Remington.

The author estimates he took over thirty longbeards while carrying his much-used Ithaca model 37 Turkey slayer.

A good aftermarket choke can dial in turkey loads for a tight, long-distance pattern.

"You must find a gobbler before you call him," I'd say.

Generally, and in usually very short order, I made my point by finding a big strutter at the far end of a Sendero or across a four-hundred-acre wheat field. I never hunt turkeys without binoculars. Do I need them every time? No. But like a personal defense pistol, when you need it, you tend to need it badly.

TURKEY GUNS

Today's turkey hunter has many firearm options which were unavailable to our fathers and grandfathers. In the past, their favorite waterfowl shotgun probably pulled double duty when – or if, in some instances - turkey season rolled around. But most firearms manufacturers today offer a shotgun package or two that targets the specific needs of the serious turkey hunter. And, of course, all of them

will get the job done.

During my younger years, I used a Remington model 1100 autoloader and a Remington 870 pump shotgun for turkey. I started with standard 12-gauge 2 3\4-inch loads until the 3-inch stuff came along and made that sensible jump, but with the same model shotguns. Somewhere along the line, I bought a short-barreled Ithaca Model 37 12-gauge pump gun that has accounted for a few dozen longbeards. I will never part with it, but a few years ago, I found a better mouse trap offered by Remington Firearms, which is precisely the turkey gun I would have designed if I could customize one from the ground up. Let me introduce you to my new go-to turkey medicine, the Remington V3 Turkey Pro.

The V3 is a 12-gauge autoloader that handles the 3-inch turkey loads on the market. It has a sleek design that nestles perfectly into the cheek and shoulder and features a shorter 22-inch barrel, which points like a dream. Since I wear camo gloves while hunting, which can sometimes dampen the feeling in your fingers, I really appreciate the V3's oversized bolt handle and enlarged safety mechanism. The shotgun has a fiber-optic front sight with a steel mid-bead for accurate sighting on an incoming gobbler. At the shot, even today's hard-hitting magnum 3-inch loads are tamed considerably by its SuperCell recoil pad. Remington also equipped the V3 Turkey Pro with a TRUGLO Headbanger choke tube for superior patterns. This coming year, the V3 will be offered in a popular Kryptek camo pattern, putting the finishing touch on what is, in my opinion, the finest shotgun ever made for the serious turkey hunter.

The final and critical last step in putting a big gobbler on the ground is the shotshell. And today's turkey hunter has an incredible selection of premium ammo.

Ammunition explicitly designed for turkey hunting has seen some real breakthroughs recently. Over the past decade, my preferred turkey load has been the Remington extra hard lead Nitro Turkey shot. I have taken gobblers with just about every shot size out there, but I have leaned most heavily on Rem-

The author will be shooting two shotguns this spring: The Remington V3 Turkey Pro that comes with the TruGlo Headbanger choke tube and a new Remington 870 SPS Turkey model that comes standard with an Extra Full Rem Turkey Choke.

ington Nitro Turkey in 12-gauge 3-inch shooting No. 5 pellets. I've been satisfied with the pattern density on paper and longbeards. Plain and simple, it's a load that I have confidence in from successful field experience.

But like so much other gear related to the hunt for turkeys, ammo has also seen constant and vast improvements. And nothing has been a more significant game-changer in turkey ammunition than the new tungsten alloy ammo that is taking today's market by storm. Commonly referred to as TSS, tungsten alloy is 56% denser than lead. The advantage is a smaller but harder pellet, a hell of a *lot more pellets* per load versus lead, and increased terminal velocity, which all result in cleaner kills. For instance, my 12-gauge No. 5 3-inch shot gives me roughly 410 pellets in the air. The Remington Premier TSS in No. 9 shot gives me 800 pellets with better terminal velocity.

I took two big birds in central Texas the same morning last year using the loads described above. The bird I took with the TSS was hung up at 45 yards,

but a load of TSS No. 9 shot (yes, No. 9 shot) folded him up without a flutter, and his head was completely shot to pieces. Impressed was not a strong enough word.

TSS loads provide the ability to use smaller gauge shotguns, including 20-gauge, 28-gauge, and even .410 bore. Believing bigger is still better for these hardy birds, I'll still stick with my 12-gauge 3-inch standby, but I will be experimenting even more with the TSS option on both the range and in the field this spring. I think the writing may be on the wall with TSS. It makes more sense at every performance level.

PATTERNING

Patterning a turkey shotgun is a far cry from regulating a fine double rifle, but it is a critical step in getting peak performance when it's 'trigger time' in the turkey woods.

A quality turkey shotgun with a mid-bead and front bead correctly aligned will certainly shoot in the direction it is pointed. Your shot will then spread out until the target is reached at whatever range it is from your barrel. Simple

enough, but doubtfully as good as it *could* be.

If you are shooting a red-dot-style scope, which many hunters are using today, like a rifle scope, it must be zeroed, so the majority of your shot pattern impacts the center of your bulls-eye target, or the one I prefer, the life-size turkey neck and head target. It's not as exacting a process as having your rifle bullets touch inside the 10-ring, but you will easily see the necessary adjustments by seeing where the most pellets impact the target. That will be your "turkey bullseye."

Now all you need is a variety of different turkey loads and a good supply of targets.

I generally pattern my turkey shotgun at 30 yards. Let's assume you are steady on your shot, whether you're sighting down the barrel or using a red-dot scope. Now the fun — and the work — begins.

There is a tremendous variety of turkey-specific loads on the market today. They can range from 2 ¾- to 3 1/2-inch magnum loads in various shot pellet sizes. I know hunters who bought a box of shells 40 years ago with a photo of a turkey on the box, took it hunting and killed a gobbler with it. Guess what? They are still shooting the same load today.

But that reminds me of the fisherman who is leaving the lake, who tells a guy just launching his boat, "Hey buddy, all they are hitting today is spinner baits," and the other guy says, "better than crankbaits?" to which the first replies, "Who knows? I only used spinner baits!"

Experimenting with a variety of loads and shot sizes will, in short order, show you exactly which pattern delivers the most lethal load of pellets into the "kill zone."

Another variable, but not a *major* concern, is your shotgun's barrel length. Honestly, at acceptable ranges for turkey (and you must know what that is for your setup and shooting ability), I have noticed little, if any difference, with the shorter-barrel shotguns I prefer and Granddad's Long Tom 30-inch barrel turkey medicine. But again, time on the target range will provide the answers you seek.

Something that can indeed affect your pattern, especially at longer ranges, is a shotgun choke. A choke is a tapered constriction of a shotgun barrel at its muzzle end. Its purpose is to shape the spread of the 'shot cloud' or string to gain better range and accuracy while delivering the optimum pattern of pellet density, for the particular target, depending on its size and range. Chokes are screw-in types selected for a particular application or fixed and integral to the barrel.

The overwhelming majority of turkey hunters, myself included, choose either a fixed full-choke barrel, or purchase a screw-in choke specifically designed for the challenge of turkey hunting. There are endless options from manufacturers today, and most will improve your patterns and killing efficiency.

I will be shooting two shotguns this spring: The Remington V3 Turkey Pro that comes with the TruGlo Headbanger choke tube and a new Remington 870 SPS Turkey model that comes standard with an Extra Full Rem Turkey Choke. Both have patterned beautifully, and I know exactly what they will deliver at various ranges. Again, proper dedication to range time and load experimentation is the key to success in the turkey woods.

CONCLUSION

For many years, I guided spring hunts nearly every day of the season somewhere, and I generally enjoyed every minute of it. But now, time does not allow me the luxury of unlimited days. Today, I save those precious spring days for myself or close friends and feel I have earned and certainly appreciate that gift.

I will never lose my sense of excitement watching and listening to a springtime gobbler close in on my calling. It is truly the sport of my youth, my present, and, God willing, my last years. I will be a turkey hunter as long as I can walk and strike a slate. And if heaven is what I hope, green spring fields will be alive with gobblers — no floating on clouds and playing harps for me.

And I'm also glad Ben Franklin lost in his bid to make the wild turkey our national symbol. I just can't wrap my brain around the thought of sitting down at the Thanksgiving table, folding my hands, and saying, "Lord, Thank You for bringing us together today, especially for this delicious bald eagle we are about to enjoy."

Sorry, Ben! GD

There's only one way to find out how your turkey gun shoots: Get to the range and shoot some patterns.

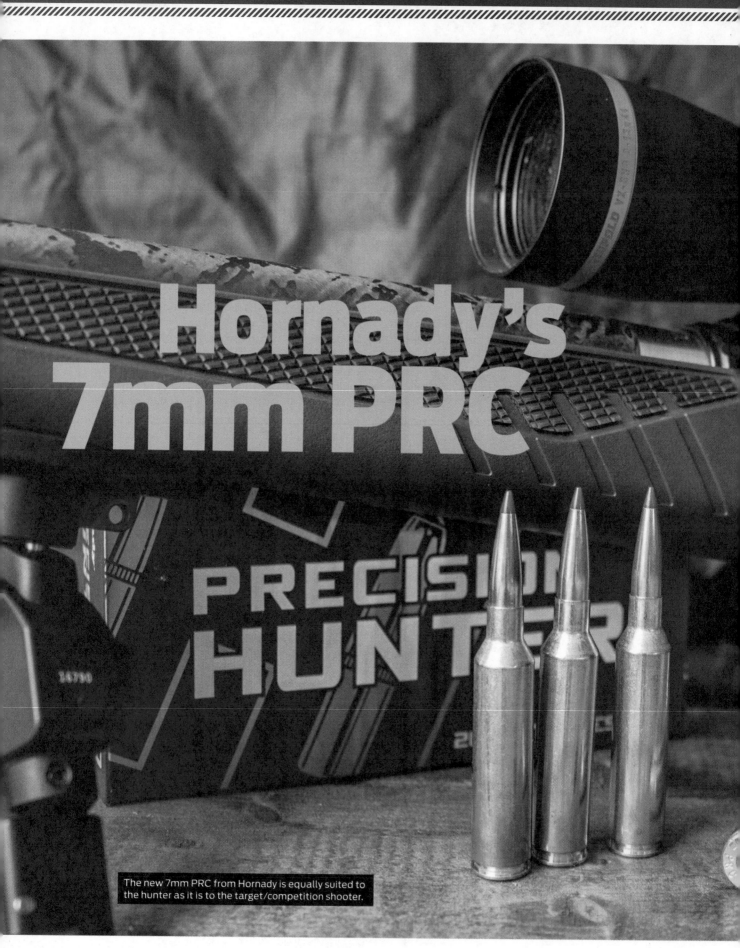

Hornady's 7mm PRC

The new 7mm PRC from Hornady is equally suited to the hunter as it is to the target/competition shooter.

A dual-purpose cartridge with all sorts of appeal.

> PHIL MASSARO

"It's all been done."

I've heard this for most of my life, whether the topic was rock music, movies, or cartridges. My dad still asks rhetorically, "how many different ways can they come up with to launch a bullet?" I must admit that — in the not-too-distant past — I subscribed to that theory myself, as well as more recently "get off my lawn," but the last few years have proven me wrong on more than one occasion. The latest cartridge to cause me to doubt that oft-repeated declaration is Hornady's 7mm PRC.

The folks at Hornady are certainly no strangers to cartridge development; they are responsible for the uber-popular 6.5 Creedmoor, the .375 Ruger, the .204 Ruger, the .480 Ruger, and the .17 Hornady Magnum Rimfire. With the popularity of long-range shooting, and in particular the Precision Rifle Series competition, Hornady's engineers looked for a cartridge to reach even farther than the 6.5 Creedmoor. Looking to the .300 Ruger Compact Magnum — itself based on the highly successful .375 Ruger — as a platform, Hornady cooked up a cartridge that could offer a higher muzzle velocity than its own highly popular 6.5 Creedmoor yet would still fit in a short-action rifle magazine: the 6.5 PRC.

The formula certainly makes sense; they'd used the .532-inch base and belt diameter of the proven Holland & Holland belted magnums yet relied on the shoulder for headspacing instead of a belt. The rimless, beltless design improves chamber concentricity out of the gate, and using the shoulder for headspacing eliminates the case stretching often associated with the H&H belted design. For those shooters who frequent the range regularly — a common trait among the long-range and competition shooters — the extended case life will make a difference, especially when compared to the hunter who doesn't expend the amount of ammunition that a competition shooter will. With a case length of 2.030 inches and a 30-degree shoulder, the 6.5 PRC is much more reminiscent of the Winchester Short Magnum family of cartridges than the .308 Winchester-esque 6.5 Creedmoor. The 6.5 PRC caught on quickly, with many competition shooters flocking to the new design. It seemed that Hornady engineers might have out-designed their Creedmoor.

The following year, Hornady announced the release of the .300 PRC, but it was more than just the 6.5 PRC case necked up to hold America's beloved .30-caliber bullets. It's a much longer cartridge, with a case length measuring 2.58 inches, and a cartridge overall length of 3.700 inches, requiring at

The Hornady 7mm PRC Match load sees a 180-grain ELD Match bullet cruising at 2,975 fps; this high BC bullet is perfect for long-range work.

Massaro used the 7mm PRC in the Savage Impulse Mountain Hunter to take this pronghorn antelope at the Lander One Shot Antelope Challenge. A 330-yard shot from the prone position put the buck down immediately.

least a magnum-length receiver. The 30-degree shoulder was retained, as was the .532-inch base, but where the 6.5 PRC used the same 140- to 147-grain bullets common to the 6.5 Creedmoor and .260 Remington, the .300 PRC would be centered around heavy-for-caliber bullets. Using the 212-grain ELD-X soft-point hunting bullet, and the 225-grain ELD Match target bullet, the .300 PRC is designed for long-range work. These projectiles retain a healthy percentage of their energy and offer a flat trajectory, though both will come at the expense of heavier recoil. If you're a dedicated long-range shooter or a hunter of larger game species at longer ranges, the .300 PRC makes sense, though many feel it's simply too much gun for the most common game species like the whitetail deer.

2022 saw the release of the 7mm PRC and like the story of Goldilocks, who found one bed too soft, the next too hard, and the third just right, this is the one

I consider to be 'just right' among the PRC family. Sitting comfortably in a standard long-action receiver, the 7mm PRC shares the 3.340-inch cartridge overall length of the .30-'06 Springfield, 7mm Remington Magnum, and .300 Winchester Magnum. The case is shorter than many other cartridges in this class — measuring 2.280 inches, whereas so many come in around the 2.5-inch mark — and that is intentional. To utilize projectiles that will deliver the best possible downrange performance, the case must be shortened for a couple of reasons.

First, the case mouth must sit on the

Like many new cartridge designs, the 7mm PRC uses a shorter case to allow for longer ogive bullets to be seated with the shank/boattail joint of the bullet at the neck/shoulder junction of the case.

shank or parallel sides of the bullet, which attains the maximum diameter yet fits in the magazine of the rifle for which the cartridge is designed. When you look at some of our favorite cartridges, for example, the .300 Winchester Magnum and 7mm Remington Magnum, the case capacity has been increased by removing much of the taper and moving the shoulder junction forward. While this certainly achieves the goal, it also reduces the available real estate within the magazine. In the early 1960s, when these cartridges were conceived, the projectiles of the day did not have the long, sleek profile that the bullets have six decades later; simply put, long-range hunting and shooting, which is so common today, was a rarity at that time. Speed (and striking energy) was more important than the Ballistic Coefficient, as the hunting ranges were assuredly shorter.

Secondly, increasing case capacity just to seat a bullet deep into the case is counterproductive. Looking at the 7mm Remington Magnum, the maximum cartridge overall length is 3.29 inches, with a neck length of .271 inches, slightly less than one caliber. This leaves room for .79 inch of bullet outside the case and provides room for 1.061 inches of bullet length before the neck/shoulder junction is reached and the case capacity begins to be compromised. With a bullet of lower BC value, where the ogive's curve is steeper and more pronounced, shortening the bullet's length, this might not pose much of an issue. But when dealing with a high BC bullet like Hornady's ELD-X or ELD Match, over a half-inch of the bullet can be shoved down into the case. Why extend a case for additional capacity only to take it back when you seat a long bullet? The answer hearkens back to the original design era: those bullets

just weren't available in the early 1960s.

During the 7mm PRC's development, Hornady engineers considered these factors and built the case around the longer bullets and long-action magazine length. Like the 6.5 PRC and .300 PRC, the 7mm variant retains the 30-degree shoulder of its siblings and the .532-inch case head diameter, with a neck length of .287 (just over the desired one-caliber length). Having no belt, the headspace is handled by the shoulder, so chamber concentricity is improved — at least when it comes to factory ammunition — and the case stretching issues of the H&H belted design is avoided altogether.

Even though the word "magnum" does not appear in the cartridge's name, the 7mm PRC delivers magnum performance. At the time of this writing, three factory loads are available for the 7mm PRC, all from Hornady. The Match load sees a 180-grain ELD Match bullet driven to a muzzle velocity of 2,975 fps, the Precision Hunter load has a 175-grain ELD-X bullet cruising along at an even 3,000 fps, and the Outfitter ammo series uses the lead-free 160-grain CX copper-

alloy monometal bullet at the same 3,000 fps velocity. Comparing that to what I feel is the most popular of the 7mm magnum cartridges — the 7mm Remington Magnum — you'll see a slight velocity advantage in favor of the new 7mm PRC. But there is more to it than just velocity numbers, as you'll see in just a bit.

BOOTS ON THE GROUND
I had the privilege of spending significant time in late summer/early autumn 2022 with the 7mm PRC in target shooting and hunting situations. My first experience was at the fabled FTW Ranch in Barksdale, Texas, where my friend Tim Fallon has assembled one of the best shooting instruction schools I've ever experienced; we were enrolled in the S.A.A.M. (Sportsman's All-Weather All-Terrain Marksmanship) Precision course. It was the first unveiling of the new 7mm PRC cartridge, and we'd be putting it through its paces in a Remington Model 700 Long Range rifle.

Now, the gents at FTW will engender all sorts of confidence in any shooter, but they will also show you the shortcomings

With velocities better than the popular 7mm Remington Magnum, the Hornady 7mm PRC won't have issues with headspace or case stretching and is a fantastic all-around choice for North American hunting. Photo: Hornady

The author used the Savage Impulse Mountain Hunter and the Hornady 7mm PRC Precision Hunter ammunition to take this black bear in British Columbia.

of your gear in a hurry, whether it's the rifle, scope, ammunition or even the chosen cartridge. Most of your stay in Barksdale will be spent on your belly, in the prone position, becoming one with your rifle; this is a good thing. From the confirmation of the rifle's zero at 100 yards to the initial plate engagements at 250 yards to the "let-me-talk-you-to-that-one-mile-plate" scenario, the SAAM course will make you a better shooter. It will also show you the true potential of your cartridge; in this instance, it was the 7mm PRC loaded with the 180-grain ELD Match load. With an impressive G1 Ballistic Coefficient of .796 and a G7 BC of .401, the ELD Match bullet performed very well in the varying winds of the canyons on the FTW Ranch. We were provided range cards with the

The 7mm PRC headstamp; the author believes this one will be around for quite some time. Photo: Hornady

7mm PRC trajectory, which worked out perfectly, and the sleek bullet performed exceptionally in the wind.

Over two days, we took the cartridge out to 1,400 yards consistently — with some of my colleagues shooting beyond a mile — and I had the chance to use it at the famous Crusader station. With all the students lined up, the instructors would indicate a pair of steel targets at different ranges from 250 to 550 yards and located in a manner where the shooter would have to quickly adjust their positioning to make the shot. Oh, and you have 10 seconds from the report of your first shot to make contact with the second. Miss the first, and you must re-engage. The idea is to best simulate a hunting situation, and I'll

testify to how difficult it can be. I didn't get Best in Class, but the 7mm PRC and I placed respectably, with the speedy cartridge making those shots where I'd use the reticle for holdover much easier. And, despite being in the prone position for a considerable amount of time, I didn't have a sore shoulder at all.

The following month, I had a two-week journey with the 7mm PRC in a straight-pull Savage Impulse Mountain Hunter rifle, first on a prestigious pronghorn antelope hunt in Wyoming and then on a combination hunt in British Columbia.

The Lander One Shot Antelope Challenge is an annual hunt held each year since the early 1940s (with the exception of a couple of years during World

War II) and absolutely reeks of tradition. There are wonderful ceremonies with the Shoshone Indian tribe, shooting competitions, and, of course, the opening day antelope hunt. Three-man teams are entered into the competition, which is based on taking a legal antelope with just one shot in the least amount of time. Miss, and you're disqualified; if you require a second shot, you're disqualified; the team that takes three bucks in the least amount of time is crowned the winner. The event was attended by Wyoming Governor Mark Gordon, who was a good sport and a lot of fun, and the overall atmosphere was fantastic.

I was paired with guide Mike Lilygren, who heads Maven Optics, native to Lander, Wyoming, and it wasn't long after legal light that we spotted a decent buck working a fence line. Now, the One Shot Challenge doesn't allow for any rest or aid, be it a bipod, sling, leaning over a pack, etc.; you must improvise by kneeling, sitting cross-legged, or, as I did, using a couple of strategically placed stones as an improvised rest. Lilygren and I low-crawled into a slight depression, barely out of sight of the antelope, and I got prone and as steady as I could on a rock. Mike ranged the goat at

330 yards, and a single 175-grain ELD-X had me on the board at twenty minutes after legal light. With no wind to speak of, I simply dialed the Leupold's compensated elevation turret to the appropriate range and broke the Savage's trigger. Our team didn't win, as one member took out a sage bush with his first shot, but we all had a good time.

The following week saw me in British Columbia with tags for elk, moose, and black bear in hand. It also saw some of the warmest and most unseasonal weather late September has ever offered. I was paired with Leupold's Shawn Skipper — a good friend and my hunting partner on many adventures — who had the same high opinion of the 7mm PRC I did, and we spent the afternoon of our arrival day confirming zero. Day one yielded neither moose nor elk, but our midday travels between glassing points did offer a good black bear; not being the guy to kick sand in the face of good fortune, I took the boar cleanly at 75 yards. The scenario repeated itself the next day, with a bear for Skipper, though this one played hide-and-seek more than mine. Skipper loosed a 175-grain ELD-X, and slightly less than 100 yards away, we heard the death bel-

The 7mm PRC uses the .532-inch rim diameter, common to the Holland & Holland belted cases, so rifle construction is affordable.

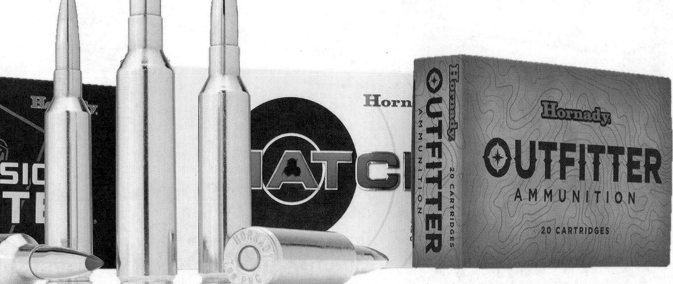

Hornady offers three factory loads for the 7mm PRC: the ELD-X in the Precision Hunter, the ELD Match in the Match ammo line, and the CX bullet in the Outfitter line. Photo: Hornady

low of his boar. And sadly, that wrapped up our week, as the heat essentially shut down the elk and moose hunting.

In all three instances, the shots completely passed through each animal; there were no recovered bullets to measure or weigh. And all three kills were quick, as you'd expect from a 7mm magnum cartridge at normal hunting ranges. One of the members of our group used the 7mm PRC with the 160-grain CX bullet to take a bull moose at the end of the week; the shot was at less than 100 yards, and the bull went down without issue.

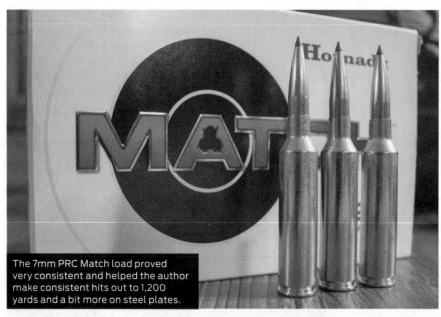

The 7mm PRC Match load proved very consistent and helped the author make consistent hits out to 1,200 yards and a bit more on steel plates.

IN COMPARISON

Why would anyone want to abandon the 7mm Remington Magnum, 7mm STW, or 7mm Weatherby Magnum for the new 7mm PRC? Well, there are some good talking points that would indicate it might be a good idea. First, the 7mm PRC is beltless and rimless, so compared to the other three cartridges I mentioned, you'll see better chamber concentricity with factory-spec ammunition. Better chamber concentricity can lead to an improvement in accuracy, and improved accuracy is always a good thing. Because the 7mm PRC doesn't have the Holland & Holland belt (which is unnecessary on most of our magnum cartridges with pronounced shoulders), the case-stretching issues are avoided. I've seen 7mm Remington Magnum cases stretch as much as .020 inch on the first firing, and when those belted cases fail, it is as often as not in the area just above the belt as it is in the case mouth. A rimless, beltless design alleviates a good portion of those issues.

The 7mm PRC delivers higher veloci-

Massaro had the opportunity to put the 7mm PRC through its paces at long range at the FTW Ranch SAAM course, using a Remington Model 700 to punch steel at 1,400 yards.

Massaro and Leupold's Shawn Skipper were paired up in British Columbia, where Skipper used the 7mm PRC for this good male black bear.

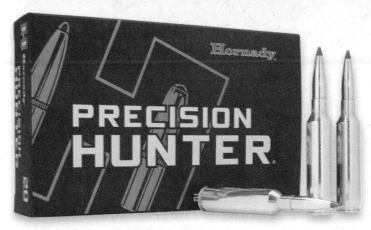

There aren't too many game animals that couldn't be confidently hunted with a 175-grain ELD-X delivered from the 7mm PRC, shown here in the Hornady Precision Hunter line. Photo: Hornady

ties than the 7mm Remington Magnum yet is only slightly slower than the 28 Nosler, 7mm STW, and 7mm Remington Ultra Magnum, depending on the manufacturer. Driving that 175-grain ELD-X to an even 3,000 fps, you have just shy of 3,500 ft-lbs at a tolerable recoil level. While I spend considerable time with big-bore rifles and cartridges, some of the speedy designs can beat you up quickly, especially in an ill-fitting rifle. The 7mm PRC was not unpleasant to shoot in any

position, and I found it to have less felt recoil than the average 7mm Remington Magnum.

Looking at the hunting trajectory of the 7mm PRC, you'll see that when the 175-grain ELD-X load is zeroed at 200 yards, you'll need 6 inches of elevation to hit at 300 yards, 17.2 inches of holdover at 400 yards, and 34.2 inches at 500 yards, where that load will retain over 2,100 ft-lbs of energy. In fact, the Precision Hunter load with the 175-grain ELD-X

will have over 1,200 ft-lbs of energy at 1,000 yards for those who would consider taking an animal at that distance — though I certainly would not. Point is, for those who pursue those species commonly taken at long range, the 7mm PRC ranks among the finest choices available.

The features that best set the 7mm PRC apart are inside the barrel: the 1:8 twist rate will properly stabilize the longest 7mm projectiles, and the longer throat allows the highest BC projectiles to be seated correctly, with the least amount of bullet driven into the case. This just cannot be done with the current SAAMI configurations of the 28 Nosler, 7mm Remington Magnum, 7mm Weatherby Magnum, and the like. The 28 Nosler has a larger case capacity and more velocity, but the 175-grain AccuBond Long Range doesn't have the Ballistic Coefficient that the 175 ELD-X possesses (G1 .689 for the ELD-X and G1 .672 for the ABLR), and for long-range target work, that will come into play. Yet, for those who wish to use the cartridge at more common distances, the 7mm PRC can be handloaded to

Though the Hornady factory ammunition has a whole lot to offer, handloading the 7mm PRC extends the cartridge's versatility.

use the lighter bullet weights, giving yet another dimension to the new cartridge.

HANDLOADING THE 7MM PRC

Should you choose to handload for the 7mm PRC, you'll need a large rifle magnum primer and a slow-burning powder. In my experiments, Alliant's Reloder 25 and Reloder 26, and Hodgdon's H4831SC gave the best results across the bullet weight spectrum. My Savage Impulse Mountain Hunter really liked the Badlands Precision Bulldozer 2 140-grain monometal, the Swift Scirocco II 150-grain bonded core bullet, the 160-grain Federal Trophy Bonded Tip, and the 165-grain Sierra Tipped GameKing. Each bullet would print three-shot sub-MOA groups — with the Badlands Precision giving just under 1/2 MOA accuracy — and I could certainly find an application for each in the hunting fields. Were I pressed to choose a powder for the 7mm PRC, I'd pick Reloder 25 or 26, and I've long been a devotee of the Federal Gold Medal Match primers, as they've given me the

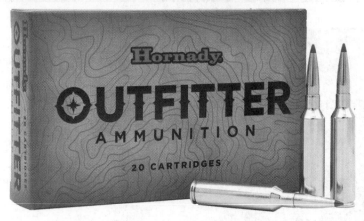

For the monometal lovers, Hornady offers the 160-grain CX bullet at 3,000 fps in the 7mm PRC, in the Outfitter ammo line, with nickel-plated cases. Photo: Hornady

most consistent results over the years. The GM215M large rifle magnum primer has been very good to me.

You'll definitely want a VLD-profile seating stem for your seater die, as the 7mm PRC's longer, high-BC bullets can be damaged with a regular seating stem. If you're loading for the long-range game, make sure you put a nice chamfer on the inside of the case mouth to prevent marring the bullet jacket during the seating

process; a jacket that's been scratched or scuffed can fly differently past 1,000 yards.

Should you choose the 7mm PRC for a target cartridge, I'd highly recommend a tool like the Redding Instant Indicator and Bullet Comparator, so you can see how much your fired case shoulders have moved in comparison to SAAMI specs and minimize the amount of shoulder bump needed for the cases for your particular rifle. Couple the Comparator's reading with the correlative Competition Shellholder — which are compensated in depth increments of .002 — and you can minimize the distance you move the case's shoulder while still resizing the diameter of the case body and neck. I've seen these tools significantly improve group size and extend case life.

A SEAT AT THE TABLE

It is never easy to predict which new releases will survive over time; I never would've thought the .260 Remington would become nearly obscure, nor would I have predicted that the 6.5 Creedmoor would skyrocket in popularity after its slow start. I have become extremely fond of the 6.8 Western, and while it seems it has steadily increased in popularity, it sits in that same mid-caliber magnum territory that the 7mm PRC will have to occupy.

Considering the devoted following that the .300 Winchester Magnum, 7mm Remington Magnum, .270 Winchester and .30-'06 Springfield still enjoy, hunters might be difficult to convince that any new-fangled cartridge offers a true advantage over their tried-and-true favorite. But, with the possible exception of the Ought-Six, all of these were once considered "new-fangled," at least for their era. O'Connor championed the .270 Winchester in the 1920s, which gave it a big shot in the arm, and the .300 Winchester Magnum and 7mm Remington Magnum rode on the coattails of the late 1950s magnum-mania. Still, the comparisons to the cartridges that came before were inevitable. Now that those cartridges are household names, rounds such as the 28 Nosler, 6.8 Western, and 7mm PRC must prove themselves.

While the 6.8 Western assuredly offers an advantage over the existing .277-caliber cartridges in bullet weight — giving

all sorts of hunting appeal — the 7mm PRC needs some distance to show an improvement in performance over other 7mm magnums. There is a definite market for shooters who want a single rifle capable of giving good terminal performance at all reasonable hunting distances and serving as a perfectly viable target cartridge for shots within your own zip code. I feel the 7mm PRC is one of the best possible choices to fill that niche.

Odds are a devotee of the 7mm Remington Magnum isn't using that cartridge for long-range target work and might not have cause to switch to the 7mm PRC for their hunting needs, but if I were in the market for an all-around 7mm magnum, you bet I'd look long and hard at the 7mm PRC. Based on my experiences with it in the field and at the range, this one's going to be a very popular choice for decades to come. **GD**

The author was very pleased with the long-range target capabilities of the 7mm PRC; the SAAM course presents a complex situation that will test the mettle of any shooter, rifle, or cartridge combination.

Unknown by its correct nomenclature until now, the Indonesian M95/51 .303 British modification of the 6.5x53mm Dutch Model 1895 Mannlicher was frequently coined an oddball, with made-up terminology used by dealers, collectors, or anyone who happened upon one. This sharp-looking refurbished bolt-action rifle is curiously interesting to the modern military surplus collector or shooter. Upper gun: 1983 import. Lower: 1962 import. Author Collection

D uring the communist troubles of the Malayan Emergency from 1948 to 1960, the term "jungle carbine" became widely associated with the No.5 Enfield. A newly independent Republic of Indonesia faced a turbulent decade throughout the 1950s rife with insurgencies and other political instability. In 1951, a long obsolete, 50-plus-year-old bolt action rifle was transformed into one of the sleekest, .303 British-caliber military carbines ever conceived for jungle warfare. In 2019, the haze of its mysterious, overlooked, 70-plus-year past was finally clearing up, with information located not far off its beaten path!

The 1960s were the "platinum decade" for military surplus fans when nearly every gun publication displayed flashy, informative advertisements of countless obsolete, often exotic rifles and pistols, holding surprises at every turn. Interarmco's red, white, and black Hunter's Lodge one- and two-page spreads unforgettably hosted by the bearded "Ye Olde Hunter" caught my imagination from age ten on up. Times were different, but this Alexandria, Virginia, firm was the success story of surplus guru Sam Cummings, whose arms scouts combed the world, cutting deals for surplus military arms and ammunition.

In August 1962, several gun periodicals carried a half-page advertisement: "The Far East Cracked at Last," followed by "Cal. .303 British 95 Mannlicher Jungle Carbine." Hailing from Indonesia, no one in the United States had ever observed these puzzling .303 carbines, and its short-rifle variant was a radical departure from the norm. The former was labeled with the unofficially sanctioned Jungle Carbine moniker due to its similar Enfield-like cosmetics. Unbelievably, only since the late 2010s did its identity become a reality, thanks to a long-time Indonesian friend of mine. A stroke of luck uncovered partial but fragile documents, disintegrating from age, in the dilapidated Dutch colonial arsenal's brick

A Riddle of the Cold War Era Deciphered!

GEORGE LAYMAN

Indonesia's Enigmatic
M95/51
Jungle Carbine

annex in Bandung, Java. Everything was in disarray for more than seven decades, with the shabby structure slated for demolition in 2020. However, a brief synopsis of the carbine's platform, the Dutch Mannlicher 1895, is appropriate.

KNOWN EARLY HISTORY
The Netherlands adopted and issued the 6.5x53R Mannlicher Repetier Geweer 1895 bolt-action rifle and carbine in the year of its namesake until 1940, with an estimated 470,000 guns produced. Identical in design and caliber to the earlier Romanian Mannlicher Model 1893, the G 95 is not to be confused with the straight-pull 1895 Austrian Mannlicher. The diversity of Holland's 1895 carbines was quite prolific, given the size of its army. Still, the wild card was sizeable military and police forces in two distant colonies — one in South East Asia, another in Dutch Guiana (Surinam) in South America. Compounding the confusion, the carbines were gradually upgraded as Old and New models (*Oud* and *Nieuw*), with those in the Netherlands proper having numerical designators, where the Dutch East Indies army or *Konilijk Nederlander Indische Leger* (KNIL) labeled them by type, i.e., *Artillerie, Genie* (engineer), Police (*Marchausee*), etc.

The tropical carbines were supplied with or without handguards and had drilled gas ports on both receiver sides as a reduction measure for pressures generated by the hot, humid climate. In addition, the bolts on new model

The original Model 1895 Dutch Mannlicher 6.5mm carbines were used by military reserves in Indonesia and by the National Police until 1955 in the original caliber. In this 1947 photograph, are Indonesian police recruits training during range practice with Artillerie or Engineer carbines. Photo: Tropen Museum

In 1951, when Indonesia began converting the 6.5mm M95 carbine to .303 British, it designed it as close as possible to the already established Enfield No.5, which was unofficially nicknamed the "Jungle Carbine." Aside from the caliber and the recoil pad, this duo has little in common. The M95/51 is the more streamlined of the two. However, practicality deems the Enfield a far better combat choice, given its detachable, 10-shot magazine. The M95/51 is relegated to single-shot status without the easily lost, five-round en-bloc clip. Additionally, the No.5 Enfield Jungle Carbine magazine need not be removed for reloading, and the shooter can use a stripper clip or load by hand from the top. Spare 10-shot magazines can also be carried. Jude Steele Collection

Aside from the original steel forearm nose cap, something gave this carbine a hint of suspicion as one of the original .303 conversions of 1941. Minus any evidence of a "scrubbed" Indonesian PSM Arsenal star on the chamber, this convinced collector Jude Steele and the author that it is one of the converted 1941 Australian M95 Dutch Mannlicher reworks. One of the many torn pages of the recovered documents specified an "N1" cartouche over the chamber, or a dotted circle of five and six punch marks as shown, stated such guns were converted to .303 British at either Paddington or Small Arms Factory Lithgow, Australia, before delivery to the KNIL. Jude Steele Collection

A pre-war photograph of a Dutch KNIL officer and constabulary unit with carbines. The local Indonesians proudly show their short sword or "Klewang," which was preferred over a bayonet for close-in combat. Photo: Tropen Museum

abruptly terminating shipments of supplies to the region. The lack of cartridge components required for indigenous ammunition production and repair parts for the *Artillerie Constructie Winkel* (ACW) or Artillery Manufacturing Works put the isolated colony in dire straits. Life had been good for decades in the Dutch East Indies until the Imperial Japanese army arrived.

Japan's expansionism became a sobering reality for the resource-rich Dutch colony. Following the declaration of war with Japan on December 8, 1941, an expedient minor arms upgrade that began six months earlier was completed. A limited number of 6.5mm M95 rifles and carbines were selected for conversion to the geographically widespread .303 British cartridge. By August 1941, Australia was to provide the KNIL with .303 British ammunition, but some confusion regarding this will be seen.

Additionally, a neutral, pre-December 7 United States saw Winchester already providing numerous calibers of small arms ammunition for the isolated colony. Furthermore, despite a contract of 70,000 .30-06-caliber Johnson semi-automatic rifles, few arrived with less than half completed. Earlier in June 1941, Australia's defense ministry met with Dutch Lt. General Gerardus Berenschot's officers and agreed to convert 3,775 Model 1895 Mannlicher rifles and carbines to .303 British. The production staff from Lithgow suggested that only 1,315 M1895 rifles and 2,460 carbines could be completed in the allocated timeframe.

NEW INFO DISCOVERED

Five years ago, the nearly discarded, large stack of pertinent, sticky old documentation in poor condition was fortunately discovered. Portions of it explained the reasoning behind this conversion venture.

Berenschot's logistics officers miscalculated the projected shortages of 6.5x53mm ammunition, primarily war reserve stocks. Though 3,775 conversions were minimal at best, re-chambering to the easily obtainable .303 cartridge was practical (Australia was concerned about Japanese incursions on its homeland). Pre-dating the conversion plan,

carbines were turned down. The straight-bolt rifles were mainly issued to Dutch regulars, with carbines often supplied to the smaller-statured Indonesian members of the KNIL.

Austria's Steyr OEWG manufactured the Model 1895 for the Netherlands

until 1904, following Dutch licensing for domestic production at Hembrug Armory in Zaandam, Holland. Geopolitical circumstances gave this near-obsolete military arm a second wind. Germany's occupation of the Netherlands on May 15, 1940, affected KNIL's self-sufficiency,

Two Interarmco/Hunter's Lodge M95/51 carbines; 1952 s/n 1083 and 1953 s/n 4335, the latter missing its sight blade, shown with a No.5 Enfield Jungle Carbine. The M95/51 rubber recoil pad versions have serial-numbered buttplate bases, like the conventional steel buttplate guns. Fortunately, these 1962 M95/51 imports came complete with the Indonesian PSM star on both the receiver ring and above the chamber beneath the handguard. Author and Jude Steele Collections

Uncommon examples of the M95/51 Carbines are those with a year stamped on the upper chamber. The example here, originally delivered and dated 1914, has a 1952 conversion, is re-serialized as A 709, and could have been a rifle at one time. The year "1937," marked over the upper chamber, tells us it is one of the 6.5x53mm Model 95 guns refurbished and shortened during the pre-war contingency upgrade of the mid to late-1930s. Author Collection

the late 1930s saw the KNIL conduct a "war emergency" refurbishment of several-thousand Dutch Model 95 rifles, many re-barreled to carbine length. (A year stamp typically identifies such guns over the upper chamber.) The KNIL was familiar with the .303 British, using it in the Vickers machine guns and other arms. Fortunately, the 6.5x53mm Dutch and the .303 British have similar head and rim dimensions, the latter compatible with the 6.5x53 en-bloc clip.

Also, in June, Berenschot requested 1.5 million rounds of .303 British ammunition to be included for delivery in August. The payment was substituted by a commodities exchange of natural resources such as rubber, tea, and cinchona that Australia needed. My Dutch-Indonesian colleague, Jan Roeningen, explained why the entire agreement lacked precise details from June to December 1941. The single master copy in English & Dutch, specifying all particulars of the ammunition and conversions, was destroyed in General Berenschot's fatal plane crash in October.

Former New Zealander Bruce Carlsen's father worked at SAF Lithgow before World War II. He kept a diary that states that, on September 9, 1941, the KNIL guns were delivered to Sydney, Australia's Paddington ordnance workshop. Under the supervision of Captain George Brooke, all guns were to be disassembled, with only the barrels sent to the Small Arms Factory Lithgow for conversion to .303 British. Carlsen notes that re-chambered rifle barrels were recorded marked with solely an "N1" with carbines having a "Circular" dotted punch mark over the chamber minus normal proofing cartouches. They were shipped from Sydney in November for return to ACW in Bandung. Many historians believe that the guns never made it back

to Indonesia, and the freighter sunk due to Japanese activity in the region. As will be seen, the ship arrived before the KNIL surrendered to Japan's Imperial army on March 10, 1942.

The three-plus-year Japanese occupation was brutal for incarcerated Dutch nationals who didn't escape to Australia. The Imperial army used ACW for overhauling its weapons, renaming it *Dai Ichi Kozo* (First Manufacturing). Following the war's end in 1945, the Dutch re-christened *Leger Productie Bedrijven* (LPB) or Army Production Companies. My colleague Jan stressed that a violent independence movement arose after the Japanese occupation from 1945 to 1949 in the war-weary country. In 1946, British General Louis Earl Mountbat-

Most of the ODIN M95/51 carbines in .303 caliber were of the steel buttplate category, as those having the classical Enfield Jungle Carbine-style rubber buttpad were far fewer in number. This example, s/n A1611, has all matching parts aside from the bolt and magazine assembly. It lacks the triggerguard locking screws, usually standard on rubber buttpad versions. The pad lacks a ribbed configuration and has lost its pliability due to exposure to hot, humid temperatures. Author Collection

The rarest Indonesian M95/51 conversion gun is the short-rifle, which first arrived in the United States with the Hunter's Lodge carbines. These uniquely modified rifles were made in 1954 and 1955, and all work was completed at the PSM plant in Bandung. The fragmented, incomplete production log states they were discontinued at the 3,900 to 4,000 mark. This version, with a shorter, 26-inch barrel, turned-down bolt, and rubber buttpad, made for a handier, contemporary-appearing rifle. Some were sold with the older, straight bolt stem, likely by the importer. The machined, scalloped left receiver wall is a clue of a significant modification to older rifles undertaken. Thus, all markings aside from the serial number were neatly stamped within. Jude Steele Collection

ten assumed command of the region to maintain order. Annoyed by the insistence of the United States and Australia supporting Indonesian independence, the querulous Dutch had finally tired of resisting, with Queen Julianna granting sovereignty to the new Republic of Indonesia on December 27, 1949. Specific military equipment, including small arms, ammunition, and repair parts, was left in place.

Regarding the doubts about the 1941 .303 Dutch Mannlicher 95 conversions, evidence attesting to this was discovered in the late Winter of 1950, before the official turnover of military equipment to an independent Indonesia. Jan noted that surviving KNIL property books annotate multiple counts of military arms conducted in March and April 1950. Excluding 6.5x53-caliber rifles and carbines, the KNIL ledgers indicated in a "*modification/remarks*

column" a typed notation stating, "*1,486-Nederlands Mannlicher 1895, kaliber 7.7 Brits - Australische conversie / 'A' conversie karabijnen/geweren.*" (sic) or, 1,486 Dutch Mannlicher 1895, caliber .303 British-Australian conversion / 'A' Conversion Carbines/Rifles, as being; "On Hand," (no mention of rifle versus carbine numbers).

The KNIL recorded this in the Dutch language, sufficient evidence that this was all that remained. Indeed, independence-minded natives helped themselves to everything and anything unsecured that would shoot at the war's end, not to mention guns taken by the Imperial Japanese army earlier on, deploying to other locales in the Southeast Asia/Pacific region.*

The Lithgow-converted guns were recorded on post-war inventories. Less than 1,500 is a noticeable reduction from the original 3,775. However, a replay of the past would again become a reality. With Great Britain pursuing communist guerillas during the Malayan Emergency, stocks of .303 British ammunition were commonly encountered. Despite obsolescence, the Dutch 6.5x53mm was completely phased out by 1955, but significant ammunition stores remained scattered throughout Indonesia.

In 1950, the new President Sukarno welcomed contemporary foreign military assistance. Australia, in particular, was Indonesia's strongest supporter of its independence and had superb relations with the country but was shunned and

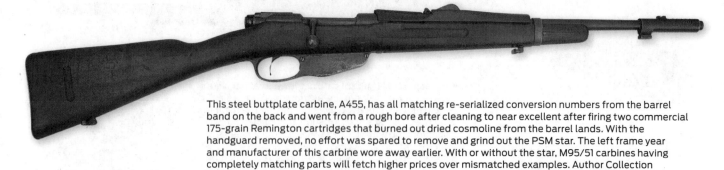

This steel buttplate carbine, A455, has all matching re-serialized conversion numbers from the barrel band on the back and went from a rough bore after cleaning to near excellent after firing two commercial 175-grain Remington cartridges that burned out dried cosmoline from the barrel lands. With the handguard removed, no effort was spared to remove and grind out the PSM star. The left frame year and manufacturer of this carbine wore away earlier. With or without the star, M95/51 carbines having completely matching parts will fetch higher prices over mismatched examples. Author Collection

boycotted by the Dutch after WWII for its pro-independence stance. New weaponry began replacing the post-war hodgepodge of surrendered Japanese ordnance and other small arms. Unfortunately, rifles with completely interchangeable ammunition remained in short supply, especially for the new rural military reservists and *"Polisi Nasional Indonesia"* units in out-of-the-way areas of the vast archipelago. The idea of the old 1941 Australian program became a partial solution.

Recommendations from Australian advisors, Dutch-educated former KNIL Indonesian officers, including Generals Abdul Nasution and Gatot Soebroto, local skilled machinists, and officers of Java's Silliwangi Division, agreed that the *"konversi bahasa 7.7 Australia"* (7.7x56mm the metric definition of the .303) still held water. This time, an abundance of Geweer M95 carbines and rifles would see work performed locally.

On April 29, 1950, the Netherlands transferred the LFB armory's weapons and machinery to the Indonesian military. Thus, it became the *Pabrik Senjata dan Meslu* (Arms and Munitions Factory), or PSM. In 1989, Jan located a partial information trove labeled "1951-55 conversion production log books," or; *Buku log Direktif Konversi Edsi Pertama 1951-55,* emphasizing large quantities of parts and component swapping that frequently occurred. The precise numbers of parts used and other details were missing.

The re-boring of 6.5mm barrels to .303 British became PSM's first successful small arms project. However, in June 1950, 12 members of PSM traveled to Australia with 800 6.5 barrels to conduct a test run of the program. After completion, the barrels numbered 1 to 800 were stamped on the lower chamber. The Indonesian team was loaned specific Lithgow equipment required for the conversion. Nine Australian technicians accompanied them on their return, assisting in setting up and training the Indonesian workforce. Fortunately, surviving records list 13,999 conversions, of which 9,094 were M95 carbines and approximately 4,905 modified short-rifles to be reworked. Another information coup was an incomplete string-bound 60-page Indonesian manual dated 30.3.1951, RE: Plans & Procedure Directives, stating, "… only best quality guns, or those with serviceable parts and components, in highest grade condition must carefully be selected for inspection before disassembly for conversion…." (sic)

Numerous details of the 95/51 conversion remained unknown outside Indonesia and largely forgotten. Poor archival maintenance caused most documents to become fragile and stained, mostly disintegrating on touch, all dated March 1951 to September 1955.**

DOCUMENTS REVEAL UNKNOWN HISTORY

As a blueprint assessment technician, Jan visited the old Dutch Annex twice, working at PINDAD 27 years earlier (PINDAD replaced PSM). Returning in 2019 was a huge favor when I asked, but unlike 20 years earlier, much disappeared through water leakage and storms. Several pages — strewn about yet still

This Steyr 1896 carbine, converted in 1953 with its "A" prefix followed by a punch dot, is sporadically observed on a per-gun basis and noted in the log directive, which states that guns were marked as such at the Surabaya factory until eventually, this step was eliminated. Jude Steele Collection

intact — were photographed, with many hand-drawn sketches of compensators having "95/51" scribbled, a significance not yet understood with scattered notes challenging to read. The icing on the cake, overlooked years earlier, was a satisfactorily preserved serialization column ledger stuck to a corroded drawer that at

The most noticeable feature of the M95/51 is the varied compensator styles. Both compensator production and marking were done in two locations — the main PSM factory in Bandung and the older Surabaya armory 478 miles away in Eastern Java. The earliest 1951 production guns had the banded, diametrical stop mark, or witness cut, behind the front sight base. Essentially, this is where the compensator has its rear internal shroud stop point. Above the bayonet lug platform, the tapered pins were force-inserted just ahead of the front sight base, equating to 2 inches from the front of the device to the muzzle of the barrel inside the compensator. Scarce carbines such as s/n A. 65 differ immensely with only the caliber and serial number; both marked vertically in line with the barrel, minus the Pancasila Star.

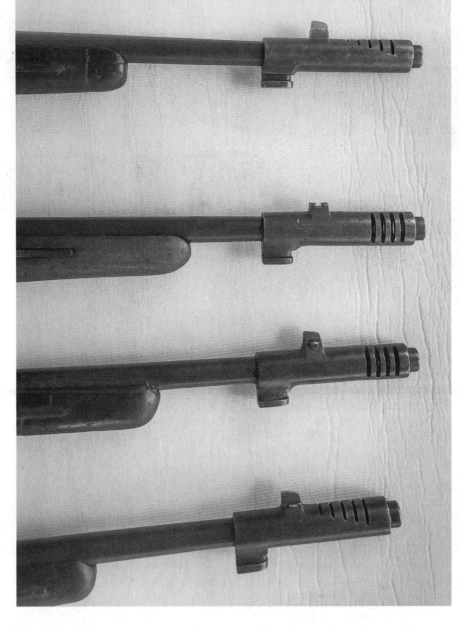

Using the original Model 1895 terminology, 1951 being the first production year, local designation confirms it as "M95/51 Karabin/Senapan-Pendek" (carbine/short-rifle). Strangely, modern-day career Indonesian military or police personnel don't recognize the term. Inquiring with historians at PINDAD about M95/51 archive data, Jan was told it was "Certainly an early PSM project, but a scrapped gun of no concern." Their complete disinterest compelled him to locate all the information independently. Imports of 1962 show several rifles appearing unissued, with a few carbines — essentially a mixture of refurbished guns and parts that don't identify with original 1895 Dutch variations. The receiver rings were marked "Cal. 7.7" at the top, over a geometrical star, with tiny, stylized letters of "PSM" in the center of the pentagon.

The production year is beneath the star, with carbines having an "A" prefix before the new serial number. The ledger's preface page noted this barely legible statement: "… *the letter 'A' identifies model 95-51 karabin, as a symbol to honor Australian help to our nation* …" *(sic)* — thus, the meaning of the "A" prefix. Handguard removal revealed a second PSM star marking, meaning the barrel was converted in Indonesia. Where absent, it indicates they are one of the 800 barrels converted and serial numbered in Australia during the 1950 test run. Removal of the stock reveals the serial number on such guns.

Another noticeable addition to the M95/51 carbines and rifles is what appears as an in-the-white replacement bolt-head, with a two-digit number not matching any other numbers. I was told that a bolt-conversion directive interjected the German word for "bolt head." Written in Indonesian, it stated, "… bolts will be replaced with a new '*Verschlusskopf*' (bolt head) due to excessive…[illegible] … [illegible] …" (sic). The remaining paragraph was also illegible. I conjecture that it continued as '… wear or pitting on original bolt faces requires the thicker .303 rim [and] slight enlargement of the extractor.' If correct, such attentiveness took a very knowledgeable individual to address this.

A pitted, worn bolt face can be a hid-

long last provided the official designation of these conversions by the Indonesian military. Never known in the United States, it is the *sine qua non* of today's military surplus bolt-action world!

Fortunately, numerous pages were intact. Hence this first post-independence arm was christened the "*Model Sembilan Puluh Lima/Lima Puluh Satu Senapan Pendek-Karabin Konversi 7.7/Australia,*" or *Model 95/51 Carbine- Short-rifle, 7.7/ Australian Conversion,* indeed alien terminology to American arms scholars. Still, finally, the accurate description of this carbine and short-rifle is known at long last!

Deciphering Jungle Carbine Serial Numbers

These three ODIN import M95/51 carbines display subtle but noticeable differences. Most apparent are the font sizes and how they were stamped, which tells us they were marked by different workmen with various stamping dies. Two of the three alpha-numeric die sets obtained from Australia had been broken by 1953.

Below is a partial chart of 1951–1955 carbine conversion production years and quantities. Though incomplete, the remaining original documents show months and numbers, but space limitations do not permit more than a sampling.

All three guns have matching serial numbers. The production months for these 1952-produced carbines are February for A455, March for A709, and July for A1611 at the far right. Close observation of the bolt stem flats reveals file marks indicating that the original serial was scrubbed before re-numbering for accounting/identification purposes. A 1962-imported Dutch Mannlicher M95/51 "Jungle Carbine" (top) compared to a steel buttplate carbine imported in 1983 (bottom) visibly displays what oc-curs when even minimal maintenance is overlooked. The cosmoline-like preser-vative dried into the wood, creating an epoxy-like stain, given long periods of extreme humidity exposure in Sumatra's climate. This rarely seen 1954-marked carbine was close to the end of produc-tion and is a scarce year to locate. Though a mismatch, it is one of the few with the Indonesian star on the bolt. The elusive "N1" mark over the chamber on this car-bine tells us it was once a rifle part of the 1941 Australian re-bored barrels. Jude Steele Collection, Photos: Stephen Eisel

den hazard on any older bolt-action rifle, incipient to hairline cracks. The PSM staff used original Mannlicher 1895 schematic illustrations in German, possibly under-stood by Dutch speakers but problematic for Indonesian machinists/engineers un-less previously familiar with this weapon.

UNUSUAL FEATURES

When firing these re-chambered guns, they display a bizarre feature: spent cases reveal a double neck! This anomaly is likely due to a worn or undersized chamber reamer. (The 6.5x53 neck length is .297 instead of .332 of the .303 British.) Hence, a portion of the remaining metal in the throat was not entirely removed. Besides the gas escape from the receiver, an M95/51 carbine's most recognizable feature is the muzzle brake/compensa-tor. PSM engineers designed this clever, ported device to reduce recoil, and it is generally secured to the barrel by two tapered pins above the bayonet lug. The

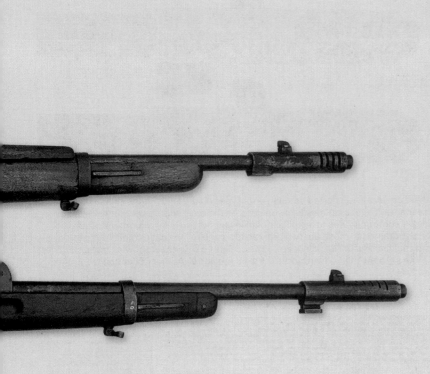

1951–1955 CARBINE CONVERSION

PRODUCTION YEARS	QUANTITIES
January to September 1951	Serial numbers January A.01 to A110-/ February A111 to A131 / March A134 to A140 (A.132 and A.133 are not recorded) [Serial numbers 1 through 90 have banded witness marks behind the front sight base but are devoid of a compensator]. Monthly production quantities were very inconsistent in 1951.
January to December 1952	Serial numbers A111 to A3799 (the exact final production number page is missing from the PSM register.)
January to December 1953	Serial numbers A3800 to A8989
March 1954 to January 1955	Serial numbers A8990 to A9094 (Surviving records show these two years merged on one running ledger; there is some overlap due to missing pages. However, the year 1955 is found on these final carbines from January of its final production month and are extremely rare, doubling their value if in very good to excellent condition with matching numbers. The M95/51 short-rifle serial numbers are a separate range: 4-0001 to 4-003975 with Model 1954 guns completed until September 1955. The four-dash prefix was retained on guns dated and manufactured in 1955. (Overlapping here is possible. June through September 1955, production guns have serial numbers out of sequence. The pages in production logs are missing regarding this.)

pins were then smoothly machined flush. Australian technicians recommended the compensator addition during their stay at PSM. On November 13, 1950, the Indonesian staff independently completed the first barrel conversions.

An odd trait of the compensators is the inconsistency of the ported vents, cut by a slide slit saw, and many differ immensely. Some have upper or side-slotted vents, others drilled circular vents. In reality, recoil is noticeably reduced, much less, in fact, than the heavier Enfield No.5 Jungle Carbine. A footnote in the string-bound ledger states that 2,970 carbines have the "cup style" Enfield rubber recoil pad buttplate. Additionally, a parts inventory leaf states that, in October 1952, an Australian depot shipped a small supply of original No.5 Enfield Jungle Carbine rubber recoil buttplates (made at Fazakerly, UK). The nine Australians assisted the PSM staff in reworking a steel stamping machine to create a similar buttplate tailored to the Mannlicher G95 buttstock. The PSM hard rubber pads have either ribbed or smooth pads.

The surviving documents reveal that the compensator assembly and markings on receivers and actions also took place at the old Surabaya plant, 478 miles from the main PSM factory. The Surabaya factory was used until 1932, when operations relocated to Bandung — another reason for the erratic quality of markings on some M95/51 carbines. Buttstocks on most resemble original M95 Police, with Cavalry carbines having rounded forearm tips requiring less labor than shortening a rifle stock. (On some guns, the original steel forearm cap is left as-is.)

Indonesia's shortage of arms of interchangeable calibers existed until 1956. However, the M95/51 remained in issue until the 1960s. In today's market, the last batch of ODIN imports in both original 6.5 Dutch and modified .303 British calibers are all over the map condition-wise. Ironically, many have bores remaining dark after several brush scrubs. But after three or four rounds, dried grease is burned out, and the bore condition can improve (however, rifling on most is very shallow).

The ODIN imports have another downside, unlike the 1962 imports. The PSM/Indonesian Star (Pancasila) is ground off on the receiver and barrel.

THE COLLECTOR'S MARKET

The M95/51 was supposedly withdrawn from service in 1961 and sold as surplus in 1962, with most American buyers believing they were gone forever. It was a complete surprise when more were discovered in 1976–79 in northern Sumatra, where Acehnese insurgents

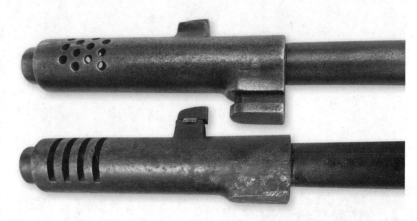

Overall, there are two basic ported compensator types on the M95/51; the circular and the slit-sawn variants. The example sans bayonet lug on the base was possibly uninstalled or disengaged at some point due to insufficient fluxing during sweating. Faintly visible on the lug's base, as common to most, are two tapered locking pins, the bases machined near invisibly flush at the final finish. The pair have been highlighted with chalk showing placement location. Both securely fit into twin slotted cuts on the barrel. Author Collection

Shown is the advertisement that started a new area of military surplus arms. The August 1962 Hunter's Lodge advertisement shown in major gun periodicals was offered in two different .303-caliber carbines and a rifle, neither of which originated in the U.K. or its dominions. Also included was the long obsolete 9.4mm 1874 Dutch revolver that was 40 years old by World War I yet still in use in the Dutch East Indies. From the age of 12, this sharp-looking, very un-Enfield "jungle carbine" became an immediate must-have for the author but took him nearly 45 years to locate.

Unlike the Hunter's Lodge advertisement stating "special flash hider-compensator," the photo reveals this is no flash hider in any sense! At 60 yards, 1952 British 180-grain Mk VII .303 surplus ball used in two different M95/51 carbines produced identical results, both keyholing, which was not the fault of an improper twist but perhaps by worn, shallow rifling not stabilizing the projectile. Jude Steele/Author Photos

Lighter than the Enfield of its name-sake, the handy Indonesian M95/51 .303 Jungle Carbine has been seen as late as the 1990s in the hands of Dutch or Australian ex-pats in areas of New Guinea for hunting medium-size game. Many of these carbines are still available in various places throughout the region. Photo: Dianna Kelly

carried numerous old .303 conversions during the Free Aceh Movement. These guns came from an overlooked storage cache at Palembang in the south and spent years without maintenance before being located and ultimately imported. The Suharto government scrubbed the star before export.

Condition-wise, the 1962 M95/51 batches significantly outdid the last 1980's lot, but fortunately, the appearance of the second batch increased shooter and collector availability. The Dutch/ Indonesian M95/51 may be one of the most-streamlined military bolt actions ever rebuilt from a long-obsolete design, but cosmetics outweigh performance; without the proper en-bloc clip, it's no more than a single-shot rifle.

CONCLUSION

Historically, these 1950s non-British-made .303-caliber guns were used in several violent conflicts of the 1950s to the 1970s and beyond, from the first and second communist Malayan Emergency, the Western Papua Dispute, Indonesia-Malaysia Confrontation, the Borneo troubles of the 1970s, to Indonesia's communist PKI fiasco — truly a firearm of several virulent periods throughout the Cold War. The M95/51 carbine and short-rifles are, unquestionably, an awakened sleeper, somewhat misunderstood by the most advanced student of the military surplus world. Still, most importantly, we military gun collectors now know their proper terminology!

I am indebted to Jan Roeningen of Balikpapan, Indonesia, a great friend since 1970 whom I met while I was in the U.S. Army on a TDY mission in Borneo. His assistance was priceless in breaking the mysterious M95/51 riddle. I sincerely appreciate Bruce Carlsen for sharing his father's 1941 work diary notes. And thanks to my cousin Jude Steele for photographing his carbines and 1954 short-rifle. ⑨Ⓓ

---

* The Japanese used the term *Dai Ichi Kozo* to repair their weapons and re-bore and re-chamber unknown numbers of Dutch Geweer 95 6.5 rifles to their rimless 7.7x58 Japanese cartridge. That included possibly some of the 1941 Australian .303 conversions, as the two cartridges have some similarities. Some 7.7 Japanese-caliber Dutch M95 conversions were captured by U.S. Marines on Guadalcanal, significantly magnifying this phenomenon.

** The author's contact, Jan, verified the partial 1954 and 1955 output and QA registers had shown few converted carbines were made in these years, ending in January 1955. The highest production was in 1952 and 1953. Quantity-wise, only one-quarter of M95/51 carbine production has steel cup rubber buttpads. Some ODIN-import carbines have no muzzle compensator, with the vertically marked caliber and serial number markings, sans date and star, a mixture of the 800 Australian test barrels from 1950 and some from the 1941 batch. Only those barrels reworked in Indonesia have the star over the chamber.

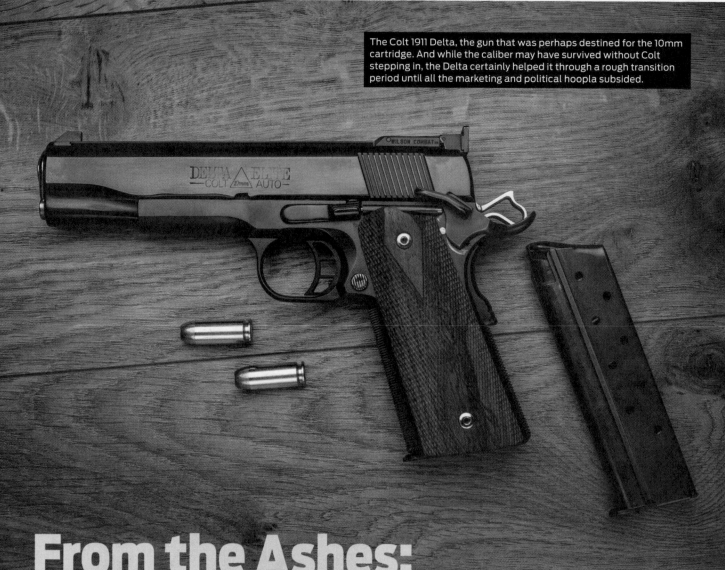

The Colt 1911 Delta, the gun that was perhaps destined for the 10mm cartridge. And while the caliber may have survived without Colt stepping in, the Delta certainly helped it through a rough transition period until all the marketing and political hoopla subsided.

From the Ashes:
The 10mm Auto

Delivering horsepower in spades, the 10mm is the business on pork, deer, and more.

❯DICK WILLIAMS

With its 6-inch barrel and slide, the Glock 40 Gen 4 looked and handled more like the handguns the author had previously carried afield. He expressed no complaints about its light weight.

Bob Radecki's big buck taken on a winter deer hunt in the Midwest with a standard-size Glock 40 in 10mm.

Few calibers have experienced the roller coaster ride like the 10mm did in its early years. When first introduced in the 1980s, it was endorsed by Jeff Cooper, arguably the defensive handgun guru of the late 20th century. Many referred to the new caliber as "the perfect Ten!" To further enhance its appeal, a new company had been formed to manufacture a pistol that would handle the powerhouse semi-auto round: Dornaus & Dixon. The caliber and the new pistol (the Bren Ten) were a collaboration between Dornaus & Dixon and Cooper.

THE EARLY YEARS

When Dornaus & Dixon went bankrupt, it was not the death knell for the 10mm cartridge. Colt's 1911 was, and still is, a superb platform for the then-new poster child magnum of defensive pistol craft. Lightweight, high-capacity polymer frame striker-fired pistols were in their infancy and perhaps not ready to tackle the 10mm, but both Smith & Wesson and

Colt were fully qualified. After the FBI's famous "Miami Massacre" in the late 1980s and the agency's decision to adopt the new 10mm cartridge, interest in the caliber again skyrocketed. For various reasons, the prestigious law enforcement organization changed its mind and switched to another caliber. I believe Colt kept the 10mm alive when it produced a 10mm-caliber 1911 called the "Delta Elite." A Colt Delta and an early Smith & Wesson Model 1006 were my first ventures into the world of 10mm handguns.

The Delta Elite was a solidly built, full-size Colt 1911 meant for hard work but lacking in some refinements that graced customized 1911s of that era. The S&W 1006 was about the same size as the Delta (both used single-stack magazines), but the Smith could be fired single and double action.

I was enthralled with custom 1911s then and sent the Colt to Smoking Hole Pistol for some fancy embellishments. Upon return, the gun ran flawlessly with one exception. It had been fitted with an oversized thumb safety which was in vogue then, and when I thumbed the safety off and tried to shoot with my thumb remaining on top of the safety lever, I could not depress the grip safety. This was not uncommon back then and had been reported earlier by Jeff Cooper from Gunsite. Aside from that, both guns ran smoothly. The only flaw with the 1006 was that I had trouble maintaining accuracy when firing the first shot double action. I enjoyed time spent with the two 10mms but ultimately relegated the Colt to a "Safe Queen" and traded the Smith for another "must-have" handgun.

10MM RESURGENCE

Today, after some lean years, the 10mm caliber has staged a resurgence. You don't see many being selected for concealed carry in heavily populated areas because of the gun's size, plus the 10's power doesn't lend itself to compact guns. But like the .41 and .44 Magnums in the revolver days, some see enough advantages in its enhanced power to warrant packing one for daily carry. And with the caliber chambered in lighter-weight, striker-fired pistols by respected manufacturers today, it's worth another look.

For this article and a planned pig hunt, I obtained three sample 10mm handguns. Two were striker-fired pistols: a Glock Model 40 Gen 4 and a Springfield XD Elite, topped with red-dot sights, today's current accessory rage. The XD had a standard 4.5-inch barrel, while the Glock Model 40 slide and barrel were 6 inches. The third gun was a TISAS full-size 1911 with a 5-inch barrel/slide and adjustable iron sights. Dragging my Smoking Hole Colt Delta from the vault gave me four guns to compare.

All four pistols proved 100% reliable in functioning, except for the customized Colt that required me to shoot with my thumb underneath the safety lever. All produced 1.75- to 4-inch groups at 25 yards depending on what ammo they preferred and my level of competency on a particular day. As expected, the dots had an edge in accuracy (again, depending on the ammo used). Still, the TISAS

Extremely high quality and an affordable price are two hallmarks of the TISAS 1911 chambered in 10mm.

The new "Hog Hammer" from FCG was not available in time for the hog hunt but immediately caught the author's fancy upon returning to Gunsite.

yielded more than acceptable iron sight accuracy, as later proved in our "field tests." No machine rest was used in the accuracy testing; it was a matter of resting the forearms on a range bag placed on a table — about as stable a position as I can ever achieve when hunting. It doesn't tell me how accurate the gun is but instead how well it will perform in my hands in real-world conditions.

I've been a happy 1911 fan for 60 years

but never fired one with a red dot. Still, I've recently started using these new-fangled optics on hunting handguns with noticeably improved results at ranges past 25 yards. My experience shooting bulls-eye competition in my early adult years convinced me that a well-built 1911 will perform with (perhaps outperform?) the best handguns. I suspect most handgunners' results would vary depending on which gun fit the shooter best or which

The author (right) and DoubleTap CEO Mike McNett on an earlier pig hunt with a custom Springfield 10mm 1911 at the Fort Rock Ranch.

If you carry a Springfield 10mm daily, you'll have no adjustments to make should you wander off the pavement and into a more rural environment.

gun they had used the most.

While our field test crew had been assembled based chiefly on their social skills (after all, it was a pig-hunting trip with good friends), all were experienced handgun shooters. Two were instructors at Gunsite Academy, and one was a police firearms instructor in California. Our group also included Bob Radecki, Glock's National Sales Manager. All had experience in handgun hunting. As expected, Radecki used his standard-size Glock 40 topped with a red dot. Our lady Gunsite instructor and retired police officer Aimee Grant used the Glock. The other Gunsite instructor, still an active duty police officer in central California, chose the red-dot-equipped long-slide Glock. The southern California firearms instructor picked the TISAS 1911 with iron sights.

All ammo was provided by Double-Tap and loaded with 200-grain hard-cast bullets except for some 200-grain Controlled Expansion loads used in an earlier deer hunt. While deer are reason-

Gunsite instructor Aimee Grant nails her Fort Rock Ranch pig with a single round from her Glock 10mm.

ably close in body size to pigs, they are thinner-skinned animals without the gristle armor plates carried by the larger boars. Since the pig-hunting ranch did have some Russian boars known for their attitude, we opted for maximum penetration in case we encountered the mythical Hogzilla. (As an interesting side note, DoubleTap's CEO and founder, Mike McNett, is an avid 1911 10mm fan and started the company a couple of decades ago with 10mm loads. Perhaps he knew something then that the rest of us didn't!)

Our hunt occurred on Fort Rock Ranch, located on Interstate 40, a few miles east of Kingman, Arizona. Owner Scott Dunton stocks the ranch with various pig species, plus a few bison, Asian buffalos, and various sheep. A two-day, guided pig hunt is not the equivalent of a 6-month safari across Africa with Teddy Roosevelt. Still, it makes for a fun weekend, a great first hunt for kids, can be scheduled year-round and includes exceptionally comfortable accommoda-

tions. Another factor that pleased me is that Scott is heavily committed to hunting activities supporting American veterans.

PORK SHOPPING WITH THE TEN
By late Friday afternoon, when all hunters were satisfied that their weapons were properly dialed in with the DoubleTap hardcast bullet loads, there was enough daylight left for a quick hunt. While pigs are not hard for the guides to find on the ranch, shooting skills are strictly the responsibility of the individual hunter. The first kill went to Bob Radecki. He set the bar high with a one-shot, dropped-on-the-spot kill using his Glock. That night we toasted his shooting skill and wrote songs about his hunting prowess.

The following day, the remaining hunters ventured forth with our young guide to fill the freezers. Nothing changed; our guide found pigs in different places, and the level of shooting skill displayed was high. By early afternoon, another three

pigs were down, dropped on the spot with one clean shot each. I've been on many handgun pig hunts, but I've never seen four consecutive pigs taken without at least one or two running off some distance before expiring. Admittedly, the 10mm is a superior performer, but as always, there is no substitute for marksmanship. So much for high-capacity magazines!

Given the background experience of the participating hunters, I was not surprised that Glock was the primary weapon selected. But considering the operating similarities of the two striker-fired pistols available, I expected (and hoped) to see the Springfield XD Elite in action. Had I not been the self-designated photographer with some pork still in the freezer, I would have used the XD. The Springfield feels larger than the other pistols (except the long-slide Glock) and more compatible in terms of ergonomics. Both of these characteristics can prove beneficial in a self-loading pistol when stepping up in power to a cartridge like the 10mm.

In addition, at least for me, the Springfield's trigger seemed easier to keep the gun aligned on target throughout the long trigger pull. This is in no way a negative comment on Glock. My number one gun approved for concealed carry in California is a GEN 2 Glock Model 19, and it is a superb weapon for fast defensive use. But the ergonomics of the red-dot-equipped Springfield make a difference in the precise placement of longer-range shots.

HANDGUN CHOICE AND EDC

I've not paid much attention to revolvers chambered in 10mm simply because the cartridge was inspired and created with self-defense in mind and semi-autos as the designated platform. When it comes to defensive scenarios, autoloaders have a significant advantage in fast reloads. Even so, I love hunting with a single-action revolver. For those comfortable carrying these old-fashioned "wheelguns" and whose travels take them beyond the downtown streets of Metropolis, Ruger's Blackhawk will handle the 10mm's power in a relatively compact and slender single action. And while the single action is a slow revolver to reload, it does allow you to utilize partial reloads of one or two rounds during a break in the action.

During our sessions with single-action revolvers at Gunsite Academy, we use the "reload as you shoot" technique. Double-action revolvers require moon clips to properly headspace the rimless 10mm cases. Reloads are an all-or-nothing proposition, which can result in you throwing away unfired rounds remaining in the moon clip. Bad tactics!

Two fairly recent Gunsite classes have resulted in my re-evaluation of the 10mm cartridge for everyday carry. The first was "Vehicle Defense," which is not about defending your vehicle but rather using your vehicle to protect yourself. Americans spend a great deal of time in and around automobiles. If a threat presents itself while you're behind the wheel, the preferred solution is to hit the gas and use all those horses to escape. If flight is not an option, any available vehicle can and should be used for cover. If the encounter degenerates into a gunfight, having a 10mm could turn the tide by converting the bad guy's "cover" into "concealment" with penetration abilities well beyond that of a typical street-approved handgun.

The other class was "Active Shooter." One of the scenarios in this class involved

TABLE 1. TISAS 1911 WITH IRON SIGHTS

LOAD	AVG. VELOCITY (FPS)	AVG. GROUP (IN.)
180-gr. FMJ	1,205	4.0
DTAP 155 gr.	1,278	3.5
Federal 180 gr.	1,309	2.5
DTAP 200-gr. hardcast	1,181	—

Five-shot groups at 25 yards. Chrony Chronograph 10 feet from the muzzle.
Ambient Temperature: 43 degrees F.

J.D. Donnellon (left) and John Hall put some pork chops in the freezer. Both pigs dropped on the spot.

suicidal terrorists armed with rifles working through a shopping center, shooting everyone encountered. Given the time spent in shopping centers, particularly by teens, we're talking about a "target-rich" environment for terrorists. Since the sounds of gunshots carry, you might receive an early enough warning to leave the mall. If the shooters block your exit path, you might take comfort in having a 10mm with a red dot capable of making precise, longer-range shots.

After the hunt, our happy group of pig hunters returned to Gunsite, where I spent some time with the new semi-custom/production 1911 chambered in 10mm called the "Hog Hammer." Dave Fink of Finks Custom Gunsmithing, the resident smithy at Gunsite, built the gun. The pistol is a forged and hand-fitted government model 1911 Series 70 with several features of interest to handgun hunters and armed citizens. Most noticeable is the two-tone smooth satin Cerakote finish that defies the degradation effects of nasty weather and clumsy hunt-

ers. The match trigger and barrel, along with a full-blown reliability package, will be appreciated by citizens from all walks of life. The Holoson red-dot sight is fitted (with no adaptor plate) to the slide and co-witnessed with excellent adjustable sights. Could this combination of gun and caliber be the mythical "Handgun for All Seasons?" Unfortunately, it was unavailable for our hunt, but I promise a thorough investigation.

CONCLUSION

Since the 10mm was introduced almost four decades ago, the number of citizens who carry weapons daily has grown

unbelievably. That does nothing to account for the enhanced popularity of the "perfect 10." For those seeking to protect themselves from typical street crimes, the more compact 9mm handguns are still the dominant choice. But for those who don't live in densely populated areas where total concealment of one's firearm is perhaps as important as 100% reliability, the 10mm is making converts. Rural residents encounter animal threats, some of which are of a size that suggests a larger caliber than the nine. If your state allows open carry, concealment is a much lesser concern. I say "lesser concern" rather than "no

TABLE 2. GLOCK 40 LONG-SLIDE WITH RED-DOT

LOAD	AVG. VELOCITY (FPS)	AVG. GROUP (IN.)
180-gr. FMJ	1,209	2.5
DTAP 155 gr.	1,269	2.0
Federal 180 gr.	1,279	4.0
DTAP 200-gr. hardcast	1,175	—

Five-shot groups at 25 yards. Chrony Chronograph 10 feet from the muzzle.
Ambient Temperature: 43 degrees F.

Once you try shooting from a moving vehicle, you'll wonder if the cops and robbers ever hit anything in those great car chases shown in the movies. But on the off chance they had to shoot through a vehicle, it's hard to imagine they wouldn't have wished for a 10mm.

If you prefer revolvers, Ruger makes the 10mm in both single- and double-action, as an alternative to the 1911-style autoloader.

TABLE 3. SPRINGFIELD XD WITH RED-DOT

LOAD	AVG. VELOCITY (FPS)	AVG. GROUP (IN.)
180-gr. FMJ	1,193	3.0
DTAP 155 gr.	1,279	1.75
Federal 180 gr.	1,239	3.75

Five-shot groups at 25 yards. Chrony Chronograph 10 feet from the muzzle.
Ambient Temperature: 43 degrees F.

concern" because while a visible firearm might deter a criminal, it identifies you immediately as a primary threat to his nefarious plan. Engagements can also occur at longer ranges where shooting proficiency can significantly improve using a larger handgun rather than an ultracompact. Crimes like rape, robbery, and carjacking are close encounters, typically occurring at contact distance where the only barrier between you and the bad guy might be your car's window. An active shooter event might involve longer distances and barriers being used as cover. In a contest requiring penetration, the 10mm wins.

No one can predict the events that will take place in a gunfight. Murphy's Law says that whatever you think will happen will likely be the wrong guess.

As always, you must examine your needs and circumstances and choose a weapon/caliber that will work best for you. I don't think you'll see any long-slide Glock Model 40s carried in a pair of skinny jeans or used at a competitive speed shooting match involving concealed carry. But when it comes to finality, the 10mm makes a strong candidate for numerous scenarios. GD

Hunting with

Falling Block Single Shots

> CRAIG BODDINGTON

In the Mozambique swamps, hunting buffalos with a Ruger No. 1 in .450/.400-3-in., Boddington is comfortable with a big falling block, but not if hunting alone!

Discontinued in 1918, Winchester's Model 1885 was the last classic American single-shot centerfire rifle. There would be no more until Bill Ruger brought out his No. 1, 50 years later. To my eye, the No. 1 was (and is) the best-looking production rifle ever. The initial reception was mostly favorable, but the *concept* of a single-shot hunting rifle baffled some. "I am convinced the single shot rifle is — on game — at best impractical; at worst, it is unethical," writes Les Bowman in *Gunsport*, April 1967.

The brand-new and gorgeous Rigby falling block single shot is based on a Farquharson-type action. The initial rifles are chambered to the also-new .416 Rigby No. 2, a rimmed version of the famous .416 Rigby.

DEVELOPMENT

Practical breechloaders came into common use in the 1840s, but muzzleloaders remained dominant until the self-contained metallic cartridge. By this time, reliable repeating actions also existed, but early repeaters were limited in cartridge dimensions they could accept, reducing range and power.

In the late 19th Century, long-range competition was a popular sport, possibly more popular than today; it was easier to find space for 1,000-yard ranges. By then, even whitetails were scarce. Eastern hunters didn't need powerful rifles, but the American West beckoned with elk, bison, and big bears. The big single shot was the answer for distant targets and larger game. It had no restriction on case length, was stronger than early repeaters, and quickly made the leap from black-powder to smokeless. Even so, its time in the sun was short: The single shot was the dominant sporting rifle action only from the 1870s into the 1890s.

The mechanics are simple: A solid breechblock locks behind the chamber. In America, England, and Europe, numerous actions and variations developed. Some breechblocks swung into place (Snider and Springfield), others tilted (Martini and Peabody), and some were rolling (Remington). One of the most robust and long-lasting designs is the falling block, also called the "dropping block." The premise is simple and incredibly strong. A finger lever lowers a massive breechblock, exposing the chamber for loading. The same lever raises the block into battery.

From the 1890s, one of the most famous photos of Frederick Selous, reading by his wagon, with two Kori bustards and a Holland & Holland falling block on the Holland-Woodward patent.

This Zambezi Valley buffalo was the first to fall to Hornady's modern .450/.400-3-in. load, in the first Ruger No. 1 so chambered. The bull was down in 80 yards; no second shot was required.

It takes a bit of dexterity to load a scoped falling block; the ocular bell will always obscure some of the chamber.

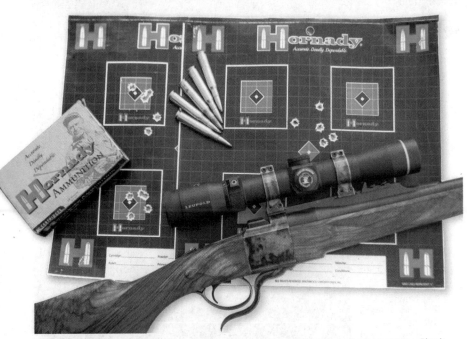

The Dakota Model 10 is one of several modern variations of the Farquharson action. Sleek and elegant, it's a fine hunting rifle. Boddington's is in .275 Rigby (7x57). Like most classic single shots, it's an extractor-only rifle.

Christian Sharps developed his famous action in 1848. Initially loaded with paper or linen blackpowder cartridges ignited by percussion caps, the Sharps saw widespread use in the Civil War. After the war, the action was quickly converted to metallic cartridges, the nipple under the hammer replaced by a firing pin. The Sharps was accurate and housed big, powerful blackpowder cartridges. It gets much credit for the demise of the American bison, but although highly respected, Sharps rifles were expensive and thus uncommon.

HAMMERS AND EJECTORS

The Sharps was an exposed hammer design, as was our trapdoor Springfield and many others. The Scottish Farquharson, patented in 1872, was among the first internal hammer (hammerless) actions. The Farquharson is a strong action with clean and elegant lines. Widely copied and heavily modified, the "Farkie" was the inspiration for numerous modern rifles, including the Dakota Model 10, new falling blocks by both John Rigby and Westley Richards in England, and, of course, the Ruger No. 1.

The last Sharps rifle, the Sharps-Borchardt Model 1878, used a hammerless action. With bison hunting ending, sales weren't enough to save the Sharps company. Manufacturing ceased in 1881 when only the northern bison herd remained.

The bison were gone, and lever-action repeaters were coming on fast, but the bolt-action rifle was still in the womb when Winchester bought young John Browning's design for a new single shot. Winchester's 1885 would be the most successful of all classic single-shot sporting rifles. Offered in High Wall for larger cartridges, Low Wall for smaller ones, it was chambered to more cartridges than any production rifle (until the Ruger No. 1), with 140,000 produced. Faithful reproductions have long been available from Browning, Winchester, and Uberti.

The 1885 is probably the most advanced exposed hammer design, self-cocking in that dropping the lever lowers the breechblock and rolls the in-line hammer to full cock. Unlike most pre-Ruger single shots that are extractor-only, the High Wall has an ejector with a

"Deflector" that can be adjusted for left or right deflection or "retain" for extraction only.

The 1885's hammer must be lowered to half-cock if you decide not to fire immediately. This feature is a primary difference between hammerless and exposed hammer designs. Once loaded, the former is cocked and ready to fire, remembering only the manual safety (if present). With hammer guns, a half-cock position serves as the safety.

Either way, exposed hammer guns require more time and motion to ready for firing. With cold or wet hands, there's always the chance the hammer can get away from you, mitigated by practice. But that's not all. Riflescopes were used during our Civil War and employed by some bison hunters. Col. Richard Dodge (*Hunting Grounds of the Great West*, 1877) used scoped Sharps rifles. Neither Dodge nor John Moses Browning envisioned a time when riflescopes would be universally used. With a scope conventionally mounted low over the receiver, exposed hammers are a mess. Sometimes there's barely enough room under the ocular bell to scrabble for the hammer. Speaking purely of scoped hunting rifles, hammerless designs are superior.

Ejection versus extraction is a different story. Again, most classic single shots were extractor-only. Often, one must manually pluck the case from the chamber. This depends on the extractor and also on the cartridge. Tapered cases are more likely to fall out of the chamber, much like a non-ejecting double rifle: Train to open the action, tilt the barrel sharply upward, and allow cases to drop. However, the occasional case will hang up, and you must reach into the maw with your thumb and forefinger. Practice and familiarity count, but plucking out the case is more difficult with a scoped rifle because the ocular bell usually blocks some access to the chamber.

Only Bill Ruger figured out how to put a strong, goof-proof ejection system into a Farquharson-type action. Dad and I got our first No. 1 before 1970 and had many since, so I have 50 years of experience with the Ruger. The fired case will eject clear.

Over the years, I've done quite a bit

The John Browning-designed Winchester 1885 is probably the most advanced exposed hammer falling block. This example is a Uberti reproduction in .303 British, used to take a cull whitetail on Boddington's Kansas farm.

Boddington and Lee Newton with a fine Kansas whitetail. Newton, an avid Ruger collector, used a No. 1 with spectacular wood chambered to .280 Ackley Improved.

of hunting with the sleek Dakota Model 10, also a Farquharson variation. Always wanted one, and have one now; one of the best rifles I own, slim and gorgeous, roll-marked .275 Rigby (7x57). Like most Farquharson-type actions, it is extractor-only. I've hunted with it quite a bit and find myself scrabbling between scope and tang. The smaller the cartridge, the more

dexterity is required. Large-caliber cases are easier to grab and, because of sheer weight, more consistent in dropping out!

ACROSS THE POND

Bristol gunmaker George Gibbs (of .505 Gibbs fame) acquired the Farquharson patent in 1875. Gibbs-Farquharson rifles are rare; Gibbs made less than a

Winchester's exposed hammer Model 1885 was probably the most successful classic single shot, with faithful modern versions readily available. This example is a Uberti Courteney in .303 British, a tribute to Frederick Courteney Selous, who loved his falling block single shots.

Two-piece stocks are often problematic for accuracy, so results vary. This Ruger Medium Sporter, .300 H&H with a 26-inch barrel, is the most accurate No. 1 Boddington has owned in a big-game cartridge.

popular among European hunters, partly because Europe has no large or dangerous game. Things were different in the British Empire. Africa was still being explored, and the Indian subcontinent held a greater variety of dangerous game than Africa. The Martini-Henry in .577/.450 was almost universal, and some used various other single shots in appropriate chamberings. The abundance of large and dangerous game on both continents led to the development of the double rifle for that life-saving second shot. After 1900, the bolt action or "magazine rifle," began to take over. But, in the latter days of blackpowder and the first decade of smokeless, the double bested the single shot in Britain's far-flung colonies.

There were exceptions. Frederick Courteney Selous, arguably the greatest of all early African hunters, loved his single shots. Selous (1851–1917) started his elephant hunting with large-bore blackpowder muzzleloaders. He wrote that the brutal recoil affected his shooting for the rest of his life. No wonder he loved the light, smooth-handling single shots. He used a Gibbs-Farquharson in blackpowder .461 Gibbs for much of his career, but he was a bit of a gun guy and, in later years, a Holland & Holland man.

The most famous photo of him, next to his wagon with two Kori bustards, shows an H&H single shot, Woodward patent. In Mozambique and Namibia in 2011, I was fortunate to hunt with another H&H falling block, also a Woodward patent. Made for Selous in 1898, it was chambered to 6.5x53R. Part of Bill Jones' collection, it was sweet-handling and accurate. I used it for gemsbok, and black-faced impala and Bill used it for zebra and wildebeest, also taking a buffalo with the little rifle, one shot, proving the legendary efficiency of the 156-grain 6.5mm solid.

Selous was not an exclusive single-shot guy. He owned bolt actions and waxed eloquently about the .375 H&H Magnum, saying that if he'd had it in his elephant hunting days, he'd have taken "thrice as many." On campaign in East Africa, he carried a non-regulation falling block. On January 4, 1917, he was killed by a German sniper on the banks of the Rufiji River in what is now the Selous Game

thousand through 1910. After the patent expired, the Belgian firm of Auguste Francotte produced faithful copies of the Gibbs-Farquharson action. Used by several English gunmakers, most British "Farkies" are likely based on the Belgian action. W.J. Jeffery started using this action in 1895. In 1904 they scaled it up to house the big .600 Nitro Express.

Jeffery cataloged these rifles until 1927, but the numbers were small. There were other action variations, both British and European. Holland & Holland used a similar action on a Holland-Woodward patent. Greener, H&H, and others made quite a few on Field's falling block with a side lever.

Many variations of single shots were

Reserve. Five days past his 65th birthday, we'd like to think he was carrying his falling block.

BILL RUGER'S SINGLE-SHOT CHALLENGE

On both sides of the Atlantic, interest shifted to repeaters; they were less expensive to make, yet wonderfully accurate. After 1912, Jeffery's catalog said this about its Farquharson falling block: "Now made to order only, having been superseded by the Magazine Rifle." Winchester's last 1885s shipped in 1920. Nearly a half-century later came the Ruger No. 1.

In 1967 Bill Ruger's company was just 20 years old, but he'd been on a winning streak with well-made — and well-priced — firearms that shooters loved. The No. 1 was a pet project. Ruger owned Farkies, admired the action and the concept, and thought he could build it at a lower cost and add a better extraction/ejection system.

For Sturm, Ruger & Co, the No. 1 was a departure. More expensive than most Ruger products, clearly top-of-line and in a platform not manufactured for decades. It wasn't the price, still Ruger-reasonable, but the concept: After generations of repeaters, did a single-shot hunting rifle fit in, and would we accept it? The rifle was gorgeous, functioned perfectly, and shot straight. My friend and noted Ruger collector Lee Newton made a scrapbook with all the early stories about the Number One. Most initial reviews were euphoric. Privately, many pundits wondered if Bill Ruger had lost his mind. A single-shot hunting rifle in the 1960s?

Not especially prolific and pre-Internet, little-known today, Les Bowman was a Wyoming rancher, outfitter, and one of the more knowledgeable gun writers of his day. Bill Ruger was furious, but Les Bowman may have written the most honest, straight-from-the-heart first-year assessment of the No. 1. That was the question: Was a single shot sensible? Or, absent a quick follow-up shot, was it impractical and possibly unethical?

Implied was the rifleman's challenge: One shot, one kill. Always the goal, but sometimes more than one shot is needed. The public spoke, and the No. 1 flew. Sales

Boddington's Dakota Model 10 falling block, in .275 Rigby, on a roebuck hunt in Scotland.

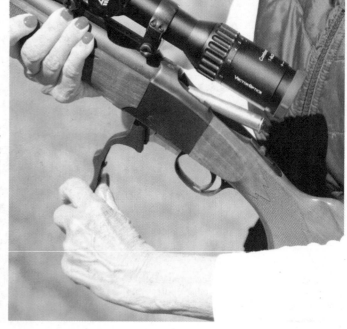

The Ruger No. 1 is among very few falling block single shots equipped with a strong, almost foolproof ejector. Although the difference is minuscule, it takes longer to reload an extractor gun, especially if scoped.

have never been huge, but the No. 1 has been at the top of the Ruger line for 55 years. It has spawned many other rifles that speak to the single-shot challenge. Less-costly break-open rifles like the T/C and H&R's Handi-Gun; innumerable re-introductions of classic single shots, from Remington rolling blocks, to Sharps, to 1885s; to higher-end Farquharson clones like the Dakota Model 10; and on up the scale to new falling block single shots from Rigby and Westley Richards.

PRACTICAL OR UNETHICAL?

It's easy to say that "one shot should be enough." In practice, it doesn't always work that way. There are two considerations when hunting with a single

Single-shot rifles may not be ideal for horseback hunts because, absent a magazine, they must be empty, which is awkward in a fast encounter. Boddington used his No. 1 in .375 Ruger on a horseback kudu hunt in South Africa.

shot: Only that first shot can be counted upon. And the single shot is either fully loaded or empty. There is no magazine in reserve. Both deserve discussion.

Reality: Nobody can reliably reload a single shot fast enough to react to all situations. However, the same truth applies to all repeaters. Sometimes, with rapid movement, vegetation, and other animals, there isn't time for a second shot, no matter what you're packing. And, no matter what you're shooting, sometimes one shot isn't enough.

With a single, you *know* you can only rely on one shot. This makes you extra careful, a crucial psychological thing. Knowing there's only one shot, hunters with single shots expend it wisely. I know I do! That said, it isn't always enough, but a *rapid* second shot isn't always necessary, and with a repeater, it's often fired too quickly. Before hunting with a single shot, one should practice rapid reloading and figuring out how to keep additional

This Texas "management buck" dropped in its tracks to a single shot from Boddington's Dakota M10 in .275 Rigby.

A fine nyala, taken with a Ruger No. 1 in .300 H&H.

cartridges close at hand.

But, even with long expertise and cartridges between the fingers or in a wrist bandolier, nobody will be fast enough all the time. I don't worry about that too much anymore. Sometimes you have lots of time to fumble for another cartridge; sometimes, none. In 50 years of hunting with falling block single shots, there has never been a time when I've lost a wounded animal for lack of a faster second shot.

So, with apologies to the unsung great Les Bowman, I don't find any ethical considerations. You know you have just one shot. You do the best you can with it. Then you reload.

There are practical considerations. Since the single shot is either loaded or empty, there are situations where the lack of a magazine causes concern. One is horseback hunting. Obviously, you cannot put a loaded rifle in a saddle scabbard, so you're grabbing an empty rifle and must fumble for a cartridge in a fast-breaking encounter. Where legal, many of us ride around our hunting areas in vehicles with chamber clear, magazine loaded. You can't

Lacking a magazine, single shots must be completely empty when carried in a vehicle. That isn't a major problem; you learn to keep a cartridge handy!

do that with a single shot!

Let's turn to dangerous game. Fred Selous shot more dangerous game than anyone reading (or writing) this will ever see. The single shot didn't bother him. Generally speaking, it doesn't bother me, but there's a big difference. Selous shot most of his dangerous game alone or with unarmed trackers. Me, rarely! A Zambezi Valley story is that a resident hunter went missing. They found him dead, killed by a buffalo, his falling block close by, and fired cartridge in the chamber. The buffalo was long gone, so nothing else is known.

I have taken African and Asian buffalos with single-shot rifles, all falling blocks, mostly No. 1s, several with Dakota M10s. Never a problem, often one-shot kills. On follow-ups, also no problems, *but I wasn't alone.* We, as visiting hunters,

A fine black-faced impala, taken with a gorgeous Holland & Holland 6.5x53R, built in 1898 for Frederick Selous, part of Bill Jones' collection. This rifle is on the Holland-Woodward patent, similar in appearance to the Farquharson action but not the same.

rarely are. Somebody else usually covers us with a big double or bolt gun.

It is foolish to hunt dangerous game alone with a single shot and a poor choice for a PH, whose job is to protect the party. Hunting buffalo with an accurate single shot is OK for you and me. It's an excellent choice for leopard because there will never be more than one shot; best make it good. Despite ideal chamberings, I have not hunted elephants, lions, or the big bears with my singles. I could, but I probably would not. My experience has been that fast second shots are often called for in all three cases. Since we aren't hunting alone, the danger is increased little, but carrying a single shot invites collaboration, which otherwise might not be necessary.

In the main, hunting with single shots is fun. Knowledge of that one certain shot slows you down, and it's usually enough. There are also pragmatic reasons for choosing one. Absent a repeating action, a falling block rifle is about four inches shorter than a repeater with equal barrel length. So, you get the extra velocity of a longer barrel for free. My Ruger Medium Sporter with a 26-inch barrel is the same overall length as my .270 bolt action with a 22-inch barrel. As with all rifles, accuracy varies but is plenty good enough and sometimes spectacular. I love the simplicity and safety: The single shot is loaded or unloaded, the chamber yawning before you, easy to check. As a rifle freak, I love rifles that look good, handle well, and shoot straight. That's a good description of the falling block single shot — as it was a century ago and as it is today.

The single shot isn't for everyone, perhaps not for everything. But, as usual, Bill Ruger was right. There were hunters out there who appreciated his single-shot challenge. A half-century later, there are still plenty of us, and it is a practical and ethical option. GD

This gemsbok fell to a Holland & Holland falling block in 6.5x53R. The rifle was built for Frederick Selous in 1898, on the Holland-Woodward pattern, similar in appearance to the Farquharson but with mechanical differences.

Custom & Engraved Guns

❯TOM TURPIN

It seems that the custom gun trade may not be fully recovered from the Covid pandemic's impact even at this late date. However, I've not seen enough hard evidence to convince me that such is the case. Instead, I've based my opinions primarily on comments I've picked up during BS sessions with a few trade expert friends.

Over the years, I've learned that my pals have likely forgotten more about custom guns than I'll ever know. Unlike more than a few "experts" I have known in the past, my pals know all there is to know about custom guns and then some.

Our Annual Review of the Finest Examples of Beauty and Artistry in the World of the Custom Gun

All photos by Mark Hoechst unless otherwise noted.

Ben Piper
SAVAGE MODEL 99

Savage Model 99 in .250 Savage by gun maker Ben Piper and engraver Derek Fernelius. Photos by Tom Alexander

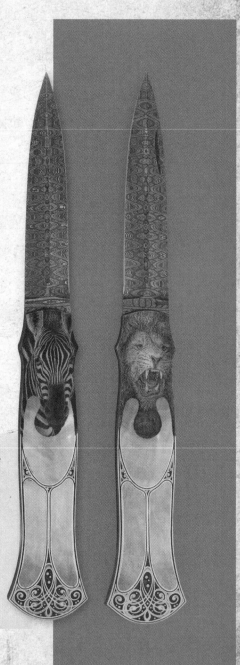

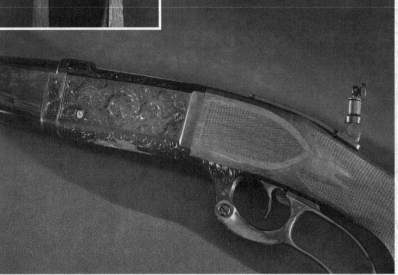

Warren Osborne & Brian Hochstrat
ENGRAVED KNIFE

This beautiful folder by knife maker Warren Osborne and engraver Brian Hochstrat won the Best Engraved Knife award at the Firearms Engravers Guild of America (FEGA) 2023 Show. An amazing piece showcasing the artistry and extraordinary attention to detail by Master Engraver Brian Hochstrat.

Lee Griffiths

COLT HAMMERLESS

This Colt Hammerless engraved by Master Engraver Lee Griffiths was judged the winner of Best Engraved Handgun at the FEGA 2023 Show.

During the pandemic, many of the annual trade shows were canceled, and those that weren't were poorly attended. These closures affected everyone in business, particularly small business owners/operators. The top-tier makers and engravers were best equipped to weather the Covid-generated storm. Those top guys and gals had a pretty healthy backlog of work, and none of their clientele had hinted at canceling orders or cutting back on future jobs.

The mid- and economy-level makers showed little differences in presumed Covid-related cancellations of existing orders or not following through on promised ones. I've also heard rumors about a few shops closing their doors, but I could never determine if the closures were Covid-related or something else. (By the way, the terms top-tier, mid-level, and economy level are not officially accepted terms used by anyone I know except me.)

Marty Rabeno
WINCHESTER HIGHWALL

This beautiful Winchester Highwall, engraved by Master Engraver Marty Rabeno, earned second place for the Engravers Choice Award at the FEGA 2023 Show.

To my knowledge, none of the major shows this year were canceled. The Engravers Guild did its thing in Las Vegas and the Gunmakers in Dallas, both their usual show locations. Personally, I quit the show circuit several years back, but I still have my spies keeping me informed. All of the information I've received from the Guilds has been positive — good news. Time will tell us the accuracy of our info.

Those of us smitten by the custom gun bug live in a golden age. I ordered my first custom rifle in the late 1960s and have had at least one on order ever since. I've used my custom guns for sport shooting and as serious collectibles. I've even written a few books on the subject. I know many of our makers and engravers personally and have spent time in their shops, watching them do their thing.

Tom Harvey
MODEL 42 WINCHESTER

Starting with a highly desirable palate of a Model 42 Winchester in .410, Master Engraver Tom Harvey converted it into a masterpiece. The result was awarded Best Engraved Shotgun at the FEGA 2023 Show, as it is a superb example of artistry on metal.

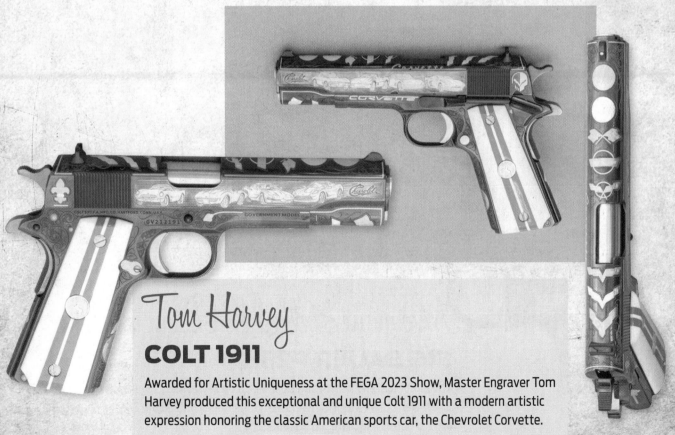

Tom Harvey
COLT 1911

Awarded for Artistic Uniqueness at the FEGA 2023 Show, Master Engraver Tom Harvey produced this exceptional and unique Colt 1911 with a modern artistic expression honoring the classic American sports car, the Chevrolet Corvette.

Sam Welch

ENGRAVED 1873 WINCHESTER

This 1873 Winchester in .38 WCF from the vise of veteran Master Engraver Sam Welch was awarded Best Engraved Rifle and received the Engravers Choice Award at the FEGA 2023 Show. This rifle embodies Sam's dedication to time-honored tradition, craftsmanship, and artistry.

Marianne Kelley & Layne Zuelke

SIG SAUER P238

The Best Modern Firearm and Best Metal on Metal Inlay Awards at the FEGA 2023 Show went to Master Engravers Marianne Kelley and Layne Zuelke, contributing artist, for this exquisite SIG Sauer P238.

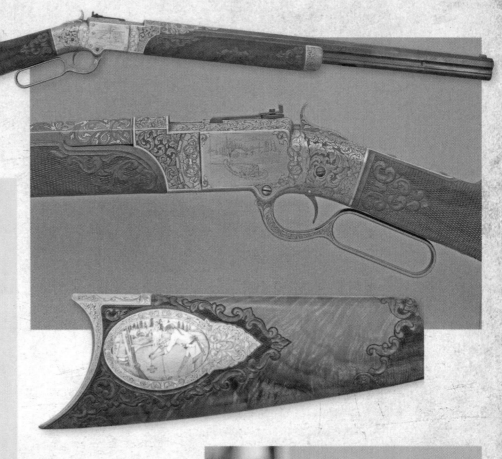

Paul Lindke-Ron Smith

VOLCANIC RIFLE

In the ACGG/FEGA combined category, this Volcanic Rifle by Paul Lindke, gun maker, and Ron Smith, Master Engraver, is the extraordinary result of a collaboration by two veteran artisans. The resulting rifle doesn't get any better than this example.

Paul Lindke

SHARPS SINGLE SHOT

Taking the Best Single Shot Award at the FEGA 2023 Show was this remarkable Sharps Rifle by Paul Lindke.

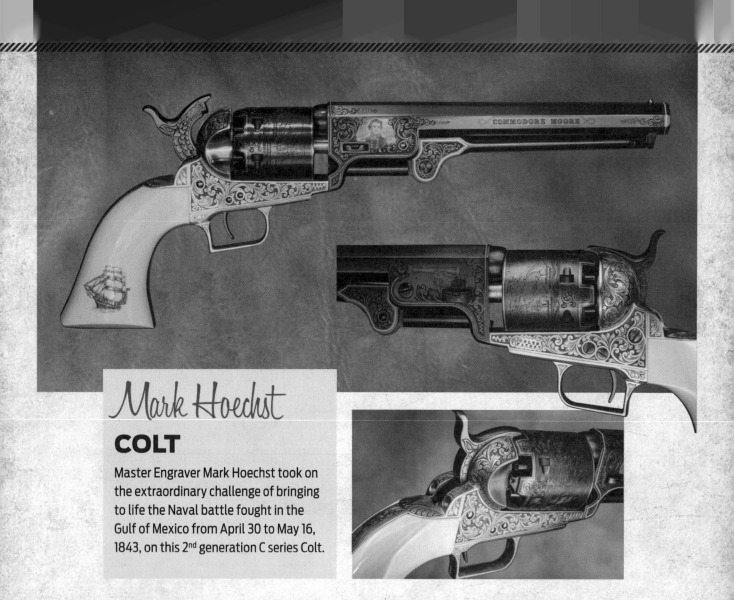

Mark Hoechst

COLT

Master Engraver Mark Hoechst took on the extraordinary challenge of bringing to life the Naval battle fought in the Gulf of Mexico from April 30 to May 16, 1843, on this 2nd generation C series Colt.

Diane Scalese

RUGER BEARCAR GAMBLER'S SET

Taking third place for the Engravers Choice Award at the FEGA 2023 Show was this elegant Ruger Bearcat Gambler set, which showcases the artistry of Diane Scalese.

Reto Buehler-Gary Goudy

'09 ARGENTINE

Reto Buehler/Gary Goudy 9.3x64 Brenneke on a 09 Argentine action. Seldom encountered in the U.S., the 9.3x64 Brenneke is an excellent big game cartridge comparable to the venerable .375 H&H. Swiss-born gun maker Reto Buehler was selected as the metalsmith on this project because he was intimately familiar with this cartridge. The stock work was done by the author's old pal Gary Goudy, and this rifle perfectly embodies the concept of a "custom afield" and is a favorite of Turpin.

I truly believe that the finest custom firearms ever crafted are being created right now. The Europeans, mainly the English, probably craft the finest shotguns made. However, it's not even close regarding custom rifles (and, to a lesser extent, custom handguns) — it's a one-horse race. Small one- or two-man shops in North America, mainly in the USA, but Canada has a couple as well, take the gold.

Yes, the best is expensive, no doubt about that. However, a careful collector not pressured by a fire sale liquidation requirement can often profit a few bucks if circumstances require a sale. That eases the pain a bit! **GD**

Topped with a Trijicon SRO red-dot sight and shooting Hornady's 240-grain XTP Custom ammo, the .44 Mag Taurus Raging Hunter is highly accurate, as this 50-yard group shows.

The Taurus Raging Hunter

Mr. Whitetail sings the praises of affordable handcannons for deer hunting and more.

❯ LARRY WEISHUHN

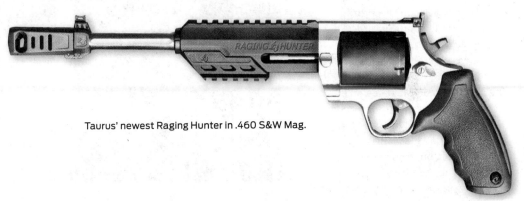

Taurus' newest Raging Hunter in .460 S&W Mag.

"Ever hunted deer with a handgun?" I asked. Brandon Houston nodded his head in the negative. "Well, it's time you did!" Before he could say anything, I continued, "As part of my lease agreement, my guests or I have to take nine does this season. You've been appointed to take at least one with my Taurus Raging Hunter handgun!" Brandon smiled and nodded approvingly.

Moments before, hunting Brandon's property, I had shot a hundred-pound wild hog with my .44 Mag Taurus Raging Hunter. The Hornady 240-grain XTP dropped it in its tracks. Brandon had filmed my hunt for an upcoming episode of *The Journey;* I had seen a glint of interest in his eyes earlier, loading the double-action revolver for that afternoon's hunt. No doubt he was keen on hunting with a handgun. That night, I explained how I shot my double-action revolvers single-action-style to reduce trigger pull. I showed him how to access the cylinder for loading and removing spent cases using Taurus' cylinder releases. And I explained how I used Trijicon's SRO red-dot sights for quicker target acquisition than long-eye relief scopes.

I took Brandon to the range at my hunting lease a few days later. He soon put bullets within 3 inches or smaller groups at 25 yards. That was sufficient because I knew we could get within that distance of a doe. Hidden in a ground blind later that afternoon, Brandon shot his first deer with a revolver. He was hooked! Two days later, I sent my .44 Mag. 6.75-inch-barrel Raging Hunter and a couple of boxes of Hornady 240-grain XTP ammo home with him to use on hogs and deer. "You're welcome to keep my .44 Mag until you get your own Raging Hunter," I said, knowing he would be ordering one from his local gun shop as soon as he returned home.

Several weeks earlier, I had lent my .357 Mag Taurus Raging Hunter to Luke Clayton to use on wild hogs; Luke and I have done a weekly outdoor radio show for the past fifteen years. Earlier in the year, I had procured four Raging Hunters, one each in .357 Mag., .44 Mag., .454 Casull Mag. and .460 S&W Mag. I shot all four at my range shortly after getting them. Thus, in Luke's case, I knew the .357 Mag — attractive in Taurus' "two-tone" black and silver format — was highly accurate out to 50 yards. I did not attempt to shoot beyond.

From a solid rest, I shot several loads through the .357 Mag. The two my Raging Hunter liked best, based on group size, were Hornady's Custom 158-grain JHP/XTP and Handgun Hunter 130-grain Mono Flex HP loads. Thankfully, I had six boxes of both in my ammo cabinet. With the Custom load, which it slightly preferred, at 50 yards using a 2.5 MOA SRO sight, I could consistently group all seven rounds within a hair over 2 1/2 inches. I felt the round's 460 ft-lbs of retained energy at that range was sufficient to kill a hog. If I were using the .357 Mag. to hunt deer, I would limit my shots to 50 yards. Luke planned on using it exclusively on hogs, and his shots would be less than 25 yards. He's used the combination on several wild hogs.

With my .357 Mag and .44 Mag Taurus revolvers in the hands of friends, I turned to my .454 Casull. I topped it with a Trijicon SRO 2.5-MOA red-dot sight. Mounting this sight was simple, thanks to the integral Picatinny rail. The rail sys-

Taurus' Raging Hunter in .44 Mag. is accurate, fun to shoot and works excellent on game.

The .454 Casull is one of Weishuhn's favorite handgun rounds and has helped him account for big game, from whitetails to monstrous Alaskan Brown Bears.

The author with a doe he took using the .44 Mag. Taurus.

Taurus Raging Hunter revolvers are chambered in .357 Mag., .44 Mag., .45 Colt, .454 Casull and .460 S&W Mag., here compared to a .30-06 round.

Larry's daughter Theresa Tigrett with a wild hog she shot with the Raging Hunter .454 Casull and 300-grain XTP Hornady Custom.

Above: Larry's .454 Casull Taurus Raging Hunter shot at 100 yards with the 300-grain Hornady XTP Custom load.

Left: After carrying his .454 Casull on numerous hunts, the author decided to ensure it was still sighted in. This shot was from 100 yards using Hornady 240-grain XTP.

can be a "handful." The Raging Hunter's stainless barrel assembly is ported within a shroud. Thanks to the porting system, the .454 Casull's recoil is manageable and not unpleasant. Taurus' signature "recoil absorber grip" dramatically reduces felt recoil.

In the past, I've taken numerous whitetails, mule deer and elk, plus a bison and a sizable Alaskan Brown Bear with the .454 Casull. It's one of my all-time favorite handgun rounds. I also must admit that I love the .44 Mag and the .460 S&W Mag.

Factory Raging Hunters have fairly heavy trigger pulls, north of 10 pounds shooting double action and about 8 pounds shooting hammer-cocked, single action. After shooting numerous rounds with the factory trigger pull (no creep), I got "used to it," particularly in my .44 Mag. Knowing I wanted to do considerable hunting with the .454 Casull, I had a pistolsmith friend do a trigger job. It's now in the neighborhood of 3 pounds, fired hammer-cocked. I plan on having him work on the .44 Mag and .460 S&W Mag during hunting's off-season for big game.

At my range, I shot Hornady .454 Casull 240-grain XTP MAG, 300-grain XTP Mag, and 200-grain Monoflex Handgun Hunter at 50 and 100 yards in five-shot groups (the cylinder holds five rounds). All three handguns were accurate, essentially 3-inch (average) groups at 100 yards. The smallest were 1.5-inch groups with 240- and 300-grain XTP MAG loads. Remember, the red dot covers 2.5 inches at 100 yards. My best groups with the 200-grain Monoflex Handgun Hunter loads were just over 3 inches. Such groups at 100 yards, considering their substantial downrange energy, make all three lethal for elk, deer, bears, hogs, and javelina-sized animals. I used the 200-grain Handgun Hunter loads for javelina while hunting the brush country of South Texas. There, I stalked to within 40 yards and got a solid rest in the crux of an ancient mesquite. The javelina, shot through both shoulders, collapsed on the spot. The bullet exited after doing extreme damage to the vital organs.

Several weeks later, I was hunting with Double AA Outfitters, owned by long-

tem, too, would make it easy to mount an extended eye relief scope. I truly appreciate when the scope base or sight mount is part of a hunting handgun. With an integral rail in place, I do not have to be concerned about finding bases or the base loosening from recoil.

The Taurus' rail also adds a bit of weight. The .357 Mag. weighs 53 ounces, the .44 Mag. is 55 ounces, and the .454 Casull with an 8.375-inch barrel is 57

ounces. The big-bore .460 S&W Mag. weighs 63.6 ounces sans SRO sight and ammo. Raging Hunters are available in several barrel lengths, including 5.125, 6.75, and 8.375 inches. Weight and overall length vary.

I have fortunately never been "recoil conscious" when it comes to shooting hunting handguns. But having shot several .454 Casull single and double actions, I know the cartridge's recoil

time friend Craig Archer and headed by his brother David, when we spotted an old 3x3 whitetail buck across a canyon. Before we could get within a reasonable range, the buck disappeared. We returned to the vehicle and drove to the other side of the canyon to rattle. However, before I could start rattling, the 6-point reappeared. When he stopped at 70 yards, I placed the red dot on his quartering-to left shoulder and, taking a deep breath and exhaling to steady myself, pulled the trigger, sending the 240-grain Hornady XTP. The old buck dropped in his tracks. I could not have been more pleased!

Later, I recovered the spent bullet, finding it just under the skin of the opposite hindquarter after traveling through about 40 inches of tissue and bone. It had passed through the scapula, ribs, and femur.

Later, while hunting antlerless whitetails with the .454 Casull, I used 240- and 300-grain XTP MAG Hornady Custom loads. The first doe stood broadside 50 yards distant. The bullet took her squarely through the shoulders. My second doe was almost exactly 100 yards away. She dropped in her tracks; the 300-grain XTP MAG penetrated both shoulders and spine before exiting.

With the deer properly cared for, I headed to the range and replaced .454 Casull ammo with .45 Colt, which can also be shot in the Casull chamber. Shooting at 25 yards, I placed five shots easily within a 3-inch circle. I will use that .45 Colt load on wild hogs in the future.

This brings us to the .460 S&W Magnum Raging Hunter, a fabulous big game hunting round. Should I again hunt Alaskan Brown bears or dangerous game in Africa, the .460 S&W Mag. would be my choice. The largest animal I have taken with that beefy cartridge was a monstrous-bodied bison.

Maybe it's just me, but shooting the

This doe fell to Weishuhn's .454 Casull.

The .454 Casull Taurus Raging Hunter brought down an old six-point whitetail.

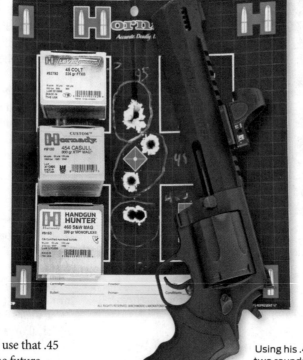

Using his .460 S&W Mag. Taurus, the author shot two rounds each of .45 Colt, .454 Casull, and .460 S&W Mag. at 50 yards. This shows the results.

.460 S&W Mag. is a "double handful" in terms of recoil. Even so, with Taurus' ported barrel and recoil-absorbing grip, I can shoot three cylinders full (fifteen rounds) before I need to set it aside for

a break. I've been unable to do the same with any other manufacturer's gun chambered for the same round.

I enjoy hunting with the .460 S&W Mag Taurus Raging Hunter, but it is not a round I would recommend someone new to handgun hunting start with. However, on second thought, the fantastic thing about revolvers chambered for the .460 S&W Mag. is that you can shoot .454 Casull and .45 Colt ammunition in the same chamber. So, starting with a revolver chambered in .460 S&W Mag. may not be such a bad idea after all!

I shot that big Raging Hunter at the bench with .45 Colt, .454 Casull, and .460 S&W Mag. sighted in dead-on at 100 yards (the .454 Casull load was a 240-grain Hornady XTP MAG). At 50 yards, I shot two rounds each of Hornady's LEVERevolution 225-grain FTX .45 Colt, Hornady 300-grain XTP MAG and Hornady Handgun Hunter .460 S&W Mag 200-grain Monoflex holding on the target's center diamond.

The two .45 Colt loads hit 1 1/2 inches above the center diamond, creating one ragged hole. The .454 Casull 300-grain XTP struck the target just to the top-right of the center diamond and the second very slightly left. The 200-grain Monoflex bullets smacked the target nearly 2 inches low, directly under the center diamond. The second shot cut the hole of the first. From this, I would have no qualms about using any of these rounds without any sight adjustment out to 50 yards on whitetails. The 4-inch vertical in-line "grouping" of all six shots would have struck nicely within a deer's 8-inch vital zone of heart and lungs.

One of the many things I like about the Raging Hunter revolvers, beyond their real-world price (ranging from about $700 to $800) and their accuracy, is their non-glare matte finish. I can

A few days later, I got a call from the local FFL dealer. "*Get down here! You got something really interesting from Taurus!*" I hurried to his store. After completing the appropriate paperwork and being approved, I was handed a large-framed black and silver double-action revolver. The revolver's 10-inch barrel, of which 4 inches extends beyond the shroud, and is four-fluted, ends with a flash suppressor-style porting system. The barrel shroud held Picatinny rails above and below the barrel. The fiber-optic open sights were easily seen. A quick look confirmed the large-cylinder revolver was chambered in .460 S&W Mag. Overall, the package had a somewhat futuristic appearance, which is popular today. I could hardly wait to shoot it!

That night, I called Osborn. He told me the new Raging Hunter I'd received would be introduced at the upcoming 2023 SHOT Show. When asked my opinion of the gun, I said I would let him know as soon as I shot it. The next morning, long before daylight, I headed to a whitetail and javelina hunt in South Texas brush country. Arriving in camp, I set up a target at 25 yards, then loaded five 200-grain Monoflex Hornady Handgun Hunter rounds. From a reasonable rest, I shot the new revolver single-action style.

My eyes are no longer fond of open sights, but there had been no time to mount a red-dot sight before leaving for the hunt. The fiber-optic sights were greatly appreciated. All five shots were kept easily within a 3-inch group. I was ready to hunt javelina.

It had been a "no deer morning." On the way back to camp, I spotted a small herd of javelinas and stalked within 20 yards of a toothsome boar. With the big revolver resting on tripod shooting sticks, I cocked the hammer and started my trigger pull — heavy, but no creep, and crisp. The Taurus raged, and the chosen javelina went down, shot through both shoulders. That evening, I sent Cody a message. "*Love the new Raging Hunter! Javelina down! Need to do more research. Please send more bullets!*" GD

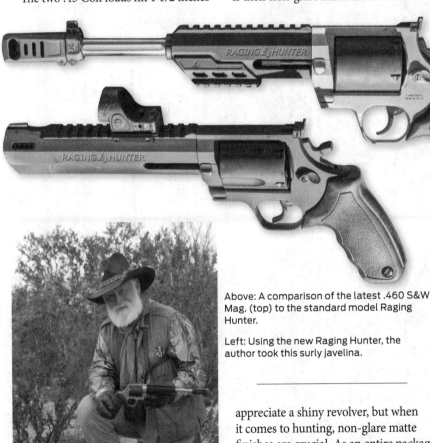

Above: A comparison of the latest .460 S&W Mag. (top) to the standard model Raging Hunter.

Left: Using the new Raging Hunter, the author took this surly javelina.

appreciate a shiny revolver, but when it comes to hunting, non-glare matte finishes are crucial. As an entire package, why the Taurus Raging Hunter received the American Hunter 2019 Handgun of the Year Golden Bullseye Award is easily understood.

Before this article was due, I got a message from Taurus' Cody Osborn: "*Sending you another Raging Hunter. Let me know what you think.*"

With these five cartridges, you can successfully hunt game animals, from hares to hippos. Photo: Massaro Media Group

5 Cartridges to Hunt the World

A Professional Hunter Weighs In

❯ JAY LEYENDECKER

Hunters are natural dreamers. Our minds often drift to far-off lands or at least what's happening on the back forty while we're away. Naturally, the next question to come to mind is which rifle to use while in such a dream state. It invokes thoughts like caliber choices for gaur in India or stone sheep in British Columbia. My most important question as of late has been, which gun and caliber should I begin training my young five-year-old daughter with? Dreams often become realities, the rifles very real. We want the hunt to be perfect, as we've dreamt of it so many times before. We want the memory to be perfect.

The truth is, many rifles can tackle the same species with equal results, so how do you pick? How do you choose the five guns to hunt the world successfully? The question is much more difficult than I initially believed. What are the parameters? One, the calibers must be able to handle a wide variety of game, from cottontail rabbits to elephants. The ammunition must be available, and the cartridge effective at reasonable distances. All these factors were considered in my five choices.

The .22 Long Rifle makes a great training tool for new hunters and shooters. Photo: Massaro Media Group

.22 LONG RIFLE

We'll begin with the smallest of the lot, but quite possibly the most important, the caliber 95% of us cut our teeth on as youngsters hunting jackrabbits, squirrels, and cottontails — the king of calibers, the .22 long rifle.

In 1871, American firearms manufacturer J. Stevens Arms & Tool Company introduced the .22 Long Rifle cartridge. It is based on the .22 Short of 1857 and combined the .22 Long case of 1871 with a 40-grain bullet, giving it a longer overall length, a higher muzzle velocity, and superior performance as a hunting and target round. The 40-grain bullets have a muzzle velocity of 1,200 fps, generating about 131 ft-lbs of energy. The .22 LR uses a heeled bullet, which means it's the same diameter as the case and has a narrower "heel" portion that fits in the case. It's one of the few cartridges accepted equally by many rifles and handguns. The .22 Long Rifle will be on every gun store shelf across the planet, and its availability earns its seat as one of the five kings. It is without question the single most circulated cartridge across the world.

When I think of the .22 Long Rifle, I am instantly taken back 30-plus years to the thousands of hours of my youth driving down the south Texas Senderos with my grandfather and younger brother. Early afternoons, we'd find a stock tank to bass fish, and as the day wore on, we'd hunt cottontails and rattlesnakes for the pot. The cottontails were typically given to needy families in my hometown of

The author as a young boy, having used his .22 LR to sort out a South Texas buzzworm.

Laredo. Still, often enough, we'd keep one for ourselves, grill it, and put it into a stew or *guisado*.

Rattlesnakes were my passion at seven years old. For a boy in south Texas toting a .22 lever action, it may have well been a dinosaur that I was hunting! I can think of many occasions when we walked up to a huge snake with my grandfather's hands on my shoulders, as the diamond-back would get coiled and aggressive.

I'd get calmly directed where to shoot, aim, and make my shot. Some of the best memories of my life involved the .22, and it's the caliber that began my training, which led me across the world. What more spectacular choice could there be than the .22 Long Rifle? For many of us, it was our foundation.

.223 REMINGTON

Like Hemingway's writing style, I believe in simplicity and what works. What has endured the sands of time? What can be found on every ammo shelf? My preferred calibers have often been accused of being plain-Vanilla. (Luckily, my personality is more like Rocky Road, and my lovely wife would agree!) With that said, my second choice for a caliber to hunt the world is the timeless .223. It's a military-approved cartridge, a fine round for hunting and target shooting, and is probably the most-fired caliber in the world. It's important, it's significant, and it's wildly lethal in capable hands.

The cartridge's development, which began in 1957 and would eventually become the .223 Remington, was due to the need for a lightweight combat rifle. The cartridge and rifle were developed by Fairchild Industries, Remington Arms, and several engineers working toward a goal spelled out by the U.S. Army. The goal was to create a cartridge which could fire a 55-grain projectile with a muzzle velocity of 3,300 fps and was accurate to 500 yards.

In September 1963, the .223 Remington cartridge was officially accepted by the military and named "Cartridge, 5.56 mm ball, M193." The following year, the ArmaLite AR-15 was adopted by the

Born for the military, the .223 Remington has many practical applications in hunting. Photo: Massaro Media Group

Dating back to the 19th century, the .22 Long Rifle remains the popular rimfire cartridge. Photo: Massaro Media Group

The author proudly poses with his younger brother and grandfather, holding his first whitetail buck.

United States Army as the M16 rifle, and it would later become the standard U.S. military rifle. The specification included a Remington-designed bullet and IMR-4475 powder, which resulted in a muzzle velocity of 3,250 fps and a chamber pressure of 52,000 psi. In the spring of 1962, Remington submitted the specifications of the .223 Remington to the Sporting Arms and Ammunition Manufacturers' Institute (SAAMI). In December 1963, it introduced its first rifle chambered for the .223 Remington — the Model 760. Thought the .223 Remington is dentical in exterior dimensions to the 5.56 NATO, the .223 Remington rifles have a slightly different throat configuration.

I grew up on the .223 and took my first javelina, whitetail doe, and buck with that cartridge. I remember those hunts vividly. One afternoon, just after lunch, my grandfather decided to pull me out of school early. I'm still not sure he had my mother's permission. With a smile, all he said as we walked up to his old dodge was, "Load up, Grandson. We're going to go look for a buck today." I couldn't

A good .300 Winchester Magnum will suffice for many hunting situations. Photo: Massaro Media Group

Leyendecker guided his client to this good Botswana blue wildebeest; one well-placed .300 Winchester Magnum did the job perfectly.

The lovely Mrs. Leyendecker used a .300 Winchester Magnum to take this Texas whitetail; though some may consider it heavy for deer, it worked.

believe it. My time had come during a school day! I had taken most indigenous species by that time but never a buck.

We bumped down an old caliche road where we fed corn in a stand of Huisache and Retama trees. My zany Uncle Albert, my grandfather's brother, had joined us after picking up my younger brother, Jonathan, from school. Uncle Al and Jono tore off in one direction, looking for a pig for the pit. My grandfather and I climbed into the tower blind. Hunting was still innocent, pure, and un-technical in those days.

As we sat and waited, numerous does slowly emerged from the thick brush country. A pack of javelinas came down the road gobbling up the corn like a herd of vacuum cleaners. A couple of young bucks wandered in. Then, I suddenly saw a heavier-bodied deer and looked over at my grandfather, who already had his binoculars on him. He then passed me the binos and asked me to look through them, which I did. As I looked through "the glasses," he asked, "Do you

like him?" I put the binos in my lap and looked back at my grandfather. I must've looked as though I was in shock, but I was able to mutter two words, "Yes, sir." "Then go ahead and shoot him, Grandson," he said. I could hardly contain myself. He allowed me to grab the rifle and stick it out the blind window all on my own and take it off safety. He softly and calmly whispered, "Put the crosshairs right behind the shoulder and squeeze the trigger; we have all the time in the world." His voice naturally calmed me, "We have all the time in the world." I have since used that phrase hundreds of times while guiding others, even when we didn't have time.

The rifle went off. The buck ran, and Papa said behind a big smile, "Well, you got him. Let's give him a minute and get reorganized; then we will go see if we can find some sign." My grandfather was a tremendous hunter; at the time, I didn't know how blessed I was to have had him. After climbing out of the blind, he put one finger over his lips, made the "shhh"

sound, and mouthed the words, "No talking." We quietly arrived at the spot where the buck was standing. He pointed at the ground, and I couldn't see the tracks, but he could. He immediately took the lead and whispered, "Rifle barrel up, Jay. Rifle safe?"

"Yes, sir," I replied and showed him.

"Good. Don't shoot at all, no matter what happens, and if you need to shoot, I will help you. Rifle barrel down and away at all times," he said sternly. He followed the spoor quickly, abruptly stopped, turned around, and said, "Let's go back to where we started. I want to see if you can follow him up to where we left off, maybe a little further." Little did I know then that my grandfather had already seen the buck down but wanted me to track him myself. At this stage, I was a little concerned, thinking I might not find him.

I followed the tracks one by one and went another five to 10 steps beyond where he had stopped and turned back and saw some blood. I continued on another few paces, and saw the most

The .375 Holland & Holland Magnum is one of the most versatile cartridges ever created. Photo: Massaro Media Group

The .300 Winchester Magnum has become a staple among traveling hunters, offering flexibility. Photo: Massaro Media Group

remarkable sight of my life: the white underside of a whitetail buck beneath a large mesquite tree. I looked up at my grandfather, who was looking down at me, melting. As I walked up to it, I was in complete disbelief. I knelt and picked up his antlers — a solid typical eight-point

buck. It's something I'll never forget and one of my greatest memories with my grandfather. The .223 will forever hold a special place in my heart as it was the rifle I used for all my firsts — my first whitetail buck, doe, and javelina; that's a lot of firsts in a young man's life.

I still own the rifle to this day, and if she chooses to become a hunter, my daughter will likely take her first with it as well.

.300 WINCHESTER MAGNUM
Now for one of my favorite calibers:

the .300 Winchester Magnum. It can effectively take down most game on this planet, so long as it is paired with the proper bullet. It is the most versatile non-dangerous big game round in existence. It's capable of extreme ranges with more than enough energy to accomplish whatever one may ask within reason. It is a 'go-to' in my arsenal, guiding thousands of hunters to various big game species. I am never unhappy when a client has a .300 Win. Mag. in tow.

Released in 1963, the .300 Winchester Magnum is based on the belted .375 Holland & Holland Mag., blown out, shortened, and necked down to .30 caliber. Its traditional 180-grain bullet has a velocity of nearly 3,000 fps and just over 3,400 ft-lbs of energy. Like the previous two calibers, .300 Win. Mag. ammunition is readily available at any arms store.

Should a hunter come into an unfortunate situation, they can easily find ammunition and continue their hunt. This comfort alone is worth its weight in gold and is always an essential aspect of what gun I use on a hunt or recommend.

A recent and fond memory of mine with the .300 Winchester is of a particular buck my lovely wife, Karina, and I had been hunting for quite some time. He was perfect, a 7 1/2-year-old brute, a typical 10-point with a 4-inch drop tine on his left antler; it was a dream buck most of us wish would amble by just once. The buck lived in a particularly dense part of the ranch and was nocturnal; he would come out at last light and never would stick around for long. When we got serious and began our quest to hunt him, he changed locations. When we zigged, he zagged, and when we zagged, he zigged.

We played quite the cat and mouse game until one sweltering October afternoon.

We had a few deer and a pack of javelinas feeding on the upwind roads. As I was glassing, Karina whispered, "there's a buck." As I turned to get into a better position, I immediately saw it was him. We waited for him to get into a position where Karina could maneuver my .300 Winchester out of the blind window without making a sound. Then he walked directly toward the blind, not offering us a shot opportunity. It seemed like an eternity, but we had all the time in the world. And, boy, did it feel like an eternity! He turned broadside, and I gave Karina the green-light to shoot if she felt comfortable. Old drop-tine kicked his hind legs and tore into the brush at breakneck speed. The shot looked good; the buck reacted well. We slowly exited the blind

Leyendecker used his .375 H&H to take this big-bodied sable bull; the cartridge is equally at home on the plains as it is when pursuing buffalo in the bushveld.

and picked up tracks right away. After a short follow-up, we found the big boy down. Not sure who was more excited — Karina or me.

.375 HOLLAND & HOLLAND MAGNUM

And now the golden child, God's cartridge, the blue-eyed boy, whatever nickname you'd like to use for the special one, please insert here, the emperor's crown goes to the .375 Holland & Holland Magnum. My capital pick is, without a doubt, the single most important caliber. It's capable of taking the largest game species. If I had to pick one caliber to hunt the world with forever, it would be the .375 H&H.

The caliber was born to the world in 1912 in London by famed gun maker Holland & Holland, launching a 300-grain bullet of nominal diameter at 2,500 fps. I have used the .375 successfully in numerous African countries and North America. Its manageable recoil allows it to be used by all shapes, sizes, and heights of hunters. It is not the best

stopper, but it is highly effective.

One fantastic hunt I remember well, I had a lady client who stood just over 5-foot tall and weighed maybe 110 pounds, who carried a .375 H&H. The quarry was the elephant. We had been looking for a good bull for about seven or eight days when we stumbled upon a massive tusker one early afternoon. We made a splendid stalk, but the bull came right toward us in heavy mopane, not giving us a shot. He sensed something was not quite right and spun to walk away. However, for whatever reason, he wanted to get behind us. We continued to walk parallel with him. He knew we were there and began to get agitated.

Once he had had enough, he came at us, making a helluva racket trumpeting and crashing through the mopane scrub. We set the sticks for her to get ready. The bull broke from cover at less than ten paces with his ears splayed out and bowed up posture. A beautiful display of a mature bull elephant trying to look bigger and more intimidating than he already is. As he stood before us in per-

formance, I told her to take him between the eyes, as the way he positioned his head at that angle, it was the only shot to take. The rifle bellowed, and the elephant in classic brain shot form, threw his head back and went down all in one motion. He never moved again.

It was a superb display of the capability of the .375 H&H Magnum. The 300-grain Trophy Bonded Sledgehammer solid made it through 4 feet of meat and honeycombed bone to reach its destination, claiming the world's largest land mammal effortlessly.

THE .500 NITRO EXPRESS

This piece wouldn't be complete without a cartridge suited for the two-pipe, that bacon-saver, the double rifle. My choice would be the .500 Nitro Express. Those who know me know I have a particular fondness for the .500 Jeffery, and it may be a surprise that I don't list it in my top five. Even so, I hold to my belief that ammo availability in the direst of circumstances is a priority. The fact remains that there are more .500 NE rifles currently

The .500 Nitro Express is a great choice when the game is dangerous and the distances are short. Photo: Massaro Media Group

Leyendecker used a .500 NE double rifle to guide his client to this Cape buffalo bull.

operating in Africa than .500 Jefferys. Therefore, the .500 NE gets the nod.

The .500 NE is a very capable cartridge, which can make quick work of the world's largest game species. This caliber is a stopper and ideal medicine for elephants, rhinos, buffalos and hippos. Furthermore, it's housed in a double rifle, and a big double is a priceless piece of equipment for dangerous game hunters worldwide.

Developed around 1860, the .500 Nitro Express was originally a blackpowder cartridge, the .500 Express. With the advent of cordite in 1889, the traditional blackpowder rifles had to be either powered down or a completely new rifle built due to the cordite's high pressure. Cordite contains nitroglycerine, where the name Nitro Express is derived, the latter part of the name coming from the comparison to an Express train.

The difference in stopping power between the blackpowder cartridge and the cordite version was worlds apart,

and after the First World War, the Nitro Express became a staple in Africa and India. The traditional 570-grain bullet travels at 2,200 fps with about 5,800 ft-lbs of energy behind it. It is a necessary and formidable caliber after the largest and most dangerous big game.

On a recent safari, I carried a .500 NE as a backup rifle for my buffalo hunter. My client shot a beautiful buffalo bull that required a bit of follow-up. Once we caught up to the cantankerous beast, we got a shot into him that took him off his feet at a range of about 50 yards. We moved in slowly, for as famed professional hunter Tony Dyer once said, "It's the dead ones that get up and kill you." As we neared the downed bull, he rolled over and was sternal.

I instructed my client to shoot immediately. We were under 7 yards from the buffalo. As he shot and the buffalo sprung to its feet, Professional Hunter Van Zyl Du Toit and I fired. As everyone was reloading, I still had my second

round readily available and had the ivory bead fixed on the bull's brain. Luckily, the buffalo stumbled and fell over. I positioned my client to give the bull a *coupe de grace* as the buff attempted to roll back on its legs. The bull was out for the count. In this situation, had the bull not stumbled, we would have had a scenario where two out of three were reloading, and only one was ready for an immediate shot, the big double. Once again, the .500 NE proved its place on the top five list.

There is nothing particularly interesting or different in this lineup of king cartridges. I don't believe in the latest and greatest and have a deep love for the cartridges of yesteryear that have remained steadfast and reliable through time. Some calibers never go out of fashion, and this list is a perfect example of that — calibers that work and truly need no introduction. The five listed are reliable, capable, available, dependable, and, to a degree, nostalgic. **GD**

AR-18: Evolution of Stoner's Rifle

> JOSH WAYNER

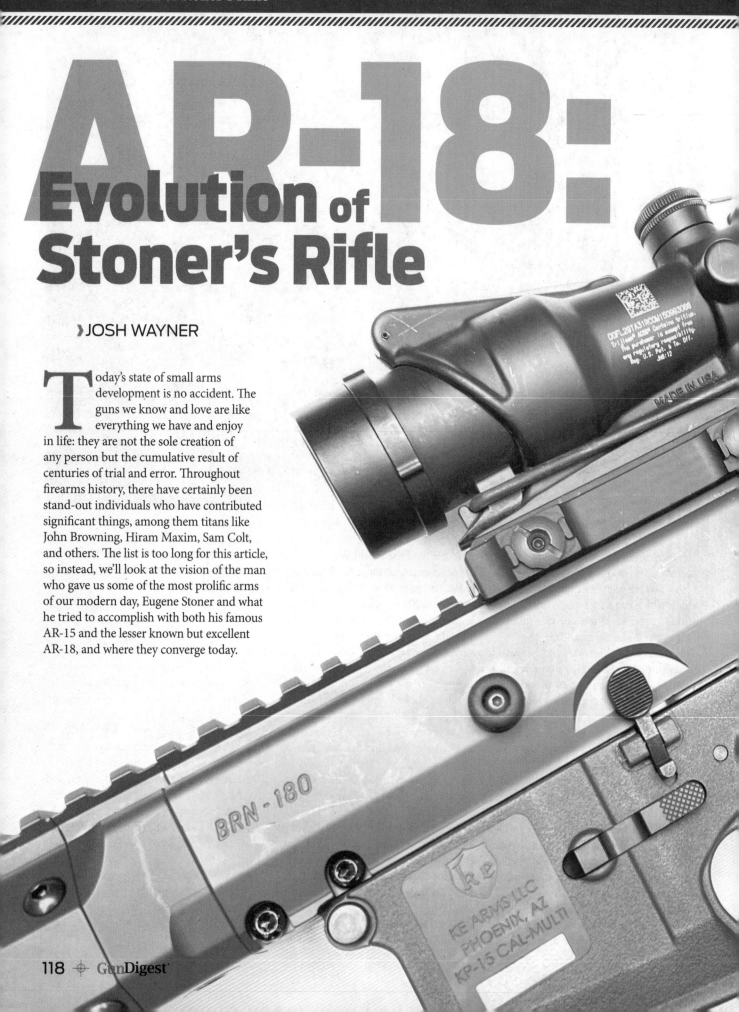

Today's state of small arms development is no accident. The guns we know and love are like everything we have and enjoy in life: they are not the sole creation of any person but the cumulative result of centuries of trial and error. Throughout firearms history, there have certainly been stand-out individuals who have contributed significant things, among them titans like John Browning, Hiram Maxim, Sam Colt, and others. The list is too long for this article, so instead, we'll look at the vision of the man who gave us some of the most prolific arms of our modern day, Eugene Stoner and what he tried to accomplish with both his famous AR-15 and the lesser known but excellent AR-18, and where they converge today.

The AR-18's folding stock is difficult to replace, so this one used a FAL-style folder. Photo: Brian Meyer

A MAN WITH A PLAN

Before we review Brownell's fantastic reproduction, the BRN-180, we need to look at what Stoner was trying to accomplish when he set about creating his guns. Without getting too far down the rabbit hole of the man's life, Stoner was decidedly ahead of his time in many ways. But he took a backseat in others regarding certain aspects of his designs. Mikhail Kalashnikov – developer of the Russian AK-47 - was not exactly impressed when he reviewed captured American M16s taken from the field in Southeast Asia. As the story goes, he thought the design was akin to a joke.

But Stoner's designs were quite advanced for their day, not just in the way they worked but also in the materials. Stoner was the first designer to develop products made from space-age materials like polymer and aluminum instead of steel and wood. The overarching theme of Stoner's first rifles was that they should be lightweight so shooters could carry equipment with less fatigue and maintenance. This task was not readily accomplished; it was a downright disaster. Stoner's first major 'success' was the military's adoption of the early AR-15 as the M16, but this victory was rife with difficulty. The supposedly space-age rifle system was running into tremendous problems in Vietnam. That such an advanced country with a nuclear arsenal rivaling any in the world could not produce the basic arm of a soldier was incredulous to many people, including politicians and gun writers.

The AR-18 was designed for manufacture by unskilled labor. Made chiefly of stamped metal, the number of machining operations was minimized. Photo: Brian Meyer

The real issues came down to the materials used in the M16 and that it wasn't Stoner's final version of his weapons family. The M16 was not rugged enough for the environment it was being asked to fight in; it lacked features common to inexpensive guns like the AK-47, such as a chrome-lined barrel and a reliable piston gas system. The M16 was a direct gas design, blowing powder residue directly into the receiver. Due to a last-minute change in the powder type, the M16 was prone to excessive corrosion and rusting. The guns were falling apart. Soldiers took to various methods to keep them running, including oiling up ammunition and carrying cleaning rods taped to the upper receiver so they could punch out stuck casings in the chamber. That was not a good look for the design, but over time it was remedied, and today the AR-15 is the most popular civilian rifle in the country. It is head and shoulders above what was first issued.

Stoner never intended to stop with the M16. He envisioned an entire suite of modular small arms, different uppers, lowers, belt-fed light machine guns, and many other variations. Today, we have realized that vision. Indeed, you can get any upper you want in any caliber you want for your AR-15, including belt-fed versions and other cool stuff. The sky is the limit.

THE AR-18 EVOLUTION

Stoner's initial work on the M16 eventually stopped, and his attention shifted to other products, most of which never became commercially successful in America. One of these designs produced by ArmaLite was the AR-18, which was highly successful in its own right but never achieved much fame as a stand-alone design. It became the basis of many

other types of rifles, most of which were proprietary designs and not interchangeable. The basis of the AR-18 is a short-stroke piston and compact bolt carrier, as opposed to the AR-15's direct gas system and long buffer tube. Thus, the AR-18 could have a folding stock. It had very little reciprocating mass, making for a very easy-to-shoot rifle.

Though the AR-18 never really achieved the success it deserved, it was in almost every way a superior rifle to the AR-15. But in the realities of Cold War America, these rapid small arms changes would only complicate the situation where fighting was taking place. The AR-15/M16 was going to stay, and ArmaLite went looking for buyers for the AR-18. It succeeded in finding a few end users, and the rifle only achieved lasting fame in the hands of the Irish Republican Army, which procured enough of them to cause the occupying British headaches for decades. In the end, only around 25,000 were produced in fully automatic and semi-auto variants, a footnote in the history of small arms design. However,

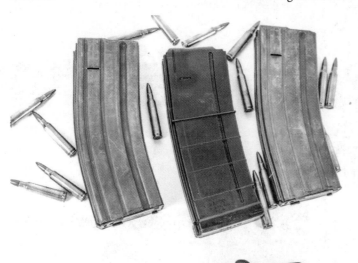

One major design flaw is that the AR-18 cannot use AR-15 mags. Photo: Brian Meyer

Compact, light, and hard-hitting, the BRN-180 with KE Arms lower is all the rifle you need. Add a SilencerCo suppressor, Armageddon Gear high-temp cover, Winkler Combat Axe, and other goodies, and you'll have a great time wherever you go.

The BRN-180 can ride in a dedicated, folding stock lower.

Eugene Stoner's designs have come a long way but haven't strayed too far from their source. These rifles can be built (minus a few odds and ends) directly from the Brownells catalog. The Brownell's Retro M16-A1 is reminiscent of the original guns used in the early days of Stoner's design career. The modern, fully kitted-out AR in the middle shows what this platform can become with some imagination. The BRN-180 build is the child of several Stoner-inspired concepts, itself a perfect blend of AR modularity and AR-18 simplicity.

the offshoot products, including the British SA80, Japanese Type 89, FN SCAR and FS2000, H&K G36, Steyr AUG, and many more, are direct descendants of the AR-18. ArmaLite's design had merit, but not in the hands of the company that developed it.

As the years passed, various attempts were made to homogenize the AR-15 lower into a less complex, easier-to-maintain unit. Colt, which at the time was manufacturing the M16 for use in Vietnam, produced the prototype of a one-piece polymer lower receiver. It was ultimately not a success, but it showed that the design could be continually worked on and improved. Of course, this one-piece lower never saw use outside the prototype phase, but it allowed in-

The railed handguard features a full-length 1913 interface. The rest of the handguard is covered in MLOK attachment points. Note that the handguard is very close to the barrel, so you must watch your MLOK accessories, as the locking screws can be too long to touch the barrel. Many people ignore this, which has led to poor accuracy results.

sight into the direction the AR-15 would go. Today, we see a vast proliferation of one-piece lowers, most notably from KE Arms. The KE Arms lowers are simple, strong, and, more importantly, light-

weight. While we will never fully know what Stoner intended for the end-stage evolution of the AR-15, we can certainly use our imaginations, which is just what we're going to be doing as you read on.

THE BROWNELLS BRN-180

Over the last five or so years, Brownells has been a major player in bringing interesting designs to market. It had a very popular Retro line of AR rifles that were about as close to the original models as you could get, including some truly fascinating versions made to replicate some of the AR prototypes. In that timeframe, Brownells brought out what is now one of its most iconic products, the BRN-180. I called Brownells' Paul Levy, and we chatted about the BRN-180, where it is, where it is going, and a bit of its history. The BRN-180 upper's development timeline was relatively short, although it was a completely new design in its own right, making that feat even more impressive.

"We started looking at other designs for inspirations, and the 180 came up," Levy said. "Stamping was not feasible, it would cost too much. The idea was to put the 180 upper on an AR lower, and Dean Sylvester at Primary Weapon Systems and Paul Noonan at Foxtrot Mike Products were contacted, and a design was mocked up."

With the groundwork of the standard AR-15 already laid out, the dimensions of the new 180 upper were more or less already decided. The AR-18 is a longer action with different dimensions than the BRN 180. The two are incompatible. However, unknowingly, this marriage of AR-15 to AR-18 would bring out the absolute best of both systems and combine them into the cleanest, most efficient upper available today. What Brownells has brought to market with the BRN-180 is nothing short of extraordinary. This collaboration resulted in a multi-piece upper receiver with a bolt carrier that rides along two guide rods. The bolt carrier is compact and surprisingly low in mass. The gas piston system is stunningly compact; the receiver and handguard have a narrow profile, making the completed rifle feel handy and quick. It's not bulky or uncomfortable in any place, which I feel Stoner would have appreciated. As a reimagining of an existing design, it's a dream come true and is arguably better across the board than any other AR-18 descendant.

The BRN-180 can mount virtually all modern optics. Ensure your scope mount doesn't stick out too far on the sides, as the charging handle must be clear of any obstruction to move freely.

The BRN-180's operating components are compact and clean-running. The low bolt carrier mass makes a huge difference in felt recoil. While the AR-15 is not a bruiser by any stretch, the difference is tangible between uppers if you swap them onto the same lower.

The author with the BRN-180; while its silhouette may seem to conjure an AR-15, it is a different animal altogether.

many things about what Stoner would do today.

The distinct difference between the original AR-18 and the Brownells BRN180 is that the former was a true standalone design made to work with minimal machine time, something of a modern Grease Gun or STEN in terms of stamped parts and simplicity. The BRN180, while heavily based on the operating system of the AR-18, is designed to work with the AR-15 as a self-contained upper receiver. It is not stamped, instead being completely machined. The major point here is the the AR-18 was not just a firearm mechanism, but a design theory that integrated certain methods and materials. The BRN180 is more or less a supplemental design

Brownells also sells the lower KE Arms developed for the 'What Would Stoner Do' (WWSD) rifle project. While this topic has been discussed for quite some time, this is the first product series that addresses it in a way you can spend money on. The concept behind the lower (also available as a complete rifle) was the idea Stoner had in mind: using the most advanced materials and methods in his day. In our modern era, we should seek to keep that going. The folks at InRange TV and KE Arms conceived the discussion on that particular product series, and they surmised

The BRN-180 upper on a standard Brownells BRN4 H&K-style lower. You can add the upper to any standard AR lower, folding stock or not.

that takes the benefits of the AR-18 and applies them to the AR-15. As a result, the original AR-18 and today's BRN180 are not compatible with one another.

THE BUILD

I disagreed with some assertions posed by the hosts of the show, namely that the final commercial rifle for sale in modern times would have been based on the AR-15 rather than the AR-18. Stoner's designs had moved past the AR-15; while space-age in 1955, it was inefficient and had many prob-lematic elements,

namely the action with its buffer assembly and direct gas operation.

The WWSD rifles would certainly not have been AR-15s if Stoner himself had been there to do it. I agree with the one-piece lower and lack of iron sights, considering that modern optics are incredibly rugged and one-piece lowers reduce weight and complexity.

Adding the BRN-180 upper to the KE WWSD lower was a no-brainer, and I built one in classy OD Green. I added a Trijicon TA31 ACOG sight, SilencerCo Hybrid 46M suppressor on an ASR quick-detach mount, and as few other goodies as I could manage while making the rifle functional. I wanted it as slender and light as possible while making

it easy to shoot and handle.

The upper and lower came ready to slap together, and it took me all of ten minutes to install the optic, low-profile Geissele MLOK grip panels, Magpul vertical grip, and ASR mount. It was one of the fastest builds of my writing career. Once it was all set, I took it out to make some noise.

Shooting this rifle is a joy, plain and simple. If you were to look up 'soft shooting' in the dictionary, you would inevitably find the BRN-180 under the definition. With a suppressor attached, the rifle has essentially no recoil. The low bolt carrier mass combined with the 5.56mm cartridge truly makes the firing experience feel like nothing else. Not only is it soft shooting, but it's incredibly fast and stays on target. The bolt travel distance is roughly the same as a standard AR-15, although it stays on target

The BRN-180 receiver is thick-walled and extremely rigid.

BRN-180
Compatibility

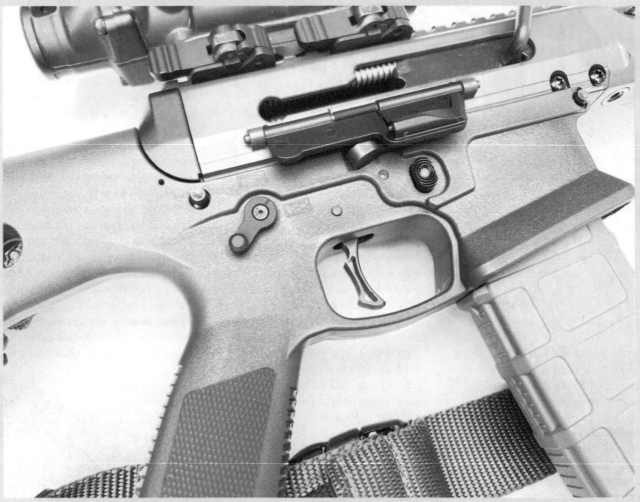

The WWSD KE lower has an excellent trigger, functional short-throw safety, and an ambidextrous bolt release.

The BRN-180 is a drop-in upper for standard AR-15 lowers. It can work on just about any footprint that shares these dimensions. The upper does not require a buffer tube, but you should not feel the need to move to a folding stock automatically. I've used both, and there are benefits to each. If you have a standard lower and want to keep it as-is for use with your other uppers, there is no reason to go with a side-folding stock. This is especially useful if you're like me and have lots of uppers going on several lowers. It makes things much easier. If you want a folding stock, Brownells has a line of BRN-180 lowers that feature 1913 rails and no buffer tube should you wish to make a dedicated lower for your BRN-180 upper.

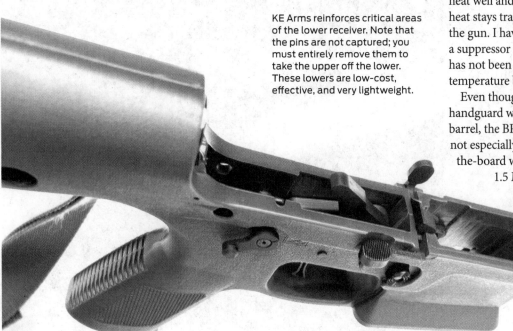

KE Arms reinforces critical areas of the lower receiver. Note that the pins are not captured; you must entirely remove them to take the upper off the lower. These lowers are low-cost, effective, and very lightweight.

much easier. Split times with this rifle are impossibly fast. I could stay entirely in the A-zone at 25 yards with this rifle firing six shots in under a second. When I say it doesn't move, *it doesn't move*.

What is more impressive is how easy it is to use with a suppressor. This is a Gen 2 upper on the test rifle, and it comes with a means to manually adjust the gas piston, although I found that unnecessary on my sample. It runs exceptionally clean. The action is fully enclosed, and unlike the AR-15, it doesn't have a port at the rear for the charging handle. Working the action is accomplished using the charging handle mounted to the side of the bolt carrier, just like you would find on an AK or the original AR-18. As a result, you don't get any gas blowing back into your shooting eye — probably the most notable feature when firing the gun rapidly with a suppressor attached. Optics like the ACOG require you to get relatively close to the lens for a complete sight picture; firing a standard AR with the ACOG mounted similarly can get uncomfortable. I can't tell you how often I've gotten dry eye from shooting suppressed ARs. It was a breath of fresh air not to worry about that.

Another substantial benefit of the BRN-180 is that it runs exceptionally clean. The piston operation system

ensures that no hot gas is blown back directly into the action, so the upper receiver stays as clean as you could hope during the entire course of fire. Having worked with both generations of BRN-180 and in rifle and pistol format, this is a huge benefit. Suppressors are quite dirty to use, and most AR-pattern rifles I have fired suppressed need to be thoroughly cleaned relatively often because of the amount of carbon that builds up in the receiver. This is just not so with the BRN-180. Because the action stays so clean, it also remains reliable. Even after firing 500 rounds combined of Federal M193 and a mixed bag of other Federal loads, it was only perhaps 5 percent as dirty as an AR-15 in the same firing schedule.

A notable difference between the AR-15 and the BRN-180 is where heat develops and how that heat is radiated through the handguard. The BRN-180's handguard is relatively thick-walled and quite close to the barrel. There is not much space underneath the handguard. Many people are accustomed to shooting the AR-15 with quite a bit of open air around the barrel — between it and the handguard. However, the BRN-180 bleeds most of its heat directly into the handguards. I have used fabric covers that mitigate this; however, these are only a stopgap measure. While they absorb

heat well and keep your hands safe, most heat stays trapped underneath, heating the gun. I have noticed stringing when a suppressor is mounted, and the gun has not been allowed to cool to room temperature between strings.

Even though it is a relatively slender handguard with little space around the barrel, the BRN-180's barrel profile is not especially thick. Accuracy across-the-board with Federal M193 is around 1.5 MOA when cool and 2 1/2 MOA when hot. Vertical stringing, while minor, occurs in groups after around two 30-round magazines. I've noticed this issue with all BRN-180 models I have worked with, and it's a relatively common problem with piston rifles in general. However, it's not problematic for a rifle like the BRN-180, designed for recreational shooting and ruggedness. The BRN-180 is not expressly designed as a target upper; it is firmly in the sport/utility camp.

CONCLUSION

Over the years, there have been many exceptional firearm designs that have never achieved actual fruition. In the case of the AR-18, it was simply not the rifle for its time. However, what Brownells and friends accomplished with the BRN-180 truly bridged the gap between what could have been and should have been. The BRN-180 is still a relatively young design. It is, without a doubt, one of the most reliable, self-contained uppers I have ever used, if not the most reliable. Over many years, I've worked with the first- and second-generation models and have put 10,000 to 15,000 rounds through them without a single feeding or firing issue. This design's pure utility to the AR-15 lower cannot be understated! I think Stoner would be proud to see that his ideas are still being tweaked and worked on today. While we stand on the shoulders of giants like him, I believe they are happy that we continue their work. **GD**

Founder Harris Holland.

On February 1, 2021, Holland & Holland (H&H), long revered for its high-quality rifles in big game calibers, was acquired by the Beretta Holding Group from its previous owner, Chanel. For the previous three decades, the French company tried to redefine and reinvent the venerable old gun maker into a fashion-focused entity, with questionable success. Quoting one of Chanel's directors, the French fashion giant tried to turn the English company into "the Ralph Lauren of the shooting world." Ultimately, it failed and sold the company to a renowned family-owned enterprise that has crafted guns for the past 500 years.

Since 1893, Holland & Holland's London factory has produced some of the world's finest and most reliable sporting shotguns and rifles. H&H guns are handmade by integrating both traditional and contemporary techniques. Time-honored gun-making skills and state-of-the-art machinery combine perfectly to instill quality and artistry into every shotgun and rifle. For many owners, these are not just guns ... they are pieces of art to be treasured for generations.

JOE COOGAN

The venerable London gun company is re-armed with its sights set on a bright future.

Holland & Holland
Returns to its
Prized Purpose

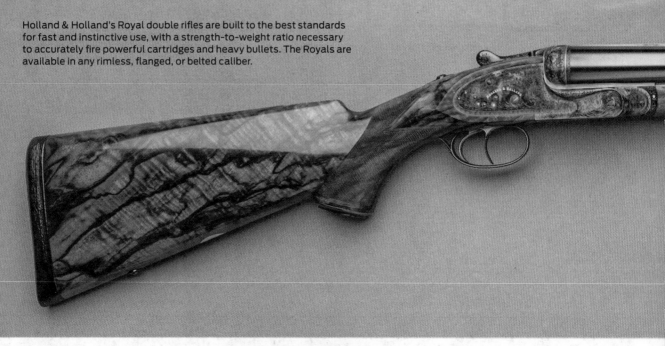

Holland & Holland's Royal double rifles are built to the best standards for fast and instinctive use, with a strength-to-weight ratio necessary to accurately fire powerful cartridges and heavy bullets. The Royals are available in any rimless, flanged, or belted caliber.

A disassembled .700 H&H NE Royal de Luxe is displayed in its three main components; the barrels, forend, sidelock action, and buttstock. The rifle sports 26-inch barrels, the finest deluxe-grade Turkish walnut stocks and ornate engraving masterfully executed by the renowned Brown brothers of Swindon, England.

"We have an exciting future ahead of us, and this new era sees the company re-establishing itself as the hallmark of fine English gun making," said Mike Jones, H&H's marketing manager. "Last year, we undertook a full strategic business review alongside an extensive brand positioning exercise to put us firmly back on track."

Holland & Holland's DNA has always been that of a pure gun company, one of the best, in fact. If you wanted its artisans to build you a gun, they dedicated themselves to that purpose by being masters at determining and satisfying the customer's wants and needs. They'd say whether they could do it, how they could do it, and when they could do it. The customer was involved from the first moment, and the excitement of initiating a new build was maintained throughout the process. There were no surprises or deviations to limit the production of high-quality products with value built into the brand. Excellent customer rela-tions were cultivated by maintaining personal relationships that began with a one-on-one relationship with the man behind the counter.

THE .700 H&H

No finer example of Holland & Holland's working relationship with a customer exists than the consummate gun collector and big game hunter William Feldstein, who walked into 33 Bruton St., London, in 1985 with a check to cover the cost of

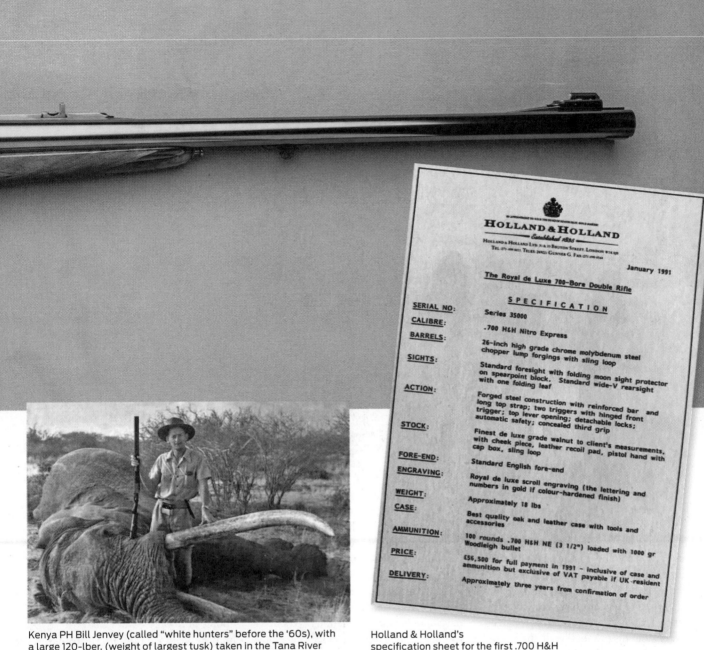

Kenya PH Bill Jenvey (called "white hunters" before the '60s), with a large 120-lber. (weight of largest tusk) taken in the Tana River region of northeastern Kenya. Jenvey holds his backup gun, an H&H Royal sidelock double rifle in .500/465 NE.

Holland & Holland's specification sheet for the first .700 H&H NE double sidelock rifle delivered in January 1991. Considered the most powerful sporting firearm in the world, recoil management for the .700 H&H NE requires that the rifle weighs around 18 pounds.

a huge gun order. Feldstein, known to all London gun makers, could have gone to any of them, but he chose Holland & Holland to build him a set of five bespoke British large-bore Nitro Express double rifles. These five tailor-made rifles would be made to his specifications, with the .600 NE anchoring the set. Feldstein had no doubts about Holland & Holland being the company to fulfill the order and his dreams.

Feldstein's philosophy about the artistry and function of fine double rifles was summed up in a letter he wrote to a friend with whom he'd done several safaris. "Most men who purchase English best double rifles do not hunt with them because of their value. I believe to the contrary. Skilled craftsmen have devoted 1400 to 1500 hours of their time … is it not our responsibility as a tribute to their artistry to take the rifles into the field and use them in the manner for which they were built?"

Feldstein met with David Winks, Holland & Holland's showroom manager. After hearing Feldstein's request, Winks regrettably explained that H&H couldn't entertain the complete order. In 1975, H&H directors had decided to build the company's last .600 NE and announced and certified that rifle as such. The board of directors refused to budge on its decision with an unequivocal "no." Feldstein finally accepted the board's decision but was still resolute in his desire for an ultra-

An fine example of Holland & Holland's deep scroll engraving bordering a game scene depicted on the Royal's elegant and bolstered sidelock action. The back action locks allow for a solid bar to add rigidity and weight where needed. The Royal double rifles feature articulated front triggers to prevent finger bruising.

large-bore bespoke H&H rifle to crown his collection.

"Okay, then build me a .700 NE," Feldstein suggested. When the laughter and mirth died down, the board calmly explained why they would hesitate to consider his .700 order request.

Through Feldstein's dogged persistence, H&H's directors eventually agreed to consider his proposal. Still, they were extremely wary of undertaking a scheme they considered impulsive and stipulated conditions that would have proved daunting to a man of lesser means and determination. Their reply to Feldstein came down to, "Design the cartridge, give us the specs, and we'll talk again."

The company agreed to the project only after Feldstein had financed the development and production of 5,000 rounds of .700 H&H cartridges. By January 1990, a beautifully engraved double sidelock Holland & Holland Royal de Luxe prototype in .700 H&H was completed. The range tests verified what the designers had calculated regarding recoil: "about on par with a light 10-pound .500 Jeffery magazine rifle with the character of a faster recoiling eight-bore."

The field test for the new .700 H&H double gun was a 21-day safari to hunt elephants in Ethiopia. Feldstein, accompanied by PH Nassos Russos,

Holland & Holland's

1874	1880	1890	1899	1905	1907
.295 Rook introduced	.297/250 Rook introduced	.500/450 Nitro Express introduced	.375 Flanged Nitro Express introduced	.400/375 Belted Nitro Express introduced	.500/465 Nitro Express introduced

From left: The .700 H&H NE accommodates a bullet weighing 1000 grains; bullets in the .577 NE weigh 750 grains, the .500 NE 570 grains, the .375 H&H Magnum 300 grains, and the .300 H&H Magnum 200 grains.

collected an elephant on the third day while hunting the productive Garafurda area. Both cartridge and rifle performed as expected, and Feldstein was ecstatic, claiming "the fantasy and dream have become a reality."

In hindsight, the original price of $115,000 for a .700 H&H was quite a deal, whereas today, you can expect to spend $315,000 for a bare-bones double rifle and upwards of that amount depending on your order requirements. H&H has built 17 double rifles in .700 caliber, with number 18 in current production.

MORE THAN JUST AMMO

My awareness of Holland & Holland goes back to the mid-'50s when my father purchased a Remington Model 721 rifle chambered in a caliber that Holland & Holland originally called the "Super-Thirty." Introduced in 1925, the Super-Thirty cartridge, later called the .300 Holland & Holland Magnum, was designed around a necked-down .375 H&H Mag. belted case. Not only did it cut an impressive figure with its slope-shouldered profile, but it was a real performer able to reach out 200 yards or more effectively. The .30-caliber cartridge has capably proved itself worldwide, accounting for game from the size of moose in North America to the 2,000-pound eland in Africa. Since its introduction, the venerable cartridge has stood the test of time throughout the world's game fields.

When my family moved to Kenya in the '60s, that rifle/caliber combo was the ticket for the plains game we hunted. That's when I discovered the name Hol-

Sara Johnson (right) of Houston, Texas, with an exceptional Botswana gemsbok she collected using her brother Kley's (left) bespoke H&H bolt-action magazine rifle, chambered in .300 H&H Magnum, a respected and inherently accurate rifle/caliber combination.

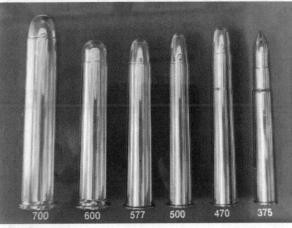

700 600 577 500 470 375

A selection of popular big-bore cartridges typically chambered in H&H guns.

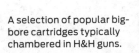

Cartridge Introductions

1912	1912	1920	1925	1929	1955	1991	2003	2003
.275 H&H Magnum introduced in belted and rimmed versions	.375 H&H Magnum introduced in belted and rimmed versions	.240 Apex introduced in belted and rimmed versions	.300 H&H Magnum introduced in belted and rimmed versions	.600/577 Rewa introduced	.244 H&H Magnum introduced	.700 Nitro Express introduced	.400 H&H Magnum introduced	.465 H&H Magnum introduced

land & Holland signified far more than an excellent, field-proven cartridge — it's one of the oldest and most respected names in the world of gun making. Owning an H&H rifle is a dream for many, and carrying one brings respect and prestige among the world's knowledgeable big game hunters.

When I began work as a professional hunter in Botswana, one of my first clients arrived in Maun with a beautifully cased H&H Royal in .500/.465 Nitro Express. Dutifully proud, my client stood back to watch as I reverently opened the case to admire the deeply engraved artwork and beautifully figured stock of a magnificent rifle. But I soon found that my client's lofty esteem of the rifle's capabilities did not match his shooting ability. Regarding the rifle as if it were a magic wand, he thought it needed only to be waved in the general direction of game, which would drop at the sound of the shot. Sadly, this was not the case, and lifting him from his shooting slump was challenging.

"But it's a Holland & Holland; how can I miss with it?" he appealed naively.

As a dangerous game gun, it was even more critical that his shooting improve before we tackled the game that might strike back. My constant and repeated reminders for him to hold the rifle steady to the point of aim and squeeze the trigger eventually edged his shots closer to the bulls-eye. He soon began to see the benefits of the rifle's inherent accuracy. No matter how magnificent a rifle might look or its inherent accuracy, effective and accurate shots at game still depend on the shooter's ability to apply gun handling skills to achieve desired results. The client eventually got it and enjoyed collecting a fine tusker with his H&H Royal de Lux.

HOLLAND & HOLLAND'S BEGINNING
Harris Holland began gun making in 1835. While the company's background is unclear, it is known that Holland owned a lucrative tobacco wholesale business in London before delving into gun making. His interest in shooting saw him frequently participating in pigeon shoots at important London clubs and leasing an expensive grouse Moor in Yorkshire.

Being a recognized and accomplished shot, his friends encouraged him to start his own gun-making business. When he did, his approach was rather unorthodox, to say the least, for Harris completely skipped the all-important apprenticeship training. London Best makers such as Boss, Lang, and Lancaster had all served apprenticeships with Joseph Manton, while others such as Beesley, Grant, and Atkin apprenticed under Purdey or Boss.

The company's early guns were likely built to Holland's specifications by other makers in the trade and bore only the inscription *H. Holland* without an address. Exactly when he started manufacturing his guns is unknown, but it is estimated to have been sometime in the 1850s. Holland invited his nephew, Henry Holland, to join the company in 1861 when Henry served his apprenticeship. Henry excelled at the craft and, in 1876, became a partner, which initiated the company's name change to Holland & Holland.

By 1883, H&H dominated the trials organized by the magazine *The Field*, sweeping the rifle categories to set a new standard of excellence for competition among English gun makers. During this time, Henry secured 47 firearms-related patents for Holland & Holland.

Three essential qualities define a Holland & Holland game gun: ease of handling, absolute reliability, and effortless maintenance. Hand-detachable sidelocks can be easily removed for cleaning using a discrete release lever.

Skilled master craftsmen fit each H&H double rifle with individually regulated chopper-lump barrels, detachable sidelock action, bolts, and ejectors. Each finished gun has received between 1,400 and 1,500 hours of expert hands-on work.

THE ROYAL

But the crowning achievement of the partnership was the Royal side-by-side sidelock. Initially, the Royal had problems with an asymmetrical design with one lock cocked upon opening and the other upon closing, which tended to promote weakness on one side. That problem was resolved by the simple solution of duplicating the right-hand lock. Donald Dallas, writing in *Holland & Holland: The Royal Gunmaker*, says it was introduced "in the spring of 1885 and has continued in production ever since as the flagship of Holland & Holland."

That same year, the trademark "The Royal" and Holland & Holland's patents were granted for the Paradox gun, a shotgun with rifling in the front two inches of the barrel. By the latter part of the 1880s, H&H's success was such that it sold an average of 400 shotguns and rifles yearly — probably the largest trade in sporting rifles in Britain.

At that time, its premises were located at 98 New Bond Street, which was too small to allow for the large-scale manufacture that was becoming necessary. Henry decided to use profits from the business to build a new factory, thus revolutionizing the brand from retailers to builders of guns on a much larger scale. It would also allow for greater quality control.

The first factory was located at 527 Harrow Road — a location chosen for its proximity to the shooting and testing ground at Kensal Rise and nearby train stations. At the time, there was little building in this area, so the land was cheap, and there was much open countryside. Construction began on the new factory in 1892 by builders Holland & Hannen — a curious coincidence, but with no relation to Harris or Henry. By the Spring of 1893, work was completed, and the building drew universal admiration for the specifically-designed

structure with many windows to allow as much natural light as possible.

The Field published a detailed article about the factory on May 27, 1893, writing:

"In all upwards of 100 men are employed by Messrs. Holland & Holland upon the highest clay of work alone; and in order to secure the intelligent services of the best artificers, and to turn out work the firm need not be ashamed of, everything that money can procure, or experience suggests, appears to be provided. This is the most perfect and complete factory we have yet seen in London."

In 1908, H&H patented the detachable lock feature with a small lever for sidelock shotguns. The last significant development in the evolution of the side-by-side sidelock gun occurred in 1922 when H&H patented an assisted-opening mechanism. Its self-opening Royal side-by-side gun was an innovation that influenced the gun-making of double-barreled shotguns

Building an H&H Rifle

The production of a Holland & Holland gun begins with the barrels that start life as two lengths of steel. The tubes are meticulously drilled, turned, reamed, joined, and polished to ensure a perfect line. Barrel-makers guarantee that each one is perfectly round and concentric.

Quality actions only leave the factory after firing tens of thousands of shots. Every mechanical part works according to the best engineering principles; stress and wear are minimized while operation remains flawless.

Hand engraving is a true celebration of ancient art. H&H's iconic Royal engraving showcases deep foliate scrolls that enhance the appearance of the actions and locks. Bespoke engraving can incorporate detailed game scenes, personal designs, and precious metal inlays.

Stocks are made from the finest Turkish walnut, a beautifully strong wood that is dried for up to two years to prevent warpage. Utilizing only the best blanks, craftsmen carve, cut, chisel, and shape the wood to fit the bespoke measurements of the customer. Hand inletting ensures perfect function; hand-rubbing seals the grain with a durable natural finish, wherein the hand's heat helps the oil settle

and builds up essential layers of protection. The result is a beautiful, comfortable, ergonomic, and hard-wearing stock that connects the shooter with the gun.

"Finishing" a gun brings together all the work of every craftsman. Once the final touches — from ejector timing to trigger pulls and lacquering the metal to checkering and polishing wood — are complete, the gun is ready to leave the factory and begin its life in the field.

and rifles throughout the world.

Holland & Holland's Royal, which saw improvements applied over a century, became the classic London Best Gun. This design has been copied but never bettered by any gun makers. With a rock-solid sidelock mechanism, reliable ejectors and a self-opening mechanism, the Royal Game Gun was elegant, accurate, and fast in the field. An H&H Royal was one of the best bespoke guns to own and was considered the ultimate firearm, tailored to each shooter.

Each Royal features individually regulated chopper-lump barrels, a time-proven sidelock mechanism, bolts, and ejectors. The front trigger is articulated to help prevent finger bruising, and the patented ejector system is simple and exceptionally reliable. The reinforced action incorporates locks at the back of the action to create a solid bar, adding weight and rigidity where it is most needed. The Royal

double rifle, designed for close work when the next shot might mean the difference between life and death, was available in any rimless, flanged, or belted caliber.

In the 1930s, Holland & Holland introduced the Dominion model in both shotgun and double rifle format, which was available at affordable prices compared to the best Royal models offered by the company. The name Dominion was about the British Dominions, which included countries such as South Africa, Australia, New Zealand, and Newfoundland. The Dominion guns targeted a broader customer base, mainly administrators, military officers, and sportsmen.

These rifles are very distinctive in style and embody a certain appeal. Featuring swept-back and slightly dipped back-action locks, they are robust and are real workhorse rifles. Dominion shotguns and rifles are still regularly seen in the field today, a testament to the design's strength.

The late Soren Lindstrom holds his Holland & Holland .500 NE Dominion-grade, boxlock double rifle. Dominions were introduced in the 1930s in both shotgun and double rifle formats. The name Dominion refers to the British Dominions, which included countries such as South Africa, Australia, New Zealand, and Newfoundland.

A cased H&H Royal sidelock double rifle with accessories. The gun features color-casehardened sidelocks with scroll engraving and a beautifully figured top-grade Turkish walnut stock that was dried for two years to prevent warpage.

As the name Dominion suggests, the gun was built for use in remote areas where reliability was crucial to survival.

Following World War II, under the leadership of the new owner and Managing Director, Malcolm Lyell, company representatives traveled to India to locate and buy guns from the famous collections of the princes and maharajahs, developing an essential market for pre-owned guns bought by second owners. The '50s and '60s were reasonably profitable for the company. Still, times were changing, with ammo availability for double guns becoming scarce and the introduction of more economic big-bore magazine rifles and ammo suitable for the largest game gaining momentum.

In 1989, the French luxury group Chanel bought all remaining shares in H&H. The original factory building, in use since 1898, was renovated and equipped with modern technology. During Chanel's reign, naysayers claimed that sales of high-end shotguns and rifles had seen better days and were in a slump. Some pointed out that a generation of significant collectors was fading away, with their collections flooding the market and reducing prices and values. Others felt the Holland & Holland name meant little to those outside the shooting world.

Despite this pessimism, Chanel poured money into modernizing the production facilities on Harrow Road, including an investment in computers and CNC machinery to the tune of millions of dollars. Guns like the Royal over/under and side-by-side were improved and reintroduced, becoming available from 4-bore to .360 inch. Back then, a hand-built gun from H&H could cost around $75,000 for a shotgun and close to $120,000 for some rifles, with prices roughly doubling with luxury engraving. The waiting period was two to three years between ordering and delivery. But sales continued to decline, and, during this time, the company's London flagship store, for many years located at 33 Bruton Street, was closed, as was the gun room in New York City.

A NEW DAY DAWNS

In 2004, rumors began to circulate that the company was again up for sale, but it would take nearly 20 years before a final deal could be made with the Beretta

Holland & Holland's new London flagship gun room, located on St. James Street, offers customers personal services that include gunsmithing, gun fitting, valuations and histories in a well-appointed, comfortable setting.

Holland & Holland's Future

The whole ethos of Holland & Holland is based around its new tagline, "Perfecting the art of shooting since 1835," the result of last year's strategic planning. The company is implementing a 10-year product strategy, starting with launching a new shotgun in late 2023. The rebrand will include hosting VIP events in the U.S. in support of that introduction and a re-launch of a hunting clothing and accessories line in late 2023.

Early in 2024, H&H plans to launch a new bolt-action rifle that will be unveiled at the 2024 Dallas Safari Club Show. Beyond building fine shotguns and rifles and best-in-class clothing and accessories, H&H's aim, along with its Beretta Group partners, is to initiate innovative ammunition solutions, grow brand partner networks, and deliver the very best in customer service with a dedicated team of specialists.

Group. Headquartered in Gardone Val Trompia near Brescia, Italy, Beretta Holding is an Italian holding company for the industrial group that holds direct or indirect participation in 26 companies. With its centuries-old history and background, there is no doubt Beretta knows more about guns and corporate survival in a changing environment than any other company.

Today, Holland & Holland's new London flagship gun room is located on St. James Street and is available for visits by appointment during business hours throughout the week. The company's U.S. gun room is located at University Park, Dallas, Texas, where a selection of new and pre-owned shotguns, rifles, leather goods, and gun accessories are displayed. The new gun rooms enable H&H to offer customers genuine personal service that includes gunsmithing, gun fitting, valuations, and histories in a setting that reflects the splendor and richness for which

the name Holland & Holland is known.

Holland & Holland's new tagline, "Perfecting the art of shooting since 1835," incorporates the pursuit of perfection in gun making, craftsmanship, and the skill and art of shooting and hunting. This is consistent with the world-class instruction and service that H&H provides at its shooting grounds, including locally sourced game recipes served at the shooting grounds' exclusive restaurant.

Beretta's President & CEO, Franco Gussalli Beretta, said, "Holland & Holland is a project that is much more complex because we absolutely want to keep the strong English identity of the brand, and which is the reason we acquired it. As far as the firearms are concerned, they are and will be completely produced in the London factory and we are reinvesting to have the products and the shop upgraded. The shooting range is also a big asset. We are also analyzing the famous Holland & Holland ammu-

nition's heritage and we will soon make some decisions about the right strategy to take."

There is no question that Holland & Holland plans to remain London's premier gun maker, with all its shotguns and rifles manufactured and assembled in their entirety in England at the London factory. Being part of the Beretta Group allows it to collaborate with partners within the group to innovate and share knowledge. This is a competitive advantage over the competition as Holland & Holland continues to invest in a team of talented craftsmen and apprentices to ensure the long-term continuity of gun-crafting skills. Beretta has a deep-rooted respect for H&H's history, which it, along with the London company, is proud to protect. Holland & Holland plans to build on its prestige within the field sports in preparation for the company's next chapter, looking forward to its 200th anniversary in 2035. **GD**

The Sauer SL5 and the author's test fodder. This combination takes long-range shotgunning for game to a whole new level.

Terminal Tungsten!

When it comes to the latest generation of tungsten shot and long-range shotgunning, prepare to have your mind blown.

❯ L.P.BREZNY

It was late fall in 1971 when I found myself with a small group of eccentric goose hunters digging into deep snow banks along a country road. We were hunting land that bordered the federally controlled Rochester, Minnesota, waterfowl refuge. Clad in down-stuffed snow white camo, these hunters were excited to get their front sight on a passing giant Canada goose. Thought once extinct, the birds had been located on the refuge several years before and were reproducing in huntable numbers.

With six-foot wingspans and weighing more than 21 pounds, they were the big game of the sky, and even at 11 below zero, hunters would fort up in small tents or 4X4 trucks while holding down a small piece of refuge space in the hopes of a fly-by.

This was during the old-school lead shot load development days when I'd use the 10-gauge magnum almost exclusively. We used star-crimped 3.5-inch hulls, smoothing out the hull to create a 4-inch hull, then crimping the edge. We'd then load a couple of ounces or more of No. 4 buckshot into a bed of Cream O' Wheat breakfast cereal. The buckshot was high-antimony blended lead (Western) and custom plated by a local foundry with a thick coating of copper. We used long, one-piece plastic wads designed by Ballistics Products out of Minnesota; Blue Dot (HM 90) with Federal magnum primers was the engine that drove the whole payload to 100 yards with very workable effectiveness.

Ten years of hard-nosed research and testing nabbed the attention of Federal Cartridge and several tiny mom-and-pop outfits. In effect, Minnesota had become the heart of high-performance long-range smoothbore development and still holds that title today through Ballistics Products and Federal Cartridge at Anoka, Minnesota.

The mere mention of steel shot struck fear in the hearts of waterfowl hunters back then. In truth, with all its issues, the move turned out to be positive, but not until after another decade of hard engineering work. Mike Jordan at Winchester and Mike Larsen and Bill Stevens at Federal laid the groundwork with Federal's engineers, then followed up with efforts by Ross Metzger, an engineer at Sperry, and the Army Corps of Engineers to turn the tide in favor of workable iron shot loads downrange.

Another product I evaluated was produced with the help of Minnesota Steel Shot, LLC and Ballistics Products to a lesser degree, making up a 10-gauge load of steel .22-caliber ball bearings packed to the count of 54 pellets into the B card crimped 10-gauge hull. When taken afield at Rochester, Minnesota, the first goose that rolled out of a flock with a 70-yard pass shot caught the attention of both Federal and state wardens. No one had these loads, as Remington was still trying to get the new #1 steel 12-gauge goose load to work past 40 yards. When the fish cops arrived, I hauled out my dummy sample of a steel shot 10-gauge goose load of eight 10-penny spikes pointed straight out of the hull. I thought we were going to lose a warden to a heart attack. After a bit, we showed them a .22-caliber iron shot load, and at that point, a couple of disappointed officers put the tag books away.

Knowledge breeds success, and during several decades I gained a solid idea about the velocity and kinetic energy required to bring game down cleanly, whether ducks, geese, turkeys, or even hogs and coyotes at about any reasonable range. I had handloads in 10 and 12

A 75-yard dead coyote! Tungsten T load with Super Performance Remington 870.

Remington 870 Performance 10-bore long-range shotgun.

gauge effective from 70 to 110 yards on most targets. The key was pellet mass, velocity, and retained energy. Note, I do not advocate "sky-busting" game birds at ranges beyond which you have a proven lethal load, and the same goes for turkeys, hogs, and predators. You must extensively test your gun and load through careful patterning. Know your load's performance at all reasonable ranges and stick to ethical limits.

Tom Armbrust at Ballistics Research, and MEC of Henry, Illinois, had cracked several hundred loads for me when studying safe working chamber pressures. Dr. Oehler, the man who invented the only chronograph used by the U.S. Army to measure the velocity of the 120mm tank gun on the M1-Abrams, sent me a Chronotech Model 33 that could measure shotshell pellet velocities in flight. Now I had the real deal in applied ballistics research and testing.

NEW GENERATION TUNGSTEN SHOT

The exact type of shot used is critical when load developers want a more effective payload punch at long ranges. Lead shot was good in its day; steel was nasty stuff to work with, but because of it, the new age of pure .18-density tungsten and even tungsten-blended shot raised the performance standards of modern shotshell loads by a vast margin.

As a shot-building material, tungsten is the second heaviest material known on earth, according to the periodic tables. (Pure depleted Uranium is heavier in mass, density, and retained weight.) When the product is heavier (in terms of density), a small size in a round ball (shot) can produce the same results as a much larger pellet size in lighter weight material — in this case, steel shot.

In effect, a tight mass of #9 (pepper/dust) tungsten shot carries several hundred individual pellets more than an equal 1-ounce load of a larger steel shot size. One pellet of #9 tungsten would require a #2 steel pellet to equal its effectiveness in the weight velocity retention department alone. One ounce of #9 tungsten "dust" will equal about 365 pellets in the pattern; the #2 steel at the same load

TABLE A - #9 HIGH-DENSITY "TUNGSTEN" SHOT

An allowance was made for the true MV and choke increase. Extremely small sample but the results are indicative. Gun: .410 with 3-in. shell, approx. 15/16 oz. shot.

PELLET WEIGHT (GRS): ~ 1.22 RANGE YARDS	PELLET DIAMETER,INS.: VELOCITY FT/SEC	NOM. 0.080 ENERGY FT-LBS	TOF SEC	DROP INS	WIND DEF IN/ 10MPH	45MPH LEAD FEET
0	1,125	3.4	0.0000	0.0	0.0	0
5	1,036	2.9	0.0149	0.0	-0.1	1.0
10	960	2.5	0.0300	0.2	0.2	2.0
15	894	2.2	0.0463	0.4	0.7	3.1
20	837	1.9	0.0637	0.7	1.4	4.2
25	786	1.7	0.0823	1.2	2.3	5.4
30	742	1.5	0.1020	1.8	3.4	6.7
35	704	1.3	0.1229	2.5	4.6	8.1
40	667	1.2	0.1448	3.4	6.2	9.6
45	632	1.1	0.1680	4.6	8.0	11.1
50	600	1.0	0.1925	5.9	10.2	12.7
55	569	0.9	0.2182	7.5	12.6	14.4
60	540	0.8	0.2454	9.3	15.5	16.2

TABLE B – #T STEEL

PELLET WEIGHT (GRS): 8.327 EFFECTIVE SD: 0.0297
PELLET DIAMETER, INCHES: 0.200 STANDARD SD: 0.0297

RANGE YARDS	VELOCITY FT/SEC	ENERGY FT-LBS	TOF SEC	DROP INS	WIND DEF IN/10MPH	45MPH LEAD FEET
0	1,300	31.2	0.0000	0.0	0.0	0
5	1,191	26.2	0.0129	0.0	-0.1	0.9
10	1,099	22.3	0.0261	0.1	0.2	1.7
15	1,021	19.3	0.0403	0.3	0.7	2.7
20	953	16.8	0.0556	0.5	1.3	3.7
25	893	14.7	0.0720	0.9	2.1	4.7
30	841	13.1	0.0894	1.3	3.1	5.9
35	794	11.7	0.1078	1.9	4.3	7.1
40	752	10.5	0.1273	2.6	5.7	8.4
45	716	9.5	0.1478	3.5	7.2	9.8
50	682	8.6	0.1693	4.5	8.9	11.2
55	650	7.8	0.1919	5.8	10.9	12.7
60	619	7.1	0.2157	7.2	13.3	14.2
65	589	6.4	0.2406	8.8	15.9	15.9
70	562	5.8	0.2668	10.7	18.8	17.6
75	536	5.3	0.2942	12.9	22.2	19.4

Today's long-range performance shotshells, such as these TSS loads, give wingshooters a powerful, ethical solution that meets environmental standards.

weight would count to only 90 pellets moving downrange. That fact makes it not even close in terms of overall pattern printing long-range performance, and we have not even come close to what is out there in pure tungsten pellet sizes for the heavy work downrange.

Large tungsten shot in T .20 caliber will reach 100 yards at a target contact velocity of 700 fps. That is 100 fps faster than is required for good penetration in larger game animals. T-shot tungsten will do significant damage to an excess of 150 yards range. Now, match this to T steel of the same shot size, and we see that the iron shot pellet of T is all washed up at 65 yards in terms of the baseline 600 fps terminal velocity required of any shot type in adequate soft target penetration.

Adding the fact that tungsten, in a small, dense pellet — one that makes use of a less frontal area, fights off drag (friction effect slowing down the shot) — we see that even the fine #9 tungsten dust is cutting deep penetration results at ranges as great as 60 yards or more because it is heavy and carries a minimal frontal area. Because I've shot an assortment of game with a wide range of different brands in pure tungsten, I can assure you that the downrange results are mindblowing when you're behind the shotgun.

At this point, it is only fair to include other shot types than tungsten, for significant development has occurred with Bismuth, ITX, blended tungsten (Hevi-Shot), Heavy Weight by Federal, and Xtream high-density shot by Winchester. Kent Cartridge and its polymer high-density shot are also selling well.

CORRECT CHOKING FOR THE LONG-RANGE SHOTGUNNER

Forget the old standard discussion about choke sizes and when and where to use them. Long-range shotgun shooters live in a different universe when choking down a payload of smoothbore shot. In our long-distance world, chokes have very different sizing, and while the standard .40-point full choke in a 12 gauge is primary for most shotgunning, it is the end of the line when moving into sending smoothbore shot into the next zip code. Now, a .60-point ultra-tight super full turkey, duck/goose, or hog-harvesting

steel choke tube is more in line with payload control beyond the 40-yard mark.

We want a slug (tight mass) of shot moving across the first 25 yards downrange with most of it still inside its full-length plastic wad and only opening to the size of a coffee can cover by the time it reaches 40 yards. At 40 yards, it starts its assigned task: holding that payload together for the next 40 yards as a workable game-harvesting pattern. Chokes that accomplish this are in a performance class by themselves and not often found in the factory-packaged box with a new shotgun. I say "not often" because I will present one maker in long-range fire-

power that only sells specialized chokes with its product. Standard everyday styles of choke tubes need not apply.

Long-range chokes are almost always designed as extended models. That means the working end of the choke is beyond the choke threads and main muzzle of the barrel body. All that work area extends beyond the shotgun's muzzle because the stresses associated with choking down shot materials like steel or various tungsten composites create massive muzzle strain. I measured it with strain gauges on test gun muzzles while evaluating the new super-hard shot materials.

TSS T shot fired from a Super Performance 870 Remington for 37.8% on target at 100 yards.

TABLE C — "TSS" T SHOT
PELLET WEIGHT (GRS): 18.520   **EFFECTIVE SD:** 0.0676   **PELLET DIAMETER, INCHES:** 0.1978 average

RANGE YARDS	VELOCITY FT/SEC	ENERGY FT-LBS	TOF SEC	DROP INS	WIND DEF IN/10MPH	45MPH LEAD FEET
0	1,231	62.3	0.0000	0.0	0.0	0
10	1,144	53.9	0.0262	0.1	0.0	1.7
20	1,069	47.0	0.0534	0.5	0.5	3.5
30	1,003	41.4	0.0824	1.2	1.3	5.4
40	945	36.7	0.1133	2.3	2.4	7.5
50	893	32.8	0.1460	3.7	3.9	9.6
60	847	29.5	0.1806	5.6	5.6	11.9
70	805	26.7	0.2170	7.9	7.7	14.3
80	767	24.2	0.2552	10.8	10.1	16.8
90	734	22.1	0.2953	14.3	12.8	19.5
100	703	20.3	0.3371	18.4	15.8	22.2

The author conducted long-range testing with the Remington Super Performance and tungsten-packed gunning system.

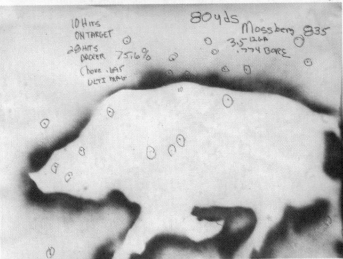

Mossberg 835 pump action that uses the same chokes as the Remington Super Performance and a dead-on pattern shot to 80 yards on a 100-pound pig target. Tungsten T's are beyond belief.

Adam Ziegler of Backridge Ammunition with a boar hog. Ziegler was shooting T tungsten and using a Super Performance 870 10-gauge bore, and the range was about 55 yards. This boar was hard won during a wet and dangerous South Carolina swamp hunt.

GUNS AND CHOKES FOR LONG RANGE

The choke design selected matched several shotguns used for this review, and I will list them accordingly. First off is the newly-introduced German Sauer SL5 blowback recoil autoloader in 12 gauge. There is a turkey model and a long-distance waterfowl variant. My test shotgun had a 20-inch barrel with a Benelli-style Cryo forward thread extended choke tube design. Right out of the box, the shotgun has a custom Carlson turkey/long-range choke at .660 constriction and another hard MAX I M .695 tube choked for super hard steel. The Germans set this shotgun up for the future of new-generation steel and tungsten shot.

Gun number two in my stable of test firearms included the new Remington Wildcat 870 10-gauge bore using a 3-inch 12-gauge chamber setup. The chokes were all 10 gauge with thread patterns to the exact measurements as the current Mossberg 835 and 935 models. In other words, 12-gauge guns with 10-gauge bores and chokes. As to the why of all this, please stand by because performance says it all. Nothing can touch the Wildcat 870's 70- to 100-yard performance profile. While compiling this material, two different handmade custom barrels were used on a pair of 870s built and designed by Adam Ziegler of Backridge Ammunition.

Chokes were offered after a hands-on visit to Kicks Chokes in Georgia and an offer from Adam Ziegler, which returned a tube set from Kelly Haydel of Haydel Game Calls, and several of my own Mossberg tubes as well. In effect, I was well covered with extended super chokes designed for just the work I had outlined for the project.

With the large selection of high-performance Trulock Cryo Benelli chokes, including my Benelli Super Black Eagle for testing was a logical decision. In prior years, this 28-inch barreled duck gun also served as a turkey getter and held a solid record on ducks and geese. With the Carlson Hevi-Shot extended choke tubes locked into place, this gun and choke combination retained a solid reputation as a first-class game-harvesting machine.

I also included my old standby Remington 870, mounting a 21-inch slug/buckshot barrel, a Weaver rail, and scoped with a Bushnell turkey scope. This gun was relegated to target work instead of hunting. The choke system is now out of production since Hevi-Shot has been sold to Vista Corp/Federal Cartridge. I gave the old-school Hevi-Shot long-range waterfowl model and a second Hevi-Shot tube in the .60 turkey choke constriction the nod based on many years of service. The performance with these choke tubes over 26 years has been nothing but off the charts for extended-range shooting.

PATTERN EFFECT

Lacking patterning work, the hunter, researcher, or general shooter has no idea what is taking place downrange regarding where those pellets of shot are going. While it's easy to predict how a pattern will look at 40 yards or closer, all bets are off when the range is stretched to 50, 60, 70, or even 100 yards.

One key to obtaining workable long-range patterns is using the correct shot type. Two decades ago, with the introduction of tungsten blends, I saw significant performance increases when hunting Canada geese — during industry-sponsored events and hunts set up by local friends and associates here in South Dakota. Pattern tests were required even when the shotshell product was costly. Some tungsten load tests were $12 or

more per round, and the industry offered few for testing.

Pattern work proceeded with two primary shotguns, the Backridge-designed Remington 870 3-inch chambered and back bored to 10 gauge, using paired 10-gauge Mossberg thread pattern chokes. The second was the German Sauer SL5 3-inch 12-gauge autoloading turkey gun, which I used to shoot the first of three separate test runs with loads on paper ranging from 50 to 100 yards. Why three tests? Because the first can be a stroke of luck if positive results are

obtained, and a second starts to formulate a better picture of load performance, while a third sets the results in stone, being good, bad, or just flat-out ugly. While gun writers often shoot a single series of patterns, payload performance is far too random to trust those results completely. Also, for extended shotgun performance much past 40 yards, many things start to come into play in pattern performance. Tungsten shot density has been the game changer in many cases, but when selected chokes and excellent barrels are also involved, some good stuff starts to happen.

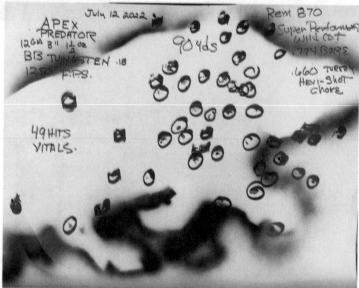

Remington 870 Super Performance 10-gauge (bore) with a 90-yard BB APEX tungsten shot pattern. 12-gauge 3-inch 1 1/4 oz., 1,250 fps muzzle velocity.

This 70-yard duck target was peppered with a #2 TSS tungsten shot load.

You've got to hunt many turkeys with different tungsten-loaded guns to understand how effective this stuff can be.

The author with a 72-yard turkey target that took 53 total hits. In the 1970s, the record hits with a 10-gauge shooting 2 1/4 oz. #4s was 40 hits at 40 yards.

TABLE D — #7½ TSS SHOT

PELLET WEIGHT (GRS): 2.010   EFFECTIVE SD: 0.0318
PELLET DIAMETER, INCHES: 0.095   STANDARD SD: 0.0318

RANGE YARDS	VELOCITY FT/SEC	ENERGY FT-LBS	TOF SEC	DROP INS	WIND DEF IN/10MPH	45 MPH LEAD FEET
0	1,220	6.6	0.0000	0.0	0.0	0.0
10	1,052	4.9	0.0275	0.1	0.2	1.8
20	925	3.8	0.0581	0.6	1.2	3.8
30	825	3.0	0.0927	1.5	2.9	6.1
40	745	2.5	0.1311	2.8	5.3	8.7
50	680	2.1	0.1734	4.8	8.3	11.4
60	621	1.7	0.2198	7.6	12.4	14.5

The tables I have included in this review indicate that in every test firing, enough shot reached the vitals of birds and hogs to kill them. Even to 100 yards, when shooting tungsten T shot in .21 caliber, the pellets retained over 100 fps more energy than is required on the target and shot predictable patterns. When viewing the tables included here, the load becomes ineffective when the shot reaches velocities below 600 fps. All 100-yard test patterns were shot using the Remington 870 10 bore and Kicks chokes, and I had hit on this as the best solution to ultra-long-range shooting.

The test gun had been set up for ducks and geese; therefore, no additional modifications were made (as was the case with the 12-gauge turkey guns used for this article).

DOWNRANGE EFFECTS

Shooting paper targets is required to make headway on performance standards. However, performance on wild game is the most critical element when undertaking a review of this type. Sending loads that are nothing but game cripplers is not an option.

With the much-appreciated assistance of Backridge Ammunition and TSS Tungsten Super Slam loads, I got the most out of my field application during the test shooting on long-range game targets. TSS Super Slam is the only ammunition company that offers pure .18 tungsten shot pellet sizes in T (.21-caliber ball), and it was the go-to company when moving my shooting distance as far as 100 yards.

While APEX Ammunition also offers BB tungsten, the package comprised #2, BB, and T shot as triple-threat field ordnance. Except for the #7.5, 2 3/4-inch load manufactured by Backridge Ammunition, everything else selected for fieldwork was based on the 12-gauge 3-inch magnum tungsten load.

TURKEYS!

One of the primary targets being addressed by tungsten shot shooters today is the wild turkey. Even shot sizes as small as #9 "dust" can produce lethal hits at massively extended range limits. I elected to go with Backridge-developed

#7.5 tungsten shot loads in a lightweight 1-ounce payload. I found them to pattern well, and with computer ballistics, there was every indication that #7.5 was the best of all worlds in the 12-bore as a turkey-harvesting shot size selection.

Early hunting during the fall of 2022 was nothing to write home about. With the short-barreled Sauer SL 5 as my choice in shotguns, I had been cutting and running all manner of terrain when on day eleven, with clean, cool weather, I hit on a solid gobble return deep in a shallow draw that was studded with scrub oak and pine trees. With several moves straight at the gobbling bird, I discovered an old hen had spotted me and was cutting up a storm as she strutted around me while I tried to cover against a tiny scrub oak tree trunk. About the same time, the target gobbler went silent, but to the rear of my position, a second gobbler answered the yelping hen, and, as the sound of the bird grew closer, it was gun up, game on, and I dropped the safety latch on the SL 5.

A 2 3/4-inch 7.5 Backridge research test tungsten load was chambered in the gun. Using the HUD display Tru-Glo sight, I picked up my target about 130 yards out, angling toward me with the hen between myself and the gobbler. When the gobbler closed to about 50 yards, it turned and looked straight at me. Now it was game on or lose the shot. With the 3-MOA red dot covering the middle of the bird's neck, I dropped five pounds of the German SL5's trigger. There was no delayed flopping reaction at the shot, but the bird dropped straight down and out of sight. It was a 24-pound gobbler and a solid test base for the new .18 tungsten fine shot loads. Using a small rangefinding unit, I ranged the birds' location back to the tree I had used for cover and found that the shot had measured precisely 67 yards.

Several days later, it was game on again, but I was hunting the rock-faced high country in the South Dakota Black Hills. A buddy told me there was bird activity in the area early in the morning and that the ledge above a deep canyon was a strut zone.

Setting up in a low-depression rock hole, I sent a few yelps down the line of

Brezny with some Specks (white-fronted or "specklebelly" geese) during testing of Hevi-Shot and other new developments using tungsten-based pellets.

A good gobbler which the author clobbered with the new long-range Tungsten loads. Success at a distance!

rim rock and didn't get a response, but a gobbler did step straight up out of a shallow draw. With the range estimated at 55 yards and nothing but air between the bird and me, it was "Quick Draw McGraw" time. Off-hand shooting and standing in the shallow stone trench, I sent a load of Federal 3-inch magnum 2-oz. 7X9 .18 tungsten at the bird again by the Sauer SL 5. Like the first gobbler, it was game over in a flash, and another stone-dead bird went down. I do not believe that bird ever heard the shot that killed it.

The load I used was from the same lot-numbered box that had produced just about the best pattern at 72 yards I have ever seen come out of a smoothbore barrel. With 53 hits — 27 of those in the vitals — I had no hesitation about dropping the firing pin at the indicated range. The actual ranged distance for that shot turned out to be 54 yards.

I harvested an additional turkey out on open prairie grass at 49 yards and a coyote taken with the 870 Wildcat 10 bore using Backridge loaded TSS LLC 3-inch Ts at just under 60 yards. Topping off the list, I killed a 200-pound boar tusker in the South Carolina swamps using the tungsten Ts, which punctuated the whole series of events.

We are seeing a whole new age of smoothbore payload performance. To reiterate, I do not advocate long-range sky-busting or taking unethical shots at game beyond ranges where you have established a high probability of humane kills based on testing and patterning. However, crippling can be reduced with

TABLE F

Series 1 Choke Performance Tables: Head/Neck Target Turkey – Choke Trulock .650

LOAD	RANGE (YDS.)	PELLET HITS
1 oz. #8 TSS Tungsten Super Slam	60	31
1 oz. #7 TSS Tungsten Super Slam	60	38
1 oz. #9 TSS Tungsten Super Slam	70	16
2 oz. Duplex # 7-9 TSS		
Federal Cartridge 3-in. Magnum	72	53*
1 7/8 oz. #6 lead Winchester Long Beard /Trulock Crio .660	50	46
**1¾ oz. #9 Rem TSS w/ Kick .600 choke and 870 Rem.	60	34
1¾ oz. #9 Remington .650 Trulock Crio Remington Experimental	60	37

*53 pellet-count load is a possible record.
**Note: Remington experimental process sample loads could differ from production-level shotshell loads. These are pre-retail samples.
Test guns: Sauer SL5, Ziegler Rem Super Performance 870, Remington Turkey Special 870 Super Mag factory model
Shooting conditions: Air temp 55-73 F; Wind following or 30° angle left-right to left, 5-10 m.p.h.; Altitude 3,200 ft. above sea level; Sights zeroed for a 3-in. holdover for pellet drop at long range; Sights: Sauer SL5 12 gauge, Remington 870 12-gauge Turkey Super Magnum: TruGlo 3 MOA red dot HUD sight; Remington 870 TurkeyBushnell Banner 4X with a turkey subtension reticle and red laser alignment-targeting system.

Series 2 Pig/Turkey Head Targets — 80 yards

GUN/CHOKE	TARGET	LOAD	RANGE (YDS.)	SHOTSHELL PELLETS	VITAL HITS (QTY./%)
Backridge 870/Kicks .600	Turkey head/ neck	T tungsten TSS/LLC Super Slam Varmint/Big Game	80	37	10/40.5
*Mossberg 3 ½-in. 835 Factory Stock Shotgun/ Mossberg .695 Ulti Mag.	Pig full body	T tungsten TSS/LLC Super Slam Varmint/Big Game	80	37	10/75.6
Backridge 870 /Kicks .600	Pig full body	T tungsten TSS/LLC Super Slam Varmint/Big Game	90	37	8/54
Backridge 870 /Kicks .600	Mallard duck	APEX 3-in. BB tungsten	75	N/A	11
Backridge 870 /Kicks .600	Mallard duck	12 2 ¾-in. 1 oz. #7 tungsten	60	N/A	26
Remington 870/ Hevi Shot turkey full .60 with turkey scope sights.	Turkey head/ neck	Backridge 3-in. magnum #9 tungsten.	65	N/A	31

*Note: A Mossberg 835 was used as the choke system in 10 gauge, and the bore is also .774 10 gauge. (Same as the Backridge 870 barrel design.)

Series #3 Pig Targets 80-100 Yards
TABLE A. – Load Backridge TSS Super Slam T (.22 caliber) shot tungsten, 37 pellets. Backridge 870 Super Performance 10-gauge bore, 12-gauge 3-in. chamber. Kicks .600 choke.

TARGET #	RANGE (YDS.)	HITS ON PAPER	VITAL HITS
1	80	34	10
2	80	29	7
3	90	20	5
4	100	17	5
5	100	19	7
6	100	21	8
7	100	26	5

the new generation of super-density shot. There is also the question of safety when tungsten is used. It's critical to ensure your backstop when using this new shot. Keep this in mind at all times when using tungsten shot ammunition.

No, this is not your daddy's grade of smoothbore ammunition. Tungsten is a game changer and a deadly long-range option in the field. GD

Great Britain's Palindrome Trifecta

The Holy Trinity of the .303, .404, and .505

> PHIL SHOEMAKER

S oon after the close of the Napoleonic Wars in the early 1800s, Great Britain eventually expanded its domination to include over a quarter of the globe. It often bragged that "the sun never set on the British Empire." Explorer David Livingston proposed that the "Three Cs, Commerce, Christianity and Capital" were the best means for Great Britain to redeem the African continent. However, as China is currently reminding us, redemption has never been the goal of colonization. Three other "Cs"; Colonization, Conquest and widespread plunder of resources for Capital became the management theme for colonies under Great Britain's rule. All three required prodigious application of modern military might and weaponry, which the burgeoning English gun trade was more than willing and capable of providing.

32
CARTRIDGES
·303 INCH
Mk 7
↑
C.I.A. (P)
P.O.F.

The British cartridges .303 British, .404 Jeffery, and .505 Gibbs represent the author's notable "palindrome" trinity.

The .404 Jeffery belonged to the author's Grandfather.

The English firearms trade had been expanding since 1672 when the Royal African Company of England had received its exclusive charter for the lucrative trading rights on the African continent. The industrial town of Birmingham began supplying thousands upon thousands of flintlock muskets to be shipped to Africa in exchange for slaves who, in turn, were shipped to English colonies in the West Indies and America to be traded for cotton, molasses, and tobacco, which were convenient byproducts of the slave trade. Those were then shipped back through Liverpool to be turned into rum and cloth. The statement that "every brick of this infernal town is cemented with African blood" was as true of Birmingham as of Liverpool.

THE .303 BRITISH

A vibrant firearms industry grew and thrived in England over the next two centuries. After retiring its muzzleloading "Brown Bess," the rugged and reliable .577/.450 Martini-Enfield served the

empire with distinction. In 1888, a new bolt-action repeating rifle, the Lee-Metford, was adopted. Chambered in a new small bore, rimmed, .303 caliber (which denoted the bore diameter rather than its .311-.314-inch groove diameter). It was loaded with 71.5 grains of RFG blackpowder and launched a round-nosed 215-grain cupro-nickel jacketed bullet at 1,850 fps. In 1892, the adoption of a new smokeless cordite powder increased its muzzle velocity to 2,000 fps.

Three years later, it became apparent that the segmented Metford rifling could not withstand cordite powder's extra heat and velocity. A more durable Enfield style of rifling was adopted. In 1910, a lighter weight, more modern 174-gr. spitzer bullet with a muzzle velocity of 2,440 fps was adopted. That load, along with the .303 Magazine Lee-Enfield, remained in service through two World Wars until eventually being phased out by the L1A1 SLR chambered for 7.62 NATO in the

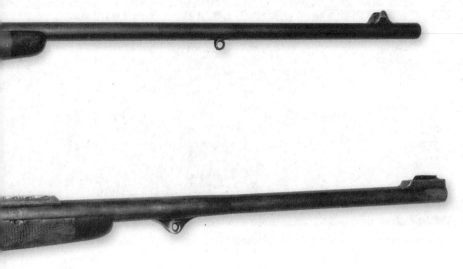

The author's .303 Lee-Speed and .404 Jeffery.

Shoemaker's .303 Lee-Speed.

late 1950s. The .303 remained in active service with India throughout its 1962 war with China and with the Canadian Rangers, an armed forces reserve, until 2017. By any measure, the .303 British is one of the world's most successful and enduring military cartridges.

Alongside a distinguished military career, the .303 also filled an insatiable demand for sporting weaponry. As untold wealth from its far-flung colonies poured into Great Britain, its citizens began looking for ways to spend it. Travel was a popular pastime for people living on islands. With a quarter of the globe now under their rule and ships leaving weekly, the great hunting fields in Africa, Australia, India, and North America became popular destinations.

Demand was such that virtually every Birmingham and London gun maker offered some version or another of either a Lee-Enfield or Lee-Metford sporting rifle chambered in the .303. The Lee-Speed was named after inventor James Paris Lee and Joseph Speed, the manager of the Royal Small Arms factory where the military versions were built. Lee-Speed sporting carbines and rifles were produced by both BSA (Birmingham Small Arms) and LSA (London Small Arms) companies and offered in varying grades from the simplest and cheapest "Colonial Grade" for 5 guineas up to the best, No. 1 Pattern Lee-Speed "Shot and Regulated" by the top London factories for 12 guineas. Along with national pride, the fact they were half the price of a Rigby sporting rifle or an imported .256 Mannicher, 7x57 Mauser, made them quite attractive for the various explorers, remittance men and ner-do-wells heading off for adventures in the colonies.

The Lee-Speed .303 became a trusted companion for numerous celebrated and published hunters such as Alexander Lake, American scout Fredrick Russell Burnham, Fredrick Courteney Selous and Col. J.H. Patterson, who used one in 1898 to sort out the man-eating lions that

The .404 Jeffery rifle the author used for hunting Alaskan brown bears. The .404 Jeffery is a rimless version of its highly regarded and popular rimmed .450/400 3" Nitro Express.

nearly halted the Kenya-Uganda railway and WDM Bell. Bell began his long and illustrious career at age 16, hunting lions for the same Uganda railroad with his favorite single-shot .303. A few years later, after meat hunting to supply gold miners in the Canadian Yukon territories, Bell returned to the Dark Continent to fight in the Boer war and in 1902, immediately after those hostilities, he began his now legendary elephant hunting career by harvesting the tusks of 63 large bulls with a pair of .303 Lee-Speeds.

Lee-Speeds and de-commissioned surplus military Lee-Enfields were widespread throughout the English domain. The remote border between the Yukon and Alaskan territories has always been porous in North America. I have run across quite a few surplus Lee-Enfields and Lee-Speeds in Alaska. With modern ammunition, they remain a solid, reliable, and well-proven hunting tool. I owned and hunted with one for several years. The only drawback I found was that due to slightly oversized chambers, which enhanced reliability, reloading was more difficult due to the compromised case life. That was a small price to pay for a lightweight, highly reliable, and excellent-handling rifle. Performance-wise, the British .303 slightly bests the .30/40 Krag and is more comparable with the .300 Savage and the .308 Winchester — all of which remain proven performers on large game.

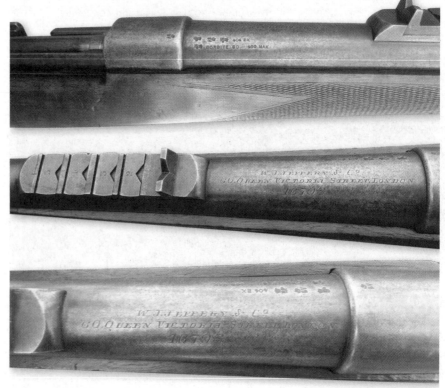

Jeffery barrel markings.

JEFFERY'S ICONIC .404

In 1905, seventeen years after the initial adoption of the .303, the London firm of William Jackman Jeffery introduced a rimless version of its highly regarded and popular rimmed .450/400 3" Nitro Express. Designed to feed in a Mauser bolt action, the new .404 Jeffery was proofed with the same 60 grains of cordite behind a 400-gr. bullet as the .450/400. Jeffery was most certainly aware that its competitor Rigby had an exclusive contract to import

Mauser rifles and was then using a slightly larger magnum action with a stepped front receiver ring and a slanted magazine box for its new .400/350 rimmed cartridge. Rather than purchase actions from a competitor, Jeffery designed a cartridge that would (just barely) fit into a standard-length military Mauser action. Offering its new .404 Jeffery, the first large-bore cartridge designed to work through a magazine-fed repeating rifle, positioned Jeffery years ahead of its competition.

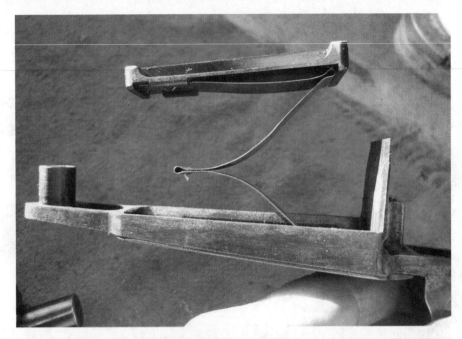

Magazine cut for the original Jeffery .404.

lege also produced civil and political unrest. Hoping to keep all ammunition that could be used in the old .577/450 rifles out of the hands of insurgents, the Crown banned all .450-caliber rifles throughout the colony. English gun makers quickly responded by introducing a surfeit of larger-bore calibers such as the .500/465 H&H, .470 Nitro, .475 3 1/4", .475 No. 2, .476 WR, and .505 Gibbs to fill the niche.

Jeffery's solution to the problem with its .404 was elegant: Slightly enlarging the caliber of the new cartridge to .423 inch, rather than the .410 diameter used in the .450/400, making it even closer in performance to the popular and proven .450. However, why it christened it the .404 is anyone's guess, but I suspect it may have had something to do with the verbal ring and popularity of the .303. Whatever the reason for its name, Jeffery's .404, like its progenitor and double rifle counterpart, the .450/400, quickly earned a sterling reputation throughout the vast game fields of the English empire.

To its credit, Jeffery chose not to make the cartridge proprietary; as Wesley Richards had done with its .425 (which looks suspiciously like a shortened .404 with a rebated rim), and John Rigby chose to do with its impressively massive .416. The Jeffery .404 was freely available to any company that chose to use it. It could be chambered in most Mauser-type actions, as well as the large P14 Enfield. Hundreds of inexpensive .404 rifles were built and sold to the various game departments across the African continent, busy with "animal control" projects. Additionally, farmers and a new breed of "White Hunters," as today's PHs were referred to, quickly recognized its advantages.

John Taylor, a professional ivory hunter for over thirty years and author of *African Rifles and Cartridges*, is the most quoted authority and an unabashed fan of the .404. He claimed it had all the power necessary to make it a perfectly safe weapon and, weighing only 8 1/2 pounds, was light and handy enough to carry it all day easily. He wrote, "Just because a .400 looks small when compared with an 8-bore, or even a .577, is no argument. Sure, it's small by comparison; but practical experience has shown that it's a

Timing played an essential role in the development and naming of Jeffery's .404. India, Britain's "Jewel in the Crown," was not only its most profitable and indispensable colony, but it was also the most popular hunting destination. English nobility commonly spent months on extended Shikars hunting tigers, elephants, rhinos, guar, bears, and buffalos. British officers and civil servants, on their way to serve the crown, typically purchased armament in London before embarking on

their journey but Indian firearm dealers in the major cities of Calcutta and Delhi — like Manton & Company and R.B. Rodda — imported and sold thousands of high-grade English rifles. However, it was the extensive orders from India's innumerable Maharajas, Nawabs, Nizams, Jam Sahebs and Princes, who were some of the wealthiest people in the world then, that energized and subsidized the British firearms industry.

Highly concentrated wealth and privi-

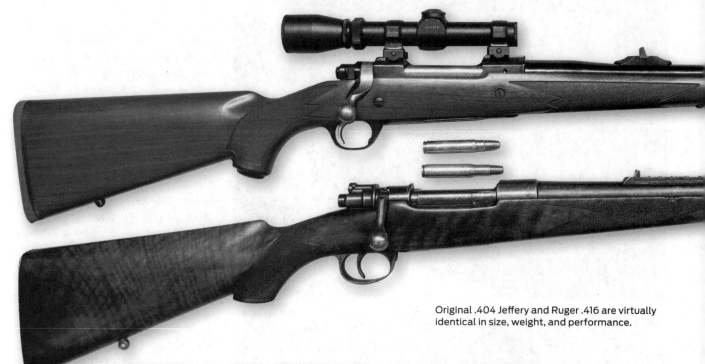

Original .404 Jeffery and Ruger .416 are virtually identical in size, weight, and performance.

The steel insert in front of the magazine box on the .404.

simply splendid weapon for all heavy and dangerous game anywhere – particularly when in the hands of an experienced hunter." He also mentioned that the H.V. 300-gr. load at 2,600 fps was wonderfully deadly on lions.

For many years, I owned and hunted with an early Jeffery .404 rifle specifically purchased for an Alaskan brown bear hunt. According to Jeffery's records, it was one of a group of ten that had been outsourced and built on a standard M98 Mauser action. Manufactured in 1905, it was delivered to its owner the following January. The stock had been hewed from a dense, well-seasoned blank of walnut as, after over a century of use, it showed no splits or cracks. The front and sides of the original military Mauser magazine box had been completely milled away, and the rear plate thinned as much as practical. The stock was inlet just wide enough to allow the proper geometry for reliable feeding. The feed ramp was machined, steepened, and polished, and a steel plate inlet into the stock below it to keep the bullets from battering the wood during recoil. The ejector had been cut back, and the top of the receiver opened up both at the front and rear to allow easy loading and unobstructed ejection. It worked perfectly.

After using the rifle in Alaska for a few seasons, it became apparent that it had been built for serious use. It weighed an even 8 1/2 pounds and, even with its original steel buttplate, recoil was not unpleasant with factory Kynoch loads. Like so many English rifles of the era, the balance was impeccable. The 24-inch barrel retained most of its diameter toward the rear until past the parade sights and then exhibited a convex taper, which kept the weight centrally located. It was a lithe, lively, and lethal combination. It was no wonder that various game departments across the African continent adopted it for game rangers and scouts.

When I received the rifle, it had been used by the grandsons of the original owner. It came with nearly 30 rounds of once-fired Kynoch brass, a few old yellow and red boxes of factory ammunition, and two sealed, paper-wrapped cartons of Kynoch ammo. Each carton contained ten packets of five rounds, each with a sticker stating, "Important: Muzzle velocity increased to 2,225 ft./sec. Rifles sighted for cordite cartridges should be re-zeroed."

The old Kynoch ammo fed perfectly, but whether it had deteriorated slightly from age or velocities had been obtained from longer barrels, it averaged around

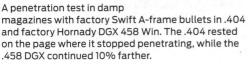

A penetration test in damp
magazines with factory Swift A-frame bullets in .404
and factory Hornady DGX 458 Win. The .404 rested
on the page where it stopped penetrating, while the
.458 DGX continued 10% farther.

2,150 fps. That matched the originally
published velocities of the .404 with 60
gr. of cordite, and I knew from experience that that was perfectly adequate. But
for seriously hunting our giant brown
bears, I wanted a little fresher ammunition. At the time, I was also writing for
Wolfe publishing company, and ammunition companies Hornady, Swift, and

Norma willingly sent me boxes of their
modern loads to test.

The Jeffery case has slightly less capacity than the .416 Rigby, and some modern
loads chronographed close to 2,300 fps.
They also had considerably more recoil! I
began to reconsider the usefulness of the
steel buttplate and the effect a heavier recoil might inflict on a hundred-year-old

rifle with no extra recoil lug, cross bolt,
or steel bedding.

I decided to reload using 71 gr. RL-15
and either the 400-gr. Hornady DGX or
the Swift A–Frame bullet. The Hornady
was slightly faster (2,150 fps) than the
softer Swifts (2,125 fps), but both shot
close enough to the point of impact
with the original sights. Performance

The .303 British, .404 Jeffery, and a more contemporary rifle in the awesome .505 Gibbs.

and results, while maybe not quite as convincing as my familiar old .458, were excellent.

THE MASSIVE .505 GIBBS

The third and largest of our palindromes was also the last introduced. Like the .404 Jeffery, there is some confusion about the original time of introduction of the .505 Gibbs. The third volume of Hoyem's *History of Small Arms Ammunition* lists it as 1913, while Frank Barnes' *Cartridges of the World* has it as 1911. The discrepancy appears to be a matter of defining whether "introduced" means developed or produced.

As mentioned, Rigby held exclusive rights to import Mauser rifles and actions into Great Britain until 1912. Immediately after Rigby lost the contract, many English rifle builders began ordering barreled actions directly from

Mauser. George Gibbs lists its first .505, serial no. B6413 and built on the largest No. 20 Magnum action, as sold in 1913. However, as with all Mauser imports, the action also carried the Mauser serial no. 53501, which places it within the series of actions made in 1912. Gibbs also lists a second .505 exported to the U.S. in 1913. Records show that Gibbs produced fewer than a hundred of the powerful, oversized .505 rifles using Mauser actions and that they were still using actions produced in 1912 as late as 1924. Most .505's were sold between 1924 and 1939.

During the Gibbs heyday, from the roaring 1920s until the start of WWII, American custom gun makers like Griffin & Howe, Hoffman Arms, and Seymour Griffin turned out a few magnificent rifles built for the .505. One confounding rifle, sold by Gibbs in 1924, was received from Rigby as a barreled

action (apparently virtually all were) with a 1901 vintage Mauser serial number. Jon Speed's excellent series of books on Mauser rifles claims that many special order actions originally came with their own range of serial numbers. Harald Wolf, the highly gifted and knowledgeable German rifle builder, claims that Jeffery's records prove that they purchased all their actions barreled, proofed and supplied with ammunition from outside sources.

The .505 case is nothing if not imposing. It is the largest — both in length and width — commercial cartridge designed for bolt-action sporting rifles. It earned an equally oversized myth and reputation far exceeding its actual use. Although the pre-WWI rifles were designed with a 28-inch barrel and 1:16-inch twist intended for a 600-grain bullet at 2,100 fps, all later rifles came with 1:19 twists and a

published velocity of 2,300 fps using 95 grains of cordite and a 525-gr. bullet.

African legends Philip Percival and John Hunter spoke glowingly of their .505 Gibbs, and Ernest Hemmingway's semi-fictional book, *The Short Happy Life of Francis Macomber,* further etched the .505 Gibbs in many peoples' conscience. John Taylor mentioned his experience with it and claimed that the only ammunition available came from Germany. He wrote that he only killed a few buffalos and rhinos with a rifle borrowed from a friend. "It was a magnificent weapon, if you like a magazine, and has adequate power for all emergencies, so much so, in fact, that it would comfortably stand a reduction in barrel length to around 22", which would make it a much handier weapon in thick cover," he wrote.

More recently, hunter John Kingsley-Heath found his original Gibbs unwieldy with its massive action and "Long Tom" barrel. His biggest problem, however, was the poor performance of old and infirm

The author with a bear hunter and the big .505 Gibbs.

ammunition. Even with the long barrel, he claimed the velocity as only 2,060 fps with the 525-gr. FMJ bullet and that they penetrated horribly, most likely due to age deterioration and the relatively thin, softer jacket of outdated German ammunition.

Unwieldy, long barrels, especially on bolt-action rifles designed for hunting dangerous game, have always presented a problem. Correct feeding and ammunition issues are of even greater importance. When a single company like Gibbs was building rifles for a single brand of ammunition, there were few problems. I have been told by numerous modern gun makers that there are no modern SAAMI specifications for many of the older English calibers. This leads to cascading series of problems for rifle builders. Kevin "Doctari" Robertson had serious feeding issues with his custom .505 due to incorrect magazine geometry. When Utah gun builder D'Arcy Echols was commissioned to build a pair of .505 rifles for clients, he found it impossible to obtain properly dimensioned magazine boxes to fit the massive .505 case. He was forced to build his own. He then encountered a nightmare of differing rim groove diameters and thicknesses between brass and factory ammunition manufacturers. That made feeding problematic and, in some cases, entirely impossible. An extractor properly cut for a .530 groove diameter would not feed or even chamber factory ammunition made by a different manufacturer with a .550 groove diameter as it would cause the extractor to bind on the receiver. An extractor properly fit for the .550 groove diameter was unreliable with ammunition with the .530 diameter. When one needs a .505, reliability is paramount.

When I bought my .505 in 1997, it reinforced that education always comes at a price. It had been locally assembled using a large Korean Bauska action, a .510 dia. chromed-lined military .50 BMG barrel, and bedded in an MPI synthetic stock. I wrote about my trials and tribulations with it in the August 1999 *Handloader* magazine. Eventually, I got it up and running reliably with help from a few knowledgeable and capable machinists and gun-making friends. Jim Brockman fitted

The author's .505 with a Brockman peep sight.

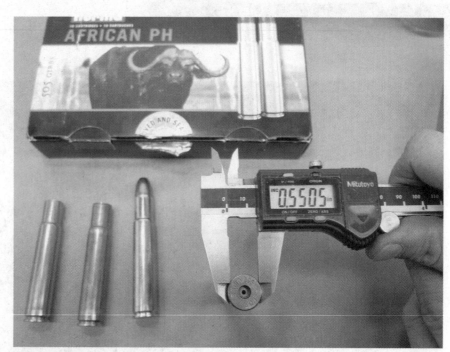

Differing rim diameters on .505 Gibbs cartridges.

it with one of his rugged peep sights, just as many of the original early Gibbs .505 rifles had been. He also replaced the MPI stock with a tough, laminated wood stock designed in the slim, English style. At the beginning of each season, I often vacillated between the slim, lithe English style or the beefier, easier-to-control synthetic stock. As my gun-building friend Lon Paul points out, it's basically like a manly

version of playing "Barbie dolls" where I could switch outfits, depending on where I planned on using them.

The rifle ended up with a handy, well-balanced 21-inch barrel, and I experimented with numerous bullets from 450-gr. .510-inch-diameter Alaska Bullet Works at 2,200 fps to heavy 680-gr. hardcast .512-inch bullets that easily bested the energy level of the .577 Nitro Express

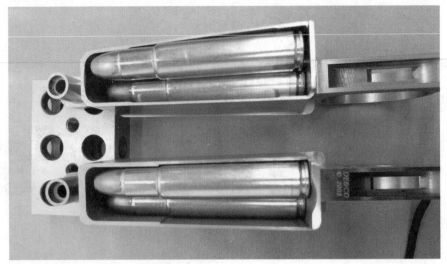

Proper magazine geometry for the .505 Gibbs.

Grandpaw's Jeffery

BY REGE PODRAZA

It rested between the Ivory
That hung on Grandpa's wall
It's finally checked and yellowed
Like the tusks it helped to fall

Its barrel smooth and polished
From a hundred bearers' hands
It reflected the light warmly
Like campfires flickering brands

The stock of English walnut
Chewed and clawed a bit
It still showed a trace of checkering
and a dent where a horn had hit

Stamped on the barrel lightly
Was a name and not much more
A single word "Jeffery"
"Jeffery .404"

If that rifle could only talk
And take us back once again

With grandpa in Africa
A time of Buffalo, Elephants and men

But that day has set its sun
And the rifle speaks no more
Oh what I'd give for one last time
To hear its mighty roar

Grandpa's "Jeffery"
His "Jeffery .404"

(650-gr. bullets at 1,950 fps). The accuracy with .505-diameter 525-gr. Barnes and Woodleigh bullets was certainly acceptable, but I finally settled on the .510-inch 535-gr. Woodleighs ahead of 130 grains IMR-4831. That was a stiff but controllable load and virtually matched the originally claimed factory ballistics. Not surprisingly, it also proved to be a highly effective charge stopper.

In the fall of 1998, I had a senior bear-hunting client wound a massive old brown bear that escaped into a thick patch of brush. We weren't far from camp, and I had a young apprentice guide, Brad, with me. While Brad walked the client back to camp, I began sorting out the trail. Within half an hour, Brad and another experienced guide, Tim, caught up with me, and we began unraveling the maze of bear trails. Tim and Brad followed a trail near the river while I took a parallel track farther inland. I was examining a suspicious dark form in the brush 15 yards ahead of me when Tim called out, "There he is!" and fired his .375. The dark object instantly became animated and spun around as, out of the corner of my eye, I could see Tim frantically dancing with his rifle, yelling, "My rifle's jammed!"

I quickly fired.

My first shot struck just in front of the bear's hip and dropped him, but he immediately popped back up and charged. My second shot, at less than 10 yards, struck him on the point of the shoulder and put him right down. As I

was recovering from recoil and chambering another round, I could see he was attempting to get back up, so I ran a few quick steps forward and put the third and finishing shot down between his shoulder blades.

Although the .505's performance had been spectacular, I vividly remember how slow the recovery from recoil and operating the long bolt was compared to the much quicker recovery time when using the .404 or even my .458. It was fortunate that all the shots had been well-placed.

From my limited experience and the expert opinions of numerous African PHs, there is little doubt that a heavy blow from a bolt-action .505 imparts a significantly greater impact on game than the lesser calibers. But it comes with the price of a bulkier, heavier rifle, with a much stiffer and longer recoil and limited ammunition availability. This is likely why the big .505 Gibbs is the least popular of the palindromes.

The .303 was undoubtedly the most prolific and, in English, the most popular palindromes. But its sharply tapered, rimmed case is an anachronistic throwback to an earlier era and limits its use in modern bolt-action rifles. But, at least for nostalgic reasons, the .303 remains a useful and valid hunting caliber in lever actions and single shots.

Technically, for all those Ailihphiliacs reading this, Jeffery did introduce another palindrome caliber, the .333. It was also introduced around the same time in the early 1900s and offered in a rimless and a flanged version for double rifles. According to John Taylor, it achieved some degree of popularity in Africa. That is unsurprising, as the .333 Jeffery utilizes a shortened version of the rimless, beltless .404 case with a slightly larger powder capacity than the modern .338 Winchester. Both it and the .338 deserve comparison in a feature of their own.

The palindrome that has not just survived, but has continued to flourish in popularity, is the .404 Jeffery. It feeds well and will fit into any action capable of holding the .375 H&H, yet offers controllability, a significant increase in power, and the important and distinguished benefit of nostalgia. **GD**

The **Heartbeat** of **Today's**

The Accura V2 has remained a popular frontstuffer with consumers, adaptable to hunting situations.

Muzzleloader Industry

Today's smokepoles take muzzleloader hunting and shooting enjoyment to new levels!

❯BRAD FENSON

The rising sun was a perfect reminder of why I love to hunt. The eastern horizon blew up in orange, lavender, and crimson splinters to backlight the Nebraska Sandhills. A huge whitetail buck scent-trailed a doe, unaware of our presence. Taking full advantage of the rut-crazed buck, we crossed the fence and hustled to a rise where the buck had disappeared a minute before.

As we slowed and tiptoed the last few yards, big antlers came into view. A quick range confirmed the buck was 156 yards away, where he had caught up to the estrous doe. Another buck was trying hard to look dominant but wouldn't stand a chance against the old veteran of the deer plains. The rutting turmoil provided enough time to set my shooting sticks and level the crosshair on the big buck. As the deer appeared in the scope, I cocked the hammer on my Traditions NitroFire muzzleloader and gently squeezed the trigger. At the shot, the buck lurched forward with its head down and ran 30 yards before falling over and sliding down the hill. It was a special day for me, taking my first buck with the newest muzzleloader technologies to hit the market.

With modern accessories, the Accura V2 is accurate, easy to use and maintain, and loaded through the end of the barrel.

Muzzleloaders available to the consumer today are nothing short of outstanding. The modern inline has come a long way since Tony Knight introduced the MK-85 almost 40 years ago. However, many other makes and models have also proven reliable over time. Old favorites and new rifles to offer changes in design and performance might mean it is time for some to upgrade. The First-World problem is deciding if you want to stick with the comfort of your old reliable front-stuffer or go with increased convenience and maybe even improved accuracy.

Inline muzzleloaders produced 30 years ago have proven their weight in venison, but it may be time to consider an upgrade. Many seasoned hunters started with a Weaver K-4 riflescope, which was revolutionary when brought to market. However, modern optics have advanced to the point where the early options can't hold a candle to modern performance, light transmission, and clarity. Even early-generation Leupold optics pale compared to modern HD glass with improved coatings. Inline muzzleloaders have new ignition, powder, projectiles, and performance options. For those who do not like cleaning and maintenance, there are some tremendous new rifles to lower your angst.

Here's a rundown of muzzleloading products, new and old, for consideration.

FIRESTICK

Federal engineers had been working on a new powder and loading system and introduced the FireStick. This encapsulated propellant simplifies loading and is impermeable to the elements, especially moisture. It allows a break-action muzzleloader to be charged or uncharged within seconds. The extruded propellant is cut to maximize surface area, which allows it to ignite and burn rapidly and efficiently. The FireStick is formed with a recess on the back to insert a 209 primer for ignition, making it safe and waterproof. Several ground-breaking advances arose with the FireStick, including a new Hodgdon blackpowder substitute called Triple 8. A FireStick looks similar to a 16-gauge shotshell but only contains powder.

Traditions Performance Firearms was the first company to manufacture a muzzleloader to take advantage of the FireStick technology. Traditions called the new smokepole the NitroFire, and it was the first of its kind in the muzzleloader world. It was designed to load a bullet down the barrel, which sits on a shelf and allows the capsulated powder to load directly under the projectile through the breech. There is no breech plug, and the design provides a fast, safe, accurate, and consistent shooting system that is easy to maintain.

The NitroFire proved highly accurate and

A trip to the far north is an excellent test for any muzzleloader, with damp conditions and nowhere to go for help, accessories, more powder, or bullets. You must be able to trust what is in your hands.

There are plenty of options on the market for propellants, and time on the range can provide insight into what your favorite muzzleloader likes and shoots best.

consistent at the range, and harvesting a buck at 156 yards certified the advantages. Before the hunt, I put the rifle through its paces. A chronograph was set up 10 feet from the barrel to record the velocity of five shots, with Federal Premium Muzzleloader 209 primers as the ignition source.

Traditions' Smackdown Carnivore 250-grain bullet with sabot produced the following results.

High velocity: 1,997 fps
Low velocity: 1,953 fps
Mean velocity: 1,973 fps
Variance: 44 fps

Three groups of three shots at 100 yards were used to measure the accuracy of the NitroFire with a 100-grain FireStick and Traditions Smackdown Carnivore 250-grain bullet.

Smallest group: .375 inch
Largest group: 1.625 inches

Average group: 1.167 inches

The accuracy was impressive, and the system provided many advantages to a muzzleloader hunter or shooter while increasing safety. The newest Traditions NitroFire .50 caliber has a VAPR barrel with a faster 1:24 twist. The faster twist stabilizes bullets to increase accuracy and range and equates to tighter groups at extended ranges. New firearms are continually upgraded, and it's not uncommon to see new models hit the market every year.

A historical perspective helps to recognize the significance of new muzzleloading technologies and benefits for hunters and shooters. The NitroFire, FireStick, and Triple 8 powder represent milestones in the muzzleloader industry. In 1808, Jean Samuel Pauly designed and patented an inline action, where the cock of the sidelock was replaced by a cylindrical hammer driven by a coil spring. Six years later, in 1814, English-born American artist Joshua Shaw refined the percussion cap design with a copper cup filled with fulminates. In more current times, in 1975, Pyrodex was one of the first reliable blackpowder substitutes introduced and offered to shooters.

PAY ATTENTION TO THE .45 CALIBER

Anyone following the advancements of smokepoles will notice an increase in options with the .45-caliber rifles. Traditions recently introduced a new model of its StrikerFire in .45 caliber. The smaller diameter bullet has an even faster barrel twist than the .50 caliber at 1:20 inches. The Vortek StrikerFire was the first hammerless muzzleloader to hit the market and offers fast, silent lockdown. The silent cocking button slides forward until it locks, putting the gun in fire mode and ready to shoot. A red dot is uncovered when the slide is locked, letting you know the gun is ready to fire. It's uncocked by pushing the spring release button behind the slide to let the mechanism glide back to the safe position. No external hammer offers faster lock time and a more silent operation.

LONG-DISTANCE SHOOTING

A .50-caliber LDR, or Long Distance Rifle, has been available in the

StrikerFire lineup for several years. The .45 caliber is the newest model offering long-range shooters both ballistic and barrel technical advantages. The StrikerFire is a traditional inline muzzleloader that uses standard blackpowder equivalent charges and a sabot and bullet. It offers advantages without the need for extreme powder charges.

CONSUMER FAVORITES

Traditions has two long-standing models that remain popular with consumers. The Pursuit and Buckstalker have proven longevity in the market and offer value

and performance. The Pursuit XT is the newest rendition with upgrades such as the Elite XT trigger system, rebounding hammer, and manual cross-block trigger safety. These improvements, along with standard features such as a 26-inch Chromoly steel barrel, Dual Safety System, and Accelerator Breech Plug Speed Load System, make the front-stuffer perfect for accuracy beyond 200 yards. The Buckstalker XT has similar upgrades and history. We shot it for accuracy and had groups sub-MOA to 1.75 inches.

If you like the old-style muzzleloaders, the Traditions sidelock rifles offer modern technologies with a historical look and feel. You can build your own Hawken Rifle from a Traditions kit or purchase a percussion or flintlock ignition rifle.

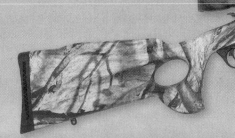

The Pursuit line of Traditions muzzleloaders has been a consumer favorite. The XLT Accelerator offers upgrades to technology and components.

KNIGHT RIFLES AND MUZZLELOADER RESURGENCE

The muzzleloader market continues to change. Tony Knight developed the modern inline muzzleloader. The MK-85 was the first production rifle to offer consistent inline ignition, accuracy, and safety with a No. 11 percussion cap. Knight generated interest in a fading segment of the shooting and hunting community, and there was an immediate resurgence in the popularity of smokepoles. New muzzleloader manufacturers quickly developed products, took advantage of the market, and raced to design better systems and components to improve accuracy and consistency.

I was fortunate to hunt with Tony Knight, who revolutionized modern muzzleloader technology. Tony brought several models of his Knight muzzleloaders to camp, and we were given a quick rundown of features, loading tips, and techniques. The .52-caliber Long Range Hunter proved to be exciting and accurate. However, I opted to hunt with the .50-caliber Disc Extreme. The Ultimate Slam Series polymer-tipped bullets were fresh out of production, and we were the first to put them to work in the field. The 250-grain boattail loaded easily and produced accurate results.

Knight Rifles were well known for using Green Mountain barrels that stole the show at shooting competitions. The company has changed hands several times, but consumers still provide a loyal following. The company saw several transitions, but Knight still offers made-in-American rifles. The Knight Disc Extreme was new to the market in 2011, an upgraded model of the original Disc rifle, and is still in the lineup today. The Extreme offered features and unique designs available only through Knight, such as a plastic disc jacket for a 209 primer and stock and caliber options, making it easy to shoot, clean, and maintain. The Disc Extreme has a look and feel of any modern centerfire rifle with the reliability of an old friend.

CLASSIC LOOK AND FEEL

The Knight Mountaineer is another long-standing favorite from the company, with excellent curb appeal and accuracy. Suppose you need a muzzleloader with laminated wood stock and outstanding accuracy. In that case, the Mountaineer is hard to overlook. This muzzleloader looks and feels like a centerfire rifle with a 200-yard accuracy guarantee. The trigger is crisp, and it sports a tight-fitting action and components. This rifle consistently shot sub-MOA groups at 100 yards.

LONG-RANGE KNIGHT

The newest Knight rifle, the Peregrine, will compete in the long-range muzzleloader category. We were not able to get a rifle for testing. However, the company claims the rifle produces a muzzle velocity of up to 3,000 fps. Knight guarantees every Peregrine will be MOA accurate at 500 yards. The Peregrine is a .40 caliber, with a faster twist rate than most rifles at 1:16 inches, which should deliver good speed and accuracy in a long-range muzzleloader. The rifle uses a breech plug design with a 28-inch fluted barrel. Modern Knight Rifles are built with a

The term "smokepole" might change with the new propellants that are coming out, producing less fouling, requiring less cleaning effort, and producing less smoke.

Timney match-grade trigger and are 100% American-made.

CVA NEW AND OLD STANDARDS

Connecticut Valley Arms, or CVA, has been building muzzleloaders since 1971 and continues to raise the bar in design and technology to offer hunters and shooters options with consistent and accurate results. I had dreamed of hunting Dall sheep since I was a young boy. With a new CVA ACCURA V2 in hand, I headed for the Mackenzie Mountains in Canada's Northwest Territories. Weeks on the range had me shooting sub-MOA groups at 200 yards. The rifle was accurate, consistent, and easy to use and maintain. After days of packing, I shot my dream ram at 213 yards with a single, well-placed shot. From that day forward, I followed the introduction of new technologies and advances in all CVA muzzleloaders.

LONG-TERM LOVE AFFAIR

CVA's best-selling rifle is the Optima .50 caliber, first introduced in 2003. History has proven that hunters and shooters embraced the Optima, and newer versions developed as new technologies were available. Dependability, accuracy, simplicity, and quality have created loyal followers. To take advantage of the popularity of the Optima and offer more

value, CVA introduced the Optima V2 in early 2013. The "Version 2" Optima came about after the popularity of CVA's AC-CURA V2. Both rifles feature the same trigger guard-actuated breeching lever, internal parts, a balanced trigger, and a Quick Release breech plug.

Shooting the Optima V2 proved why it remains popular. Today, several models of Optima V2 are sold as economical rifles with quality components. The rifle is value-driven and shoots groups of .70 to 2.50 inches, depending on the shooter, the bullet, and the load.

CVA has updated its most popular rifles with newer components and technologies at value prices. CVA has

mastered the breech plug by creating one that is easy to remove and clean using just your fingers. Even after prolonged shooting, the breech plug threads out easily, never seizing due to blowback and fouling — specially designed O-rings prevent blowback into the threads or primer chamber. The breech design ensures consistent ignition, keeping your primer and powder moisture-free. Safety features built into the breech mean that if it is not entirely threaded into the barrel, the shooter cannot close the break-action of the rifle. The ease at which the breech is removed or reinstalled makes it one of the fastest muzzleloaders on the market to clean and maintain.

The NitroFire rifle and FireStick propellant provided repeatable accuracy that tore the center of the target out.

After dreaming about shooting a Dall's sheep for most of his life, the author harvested an old ram with an Accura V2 muzzleloader.

LONG-RANGE ADVANTAGE

Long-range shooting continues to grow in popularity, including among muzzleloader enthusiasts. CVA embraced the surge and introduced the Paramount in a .45-caliber bolt-action gun that can handle extreme propellant charges, producing velocities of 2,200 fps. The Paramount ignition uses a hotter Large Rifle primer to burn the higher volume powder charges of the muzzleloader. The Paramount Pro was the next model in the line and included a threaded barrel for a muzzle brake to help reduce recoil.

The CVA Paramount HTR is the latest addition to the Paramount Series and is offered in .40 and .45 calibers. This series is best described by its precision and long-range capabilities. The HTR .45 caliber shoots a 285-grain bullet at 2,560 fps, comparable to several .30-cali-

Nothing beats time on the range to shoot different bullets and find out what your rifle likes best.

The NitroFire is easy to charge with a FireStick by inserting a primer into the breech. The bullet is loaded down the barrel, and the charge fits tightly in the breech.

ber centerfire cartridges. After shooting the Paramount, I noted the range and accuracy. As an alternative to shooting three bullets at 100 yards and measuring the group size, steel targets were shot and hit at 200, 300, 400, and 500 yards. CVA has worked closely with PowerBelt bullets to create projectiles for long-range performance.

Ballistically stable bullets are another milestone within the muzzleloader industry. It was in 1853 that Sir Joseph Whitworth developed a new elongated muzzleloader bullet. The .451-caliber projectile was 3-1/2 times as long as wide, weighing 520 grains. It was the first proper look at the ballistic coefficient.

BEST-SELLING

CVA is the best-selling muzzleloader in North America, with a diverse lineup of rifles to support the different facets of the hunting and shooting fraternity.

A CHANGING INDUSTRY

Thompson Center (T/C) produced muzzleloaders for many years and led innovation. T/C developed the first muzzleloader to use a 209 primer and changed breech plug designs for quick, dependable insertion and removal of the ignition source. Multiple players in a growing industry spurred innovation and competition, which was great for hunters and shooters.

Savage, Remington, and others pushed the limits in performance but could not stay in the industry's muzzleloader manufacturing side. It is important to note that reduced competition does not mean fewer great products to choose from in modern times.

THE MAINSTAY

Traditions Performance Firearms, CVA, and Knight Rifles have all proven the test of time. Lineups include old favorites and new models that push the performance envelope. The marketplace offers several categories of muzzleloaders, including traditional Hawken rifles with flint or percussion ignition. The modern inline muzzleloaders have changed drastically, and the old faithful ones are of great value and perform exceptionally well. The new long-range muzzleloaders would have been unimaginable 20 years ago and speak to the research and development to build products to revolutionize front-stuffers once again.

ACCURACY

Accuracy tests can be misleading, as every shooter has different capabilities. Most muzzleloaders will have a powder charge and bullet that outperforms all others. Experimenting at the range starting with 70 or 80 grains of powder and working up can show valuable results. Using different propellants and projectiles at the distances you intend to hunt is still the best way to determine an ethical

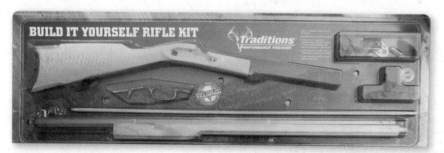

The kit rifles from Traditions are fun to build and provide a firsthand understanding of how different ignition systems work.

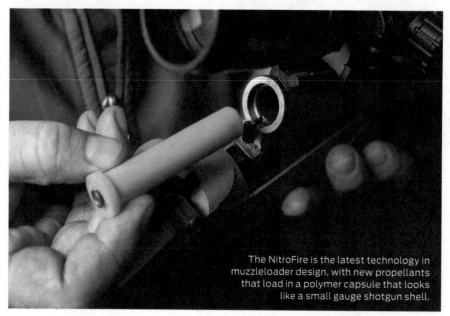

The NitroFire is the latest technology in muzzleloader design, with new propellants that load in a polymer capsule that looks like a small gauge shotgun shell.

shot and how to achieve maximum performance from any muzzleloader.

COLLECTOR'S CORNER

Avid muzzleloader collectors are always on the watch for old favorites that appear in used markets as hunters and shooters upgrade. There are several big-name companies that no longer produce muzzleloaders. Many of the rifles produced over the years are considered keepsakes.

Thompson/Center (T/C) released the first muzzleloader to use a 209 shotgun primer for ignition in an inline muzzleloader. The T/C Encore rifle was modified to become the first 209 primer, break-action muzzleloader. The hot, consistent ignition burned magnum powder charges faster, providing increased velocities — the new design also made for easier cleaning. T/C took things a step further with the Speed Breech quick-release breech plug. The new breech plug design allowed it to be removed by turning it 90 degrees, eliminating the need

for a tool or struggle with seized breech plugs.

T/C was a significant player in the muzzleloader industry for decades. However, the various muzzleloaders are no longer produced. Many T/C models are in the market, and the brand still has a strong following.

The CVA break-action Apex was a great combination rifle with interchangeable barrels for muzzleloaders and centerfire calibers. In 2009, CVA introduced its Electra, an electronic-ignition muzzleloader. The trigger is a micro switch that transfers an electric charge when depressed. It used an electric spark created by a 9-volt battery to ignite the powder, making the time between pulling the trigger and the bullet's exit from the barrel nearly instantaneous.

Traditions Performance Firearms was one of the first companies to improve the velocity, downrange energy, and effective muzzleloader range by going to a 30-inch barrel on its Vortek Ultralight LDR (Long Distance Rifle). The extra barrel length allowed magnum powder charges to burn completely in the barrel, maximizing the energy and consistency of the propellant. The Traditions Vortek StrikerFire was the first hammerless muzzleloader. A simple, silent cocking button slides the striker button forward until it locks, putting the gun in fire mode.

Savage introduced the 10ML-II as the first muzzleloader to use smokeless powder. About 50,000 firearms were purchased, but as of October 2010, Savage quit manufacturing the 10ML-II muzzleloader. Using smokeless powders in a muzzleloader was a radical step that did cause issues. Gun barrels blew up, and shooters suffered hearing damage and burns, leading to multiple lawsuits. Savage maintained that the problems were user errors and that the muzzleloader was safe when used correctly. The company held to its claim that the firearm had no defects and was designed following industry standards. There are thousands of Savage muzzleloader rifles still being used, and the people that love them still sing their praise.

In 2013, LHR Sporting Arms, LLC introduced the Redemption muzzleloader. The rifle had the first external-threaded

Modern Muzzleloader Timeline

1610 – Marin le Bourgeois develops the first flintlock for King Louis XIII of France.

The 1700s – The long rifle, or Kentucky long rifle, developed by Martin Meylin in Pennsylvania in the 1700s, was among the first muzzleloaders to have rifling. The spiral grooves in the rifle bore stabilized projectiles in flight and extended their range. The rifled barrels were a drastic leap forward from the smoothbore muskets, which had only an effective range of 50 yards. With improved ignitions, propellants, projectiles, and design, muzzleloaders have evolved by leaps and bounds.

1807 – Reverend Alexander Forsyth patents the first percussion ignition muzzleloader.

1823 – Jacob and Samuel Hawken designed a muzzleloader that hunters of the day envied.

1985 – Tony Knight forced massive changes with the MK-85. Everyone wanted a new inline muzzleloader, and companies raced to build a better mousetrap. It was a bubble that burst in terms of longevity for some companies.

1990 – Del Ramsey created the Muzzleloading Magnum sabots to shoot modern jacketed or lead pistol bullets in modern muzzleloaders.

Getting to hunt with Tony Knight was like going to muzzleloader school with the brains behind the modern inline rifle. Sharing time with the man and having him share knowledge was priceless.

breech that put the threads on the outside of the barrel and sealed blowback inside to eliminate seized breech threads and simplify cleanup. The concepts were sound but never garnered much attention. There was enormous potential with LHR engineers having a significant history in the industry and rifle designs. Some LHR rifles are on the market, and collectors will know their history and value.

The Remington Ultimate Muzzleloader, built on a model 700 action, uses primed centerfire brass casings for an ignition source. This rifle was one of the first production long-range muzzleloaders available. The design and technology came from Ultimate Firearms, Inc. of Michigan, also known for producing the Johnston Muzzleloader, which had been building long-range front-stuffers for years. The company uses primed pistol brass for an ignition source, hot enough to burn 200 grains of powder, thereby increasing velocity and range. These accurate rifles grabbed an immediate following from model 700 enthusiasts and long-range muzzleloader shooters. There are enough of them floating around the market that anyone interested could still

add one to a collection.

In 2018, SilencerCo. developed the first integrally suppressed muzzleloader. The Maxim 50 is a .50-caliber, break-action muzzleloader with a suppressor permanently affixed to the barrel. It's a Traditions Vortek StrikerFire inline muzzleloader with a SilencerCo. suppressor. The Maxim 50, in most cases, can be owned without the requirement of an ATF Form 4 or the tax stamp and waiting period.

EMBRACE TODAY'S MARKET
There have been radical changes to the muzzleloader world in the last two decades, and the march forward has no end. The biggest challenge for hunters and shooters is finding a gun safe big enough to store all the options.

Research and development teams continually seek to advance and introduce new designs and technologies. Hunters and shooters are the winners, with precision muzzleloaders that are easier to clean and maintain. Take the time to look into new models from Traditions, CVA, and Knight, who remain the key players in the muzzleloader game.

Modern muzzleloaders are more accurate and easier than ever to use and

The StrikerFire was the first muzzleloader without a hammer, using a push-button cocking device that is quick and easy to find.

maintain. However, you must shoot and practice from close to long range to know what any smokepole will do. When that big buck steps out and gives you the shot, you'll be ready. **GD**

The new 6.8 Western is a fresh twist on the .270-class cartridges but uses heavy-for-caliber bullets, like in this 175-grain Browning load.

Are Deer Rifles Suitable for Elk Hunting?

A recipe for success when using standard deer guns to hunt the monarch of the West.

❯ COLTON HEWARD

Heated debates about cartridges and their killing capabilities, or lack thereof, have been topics of campfire banter for decades. However, one ideology that few will disagree with is that a mature bull elk is a formidable foe that requires precision and ample knockdown power. Certain cartridges are undoubtedly more qualified than others to hunt elk, but that doesn't mean your trusty deer rifle can't get the job done. Below is a recipe to successfully hunt the mighty wapiti, regardless of which rifle you take into the woods.

The author admires a mature New Mexico bull that quickly succumbed to a single shot from a Browning X-Bolt Mountain Pro chambered in 6.8 Western.

Growing up in the West, I've taken the opportunity to hunt elk for granted. I killed my first elk at 12 years old and have punched many tags in the last 21 years. I have also spent the last 11 years as a hunting guide in Northern Utah. These experiences have allowed me to witness 75+ mature bulls — and a couple of hundred cow elk — hit the dirt. My approach to effective elk cartridges has always been "the bigger, the better," but that doesn't always hold, and my views have slowly shifted with time. There is much more to killing elk than just "carrying a big stick."

LESSONS LEARNED

Hunting is a revolving educational experience in which I strive to be an astute student. In late October, I found myself in a remote corner of Colorado preparing for an upcoming mule deer hunt. With camp set up and firewood cut, we set out to verify our rifles' zeros on the eve of opening day. Two trucks toting Pennsylvania license plates pulled up as we finished shooting, and seven blaze orange-clad hunters piled out. They were friendly folks, and we struck up a conversation while they sighted in their rifles. For five of them, it was their first elk hunting adventure, while the other two, a gentleman in his 70s and his son in his late 40s, had been coming west for years. Three hunters were shooting .30-06s, two the 6.5 PRC, and another a .270 Win. When it was the senior group leader's turn to shoot, he pulled out a well-used but manicured Winchester Pre-64 Model 70 chambered in .257 Roberts.

"A little light for a big bull, isn't it?" I chuckled. "I've killed dozens of elk who would whole-heartedly disagree," the gentleman piped back. He steadied his rifle and fired two nearly touching shots into the target at 100 yards. "That'll do. I don't shoot them much farther than that anyway," he said. True to his persona, he was shooting 117-grain Remington Core-Lokt ammunition from a weathered box that

The snow flurries couldn't wipe the smile off the author's face after tagging a mature bull. Many deer rifles can take elk like this with today's well-constructed bullets and proficiency with your rifle.

Hornady's Precision Hunter ammunition line utilizes the company's ELD-X bullet. This well-constructed cup-and-core projectile has been the demise of many big bulls across the West.

appeared older than me. While his setup was lighter than I would use, I understood why this rifle had treated him well for so many years.

ABSOLUTE TRUTHS

This experience drove home three absolute truths about the ethics of killing an elk. First and foremost, he was comfortable with his rifle and shot it well. No matter your caliber of choice, if you cannot precisely place a bullet in the kill zone, your lead-slinging elk cannon is nothing but a boat anchor slung over

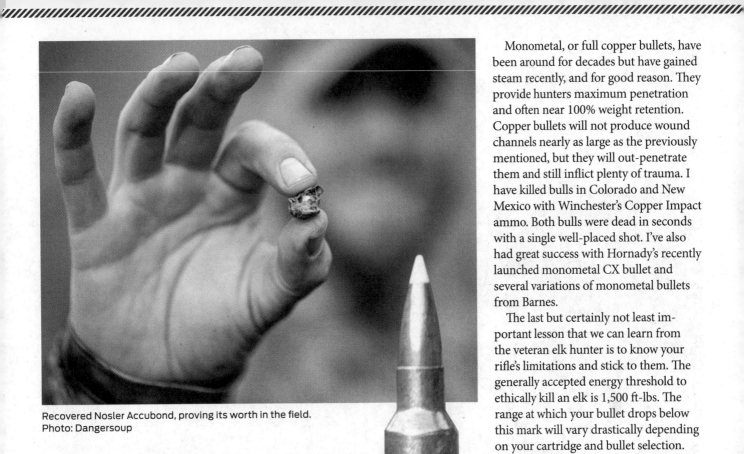

Recovered Nosler Accubond, proving its worth in the field.
Photo: Dangersoup

Nosler's proven deadly Accubond bullet is a favorite among many elk hunting enthusiasts. Photo: Dangersoup

your shoulder. Do whatever it takes to become proficient with the rifle you take into the elk woods and practice often. Take your practice one step further and shoot from various shooting positions and use a variety of shooting aids. I hate to be the bearer of bad news, but the chances of shooting an elk from a bench are slim.

Second, the gentleman was shooting a well-constructed bullet designed to penetrate through muscle and bone. Your bullet selection, especially with smaller cartridges, can mean the difference between the agony of wounding an animal and a punched tag. The market is flooded with an overwhelming number of bullets to choose from, and depending on what caliber you are shooting, some will perform better than others on elk.

His bullet of choice, the Remington Core-Lokt, is a "cup and core" type designed to rapidly expand and penetrate due to its thin copper jacket and dense lead core. Hornady's ELD-X and Sierra GameKing bullets are similarly designed to expand on impact while retaining a good portion of their weight to drive home through obstructive bone.

Bonded bullets are another highly effective bullet in the elk woods, utilizing an electrochemically fused bond between the bullet jacket and lead core. This bond slows bullet expansion and guarantees maximum penetration via high bullet weight retention. Nosler's renowned Accubond bullet is a favorite among elk hunters for many reasons, most importantly because it's proven itself time and time again as extremely capable and efficient on elk. Other popular bonded bullets include the Federal Terminal Ascent and the Swift Scirocco.

Monometal, or full copper bullets, have been around for decades but have gained steam recently, and for good reason. They provide hunters maximum penetration and often near 100% weight retention. Copper bullets will not produce wound channels nearly as large as the previously mentioned, but they will out-penetrate them and still inflict plenty of trauma. I have killed bulls in Colorado and New Mexico with Winchester's Copper Impact ammo. Both bulls were dead in seconds with a single well-placed shot. I've also had great success with Hornady's recently launched monometal CX bullet and several variations of monometal bullets from Barnes.

The last but certainly not least important lesson that we can learn from the veteran elk hunter is to know your rifle's limitations and stick to them. The generally accepted energy threshold to ethically kill an elk is 1,500 ft-lbs. The range at which your bullet drops below this mark will vary drastically depending on your cartridge and bullet selection. For the .257 Roberts that the gentleman was shooting, his bullet drops below this mark at just under 200 yards. Given that he rarely shoots beyond 100 yards, it's easy to understand why that caliber/load combination has enough knockdown power to quickly and efficiently kill an elk inside 200 yards. On the flip side, a .300 Win. Mag., shooting Nosler's 180-gr. Accubond does not dip below the 1,500 ft-lbs benchmark until just beyond 600 yards. I'm not saying that you should or should not shoot at that distance, but the difference in downrange energy between these two is night and day.

Another relevant example that needs to be addressed (due to its healthy dose of hazing within the elk hunting community) is the terminal performance of the 6.5 Creedmoor. The reality is that most problems elk hunters face when using the 6.5 Creedmoor are self-inflicted, lacking an understanding of the cartridge's capabilities. For example, Hornady's Precision Hunter ammunition, loaded with a 143-gr. ELD-X bullet, drops below that 1,500 ft-lbs mark around 400 yards. Inside that range, the cartridge is extremely capable of killing elk; I have seen it many

The author settles his crosshairs on a mature Colorado bull in the early morning.

times. Shooting beyond that distance, you are rolling the dice on the terminal performance of a good shot, let alone a less-than-ideal shot placement.

Plain and simple, a mature bull elk is 700+ pounds of raw muscle and sheer determination to survive in some of the most rugged environments in North America. Being proficient with your rifle, using a well-constructed bullet, and knowing your rifle's limitations will substantially increase your odds of success when you go toe-to-toe with one of these monarchs.

Jack O'Connor's favorite — the .270 Winchester — is even better as an elk cartridge using modern projectiles like Federal's Terminal Ascent.

CARTRIDGE SELECTION

All cartridges have pros and cons that must be considered when hunting elk and will differ from hunter to hunter. In true battle satire, I have broken down a list of popular and proven elk hunting cartridges into three weight classes: welterweight, middleweight, and heavyweight. The cartridges included are not inclusive but represent various

options ranging from vintage classics to the latest and greatest hotrods released in recent years.

WELTERWEIGHT

Many of the most popular deer hunting cartridges fall into the welterweight category, encompassing all cartridges built on the .243-, .257-, and .264-caliber platforms. The typical welterweights

include .243 Winchester, .25-06 Remington, 6.5 Creedmoor, 6.5 Weatherby RPM, and 6.5 PRC. All can kill an elk, but each requires immense attention to detail, marksmanship, and a deep-penetrating bullet. While I would not buy a rifle chambered in one of these cartridges to specifically go elk hunting, they can serve as a dual-purpose deer and elk rifle when needed.

The biggest advantage to using welter-weight cartridges is their lack of recoil and ability to rapidly re-acquire your target for a follow-up shot. This matters because none of them will immediately knock a bull off its feet, and a second or third shot is often required regardless of what you are shooting. Less recoil also minimizes "flinching" and equates to more precise shots, which is crucial when shooting elk.

I like to shoot elk on the shoulder and break them down. That makes for a quick tracking job. However, when using lighter cartridges, make an adjustment and push your crosshairs back 4 inches behind the crease of the shoulder and squeeze the trigger. That maximizes penetration and steers you away from the dense shoulder bone. Executing this shot with a well-constructed bullet will easily punch through both lungs and put the elk down quickly. Remember that even with a perfect shot, an elk may not react to the shot. I've seen many elk get shot with lighter cartridges and not react to the bullet impact. Often, they run out of sight. Upon further inspection to double-check for blood and verify the miss, we find them lying dead less than a hundred yards from the original impact. Always check for blood.

It is also worth noting that, with very few exceptions, most of these cartridges are intended to shoot elk inside 300 yards. The 6.5 Creedmoor can extend to 400 yards and the 6.5 PRC to just over 500 before dipping below 1,500 ft-lbs, but always be cognizant of their limitations and do your best to stay well within them. Just because you can regularly ring steel with them at 750 yards does not mean you should be flinging lead at an elk at that distance.

The first time you lay hands on a bull's antlers is a special experience. If you can't afford a new dedicated elk gun, your deer rifle will work — you just need to understand its limitations.

Monometal bullets, such as Hornady's new CX bullet found in the Outfitter ammunition line, are tried and proven in the elk woods.

MIDDLEWEIGHT

There is a plethora of extremely capable .277- and .284-caliber cartridges in the market. These middleweights offer elk hunters a substantial advantage in knock-down power by jumping dramatically in bullet weight from their welterweight relatives. The most common bullet weights drift between 140 and 175 grains. The heavier bullets and increased speeds also extend these cartridges' effective range.

Classic middleweight cartridges include the .270 Winchester, 7mm Remington Magnum, and .280 Remington. The .270 Win., thanks to legendary gun writer Jack O'Connor's exploits, is revered as one of the greatest hunting cartridges ever. His "No. 1" rifle was a Winchester custom Model 70 chambered in .270 Win. He openly advocated for the .270 and successfully killed many elk with that rifle. Interestingly enough, in much of O'Connor's writing, he, too, urged hunters to stay clear of the shoulder and pick shots wisely on elk-sized game.

While the .270 Win. and 7mm Rem. Mag. are still relevant and capable cartridges, the middleweight division has seen several new offerings that outperform these classics. New cartridges always take much flack over their validity, but you can't argue with the downrange numbers. New rounds — such as the 6.8 Western, 7mm PRC, and the 28 Nosler — outperform their classic counterparts. They separate themselves from the pack the farther you extend your effective range. For example, the .270 Win., shooting a 150-grain Nosler Accubond, drops below 1,500 ft-lbs of energy at 500 yards and has 48.4 inches of bullet drop. The 6.8 Western, shooting a 165-grain Nosler Accubond, still packs 1,856 ft-lbs at 500 yards and only 36 inches of drop. The same comparison could be made between the 7mm Rem. Mag. and both the 28 Nosler and 7mm PRC.

Another noticeable advantage these middleweight cartridges offer is a wide variety of bullet options. Any bullets above from these cartridges can take a rut-crazed bull cleanly. Middleweight cartridges will have more recoil than the welterweights, but with a good muzzle brake or suppressor, the additional recoil

Winchester's Copper Impact ammunition dispatched this bull in seconds with a single 162-grain projectile through the vitals.

is minimal and well worth the added performance.

Growing up, I had the opportunity to punch many elk tags thanks to my 7mm Remington Mag. shooting 140-grain Barnes TSX bullets. This rifle will always have a special place in my safe, but it rarely sees the light of day anymore. My last two bulls fell to a single shot from the 6.8 Western, shooting 162-gr. Winchester Copper Impact ammo. In Africa, I've taken the elk-sized kudu with the 7mm PRC and it performed as expected with another quick one-shot kill. These new cartridges are not the end-all answer to the perfect elk hunting rifle, but they unquestionably give hunters an advantage in terminal performance, especially at extended distances that are very common when hunting the West.

HEAVYWEIGHT

The heavyweight division is stacked with many .308- and .338-caliber cartridges that have long been touted as the most

versatile rifle rounds for elk. Plain and simple, these heavyweights can take any animal in North America, given proper bullet selection. Classic .30-caliber choices include the .30-06 Springfield, .308 Winchester, and .300 Winchester Magnum. There has also been an onslaught of new .30-cal. cartridges launched, the most popular being the .300 PRC and the 30 Nosler. The .338-caliber has also amassed several noteworthy cartridges, including the .338 Ultra Mag., 33 Nosler, and .338 Weatherby RPM. If you are looking for the hardest-hitting, most-powerful rifles to take into the elk woods, these heavyweight cartridges are your huckleberry.

The additional downrange energy is impressive. On many occasions, I've seen massive bulls knocked clean over without as much as a twitch from the heavyweight rounds. But everything comes at a price. Recoil, especially without a brake or suppressor, can be downright uncomfortable. Additional recoil makes follow-up shots more difficult, as the rifle's jump will take you off your target. But, if you can manage the recoil and execute a precise shot with a heavyweight cartridge, you will reap the benefits of devastating terminal performance.

The wide variety of cartridges in the heavyweight class gives you an array of bullet options, ranging from 150 to 225 grains or more — plenty to harvest a massive bull. Given a heavier bullet with a high ballistic coefficient, it's not uncommon for many of these cartridges to produce downrange energy north of 1,500 ft-lbs *well beyond 800 yards*, especially in the newer cartridges. Again, I'm not advocating shooting elk at that distance, but it certainly means that at 300 or 400 yards, your bullet still has the energy of a freight train.

Several years ago, I built a custom 30 Nosler which, with a 210-grain Accubond, hits animals like the Hammer of Thor. I have killed everything from eland in Africa to elk, deer, and antelope in the States using it with zero problems. With a radial muzzle brake, the recoil is manageable enough that even my wife enjoys shooting it.

Heavyweight cartridges might not be for everyone, but they undoubtedly pack the greatest downrange performance of the lot. However, their performance will not trump a marginal shot. Do not sacrifice precision for power when squeezing the trigger on a big bull. And for the love of all that is good, regardless of your rifle, keep shooting until that bull is on the dirt! Do not hesitate to send an insurance shot into the downed bull to ensure it is anchored. I cannot count the number of times that I have seen a bull collapse from the shot, only to jump back up minutes later, never to be seen again. This situation is often the result of a high shot that shocked the spinal column, temporarily paralyzing the bull but not breaking any bone. Such heartbreak is easily avoided with a quick follow-up shot.

Elk do not come easily; each one is earned in its own way. Whether you head into the elk woods with your "old reliable" deer rifle or spend some money and purchase one chambered in a hot new cartridge, do yourself and the elk a favor and heed the absolute truths that the veteran elk hunter in Colorado exemplified. Be confident and proficient with your rifle, know its limitations and stick to them, and shoot a well-constructed bullet. You still have to locate the elk and close the distance, but this is a recipe for success to quickly and ethically kill the elk of your dreams.

Embrace the entire experience and the special places that elk hunting takes you. Few things are more exhilarating than hearing an elk bugle, and few delicacies are better than those from a freezer full of elk meat. With the correct elk cartridge, both can be yours next season! **GD**

The author considers the .300 Winchester Magnum to be in the heavyweight class for elk, and it will speak with authority. Photo: Massaro Media Group

The author packed up and headed out with the last load of a hard-earned bull.

Modern Squirrel Guns

Whether you like sniping from a distance or following a dog right up to the tree, squirrel hunting guns have never been better.

❯ WILL BRANTLEY

Squirrel hunting has an enduring association with hillbillies and backwoods bumpkins, and that's perhaps why there are so few detailed discussions of good squirrel guns. After all, any old .22 rifle or single-barrel shotgun plucked from the corner of a farmhouse closet will do just fine for tree rats, right?

Actually, no. Maybe squirrel hunting isn't as popular as it once was, but a faction of us still enjoy sneaking through the hills and hollers in pursuit of the arboreal rodents. Are we hillbillies and bumpkins? Probably so; we aren't offended if you want to call us that. But if you try to tell us that any old iron will work as a squirrel gun, we'll set you straight. Today's squirrel hunters can be pretty particular about their guns, and for good reason. We still revere the classics, but we also know modern hunters have some excellent modern choices.

Squirrels taken with the CZ 457 Varmint in .17 HMR and 20-grain CCI Gamepoint. The soft-point bullet is a little more destructive, so headshots are required, but it's an excellent all-around hunting load.

BUSHYTAIL BACKGROUND

I grew up in western Kentucky, where the gray squirrel is the state animal, and I still live here today. Though at 40, I'm young enough to have always had good deer and turkey hunting close by, squirrel hunting was the most popular game in town when I was a kid. Maybe I couldn't take you back to the *exact* shagbark hickory tree where I shot my first squirrel at age 7, but I could get you pretty close to it. I hunt that ridge to this day with my son (who's almost 9 as I write this).

I shot that first squirrel with a Remington 514, a single-shot, bolt-action .22 rifle that had been my dad's first gun when he was a kid. The front sight bead was broken off, and the extractor didn't work, meaning that every spent .22 rimfire case had to be manually plucked from the chamber, often with the blade of a pocket knife,

tree, chasing each other as if they were following the stripes of a candy cane. One of the squirrels stopped on the trunk and looked at us standing there, Dad and me, and began to flick its tail and bark in alarm.

"Take your time," Dad whispered.

The Remington rifle cracked, and the squirrel fell. The feeling I had could've as well been the first hit of a drug and would later cause me to miss sleep and school, skip out on sports and parties, and — if I really get philosophical — shape an entire life's trajectory.

I was lucky to have killed that squirrel because my rifle was a real piece of junk, and Dad

wasn't much for coddling after I'd had my opportunity. He carried a 16-gauge Model 37 Winchester, which he called "Brother Win," and the rimfire's report had scarcely settled before he began pounding the treetops with No. 6 lead. Empty, green "high-brass" hulls popped out of the gun one after the other as he reloaded, and dead squirrels hit the ground with a thud. Some of those hulls are probably still there on that ridge, squashed under the duff and with rusted brass, but there nonetheless.

I'd gotten a squirrel, but I was clearly under-gunned — a good lesson for a boy. Like most little kids learning to hunt, I was terrified of the recoil from

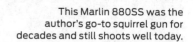

This Marlin 880SS was the author's go-to squirrel gun for decades and still shoots well today.

regardless of whether you'd just missed and were trying to reload quickly.

Dad and I snuck within 20 yards of the hickory tree that morning. Several squirrels (could've been three of them or 30) were working up in the canopy, chewing through the husks of the fall mast to get at the meat inside and letting the "cuttings" rain to the ground. All the gnawing of sharp teeth against husks, falling nuts, and thrashing leaves creates a commotion that can be heard from 100 yards or farther on a still morning, and I get fired up just thinking and writing about it to this very day.

In that situation, with so many squirrels vying for space and food in one tree, it doesn't take long for one of them to get upset over what another is doing and for a scuffle to break out. That's what happened that morning when a pair of young grays came spiraling down the

The author's favorite style of squirrel hunting happens in the early fall. It calls for precise headshots from a good rimfire rifle.

"big guns" like my dad's 16 gauge. But I remember him telling me, "You'd kill a lot more squirrels if you'd toughen up and try a shotgun." So, I did.

Dad had a Savage 24 combo gun, with a 20-gauge barrel underneath, that I used for a while, but it never did pattern all that well. I soon took to carrying Brother Win myself and the high-brass 16-gauge shells that Dad used. It was choked full and threw a pattern tight enough for turkeys, so it was hell on squirrels. But the recoil was vicious.

I got a youth model Browning BPS 20 gauge for Christmas a couple of years later, and killing limits of squirrels with that became almost easy. Dad seemed to notice, too, so the following Christmas, I found my first serious squirrel rifle

under the tree. It was a Marlin 880SS, with a synthetic stock and stainless-steel micro-grooved barrel that wasn't quite a bull barrel but was fairly heavy. Bolt-action Marlin .22s of the time were usually very accurate, especially for the price, and that one was no exception. I hunted with it for a season or two with iron sights, and it was a different tool altogether than the hand-me-down Remington 514.

I had a neighbor who gave me permission to hunt the woodlot behind his house on the condition that I'd give him my young gray squirrels because he liked them fried up for breakfast. But he flatly rejected the first limit of six I brought to him because I'd shot them through the shoulders, the middle, and just about everywhere else. "Lord, what a mess," he said. "You're going to have to skin those yourself. If you want me to take them, you bet-

ter start hitting them in the head."

I took it as a challenge and saved some chore money to buy a 4x scope and rings for my .22. Once sighted in, I could put five 37-grain high-velocity hollowpoints into a group the size of a quarter at 25 yards. I could hit gray squirrels in the head with it, too, which made for a cleaner skinning chore and a really satisfying hunt. That Marlin was my go-to squirrel gun for the next 25 years. Consistently headshooting squirrels became my foundation for building hunting and woodsmanship skills that have since served me on big game hunts worldwide.

A MAGNUM UPGRADE
I still have my 880SS, topped with the same 4x Tasco scope I bought at Walmart. I've rarely had to adjust the scope more than a click or two, and I don't know how many hundreds of squirrels I've shot with it. But it's no

Collecting supper in the hardwoods with a good rifle and sneaky attitude.

longer my go-to rifle because I replaced it five seasons ago with a CZ 457 Varmint chambered in .17 HMR.

Introduced in 2002, the .17 Hornady Magnum Rimfire is one of the most successful new cartridges of the past 20 years. It's based on a .22 WMR case necked down to accept .172-inch-diameter bullets, most of which are polymer-tipped, weigh 17 grains, and leave the muzzle at nearly 2,600 fps. The round is flat-shooting and quickly earned a reputation for incredible accuracy. But most consider it more of a varmint round than a small game hunting cartridge since the tiny, tipped bullets are explosive against 14-ounce gray squirrels and ruin too much good meat to make body shots acceptable.

But the 17-grain grenades aren't your only option. CCI loads a 20-grain soft point (called the Gamepoint) and a 20-grain Full Metal Jacket in .17 HMR, which shoot exceptionally well from my CZ. The Gamepoint is an excellent all-around hunting load I've used on several coyotes, foxes, and bobcats. It's a little vicious on squirrels at close range, but at 50 yards and beyond, the usual result is

The author's hunting buddy Ryan takes aim with his Ruger American chambered in .22 WMR.

So long as they shoot well, there's still plenty of room in the squirrel woods for classic .22s like the author's vintage Marlin 39A.

a tiny entry hole and an exit the size of a nickel. You still need to strive for headshots, but a squirrel isn't usually rendered inedible if you hit it through the shoulders.

Though I wouldn't use the FMJ round on larger critters, it's a perfect small game load that I've hunted with extensively over the past couple of seasons. It pierces a tiny hole through squirrels, regardless of shot placement, and destroys less meat than a high-velocity .22 LR hollowpoint.

I had verified the .17 HMR's reputation for accuracy a few times with other guns that I had on loan for assignment, but the CZ I called in for a review was exceptional, so I bought it. It is heavy, with a .866"-diameter barrel and walnut stock.

The squirrel woods are a great place to break out a classic rifle like this vintage Marlin 39AS.

Specialized Shotguns

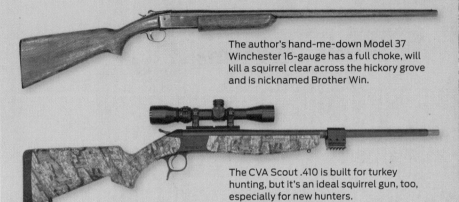

The author's hand-me-down Model 37 Winchester 16-gauge has a full choke, will kill a squirrel clear across the hickory grove and is nicknamed Brother Win.

The CVA Scout .410 is built for turkey hunting, but it's an ideal squirrel gun, too, especially for new hunters.

The author's son, Anse, shows off a limit of Kentucky squirrels he killed with his CVA .410 Scout.

I no longer use shotguns for squirrels because I enjoy hunting with rifles more, and I don't care for picking lead shot out of my squirrel and dumplings. Still, scatterguns are practical hunting tools, especially with dogs, where the shots are likely to be close and the squirrels on the move. The modern crop of single-shot .410 turkey guns is particularly suited for young squirrel hunters learning the ropes. I've seen that firsthand.

My son, Anse, has been shooting guns since he was four and has never had a negative experience with recoil. Still, he's like most little kids in that he doesn't want to shoot anything that "kicks." I started him out with a Savage Rascal .22, which certainly doesn't kick, but killing squirrels with a rimfire can be difficult enough for experienced adult hunters, much less young beginners.

So when he was six, I got Anse a CVA Scout, a single-shot .410 equipped with a Jeb's turkey tube and optic base. I put a low-power shotgun scope on it, and after a few practice shots at home with light-recoiling, 2-1/2-inch shells, Anse killed his first squirrel with that little shotgun the very first afternoon out. We load it with 3-inch loads of No. 6 lead when we're hunting (he never notices the extra recoil), and we wait for close shots inside 30 yards. The setup is just what the doctor ordered for boosting a kid's confidence in the woods.

There are several similar single-shot .410 turkey guns on the market (though the Scout is my favorite), all of which are lightweight, tight-choked, and ready for an optic, making them about as ideal for squirrels in the fall as they are for gobblers in the spring.

With a 2-10x40mm Leupold VX-3, mine weighs shy of 9 pounds. But it will put five .17-caliber bullets into a tiny, ragged hole at 50 yards, and it is not finicky about what I feed it. My son calls it "Big Blister," for the effect it typically has on a squirrel's noggin.

Of course, the .17 HMR isn't the only magnum rimfire cartridge suitable for squirrels. My buddy Ryan, whom I've known since college, might be one of the few people who's even more obsessive

than I am about headshooting squirrels. He prefers the .22 WMR through his Ruger American, which, he reminds me often, isn't as pretty or expensive as my CZ but shoots nearly as well.

The .22 magnum has a reputation for inaccuracy and killing power out of proportion to its size. Maybe the former was true with some guns once upon a time, but it's not true today. Every modern .22 WMR bolt action I've reviewed has been exceptionally accurate. Ryan doctored

the trigger on his Ruger and has it topped with a Vortex 3-9x40 Diamondback Tactical scope. It won't *quite* shoot with my CZ .17 (sorry, buddy, this is my story), but it's close — and will outshoot my old Marlin all day. I've watched Ryan headshoot squirrels with it from a legitimate 100 yards.

Anecdotally speaking, the .22 WMR is more meat destructive than the .17, but as with the .17, much of that can be fixed with proper bullets. Most .22 WMR

A scope helps for aging eyes and precision shooting, but hunters can get away with open sights, especially when hunting over dogs.

ammunition sold is a 40-grain hollow-point traveling 1,900 fps. It's bad news on squirrels hit through the ribs, and the lighter stuff, like Hornady's 30-grain V-Max, is even worse.

But there are plenty of better options, including CCI's 40-grain Gamepoint, a jacketed soft point and Ryan's go-to hunting load (it's the same bullet I like in a .17, too, just twice the size). Winchester Super-X has a 40-grain FMJ, and CCI and Fiocchi both have 40-grain Total Metal Jacket loads, all of which should be ideal for squirrels and meat preservation (but I haven't personally hunted with them).

Still, these magnum calibers are expensive to shoot; .17 HMR costs about 40 cents per round these days. And to boot, you've got to have special bullets to get your squirrel dinner. Why would any frugal hillbilly pay that when a good .22 LR hunting load costs 11 or 12 cents a round?

Well, if you hunt big, mature timber as we do, where the shots can be 75+ yards, and you enjoy the precision shooting aspect of squirrel hunting, magnum rimfire

cartridges can provide some decisive advantages. A .22 LR sighted in at 25 yards will hit about an inch high at 50 yards. That's just enough to sail over a squirrel's ears if you're holding on its eyes. The same bullet falls 2-1/2 inches low at 100 yards — plenty enough to miss a squirrel altogether, even if you're aiming right in the middle of it.

The .17 HMR, meanwhile, if sighted in at 100 yards, will be about a half-inch low at 20 yards and a half-inch high at 75. Later in the season, when squirrels are foraging on the ground, a 100-yard shot from one white oak ridge to the next is not unheard of. My .17 allows me to aim for a squirrel's head from about any distance I'm likely to hit it and do just that — if I do my part. That makes hunting with it that much more fun, and having fun is why I love squirrel hunting so much.

THE CLASSIC .22

Maybe you don't hunt much in big, tall timber, however. A lot of squirrel hunting, especially in the Midwest, happens in woodlots where the trees are shorter and

the shots closer. Hunting over dogs in the winter, when the leaves are down, might be the most popular style of squirrel hunting going these days. It involves a lot of walking and relatively easy, close-range shooting.

Many squirrel doggers prefer small-bore shotguns, but if I were hunting with dogs often and shopping for a new gun, I'd be especially interested in the modern crop of lightweight precision .22s such as the Bergara BMR Carbon (which weighs just 5 pounds!) or Ruger's Target version of the classic 10/22, with an aluminum alloy barrel sleeve that also drops its weight to 5 pounds.

Hunting with dogs provides an excellent opportunity to carry a classic lever gun, too, like the 1950s model Marlin 39AS I found on the used rack at the local gun shop a couple of winters ago. I put a Weaver scope base and 3x9 on mine, but for hunting over dogs, provided your eyesight is up to it (mine's marginal), open sights work just fine. Rumor has it that a new Ruger-made version of that discontinued Marlin .22 is in the works, and I'd love to see it.

In the meantime, a few very nice .22 lever guns are still in production. My brother has a Browning BL-22 that weighs just 5 pounds but has a grooved receiver for scope rings and will shoot right with my Marlin 880SS. It's also a smooth operator with a short-throw lever that will cycle .22 Shorts (and Longs) as well as Long Rifle cartridges. Some old-school squirrel hunters still prefer the .22 Short for close-in work because it destroys the absolute minimum of meat (though they're not exactly common on store shelves anymore).

Of course, no discussion of lever-action .22s can be had without mentioning Henry's extensive lineup, including the Classic, which weighs just 5-1/4 pounds and has a grooved receiver for mounting a scope. My buddy Nathaniel "Potroast" Pendley, whose father, Michael Pendley, is a renowned wild game chef and cooking writer, carries this exact rifle whether he's slipping through the hickories in September or following his Mountain Feist in December. Henry's lever guns are also available in .17 HMR and .22 WMR, including 24-inch threaded-barrel versions.

Really, there aren't too many .22s made these days that would be a poor choice for squirrel hunting. But today's hillbillies and bumpkins are loyal to their favorite squirrel rifles, which might change depending on the season and hunting style. It's best to have a few different ones in the safe — or even leaning in the corners of the farmhouse closet. GD

The .17 Mach 2

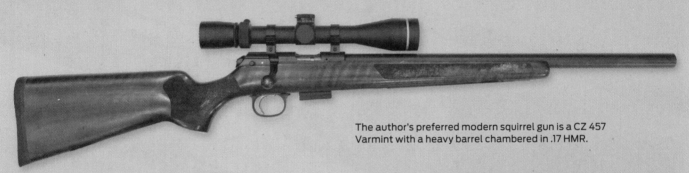

The author's preferred modern squirrel gun is a CZ 457 Varmint with a heavy barrel chambered in .17 HMR.

I have a couple of squirrel-hunting buddies who are dedicated .17 Mach 2 users. This cartridge was another Hornady introduction that followed the successful .17 HMR. It's based on the .22 Long Rifle Stinger case (which is .100 inch longer than a standard LR case) and necked down for the same .172-inch bullets used in the HMR.

The Mach 2 leaves the muzzle at about 2,100 fps, resulting in a slighter flatter trajectory than a 40-grain .22 WMR but far less meat destructive than it or the .17 HMR. In theory, it should've caught on as the perfect squirrel rifle round, but it never did, maybe because there aren't enough serious squirrel hunters left. In fact, the .17 HM2 almost disappeared entirely. My buddy Ricky King, who uses a .17 HM2 Anschutz for his squirrel sniping, worried that he wouldn't be able to find ammo for his gun at all, and that was well before the shortages of the past few years.

Fortunately for him and other .17 HM2 fans, the round had a resurgence in 2018 that continues today. A few factory ammo options are available, including the 17-grain V-Max in both Hornady and CCI loadings and the 17-grain CCI VNT. A few rifle options are available, too, including the semi-auto Savage A17 and high-end rifles from Vudoo Gun works and Anschutz.

My hunting experience with the .17 HM2 is admittedly limited, but I've not been impressed with what I have seen. It is accurate and fun to shoot, adequate for headshooting squirrels

Based on a CCI Stinger case, the .17 Mach 2 can be considered the little brother of the .17 HMR. *PC: Massaro Media Group*

(though I would expect as much from the expensive rifles I've tried). But you better headshoot them because the .17 HM2 is not a great game-getter. Squirrels are tough critters for their size, and I've seen multiple instances of them being hit well (but not in the head) with the .17 HM2 and then escaping into dens where they no doubt died later. Those things sometimes happen when you're hunting; they seem to happen too often with that particular round. I've never warmed up to it for that very reason, and perhaps that's why it never caught on with squirrel hunters any better than it did.

With the widespread distribution of Remington ammunition, many gun makers have rallied to the cause to provide quality, accurate rifles for field use. Illustrated here is the CZ Varmint rig, complete with a Leupold 6X scope in CZ rings chambered in the high-stepping .222 Remington.

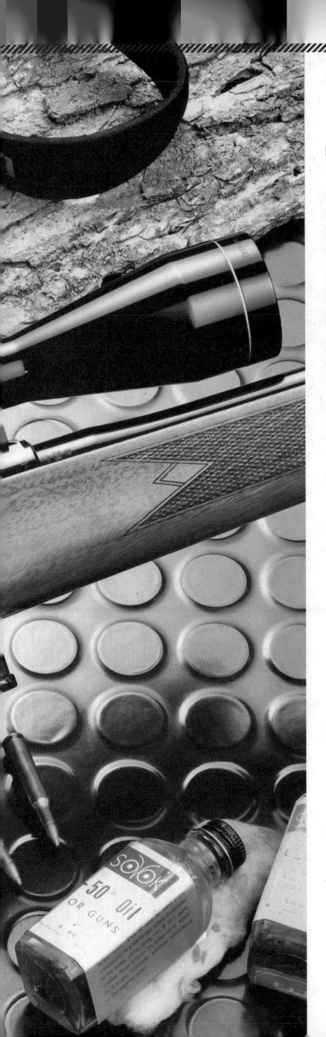

Those Cartridges Named Remington

From yesteryear's endearing classics to today's hottest numbers, Remington has a cartridge for you.

❯ STAN TRZONIEC

A s a sportsman and outdoor writer, the name Remington has meant a lot to me. As a young hunter, I remember the days in New York State at my uncle's farm hunting small game with nothing more than a single-shot .22 rimfire rifle and purchasing ammo under the Remington name at the local farm store at four bits or less in 1950. Interestingly, as soon as the local farmers knew the sharpshooting nephew of Uncle Frank was around, they contributed additional ammo to help cull the woodchuck population on their farms. My friend "Little Jimmy" and I had a summer filled with hunting, fishing in the brook, and having a good time.

The Cooper Model 21 chambered in the .221 Remington Fireball with some custom touches added, such as *fleur-de-lis* checkering and fancy wood, and topped off with a quality Redfield scope.

As I grew up and was old enough to support my hunting with a new rifle (new to me, but used), I acquired a Remington Model 722 in .257 Roberts with a well-worn stock and a Weaver scope. After minor stock refinishing, that gun served me well for far-distant woodchucks with 75-grain bullets. It also took deer with heavier loads. If nothing else, it was a learning experience: use a .22-caliber centerfire for chucks; the .257 for deer! Since I did not reload ammunition then, the stuff in the green boxes was at the forefront of my purchases, depending on my location and budget.

Moving into the outdoor writing field was another Remington party of product information, use, and writing workshops. Rifles and ammunition were there to use for magazine reports and hunting trips. At that time, reloading started to enter the picture heavily, so brass, bullets, and primers were available. Since Ilion, New York, was all within a few hours' drive, there were jaunts to record the manufacturing of the Remington guns, plus side trips to the famed Custom Shop when I needed information. Additional excursions to Lonoke, Arkansas, broadened

Remington factory ammunition has now reached the point where you can almost take accuracy as second nature. This .222 Remington group fired from a Model 700 shows three shots under three-quarters of an inch at 100 yards.

my base on the many ammunition manufacturing operations, which I found very interesting. Even though the Remington brand has endured some hard times, the Vista Group has taken over, assuring a steady supply of new Remington ammunition and related products.

SMOKELESS BEGINNINGS

So where did all this start with smokeless ammunition? Winchester began all this in or around early 1895 in conjunction with its famed Model 1894 lever-action rifle as the first small-bore American sporting cartridge. Remington got into the fray in 1906 by introducing the Model 8 autoloading rifle chambered for the .25 Remington, followed later with the same rifle chambered in the .25 and .30 Remington cartridges. These developments spurred on a new era of cartridges that separated themselves from the blackpowder era, especially when Remington merged with the United Metallic Cartridge (UMC) company in 1912.

From there, the parent company started to grow and, over the years, went under the management names of DuPont, RACI Acquisitions, Cerberus Capital Management, and finally, into the umbrella of the Freedom Group. Yet despite all this growth and various acquisitions, the Remington Outdoor Group failed to survive, later to be auctioned off to Vista Outdoor. A delay ensued in the ammunition production at the Lonoke, Arkansas facility. Now, after months of getting back on its feet, Remington is back in the ammunition business again and very seriously.

Over the last century-plus, Remington has turned out dozens of cartridges under its brand name, from the smallest .17 caliber to the most powerful magnums. All fit into specific hunting niches, from varmints to big game. We'll start with Big Green's entries into the .17 caliber and move up from there.

.17 REMINGTON

At one time, there was no shortage of .17-caliber variants. Way back, Parker

The 6mm Remington remains a viable cartridge for varmint or plains game. Based on the 7X57mm case necked down and starting as the original .244 Remington, it was later updated to a new twist rate and was soon chambered in several popular rifles.

Otto Ackley, aka "P.O.," had dibs on the .17 Pee Wee, which was nothing more than a .30-caliber M1 case necked down. From there, the .17 Woodsman, .17 Javelina, and others were floating around before the .17 Remington cinched the .172-inch market with a true Model 700 production gun for the diehard varmint shooter. Here, Remington should get some credit for its investment as the .17 will appear only to a small segment of the shooting population, but in a small way, the gamble did pay off. By having a factory rifle and ammunition available for those who did not want to contend with the numerous wildcats and custom rifles needed to get into field shooting, this .17 quickly gained popularity.

Based on the .223 case necked down with the shoulder moved back slightly, the .17 Remington is an efficient cartridge when you look at the stats. With my rifle, 23.5 grains of H-335, and a Hornady 25-grain hollowpoint, you can hit almost 4,100 fps and groups just under an inch with no sweat. Back it down to 23.0 grains of IMR-4895, and you get around 3,700 fps with impressive quarter-inch groups at the century mark. You should be careful reloading the .17, as tiny variations in powder charges could raise the pressure reading drastically.

With these ballistics, it's no wonder why small game hunters adapted the .17 Remington with open arms. My experience on small game out to 250 yards or more was enlightening when I did my part, and there was a light crosswind. If your scope could resolve the details, little recoil with almost non-existent muzzle jump made the hits visible to the shooter.

Regrettably, the newer .17 Remington Fireball introduced in 2008 replaced the parent cartridge as the go-to .17-caliber round for varmint enthusiasts.

.221 FIREBALL

Based on the shortened version of the popular .222 Remington, the .221 Fireball originally started as a pistol cartridge in the XP-100 in 1963. While the pistol fell to the wayside, the cartridge always seemed to be hiding in the shadows until companies like Cooper, Thompson Center, CZ-USA, and others, brought it back into the limelight. Remington even chambered the round in its Classic series of Model 700s in 2002. For the varmint shooter, it was a no-brainer as bullets in the .224 caliber are out there by the dozens, brass is available in limited quantities from Remington, Lapua, Norma and Nosler, and with a case that beckons for the suitable powder with economy to boot, accuracy and distance are assured.

During its lifetime, the Fireball was a favorite of small game and varmint hunters as the potential for sub-MOA groups is well within the realm of the factory and handloaded ammunition. For my use, Cooper Arms still offers a rifle for the round, and I had one made for me that I use in the fields here in New England with great success.

Undoubtedly, the .221 Fireball is an accurate cartridge with which

to work. Witness the small groups in the Cooper loaded with 15.8 grains of IMR-4227 that show velocities of 3,000 fps or better with a 50-grain Hornady V-Max bullet. On the flip side, Remington factory loads come pretty close to matching that with an average velocity of 2,893 fps with three-quarter-inch groups at 100 yards. Either way, it's a winner!

.222 REMINGTON

Next to my prized Ruger No. 1 chambered for the .219 Donaldson Wasp, the .222 Remington follows a very close and tight second. Like many of the traditional Remington entries, the "Triple Deuce" was introduced almost 75 years ago by Mike Walker — a dedicated Remington employee. In appearance, this cartridge is not based on anything else in the line; in short, it's

an original design made for the benchrest circuit. It looks like a miniature .30-06 Springfield; in power, it falls between the .218 Bee and the .220 Swift.

Remington introduced it to partner with the new Model 722 bolt-action rifle. Later, it was a perfect match for the updated Model 700 series and, for a few decades, was *the* varmint cartridge. My enthusiasm went as far as having a custom Model 700 made for me to take woodchucks at more than average distances — which it did handily. Today, it's tough to find a rifle maker or an ammunition manufacturer that doesn't include the .222 in its product line.

In testing the .222, I used one bullet (Hornady 52-gr. A-Max), one gun (a Remington 40XBBR rifle), and 17 powders. Groups varied from .365 inch to 1.4 inches with velocities topping 3,551 fps chock full of Accurate XMR-2015 propellant. With my pet Model 700, groups were outstanding, with the best coming in at .375 inch at 100 yards; factory loads hit around .700 inch at 3,197 fps.

In looking at a Remington press release right in front of me dated March 30, 1950, Mr. R.C. Swan, in a letter to his jobbers, mentioned that the new .222 was "developed exclusively by Remington" and "There is nothing like it!"

To me, that says it even today.

A Remington Model 700 chambered in the .223 Remington with a Redfield 3-9x40mm scope.

It's hard to beat the accuracy of the Remington .223 Match ammunition, as this target shows. One of several offerings by the parent company, due to its popularity, it has a broad following with other major brands in the industry.

these days of shortages. Additionally, the wide availability of .22-caliber bullets in various bullet weights adds to the flexibility of the cartridge and its accuracy — especially with the use of 55-grain bullets in 1:12 twist-rate barrels. For the handloader, the .223 is economical to reload, the listing of modern powders seems never to end, and with the number of various primers on the market, one could make the .223 Remington a true labor of love over a lifetime of shooting. Regarding factory loads, I can't find any manufacturer that *doesn't* include the .223 Remington with various loads and bullet weights.

Over a long wait of 30 years, Browning finally brought back its B78 High Wall single-shot rifle, which was the right combination for the .223 Remington and my hunting style. With that gun, a Hornady 55-grain bullet, and powders like Vihtavuori R-135, H-335, or BL(C)-2, my groups are always in the sub-minute of angle range with velocities over 3,000 fps.

.223 REMINGTON

If there was ever a more popular varmint round for the masses than the .223 Remington, I have yet to find it. Sure, there are other .22-caliber offerings, but with the advent of the AR platform and newer rifles with up-to-date hammer-forged barrels, this cartridge is still hard to find in most gun or box stores.

Initially designed for the military in 1957, it was not long before the general shooting public noticed the cartridge's advantages. Since the .222 Remington and its magnum counterpart were on

the wane, the .223 took their place with gusto as a sporting round with a slightly shorter case than the magnum version and more power to boot. Noting this, and while the case lengths appear very close, do not ever fire the .223 in a rifle chambered for the .222 Remington Magnum. Nor should you ever shoot the 5.56X45 NATO in a .223 Remington chamber, as it will damage the rifle and possibly injure you.

Its rise to popularity was no doubt due to the ample supply of once-fired military brass, something we can all relate to in

.22-250 REMINGTON

I have always enjoyed the allure of the single-shot rifle for varmints, so I placed the order when the Ruger No. 1 became available in 1976 for the .22-250 Remington. That gun and cartridge have given me years of pleasure without a hitch, and I still have and use it today.

Like many varmint cartridges, the .22-250 Remington can be modestly upgraded in the Ackley Improved version on the right. Take note of the shoulder angle and a slight increase in the case capacity with about a 10% increase in velocity.

Based on the necked-down version of the .250-3000 Savage, the cartridge was also known as the .22-250 Varminter and initially was the work of J.E. Gebby and J.B. Smith in 1937; later to be commercialized by Remington some 30 years later in 1967. Looking at comparisons, this cartridge is slightly less powerful than the .220 Swift but overall is more versatile using either reduced or full-house loads and bullet weights from 35 to 80 grains. In popularity, only the .223 Remington surpasses it.

When it comes to personal experience, not only has the Ruger No. 1 been a companion in the field, but as an outdoor writer, I've had the opportunity to use the .22-250 in guns offered by Remington, Browning, Winchester, and others not only in New England but on hunts in the west. For beyond 300 yards and using favored 55-grain bullets, the wily woodchuck hasn't a prayer here in the East. For powders, while new entries like Varget give excellent results, the old timers like IMR-3031 or (the now obsolete)IMR-4320 — in concert with benchrest primers and neck sizing the once-fired cases — still produce sub-minute groups at 3,400 fps and more.

The author considers the .22-250 Ackley Improved an easy wildcat to reload. Once you have a rifle chambered for the Improved, shoot the parent .22-250 Remington ammunition, and you have a fireformed case ready for loading.

For consumer convenience, the .22-250 Remington is hard to beat. In checking my references, finding a rifle, ammunition, or component manufacturer that doesn't make a product to fit this cartridge is difficult. In short, whether you're a beginner or a seasoned small game hunter, the .22-250 has the accuracy, versatility, and availability to suit all.

6MM REMINGTON

If you want a controversial cartridge to discuss over the campfire, this is the one! The 6mms were born to the sportsmen of the hunting fraternity in 1955. It started with Winchester's idea of what 6mm should be, and the company aimed its idea at deer hunters with the .243 Winchester. On the other side, based on the

.257 Roberts case necked down to 6mm, Remington brought on the .244 Remington with the sole idea of a varmint cartridge. Still, it soon revamped that thought after the 1:12-inch twist did not stabilize heavier 100-grain bullets. Later, with a minor course correction, the twist was changed to 1:9, changed the name to the 6mm Remington in 1963, and the cartridge moved on to be chambered in its Model 722A, 700 BDL, Model Seven, and the semi-auto Model Six.

With a larger case capacity, the 6mm Remington does have a slight advantage over its rival when pushed to the limits, but not that much as to influence you on the choice of rifle. My experience with the 6mm started with a Ruger M77. Later, the cartridge started to shine when I reloaded it for a Remington Model 700 "Varmint" model, complete with a heavy barrel for my woodchuck forays in the Empire State.

Running the gamut of bullets from 55 to 75 grains, out of the 20 loads I tested,

On an antelope hunt, Tzroniec took a Model 70 chambered for the .257 Roberts and connected with a nice antelope and mule deer. The author found the Roberts a versatile cartridge and useful as a "one-rifle" tool for any plains game.

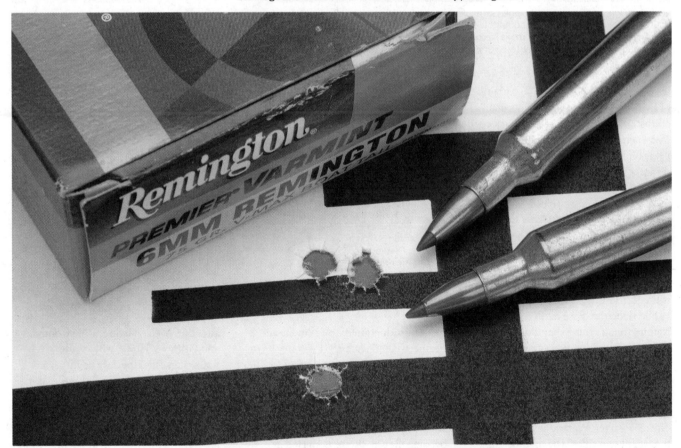

The 6mm Remington has plenty to show regarding velocity and accuracy, using a range of bullet weights from 68 to 108 grains for various game. In the spring, the author uses his Model 700 with the 6mm Remington varmint loads for hunting woodchucks over the freshly cut fields in New York State.

While you will not find the .257 Roberts on every gun rack in the country, rifle makers like Kimber offer this semi-production/custom rifle with all the trimmings that make it a pleasure to own. Topped with a quality scope, under minute-of-angle groups are the norm.

the Speer hollowpoint over 46.0 grains of IMR-4350 printed three shots in an almost one-shot group measuring a curt .225-inch at a tick under 3,200 fps. Since I was looking for more velocity for those distant chucks, one standout load used a Nosler 55-grain spitzer with 53.0 grains of W-760 (compressed) for less than half-inch groups at 4,077 fps. After the first cutting, nothing was safe on the field past the barn.

Finally, if you like to shoot wildcat cartridges, a variant on the 6mm Remington is the .22/6mm Texas Trophy Hunter. While velocities close in on the 6mm Remington, it's fun to handload and shoot. And besides, you can have bragging rights at the range with a new rifle. That makes it all worthwhile.

.257 ROBERTS

The .257 Roberts cartridge comes under the tale of two rifles. The first was the Remington Classic Limited Edition based on the Model 700; the second was

With the .257 Roberts, one can expect better-than-average accuracy in factory ammo and handloads. This tight group is from a Remington Classic rifle with the Remington 100-grain loading.

the reintroduction of the Winchester Featherweight, circa 1981 — one sits in my gun rack — both chambered for the .257 Roberts.

Based on the 7x57 Mauser necked down to .25 caliber with a 15-degree shoulder, the concept for what would become the .257 Roberts started as early as 1909. As the cartridge grew in popularity, Mr. Ned Roberts seemingly got the

attention of the Niedner Rifle Company and Griffin & Howe, which, after a few years, suggested the case be increased by roughly 1/16 of an inch, thus making it unsuitable to use in older rifles of the time.

Interesting to note is that Mr. Griffin got Remington Arms to look at the new cartridge in 1934. Remington changed the shoulder angle to 20 degrees and made some other minor changes to manufacture it on a larger scale. First called the .25 Roberts, then the .257 Remington Roberts, it finally became the .257 Roberts. Additionally, at that time, the cartridge came under reams of discussion as others in the group said the Roberts was not that much better than the .250 Savage. Maybe yes, maybe no, but on the side of the Roberts, it could handle the 117-grain bullet at a higher velocity with a slightly heavier 120-grain bullet as an option.

Looking at the numbers places the Roberts as a thoroughly classic cartridge in its own right and worthy of your consideration for a wide variety of game. The round is chambered by many rifle makers, both custom and production, and I've used it for pronghorn with great success, especially when Ned Roberts was looking over my shoulder. Ultimately, whether you use it in the commercial or handloaded +P version, it's still a great cartridge.

.25-'06 REMINGTON

The .25-'06 Remington has always been an extremely practical cartridge. Beautifully proportioned and sized to a bullet diameter capable of handling many chores, this cartridge does the job well. Born out of a marriage between the well-known .30-'06 Springfield and the .257-inch bullet, Remington commercialized the .25-'06 in 1969.

As an exact duplicate of the .30-'06 case, complete with a 17-degree, 30-minute shoulder and an overall length of 2.494 inches, this is truly a modern dual-purpose round. With lighter 87-grain bullets, it makes an excellent varmint tool even past 300 yards. With heavier 100- to 120-grain bullets, this .257 entry is equally suited for deer and pronghorns at those longer ranges on the prairie under the right conditions.

In 1977, I was so impressed that I ordered a Remington C-Grade rifle from its famed Custom Shop in Ilion, New York. Reasonably priced, very accurate, and well-equipped with semi-fancy wood, my records show that with a modest break-in period of only 50 rounds, the gun was capable of one-inch groups or less with Hornady's 120-grain hollowpoints over 50.7 grains of H-4831. That was good enough to set me up with partner Joe Pirani for an antelope and mule deer hunt near Jordan, Montana, with excellent results.

The popularity of the .25-'06 has boosted its availability in commercial ammunition, and like any cartridge, it responds well to handloading. In the beginning, many shooters used .30-'06 military brass necked down to .25 caliber, but depending on the parent brass, pressure levels could rise due to thicker case walls. However, relying on military brass is not necessary today as plenty of commercial product is on the market from various sources.

Bullet availability today presents no problems. This cartridge is a formable choice for any game with bullet weights from 75 grains (3,700 fps) to 120 grains (3,000 fps). With a case capacity of just over 65.0 grains of water, slower powders like H-4350, IMR-4831, RL-22, and IMR-7828 get the nod.

The .25-'06 Remington is regarded as one of the best cartridges for plains game today. Using factory ammunition or necking down the parent .30-'06 cases to .25 caliber nets you a tool for long-range shooting that is ideal for antelope and mule deer in states like Montana or Wyoming.

.280 REMINGTON

While the .280 Remington looks good on paper, it never seemed to make the grade in popularity. My association with it began at a Remington get-together some years back when the company introduced the Mountain Rifle as part of a new lineup. That rifle was a new design for the company, and just looking at and shooting it made you want to go on a hike.

Writers had a choice of cartridges, but for hunting the Axis deer on the ranch, I picked the .280 Remington. Initially introduced in 1957, the first rifle available was the Model 740 autoloader, followed by the 760 pump and the 721 and 725 bolt actions. Naturally, when the Model 700 arrived, the .280 also got the nod there.

While the .280 Remington was not setting the world on fire in sales, the company decided to

let weights. Regardless of the naysayers, it's still a fine cartridge for anything you want to hunt in North America.

Want to try the .280 Rem.? How about a Hornady 139-grain bullet seated to 3.285 inches over 53.5 grains of IMR-4350 for half-inch groups at 2,806 fps? Nice!

Additionally, for those handloaders looking for more of a challenge — hence more velocity — you might want to try your

combination for almost any type of big game in North America. With bullet weights from 100 to 175 grains, it beats out anything in its class in factory and handloaded ammunition. Since the American hunter was ready for something new, Remington had a hard time keeping up with the demand for both.

Like many

While some hunters may shy away from semi-automatics for hunting, Trzoniec found the Browning BAR very accurate in any variation and a distinct advantage for those who might be sensitive to recoil. These guns were chambered for the heavy-recoiling 7mm Remington Magnum.

rename it to the 7mm Remington Express for only a year from 1979 to 1980, ostensibly to be more with the times. This change led to more confusion for the consumer and retailer, so a year later, the name was back to the .280 Remington. In simple terms, this cartridge is actually based on the .30-06 Springfield case necked down with the shoulder moved forward to prevent it from being chambered in the .270 Winchester.

On paper, the .280 is slightly more powerful than the .270 Win., but the medal goes to the .280 only because of its versatility when loaded with heavier bul-

hand at the variant they call the .280 Ackley Improved.

7MM REMINGTON MAGNUM

Introduced to the shooting public in 1962, this 7mm entry was (and still is) one of the most popular .284-inch bores. Taking a belted .264 case and necking it up to 7mm was a good idea at the time, and it still reigns as a top, premium cartridge for long-range shooting today.

That year, Remington hit a home run with the 7mm Rem. Mag. and the introduction of the famed Model 700 rifle. Together, they made the ultimate

people, I find "magnum" recoil to be troublesome. For my hunting duties, I went with the Browning BAR rifle, which is soft on the shoulder and accurate. It proved the best for my needs in the western part of the country. I started my journey with this 7mm using the 140-grain bullet and a good dose of 64.0 grains of IMR-4350; it shot tight three-quarter-inch groups at 100 yards.

To show you the versatility of this 7mm, I moved up to the 150-, 154-, 160-, 162-, and 175-grain bullets from Sierra, Nosler, and Hornady. In all my testing, groups never strayed beyond 1-1/4 inches for three shots. With slow-burning powders like IMR-4350, IMR-4831, Norma MRP, and IMR-7828, velocities remained in the high 2,800 to lower 2,900 fps range. The big 7mm is also at home with reduced loads for practice, and 30.0 grains of SR-4759 will net you around 2,200 fps with a 160-grain bullet.

No doubt, the 7mm Remington is a popular cartridge today, no matter the rifle used and will remain in its lofty position for years to come.

.35 REMINGTON

An interesting addition to the Remington lineup, the .35 Remington is the sole remaining cartridge of a group of rimless products chambered in the Remington Model 8 semi-automatic rifle introduced in 1906. From here, this .35-caliber entry has seen chamberings in various Remingtons, including the XP-100, Model 14, Model 7600 and Model 7, plus other makers, including the Marlin 336, Stevens Model 425, Thompson-Center Contender, and the Winchester Model 70 in the late 1930s.

For the woods hunter, especially here in the East, the .35 Remington with the Marlin 336 is a perfect match. Loaded with a 170- or 200-grain bullet for deer at modest ranges and shooting through timber, many hunters still are not ashamed to carry an "almost obsolete" cartridge for their hunting needs. Besides that, others, like the .350 Remington Magnum, are high on the recoil factor. For the young country hunter just starting, the allure of the lever action combined with a soft-recoiling cartridge will make an impression that will last a lifetime.

My experience with this .35 has been with the Marlin 336 and the Thompson-Center Contender. Because of my enthusiasm for western hunting, I've

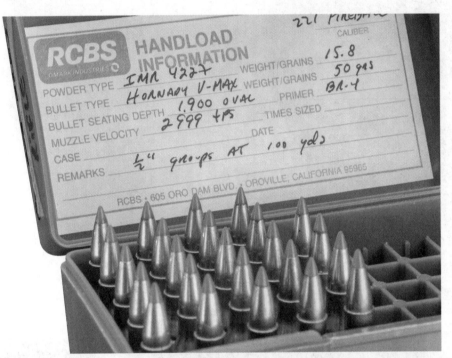

Regardless of using commercial Remington ammunition or handloads, keeping records is all part of the hobby. Once you have a good load, make a batch for the next hunting or varmint season.

At 75 yards, the .35 Remington loaded in a Marlin lever gun proves its worth in hunting and surpasses the ever-popular .30-30 Winchester. Additionally, this round can be reloaded with a lighter, 158-grain bullet for off-grid small game or varmint hunting.

The .35 Remington was available in the Thompson-Center line of single-shot pistols for a time. Carried in a shoulder holster and equipped with a scope, this is the perfect rig for the hunter on the go.

never taken either gun out in the field but shot them enough to see how they would do hunting. Regarding the Marlin, I found it versatile, especially when loaded with 158-grain .357 magnum bullets and H-322 powder to around 2,100 fps. Heavier bullets in the round-nose configuration (never use spire points in a tubular magazine) to the same velocities with LeveRevolution powder make for some accurate shooting at closer ranges for which the .35 was designed.

On the other hand, the Contender was a blast to shoot. Equipped with the 2.5x scope, this Super 14 version at 40 to 50 yards and using Sierra 158-grain soft points, 170-grain full metal jackets, and the 200-round nose bullet and Norma N200 powder, it gave the best groups around an inch or a bit under. It's not hard to understand why, after all these 115 years, the .35 Remington has the staying power that knowledgeable hunters still desire in a woods cartridge.

Back in 1987, Remington commercialized the .35 Whelen by listing it as an "authorized" factory-loaded cartridge out of Lonoke. In basic form, it is another variant of the .30-'06 cartridge, necked up to .35 caliber. Remington chambered the round a year later in its Model 700 bolt-action and Model 7600 pump-action rifles.

Trzoniec took a prototype Model 700 chambered in the .35 Whelen on a deer hunt on Anticosti Island, Canada. This deer was one of two taken with the newly chambered round.

.35 WHELEN

The coming of the .35 Whelen to my possession was a pleasant surprise. When planning a fall trip to Anticosti Island, public relations man Dick Dietz at Remington called to ask if I would like to take a prototype Model 700. Without a heartbeat came a resounding "yes," and that started my love affair with the Whelen. In short, Remington gave Whelen's "wildcat" full commercial status in the Model 700 Classic and the Model 7600, topped off with a pair of factory loadings with 200- and 250-grain bullets.

Designed in 1922 by a gunsmith named James Howe, this .35-caliber cartridge offered the shooter very close to magnum performance in a round that would fit into a standard-length rifle action. It delivered over 3,000 ft-lbs of energy. Howe was so proud of his new achievement that he named it after the dean of gun writers, Townsend Whelen. Naturally, the Whelen is no match for today's run of magnum cartridges, but for the knowledgeable hunter, it is a dream come true for most of our hunting needs when dealing with larger big game.

After the hunt, I had time to range-test the Whelen to see where the classic might fit into today's hunting world. Using bullets from 180 to 250 grains and powders such as IMR-4064 and IMR-4895, I had three-shot groups averaging 1.8 inches at 100 yards. Some groups printed a bit smaller, but on average, I was happy with the Whelen, with a mean velocity of 2,417 fps. Factory loads of 200 and 250 grains printed 1.5 inches with velocities of 2,610 and 2,301 fps, respectively.

By the way, I did come home with a pair of nice bucks for my efforts.

Over the years, Remington Arms has produced a wide array of rifle and handgun cartridges that have provided the American hunter with a choice of firepower to fit their hunting style. What I have covered here is a small portion of the long list and probably shows my favorites. **GD**

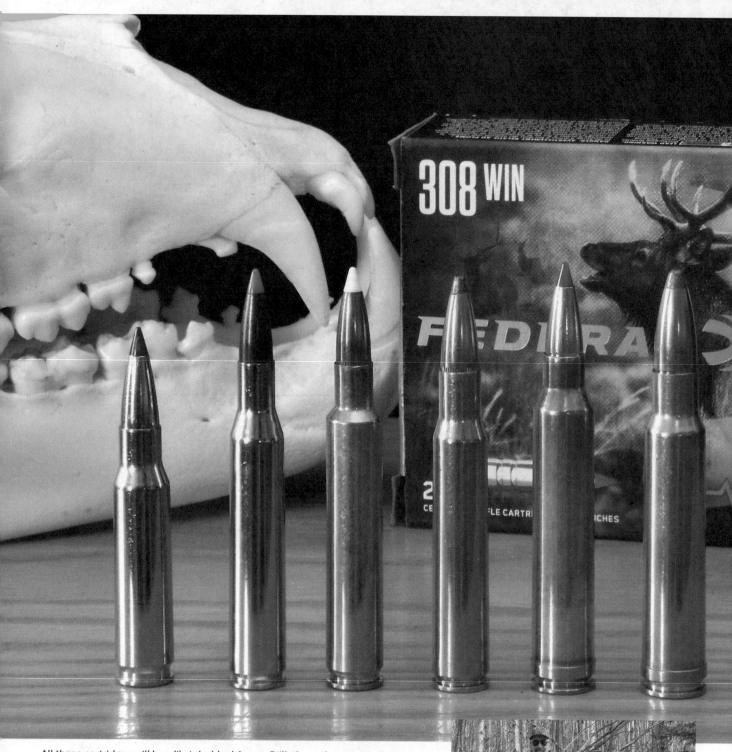

All these cartridges will handily take black bears. Still, the author argues that only the .308 Winchester checks all the boxes of potency, mild recoil, accuracy, wide ammo availability and suitability for all rifle actions. Shown are, left to right, .308 Win., .270 Win., .280 Ackley Improved, .30-'06 Springfield, .300 Win. Mag., and .338 Win. Mag. With same-weight bullets, the .308 has the mildest recoil of the bunch.

This giant black bear, which measures 7 feet, 7 inches from nose to tail, was shot with a Mossberg Patriot rifle in 308 Win. just 30 minutes after the author shot a different bear that measured 7 feet, 3 inches. While big black bears can appear menacing and sometimes aggressive, they aren't that hard to kill. The .308 Win. will handily do the job.

The Best All-Purpose Black Bear Cartridge

If you ask the author, it's the .308 Winchester.

> MIKE DICKERSON

Ask six different hunters what the best all-around rifle cartridge is for hunting black bears, and you will likely get a half-dozen answers – and most of them will be wrong. That's because an excellent choice for hunting in thick woods may not be a good choice for a spot-and-stalk hunt where shots may be longer. Hot-rod magnum cartridges might be fine for some, but many people will never shoot them well because they can't tolerate the recoil. Some hunters will vote for fine specialty cartridges they cannot find on store shelves in remote locations or during ammo shortages.

Don't get me wrong, many great cartridges will handle black bears. Despite what some would have you believe, black bears aren't all that hard to kill, and they have been taken with almost every reasonably powerful deer cartridge you can name. The bigger-is-better philosophy likely has more to do with perceptions of black bears being potentially dangerous. Black bears are usually shy and inoffensive, but that is not always the case. They attack more people than grizzlies or brown bears, mainly because there are many more black bears, with a much wider distribution. A significant percentage of black bear

attacks are purely predatory. Black bears don't measure up to grizzlies or brown bears, but the strongest human is no match for even an average-sized black bear in hand-to-paw combat, and it's wise to remember that they are quite capable of killing you.

Ruark's advice to "use enough gun" applies to black bears. That rules out most cartridges that don't use a 30-caliber bullet with its large frontal area. On the other hand, most of us don't need to hunt black bears by shooting a cartridge that will rattle our teeth. The ideal, all-purpose black bear cartridge should be potent enough and widely available, with many proven bullet options that work near or far, and be offered as a standard chambering by virtually every rifle manufacturer. In my book, one cartridge handily checks all those boxes, which is the aged but still-deadly .308 Winchester.

A BLACK BEAR HUNT OF A LIFETIME

One hunter recently told me he would never hunt black bears with such a "puny" cartridge, and he argued that the .300 Win. Mag. should be a minimum choice. I couldn't disagree more. The .308 Win. is more than enough for black bears, as demonstrated last year on a black bear hunt of a lifetime for me.

It happened on the second afternoon of a two-tag hunt for trophy black bears in far northern Alberta with W&L Guide Service. I sat quietly in a treestand overlooking a bait station, holding a Mossberg Patriot rifle chambered in .308 Win. As I scanned the terrain, a huge boar appeared seemingly from nowhere. One minute he wasn't there, and the next minute he was. He came in silently and began swatting the 55-gallon bait barrel around like a toy. It didn't take me long to make a decision. I knew he was at least a 7-foot bear and likely larger than my previous best bear, which made the record book. When he finally gave me a slightly quartering-away shot, I took it. The bear ran off in a half circle, laboring until it dropped in a thick stand of trees behind me.

The boar would be the biggest-bodied black bear I had ever shot, but that accomplishment was eclipsed just 30 minutes later. That's when I spotted an even larger bear sneaking behind me, and he already had me pegged. Watching me the entire time, he cruised by the bait, ignored it, and walked directly to the bottom of the angled wooden ladder leading to my stand. I slowly raised the Patriot, and the big bruin and I stared at each other for an eternity. He blinked first and circled back toward the bait but again began angling toward me, walking across my front while getting closer with each deliberate step and a determined stare. I know a stalking posture when I see it, and I had seen enough. When the bear's facing leg swung forward, I touched off a shot and put one in his boiler room. He ran 20 yards and piled up. Knowing that the bear was huge, I put an insurance shot into him after he stopped moving. However, a post-mortem examination revealed that the second shot was unnecessary.

The first bear measured 7 feet, 3 inches from nose to tail, and the second taped 7 feet, 7 inches — both bears of a lifetime. It's worth noting that I didn't even shoot them with one of the newer, more advanced bullets loaded in .308. I instead used Hornady's 150-grain InterLock bullet, a decidedly old-school but highly

effective design delivering impressive terminal performance. The bullet was not recovered from the biggest bear — it was a complete pass-through — but I recovered it from the first bear. That bullet had a retained weight of 90.1 grains, which isn't bad considering everything it smashed through before slamming into the big off-side shoulder bones.

IS THE .308 ENOUGH GUN?

So much for the theory that the .308 Winchester is too "puny" to handle black bears. I would wager that most black bears are shot at relatively close range, but the .308 Win. will work at longer distances, too. Consider this sampling of .308 Win. loads. Federal's 175-grain Terminal Ascent load still hits with 1,503 ft-lbs of energy at 400 yards, which is farther than most hunters will ever shoot a black bear. At the same distance, Hornady's 178-grain ELD-X Precision Hunter load impacts with 1,556 ft-lbs of

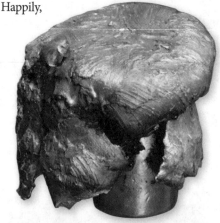

This recovered bullet demonstrates the modern terminal performance of .308 Win. loads. The author didn't shoot a bear with this Federal 175-grain Terminal Ascent bullet but shot a 200-pound fallow deer with a quartering-on shot. The bullet smashed the big shoulder bones and penetrated over 20 inches before resting in the offside hide. It's an ideal bullet for black bears.

energy, and Nosler's 168-grain AccuBond Long Range bullet strikes with 1,665 ft-lbs.

Of course, bears are not killed with calculated foot-pounds of energy. They're killed with properly placed bullets that mushroom without coming apart and penetrate deeply to disrupt vital organs. Standard cup-and-core bullets have been getting the job done on black bears for as long as these bullets have been around, and I killed my first truly big black bear, a seven-footer, on a spot-and-stalk hunt on Vancouver Island many years ago with a single heart-lung shot using a Hornady SST bullet.

These days, I prefer bullets with a somewhat tougher design because I'd much rather trail a bear with two holes in it than one.

Happily,

The Mossberg Patriot rifle the author used to take two huge black bears in Alberta. The Patriot is one of the best of the bunch in the affordable rifle category.

The .308 Winchester has long been known for its inherent accuracy. The author recently shot this group using a Benelli Lupo rifle and Federal's 175-grain Terminal Ascent load.

The latest version of the Benelli Lupo rifle tested by the author proved impressively accurate in .308 Win. With a new BE.S.T. finish, the gun is nearly impervious to the elements and is an excellent choice for a go-anywhere, do-anything rifle for black bears.

there's no shortage of .308 Win. factory ammunition loaded with tough, proven bullets that will definitively accomplish the task. These include the Nosler Partition and AccuBond, Hornady InterLock, Swift A-Frame, Norma Bondstrike, Winchester Power Max Bonded and Remington Core-Lokt, and Federal's Terminal Ascent, Fusion and Trophy Bonded Tip bullets, among others. There are also many options for those who prefer to punch game animals through the shoulders with solid copper bullets like the Barnes Tipped TSX.

If you ask the major ammo makers, they will tell you that the .308 Win. remains immensely popular despite the appearance of so many newer cartridges in recent years. Many of those cartridges offer superior ballistic performance. Still, they won't make bears any deader than the .308 Win., which consistently ranks among the top five-selling cartridges for the big ammo manufacturers. That's

reflected in the astonishingly wide range of available factory loads for the cartridge. (The last time I checked, Federal makes 16 different .308 loads. Winchester offers 18, Hornady lists 15, and Black Hills offers more than a dozen.)

Experienced handloaders know that the .308 Win. is a joy to handload using standard Large Rifle primers. With the vast array of available bullet weights and styles, options are many for the handloader to create a tailored black bear load for their chosen rifle.

AMMO IS WIDELY AVAILABLE

Another big plus for the .308 Win is that you can almost always find ammo. Even at the peak of the recent ammunition shortage, .308 Win. was easier to find in many areas than other popular cartridges. That's partly due to its military roots in the 7.62X51mm NATO form. Since its

development in the 1950s, it has been used in numerous U.S. and allied-nation firearms, making it a global standard. There are few places in the world where you can't find it.

Winchester saw the commercial possibilities for the cartridge and beat the military to the punch, introducing the .308 Winchester two years before NATO adoption of the 7.62X51mm NATO. Chambered for the popular Model 70 rifle, among others, it quickly caught on. The round has been a popular choice ever since for everything from hunting and target shooting to military and police sniping.

While the .308 has been proven time and again to be potent enough for black

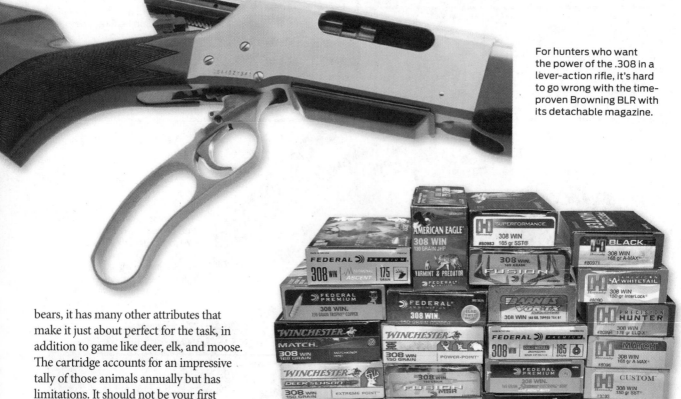

For hunters who want the power of the .308 in a lever-action rifle, it's hard to go wrong with the time-proven Browning BLR with its detachable magazine.

There are few places in the world where you can't find .308 Win. ammo, which is loaded with an amazing variety of bullet styles and weights. This is just a sampling of factory .308 Win. loads the author had on hand.

bears, it has many other attributes that make it just about perfect for the task, in addition to game like deer, elk, and moose. The cartridge accounts for an impressive tally of those animals annually but has limitations. It should not be your first choice for hunting grizzlies and brown bears, even though it can kill the great bears with good bullets and precise shot placement. The .338 Win. Mag. is generally viewed by many guides as a minimum requirement for that task, and it's hard to argue with that logic, but I would feel far more comfortable in grizzly country toting a .308 Win. than any of the handguns commonly carried for bear defense.

Of course, you might ask, "What about the ought-six?" The .30-'06 Springfield launches same-weight bullets faster than the .308 Win. — but it does so at a cost. A 7.5-pound rifle shooting a 150-grain .308 Win. bullet generates about 15.8 ft-lbs of recoil energy, which puts it at the limit that many shooters can comfortably — and accurately — shoot. In comparison, a heavier 8-pound .30-'06 rifle launching the same 150-grain bullet hits the shoulder with 17.5 ft-lbs of energy, and recoil only increases as bullet weights increase or rifle weight decreases. The story is much the same when you compare .308 Win. recoil levels with cartridges such as the .270 Win., 7mm Rem. Mag., .280 Ackley Improved, .300 Win. Mag., and .300 WSM. They will all kill black bears, but they do

so while delivering more punishment to your shoulder than the .308.

Although the .308 traces its roots to the .300 Savage, which developers at the Frankford Arsenal used in developing the T65 series of experimental cartridges, later versions were made from shortened .30-'06 cases, and the debate over .30-'06 versus .308 continues to this day. There are valid arguments on both sides, but there's no denying that the .308 Win. is, in some ways, a more efficient cartridge. With the continuous development of improved propellants and bullets, there are few jobs the .30-'06 can do that the .308 can't do equally well. The .308 will not handle bullets heavier than 200 grains as well as the .30-'06, but those bullets aren't needed for black bears — and neither is the harsher recoil of cartridges with those heavier bullets. The sweet spot for the .308 Winchester is with bullet weights in the 150- to 180-grain range.

INHERENT ACCURACY

Another reason the .308 Win. gets my vote is that the cartridge has long had a reputation for being inherently accurate. That's partly because it fits in a short action, which is stiffer and theoretically more accurate than long actions. The round is still used in some forms of competitive target shooting, such as PALMA matches, and it is one of the choices allowed in F-TR matches. I've tested several new rifle models chambered in the cartridge during the last year, and most of them delivered ½-MOA or better groups with ammunition they liked. Notably, this was with hunting ammo; match-grade .308 Win. ammo can deliver even tighter groups, but it's not a good choice for hunting bears.

Another factor in the .308's favor is the number of guns chambered for the cartridge. Because the .308 has been so popular, it's pretty easy to find good

Outdoor writer Craig Boddington, right, congratulates the author on taking two black bears of a lifetime on a hunt in northern Alberta using .308 Win. ammo.

The newest Browning X-Bolt Speed rifle in .308 Win. would be an excellent choice for hunting black bears in any terrain under any conditions.

The Hunter model from Kimber was introduced as a more affordable alternative to Kimber's higher-priced rifles. It's light and accurate and, in .308 Win., it's a good option for black bears.

deals on used guns. Many custom gun makers will happily build a rifle to your specifications in the chambering, and just about every major rifle maker offers .308-chambered rifles in styles and price categories to suit every taste and budget. Solid choices at the high end of bolt-action factory rifles include various versions of the Winchester Model 70, Browning X-Bolt, Weatherby Mark V and Ruger Hawkeye, and excellent guns like the Bergara Canyon and Benelli Lupo.

Mid-priced offerings include some of the more affordable Bergara rifles and several models from Howa, as well as the Weatherby Vanguard, Savage 110, Kimber Hunter, and Tikka T3X. There's also no shortage of more affordably priced guns. Popular choices in this category include the Mossberg Patriot, Ruger American, Winchester XPR, Franchi Momentum, Savage Axis, Mauser M18, Thompson Center Compass II and others.

If lever-action guns rock your boat — and there's much to be said for them when hunting bears in thick timber or heavy cover — you can certainly find one in .308! As of this writing, Browning offers four different BLR rifle models,

including a couple of all-stainless options. Unlike most lever guns, the BLR uses a detachable magazine, allowing for the use of modern, sharp-pointed cartridges. The Henry Long Ranger lever-action rifle also uses a detachable magazine and is available in the .308 chambering.

For those who prefer to hunt with an AR-platform rifle, there are many good AR-10 options. While they have been chambered for many potent cartridges, the .308 remains the most popular choice in AR-10s. Their main drawback is that most are heavy, weighing 8 to 10 pounds with no optic attached. There are, however, a few relatively lightweight AR-10 rifles out there, and Ruger has just shaken up the field with its new

SFAR (Small-Frame Autoloading Rifle) chambered in .308 Win. This gun's dimensions are much closer to those of an AR-15, and it weighs just 7.3 pounds, even with a heavy-profile 20-inch barrel (guns with 16-inch barrels weigh even less). Weight-wise, it's on par with many bolt-action rifles.

Whether you're hunting black bears behind hounds, putting a stalk on them from a distance, or hunting them over bait, the .308 Win. will do it all. The cartridge has been handily taking bears for more than 70 years and will likely continue for as long as centerfire rifle cartridges are made. If you do your part behind the trigger, the .308 Winchester will put bear meat in the freezer and a bearskin rug on your wall. GD

Weight Class

Chassis rifle weight for different hunting styles.

THOMAS GOMEZ

Chassis rifle systems have become increasingly popular in the world of firearms, especially among hunters. Originally built for military and law enforcement applications, chassis rifles quickly found their way to the competition world and, ultimately, the hunting field. What is a rifle chassis, and what makes it attractive to hunters?

Rifle chassis, also known as a chassis rifle system, is a rifle stock, usually made from aluminum, which incorporates the handguard, trigger guard, and buttstock into one or two units. It doesn't require bedding and typically features a v-block or a bedding block.

Most have an intuitive design that negates gunsmith- or armorer-level installation. Installation is as simple as dropping a barreled action into a chassis and tightening the action screws with a torque wrench.

HISTORY AND DEVELOPMENT

The British company Accuracy International (AI) pioneered chassis rifle systems in the 1980s with its PM/L96A1 rifle. (At the request of the Swedish military, AI would later refine the L96A1 into the L118A1/L118A2.) The L96A1 was unique because it featured an aluminum chassis core mated to the barreled action. That was augmented with polymer side panels comprising the comb, handguard, and grip. AI also developed a detachable steel box magazine to complement the system, which has become the *de facto* standard in the industry. The AICS-style mag is made by Accuracy International and Accurate Mag, Magpul, and Modular Driven Technologies, which has carved a niche making them for new high-performance calibers such as 6.5 PRC, 300 PRC, and 6mm ARC.

Chassis systems went "mainstream" around 2012. Today, consumers have top-of-the-line options from Kinetic Research Group, Modular Driven Technologies, Magpul, Masterpiece Arms, XLR Industries, Accuracy International, and Cadex Defense. In any competitive market, companies quickly expand product lines and specialize, and consumers who watched the chassis rifle evolution soon adopted the technology for competition and hunting. The attributes that make chassis optimal for law enforcement and military applications — consistent harmonics, temperature stability, modularity, and the ability to be tailored to individual body types — make them ideal for competition and hunting.

FORM FACTOR AND DESIGN

Chassis systems available today fall into two form factors. The first is similar to the original Accuracy International design, consisting of an internal aluminum chassis mated to the barreled action and augmented with polymer panels or sides. The MDT XRS and KRG Bravo are examples. The second design is a heavily machined piece of aluminum with an aluminum stock and handguard. Some companies offer this style with an AR-15 buffer tube/receiver extension and the ability to accept an AR-style pistol grip. Any chassis style can be used for hunting, though specific designs and brands are better suited.

ANALYSIS

I started using chassis rifle systems in 2016 and quickly adopted them for all my shooting applications, including hunting. My first was a Whiskey-3 from KRG, and I immediately appreciated the ability to adjust length-of-pull and comb height. The KRG chassis made my Remington 700 SPS Tactical's barreled action more consistent and

tightened my groups. The ability to customize the system with MIL-STD 1913/Picatinny, M-LOK, and ARCA rails was a plus, and I appreciated the multiple QD attachment points. What are the specific attributes that I look for? The ability to adjust comb height and length-of-pull is a priority, as well as QD attachment points and, of late, an ARCA rail to quickly leverage support equipment like bipods and tripods.

Most chassis systems are on the heavier side, though purpose-built, lightweight hunting versions like the MDT HNT26 are perfect if you need a lightweight solution. Is a heavy rifle a bad thing when it comes to a hunting rifle? For the backcountry hunter who hunts the canyons and peaks of the Rockies on foot, yes. For the hunter who travels by ATV or horse, weight doesn't matter. For the hog or varmint hunter driving around at night on ATVs with night vision and shooting feral hogs with thermal scopes off a tripod, heavy rifles steady you, making followup shots easier. Let's break down each category and discuss the optimal weight and features for the task. Along the way, I will highlight my builds and discuss the evolution and the "why" behind each.

Accuracy International PM/L96A1 rifle. Accuracy International pioneered the Chassis Rifle System.

Custom Remington 700-style barreled action mated to an MDT XRS Chassis System. IRAY USA thermal optic. This rifle was built to hunt feral hogs and coyotes at night. Note the AICS-style mag. Photo: Anthony Amantine

LIGHTWEIGHT HUNTING CHASSIS RIFLES

A lightweight rifle has many advantages. Not only is it easier to carry for the youth and elderly, but it's also an absolute necessity on a backcountry hunt by foot. Backcountry hunting involves hiking miles over rough terrain to your intended spot, where you will camp, then start hunting. It requires food, shelter, a sleep system, water treatment, a medical and survival kit, a small day pack, and all the technology required for hunting, such as binoculars, spotting scopes, rangefinders, Kestrels, GPS, ammunition, and a rifle. Not only do you have to hike all the gear in, but you must also plan on carrying out an animal if you successfully harvest one.

Lightweight rifles are not only easy to carry during your ruck into the backcountry, but they can be highly maneuverable and easy to shoulder if a game animal presents itself for a quick shot. Lighter rifles are easier to hold for standing, unsupported shots and navigating

heavy timber and fallen logs. Lightweight rifles have more recoil, which can be managed by a suppressor or muzzle brake and a recoil pad.

I am a big, strong guy who likes to do timed marathons with 50-plus pounds on my back, so for many years, I didn't mind carrying a heavy rifle in the woods. The weight could be managed by a good sling or simply attaching the rifle to my ruck during my hikes into my hunting spots. As a precision rifle instructor and long-range shooter, my hunting style was shooting from canyon to canyon or into meadows and taking 400- to 700-yard shots on big game. However, my life changed when I started hunting elk in heavy timber.

Recently, I drew an elk tag in the Santa Fe National Forest. During my scouting trips, I found that the elk were still holding in the Aspens near the tree line, and I would be walking at least 12 to 15 miles a day. Packing out mule deer from the high desert or a ponderosa forest isn't

bad if you have a sled or field butcher and a good pack to attach your rifle. Packing out an elk requires a different strategy, including cutting weight wherever possible and taking the bare minimum of ancillary gear. One area where I could shed some weight is my rifle platform. I set a weight limit of 9 lbs. and got to work.

I started with a stock Tikka T3 chambered in .270 WSM for my mountain rifle build. After a call to Oregon Mountain Rifle Co., I had a pre-fit Tikka T3/T3x carbon-fiber-wrapped barrel chambered in 6.5 PRC and an Oregon Mountain Rifle Co. Dakota Tikka trigger on the way to my mountain home in Central New Mexico. I chose the HNT26 from Modular Driven Technologies for a chassis and sent it all to Whiskey Mountain Dynamics in Edgewood, New Mexico, for assembly. For optics, I chose a TRACT TORIC UHD 2.5-15x44 Hunting Rifle Scope. The TRACT is a premium tough-as-nails, no-frill scope that has everything you need and nothing

Tikka T3 chambered in 6.5 PRC mated to a KRG Bravo Chassis System helped the author ring steel at 1,800 yards. Note the Charlie TARAC prism from TACOM HQ.

Custom Remington 700-style rifle mated to an MDT ACC Chassis System. IRAY USA thermal optic. Note the full-length ARCA rail on the MDT ACC chassis, allowing you to lock into a bipod or tripod quickly. Photo: Anthony Amantine

you don't. Loaded with a sling, the rifle weighed just under 9 lbs.

After checking the rifle with a Go/No-Go gauge, I zeroed it and confirmed the data to 1,200 yards on targets. Paired with Hornady 143-gr. ELD-X, the rifle shot .5 MOA groups, and I had no problems hitting a milk jug-sized boulder at 1,286 yards. Several weeks later, I would find myself chasing elk on the North side of the Jemez Mountains. Due to bad weather, the hunt was tough, and with abundant rain from the Summer and Fall, the elk were spread out and not clustered in the high meadows and canyons. We saw no large herds; the only elk we saw were ones we jumped that quickly appeared at 50 yards, then vanished into the thicket. Even with my scope dialed to minimum magnification, I could not instantly find my target for a decent shot. I often thought, why don't I bring a fast-handling AR-15 out here chambered in 6.5 Grendel? Paired with a red dot or LPVO (low-power variable optic), I would have enough energy for 200 yards and closer for a large-bodied animal like elk.

This idea was reinforced on my last night of the hunt. Cold and with no elk in my ruck, I settled in for a long hike back to my SUV. A small pack of coyotes shadowed me in the darkness during my hike. I had left my pistol at home to save weight, and I found that my high-powered rifle scope dialed down would not be ideal for fending off a predator at close range. I got to my vehicle without issue, thanked God for a good day in the woods, and drove home to my family. I wondered if I had taken the optimal rifle into the woods on my drive home.

Several weeks later, I would be in the Lincoln National Forest chasing mule deer with the same rifle I had used to pursue elk. The terrain was rocky canyons filled with cedar, pinon, and juniper trees. The hunt would be two days, and my friend Mark and I were only interested in filling

Remington 700 SPS Tactical, MDT LSSXL-Gen2 chassis system. This was one of the author's first chassis rifles. Note the small ARCA section.

The ultimate mountain rifle? Stock Tikka T3 chambered in .308 Winchester. TRACT 1-8 LPVO, MDT HNT26 Chassis, SilencerCo Harvester EVO. Note the small MIL-STD 1913/Picatinny rail.

A lighter stock and barreled action give you flexibility in optics and accessories options. Photo: Modular Driven Technologies

our freezers with meat. Mark tagged out the first morning harvesting a nice 6-point buck with his Tikka T3 Hunter chambered in .270 Winchester. We spied a small herd grazing on an adjacent canyon, and Mark grabbed the top of a small pine tree, rested his rifle atop his fist, and sent a projectile through the heart of his intended target. I harvested mine the following morning when we spied a small group feeding on a ridge. I slowly sat down, deployed my MDT Triple-Pull CKYE POD bipod, inhaled, exhaled, and made a perfect headshot at 180 yards on a decent meat buck. We prayed, field butchered the animal, and rucked a few miles back to the truck. Before leaving the kill site, I used my laser rangefinder and lased the surrounding mountain. In theory, my longest shot in that canyon would only have been 600 yards. On the drive home, I wondered

again if I was taking too much rifle and magnification into the woods.

Among newer releases, Nosler has mated their M21 rifle with the MDT HNT26 carbon fiber chassis system in the new Nosler Model 21 Carbon Chassis Hunter, resulting in a flexible yet accurate package which makes perfect sense for the backpacking hunter. With a 26-ounce carbon fiber chassis, the resulting rifle weighs in at just over 6 ½ pounds unscoped, and can be folded in half to measure just 37 inches. The entire design is ergonomic, and lends itself nicely to a tripod, bipod, or shooting over a pack. The M21 CCH uses a Proof Research carbon fiber wrapped barrel to further reduce weight. Fully adjustable for length of pull and comb height, The Nosler M21 CCH is a good candidate for the hunter wanting a sensible chassis rifle.

MOUNTAIN RIFLE 2.0

Over several weeks, I concluded that I was addicted to hunting elk in the timber and that if I continued sneaking through the trees, which has become my favorite style of hunting elk in the alpine country, I would need a purpose-built mountain rifle. For this task, I removed the Tikka T3/Oregon Mountain Rifle Co. carbon-fiber barreled action and TRACT 2.5-15x44 scope and swapped it out with a Tikka T3 barreled action chambered in .308 Winchester with a factory barrel that had been cut to 18 inches. For optics, I chose TRACT TORIC UHD 1-8 LPVO, which would allow me to dial down to 1 power, making close-up shots easy with the option to dial up to 8 power for 600-yard shots if necessary.

The rifle came in just under 7 lbs. Paired with 165-grain Federal Premium Ammunition, it could achieve 1 MOA groups and easily hit 10-inch gongs at 600 yards. The MDT HNT26's folding stock made the package small enough to fit in my Mystery Ranch pack. Adding a SilencerCo Harvester EVO suppressor only added 10.8 ounces to the entire package. I might add a high magnification scope and potentially a 6.5 Creedmoor-barreled action, but for now, the rifle has become my go-to rifle for hunting coyotes at the ranch and shooting feral hogs. I carry it while guiding and intend to use it in 2023 for all of my big game hunting, where conceivably, my farthest shot is 500 yards.

If I had to build the lightest chassis rifle possible, I would start with a titanium short action from Defiance, Pierce Engineering, Lone Peak Arms, or Oregon Mountain Rifle Company and spin on a Proof Research carbon-fiber-wrapped barrel in a medium sporter contour chambered in 6.8 Western or 6.5 PRC. I would mate the barreled action to an MDT HNT26 Chassis System and attach a muzzle brake. For optics, I would choose something under 25 ounces with a 30mm main tube and a "Christmas tree" reticle. Strong contenders would come from the Vortex Viper PST, Leupold VX-6HD, Leupold VX-5HD, Arken EPL4, Swarovski Z8i, and TRACT TORIC product lines. Scopes with 1-inch tubes are lighter, but 30mm tubes, MIL-hash reticles, parallax adjustment, and illumination complement my hunting style and allow me to handle most situations that can arise during a hunt. A benefit to cutting weight from the barrel, action, and chassis is that it allows for more flexibility in optics.

HEAVY HUNTING CHASSIS RIFLES

A heavy hunting rifle has many advantages. This article will define a heavy rifle as anything over 10 lbs. Heavy rifles are easier for small-statured humans to shoot, granted the gun is supported with a bipod or tripod. The rifle system, as a whole, tends to be inherently more accurate. The rifle weight lends stability and makes self-spotting and follow-up shots easier. You can add weight and adjust the balance of a chassis system by installing internal and external weights. Heavy chassis rifles are awesome for hunting plains animals such

Hunting elk in the Jemez Mountains, Santa Fe National Forest. Note the height of the MDT Triple Pull CKYE-POD bipod.

The author's first iteration of a chassis-style mountain rifle. Tikka T3, Oregon Mountain Rifle Co. carbon-fiber barrel, MDT HNT26 Chassis, MDT Triple Pull CKYE Pod, and a TRACT TORIC Hunting Scope.

Deer hunt in the Lincoln National Forest.

as pronghorn antelope, barbary sheep, oryx, and desert mule deer. Heavy rifles shine when shooting varmints and predators at long range.

Hunters who leverage night vision and thermal technology have also gravitated toward heavy chassis rifles, with the guns deployed on sturdy tripods. With night vision or thermal technology, feral hog hunters become nocturnal and look for pigs. Once found, the hunter will sneak in, set up their rifle on a sturdy carbon-fiber tripod, and take a shot. A heavy rifle shines in this role because it's easier to steady, and follow-up shots and spotting are simple due to the light recoil. Coyote hunters using night vision technology employ the same tactics but usually call animals in instead of going after them. Deploying a heavy rifle off a tripod came out of the military and law enforcement arena and continues to be refined and developed in competitions such as the Precision Rifle Series (PRS) and National Rifle League (NRL).

Except for my hunts last Fall, I have done most of my large game hunting with heavy rifles. What do I love about heavy rifles? First and foremost, the accuracy. Heavy barrels can be more accurate and deliver precise shots at long distances with quality match ammunition. Whenever I go into the woods to harvest an animal, a precise shot and a quick death are paramount. Getting steady and consistently accurate is easier for me with a heavier rifle system. I got into precision rifle to manage coyotes at our ranch in New Mexico. This ultimately led to extreme-long-range shooting and work as a precision rifle instructor. Living in the high desert West, my hunting styles consisted of long shots on plains game like pronghorn antelope, canyon-to-canyon shots on deer, or sitting on the edge of a mountain and shooting into meadows.

Heavy match-grade rifles also gave me the confidence to know that if I wounded an animal at 300 yards, then it popped up

The author's "heavy" rifle. Tikka T3, Oregon Mountain Rifle Co. carbon-fiber barrel, MDT XRS Chassis, TRACT TORIC Hunting Scope, SilencerCo Harvester EVO. Note the ARCA rail on the bottom of the handguard.

Photo: Nick Setting.

Anthony Amantine hunting predators at night with thermal and night vision optics. Anthony is a cultural leader on the cutting edge of hunting at night with emerging technology. Heavier rifles and tripods shine during night hunts. Photo: Anthony Amantine

at 700 yards, I had the equipment necessary to make that shot. As I have trended towards backcountry hunting in the wilderness, I have purpose-built lightweight rifles. Still, if I only walk 5 to 10 miles daily and pursue deer-sized animals, I'll usually go with a rifle on the heavier side. I will also opt for a heavy rifle if traveling by ATV, OHV, E-Bike, or horse. Let's look at my heavy hunting rifles.

For the last decade, I've carried either a heavy-barreled Remington 700 SPS Tactical or a Howa 1500 chambered in 6.5 Creedmoor. The barreled actions were mated to chassis systems from Kinetic Research Group and MDT. My current heavy rifle consists of the Oregon Mountain Rifle Co. Tikka T3/T3x pre-fit carbon fiber-wrapped barrel from my original mountain rifle project. The barreled action has an Oregon Mountain Rifle Co. Dakota Trigger and is mated to

an MDT XRS Chassis System from MDT. For optics, I use a TRACT TORIC UHD 2.5-15x44 Hunting Rifle Scope. I have a full-length ARCA rail on the bottom of the chassis for tripods and bipods, and the system as a whole weighs around 11.5 pounds with the SilencerCo Harvester EVO suppressor attached. Paired with Hornady 143-gr. ELD-X Precision Hunter ammo, the rifle holds .5 MOA groups, and I have pushed it out to a mile on steel targets. Unlike previous rifles, it's only used for hunting to preserve the barrel.

When guiding pronghorn antelope hunts at the ranch, I have a similar setup for clients chambered in 6.5 Creedmoor. I also have a rifle with an MDT ACC Chassis System with internal and external weight. The system, as a whole, weighs close to 20 pounds, but there is zero recoil, which is great for children with little training and time behind a rifle.

A simple, lightweight tripod is perfect for the backcountry. Photo: Modular Driven Technologies.

flexibility when building a stable shooting position.

Elk hunting in the backcountry forced me to limit what I put in my pack. Last year, the only bipod I carried on my hunts was a Triple-Pull CKYE-POD from MDT. It allowed me to take shots in the prone, seated, kneeling, or leverage the ARCA rail for spotting scopes and binoculars. Next, I'll take a heavy-duty tripod and a Triple-Pull CKYE POD while guiding and use just the Triple-Pull CKYE-POD on my hunts.

Carbon Chassis Hunter offers the hunter a very useable package which can be packed into rugged terrain.

ANCILLARY EQUIPMENT

Besides the barrel, action, chassis, and optic, there are other areas to save weight. Tripods and bipods made out of carbon fiber have been a blessing for backcountry hunters. Several companies sell decent tripods, including Really Right Stuff, Two Vets, Vortex, Leupold, Hog Saddle, Leofoto, and Feisol. If I'm guiding and not carrying a rifle, I'll take a Feisol tripod with a Pig Saddle for clients if they cannot get prone. If I'm doing a backcountry hunt, I usually take a compact, lightweight camera tripod with an ARCA mount.

I hunted with a simple Harris bipod for years but recently have been carrying a Javelin or MDT GRND-POD. The Javelin is awesome because it uses a rare earth magnet to stick to your stock so you can quickly attach or remove it. It can be carried in your pack, which mitigates snags until ready for use. The MDT GRND-POD is a lightweight bipod with a traditional form factor with significant leg adjustment. It attaches to an ARCA mount, allowing me to position the bipod anywhere on my handguard, giving me

CLOSING THOUGHTS

My daughter is getting old enough to start shooting and will be formally trained in precision rifle. Her first rifle will be a Howa Mini chambered in 6.5 Grendel mated to an MDT LSS-XL Gen 2 Chassis System. Length-of-pull and proper comb height will be easy to attain, and the system can be adjusted as she grows. The rifle will be optimized for shooting off a tripod and light enough to carry in the woods. I hope she harvests her first deer with the rifle.

Chassis rifle systems offer hunters considerable flexibility in the field. They can be tailored for any body type and optimized for bipods, tripods, night vision, and thermal technology. They can be lightweight or, with heavy barrels and weights, can be as heavy and balanced as you want. Though I love the look and feel of wood stocks, hunting in the West requires rugged and adaptable rifle systems and potentially long shots, which is why I see myself carrying a chassis-equipped rifle for the foreseeable future. **GD**

The author's guiding gear includes a heavy-duty carbon-fiber tripod and MDT Triple-Pull CKYE POD bipod. While not guiding, he takes the CKYE POD to support his rifle and spotting scope.

Among myriad bolt rifles in .30-06, Tikka's T3, here with Norma loads, is among van Zwoll's favorites.

What! You Have No .30-06?

With apologies to other rifles, a gun rack without an 06 is essentially empty. Heck, it may be un-American!

❯ WAYNE VAN ZWOLL

"Will you take $125?" I asked. The Enfield was tagged at $150. The proprietor read my eyes and divined that he'd get no more. He paused a couple of seconds for effect, then pulled a Form 4473. "Sure." It was a project rifle, but some work had been done. The replaced walnut held promise and cradled a blind magazine. The bridge had been cleaned up. The front sight could be paired with a Skinner aperture.

Not that I needed more unpaid hours at the bench.

You can still get a rifle in .30-06 without putting the children to work in a sweatshop. Now in its 113th year, this cartridge has been chambered in every rifle that will cycle it. In fact, ".30-06-length" is the standard way to describe actions that accept the 06's progeny and short belted magnums as well.

Often hailed as the best all-around big game cartridge, the .30-06 may well be. No alternative can beat its record afield or offer more loads suitable for hunting North American beasts. It also boasts an enviable record punching bullseyes, having served in National Match competition for half a century.

"Tried 6.5s yet?" he asked, handing me the pen. I had – at least most of the useful ones, from the 6.5x55 to the 6.5-.300 Weatherby. "Hotrods," he declared without naming one.

"You ever own an 06?"

Signing and dating, I said I still did. That seemed to puzzle him. "What are you going to do with two?"

Two! I'd passed *that* mark decades earlier. Some have gone down the road, but not lately. Eerily, even from great distance, a .30-06 can make you regret you sold it.

***

The roots of the .30-06 cartridge run to 1900, pre-dating Henry Ford's Model T and John Browning's .45 pistol. The Titanic hadn't been built. Idaho was yet to get its Big Burn, San Francisco, its great earthquake. Hunt-ing camps made do without Coleman lanterns and paper towels. Engineers at Springfield Armory had just begun work on an infantry rifle to replace the Krag-Jorgensen and its .30-40 cartridge.

A prototype emerged in 1901. Two years later, the Springfield Model of 1903 and its new, powerful ammunition made headlines. A 220-grain bullet clocking 2,300 fps, 100 fps faster than the Krag's, made the .30-03 a ballistic match for Ger-many's 8x57.

The Ger-man army had adopted the 1898 Mauser action on April 5 of that year and initiated '98 rifles in the Boxer Rebellion months later. These were bored to 8mm (8x57 or 7.9x57) Mauser, a cartridge first used in the *Gewehr* 88 or "Commission" rifle of modified Mannlicher design. Round-nose 226-grain .318"-diameter bullets left at 2,093 fps. The 8x57 got more muscle in 1905 when Germany replaced its original load, labeled "I" or "J" for "Infantry," with one hurling a 154-grain .323"-diameter spitzer at 2,880 fps. The designation was changed to "S" or "JS." This faster, pointed (*spitzer*) bullet prompted a redesign of bullets for the .30-03 and a slight short-ening of its case. The U.S. "Ball Cartridge, Caliber .30, Model 1906" sent a 150-grain pointed bullet at 2,700 fps. Trimmed .070 to 2.494 inches, the new hull begged a different chamber. All .30-03 rifles were recalled for re-chambering. Bullets in issued ammo would be changed twice more before WWII.

The .30-06 dwarfs the .30 Remington, introduced for hunters in 1906, and the .300 Savage, circa 1920.

The .30-40 Krag of 1892, the first smokeless U.S. infantry round, was replaced by the .30-03 in a decade.

.30 ARMY (.30-40 KRAG)
180 GRAIN SILVERTIP
SUPER SPEED
CONTROLLED EXPANDING
K 3050 C
WINCHESTER
MADE IN U.S.A.

In 1908, the .30-06 began a 32-year run in the National Matches, hailed as "the most accurate and probably the comeliest military shoulder weapon ever devised." The 1903 Springfield (and the later, less costly 03A3) would keep its Service Rifle status in 1940, as the M1 Garand, also in .30-06, made its competitive debut. Eleven years later, the Garand would earn that designation.

In 1916, the U.S. (Remington and Winchester) gave Great Britain a hand by building Pattern 1914 Enfield rifles in .30-06 after barreling some to .303 British when Vickers couldn't fulfill the contract. The P14 had evolved to fire a new .276 cartridge. But committing British troops to France, England revamped the action for the rimmed .303 that had distinguished itself in the SMLE (Short Magazine Lee-Enfield). In lieu of re-tooling production lines stateside when America entered the war, the P14 action was modified and barreled to .30-06 to become the Enfield Model of 1917. Production surpassed that of the Springfield. Before it was halted in 1918, Remington and Winchester delivered more than 545,500 Model 1917s each, Eddystone nearly 1.2 million. Government cost: $26 apiece. After the armistice, many rifles were surplused at bargain prices on the civilian market.

The 1917 Enfield action is strong, the receiver machined from a nickel-steel forging. Two burly front locking lugs easily hold .30-06 pressures. The bolt handle serves as a third or safety lug. By military standards, rifles were well-finished, too. The bolt ran smoothly; a full-length stock cradled a 26-inch barrel with clean five-groove, 1-in-10, left-hand rifling. (Later rifles had two- and four-groove barrels.) A 1917 receiver is long enough that, with modification to the bolt face, magazine and ramp, it can handle full-length magnums like the .300 Holland & Holland. Many Enfields were barreled to .300 Weatherby.

As the basis of a custom rifle, however, the Model 1917 couldn't match the leaner Springfield or Mauser. It was a big, deep action, with a dogleg bolt handle and massive rear-sight "ears." At 9 1/2 pounds, it was also heavy. And like

Above: The author shot this bull with a Springfield in .30 Gibbs, a frothy, short-necked wildcat on the .30-06 case.

Left: Heavy round-nose bullets were once the norm for hunters using the 03A3 Springfield (background).

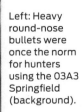

In 1920, the .300 Savage was developed to give lever-rifle enthusiasts the punch of the .30-06. It didn't.

the SMLE, it cocked on closing. These features spelled work for gun makers.

***

The Great War demonstrated the value of sleek, pointed bullets at distance. The U.S. Army replaced the .30-06's flat-base 150-grain bullet in 1926 with a 173-grain boat tail spitzer to add more reach. The modest reduction in velocity (to 2,646 fps) was more than offset by its greater weight and tapered heel, or boat tail. Both boosted its ballistic coefficient. This M1 load pestered soldiers to 5,500 yards. It increased recoil too, and its great range proved a hazard on some training grounds, prompting the Army to adopt the M2 load in 1939. While much like the original .30-06 issue ammunition, its 152-grain spitzer at 2,805 fps wore a gilding metal jacket, introduced on the M1. It functioned better in the new, gas-driven Garand rifle than did loads with heavier bullets.

When I was young, surplus military .30-06 ammo sold for a pittance. But rifle barrels didn't long endure it without diligent cleaning. Potassium chlorate primers left corrosive salts. Immediate swabbing with hot water and ammonia, then drying and oiling bores protected them, but such care was often impossible in the field. In 1901, the German company RWS (*Rheinische-Westphalisch Sprengstoff*) developed priming without potassium chlorate. Despite such advances, .30-06 service loads would have corrosive FA 70 primers as late as 1952. The only corrosive-primed domestic .30-06 ammo since? A run of Western Match with Western 8 1/2 G primers. These were also mercuric.

Remington unveiled non-corrosive Kleanbore priming in 1927. Winchester Staynless and Peters Rustless soon followed. All contained mercury fulminate. Its residue, harmless to steel, weakens brass. It would fall to German chemists to remove potassium chlorate and mercury fulminate from primers.

Bullets driven at the high speeds possible with smokeless powders of the 1890s required jackets to prevent bore fouling. Steel jackets on Krag and early .30-06 bullets had cupro-nickel coating. But these jackets also fouled bores at .30-06 speeds, especially near the relatively cool

Explorer Roald Amundsen selected a Remington Model 30S high-power rifle to arm his expedition to the Pole in the 1930s.

(Photo Credit: Remington Arms Co. Photo Collection)

The .30-06 and its rifles were hailed by hunters and explorers (here Roald Amundsen) on far frontiers.

Despite their utility, blunt bullets of high sectional density have acceded to faster spitzers in the .30-06.

TOP DOZEN CARTRIDGES IN 1939

CARTRIDGE	QUANTITY USED	PERCENTAGE OF TOTAL
.30 and .30-30	613	27
.30-06	491	21
.30-40 Krag	268	12
.300	123	5
.35	119	5
.32 Special	87	4
.303	86	4
.25-35	71	3
8mm	53	2
.348	52	2
.250-3000	47	2
.32	44	2

This Springfield 03A3 is like a restocked rifle Wayne used to kill a moose and Dall's ram in Alaska.

muzzle. "Mobilubricant" issued to soldiers on the eve of World War I softened fouling, but breech pressures bounced erratically from 51,000 to 58,000 psi, increasing back-thrust. Tin-plated jackets were worse, the tin "cold-soldering" to the case. One bullet recovered at a shooting range still wore the case neck! The Army dropped Mobilubricant and tin-plated bullets. Cupro-nickel jackets, 60% copper and 40% nickel, were better. During the 1920s, gilding metal of 90% copper, 10% zinc excelled as jacket material. It's still the dominant alloy.

***

Its success in battle, and a wash of surplus Springfields and Enfields after WWI, made the .30-06 a hit with hunters. Winchester's lever-action Model 1895 was among the early sporting rifles so chambered. Its box magazine permitted the use of pointed bullets. Announced in June 1896, the '95 first sold in .30-40 Krag, .38-72-275, and .40-72-330. The .303 British, .35 and .405 Winchester followed, the .30-03 in 1905, the .30-06 in 1908. Bolt rifles of that era — Remington's 30S, Winchester's 54, and custom sporters by the likes of Griffin & Howe — carried the '06 through the Depression. Winchester's Model 70 arrived in 1937. Before its infamous 1963 overhaul, this rifle would appear in 18 chamberings. Of 581,471 M70s shipped in that period, 208,218 were .30-06s. The cartridge also

Van Zwoll downed this BC goat with a Dakota rifle in .30-06. Repeated hits? Yes. Goats can be resilient.

Between 1937 and 1963, Winchester sold 208,218 Model 70s in .30-06. No other cartridge came close.

The .30-06 is one of the relatively few cartridges offered in Remington's 760 pump rifle and its progeny.

drove sales of Remington's 721, introduced in 1948.

Gun writer Townsend Whelen, a military man, hailed the .30-06 soon after its debut and handloaded 165-grain boat tail bullets atop 58 grains of 4350. Plaudits from other notable scribes continued through the '40s as Roy Weatherby hawked his magnums, short-belted hotrods from Winchester and Remington on their heels. Ken Waters favored 50 grains of Norma 203 behind 180-grain bullets. *Outdoor Life* shooting editor Jack O'Connor hurled 150-grain missiles with 53 grains of IMR-4320. Warren Page of *Field & Stream* and *Gun Digest* notoriety got tight groups with 180-grain bullets, 55 grains of 4350. With bullets of 180 to 220 grains, the .30-06 landed a punch that handily took any game in North America. Its 150- and 165-grain bullets shot flat with less recoil to kill deer-size game at distance. Hunters could buy '06 ammo just about anywhere.

Inherently accurate? Even lightweight Kimber rifles shoot tight groups with the ever-popular .30-06!

Old Springfield .30-06s can be accurate, as this 100-yard group, fired with Black Hills ammo, shows.

This outstanding gemsbok fell to Kim's CZ rifle in .30-06, a fine cartridge for Africa's plains game.

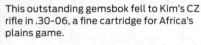

Current '06 loads include some with all-copper "controlled expansion" bullets, like the Barnes TSX.

In a 1939 survey of 2,285 Washington State elk hunters, the .30-06 ranked among the three most popular cartridges. The top dozen listed in the chart on left.

Now, ".30" here could apply to several cartridges. Presumably, it's the .30 Remington; but barrels bored for the .30-06 were once marked .30 Gov't 06, perhaps leading some hunters to record such a

rifle as a .30. (The ".300" is also problematic here. Savage's .300, appearing mainly in its popular lever rifles, was much more common than the .300 H&H Magnum. Both date to the 1920s.)

***

The .30-06 has taken most, if not all, the *world's* big game. In 1958, Grancel Fitz completed a 30-year quest to shoot all 25 North American species that were then legal to hunt. His rifle: a Griffin & Howe-built Model 30S Remington in .30-06. A half-century later, surveys I conducted among elk hunters showed the .30-06 and Remington's 7mm Magnum neck-and-neck as the most popular cartridges, trouncing runners-up (the .270 and .300 Winchester Magnum). The most enormous elk antlers claimed by a client during my days as a hunting guide came from a bull shot by a woman with a .30-06.

Yes, people of a light frame can shoot well with .30-06 rifles. An 8-pound '06 hurling a 150-grain bullet at 2,900 fps delivers about 17.6 ft-lbs of recoil. A 165-grain bullet at the same speed brings 20.1 ft-lbs. Arbitrarily, that's about the most "kick" many people can endure without flinching. Of course, much of the *felt* recoil depends on the stock design and shooting position. But the .30-06 is about as gentle a cartridge as can be designed without trimming bullet speed and punch below levels useful on tough animals at the 250-yard point-blank range now expected of hunting loads.

Many of the best alternatives to the .30-06 derive from it: The .270 Winchester came in 1925, the .280 in '57. In 1969, Remington adopted the .25-06, long a wildcat, the equally aged .35 Whelen in '87. Contemporary wildcats include the .30-06 Ackley Improved (the case shoulder blown out to 40 degrees) and the .338-06 (listed now as an A-Square cartridge). Also, for handloaders: the 6.5/06 and 8mm/06, the .375 and .400 Whelen.

On my first hunt to Alaska's mountains, I carried a re-stocked Springfield with the original .30-06 barrel. I was shooting competitively back then, so iron sights seemed no handicap. With them, I took a Dall's ram and a bull moose. Other .30-06 rifles since have brought me elk,

To War Again

The .30-06's history in machine guns predates the 1917 development of the Browning Automatic Rifle. By 1910, John Browning had invented his Heavy Water Cooled Machine Gun. But it stayed on the shelf as the BAR entered military service. However, the U.S. declaration of war on April 6, 1917, drew Browning to Springfield Armory to test his machine gun. It chattered through 20,000 rounds. The Utah genius then stunned onlookers by firing *another* 20,000. The encore: He readied a second machine gun to prove this wasn't a special sample. It roared without stop for 48 minutes, 12 seconds — no doubt well past the time the seven-member examination board decided to approve it.

The Model 1919, also in .30-06, would follow.

During the 1930s, as the Depression and political unrest in Germany threatened another war, John C. Garand developed his famous self-loading infantry rifle in .30-06. Three years after its 1936 adoption by the U.S. Army, an alternative short-recoil rifle by Melvin Johnson appeared. Its barrel retracted upon firing, then unlocked from an eight-lug bolt, which continued rearward. Bored too in 7x57 (for Chile) and .270, the 1941 Johnson was faulted in bayonet trials and for vertically stringing shots. But this rifle helped the Netherlands defend the Dutch East Indies. About 2,000 shipped before the Japanese invaded. In 1944, the U.S. Army sent the Free French 10,500 Johnson rifles and light machine guns from unfulfilled Dutch contracts.

Soon after WWII, work began on a shorter, lighter infantry and machine gun cartridge. It would appear in 1952 as the .308 Winchester, in 1957 as the 7.62x51 NATO.

mule deer, and African plains game. A lightweight Springfield in .30-06 Improved accompanied me on a wilderness hunt in Wyoming. One morning, after an elk bellowed from a Doug-fir thicket, I slipped up on the six-point, found its ribs in the 3x Leupold and finished the drama with a 180-grain Nosler Partition.

Another time, I climbed a forested slope in Wyoming's Thorofare drainage with a different Springfield in hand. My cartridge that day was the .30 Gibbs, a wildcat fashioned by Rocky Gibbs, who, in the 1950s, came up with a line of maximum-capacity cases based on the .30-06. Opening the original case neck with an expander, then reducing it in a Gibbs die to a new headspace measure and fireforming with

a reduced load yielded the desired case to be handloaded for hunting. That morning, an elk surprised me on the steep slope at 25 steps. A hasty offhand shot struck the animal high. Quickly, I cycled and fired again. But as the trigger broke, my footing gave way, and I fell backward. The bullet flew over the elk. Charitably, the beast permitted me one more try and fell to a third Nosler.

No rifle or load is lethal without careful aim.

***

While the .30-06 and its derivatives get plenty of attention from handloaders, commercial .30-06 hunting cartridges sell by the millions. My second book on rifle

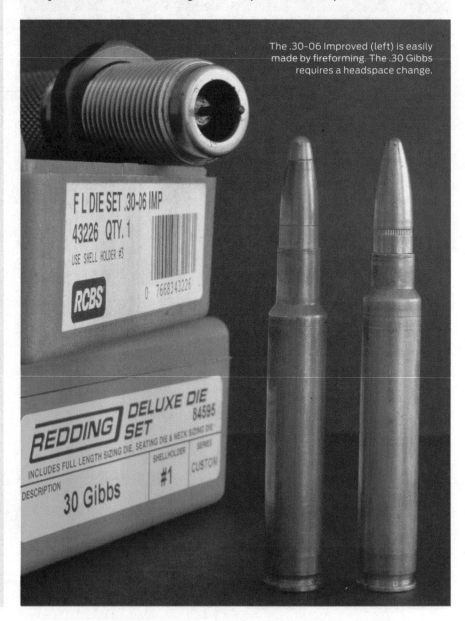

The .30-06 Improved (left) is easily made by fireforming. The .30 Gibbs requires a headspace change.

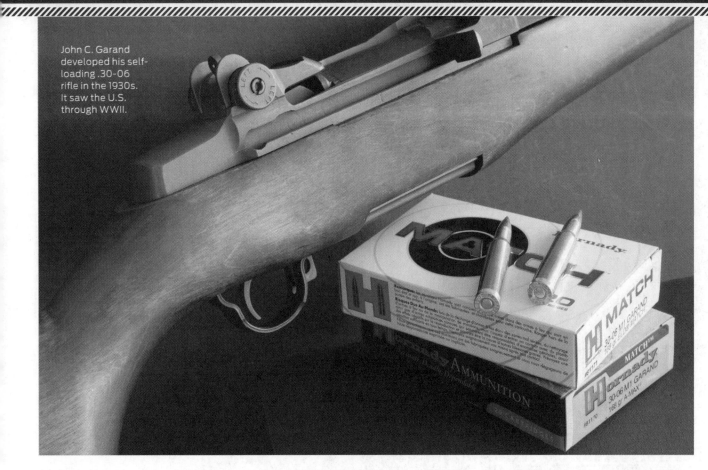

John C. Garand developed his self-loading .30-06 rifle in the 1930s. It saw the U.S. through WWII.

ballistics lists more than 100 commercial '06 loads from just a half dozen ammo companies. Their ballistic data is more or less accurate, but checks with a chronograph can be helpful. For instance, though 2,700 fps has long been the standard exit velocity for 180-grain .30-06 bullets, my chrono shows many factory loads fall shy of that mark. New powders are producing honestly higher speeds. Hornady lists a 180-grain Superformance load at 2,820 fps, 165- and 150-grain loads at 2,960 and 3,080 fps. Those figures approach what was once expected of the .300 H&H Magnum. Like other cartridges, the '06 has benefited from bullets that fly better and behave more reliably in game — that is, with sure upset over a range of impact speeds and wound channels specific to the load. "Controlled expansion" missiles, both lead-core and solid copper, drive deep and retain nearly all their weight.

The 220-grain round-nose bullet at 2,400 fps is nearly gone from .30-06 ammo rosters, though its high sectional density makes it useful for hunting big beasts in close cover. Federal still has that weight in a soft-point load. Until recently, Federal also offered a 200-grain Trophy

Bonded Bear Claw. Loaded to 2,540 fps, it opened to double its diameter, carved predictably deep channels, and kept over 90% of its weight. Alas, hunters seem intent on worshipping at the altar of high ballistic coefficient.

Jacket and core dimensions for .30-caliber bullets are held to ever tighter tolerances. Sierra keeps MatchKing jacket thickness within .0003 of a standard and limits bullet weight variation to .3 grain. Test lots that don't shoot into .250 inch at 100 yards can disqualify the entire batch. From sporting rifles, I've found Sierra's GameKings to group about as tightly as MatchKings. They rank among the most accurate hunting bullets.

Verily, closer tolerances, improved processes, and higher standards have improved loads and bullets industry-wide. "We shoot four five-shot groups to check lots," said a Hornady engineer. "Average extreme spread for .30-caliber hunting bullets must stay inside .600 at 100 yards. Our match bullets must print .800 groups at 200."

Its breech pressure now listed by SAAMI (the Sporting Arms and Ammunition Manufacturers' Institute) at 60,000

psi, the .30-06 is no cartridge for weak rifle mechanisms. Still, given modern steels, a few 19th-century actions are suitably stout. Winchester's John Browning-designed 1885 dropping block comes to mind. The .30-06 has since appeared in rifles of all types, including the slide-action Remington 760 and its progeny. The standard rifling twist is 1:10.

A compelling reason to buy a .30-06 rifle, on the off-chance you don't have one or, more likely, you feel the itch for another, is the ease of feeding it. Almost as widely distributed as Coca-Cola, .30-06 ammo is loaded in quantities that keep it affordable. Its ubiquity has ever endeared it to shooters. During Mexico's 1929 revolution, recalled Jack O'Connor in a long-ago column, he met a man visiting the U.S. to buy and smuggle arms. The fellow was looking for rifles "in just two calibers — the .30-30 and .30-06." The availability of their ammo ensured a market for both.

Nearly a century later, you'll look hard to find a more versatile or practical hunting round than the .30-06. If it has any flaws, they've escaped generations keen to chase alternatives. **GD**

Make My Next Handgun a Rimfire!

Rimfire handguns are fun, affordable, and perfect for training, small game hunting, or just a day of shooting at the range.

›MICHAEL PENDLEY

I n case you haven't noticed, ammo is still relatively hard to find. And, when you do find it, the sticker shock is enough to make you keep your handguns holstered instead of spending an enjoyable day at the range. Luckily, there's an alternative to the big-bores out there that you can still shoot for pennies per trigger pull.

That's why every shooter should own at least one rimfire handgun. It's the perfect platform for a fun day of target shooting, makes an excellent choice for small game hunting, and can keep your muscle memory in top shape when you need to pull out a big-bore handgun.

Photo: Ruger

PRACTICE, PRACTICE, THEN PRACTICE SOME MORE

If you carry a handgun for personal and family protection regularly, you know that being familiar with it on an instinctive level is the best way to be effective, should the need ever arise. How do you get to the point that you can draw, aim, and fire the handgun without thinking about it? You build muscle memory, so your hand automatically goes to the right spot without fumbling around. And you do that by firing round after round in different situations.

However, there are several limiting issues with that. Practicing with a large-caliber handgun is expensive, ammo can be hard to find, and it can be on the loud side if you have neighbors close to your practice area.

You can get around most of this by practicing with a rimfire handgun similar in size, shape, and trigger action to your everyday carry gun. Manufacturers have picked up on this trend, and many have started offering rimfire models nearly identical to their larger-caliber handguns.

BAG SOME SMALL GAME

If you're looking for a challenging way to fill your wild game larder, grab a rimfire handgun and hit the woods for squirrel, rabbit, grouse, or whatever small game your area offers.

Getting close enough for an accurate shot with a rimfire pistol or revolver will make you a better hunter and improve

Grabbing a rimfire handgun and hitting the field for small game is a fun way to improve your woodsmanship and handgun accuracy.

The Glock 44 .22 LR makes the perfect doppelganger for your full-caliber handgun. However, some folks carry it for self-defense, too. Photo: Glock

Rimfire pistols like this Glock 44 in .22 LR can complement a well-prepped bug-out bag. The author also likes the 30-round magazine of the Kel-Tec PMR-30 for this application. Photo: Glock

The addition of a slide assist like this Halo ring makes racking a round easy, even with gloves or cold, wet hands and can be an invaluable aid to shooters who don't have the hand strength to pull back the slide.

your shooting skills with any handgun. Rimfire handguns are the perfect choice for tossing in the truck or side-by-side for a day on the farm when you aren't seriously hunting but would like something light and easy to carry should you decide to.

GO PLINKING WITH THE FAMILY

Let's face it. Shooting stuff is fun. You name it: paper targets, reactive steel, stumps, dirt clods, soda cans; they're just fun. There isn't a better choice for a fun day of shooting than a rimfire handgun. You can fit enough ammo in your jacket pocket to keep an entire family plinking away for hours. And you won't have to break the bank to do it.

Rimfire handguns are the perfect platform for introducing new or young shooters to the sport. Most are easy to hold, lightweight, and have little to no recoil, allowing a new shooter to concentrate on target acquisition and trigger control without worrying about loud muzzle blast and heavy recoil.

PACK A BUG-OUT BAG

Do I expect Armageddon soon? Not really. But you don't need full-blown pandemonium for a bug-out bag to come in handy. A truck bag with extra clothes, shelf-stable food, and essentials such as rope, a first aid kit, and fire starters can be critical in many situations. Let's say

A new Buck Mark Medallion model with Vortex red-dot sight. Photo: Browning

SELF-DEFENSE

While few would choose a rimfire hand-gun as their primary defense weapon, if it comes down to a choice between a rimfire and a rock, I pick the rimfire every time. Shooters who are extremely recoil sensitive or require a small frame gun to fit their hands often choose rim-fire platforms as carry guns. Many also choose a small-frame rimfire handgun as an easy-to-conceal backup to their main carry piece.

Federal Premium has taken notice of the need for a self-protection .22 round with its new Punch Personal Defense load. It features a nickel-plated lead-core bullet propelled at extreme velocities and engineered to minimize expansion to hit critical penetration depths through even short-barrel handguns.

MAKE IT YOUR OWN

With the popularity of rimfire handguns comes a multitude of add-on gear to customize them. Bolt-on-slide assists like the Halo ring make racking a round easy, even with gloves or cold, wet hands. Many models feature rails that allow mounting red-dot or traditional scopes, making the guns more accurate for small game hunting and target shooting. Lights, lasers, upgraded

weather conditions leave you stranded in the backcountry for a few extra days. Knowing you have a bag with essential survival gear handy will ease your mind and keep you warm and fed.

A firearm can be a handy tool in a situation like that, and a rimfire handgun is an ideal choice. Consider a .22 WMR for a bit of extra punch. Short of a bear attack, it will handle just about anything that comes your way without adding a ton of size and weight, even if you pack just a couple of hundred rounds of ammo.

The Glock 44 will be instantly recognizable to shooters of larger-caliber handguns from the manufacturer thanks to an identical frame and control system to the popular Glock 19 9mm.

Browning's Buck Mark design has been around for nearly 40 years and remains a top seller thanks to the gun's excellent trigger, long sight plane, and easy-to-hold grip style.

drop-in triggers, and extended magazines are popular upgrades.

RELIABILITY

One of the most critical requirements for a firearm is that it goes bang every time you squeeze the trigger. While .22 auto-loaders weren't always known for smooth feeding reliability, manufacturers have come a long way in designing firearms that reliably feed whatever ammo they are fed. I headed down to Kentucky Gun Company for some range time to test these guns with various CCI and Federal ammo, from match grade to bulk box rounds. To test each gun, I mixed various brands and styles of ammo in a magazine. Even though I fired multiple magazines through each gun, I didn't have a single jam or misfire (perhaps these were

well-worn and proven guns), a true testament to how far rimfire handguns have come in the design department.

GLOCK 44

Released in 2019, the Glock 44 is the perfect .22 LR rimfire for those who regularly shoot a larger-bore Glock. Identical in frame size and shape to the Gen 5 Glock 19 chambered in 9mm Luger, the G44 will be instantly recognizable and comfortable for Glock shooters. The form and function of this striker-fired pistol are the same as the larger calibers, making it the ultimate training rimfire for those who choose the brand as a carry gun.

The G44 digested several CCI and Federal ammo styles without missing a beat. The trigger pull is like larger frame

Glocks: not the smoothest in the test, but serviceable and a great training aid for those who regularly shoot Glocks. Drop-in trigger kits from companies like Glock Triggers and others are an available upgrade if you prefer a smoother, crisper shooting experience. The 44 comes equipped with adjustable rear sights and two magazines.

The .22 LR Glock features a 4.02-inch non-threaded barrel, although threaded ones are available through the factory and as aftermarket components. The handgun measures 7.28 inches overall, with a height of just over 5 inches and a width of 1.25 inches. The gun tips the scales at just over 12 ounces without the magazine and just over a pound when fully loaded. Its magazine capacity is ten rounds. Like other Glocks, the 44 breaks

The Mark IV is Ruger's latest and best variation of the Standard Auto classic design thanks to its wide array of variants such as this (top) Competition model with heavy slab-sided barrel and the massive Target model. New Mark IVs offer easy breakdown for field stripping without tools. Photos: Ruger

down quickly with no tools for cleaning after a day at the range.

BROWNING BUCK MARK

Since 1985, the Buck Mark has been one of the most popular .22 rimfire semi-autos around. And that's for a good reason: The Buck Mark continues to prove itself as one of the most accurate rimfire handguns on the market. As you might suspect, in a design that's pushing 40 years old, the Buck Mark is now available in several variations with different grips, barrel lengths, sights, and overall sizes.

Barrels range from 4 inches to a whopping 11.25 inches. The rimfire handgun is on the heavier side, with some models tipping the scales at a hefty 38 ounces. The Browning gold-plated trigger breaks crisp and clean, one of the best pistols I tested. It features a single-stack, 10-round magazine, and most models have a built-in rail, making mounting scopes and red-dot sights quick and easy. Both the range gun and my personal Buck Mark ran multiple brands of ammo without a jam.

One downside of the Buck Mark is the need for tools and the relatively involved process of disassembly for cleaning. However, once you have the method down and a 3/32-inch Allen wrench, it can be done in a few minutes with careful handling. You can put thousands of rounds through one without breaking it down. This .22 pistol would be *the one* if I picked a gun with small game hunting in mind.

RUGER MARK IV

Another classic design, Ruger introduced a semi-auto .22 in 1949 as the Standard Auto. The Mark IV is the latest rendition and the best so far. With several variations, including lightweight, hunting, target and tactical models, there's a Mark IV for any shooter.

While the Ruger trigger is a bit heavy at 5 pounds, the test gun — a Mark IV 22/45 — was accurate and easy to shoot.

A Volquartsen drop-in Accurizing Kit with an adjustable match-grade trigger which breaks at 2.5 pounds is available, and it is a worthy investment. It had no problem digesting various ammunition brands on the range. The Mark IV comes with two 10-round single-stack magazines.

The standard Mark IV weighs 28.2 ounces with a 4.75-inch barrel, but other models range from 25 to 53 ounces. Even so, the classic swept-back grip makes handling and shooting it accurately like second nature. Sights are fixed front and adjustable rear, but most models either come equipped with a rail or are drilled and tapped for quick aftermarket sight attachment. Barrel lengths range from 8.4 to 14 inches.

One of the best features on the Mark IV, and a marked upgrade from previous models, is the rear takedown button that allows field stripping in seconds with no tools required.

SMITH & WESSON M&P COMPACT 22

If you regularly carry an M&P, you will instantly recognize the M&P Compact 22. The frame and grip are nearly identical, only downsized about 12% from the larger-caliber models. The result is a fun-to-shoot and easy-handling gun that will fit any size shooter.

The Compact uses blowback action with a fixed barrel. It's a single-action, hammer-operated firing mechanism. The

total length is 6.7 inches, with a barrel length of 3.6 inches. Total weight with an empty magazine comes in at 16 ounces.

On the range, the trigger on the test gun broke consistently right at 6 pounds.

Like other guns in the M&P line, the M&P22 Compact has a hinged trigger to prevent inadvertent activation. There is about 1/3 of an inch takeup if you measure travel at the hinge point with a smooth break and minimal overtravel. It has a visually loaded chamber indicator on the top of the slide, and a small curved cutout lets you see if there's a cartridge in the chamber. Sights are fixed front and adjustable rear and were easy to use at multiple distances.

The M&P Compact includes a pair of single-stack 10-round magazines, a Picatinny rail for mounting a laser or light, and a threaded barrel. Field stripping is simple and doesn't require tools. The

thumb safety is ambidextrous.

The S&W Compact digested various ammo with no hiccups or jams. Accuracy was outstanding for a short-barreled handgun.

TAURUS TX22

While Taurus' TX22 pistol doesn't exactly match its larger-caliber models, it does get close enough to feel familiar in practice. My test model was the full-size version. With an overall length of 7.06 inches, a 4.10-inch threaded barrel, and an overall width of 1.25 inches, the TX22 felt and handled like a full-frame 9mm. Taurus offers several other models of the TX22, including a compact version with a slightly smaller frame.

The TX 22 feels like a large-frame pistol and features a modified double-stack magazine holding 16 rounds instead of the standard 10-round single-stack mags found in many semi-auto rimfire handguns.

One of the first things you notice about the TX22 is the solid feel and ease of use. It's surprisingly lightweight, thanks to a forged aluminum slide and polymer frame. The Standard model weighs in at just 17.4 ounces with an empty magazine. The trigger pull is around 4 lbs., 10 oz., with a smooth feel and minimal creep. The slide is easy to rack, and the magazine release button was firm but fast to deploy. There is a Picatinny Rail for accessory mounting.

In a class that features almost entirely single-stack, 10-round magazines, a nice feature on the TX22 is a semi-double-stack 16-round magazine. While not an actual double-stack system, the mag shuffles each round, alternating slightly to the right or left, allowing for more rounds in a similar-sized magazine. The standard TX22 also ships from the factory with two mags, but some models come with a third.

Accuracy was good, but the point of impact shifted more with different ammo brands and styles than with some of the other tested guns. There were no jams or failures to fire with any of the tested ammo.

RUGER SR22

For fans of the Ruger SR9 or SR40 in the market for a rimfire handgun, the Ruger SR22 deserves a look. While grip and function aren't the same as the large-caliber guns, it is similar enough that muscle memory with the smaller firearm will transfer over to them. One of the most significant differences between the SR22 and the other semi-autos tested is that this gun has an exposed hammer and a single-action/double-action trigger. The trigger isn't one of my favorites. The single-action mode isn't bad, with a crisp, 4-pound pull, but double action can be very gritty and difficult to pull at 7 1/2 pounds with what seems like an incredibly long travel. It's worth noting that the test gun was a new, off-the-shelf model. I later shot a well-used range gun, and the trigger was much smoother. I'd say it takes a while to break in.

The SR22 is compact, weighing just over a pound thanks to an aluminum slide and polymer frame. With an overall length of 6.4 inches and a height of 4.9 inches, the gun feels larger in the hand than the weight suggests. The barrel length is 3.5 inches and is threaded.

The gun has an ambidextrous manual thumb safety, a de-cocking lever, and an ambidextrous magazine release, suitable for left- and right-handed shooters. My main issue with it was its safety. While the location and operation were comparable to other handguns tested, it's backward — up is fire, and down is safe. That takes some getting used to, particularly if you switch back and forth with other handguns.

Sights are fixed front and adjustable rear with a three-dot setup. The front and rear sights can be reversed if you don't prefer the dots. A Picatinny rail has multiple cross slots for laser and light accessories.

In single-action mode, the gun was surprisingly accurate for a 3.5-inch barrel. The SR22 had no problem digesting all CCI and Federal ammo I fed it. Factory packaging includes a pair of 10-round, single-stack magazines with finger grip extension floorplates to help shooters with larger hands.

The extremely compact SR22 features an exposed hammer that allows the shooter to use the firearm in single- and double-action shooting styles.

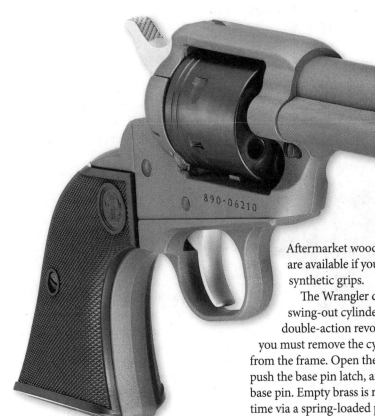

The author found the Ruger Wrangler .22 LR quite accurate. Photo: Ruger

RUGER WRANGLER

For many shooters, a revolver is the preferred choice for handguns. Accurate and utterly reliable, a rimfire revolver makes sense when situations call for a few shots at a time. If you're looking for an excellent value in a .22 LR revolver, give the Wrangler a shot. There is a model for every shooting style, with barrel lengths ranging from 3.75 to 7.5 inches. The standard barrel length is 4.75 inches. With an MSRP of $269, the Wrangler is one of the most affordable guns I tested.

Don't let the low-cost fool you. This wheelgun is a well-built, substantial piece. The test gun had an overall length of 10.25 inches and a weight of 30 ounces, giving it the feel of a larger revolver. Unlike the more costly Single Six (available with up to a 10-round cylinder), the Wrangler's capacity is limited to six. Trigger pull is crisp, with almost no creep and a break that surprises you almost every time. The accuracy was exceptional.

The Wrangler's grip features synthetic grip panels attached with a single screw in the middle to hold things together.

Aftermarket wood grip panels are available if you don't care for synthetic grips.

The Wrangler doesn't have the swing-out cylinder of Ruger's double-action revolvers. Instead, you must remove the cylinder entirely from the frame. Open the loading gate, push the base pin latch, and remove the base pin. Empty brass is removed one at a time via a spring-loaded push rod.

Sights are fixed and non-replaceable as they are molded into the frame. While not the most accurate sighting systems tested, it is serviceable and will feel familiar to longtime single-action shooters.

Overall, the Wrangler is a fun-shooting gun and a superb value for anyone looking at rimfire revolvers.

SMITH & WESSON MODEL 617

Smith & Wesson's Model 617 will be instantly recognizable to fans of the larger K-frame revolvers. With a heritage dating to 1899, these guns have been tested and proven worldwide. The full-size, stainless frame is an ideal training aid for those carrying larger-bore K-frames. The 617 features a ten-shot, swing-out cylinder, making loading and unloading a breeze.

The 617 is available in either 4- or 6-inch barrel configurations. Weights range from 39 ounces for the 4-inch to a hefty 44 ounces for the 6-inch. Add about 5 ounces to both for a fully loaded cylinder. Sights are fixed front and adjustable rear. Trigger pull, while classic Smith & Wesson smooth, is a heavy 13 pounds in double action and drops to 4.9 pounds as a single action. The standard S&W

black rubber grips provide a sure hold, and the combination of the grip style and the handgun's weight makes recoil with a .22 LR nearly unnoticeable. If you prefer wooden grips, there are many aftermarket alternatives to the factory rubber.

As you would expect from a revolver, the 617 has no problem with any .22 ammo you feed it and smoothly extracts empties.

THE OTHER RIMFIRES

While the .22 LR dominates the rimfire handgun market, other rimfire options exist. The .22 Winchester Magnum Rimfire or .22 WMR offers more punch packed into a longer and slightly wider case than the .22 LR. Typical .22 WMR bullet weights range from 30 to 50 grains, with a 40-grain bullet being the most common.

KEL-TEC PMR-30

The PMR-30 is a full-size polymer frame semi-automatic pistol chambered in .22 Mag. It's lightweight, at a feathery 13.6 oz. empty, or 18.6 oz. with a full magazine. Speaking of magazines, the PMR-30 advertises a stunning 30-round capacity. I have difficulty cramming more than 25 or 26 in by hand, but that's almost three times the capacity of most handguns we tested.

The Kel-Tec's light weight is thanks to a polymer and aluminum construction. It has an ambidextrous safety that's easy to reach and operate. The gun comes with bright, two-color fiber-optic sights, and it's drilled and tapped to accommodate a scope base. The frame has an integrated

Picatinny accessory rail, and you'll find the mag release at the base of the grip instead of the more typical frame mount. The overall length is 7.9 inches with a 4.3-inch barrel. Height is 5.8 inches, and width is 1.3 inches. The PMR-30's trigger is surprisingly light and crisp, breaking at just 4 pounds on my test gun.

This gun is just fun to shoot. Yes, it rattles a bit, but it is highly accurate and easy to hold, despite the long front-to-back length necessary to house the .22 WMR rounds. There is almost no recoil, and the slide is effort-less to rack, making the PMR-30 a viable self-defense weapon for those who have difficulty racking a round or handling the recoil in larger-caliber handguns.

If packing a bug-out bag, the PMR-30 would be my choice of handgun. The light weight, large capacity, and added power of the .22 WMR load make it an excellent choice for carrying in the backcountry, where you might run into anything from snakes, to irritable hogs, to unsavory humans.

THE .17 CALIBERS

On the other end of the rimfire spectrum is the .17 Hornady Magnum Rimfire, commonly known as the .17 HMR. First developed by Hornady in 2002, it was formed by necking down a .22 Magnum case to take a .17-caliber, 17-grain bullet at a higher velocity than the .22 LR or .22 WMR.

For single-action revolver fans, the Ruger Wrangler provides a fun, accurate wheelgun that feels similar in hand to large-frame revolvers and does it at a great value. The MSRP? Just $269.

While the steep shoulders of the tiny .17-caliber bullet make reliable feeding in a semi-auto pistol an issue, there are several revolvers on the market chambered for the cartridge.

TAURUS M17 TRACKER .17 HMR

For anyone looking for a handgun chambered in .17 HMR, the M17 Tracker from Taurus will fit the bill. While the shorter barrel doesn't benefit fully from the necked-down cartridge's increased

Firing the more powerful .22 WMR round, the Kel-Tec PMR-30 makes an outstanding backcountry and hunting sidearm thanks to its light weight, excellent trigger, and a 30-round capacity.

Accuracy varied by gun, barrel length, sight options, and shooting styles. However, all tested handguns were easy to hold on paper at varying distances, and some were surprisingly accurate.

The handguns were tested with a mix of Federal and CCI ammo ranging from match grade to bulk box rounds and handled all rounds without a single misfire or jam.

speed, it still packs a punch. It is the perfect partner gun for someone who regularly carries a rifle chambered in .17 HMR and doesn't want to worry about mixing up ammo.

The Tracker comes standard with a 6.5-inch barrel and a seven-round cylinder. The sights are fixed front, black-outlined adjustable rear. You can fire it as a single- or double-action. Its overall length is 10.75 inches, with a height of 5.3 inches, and the gun weighs 47 ounces. The Tracker is equipped with the popular Taurus rubber grip so that you can hold and shoot it in any weather. GD

Based on the ingenious design by Eugene Stoner, the AR-15 has become "America's Rifle."

Ten Guns You've Got to Own

We all have our dream guns, but these are the ones no self-respecting gun owner should ever be without.

❯BRADLEY JOHNSON

This scene has played out innumerable times. A new shooter or hunter is at a campfire or gun counter, going down the rabbit hole we all know well. A question arises, which gun should I get next? My answer is the list below, ten guns everyone should experience at some point. However, before you get your pitchforks sharpened and torches lit, this isn't a list of firearms you need for the rest of your life (though you would be well-armed). Think of this as ten guns you need to get your hands on at some point simply because they are timeless classics.

A WELL-BUILT AR-15

Eugene Stoner blessed us with an absolute classic when he designed the M16/AR-15 platform many years ago. While hundreds of manufacturers have produced the AR in many different iterations, the spectrum is broad and varied. It has been chambered in many different calibers, so I'm referring to a good-quality carbine or rifle variant in .223/5.56 NATO chambering.

What makes the AR-15 so handy? It's lightweight, easy to operate and maintain, and it shoots cheap ammo. From a self-defense standpoint, my AR-15 is the first gun I grab when things go bump in the night. With a standard-capacity magazine of 30 cartridges, it's serious firepower and relatively low recoil for faster follow-up shots. If you told me I could only have one rifle, it would likely be a well-built AR-15 in .223/5.56. Is it the perfect cartridge for taking big game in North America? Absolutely not. Much has been written about shot placement and bullet construction, but I can say that I have taken many whitetails in America

Few pistols feel better in hand than a well-built 1911.

and springboks in Africa with this chambering.

Note that I said *good quality*. There are a lot of great manufacturers, such as FN, Colt, Cobalt Kinetics, Knights Armament Corp., Barrett, and Noveske. You can't go wrong with any of these.

The popularity of the AR-15 in America is a double-edged sword. On the one hand, the platform is so modular that most people can build one in the garage. This is fantastic from a modularity standpoint because a rifle that is perfectly set up for me might be the complete opposite of what might work for you regarding trigger, barrel, stock, gas system, etc. On the other hand, this ease of building leads to some manufacturers putting together the cheapest parts they can source to sell to the consumer.

You want a name brand with a reputation for reliability, accuracy, and quality

The Ruger Mini 14 rifles offer an excellent alternative to those living in less freedom-friendly states.

fit and finish. You don't want a random, cobbled-together rifle you bought at a gun show the morning after a few dudes with a garage FFL slapped it together after polishing off a six-pack. Itseems like every election cycle many new AR-15 manufacturers appear out of nowhere. Some are good; others are not so great.

Backup/alternate: Ruger Mini-14 — If you live in one of the "ban" states, get a standard Ruger Mini-14 in 5.56/223. While some question this rifle's accuracy, the current production will hang with any off-the-shelf AR-15 variants at the same price point. How accurate? You will

still hit a man-sized torso steel target out to 400 yards all day and will certainly maintain 2 MOA with good ammo. Accuracy like that is more than acceptable for anything I will ask of such a rifle.

1911 HANDGUN

Over a hundred years ago, the legendary John Moses Browning — a genius in business and firearms design — began the development of a semi-automatic handgun for military trials that resulted in several successful designs. Still, the one that the U.S. military would adopt would be the model of 1911 produced by Colt.

It should come as no surprise that a significant contributing factor to the gun's popularity was that multiple generations of service members came home and bought what they were familiar with, leading to the 1911's widespread use.

A well-built 1911 truly is a shooting experience to behold. But, like the AR-15, popularity leads to a wide range of offerings. It can't be stressed enough: Buy quality 1911s. While this may seem snobbish, remember that the 1911 design does not lend itself well to cheap mass production. Because a gun is technically a 1911 design, it is not inherently great.

Start with quality. It will save you time and money in the long run. Where is the line of quality? The baseline offerings from Springfield Armory and Colt are an excellent starting point.

As a good friend of mine (ironically, he's in the UK gun industry) once said, the 1911 is the embodiment of America's pistol. I couldn't agree more with this statement; it's a gun every red-blooded American should own and enjoy.

Backup/alternate: Browning Hi-Power — The Hi-Power is undoubtedly one of my favorite semi-auto handguns. Some would even argue that it was the natural progression of the 1911 design. You can never go wrong with this classy 9mm semi-auto.

SMITH & WESSON MODEL 29 REVOLVER

In 1955, a match made in heaven was brokered by the God of wheelguns himself, Elmer Keith. Keith was an Idaho big game hunter and guide and one of our most influential gun writers. He used his pull to bring about a new cartridge designed around what he believed the current .44 special should have been performance-wise; enter the .44 Remington Magnum cartridge paired with the new Smith & Wesson Model 29 revolver on the N-frame.

It's a big gun, easy to control, and versatile. Keith was an avid handgun hunter and rancher. The .44 Mag. was designed with his needs in mind. You can do it all with the classic 4-inch barrel configuration (my preferred variant).

While the .44 Magnum cartridge is a reloader's dream, if you don't hand-load, there is a wide assortment of .44 Magnum and .44 Special factory loads commercially available to cover everything from hunting to self-defense. If I'm in the woods or on the water, my model 29 is on my hip. I wear mine in a Simply Rugged pancake-style holster called the Sourdough. The holster distributes the weight of this massive boat anchor of a handgun. But once you get used to the weight, you will find it a benefit regarding recoil control.

If given the restriction of only being able to own one handgun, a 4-in. blued finish Model 29 would be my choice.

Backup/alternate: Ruger Redhawk — If the Model 29 isn't your speed and you want to be slightly different, go with the Ruger Redhawk. The Redhawk is beefier, heavier, and a bit less refined in the trigger department when compared to a pre-lock S&W. The Redhawk is more robust, though, and its weight can be helpful when shooting heavy loads.

RUGER MKIV .22 PISTOL

After WWII, prolific firearm designer Bill Ruger entered the American gun scene.

Elmer Keith was right. The ultimate packing and do-all field revolver is a 4-inch Model 29 .44 magnum.

He was a fan of the Japanese Nambu pistol and its bolt design. In 1949, he introduced the gun known as the Ruger Standard Auto in .22 LR. The Standard Auto was the first generation in a series of pistols currently in the fourth iteration (Mark IV).

So what sets the MKIV apart from the others? The takedown system! Anyone who has owned a Ruger Standard Auto in the first three generations will tell you it's an amazing gun with one major drawback: disassembling it requires black magic, luck, and a rubber mallet. It isn't that bad once you learn a few tricks and get used to it, but it certainly was a significant drawback. The latest generation has a button on the back of the frame you push, and the gun hinges open for easy field stripping and cleaning.

The MKIV also has one of the cleanest triggers of any commercially available rimfire pistols today. I love guns that are good to go right out of the box. After properly sighting in an Aimpoint Micro T2 on top of mine, we frequently made hits on a 6-inch gong at 100 yards.

If you live in a freedom-loving state, buy the threaded model and get a suppressor (I highly recommend the Q Erector).

Backup/alternate: Taurus TX22 Competition — The Competition variant is my top pick of the TX22 line as it comes threaded with an optics mounting plate. I will be the first to admit I was not a fan of Taurus for many years, but this is one of the guns that made me a believer that the Taurus of today is an entirely different company putting out high-quality products. I'll purchase one next for backpacking, as it's a bit lighter than the Ruger.

THE RUGER NO. 1 SINGLE-SHOT RIFLE

You won't find an American-made rifle with more class and style than the Ruger No. 1. Get your pith helmets and tweed field coat ready. The brainchild of Bill Ruger and Leonard Brownell, the No. 1 gave Americans a single-shot rifle that is a mashup between classical British and American gun-making styles. Through the years, it has come in many configurations in stainless and blued finishes and everything from varmint rifles to true big-bore safari guns — all built on the same indestructible falling block action.

I like the No. 1A configuration best, a blued half-stock sporter variant with a beautiful Alexander Henry-style forend and banded front sight. The barrel is of light contour, and it makes for a lovely stalking rifle that makes you want to glass red stags in the Scottish highlands or kudu through the mopane brush.

They aren't winning any awards in the accuracy department, but some of my Ruger No. 1s are the most accurate rifles I have ever owned. That said, others needed a little love and were picky on ammo. My current No. 1A in .275 Rigby (7x57 Mauser) will shoot an honest 3/4-in. three-shot group all day long from a cold bore with 140-gr. Nosler Accubonds. With most other factory ammo, it's a 1.5 MOA gun. Is it going to beat any accuracy records? Absolutely not! Am I pleased with it, and will it suit my needs? Absolutely yes! What level of accuracy do you expect and need? My No. 1A in .275 Rigby is a stalking rifle for medium-sized game, and I am taking shots 250 yards and closer. For my needs, the rifle works perfectly fine.

Backup/alternate: Browning 1885 — The Browning 1885 is equally classic; if having an exposed hammer is more your speed, this is the route you want to go. It's also one of John Browning's masterpieces.

THE REMINGTON 870 PUMP SHOTGUN

If you ever want to experience a pump-action shotgun, buy a Remington 870. With production numbers in the millions, if you ask most people about their first pump-action shotgun, it was likely an 870.

The 870 is the literal definition of a workhorse; it's so reliable that it's boring. But this rugged pedestrian reliability has a charm all of its own. I am constantly adding guns

Coupled with the Aimpoint Micro red-dot optic and a threaded barrel, the new Ruger MkIV makes for the ultimate rimfire shooting experience.

to my collection, but one thing has stayed constant throughout my years of wheeling and dealing: I have always owned at least one 12-gauge Remington 870. An 18-inch cylinder bore barrel is an excellent home defense option to complement my defensive carbine and handguns. With a regular 28-inch hunting barrel installed, I give it to every new shooter and hunter who joins me in the field. If a buddy shows up to a hunt without a gun, I hand them an 870.

My advice when looking for one: if you are OK with only shooting 2 3/4-inch shells, find an older Wingmaster model. The 870 Wingmaster has a lighter receiver and generally a better fit and finish than the Express line of guns. The best part? A used Remington 870 of any variety is generally one of the best values on the market. And if you don't like buying used, they are back in production. Given its popularity over the years, parts are everywhere and not going anywhere anytime soon. Servicing or swapping out 870 parts will be affordable and accessible for generations.

Backup/alternate: Winchester Model 12 — While it doesn't have the aftermarket support of the Remington 870 and hasn't been in production for decades, the Winchester Model 12 pump action is for those who love the classics. No pump action has a tactile lockup as satisfactory as a well-worn Winchester model 12.

WINCHESTER MODEL 70 BOLT-ACTION RIFLE

In 1936, Winchester did something extraordinary: It listened to seasoned gun writers and the American shooting community and gave us the best bolt-action American sporting rifle ever produced, the Model 70.

American soldiers returning from WWI got a taste for bolt-action rifles, and Winchester responded in 1925 with the Model 54. While the Model 54 was terrific by the standards of its day, it could use a few tweaks. The main issue was that it was introduced when most American shooters were still shooting iron sights, and the bolt handle's shape and flag safety did not lend themselves well to optics.

Fast forward 11 years to 1936, when

The Ruger No. 1 series of rifles are arguably the classiest-looking single shots currently in production.

Winchester introduced the model 70, a very refined Model 54. This time, Winchester hit the nail on the head. The Model 70 was named the "Rifleman's Rifle" for good reason.

There are three main categories of Winchester Model 70. (Collectors, you can put your pitchforks away as I'm giving the cliff notes version of the generations.) The most desirable from a collectible standpoint is the pre-64 series. This is a 1936-1964 production. These rifles had controlled-round feed bolts and are considered the gold standard among American-made bolt guns. Then

you have post-64 push-feed rifles. These went through multiple generations but are generally characterized by the lack of a Mauser-type claw extractor. Next came the post-64 controlled-round feeds. These are produced today and are called such because though production is post-64, they have a Mauser-type claw extractor found on the pre-64 guns.

Literal volumes have been written over the years, arguing the merits and benefits of each series. I will let you in on a secret, though: they're all great. Even the post-64 push-feed Model 70s, which don't hold the serious collector value of the earlier guns, are amazing deals and generally very accurate rifles. The pre-64 models are a throwback to the best in American gun making, but they aren't any more accurate than later generations. A current production Winchester Model 70, produced by FN, is on my short list of firearms I can't wait to snag next.

Backup/alternate: Mauser 98 — This one deserves an article all of its own, but rest assured, anything pre-war commercial Mauser or post-war FN on a commercial Mauser action is generally a great gun.

BROWNING A5 SEMI-AUTO SHOTGUN

The Browning A5 was in production for almost a century. What's funny about this shotgun is that it's the model that put FN on the map. When John Browning offered the design to Winchester, his long-time partner, it declined to buy it, stating that the automatic shotgun would not sell. So, he brought the design to a little-known, small Belgian firearms manufacturer, FN (Fabrique Nationale), and the rest is history.

The A5 is highly recognizable from its "humpback" design, housing a long recoil operating system that oozes

classic cool and makes you want to wear waxed canvas in a duck blind. Like many popular shotgun designs, it has gone through multiple iterations and has been produced in 12, 20, and 16 gauge.

The Browning A5 variant that makes me smile the most is the Sweet 16. If there ever was a true classic American autoloader that defined wingshooting upland birds, this was it. It's the one I pick for most of my wingshooting, from doves to Canada geese and everything in between. The Sweet 16 sports an actual 16-gauge-sized frame. Sometimes, when a gun company wants to introduce a 16 ga., it puts a 16-ga. barrel and parts on a 12-ga. receiver. That takes away the advantage of running a 16 gauge which, to me, is

The Remington 870 is possibly the most popular pump-action shotgun ever produced. Everyone should own at least one.

The Mauser 98 and its many iterations is the original controlled-round feed system for those who appreciate the classics.

If you are interested in hunting big game anywhere in the world, get a Winchester Model 70. It's the gold standard to which other bolt-action hunting rifles are held.

The Winchester Model 12 epitomizes the gentleman's pump gun.

lighter weight.

Like the Winchester post- and pre-64 model 70s, the Browning A5 has two main series — Belgian-made and later Japanese-made. The Belgian ones bring more money and have a higher collector value, but the Japanese-produced A5s are every bit as good, if not better, mechanically. Buy the one you can strike a deal on and take it in the field; they are all great.

Backup/alternate: Remington Model 11 — While it was not in production for as many years, Remington had a license to produce the Browning design. These Model 11s do not have interchangeable parts with the Browning A5 but look similar and are rock solid. The 12-ga. models can generally be had for a steal.

MARLIN 39

I can remember this moment as clearly as day. I was maybe 11, and my mom brought us into town. Naturally, I found my way to the gun magazines and started reading. I can't remember the publication or author, but there it was, the Marlin 39 in a featured piece. The photo had a Marlin 39 .22 rifle set against some barnboard with a red plaid hunting jacket, a Case trapper pocket knife, a brass compass, a few traps, and a fox tail. I was immediately taken in by what I read about this classic American rimfire rifle. I had to have one.

Unfortunately, I soon found out that the Marlin 39s have quite the following, but I would not end up with my first one until I was a freshman in college. I then proceeded to hunt small game every weekend I legally could, and it was a constant companion on the trapline and on summer camping trips.

What made this rifle so handy with such appeal? For starters, it was a shooter. I only have a peep sight on mine, but putting ten shots into a quarter-sized group at 50 yards is easily achievable. The Marlin 39 is not a "youth"-sized rifle. It is a full-sized gun that happens to be chambered in .22 LR. These guns are not lightweight in the standard configuration by any means, but if you are Sasquatch-sized like me, you will appreciate the full size. Working the action feels like you are winding the finest precision pocket watch.

Here's the best part, it's a takedown! Remove one captive screw in the receiver, and the rifle breaks in half for easy transport or cleaning. I carry mine in a Skinner takedown rifle bag, and away it goes into the field.

Marlin produced this rifle for over a century before the company's recent sale to Ruger. I hope Ruger brings it back, as it is my favorite lever-action rimfire ever produced.

Backup/alternate: Winchester 9422 — While not a takedown, this alternate gets an honorable mention as it's a great rifle to add to the collection. The Winchester 9422 is a classic and came in a .22 WMR variant.

WINCHESTER 94 LEVER-ACTION RIFLE

The end of the 19th century was a wild time for gun design. John Browning wanted to make a lever-action rifle chambered in the then-new smokeless rifle cartridges. He used the locking system that was already a success from the 1886

Of all the Browning A5 variants, the author favors the Sweet Sixteen model the most.

and 1892 models and adapted it into what we now have as the Model 94.

The Model 94 is the quintessential brush gun. The standard 20-inch barrel carbine configuration, chambered in .30-30 Win., has put deer in the cooler for over a century. There is no other rifle I can think of that is as comfortable to carry. If you want to experience a fantastic brush gun that is relatively low recoil, lightweight, handy and quick to shoulder, the Winchester 94 should be the first gun you try.

The 94 was in production until 2006, when Winchester closed its New Haven plant. Luckily for us, Browning, which now owns Winchester, is producing them again at the Miroku plant in Japan, and they are as good as the older ones.

The Browning A5 is America's autoloading shotgun. Almost 100 years of production doesn't happen by mistake.

While it might not have the romantic Old West history of the Winchester, the Marlin 336 lever action is no slouch in the classics department and has been serving for over half a century.

Backup/alternate: Marlin 336 — While the Marlin 336 does not have the longevity and Old West mystique of the Winchester 94, it is arguably a better rifle in some regards. That's especially true if you wish to mount a magnified optic. The Winchester 94 is not forgiving regarding optics mounting options due to the top eject receiver,unless you get the angled eject variant, whereas the Marlin 336 has a side ejection port and a solid top receiver. The deciding factor between these two should be whether you wish to mount an optic.

CONCLUSION

While you should never restrict yourself to ten guns, these are the ones you should consider owning and shooting at some point. Remember, they're best experienced in the field and range. A gun in a safe doesn't build nearly as many memories as one that gets shot and carried. **GD**

If you want the ultimate takedown .22 lever action to walk an oak bottom with, the Marlin 39 is for you.

No gun will ever feel as comfortable in hand as a Winchester 94 lever action.

Bell of Africa!

W.D.M. Bell led an extraordinary life of African hunting adventure and proved the importance of shot placement!

> JOHN WALLACE

Apart from it being the frontispiece of the posthumously published *Bell of Africa*, only guesswork suggests that this might be the sole painting Bell had hung in the Royal Academy, an honor plutocracy or pedigree cannot buy. The author would love to hear from anyone who knows.

Most of us know of W.D.M. Bell as a giant from an unrepeatable era when the modern rifle met Africa, much as it was before the governments came. Perhaps the last great hunter we can consider an explorer, Bell ran yearlong safaris without white companions, forming bonds with terrifyingly homicidal people he counted among his closest friends.

Karamojo Bell is perhaps most well-known for using the .257 Rigby, 7mm Mauser on his infamous elephant hunts.

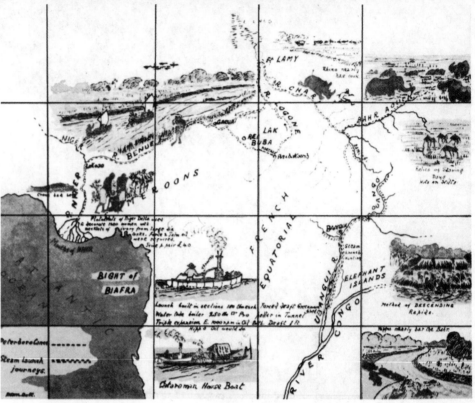

Drawing by Bell

FORMATIVE YEARS

Walter Dalrymple Maitland Bell was born in Linlithgowshire, Scotland, in 1880, to a family wealthy in coal and oil shale. Orphaned in early childhood, his trustees and all elder brothers always mistrusted what surely seemed outlandish business ventures.

He ran away from several schools at age 8, hitting his school captain on the head with a cricket bat. So hallowed a place does cricket hold among the cultivated classes that similar abuse of a baseball bat bears no comparison.

In that sternly Presbyterian age, Walter's becoming a gentleman of leisure was not considered. His guardians sent him to sea as a sailing ship line apprentice. Although the officer track was a hard life, subservience to authority was the wrong kind of hard for Bell. So he jumped ship in Australia and worked his passage home.

His subsequent escape was from a tutor in Germany. His kayak, built from drawings in Nansen's book, came to grief on a mill weir, but he made what POWs of a later age would call a home run. The campaign of attrition continued until they agreed that to Africa he must go. He was sixteen years old.

BECOMING BELL OF AFRICA

Bell arrived in Mombasa with a second-hand .303 Martini-Metford from Daniel Fraser of Edinburgh. He intended to join one of the large caravans of Swahili coastal natives and Zanzibar Arabs but found no demand for his services. That was partly due to their having no idea how superior modern firearms were over crude muzzleloaders. Britain held a protectorate over Zanzibar, but those caravans, still involved in slaving, dreaded a witness from a nation committed to abolition. So Bell joined the Uganda Railway, whose Indian and African workers were held to be in danger from hostile natives and lions.

Two years later, the grim story of the two untypical maneaters of Tsavo may not fully stand up to investigation. Bell became convinced that the ordinary lion posed little threat to such unnatural prey. He learned a lot, notably confidence in the bush and appreciation of people many dismissed as inferiors. But he shot no lions with his Martini, which extracted shells very unreliably in the daytime heat.

So he traded that rifle for a Greek trader's .450

Karamoja warrior.

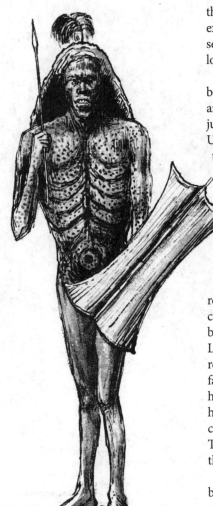

Longelly-nyung, W.D.M. Bell's bloodbrother.
Drawings by Bell

Winchester Single Shot. Unfortunately, the only ammunition available had extremely hollow points, which failed severely on a lion, disintegrating on the lower jaw and shoulder.

A few years later, lion hunting in Kenya became a fashionable accomplishment and a form of demise. Bell was never injured or seriously charged by an animal. Unwounded ones, notably elephants, certainly can and will kill you. Still, Bell believed that a hard-hit one more often dashes in whatever direction takes its fancy. If the hunter is unlucky, it engages what bomber pilots term a target of opportunity. With that lion, Bell was two feet from the wrong place.

His next gun was a Lee-Metford, a reliable magazine rifle for which he never ceased considering the jacketed military bullet among the best for elephants. Lacking the means to fit out a safari, he resigned to join a German explorer who failed to show up. Infected with malaria, he returned to Scotland, but even his hard-won knowledge of Africa failed to convince his trustees to finance a safari. They relented, however, to the extent of the Yukon gold rush.

Bell made light of the Chilcoot Pass by not bringing the food stocks a mining syndicate would require and found the notorious White Horse Rapids behaving themselves. But in Dawson, food could not be bought. Rather than the backbreaking tedium of wage labor in permafrost mining, he turned to the meat-hunting business.

His hunted moose and deer were frozen in a remote cabin with his .360 Farquharson rifle and a .45 Colt revolver borrowed from his partner to eke out its irreplaceable cartridges. The latter took sled loads of meat into town and banked the proceeds, which in gold-rich and food-poor Dawson must have been considerable. Disaster came when that partner, whom Bell knew only as "Bill," disappeared. Bill's reticence about the bank account and his reclaiming the Colt for protection from wolves weighed against him. Bell thought fraud to be the likely explanation but drew no firm conclusion. People disappeared on the Yukon, and the wolves were unquestionably about.

Impoverished again, Bell sold the Farquharson and left to enlist in the newly commenced Boer War. He found the lifestyle in "the last of the gentlemen's wars" congenial rather than adventurous, although one of his paintings shows him in flight, as his horse was shot at high speed. He became a prisoner but escaped, possibly because the Boers saw little point in keeping him. Peace brought a new era. Aged twenty-one, he controlled his financial affairs.

Drawing by Bell

Walter Dalrymple Maitland Bell, known to most as "W.D.M. Bell" or "Karamojo Bell," penned several all-time great African safari books, including *The Wanderings of An Elephant Hunter*, *Karamojo Safari*, and *Bell of Africa*.

Skull of Bull Elephant killed in UNYORO, UGANDA. Sawn down middle to shew Brain. In this skull the brain measured 12" x 6". He was not very old. Tusks weighed 81 x 78

This may be the most crucial picture the aspiring elephant hunter will ever see. The false cranial dome is soft and spongy but contains no vital parts, while the hard tusk sockets are a barrier that must be avoided.

BELL AND THE ELEPHANT

The hunter fortunate enough to afford an elephant hunt today cannot be reckoned as lucky as Bell. Guidance and instructions from his Professional Hunter have the force of law. He may be denied any rifle Bell favored to follow up his wounded animal or to take what the laymen would consider a golden opportunity. Even nowadays, the Professional's expertise on elephants may owe more to Bell than any other.

Bell had to devise his techniques and make mistakes with elephants and natives. It is saddening that elephant hunting now requires one to defend it. He did not, as some say, kill more elephants than anyone else. His often-quoted 1,011 kills preceded some hunting in West and Central Africa, raising the total considerably. Some killed far more "on control," including a thousand a year throughout the 66 years of the Uganda Protectorate. Elephants being polygamous, population reduction was best accomplished by killing females and calves rather than the elderly bulls — with their breeding days

behind them — that Bell singled out.

Estimates of a natural population of ten million seem conjectural. In 1979, the most-credited figures were as imprecise as 1.3 to 3 million — improved census techniques confirmed up to 609,000 in 1989, declining to 415,000 in 2016. *(Editor's Note: Habitat loss and human-elephant conflict has played a major role in the decline of the elephant's numbers, with sport hunting taking less than any natural causes of death.)*

Something had to be done. But the most credible part of the decline occurred with legal ivory hunting, of-

ficial culling, and recreational hunting significantly declining. Most countries have severely limited hunting to placate the camera tourists or support the market price of a hunt like de Beers with diamonds. East and southern Africa have achieved modest increases due in part to the somewhat reduced role of the Kalashnikov in politics and suppression of the international ivory trade. Computer Numerical Controlled (CNC) carving machinery has undoubtedly harmed elephant populations more than the sporting rifle.

We must remember, too, that hunting

and control have enabled millions of an increasing human population to live on the land. Tourist income can compensate a native farmer for occasional wipeout by locusts but not for being occasionally killed.

Just sixteen years into the existence of smokeless rifles, the state-of-the-art elephant gun was the Nitro Express double, of .450 to .600 caliber, with jacketed solids. Also, 8-gauge cartridge rifles, good weapons in certain circumstances, retained some favor. But Bell had fired heavy rifles at his friend Fraser's range. He found heavy recoil objectionable and conducive to flinching. I believe he would have overcome this, as he overcame many other things. But his experience before elephant hunting (perhaps not rhinoceros) convinced him that bullet placement far outweighed energy. Bell preferred the almost universal round-nosed military bullet of moderate velocity, 3½- to 4-calibers long and non-expanding to comply with the Hague Convention. The legendary reliability and speed of the double might apply to two shots. Still, a fragment of debris could fatally impede the third, and African foliage can drip mud or shower twigs. Unlike doubles, military actions were designed for the incessant dry firing Bell considered indispensable to accuracy.

Was he right about the effect of perfectly placed solids? He records rare occasions when an elephant, stunned by a near miss at the brain, woke up with embarrassing suddenness. It is hard to doubt that, as many great hunters have said, fingertip-sized express bullets could buy some margin for error.

One of Bell's tiny bullets through the low-set heart, or even the concentration of great arteries above it, would kill without distress or commotion. The modest report of the .303 or later Mausers and Mannlichers often set the herd moving, but not in the panic flight that no hunter could keep up with.

Headshots produced no commotion but must have caused some self-questioning on caliber, as the elephants, other than moderately paced retreat, took no notice. Bell's typically methodical reaction was to have his boys saw through an elephant skull down the middle, after which he found himself misinformed on the location of the brain. What looked like a perfect cranial dome was a resilient honeycomb of bone and delicate air passages. Hit in the brain, actually lower and farther back, the elephant would die quickly and quietly, usually on its knees, facilitating the extraction of the tusks.

The easiest brain shot was side-on, mid-way between earhole and eye. But an alerted elephant faces you, so the classic brain shot is frontal, with only thin bone behind the nasal passages. More dangerous, in an elephant charging or threatening with trunk upraised, was through the palate into the brain. An alternative, when less instantaneous death was acceptable, was the point where the windpipe clears the ribcage. Later he developed what is still called the Bell Shot, from the three-quarters rear into the brain via the neck.

The lunatic Pyjale spears an elephant and makes trouble for everyone. Drawing by Bell

Bell held that the hunter charged by an elephant must not run or try to dodge but must keep firing well-placed shots. I never found my purely nostalgic .300 H&H unpleasant in recoil. Still, I was aware of a momentary loss of sight picture between shots, yet my 6.5x54 Mannlicher-Schoenauer left me as uninterrupted as a .22.

All his African hunting was done with iron sights, evolving to a bead and wide-V rear sight. He found conventional aperture sights too slow but was a late convert to a large-diameter ghost ring.

It is sometimes said that Bell did not recommend his weaponry or methods for the newcomer to Africa. I find no firm discouragement for the hunter prepared to learn, although he suggests mastering the heart shot before attempting the brain.

As to circumstances, his lines are easily read between. In theory, you could snipe an elephant in perfect safety from long range with something like a scoped .460 Weatherby if you fancied that kind of thing. In practice, it is far more often necessary to hunt in the forest, elephant grass or scrub, where this huge animal is a master of concealment. Bell describes being among elephants in dense cover, unaware of how many were at single-figure distances or what part of the elephant he saw. No newcomer should need a specific warning against that.

Not all mathematics is tedious. A 1% chance of death may be invigorating to the once-in-a-lifetime hunter. Doing it twice gives a 0.99^2, i.e., a 98.1% chance of survival. (That it is not 98% is due to the possibility of "game over" in the first attempt.) But take the same risk 1,011 times, and your 0.99^{1011} is a 0.0039% chance of coming out alive. Bell clearly worked out far better chances than 99%.

KARAMOJO BELL

With his hunting technique sorted out, Bell enjoyed Uganda and found an adequate ivory supply. Some say he had to turn in his ivory to the government — it was more probably the British East Africa Company — for an acceptable price. Still, it was probably resentment of restrictions that led him to obtain from a British Agent permission to enter the

The Bell Shot, through the neck and into the brain, was easy to misjudge. But taken at a fleeing elephant, it was unlikely to turn on the hunter. Drawing by Bell

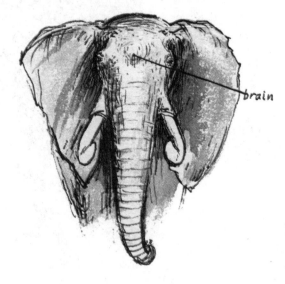

The location of the brain when viewed from the front.

unadministered territory of Karamojo, which became his nickname. I believe it was used in his absence rather than as a form of address. Like Machine Gun Kelly or Thugee Sleeman, who suppressed that murder cult in India, it is unlikely that people said, "Hey, Karamojo..."

In 1903, Karamoja was an almost excessively interesting place. The tribes, in a state of perpetual warfare, were far more primitive than the obsessively disciplined Zulu. Killing someone, almost anyone, conferred rights over the girls of the tribe, which brings savagery into disrepute. A male victim earned a tattoo on one's right side and a female on the left.

Bell found local traders obstructive regarding supplies, recruitment and livestock. But he typically concedes that although black life was considered cheap then, no attempt on his was made. The Swahili and Arab caravans hunted little ivory, obtaining it instead from natives whose snares and weighted-spear deadfalls often inflicted lingering death. What they traded for ivory and slaves was intervention in the incessant tribal wars. Many of the Swahili enforcers and bearers were slaves or in debt-peonage to people who knew where their families lived in Zanzibar.

Bell made friends with a remarkable man, Shundi, formerly a Kavirondo slave in Zanzibar, who had risen by force of character to eminence among the slavers, and faced up with better grace than most to the fact that the bad old days were passing. A slave of Shundi's acquired the heaviest tusk you will ever see, 226 pounds after loss by drying, now in London's Natural History Museum. Bell shot much lighter tusks of comparable outer dimensions, for the nerve cavity narrows and shortens after external growth slows.

The Karamoja detested the caravans and, by carefully planned treachery, occasionally wiped them out to the last man. Firearms were little feared, as you could throw yourself down on seeing the smoke and charge while the victim plied his ramrod. Stragglers became tattooing opportunities, written off as a business expense.

Bell gained some foothold in Karamoja and the adjacent Dabossa through what Jack London termed the great meat hunger. Then a stroke of inspiration arose from the Karamoja rarely sold female livestock, possibly to preserve the difference between cattle-rich magnates and the poorest hunters. Bell offered a heifer, the first step towards wealth, for information leading to ivory.

He found the Karamoja far friendlier

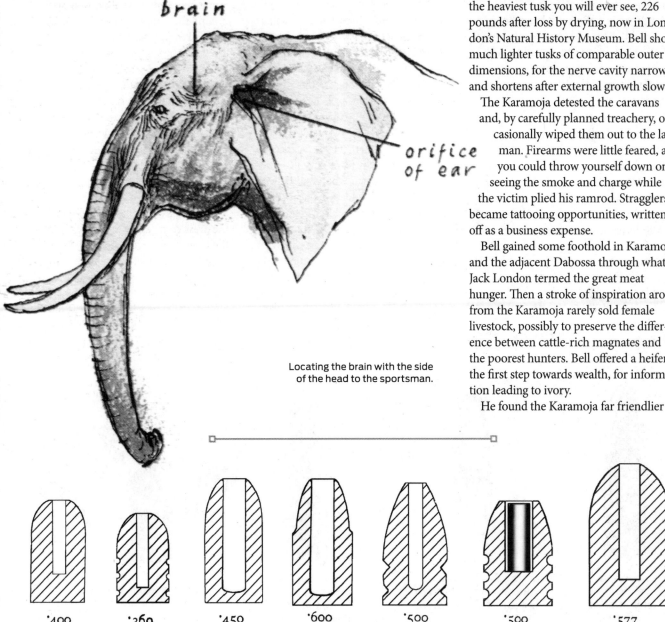

Locating the brain with the side of the head to the sportsman.

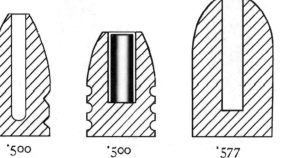

'400   '360   '450   '600   '500   '500   '577

Most early British blackpowder express rifles used hollow bullets. Solids in a well-chosen alloy are superior for almost any purpose, but not all rifles had rifling fast enough to stabilize them.

than anticipated but volatile. There was never much future in armed self-defense, but he found it best to carry matters with a high hand. One Karamoja began spearing the waterproof sheet used for watering Bell's animals, and Bell shattered the spear with a shot from his shoulder-stocked Mauser pistol.

Probably his greatest danger came when his headman remarked upon the absence of women in an ostensibly friendly crowd. Bell realized that each of his men was being "marked" by several spearmen, and the signal that doomed caravans was moments away.

Fortunately, a herd of zebra galloped past, and Bell killed a large number with his 10-shot Lee-Enfield, reloading with a charged magazine in case they realized that counting to 10 meant anything. Whether it was the meat, this new level of lethality, or his never turning firearms on humans, they became staunch friends.

Another Karamoja, Pyjale, became Bell's long-term tracker and friend. Although not as civilized as the average tribal African,

W.D.M. Bell's 1915 pilot's license.

Bell described him as not merely clever but of an intellectual, thoughtful, and modest countenance. However, Pyjale thought himself superior to Africans who wore clothes — any clothes — and slept on mattresses. Pyjale was tattooed, Bell was relieved to note, only on the right. Writing after his ivory-hunting days, Bell considered this a closer relationship than he had known with any other man.

Another Karamoja friend had a better claim to be a monster. A famous spear fighter and rich in cattle, he was ugly and tattooed everywhere, given to wild emotion. He insisted on blood-brotherhood, but even when Africa had only bacteria to worry about, Bell was relieved to persuade him that a handshake was more prestigious than eating meat smeared with one another's blood. They exchanged names, the African becoming Longelly-nyung, or "Red Man." He never accepted any reward for his influence, which was between friends. One hears of worse closer to home.

Bell allowed his boys to bring "wives," partly to facilitate his prohibition of dalliance with village women. Occasionally he saw single girls of rare grace and beauty. When he asked if no man want-

ed one, Pyjale, whose vocabulary possibly didn't run to "temporarily," explained that all men did, clarified in terms unsuitable for these pages.

Were there relationships? Bell doesn't tell us. None of the great explorers do, except Sir Samuel Baker, who contrived to rustle the future Lady Baker from a Turkish slave market. He had come without the necessary cash, which surely does him credit.

Bell never ceases speaking of his boys' fidelity, energy, and cheerfulness; being on Bell's safari was quite something. Some of his finest evenings were spent around the campfires as the chronicler chanted the day's addition to their story. They may be singing it yet.

AFTER KARAMOJA

After four Karamoja safaris, Bell hunted elsewhere with white companions. Despite his cricket-bat incident, we see none of the interpersonal conflicts Hollywood seems to require.

First, he took several of his best men by Thomas Cook steamer to Djibouti (excluding Pyjale, who couldn't have met the dress code) and across Abyssinia via the Gelo River to the Sudd marshes. The elephants were there, in a maze of minor waterways and overgrown islands, and if there remains a living fossil to match Shundi's, that may be the place. But with native canoes lashed together in threes, many supplies had to be abandoned, and

Section showing lead interior. 215 grs.

.303 Nickel Bullet after passing through 45 in. of solid wood.

Showing lead core and nickel-covered *base*. The Tweedie Patent. 215 grs.

Soft-nosed Tweedie Bullet after passing through wood 12 in. thick.

The round-nosed MkVI military .303 and a soft point of the period.

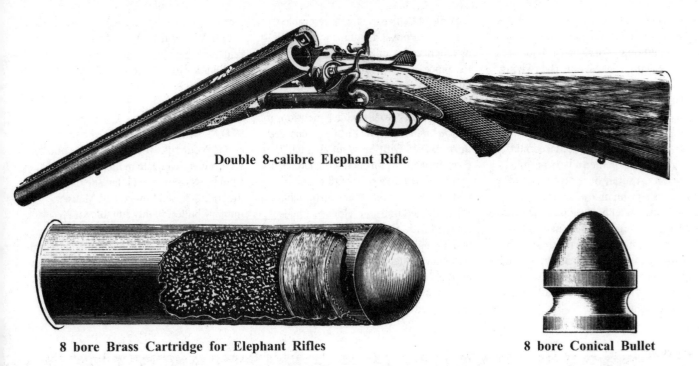

Double 8-calibre Elephant Rifle

8 bore Brass Cartridge for Elephant Rifles

8 bore Conical Bullet

The brass-cased 8 gauge, rifled or smooth, was a capable elephant gun in some circumstances when the hardest possible bullets were used. For carnivores, pure soft lead was far superior to hollowpoints.

Bell's final choice of an elephant rifle was the .318 Westley Richards. Even today, it would be hard to beat.

he could not bring out as much as he otherwise could.

Bell reappeared in a most unusual place. In exchange for a railway right-of-way, the Anglo-Egyptian Sudan leased the Lado Enclave to King Leopold of Belgium's curiously non-governmental colony, the Congo Free State. The lease, optimistically aimed at an organized handover, was for Leopold's lifetime plus six months. An international scandal over forced labor (really forced, by amputation) provoked a Belgian governmental takeover just before Leopold's death, and perhaps damnation, in 1908. There was an interval when the Lado, with vast elephant herds, had no government.

Then followed an influx of fortune-hunters, often new to hunting and the rifle, and widespread mistreatment of the natives. Bell at least started with a license from the Belgian *chef de poste*, whom he considered a wonderful gentleman. For its brief duration, this was probably Bell's most productive period.

After an unsuccessful diversion into whaling (what else?), Bell proceeded to Liberia. This was unsatisfactory from the ivory point of view, as most of the elephants were the diminutive forest specie, but the episode demonstrates one of Bell's endearing characteristics.

There is a long British tradition of affinity with the most frightful brown Vikings. It is strongest with the Scots, although I can't imagine why. Bell was ex-

ceptional in liking the formally dressed, part-way civilized Africans of the coasts, whom many explorers despised. He met American ex-slaves who were agreeable and helpful and seemed to have approved of the firm, but not oppressive, straightening out of white men who would trade upon racial superiority. The Liberians themselves kept slaves from the interior. But so low was their fertility (from alcoholism Bell says) that they bought and adopted indigenous children and treated them with great kindness. Evening parties began with utmost decorum, although "things indescribable happened." Having described alcoholism with the Belgians, I suppose Bell meant something else.

A long safari followed on the French Equatorial African rivers using a 35-foot steam launch, shipped out from the Clyde in pieces. No mere "African Queen," she had a modern triple-expansion engine and struck Bell as the ideal way to travel.

THE GREAT WAR

Bell enlisted in the Royal Flying Corps, training on the Maurice Farman Longhorn, which, while somewhat advanced upon the Wrights' Flyer, didn't look it. He made one forced landing on the sewage farm adjoining Brooklands Aerodrome, which, although not as bad as it looks in *Those Magnificent Men in Their Flying Machines*, was pretty bad.

His first active duty was reconnaissance in Tanganyika, using only marginally more advanced aircraft. He was transferred to Salonika in Macedonia, where my grandfather, a horse-artillery driver, must surely have seen him. On one occasion, an unknown fast fighter put several bullet holes in his machine. He and a comrade shot it down before identifying the solitary French SPAD in the theater, sent to eliminate an untouchable German reconnaissance aircraft. Fortunately, the pilot was unhurt, except for paroxysms of fury.

Some of Bell's early flying resembled the movie aforesaid, but his war ended as a flight commander in Bristol Fighters in France, which was the major league. He was not among the great aces of the war but earned his keep, receiving the Military Cross twice and five mentions in dispatches. He was medically discharged in April 1918 with "nervous asthma," a proper diagnosis for men who had used themselves up in a service that always had higher mortality than the trenches.

Bell denied one marvelous feat he is credited with: shooting down an aircraft with a single shot before his gun jammed. He believed that the German, in an obsolete aircraft, seized upon the excuse to do a forced landing where his aircraft was immediately pasted by French artil-

lery to obtain a replacement better for his health. Why is this important? If Bell was reluctant to let his military superiors gild his lilies for him, it adds credibility to his accounts of African adventures.

BELL'S RIFLES

W.D.M. Bell surely believed that to choose your rifle, you should first choose your bullet. Even late in life, aware of solid brass or bronze bullets, he thought the round-nosed Enfield and Mauser military bullets highly suitable for elephants.

These were considered a humanitarian measure in war after the terrible shattering of heavy lead bullets like the Martini-Henry's. Penetrating a great distance in flesh and bone, the "new bullets" usually

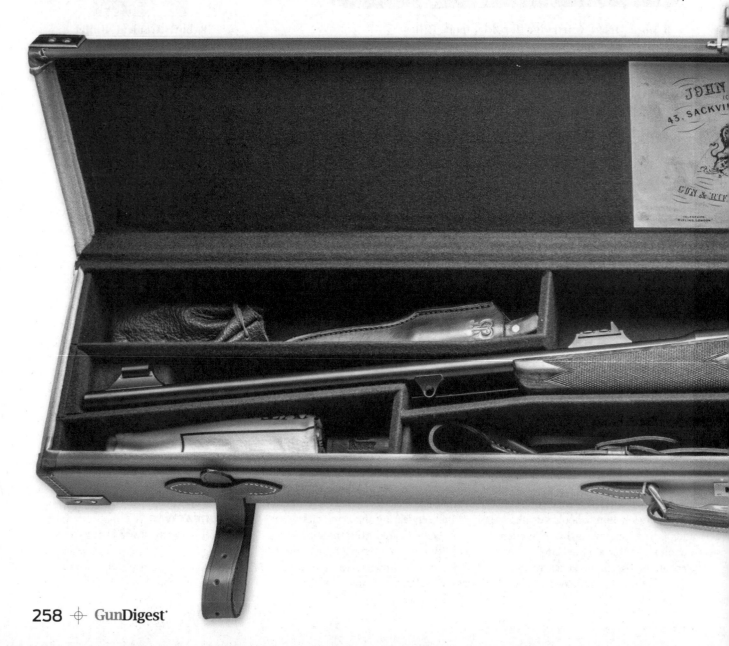

exited cleanly. On the relatively sterile South African veld, it was not uncommon for bandaged wounds to heal on the march, as long as the horse did the marching.

That changed abruptly early in the century, as nations adopted lighter pointed bullets for better velocity retention. Rearward weight distribution usually causes tumbling on impact, unpredictable paths and break-up. The British MkVII, with an aluminum or wood-pulp nose filler, was particularly unstable. A retrograde step for the injured in war, they also threatened disaster on dangerous game. Some ex-servicemen resettled in Africa and died using a good rifle with which they were familiar.

Ironically, Bell's Martini-Metford could have suited his elephant-hunting style. These were simply .577/.450 actions re-barreled for sportsmen or colonial troops with Metford and later Enfield barrels made for the Lee bolt action. While several factors can impede extraction, the earliest .303 Martinis kept the .577/.450 breechblock, the face of which sometimes became slightly concave. Heat increases the pressure generated by cordite, explaining Bell's trouble-free extraction in the night's cool or Fraser's range.

Bell's Winchester Single Shot was probably a .45-70 or .45-90 and unlikely, at that time, to use smokeless loads. The heavier .45-70 bullets should have dealt with the lions. But Bell had only hollowpoint bullets, which like the almost thimble-shaped British express bullets around the time of his birth, inflict ugly but not incapacitating injuries.

Bell's Farquharson would have been an excellent rifle. But if we believe the introduction dates, it used the .360 2-1/4 in. Express, which by that time probably had its smokeless loading. Most modern shooters consider it a suitable deer cartridge, marginal for moose. His 160 rounds probably remain the first and last seen on the Yukon, suggesting that commercial meat hunting was unplanned.

His sporting Lee-Enfields, among the most unjammable rifles, served him well. But his Rigby sporting Mausers probably killed more elephants than all others put together. The .275 Rigby is Rigby's name for the 7x57 Mauser.

Bell is forever associated with the

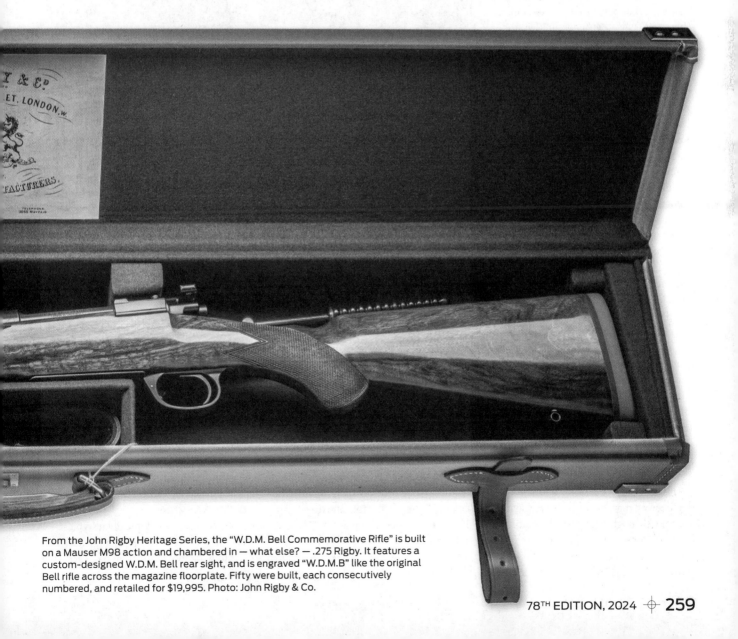

From the John Rigby Heritage Series, the "W.D.M. Bell Commemorative Rifle" is built on a Mauser M98 action and chambered in — what else? — .275 Rigby. It features a custom-designed W.D.M. Bell rear sight, and is engraved "W.D.M.B" like the original Bell rifle across the magazine floorplate. Fifty were built, each consecutively numbered, and retailed for $19,995. Photo: John Rigby & Co.

6.5x54 rotary magazine Mannlicher-Schoenauer, but it accounted for relatively few elephants, mainly because of an unreliable batch of Austrian cartridges. No other rifle evoked quite his delight at "the oily little rascal" delivered to him in the bush. Being carbine length, he got the weight down to 5-1/2 pounds by trimming the woodwork, admirably suited to pursuing a moving herd.

He also had a similar Mannlicher box magazine long rifle chambered for the rimmed 6.5x53R cartridge. He used this exclusively for camp meat, having only soft-point cartridges. Otherwise, I see no reason it would have performed worse on elephants than the Mannlicher-Schoenauer.

Another meat rifle was the .22 Savage Hi-Power lever action with a rotary magazine that permitted pointed bullets. These bullets were heavier at 70 grains and more heavily jacketed than most .22 centerfires today, making them suitable for medium-sized deer.

This brings us to one of Bell's most surprising verdicts on game. In striking contrast to so many highly regarded authorities, he denies that the African buffalo is a particularly dangerous or aggressive adversary. He allows that it can nurse its wounds, imperceptible in surprisingly slight cover by the trail. But he seems skeptical of its laying a deliberate ambush with payback in mind. He once witnessed something like the U.S. buffalo stand when another hunter wanted to steer some recently reformed cannibals from backsliding during a famine. The result was that 23 buffalo died unresentfully to 27 chest shots from the little Savage. Another time Bell saw Karamoja warriors charge a herd with spears and kill a large number with no apparent signs of the buffalo's ferocity. This is probably Bell at his least convincing on animal behavior, and yet how many naysayers have killed six or seven hundred buffalo? I would stake something less than my life on all being possible in the right circumstances.

The C96 Mauser pistol is another engineering marvel, far better at staying accurate through a long life than a tilting-barrel automatic. But its impressive energy figures far exceed the stopping power of its tiny 7.63mm bullet. I suspect

The chest skin of a deer caught this 6.5x54 soft-point bullet after passing through its entire body length. That shot could not have been taken with the .220 Swift.

Matching bullet shape to the chamber throat is not always critical. This caliper is set to a land diameter of .256 inch.

that some of the dervishes Winston Churchill killed in his cavalry charge unkilled themselves later. Bell's C96 used Mauser's very superior 9mm export cartridge. Like Churchill, he bought a 1911. That was in 1913.

His final choice of elephant rifle was the .318 Westley Richards, firing a 250-grain .330"-diameter bullet. A few unexplained "misses" with the 7x57 promptly disappeared, suggesting undiagnosed bullet failures.

He wished it had a higher powder capacity but makes no mention of the Holland & Holland Magnums, possibly from his belief that length risked short-stroking the bolt under stress. The modern short magnums might have appealed.

In late life, Bell's thinking took a different turn. For the Scottish red deer, he favored "The Neck Shot," the title of his 1950 *American Rifleman* article. Acceptable with the Savage, he was a convert to his .220 Swift Winchester 54. Any hit in the neck, even without touching verte-

brae or arteries, became instantly lethal. It is a handy shot for deer that may be couched in heather or approached on a rounded hilltop.

To Tanganyika with the RFC, Bell took what he or his posthumous editors term a semi-automatic Farquharson, obtained from the inventor, but was surely a Farquhar-Hill. Armies had long known that the semi-automatic rifle would be the ordinary soldier's weapon when compact and reliable enough for service. The Farquhar-Hill had recently been adapted from long-recoil to gas operation, with drum magazines up to 65 rounds, and the aviator did not have to keep it mud-free or carry it about. Bell undoubtedly anticipated aerial combat, but no enemy aircraft in Africa existed.

OUT OF AFRICA

In 1919 came Bell's typically untypical marriage to Kate Soares, of a formerly Hindu Goanese family that had successfully gone native in Britain. The Bells

The Mannlicher-Schoenauer action combined the finest magazine on any sporting rifle with the most humdrum bolt, inherited from the German Commission 1888. Late in life, Bell preferred the faster striker fall of his Winchester 54.

The Mannlicher-Schoenauer rotary magazine is dismantled in seconds with no tool but a bullet point. With investment casting available, why aren't they all like that?

bought a Highland estate, Corriemoillie, in Ross-shire. Local gossip says he shot more red deer than the estate could support. There are ways of achieving such things.

Kate never became an intrepid and trousered huntress like Lady Baker, nor accompanied Bell on safari. But she shared his ambition to own a large ocean racing yacht. We may save hunting biography space on the story of *Trenchemer*, or Cut-the-Sea, with as much anarchic brilliance as anything Bell did. He also hung a painting in the Royal Academy, an honor plutocracy or pedigree cannot buy. It was sold for 50 guineas, a sum he chose while fearing ridicule.

Bell lived quietly at Corriemoillie through World War II, serving in the Home Guard. A figure of comedy nowadays, the War to End All Wars, more recent than Desert Storm, meant that more units than Ross-shire included old men you do not want hunting you.

Bell died childless in 1954, Kate in 1957, and Pyjale in Africa in 1956. Bell ranks high in select company: those who cannot bear to lead ordinary lives. GD

The .318 Westley Richards has a 250-grain bullet of high Sectional Density, capable of great penetration. *Photo: Massaro Media Group*

Tony Galazan and C.S.M.C.

Connecticut Shotgun Manufacturing Company — a gun company like no other.

›TERRY WIELAND

T en years ago, in the spring of 2013, I paid a visit to Tony Galazan's shotgun-making operation in New Britain, Connecticut. On one side of the long, low industrial building, there was a door, and beside the door was parked a van, and around the van was painted a rectangle on the asphalt.

This was a reserved spot, and only that van — the "gun van" — was allowed to occupy it. Inside the door was a rack holding a dozen guns, fresh from the factory and ready for testing. Each afternoon, Tony would pack the guns from that rack in the van and drive off alone to his private shooting range in the country.

The C.S.M.C. Revelation 20-gauge over/under was given a *Gray's* Best Award in 2019. The gun combines elegant good looks with smooth handling and silky operation at a remarkably low price.

The A-10 American is available as a fully outfitted trap or sporting gun, with adjustable stock and buttplate, high rib, interchangeable chokes, and so on. Tony Galazan still test fires all of C.S.M.C.'s high-grade guns.

While I was visiting, I joined Tony on these daily excursions. As well as the guns, the van contained carton after carton of shotshells. When we reached the farm, we would each take a gun and a couple of boxes of shells, pick out a clay thrower and shoot. And shoot. And shoot. We weren't concerned about hit-ting the clays. What we were testing was the operation of each gun. How the top lever worked: Did it open readily? Did it open *too* readily? Were the barrels too stiff? Were the trigger pulls right? Were they crisp? Did the barrel selector work properly, whether top-bottom or bottom-top and did the ejectors work correctly every time and deposit the empties side by side in the grass?

Detailed notes were kept on each gun, attached to the triggerguards. When we got back, the guns went onto an "In" rack and, from there, back into the finishing shop to have every minor problem corrected. And after that? They

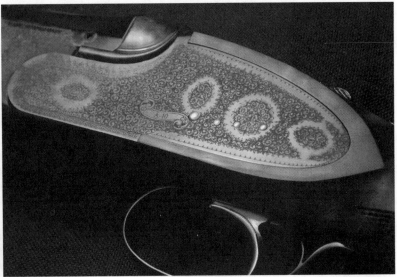

The C.S.M.C. A-10 American received a *Gray's* Best Award in 2012. It is a genuine detachable sidelock over/under, with rose-and-scroll engraving reminiscent of the Boss.

returned to the "Out" rack for another trip to the farm to be put through their paces again. Until a gun passed through Tony's expert hands without displaying the slightest problem, it would not be shipped to the customer.

A year later, I was in England, visiting Holland & Holland's range at Northwood, outside London, when the managing director, Daryl Greatrex, arrived with a Range Rover and a half-dozen finished guns from the factory on Harrow Road. He invited me to join him as he put each gun through the grueling procedure. There were side-by-sides and over/unders, and we forewent the

formality of a clay thrower, just standing there in the early-morning October chill, shooting into the air, noting the top-lever operation, opening and closing, trigger pulls, ejector timing. Each H&H gun, as I recall, was required to fire 250 rounds without a hitch before it was sent home to its new owner, and Daryl, the head of the whole operation, insisted on testing each one himself.

Not every gun maker performs this tedious and time-consuming operation, nor even every high-quality gun maker. But every one of them *should* do it. It separates the Purdeys, the Holland & Hollands, and the Tony Galazans from all the rest.

***

Almost exactly twenty years earlier, in 1993, I'd become the shooting editor of *Gray's Sporting Journal*. At the behest of my friend Michael McIntosh, one of my first ventures was a trip to Connecticut to visit Tony Galazan. I'd met him at a Safari Club convention a year or two earlier, introduced by Robert M. Lee, one of America's two or three wealthiest and most discriminating gun collectors and buyers of the finest guns. I mention all this not to drop names but to illustrate the circles in which Tony Galazan was moving, even as early as the 1990s.

Galazan now owns Auguste Francotte, one of the great names in Belgian fine gun making. The Francotte guns are manufactured, in all their European finery, in New Britain, and the workmanship is equal to the originals in every way, from fit and finish to extraordinary engraving. Francotte guns are, of course, a purely custom proposition.

When I arrived in Connecticut in 1994, I found a somewhat dilapidated former garage surrounded by a chain link fence in a not particularly good part of town. This, however, belied what I found inside: Like all good gun shops, it was redolent of gun oil, and guns and gun parts were everywhere. In one separate room was a long bench in the European fashion with a half-dozen Austrian gun makers hard at work producing the A.H. Fox guns — the undertaking that brought Tony to the attention of the gun world.

The brief fashion for reproduction guns began in the 1980s with the famous but short-lived Parker Reproduction. Tony Galazan, one of those peculiar mechanical genii fascinated by anything that

"The Galazan" is immediately identifiable by its extended forend iron. It is Tony's top-of-the-line and exudes quality from its flat-topped English checkering to its French-fitted case. From the beginning, Galazan has assembled all the old hand skills, from checkering to action-filing to engraving, in his shop in New Britain. Naturally, he can also supply the accouterments required of a fine cased gun. No company comparable to C.S.M.C. has ever existed in the U.S.

whirrs and clinks and hums, got his start in the gun business trading vintage Parkers, which led him into serious gun making. Exactly where the idea originated of making the A.H. Fox, the gun that McIntosh himself believed was the best shotgun ever made in America, is not clear. However, by a lucky coincidence, Michael was in the process of writing a book about the Fox. It was published in 1992, sold out almost immediately, and was revised and expanded — with a chapter devoted to Tony Galazan and the new Fox — and published in 1994.

Because he made a deal with Savage, owner of the Fox name, to make the guns, they are technically not reproductions but renewed production by a different company, just as had happened several times with the original Foxes over the course of half a century. In the 1990s, there were a few genuinely influential shotgun writers in America, and Michael McIntosh was one of them. (By a rather disturbing coincidence, I was on my way to visit Galazan at his new, vastly expanded factory in 2010 when I heard about Michael's death.) At any rate, McIntosh helped Galazan in many ways and undoubtedly sold a lot of the new 20-gauge Foxes, which began, as I recall, at about $5,000. That was big money in 1994 for a shotgun. At least, it looked big to me.

As Michael recounted it, every part of the new Fox was made in the United States of America. For those who insisted, it imported Krupp barrel billets from Germany (as had the original Fox) but

C.S.M.C. has pioneered the application of some seriously untraditional finishes for seriously untraditional clients. This Galazan combines killer whales, porpoises, sharks, and ducks, all done in enamel with exquisite gold inlay and a gold-inlaid seahorse. You will not see a gun like this just anywhere, but Galazan is ready to try many different things. The company has even applied portraits of clients' dogs in enamel.

finished them here; the Turkish walnut was, of course, imported, but Tony's craftsmen shaped the blanks into exquisite custom stocks. Otherwise, everything was made in Tony's factory, down to and including screws and springs.

As it turned out, for the Connecticut Shotgun Manufacturing Company (C.S.M.C.), the A.H. Fox was just the beginning.

To Tony Galazan, making the guns was only part of the fascination. He made a mission of supplying all the hard-to-find items required by serious gun lovers, including English cleaning rods, leather trunk-style cases, and even reproduction trade labels to put in the cases to identify that lovely old Lancaster or Woodward. And the tools: Properly sized sets of London turnscrews, stuck-case extractors, and chamber brushes. This sideline — recognizable to any marketer as a shrewd promotional move — grew into a substantial part of his business. He became the guy you called when you needed some arcane item from the dim, distant past, and Tony would either find it for you or make you one. And if he made one for you, he'd keep on making them for others.

By the time I made my fourth visit in 2013, the company had grown to be one of the largest niche gun makers in the country. It dwelt in a new factory building replete with the latest CNC and laser machinery, occupied several acres of land in New Britain, and employed close to a hundred people.

To say that C.S.M.C. is unlike any other gun company somewhat understates the case: Galazan has managed to combine in just one company many of the features and attitudes found in a combination of companies — manufacturers, retailers, and custom gunsmiths.

Connecticut Shotgun has no dealers: It sells directly to the customer, whether a high-priced custom-made gun or a lower-priced off-the-rack one. Since trades are a big part of the retail gun business, the company takes in trades and sells them through its used-gun showroom. And what a showroom it is! Outfitted like a cross between a private club and the gun room on a wealthy estate, an aficionado can lurk there for

The used-gun showroom at the C.S.M.C. facility in New Britain is as traditional and comfortable as anyone could wish, evoking thoughts of oiled wood paneling, leather chairs, and fine cigars. It all goes well with the Purdeys and Bosses that the company takes in trade and sells to other clients. Tony Galazan has successfully combined manufacturing with direct sales to clients and trading in high-quality guns, all in one company.

hours, handling Purdeys and Woodwards, Krieghoffs and Fabbris. While I was there once, a walk-in client casually dropped over two hundred grand on a Boss O/U .410.

Since it began making the Fox, C.S.M.C. has established itself as the premier maker of high-quality shotguns in America. One result has been acquiring the rights to manufacture other big names from the old days, including the Parker and the Winchester Model 21. After Parker Reproductions died in the 1980s, the banner was taken up by Remington (owner of the Parker name) and Winchester. Still, amid the corporate turmoil, both ended up contracting the manufacturing to Galazan. The Winchester 21 is a bit different in that the Olin group still owns the name (as I understand it). So, in effect, Galazan is the 21's factory production.

As of its latest catalog, C.S.M.C. is also making the L.C. Smith and the Lefever, two more respected names in American gun making. Naturally, C.S.M.C. is also the source for parts for all of these — you should see the parts department — as well as "factory" repairs.

Another big name, now owned outright by C.S.M.C., is August Francotte of Belgium. Tony acquired it some years ago, so if you want a genuine European sidelock game gun wholly manufactured in the United States, you can order a Francotte from New Britain, Connecticut.

But Tony Galazan was never content to produce existing designs. Today's most significant part of his business is making his own guns, of his own design, bearing the C.S.M.C. name. These include over/unders and side-by-sides, boxlocks and sidelocks, ranging in price from a few thousand dollars to upwards of $100,000, depending on the model and the (sometimes extravagant) custom features. Among the models introduced in the past twenty years is the RBL boxlock side-by-side, the A-10 American sidelock over/under, and various models of boxlock over/under. Being primarily a custom shop, especially regarding higher-grade guns, almost anything is possible.

To take the A-10 American as an example — and Tony considers the A-10 his greatest accomplishment — it's available in a game gun configuration or as a no-holds-barred trap or sporting arm. As a genuine sidelock over/under, it's uniquely American, but, for that matter, there are not many O/U sidelocks made anywhere else. Purdey is producing the Woodward again, Holland & Holland has its Royal, Beretta the SO series, and the Boss — the original, dating from 1909.

The Boss, designed by John Robertson, has set the standard for style in over/unders from the beginning, and Tony adapted some of those features in the model he calls simply "The Galazan." This is immediately identifiable by the extended forend iron — a complex feature to make, but one that breaks up the boxy, up-and-down lines of an over/under and gives it a grace all its own. Prices for the "Galazan" start around $75,000 — these all have to be general estimates — and climb into the hundred-thousand range, putting them in the same stratospheric region as the Purdey and Fabbri.

At the same time, Galazan has not neglected those who hunger for a fine gun but can't afford the very finest. His

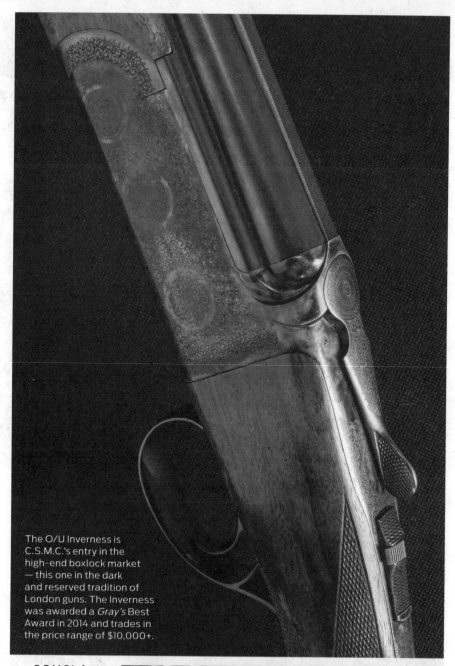

The O/U Inverness is C.S.M.C.'s entry in the high-end boxlock market — this one in the dark and reserved tradition of London guns. The Inverness was awarded a *Gray's* Best Award in 2014 and trades in the price range of $10,000+.

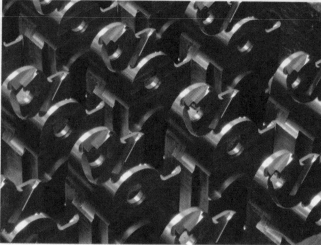

C.S.M.C.'s factory is outfitted with modern CNC machinery that allows the company to produce action frames in various sizes and configurations in economical quantities. They are close to allowable tolerances, leaving a minimum of metal to be removed by the makers who fit them, as they should be, by hand.

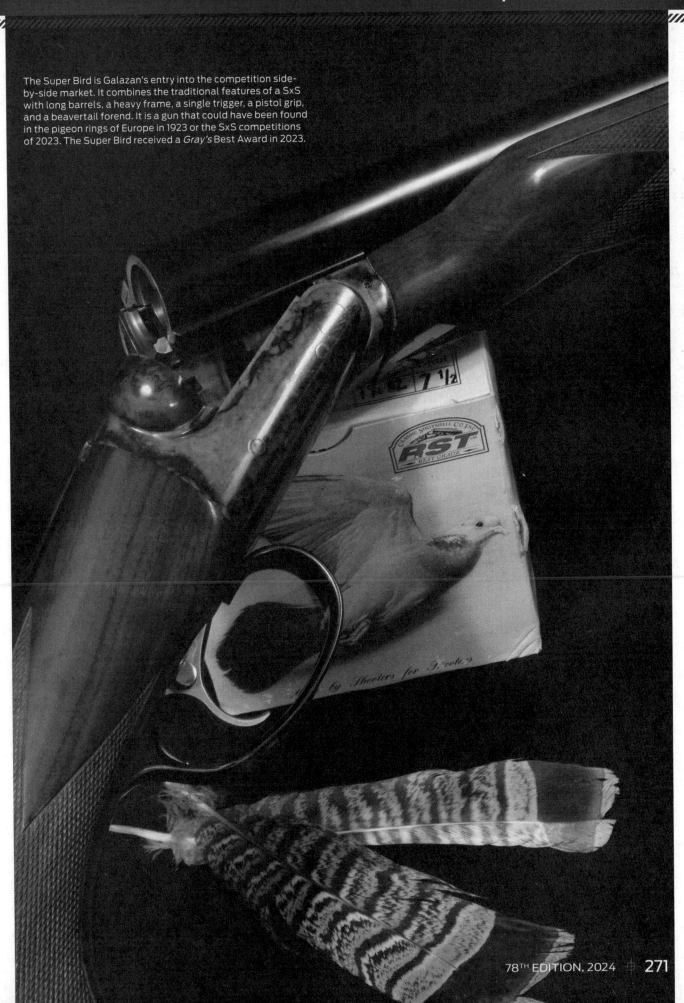

The Super Bird is Galazan's entry into the competition side-by-side market. It combines the traditional features of a SxS with long barrels, a heavy frame, a single trigger, a pistol grip, and a beavertail forend. It is a gun that could have been found in the pigeon rings of Europe in 1923 or the SxS competitions of 2023. The Super Bird received a *Gray's* Best Award in 2023.

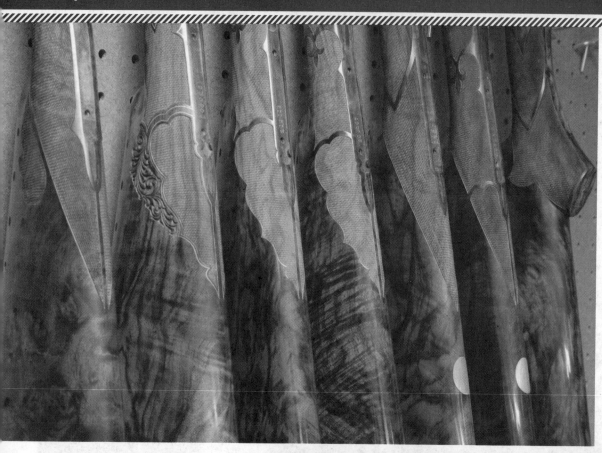

In terms of walnut quality and level of workmanship, the stocking shop would fit right in, in London, in 1935 — or 1895, for that matter. Some things cannot be left to machines.

Revelation, introduced in 2018, starts at around $3,000 and is a bargain at that price by any standard.

As a significant player in the trap and sporting game, C.S.M.C., like the other big names, attends major shoots like the Grand American and does so with a fully equipped bus to fill every need of a competitor on the line shooting a Tony Galazan gun. Big-name country singers tour the land in buses that are not as flashy as Tony's, which even sports a clay-throwing facility on its roof.

Lest you think Connecticut Shotgun caters only to the monied classes, there is a subsidiary company called Standard Manufacturing, and its line of products is, in many ways, the polar opposite of its parent. It produces such oddball black gun designs as a tactical double-barreled pump gun, complete with door-breaching extensions on the muzzles, and a .22 LR with a 50-round drum magazine for anyone who just likes the look of a Tommy gun.

Standard's latest creation, out of the ordinary for the company, is a reproduction of the Colt Woodsman .22 semi-auto, which it calls the SG22. This rimfire is not a black gun; it comes in either

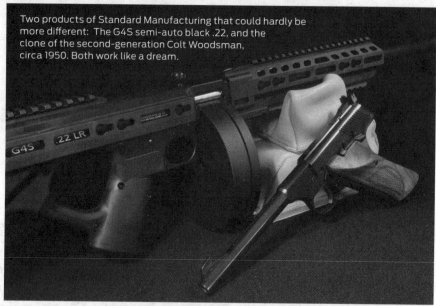

Two products of Standard Manufacturing that could hardly be more different: The G4S semi-auto black .22, and the clone of the second-generation Colt Woodsman, circa 1950. Both work like a dream.

From C.S.M.C.'s sister company, Standard Manufacturing, the G4S .22 is a semi-auto with all the cachet of a Tommy gun without the paperwork. The drum magazine holds 50 rounds.

polished blue or case-colored, plain or engraved, with walnut grips. It's a clone of the second-generation Woodsman, circa 1950, and is so exact that its magazines are interchangeable with the original. An added touch for the aficionado: Its magazine is the highly collectible "tombstone" that came only with the elite Match Target. It's the little things.

***

Over the past 30 years, C.S.M.C. has grown, as has its line of guns, to the point where it is hopeless to try to summarize everything in one article — much like

trying to tell the whole story of Colt or Winchester. The remarkable thing about the company is not just the fact that it produces extraordinary guns but how it does it. A few years ago, in conversation with a gun maker from Europe, I mentioned Tony's myriad processes — traditional and radical — and he told me that some of the best European gun makers are sending their employees over to spend time at the C.S.M.C. factory to study Tony's methods and learn how it's done.

More recently, an acquaintance who used to work for Beretta told me about wandering the aisles at a show with one of the Beretta family. They stopped and chatted with Tony Galazan for a while, admired some of his guns, and as they moved away, Signore Beretta said, "He's the real deal."

In the world of gun making, one cannot find praise much higher than that. **GD**

The SG22 is Standard Manufacturing's clone of the second-generation Colt Woodsman circa 1950.

A Dakota Traveler in .300 H&H, reworked into a truly deluxe rifle by C.S.M.C.'s craftsmen. The retail price is around $32,000, so it's not for everyone. But anyone can admire it.

MAKE ~THE~ SHOT!

Buffalo Bill's Wild West Show appeared all over the United States and throughout Europe.

Ad and Plinky Toepperwein shot demonstrations together for decades. Photo: Winchester

A History of Exhibition Shooting, Then and Now

❯ W. F. "BILL" VANDERPOOL

The shooter nodded, and the teenage boy threw the final 2 1/2-inch glass ball into the air. It ended six days of shooting, and 'Doc' W. F. Carver shattered it. Shooting ten or more hours a day, Doc hit 59,340 of 60,000 targets thrown. He did it with a .22 rifle.

In the last quarter of the 19th century and well into the 20th, exhibition shooters were the country's rock stars. Dr. A. H. Ruth, A. H. Bogardus, Frank Butler and his wife, Phoebe Mosey — later known as Annie Oakley — and many others traveled the country and the world, thrilling crowds, breaking records and later representing firearms and ammunition companies.

Captain Adam H. Bogardus was one of the earliest exhibition shooters. He started as a market hunter in the late 1860s in his home state of Illinois, then started giving shows. In 1869, it was said that he shot 500 live pigeons in 528 minutes with a muzzle-loader he loaded himself! But shooting live pigeons attracted bad press, so he invented and patented a hollow glass ball and a spring-loaded trap to throw them.

Some of these balls had feathers inside and were tinted to be seen against the sky. In 1877, just before retiring, he put on one more shoot, attempting to hit 5,000 glass balls in 500 minutes. He used a double-barreled shotgun with an extra set of barrels and switched sets every 50 rounds. The extra barrel set was cooled in buckets of water. By the 4,700th round, he had to sit in a chair to shoot. He fired his last shot (5,156) at 480 minutes.

While she started assisting her husband, Frank Butler, with his act, Annie Oakley soon became the star attraction.

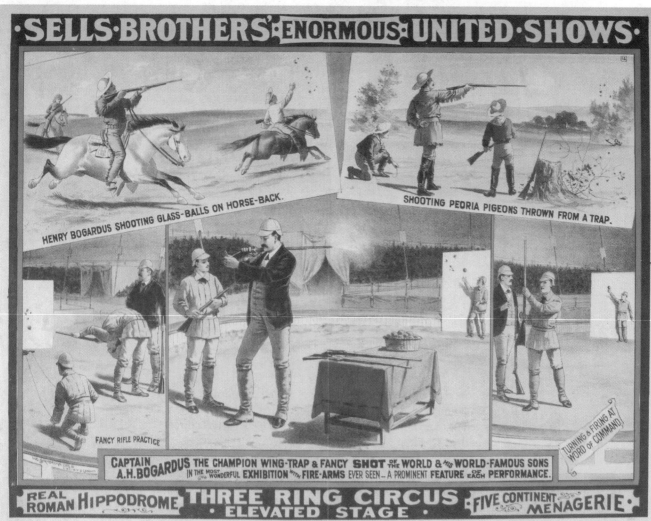

Captain A. H. Bogardus was one of the earliest professional exhibition shooters.

William Cody was a master of showmanship, giving audiences a glimpse of what they believed was the "Real West."

BURKE-KORETKE
PHOTO CHICAGO

A former dentist, William F. 'Doc' Carver learned to shoot "out West" and turned his skills into a living. He was about 17 years younger than Bogardus, and after gaining a reputation, he toured his show around Europe. Returning in 1878, he published an autobiography entitled *Life of Dr. Wm. F. Carver of California; Champion Rifle Shot of the World.* It was a heavily fictionalized version of his life. Doc had been challenging Bogardus to competitions, and, finally, in 1883, the Captain agreed, and they met for a live pigeon match in Louisville, Kentucky. More than a thousand spectators watched Carver beat Bogardus by one bird. Subsequently, they met for several shoots, both live and clay pigeon, where

Carver won 19 out of 25 matches.

In 1883, Carver joined "Buffalo Bill" Cody in a Wild West show, but the partnership lasted only about a year. He performed in 1885 to shoot 60,000 flying targets in six days. In four days, he fired at 64,881 targets, hitting 60,016. Carver finished his career with a "diving horse" show, traveling nationwide. He died in 1927.

In 1875, Frank Butler was already a well-known marksman and "trick" shooter when he appeared in Cincinnati, Ohio, to put on a shooting demonstration. A match was proposed, with the town putting up its best shot. A local newspaper sponsored the $100 prize. But Frank would soon be beaten by a five-foot-tall, 15-year-old girl named Phoebe Ann Mosey. A year later, they married and started a more than 50-year partnership. Frank continued putting on shows with a male partner until the man became ill, and Frank used Phoebe, now called Annie Oakley, to hold or throw the targets. Then, she started shooting on a dare, and they became a team. As Annie's skill became apparent, she became the star, and Frank became her manager. They joined Buffalo Bill Cody's Wild West Show in 1885, touring in the U.S. and Europe, where she performed before royalty, including Queen Victoria.

William Cody, an excellent shot, would hit thrown glass targets with one of his Winchester 1873 rifles in .44-40 caliber. That he used shot loads was due less to questions of marksmanship and more about the safety of the audience and the roofs of such venues as Madison Square Garden. Cody's genius combined marksmanship with showmanship, adding runaway stagecoaches, "wild" Indians, and bronco busters for crowds worldwide who longed to glimpse the "real" West.

The Encyclopedia Britannica described one of Annie Oakley's shows. "Oakley never failed to delight her audiences, and her feats of marksmanship were truly incredible. At 30 paces, she could split a playing card held edgewise; she hit dimes tossed in the air, she shot cigarettes from her husband's lips, and, a playing card being thrown in the air, she riddled it before it touched the ground." They left Cody's show in 1901, shot with other

In 1907, Ad Toepperwein fired Winchester Model 03 rifles to shoot 72,500 targets with *nine misses*. He fired at the 2 1/4-inch wood blocks for ten days.

Plinky Toepperwein continued shooting into her 60s.

Ed McGivern is shown hitting a thrown target in one of his countless demonstrations. He got much pleasure from teaching law enforcement officers.

groups, and then fully retired. However, in 1922, she hit 100 clay targets in a row at 16 yards at age 62. Annie Oakley died on November 3, 1926. Frank Butler died 18 days later.

Exhibition shooting continued into the 1900s, and perhaps the most popular couple then was the Toepperweins, Ad and "Plinky," who wound up representing Winchester in their wonderful shoots around the country. Ad started his shooting shows in a traveling circus and on the vaudeville circuit. In 1901, he was hired by Winchester to promote its products.

Dot and Ernie Lind represented Western Ammo in their entertaining shoots.

During a 1902 visit to the factory, he met his future wife and shooting partner, Elizabeth, known the balance of her life as "Plinky." The pair shot together, and although Plinky had never fired a gun before their marriage, it was later debated who was the better shot. Ad shot for Winchester at the 1904 World's Fair in St. Louis, hitting 3,507 straight 2 1/4-inch targets. In 1907 in San Antonio, he used Winchester Model 03 .22 rimfire rifles to shoot at 72,500 targets with nine misses! The targets were 2 1/4-inch wood blocks, which took him ten days of shooting.

Ad and Plinky continued their shows for years. They used handguns, rifles, and shotguns on various targets, including Plinky shooting sticks of chalk that Ad held between his fingers and a cigarette between his lips. Ad was famous for drawing pictures on metal sheets with bullet holes, and some of his examples have been sold for thousands of dollars today. A video of a 1941 show is still available. He died in 1962 at age 93.

Winchester's next exhibition shooter was Herb Parsons. While in high school, Herb watched a shoot by Ad Toepperwein and was hooked. Already an accomplished shot, he later became a salesman for Winchester, and when Ad wanted to retire, Herb took his place. Herb Parsons' show was a constant stream of difficult shots and amusing banter that enthralled the crowds. He shot rimfire and centerfire rifles and shotguns and was well known for making a salad the hard way, with rifles and shotguns blowing lettuce and other vegetables into shreds. Herb Parsons passed

Ernie Lind demonstrates his speed shot with his favorite .35l Winchester.

away from complications of surgery at age 51. Some of his shots, and his banter, have never been duplicated.

In the 1930s, Ed McGivern was considered the best handgun shot living. His exploits in shooting the Smith & Wesson and the single-action Colt revolver with speed and accuracy were legendary. He could hit a playing card with six shots in less than one second, and routinely nailed aerial targets, often in some rather awkward positions. Ed donated a lot of time training law enforcement officers in his home state of Montana and elsewhere. His book, *Fast and Fancy Revolver Shooting* is a classic, and reprints are still available.

Contemporaries of Herb Parsons and Ed McGivern included Ernie and Dot

The author, right, first met Bill Jordan at a police match in Florida. They would later become good friends.

Jerry Miculek, with his wife Kay and daughter Lena, are carrying on the tradition of exhibition shooting while winning countless firearms competitions. They all hold numerous records. Their videos are both entertaining and instructive.

Lind (Western), Billy Hill (Remington), and Dave Flanningan (Peters). And later, Remington set up a stable of shooters traveling the country. (In 1971, Ernie Lind wrote *The Complete Book of Trick & Fancy Shooting*, still available today.)

These old timers were soon followed by Bill Jordan, a tall, slow-speaking retired Border Patrolman. I had the privilege of seeing one of Bill's exhibitions in Florida in 1967 during a police competition. Bill represented the National Rifle Association in many events and was one of NRA's most popular spokespersons. His feats in revolver shooting were amazing, and when an outdoor venue wasn't available, his wax bullets did the job indoors. He often placed a matchbox on the back

of his shooting hand, drew, and hit the box before it touched the ground. He claimed that he once shot so fast he shot himself in the back of his gunhand! — a Jordan joke. Bill also wrote the classic book, *No Second Place Winner* and authored numerous articles for gun magazines. He was a gentleman with a sense of humor and became a good friend.

Modern firearms companies have continued using exhibition shooters to demonstrate their products. The late Tom Knapp represented several gun and ammo companies. His deep voice and great humor will be missed, as will John Satterwhite, an extraordinary skeet shooter who was a World Champion and an Olympic shooter. His videos on

Jelly Bryce joined the Bureau as a Special Agent but eventually became a supervisor. His firearms demonstrations around the country became so demanding that he requested Hoover to set up a stable of shooters to relieve his workload.

This PR shot shows various aspects of the FBI's demonstrations. Photo: FBI

exhibition shooting are amazing.

Another well-known shooter was Joe Bowman. Joe started with live shooting demonstrations and was an advisor to many movie stars. He would shoot aspirin tablets at 30 paces and split a playing card at 20. In later life, it seemed he concentrated on "gun handling," drawing and spinning his pair of Ruger revolvers at trade shows and other venues. I often saw Joe, "The Straight Shooter," at the SHOT Show. In all the many times we talked, I never knew until after he died in 2009 that he was a WWII veteran awarded three Bronze Stars and a Purple Heart in France.

Bob Munden was an exhibition shooter who claimed 18 world records in speed shooting. He started at age 11. After winning many fast-draw contests in California, he eventually started giving shooting shows around the country. He and his wife Becky toured with their two daughters in tow. He was named "The Fastest Man with a Gun Who Ever Lived." The show was called "Six Gun Magic." He appeared in numerous videos, and his shooting ability was apparent, as was his famous ego.

Perhaps the principal flag bearer of

After his Unit Chief discovered the author had been a cowboy, the "Western Marshal" act was born. The borrowed horse was not amused.

The author spent years taking his turn shooting for the famous FBI Tours at FBI HQ. Photo: FBI

Special Agent John Cox practices the "Blocked Sights" shot before the demonstration. To try this, you can use a 3 x 5 card. Photo: FBI

today's exhibition shooters is Jerry Miculek. Jerry, with his wife Kay and now his daughter, Lena, are the heirs apparent. While the trio is heavily into competition with rifles, pistols, and shotguns, Jerry has set records with all three types of firearms. You can watch videos of Jerry firing a S&W 625, 12 shots with reload in 2:99 seconds and eight rounds from a Model 627 in one second even! In 2013, Jerry hit a target at 200 yards while holding a revolver upside down, using his little finger. And new records continue. The Miculeks are excellent representatives of the firearms family.

But professional shooters aren't carrying the torch alone. Law enforcement officers and agencies use firearms demos to attract recruits and to promote firearms safety (although I recently watched an old black and white film of the LAPD shooting team that included shooting cigarettes out of the mouths of other team members! Don't try this at home.)

Delf "Jelly" Bryce was a famous Oklahoma lawman with extraordinary hand-eye coordination. That and hours of firearms practice made him a way above-average shot. This ability proved invaluable in his career, first as an Oklahoma City detective and later as an FBI agent on J. Edgar Hoover's "Heavy Squad," also known within the Bureau as the "Baseball Team," chasing gangsters in the mid-'30s. But Jelly used his skills in other ways. He would give firearms demonstrations throughout his Bureau career for law enforcement events and the public. His FBI file held countless letters of commendation for his efforts.

Bryce often used a .38, a pump shotgun, and a .220 Swift rifle. As Ron Owens describes in his biography of Jelly, "Bryce would hold his arms out in front of him at shoulder level, an unloaded pump shotgun lying on his outstretched palms. Three clay pigeons would be balanced on the stock, and he would hold three rounds in his left hand. He would flip the three targets up in the air, load the shotgun and shoot all three targets before they hit the ground." In 1945, Jelly appeared in an issue of *Life Magazine* in a spread showing his fast-draw talent in time-lapse photographs.

In 1937, the FBI started giving tours to the public at its Washington, D.C. headquarters in the Department of Justice building. The public would walk along the corridors, watching evidence technicians reading fingerprints or filing documents. At the end of the tour, they would head to the basement firing range and watch a Special Agent fire the revolver and Thompson submachine gun. The FBI tour became the most popular tour in Washington, and they continued when the FBI moved across the street to the J. Edgar Hoover Building. The tours were discontinued after 9-11 for security reasons.

When the FBI's National Academy (an 11-week school for police officers) was moved to Quantico, Virginia, the classes were increased to four per year of 250 students each. Families and friends attended the graduations, and it was decided that the Firearms Training Unit (FTU) would put on a demonstration of firearms skills for them. At first, the instructors shot the qualification course — four or more shooters at a time — and each shooter was expected to fire a "Possible," a perfect score. FTU members

A Special Agent makes the "Two Gun" shot during a National Academy demonstration.

also fired the shotgun and Thompson submachine gun at bobber targets and then some "novelty shots" such as using two revolvers to hit two clay pigeons at once, shooting the revolver upside down, firing backward using a diamond ring, and splitting a bullet on an axe blade to break two pigeons. But by the time this author joined the unit, the demonstration was increasing in scope.

Taking a tip from Bill Cody, much showmanship was added. Bobber targets were made of plasterboard so that the bullets would blow dust and powder. The Thompson shooters arrived in a 1930s sedan wearing pin-striped suits and Fedora hats. Background music was added, and some instructors were qualified in helicopter repelling to represent the Bureau's SWAT teams, sliding down the ropes of the hovering chopper to fire M16s with tracers. Water-filled milk jugs were exploded by a sniper at 200 yards, and a final shot exploded a stick of dynamite as it was explained to the audience that this was an "FBI bullet."

The FTU Unit Chief discovered that your author worked as a cowboy as a youngster, and the "Western Marshal"

Good eyesight helps split a card in half. So does a wheelgun loaded with wadcutters.

was added. I'd arrive on a borrowed horse to the theme of *The Good, the Bad, and the Ugly* and hit water jugs with a .45 single action loaded with blackpowder. Inasmuch as we couldn't get the horse on the helicopter, we had to give up this role on the "SWAT team."

The FTU had to discontinue the demos a few years ago due to budget and manpower limitations. But Buffalo Bill would have been proud.

In January of 1984, Special Agent Danny Coulson, head of the new Hostage Rescue Team (HRT), was called to Judge William Webster's office at FBI Headquarters. The team was ready to go operational. Director Webster advised Coulson that he wanted a press

conference held to announce the team's formation and to show the public the team's unique abilities. Coulson protested, thinking the team should be kept secret, but the Director asked, "Who do you work for, Danny?" Coulson replied, "You, sir," and the preparations commenced. It would be a one-time event and had to be a stunner.

On the day of the demo, two of the team's snipers fired at targets 200 yards downrange. Then two other snipers took shots from the roof of a nine-story dormitory, across the road, over the rifle deck, and made their hits. A team of four operators fast-roped from a helicopter. The press corps was impressed.

The press corps was then led into the

indoor range. In preparation, the exit signs had been covered. A table, chair, and two cartoon "bad guy" targets had been placed in front of the steel backstop. I had a couple of experimental cardboard bullet traps that I placed directly in front of the steel to prevent the loud impact of the bullets. Assistant Director 'Buck' Revell sat in the chair, and the press stood nearby in total darkness. I couldn't hear the two operators, armed with suppressed MP5 SDs and subsonic ammo, enter, but I could hear brass hitting the concrete floor. When the lights came on, the operators were gone, and Buck still sat behind the desk, bullet holes in the heads of the targets next to him. (Lots of reaction from the

Exploding milk jugs was not a difficult shot but was spectacular.

press, but more when they discovered "Free Puerto Rico" stickers on their arms or camera bags. One of the operators was from the PR.)

The finale came at "Tire City," the HRT shooting house. One of the reporters wanted to be a "hostage," and Danny agreed, then asked, "What's your blood type?" The reporter didn't know that it would be an explosive entry, the entry team using explosive charges to breach the door. The other reporters asked him how he felt when the exercise was over. He replied, "Terrible, but I got a hell of a story!"

BECOMING AN EXHIBITION SHOOTER

In the early 1960s, I was a state vice investigator on the West Coast of Florida, busting moonshine stills and helping raid gambling joints. I was once asked to put on a firearms demonstration for kids and their families for a charity event. A little research (where was Google when you needed it?) and a basic novelty shoot was born. A supply of "Bustible Bullseyes" was obtained, and with some clay pigeons and balloons with talcum powder inside, reactive targets provided the entertainment. Shots included shooting the revolver sideways and upside down, splitting a bullet on an axe blade, and shooting a target backward using a small mirror to sight. (I couldn't afford a diamond ring.) The ranges were modest, with more showmanship than marksmanship, but the crowd enjoyed it.

You can shoot your own demonstration. For practice, use paper targets to see your hits and misses. Emphasize safety in handling the firearm(s). Keep the distance modest, perhaps 7 yards, and consider using a revolver with wadcutters. Holding the gun one-handed, shoot one shot each with the firearm upright, turned to 9- and 3-o'clock and finally upside down, using the little finger to pull the trigger. Sight alignment remains the same, but your sight picture might have to be adjusted somewhat.

To shoot between your legs, lay the handgun on the ground, facing downrange. Straddle it, facing the audience, and bend over, picking it up while keeping it always pointed downrange. Lay it on the ground after the shot rather than

FBI Firearms Training Unit instructors were certified in helo rappel to represent SWAT team members.

reholstering it facing the audience. The gun is upside down, but your sight picture is the same. You better not try this if you are over 60.

For the axe shot, position two clay pigeons touching on either side of the axe blade. Balloons are easier. Put in a little talcum powder for effect. FTU cut the ax handle to bolt it to a cross piece. It helps to highlight the axe blade's edge with chalk to see it better. Remember, you don't have to cut the bullet precisely in half. A mere shaving of lead will break the pigeon or balloon.

The mirror/ring shot requires more practice. Standing sideways to the target with the revolver pointed downrange, cradle your arms at your shoulders like you are holding a baby. Hold the mirror or ring in your weak hand. Align the sights and shift your shoulders to see the sights on the target. Readjust as required and take the shot. If you use a diamond ring, it has to be held much closer to the eye. Dry fire a lot before trying this before an audience. The demo drags if the audience has to wait too long.

You can split a playing card with a bullet. Try tacking it on the end of a horizontal 2 X 4, with most of the card below the wood. You can use the end of the wood to help obtain the sight picture, holding it just below the wood. Or you can shift your position slightly to make the edge of the card appear thicker. Again, you do not have to hit the card exactly.

You can fire a handgun with blocked sights and still hit the target. Place a white 3 X 5 card around the barrel in front of the front sight. Shoot with both eyes open. With some practice, you can see the sights with your master eye and the target with your other, superimposing them to make the shot. While you can use a 3 x 5 taped into place, the FTU had white painted metal cards with a spring clip to hold to the barrel.

Perhaps one of the most challenging shots is the "Two Gun." Hold a gun in each hand, with your arms spread just enough to see each set of sights without moving your head, just the eyes. Obtain each sight picture by shifting the eyes only and check the weak hand target last. The shot is best described as a "controlled jerk." If you try to shoot this normally, one gun will fire before the other, moving your sights. But not too much jerk, please. Of course, single action is much easier for this.

Novelty shooting is not limited to handguns. Anyone even reasonably proficient with a shotgun can make this spectacular shot. Set a one-gallon paint can filled with water on a solid surface. The lid should be in place. Place a second empty can on top of the first. Shoot the bottom one with a rifled slug and the second, which by now is heading straight up, with one or more loads of No. 9. Don't try this at home, but it is impressive.

Remember: Exhibition shooting is part marksmanship and part showmanship. Emphasize safety, and have fun. GD

The author is a 31-one-year law enforcement veteran, an Endowment Member of the NRA, and served on NRA's Law Enforcement Assistance Committee. He is the author of the book, Guns of the FBI, *available at GunDigestStore.com.*

A diamond ring or a small mirror can be used for a ring shot. Make sure it is a real diamond, especially if you borrow one from someone in the audience!

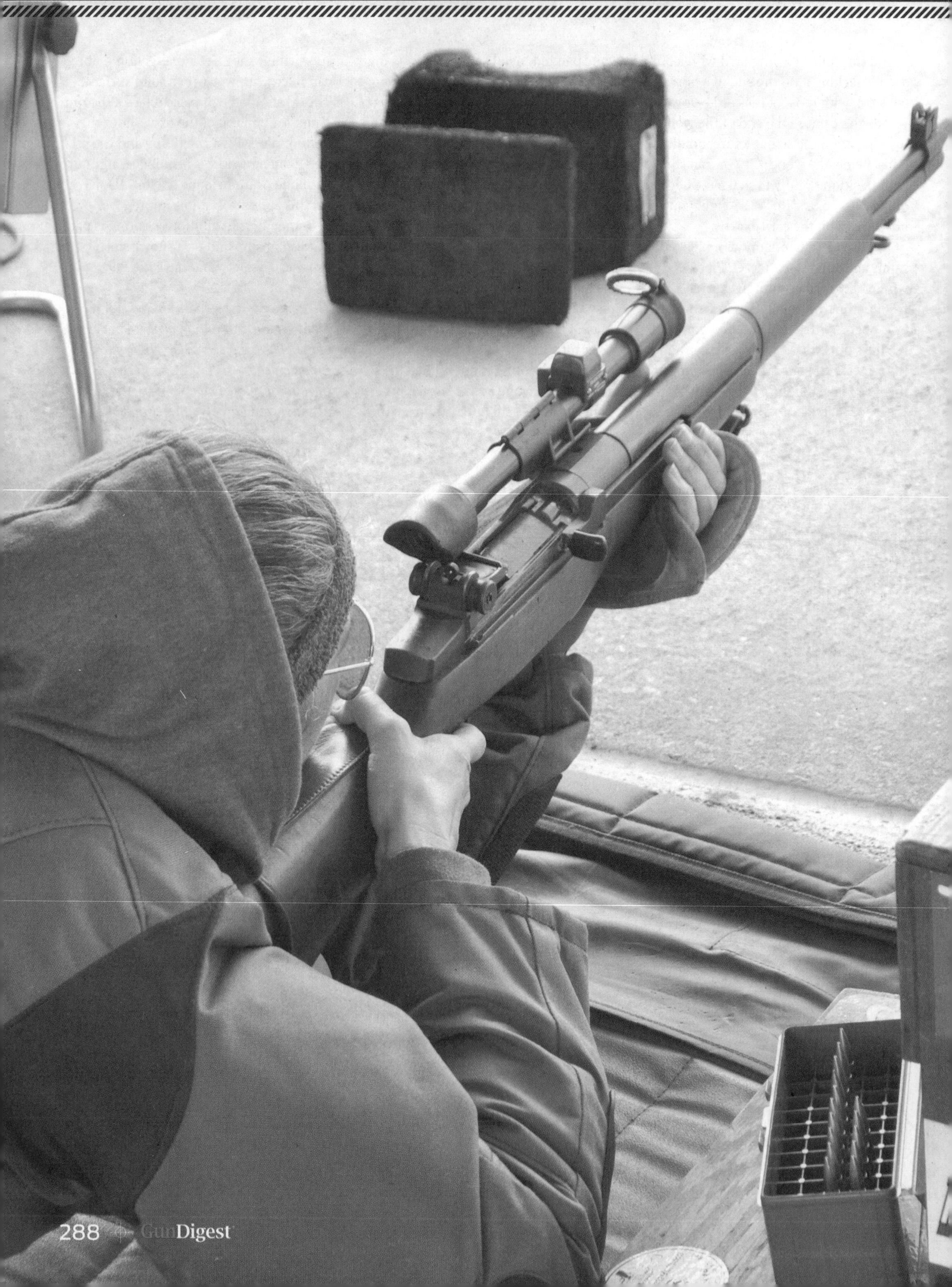

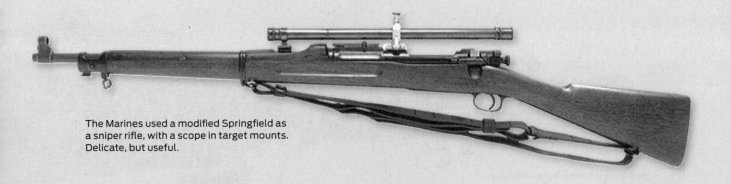

The Marines used a modified Springfield as a sniper rifle, with a scope in target mounts. Delicate, but useful.

SNIPER RIFLES: The M1C and M1D Garands

The first sniper rifle, the Springfield '03 with a Warner & Swasey scope, was used in WWI.

❯ PATRICK SWEENEY

While not the easiest variants to find, the Garand sniper rifles are popular among long-range shooters who compete in the Civilian Marksmanship Program's (CMP) Vintage Sniper Matches. Photo: CMP Archives

During WWII, it was obvious that more accuracy was needed in some instances. That is, sniper rifles. It's another instance of learning lessons from a previous war, forgetting them, and having to do it all over again. All the lessons learned in WWI were allowed to fade, and with Pearl Harbor, the Army had to get back up to speed. The Garand would be the new sniper rifle if the military could solve its problems with scopes. Until then, the existing rifle, the Springfield '03, would have to do. The conversion to sniper rifle was relatively simple by today's standards but a massive task in those days. But, by drilling and tapping the top of the receiver and installing a base and rings, the Army could wrestle together a rifle with a magnifying scope.

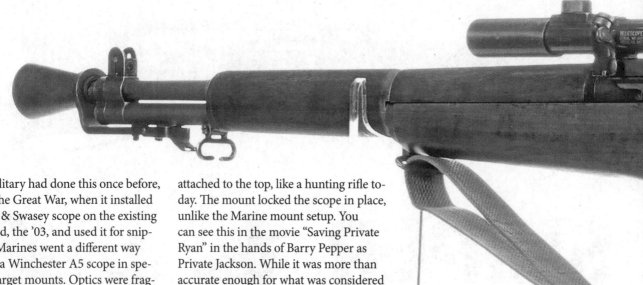

The military had done this once before, back in The Great War, when it installed a Warner & Swasey scope on the existing Springfield, the '03, and used it for sniping. The Marines went a different way and used a Winchester A5 scope in specialized target mounts. Optics were fragile then, and the mount for the Marines' rifle did not securely clamp the scope tube. Instead, the scope slid back and forth in the mount. On recoil, the rifle moved back, and the scope slid forward. The rifleman had to move the scope back to the rear position for each shot.

The existing WWII sniper rifle, the Springfield 03A4, was an updated (Remington upgraded the '03 with stamped parts) bolt-action rifle with a scope attached to the top, like a hunting rifle today. The mount locked the scope in place, unlike the Marine mount setup. You can see this in the movie "Saving Private Ryan" in the hands of Barry Pepper as Private Jackson. While it was more than accurate enough for what was considered sniping by the U.S. Army, it was still a bolt-action rifle. (The Western Front was not like the Eastern. In the East, snipers hunted each other and were considered high-value targets. In the West, the 03A4 was used more as a DMR.)

Let's consider accuracy. The existing Springfield '03 was inherently accurate. You'd get good groups if you mounted one in a machine rest and fired it. What hindered it was the sights. And its handi-

The M1C's mount was attached to the receiver and required holes drilled and tapped. Photo: Rock Island Auction Company

The Garand's scope offset to avoid clip insertion and ejection is apparent here. That meant a leather cheekpiece had to be tied to the stock, a small price to pay.

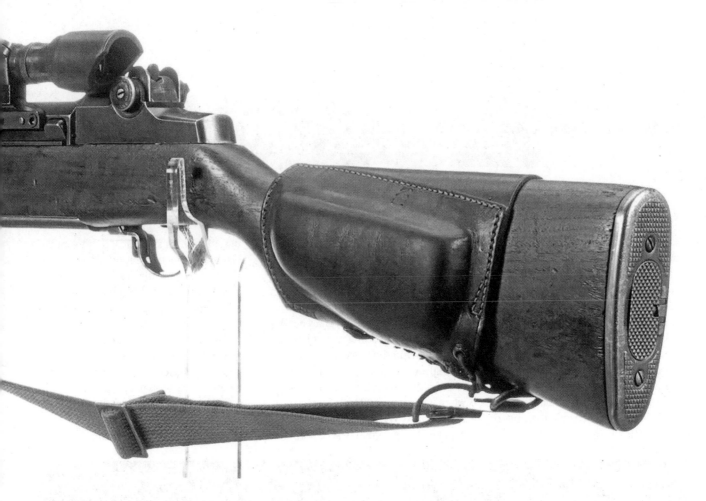

The Germans had lots of experience with snipers in the trenches and kept that knowledge current for WWII.

ness. The sights were the late 19th-century idea of good target-shooting sights. The "combat" sight was a notch and post. So, you had a .30-06 rifle meant for 1,000 yards but used what amounted to pistol sights. If you wanted more precision, you had to stand up the rear sight, adjust the slider to the range, and use the peep sight. As far from your face as it was, that ended up being slow, awkward, and not combat-friendly.

The Garand, as a rifle, was equally accurate. The '03 handiness? Well, a relatively lightweight .30-06 with a steel buttplate is not what you want to shoot a lot. The '03 tips the scales at about 8.5 pounds. The Garand is about 9.5 pounds. Add a pound of weight, and then soften the felt recoil by making it a self-loading, gas-operated rifle, and you have a much more pleasant experience. And while "pleasant" is not in the military's basic vocabulary, it does matter when you are trying to build skills.

The big deal for accuracy was the Garand's sighting system. Placing the aperture near the aiming eye improves accuracy in several ways. First, the sight radius is longer, and that adds precision. Second, with the aperture close to the eye, the shooter does not have to move around as much behind the stock to get aligned with the rear sight.

The last part may seem like magic in the modern era with so many AR-15-experienced shooters using scopes or red-dot optics. If you relax and let your eye and brain work naturally, your eye will find the center of the aperture. Get comfortably behind the sight, focus on the front blade, and you will center it in the rear aperture.

As a result, despite both rifles having similar inherent accuracy, the Garand is much easier to shoot accurately than the Springfield. The value of an aperture sight was recognized quickly, and as a result, when it came time to scale up rifle production in WWII, something interesting happened. Remington, tasked with mak- ing sufficient Springfields to supplant the Garand production, reported to the War Department that the design was hopeless and the rifle had to be modernized. The War Department agreed, and Remington updated everything on the '03, making as many parts as possible, including heavy-gauge steel stampings, welded assemblies, and updated steel alloys. And it junked the elaborate '03 rear sight and installed a simpler aperture sight mounted on the rear receiver bridge.

The idea of the distances snipers can

The M1D mount was attached to the barrel, so any Garand could be built or rebuilt as an M1D if you had the special barrel. And the scopes were, of course, serial numbered.

TELESCOPE M84
SERIAL NO. 30125

The M1D used a special barrel, no mods to the receiver, and was a better setup. Photo: Rock Island Auction Company

connect on these days would have been fantastical to GIs in the 1940s. A 1,000-yard shot was seen as a target-range distance on a six-foot-sized target. They were concerned with hitting a partial target, like a helmet, at 200 yards. For that, a magnifying scope would be handy.

The demand for a more accurate Garand with a scope was strong enough that the Army did what it could. Let's look at this from a technical perspective. First of all, there's the en-bloc clip. It has to go straight into the receiver. And after the last round is fired, it has to come straight out. You can't have a scope in the way. The Springfield had the scope on top, so it could not be reloaded with a stripper clip. The user had to thumb individual rounds into the magazine, fitting them under the scope. So, in a fast-moving, target-rich environment, you, the sniper, were armed with a bolt-action rifle, and when you had used your five rounds, you were out of action, behind cover for a minute or two, thumbing rounds into the magazine.

Meanwhile, your squad mates were hammering away: eight rounds, reload, and eight more.

On the M1 Garand, the scope had to be mounted to the side of the bore axis.

Add a padded leather cheekpiece, and the soldier it was issued to could use the optics and still have a self-loading rifle. There were two prototype designs to consider: the M1E7 and M1E8. The E7 used a Griffin & Howe side mount. This mount placed the scope to the side, and it was a known and well-regarded mount to add optics to a Garand. The M1C, as it was designated when adopted, used a Griffin & Howe mount with five holes in the mount and receiver. Three of the receiver holes were tapped, and two were left untapped. The three tapped holes were for the screws that held it on, and the other two were for tapered pins. The pins did two things: they provided mount location repeatability should it be removed and shear strength to keep the mount from loosening and coming off from the recoil of multiple shots fired.

The M1E8 did things differently. On the E8, the barrel was the mounting location, the mount clamped on a modified barrel, and there was a large knurled thumbscrew to tighten it in place.

For various reasons, the E7 was adopted as the M1C and put into production late in the war. Things did not go smoothly. The initial attempts had the non-heat-treated receivers drilled and tapped, the mount af-

fixed, and the receiver heat-treated. When I first read that, a shudder ran through me. Two pieces of steel of different sizes and thicknesses, and almost certainly of different alloys, being bolted together and *then* heat-treated? The warpage must have been epic. After that attempt, the receivers were drilled and tapped, heat-treated, and the mounts fastened. While production was approved with a finalized design in June 1944, it wasn't until later that year that Springfield began production.

The M1C was made only on Springfield rifles, which only converted certain blocks of serial numbers. While those blocks fell within the 3,100,000 and 3,800,000 serial number range, the total number of M1C rifles made during WWII was about 8,000. Rare, indeed.

M1C production took so long that the sniper rifle saw little, if any, action in WWII. With its Lyman Alaskan scope (and all of its 2X magnification), it would have been very useful in the M81 with a crosshair or the M82 with a tapered-post reticle.

The E8, designed by Garand himself, was adopted as a substitute standard in September 1944, so the services would have a backup. Well, that was the official explanation. Me? I suspect those in

How to Match-Condition a Garand

When it comes to improving your Garand's accuracy and making it match-ready, I'm going to give you the tidbits of what not to do, what to look out for, and how to avoid problems based on my gunsmithing work on Garands, and from dealing with customers who got themselves in trouble. Taking a page from professional painters, most of the work is in the prep. The actual painting is the easy part. In other words, read and study before you apply power tools to or epoxy your Garand.

BEDDING THE STOCK

One of the best things you can do to improve your Garand's accuracy is bedding the stock. But heed warnings about using modeling clay and release agent seriously. If you don't, your Garand's action will almost certainly bond permanently to the stock, and you won't be able to remove the trigger assembly or get the action out. To start, disassemble every part of the trigger assembly and all the receiver parts. Then fill every gap where bedding epoxy is not supposed to go with modeling clay and smooth it flush with the surrounding surface.

Don't assume, "The epoxy won't get there" or "I've got the secret gel mix, and it won't flow to the wrong spot." Those are the famous words of customers who ended up in the shop.

Once the modeling putty is in place, apply the release agent. Let it dry, perhaps overnight. Then, inspect the coating with a close eye and a bright light. If you see any spots, lines, or joints where the release agent is missing or looks thin, apply more. Applying two coats is not a bad idea.

You need not attend Camp Perry to get practice. Many local clubs will have matches you can use your Garand in, but Camp Perry is the holy grail of Garand shooting.

"But two coats make it thick, and I want a tight fit," some will say. It will be plenty tight enough, even with two coats.

When you press the receiver in, followed by the trigger assembly to lock it partially but not fully closed, epoxy will ooze out. Now is the time to use a wooden scraper and scrape the excess off. Do a good job here, as it's much easier to scrape liquid epoxy off than to cut, grind, sand, or otherwise remove hardened epoxy that you left oozed.

Then, once the epoxy is set (let it set for the whole time according to the packaging; there is nothing to be gained by taking things apart early), remove the receiver and trigger housing and inspect the interior for gaps. If there are voids, gaps, or missing epoxy spots, now is the time to address them. Use a degreasing agent on the epoxy, rough the voided spot and the area around it, mix more epoxy, and apply it. Re-apply more release agent and reassemble the receiver and trigger housing as before.

Once set, take it apart again and inspect it. Is epoxy in all the right places? Now scrub the release agent off and clean out the modeling clay. Check the parts for a correct fit. If they fit, you are halfway there.

HANDGUARD FIT

The forward handguard is important. Do not get lazy or sloppy in fitting it to the steel ring to which it needs to be secured. Inspect the handguard fit every time you go to a match, as it must not touch the barrel. If it has been misaligned, straighten it and think to yourself how that could have happened, and don't do that again.

PRO TRIGGER JOBS ONLY

Leave the trigger alone. Yes, the Garand trigger is good, and yes, it can be improved. But stoning the surfaces yourself is an invitation to problems. Get it wrong, and you'll have a doubling or slam-fire rifle and get hurt sooner or later. And even if you aren't hurt, you'll get disinvited from the shooting range.

If you must have a better trigger, have someone who does it for a living attend to its improvement. You will avoid the hassle of an inoperative rifle and the cost of new parts. And, if you attend Camp

Photo: CMP Archives

Perry or shoot in an official match, you will have a trigger that will pass the trigger pull weight test. Yes, at matches above the club level (and even at some clubs), your trigger pull will be weighed, and if it's less than a specified amount, you will not get to shoot. Or, you get to shoot, but not for score/match standings.

RELOAD, THEN PRACTICE

Ammo only does so much. You can spend a lot of time and effort improving your ammunition, but your skills and the mechanical precision of your rifle will still limit it. What you especially don't want to do is exceed the loading limits for the Garand. You'll harm your rifle and gain nothing for it. Stay within specs and load for quality, not production speed or output volume.

CRITERION BARREL

Don't look to parts to improve your scores. Buying an NM or National Match sight set or a National Match op rod, and expecting some big jump up in your scores, or significantly smaller groups, is kidding yourself. Unless the original parts are seriously worn or out of spec, the improvements will be marginal.

One big jump up in accuracy will come from a new barrel, especially a match barrel from Criterion. Have Criterion install it properly. The bore will be better than any barrel made during the Garand's heyday. A matching-period barrel on an otherwise collectible Garand? Don't mess with it. Buy a beater. A rebuild, a non-period barrel on a mixmaster? Don't feel guilty about putting a new, better barrel in it for shooting. You can always have the old barrel

plugged back in if you want a collectible.

EXPERT REBUILDS ONLY

Experts are worth it. Yes, there is a certain pride — and knowledge gained — by doing things yourself. But know your limitations, and where an expert would do it better, have them do it.

PRACTICE MORE

The best way to improve is to practice. Yes, it means using up a barrel and adding wear to the parts, but if you want to get good, you must put in the time. For serious shooters, this means two Garands. The "weekend" Garand, which looks good, is period-correct, and they can take it to the club on weekends and put a few clips through it. The serious one, the "shooting" Garand, is built on a pitted receiver with

Practice, that's the way. Get out and put in some trigger time. Yes, it wears the barrel, but it is the only way.

lots of mileage. Maybe it has been re-Parkerized, but it has a new match barrel, and everything is fitted properly. Since the barrel isn't a USGI, they can run it as much as they want and replace it when it shows wear. If it wears too much, you can have a new piston brazed onto the op rod and even a larger one if the gas cylinder is starting to enlarge.

This is true in shooting, car racing, and any skill-building enterprise or sporting competition. If you want to get better, you have to put the time in, which means putting wear and tear on the tools of the trade.

So, get to it.

Note: Besides these seven tips, you can learn more from USAMTU manuals, online videos, instructions from Brownells, and people who have done it. Don't listen to the guy at your club "who knows everything," but you suspect he hasn't done a tenth of it. GD

Buying parts to improve your score won't do much but hammer your wallet. These NM sights are cool but will only add a few more points to your score. Better to practice.

The British No. 4 was also made into a sniper version, but it required the receiver to be drilled and tapped (like the M1C), and a special mount with oversized thumbscrews held the scope.

charge got it wrong at the start and didn't want to admit it. Yes, the adoption of an existing scope mount system seemed prudent. But the heat-treatment mistake cost time. Plus, once you drilled and tapped a receiver to be an M1C, that's what it was. If you needed more, you had to make more from scratch, as drilling and tapping an already heat-treated receiver would have been a game of chance.

The M1D, on the other hand, was just another barrel. Once the tooling was set up to make the modified chamber area of the M1D barrel, you could make as many as you needed for years to come and stash them in inventory. If you needed more M1Ds, you swapped barrels in existing rifles. And, if something better for sniping came along, an M1D barrel, under a regular handguard, was just another M1 rifle.

Both the M1C and the M1D were issued with a laced-on leather cheekpiece that was padded to provide a solid cheek weld for the shooter, which aligned with the left-canted scope. The flash hider, M2, clipped onto the muzzle and gas

cylinder like the grenade launcher but did not compress the poppet valve since there was no change in the gas flow when firing Ball ammo.

The Springfield 03A4 was not numerous, with some 28,000 made. But it served long enough to do well in WWII and see action in Korea. However, Korea changed things.

Just as with regular M1 inventory, the Army realized it needed more sniper rifles. So Springfield assembled them from existing receivers, but drilling and tapping receivers to make M1C rifles was a non-starter. So, the plant made new M1D barrels and installed them into existing rifles. This poses a problem for collectors. While the M1C rifles are M1C (I suspect there are more than a few fakes), the M1D could legitimately be any rifle. If Springfield grabbed an in-spec 1942 receiver and built it into an M1D in 1952, it was and is a legitimate M1D. Sigh.

The M1D suffered the same fate as the M1C, being too late to do much, if anything, in the war for which it was built. By the late 1950s, the new rifle,

This article is an excerpt from *The Gun Digest Book of the M1 Garand*, available at GunDigestStore.com.

the M14, was set up to accept a scope mount (not designed yet, but one step at a time, right?) without going to extra measures. **GD**

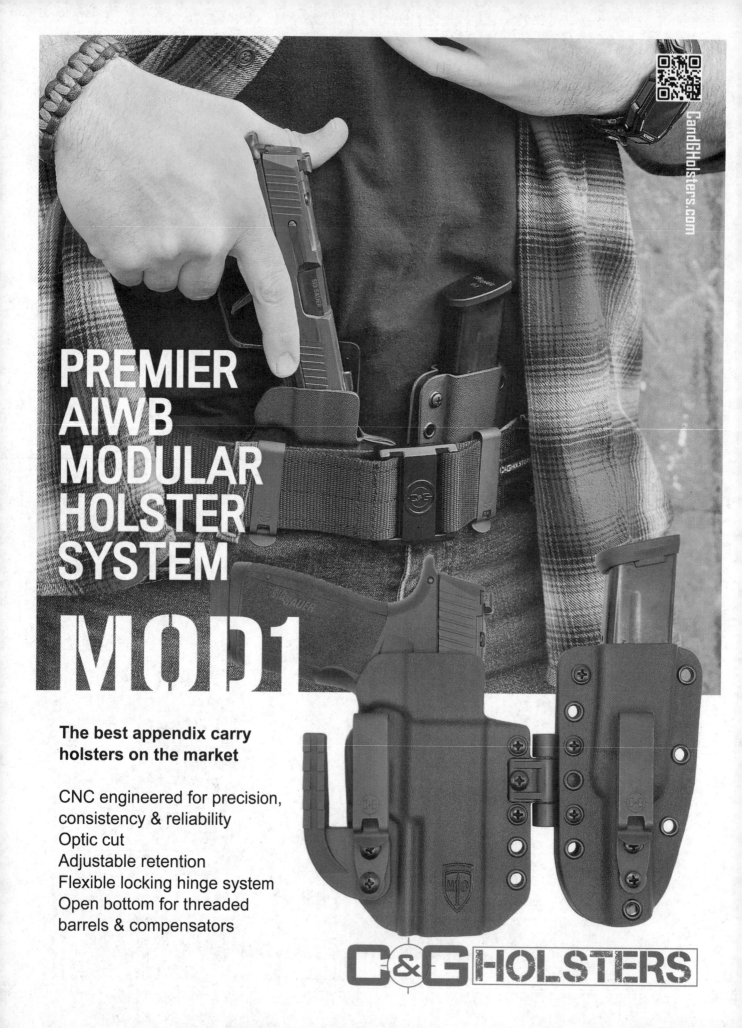

FDR-9

Following the success of the FDR-15 F-1 Firearms has decided to expand this series and introduce a 9MM FDR. This little Saturday-night special is soft in recoil, easy to suppress and is designed to take double-stack Glock mags. Make the FDR-9 your next reason to visit the gun range.

HATSAN USA

JET & JETII

HUNTING POWER + TARGET ACCURACY
LIGHTWEIGHT + COMPACT

SCAN FOR MORE DETAILS

A TWO-IN-ONE PISTOL AND CARBINE RIFLE

Adjustable Cheek Rest and Telescoping Buttstock

Detachable Buttstock

OPTICS NOT INCLUDED

3 Integrated Sights for Pistol or Rifle Mode

Full Length 11mm Dovetail Optics Rail

Pistol Grip

PCP Power (Pre-Charged Pneumatic) 80cc Fills to 250 BAR (40cc on JET I)

hatsanairgunsusa.com

SWAMPFOX
TACTICAL OPTICS

RAIDER
1X20 MICRO PRISM

- T2 footprint with included 1.1" and 1.6" mounts
- Shake N' Wake for grab-and-go readiness
- Etched reticle available in RED or GREEN illumination
- Expansive eye relief

BULLET RISE
COMPENSATION RETICLE

The BRC reticle from Swampfox is optimized to counter the mechanical offset at close distances, effectively compensating for the "bullet rise" caused by the scope's height over bore. This results in dedicated holds at 5, 10, and 15 yards, providing enhanced accuracy and precision in close-range targeting scenarios.

LEARN MORE

LPVOS | DOT SIGHTS | PRISMS | PRECISION SCOPES
HTTPS://WWW.SWAMPFOXOPTICS.COM

Springfield Armory 1911 DS Prodigy

Sadowski reviews a pair of performance-driven 1911s — 2011-style double stacks! — from Springfield Armory.

❯ROBERT A. SADOWSKI

A ny double-stack, hammer-fired 1911-style pistol has become known as a "2011." And Springfield Armory flipped the 2011's script with the introduction of the 1911 DS Prodigy in a 4.25-inch barrel Commander-size model and a 5-inch barrel full-size variant. Not only is the full-size version ready to rumble through stages at match competitions, but the more compact 4.25-inch Prodigy takes concealed carry to a whole new level of 1911 performance.

If you compete, you probably already know that STI, which has since morphed into Staccato, coined the 2011 name decades ago, transforming competition shooting and the pistols used. An authentic 2011 is a 1911-style platform with a steel slide and frame, less the grip portion. A polymer grip module bolts onto the steel frame to provide room for the thicker, double-stack magazine. By comparison, the standard 1911 platform uses a single-stack mag, and the grip is integral to the frame.

The sole purpose of double-stack 2011s was and still is to shoot fast and accurately at steel or cardboard targets. They are high-performance, high-end, custom race guns — so expensive you might have to sell an organ. However, with the new Prodigy line, Springfield Armory enables shooters to get into a 9mm double-stack for a lot less, so you can keep your kidney.

Each 1911 DS (DS stands for Double Stack) pistol employs a steel slide and frame comprising the slide rails, the recoil spring inside the dustcover, and the fire-control components. To this, the polymer module is bolted. While that may sound like Springfield Frankensteined the 1911 DS, the polymer grip module blends seamlessly with the steel components. The grip has more girth than a standard 1911 but feels less chubby than some striker-fired double-stack pistol grips. The grip's texture is like fine sandpaper. I found myself wanting to grip the pistol; it just feels good in the hand. The triggerguard is undercut for a higher grip and less muzzle flip, and the magazine well is flared, so it slurps up the tapered double-stack magazines fast when reloading.

Springfield Armory's DS Progidy is a 2011-style pistol (double-stack 1911) that is not only fast shooting and accurate but affordable. Here the author reviews two versions, the full-size 5-inch with open sights (top) and the Commander-sized 4.25-inch model with a red-dot sight.

Left: Course slide serrations fore and aft allow effortless slide racking, especially when doing a press check.

Below: A full-length guide rod ensures the Prodigy runs and cycles smoothly.

Notice how the magazine tapers to a single stack at the top. That taper makes for a smooth and fast reload.

The pistols use a bushing-less bull barrel that flares at the muzzle and mates with the inside of the slide. It's made with an integral feed ramp, so 9mm cartridges feed smoothly and reliably. The case is also fully supported. Like other Springfield Armory models with this barrel setup, it requires a hex wrench for disassembly (Springfield supplies the wrench). The slide has a traditional dome shape, and coarse slide serrations fore and aft, offering plenty of traction to rack the slide and do a press check. The slide-to-frame fit is tight with no wiggle. Racking the slide or doing a press check, I discovered how smooth and slick it was to manipulate. The Prodigy has a two-piece guide rod that acts like a full-length rod. The back half of the rod is like a GI-length rod but threaded on the end to mate with the second piece. It provides smoother recoil.

The sights are another feature where Springfield pushed the pistol squarely into the 21st century. The front sight post is dovetailed to the slide and houses a green fiber tube, so the front sight pops when aiming. The rear sight is flush with the rear of the slide and serrated to cut glare. It has a U-notch groove. OK, that may seem pretty vanilla, so here is the innovative part: Springfield partnered with Agency Arms to develop an interchangeable optics plate system. The rear sight is part of the optics plate. What I like about this setup is that the plate is half-dovetailed into the slide, which takes the shear force during recoil rather than the screws holding the optic to the gun. The pistols have a Trijicon RMR-footprint optics adapter plate, popular with several other red-dot sight manufacturers.

Controls consist of an extended ambidextrous thumb safety that crisply clicks on and off. The slide stop is inset into the nearly full-length dustcover, yet can be used to rest your support hand thumb. The magazine release button is serrated and slightly extended to make reloads a hair faster than a standard one. The trigger is a three-hole aluminum affair with a curved, serrated face and is adjustable for overtravel. The polymer grip module guides the trigger, making the rearward press smooth. The grip safety has a decent speed bump and an upswept beavertail that keeps beefy hands from being bitten by hammer and slide.

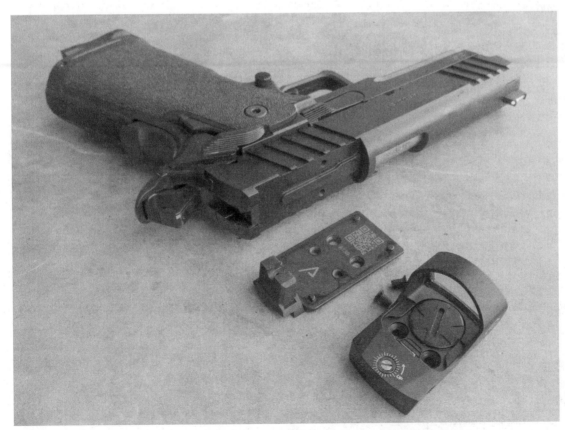

Springfield partnered with Agency Arms to develop an interchangeable optics plate system on the DS pistols, and the rear sight is part of the optics plate.

The 4.25-inch-barreled Prodigy has soft recoil and cycles like butter. With the Crimson Trace red-dot optic, shots can be surgical.

The most finicky component in a 2011 platform is the magazine. Springfield uses DuraMag to build the 17-round flush fit and 20-round extended mags. Springfield also offers a 26-rounder. The floor plate is polymer, and the magazine tube is steel. There are three witness holes at 5, 10, and 17 rounds on the flush fit mag and an extra hole at the 20-round mark on the 20-round extended magazine. Springfield Prodigy magazines will function in Staccato P guns and vice versa.

I function-tested both a 4.25- and 5-inch DS Prodigy. Both models are available with iron sights and optics ready or with a factory-mounted Springfield Hex Dragonfly red dot. I ran iron sights on the 5-inch Prodigy; on the 4.25-inch model, I mounted a Crimson Trace CTS-1250 compact reflex sight with a round 3.25 MOA red aiming dot. The tall Prodigy sights co-witness with the Crimson Trace, and in the event the battery gives up the ghost, you can still use the irons.

I started with speed shooting some Failure to Stop or Mozambique Drills on plain cardboard IPSC/USPSA targets and immediately noticed how smoothly the pistols cycled. The recoil pulse in the 4.25-inch model was soft, and the pistol's weight enables you to stay on target. The recoil pulse on the 5-inch gun was not as soft, but it was still easy to control. I found these handguns forgiving, which makes you a better shot. I shoot many compact- and full-size striker-fire pistols, so the transition to the Prodigy's grip felt familiar. However, the trigger was different — in a good way. There was slight takeup on both models until I hit the wall, and the trigger broke at 5.3 pounds on average. Could the pull weight be better? Sure. I want a clean 3.5 to 4 pounds, but that's just me being hyper-critical. Trigger reset is fast, enabling quicker follow-up shots.

I shouldn't complain about the trigger pull since I was shooting 5-shot groups at 25 yards that average 1.2 inches with the

PERFORMANCE: SPRINGFIELD ARMORY 1911 DS PRODIGY 5 INCH*

LOAD	VELOCITY (FPS)	MUZZLE ENERGY (FT-LBS)	BEST ACCURACY (IN.)	AVERAGE ACCURACY (IN.)
9mm Remington HTP 147-gr. JHP	920	276	2.0	2.27
9mm Federal American Eagle 115-gr. FMJ	1,152	339	1.19	1.38
9mm SIG V-Crown 124-gr. JHP	1,038	297	2.27	2.29
9mm Winchester Active Duty 115-gr. Ball	1,272	413	1.34	1.45

*Best five-shot groups at 25 yards. springfield-armory.com

Each Prodigy DS shot accurately; the author's best group with the Commander-sized 2011 was .7 inch.

SPECIFICATIONS

Springfield Armory
Model: 1911 DS Prodigy 4.25 Inch
Caliber: 9mm
Action Type: Semi-auto, short-recoil-operated, SAO trigger
Overall Length: 7.8 in.
Overall Height: 5.5 in.
Maximum Width: 1.2 in.
Weight Unloaded: 32.5 oz.
Barrel Length: 4.25 in. forged stainless steel, match grade, bull
Frame Finish/Material: Matte black Cerakote/steel
Slide Finish/Material: Matte black Cerakote/steel
Grip: Textured polymer
Magazine: 17+1 and 20+1
Sights: Green fiber-optic front, black serrated U-notch rear
MSRP: $1,499
springfield-armory.com

4.25-inch red dot-equipped pistol and 2 inches with the 5-inch pistol's iron sights.

Shooting the 4.25-inch gun was an exercise in precision. A red-dot optic provides a distinct advantage in accuracy. The data from Remington HTP and SIG V-Crown defense ammo showed that my best groups were 1.1 and .97 inches, respectively. Sure, that was using a rest, but shooting offhand, I easily clustered holes center of mass. It liked the inexpensive Federal American Eagle ammo. My best group measured .7 inch! Looking at the 4.25-inch Prodigy DS through an EDC lens, I could see myself carrying it. It may be a bit heavier than a single stack, but that is manageable with the right holster and belt.

Shooting the 5-inch Prodigy old-school style, meaning iron sights, I didn't feel disadvantaged. The sights allow fast target acquisition, and the soft recoil ensures faster follow-up shots. The big version also liked the inexpensive 115-grain training ammo from Winchester and Federal, giving me a best group of 1.34 and 1.19 inches, respectively. With the 5-inch model, I almost felt like I was cheating shooting the Mozambique Drill. The heavy pistol chugged through rounds begging me to slap the go switch faster.

Both pistols ran exceptionally well. No issues of any kind were encountered.

The Prodigy is a fast-shooting pistol with an excellent trigger reset and outstanding recoil control. These pistols beg to be run fast and hard. Springfield has a couple of winners here that offer superb value and performance for the price. **GD**

PERFORMANCE: SPRINGFIELD ARMORY 1911 DS PRODIGY 4.25 INCH*

LOAD	VELOCITY (FPS)	MUZZLE ENERGY (FT-LBS)	BEST ACCURACY (IN.)	AVERAGE ACCURACY (IN.)
9mm Remington HTP 147-gr. JHP	925	279	1.1	1.27
9mm Federal American Eagle 115-gr. FMJ	1,140	332	0.7	1.02
9mm SIG V-Crown 124-gr. JHP	1,031	293	0.97	1.2
9mm Winchester Active Duty 115-gr. Ball	1,229	386	1.02	1.06

*Best five-shot groups at 25 yards. springfield-armory.com

Franchi
Momentum Elite
VARMINT EDITION

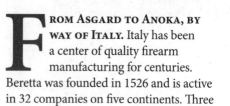

›STEVE GASH

ROM ASGARD TO ANOKA, BY WAY OF ITALY. Italy has been a center of quality firearm manufacturing for centuries. Beretta was founded in 1526 and is active in 32 companies on five continents. Three major names in its firearms portfolio are Beretta, Benelli, and Franchi. Interestingly, while each company is a part of Beretta Holdings, each entity is separate and competes with each other in specific market segments.

The name Franchi is best associated with fine shotguns, but in 2018, it introduced its first rifle, the Momentum. It was a feature-packed three-lug bolt action and proved accurate and dependable. I have a Momentum in .308

Winchester, and on a recent Texas Hill Country hunt for deer, javelinas, and varmints, I fired nine rounds and collected nine critters — an auspicious beginning.

Never one to rest on its laurels, Franchi continued to develop the Momentum platform, and in 2022, the Momentum Elite was born. It is available in several versions, chambered for many popular cartridges, including the .308 Winchester and the perennial over-achiever, the 6.5 Creedmoor.

THE VARMINT MOMENTUM

A uniquely specialized Momentum Elite is the Varmint Edition, chambered for the .223 Remington, .22-250 Remington, and the new .224 Valkyrie. It's packed with features that make it perfect for varmint sniping.

I unexpectedly came into a new Elite Varmint Edition last summer. Franchi had a shooting contest with the new Momentum rifles at a company gathering of writers. There were three targets, and each contestant was given five rounds. The course of fire was as follows: one shot at two steel targets, one at 200 yards, and one at 300 yards. Actually, with the Momentum, these were downright easy. But the third target was challenging. It looked like a pop can at 400 yards and was filled with some explosives, so if you hit it, it went "boom!" If you didn't hit it, you were eliminated.

I missed the can with my third and fourth rounds, then held a little into the wind with my last round and hit the can – boom! Three other shooters also hit the boom can, and later after dinner, our names were put in a hat, and a name was drawn out. I was the lucky winner, and the prize was any Momentum of the winner's choice! It didn't take me long to choose the new Varmint model chambered in the uniquely designed .224 Valkyrie. I wasn't the only shooter in the U.S. who wanted a new Momentum in the Valkyrie, as it was some time before my prize became available. But it was well worth the wait.

The Momentum Varmint rifles have cold hammer-forged, 24-inch barrels, with fluting forward of the forend, and come with a 2-inch, removable muzzle brake (the muzzle is threaded 5/8-24).

The Momentum Elite is drilled and tapped for Rem. M700-pattern scope bases. The test rifle was sighted with a new S1 Sightron 4-12x40 G2 scope, which proved excellent in range tests.

The Momentum bolt has three locking lugs and is hard chrome plated for wear resistance and lubricity. The extractor is a sliding plate, and the ejector is the spring-loaded plunger type.

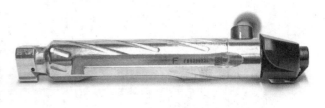

The Momentum bolt is fluted along its length.

Barrel lengths on some other versions of the Momentum are 22 inches in length, depending on the caliber. The .224 Valkyrie model's rifling twist is a fast 1:7 inches, so it's rarin' to go with bullet weights up to 90 grains. For top accuracy, the barrel is free-floated its entire length.

The Momentum has what Franchi calls the Relia Bolt. It is one-piece, chrome-plated, and features three locking lugs, which produce a bolt lift of about 60°. And, unlike some three-lug actions, the Momentum's bolt lift is not noticeably heavier than a two-lug action. It was easy to work the bolt, and it slid back and forth smooth as silk. The bolt body has spiral flutes, and the bolt handle knob is nicely contoured. The bolt body mics a hefty .86 inch, with a sliding plate extractor and a plunger-style ejector on the bolt face. The two-position safety button is

The bottom of the Momentum Elite wears the big red Franchi "F" brand.

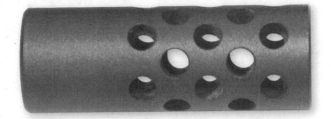

The rifle has an easily removable muzzle brake, and a thread protector is provided.

at the right rear of the receiver. When in the "on" position, the bolt is not locked, so the chamber can be unloaded safely. A bolt-release lever is found at the left rear of the action. The bolt shroud has a cocking indicator you can see or feel — another neat safety feature. The receiver and barrel have a great-looking Cerakote Midnight bronze finish.

The single-stage Relia Trigger on my rifle broke cleanly at 1 pound, 4.3 ounces, and was as *crisp* as a breaking, well, you know. (When was the last time you heard of an out-of-the-box factory trigger this nice?) Yeah, the trigger is user-adjustable, but it was so excellent from the factory I figured I'd better leave well enough alone.

The rifle comes with two detachable box magazines. The 4-round magazine fits almost flush with the bottom of the stock, while the 7-round mag sticks out slightly more. Both snapped in and out slick as can be, were easy to load, and feeding from both was 100%. The magazine release button is located at the front of the triggerguard. The overall length of my Momentum was 44 3/4 inches, and as received, the rifle weighed 9 pounds, 1 ounce.

Above: The Momentum feeds from a removable box magazine, and 4- and 7-round magazines are provided.

Right: The Momentum's cheekpiece is removable, and different height combs are available. The "low" insert is installed here, with the "high" insert in front.

The popularity of the .224 Valkyrie cartridge is enhanced by the many powders suitable for tailor-made handloads.

A vast array of .22-caliber bullets, including heavy-for-caliber ones, are suitable for the .224 Valkyrie. These include (from left) Barnes 70-grain TSX-BT, Hornady 70-grain GMX, Hornady 73-grain ELD Match, Hornady 75-grain ELD Match, Hornady 80-grain ELD Match, Hornady 88-grain ELD Match, Nosler 55-grain Ballistic Tip, Nosler 60-grain Ballistic Tip, Nosler 60-grain Partition, and Nosler 64-grain Bonded Solid Base.

This Momentum sports a synthetic stock Franchi calls the Evolved Egonnom-X. It has the Optifade camo finish, and it's quite a looker. The cheekpiece is a black composite and was too high for me. But not to worry, it is removable, and other heights are available. Just grab the rear end of the cheekpiece, pull up, and … it's out. I quickly snapped a "low" cheekpiece into place.

The stock's camo pattern is attractive and should be a welcome addition to any varmint hunter's setup. Franchi engineers didn't just stick any old stock on the new Varmint rifle. It's a very sturdy and stable synthetic and is carefully designed. They studied the way shooters held rifles and determined that there were five common shooting positions. The Momentum stock has "gripping panels" in all the right places for those five positions. It has built-in sling swivel attachment points fore and aft. Although the .224 Valkyrie doesn't kick much, the Momentum stock has Franchi's TSA recoil pad.

Let me relate another example of Franchi's attention to detail. Before the Texas hunt, we writers shot about a dozen original Momentum rifles, all in .308 Winchester. Some rifles didn't shoot as accurately as others, which some writers attributed to the stock touching the barrel, affecting accuracy. The Franchi representative noted this, and the syn-

thetic stock was re-designed to provide adequate barrel-stock clearance and stiffness. Subsequent Momentum rifles uniformly shot very well. This was at no small cost to Franchi, but it markedly improved an already good product.

The top of the receiver comes with a Picatinny rail attached, which accepts most Weaver-type rings. I mounted a big target scope on it, but it was too high for me. The Momentum receiver is drilled and tapped for Remington Model 700 two-piece mounts, so this was no problem. I removed the Picatinny rail and installed No. 35 (front) and 36 (rear) Weaver bases. Then I mounted a new Sightron S1 G2 4-12x40 scope with the Duplex reticle in Leupold medium-height rings. This optics setup and the lower cheekpiece leveled things out satisfactorily and worked well through lots of test firing. With this excellent scope attached, the rig weighed 10 pounds, 4.1 ounces, and became a prairie dog's worst nightmare.

THE FLIGHT OF THE VALKYRIE
Federal has a way of creating innovative, totally off-the-wall products to tantalize us shooters. A perfect example is the .224 Valkyrie, introduced in 2017. The name is based on Norse mythology and comes from the epic English poem "Beowulf," thought to have been written between

Handloads with CFE 223 powder from Hodgdon delivered excellent accuracy with several bullet combinations.

975 and 1025 A.D. In the poem, the god Odin ruled over his kingdom Asgard, and the Valkyries were maidens sent by Odin to the battlefields to select the slain worthy to go to the afterlife in Odin's magnificent palace called Valhalla. Thus, Valkyrie means "chooser of the dead." (Pay attention, there'll be a quiz later.)

Presumably, the cartridge name refers to the critters shot with it. I'm just guessing here, but you must admit, it's a catchy moniker. Consider this: We are all aware of the tremendous (and well-deserved) success of the 6.5 Creedmoor due to its tight chamber and cartridge case dimensions. The Valkyrie case mimics these case and chamber principles to the letter and is a powerful, efficient, and accurate round. It is equally applicable to bolt actions as well as AR platforms.

The Valkyrie case is based on the Remington 6.8 SPC, necked down to .22 caliber, with the same body diameter. So, 6.8 magazines are required for ARs. In addition, the Valkyrie's shoulder is pushed back somewhat to make room for today's long, skinny, high-ballistic coefficient (BC) bullets. The rim diameter is .422 inch — the same as the 6.8 SPC.

The designers of the Valkyrie case certainly did their homework. It holds plenty of powder for its bullet diameter and weight. And to stabilize these pencil projectiles, a fast 1:7-inch twist is standard. At the same time, the .224 gets the most out of 77- to 90-grain bullets, and lightweight (55- to 62-grain) ones shoot just fine. There is no such thing as "over stabilization" these days. Today's bullets are so good that this is not a problem. A 1:9-inch twist is required for 69-grain bullets and an 8-inch spin for 80-grainers. The Valkyrie is the next step up in what we might call the "twist wars." (History buffs will recall that the .25-35 Winchester, introduced in 1895, had a 1:8-inch twist.)

It's also important to note that the longer and heavier bullets appropriate to the Valkyrie have ridiculously high BCs, unheard of a few decades ago. Example: The Sierra 90-grain MatchKing has a BC of .563. This BC is slightly higher than the Hornady 130-grain 6.5mm ELD Match bullet.

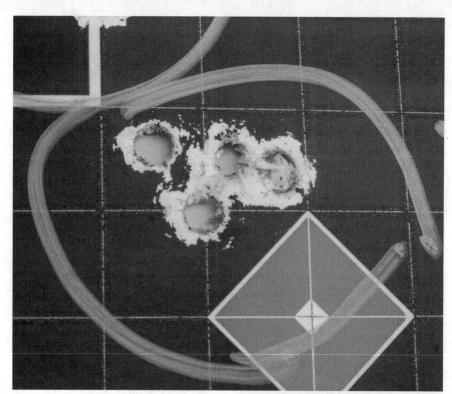

The Nosler 60-grain Ballistic Tip bullet showed varmint-ready groups with IMR-8208 XBR powder.

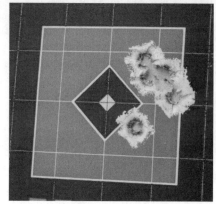

The Federal Factory load with the Fusion 90-grain soft point was accurate.

THE VALKYRIE'S QUEST

The .224 Valkyrie was slow to catch on. Still, word of its performance spread, and now, the Federal ammo folks say they're having difficulty keeping up with the demand. As you would expect, availability varies seasonally. In the Premium line, Federal has the 60-grain Nosler Ballistic Tip and 90-grain Sierra MatchKing; the American Eagle load has a 75-grain FMJ and the Fusion series with the 90-grain Fusion Soft Point. Hornady also offers three loads, the 60-grain Varmint Express, the 75-grain Black BTHP Match load (obviously intended for ARs), and the 88-grain ELD Match bullet. And Remington also makes three loads, a 60-grain Premier Accu-Tip, a 75-grain

FMJ, and a 90-grain Premier Match with the Sierra 90-grain MatchKing bullet.

I obtained seven of these loads for testing in the Momentum, and the results are shown in Table 1. I fired five-shot groups at 100 yards off a Lead Sled DFT in my shooting building. For the factory fodder, the overall average group size was .67 inch.

It's getting harder and harder for handloaders to best factory loads these days, but it's fun trying and reloading the Valkyrie is just, well, a blast. The little cartridge seems to like almost any combination of a suitable powder charge and good bullet. Dies and other tools are made by virtually all manufacturers and are usually available. I used Federal cases

TABLE 1. .224 VALKYRIE VELOCITY & ACCURACY

FRANCHI MOMENTUM ELITE VARMINT EDITION 24-INCH BARREL, 7-INCH TWIST	COL (IN.)	POWDER (TYPE)	POWDER (GRS.)	CASE	PRIMER	VEL. (FPS)	E.S. (FPS)	S.D. (FPS)	M.E. (FT-LB.)	100-YD. ACC. (IN.)
Handloads		Franchi Momentum Elite Varmint Edition								
Berger 55-gr. Flat Base Varmint	2.100	Ball-C(2)	28.6	Fed.	Fed 205	3,138	42	15	1,203	0.89
Berger 55-gr. Flat Base Varmint	2.100	Benchmark	25.2	Fed.	Fed 205	3,064	35	13	1,147	0.57
Berger 73-gr. BT Target	2.150	CFE 223	27.0	Fed.	Fed 205	2,948	35	14	1,409	0.93
Berger 80.5-gr. Full Bore Target	2.233	CFE 223	26.0	Fed.	Fed 205	2,785	26	10	1,387	0.63
Berger 85.5-gr. Long Range Hybrid Target	2.321	CFE 223	25.0	Fed.	Fed 205	2,671	27	11	1,355	1.04
Hornady 75-gr. ELD Match	2.306	CFE 223	26.5	Fed.	Fed 205	2,805	52	18	1,311	0.65
Hornady 75-gr. ELD Match	2.306	IMR 4166	24.5	Fed.	Fed 205	2,724	27	10	1,236	0.85
Nosler 55-gr. Ballistic Tip	2.146	CFE 223	29.3	Fed.	Fed 205	3,304	58	22	1,334	0.98
Nosler 60-gr. Ballistic Tip	2.180	CFE 223	26.2	Fed.	WSR	2,831	49	22	1,068	0.80
Nosler 60-gr. Ballistic Tip	2.180	IMR 4166	25.7	Fed.	Fed 205	2,850	30	11	1,082	0.98
Nosler 60-gr. Ballistic Tip	2.180	Ball-C(2)	27.2	Fed.	Fed 205	2,912	29	10	1,130	..57
Nosler 62-gr. Varmageddon FBHP	2.100	IMR 8208XBR	23.7	Fed.	Fed 205	2,753	47	16	1,044	0.71
Nosler 62-gr. Varmageddon FBHP	2.100	Benchmark	23.5	Fed.	Fed 205	2,815	36	12	1,091	0.57
Nosler 70-gr. RDF Match	2.123	CFE 223	27.5	Fed.	Fed 205	3,052	27	10	1,448	1.51
Nosler 77-gr. Custom Competition	2.167	CFE 223	27.0	Fed.	Fed 205	2,941	51	19	1,479	1.09
Sierra 69-gr. MatchKing Tipped MatchKing	2.194	CFE 223	27.8	Fed.	Fed 205	2,999	65	24	1,378	1.02
Sierra 77-gr. MatchKing Tipped MatchKing	2.245	IMR 4166	24.5	Fed.	Fed 205	2,718	66	27	1,263	1.19
Sierra 77-gr. MatchKing Tipped MatchKing	2.245	CFE 223	27.0	Fed.	Fed 205	2,851	50	21	1,263	1.06
Sierra 80-gr. MatchKing Tipped MatchKing	2.334	CFE 223	26.5	Fed.	Fed 205	2,779	21	10	1,372	1.00
Sierra 90-gr. MatchKing Tipped MatchKing	2.292	CFE 223	25.0	Fed.	Fed 205	2,593	63	25	1,344	0.92
									ave.	0.92

FACTORY LOADS			LISTED VEL. (FPS)			ACTUAL VEL. (FPS)	ED (FPS)	S.D. (FPS)	M.E. (FT-LB.)	100-YD. ACC. (IN.)
Federal Premium 60-gr. Nosler Ballistic Tip	2.169	Factory Load	3,300			3,164	35	12	1,334	0.61
Federal American Eagle 75-gr. FMJ	2.135	Factory Load	3,000			2,876	45	20	1,378	0.51
Federal Fusion 90-gr. Soft Point	2.253	Factory Load	2,700			2,548	19	8	1,298	0.71
Federal Premium Gold Medal Match, 90-gr. Sierra MK	2.252	Factory Load	2,700			2,735	52	21	1,495	0.67
Hornady Varmint Express, 60-gr. V-MAX	2.072	Factory Load	3,300			3,216	58	21	1,378	0.98
Hornady Black 75-gr. HPBT	2.253	Factory Load	3,000			2,895	27	10	1,396	0.55
Hornady 88-gr. ELD-Match	2.243	Factory Load	2,670			2,625	11	4	1,347	0.67
									ave.	0.67

Notes: Accuracy is for five-shot groups. Velocity measured 10 feet from the muzzle. All groups fired off a Lead Sled DFT rest from an indoor shooting building. Range temperatures were 42 to 58 degrees F. Sight was a Sightron S1 4-12x40 G2 scope in Leupold 1-inch rings.

There are several factory loads for the .224 Valkyrie, including these from Federal and Hornady.

SPECIFICATIONS

Model: Franchi Momentum Elite Varmint Edition
Type: Push-feed bolt-action repeater
Caliber: .224 Valkyrie, .223 Rem., and .22-250 Rem.
Magazine: Removable box, 4 and 7 rounds furnished
Barrel: 24 in. fluted, with muzzle brake, 26 in.
Twist: 1:7
Overall Length: 46.75 in.
Weight: 9 lbs., 1 oz. with scope and mount; 10 lbs., 4.1 oz.
Receiver: Carbon steel
Bolt: Three-lug, chrome-plated, fluted
Trigger: Pull weight 1 lb., 4.3 oz. user-adjustable
Sights: None, receiver drilled and tapped for scope bases, Rem. M-700 pattern; tested with Sightron S1 4-12x40 G2 in Leupold rings
Safety: Two-position on right-rear of the receiver
Finish: Bronze Cerakote, barrel and action
Stock: Synthetic, Optifade camo finish, length of pull 14 in.
Warranty: 7 years
franchiusa.com

for my test loads, but Starline also offers Valkyrie brass. I prepared test loads with RCBS dies in my Redding T-7 Turret press. Bullets were seated to the base of the case neck, primers were Federal No. 205, while one load used WSR primer. Many powders work great in the Valkyrie, but if I had to pick a favorite, it would be CFE 223. BL-C(2) and Benchmark are close behind, however. Not only does CFE 223 flow uniformly through a drum powder measure, but it also has Hodgdon's magic "copper fouling eraser" ingredients that retard jacket fouling. Loads with it are accurate.

I had good results across the bullet weight spectrum. Considering the case size, varmint-weight bullets of 55 and 60 grains shot very well and at high velocities. But one of the Valkyrie's claims to well-deserved fame is the ability to launch heavy-for-caliber bullets at relatively high velocities. That was the case in the Momentum. It shot well, and the barrel didn't foul excessively. The average group size for my 20 handloads was .92 inch, but several loads formed nice ragged holes.

The new Franchi Momentum Elite Varmint Edition is a winner and is a

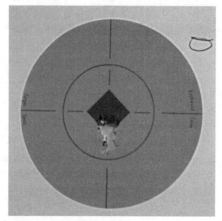

The Momentum was accurate with several factory and handloads. Above is a group made by the Nosler 60-grain Ballistic tip over 27.2 grains of Ball-C(2). The Hornady factory load printed the group with the 88-grain ELD Match bullet.

perfect platform for the powerful (for its size) and accurate Valkyrie round, with many weights and styles of bullets. Purists can have a Momentum Elite Varmint in .223 Remington (yawn) or .22-250 Remington (better), and they'd be fine, but, heck, they're like belly buttons — everybody has 'em. The Momentum is new and exciting, and it looks like the perfect home for the cleverly designed

.224 Valkyrie. And, as the saying goes, bullet holes in paper don't lie. And when you start shooting one, it's so much fun that you'll find it hard to stop.

That's my story, and I'm stickin' to it. Now, if you'll excuse me, I have to load up some Valkyrie ammo, so I can "prepare" some varmints for their trip to Valhalla. **GD**

The author prefers the stainless Taurus 605 Defender model with Hogue grips.

Taurus 605 Defender:
.357 Magnum
VERSATILITY FOR THE MASSES

❯ROBERT CAMPBELL

Among the most useful handguns for self-defense is a quality double-action revolver of medium size with a 3-inch barrel. These rugged handguns are what I like to call go anywhere, do anything handguns.

I like to have a handgun on my hip when traveling and hiking. After 50 years, packing a revolver just feels right in the wild. The revolver handles quickly with an excellent natural point, and accuracy is more than enough for the mission. Having found myself between the public and assailants more than once - not to mention a couple of attacks from dangerous animals - I demand powerful and reliable firearms. I am not eager to repeat specific battles, but if the task befalls me, I hope the outcome will again be in my favor.

THE NEW DEFENDERS

Among my favorite handguns is a relatively new revolver on the market. Taurus recently upgraded several of their revolvers to Defender status. The improvements are primarily centered on a heavy under-lugged barrel of 3-inch length rather than the standard 2-inch snubnose barrel. These may be appropriately called short-barrel revolvers rather than snubnose types. The Defender revolvers feature hand-filling grips; some are fitted with VZ grips, others with Hogue Monogrips, and others with wooden grips. Cerakote, blue and stainless steel finishes are available. The barrel features a heavy profile and a tritium front sight. A tritium insert is a rarity in revolvers, especially in this price range. The tritium dot isn't giant, but it is surrounded by an orange outline making this among the highest visibility sights in the revolver world. The Taurus' cylinder locks up solidly at the rear and with a detent in the crane. The revolver is double action with a remarkably smooth action and will compare in smoothness to any modern revolver at any price. The single-action press is crisp and smooth.

The 605 is a five-shot revolver chambered in .357 Magnum, which handles .38 Special cartridges as well. If you're not interested in using the magnum cartridge, the Taurus 856 Defender six-shot .38 Special may make a better choice. I prefer the option of Magnum loads for specific uses. The versatility of the combination of the .38 Special and .357 Magnum are proven in decades of use.

A good .38 Special for concealed carry or home defense is viable for a trained shooter. The Magnum is useful for those wishing to put effort into mastering the revolver. Magnum loads are best reserved for last-ditch efforts in animal defense when in territory that may harbor dangerous feral dogs or big cats. (Funny, you are armed at home to repel invaders while the animal considers humans the interloper. Whatever the moral quandary, I do not wish to become table fare for a mountain lion or a rag doll for a feral dog.)

My wrists are accustomed to pounding from heavy handguns, and my ears have hardened to blast. (Not entirely in jest. Even my pet barks more loudly these

Taurus also offers a dark finish.

A satin-finished revolver with wooden grips is an attractive option. The 605 Defender's heavy barrel adds balance.

This is a striking version of the 605 Defender. Note the VZ grips.

days to get my attention. So, of course, I use the best hearing protection available.) I discovered just what level of performance might be expected from such a light, handy revolver.

I am not concerned with the failure of the steel used in this revolver. While it is a lightweight handgun, the cylinder is strong enough for magnum loads. The bolt cut isn't directly over the cylinder but offset, which aids in strength. A lightweight magnum isn't going to crack

a frame or split a cylinder unless you go way too far with Elmer Keith memorial handloads. You can work wonders with handloads: A heavy cast SWC in .38 Special will outstrip factory .38 Special performance. You can even back off from full-power .357 Magnum loads with handloads offering real power without the magnum kick.

Like any good experimenter, I worked up several loads worthy of the little magnum. A caution: small parts take a

The 605 Defender is fast from leather. Whether facing assailants or dangerous animals, the Taurus 605 is a quick-handling and reliable handgun.

.38 Special Loads

MAGNUS BULLETS 198-GRAIN RNL

LOAD (GRS.)/ BRAND	VELOCITY (FPS)	15-YARD GROUP (IN.)
3.0 Titegroup	680	3.0
3.1 Unique	670	3.2
4.1 Unique	770	2.5
9.5 2400	909	2.6

Heavy loads put up in .38 Special case for .357 Magnum revolvers only.

160-GRAIN SWC MAGNUS

LOAD (GRS.)/ BRAND	VELOCITY (FPS)	15-YARD GROUP (IN.)
5.0 Unique	840	2.0
6.0 Unique	1,001	1.9

The Hornady XTP is a very accurate bullet. The XTP reliably expands to some degree, but at over 1,000 fps, expansion is better.

the revolver homes the bullets in on the target using this firing trick.

After promising results with .38 Special rounds, I fired 125-grain JHP magnum loads. The recoil is stout, as expected. It doesn't sting because the rubber Hogue grips separate your hand from the metal. In a worst-case scenario, shoving the revolver barrel into the body of an attacking bear or one of the big cats, the 605 Defender would be a lifesaver. Recoil and slow follow-up shots are too tricky for personal defense use by most standards. But then we are not running a contest to make a small cluster of fifty rounds at 20 yards but firing to save our life at a few feet. A magnum is an option.

There are modern .38 Special loads that offer excellent wound potential. Among the most useful of these is the Federal 120-grain Punch. I have been impressed by this load's performance. Another is the Federal 129-grain Hydra Shock +P. At nearly 1,000 fps, the balance of expansion and penetration is good. These loads make a reasonable choice for personal defense.

I had a small supply of the .357 Magnum Remington 125-grain Golden Saber, tailored to perform well in short-barrel magnum revolvers while offering a jump in performance over .38 Special loads. At 1,240 fps, this is a powerful loading offering good wound potential. Compared to a full-power magnum, the Golden Saber isn't difficult to control in double-action pairs. The rub is that most places show OUT OF STOCK for the stuff. If you can find it, this is the best choice for defense use in the short-barrel magnum.

I put together several loads to test in the Taurus 605 Defender .357 Magnum. I also had a small number of handloads - drat the primer supply chain - that proved helpful. Along the way, I came across a couple of exceptional loads. The Buffalo Bore .38 Special Outdoorsman

beating. My 605 Defender is as tight as new after 800 mixed loads over a year and a half of experiments. However, a light revolver is more likely to go out of time than a larger magnum.

I worked the Taurus 605 Defender on the range in combat drills and tested target accuracy. There was no point in testing ammunition performance if the revolver wasn't worth the effort. I began with factory generic practice loads in .38 Special. Firing quickly at 5

to 10 yards, the revolver is fast on target, well-balanced, and pleasant to fire. The double-action press is smooth, and the front sight offers rapid sight picture acquisition. A tip: For rapid shooting, set the high-visibility sight just a bit high over the groove that serves as the rear sight. This sight picture causes the bullet to strike high on the target, so aim a few inches below the X ring at close range and shoot for the belt buckle at 10 to 15 yards. Firing quickly in double action,

While a deformed nose also does damage, the expanded Hornady XTP, center, is most effective.

Several .38 Special loads were test fired in the Taurus 605 Defender with good results.

.357 Magnum Loads

STARLINE .357 MAGNUM BRASS 125-GRAIN XTP

LOAD (GRS.)/ BRAND	VELOCITY (FPS)	15-YARD GROUP (IN.)
6.8 Titegroup	1,121	2.4
7.5 Titegroup	1,200	2.0

158-GRAIN SWC MATTSBULLETS.COM

LOAD (GRS.)/ BRAND	VELOCITY (FPS)	15-YARD GROUP (IN.)
6.2 Unique	1,055	2.4

180-GRAIN XTP

LOAD (GRS.)/ BRAND	VELOCITY (FPS)	15-YARD GROUP (IN.)
12.0* 2400	1,050	1.9*MAX load. Work up with care.

is a modern rendition of the old Keith load with a true Keith-type SWC, a flat meplat, and a sharp-driving shoulder. At 1,060 fps, it isn't something I would like to fire in an airweight .38, but it is ideal for the 605 Defender.

Buffalo Bore also offers a slightly softer bullet in hollowpoint form, the 158-grain LSWCHP. Cast bullets are not soft lead and don't unnecessarily lead the bore. The Buffalo Bore hollowpoint offers impressive wound potential. I would be as confident with this as the Golden Saber load. If hiking, camping, or packing a revolver while hunting with a rifle, the Buffalo Bore Outdoorsman 158-grain SWC offers real promise in defensive use against animals as the hardcast SWC doesn't expand and gives you excellent penetration.

HOLSTER IDEAS

A quality revolver needs a first-class high-riding holster, offering a sharp draw and comfortable carry. The balance between retention and speed is essential in a working man's revolver holster. The Galco Combat Master is that type of holster. Quality stitching, a reinforced spine, and a design that sets the holster high on the belt line make for an excellent choice for town or country work. It complements a fine handgun. GD

Penetration and Expansion Using Water Jugs

.38 SPECIAL

FACTORY LOAD	VELOCITY (FPS)	PENETRATION (IN.)	EXPANSION (IN.)
Black Hills 100-gr. Honey Badger	1,113	20	.355
Fiocchi 110-gr. JHP +P	1,090	24	.45
Fiocchi 125-gr. XTP	1,030	20	.54
Federal 120-gr. Punch	939	18	.55
Buffalo Bore 158-gr. Lead HP	1,011	22	Nose Blown

.357 MAGNUM FACTORY LOADS

FACTORY LOAD	VELOCITY (FPS)	PENETRATION (IN.)	EXPANSION (IN.)
Remington 125-gr. Golden Saber	1,240	20	.63
Buffalo Bore 125-gr. Barnes Low Recoil	1,180	18	.64
Hornady 125-gr. XTP	1,289	22	.50
Hornady 125-gr. Critical Defense	1,283	20	.54
Hornady 130-gr. Handgun Hunter	1,260	24	.60

Mossberg Maverick 88
Youth 20 Gauge

Many people dislike 12-gauge shotgun recoil. This affordable 20 gauge is a sensible alternative.

❯ AL DOYLE

The author found the Mossberg Maverick 88 Bantam 20 Gauge youth model to be the perfect solution for a wide range of shooters with varying abilities.

Need some firearms-related inspiration and ideas? Visiting a well-stocked gun shop could be the catalyst. That's exactly what happened when I browsed at my favorite independently-owned retailer. With 250 or more firearms available, the most interesting items might not be prominently displayed, and a hidden gem was housed in an obscure rack of moderately priced single-shot and pump shotguns.

In addition to a short buttstock and two beads on the barrel, something else was different about the Maverick 88 — Mossberg's lower-priced brand — 20-gauge pump youth gun. The barrel looked shorter than normal for a hunting piece but wasn't as stubby as the 18 and 18 1/2-inch models designed for home defense. This budget-friendly pump screamed, "Check me out!" and I gave in.

In addition to the Bantam youth model, the Maverick 88 comes in many other "full-size" Security-variant flavors, such as the eight-shot FDE model (top), six-round Shotforce (middle), and Security Field Combo.

The Maverick came with a 22-inch barrel, so how did this in-betweener handle? The unpretentious gun — black synthetic stock, no rails — was incredibly well-balanced. It was the first time I handled a 20 gauge in years, and it revived a long-forgotten idea: How does a 20 gauge compare to the hugely popular 12 gauge for self-defense and especially in recoil reduction for those of small stature, advanced age, or various physical limitations that can make the 12 too much to absorb?

This Maverick came in a Mossberg box with a small Maverick label on the flap.

Low-priced birdshot, sometimes known as "promotional loads," was the starting point for this experiment. Every mass-market 12- and 20-gauge box promises a full ounce of shot in the 12-gauge shells versus 7/8 ounce of metal in the 20. Subtracting an eighth of an ounce means a 20 gauge sends 382.81 grains downrange, which is more than a trio of 115-grain 9mm bullets. The exact numbers apply to traditional-length buckshot loads, which could be a better option in a tense encounter.

I shot the Maverick with birdshot, buckshot, slugs, and a few rounds of Hevi Metal 20 gauge, which contains a full ounce of number 4 shot. Recoil was tame with all shells. The buckshot may have

been marginally "hotter" than the other options, but my 64-year-old shoulder felt zero discomfort with any rounds. The same wouldn't be said after a session with a mix of 12-gauge shells. Manageable recoil makes practice and training a pleasure. Never buy a gun, toss it in the closet, and hope for the best when a bad guy makes his move.

TESTING THE MAVERICK

One person testing any item is a small sample size, so I passed the Maverick around for others to use. The goal was for people with problems with the 12 gauge to test a 20 and see how it worked. Here are the reviews.

Small-framed (5'8", 135 pounds) 73-year-old man: "It didn't hurt me at all. The rounds cycle very easily. This would make a great trunk gun." This shooter had a detached retina that turned him into a .410 shotgun user, but he quickly ran rounds through the 20-gauge pump with ease.

14-year-old girl: "At first, I was a little nervous about it recoiling into my shoulder, but the more I shot it and kept it tight against my body, it didn't hurt badly at all. Aiming was easy, and I could hit targets. I enjoyed shooting it, and I highly recommend it."

31-year-old woman: "It is very simple to use, and I seemed to hit what I was aiming at. It didn't hurt while shooting. My right arm got sore a little later, but nowhere near as bad as my arm has gotten shooting 12-gauge shotguns. Overall, it was a pleasant experience. I would recommend it."

A 71-year-old man with decades of 12-gauge experience: "This is great. It was like it had no recoil. I'm a convert. I'm buying a 20 gauge."

29-year-old man, 5'7", 118 pounds: "I have had some health issues over the past several years, and this has made me lose a lot of weight. This has caused me to stop handling certain types of firearms. Shotguns are the main guns I no longer shoot. I was very interested to see how I could handle the 20 gauge. I was expecting to not see much of a difference over the 12 gauges I no longer shoot, but I was

A teenage (14-year-old) girl had no issues with the Maverick 20 gauge.

Besides home defense, a 20 gauge is ideal for beginners.

wrong. I sent birdshot, buckshot, and slugs downrange and was able to control everything. If you have health issues or problems controlling a 12 gauge, I would seriously consider this 20 gauge. It is much more manageable than a 12 gauge and just as easy to operate as any other pump shotgun."

It's possible to short-stroke a pump shotgun in a stressful situation, as fine motor skills can decline under pressure. The 20-gauge American-made Maverick loaded rounds smoothly and with little effort right out of the box, so that is a plus for defensive use. Twin action bars and dual extractors are the same as those used on pricier Mossberg scatterguns.

Some gun dealers understand that owning and using a 12 gauge isn't for everyone. Tom Lauritzen of Lauritzen Sports in Wild Rose, Wisconsin, recommends 20-gauge pumps. "We've sold a lot of 20 gauges since the Covid-19 pandemic," he said. "There are two contributing factors. Beginners were buying shotguns for home defense, and there were more older folks buying guns. In both cases, it was related to recoil. I have suggested 20 gauge and even .410 to recoil-sensitive customers."

The 12-gauge pump is an American icon, but the 20 gauge is popular enough for stores to carry an assortment of shells.

"12-gauge shells are more common and readily available, but buying rounds for a 20 gauge won't be a problem at all," Lauritzen said. "If you need it, a 20 gauge can be effective for sure."

There could be another reason for obtaining a 20 gauge over a pistol: Heavily left-leaning states such as Massachusetts and New Jersey make it easier (relatively speaking) to purchase a long gun over a handgun. If you're unfortunate enough to live in such places, a shotgun purchase could result in less aggravation.

The 2022 story of 80-year-old Craig Cope is Exhibit A of how a shotgun can protect an older person in a life-threatening encounter.

Cope was working alone at his Norco Market & Liquor store in Norco, California when four masked and armed intruders entered. The first was carrying an "AR-15-style" rifle. Cope reached for a shotgun and hit the rifle holder in

Clint Smith on 20-Gauge Defense

Hitting where you aim at typical home defense distances is no problem. The Maverick can handle headshots or torso shots.

There is a surprising lack of 20-ga. defensive loads on the market. However, one good option is Federal's 20-ga. No. 3 Buck from the Power Shok line.

the arm. Multiple news accounts failed to mention if Cope's firearm was a 12 or 20 gauge, but that single round left the would-be robber screaming, "He shot my arm off! He shot my arm off!" The arm was still attached to the perp's body, but his accomplices immediately lost interest in the contents of Cope's cash register and took off.

Taller people might need to add a slip-on recoil pad to obtain a longer length of pull on the youth model, but the Mossberg Maverick 88 20 gauge provides dependable, soft-shooting protection for less than $300. **GD**

Even though the 12 gauge is the standard bore at his shotgun classes, Clint Smith of Thunder Ranch in Lakeview, Oregon, sees the 20 gauge as a viable option.

"There's no problem with the 20," he said. "One of the most memorable shootings I ever saw as a cop was with a 20 gauge and birdshot. The guy's jaw was pretty much blown off."

Never acquire your gun "knowledge" from Hollywood, which gets it wrong only 98% of the time. Renegade 300-pound bikers aren't sent somersaulting through the air by a load of shot fired from 125 yards away. The shotgun is a proven performer at shorter distances, but don't be casual about aiming. "As a general rule, each yard of distance results in an inch of spread in the pattern," Smith said. "Buckshot might pattern a little tighter than birdshot. Inside the house, a shotgun is more like a rifle ... I tell my students to measure the farthest distances they might have to shoot and check the patterns from different places."

Don't lead with your gun barrel into a room, or a hidden bad guy might grab the weapon.

Many people stand straight in front of a paper target, fire a few rounds, and call it good. That's not how life works. Home invaders are mobile, so practice shooting at different angles while moving. What happens if you end up on the ground? Fire a few rounds from your butt to know what to do. If your plan includes the possibility of hunkering down behind a bed or other objects, duplicate that position while you're at the range.

Remaining in place with your gun ready can be a logical option, as those with less than youthful agility or health might not want to be stumbling around the house when danger is lurking. Regarding home defense encounters, shooting beyond 25 feet is rare. Any firearm can be useful in those situations, but shotguns often shine when things are up close and personal.

"If someone gets hit with a shotgun at 15 feet, they will have a chunk of (expletive) removed from their body," Smith noted.

Verbal drills are just as crucial as trigger time, which can be done at home. Practice dealing with the potential threat. Keep your speech short, commanding and loud, as in "Stop!" "Don't move!" and "On the floor!" You want the burglar to think you're a Marine Corps drill instructor or psychotic and off your meds for a week. That might not be as challenging as it sounds, as there will be justifiable anger when you find someone with less than honorable intentions has invaded your home.

Don't reveal too much when talking to intruders.

"You can tell them to leave the house, but I never tell people I have a gun," Smith said. "They'll find that out when they get shot."

The subject of pump shotguns brings up one of the most clueless remarks in gun circles. Everyone has heard the line, "If someone breaks in, I'll rack the slide and scare 'em off."

Smith said, "Why let them know what kind of gun I have? If you want to scare people, get a Halloween mask."

Glock 48

Glock's Most Perfect Carry Gun Yet?

›COREY GRAFF

T he Glock pistol is to Gen Xers like me what the 1911 was to Baby Boomers. In the late 1990s, when I turned legal age to buy a handgun, the Glock was the choice of law enforcement agencies nationwide. Concealed carry laws were gaining traction in state legislatures; Glock was what we bought, and Glock was what we knew.

And to borrow its marketing slogan, we honestly thought the polymer apparatus from Austria was "perfection" personified.

Of course, competitive pressures would eventually force Glock handguns to undergo their own generational changes — we're at "Gen 5" as I write this — as the polymer striker-fired handgun market flooded with Springfield Armory, Ruger, Smith & Wesson, and others. For many armed citizens, the Glock 19 mid-size compact with its massive double-stack 15+1 capacity would take on an almost cult-like following as concealed carry became "a thing." It would be hard to imagine anything better, but with the G48, I'm here to argue that Glock has managed.

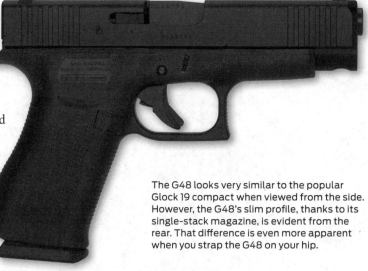

Hornady's Critical Defense 115-grain FTX shot superb groups from the Glock 48 and features a controlled-expansion bullet ideal for personal protection.

GLOCK SINGLE-STACK COMES OF AGE

What makes the Glock 48 such a natural option for concealed carry is its slim design — made possible thanks to its single-stack mag and trim slide. The little pistol represents Glock's Slimline series, which it shares with the G43 and G43x (a single-shot 9mm with a shorter grip), G36 (a subcompact single-stack 6+1 .45 Auto), and the G42 (Glock's much-ballyhooed 6+1 .380 Auto) models. (As of summer 2020, MOS or Modular Optics System versions were available in the G43XMOS and G48MOS.) The 10-shot G48's slide measures a prim .87 inch in width, compared to the G19's comparatively portly 1-inch-wide thickness (the G48's maximum thickness at the frame is 1.10 in.). That .13 inch might not seem like much, but when each day is a battle to resist the effects of gravity pulling you slowly over the hill, and each meal threatens to blast you up into a new belt size, it's a country mile.

Sure, the Glock 48 looks like the front end of a 1979 Volkswagen van, but the stuff under the hood is what matters. Despite its compact size, the G48's controls are full-size, so you won't waste

The G48 looks very similar to the popular Glock 19 compact when viewed from the side. However, the G48's slim profile, thanks to its single-stack magazine, is evident from the rear. That difference is even more apparent when you strap the G48 on your hip.

milliseconds fumbling around for the mag release button. There's a slight flare on the front interior of the magwell but not on the sides. The gun comes with two 10-round magazines, which, as some Spinal Tap fans have discovered, will take 11 rounds, but deviating from OEM mode in a carry pistol isn't recommended.

Glock doesn't list the G48 as a Gen 5 gun (Gen 5 developed as a variation of the FBI's M Pistol). Still, most of the newest features are present, including the lack of finger grooves and stippling, the 4.17-inch Glock Marksman Barrel (GMB),

front slide serrations, tough nDLC finish, reversible mag release button, and built-in beavertail grip. Southpaws take note: It does not sport ambi controls, which is one of the design compromises required to keep the pistol narrow. Yet, at just 25 ounces fully loaded, this little concealed carry handgun balances like a dream and will feel like an old hat for G19 shooters. What's more, unlike the G43, its grip is long enough to give you complete control under recoil when quickly emptying a full mag into an IDPA target — or, God forbid, if you're forced to stop a lethal threat.

The sights are typical white outline Glock, non-adjustable. I swapped them out for the XS Sights Big Dot, which makes hitting center mass at 7 yards ridiculously fast and easy.

The Glock 48 has the shorter trigger travel of the Gen 5 guns, and while no one will compare its trigger pull to a carefully honed 1911, it is an improvement over previous generations. It feels like a double-action revolver, tripping at just over 5 pounds. It would be easily defensible under a post-self-defense shooting cross-examination in court, where an anti-gun prosecutor may try to paint you as a gun nut with a "hair trigger."

"The Gen5 Glock, in my opinion, has the best 'street trigger' that any manufacturer has ever put in a pistol," says Massad Ayoob in *Deadly Force, 2nd Edition*. "It doesn't need a NY-1 module because it already gives a firm, smooth trigger pull, which meets the company's long-standing 5.5 pounds minimum pull weight recommendation."

G48 SPECS

Caliber: 9X19mm
Width: 1.10 in.
Length: 7.28 in.
Height incl. magazine: 5.04 in.
Sight radius (polymer): 5.98 in.
Barrel length: 4.17 in.
Mag. capacity: 10
Weight incl. magazine: 20.74 oz.
Weight loaded: 25.12 oz.
MSRP $580
us.glock.com

As of summer 2020, Glock's G48 Slimline could be used with reflex-style optics in a MOS version. However, as *Gun Digest* online content developer Woody Shelton points out, "Given the guns' whisper-thin widths, the slide cut is only compatible with specific micro-reflex optics, including Shield RMSc and JP Enterprises' Jpoint. In addition, the Glock 43X MOS and Glock 48 MOS also have non-standard accessory rails, meaning not every weapon light can attach to the pistols."

Of Glock's 9mm Slimline single-stacks, the G43 has a .79-inch shorter grip and four fewer rounds than the G48 (top). However, the G43X has the G43's shorter 3.41-inch barrel, the G48's grip length, and a 10-round capacity.

AT THE RANGE

From 7 yards, the G48 does everything you need: It goes bang each time you pull the trigger and chews through every type of ammo you feed it. Like an old Toyota truck, it's just plain reliable. I ran a variety of ammunition through the gun from Winchester, Hornady, and Federal. As I've come to expect from Glocks, it was boringly consistent and gave me no failures to feed, eject, or any other issues.

I did not do any accuracy testing from a solid rest. However, the two top accuracy performers shooting offhand were the Hornady Critical Defense and Federal's HST, which printed 1.30- and 2.70-inch groups, respectively. Again, this is offhand shooting with defensive training methods, not locked into a Ransom Rest or using marksmanship techniques. Regarding personal defense ammo, the armed citizen's primary concerns are reliability, accuracy, and a good bullet to stop the threat as quickly as possible without

The G48's recoil with full-power defensive ammo was controllable under rapid fire. If you've ever shot the G19, you'll feel at home with the slimmer G48.

Federal Premium's HST LE 147-grain ammo was another top performer in the Glock 48. It was accurate, completely reliable, and designed for personal protection.

endangering bystanders — that means hollowpoint. These ammo choices were accurate, each with an excellent bullet for personal defense. The Federal shoots the 115-grain FTX bullet while the Hornady is loaded with the 147-grain HST LE projectile. Bullets like these — engineered for maximum controlled penetration and tissue destruction — put the 9mm caliber on the map against old standbys such as the .45 ACP.

I also had some Winchester Active Duty MHS M1152 115-grain FMJ ball ammo, which became my preferred training load. It shoots accurately and is full power, giving you a realistic training experience.

I used an inside-the-waistband (IWB) holster from Stealth Gear USA, which is padded and comfortable. Combined with the G48's virtually weightless and compact signature, that holster means the whole package disappears on your hip. You (almost) forget it's there.

Like all Glocks, the plastic case contains a nylon cleaning brush, two magazines, a handy mag loader, and all your manuals and paperwork. Glock 48 disassembly is a breeze: Double- and triple-check that the gun is unloaded, point it in a safe direction and squeeze the trigger. Pull the slide rearward slightly and depress the slide release latch. Let

the slide come forward, pulling it up and off the frame. Remove the recoil spring and extract the barrel. Carefully clean everything per the manual and reverse the steps to reassemble.

IS IT A KEEPER?

Since the rip-roaring '90s, many companies have entered the striker-fired compact 9mm market with arguably more refined ergonomics and (some claim) better triggers. But there's a good reason brand trust pulls people like me to Glock — and that reason is *reliability*. When you want something that will fire every round and shoot those rounds with impressive accuracy right out of the box, you buy a Glock.

And while I wasn't able to pry sales figures from the notoriously secretive Glock, a perusal of online auction sites and local gun stores indicates the little G48 is selling like hotcakes. "The Slimline

series (G43X and G48) are in high demand for their versatility and increased magazine capacity as we see with the iconic G19 as well," Brandie Collins, Marketing Director for Glock, told *Gun Digest*.

With a street price of around $480, which defies today's crushing inflation, it's an expense that people new to concealed carry can swing, knowing that they'll also need to buy ammo, holsters, and possibly a new wardrobe to accommodate a concealed handgun. Some have argued that there are more refined pistols in this category, but when it comes to a handgun that I know I can bet my life on, I go to what I know works. Based on my experience, that means Glock. In hindsight, the Glock 19 compact set the bar high for concealed carry, but the G48 is superior — some might even say "perfection." The only thing I can't figure out, Glock, is why it took you so long. **GD**

Ultra Light 20
ARMS MODEL
aka, Spomer's Favorite Rifle

❯RON SPOMER

It was love at first feel.

The year was 1986. I was 33 years old and hot to trot up any mountain that promised a sheep, goat, elk, caribou — any legal game animal calling the mountain wilderness home. In pursuit of such, I'd developed a wandering eye. It would settle with lust on any lithe, trim, and beautiful rifle. The one I landed on that year was not a traditional beauty, but once I touched it … positively gorgeous.

The author quickly discovered his ULA M20 was just as effective on the plains as in the mountains. He carried it with complete confidence on a Kansas hunt that led to this 180-class 5x5 taken on the run at roughly 240 yards. By this date, 1997, the rifle wore its new paint scheme.

The old girl in all her glory. Light and right.

Above: Spomer's ULA M20 shoots a wide variety of bullets, MOA or better. His latest is a 120-gr. Barnes TSX at 3,186 fps.

Left: The 3-inch magazine box of the ULA M20 accommodates relatively long bullets.

Say hello, big boy, to the Ultra Light Arms Model 20.

The display rifle was what my friend Dwight would call "tarted up." It showed a little leg via its original, garish, green-brown-and-black-striped hide. Despite this bold step away from tradition, I lifted the rifle from its display stand at the 1986 NRA Convention and fell in love. It sported a full-size stock and 22-inch button-rifled Douglas barrel, and the rifle felt deadly. Ridiculously quick to the shoulder and nigh perfectly aligned with my aiming eye, it balanced like a ballerina, yet hanging on target as if five pounds heavier.

I then looked at the chamber marking on the barrel and nearly drooled: 284 Win. — my ultimate mountain sheep cartridge. On the action's left side was etched Ultra Light Arms Model 20. I write "etched" because Melvin Forbes, the M20's designer and builder, had used an etching tool (think Dremel) to inscribe the letters and numbers. This was

his prototype rifle, the first of what was to become the iconic ultralight rifle of the latter years of the 20th century and the first two decades of the 21st. I didn't know that at the time, of course. I just knew that I needed to invite this new love to join me in pursuit of my old love — wilderness big game hunting.

Our first date was to the tundra peaks of British Columbia's Coast Range, the epicenter of the North American mountain goat range protected by black bears and grizzlies with enough moose scattered about to make one tread lightly through the willows. Before embarking, I'd built handloads with 58 grains of Hodgdon 4831 ignited by CCI 200 primers. The combination pushed 140-gr. Nosler Partitions 2,950 fps into

MOA clusters. Zeroed 3 inches high at 100 yards, those bullets would peak 3.5 inches high at 150 yards and drop just 4 inches below the point of aim at 315 yards. A center chest hold would suffice for anything to 300 yards. For 400-yard targets, I "held a bit of daylight" over the withers, the bullets dropping 15 inches right into the heart/lung boiler room, as the old timers used to call it back in the 1960s when I was learning the ropes.

It worked.

A heavily-horned mountain mule deer collapsed inside 200 yards. I can no longer recall the range of the mountain goat. Probably 250 yards. Close enough that a dead-on hold broke the onside shoulder. When the billy spun around, a second 140-grain Partition broke the other shoulder, anchoring the animal to the ledge. Two for two, and the party was on.

I worked up a 139-grain Hornady Interlock load that liked 56 grains of IMR-4350 to group MOA at 2,985 fps muzzle velocity. That proved itself on a little 4x4 coues whitetail at an estimated 400 yards (411 yards when stepped off to confirm.) One and done, and the 6-pound weight of the rifle — sling, Talley rings, three-round magazine fully stuffed and a 2.5-8x36 Leupold VXIII directing the aim — was on its way to glory.

That first hunting season, the lithe .284 Win. spit 11 bullets to anchor 10 animals, including five coyotes, two running flat out.

The honeymoon continued the following season. Elk, a bighorn ram, Dall's ram, caribou, one of the largest whitetails of my life and much more. I built and tested additional loads with 130- and 145-grain Speer bullets, 140-grain Sierra boattails, Nosler Ballistic Tips and a 120-grain Barnes TSX skipping off at an impressive 3,186 fps, H-414 powder doing the heavy lifting. And now, 35 years on, I remain as loyal

to the ULA M20 as my "gun writer" career permits. (Cry me a river: I'm often tasked with hunting various beasts with sundry rifles from several manufacturers.)

Yes, I've flirted with a biblical host of other rifles and cartridges, but my fidelity to the M20 remains. Were I forced to forswear all others, this is the one I'd hang onto. So I'd best explain myself and spill the beans as to how this particular collection of steel and Kevlar has been put together to perform so well.

West Virginia gun builder Melvin Forbes conceived his Ultra Light Arms M20 as the ultimate mountain rifle. I suspect he chose the .284 Winchester as it is a short-action equivalent of the .280 Remington, which is the 7mm "improvement" of the .30-06 Springfield and .270 Winchester. In short, the .284 pushes to roughly the same velocities of the same-weight bullets as the .30-06 but with higher

ballistic coefficients. This translates to flatter trajectories, reduced wind deflection, and higher retained energies. It'll throw the same 150-grain bullet mass as the .270 Win., but with a slightly lower B.C. It compensates by doing this in a shorter, lighter action. In addition, the .284 Win. stands ready to push high-B.C. 160-grain bullets at 2,800 fps and deep penetrating 175-grain slugs as fast as 2,660 fps, bullet weights and lengths .270 Winchester factory rifles are not able to stabilize.

Such is my pitch for the .284 Winchester cartridge. Now on to the rifle.

Forbes kept weight an ounce or three below 5 pounds by recreating the traditional push-feed action to do more with less. He trimmed the size to a fair-thee-well and used strong, modern steel

From an early catalog showing the original, eye-catching color scheme.

The action and bolt of the M20 have been scaled down to a minimum while retaining essential steel strength and integrity. The actions have been tested to 124,000 psi without failing.

Spomer still finds the M20 easy to carry and aim. It seems to find and hang onto targets as if on auto-pilot. Recoil is mild, helping with follow-up shots, not that they are often needed.

without sacrificing strength or safety. His trimmed-down actions have been tested to double the industry-standard chamber pressures without measurable ill effects.

The M20 bolt is a traditional, dual-lug style with a Sako-style extractor hook and plunger ejector. What appears to be a two-position, rocker safety on the right rear of the action is a three-function safety. Fully back, it locks the bolt and Timney trigger, another Forbes design. Pushed forward, it frees the rifle to fire. Pushed down while in the rear, safe position, it continues blocking the trigger but frees the bolt for removing rounds from the magazine. The bolt and locking lugs are "blueprinted" 90 degrees to the centerline of the action and barrel.

Integral to the performance of the M20 is its 18-ounce Kevlar/graphite stock. The material is absolutely stiff, water-proof, and incredibly tough, but its shape contributes mightily to rifle performance. The full, nicely rounded comb slants upward to the heel. This results in it sliding under your cheekbone during recoil, not slapping into it. Aiding this is an over-

Short and fat, the .284 Win. of 1964 hangs close to the performance of more recent short, fat cartridges like the 7mm SAUM and 7WSM.

sized, raised cheekpiece some 20% larger than those found on most rifles. It affords excellent cheek weld. The relatively open pistol grip accommodates a variety of

hand sizes without pinching. The stock's blind magazine features a 3-inch long well to accommodate the longer, high-B.C. bullets so popular these days.

Finally, and critically, the stock is full-length bedded to the barreled action. Lest floating barrel aficionados blanch, understand that floating is unnecessary when stock material is as stiff and consistent as the Ultra Light Arms' stock. Fitted evenly and tightly to the barrel, it acts as a stiffener, dampening oscillations and vibrations. The result is 100-yard impact consistency with nearly any bullet weight. I get MOA performance with most loads, sub MOA with many. I once worked up three different loads of H414 powder from 56 to 57.5 grains behind 120-grain TSX bullets. Velocity variations from four shots spread from 3,172 fps to 3,196 fps, yet bullet holes spanned just .815-inch on the 100-yard target. Thereafter, the 56.5-grain loading printed four TSX bullets into .788 inch.

My original M20 came with Talley aluminum, one-piece rings (yet another Forbes design) with integral bases. These

The short .284 Win. can shoot some of today's heaviest, longest bullets (depending on twist rate), but Spomer has had excellent success with traditional 120- to 140-grain bullets like the loaded 120-gr. TSX on the right.

Forbes literally etched the model number on this, his prototype ULA M20. Wilson Combat will soon make them.

WILSON COMBAT TO BUILD
Ultra Light Arms Rifles
Going Forward

Since I acquired my M20 Ultra Light Arms rifle, that company sold, and the new owner subsequently went out of business. Forbes reconstituted it as New Ultra Light Arms and resumed building his top-quality models. More recently, Forbes sold to Wilson Combat, which should be building Ultra Light Arms rifles going forward. Watch wilsoncombat.com for news on the production of new ULA rifles.

have remained on the rifle through a half-dozen scope changes. They add less than 3 ounces to the rifle and have done everything scope rings are hired to do without weighing half as much as the scope itself.

Finally, this rifle has the nebulous, difficult-to-articulate "feel" or magic. Something about it — likely the sum total of its weight, balance, form, and payload — makes it perform as we wish all rifles would. It carries like a thought, comes to the shoulder as if self-powered, and delivers bullets like heat-seeking missiles. And, no, it does not kick like a mule. Not even a newborn foal. The stock materials and design absorb or moderate recoil as magically as the barrel throws bullets. Men and women of all frames and sizes to whom I've loaned this rifle marvel at its moderate recoil behavior. But to enjoy it further, they are instructed to beg, borrow, or steal one of their own because this Ultra Light Arms M20 .284 Winchester is sticking with me for as long as I can carry it. Given its light weight, that'll be a long, long time. Ⓖ

Soon after obtaining his M20, Spomer stalked and dropped a heavily antlered whitetail tooth aged 13 years. A 140-gr Nosler Partition caught it amidships from 325 yards. Note the original striped paint job.

Dad's Last Gun

› ANDREW EWERT

Father and son shared a lifetime of firearms experiences. But in the end, there was one piece of unfinished business.

Beauty and the Beast? The Glock 19 Gen 5 (below) with the Browning Hi-Power. The Glock is a different pistol from a different era. While it lacks the elegant lines, fine bluing, sculpted all-steel construction, and French walnut grips of this 1970s-vintage Hi-Power, it does offer high magazine capacity in a lighter-weight package. Add reliability with modern, high-performance ammunition and easy takedown, and the Glock comes ahead.

Although they didn't share the last handgun, the author and his father, Harry Ewert, enjoyed over half a century of shooting, reloading, hunting, and acquiring firearms together. By adding a Glock 19 to the collection, the author completed their unfinished business.

As father-son relationships go, Dad's and mine lasted 64 years. We shared a lifetime of hunting, shooting, reloading, and "accumulating" all kinds of firearms, including rifles, shotguns, and handguns. We shot them all, reloaded for most of them, and added to the trove periodically when our finances aligned with our desires. And sometimes, when they didn't.

The story of Dad's last gun is a puzzle that, once assembled, was the sum of our knowledge and wisdom, somewhat belated, with a seemingly contradictory outcome if viewed after the fact. It's a story best told from the beginning.

From my early teens, hardly a day went by when my father and I didn't discuss, fantasize, and argue (sometimes heatedly) about the merits of one gun versus another. My poor mother bemoaned the perpetual subject matter in vain.

My late mother, Marilyn, and my late father, Harry, raised me well; Dad worked as an electrician, and Mom was an advertising copywriter. We lived in a modest house in a cozy, middle-class, tree-lined suburb in Wisconsin.

Under my father's tutelage, my introduction to the firearms world was gradual and measured. At age 10, Dad began taking me to gun stores and shows and introduced me to his friends steeped in firearms culture. His voluminous library of gun books (including many fine editions of *Gun Digest*), magazines, and sales literature in the basement was always open to me, on one condition (not always honored) that I *put all borrowed items back where I found them*.

Being young, curious, and fascinated with firearms, I read his collection enthusiastically and absorbed what I learned like a sponge. In time, my book knowledge would rival his. Looking back, I couldn't have asked for a better upbringing.

When I reached 12, Dad decided it was time to begin my formal firearms education. He taught me pistol craft with his classic Smith & Wesson K38 .38 Special revolver and allowed me to shoot my Marlin 39 .22 lever-action rifle, a birthday gift from his brother, under strict supervision.

During my teens, I purchased my first shotgun, a beautiful Browning Auto 5 in 20-gauge magnum, and my first handgun, a Smith & Wesson 6-1/2-inch barreled Model 28 Highway Patrolman, from the fruits of my summer and after-school jobs. At 16, I hunted ducks, geese, pheasants, and furred game with the Browning and perforated coffee cans and paper targets with .38 Special wadcutters shot from that Model 28. A while later, Dad and I took up deer hunting. There was wild game in the freezer during the winter for our family's dining pleasure.

Handguns were our first love. Over the years, we owned and shot over 50 revolvers and semi-autos by Smith & Wesson, Colt, and Ruger. The foreign models came later.

We reloaded the most popular American centerfire handgun cartridges. We graduated to casting bullets for our handguns by the thousands, in .35, .44, and .45 calibers, including some round balls for a brace of Colt second-generation percussion revolvers.

As the cliché goes, it was a great run. Human mortality proved the only limit to our shared passion.

After a long struggle with many health issues, Dad passed away peacefully at age 89. My lifelong hunting and shooting partner still is sorely missed. However, the memories remain clear, and the knowledge and wisdom acquired during our time are firmly in place.

This leads us to the unfinished business of that last handgun.

Dad and I had conservative tastes in firearms. A majority of them are classics in their category. Through our readings, we were heavily influenced by 20th-Century firearms writing greats Jack O'Connor, Elmer Keith, Charles Askins, and, later, Jeff Cooper, Skeeter Skelton, and Bill Jordan. Those were our prophets during the 1960s and '70s.

Our revolvers included that classic S&W K38, followed by an S&W Model 1950 Target Model in .44 Special, a 1950 Military and Police .45 ACP, and many other well-known Smith and Colt revolvers.

Later, we added a host of vintage European 9mm semi-autos, with the Browning Hi-Power and an early World War ll Walther P38 at the head of the class. Then there is a family of Argentine 1911A1 semi-autos, including a Colt contract pistol, a licensed copy, and an unlicensed knock-off, with indigenous design improvements, all in .45 caliber.

For the most part, blued steel and well-figured wood grips were our quality standard in sidearms. However, as the shooting world rushed ahead, we were stuck in the '70s, decades behind firearms technology. By then, the lightweight, high-capacity, double-action 9mm "Wonder Nine" was conquering the military, law enforcement, and civilian handgun markets.

Dad and I discussed this frequently before his illness. Had we missed the boat? Were we out of touch with the 21st Century? We agreed that we were. What to do about it? Our time together was running short. But we were stubborn, inflexible, and complacent with what we felt were the best handguns in the world. We owned them for years, shot them regularly, and were proficient, sometimes better, with them.

One gun, in particular, stuck in our craw: The revolutionary Glock 17, the pistol that turned the handgun world on its head. At first, it was an abomination to us. Before the Glock, we even disdained

For years, the author and his father doubted the relevancy of lightweight, high-capacity, striker-fired "Wonder Nines." Dad's last gun, this Glock 19 Gen 5, illustrates that even the most entrenched attitudes can change over time with experience.

semi-autos with aluminum frames, including the original Colt Commander (now lightweight Commander) and the S&W Model 39, America's first double-action 9mm autoloader. Why?

As we believed at the time — later proven wrong — aluminum frames were less durable than steel. And "plastic" guns? They were anathema.

Yet, in our discussions, we couldn't deny the wisdom of the lightweight frames, double-action, high-capacity magazines, well-defined sights, and improved trigger pulls these new pistols offered, at least for military and law enforcement professionals. We both

knew our beloved Colt Government Models and Browning Hi-Power were beautiful, classic, storied pistols, though heavy and hard to conceal. But we believed they were the standard in semi-auto excellence.

Eventually, we old dogs were keen to learn a new trick. Glock and others of the genre were on our minds. Then Dad's illnesses worsened, and our plans were put on hold. Though bedbound at the end, we discussed guns, what we'd learned together, and what we hadn't. During his last week of life in hospice, we ruminated about the ones that got away, the Glock in particular.

After Dad passed away, I rested all our firearms for a while. As an only child, and per his wish, his guns were now mine and had to be managed as objects of use and investments. I knew he would want me to continue with our passion, enjoy firearms, move forward, and continuously learn. For three years, I thought about our unfinished business and what I would do about it. There was substantial research, including from the pages of *Gun Digest,* the Internet, social media, and face-to-face discussions with veteran shooters. It seemed a consensus was impossible. I was bombarded with opinions and advice from a host of trusted, grey-haired pistoleros and then, for good measure, input from a handful of knowledgeable millennial shooters.

The biggest obstacle was personal. Having grown up on hammer-fired, single-action semi-autos from the John Browning stable, it was a big adjustment to accept striker-fired, double-action pistols. However, striker-fired technology was proven for many years — U.S. law enforcement and our military made the transition and weren't going back. With some reservations, striker-fired it would be.

Visits to gun shops to examine, hold, and debate the merits of one model versus another were interesting but inconclusive. My selection criteria focused on a proven design, mechanical simplicity, reliability, and ergonomics. While this would not be a target gun, a first-rate trigger and sights were prerequisites. For concealed carry, weight and size were a concern.

All the Wonder Nines felt good in my large hands; today's pistols have ergonomics down pat. The lighter weight gives my arthritic shoulders a break. Sights and triggers? Handgun manufacturers offer consumers new levels of off-the-shelf excellence in both. The magazine capacity is there if you want it.

After a year of searching, I purchased a Glock 19 Gen 5 and haven't looked back. This pistol has it all, and there's no shortage of aftermarket accessories. To me, the jump into the 21st Century was exhilarating.

The G19 pistol has been reviewed extensively. It's an excellent compromise in size, weight, firepower, and concealability, incorporating all the advancements in semi-automatic handguns over the past 50 years.

Out of the box, fired offhand at 25 yards, the Glock is accurate, reliable with all ammunition, balances right, and is very natural and comfortable to shoot. These attributes are reinforced at close range and with higher fire rates. Takedown for cleaning and routine maintenance is shockingly easy. Other pistols would have sufficed, but this is the one we — myself as purchaser and my father, through me as his proxy — chose.

I know Dad would have approved of the choice. I only wish he was around to share the joys of its ownership and use. No, it's not the finely blued, sculpted steel and quality-checkered walnut grips we valued on handguns. But it is a marvelous shooting tool, built for a purpose. If you judge a handgun by form-follows-function design, the Glock is a work of art.

This newcomer to our collection does not diminish the legacy of the Browning masterpieces we've owned and shot for most of our lives. They're still prized, in the gun safe, ready for use, and will be to the trail's end.

Dad's last gun, a Glock 19 awarded posthumously in his honor, completely contradicts what we thought a handgun should be for almost half a century. That's ironic, but so be it. The unfinished business is now complete.

Our hoard of classic firearms is a testament to Dad, my shooting and hunting partner, teacher, and best friend. It represents a lifetime of shared firearms experiences, knowledge, and shooting memories. Examining each gun, whether to shoot or hold, relive the memories, and admire, still brings tremendous enjoyment.

Dad's last gun is now a valued part of that collection. GD

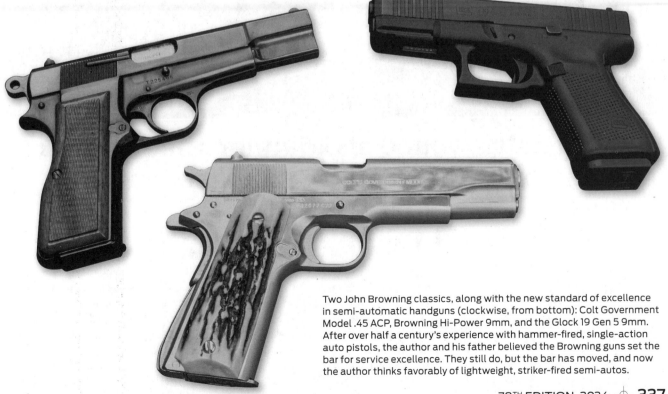

Two John Browning classics, along with the new standard of excellence in semi-automatic handguns (clockwise, from bottom): Colt Government Model .45 ACP, Browning Hi-Power 9mm, and the Glock 19 Gen 5 9mm. After over half a century's experience with hammer-fired, single-action auto pistols, the author and his father believed the Browning guns set the bar for service excellence. They still do, but the bar has moved, and now the author thinks favorably of lightweight, striker-fired semi-autos.

The Greener

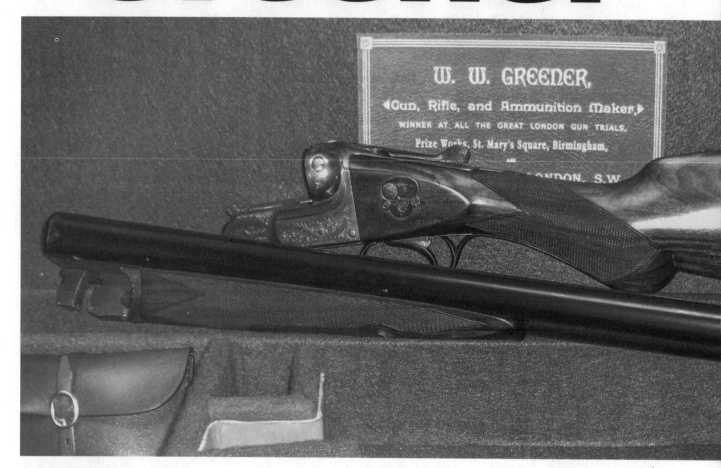

Nothing gets a young shotgunner's attention like touching off both barrels — simultaneously!

›NICK HAHN

The first shotgun I ever fired was a 20-gauge J. C. Higgins single-barrel single shot. It belonged to the wife of a close family friend, one of two hunting and shooting mentors I had as a kid. I believe Stevens made the gun, but back then, it was marketed under the J. C. Higgins label by Sears, Roebuck and Company.

As was typical of that type of single-barrel shotgun, it was very light and gave a healthy jolt with standard loads. So, to offset the recoil, my mentor loaded a few cartridges with about half an ounce of shot and reduced powder. In short, he made .410 loads in 20-gauge hulls. I shot at a tin can about 15 yards away; it was the first time I fired a shotgun. It was a

This Greener Model F35 has rather nice wood, nothing spectacular, but nicely grained.

spots after an unsuccessful hunt in one area. While driving, my uncle suddenly stopped and pointed at a tree about 30 yards away. A crow sat on the top branch. We exited the car, and he assembled his shotgun from its case, a W. W. Greener 12 gauge with double triggers and side safety.

He loaded both barrels with those wonderfully aromatic waxed green paper Remington Express loads with round yellow paper stickers on the crimp marked with the shot size. He checked to ensure the gun was on safe, then handed it to me and said to aim, take it off safe, and shoot. If I missed with the first barrel and the crow started to fly off, I was to pull the rear trigger for the second barrel. He reminded me to "lead" the crow if it was flying. Eagerly, I took the gun from his hands and attempted to do as I was told. I aligned the bead on the crow and took the safety off. Then I pulled the trigger, or at least I thought I had pulled the front trigger, but apparently, I did more than that.

The shot was thunderous and almost knocked me off my feet! I missed entirely, and the crow disappeared before I could

shoot again. My uncle laughed as I stood there somewhat dazed, staring at the Greener that kicked like a mule. He took the gun from me, thumbed the top lever, and popped two empties. In my excitement, I pulled both triggers at the same time. It was quite a shock, and I never repeated that mistake.

I later shot that wonderful Greener more successfully, pulling one trigger at a time. I discovered that it did not have a vicious kick at all. I often shot those mild, maroon-colored, low-base Remington Shur-Shot loads, and the recoil was minimal. It was a game gun and weighed about 6 1/2 pounds, the same as my uncle's other game guns. My uncle was a wealthy man and a hunting fanatic who owned many shotguns, all 12 gauges. As far as he was concerned, the 12 gauge was the only bore size worth shooting. He owned a successful company, and he concentrated on hunting for about four months each year during the hunting season. During that time, he rarely visited his office except in emergency cases, leaving the company business in the hands of his deputy.

good thing that it hardly kicked since, at age 12, I wasn't a large kid; I was kind of scrawny, about 90 pounds soaking wet!

A few months after shooting the powder-puff 20 gauge, I shot a regular 12-gauge load at a live target. I was out with an uncle, my other childhood mentor, hunting. We had been after partridge and drove to one of his "secret"

The Greener with a Copper pheasant.

The Greener in two parts.

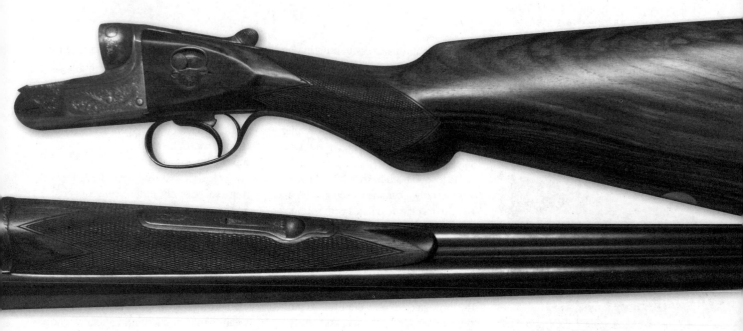

He used to jokingly say that if Clark Gable, the reigning "King of Hollywood" at that time, could take off during hunting season, so could he. (Gable was famous for having a clause in his contract with MGM Studio that specified he would not make any movies during hunting season.) My uncle may not have been the "King of Hollywood," but he had his priorities straight.

It was from this uncle that I learned about fine English and European doubles. He had a Purdey, a Holland & Holland, and some fine Belgian guns, including a Jules Bury, which he said was as good as

any English Best Gun. However, despite all these guns, it was apparent that he preferred to shoot the Greener. The two guns he shot the most were the Greener and a Belgian boxlock "Guild Gun" with no name, which he told me Francotte made. He didn't shoot his Best Guns with finer pedigrees as much.

Many years later, he surprised me with his generosity and presented me with one of his prized guns, the Holland & Holland. It was a beautiful Royal Model, and I was grateful for this unexpected and priceless gift, but to be honest, I secretly wished it had been the Greener instead. There was something about that old Greener that made it special. The Holland & Holland was a superb gun and felt like a magic wand in my hands, and it came in a fancy oak and

leather trunk case. But I had never shot it before and hadn't developed the connection and feeling I had for that old Greener. The Greener felt solid yet light and like magic, at least for me. That was many years ago, and much time had passed since that Greener gave me such a wallop.

I still remember that Greener very well. Its triggerguard tang, worn white, had the serial number followed by "Grade FH25" engraved. The bluing on the barrels was thin, especially in front of the forearm, where it was held by the forward hand. The color casehardening on the receiver was gone entirely, making the receiver appear to have a pickled gray finish. The barrel flats were stamped with Birmingham proof marks and 2 ¾" and 1 ¼ oz. Both barrels were stamped "choke," but my uncle told me that the left barrel was "half choke" while the right was "quarter choke." I knew, from reading articles about shotguns, that "half choke" meant modified and "quarter choke" was improved cylinder. The stock, though not fancy, was attractive with lightly grained wood and had that distinctive Greener trademark rounded Prince of Wales grip, which was almost a straight grip, and it had a horn buttplate. The wood finish had numerous scratches and minor dents but was otherwise still in good shape.

I cleaned the gun thoroughly each time after shooting and lightly oiled everything. I would then slip the barrels with its forearm and the receiver with its stock into their frayed, oil-stained red flannel cloth sleeves. Then I would put the two parts into the much worn and scuffed old leather leg o' mutton case in which it was kept. The top lid of the case was stamped "W. W. Greener, Ltd" with an image of an elephant, a Greener trademark. My uncle kept his other guns in the cabinet, but there was no space for all his firearms,

so the Greener and several others stayed outside. Besides, he shot the Greener the most, so he kept it handy.

Through the years, I have owned a couple of Greeners. I once had a worn-out Empire-Grade Greener that had belonged to an old duck hunter who shot it every duck season for over half a century. I got the gun more for sentimental reasons than actual use, and it was pretty beaten up, badly off-face, and its side safety did not work. It had consumed its share of heavy loads, perhaps too many. I kept it for a while, never actually shooting it before trading it for something else. I also had a very early Damascus-barreled high-grade Greener that was a nice gun and proofed for 2 3/4-inch loads, but it was not quite to my liking, so it also left my house.

My current Greener is an FH35, a grade higher than that old

one I shot as a kid. According to Greener records, it was made "between the wars" for sale in America with its factory single selective trigger and 26-inch barrels. It is a light upland gun, a few ounces lighter than my uncle's old Greener, and being a grade higher, slightly finer with more engraving and better wood on the butt-stock. It, too, has the shallow, rounded wisp of a Prince of Wales grip on a very nicely-grained stock with dark streaks.

I suspect it was initially purchased by a grouse and woodcock hunter or a bobwhite enthusiast. It came to me in an old, restored canvas and leather Brady case. I don't know whether the case was initially purchased with the gun, but the shotgun is nicely fitted to the case, which has been

This FH25 is like the old Greener the author's uncle owned. That gun had the original horn buttplate, and the wood showed just a bit more grain. Otherwise, this one is like that old gun.

This 12-bore Greener is light at 6 pounds, 4 ounces, as light or lighter than most modern 20 bores! It makes for an excellent upland gun with its 26-inch barrels and open boring.

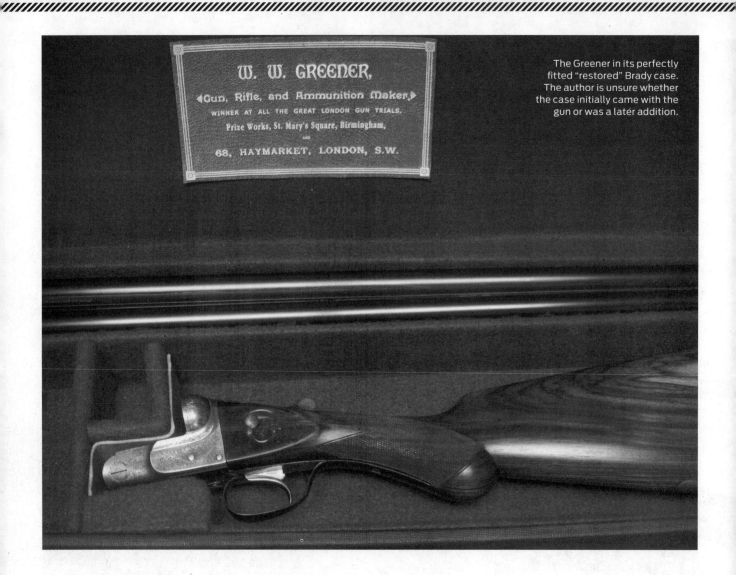

The Greener in its perfectly fitted "restored" Brady case. The author is unsure whether the case initially came with the gun or was a later addition.

relined with new fabric.

The Greener I own today is not a Best Gun. It is a Birmingham boxlock, albeit a very lovely graded model. But, just as my uncle of long ago seemed to prefer his old Greener over other, more costly and pedigreed guns, I too like this Greener a lot. It is choked cylinder in the right barrel and modified in the left, an excellent combination for upland gunning. I haven't shot it much, not as much as I once shot my uncle's old FH25. But I did take it out after quail and dove a few times, and it did its job perfectly, as long as I did my part.

Since my introduction to shotguns with my uncle's old Greener gave me such a violent jolt, I have always been partial to Greener shotguns. Some dislike the Greener cross-bolt, considering it an unnecessary appendage. Others don't like the side safety. Yet others claim Greeners

are nothing but Birmingham "working guns," not as finely made as London guns. I find it to be quite the opposite. In my experience, Greeners are as well made as any London gun. Granted, their basic models, like the Empire Grade, are not as finely finished as the London "best guns," but they don't cost the price of a small house!

Like the Royal Grade, the top-grade Greener boxlocks are as finely made as any London Best sidelock. And Greener made very fine sidelocks that are as good as the London counterparts and cost as much. However, the boxlock gave Greener worldwide fame; the proprietary boxlock action called "Facile Princeps" with its famous Greener top lock and side safety.

A Greener will last as long as any London gun, maybe even outlast it. Not surprisingly, when Winchester held a

torture test for its Model 21, shooting thousands of rounds of unreasonably heavy overloads, all other guns, including London Best Guns, broke down early on. Only the Greener hung on for a while longer, although it couldn't keep up with the tank-like, overbuilt Model 21.

But my fondness for the Greener is not based on its strength. It is simply that it was a Greener that I shot first as a kid. So for me, a Greener will always hold a special place. **GD**

My Ruger Hawkeye .257 Roberts Is A Keeper

›JIM HOUSE

The Ruger Hawkeye 77 .257 Roberts is an elegant sporter.

I now jokingly refer to myself as a dinosaur, meaning I've started using things like a Parker 51 fountain pen and a Buck 119 Special knife. That also means I like my bolt- or lever-action rifles made of metal and wood and am happiest when my rifle is a classic sporter and wears iron sights.

My first centerfire rifle was a Mauser 98, which I turned into a sporter configuration. That rifle was eventually traded for a handgun I wanted, but I never lost my love for rifles designed with the features of the Mauser 98 action. I have some rifles with push-feed actions, and they work perfectly, but there is something special about the Mauser.

The Ruger Hawkeye has a versatile three-position safety that allows you to open the bolt with the safety on.

When it came time to add a rifle in .257 Roberts caliber for reloading work, I wanted one with the classic features of the 98. At that time, the obvious choice was a Ruger Model 77 Hawkeye. I already had a Model 77 Mark II in 7x57 caliber, and almost all features of the newer Hawkeye were identical. Since the Model 77's introduction in 1968, the Ruger bolt actions have had classic lines, Mauser-type claws, non-rotating extractors, and dual-locking lugs.

By the time the Mark II came along in 1991, the original tang-mounted sliding safety had been replaced by a three-positon wing safety on the right-hand side at the rear of the receiver. In the rear position, the safety is "on," and the bolt is closed and locked. In the middle position, the safety is "on," but the bolt can be opened. While forward, the rifle can be fired. This arrangement is like the Winchester Model 70, and it would be difficult to imagine a more reliable or desirable type of safety that locks the bolt and firing pin. The Ruger Model 77 Hawkeye is available in numerous configurations and calibers, but the classic Hunter version suits me.

Taking a cartridge case designed for one caliber and changing the neck size to

A .257 Roberts is an excellent choice for many types of hunting.

hold bullets of larger or smaller diameters has long been a common practice. A case that has been around since 1892 is the 7mm Mauser or 7x57. Its bullet diameter (bore or groove diameter) is .284 inch, but between the lands is .275 inch. Thus, the cartridge became known in Britain by that designation, and the .275 Rigby was soon world famous.

The 7x57 was loaded with a 173-grain round-nose full metal jacketed bullet with a muzzle velocity of approximately

2,300 fps. That is not spectacular by modern standards, but the bullets penetrated exceptionally well, as W.D.M. Bell proved using that load for elephants. Jim Corbett used the cartridge in sporting form extensively with his Rigby rifle in India, eradicating man-eating leopards and tigers.

With a cartridge case as world-famous as the 7mm Mauser, it was only natural to be given the "neck treatment." Necking it up produced the 8x57 Mauser that became a worldwide military cartridge. And by necking it down to hold .257-inch diameter bullets, Ned Roberts created a wildcat cartridge that Remington would eventually standardize in 1934 as the .257 Roberts. For many years, the .257 Roberts was a popular sporting cartridge chambered in several popular rifles, such as the Winchester Model 70 and Remington 722. Many custom rifles were also chambered for the round.

For many years, Warren Page was the shooting editor for *Field & Stream*, a *Gun Digest* contributor, and an avid competitor and experimenter. One of his projects involved necking the .308 Winchester to hold bullets of 6mm diameter — resulting in a cartridge close to the present .243 Winchester. Not to be outdone, Remington necked the .257 Roberts case to hold 6mm bullets and created the .244 Remington having a 1:12-inch twist. The .243, which has a 1 in 10-inch twist, was initially available with 80- and 100-grain bullets, the former intended for varmints and the latter for medium game. Reming-ton loaded the .244 with 70- and 90-grain bullets.

The .243 was deemed by many as the more versatile cartridge, eventually leading Remington to change the twist rate to 1:10 and renaming the .244 the 6mm Remington. More than any others, these 6mm calibers led to the .257 Roberts' decrease in popularity.

The advantages of the .257 Roberts over cartridges like the .30-06 Springfield, .270 Winchester, and 7mm Remington Magnum include reduced recoil while still giving relatively flat trajectory and adequate performance on varmints, predators, and medium game. However, when the .243 Winchester and .244 Remington were introduced in 1955, they quickly decreased interest in the .257 Roberts and .250 Savage calibers. The newer cartridges are more desirable for hunting varmints and predators, but the advantage, if any, for use on medium game is imaginary. Be that as it may, rifle makers produce goods to sell, so very few factory rifles are available in .257 Roberts.

I always admired Page's writing, and while working on reloading projects, I deemed it necessary to get a rifle in .257 Roberts. My choice then was the Ruger Hawkeye, so I had my local dealer order one. When it came, I completed the paperwork and admired the elegant rifle. Currently, the Ruger Hawkeye has

Cartridges in the magazine can be removed by depressing the floorplate release.

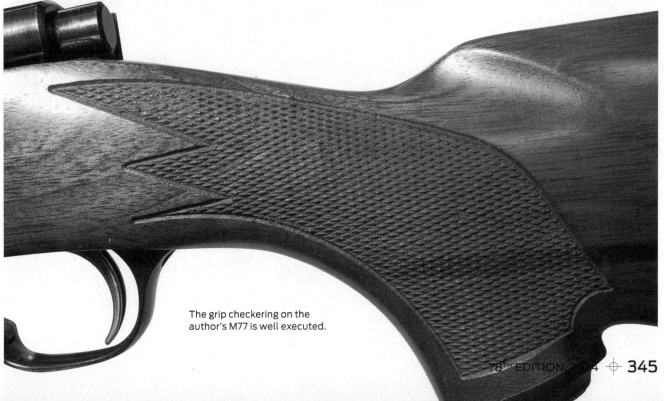

The grip checkering on the author's M77 is well executed.

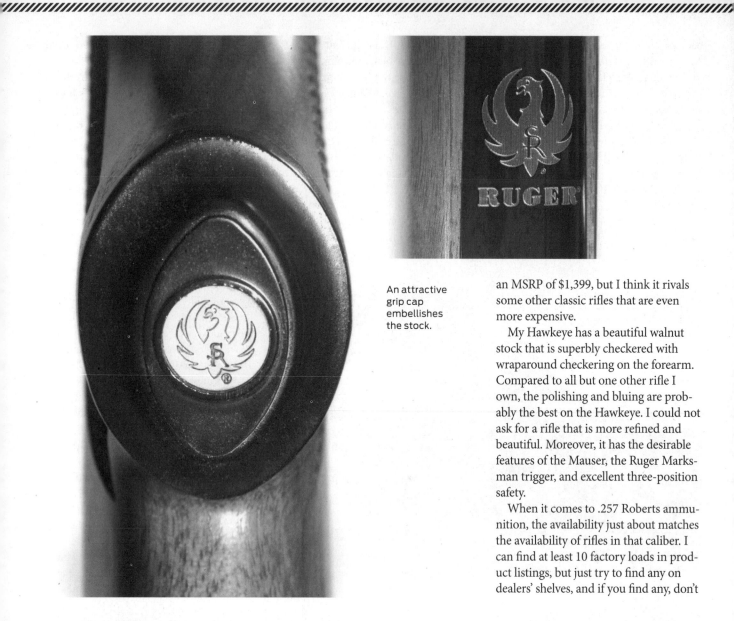

An attractive grip cap embellishes the stock.

an MSRP of $1,399, but I think it rivals some other classic rifles that are even more expensive.

My Hawkeye has a beautiful walnut stock that is superbly checkered with wraparound checkering on the forearm. Compared to all but one other rifle I own, the polishing and bluing are probably the best on the Hawkeye. I could not ask for a rifle that is more refined and beautiful. Moreover, it has the desirable features of the Mauser, the Ruger Marksman trigger, and excellent three-position safety.

When it comes to .257 Roberts ammunition, the availability just about matches the availability of rifles in that caliber. I can find at least 10 factory loads in product listings, but just try to find any on dealers' shelves, and if you find any, don't

Handloads utilizing the 60-grain Hornady flat point (left) to the 120-grain Speer (right) can make a .257 Roberts extremely versatile.

Factory loads in .257 Roberts caliber are effective but somewhat limited.

look at the price tags. One factory option is the traditional 117-grain load with velocities of approximately 2,700 fps. Such a load is quite adequate for deer-size game under most conditions.

However, more exotic loads are listed by several companies. For example, Nosler lists ammo featuring the 110-grain AccuBond at 3,050 fps, 115-grain Nosler Ballistic Tip at 2,925 fps, and 100-grain Partition at 3,000 fps. Hornady has a Superformance load with the 117-grain SST bullet listed at 2,945 fps. Such loads transform the .257 Roberts into a good performer on medium game at rather long ranges.

Although some wonderful .257 Roberts loads may be listed in catalogs, my handloads add so much to the versatility and performance of the rifle. I've used bullets ranging from the 60-grain Hornady flat point intended for use in the .25-20 to the Speer 120-grain spitzer boattail. The 60-grain bullets loaded to about 2,000 fps will group into a ragged hole and work well (and quietly) on varmints.

The range of bullets available in .257-inch diameter includes a great many styles. My favorite varmint load is the 75-grain Sierra hollowpoint with enough IMR-4064 or Hodgdon Varget to give just over 3,000 fps velocity. That load prints five-shot groups at 100 yards that consistently measure well under an inch, the smallest I obtained with the Ruger. The 75-grain V-Max gives comparable groups when loaded at 3,000-3,100 fps. For larger game, handloads with bullets in the 100- to 120-grain range perform well, my favorite being the 115-grain Nosler Ballistic Tip. A load with the 117-grain Sierra SPBT has a velocity of approximately 2,700 fps with IMR-4955 and has performed well.

Despite the .243 Winchester, 6.5mm Creedmoor, and other newer cartridges, my .257 Roberts has not lost any of its versatility or capability. The Ruger Hawkeye Model 77 is an elegant rifle with excellent performance. If it were necessary to dispense with some of my centerfire rifles, the Ruger .257 Roberts would be among the last to go. I don't shoot a "system," and I don't "run" ammunition, but my Ruger Hawkeye is a keeper. GD

Some of the author's favorite loads use (left to right) 60-grain Hornady, 75-grain Sierra, 100-grain Speer, 117-grain Sierra, and 120-grain Speer Grand Slam bullets.

- REPORTS -
from the Field
RIFLES

❯WAYNE VAN ZWOLL

Line extensions and models chambered for the newest rifle cartridges lead this year's crop.

Ruger's new series of lever rifles on the 1895 Marlin design accepts a variety of .45-70 ammo.

With stacks of existing orders to fill, ammunition factories needed no further business. But loath to enter a new year without new product, Remington engineers readied the.360 Buckhammer for its debut at January's 2023 SHOT Show, where Hornady's 7mm PRC had already set tongues to wagging. Even with pallets of ammo on backorder, new cartridges begged matching firearms. The predictable response from gun makers: line extensions. As the 6.5

The Nexus is the first rifle produced entirely in-house (vertical integration) by Gunwerks in Cody, Wyoming.

Creedmoor required only fresh barrel blanks and reamers for rifles friendly to the .308, so the 7 PRC was an easy fit in rifles barreled to 6.5 PRC. Lever rifles suited to the .30-30 smoothly gobbled the .360 Buckhammer, Henry quickly stepping to the front of that line.

Weatherby's .338 RPM (Rebated Precision Magnum) came as no surprise on the heels of the 6.5 RPM. The case wholly and efficiently fills .30-06 Howa and six-lug Weatherby Mark V receivers. As bullets from the 6.5 RPM fly flatter and hit harder than those from the 6.5-06, so this .33 out-muscles the .338-06 — which Weatherby once chambered briefly.

New .45-70 rifles include Ruger's three fresh renditions of the 1895 Marlin. Gun makers overseas build fetching reproductions of Winchester's 1892 and 1886, sold stateside by Taylor's and Cimarron and refined by Doug Turnbull.

ANSCHUTZ

After three years of development, there's the Anschutz Model 1761 series in .22 LR, .22 WMR, and .17 HMR. The 1761's bolt is shorter, with a light, single-spring firing pin. It has three mid-body lugs and a 60-degree, bearing-assisted lift. It's priced from $1,775 to $2,195.

Anschutz recently added Fortner straight-pull rifles to its catalog. These 7.5-pound walnut-stocked sporters, in .22 LR, .17 HMR and .17 Mach 2, have detachable magazines like their turn-bolt stablemates. Prices: $4,195 to $4,295. *anschutznorthamerica.com*

BENELLI

The Lupo bolt-action centerfire rifle is offered in eight chamberings for 2023, including 6mm Creedmoor and 6.5 PRC. Introduced at $1,699, the Lupo now has a pricier version with a Gore Optifade stock finish. A new, checkered-walnut rifle with deeply blued steel lists at $2,199. *benelliusa.com*

BERGARA

For 2023, Bergara has introduced carbon-fiber (CF) barrels in the B14 line. The HMR Carbon Wilderness in 6.5 PRC, .308, and .300 Winchester weighs just 7.2 pounds and costs $1,599. The 6.4-pound Ridge Carbon Wilderness is tagged at $1,399.

Bergara's Premier series has grown. It includes Canyon, Divide, Mountain and MG Lite rifles with the same twin-lug bolt action but different stocks and braked barrels. Canyon and Mountain versions have steel barrels, composite stocks, list for $2,475 and $2,279. Chamberings include the 6.5, .300 PRC, and the 28 Nosler (.375 H&H in the Canyon). The Divide has a CF barrel and prone-style AG Composites stock with an adjustable comb. At $2,965, it's about $330 less costly than the 6.6-pound MG Lite, a "chassis" rifle with a folding buttstock and ARCA-Swiss forend. Like the Canyon, it feeds from an AICS magazine and accepts Remington 700 scope bases.

Bergara now lists bolt-action rimfires. The B14R in .22 LR, .22 WMR, and .17 HMR comes with a steel or CF barrel of 9.2 and 8.1 pounds, respectively, for $1,229 and $1,329. The BMR weighs 5.5

A classy new Anschutz 1761 in .22 LR, . 22 WMR, and .17 HMR is nudging aside the Model 64 series.

Bighorn Armory's Model 89 in powerful .500 S&W includes features of Winchester's 1886 and 1892.

ing 3,696 ft-lbs of energy. *blaser-usa.com*

and 5.0 pounds with those barrel options, costing $619 and $719. *bergarausa.com*

BIGHORN ARMORY

New at Bighorn Armory: Black Thunder, a "tactical lever gun" in .500 S&W. A big brake caps a 16-inch barrel, wearing a Picatinny rail for a scout scope. Iron sights and a black laminated stock bring the price to $2,899. *bighornarmory.com*

BLASER

Eighty percent of Blaser-branded firearms are versions of the R 8 — bored for 48 cartridges to the size of the .338 Lapua and .500 Jeffery! The R 8 "Silence" features a barrel-length suppressor, the "Ultimate" an adjustable stock. For women, there's an R8 "Intuition" with additional cast-off. Blaser's latest engineering feat: a rimfire conversion that turns any R 8 into a .22! I pulled the 6.5 PRC barrel from a new R 8, inserted the .22 LR barrel and popped in a rimfire magazine. The bolt-head

swap was hassle-free. With a Burris 3-9x scope in Blaser rings and Eley ammo, the rifle printed a .6-inch five-shot group at 50 yards. After a switch back to 6.5 PRC, I landed five Hornady bullets in a knot that size at 100! Listing for about $1,450, the kit isn't cheap. But it works without fault.

Blaser has a new hunting cartridge, too. The 8.5x55 is ballistically a frothy .338-06. "It excels in 42cm (16.5-inch) and 47cm (18.5-inch) suppressed barrels," said Blaser engineers. Norma loads it with 230-grain bullets at 2,960 fps deliver-

BROWNING

Four new X-Bolt rifles join Browning's flagship centerfire line for 2023. The X-Bolt Speed series has a 6.1-pound suppressor-ready version in Bronze Cerakote that features fluted 18- to 22-inch barrels in 12 chamberings, .204 Ruger to .300 Winchester and .300 PRC, including the long-legged 28 Nosler and 6.8 Western. The detachable five-shot magazine fits the belly of an Ovix-finished composite stock. Price: $1,430 to $1,530. The other new X-Bolts feature adjustable target stocks designed

Here in lovely walnut: a Blaser R8 converted to rimfire with .22 LR barrel, bolt head, and magazine.

Blaser R8 bolt heads easily change from centerfire (left, for the 6.5 PRC) to rimfire for the .22 LR.

for long-range shooting.

They have heavier, stiffer short-action receivers, 10-shot detachable magazines, extended bolt knobs and 26-inch fluted barrels in 6mm Creedmoor, 6mm GT, 6.5 Creedmoor, and .308. The 10.8-pound Target Pro McMillan with A3-5 McMillan stock and Recoil Hawg brake list for $4,130.

The X-Bolt Target Max is similar but with a MAX composite stock. It scales a pound less and seems a bargain at $1,730.

An X-Bolt Target Max Lite has a "heavy

Browning's X-Bolt Eclipse with thumbhole stock is one of a growing clan for flat-shooting cartridges.

CVA's reasonably priced Cascade rifle offers chamberings to .300 Win. Here: the Graphite version.

Franchi's Momentum bolt rifle is offered in many configurations and chamberings.

sporter" instead of a bull barrel and comes in at 9.1 pounds. MSRP: $1,780. *browning.com*

CHRISTENSEN ARMS

Roland Christensen's carbon-fiber barrels astonished shooters when they proved viable a quarter-century ago. Now, the Christensen shop fashions lightweight CF-barreled rifles on Remington 700-pattern actions. CNC machined to gnat's-lash tolerances, they have surface-ground lugs and fluted, nitrided bolt bodies. Magnum actions have dual ejectors. Receivers are pillar-bedded to CF hunting- and adjustable target-style stocks. The Ridgeline Scout, new last year, comes in powerful chamberings but scales less than 6

Christensen pioneered carbon-fiber rifle barrels. This 6-pound Christensen Ridgeline rifle wears one.

pounds. The rail is receiver-mounted, not on the barrel. MSRP: $2,200. The Mesa Elevated II, even lighter at 5.5 pounds, is priced from $1,695 and includes the removable, barrel-diameter brake standard on Mesa FFTs. For 2023, this series gets two Optifade stock finishes. *chris-tensenarms.com*

CVA

For '23, CVA gives us a Cascade XT ("Xtreme") with a stiff 22- or 24-inch barrel, fluted and braked and bored for seven short- and long-action cartridges, 6.5 Creedmoor to .300 Winchester — including the straight-case .350 Legend and .450 Bushmaster. An extended bolt knob helps with cycling. The steel has a black Cerakote finish, the stock Realtree Hillside camo. MSRP: $850. CVA is adding the .270 and .30-06 to the growing roster of cartridges for the Cascade in Flat Dark Earth/Veil Wideland camo ($775). *cva.com*

FRANCHI

As introduced three years ago, the Momentum bolt-action rifle in 6.5 Cm, .308, .300 Winchester, and .350 Legend boasts a three-lug bolt and feeds from an internal box over a hinged floorplate. An Elite version appeared in 2022. Price hikes have put the standard rifle at $799, the Elite (also in 6.5 PRC but not in .350) at $999.

Meantime, two new Elites have joined them. The Varmint with modular cheekpiece and a heavy-fluted barrel comes in .223, .22-250, .224 Valkyrie, 6.5 Cm, and .308. Price: $1,179. The All-Terrain, with iron sights and extended Picatinny rail, has a "scout rifle" form. It's chambered in .223 and .308 and retails at $1,449. Franchi offers Cerakoted metal on its Momentum and three camo stock finishes. I like the Pic rails and the palm-friendly bolt knob. Not so much the molded sling swivel tabs. *franchiusa.com*

H-S PRECISION

"It's a nimble version of our PLR," said H-S marketing VP Josh Cluff, describing the PLC Long Range Carbon Fiber Rifle. "A lightweight with the features and accuracy of our long-range rifles with fluted steel barrels."

H-S Precision is unique in making every major part of all its super-accurate long-range rifles in-house.

Henry is shipping these two new .22 Small Game Rifles with big loops, walnut stocks, Skinner sights.

To help shooters direct that CF barrel, H-S designed an adjustable prone version of the proven PLR stock. The H-S team cut ounces by reducing the weighty resin in the barrel. My first groups with a sample rifle in .300 PRC hovered at 1/2-minute — guaranteed on all Pro-Series rifles. A host of chamberings range from hot .22s to long-range magnums. Stainless twin-lug actions are CNC'd to fly-wing tolerances. H-S triggers adjust down to a crisp 2.5 pounds. Cut-rifled stainless barrels and hand-laid stocks with alloy bedding blocks come from H-S's shop. *hsprecision.com*

The Henry Homesteader Carbine 9mm. No lever!

Marlin's 336, from 1948, gets new life in 2023 at Ruger, with walnut and traditional sights, in .30-30 and .35 Remington.

Howa's sturdy, reliable bolt rifles now include this stainless Walnut Hunter in popular chamberings.

Mauser's Model 18 Savannah is the latest version of an affordable but excellent rifle for U.S. hunters.

HENRY REPEATING ARMS

The most recent Henry of traditional design is the first from any manufacturer to chamber the .360 Remington. This new straight-wall cartridge on the .30-30 case outperforms the .350 Legend.

Henry's other new rifle has no lever loop or exposed hammer! The Homesteader 9mm carbine is a blowback-driven autoloader. It has a tang safety and a charging handle that can be installed easily on either side. It's also southpaw-friendly with a central magazine release forward of the detachable box. (Besides the 5- and 10-shot magazines provided, the carbine accepts adapters for those from Glock, SIG, and S&W.) The 16-inch threaded barrel has an adjustable ghost ring rear sight and a bold post in the front. In a rifle, the 9mm is a mild cartridge. Still, a reciprocating forend weight in this Henry reduces recoil, so you stay on target for fast follow-ups. Also keeping you in control: stippling on the attractively shaped two-piece walnut stock. Its installed studs accept popular QD sling swivels. The alloy receiver is drilled

Ruger's first Marlin, the SBS (stainless, big loop) in .45-70, differs in details from the original 1895.

Hornady ammunition gave Wayne this 100-yard group with the SBS – fine accuracy from *any* sporter!

Marlin .45-70 325 Hor. FTX 100 yds.

Nimble, economical but strong and accurate, Mossberg's Patriot comes in chamberings to .375 Ruger.

barrel, a Picatinny rail, and a featherweight synthetic stock in Kryptek camo. Price: $1,399. *legacysports.com*

Nosler's recent 21 now comes in Carbon Chassis form. It has a CF barrel and a folding CF stock with an ARCA rail. Weight: 7 pounds. Chamberings: 6.5 Cm, 6.5 PRC, 28 Nosler, .300 Winchester.

MARLIN

The first "new" Ruger-made Marlin rifle would appear in January 2022. A descendant of the Model 1895 Marlin, this .45-70 SBL (stainless, big loop) is distinctive. The action on my sample cycles like earlier Marlins. But the stainless steel oversized lever, threaded muzzle, extended Picatinny rail, Skinner rear aperture, and fiber-optic tritium-assisted front sights are all 21st-century. So, too, the

for a Weaver scope base. The Homesteader weighs 6.6 pounds and retails for $928. *henryrifles.com*

HOWA

The new Carbon Elevate bolt rifle has the standard (stout, simple, smooth) Howa twin-lug action but with a CF stock and barrel. It weighs little more than the equally fresh 4.6-pound Carbon Stalker with a Mini Action in 6mm ARC and kin. Seven chamberings in long and short actions bump the Carbon Stalker to 6.1 pounds. Unlike the Mini with its detachable box, these have hinged floorplates. The Super Lite, a 4.5-pound rifle with a flush detachable magazine, boasts an action Howa hails as slightly smaller than a standard short action but able to handle two short-action cartridges: the 6.5 Creedmoor and .308. It has a 20-inch

fluted, nickeled bolt. The trimmer forend and crisp stock detailing (lost during Remington's production) returned, enhanced by a better finish. Ruger laser-engraved Marlin's horse-and-rider logo on the grip heel and changed the black stock-belly bulls-eye to red. Rifling is hammer-forged, an "RM" serial prefix and "Mayodan, NC" added to the inscription on the 19-inch barrel.

Accurate? My rifle put three Hornady FTX bullets into a 3/4-inch delta at 100 yards! The SBS lists for $1,399. It's been followed by a new Trapper, also stainless but with a satin finish and shorter 16-inch barrel and a five-shot magazine. There's no Pic rail, and the

sights differ. Then there's the new Guide Gun, essentially an SBL in blued alloy steel with brown laminated stock, bead-blasted metal, and open sights. At $1,239, it lists for $210 less than the Trapper. Both these rifles are bored to .45-70. Ruger just announced the Marlin 336. And the 1894 rifle is in the works, with a checkered walnut stock and blued chrome-moly steel; the 336 in .30-30 and .35 Remington is due first. It has a pistol-grip wrist. As its 20-inch barrel isn't threaded, the rifle wears traditional bands at the forend and muzzle. It sports open sights. *marlinfirearms.com*

A new Remington Alpha 1 rifle is in the prototype stage at RemArms, in an equally new Georgia factory.

MAUSER

An ultra-refined, limited-edition 98 has just been announced for 2023. The Model '98 action serves another L&O company as well: the London house of Rigby, whose magazine rifles have long been based on that mechanism — even when the Germans and Brits were at war!

More recent, affordable Mausers include Models 12 and 18 (for debut years 2012 and '18). The "M" has now been scrubbed from the M18 designation; it's now simply Mauser 18. It's an entry-level rifle, but intelligently designed, skillfully rendered. It has a full-diameter three-lug bolt with dual ejectors, a three-detent safety, a trigger that adjusts down to 2.3 pounds and a receiver that accepts Remington 700 scope mount bases. The bolt cycles piston-slick.

The new Model 18 Savannah is chambered for nine cartridges, .223 to .300 Winchester. Its fetching tan synthetic

Rock River Arms, celebrated for its AR-style rifles, is now producing the RBG bolt action in 6.5 Cm and .308.

The Model 100 is Sako's latest, most advanced rifle. It is a modular, interchangeable barrel system, so popular in Europe.

stock brings the rifle on target fast and steadies it there. At $850, it's an outstanding buy! *mauser.com*

MOSSBERG

For deer hunters where shotgun-only restrictions have been relaxed to permit straight-wall rifle cartridges, Mossberg's Patriot series now includes rifles in .350 Legend. Walnut- and synthetic-stocked models in 7mm, .300, and .338 Magnum with 24-inch threaded barrels also appear in Combo scope-and-rifle pairings. MVP Scout, Patrol, Predator and Light Chassis rifles have AR-style detachable magazines. The MVP LR's prone-style stock wears an adjustable comb. The MVP .300 Blackout Patrol features a threaded, braked 16.3-inch barrel. Bolt fluting, a fiber-optic sight and a Picatinny rail are standard. The Patriot Predator in .450 Bushmaster has a threaded 16.3-inch barrel under iron sights and a stock finished in Flat Dark Earth or True Timber Strata camo. *mossberg.com*

NOSLER

Its new Model 21 rifle, claims Nosler, "blends the best of the Mack Brothers' 1918 EVO action" with the features of the well-known Nosler 48 series. A fluted one-piece bolt with an M16-type extractor runs in a receiver shaped by a wire EDM machine. A TriggerTech trigger, adjustable down to 2.5 pounds, is standard. So, too, a Shilen match-grade barrel. Chamberings run from 6.5 Creedmoor to .375 H&H. The gray-Cerakoted barreled action snugs into a McMillan CF stock. MSRP: $2,795.

A Carbon Chassis Hunter, Nosler's first chassis rifle, is new for '23. It features a magnesium alloy frame and a folding, foam-filled CF stock with an adjustable comb and length of pull. There's V-block bedding and an integral ARCA rail up front. The CF-wrapped barrel comes in 6.5 Creedmoor and 6.5 PRC (short action), also 28 Nosler and .300 Winchester (long action). Overall weights: 6.9 and 7.1 pounds. A TriggerTech trigger adjusts down to 2.5 pounds. At $5,395, the Model 21 Carbon Chassis Hunter is pricy but should appeal to long-range enthusiasts tired of carbon-free rifles that feel like rail ties at day's end. *nosler.com*

REMINGTON

First on the production schedule at the new RemArms plant: reviving the Model 700, Remington's flagship bolt-action since its 1962 debut. At this writing, the Alpha 1 is in the prototype stage. Designers have given it a one-piece fluted bolt body with two locking lugs. The handle is dovetailed and brazed in place. In place of the "snap-ring" extractor typical to the 700s, it has a strong claw held by a ball detent in a locking lug. The bolt can be easily hand-stripped. Instead of a stamped under-trigger lever that could be rendered inoperable by grit or cold-hardened grease, the bolt release on the new rifle is a button on the receiver's left side. The two-position safety is like its forebear's and allows cycling when "on." The magazine box is longer — 2.974 inches inside — for long bullets favored by shooters who want to reach far. The Alpha 1 rifle should appear soon! *remarms.com*

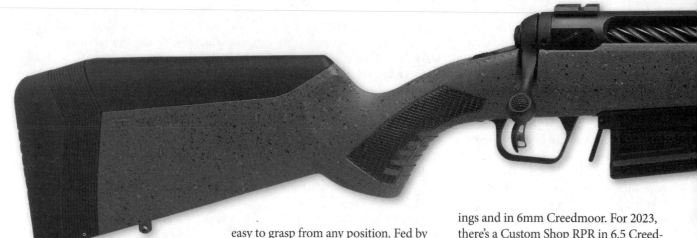

ROCK RIVER ARMS
In 6.5 Creed or .308, the RBG (Rock Bolt Gun) stands out in a distinguished stable of Rock River AR-type autoloaders. A chassis rifle, it features a proprietary stainless short action and air-gauged, fluted, stainless, cryogenically treated Wilson barrel (20, 22 or 24 inches). The receiver's Picatinny rail has 20 minutes of gain for long-range zeros without exceeding the limit of a scope's elevation dial. The knurled, oversize bolt knob is easy to grasp from any position. Fed by a Magpul-compatible AICS detachable box, the RBG features a TriggerTech trigger. The buttstock is adjustable; it and the forestock have multiple fixtures for sling and bipod attachment. Chassis (stock) colors: tan, green, or black. The RBG weighs 10.5 pounds and lists for $4,450. *rockriverarms.com*

RUGER
Long-range shooting continues to prompt new rifle offerings at Ruger. The Ruger Precision Rifle (RPR) recently became available in magnum chamberings and in 6mm Creedmoor. For 2023, there's a Custom Shop RPR in 6.5 Creedmoor. Its thick, stainless 26-inch barrel, .850 at the threaded muzzle, wears an APA brake. The 5R cold hammer-forged rifling is pitched 1:7.5 for long bullets. Cerakoted gray, this Custom Shop rifle weighs 12.8 pounds and lists for $2,499.

Also for shooting far: Ruger's Long-Range Hunter and Long-Range Target in the Hawkeye series of bolt rifles. Hawkeyes have non-rotating Mauser extractors, fixed ejectors, three-position safeties. Picatinny rails with 20 minutes of gain add reach to elevation dials. Seven sub-models of the popular American

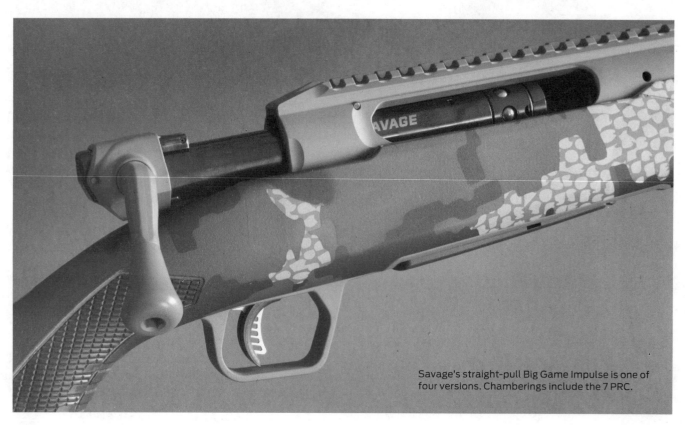

Savage's straight-pull Big Game Impulse is one of four versions. Chamberings include the 7 PRC.

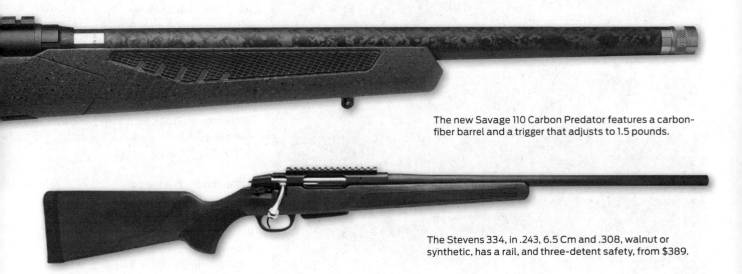

The new Savage 110 Carbon Predator features a carbon-fiber barrel and a trigger that adjusts to 1.5 pounds.

The Stevens 334, in .243, 6.5 Cm and .308, walnut or synthetic, has a rail, and three-detent safety, from $389.

bolt rifle start at just $489. Its long list of chamberings, .223 to .300 Winchester, now includes the straight-walled .350 Legend and .450 Bushmaster, also the 6.5 PRC and .25-06.

Ruger now offers five rimfire Americans in .22 LR, .22 WMR and .17 HMR. Fresh 77-Series rifles come in .17 WSM as well as .17 and .22 Hornet, .357 and .44 Magnum. The Scout rifle now comes in .350 Legend. *ruger.com*

SAKO
For 2023, Sako has introduced the Model 100 Explorer, with a two-piece adjustable stock, CF or wood. It's barreled to 11 cartridges, .243 to .375 H&H. The detachable steel box can be top-loaded in the rifle. The bolt has a diamond-like machine-tool coating; the receiver and barrel boast weather- and scuff-proof Cerakote Elite treatment. Barrel interchangeability makes it unique. *sako.fi*

SAVAGE
For 2023, the straight-pull Savage Impulse comes in a new Mountain Hunter version with a Proof Research carbon-fiber barrel. It's the fourth Impulse, following last year's 13.7-pound Elite Precision with a braked stainless barrel in an adjustable chassis stock and vertical grip. With 20 minutes of gain, the rail suits the Elite Precision's seven long-range chamberings, 6mm Creed to .338 Lapua.

My sample Impulse was the Big Game sub-model in .300 Winchester. (It also comes in .243, 6.5 Cm, .308, .30-06, and .300 WSM.) Fed from a flush, detachable magazine, this .300 cycled smoothly and reliably and shot 3/4-inch groups for me. Its siblings: the Impulse Hog Hunter, in the same chamberings, less the .243 and .300 WSM, and the Impulse Predator in .22-250, .243, 6.5 Cm and .308. AICS magazines feed these rifles. All Impulses have Savage's new Hexlock system: a straight-pull bolt with a ring of ball bearings that engage a circumferential groove in a barrel extension. Pushing the bolt handle ahead forces these six bearings into battery; pivoting it back frees them. A release button on the bolt shroud lets you cycle a cocked action.

Now in its third year, the Impulse gets plaudits as an affordable option to straight-pull rifles from Europe. The Big Game and new Mountain Hunter will be the first Impulses to chamber the 7 PRC cartridge, which has also been added to the cartridge rosters for nine versions of the Savage 110. The newest is the Carbon Predator, with "granite textured" AccuStock and a CF barrel from Proof Research. The AccuTrigger adjusts to 1.5 pounds; the magazine is an AICS box.

In rimfires, Savage is trotting out the A22 Takedown, an autoloader with an 18-inch barrel, low-profile sights, a Picatinny rail and a 10-shot rotary magazine.

The affordable Stevens line boasts a new entry, too: the Model 334 bolt rifle in chrome-moly steel. The receiver, drilled to accept scope mounts for the Savage 110, has an integral recoil lug and wears a steel Picatinny rail. A three-shot detachable box feeds the low-lift, three-lug bolt. A three-position safety complements an adjustable two-stage trigger. Barrels are 20 inches long in .243 and .308 and 22 inches in 6.5 Cm. The 334 retails at $389 (in a synthetic stock) and $489 (in walnut). *savagearms.com*

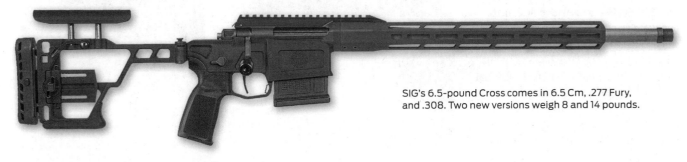

SIG's 6.5-pound Cross comes in 6.5 Cm, .277 Fury, and .308. Two new versions weigh 8 and 14 pounds.

AICS magazine. Its hinged buttstock adjusts for length and comb height. The two-stage match trigger helps shooters wring tight groups from the 1:8 rifling in the 24-inch stainless steel barrel. This rifle lists at $1,779. The 10-shot Cross PRS, in 6.5 Cm and .308, is designed for long-range matches, with a thicker barrel that brings rifle weight to 14.2 pounds. MSRP: $2,499. *sigsauer.com*

SPRINGFIELD ARMORY

Named for the Springfield, Massachusetts armory that served militias in our Revolutionary War, Springfield Armory is now a firearms manufacturer in Geneseo, Illinois. Its well-known M1A, essentially a civilian version of the M-14 infantry rifle, comes in many forms, now in 6.5 Creedmoor.

Springfield fielded its first bolt rifle, the Waypoint, in 2020. The stainless receiver has a Remington 700 "footprint" but an integral recoil lug. Its fluted, nitrided, two-lug bolt glides in EDM-cut races. Dual cocking cams help with the 90-degree lift. The TriggerTech trigger adjusts down to 2.5 pounds. The lock time of this rifle is speedy: 1.9 milliseconds. A detachable AICS single-stack box feeds from the cen-

Springfield's first bolt rifle, the CF-barreled Waypoint, has a comfy stock, a 1.9-millisecond lock time.

SIG

The Cross bolt-action rifle is so named for SIG's marketing focus: hunters and long-range target shooters. Though the Cross's folding steel buttstock and AR-style alloy fore-stock with M-LOK slots hardly bring traditional hunting rifles to mind, the 6.5 Cm has become a popular hunting cartridge.

The first Cross, introduced in 2020, was a 6.5-pound rifle chambered in .308 and .277 Fury — a cartridge designed by SIG to send 140-grain .277 bullets at 3,000 fps from 16-inch barrels for military tasks. (The Fury has a stout but costly two-part hull with a steel head that can bottle 80,000 psi.) Now there are two more Cross rifles. An 8-pound version in 6.5 Cm has a one-piece alloy receiver with a removable Pic rail and five-shot

The Springfield Waypoint has a Remington 700 footprint, dual cocking cams, and a TriggerTech trigger.

terline. The Waypoint offers button-rifled BSF carbon-fiber and fluted stainless barrels in 6mm Cm, 6.5 Cm, 6.5 PRC, and .308. Twist rates are sharp for long bullets: 1:7.5 for the 6mm, 1:8 for 6.5s, 1:10 for the .308. A slim radial brake tames recoil. The pillar-bedded CF stock from AG Composites has a steep, full grip and tall comb. M-Lok slots are standard. An adjustable-comb stock is an option. You can specify an Evergreen or Ridgeline camo finish. The barrel shank, receiver, bottom metal, and brake are Cerakoted. The average group size for three-shot groups from my sample Waypoint (with Hornady 6.5 PRC loads, 147-grain ELD Match bullets) was .69 inch. The current MSRP for the Waypoint: $2,173 to $2,670. *springfield-armory.com*

TAYLOR'S & CO.

In 2023, the 150th anniversary of the .44-40 and .45-70 cartridges, Winchester's 1873 and the Trapdoor Springfield come to mind. With its true-to-original reproductions, Taylor's also offers traditional rifles with modern features that make them practical. I hunted recently with a Taylor's 1886 carbine. Case-colored steel and checkered walnut, with the heart of the original, it deviated with modern sights, a slightly broader forend, a heavy half-octagon barrel and an oversize lever. It shot golf-ball-size groups and handily

Taylor's & Co. imports this fetching Italian-made, refined 1886 Winchester. It can fire powerful loads.

actions but sends 127-grain bullets at over 3,200 fps. The 2.0 Ti Carbon with a titanium receiver and CF barrel weighs as little as 5 pounds!

Four other carbon-barreled Mark Vs include the Carbon Mark Elite, stocked for prone shooting at distance. Only the Mark V Deluxe and Camilla Deluxe (stocked for women) wear walnut. The stability and durability of synthetic stocks, and attractive new finishes, have endeared them to hunters. The Dangerous Game rifle, in six chamberings, is the only Mark V with

took a white-tail buck.

Winchester's 1892 is the heart of Taylor's 1892 Alaskan Takedown, with a synthetic stock and a rail. Taylor's also carries period-correct Malcolm scopes and other accessories. *taylorsfirearms.com*

WEATHERBY

The Mark V action is the soul of 23 Weatherby rifle models. About half feature the trim six-lug Mark V, which historically has accounted for 20% of sales. The 6-pound Backcountry in 6.5 RPM has surely figured in that shift. The RPM fits standard bolt faces and .30-06-length

sights (from New England Custom Gun). Weatherby still lists its Vanguard rifles, on sturdy Howa actions, from just under $700. *weatherby.com*

WINCHESTER

For 2023, Winchester has three new rimfires. Wood-stocked Wildcat Sporter and Sporter SR rifles follow the first, synthetic-stocked version. This stock is a tad longer, but the action is the same blowback autoloader with a polymer receiver and integral rail. A rotary 10-shot magazine feeds the 18-inch button-rifled barrel. An adjustable ghost ring sight pairs with a ramped front. This 4.5-pound rifle lists for $350. The new Wildcat Sporter SR is identical, save for its 16.5-inch threaded barrel, which takes 3 ounces off the weight and bumps the price to $370. The other new Winchester .22 is the bolt-action Xpert, with Wildcat dimensions and magazine, a polymer stock that can be lengthened with a spacer. MSRP: $320. *winchesterguns.com* GD

Winchester's new Xpert is a bolt-action .22 with the magazine and profile of the autoloading Wildcat.

Half of Weatherby Mark Vs sold are now the lightweight six-lug version — many fire Weatherby's 6.5 RPM.

The SIG Sauer MCX-Spear.

- REPORTS -
from the Field
AR-STYLE RIFLES

It's hard to imagine a more-successful firearms segment than the AR-15 and its variants, according to recent purchasing compilations.

❯ TODD WOODARD

The seamless transition between the upper receiver and M-LOK handguard on the Blackout Defense Quantum DTL is clean and attractive.

National Shooting Sports Foundation (NSSF) President and CEO Joseph Bartozzi — probably the one person best situated to know how many widgets have been made in the firearms industry — has called the AR-15 the "most popular rifle sold in America" and a "commonly-owned firearm." The numbers to back up Bartozzi's opinions are eye-popping: about 20 million AR-15-style rifles are circulating in the U.S., up from around 8.5 million since the federal assault weapons ban expired in 2004.

After the ban expired in 2004, the net import and manufacturing of AR-style guns jumped from 314,000 that year to more than 1 million in 2009, according to the firearms production reports by the NSSF. The AR production rate has con-sistently stayed above 1 million annually since 2012, surpassing 2.2 million rifles yearly in 2013 and 2016. Everyone wants an AR these days.

And why not? I've owned more than a dozen in 5.56, 5.7x28, and .308 Win. I've found stuff on each I didn't like, leading me to sell the ones I didn't favor and buy another. A decade ago, I settled on a then-discontinued Daniel Defense DDM4V7LW chambered in 5.56 NATO because it shot well, was lightweight, and I got it for a reasonable price. Since then, I've added a Magpul CTR buttstock, bolted on a Magpul MIAD Grip, attached a GG&G 45-degree offset accessory rail for a red dot, and screwed on a Magpul B.A.D. Lever. I expect to drop in a Geissele Super Semi-Automatic Enhanced trigger next.

A smaller-diameter M-LOK handguard is out there, too.

I mention these upgrades not to tout the parts themselves, but the platform's ability to absorb such parts — and many manufacturers offer what are effectively custom parts guns on demand. You buy a basic rifle online and specify whatever handguard, stock, trigger, or any other part you want and can afford, and the maker builds the gun and ships it to your FFL. You pick it up and are happy. Or you can build your own. Or you can shop factory guns and find that the options are so manifold that your head spins. With patience, the prospective AR buyer can shop and probably find a gun that's 90% of everything he or she wants, or maybe approaching 100%, depending on your wishlist.

The Daniel Defense M4A1 RIII.

The AR platform continues to be refined, improved, and expanded, further proven by this edition's catalog listings.

BLACKOUT DEFENSE

Blackout Defense's newest gun is the Quantum DTL, which stands for Dual Taper Lock — a method of mounting the barrel and handguard that is self-centered and resistant to axial movement. Tapers are well known across industries to be one of the best self-centering mechanical fasteners for critical, continuous loads and loads under thermal expansion. The DTL system uses two tapers and two interlocking barrel nuts. The taper on the custom barrel extension mates with a taper on the I.D. of the first barrel nut; the second taper on the barrel profile mates with a taper on the I.D. of the second barrel nut. This guarantees the centricity of the barrel and upper bores while stabilizing the chamber. It also provides an exceptionally rigid base for mounting the handguard that does not result in handguard deflection.

The barrel in the DTL system features a heavy profile and precision-machined thermal expansion rings. These rings encourage the barrel to expand in the bore's direction rather than deflect and shift MOA under extreme heat.

There's a seamless transition between the upper receiver and M-LOK handguard. Blackout Defense's Presslock Technology utilizes a compression

pad to ensure a tight, rattle-free fitment, eliminating carrier tilt. The 16-inch barrel is topped off with the Horizon Compensator, a muzzle device that reduces recoil, including in compromised or angled shooting positions. The lower features an ambidextrous safety selector and weight-reducing relief cuts. The flat-faced Zero Short Reset Trigger matches the firearm's lines and eliminates pre- and post-travel. A Magpul SL collapsible stock and Magpul MOE pistol grip keep weight down and are popular upgrades on the AR-15 platform. Quantum DTLs are chambered in .223 Wylde. Barrel lengths are 13.9, 14.5, and 16 inches, with a mid-length gas system. Weight: 6.875 pounds. MSRPs start at $2,279. *blackoutdefense.com*

BUSHMASTER FIREARMS

It's good to see Bushmaster ARs available again after the company was purchased out of Remington Outdoor's bankruptcy parts sale in 2020. Bushmaster calls the

M4 Patrolman's MOE a "cornerstone to [its] iconic line of rifles." The company is "not an affiliate with any other firearms

manufacturing companies," according to a company release. Its website lists several AR variants, including the M4 Patrolman's line, QRC, Bravo Zulu, and ACR. But about the ACR specifically, "Bushmaster Firearms recognizes the current market demand for the ACR platform and intends to reintroduce it to our catalog with all promised accessories and options." The ACR listed on the

website is $6,000 and is "in new condition from old Remington stock."

As the core of the Bushmaster lineup, the 5.56-chambered M4 Patrolman's rifle series is the hard-use duty AR for which Bushmaster is best known. It has a 16-inch barrel made from 4150 CMV steel and is finished with salt bath nitride. It has a carbine-length gas system, an F-marked A2 front, a 7075 forged XM15-E2S lower receiver, and a 7075 forged A4 flat-top upper receiver. Magpul parts are highlighted on the rifle, including the company's MOE SL handguard, CTR carbine stock, MOE grip, and MOE enhanced triggerguard. The Mil-Spec trigger and A2 flash hider complete the package. Magazines are 10- or 30-round aluminum BFI units. MSRP: $1,018. *bushmaster.com*

Daniel Defense took its battle-tested DD4 and M4A1 designs and made them more operator friendly by adding an ambidextrous lower and swapping out the RIS II rail system with its new RIS III M-LOK system, which is lighter than a Picatinny arrangement.

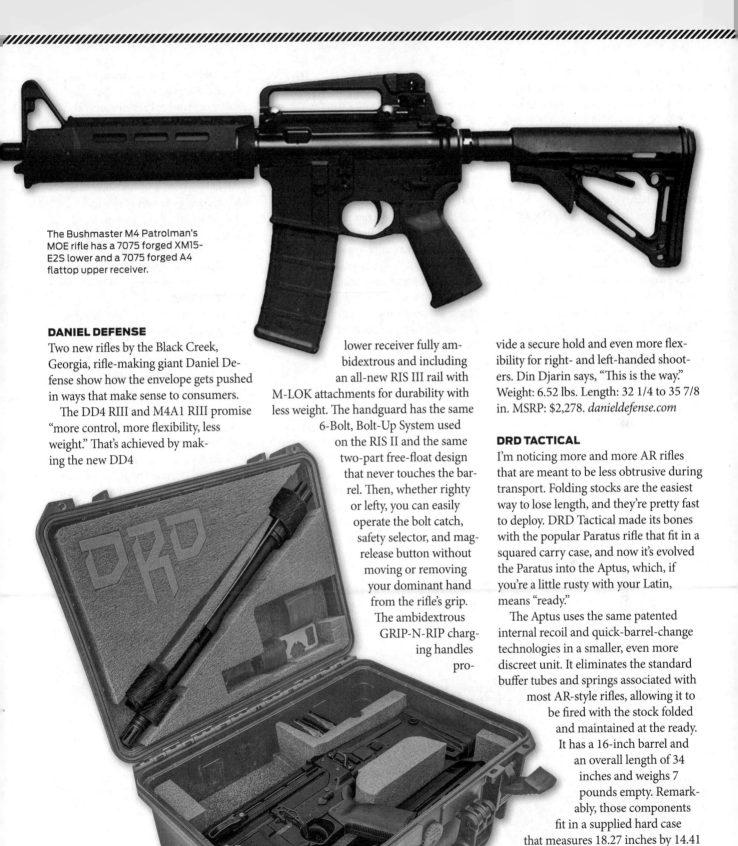

The Bushmaster M4 Patrolman's MOE rifle has a 7075 forged XM15-E2S lower and a 7075 forged A4 flattop upper receiver.

DANIEL DEFENSE

Two new rifles by the Black Creek, Georgia, rifle-making giant Daniel Defense show how the envelope gets pushed in ways that make sense to consumers.

The DD4 RIII and M4A1 RIII promise "more control, more flexibility, less weight." That's achieved by making the new DD4 lower receiver fully ambidextrous and including an all-new RIS III rail with M-LOK attachments for durability with less weight. The handguard has the same 6-Bolt, Bolt-Up System used on the RIS II and the same two-part free-float design that never touches the barrel. Then, whether righty or lefty, you can easily operate the bolt catch, safety selector, and mag-release button without moving or removing your dominant hand from the rifle's grip. The ambidextrous GRIP-N-RIP charging handles pro-vide a secure hold and even more flexibility for right- and left-handed shooters. Din Djarin says, "This is the way." Weight: 6.52 lbs. Length: 32 1/4 to 35 7/8 in. MSRP: $2,278. danieldefense.com

DRD TACTICAL

I'm noticing more and more AR rifles that are meant to be less obtrusive during transport. Folding stocks are the easiest way to lose length, and they're pretty fast to deploy. DRD Tactical made its bones with the popular Paratus rifle that fit in a squared carry case, and now it's evolved the Paratus into the Aptus, which, if you're a little rusty with your Latin, means "ready."

The Aptus uses the same patented internal recoil and quick-barrel-change technologies in a smaller, even more discreet unit. It eliminates the standard buffer tubes and springs associated with most AR-style rifles, allowing it to be fired with the stock folded and maintained at the ready. It has a 16-inch barrel and an overall length of 34 inches and weighs 7 pounds empty. Remarkably, those components fit in a supplied hard case that measures 18.27 inches by 14.41 inches, or they'll slide into an equally discreet backpack. When you're ready to shoot, the Aptus can go from the box to line-ready in about a minute without tools if you practice. Another neat feature is that you only need to swap the barrels to change chamberings, not buy an ad-

DRD Tactical's Aptus and Kivaari carry cases can be hard- or soft-sided, depending on your transport needs.

ditional upper. It's available in 5.56mm (1:7 twist) or .300 Blackout (1:8 twist). The takedown system is durable, too. There's also a chambering in .338 Lapua Magnum in the Kivaari rifle line. Aptus MSRP: $2,950. Kivaari MSRP: $5,650. *drdtactical.com*

FN AMERICA

FN America's third-generation Designated Marksman Rifle (DMR) is now available in several new colors — matte black anodize, flat dark earth (FDE), or tungsten gray Cerakote. More important, the FN 15 DMR3 has a new 18-inch barrel, SureFire ProComp muzzle brake and Geissele two-stage trigger. The 18-inch Hybrid-profile barrel balances rigidity with accuracy and is light enough for quick maneuverability.

The cold hammer-forged barrel is chrome-lined with a 1:8 twist and is made from FN's proprietary machine gun barrel steel. The rifle-length gas system has a pinned low-profile gas block. The 14 5/8-inch aluminum handguard uses Hodge Defense's wedge-lock technology, allowing for a fully free-floated barrel. Its continuous MIL-STD Picatinny rail at 12 o'clock and multiple M-LOK attachment

slots allow users to customize the setup for optics and other accessories. Inside, there's an M16-style bolt carrier group with a high-pressure/magnetic-particle-inspected and certified bolt. As befits a DMR item, the Geissele two-stage precision G2S trigger allows for exceptional trigger control, with the first-stage trigger pull ranging from 4.25 to 4.75 pounds and the second stage ranging from 2.75 to 3 pounds. The DMRs are finished with FN's custom furniture, including an ergonomic pistol grip, six-position collapsible carbine stock and 30-round magazine, and Radian Raptor-LT ambidextrous charging handle and Radian Talon ambidextrous safety selector. MSRP: $2,439. *fnamerica.com*

FOLDAR

The 2023 FoldAR Basic-Series Rifle is not only small. It has also been upgraded to include a quick-change barrel system, allowing the owner to swap cartridges and barrels lengths faster and more reliably. Another plus is the modular handguard, giving armorers three different lengths to choose from, reduced weight, and room to experiment with aftermarket gas blocks.

B-Series Rifles are configured with Mil-Spec components in the bolt carrier group, grip, trigger, carbine stock, and non-adjustable gas block. The sexy part is, of course, FoldAR's patented folding upper. Deployment and stowage take only seconds, and the process is simple and reliable. With a 16-inch barrel, the FoldAR's overall length is 32.9 inches, its folded length is 17.6 inches, and its folded width is 4.25 inches. Whether folded or extended, the FoldAR weighs 6.15 pounds. MSRP: $1,799. *foldar.com*

JP ENTERPRISES

I don't know if calling JP Enterprises a *couture* gun builder is fair or accurate, but I think the word from fashion fits here. The company is famous for its build-to-order guns that cost as much as a lady's *couture* pumps, but the rifles are much more useful unless you're Dylan Mulvaney. Less well-known are the company's Pre-Configured JP Rifles or Ready Rifles. Ready Rifles are set configurations representing JP's most popular builds, with purpose-driven selections to run the gamut of sporting and duty needs. Each is identical to a one-off custom build, and any JP Ready Rifle model can also be

Inside the gorgeous new skins of the FN DMR series are serious accuracy innards, such as a Geissele two-stage precision G2S trigger.

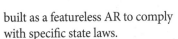

The FoldAR's overall length is 32.9 inches, represented by the silhouetted piece of the gun. Its folded length is a scant 17.6 inches.

built as a featureless AR to comply with specific state laws.

The downside is that to ensure availability, JP does not allow changes or substitutions — unless you want to incur custom-build prices. But if you want a top-notch AR with top-tier components, you might be ready for a JP Ready Rifle. MSRP: starting at $1,650. *jprifles.com*

ROCK RIVER ARMS

Rock River Arms' new premium AR-15 platform rifles are called the Ascendant. No, these aren't Stargate's diaphanous Ascended Beings but are instead best-in-caliber AR-platform rifles for shooters who demand premium performance without the hassle of figuring out how to get there.

The Ascendant All-Terrain Hunter (ATH) rifles launch the Ascendant program in .223 Wylde, .350 Legend,

and .450 Bushmaster. Each Ascendant ATH barrel is made of cryogenically treated 416R stainless steel and is media blasted to a matte finish to reduce glare in the field. RRA used its lightweight handguard to minimize weight, and a full-length Picatinny top rail is integrated, providing room for mounting IR or thermal optics ahead of the scope if nighttime hog hunting is on your dance card. RRA chose TriggerTech's Diamond Single-Stage AR-15 cartridge trigger, which has extremely short overtravel and is adjustable from 1.5 to 4 pounds of pull.

Each Ascendant ATH rifle comes with one of two Vortex variable-power

optics: the Viper HS 4-16x44mm or the Strike Eagle 1-6x24mm. Magpul's new PRS Lite stock allows the shooter to achieve a comfortable, custom fit with its adjustable length-of-pull and cheek riser height. Its length is 38 1/8-inch (collapsed), and the ATH weighs 9.4 pounds with optics. The rifles offer an Accuracy Guarantee of 3/4 MOA with premium ammo, and the package comes with one 20-round metal magazine, a 42-inch soft case, a manual, and a warranty. MSRP: $3,235. *rockriverarms.com*

The CTAC is one of JP Enterprises' Small-Frame Ready Rifles. It makes a flexible platform for target shooting, home defense, or getting a start in 3-Gun. It needs only your choice of optics or iron sights and is ready for whatever shooting discipline fits you.

From top are the Rock River Arms Ascendant rifles in .350 Legend, .223 Wylde chamber for 5.56 NATO/.223 Remington, and .450 Bushmaster, respectively. The optics and mounts are part of the packages.

A side-folding stock reduces the Spear's carry length for easier transport.

A new side-charging handle on the left side of the Spear's frame is non-reciprocating; it will not move back and forth while firing, and it will not knock the gun out of battery.

Jason St. John, director of government products at SIG Sauer, said the Spear military contract calls for SIG to supply a total of 400,000 weapons and 1 billion rounds of ammunition.

SIG SAUER

SIG's new MCX-Spear 277 rifle was announced in early 2022 to replace the current M4 rifle platform for the U.S. military, and a special edition commercial variant became available in 2023. The first-run rifle is a ridiculous $7,999. But collectors have a different way of looking at the world, and maybe that first-run price is a bargain for some. To wit:

"This is a rare opportunity for passionate consumers to own a piece of history," said Ron Cohen, President and CEO of SIG Sauer, Inc. "This first production run MCX-Spear, and all of the revolutionary technology behind its development is being offered to the commercial market in a configuration that is a near match to our NGSW-R [Next Generation Squad Weapon System-Rifle] submission."

The MCX-SPEAR is an adaptable multi-caliber rifle (.277 SIG Fury, 6.5 Creedmoor, and 7.62 NATO with barrel changes) featuring rear and side non-reciprocating charging handles, six-position folding stock, ambidextrous fire control, bolt-catch, and mag release, two-stage match trigger, two-position adjustable gas piston, a lightened free-float M-LOK handguard, and a full-length Picatinny rail. It ships with two 20-round magazines and a SIG SLX Suppressor.

The special edition MCX-Spear is chambered in .277 SIG Fury, the commercial variant of the U.S. Army's 6.8x51 hybrid ammunition, with a steel case head and a brass upper case body.

"The revolutionary SIG Fury ammunition is the most technically advanced leap in small arms ammunition in over 150 years. It turns your intermediate rifle platform into magnum performance without the added weight or length while still using 20-round magazines," said Cohen.

SIG's .277 Fury ammunition is the commercial variant of the 6.8x51 hybrid military round available in the hybrid case technology submitted to the U.S. Army NGSW program. The proprietary case consists of three parts: a stainless steel base, a lock washer, and an upper case of brass. It produces 80,000 psi in the chamber compared to the .308 Winchester's 62,000 psi. Also available is a .277 SIG Fury FMJ traditional cartridge. *sigsauer.com* **GD**

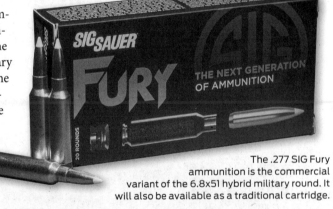

The .277 SIG Fury ammunition is the commercial variant of the 6.8x51 hybrid military round. It will also be available as a traditional cartridge.

The SIG MCX-Spear in .277 Fury.

- REPORTS - from the Field SEMI-AUTO PISTOLS

Beefy double-stack 1911s and reintroductions of classics are among this year's autoloading pistols.

›ROBERT SADOWSKI

The Browning Buck Mark Field Target Vision.

Springfield Prodigy DS (double stack).

What do you call a double-stack 1911-platform pistol? Is it a 2011 or a 2311? If you are Staccato and Springfield Armory, it's a 2011, but according to EAA and Oracle, it's a 2311. Either way, double-stack 1911s are the latest trend in pistols. While not exactly new — double-stack 1911s have been produced off and on for decades — some of the newly introduced models are quite affordable, and that is new. Striker-fire platforms continue to thrive, and the new Armscor/RIA model RIA 5.0 uses an innovative system. At the same time, the KIGER-9C PRO from Anderson is designed for concealed carry and is feature-rich. Beretta is back, too, with tricked-out model 92s and Cheetahs. Finally, Turkish pistol manufacturers continue to produce excellent 1911s and striker-fired models that perform at affordable prices. Here are the particulars.

ANDERSON

Anderson's KIGER-9C PRO (MSRP $539) is a polymer-frame, striker-fire compact 9mm pistol designed for concealed carry. The polymer frame has acres of texture for a sure grip, an aggressively lightened slide and a flat trigger, and it comes optics-ready. It features a 3.9-inch barrel, 15+1 round capacity, and a 5.5-pound trigger pull. *andersonmanufacturing.com*

ARMSCOR/ROCK ISLAND ARSENAL

The RIA 5.0 ST (MSRP $999) is a full-size, competition-ready pistol with a patented RVS recoil system that maximizes barrel mass and linear movement for softer felt recoil. This 9mm also has a deeper bore axis for less muzzle flip, a striker-fire trigger, a two-piece modular grip, 17+1 capacity, and comes optics-ready. *armscor.com*

BERETTA

Beretta's 92X series now includes the 92Xi (MSRP $949), a single-action-only version of the 92X series of performance-ready pistols with frame-mount thumb safety and straight, Vertec-style grip frame. It comes with a fiber-optic front sight and MRDS optic mounting system and is available in 9mm.

Beretta has revived the Cheetah platform and updated the design with better ergonomics for modern-day carry. The new 80X Cheetah (MSRP $799) features include a smaller Vertec-style grip, the X-treme S Double/Single trigger, a skeletonized hammer, a 13+1-round capacity, and it comes optics-ready. Available in .380 Auto and black or two-tone bronze/black finishes. *beretta.com*

BRG-USA

Turkish 9mm striker-fire handguns are becoming increasingly common and offer much value for the price. A newcomer is the BRG9 Elite (MSRP $259), a 9mm polymer-frame striker-fire with a 4-inch barrel and a 16+1 capacity. Plus, it has interchangeable backstraps and is optics-ready. The flat trigger has an average 5-pound pull that is crisp with a fast reset.

The BRG9 Tactical (MSRP $499) has everything the Elite model offers plus a 3.5-pound match trigger, threaded barrel, magwell, two 18-round magazines and one 20-round magazine. *brg-usa.com*

The Anderson KIGER-9C PRO.

The RIA 5.0 ST.

The BRG9 Tactical.

The reintroduced Beretta 80X Cheetah.

Browning Buck Mark Micro Bull.

The Browning 1911-22 Black Label Compact Copper.

The Canik MC9.

Canik's SFx Rival-S.

BROWNING

The new Buck Mark pistols include short-barrel models suitable as kit guns and target models designed to topple steel plates or cluster holes in tight groups on paper. The Buck Mark Micro Bull and Micro Bull Suppressor Ready (MSRP $340) have 4-inch barrels, Pro-Target adjustable sights, and textured polymer grip panels. The Buck Mark Field Target Tungsten (MSRP $580) features a tungsten Cerakote finish, Pro-Target adjustable rear sight, and a 5.5-inch barrel with a full-length top Pica-tinny rail. The Buck Mark Field Target Vision (MSRP $940) is tricked out with the lightweight Vision barrel with an aluminum outer sleeve, an under-barrel rail equipped with a Crimson Trace Rail Master Pro Universal red laser and tactical light, Pro-Target adjustable sights, and full-length Picatinny optics rail. The Buck Mark Plus Vision Triad (MSRP $799) has the alloy-sleeved steel Vision barrel, Picatinny optics rail, suppressor-ready threaded barrel, and muzzle brake. The Buck Mark Plus Vision Blue Shoal (MSRP $799) is similar but with a blue-finished alloy barrel sleeve and threaded muzzle.

Browning's 1911-style pistols in .22 LR, the 1911-22 (MSRP $799), and .380 Auto, 1911-380 (MSRP $950), are now available in three new finishes: a two-tone copper Cerakote slide and black-alloy frame, a Polar Blue Cerakote slide and black frame, and a Crushed Orchid Cerakote slide and black frame. *browning.com*

CANIK

The new MC9 (MSRP $439) from Canik is based on the popular Mete series of striker-fired 9mm pistols. It's designed for concealed carry, sports a 3.1-inch barrel, and has an overall length of 6.1 inches. It comes with a flush-fit 12-round mag and an extended 15-round magazine. Plus, the slide comes optics-ready. Available in FDE, black, and two-tone finishes.

Bucking the normal is Canik's SFx Rival-S (MSRP $899), a steel-frame version of its full-size Rival model. The steel-frame model shifts the weight to the palm of your hand for quick follow-up shots. This new metal gun also includes all the features of the polymer-framed Canik, including a flat-faced trigger, an optics-cut slide, a removable metal magwell, and an aggressively textured slide. Available in 9mm. *canikusa.com*

CZ-USA

CZ has souped up its newest striker-fire, the P-10, and the iconic CZ 75, to offer four new competition-ready models. The CZ P-10 C OR SR (MSRP $499) is a compact P-10 9mm with a threaded 4.6-inch barrel, 3-dot RMR co-witness-height sight, optics-ready slide, and flat-face trigger. The grip is compact yet holds a 17-round magazine. The CZ P-10 F OR SR (same MSRP) is the full-size brother of the compact model sporting a 5.1-inch threaded barrel and a full-size grip that holds a 21-round magazine.

The CZ TS 2 Orange (MSRP $2,199) provides a new level of competition sophistication to the classic CZ 75 with a 5.2-inch bull barrel, hand-fitted barrel-to-slide and slide-to-frame, modified recoil spring guide, and orange finish aluminum checkered grips and magazine funnel. It's available in 9mm and .40 S&W.

The CZC A01-SD OR (MSRP $2,699) is built from scratch at the CZ Custom Shop. It has a hammer-forged, CNC-machined and blued frame. The full dust cover offers excellent balance and shot recovery. It also has a deep beavertail, undercut triggerguard, raised 25 LPI checkering, and an internal magwell. Available in 9mm. *cz-usa.com*

EAA

EAA imports the Girsan Witness 2311 (MSRP starting at $999) from Turkey. This double-stack 1911 platform uses a polymer grip to house the super-size magazines. The available barrel lengths include 4.25, 5, and 6 inches. It's chambered in 9mm (17+1 capacity), .45

The CZ TS 2 Orange.

The CZ P-10 C OR SR.

The EAA MC P35 OPS.

The EAA Girsan Witness 2311.

Auto (11+1 capacity), and 10mm Auto (15+1 capacity).

Girsan also makes a knockoff of the iconic Browning Hi-Power, and new additions to the line include the MC P35 PI (MSRP $630) — a compact version of the full-size pistol with a shorter 3.8-inch barrel. A competition-ready model, the MC P35 Match/OPS (MSRP $776) also features a fiber-optic front sight, an all-steel frame and slide, an extended beavertail, a beveled magwell, and a flat trigger. The MC P35 OPS (MSRP $956) is similar, except it comes with a factory-installed red-dot sight. *eaacorp.com*

FN

The Edge lineup of Model 509 compensated pistols now includes The 509 CC Edge (MSRP $1,569) with a 4.25-inch barrel, flat-face trigger, optic-cut slide, and 10-, 12- and 15-round magazines.

Two new big-bore striker-fired pistols include the FN 510 Tactical, chambered in 10mm Auto, and the FN 545 Tactical, in .45 ACP. These pistols take a design cue from the FN 509 Tactical and also feature a threaded barrel for muzzle devices, a receiver cut for red-dot optics and suppressor-height night sights. Each has a standard 15-round capacity and 22+1 rounds of 10mm or 18+1 rounds of .45 ACP with the extended magazines. *fnamerica.com*

GLOCK

Remember how annoyed you were when Glock introduced the G47 for the U.S. Customs and Border Protection in 2019 and said it was only available to law enforcement? Well, the

The FN 509 CC Edge.

Hi-Point's JXP 10.

The FN 510 Tactical.

G47 MOS (MSRP $620) is nearly the same gun used by Customs and Border Patrol, and, yes, it's available to civilians. The best way to describe the 9mm-chambered G47 MOS is that the slide is the same length as a G17 and is mated to a G45 Gen5 frame. It comes equipped with interchangeable backstraps and is a MOS variant, meaning the slide is machined for a red-dot sight. I've been running an Ameriglo

Haven red-dot sight with a 3.5 MOA dot, and the pair allows me to be surgical with shots.

Glock is also merging the big-bore G20 and G21 pistols into Gen5. The G20 MOS, 10mm Auto, is now available with all the Gen5 features, and since it is a MOS variant, it is optic-ready. The G21 MOS in .45 Auto is also Gen5-equipped and comes optics-ready. *glock.com*

HI-POINT

The JXP 10 (MSRP $219) is not the most beautiful pistol, but if it is like any other Hi-Point handgun, it will go bang every time you pull the trigger. This new model is chambered for the potent 10mm Auto and has a 5.2-inch threaded barrel. It weighs 49 ounces, and the capacity is 10+1 rounds. *hi-pointfirearms.com*

ORACLE ARMS

You have undoubtedly heard of the 2011 platform, a 1911 set up to feed from a

The Oracle Arms 2311.

double-stack magazine. But have you heard of a 2311? The Oracle Arms 2311 (MSRP $1,699-$3,000) takes design cues from the 2011 platform and the SIG P320. It's a single-action, hammer-fired pistol with a grip module compatible with SIG P320 mags. Other features include ambidextrous safety levers, a cavernous magwell, and an extra-long beavertail. The 2311 will be available in several models ranging from compact to competition variants. *oraclearms.com*

Ruger's new Security-380.

The Savage 1911.

RUGER

The Security-380 (MSRP $369) from Ruger shares a lot with the Security-9 pistol but comes in a smaller package and a caliber that's easier to control — .380 Auto. Features include Ruger's Lite Rack System, which consists of slide serrations, cocking ears, and a lighter recoil spring. Capacity 15+1. *ruger.com*

SAVAGE

Savage is now making its version of the classic full-size 1911 platform. The Savage 1911 (MSRP $1,349-$1,499) can be had in three finish options — blued, two-tone, and stainless — and two frame styles — with a Picatinny rail and without. These Government-size 1911s are chambered in either 9mm or .45 Auto with 5-inch stainless steel barrels, GI-style bushings, and dual-recoil spring systems for softer and smoother recoil. Sights are Novak Lo-Mount black rear and white dot front. They come equipped with VZ G10 grips and ambidextrous thumb safeties. *savagearms.com*

SIG SAUER

SIG has super-sized the P365 with the new P365-XMACRO TACOPS (MSRP $750). It features a P365XL-length slide, a 3.7-inch barrel, an enhanced slide catch lever, and a metal flared detachable magwell. It comes with four magazines and has XRAY3 night sights.

Also new to the p365-x line is the P365X-XMACRO ROMEOZero Elite (MSRP $1,049) with an integrated compensator that reduces muzzle flip, a flat trigger, and a ROMEOZero Elite red-dot optic. The ROSE P365-380 (MSRP $749) and P365-XL (MSRP $899) are special-edition P365 pistols with laser-engraved grip modules and matte rose-colored controls. The Rose is designed for women and includes access to an online community to help encourage and inspire ladies with help and support as they become more confident and comfortable shooters.

SIG continues to grow the P320 with the new P320 Spectre Comp Blackout (MSRP $1,549), which has laser-engraved grip modules and a custom-designed slide on the proven TXG tungsten-infused grip module. This gun is ready for competition, carry, and everything in between. It features a single port compensator that significantly reduces muzzle flip, has XRAY night sights, and is optics-ready.

SIG's rimfire P322 Coyote (MSRP $549) is outfitted with a coyote finish grip module and slide. *sigsauer.com*

SMITH & WESSON

Smith & Wesson has morphed the full-size M&P platform to create the M&P 5.7 pistol (MSRP $699) chambered in the hot 5.7x28mm cartridge. The engineering work required to handle this round required S&W to design a new gas-operated, locked-breech, rotating Tempo Barrel System. This new 5-inch barrel provides quicker extraction once the bullet passes the gas port, optimizing ballistics. The M&P 5.7 has a 22-round capacity and comes with two magazines. The slide is cut for a red-dot optic.

The Equalizer (MSRP $599) is the next evolution of the S&W concealed carry pistol. This micro-compact 9mm features EZ technology, such as an easy-to-rack slide, low recoil impulse, and single-action trigger. Magazine capacity is 10, 13 or 15 rounds. It's optics-ready and sports snag-free fixed sights.

Are you looking to compete with a pistol out of the box? The new Performance Center M&P 9 M2.0 Competitor (MSRP $999) is your ticket. The Competitor has a metal frame and comes equipped with a 5-inch barrel. The light, crisp trigger and lightening cuts in the slide offer a soft recoil. The magwell slurps up 10- or 17-round magazines. The slide is cut for optics and has a fiber-optic front sight and blacked-out serrated rear. Comes with four magazines. *smithwesson.com*

SPRINGFIELD ARMORY

Springfield Armory took the proven 1911 platform and enhanced it with a double-stack magazine, then cut the slide to mount a red-dot optic, then called it the Prodigy (MSRP $1,499; $1,699 with red-dot optic). Its mag capacity is hefty, considering it's a 1911: 17 rounds with the flush-fit magazine and 20 and 26 rounds with the extended mag. If you're looking for a work-hard,

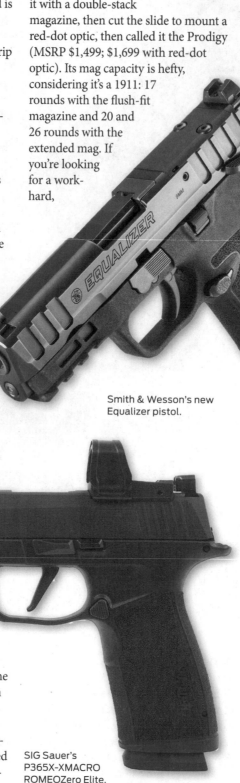

Smith & Wesson Performance Center M&P 9 M2.0 Competitor.

Smith & Wesson's new Equalizer pistol.

SIG Sauer's P365X-XMACRO ROMEOZero Elite.

compete-hard 9mm with a single-action 1911-style trigger, this might be your pistol. *springfield-armory.com*

STACCATO

Staccato is a pioneer in the 2011 double-stack platform and produces some excellent pistols for defense and competition. The Staccato CS (MSRP $2,499) is a compact 9mm 23 ounces unloaded and equipped with a 3.5-inch barrel. It has a new grip that's narrower than its big brother models. It's designed for easy carry — even appendix style — and is optics-ready. The magazine holds 16 rounds. The black-anodized aluminum curved trigger breaks at a crisp 4 to 4.5 pounds. And there are plenty of slide serrations to run the CS fast like its larger versions. *staccato2011.com*

STOEGER

Who makes a .40 S&W-caliber pistol these days? Stoeger does. The famous shotgun maker now offers the STR-40 (MSRP $449) chambered in .40 S&W with a 12-round magazine, and it comes optics-ready! *stoegerindustries.com*

TAURUS

Taurus has introduced an XL size to the GX4 series with the GX4XL (MSRP $429). This 9mm striker-fire has a 1-inch

longer barrel than the GX4 and still keeps the 10-, 11-, or 13-round magazine capacity, flat-face trigger, and modular backstraps.

The GX4XL T.O.R.O. (Taurus Optic Ready Option) model (MSRP $459) has the slide cut for an optics mounting system. A variant with a factory-installed Riton red-dot optic and BUIS (MSRP $549) is also available.

The TX22 Competition SCR (MSRP $589) is the next iteration of Taurus' TX22 platform. SCR stands for Steel Challenge Ready and features the TandemKross Game Changer PRO squared compensator for added weight and a custom bull barrel for enhanced accuracy. The TX22 .22 LR rimfire pistol is a blast to shoot, and now it comes in a smaller package. The TX22 Compact (MSRP $330) has a 3-inch barrel, slide cut for a red dot, and a 13-round capacity. Its overall length is 6.7 inches. A factory-mounted Riton red-dot variant (MSRP $390) is in the lineup. *taurususa.com*

The Walther P99 AS Final Edition.

The Tisas Raider.

The Staccato CS.

Stoeger's STR-40.

TISAS

Tisas is another firearm manufacturer from Turkey with a niche in the 1911 platform. I've run the Tisas 10mm Auto and the retro-cool M1911A1 pistols and have been quite impressed with their performance, accuracy, and quality. The newest 1911 is the Raider (MSRP

$760), a near clone of the M45A1 service pistol used by Marine Corps Special Operations. It is chambered in .45 Auto and has a Picatinny rail and G10 grips. *tisasusa.com*

WALTHER

Walther is shuttering the classic P99 AS with one final variant, the P99 AS Final Edition (MSRP $849). Features include an OD finish polymer frame, matte black slide, and chambered in 9mm. *walther-arms.com* GD

- REPORTS -
from the Field
REVOLVERS
& OTHERS

Super fun .22 wheelgun plinkers and a stunningly engraved Colt Python are among this year's revolvers.

›SHANE JAHN

Taurus Raging Hunter in .500 S&W and Bond Arms Stubby .22 LR. The largest and smallest of new wheelguns and derringers.

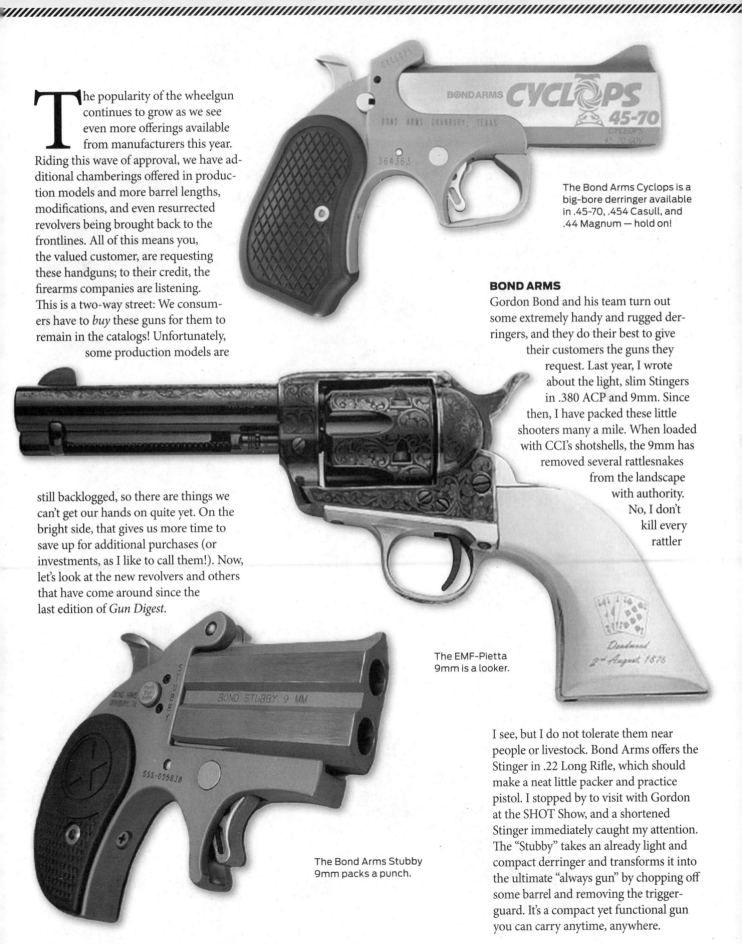

The popularity of the wheelgun continues to grow as we see even more offerings available from manufacturers this year. Riding this wave of approval, we have additional chamberings offered in production models and more barrel lengths, modifications, and even resurrected revolvers being brought back to the frontlines. All of this means you, the valued customer, are requesting these handguns; to their credit, the firearms companies are listening. This is a two-way street: We consumers have to *buy* these guns for them to remain in the catalogs! Unfortunately, some production models are

The Bond Arms Cyclops is a big-bore derringer available in .45-70, .454 Casull, and .44 Magnum — hold on!

BOND ARMS

Gordon Bond and his team turn out some extremely handy and rugged derringers, and they do their best to give their customers the guns they request. Last year, I wrote about the light, slim Stingers in .380 ACP and 9mm. Since then, I have packed these little shooters many a mile. When loaded with CCI's shotshells, the 9mm has removed several rattlesnakes from the landscape with authority. No, I don't kill every rattler

still backlogged, so there are things we can't get our hands on quite yet. On the bright side, that gives us more time to save up for additional purchases (or investments, as I like to call them!). Now, let's look at the new revolvers and others that have come around since the last edition of *Gun Digest*.

The EMF-Pietta 9mm is a looker.

The Bond Arms Stubby 9mm packs a punch.

I see, but I do not tolerate them near people or livestock. Bond Arms offers the Stinger in .22 Long Rifle, which should make a neat little packer and practice pistol. I stopped by to visit with Gordon at the SHOT Show, and a shortened Stinger immediately caught my attention. The "Stubby" takes an already light and compact derringer and transforms it into the ultimate "always gun" by chopping off some barrel and removing the triggerguard. It's a compact yet functional gun you can carry anytime, anywhere.

For a .22 LR in a slightly larger package, the Rawhide is a 21-ounce derringer sans triggerguard that is a great companion to its bigger brothers in .38 Special/.357 Magnum. The Honey B model offers a slightly larger grip by combining the Stinger with B6 Resin grips in a lightweight derringer. It's offered in .22 LR, .380 ACP, and 9mm. To step it up a notch, the Rowdy XL in .45 Colt/.410 with a 3.5-inch barrel and B6 grips for better hold is available in a two-shot handgun weighing 22 ounces.

For those who turn up their noses at the small calibers, hold on - literally! Bond Arms has the one-shot Cyclops in .45-70 Government. Additional chamberings will be offered in .454 Casull, .44 Magnum, and .50 Action Express. *bondarms.com*

COLT
The King Cobra Target .22 LR is a welcomed addition to Colt's revolver lineup. This 10-shooter is stainless and offered in 4- and 6-inch barrels. So far, it's been one of those guns we must patiently await. I've had an order in for months, and the folks at Colt tell me I might finally get it in the summer of '23. I do think the wait will be worth it!

Colt's robust .44 Magnum Anaconda, previously offered in 6- and 8-inch barrels, is now available in the easy-packing 4-inch model. The 6-inch Anaconda I've had the pleasure to shoot was very accurate, and I expect the same quality and accuracy in this convenient, shorter-barreled version. *colt.com*

The Rossi RM66 is a 6-inch .357 Magnum stainless steel revolver with adjustable sights.

Korth Silver DLC Mongoose.

The Korth Vintage is available with a 4- or 6-inch half-lug barrel in .357 Magnum.

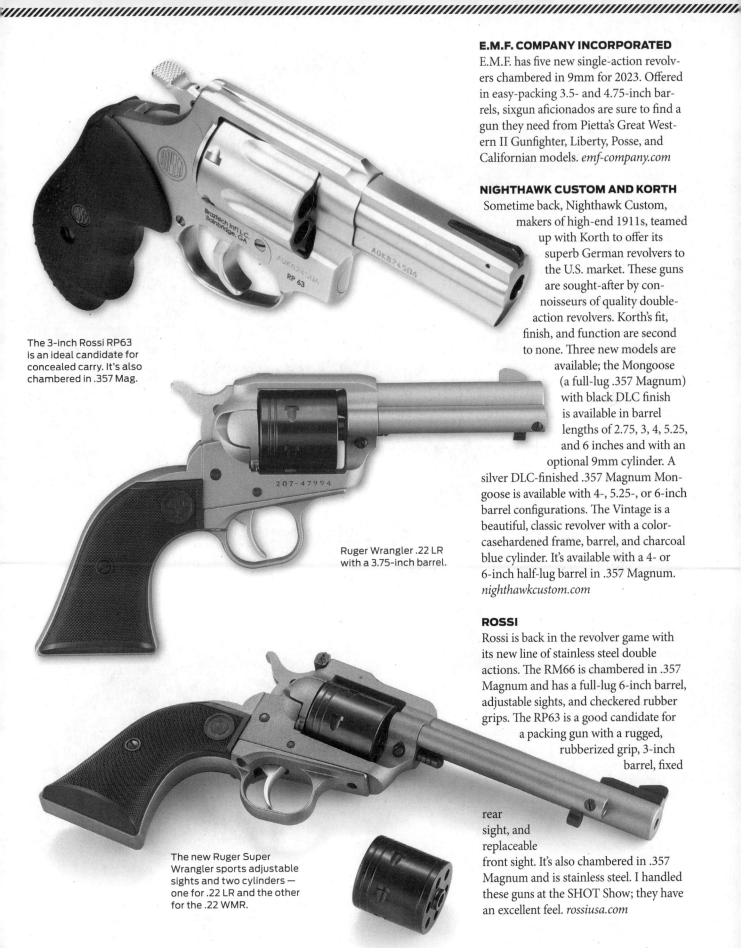

The 3-inch Rossi RP63 is an ideal candidate for concealed carry. It's also chambered in .357 Mag.

Ruger Wrangler .22 LR with a 3.75-inch barrel.

The new Ruger Super Wrangler sports adjustable sights and two cylinders — one for .22 LR and the other for the .22 WMR.

E.M.F. COMPANY INCORPORATED

E.M.F. has five new single-action revolvers chambered in 9mm for 2023. Offered in easy-packing 3.5- and 4.75-inch barrels, sixgun aficionados are sure to find a gun they need from Pietta's Great Western II Gunfighter, Liberty, Posse, and Californian models. *emf-company.com*

NIGHTHAWK CUSTOM AND KORTH

Sometime back, Nighthawk Custom, makers of high-end 1911s, teamed up with Korth to offer its superb German revolvers to the U.S. market. These guns are sought-after by connoisseurs of quality double-action revolvers. Korth's fit, finish, and function are second to none. Three new models are available; the Mongoose (a full-lug .357 Magnum) with black DLC finish is available in barrel lengths of 2.75, 3, 4, 5.25, and 6 inches and with an optional 9mm cylinder. A silver DLC-finished .357 Magnum Mongoose is available with 4-, 5.25-, or 6-inch barrel configurations. The Vintage is a beautiful, classic revolver with a color-casehardened frame, barrel, and charcoal blue cylinder. It's available with a 4- or 6-inch half-lug barrel in .357 Magnum. *nighthawkcustom.com*

ROSSI

Rossi is back in the revolver game with its new line of stainless steel double actions. The RM66 is chambered in .357 Magnum and has a full-lug 6-inch barrel, adjustable sights, and checkered rubber grips. The RP63 is a good candidate for a packing gun with a rugged, rubberized grip, 3-inch barrel, fixed rear sight, and replaceable front sight. It's also chambered in .357 Magnum and is stainless steel. I handled these guns at the SHOT Show; they have an excellent feel. *rossiusa.com*

RUGER

Ruger continuously delivers new products for the shooting public, especially handguns. The affordable Wrangler .22 LR line must be doing well because new additions have been offered from the get-go. This year's come in new barrel lengths of 3.75, 6.5, and 7.5 inches. These little guns are fun to shoot and another great way of introducing new shooters to the sport. My 10-year-old daughter loves plinking with her Wrangler Birdshead. Now I have to decide which of the new barrel lengths I need. Heck, at the low cost of these sixguns, there's no reason not to own them all! Ruger also introduced the Super Wrangler family of single-action revolvers. These feature adjustable sights, a 5.5-inch barrel, and a steel cylinder frame. The Super Wrangler is a convertible model that ships with two cylinders, one for inexpensive .22 LR and one for powerful .22 WMR ammunition. *ruger.com*

TAYLOR'S & COMPANY

The 1873-styled Single Action Army is one of those guns everyone must own. They are classic in design, feel, and function. Taylor's is now offering the TC9 SA 1873 in 9mm. This is an excellent idea because it offers affordable ammunition availability for the range. It adds a lower-recoil option that is fun to shoot and beneficial for introducing new shooters to this proven handgun platform.

Folks unfamiliar with the SAA revolver are impressed by the "feel" and accuracy of these guns. The 9mm is no cream puff with appropriate ammunition, and it makes perfect sense for the cartridge to be available in an Old West-style gun. I offered some shooters the opportunity to try one of the SA revolvers at the range a few months back, and two of those people promptly ordered

Taurus 460 Two Tone with a 10-inch barrel and all the goodies.

The Taylor's & Company TC9 is a single action chambered in 9mm.

Taurus Executive Grade Judge in .45 Colt/.410 revolver now with a hand-polished satin finish, smooth action, presentation-grade wood grips, and brass bead front sight on a 3-inch barrel.

The Taurus Raging Hunter Two Tone.

The engraved Colt Python is a Lipsey's exclusive in partnership with Tyler Gun Works.

a compensator to tame the potent .460 S&W round and a bottom Picatinny rail to attach bipods and shooting sticks. A top rail allows for additional sight/scope options. As a side note, you can fire .454 Casull and .45 Colt rounds in the .460 S&W revolvers, making it a three-for-one addition to your handgun-hunting arsenal. Taurus has also added the powerful .500 S&W Magnum with the debut of the Raging Hunter 500. This 5-shot revolver can be had in matte black or two-tone in barrel lengths from 5.12, 6.75, and 8.37 inches. I'll be testing one soon and can't wait to take this big thumper to the field! The Raging Hunter 460 provides the same finish/barrel length options chambered in the .460 S&W. *taurususa.com*

TYLER GUN WORKS AND LIPSEY'S

Bobby Tyler and his crew are turning out some fine custom and semi-custom revolvers from his shop in the Texas Panhandle. Function, fit, and finish are top-shelf. Tyler Gun Works website (*tylergunworks.com*) rolled out spec-your-own options for customizable in-stock revolvers. With a few simple clicks on your computer or phone, you can build a revolver to fit your needs, liking, and budget. Tyler also partnered with Lipsey's to offer an affordable TGW Premier Grade Engraved 3-inch Colt Python with stag stocks. As soon as I saw it, this gun rose to the top of my "gotta have one" list. The classy sixgun is available at *lipseys.com*. **GD**

one of their own! I am anxiously awaiting the arrival of a TC9 for review and expect it will be a fine shooter, just like a recent Taylor's & Co. Gunfighter Defender I tested. It's worth mentioning that the Taylor-Tuned action option is worth the nominal expense for a light, crisp trigger pull. *taylorsfirearms.com*

TAURUS

Taurus introduced its Defender 856 T.O.R.O. in a stainless steel or matte black optics-ready revolver in .38 Special +P with an easy-packing 3-inch barrel. And there's an almost identical 605 T.O.R.O. chambered in .357 Magnum. These revolvers' optics plates are compatible with the Holosun K footprint. Next up in the defensive handgun line is the Executive Grade Judge. Taurus took its popular .45 Colt/.410 revolver and gave it a hand-polished satin finish, smooth action, presentation-grade wood grips, and brass bead front sight on a 3-inch barrel.

Handgun hunters will find interest in the additions to the Raging Hunter line with the .460 S&W Two Tone with a 10.5-inch barrel. This big revolver has

- REPORTS -
from the Field
SHOTGUNS

Now more than ever, a shotgun exists to suit every taste.

> KRISTIN ALBERTS

Four years into the rip-roaring 2020s, the shotgun industry buzzwords continue to evolve. Optics-ready. Tactical-style. Hunt-specific. While this may sound like we're headed for an apocalyptic scattergun design shift, good news remains for those still adoring classic hardwood, blued steel, and practical do-all firearms.

Feel the need for an optics-topped, camouflaged, wieldy, sub-gauge Gobbler buster? You'll find not only one but multiple such offerings on these pages. Opting for a pure class break-action double with high-grade walnut, incredible attention to detail, and the most intricate engraving money can buy? That quality of gun building has not been forsaken. Got a spot behind the bedpost for a blacked-out, short-barreled, home

The Beretta 687 EELL Diamond Pigeon comes in a beautiful case.

defense weapon topped with door-breaching chokes and flashlight rails for those nighttime adventures? Like it or not, you'll find those here too.

The magnum 28-gauge continues its

expansion with shotgun and ammunition introductions, even amidst what seems to be the despondent "new normal" of wondering when factory ammunition shortages will cease. Speaking of shotshells, where has all the .410 ammunition gone? We have more lever-action .410 shotguns than ever before, with new additions forthcoming from overseas. There's even a high-capacity bullpup baby bore below. Meanwhile, Turkey — the country, not the gobbling long-beard — is producing more budget-priced shotguns than ever before. Fret not, though, for the good ol' US-of-A is still home to some fine and dedicated firearms manufacturers.

The year that sees us celebrating the 50th Anniversary of Browning's Citori — yes, that makes us all feel aged — is also

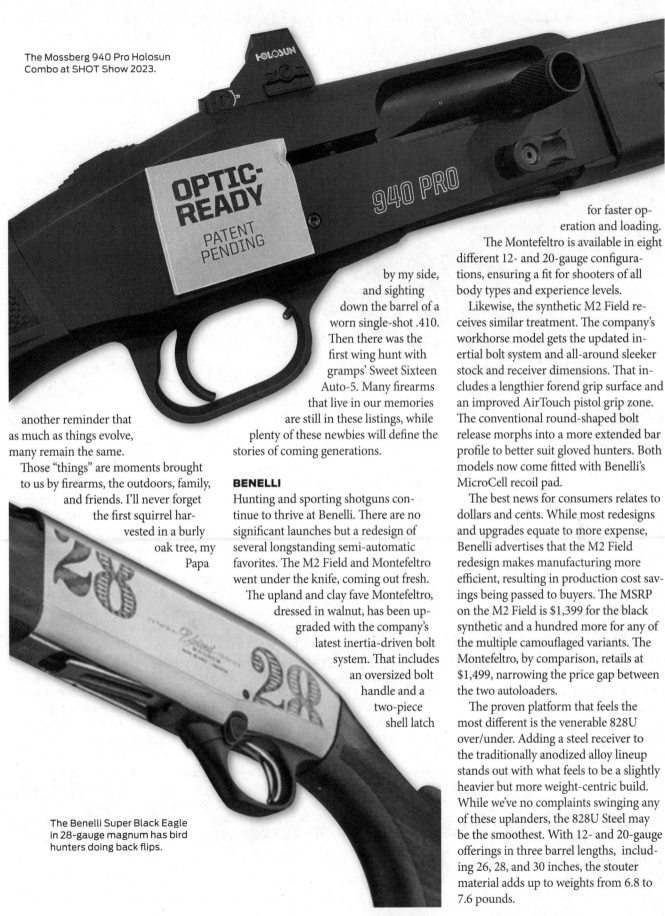

The Mossberg 940 Pro Holosun Combo at SHOT Show 2023.

OPTIC-READY

PATENT PENDING

940 PRO

The Benelli Super Black Eagle in 28-gauge magnum has bird hunters doing back flips.

another reminder that as much as things evolve, many remain the same.

Those "things" are moments brought to us by firearms, the outdoors, family, and friends. I'll never forget the first squirrel harvested in a burly oak tree, my Papa by my side, and sighting down the barrel of a worn single-shot .410. Then there was the first wing hunt with gramps' Sweet Sixteen Auto-5. Many firearms that live in our memories are still in these listings, while plenty of these newbies will define the stories of coming generations.

BENELLI

Hunting and sporting shotguns continue to thrive at Benelli. There are no significant launches but a redesign of several longstanding semi-automatic favorites. The M2 Field and Montefeltro went under the knife, coming out fresh.

The upland and clay fave Montefeltro, dressed in walnut, has been upgraded with the company's latest inertia-driven bolt system. That includes an oversized bolt handle and a two-piece shell latch for faster operation and loading.

The Montefeltro is available in eight different 12- and 20-gauge configurations, ensuring a fit for shooters of all body types and experience levels.

Likewise, the synthetic M2 Field receives similar treatment. The company's workhorse model gets the updated inertial bolt system and all-around sleeker stock and receiver dimensions. That includes a lengthier forend grip surface and an improved AirTouch pistol grip zone. The conventional round-shaped bolt release morphs into a more extended bar profile to better suit gloved hunters. Both models now come fitted with Benelli's MicroCell recoil pad.

The best news for consumers relates to dollars and cents. While most redesigns and upgrades equate to more expense, Benelli advertises that the M2 Field redesign makes manufacturing more efficient, resulting in production cost savings being passed to buyers. The MSRP on the M2 Field is $1,399 for the black synthetic and a hundred more for any of the multiple camouflaged variants. The Montefeltro, by comparison, retails at $1,499, narrowing the price gap between the two autoloaders.

The proven platform that feels the most different is the venerable 828U over/under. Adding a steel receiver to the traditionally anodized alloy lineup stands out with what feels to be a slightly heavier but more weight-centric build. While we've no complaints swinging any of these uplanders, the 828U Steel may be the smoothest. With 12- and 20-gauge offerings in three barrel lengths, including 26, 28, and 30 inches, the stouter material adds up to weights from 6.8 to 7.6 pounds.

In a move toward ultimate durability, Benelli adds the 828U Steel to the BE.S.T (short for Benelli Surface Treatment) lineup. That means the inclusion of the company's corrosion-resistant steel treatment. The 828U Steel BE.S.T includes AA-grade walnut furniture, the Progressive Comfort recoil reduction system, and five Crio chokes for $3,399. It joins the existing 828Us: Upland Performance Shop, Standard, and Sport. *benelliusa.com*

BERETTA

Whether busting clays, pursuing birds or competing with scatterguns, Beretta always seems to have a suitable selection. The biggest news is the sveltest offering. Beretta's

sideplates with exquisite hand-engraving. The wild game scenes and floral motifs are well-worthy of the engraver's signature. Select Grade-3 walnut is the stock material of choice and is hand-fit as the buttplate. Available in four gauges — including 28-ga. and .410 bore — along with three barrel

unique nickel-plated receiver with bolt "28" numeral-specific engraving. The youngest magnum retails for $1,829 and joins related-chambered arms from other manufacturers, including Benelli and Krieghoff, with more sure to join the fray. *beretta.com*

BROWNING

The list of scatterguns under the Buckmark brand continues to grow. The many variants, color combinations, camouflage options, actions, and hunt styles could

Benelli adds the 828U Steel to the BE.S.T (short for Benelli Surface Treatment) lineup. That means the inclusion of the company's corrosion-resistant steel treatment.

Ultraleggero over/under claims to be the lightest steel-receiver model on the market. How can steel be light, you ask? Good question. The company uses a skeletonized receiver fitted with techno-polymer inserts to shave weight. The result is a unique sideplate-style 12 gauge. Though we've yet to disassemble one, users with a 3D printer can download and "print" custom sideplates. Shooters can choose either 26- or 28-inch Steelium barrels with a 6x6 rib. The "Extralight" recoil pad brings scale numbers as low as 6.4 pounds. The retail price is set just below $3K.

Upland hunters with refined taste and financial reserves should take a gander at Beretta's latest addition to the 698 EELL line — the Diamond Pigeon. The low-profile boxlock O/U shows full

lengths, the Diamond Pigeon can be had in either Sporting or Field models for roughly $7,550 at retail.

The last bit of intelligence coming from Beretta is perhaps the most overlooked. I've long been in the sub-gauge fan club, especially the sweet little 28 gauge. Low recoil, surprising performance, and sleek guns drive the appeal. Yet behind those scenes, a "magnum" 28 has been brewing for years. While the standard 28 we all know and love has become the standardized 2.75-inch hull, firearms and ammunition companies are moving toward 3-inchers. Thus, we discovered Beretta showing off its A400 Upland 28 with, you guessed it, a 3-inch chamber. The gas-operated repeater has 28-inch barrels, an Extralight recoil pad, and a

nearly fill a wishbook catalog. Browning upped the ante on aesthetics and practical finish additions, albeit without significant model introductions.

The venerable A5 humpback semi-autos come dressed with Cerakote and camouflage, now including the striking Wicked Wing package. Wicked Wing also spreads to the semi-automatic Maxus II and Cynergy hunting line of over/unders.

Of significant note is the 50th birthday of the Citori over/under family. Yes, that makes us all feel old, but Browning commemorated the anniversary with a special High Grade 50th Anniversary Citori. High-grade walnut? Check. Extensive engraving? Check. Gold accents? Checkmate. The guns are part of a limited run,

The Browning A5 Wicked Wing with Cerakote and vintage camo.

Beretta's latest addition to the 698 EELL line is the Diamond Pigeon. The low-profile boxlock O/U shows full sideplates with exquisite hand-engraving.

sure to be prized by collectors and sporting shooters.

Those who eschew the glitz and glamour of limited editions shall likely be enticed by the most surprising Browning launch — the Citori composite. This composite-stocked variant mates a blacked-out stock with matte-blued metalwork. Though I've been accused of being a crow in terms of my affinity for fancy walnut and engraved steel, even I can admit the newbies' practicality. Those no-glare looks, partnered with proven Citori pedigree, equal one utilitarian workhorse. *browning.com*

CAESER GUERINI

Each year, drool-worthy doubles emerge from Brescia, Italy courtesy of Caesar Guerini USA. Pick your poison. This year, it's the still hard-to-find Invictus IX, an Elite-level dealer exclusive. That deep relief master hand-engraving will stop you in your tracks, and if it doesn't, I'm not sure we can be friends. All kidding aside, the Invictus IX has been touted as one of the most robust and most modular over/unders ever built. The barrel and receiver lockup design, replaceable action parts, and proprietary cams eliminate that dreaded "off face" slop that dooms many well-loved O/Us. Such wonder comes at a cost, so best find yourself a chair before I tell you the

ninth iteration of Invictus retails from $20K.

In more accessible Guerini headlines, the company adds to its Ellipse series of round body-action over/unders. The Ellipse Curve Gold represents a classy run showing a hand-polished coin finish receiver with gold inlay and extensive engraving. The company's Invisalloy surface treatment adds durability. European walnut stocks, hand checkered at 26 LPI, are neatly finished with a matched wooden buttplate, itself also checkered. Both left-hand and combo 20-ga./28-ga. sets are available by special order, while the case model lists at $8,900. *gueriniusa.com*

Beretta's Ultraleggero over/under claims to be the lightest steel-receiver model on the market.

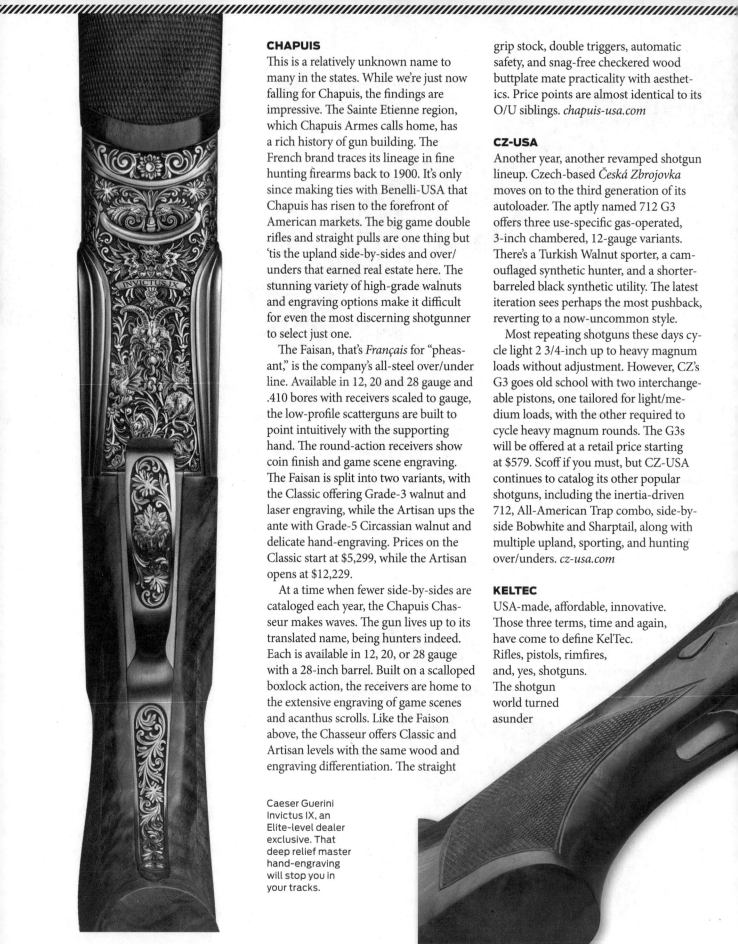

CHAPUIS

This is a relatively unknown name to many in the states. While we're just now falling for Chapuis, the findings are impressive. The Sainte Etienne region, which Chapuis Armes calls home, has a rich history of gun building. The French brand traces its lineage in fine hunting firearms back to 1900. It's only since making ties with Benelli-USA that Chapuis has risen to the forefront of American markets. The big game double rifles and straight pulls are one thing but 'tis the upland side-by-sides and over/unders that earned real estate here. The stunning variety of high-grade walnuts and engraving options make it difficult for even the most discerning shotgunner to select just one.

The Faisan, that's *Français* for "pheasant," is the company's all-steel over/under line. Available in 12, 20 and 28 gauge and .410 bores with receivers scaled to gauge, the low-profile scatterguns are built to point intuitively with the supporting hand. The round-action receivers show coin finish and game scene engraving. The Faisan is split into two variants, with the Classic offering Grade-3 walnut and laser engraving, while the Artisan ups the ante with Grade-5 Circassian walnut and delicate hand-engraving. Prices on the Classic start at $5,299, while the Artisan opens at $12,229.

At a time when fewer side-by-sides are cataloged each year, the Chapuis Chasseur makes waves. The gun lives up to its translated name, being hunters indeed. Each is available in 12, 20, or 28 gauge with a 28-inch barrel. Built on a scalloped boxlock action, the receivers are home to the extensive engraving of game scenes and acanthus scrolls. Like the Faison above, the Chasseur offers Classic and Artisan levels with the same wood and engraving differentiation. The straight

grip stock, double triggers, automatic safety, and snag-free checkered wood buttplate mate practicality with aesthetics. Price points are almost identical to its O/U siblings. *chapuis-usa.com*

CZ-USA

Another year, another revamped shotgun lineup. Czech-based *Česká Zbrojovka* moves on to the third generation of its autoloader. The aptly named 712 G3 offers three use-specific gas-operated, 3-inch chambered, 12-gauge variants. There's a Turkish Walnut sporter, a camouflaged synthetic hunter, and a shorter-barreled black synthetic utility. The latest iteration sees perhaps the most pushback, reverting to a now-uncommon style.

Most repeating shotguns these days cycle light 2 3/4-inch up to heavy magnum loads without adjustment. However, CZ's G3 goes old school with two interchangeable pistons, one tailored for light/medium loads, with the other required to cycle heavy magnum rounds. The G3s will be offered at a retail price starting at $579. Scoff if you must, but CZ-USA continues to catalog its other popular shotguns, including the inertia-driven 712, All-American Trap combo, side-by-side Bobwhite and Sharptail, along with multiple upland, sporting, and hunting over/unders. *cz-usa.com*

KELTEC

USA-made, affordable, innovative. Those three terms, time and again, have come to define KelTec. Rifles, pistols, rimfires, and, yes, shotguns. The shotgun world turned asunder

Caeser Guerini Invictus IX, an Elite-level dealer exclusive. That deep relief master hand-engraving will stop you in your tracks.

when KelTec launched the radical dual-magazine pump-action KSG 12 gauge with a crazy 15-round capacity. Years passed, and the hubbub subsided.

But now, it's back, as the company debuted its baby-bore version. Meet the KSG410. The bullpup slide action mates an 18.5-inch barrel to two magazine tubes, packing 11 3-inch shells. The metrics are miniature, with an overall length of 26 inches, weighing just over five pounds, and get this, only 1.7 inches wide. The micro-mini is touted as "recoil-less," which may be close to the truth. With a retail price under five bills, it's hard not to want this one. The hardest part, no doubt, will be keeping the high-capacity baby beast fed in ammunition. *keltecweapons.com*

MOSSBERG

It's all systems go at O.F. Mossberg & Sons. Most industry focus falls on Mossberg's Patriot Tactical LR center-fire rifle, but the list of new shotguns includes more than a half-dozen expand-ed, upgraded, and combination models. That thick catalog includes the latest repeaters, pumps, over/unders, Bantams, and even budget Mavericks.

Mossberg's International Gold Reserve Black Label is a long name for the company's premium O/U offering. With sharp looks and features to match, the expanded Black Label — now available in 12 and 20 gauge — offers serious clay busting and upland performance at relatively friendly prices, especially compared to competitors.

The theme this year is optics-readiness. More turkey hunters — and home defenders — are opting to mount red-dot and reflex sights, and Mossberg keeps its finger on every-day users' pulse. It now offers variants on the Model 500 pump, magnum Model 835, and semi-auto 940 Pro lines with receivers machined to mount RMSc-pattern optics directly. The 500s can now be had in 28 gauge or .410 bore, while the 835 Ulti-Mag chambers 3.5-inch magnum 12 gauge. Want a turnkey rig? Mossberg sells 940 Pro Turkey models with the receiver cutout and an 18.5-inch barreled Pro Tactical, including the ideal Holosun micro dot sight. Traditionalists will appreciate Mossberg's addition of a walnut-stocked version of the 940 Pro Field, which still includes LOP spacers while providing the classic wood aesthetic.

Looking for what may be the most inexpensive, do-all shotgun yet? Mossberg's ultra-budget Maverick lineup grows as well. The pump-driven 88 receives three newbies, including 12 and 20 gauges, all wearing Mossy Oak Bottomland camouflage. Though affordable, the 88s use twin action bars, dual extractors, steel-to-steel lockup, and an anti-jam elevator for reliable operation. A 22-inch Bantam model shortens the length of pull (LOP) to 12 inches for young shooters. The retail price is a refreshing $293. While only the Modified choke tube is included, Maverick 88 accessories interchange with most from the parent company's 500.

Mossberg may not have the reputation of the sexiest brand, but say what you will, it offers some of the best-selling and best bang-for-your-buck firearms on the market, whether you're into hunting, home defense, competition, target shooting, or some magical combination thereof. *mossberg.com*

REMARMS

The times are a-changin'. Yes, that title says RemArms, which has come to be the name of once-dominant Remington. While the ammunition company uses the full moniker, the now-unrelated gun builder RemArms has been quietly retooling and producing its first firearms. Along with a much-lauded Model 700 Alpha centerfire, RemArms is working back towards shotgun glory.

Name the most well-known shotgun models of all time, and surely the 870 makes that list. Though getting details from RemArms has proven akin to joys like tooth pulling, we have discovered an 870 rebirth. What was once a budget, albeit quality-maligned Express line, is now an improved and renamed 870 Fieldmaster and Fieldmaster Synthetic. The former wears standard American Walnut furniture and a matte metal finish that is advertised to be more

The Browning High Grade 50th Anniversary Citori is a fitting tribute to the successful O/U model.

The Model 870 is back in the RemArms 870 FieldMaster.

corrosion-resistant than its rust-as-you-watch predecessor. Likewise, the Synthetic version shares the improved coating, while its black synthetic stocks help save dollars and cents. With multiple variants in 12 and 20 gauge, retail prices vary greatly, but in general, the new RemArms 870 Fieldmasters come in roughly $100 more than the old Express, yet still at an affordable price point. If their improvements stand up to the test of time and rugged use, that will be money well spent. And we'll all celebrate the return of a too-long-absent American legend. *remarms.com*

ROCK ISLAND ARMORY

The small world of handheld shorty shotguns is once again front and center. Mossberg's Shockwave proved the legs to go the distance while the late Remington's TAC-14 has faded away. The platform gets rejuvenated with Rock Island Armory joining the fray. In one fell swoop, the company adds not one but two such designs to its RIA-USA group.

The PF14 and VRPF14 are 14-inch barreled, handheld, 12-gauge pump-action shotguns. The former feeds via a tubular magazine, while the latter accepts the same dropbox magazines as the company's other VR Series. No matter the model selection, both use the identical black synthetic, angular F-Grip furniture that culminates to an overall length of only 26.1 inches.

Because of its metrics and stock, or lack thereof, the design is technically not (read, *legally*) considered a shotgun. These bangers are classified simply as "firearms." we'll include them here by nature of their shotshell diet.

Whether home defense, self-defense or a riot of fun at the range, snubbed-up pumps prove a continued draw, especially when shorty shotshells are available on the shelf. At $369 and $449, respectively, entry into this world has seldom been so affordable. *armscor.com*

STEVENS

Is it a Savage? Is it a Stevens? The answer, verified with Savage Arms brass, is a little of both. The preferred name is "Stevens by Savage," but no matter what you call it, the budget division of Savage ownership grows yet again. The Model 560 Field marks the first semi-automatic in the current family of cost-conscious scatterguns. The 560 is a gas-operated 12-gauge 3-inch-chambered repeater. The 28-inch ventilated rib barrel is hard chrome-lined and tipped with a red fiber-optic front sight. Oversized controls come standard, quickly becoming popular with hunters and speed shooters.

The primary differentiation between the two brand names is revealed with Stevens' made-in-Turkey manufacture, true from barrel production to the Turkish Walnut dress. In a thoughtful

Meet the KelTec KSG410. The bullpup slide action mates an 18.5-inch barrel to two magazine tubes, packing 11 3-inch shells. The metrics are miniature, with an overall length of 26 inches, weighing just over five pounds, and get this, only 1.7 inches wide.

Mossberg's 940 Pro Holosun Combo is a ready-to-run tactical or home defense shotgun that's competition-ready, too.

move, the company launches standard and compact versions simultaneously at $499 retail. With an aluminum alloy receiver, the full-size version weighs only 6.6 pounds and swings quickly. Though durability and reliability have yet to be tested, it's refreshing to see checkered hardwood stocks on an affordable semi-automatic, as well as the backing of a proven American entity like Savage Arms.

The 560 Field joins a quickly burgeoning line of Stevens shotties, including 301 single shots, 320 pumps, and 555 over/unders. They have covered many specialties, including Trap, Sporting, Security, Turkey, and Tactical-specific variants. *savagearms.com*

The Stevens Model 560 Field is a gas-operated 12-gauge 3-inch-chambered repeater.

The Syren Julia has a stunning case-color finish, Invisalloy protective finish, 26 LPI checkering, and Deluxe-grade walnut stocks with a matched wooden buttplate.

STOEGER

This is the year of total re-design at Stoeger. The name recognized as the budget brand under Benelli-USA's umbrella scraps the old in exchange for customer-wished changes and cost-saving manufacturing moves. The retooling covers both longstanding pump actions and semi-automatics.

Stoeger's M3000, M3020, and M3500 all see a blend of cosmetic and internal refreshing. For instance, Stoeger joins the list of companies shifting to oversized controls. Likewise, the move to enlarged and beveled loading ports falls in line with the norm on repeaters these days. Furniture dimensions get downsized with slimmer, trimmer measurements and less bulky magazine caps. Improved recoil pads and a less boxy appearance will be welcome additions to many models.

Even the pocketbook-friendly pump lines — P3000 and P3500 — get freshened up. The checkered synthetic stocks now have integrated swivel studs and slimmer stock lines. The slide guns tout twin steel action bars and an improved rotating bolt head, all geared toward a no-stick slide action. In addition, the barrel extension reaches deeper into the receiver for greater longevity of the action.

Though I've yet to pull the trigger on any of these redesigns, the upgrades sound sensible on paper. Anything that adds to the durability and creature comforts should be a win.

Though Stoeger Industries must have been buzzing with the many product line rebuilds, it still had time to assemble a fresh model. The M3K is a race-ready semi-automatic built specifically for 3-Gun competitors. The inertia-driven 12 gauge wears a 24-inch barrel, oversized controls, an enlarged loading port, an elongated carrier, an integrated cheek pad, and sweet blue anodized trim. Its sub-$675 retail price point makes it accessible for first-timers to dip their toes into the sport. *stoegerindustries.com*

SYREN

Technically, Syren is a division of Caesar Guerini, but for all practical purposes, it flies as a standalone mark dedicated to women. The company's lines of scatterguns are specifically tailored to the lady competitor, huntress, and shotgun enthusiast. That includes such models as the competition-ready O/U Elos N2 Elevate Trap Combo, Elos N2 Sporting, Elos D2 Field, Tempio Trap and Sporting, camouflaged semi-auto XLR5 Waterfowler, L4S Sporting repeater, and Tempio Light field gun. Dimensions, including length of pull, cast, pitch, and specific stock metrics, are tailored to a feminine physique. That does not mean, however, sacrificing features, performance, or warranty.

The latest addition, "Julia," is perhaps the loveliest with a stunning case-color finish, Invisalloy protective finish, 26 LPI checkering, and Deluxe-grade walnut stocks with a matched wooden buttplate. First came the Julia Sporting, joined this time by the Julia Field. Both are instantly recognizable, as the side plate action shows fantasy-style engraving depicting a woman's face evolving from a floral scroll. *syrenusa.com* GD

REPORTS -
from the Field
MUZZLELOADERS

❯BRAD FENSON

Refinements to existing lines and long-range smokepoles that push the distance limits are on tap this year!

Muzzleloader enthusiasts have many options to place a bullet downrange with surgical accuracy. Modern muzzleloaders are carefully engineered to provide performance beyond expectation. For many years, I assessed new muzzleloaders. I had a team of experienced shooters, and blackpowder enthusiasts put each model through its paces. One thing that always stood out was the quality and craftsmanship of muzzleloader barrels, evident as we inspected the lands and grooves with borescopes. A firearms forensic expert commented on the quality and how they would rival any centerfire barrel.

Muzzleloaders are built to shoot accurately and consistently. All muzzleloading rifle components are designed for quality and ease of use. The only excuse for not being on target is shooter error. Using a water-based cleaning product on a solvent-based propellant can rob you of accuracy. Attention to detail is still required, and approaching each shot like it's the last is what produces consistency.

It was not many years ago that muzzleloaders were considered short-range rifles. Advancements in everything from bullets to ignition have created the perfect storm for following the rest of the shooting world into long-range. Pay attention to the caliber, barrel twist rate, bullet design, and muzzle brake for determining options.

With modern technologies, muzzle-loading has never been more effortless, and hunters can shoot farther with consistent accuracy. Hunters and shooters not using modern, quality optics will discover that they need exceptional glass to keep up with the research and developments in muzzleloaders. Long barrels, magnum charges, elongated bullets, and muzzle brakes are standard today. Recently, more interest in .45-caliber rifles and bullets has been seen. The smaller-diameter, lighter bullets lend themselves well to long-range accuracy. With changes to propellants, there is more emphasis on having the correct cleaning supplies, as water- and oil-based cleaners are required for specific powders. The good news is that new propellants make cleaning and maintenance of smokepoles effortless compared to even a decade ago.

Increased bullet performance for muzzleloader hunters now aligns with premium centerfire ammunition. Not only is it easier to be on target, but the projectiles' lethality continues to improve.

CVA

This year, CVA's Paramount Pro V2 has two new models, including a .45- and a .50-caliber rifle, both with threaded, 26-inch free-floating Cerakote/nitride stainless steel barrels. These long-range muzzleloaders are ready for a muzzle brake and come with custom-like triggers. MSRPs range from $1,920 to $2,065.

One new model in the Paramount line is a .45 caliber with a 1:22-inch twist. The stock wears Realtree Hillside and it sports a long 26-inch threaded 3/4x20 barrel. MSRP: $1,290.

These rifles were developed and designed to handle "super-magnum" propellant charges — and thus provide the higher velocities necessary for killing shots at 300 yards and beyond. The Paramount produces velocities over 2,200

FPS, but this is worth nothing without the accuracy to put those shots where they belong. Like all premium CVAs, the Paramount line features a custom-quality, free-floating Bergara barrel. Paired with PowerBelt's ELR bullets, which are specially designed for the Paramount, this barrel can produce incredibly tight groups at previously unimaginable ranges for a muzzleloader.

The stock supports the barrel on an internal aluminum chassis for maximum comfort and stability. It offers full ergonomic adjustability of both length-of-pull and comb height. Also standard with the Paramount is CVA's VariFlame Breech Plug, which uses the hotter and more consistent Large Rifle Primer by utilizing the VariFlame technology by Cecil Epps, rather than the 209 shotshell primer.

An accessory pack, including PowerBelt ELR bullets, VariFlame primer casings, a loading tool for VariFlame casings, a collapsible loading rod, a cleaning/range rod, and a Quake CLAW sling come standard with every Paramount rifle.

A new model in the Accura line is the MR-X, a .50 caliber with a 1:28-in. MR-X Cerakote Sniper Gray/nitride/True Timber Strata combination. Its 26-in. threaded 3/4x24 barrel is itchin' for a muzzle brake if you plan to touch off the magnum charges. The MR-X offers features never before seen in production muzzleloaders like quick takedown design for easy cleaning and compact transport, a carbon-fiber collapsible loading rod that eliminates the accuracy-robbing necessity of hanging a ramrod under the barrel, an adjustable comb for perfect eye-to-sight alignment with open sights or optics, fast rifling twists for optimal performance with modern projectiles and propellants, and a threaded muzzle that allows the use of CVA's Paramount Muzzle Brake for magnum charge shooting with minimal recoil. And most importantly, the new Accura LR-X and MR-X are available in the super-fast and flat-shooting .45 caliber, as well as the .50 caliber for states or seasons that require it.

There are eight new models in the Optima V2 line this year as well. They span the gamut from .50-caliber 28-inch-barreled LR models with burnt bronze Cerakote

and Realtree-camo'd stocks, to 26-inch-barreled versions, slightly handier in the woods. Equipped with a 26- or 28-inch barrel, the Optima V2 is easy to maneuver in the treestand and comfortable to carry in the mountains. They're modeled after CVA's top-of-the-line Accura V2 rifles and pistols that feature the same triggerguard-actuated breeching lever, internal parts, and trigger. All Optima V2 rifle models feature stainless steel or nitride-treated stainless steel barrels. Add in CVA's Quick-Release Breech Plug (finger-removable), ambidextrous stock, and a CrushZone recoil pad. Furthermore, it comes standard with a DuraSight DEAD-ON one-piece scope mount, DuraSight fiber-optic sights, and CVA's solid-aluminum PalmSaver ramrod.

The Wolf V2 is CVA's newest and most affordable break-action muzzle-loader, and it's packed with features such as a fully ambidextrous LOP-adjustable stock, which makes it the perfect gun for righties, lefties, adults, and children. It also has CVA's Quick-Release Breech Plug — the only tool-free removal breech plug on the market today. Even after 20 or more shots, the breech plug comes out with just a twist of the fingers. Try that with any other "speed breech" system. Plus, the break-action breech opens easily with just a touch of the breeching button located in the front of the triggerguard. The Wolf V2's barrel is compact, quick-pointing, and made of corrosion-resistant stainless steel, not blued carbon steel like other similarly priced guns. CVA's solid aluminum PalmSaver ramrod is standard equipment for all Wolf V2 models. *cva.com*

HORNADY

Hornady's .50-cal. .499-inch Bore Driver ELD-X 340-gr. bullet comes 12 to a box. The stuff is fast and easy to load and delivers some impressive muzzleloader performance. A polymer base (not a sabot) seals the bore at the system's heart. Hornady says the design maximizes energy transfer and accuracy. Atop the base is an ELD-X or FTX bullet featuring a rugged gilding metal jacket coupled with a polymer tip and an InterLock ring, all designed to maximum lethality. *hornady.com*

KNIGHT

The newest Knight rifle is the Peregrine, built to compete in the long-range muzzleloader group. Knight claims the rifle produces a muzzle velocity of up to 3,000 fps. It guarantees every Peregrine will be MOA accurate at 500 yards. The Peregrine is a .40 caliber, with a faster twist rate than most rifles at 1:16 inches. The rifle uses a breech plug design with a 28-inch Green Mountain stainless helical-fluted barrel. Modern Knight rifles are built with Timney match-grade triggers and are 100% American-made. The rifle weighs 7.4 lbs, has an overall length of 46.25 inches, and its stock is a solid carbon fiber with an aluminum bedding block for a free-floating barrel. It's a looker, too, with Sage Brush Camo print. The ignition system is a bare primer tungsten carbide inserted breech plug. Included is a Lee Hand Press with adjustable sizing die for bullets. This model is designed and built for increased velocities and accuracy at greater distances. MSRP: $1,569.99. *muzzleloaders.com*

TRADITIONS

Traditions recently introduced a new model of its StrikerFire in .45 caliber with a VAPR barrel (the smaller diameter bullet has an even faster 1:20-inch barrel twist than the .50 caliber). The Vortek StrikerFire was the first hammerless muzzleloader to hit the market and offers fast, silent lockdown. The cocking button slides forward until it locks, putting the gun in fire mode and ready to shoot. A red dot is uncovered when the slide is locked, letting you know the gun is ready to fire. The modern frontstuffer is uncocked by pushing the spring release button behind the slide to let the mechanism glide back to the safe position. No external hammer offers faster lock time and a more silent operation.

A .50-caliber LDR, or Long-Distance Rifle, has been available in the StrikerFire lineup for several years. The .45 caliber is the newest model offering long-range shooters untapped ballistic and technical advantages. The StrikerFire is still a traditional inline muzzleloader that uses standard blackpowder equivalent charges and a sabot and bullet. It offers excellent power and range without having to use extreme powder charges.

Traditions has two longstanding models that remain popular amongst consumers. The Pursuit and Buckstalker have proven longevity in the market and offer value and performance. The Pursuit XT is the newest rendition with upgrades like the Elite XT Trigger System, rebounding hammer, and manual cross-block trigger safety. These upgrades and standard features, such as a 26-inch Chromoly steel barrel, Dual Safety System, and Accelerator Breech Plug Speed Load System, make the frontstuffer perfect for accuracy beyond 200 yards. *traditionsfirearms.com* GD

- REPORTS -
from the Field
OPTICS

Competition is alive and well in the optics industry, as evidenced by new products for hunters, competitive and recreational shooters, law enforcement/military, and the growing number of people expanding the personal-defense universe.

❯ JOE ARTERBURN

Vortex Optics' new Triumph 10x42 Binocular.

A quick spin through new offerings by optics manufacturers follows trends seen in the shooting industry, such as increased interest in long-distance shooting (magnification ranges reaching wider and higher), backcountry hunting (lighter, more compact), military/law enforcement/concealed carry (small, light, and fast red-dot sights) and technical advancements in rangefinders communicating ballistic data for instant, accurate shot placement.

The winners of this competition to produce the brightest and the best — and the most value for the buck — are shooters like you and me, looking to avail ourselves of the latest, greatest developments that keep coming, especially at prices that don't drive us away.

AIMPOINT

Aimpoint launched its Duty RDS Red-Dot Sight, a new high-grade reflex optic designed to meet the demands of law enforcement agencies and the self-defense-minded. Compact and budget-friendly, the Duty RDS has a bright 2-MOA dot designed for short- to medium-range target engagements and has waterproof flush-mounted windage and elevation adjustments, so there is no need for protective — and obtrusive — caps. Brightness intensity is set with a new digital keypad for easy use while wearing gloves.

A pressure-forged aluminum alloy housing handles abuse and drastic temperature changes; plus, it is vibration- and shock-resistant and submersible up to 80 feet. It's powered by a single, commonly available CR2032 battery, which provides more than three years of constant-on power at daylight position 7 and even longer on night-vision compatible settings. (It's compatible with all generations of night vision.) Flip-up lens covers allow use with caps closed in an emergency or to aim into the sunlight. MSRP: $499. *aimpoint.us*

BURRIS

Burris' new Veracity PH 4-20x50mm riflescope features a heads-up display that shows dialed distance, wind hold, rifle cant, and battery level, which, when coupled via Bluetooth with the user-configurable BurrisConnect App, provides information valuable to precise aiming right in your field of view. Designed to do the math for precise shot placement, this scope allows

you to concentrate on getting the shot rather than working through ballistic and data sheets. It features Burris' PĒK (Programmable Elevation Knob) — pronounced "peak" — system and a digital position sensor in the scope's clickless elevation turret for 1/10 MOA equivalent adjustability for exact dial-in to distance in yards or meters. Once downloaded, the BurrisConnect App does not need wifi or cell service, so you won't be left high and dry and information-less in the boonies.

The Wind MOA FFP reticle is a front focal plane design, so hold-off and hold-over compensation is accurate at any magnification. Side focus/parallax adjustment ensures the image matches the reticle focal point from 50 yards to infinity. MSRP: $1,200.

Burris also debuted its Xtreme Tactical Pro (XTR Pro) line of riflescopes with the 5.5-30x56mm. It has new illuminated reticle designs in what Burris says is the best glass and mechanical system ever featured in its optics. Built on the success of Burris' popular XTR III line with tactical and competition shooters in mind, the XTR Pro features three front focal plane reticle designs with both red and

The Burris Veracity PH 4-20x50mm riflescope features a heads-up display that shows dialed distance, wind hold, rifle cant, and battery level.

green illumination options. A toolless Zero Click-Stop elevation turret provides quick zero adjustments, and you can swap between two Quick Detach turret caps — the Burris QD Race Dial (designed for PRS and NRL shooters) and the

standard QD Dial. Other features include the innovative Horus TREMOR5 reticle and Burris' Throw Lever for faster, easier magnification changes. MSRP: $2,639. *burrisoptics.com*

BUSHNELL

Designed as a competition-ready pistol sight in conjunction with world-champion shooter K.C. Eusebio, Bushnell's new large-lens RXM-300 can fit any firearm for virtually any situation, from competition to hunting to self-defense. The 4-MOA LED dot has 12 brightness settings for visibility from bright daylight to night-vision situations.

Features include user-selectable auto-ambient intensity; shake-awake auto-on (with optional disable and button lockout); extra-large lens with protective hood; detented 1-MOA windage/elevation adjustments; and 35,000-hour battery life on mid-settings. MSRP: $299.99.

Building off the success of its popular Match Pro, Bushnell introduced the Match Pro ED 5-30X56 first focal plane riflescope with enhancements new and experienced long-range shooters will

The Aimpoint Duty RDS is night-vision compatible.

The new Burris XTR Pro 5.5-30x56mm riflescope.

appreciate. The increased magnification ratio provides more versatility, and the large 34mm tube increases the elevation range to 30 MIL or 103 MOA. Both turrets lock, and the elevation turret has an Easy Set zero stop and pop-up revolution indicator for repeatable confidence in returning to zero. The removable three-position power change lever can be configured for left- or right-handed shooters.

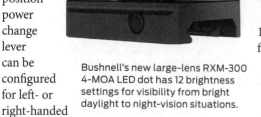

Bushnell's new large-lens RXM-300 4-MOA LED dot has 12 brightness settings for visibility from bright daylight to night-vision situations.

It has 11 brightness settings with alternating off intervals and a six-hour auto-off timer to preserve battery life. The new DM2 reticle, based on the popular Deploy MIL, has been updated to a .2-MIL-GRID-style reticle for crisp detail against various backdrops. Though rated for centerfire, its close-range 15-yard parallax side-focus also makes it ideal for rimfire plinking and NRL22 and PRS Rimfire competitions. MSRP: $699.99. *bushnell.com*

GERMAN PRECISION OPTICS (GPO)

The first thing you'll notice about GPO's new laser rangefinding Rangeguide binoculars is the size and weight, or more accurately, the lack of size and weight. Standing 5.4 inches tall and weighing 24.3 ounces (thanks to the light magnesium frame), GPO claims these are the world's most compact rangefinding binoculars at this quality level.

Depending on the target, it can accurately range to 3,062 yards with inclination/declination compensation. It'll reliably range a tree at 1,093 yards and a deer to 766 yards (to 1.75 miles on highly reflective targets). It uses an eye-safe Class 1 laser for a .25-second response time with true-angle technology. The display is easily seen via an orange OLED with nine adjustable brightness levels. It also measures humidity and air pressure. Diopter focus and orange display focus adjustments are on the ocular tube's left and right sides for convenience. The cut-brass-geared focus-wheel system provides tight, consistent turning without free play. MSRP: 8x32, $1,099.99; 10x32, $1,149.99.

GPO also introduced its new 15-45x60 Tactical Spotting Scope, featuring the same reticle found in the company's popular new first focal plane GPOTAC 4.5-27x50i FFP Tactical riflescope, which makes using them in tandem a clever shooting combination. GPO says spotting and adjusting long-range shots without a reticle wastes rounds. You can make calculations and adjustments quickly and accurately by matching reticles in the riflescope and spotting scope. Light and compact, measuring just 10.95 x 5.4 x 3.3 inches and weighing a mere 2.75 lbs, its MSRP is $1,299.99.

The GPO Spectra Reflex Sight marks the company's entrance into the reflex sight market.

German Precision Optics' Rangeguide might be the lightest and most compact ranging binos on the market.

The GPO Spectra Reflex Sight, GPO's entrance into the reflex sight market, uses next-generation red-dot technology to provide fast target acquisition for pistols, MSRs, and other firearms. A built-in photo sensor automatically adjusts the brightness of the 3mm red dot to match light conditions. A built-in motion sensor switches it on and off, eliminating the need for easily damaged rubber push buttons and extending battery life up to 40,000 hours. It measures just .90-inch tall, 1.04 inches wide, 1.6 inches long, and weighs .78 ounce. MSRP: $379.99. *gpo-usa. com*

HI-LUX OPTICS

Shooters can quickly acquire and engage targets at close quarters at 1X magnification with the fiber-optic-illuminated center point of Hi-Lux Optics' new CMR8 1-8X24 Low Power Variable Scope and yet at up to 8X have precise holdovers to 600 yards with the second focal plane Hybrid BDC reticle. Housed in an aircraft aluminum-grade 30mm tube, Hi-Lux says the crisp, clear optics provide a distortion-free image and a wide field of view. MSRP: $399. *hi-luxoptics.com*

KONUS

The new 30mm-tubed Armada riflescopes from Konus feature a patented

GPO's first focal plane GPOTAC 4.5-27x50i FFP Tactical spotting scope measures just 10.95 x 5.4 x 3.3 inches and weighs a mere 2.75 lbs. Best of all? The MSRP is $1,299.99.

New Konus Armada 30mm riflescopes use an innovative parallax-correction system.

Konus' Absolute riflescope offers a jaw-dropping 5-40x magnification range, and its 56mm objective should scoop massive amounts of light.

parallax-correction system that it says delivers enhanced accuracy via exclusive technology. That tech purportedly allows you to know exactly how far you are from the target as opposed to approximations of distance from other parallax systems. The engraved second plane reticle illuminates in blue and red (with push-button illumination control) for quick target acquisition in any lighting condition. The push-pull locking turrets provide precise 1/4-MOA adjustments on the 4-16x50 model and 1/8 MOA on the 6-24x56. Other features include fast-focus ocular and anti-canting level bubble. The 4-16x50 model (MSRP: $566.99) features a German-4 reticle; the 6-24x56 (MSRP: $642.99), a fine-crosshair reticle, is particularly suitable for long-distance shooters.

Konus also released the new Absolute 5-40x56 riflescope, providing competitive shooters with a wide magnification range. Designed with pro shooters in mind, it features the parallax wheel and illumination switch on the same side knob, a 30mm tube, a newly designed erector tube system for increased reliability under heavy recoil, 1/8-MOA adjustments via high-precision lockable turrets that are resettable to zero, and a removable zoom lever. Also, the second focal plane 550-ballistic reticle, which is laser-etched and dual-illuminated, is especially thin to avoid impairing target acquisition. MSRP: $1,186.99 *konusscopes.com*

LEUPOLD

Leupold's new Mark 5 HD 2-10x30 riflescope further expands the popular and award-winning made-in-USA Mark 5HD family of scopes in a shorter, lighter version ideal for carbines and designated marksman rifles. There are three models, all first focal plane, one with a TMR reticle and milliradian adjustments, one with an

Hi-Lux Optics' new CMR8 1-8X24 Low Power Variable Scope gives an actual 1x field of view, up to 8X — with precise holdovers to 600 yards with the second focal plane Hybrid BDC reticle.

illuminated TMR reticle and milliradian adjustments, and one with the PR1-MOA reticle and MOA adjustments. Three-Turn ZeroLock adjustments and side focus are uncommon in 2-10x scopes. MSRP: $1,999.99 to $2,499.99. *leupold.com*

MAVEN

Maven's company's latest offering for long-range hunting is the RS3.2 5-30x50 first focal plane riflescope, a new and improved version of the popular RS.3 long-range scope. The new version's design is expanded with a larger, more tactile elevation turret, improved zero stop, and a capped windage turret. With expansive magnification range and detailed reticle options, this scope feels right for hunting western big game species or anywhere medium- to long-range shooting may figure into the scenario. Additional features include side parallax adjustment, a smooth focus mechanism, precision-milled adjustments, solid click detents, durable anodizing, and custom turret options. MSRP: $1,600.

The CS.1S 15-45x65 Spotting Scope is a new variation of Maven's award-winning CS.1 spotter, equipped with a straight eyepiece, a direct

Leupold's new Mark 5 HD 2-10x30 riflescope expands the made-in-USA Mark 5HD family of scopes in a shorter, lighter version ideal for carbines and designated marksman rifles.

Maven's new RS3.2 5-30x50 first focal plane riflescope for long-range shooting.

response to customer feedback. Never fear, this new version is also available with an angled eyepiece. The lightweight magnesium and aluminum frame is compact, measuring 12.3 inches and weighing only 40.4 ounces. So, it's easy to convince yourself to take it along where you'd likely leave heavier, bulkier scopes behind. MSRP: $800. *mavenoptics.com*

MEOPTA

Meopta, producing high-end European optics for almost 90 years, has introduced the MeoSight IV red-dot reflex sight, its smallest — weighing just 1.2 ounces. With an ultra-low profile, there is little to protrude during concealed carry and little to snag upon drawing or reholstering. Not just for handguns, it also provides fast, accurate close-quarter target acquisition when used on rifles, whether mounted to a primary riflescope or directly to an accessory rail. Premium, scratch-resistant 1x optics, wide sight picture, and a 3-MOA brightness-adjustable dot facilitate fast, accurate shooting. Auto-off preserves battery life. MSRP: $299.

And Meopta's MeoSport R-3 3-15x50 RD gives hunters and shooters an option for a lower-profile 30mm riflescope with Meopta's quality but at an easy-to-take price. The illuminated red-dot reticle lets you get on target fast and accurately, even in low light. You get handy side focus from 10 yards to infinity, exposed windage, and elevation adjustments

with zero-reset turrets. MSRP: $499.99. *meoptasportoptics.com*

RITON

The newest addition to the Riton line is the 3 Primal 3-18x50 Riflescope, the company's first-ever crossover optic. It's a versatile design to meet the needs of hunters and long-range shooters, with a wide magnification range to cover virtually all hunting and shooting situations. The LRH (Long Range/Hunter) first focal plane illuminated reticle (with six brightness levels) provides accurate holdovers and wind holds throughout the magnification range. Features include a 30mm tube, exposed zero-resettable/zero-stop turrets with 1/10-MRAD windage and elevation adjustments, integrated two-location removable throw levers, and a fast-focus eyepiece. MSRP: $659.99.

Riton also came out with its long-awaited first focal plane, 5 Tactix 1-10x24, designed to do it all from 1x-power red-dot capability (with six levels of red illumination) for fast target acquisition to 10x-power for long-range precision shooting. Features include capped, zero-resettable turrets and throw levers in three heights (14mm, 11mm, 8mm, plus a flush mount), 1/10-MRAD

windage and elevation adjustments, and a fast-focus eyepiece. MSRP: $959.99. *ritonoptics.com*

SIGHTMARK

The Wraith Mini 2-16x5 Thermal Riflescope is Sightmark's continued evolution in digital night-vision thermal optics — an all-day, all-night hunting-optic solution with crisp imaging and heat signature detection out to 1,400 yards. Five thermal color palette modes and nine reticle colors make it versatile to suit any time of day or any hunting situation.

The Wraith Mini 2-16x5 Thermal Riflescope from Sightmark with crisp imaging and heat signature detection to 1,400 yards.

The OLED display provides rich color and temperature operation. At the same time, five configurable profiles allow it to hold multiple zeroes for different firearms, eliminating the need to re-zero every time it's mounted on a different gun. The built-in camera with audio recording will preserve hunt memories. The 2x optical zoom with 1-8 digital zoom and high-resolution display provide long-distance detection and close- to mid-range target engagements. MSRP: $2,000. *sightmark.com*

STEINER

Steiner announced a new line of T6Xi riflescopes, featuring advanced German optical engineering with made-in-America manufacturing, in four models: 5-30x56, for long-range and precision

The CS.1S 15-45x65 Spotting Scope from Maven measures 12.3 inches and weighs only 40.4 ounces.

shooting; 3-18x56 and 2.5-15x50 for near- to extended-ranges; and 1-6x24, for close-quarter to mid-range shooting. The first focal plane series builds on Steiner's legendary T5Xi optics developed for tactical and competitive shooting. Low-profile Never-Lost turrets feature windage and elevation locks plus a second rotation indicator to simplify adjustments in shooting scenarios, showing each MIL of elevation through a window on the elevation turret. MSRP: $1,954.99-$2,874.99. *steiner-optics. com*

Riton's 5 Tactix 1-10x24 is designed to do everything from 1x-power red-dot for fast target acquisition to 10x-power for long-range precision shooting.

SWAROVSKI

If you'd seen the thermal image of the coyote I saw right down to the February-thick bristly fur and tail, you'd also be impressed with the tM 35 thermal imaging device that clips to your Swarovski riflescope. It's compatible with Swarovski Z8i, Z6(i), Z5(i), and Z3 riflescopes (and like-sized other scopes). No changing out scopes, no re-sighting, no change of impact; attach it to the end of the scope with the optional tMA Thermal Monocular Adapter.

The optics are top-notch, and the thermal-imaging technology produces incredible detail in low- or no-light conditions since the thermal imaging reacts to thermal radiation and does not require ambient light. The automatic switch on/off timer activates when you take aim and deactivates after it is set down, saving the battery and avoiding unnecessary movement to turn it on. Automatic adjustment adapts display brightness to ambient light conditions. It features white hot and black hot modes to provide more image detail, depending

The Meopta MeoSight IV red-dot reflex sight weighs just 1.2 ounces. With an ultra-low profile, there is little to protrude during concealed carry.

on the environment. A rechargeable battery provides seven hours of continuous operation. MSRP: $5,554.

On the Wyoming coyote hunt, we also used Swarovski's new STC compact spotting scope, the straight-eyepiece version, but the ATC variant features an angled eyepiece. (Both are available with green or orange armored coating.) Suffice it to say, Swarovski packed many quality features in these 17-40X scopes, particularly considering they weigh just under 35 ounces and the straight model measures 11.2 inches; the angled, just 10.2. So there goes the weight-and-bulk excuse for not packing a spotting scope. MSRP: $2,721. *swarovskioptik.com*

TRIJICON

For more than four decades, Trijicon has been developing riflescopes and sights — any-light aiming systems — with innovations for hunters, shooters, the military, and law enforcement. Never resting on its laurels, Trijicon announced that all ACOG (Advanced

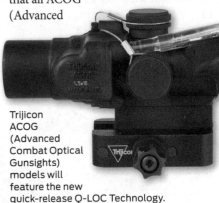

Trijicon ACOG (Advanced Combat Optical Gunsights) models will feature the new quick-release Q-LOC Technology.

Combat Optical Gunsights) models will feature the new quick-release Q-LOC Technology. That expands Q-LOC, already offered in Trijicon reflex and thermal optics and riflescopes, to include Compact ACOGs in 1.5x16S, 1.5x24, 2x20, 3x24, 3x30, 3x24 Crossbow, and 3X30/RMR Combo.

The patented made-in-

Riton considers its 3 Primal 3-18x50 Riflescope a crossover optic — the LRH (Long Range/Hunter) first focal plane illuminated reticle (with six brightness levels) provides accurate holdovers and wind holds throughout the magnification range.

Steiner announced a new line of T6Xi riflescopes featuring advanced German optical engineering with made-in-America manufacturing in four models. This is the 5-30x56 for long-range and precision shooting.

IN-DISPLAY WIND/DROP SOLUTIONS

Vortex's Razor HD 4000 GB Ballistic Laser Rangefinder handles tasks to 4,000 yards. Combine it with the GeoBallistic app.

USA Q-LOC features multiple recoil lugs to ensure solid engagement to the rail, yet, it can be easily removed and re-attached without concern of losing your zero. Heavy-duty springs ensure retention under brutal, repeated recoil and afford easy one-handed operation. Compact knobs minimize gear snags.

Also, Trijicon's 1.5x16S and 2x20 ACOGs now feature Trijicon Advanced Combat Reticles (TAC-R) with Rapid Target Reticle .223, battery-free center-dot illumination, and BDC holds to 700 yards. Rapid Target Reticle 9mm PCC, a match for pistol-caliber carbines with BDC, holds to 300 yards. *trijicon.com*

The Defender-CCW Micro-Compact Red-Dot is another big launch for Vortex. Its distortion-free aspherical-lens sight window is the largest of its class for both eyes-open shooting and enhanced peripheral vision. It's motion-activated for instant readiness and adjustable brightness on your choice of 3- or 6-MOA red-dot reticle.

VORTEX

With the Triumph HD 10x42 roof prism binocular, Vortex has unveiled a new budget-friendly line of binos that'll likely take off in a big way. These are the ones to stow in your vehicle, backpack, bug-out bag, or anywhere to have them when needed. With Vortex-quality resolution and contrast, plus brightness and clarity, they'll let you peer into the nooks, crannies, and shadows. Adaptable for use on a tripod or window mount. MSRP: $149.99. For Vortex quality, that's a deal.

The Defender-CCW Micro-Compact Red-Dot is another big Vortex launch focusing on the growing CCW market. People who prioritize personal protection, whether packing a full-size, subcompact or even micro-compact handgun for self-defense, are going to like the ultra-compact size and slim profile (and negligible weight) as well as the distortion-free aspherical-lens sight window, which is the largest of its class for both-eyes-open shooting and enhanced peripheral vision. It's motion-activated for instant readiness and adjustable brightness on your choice of 3- or 6-MOA red-dot reticle. MSRP: $349.99.

Vortex designed the Razor HD 4000 GB Ballistic Laser Rangefinder to provide all the range, ballistics, and environmental data needed to make precise shots on game or long-range shots on paper or steel targets to 4,000 yards. Fast and precise, it'll provide first-shot confidence

Swarovski's new STC compact spotting scope in 17-40X magnification ranges, weighs just under 35 ounces, and the straight model measures 11.2 inches; the angled, just 10.2.

at the push of a button and pairs with the GeoBallistic app. MSRP: $1,199.99. *vortexoptics.com*

ZEISS

Expanding its popular long-range precision scope line, Zeiss introduced the LRP S3 first focal plane riflescope for long-range precision shooting and hunting, with an impressive range of elevation travel. With up to 160 MOA or 46.5 MRAD of total elevation travel for the 4-25x50 model and 110 MOA or 32

The Swarovski tM 35 thermal imaging device is compatible with Swarovski Z8i, Z6(i), Z5(i) and Z3 riflescopes (and like-sized other scopes).

MRAD for the 6-36x56 model, the LRP S3 helps ensure bullet impact on distant targets. With ballistic stop providing a true return to zero and an external locking windage turret, shooters can make immediate corrections for wind.

The daylight-visible illuminated (red or green) smart reticle is quick and precise to read, with minimum target coverage. It has a compact 34mm aluminum monobloc main tube. MSRP: $2,299.99-$2,499.99. *zeiss.com* **GD**

Zeiss introduced the LRP S3 first focal plane riflescope for long-range precision shooting and hunting, with an impressive range of elevation travel. With up to 160 MOA or 46.5 MRAD of total elevation travel for the 4-25x50 model and 110 MOA or 32 MRAD for the 6-36x56 model.

- REPORTS -
from the Field
AIRGUNS

From backyard plinkers to heavy thumpers capable of taking predators, today's crop of airguns has something for everybody.

❯ JIM HOUSE

A good tool for budding target shooters is the Daisy 599.

Before the days of cell phones, digital cameras, tablets, and television, there was radio. I remember those days during the 1940s when the evening news was presented by Gabriel Heatter, who started the broadcast with "There's good news tonight!" That statement was his nightly greeting whether the news was good during those WWII years or not. Recalling those radio newscasts of long ago establishes me as an old timer, but I used an airgun even then. I have not heard those words at the beginning of a news program recently, but concerning the subject of this piece, there's good news for those of us who enjoy using airguns.

My use of an airgun began when Gabriel Heatter was a popular newsman who dealt with the news rather than a lengthy social commentary. That first airgun was a Daisy Model 38, a single shot cocked like a single-barrel shotgun rather than with a lever. A BB dropped in the muzzle completed the loading process. Although drastically archaic by today's standards, I learned a lot with that little gun with fixed sights and no safety.

Somewhere in my teens, I got a Benjamin Model 310 multi-pump that was also a single shot that launched BBs but at approximately three times the velocity of the little Daisy. My knowledge of airguns grew from using that rifle. Over the many intervening years, my interests and experience blossomed to include additional multi-pumps, break actions, and pre-charged pneumatic (PCP) models, such as were not dreamed of in my youth.

If you want to have a classic multi-pump, you can get one. If you want to shoot BBs from a full-auto submachine gun, you can get one. If you want to shoot a pre-charged pneumatic of .177 to .50 caliber with a suppressor attached, you can get one, also. Providing some organization of the topic is difficult because of numerous manufacturers and suppliers' bewildering array of products. There are, of course, some new models, but a lot of previously existing ones are offered with new options.

AIR ARMS

If you have a successful design, it is possible to configure the primary mechanism to give several variants. Such is the case with Air Arms and the PCP 510 series. The lineup includes the S510 PCP, featuring a beautifully shaped stock in poplar, walnut, or laminated forms. Also included are the 510 Tactical and the S510 TDR, a takedown model. All these models are available in .177 and 22 calibers with velocities of 1,035 and 950 fps, respectively. The Ultimate Sporter comes in .25 caliber with a velocity of 915 fps. For those seeking an elegant PCP of considerable power, the Air Arms models should be considered. *air-arms.co.uk*

AIRFORCE

Long a producer of big-bore airguns for hunting, AirForce continues to offer the highly regarded Texan series available in several configurations with various features. The basic rifle is produced in .25, .308, .357, .457, and .50 calibers. These rifles are single shots with features such as an overall length of 48 inches, a weight of 7.65 pounds, and 24-inch barrels. They also have two-stage triggers and are powered by a 490cc tank that can be pressurized up to 3,000 psi.

Performance depends on pellet weight, but in .25 caliber, the velocity can be up to 1,000 fps producing a muzzle energy of up to 190 ft-lbs making the rifle an excellent choice for varmints. In .50 caliber, the muzzle energy can reach 600 ft-lbs. The .308- and .357-caliber models give energies intermediate between these levels. An AirForce Texan model is available for whatever you may want to hunt with an airgun. For those who prefer a more compact airgun, the AirForce TalonP is available in .25 caliber. *airforceairguns.com*

AIR VENTURI

Known by the title Seneca, Air Venturi produces some of the most advanced airguns. A big bore, the Dragon Claw, is available in .50 caliber, and this behemoth rifle can produce up to 230 ft-lbs of energy. This is a likely choice for those who want to launch heavy slugs. Although a large airgun, the Seneca has an overall configuration that has a traditional look. The rifle has open sights and can be operated on two power levels. The stock and forearm are made of checkered hardwood and nicely shaped.

Made on the same overall pattern, the Seneca Wing Shot II shotgun is a different sort of airgun. It is not only a shotgun; by removing the screw-in choke tube, the smooth-bore barrel can launch .50-caliber round balls or flat-nose slugs with velocities up to 760 fps yielding over 245 ft-lbs of energy. The manufacturer states that the velocity of a charge of No. 8 shot is 1,130 fps. Moreover, the versatile Wing Shot II can also fire arrow bolts. In addition to the single-barrel model, a double gun, the Double Shot, is also available that shoots round balls, shot, or air bolts.

Elegant and powerful, the Winchester 70 is available in .35 and .45 calibers.

The Gamo Arrow PCP is an economical choice in a .22 for small game and varmints.

It is good to see the Dragonfly Mk 2 entry in the multi-pump category from Seneca. The rifle has excellent wood furniture and comes in .177 and .22 calibers. Provided with quality open sights, the Dragonfly Mk 2 performed well during my testing. Velocities are specified as 850 fps for the .177 and 730 fps for the .22 making these rifles sufficiently powerful for pest control.

At the opposite end of the airgun spectrum, Air Venturi offers the Springfield Armory M1 Carbine, which fires BBs powered by a CO_2 cylinder. The velocity is 425 fps, and the magazine capacity is 15 rounds with up to 40 shots per cylinder. This attractive, realistic little BB gun should be fun for pop can plinking or rolling pine cones. The Hellboy is an AR-style semi-automatic BB rifle, and also offered is a replica of a Colt 1873 that can fire either BBs or .177 pellets. Also

This BB-firing Winchester 1911 has the size, weight, and functions of a real .45 Auto.

Daisy's premier offerings are the Avanti Model 753S and Daisy 599 single-shot target rifles. Powered by a single pump, the 753S gives .177 pellets a velocity of approximately 495 fps. It features a Lothar Walther rifled barrel and a click-adjustable receiver rear sight and globe front sight that accepts inserts of different types.

Like many other suppliers, Daisy offers pistols powered by CO_2 that launch BBs. These are fun little guns that provide much practice

adequate for those desiring something with greater power. The .35-caliber TC-35 has a muzzle velocity of 1,000 fps with a barrel length of 28 inches and an overall length of 47.75 inches. It weighs 8.7 pounds. At the same time, the .45-caliber TC-45 has the exact dimensions and weight but is listed as having a muzzle velocity of 900 fps. Neither rifle is furnished with sights, but they come with a scope rail. *gamousa.com*

under the Springfield label are several BB pistols. The classic Beeman R7 and R9 break-action air rifles are available from Air Venturi. *airventuri.com*

GAMO USA-DAISY

Long the purveyor of BB guns, Daisy is still a big player in that market. The tried and true Red Ryder is still available in two sizes to accommodate shooters of small stature and those of adult size. Also offered is the Model 105, a small, lever-cocking model. The Model 2840 cocks with a single stroke of the forearm that serves as the pump lever and is a repeater with BBs or can be single-loaded with .177 pellets. (Although it does not have a rifled barrel, the skirted pellets tend to fly straight and give better accuracy than BBs.)

economically. The Model 426 closely resembles the Ruger SR22 rimfire autoloader. This and many other models from other sources need to be used carefully.

In the Gamo line, the products are of the higher power types. In traditional style are the Arrow PCP models in .177 and .22 calibers. The Big Bore TC-35 and TC-45 should be

The AirForce Texan is a good choice for those with serious hunting aspirations.

The Benjamin Marauder provides a good entry into PCP rifles.

Crosman's 362 is an inexpensive but capable multi-pump.

HATSAN USA

Offering a wide variety of airguns, Hatsan USA has a couple of models that offer maximum versatility. The Hydra QE is available with a combination barrel and receiver module that is user interchangeable. As a result, the shooter can change the rifle from .177 to .22 or .25 caliber by switching modules depending on the intended use. Velocities given by the Hydra QE are listed as 1,150, 1,000, and 900 fps for the three calibers. These models feature Hatsan's developments known as Versa Cal and QuietEnergy, along with a choked steel barrel.

Two of Hatsan's versatile products are the Jet and Jet II. These convert from pistols to short-barreled rifles using a removable and adjustable buttstock. The PCP models come in .177, .22, and .25 calibers. Sights are furnished, and a rail is provided for attaching optional optics, lights, etc. The Jet and Jet II utilize rotary magazines holding six, seven, or eight pellets, depending on caliber. The Jet II uses dual air cylinders, and from the 7.9-inch barrel, the velocities are listed as 788, 700, and 610 fps for the .177, .22, and .25 calibers, respectively, making them suitable for dispatching small varmints.

Another interesting product from Hatsan is the PCP Model AT44PA-10 QES, a pump-action repeater with a sliding forearm. This rifle is available in .177, .22, and .25 calibers with listed velocities of 1,150, 1,000, and 900 fps, respectively. Rotary magazines holding 10 pellets in the smaller calibers and nine pellets in

.25 caliber are utilized. With a muzzle energy of up to 40 ft-lbs, the .25 caliber could even be used carefully on predators. Interestingly, the Model AT44PA-10 QES is also offered in a longer version with approximately 4 inches of added barrel length with velocities listed at about 100 fps higher than the standard model. The standard model is 45.5 inches long, has a barrel length of 19.4 inches and weighs 8.6 pounds. For the longer version, you can add approximately 4 inches to the lengths, and it is listed as

For those who want a CO_2 pistol with power for small pests, the Crosman 2240 is excellent.

Among the PCP rifles for heavy-duty airgunning, the Hatsan Hydra is a good choice.

weighing 9.9 pounds. Both models have stocks made of black polymer with a thumbhole and pistol grip configuration.

In addition to the models just discussed, Hatsan USA also offers several others, among which is the BT655B, a PCP that is available in .177, .22, and .25 calibers. This interesting rifle gives a muzzle energy of up to 65 ft-lbs. It comes with no sights, but it is scope-ready and should be a suitable hunting tool. The Gladius PCP can be had in standard and long models, and the Hatsun USA line includes several others. *hatsanusa.com*

UMAREX

Long one of the major players in the airgun game, Umarex offers products that cover the entire field of airgunning. On the one hand, there is the Hammer, a .50-caliber PCP that launches a 550-grain slug at up to 760 fps producing over 700 ft-lbs of energy! On the other hand are myriad CO_2 pistol

The ever-popular break-action rifle is well-represented by the Beeman R9.

replicas of too many firearms to list individually. However, Colt, Ruger, Smith & Wesson, Heckler & Koch, Beretta, Glock, Walther, et al. are all represented. The majority are BB pistols, but some shoot .177 pellets. Generally, muzzle velocity is in the 400-425 fps range, so the pistols must be handled carefully. Whether your favorite handgun is a Luger P08, Colt 1911,

chine guns and the famous Ruger 10/22. *umarex.com*

VELOCITY OUTDOOR

Velocity Outdoor is the parent company for Benjamin and Crosman airguns and other sporting goods. It is good to see that several products produced for many years are still available. The bolt-action repeater Benjamin Marauder has been around for a while but still represents a good value in a high-performance PCP

The Seneca Dragon Claw from Air Venturi is a powerful rifle with dual air reservoirs.

Beretta 92, or a Colt Single Action, you can find a replica.

Another of the successful product lines from Umarex is the Gauntlet PCP rifle, available in .22 or .25 caliber. The rifle measures approximately 47 inches in length and weighs 9.25 pounds. It does not have open sights, but a scope rail is provided. Velocities are specified as approximately 900-950 fps for the .22 and 890 fps for the .25. The price tag? Only $254.99, so you can get a PCP that performs well at a budget price. Also available are models in the Ruger Air Hawk series of break actions, including the Magnum version in .22 caliber. Although they will not be listed in this overview, products from Umarex include numerous models resembling subma-

air rifle. In .177, .22, and .25 calibers with a wood stock, velocities are listed as 1,100, 1,000, and 900 fps, respectively. However, a semi-automatic version of the Marauder is offered in .22 caliber. The Marauder has a muzzle velocity of up to 950 fps thanks to a tank pressure of up to 3,000 psi. It features a 10-shot rotary magazine, measures 42.8 inches in length, and weighs 7.2 pounds. Muzzle energy produced can be up to 26 ft-lbs.

The Benjamin Craftsman group includes the Akela, available in .177 and .22 calibers with listed velocities of 1,100 and 1,000 fps, respectively. Also included are the Cayden .22 and Kratos in .22 and .25 calibers. The Craftsman series features

wood stocks and scope rails but no sights. Several models of the Benjamin Trail break-action rifles continue to be available, as are the PCP Armada series.

Crosman began operations in 1923, and to commemorate the 100th anniversary, a special version of the .22-caliber Model 362 multi-pump is being produced. It features a very attractive wood stock with checkering and a gold-colored medallion inlaid into the buttstock. Also offered is a particular version of the multi-pump .177-caliber Model 2100. It features a gold-colored receiver and a medallion inlaid in a synthetic stock. Both of these rifles should appeal to the collector of distinctive airguns.

As one who has used the basic Model 362 and has much experience with the Model 2100, I can heartily concur with the models selected to be introduced as commemoratives. My standard Model 362 with a black polymer stock has been extensively tested and performs admirably. It is accurate,

The Seneca Dragonfly Mk 2 is a serious contender for those who like multi-pump rifles.

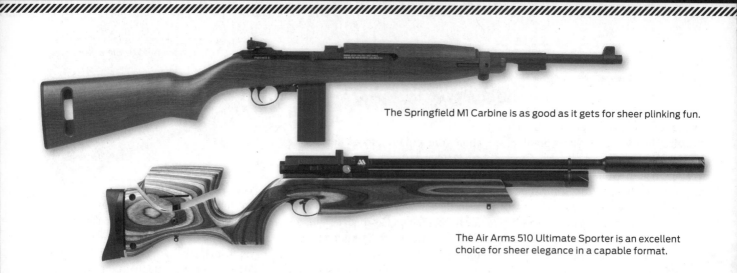

The Springfield M1 Carbine is as good as it gets for sheer plinking fun.

The Air Arms 510 Ultimate Sporter is an excellent choice for sheer elegance in a capable format.

and the velocities are uniform for each number of pumps from two to eight.

The extensive Crosman line continues to include the Model 1077 RepeatAir in several versions and two variants of the multi-pump 760. A spring-powered break action, the Optimus, comes in .177 and .22 calibers. A few years ago, Crosman transitioned to break-action models powered by a gas cylinder containing nitrogen, and the current Shockwave, Fire, and Vantage models utilize that power source. The Mag-Fire series includes several rotary magazine models powered by Crosman's Nitro Piston technology.

Other offerings from Crossman include variants that fire BBs in full-auto mode and an extensive line of CO_2-powered pistols in numerous configurations. It's also nice to see that those who like to shoot revolvers have not been forgotten. The newest example, the Fortify, holds up to 18 BBs and has the attractive shape of a single action. At the other end of the CO_2 pistol spectrum are the single-shot Model 2300T and 2300S target pistols in .177 caliber and the Model 2240 single-shot in .22 caliber. With a velocity of up to 460 fps with .22-caliber pellets, the Model 2240 produces sig-

nificant power for a pistol. Still, it's also a favorite among enthusiasts who like to modify the pistol for even greater power. *velocity-outdoor.com*

WINCHESTER

Under the Winchester label are offered two PCP rifles, the Winchester 70-35 and 70-45, with the caliber indicated after the 70. The .35-caliber model produces 12 shots

The Colt Single Action provides realism for fun shooting.

with approximately full power, whereas the .45-caliber rifle is listed as giving five shots with full power. A six-shot rotary magazine is used with the 70-35, and a five-shot magazine holds pellets for the .45. Interestingly, for the .35-cal. model, Winchester pellets weigh 127 grains, and the muzzle energy is listed as 120 ft-lbs; pellets for the .45-caliber rifle are listed as 140 grains with a muzzle energy of 150-

180 ft-lbs. Rifles such as the Winchester models are suitable for hunting species at least up to coyote size.

Also offered with the Winchester label is a pistol that fires BBs. It's a full-size replica of the Colt 1911 powered by CO_2 and has a magazine within the grip that holds 16 BBs. When fired, the pistol produces a blowback action of the slide. It provides much realism during those shoot-for-fun sessions. However, I once handed one to a park officer along with a genuine .45 Auto and asked him to tell me quickly which hand held the firearm. He could not do it. Be careful! *winchesterairrifles.com*

CONCLUSION

Growing up as I did with a Daisy BB gun and a Benjamin multi-pump, it would have been unimaginable that the airgun field would develop into models for hunting medium game or launching BBs in full-auto mode. Replicas provide realistic action and are entertaining and useful for training purposes. For airgunners like me, as Gabriel Heatter would have said, "There's good news tonight!" **GD**

If medium game hunting is on the agenda, the Umarex Hammer would be a good companion. It sends a 550-grain slug at up to 760 fps producing over 700 ft-lbs of energy!

- REPORTS -
from the Field
AMMUNITION

Ammo's back in stock with new releases in the centerfire rifle, rimfire and handgun categories for hunting, self-defense, and target!

> PHIL MASSARO

Hornady's new 7mm PRC sits between the short-action 6.5 PRC and the magnum-length .300 PRC and offers a fantastic balance of high BC projectiles, magnum velocity, and user-friendliness (read manageable recoil).

There is lots of good news on the ammunition front, especially compared to the last few years when the ammo drought had us all down in the dumps. Not only is the commonly pursued ammunition becoming readily available again, but there are also interesting new releases for handguns, shotguns, and rifles. We have a couple of new rifle cartridges to examine, some older ones getting another lease on life, and cross-brand mating, which might make you happy. Let's delve into the ammunition releases for the year.

AGUILA

Mexico's Aguila Ammunition announces the introduction of its 124-grain 9mm Luger ammo, loaded with a jacketed hollowpoint bullet. With a muzzle velocity of 1,150 fps, Aguila now offers a suitable defensive round for those who rely on the 9mm for defensive purposes. The new load has been tested in various handguns, from full-size models to micro-compact designs. Available in 50-round boxes or 500-count cases. *aguilaammo.com*

BARNES

New for 2023, Barnes offers an ammunition line that will put smiles on the faces of lever-action fans: the Pioneer line. It takes full advantage of the lead-free Barnes bullets — in this case, either the TSX FN flat-nose all-copper bullets or the Barnes Original line, which hearkens back to Fred Barnes' favored heavy-for-caliber cup-and-core designs. Options include .30-30 Winchester, loaded with the 150-grain TSX FN (lead-free), 190-grain Barnes Original (lead core), .357 Remington Magnum loaded with the 140-grain XPB or 180-grain Barnes Original, .45 Colt with 200-grain XPB or 250-grain Barnes Original, .45-70 Government loaded with the 300-grain TSX FN or the 400-grain Barnes Original. Sold in 20-round boxes. *barnesbullets.com*

BERGER

Famous for its high Ballistic Coefficient designs and highly uniform J4 jackets, Berger has announced the line extension of the Elite Hunter rifle ammunition. Using heavyweight bullets for each car-

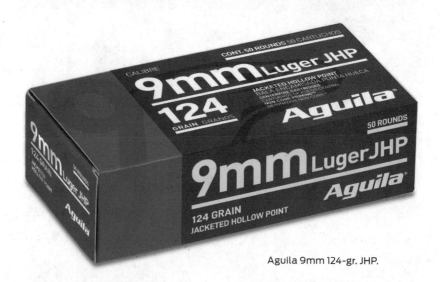

Aguila 9mm 124-gr. JHP.

Barnes Pioneer ammo.

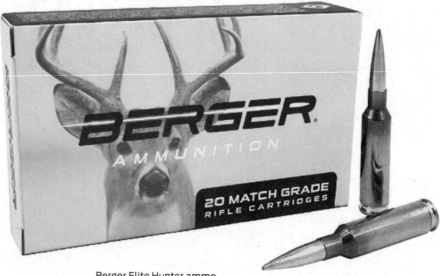

Berger Elite Hunter ammo.

tridge, Berger wrings the most retained energy at long ranges. The Elite Hunter hollowpoint bullet uses a hybrid ogive, combining the best features of a secant and tangent curve to give the best blend of resistance to atmospheric drag and positive rifling engagement in the throat. The thin jacket allows for almost immediate energy transfer, relying on hydrostatic shock for a quick, humane kill.

This year, Berger loads the 6mm Creedmoor with the 108-grain Elite Hunter, the 6.5 Creedmoor and 6.5 PRC cartridges with the 140-grain Elite Hunter, and a beastly 245-grain Elite Hunter in the .300 PRC. That 245-grain slug has a G1 BC of .807! Sold in 20-count boxes. *bergerbullets.com*

BLACK HILLS AMMUNITION

My first experience shooting Black Hills ammunition was on a mule deer hunt in South Dakota, using a Kimber in 6.5 Creedmoor, and I came away very impressed. This year, the Black Hills Gold line of ammo is expanded to include the 6mm ARC and 6.5 PRC, loaded with 103- and 143-grain ELD-X bullets, respectively. These sleek, dependable hunting bullets are cruising at 2,600 fps out of the 6 ARC and 2,900 fps out of the 6.5 PRC. Sold in 20-count boxes.

The Black Hills Honey Badger handgun ammunition line has been expanded to include the formidable 10mm Auto cartridge, featuring the 115-grain Honey Badger copper monometal at a listed

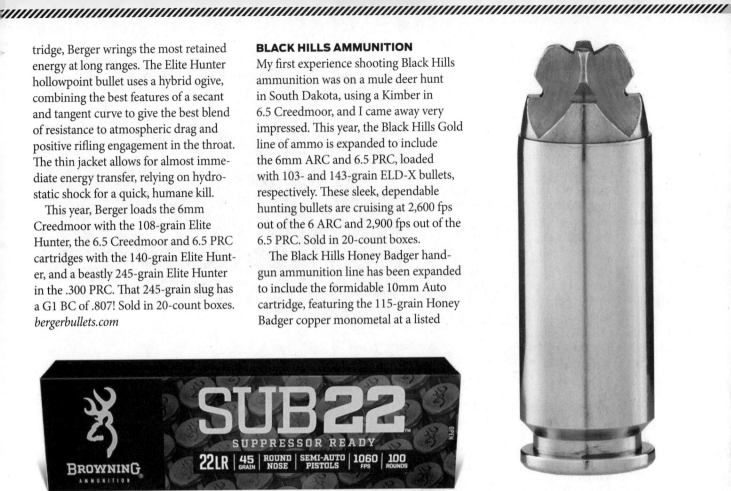

Black Hills Honey Badger 10mm.

muzzle velocity of 1,600 fps for 654 ft-lbs of muzzle energy. This bullet does not expand; rather, it resembles a screwdriver bit and will wreak havoc in a fluid-rich medium. *black-hills.com*

BROWNING

The BuckMark is on a whole bunch of new ammunition products this year, including centerfire rifle and rimfire lines. Starting with the smallest, Browning's new Sub22 rimfire ammo is a .22 Long Rifle load designed for use with suppressed rimfire rifles. The 45-grain black copper jacketed projectile has a listed muzzle velocity of 1,060 fps, starting at subsonic speed. Sold in 100-count boxes.

The Browning Silver Series ammunition uses an innovative nickel-plating process to offer a plated rifle bullet. Using heavy-for-caliber bullets, the Silver Series from Browning offers ammunition suitable for nearly all North American species. Available in .243 Winchester (100 grain), 6.5 Creedmoor (129 grain), .270

Browning Sub22.

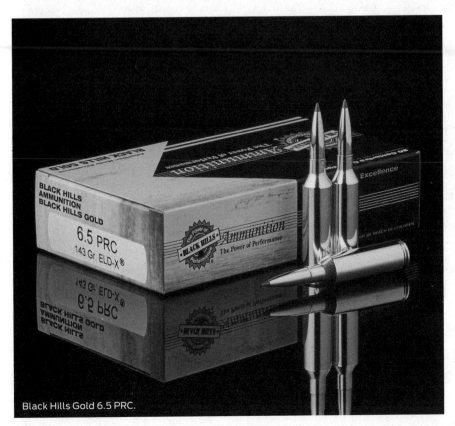

Black Hills Gold 6.5 PRC.

Winchester (150 grain), 6.8 Western (170 grain), 7mm Remington Magnum (175 grain), .30-30 Winchester (170 grain), .308 Winchester, .30-'06 Springfield, and .300 Winchester Magnum (all 180 grain), and .350 Legend (180 grain), in 20-count boxes.

The Browning MaxPoint line is an embellishment of the BXR ammunition concept, with a revised projectile at heavier bullet weights for increased penetration and recovered bullet weight retention. The excellent corrosion-resistant nickel-plated casings are still there (headstamped with the famous Buckmark), as is the large polymer Matrix Tip. Still, with the increase in bullet weight, there should be a considerable reduction in premature bullet breakup, as the increased Sectional Density will help keep things together after impact on your game animal. The Max-Point is still intended for those hunters who pursue whitetail deer, mule deer and pronghorn antelope, species more susceptible to the hydraulic shock created by a rapidly expanding bullet, yet still require that projectile to reach (and destroy) as much vital tissue as possible. Browning's new MaxPoint projectile does just that. MaxPoint ammunition is available in .243 Winchester at 95 grains, 6.5 Creedmoor and 6.5 PRC at 140 grains, .270 Winchester at 150 grains, 6.8 Western at 170 grains, .308 Winchester at 168 grains, and in .30-'06 Springfield, .300 WSM and .300 Winchester Magnum at 180 grains. MaxPoint is sold in 20-round boxes. *browningammo.com*

BUFFALO BORE AMMUNITION

For 2023, Buffalo Bore in-

Browning .308 MaxPoint.

Browning Silver Series.

troduces some new handgun ammunition to its lineup. The diminutive .25 ACP gets a couple of fresh offerings, including a 60-grain hardcast bullet at 850 fps and a 50-grain FMJ RN load at 875 fps. *buffalobore.com*

CCI

Idaho's CCI — the brainchild of Dick Speer and Arvid Nelson — has long been famous for its rimfire ammunition. Since joining the Vista Outdoor Group, CCI has continued to release innovative products. CCI released its Clean-22 Hyper Velocity this year, adding to the polymer-coated lead rimfire cartridges line. Coating a lead bullet reduces the vaporized lead in an indoor shooting range and minimizes lead fouling in the barrel. The Clean-22 line has proven to be a great choice for both a target situation and hunting small game animals; it is economical, accurate, and effective.

Clean-22 Hyper Velocity uses a purple-coated 31-grain lead bullet with a round-nose profile at a muzzle velocity of 1,550 fps — a speedy combination capable of taking headshots at squirrels at the tops of the tallest trees. A light bullet in the .22 Long Rifle at a higher velocity is not a new concept at CCI. The Stinger uses an elongated case and a 32-grain bullet at a muzzle velocity of 1,640 fps and has long been a favorite of shooters and hunters; the Clean-22 Hyper Velocity will be on par with the Stinger. According to CCI's testing, it greatly reduces the amount of fouling in the suppressor — up to an 80% reduction — and will save the shooter time when cleaning a suppressor. *cci-ammunition.com*

CHOICE AMMUNITION

When is a factory load not a factory load? When it is handloaded at a professional level from the guys at Choice Ammunition in Victor, Montana. Offering many options not available in factory configurations, Choice has made many hunters and target shooters happy. For 2023, they offer varying projectiles in the 7mm PRC, including bullets from Berger, Barnes, and Nosler. They've also extended their line of low-recoil ammunition to include the .243 Winchester, 6.5 Creedmoor, .270 Winchester, 7mm-08 Remington, and .308 Winchester. With the re-release of the Marlin 1895 and 336, Choice is ramping up production of .30-30 Winchester, .35 Remington, and .45-70 Government. And the ammo maker has updated

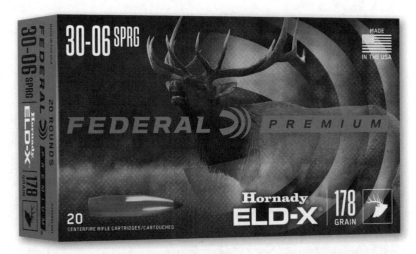

Federal Premium with Hornady ELD-X bullet.

Choice ammo.

Choice ammo.

its Bear Defense Load — my Ruger Blackhawk .45 Colt loves that load — with a harder formula and a black Hi-Tek coating. It's now available in 9mm Luger, .38 Special, .357 Magnum, 10mm Auto, .41 Remington Magnum, .44 Remington Magnum, and .45 Colt. *choiceammunition.com*

FEDERAL

There are lots of new products coming out of Anoka this year, as Federal continues to be an leader in the ammunition industry. First up is the inclusion of Hornady's ELD-X bullet in its rifle ammunition. Yes, that is correct, Federal now loads the ELD-X in its ammo, and I feel that's a good thing. The ELD-X is a cup-and-core bullet with a heat-resistant polymer tip, delivering match-grade accuracy. Loaded in nickel-plated cases, the ELD-X line includes .243 Winchester at 90 grains, 6.5 Creedmoor and 6.5 PRC at 143 grains, .270 Winchester at 145 grains, 7mm Remington Magnum at 162 grains, .308 Winchester and .30-'06 Springfield at 178 grains, and .300 WSM and .300 Winchester Magnum at 200 grains, in 20-round count boxes.

Next, we see Gold Medal CenterStrike match ammo, loaded in .223 Remington with 77-grain CenterStrike, 6.5 Creedmoor with 140-grain CenterStrike, and .308 Winchester, loaded with 168- and 175-grain CenterStrike. The new CenterStrike is a proprietary open-tip match bullet for consistent long-range performance and will make a viable option for those who enjoy high-volume long-distance shooting. Sold in 20-count boxes.

Buckshot fans will be happy that Federal offers a No. 1 buckshot load this year. With 16 pellets leaving the muzzle at 1,325 fps, the Federal Premium Buckshot No. 1 Buck ammo splits the difference between the No. 4 buck and the larger 00 and 0 buck, giving a great blend of pattern density and striking energy. Testing has shown that copper-plated shot penetrates between 15 and 18 inches in ballistic gelatin. The buffering in the shot column keeps the shot as concentric as possible, leading to consistent patterns. Having a diameter of .30 inch, the copper-plated No. 1 buckshot is buffered within the shotshell to resist deformation.

It's sold in packs of five shells.

Fans of the 28-gauge shotgun — and that will assuredly include the author — will be pleased to see that Federal has now included the Twenty-Eight in the Black Cloud shotshell line. Mixing Flites-topper and Premium steel pellets into a 3/4-ounce payload in a 3-inch magnum shell spells trouble for waterfowl. Leaving the muzzle at 1,400 fps, this Black Cloud load will extend the abilities of the 28-gauge guns, giving plenty of lethality with significantly reduced recoil. They are sold in boxes of 25 shells.

Federal is also announcing the release of Power Point ammunition for the new .360 Buckhammer (see the Remington section below) featuring 180- and 200-grain softpoint projectiles. With a round-nose profile, the Power Point .360 Buckhammer will make a great addition to the ammunition choices for this new straight-walled, rimmed cartridge. Loaded to 2,400 fps and 2,200 fps, this cartridge will perform similarly to the .30-30 Winchester with heavier bullets yet less recoil. Sold in 20-count boxes.

The Punch handgun line has been extended to include the .30 Super Carry. That Federal has designed the projectile and cartridge from a blank slate only enhances the project. Using a skived, jacketed hollowpoint with a soft lead core, the Punch projectile is a wonderful blend of expansion and penetration in various mediums, made available at an attractive price point. For the .30 Super Carry, Federal loads a 103-grain JHP, giving a performance level on par with the 9mm Luger, but with three more rounds in the magazine. Sold in 20-count boxes. *federalpremium.com*

FIOCCHI

Fiocchi announced the lead-free Knock-Down centerfire rifle ammunition line, featuring an all-copper hollowpoint bullet. This design not only adheres to the laws and regulations of those areas which prohibit lead ammunition but will leave a minimum of copper fouling in your rifle's bore. Fiocchi has chosen an all-copper bullet design for deep penetration yet with reliable expansion, and the KnockDown line is offered in .243 Winchester (80 grains), 6.5 Creedmoor (120

Federal Black Cloud 28 gauge.

Federal Power Shok .360 Buckhammer.

grains), .270 Winchester (130 grains), 7mm-08 Remington (140 grains), 7mm Remington Magnum (160 grains), .308 Winchester and .30-'06 Springfield (both at 150 grains), and .300 Winchester Magnum (165 grains). *fiocchiusa.com*

HEVI-SHOT

HEVI-Shot has taken its waterfowl shotshell line to the next step in the HEVI-Metal Xtreme series. The Xtreme series uses a blend of 30% tungsten and 70% precision steel shot to give the dogs plenty to work on. The non-toxic shot material is legal in all waterfowl situations. HEVI-Shot has incorporated a hotter 209 primer and a clean-burning propellant to ensure ignition in the most inclement weather. The Flightcontrol Flex wad keeps the pattern good and dense and works perfectly with just about any choke rated for steel shot, ported or not. Weighing 12g/cc, the tungsten shot will hit over 50% harder than any steel shot, and as it is loaded at the front of the shot column, you'll be plucking feathers in no time. HEVI-Shot offers the HEVI-Metal Xtreme in 12-gauge, 3-in. magnum at 1 1/4 ounces shot weight, blending No. 4 tungsten and No. 1 steel at 1,450 fps or No. 6 tungsten and No. 3 steel at 1,450 fps; or in 20-gauge, 3-inch magnum at 1 1/16 ounces shot weight, mixing No. 4 tungsten and No. 1 steel at 1,350 fps or

Fiocchi Knockdown.

HEVI-Metal Xtreme
from HEVI-Shot.

Hornady's Bore Driver ELD-X.

No. 6 tungsten and No. 3 steel at 1,350 fps. All loads are sold in 25-count boxes. *hevishot.com*

HORNADY

Hornady brings a brand-new cartridge to the table this year, one equally well-suited for the hunter as it is for the long-range target shooter. The new 7mm PRC sits between the short-action 6.5 PRC and the magnum-length action .300 PRC but offers a fantastic balance of high BC projectiles, magnum velocity, and user-friendliness (read manageable recoil). You can read my in-depth feature article on the 7mm PRC at the front of this esteemed tome, but I'll also give you the boiled-down version here.

Hornady shortened the .300 PRC to 2.280 inches while maintaining a cartridge length of 3.34 inches to fit the case in a long-action receiver. At the same time, that left plenty of space for the long, sleek bullets that work so well at longer ranges. The case is beltless and rimless, using a 30-degree shoulder for headspacing and good chamber concentricity. Three loads are available from Hornady: a 160-grain CX in the Outfitter line at 3,000 fps, a 175-grain ELD-X at the same velocity, and a 180-grain ELD Match at 2,975 fps. This equates to a flat-shooting, hard-hitting cartridge, without any of the case stretching issues of the belted cases, fully capable of punching steel at a mile or making an all-around hunting cartridge for nearly all of North America.

New for 2023, Hornady has announced its .50-caliber Bore Driver ELD-X bullet, taking muzzleloading rifles to a new level. Using a bullet diameter of .499 inch, the Bore Driver ELD-X features a large polymer tip and a polymer base of bore diameter, which seals the burning gasses behind the bullet. The Bore Driver ELD-X weighs 340 grains, has a G1 Ballistic Coefficient of .315, and a Sectional Density of .194. The weight of the ELD-X makes it a good choice for larger game species, like elk, moose, and bears.

The Bore Driver ELD-X uses an internal Inter-Lock groove to lock the jacket and core together to slow expansion while maintaining the bullet's integrity. The polymer base locks into the boat tail base of the bullet, eliminating the need for a sabot and reducing the force needed to load the bullet. Also, Hornady offers special brass ramrod tips that match the profile of the Bore Driver ELD-X to minimize the chances of damaging the projectile as you load the rifle. A concentric, drawn-copper jacket helps enhance accuracy, and this bullet has given up to 21 inches of penetration in ballistic gel in laboratory tests. Sold in 12-count boxes. *hornady.com*

NORMA

Hailing from Amotfors, Sweden — famous for its population of albino moose — the outfit of Norma has a remarkable history, surviving war and more, and now thriving into the 21st century. I've been blessed enough to have toured the factory twice and have yet to see a more sophisticated or well-organized operation. I've been privy to many of its new releases, from bullets to cartridges, and have an unabashed soft spot for the company.

A few years back, Norma released a series of proprietary projectiles that worked very well in their respective applications. EcoStrike was the lead-free bullet with a green polymer tip, weighing in at lighter weights than the norm. This bullet worked very well but was not very economical to produce. For 2023, Norma announced a reboot of the EcoStrike, with manufacturing techniques allowing the consumer to obtain this projectile at a lower price point without sacrificing any terminal performance or precision. I have had nothing but good results with the original EcoStrike, having used it for my largest European wild boar in Poland — with the 232-grain 9.3x62 load — and whitetail deer here in the United States. If you like a lead-free bullet, give the EcoStrike a long look.

The Xtreme LR-22 might just be the culmination of an idea I've long championed: using a .22 LR as a tool for training for long-range shooting. Norma has designed a unique bullet for this load, using a "rocket base" and an elongated nose profile to minimize atmospheric drag for shooting at longer ranges. Sending a 43-grain lead bullet at a muzzle velocity of 1,165 fps, this load is designed for use at distances out to 300 yards and beyond,

Norma Xtreme LR-22.

Remington Core-Lokt Copper.

Remington Golden Saber.

making it an excellent training tool for a shooter new to the ELR (Extended Long Range) world — or as a means of practice for an experienced long-range shooter who might not have the distance needed at their disposal. In fact, long-range rimfire competitions are quickly gaining popularity. At a fraction of the cost and with little or no recoil or report, using a .22 LR for precision shooting makes perfect sense. Sold in boxes of 50 or 500. *norma-ammunition.com*

REMINGTON

Now part of the Vista Outdoor Group, Remington Ammunition has been busy as of late. For 2023, it has released

Winchester Big Bore.

Speer Gold-Dot Carbine.

the new .360 Buckhammer, a rimmed, straight-wall cartridge designed for use in lever-action and single-shot rifles, adhering to an amalgam of laws in place across several Midwestern states. Based on the .30-30 Winchester case, the .360 Buckhammer has a case length of 1.8 inches and uses a bullet of .358-inch diameter. Big Green loads both the 180- and 200-grain Core-Lokt round-nose bullet, making the .360 Buckhammer safe for use in rifles with tubular magazines. The 180-grain load has a muzzle velocity of 2,400 fps, while the heavier 200-grain

Winchester .400 Legend.

load gives 2,200 fps, creating a velocity advantage over the .35 Remington.

Some will ask why we aren't simply using the .35 Remington cartridge; the older cartridge uses a case length of 1.920 inches (too long for some of those states' regulations) and is also a bottlenecked design. It is safe to say the .360 Buckhammer was designed to fill the needs of hunters in those regulated areas. Remington indicates that velocities, energies, and trajectories are on par with the .30-30 Winchester, and recoil is commensurate; the .360 Buckhammer should be right at home among lever-gun shooters. They are sold in 20-count boxes.

In its first union with a sister company, Remington announces the Premier Long Range ammunition line, loaded with the Speer Impact bullet. Long overlooked, the Speer Impact is a quality bonded core bullet that uses a boattail design, and the SlipStream polymer tip made famous in the Federal Premium line. That tip will allow for reliable expansion at velocities 200 fps lower than a standard tip. Yet, the Impact's construction holds the projectile together when distances are short and velocities high. Available in 6.5 Creedmoor (140 grains), .270 Winchester (150 grains), 7mm Remington Magnum (175 grains), .308 Winchester and .30-'06 Springfield (172 grains), and .300 Winchester Magnum and .300 Remington Ultra Magnum (190 grains). Sold in 20-count boxes.

Adding to the Core-Lokt lineup, Big Green has announced the Core-Lokt Copper line of lead-free projectiles in its centerfire ammunition. Using a pure copper hollowpoint bullet will guarantee deep penetration and high weight retention. Can it still be Core-Lokt if there is no core to lock? I'm not sure, but I know that many hunters happily rely on lead-free ammo, whether required by law or not. Core-Lokt Copper is available in .243 Winchester at 85 grains, .270 Winchester at 130 grains, .300 AAC Blackout at 120 grains, .308 Winchester and .30-06 Springfield at 150 grains, and .300 Winchester Magnum at 180 grains. Sold in 20-count boxes.

Lovers of the .35 Remington — and there are many — will be happy to know that Remington has announced it's bringing back the 150-grain load for that classic cartridge. Using the Remington Core-Lokt bullet at a muzzle velocity of 2,300 fps offers owners of a beloved lever-action rifle — and, by the way, new Marlin 336s available again this year — the classic .35 Remington deer load. Sold in 20-count boxes.

The 10mm Auto is making a comeback as of late, and Remington has announced the release of the Golden Saber ammo in the Big Ten. There are three loads, all using a 180-grain bullet. Two feature the standard Golden Saber 180-grain jacketed hollowpoint, one designed for regular handguns and another for compact handguns. The third features a 180-grain Golden Saber Bonded bullet for the utmost in deep penetration. The three loads are all advertised at 1,150 fps, though I expect the compact guns to generate a lower velocity. *remington.com*

SPEER

Speer introduces the Gold Dot Carbine ammunition. Featuring the Speer G2 bullet — its hollowpoint cavity filled with an elastomer — the ammo is optimized to run flawlessly through the pistol-caliber carbines that have become so popular. The first offering is a 135-grain 9mm Luger load, sold in 50-count boxes, which should hit shelves by mid-2023. *speer.com*

WINCHESTER

Over at Winchester, things are abuzz with a new cartridge and all sorts of ultramodern ammunition. The new .400 Legend cartridge gives big game hunters a bit more horsepower than the .350 Legend offers while delivering 20% less recoil than the .450 Bushmaster. Using the same straight-walled case/rebated rim formula as the .350 Legend, the .400 Legend has a case length of 1.650 inches — helping to adhere to the varying game laws in the Midwest that restrict case length in certain instances. Using a 215-grain bullet of .4005-inch diameter at a muzzle velocity of 2,250 fps, the .400 Legend delivers just over 2,400 ft-lbs at the muzzle, and the wide frontal diameter will result in a larger wound channel. This is looking like a great choice for those pursuing larger game species in

thicker cover at common woods distances. It'll deliver 20% more energy than the common .30-30 Winchester, with better penetration.

Winchester's Big Bore handgun ammunition uses a semi-jacketed hollow-point projectile in bullet weights on the heavier side for each caliber. This will give the deep penetration needed in a hunting situation and provide uniform expansion resulting from the shorter jacket. The concave dish at the meplat immediately transfers energy at the front without being overly frangible. It relies on the higher Sectional Density and short jacket to control the bullet's expansion. Big Bore is available in .357 Remington Magnum with 158-grain JHP, 10mm

Winchester M1 Garand ammo.

Auto with 200-grain JHP, .44 Remington Magnum with 240-grain JHP, and .45 Colt with 250-grain JHP, all in 20-round boxes.

For those who enjoy hunting with a .35 Whelen — and what's not to like? — Winchester once again offers ammunition for it. In the company's Power Point line, the Whelen is loaded with a 200-grain softpoint bullet to 2,800 fps, generating just under 3,500 ft-lbs of energy. Sold in 20-count boxes, you can dust off the Whelen and head to the range and woods this fall.

Winchester's Bismuth shotshell line will have waterfowl considering night flights. Denser than steel shot, Bismuth is a non-toxic alternative that is very effective for ducks and geese. There are two 12-gauge loads, each holding 1 3/8 ounces of shot, giving the shooter the option of No. 1 or No. 4 shot at 1,450 fps. The 20-gauge load contains one ounce of No. 4 at 1,300 fps. A two-piece wad gives tight patterns and a good gas seal in the scattergun's bore. All are sold in 25-count boxes.

Winchester also announced the M1 Garand line, replicating the Ball M2 military ammunition. The .30-'06 Springfield, loaded with a 150-grain

Winchester Bismuth.

full metal jacket spitzer bullet, made an indelible mark on the world in the Second World War, and many shooters enjoy shooting the M1 Garand rifle to this day. The ammo is optimized to run correctly in Garands without posing a potential issue for the gun's operating rod. Driving that 150-grain FMJ to a muzzle velocity of 2,740 fps, you'll hear that musical 'ping' before you know it. *winchester.com* **GD**

- REPORTS -
from the Field
RELOADING

Supply chains are improving, and some neat options are on tap for reloaders.

❯PHIL MASSARO

Hornady ELD Match.

Winchester StaBALL HD powder.

Alliant's new TS-11 powder.

Well, things have certainly improved since last we met, as reloading components have become much more readily available, and the press arms are again in motion. This year, we've got new powders, new projectiles, and all sorts of new tools. Let's dive right in to see what we've got on our hands.

ALLIANT

Adding to the Reloder family of powders, Alliant has announced Reloder TS11, a rifle powder on the faster side of the burn rate scale, engineered for temperature insensitivity. It is perfect for short-range benchrest cartridges and varmint work and makes a solid choice for those who want consistent results, whether in pursuit of winter foxes and coyotes or sniping woodchucks and prairie dogs in the summer heat. TS11 (TS stands for Temperature Stable) burns cleaner, features a de-coppering agent to help minimize the mess in your barrel, and is REACH compliant. TS11 is available in both 1- and 8-pound canisters. *alliant-powder.com*

FEDERAL PREMIUM

Federal has made its Podium wad — the same one used in its High All Over shotshells — available as a reloading component this year. The cylinder-shaped design offers stability and compression to keep your shot column just as it should be and your shot free of deformation. It is available in 1- and 1 1/8-ounce configurations and will work with most polymer-tapered hulls. 12-gauge only. Available in 500-count bags. *federalpremium.com*

FORSTER PRODUCTS

Famous for its Co-Ax press, which snaps the dies in place, relying upon the lock ring rather than the die body threads, Forster announces a pair of new products this year. First, the Co-Ax gets a bigger brother in the Co-Ax XL press. While the original Co-Ax remains a great reloading press, there are some cartridges that it cannot handle. Among these are the big Nitro Express cartridges requiring the larger die bodies and the big honkin' .50 BMG. These are the cartridges for which

Forster has developed the Co-Ax XL press. While details aren't fully ironed out at the time of this writing, you'll want to keep an eye on this if you're a fan of the big boomers. *forsterproducts.com*

HODGDON

While so many of us were saddened to hear of the passing of Bob Hodgdon, his legacy continues on in the company that bore his name for the last three-quarters of a century. Hodgdon was responsible for so many great powder options over the years and strived to keep not only his brand alive but the Winchester and IMR powder brands as well. Each year, I look forward to the annual *Hodgdon Reloading Manual*; no, it isn't a hardcover tome, but it is teeming with insightful articles and valuable load data. 2023 marks the 20th anniversary of the manual, and for under $15, you can't go wrong. At 192 pages, with over 6,000 loads and feature articles on new powders and cartridges, including the 7mm PRC, 22 GT, and Winchester's StaBALL HD and StaBALL Match, it's a must-read. *hodgdon.com*

HORNADY

Hornady has introduced a new ELD Match bullet: the 134-grain .257-inch diameter. With a G1 Ballistic Coefficient of .645 and a G7 BC of .327, the heavy-for-caliber bullet will take the quarter-bore cartridges to a new level of long-range shooting performance. Using the proprietary Heat Shield polymer tip — engineered to resist melting from the heat of atmospheric drag — the ELD Match line has proven to be a fantastic means of ringing truly distant steel. Sold in 100-count boxes.

Hornady has also released the Precision Lab Scale, a complex unit capable of handling all your reloading needs. With a 3,000-grain capacity and a display indicating weights down to .1 grain, the scale has high and low sensitivity modes and can even print a report to a spreadsheet, so you can keep all your reloading notes organized. Whether you're weighing powder charges for precision shooting, bullets for uniformity, or loading cartridges, the Precision Lab Scale can handle it all. *hornady.com*

Federal Premium's Podium Wad is now available as a reloading component.

LEE PRECISION

Lee updates its Pro 1000 progressive press in the 2023 Pro 1000. The three-station progressive press has received a facelift, making things much easier. Lee's Breech Lock dies are mounted into the new Smart Lock bushings, allowing quick and effortless changes with the 1/4-inch hex wrench (included). Lee improved cartridge ejection and added a collection bin for your fresh cartridges. Primers and powder are only dispensed if a case is present at the station (saving you from cleaning up a mess). If you're new to progressive presses, the 2023 Pro 1000 is a smart and affordable way to get your feet wet. Available in .32 S&W Short

Hodgdon Manual 2023.

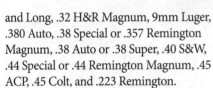

RCBS Supreme Dies.

and Long, .32 H&R Magnum, 9mm Luger, .380 Auto, .38 Special or .357 Remington Magnum, .38 Auto or .38 Super, .40 S&W, .44 Special or .44 Remington Magnum, .45 ACP, .45 Colt, and .223 Remington.

Lee also extended its Factory Crimp Die lineup to include several new cartridges, including the .30 Super Carry, 6mm GT, 8.6 Blackout, .338 Weatherby RPM, and (my favorite) the .404 Jeffery. Long famous for its segmented crimp — which will not crumple a case like a roll crimp will — the Lee Factory Crimp Die is one of those dirty little secrets reloaders use to get the best performance from their handloads. In some applications, the Lee Factory Crimp die will help even out pressures and velocities, even when using a bullet without a cannelure or crimping groove. *leeprecision.com*

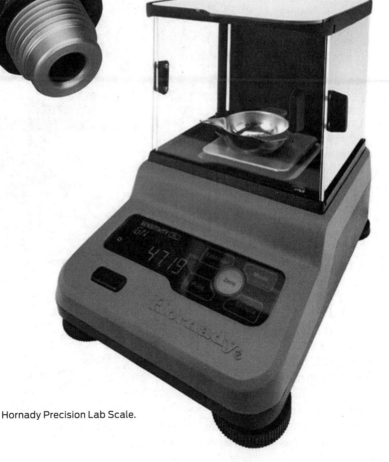

Hornady Precision Lab Scale.

RCBS

Fresh die sets are what's on the menu over at RCBS for new cartridges, such as .360 Buckhammer, 7mm PRC, and .338 Weatherby RPM. RCBS's Supreme dies are a complete package, with a full-length resizing die, seating die, proper shellholder, and a chamber case-length gauge. Available in eight popular choices, including .223 Remington, .243 Winchester, 6mm Creedmoor, 6.5 Creedmoor, .300 AAC Blackout, .308 Winchester, .30-'06 Springfield, and .300 Winchester Magnum. *RCBS.com*

REDDING RELOADING EQUIPMENT

For 2023, Redding has some nice line extensions and new products for the reloader who appreciates the utmost in precision. Redding's Master Hunter die sets have been expanded to include Category II rounds (read less-popular cartridges), including the .22 Creedmoor, 6mm Creedmoor, 6.5 PRC, 6.8 Western, .280 Remington, 7mm PRC, .300 PRC, and .33 Nosler. Featuring a carbide expander ball and Competition Seating die (with micrometer), the Master Hunter die set is a great value for those who want to take their handloads to a new level. These die sets are also available with a neck-sizing die as an upgrade.

Redding also offers its Standard dies sets for new cartridges, including the 7mm PRC and 8.6 Blackout, in addition to Custom Caliber dies sets for the 6mm ARC, .338 Weatherby RPM, and .30 Super Carry. *redding-reloading.com*

WINCHESTER POWDER

There are two new powders on the market from Winchester, and you might find they fill a niche. StaBALL Match and StaBALL HV are temperature-insensitive and REACH-compliant ball powders. They contain a copper fouling eliminator and will meter wonderfully through a powder thrower or electronic dispenser. Ball powders take up less room in the case, as the grain structure is smaller, making them a perfect choice for longer projectiles, which must be seated deeper into the case.

StaBALL Match has a burn rate similar to (but not interchangeable with) VARGET and will work well in similar applications, such as the .223 Remington, .22-250 Remington, .308 Winchester, and .30-'06 Springfield. StaBALL HD is close in burn rate (again, not interchangeable with) RETUMBO and will be a popular choice in the largest and speediest cartridges like the 6.5 PRC, 7mm Remington Magnum, and .300 PRC. Considering the voids in the powder market of the last few years — and what seems to be a continuing void in the case of RETUMBO — having a couple of new options is a good thing. Available in 1- and 8-pound canisters. *winchesterpowder.com* **GD**

Winchester StaBALL Match powder.

RCBS case-length gauge.

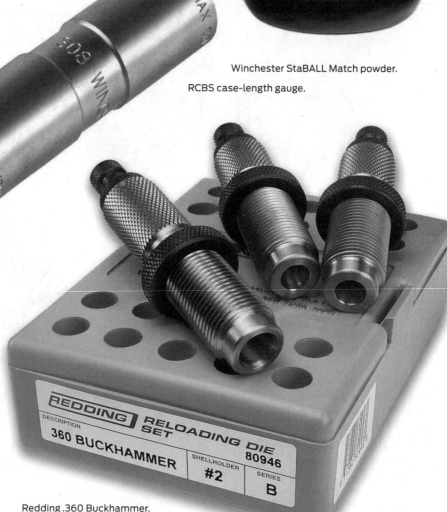

Redding .360 Buckhammer.

AUTO-ORDNANCE 1927A-1 THOMPSON
Caliber: .45 ACP. Barrel: 16.5 in. Weight: 13 lbs. Length: About 41 in. overall (Deluxe). Stock: Walnut stock and vertical fore-end. Sights: Blade front, open rear adjustable for windage. Features: Recreation of Thompson Model 1927. Semi-auto only. Deluxe model has finned barrel, adjustable rear sight and compensator; Standard model has plain barrel and military sight. Available with 100-round drum or 30-round stick magazine. Made in USA by Auto-Ordnance Corp., a division of Kahr Arms.
Price: Deluxe w/stick magazine **$1,551.00**
Price: Deluxe w/drum magazine **$2,583.00**
Price: Lightweight model w/stick mag **$1,403.00**

AUTO-ORDNANCE CASE HARDENED THOMPSON
Calibers: 45 ACP. Capacity: 20-round stick magazine. Barrel: 18-in. finned. Weight: 13 lbs. Length: 41 in. Stock: Walnut, fixed buttstock with vertical foregrip. Sights: Blade front with open, adjustable rear. Features: Hand-machined semi-automatic example of the original Thomson submachine gun, using blued steel and hard wood stocks. The Case Hardened line of Tommy Guns are meant to be a work of art built around a 1927 pattern Thompson. American made.
Price: **$1,872.00**

AUTO ORDNANCE M1 CARBINE
Caliber: .30 Carbine (15-shot magazine). Barrel: 18 in. Weight: 5.4 to 5.8 lbs. Length: 36.5 in. Stock: Wood or polymer. Sights: Blade front, flip-style rear. Features: A faithful recreation of the military carbine.
Price: **$1,036.00**
Price: Folding stock **$1,137.00**

BARRETT MODEL 82A-1 SEMI-AUTOMATIC
Calibers: .416 Barrett, 50 BMG. Capacity: 10-shot detachable box magazine. Barrel: 29 in. Weight: 28.5 lbs. Length: 57 in. overall. Stock: Composition with energy-absorbing recoil pad. Sights: Scope optional. Features: Semiautomatic, recoil operated with recoiling barrel. Three-lug locking bolt; muzzle brake. Adjustable bipod. Introduced 1985. Made in USA by Barrett Firearms.
Price: **$9,119.00**

BARRETT M107A1
Caliber: 50 BMG. Capacity: 10-round detachable magazine. Barrels: 20 or 29 in. Sights: 27-in. optics rail with flip-up iron sights. Weight: 30.9 lbs. Finish: Flat Dark Earth. Features: Four-port cylindrical muzzle brake. Quick-detachable Barrett QDL Suppressor. Adjustable bipod and monopod.
Price: **$12,281.00**

BERETTA CX4 STORM CARBINE
Calibers: 9mm, 40 S&W, .45 ACP. Barrel: 16.6 in. Stock: Black synthetic

with thumbhole. Sights: Ghost ring. Features: Blowback single action, ambidextrous controls, Picatinny quad rail system. Reintroduced in 2017.
Price: **$700.00**

BROWNING BAR SAFARI MARK II
Calibers: Safari: .25-06 Rem., .270 Win., 7mm Rem. Mag., .30-06, .308 Win., .300 Win. Mag., .338 Win. Mag. Barrels: 22–24 in. round tapered. Weights: 7.4–8.2 lbs. Lengths: 43–45 in. overall. Stock: French walnut pistol grip stock and forend, hand checkered. Sights: No sights. Features: Has new bolt release lever; removable trigger assembly with larger triggerguard; redesigned gas and buffer systems. Detachable 4-round box magazine. The scroll-engraved receiver is tapped for scope mounting. The BOSS version was discontinued. Mark II Safari was introduced in 1993. Made in Belgium.
Price: BAR MK II Safari **$1,230.00**

BROWNING BAR MK III SERIES
Calibers: .243 Win., 7mm-08, .270 Win., .270 WSM, 7mm Rem., .308 Win, .30-06, .300 Win. Mag., .300 WSM. Capacities: Detachable 4 or 5-shot magazine. Barrel: 22, 23 or 24 in.es. Stock: Grade II checkered walnut, shim adjustable. Camo stock with composite gripping surfaces available. Stalker model has composite stock. Weight: 7.5 lbs. Features: Satin nickel alloy with high relief engraving, stylized fore-end.
Price: .... **$1,340.00–$1,440.00**
Price: Left Hand .... **$1,380.00–$1,480.00**
Price: Camo **$1,380.00**
Price: Stalker .... **$1,340.00–$1,440.00**
Price: Left-hand BAR MK3 Stalker .... **$1,380.00–$1,480.00**
Price: Smoked Bronze Cerakote and OVIX camo .... **$1,719.00–$1,829.00**

BROWNING BAR MK 3 DBM SERIES
Caliber: 308 Win. Capacity: 10-round "detachable box magazine," so named for the DBM series. Barrel: 18-in. fluted blued. Length: 40-1/8 in. Weight: 7 lbs. 6 oz. Stock: Choice of two model variants. DBM Wood uses Grade II Turkish Walnut with oil finish. DBM Stalker uses black synthetic. Features: Picatinny top rail for optics mounting. Other features comparable to standard BAR Mk 3.
Price: BAR MK3 DBM Wood **$1,590.00**
Price: BAR MK3 DBM Stalker **$1,560.00**
Price: Left-hand BAR MK3 DBM Wood **$1,570.00**
Price: Left-hand BAR MK3 DBM Stalker **$1,540.00**

CENTURY INTERNATIONAL AES-10B
Caliber: 7.62x39mm. Capacity: 30-shot magazine. Barrel: 23.2 in. Weight: NA. Length: 41.5 in. overall. Stock: Wood grip, fore-end. Sights: Fixed notch rear, windage-adjustable post front. Features: RPK-style, accepts standard double-stack AK-type mags. Side-mounted scope mount, integral carry handle, bipod. Imported by Century Arms Int'l.
Price: AES-10, From **$1,735.00**

DSA SA58 STANDARD
Caliber: .308 Win. Barrel: 21 in. bipod cut w/threaded flash hider. Weight: 8.75 lbs. Length: 43 in. Stock: Synthetic, X-Series or optional folding para stock. Sights: Elevation-adjustable post front, windage-adjustable rear peep. Features: Fully adjustable short gas system, high-grade steel or 416

stainless upper receiver. Many variants available. Made in USA by DSA, Inc.
Price: From **$1,800.00**

DSA SA58 CARBINE

Caliber: .308 Win. Barrel: 16.25 in. bipod cut w/threaded flash hider. Features: Carbine variation of FAL-style rifle. Other features identical to SA58 Standard model. Made in USA by DSA, Inc.
Price: **$1,700.00**

EXCEL ARMS X-SERIES

Caliber: .22 LR, 5.7x28mm (10 or 25-round); .30 Carbine (10 or 20-round magazine). 9mm (10 or 17 rounds). Barrel: 18 in. Weight: 6.25 lbs. Length: 34 to 38 in. Features: Available with or without adjustable iron sights. Blow-back action (5.57x28) or delayed blow-back (.30 Carbine).
Price: .22 LR **$504.00**
Price: 5.7x28 or 9mm........ **$795.00–$916.00**

HECKLER & KOCH MODEL USC

Caliber: .45 ACP. Capacity: 10-round magazine. Barrel: 16 in. Weight: 6.13 lbs. Length: 35.4 in. Features: Polymer construction, adjustable rear sight, ambidextrous safety/selector, optional Picatinny rail. Civilian version of HK UMP submachine gun.
Price: **$1,499.00**

HENRY HOMESTEADER CARBINE

Calibers: 9mm Luger. Barrel: 16.3 in. round-blued steel. Weight: 6.6 lbs. Stock: American walnut. Features: Henry's first semi-automatic PPC-style rifle. Hard-anodized black receiver finish. Adjustable aperture rear sight and post front. Threaded barrel. Ambidextrous bolt handle. Swivel studs. Tang safety. All models include 5- and 10-round Henry proprietary magazines. Additional magazines and adapters sold separately.
Price: w/ Henry magazine **$928.00**
Price: w/ addition of Glock mag well **$956.00**
Price: w/ addition of Sig/S&W M&P mag well **$956.00**

INLAND M1 1945 CARBINE

Caliber: .30 Carbine. Capacity: 15 rounds. Barrel: 18 in. Weight: 5 lbs. 3 oz. Features: A faithful reproduction of the last model that Inland manufactured in 1945, featuring a type 3 bayonet lug/barrel band, adjustable rear sight, push button safety, and walnut stock. Scout Model has 16.5-in. barrel, flash hider, synthetic stock with accessory rail. Made in the USA.
Price: **$1,299.00**
Price: Scout Model **$1,449.00**

KALASHNIKOV USA

Caliber: 7.62x39mm. Capacity: 30-round magazine. AK-47 series made in the USA in several variants and styles. Barrel: 16.25 in. Weight: 7.52 lbs.
Price: KR-9 Side-folding stock **$1,249.00**
Price: US132S Synthetic stock **$799.00**
Price: US132W Wood carbine **$836.00**

RUGER PC CARBINE

Calibers: 9mm or 40 S&W. Capacity: 17 (9mm), 15 (40 S&W) pistol magazines.10-round state-compliant versions available. Barrel: 16-in. cold-hammer forged, threaded, fluted. Sights: Standard model with iron sights; chassis models with Picatinny optics rail. Length: 32.25–35.5 in. Weight: 7.3 lbs. Stock: Choice of synthetic, fixed, or adjustable aluminum chassis furniture. Features: Aluminum alloy receiver, hardcoat anodized. Utilizes 10/22 trigger components with light, crisp pull. Ergonomic pistol grip with extended trigger reach for precise control. Interchangeable magazine wells for use with common Ruger and Glock magazines.
Price: **$649.00**
Price: With handguard........ **$729.00**
Price: Adjustable Chassis **$799.00**
Price: State Compliant **$799.00**
Price: Distributor Exclusives .... **$779.00–$899.00**

RUGER MINI-14 RANCH RIFLE

Calibers: .223 Rem., .300 Blackout (Tactical Rifle). Capacity: 5-shot or 20-shot detachable box magazine. Barrel: 18.5 in. Rifling twist 1:9 in. Weights: 6.75–7 lbs. Length: 37.25 in. overall. Stocks: American hardwood, steel reinforced, or synthetic. Sights: Protected blade front, fully adjustable Ghost Ring rear. Features: Fixed piston gas-operated, positive primary extraction. New buffer system, redesigned ejector system. Ruger S100RM scope rings included on Ranch Rifle. Heavier barrels added in 2008, 20-round magazine added in 2009.
Price: Mini-14/5, Ranch Rifle, blued, wood stock **$999.00**
Price: K-Mini-14/5, Ranch Rifle, stainless, scope rings **$1,069.00**
Price: Mini-14 Tactical Rifle: Similar to Mini-14 but with 16.12 in. barrel with flash hider, black synthetic stock, adjustable sights **$1,019.00**

SIG-SAUER MPX PCC

Caliber: 9mm. 30-round capacity. Barrel: 16 in. Features: M-LOK handguard, 5-position folding telescoping stock. Weight: 6.6 lbs. Sights: none.
Price: From **$2,016.00**

SPRINGFIELD ARMORY M1A

Caliber: 7.62mm NATO (.308). Capacities: 5- or 10-shot box magazine. Barrel: 25.062 in. with flash suppressor, 22 in. without suppressor. Weight: 9.75 lbs. Length: 44.25 in. overall. Stock: American walnut with walnut-colored heat-resistant fiberglass handguard. Matching walnut handguard available. Also available with fiberglass stock. Sights: Military, square blade front, full click-adjustable aperture rear. Features: Commercial equivalent of the U.S. M-14 service rifle with no provision for automatic firing. From Springfield Armory.
Price: SOCOM 16........ **$1,987.00**
Price: Scout Squad, From **$1,850.00**
Price: Standard M1A, From **$1,685.00**
Price: Loaded Standard, From **$1,847.00**
Price: National Match, From **$2,434.00**
Price: Super Match (heavy premium barrel) about **$2,965.00**
Price: Tactical, From .... **$3,619.00–$4,046.00**

Prices given are believed to be accurate at time of publication however, many factors affect retail pricing so exact prices are not possible.

2A ARMAMENT BLR-16 RIFLES

Calibers: 5.56 NATO/.223 Rem., 16-in. barrels. 2A Armament is a subsidiary of 2A Machine, a CNC, ISO 9001 and AS 9100 certified advanced-manufacturing machining shop for the aerospace, medical, prosthetic, motorsports, semiconductor and outdoor recreation markets. Established 2009. Based in Boise, Idaho. BLR-16 Gen 2 is company's lightest rifle at 5.0 lbs. No magazine included. BLR Gen 2 Carbon has Proof Research carbon-fiber barrel, Timney 2-stage trigger, MAGPUL CTR stock, and "2A-GRAY" Cerakote finish. Palouse-Lite Rifle has forged U/L receiver. Weight: 5.3 lbs.

Price: BLR-16 GEN 2 Rifle $3,856.00
Price: BLR-16 Kuiu Vias 2.0...$2,600.00
Price: BLR-16 GEN 2 Carbon Rifle.....................................$3,675.00

2A ARMAMENT XLR-18 RIFLES

Calibers: .308 Win. Barrels: 18 in. Xanthos Lite fully assembled rifle is Cerakoted in Cobalt Grey and weighs in at 6.75 lbs. Introduced 2020. Key features include Straight Cut Xanthos Lite rail, tension lock design for attachment with an M-LOK mounting solution. Titanium parts include gas block, takedown pins, and X4 brake. Lower receiver is CNC machined 7075-T6 billet with flared mag-well, type III class 2 anodized finish, rear tensioning screw, rear takedown spring retainer, and screw-in bolt catch pin. Upper receiver has retained port door rod, M4-style feed ramps, machined T numbers in Picatinny rail. Bolt and carrier (full mass) are 8620 machined body with QPQ process, 9310 machined bolt, cryogenically treated, MPT, QPQ process. Barrel is a lightweight contour .308 profile, 4150 gun barrel steel with QPQ Nitride, black oxide extension, rifle-length gas system, .308 Match chamber, 1 in 10 twist. Other features: .750 diameter titanium gas block; titanium .308 X4 brake; BCM MOD 0 grip, BCM SOPMOD stock; Timney 2-stage, flat trigger; through-drilled titanium takedown pins.

Price: $2,659.00

2A ARMAMENT XLR-20 RIFLES

Calibers: 6.5 Creedmoor. Barrels: 20 in. Similar configuration to XLR-18 rifles. Xanthos Lite XLR-20 weight, 6.85 lbs. Barrel is 2A contour lightweight profile, 4150 barrel steel with QPQ Nitride, black oxide extension, rifle-length gas system, 6.5mm Creedmoor SAAMI Chamber, 1:8 twist.

Price: $2,725.00
Price: w/Kuiu Vias camo Cerakote finish $3,225.00

ADAMS ARMS P-SERIES RIFLES

Proprietary gas-piston operating systems mechanically actuate the bolt carrier external of the receiver. P1 model features ergonomic mid-length handguards, standard Picatinny adjustable block piston system, tactical stock and grip with QD mounts, enhanced triggerguard. Barrel lengths and chamberings: 16 in. (5.56). P2 model includes ergonomic free-float rail, P-Series Micro Block piston system. P2 barrel lengths and chamberings: 16 in. (5.56); 16 in. (.300 BLK). P3 line features Proof Research carbon-fiber-

wrapped barrel, jet comp, ergonomic free-float rail, and P-Series Micro Block piston system.

Price: P1 Rifle 16 in. $1,000.00
Price: P2 Rifle 16 in. $1,319.00
Price: Rifle .308 Win. 17 in. $2,799.00

AERO PRECISION M4E1 ENHANCED SERIES RIFLE

Chambering: .223 Wylde for .223 Rem. or 5.56 NATO. Built on Enhanced Series Upper Receiver, which has an integrated upper receiver and handguard system that's free-floated. Barrel: 16-in. .223 Wylde, mid-length, 1:8 twist, 416 stainless steel, bead blasted. Handguard: Gen 2 Enhanced Series. Gas System: Low profile gas block and mid-length gas tube. Bolt Carrier Group: M16 Cut, 8620 steel, phosphate finish, staked. Muzzle Device: Standard A2 flash hider. Stock: Magpul STR. Grip: Magpul MOE. Magazine: Magpul 30-round PMAG. Weight: approx. 7 pounds.

Price: ....$985.00–$1,090.00

ALEX PRO AR-15 RIFLES

Calibers: .204 Ruger, 22 Nosler, 5.56 NATO/, 6mm ARC, 6.5 Grendel, 6.8 SPC, .300 BLK, .350 Legend, .450 Bushmaster, 9mm Luger. Specializes in making nickel-boron bolt-carrier group and hunting-caliber AR-style rifles in both AR-15 and AR-10 sizes. Established 2013.

Price: Alpha .300 BLK $900.00
Price: APF Carbine Slim Tactical 5.56.........................$975.00
Price: APF Carbine Alpha 5.56 No Optic.......................$750.00
Price: APF Carbine Sidecharging 9mm $1,500.00
Price: APF DMR 6ARC Carbon Fiber Proof Research Barrel..............$2,000.00
Price: APF DMR Rifle 223 Wylde $2,000.00
Price: APF Varmint Sniper Green 22 Nosler $1,400.00
Price: APF Target Gray .243 Win. $1,875.00
Price: APF Hunter Texas Edition 6.8 SPC $2,000.00
Price: APF Hunter .308 Win.....................................$1,375.00
Price: APF MLR 33 Nosler.......................................$3,000.00

ALEX PRO AR-10 RIFLES

Calibers: .22-250 Rem., .243 Win. 6mm CM, 6.5 CM, .308 Win.
Price: AR-10 Target $2,550.00

ALEX PRO MLR RIFLES

Calibers: 28 Nosler, 7mm Rem. Mag., .300 PRC, .300 Win. Mag.
Price: MLR .300 Win. Mag. SST $3,200.00

ALEXANDER ARMS AR SERIES

Calibers: .17 HMR, 5.56 NATO, 6.5 Grendel, .300 AAC, .50 Beowulf.

Prices given are believed to be accurate at time of publication however, many factors affect retail pricing so exact prices are not possible.

78TH EDITION, 2024 ✦ **423**

Produces a range of AR-15-type rifles and carbines. Barrels: 16, 18, 20 or 24 in. Depending on model, features include forged flattop receiver with Picatinny rail, button-rifled stainless-steel barrels, composite free-floating handguard, A2 flash hider, M4 collapsible stock, and gas-piston operating system.

Price: .17 HMR Standard **$1,530.00**
Price: .17 HMR From **$1,150.00**
Price: .17 HMR Tactical **$1,740.00**
Price: 6.5 Grendel Hunter 18 in. **$1,560.00**
Price: .300 AAC **$1,400.00**
Price: .50 Beowulf Classic Laminate **$1,500.00**

AMERICAN TACTICAL, INC. OMNI SERIES
Calibers: 5.56 NATO, 6.5 Grendel, .300 BLK, 7.62x39. Produces a range of AR-15 type rifles and carbines. Barrels: 16, 18, 24 in. Builds include CNC-machined 7075 T6 aluminum forgings for uppers and lowers, machined to military specifications and marked "Multi-Cal" to be used with multiple calibers on the AR-15 platform. Proprietary RF85 metal treatment on some rifles.

Price: ATI Omni Hybrid Quad Rail 16 in. 5.56 .... **$449.00**
Price: ATI Omni Hybrid Maxx KeyMod 16 in. 5.56 .... **$479.00**
Price: ATI Mil-Sport OD CERAKOTE 16 in. 5.56 .... **$669.00**
Price: ATI Mil-Sport 16 in. 9mm **$969.00**
Price: ATI Mil-Sport 9mm Carbine **$899.00**
Price: AM-15 M4 Optic Ready 5.56, 16 in. **$558.00**
Price: AM-15 M4 Optic Ready 5.56, RF85, 16 in. **$773.00**

ANDERSON MANUFACTURING AM-15 RIFLES
Calibers: 5.56 NATO, 6.5 Grendel, .300 BLK, 7.62x39. This manufacturer, based in Hebron, Kentucky, produces a range of AR-15 type rifles and carbines. Barrels: 16, 18, 24 in. Builds include CNC-machined 7075 T6 aluminum forgings for uppers and lowers, machined to military specifications and marked "Multi-Cal" to be used with multiple calibers on the AR-15 platform. Proprietary RF85 metal treatment on some rifles is billed as needing "zero lubrication."

Price: AM-15 M4 Optic Ready 5.56, 16 in. **$559.00**
Price: AM-15 M4 Optic Ready 5.56, RF85, 16 in. **$775.00**
Price: AM-15 M-LOK, Magpul MOE Grip 5.56 .... **$700.00**
Price: AM-15 M4 Optic Ready 6.5 Grendel **$600.00**
Price: AM-15 M4 Optic Ready 7.62x39 .... **$790.00**
Price: AM-15 M-LOK, RF85, 300 BLK. 16 in. **$1,000.00**
Price: AM-15 Sniper M-LOK, 5.56, 24 in. barrel **$1,655.00**
Price: AM-15 Sniper M-LOK, 5.56, 24 in. RF85 .... **$1,700.00**

ANDERSON MANUFACTURING AM-10 GEN 2 RIFLES
Calibers: .308 Win., Barrels: 16, 18, 24 in. Features common to all AM-10 Gen 2 rifles include Forged 7075-T6 aluminum upper and lower receivers with Type 3 hard anodizing; 8620 steel nitrided bolt carrier; 9310 steel bolt; 4150 chrome-moly vanadium barrels, 1:10 twist rifling; standard charging handles, six-position receiver extensions, enhanced flared magwells. Models include Ranger, Battle Rifle, and Marksman XL. Introduced June 2022.

Price: Ranger .308 Win., 18 in. **$1,000.00**

Price: AM-10 M-LOK .308 Win., 18 in. **$1,200.00**
Price: AM-10 Hunter .308 Win., 18 in. **$1,500.00**
Price: AM-10 Sniper M-LOK .308 Win. 24 in. **$2,000.00**

ANDERSON MANUFACTURING AM-9 PISTOL CALIBER CARBINE
Caliber: 9mm Para. Barrel: 16-in. 4150 Chrome Moly Vanadium, 1:10 twist, 1/2-36 tpi muzzle threads. Anderson Knight Stalker Flash Hider, 15-in. Anderson M-LOK Handguard w/upper-height top Picatinny rail. Magpul furniture, K2 Grip and Black MOE stock, and PMAG 27 GL9 magazine (27 rd). Introduced 2018.

Price: AM-9 PCC **$973.00**

ARMALITE M-15 AND AR-10 COMPETITION RIFLES
Calibers: .223 Wylde (M-15) or .308 Win. (AR-10). Built for 3-Gun and practical rifle competition. Timney 4-lb. single-stage trigger, Ergo wide grip MBA-1 buttstock with adjustable cheek piece and length-of-pull. Factory ambidextrous safety and Raptor charging handle, adjustable gas block. On 13.5-in. .223 Wylde model, tunable proprietary Armalite muzzle brake is pinned and welded to create an overall length of 16 in.

Price: M-15 Competition Rifle **$2,014.00**
Price: AR-10 Competition Rifle **$2,602.00**

ARMALITE M-15 AND AR-10 TACTICAL RIFLES
Calibers: 5.56 NATO/.223 Rem., .308 Win. Slim handguard with octagonal profile, full-length MIL-STD 1913 12 o'clock rail. Adjustable gas block, Magpul MBUS flip-up sights. Non-NFA models come in barrel lengths of 14.5, 16, and 18 in. 5.56 and 16, 18, and 20 in. in .308.

Price: M-15 Tactical Rifle .... **$1,861.00–$1,881.00**
Price: AR-10 Tactical Rifle **$2,500.00**

ARMALITE M-15 AND AR-10 DEFENSIVE SPORTING RIFLES
Caliber: 5.56 NATO or .308 Win. Weight: 6.1 lbs. Forged flat-top receiver with MIL-STD 1913 rail. Optics-ready and pinned Mil-spec A2 front sight base models.

Price: M-15 Defensive Sporting Rifle **$899.00**
Price: AR-10 Defensive Sporting Rifle .308 Win. 16 in. **$1,239.00**

ARMALITE AR-10 A-SERIES SUPERSASS GEN II
Caliber: 7.62x51. SuperSASS (Semi-Automatic Sniper System) civilian model has a 15 in. Armalite Gen II M-LOK free-float handguard, Magpul PRS Gen II adjustable stock, an adjustable gas system for suppressed and un-suppressed fire. 20-in. stainless barrel, 1:10 RH twist. 11.4 lbs.

Price: AR-10 A-Series SuperSASS Gen II A10SBF **$3,799.00**

BARRETT REC7 DI DMR
Caliber: 5.56 NATO. Capacity: 20. DMR line has 18 in. 1:7.7-in. barrel. Overall length: 35.3 in. Weight: 7.9 lbs.

Price: REC7 DI DMR **$2,799.00**

BARRETT REC10
Caliber: .308 Win. Capacity: 20. Direct impingement gas system. DMR model has 16 in. barrel, 1:10 twist. Overall length: 34.5 in. Weight: 9.0 lbs. LR model has 20-in. barrel, 1:10 twist. Overall length: 41.5 in. Weight: 11.1 lbs.

Price: REC10 DMR **$2,995.00**

BLACKOUT DEFENSE QUANTUM DTL
Chamber: .223 Wylde. Barrel: 13.9, 14.5, 16 in., mid-length gas system. Pinned and welded muzzle device to exceed 16.0 in. total overall length as needed. Heavy profile, 416-R stainless steel, gun-drilled and reamed in 5R rifling and 1:8 twist. Stress relieved, precision air gauged. Dual Taper Lock (DTL) system secures and centers the barrel. Quantum-series lower receivers use patented Presslock technology with linear compression pad for a tight, rattle-free fitment, no carrier tilt. Handguard: 7-side M-LOK compatible. Stryker ambidextrous charging handle. Weight: 6.875 lbs. Black anodized is standard receiver color; several other colors are $50-$75 upcharges. Many options for gas block, charging handle, triggers, etc.

Price: .... **$2,279.00–$2,479.00**

BRAVO COMPANY MFG. BCM M4 CARBINES
Caliber: 5.56mm NATO. Capacity: 30 rounds. Barrel: 16 in., standard government profile, 1:7 twist, M4 feed ramp barrel extension. USGI

Prices given are believed to be accurate at time of publication however, many factors affect retail pricing so exact prices are not possible.

CENTERFIRE RIFLES ARs

chrome-lined bore and chamber. Mil-Spec 11595E barrel steel, manganese phosphate finish. Stock: BCM Gunfighter. Sights: Flat-top rail, post front. Weight: 6.3 lbs. Overall Length: 32.5 to 35.5 in. MOD 0 has BCM PKMR Handguard. 6.3 pounds. MOD 2 has BCM QRF Handguard. 6.5 lbs.
Price: MOD 0 ....**$1,200.00**
Price: MOD 2 ....**$1,509.00**

BRAVO COMPANY MFG. BCM RECCE CARBINES
Caliber: 5.56mm NATO. Capacity: 30 rounds. Barrels: 14.5 in., 16 in. 1:7 Twist, M4 feed ramp barrel extension. USGI chrome-lined bore and chamber. MIL-SPEC 11595E barrel steel, manganese phosphate finish. Stock: BCM. Sights: M4 feed ramp flat top with laser T-markings. Mid-length gas systems. Five models in RECCE-14 line: KMR-A and KMR-A LW, MCMR and MCMR LW, and QRF. Four additional models in RECCE-16 line: KMR-A Precision, MCMR Precision, and 300 BLK KMR-A and 300 BLK MCMR.
Price: Bravo Co. RECCE-14 KMR-A 5.56, 6 lbs....................**$1,810.00**
Price: Bravo Co. RECCE-16 KMR-A 5.56, 6.1 lbs..................**$1,500.00**

BRAVO COMPANY MFG. BCM MID16 RIFLES
Caliber: 5.56mm NATO. Mid-length gas systems. MOD 0 has PKMR handguard. MOD 2 has QRF Handguard.
Price: BCM MID16 MOD 0......................................**$1,218.00**

BRAVO COMPANY MFG. MARKSMAN RIFLES
Caliber: 5.56mm NATO. Based on the U.S. Navy MK12 Mod 0 Special Purpose Rifle (SPR), the BCM MK12 is a heavily modified DMR-type weapon. 18 in. barrels, various contours. Also includes RECCE-18 rifles. Weights: 7-9 lbs.
Price: MK12 MOD-A5 ....**$4,500.00**

BROWNELLS "WHAT WOULD STONER DO" 2020 RIFLE
Caliber: 5.56 NATO or .223 Rem (.223 Wylde chamber). Capacity: 30-round Magpul P-Mag. Barrel: 14.5 in., with titanium flash hider for OAL of 16 in., 1/2-28 tpi muzzle threads. Twist rate: 1:8, Nitride finish. Upper/Lower Receivers: KE Arms MK3 polymer receiver. Weight: 4 lbs. Trigger: SLT-1 Sear Link Technology. Overall Length: 42. Manufactured by KE Arms of Phoenix, Arizona.
Price: **$1,850.00**

BUSHMASTER M4 PATROLMAN'S MOE RIFLE
The M4 Patrolman's MOE rifle is the company's staple, with upgraded features, including Magpul furniture, a 16-in. barrel made from 4150 CMV, with a salt bath nitride finish, and a 1:7 twist rate. It comes with Magpul MOE SL handguard, CTR stock, and MOE grip in ODG. The rifle also features a Mil-spec trigger, a detachable carry handle, and an F-Marked A2 front sight. It uses PMAG Gen M2 30-round black magazines and an A2 flash hider. Made in the USA. Weight w/o magazine: 6.9 lbs. Length: 32.5 to 35.5 in.
Price: **$1,018.00**

BUSHMASTER 450 Bushmaster 20
Caliber: .450 Bushmaster. Snake Charmer muzzle brake, 20-in. barrel, 14-in. BFI free-float handguard, DM2S two-stage trigger, five-round aluminum magazine, fixed A2-style shoulder stock.
Price: **$1,103.00**

CHRISTENSEN ARMS CA5FIVE6 RIFLE
Chamber: .223 Wylde. Forged aluminum receiver set and a black nitride-finished BCG matched with a Christensen Arms carbon-fiber-wrapped 16-in. 1:8-twist stainless barrel and a carbon-aluminum hybrid handguard. Add $150 for Cerakote finish. Weight: 6.3 lbs. Sub-MOA Guarantee on all Christensen rifles. FFT model has a carbon-fiber handguard, add $200. Based in Gunnison, Utah.
Price: CA5five6 Black-Anodized 5.56 ....**$1,700.00**

CHRISTENSEN ARMS CA-15 G2 RIFLE
Chamberings: .223 Wylde, 6mm ARC. Custom-built AR-style rifle optimized for weight and accuracy. Features: Matched receiver set with contour-matching carbon-fiber handguard, black nitride-finished BCG, single-stage match-grade trigger assembly. 16-in. stainless-steel barrel, 1:8 twist. Add $400 for 16-in. carbon-fiber barrel, 1:7.5 twist. Weight: 5.8 lbs.
Price: CA-15 G2 5.56 carbon-fiber barrel **$2,400.00**

CHRISTENSEN ARMS CA-10 G2 RIFLE
Chamberings: .308 Win. (18-in. barrel, 1:10 twist) and 6.5 CM (20-in. barrel 1:8 twist) is designed for larger calibers and longer shots. Features: Aerospace-grade carbon-fiber free-floating handguard, billet aluminum receiver set, M-LOK or KeyMod fitments. Carbon-fiber barrel only. Weight: 7.2 lbs.
Price: **$3,200.00**

CHRISTENSEN ARMS CA-10 DMR RIFLE
Chambering: .308 Win. (18-in. barrel, 1:10 twist). Long-range rifle with an aluminum receiver set, proprietary barrel nut, and aerospace-grade carbon fiber handguard assembly. Comes with Christensen Arms carbon-fiber-wrapped barrel. Titanium side baffle brake, 5/8X24 threaded muzzle. Weight: 7.8 lbs.
Price: **$3,400.00**

CMMG RESOLUTE RIFLES
Calibers: .22 LR, 5.56 NATO, 5.7x28mm, 6mm ARC, 6.5 Grendel, .300 Blackout, .308 Win., 7.62x39mm, .350 Legend, 9mm Luger, .40 S&W, .45 ACP. The Mk4 is the carbine-length AR-15 direct-impingement platform. The Mk3 platform (AR-10) is based on the LR-308/DPMS Gen 1 high-pattern design. Pistol-caliber-carbine designations include MkG, MkGs, Mk9, Mk17, and Mk57. The Mk47 designation is for the 7.62x39mm chambering. Weight for the 5.56 MK4 is 6.4 lbs; length is 32.5. Add $150 for 5.7x28mm, 9mm; add $175 for Mk9 9mm with Colt-style SMG magazines.
Price: Resolute MK4 5.56x45mm NATO, 16.1 in. **$1,450.00**

CMMG ENDEAVOR RIFLES
Calibers: 5.56x45mm, 6.5 Creedmoor, .308 Win. Longer and heavier (18, 20, 24 in.) stainless barrels compared to Resolute line. Platforms: Mk3, Mk4. Lengths start at 37.8 in. for 18-in. barrel length, weight 7 lbs. Add $600 for 20-in. barrel; add $650 for 24-in. barrel
Price: Endeavor MK4 5.56x45mm NATO, 18 in. **$1,400.00**
Price: Endeavor MK3 6.5 CM, 20 in. **$2,000.00**
Price: Endeavor MK3 .308 Win., 24 in. **$2,050.00**

COLT LE6920 M4 CARBINE
Caliber: 5.56 NATO. Barrel: 16.1-in. chrome lined. Sights: Adjustable. Based on military M4. Direct gas/locking bolt operating system. Magpul MOE handguard, carbine stock, pistol grip, vertical grip.
Price: M4 Carbine...**$1,600.00**
Price: M4 Carbine Magpul.......................................**$1,200.00**

COLT M16A1 RETRO REISSUE
Caliber: 5.56 NATO. Classic design, unique triangular handguard, 20-inch pencil-profile chrome-lined barrel with a 1:12-inch twist, and recognizable carrying handle.
Price: **$2,700.00**

COLT XM177E2 RETRO CARBINE
Caliber: 5.56 NATO. Built to the Original Colt Model 629 specifications from the 1960s. 11.5-in. barrel with extended flash hider, vinyl-acetate coated aluminum buttstock reproduction, and U.S. Property-marked rollmarks.
Price: **$3,500.00**

COLT MODULAR CARBINE
Caliber: .308 Win. (7.62×51 NATO). Barrel Length: 16.1 in., chrome lined, 1:12 RH twist. Rail: 15-in. M-LOK. Length: 36.75 in. (stock extended). Weight: 8.8 lbs. Magazine: 20 rds.
Price: **$3,500.00**

DANIEL DEFENSE DD4 RIII RIFLE

Caliber: 5.56 NATO/.223. New ambidextrous DD4 lower and new 12.5-in. RIS III M-LOK rail system rather than Picatinny quad rail. Includes 6-bolt lock-up found on the RIS II, but with less weight. Ambidextrous GRIP-N-RIP Charging Handle. 16-in. cold-hammer-forged Government Profile barrel, mid-length gas system, CMV-steel, 1:7 twist. Daniel Defense Flash Suppressor, 17-4 PH stainless steel, salt bath nitride finished. Bolt Carrier Group: M16 Profile, Mil-spec MP tested, chrome lined, properly staked gas key. Daniel Defense buttstock and pistol grip. Weight: 6.52 lbs. Length: 32 1/4 to 35 7/8 in. Introduced: Spring 2022, available 2023. Made in the USA.

Price: **$2,278.00**

DANIEL DEFENSE M4A1 RIII RIFLE

Caliber: 5.56 NATO/.223. Similar to DD4 RIII but with 14.5-in. M4 barrel and pinned and welded Daniel Defense flash suppressor. Comes in FDE and black colors. Weight: 6.39 lbs. Length: 31.5 to 34.75 in.

Price: **$2,278.00**

DANIEL DEFENSE DD5 RIFLES

Calibers: 6.5 CM, .260 Rem., 7.62x51mm/.308 Win. Capacity: 20-round Magpul PMAG. Barrel: 16, 18, 20 in. 5/8×24 tpi muzzle thread, S2W barrel profile, 1:11 twist. Stock: Daniel Defense buttstock. Sights: Full-length top rail. Trigger: Daniel Defense Mil-spec. Handguard: Daniel Defense DD5 Rail 15.0, 6061-T6 aluminum, M-LOK. Weight: ~8.3 lbs. Overall Length: 33.375 to 37 in. Features: Intermediate gas system, two-position adjustable gas block, DLC-coated bolt carrier group, cold hammer chrome-lined forged barrel, Mil-spec heavy phosphate coated. 4-Bolt Connection System, ambidextrous controls (bolt catch, magazine release, safety selector, furniture, GRIP-N-RIP charging handle). Daniel Defense Superior Suppression Device, 6-position Mil-spec 7075-T6 aluminum receiver extension. Daniel Defense pistol grip, accepts all SR-25 magazines. Add $460 for Hunter model.

Price: DD5V3 (.308 Win., 16 in.)......................................**$2,650.00**
Price: DD5V4 (6.5 CM, .308 Win. 18 in.)..........................**$2,599.00**
Price: DD5V5 (6.5 CM, .260 Rem. 20 in.)...........................**$2,599.00**

DANIEL DEFENSE AR-15 RIFLES

Caliber: 5.56 NATO/.223., 6.8 SPC, .300 BLK. Non-NFA Barrels: 14.5, 16 or 18 in. Weight: 7.4 lbs. Lengths: 34.75 to 37.85 in. overall. Stock: Glass-filled polymer with SoftTouch overmolding. Sights: None. Features: Lower receiver is Mil-spec with enhanced and flared magazine well, QD swivel attachment point. Upper receiver has M4 feed ramps. Lower and upper CNC machined of 7075-T6 aluminum, hard coat anodized. Add $190 for Cerakote finishes added in 2023.

Price: DDM4V7...**$1,870.00**
Price: DDM4 V7 Matte Black **$1,907.00**
Price: DDM4V7 Pro..**$2,162.00**
Price: DDM4 V7 Pro Rattlecan **$2,396.00**

Price: DDM4 V9 ....**$2,015.00**
Price: DDM4 Hunter 6.8 ....**$1,946.00**
Price: DDM4ISR .300 Blackout **$3,390.00**
Price: DDM4V9..**$1,975.00**
Price: MK12...**$2,385.00**
Price: M4A1...**$2,240.00**

DEL-TON INC. AR-15 RIFLES

Chamberings: 5.56 NATO, .223 Wylde, 7.62x39. Del-Ton offers a complete line of AR-15-style modern sporting rifles. Dozens of variations and options. Product lines include Alpha, DT Scout, DT Sport Mod 2, Echo, Sierra, and SXT. Based in Elizabethtown, North Carolina.

Price: 5.56 models, 16, 20 in. barrels .... **$675.00–$915.00**
Price: DTI Sierra 3G, .223 Wylde, 16 in. barrel **$1,320.00**

DEL-TON INC. AR-10 RIFLES

Chambering: .308 Win. Echo optics-ready and Alpha sighted models. Upper and lower receivers: Forged 7075 T6 aluminum, integral triggerguard, 18-in. CMV 1x10 barrel, Magpul M-LOK standard length handguard, ERGO Sure Ambi grip, Magpul 20-rd. P-Mag.

Price: Alpha .308 M-LOK, 18 In. **$1,100.00**

DIAMONDBACK DB15 SERIES

Caliber: 5.56 NATO. Barrel: Diamondback Barrels 5.56, 16 in., Medium, 4150 CrMov, Black Nitride, 1:8 RH. Gas System: Carbine-Length. BCG: Shot-Peened, Magnetic Particle Inspected Mil-spec 8620 Carrier. Upper: A3 Flattop Forged 7075 T-6 Aluminum, T-Marked. Lower: 7075 T-6 Aluminum (DB-15 Carbon Lower). Handguard: 15 in. M-LOK Rail. Grip: MOE. Stock/Brace: MOE Carbine Stock. Magazine: Gen3 PMAG 30 Round. Sights: N/A. Muzzle Device: A2 Flash Hider (1/2x28). Trigger: Mil-spec. Weight: 6.6 lbs. Overall Length: 32.5 to 35.75 in. Introduced 2012.

Price: **$700.00**

DIAMONDBACK DB15 SERIES

Caliber: 5.56 NATO. Gas System: Mid-Length. Lower: Forged 7075 T-6 aluminum [Diamondback Diamond Lower] w/enhanced skeletonized trigger Guard. Handguard: Diamondback 15 in. M-LOK anti-Rrotation (S-Rail). Grip: MOE K2+. Magpul ACS-L Stock. CMC 3.5-lb. Single-stage drop-in Trigger. Weight: 7.15 lbs. Length 34 to 37.25 in.

Price: **$1,680.00**

DIAMONDBACK DB10 SERIES

Caliber: 6.5 Creedmoor, .308 Win. Barrel: Diamondback Barrels mid-length 16 in., light, 4150 CrMov, black nitride, 1:10 RH twist: Gas System: Mid-Length. BCG: Shot-Peened, Magnetic Particle Inspected Mil-spec 8620 Carrier. Upper: A3 flattop forged 7075 T-6 aluminum. Lower: Forged 7075 T-6 aluminum. Handguard: 15-in. M-LOK rail. Grip: MOE K Grip. Stock/Brace: MOE Carbine Stock. Magazine: Gen M3 PMAG 20 Rd. Muzzle Device: A2 .30 Cal Flash Hider [5/8x24]. Weight: 8.2 lbs. Length 31-1/8 in. to 33-3/4 in.

Price: DB10CCMLB .308 Win. **$1,146.00**
Price: DB1065CBGB 6.5 CM **$1,600.00**

DRD TACTICAL APTUS TAKEDOWN RIFLE
Calibers: 5.56 NATO, .223 Rem., .300 Blackout. Fits in a supplied hard case, 18.27x14.41 in., or backpack. Latin for "ready." Can go from box-to-built in 60 seconds or less without the use of tools. Also, cartridge changes can be made with barrel swaps, not additional uppers. Barrels: 5.56mm (1/7 twist) or .300 Blackout (1.8 twist), 16 in. Black hardcoat type III anodizing or NIB Battleworn finish. Operation: Semi-automatic direct impingement. Upper & lower from billet aluminum, aluminum handguard. Overall Length: 34 in. Weight Empty: 7 lbs. Non-reciprocating left-side charging handle, ambidextrous bolt catch, standard safety and magazine release. Trigger: Standard with 4.5-lb. pull. Adjustable gas block, full-length 1913 rail; M-Lok compatible, adjustable folding stock. Made in the USA.
Price: **$2,950.00**

DRD TACTICAL KIVAARI TAKEDOWN RIFLE
Caliber: .338 Lapua Magnum. Barrel: 24 in. Length: 47 in. Weight empty: 13.6 lbs. Fits in a supplied hard case, 28.87x16.77 in., or backpack.
Price: **$5,650.00**

DSARMS AR15 ZM4 5.56 RIFLES
Caliber: 5.56 NATO. Capacity: Magpul Custom G2 MOE 30-round magazine, black with flat dark earth ribs. Barrels: 14.7, 16, and 20 in., lightweight mid-length. 1:8 twist, M4 feed ramps on both barrel extension and upper receiver. Stock: B5 Systems Custom SOPMOD Stock. Weight: 6.9 lbs. Trigger: ALG Defense Advanced Combat Trigger. Overall Length: 33 to 35 in. Features: Premium match barrel machined from either 416-R stainless steel or 4150-11595 Mil-spec material, 5.56 match chamber. Enhanced A3M4 upper receiver, upgraded fire control group, ambidextrous selector switch and WarZ triggerguard, bolt catch and charging handle. Midwest Industries 15 in. Combat Series M-LOK free float handguard. Magpul Custom MIAD Modular Pistol Grip, flat dark earth with black two-tone. DSArms Enhanced FDE alloy triggerguard, SureFire Pro Comp (1/2x28 tpi).
Price: Flat Top Carbine **$665.00**
Price: Combat Companion **$870.00**
Price: A3 M4 Flat Top Carbine **$800.00**
Price: FDE **$1,150.00**
Price: Titanium **$1,150.00**

DSARMS AR15 SERVICE SERIES
Caliber: 5.56 NATO. Capacity: ASC 30-round gray alloy magazine. Barrel: 14.5 in. with permanently affixed A2 bird cage flash hider for 16 in. barrel O.A.L., or 20" A2 government profile rifle-length barrel. M4-profile, chrome-lined chamber and bore, 4150 - 11595E Mil-spec barrel steel, 1:7 twist. Stock: Mil-spec. M4 style, six-position Mil-spec buffer tube. Sights: Top rail segments. Forged front sight tower (F-Marked). Weight: 6.9 lbs. Features: Carbine-length gas system, M4 feed ramps on both barrel extension and upper receiver. Stainless-steel carbine-length gas tube, Knight's Armament Co. M4 RAS carbine-length handguard assembly. Knight's forward vertical grip. DSArms-forged A3M4 Mil-spec upper receiver, DSArms forged lower receiver, both hardcoat anodized per MIL-A-8625F, Type III, Class 2 finish. Mil-spec M16 complete bolt carrier group. Mil-spec A2-style pistol grip.
Price: **$1,200.00**

F-1 FIREARMS B.Y.O.B. BDRX-15 SKELETONIZED RIFLE
Caliber: .223 Wylde chamber for 5.56 NATO or .223 Rem., .224 Valkyrie, .300 AAC, 7.62x39mm. Modular build; user selects options on almost all components. Barrel: 16 in. (standard) or 18 in., light, medium, fluted contours, 1:8 twist. 1:10 twist on 7.62x39mm, stainless and black-nitride finishes. Upper/Lower Receivers: 7075-T6511 BDRx-15 billet receiver matched set, skeletonized. Weight: 8 lbs. Introduced 2019. 60-degree beveled mag well.
Price: **$1,800.00**

F-1 FIREARMS FDR-15 RIFLE
Caliber: 5.56 NATO. Mil-spec base model rifle with enhanced tolerances. 7075-T6511 lower, upper, and handrail with a match-grade barrel. Barrel: 16 in. medium contour, 1:8 twist.
Price: **$850.00**

F-1 FIREARMS FU KING F15 FORGED RIFLE
Caliber: 5.56 NATO. FU KING F15 forged receiver set, 13-in. M-LOK free-float handguard, 16-in. 1:8 twist stainless barrel. Black nitride bolt-carrier group, MIL-SPEC stock, grip, and charging handle. A2 flash hider.
Price: **$850.00**

F-1 FIREARMS PATRIOT FDR-15 RIFLES
Caliber: 5.56 NATO. Mil-Spec base model rifle with enhanced tolerances. 7075-T6511 lower, upper, and handrail with a match-grade barrel together capable of sub MOA. Barrel: 16 in. medium contour, 1:8 twist.
Price: **$1,170.00**

F-1 FIREARMS B.Y.O.B. BDRX-10 SKELETONIZED RIFLE
Calibers: .308 Win., 6.5 Creedmoor. Similar to BDRX-15 line. Barrels: 16, 18, 20 in., 1:10 twist, medium contour (.308, 416 stainless steel), 22 in. Criterion (6.5 CM). Add $250 for Proof Research carbine-fiber barrel. Large-frame DPMS High-profile compatible. Accepts all Mil-spec (DPMS) patterned parts as well as SR25-pattern mags.
Price: **$2,450.00**

FN 15 DMR3 RIFLE
Caliber: 5.56 NATO. The Designated Marksman Rifle (DMR) includes 18-in. barrel, SureFire ProComp muzzle brake, and Geissele two-stage trigger in matte black anodize, flat dark earth (FDE) or tungsten gray Cerakote colors. Barrel: Hybrid profile, cold hammer-forged, chrome-lined, 1:8 twist. Made from FN's proprietary machine-gun-barrel steel. Rifle-length direct-impingement gas system with pinned low-profile gas block. Hodge Defense 14 5/8-inch aluminum handguard free-float barrel. Continuous MIL-STD Picatinny rail at 12 o'clock, multiple M-LOK attachment slots. Mil-spec lower receiver, M16-style bolt carrier group. Ergonomic pistol grip, six-position collapsible carbine stock, 30-rd. magazine, Radian Raptor-LT ambidextrous charging handle and Radian Talon ambidextrous safety selector. Length: 35.2 to 38.5 in. Weight: 7.4 lbs. Introduced May 2022.
Price: **$2,439.00**

FN 15 SERIES
Caliber: 5.56x45. Capacity: 20 or 30 rounds. Barrels: 16 in., 18 in., 20 in. Features: AR-style rifle/carbine series with most standard features and options.

Prices given are believed to be accurate at time of publication however, many factors affect retail pricing so exact prices are not possible.

78TH EDITION, 2024 ⬦ 427

Price: TAC3 Duty 16 in. **$1,700.00**
Price: TAC3 Carbine **$1,800.00**
Price: SRP G2 .... **$1,529.00**
Price: Military Collector M4 and M16 .... **$1,929.00**

FN 15 TACTICAL CARBINE FDA P-LOK

Caliber: 5.56x45mm. Capacity: 30-shot PMAG. Barrel: 16-in. free-floating and chrome-lined with FN 3-prong flash hider. Stock: B5 Systems buttstock and grip. Weight: 7.2 lbs. Finish: Flat Dark Earth. Features: P-LOK handguard, M-LOK accessory mounting system, hard anodized aluminum flat-top receiver with Picatinny rail, forward assist.
Price: **$1,499.00**

FNH SCAR 16S

Caliber: 5.56mm/.223. Capacities: 10 or 30 rounds. Barrel: 16.25 in. Weight: 7.25 lbs. Lengths: 27.5–37.5 in. (extended stock). Stock: Telescoping, side-folding polymer. Adjustable cheekpiece, A2 style pistol grip. Sights: Adjustable folding front and rear. Features: Hard anodized aluminum receiver with four accessory rails. Ambidextrous safety and mag release. Charging handle can be mounted on right or left side. Semi-auto version of newest service rifle of U.S. Special Forces.
Price: **$3,840.00**

FNH SCAR 17S

Caliber: 7.62x51 NATO/.308. Capacities: 10 or 30 rounds. Barrel: 16.25 in. Weight: 8 lbs. Lengths: 28.5–38.5 in. (extended stock). Features: Other features the same as SCAR 16S.
Price: **$4,239.00**

FNH SCAR 20S

Caliber: 7.62x51mm. Capacities: 10. Barrel: 20 in. Weight: 11.2 lbs. Lengths: 40.6-42.5 in. (extended stock). Stock: Precision adjustable for LOP, adjustable cheek piece, Hogue rubber pistol grip with finger grooves. Features: Hard anodized aluminum receiver with four accessory rails, two-stage match trigger, Semi-auto version of newest service rifle of U.S. Special Forces.
Price: **$5,000.00**

FOLDAR MOBETTA B-SERIES RIFLES

Caliber: 5.56 NATO, .223 Wylde chamber. Lower Receiver: FoldAR FLDR15. FoldAR's patented folding upper offers concealability and easy carry and transport. Folded Length: 17 5/8 in. Folded Width: 4 1/4 in. Quick-change barrel system, modular M-LOK handguard of three different lengths. Barrel: 16 in., 4150 alloy steel, QPQ Melonite black nitride finish, 1:7 twist, A2 compensator, muzzle threaded 1/2-28. Mil-spec components: BCG, grip, trigger, carbine stock, and non-adjustable gas block (.750 diameter). Overall Length: 32-7/8 in. Weight: 6.15 lbs. Introduced 2023.
Price: MoBetta B-Series Rifle, 16 in. **$1,799.00**

FOLDAR MOBETTA A-SERIES RIFLES

Caliber: 5.56 NATO, .223 Wylde chamber. 300 Blackout, 6.5 Grendel.
Price: MoBetta A-Series Rifle, 16 in. **$2,299.00**

FRANKLIN ARMORY F17-L

Caliber: .17 WSM rimfire. Capacity: One 10- or 20-round magazine. Barrel: 20 in. full contour, 1:9 RH twist. 11-degree target crown. Stock: Magpul MOE. Sights: Optics-ready 12 o'clock Picatinny rail. Weight: NA. Trigger: FN Combat Trigger, 4.75–7.75 lbs. Overall Length: 30.75 in. Features: Gas piston rimfire rifle, F17 Piston. Rotating locking bolt and piston design. 12-in. TML M-Lok handguard/upper, .17 WSN salt bath nitride bolt carrier, Ergo Sure Grip. Libertas lower.
Price: **$1,829.00**

FRANKLIN ARMORY F17-X

Similar to other F17-Series models. Barrel: 16-in. M4 Contour. Sights: Fixed front & MBUS. Lower Receiver: FAI. Handguard/Upper: Magpul MOE SL M-Lok Gray. Stock: Magpul SL. Grip: Magpul K2. Stock: A2. Grip: A2. Weight: 6.7 lbs.
Price: **$1,490.00**

FRANKLIN ARMORY BFSIII M4

Caliber: 5.56mm/.223. Capacities: 30 rounds. AR-type rifles and carbines offered with the BFSIII Binary Trigger. Barrel: 16 in., LTW Contour, 1:7 RH twist, A2 muzzle device. Stock: M4. Sights: Optics ready, 12 o'clock full-length Picatinny rail. Weight: NA. Trigger: BFSIII Binary Trigger. Overall Length: 32.5 to 35.5 in. Features: Standard charging handle, low-profile gas block, 15-in. FST Handguard/Upper, salt bath nitride bolt carrier, A2 Grip. FAI-15 lower.
Price: **$1,070**

FRANKLIN ARMORY M4-HTF R3

Caliber: .350 Legend. Capacity: One 10- or 20-round magazine. Barrel: 16 in. M4 Contour, 1:12 RH twist, Aura XTD muzzle device. Stock: B5 Bravo. Grip: B5. Handguard: 15 in. FSR. Sights: Optics ready 12 o'clock full-length Picatinny rail. Weight: NA. Trigger: BFSIII Binary Trigger or custom tuned. Overall Length: NA. Features: 350 Legend was designed for use in several American states that have specific regulations for deer hunting with straight-walled centerfire cartridges. It has the same rim diameter as a 5.56 case (.378 in.), so it can use the same bolt. Rounds will fit in a modified AR magazine. MFT EVOLV charging handle, mid-length gas system, low-profile gas block, salt bath nitride bolt carrier, FAI-15 lower.
Price: **$1,290.00**

FRANKLIN ARMORY LIBERTAS-L 16

Calibers: 5.56 NATO. Similar to other Franklin Armory offerings but with billet lower. Incorporates integrated ambidextrous, anti-rotational Quick Detach sling mounts. Textured Memory Index Point, enlarged and beveled magazine well, integral over-sized triggerguard. Front of the magazine well is also textured so it can be used as a grip for forward support. Carbine length, 6-position collapsible stock. Barrel: 16 in. M4 Contour 1:7 RH twist. Handguard: 15 in. FSR. Sights: Magpul MBUS. Mid-length gas system. Stock: Magpul CTR. Grip: Ergo Ambi Sure. Add $110 for BFSIII trigger. Add $40 for 14.5-in. barrel with TRIUMVIR muzzle device pinned and welded.
Price: **$1,700**

Prices given are believed to be accurate at time of publication however, many factors affect retail pricing so exact prices are not possible.

FULTON ARMORY FAR-15 LEGACY RIFLE
Caliber: 5.56 NATO or .223 Rem. Several builds make up the Fulton Armory AR lineup, six with fixed stocks, and five with front sight posts. Legacy specs include the Upper Receiver: M16 Slick Side, with new A1 rear sight (forged, machined, anodized). Retro 601 charging handle. Parts: GI & True Mil Spec, GI Chrome M16/AR15 HPT/MPI Bolt with HD extractor spring, early slip ring. Barrel: 20 in. 1x12, "pencil" profile, match quality, chrome lined, .223/5.56 NATO hybrid match chamber. Handguard: New M16, triangular. Gas Block/Front Sight: Forged, with bayonet lug, taper pinned. Front Sight Post: A1, round. Muzzle Device: 3-prong flash suppressor. Lower Receiver: FA, with Accu-wedge (forged, machined, anodized, & Teflon coated per mil spec). Butt Stock: Fixed, A1 with A1 butt plate. Grip: A1. Trigger: Standard military, single-stage. Included accessories: FA 10-round magazine, OD cotton web sling, and owner's manual. Precision Guarantee: 1.5 MOA with Federal Gold Medal Match Ammunition. Weight: 6.75 lbs. Length: 39 in.
Price: **$1,550.00**

FULTON ARMORY FAR-15 A2 AND A4 SERVICE RIFLES
Similar to FAR-15 Legacy rifle, but with 20 in. barrel, 1x7, A2 Government Profile, match quality, chrome lined, .223/5.56 NATO Hybrid Match Chamber and 12 in. round A2 handguard with heat shields. A2 weight: 8.05 lbs. A4 lacks carrying handle and has a top receiver Picatinny rail.
Price: FAR-15 A2 ....**$1,450.00**
Price: FAR-15 A4 ....**$1,275.00**

FULTON ARMORY FAR-15 PEERLESS NM A4 SERVICE RIFLE
Similar to FAR-15 Legacy rifle, but with 20 in. 1x8 barrel, HBAR profile, match quality, stainless steel, .223/5.56 NATO hybrid match chamber. Handguard: 12 in., round A2, modified for float tube.
Price: **$1,500.00**

GEISSELE AUTOMATICS SUPER DUTY RIFLE
Chamberings: 5.56 NATO. Features a Nanoweapon-coated Surefire Closed-Tine Warcomp mounted to a 16-in. mag-phosphate cold hammer-forged, chrome-lined Geissele barrel. Twist: 1:7 in. Gas system: Geissele Length, with Geissele Super Compact Gas Block. Trigger: SSA-E X with Lightning Bow trigger, a nanocoated, two-stage unit. BCG: Machined from mil-spec 8620 steel, properly torqued and staked chrome-lined gas key. Lower: Machined from 7075-T6 aluminum with Geissele's Ultra Duty Lower Parts Kit. Ambidextrous Super Configurable safety and Ultra Precision triggerguard. Mil-spec Geissele Buffer Tube with Super-42 in H2 buffer ensures this rifle is properly tuned out of the box. 15 MK16 Super Modular Rail mates to Super Duty Upper Receiver via a center aligning tab. Sights: None. Grips: Geissele Rifle Grip. Rails: 15 in. MK16 Super Modular. Stock: B5 Enhanced Sopmod. No magazine. Colors: Luna Black, DDC (Desert Dirt Color), ODG (OD Green). Add $225 for 14.5-in. barrel with Nanocoated Surefire Closed-Tine Flash Hider, pinned and welded.
Price: **$2,100.00**

HECKLER & KOCH MODEL MR556A1
Caliber: .223 Remington/5.56 NATO. Capacity: 10+1. Barrel: 16.5 in. Weight: 8.9 lbs. Lengths: 33.9 to 37.68 in. Stock: Black synthetic adjustable. Features: Uses the gas piston system found on the HK 416 and G26, which does not introduce propellant gases and carbon fouling into the rifle's interior.
Price: **$3,500.00**

HECKLER & KOCH MODEL MR762A1
Caliber: 7.62x51mm/.308 Win. Otherwise, similar to Model MR556A1. Weight: 10 lbs. w/empty magazine. Lengths: 36 to 39.5 in. Features: Variety of optional sights are available. Stock has five adjustable positions.
Price: **$4,300.00**

HK-USA MR762A1 LONG RIFLE PACKAGE II
Caliber: 7.62x51mm. Capacity: 10- or 20-round magazines. Barrel: 16.5 in., four lands and grooves, right twist, 1:11. Stock: Fully adjustable G28 buttstock. Sights: Leupold 3-9VX-R Patrol 3-9x40 mm scope, base, mounts. Weight: 10.42 lbs. Trigger: Two stage. Overall Length: 36.5 to 40.5 in. Features: MR762 semi-auto rifle with LaRue/Harris bipod, new long 14.7 in. Modular Rail System (MRS) handguard, Blue Force Gear sling and sling mount, one 10-round and one 20-round magazine, OTIS cleaning kit, HK multi-tool, and Pelican Model 1720 case.
Price: **$7,450.00**

JP ENTERPRISES JP-15 SMALL-FRAME READY RIFLES
Caliber: .223/5.56. Mil-spec forged 7075 receiver set with Magpul MOE trigger guard. Barrel: 16- or 18-in. JP Supermatch 416R barrel, 1:8 twist, black Teflon finish. JP tactical compensator. Hogue Overmolded buttstock, A2 grip, Rapid Configuration hand guard, rifle length, with JPHG-SM QD sling mount. JP Full Mass Operating System with EnhancedBolt assembly. JP LE Enhanced Reliability Fire Control Package, 4.0 to 4.5 lbs.
Price: ....**$1,650.00–$2,400.00**

JP ENTERPRISES JP-15 LARGE-FRAME READY RIFLE
Caliber: 6.5 Creedmoor, .308 Win. Similar to JP-15 Small-Frame Ready Rifles.
Price: **$4,060.00**

JP ENTERPRISES LRP-07
Calibers: .308 Win, .260 Rem., 6.5 Creedmoor, 6mm Creedmoor. Barrels: 16–22 in., polished stainless with compensator. Buttstock: A2, ACE ARFX, Tactical Tactical Intent Carbine, Magpul MOE. Grip: Hogue Pistol Grip. Features: Machined upper and lower receivers with left-side charging system. MKIII handguard. Adjustable gas system. Subtract $200 for LTI-23 Top-Charge Upper.
Price: **$3,500.00**

Prices given are believed to be accurate at time of publication however, many factors affect retail pricing so exact prices are not possible.

78TH EDITION, 2024 ✛ 429

JP ENTERPRISES JP-15

Calibers: .223, 6.5 Grendel, .300 Blackout, .22 LR. Barrels: 18 or 24 in.
Buttstock: Synthetic modified thumbhole or laminate thumbhole. Grip: Hogue
Pistol grip. Basic AR-type general-purpose rifle with numerous options.
Price: Professional Rifle $2,100.00

JP ENTERPRISES ASF-20 AMBIDEXTROUS RIFLE

Caliber: .223/5.56, 6.5 Grendel, .300 AAC Blackout, .22 LR. Combines A-DAC
(Ambidextrous Dual Action Catch) system from Radian Weapons with JP
Ambi Mag Release. Compatible with any mil-spec pattern upper receiver.
Choice of JP Low Mass Operating System, JP Full Mass Operating System, or
JP Variable Mass Operating System. Trigger: JP Fire Control Package, 3.0 to
5.0 lbs. Ambi lower receiver introduced 2020.
Price: $2,500.00

JP ENTERPRISES LRI-20 PRECISION RIFLE

Calibers: 6mm and 6.5 Creedmoor, .260 Rem. and .308 Win. Capacity:
Magazines vary by chambering. Receiver: Machined from billet 7075-T6
upper/lower receiver set with left-side charging system on the upper
receiver. Matte-black hardcoat anodizing on aluminum components.
Barrel: JP Supermatch 416R air-gauged, button-rifled, cryogenically treated
barrel Thermo-Fit to the receiver, polished stainless, JP Compensator.
Stock: Hogue OverMolded, Magpul MOE, Magpul CTR, LUTH-AR
"Skullaton," or Mission First Tactical BATTLELINK. Handguard: JP MK III
system (Signature or Rapid configuration). Grip: Hogue pistol grip. Sights:
Optics ready top rail. Weight: NA. Trigger: JP Fire Control Package available
in weights of 3.5 to 4.5 lbs. Features: Scaled-down version of the LRP-07
available with the same caliber, barrel, handguard, metal finishing and
stock options as the CTR-02. An exaggerated bevel on the magazine well.
A new integral handguard nut stabilizes the barrel mount and front pivot-
pin joint. MicroFit Takedown Pins, lightened military-style upper design,
dust cover and forward assist paired with dedicated side-charging handle.
Thermo-Fit installation. LRI-20 upper assemblies pair with any existing LRP-
07 side-charge lower. JP adjustable gas system; JP .308 Low Mass Operating
System with JP High-Pressure Enhanced Bolt. Introduced 2019.
Price: $3,500.00

KEL-TEC RFB

Caliber: 7.62 NATO/.308. 20-round FAL-type magazine. Barrel: 18 in. with
threaded muzzle, A2-style flash hider. Weight: 8 lbs. RFB stands for Rifle
Forward-ejecting Bullpup. Features: A bullpup short-stroke gas-piston-
operated carbine with ambidextrous controls, reversible operating handle,
and mil-spec Picatinny rail. Length: 27.5 in. RFB Hunter has a 24-in. barrel;
add $200. Length: 32.5 in.
Price: RFB $1,800.00

KEL-TEC SU-16 SERIES

Caliber: 5.56 NATO/.223. Capacity: 10-round magazine. Barrels: 16 or 18.5
in. Minimum length: folded 24.9 in.; overall, 35.9 in. Weights: 4.5 to 5 lbs.
Magazine storage stock holds two proprietary 10-round magazines. The
forend covers an 18.5-in. barrel and doubles as a bipod. Adjustable sights
and an integrated Picatinny-style top rail. Offered in several rifle, carbine,
and SBR variations with A, B, C, CA, D9, D12, and E designations. Add $417 for
D9 and D12 models. Add $140 for E gas-piston model, which has a threaded
muzzle and six-position stock.
Price: $575.00

KNIGHTS ARMAMENT CO. SR-15 CARBINE

Caliber: 5.56mm NATO. Barrel: 14.5 in. Chrome-lined mil-spec, proprietary
mid-length gas system. Free-floated, hammer forged, 1:7 twist. E3 round-lug
bolt design; ambidextrous bolt release, selector, and magazine release. M-LOK
handguard. Drop-in two-stage trigger. 3-Prong Flash Eliminator. Weight: 6.55
lbs. Length: 33 to 36.5 in.
Price: $2,911.00

KNIGHTS ARMAMENT CO. SR-25 E2 COMBAT CARBINE

Caliber: 7.62mm NATO/.308 Win. Ambidextrous bolt release, selector, and
magazine release. Drop-in two-stage trigger, 7.62 QDC flash suppressor. Barrel:
16 in., hammer forged, chrome-lined, 1:10 twist, 5R cut. M-LOK handguard.
Weight: 8.4 lbs. Length: 35.75 to 39.5 in. Add $875 for E2 PC variant.
Price: $4,900.00

LARUE TACTICAL PREDATOBR 5.56 RIFLE

Caliber: 5.56 NATO. Barrels: 16.1, 18, or 20 in.; 1/8 twist rate; muzzles threaded
1/2x28. Weights: 7.5 to 9.25 lbs. Manufacturer of several models of AR-style
rifles and carbines. Many AR-type options available. Hybrid between OBR and
PredatAR 5.56x45 Rifles. May be broken down and stored into the optional
Rollup Bag and Toolbox. Handguard has locking stainless-steel QD lever
system to slide off the upper assembly in seconds. Barrel can be removed with
supplied wrench, no need to remove the gas tube, gas block, or muzzle device.
No conventional AR barrel nut; handguard bolts directly to the proprietary
upper receiver, free-floating barrel. Zero-MOA upper rail. Adjustable Port
Selector Technology gas block for sound suppressor use. LaRue Tactical
6-position Retract Action Trigger (R.A.T.) stock, A-PEG grip. Introduced 2012.
Made in the USA.
Price: $2,750.00

LARUE TACTICAL PREDATOBR 7.62 RIFLE

Caliber: 7.62 NATO. Barrels: 16.1, 18, or 20 in.; 1/8 twist rate; muzzles
threaded 5/8x24. Weights: 7.5 to 9.25 lbs. Chambering in 6.5 Creedmoor
has 20 in.; 1:7.5 twist.
Price: $4,125.00

Prices given are believed to be accurate at time of publication however, many factors affect retail pricing so exact prices are not possible.

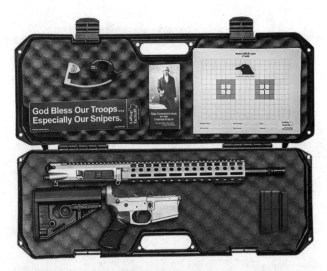

LARUE TACTICAL 16.1 IN. BLACK AND TAN 5.56
Caliber: 5.56 NATO, 6mm ARC, 6.5 Grendel. Barrels: 16.1, 18 in., 1:8 twist rate; medium-weight contour, mid-length gas tube, M4 Feed Ramps, and 1/2x28 threaded muzzle. CNC machined LaRue Billet Match Grade Upper mated to LaRue Billet. Full-floating upper handguard with M-LOK attach points, LaRue MBT trigger. LaRue Rat Stock, machined buffer tube, birdcage flash hider installed. Comes in a compact high-impact-polymer case for easy and discreet carry. Add $100 for 6.5 Grendel chambering.
Price: $2,000.00

LARUE TACTICAL PREDATAR 5.56 RIFLE
Caliber: 5.56 NATO. Chambered in .223 Wylde. Match-grade barrel, 16 and 18 in., 1:8 twist, medium-weight contour. Muzzle threaded in ½x28, with A2 flash hider. 6-position LaRue RAT Stock and LaRue A-PEG Grip. Weight: 6.25 lbs. Introduced 2011.
Price: $2,212.00

LARUE TACTICAL OBR
Calibers: 5.56 NATO/.223, 7.62 NATO/.308 Win. Barrels: 16.1, 18, or 20 in. Weights: 7.5–9.25 lbs. Features: Manufacturer of several models of AR-style rifles and carbines. Optimized Battle Rifle (OBR) series is made in both NATO calibers. Many AR-type options available. Made in the USA.
Price: OBR 5.56...$2,750.00
Price: OBR 7.62...$4,125.00

LEWIS MACHINE & TOOL RIFLES
Calibers: 5.56 NATO/.223, 7.62 NATO/.308 Win. Barrels: 16.1, 18, or 20 in. Weights: 7.5–9.25 lbs. Features: Manufactures a wide range of AR-style carbines with many options. SOPMOD stock, gas piston operating system, monolithic rail platform, tactical sights. SPM=Standard Patrol Model. MARS (Modular Ambidextrous Rifle System), fully ambidextrous. Made in the USA.

Price: Standard 16 5.56	$1,949.00
Price: SPM 16 5.56	$1,999.00
Price: DEFENDER-L 5.56	$2,150.00
Price: DEFENDER-H 7.62	$2,800.00
Price: MARS-L 5.56	$2,600.00
Price: MARS-H 7.62	$3,500.00
Price: MARS-H 6.5 DMR	$3,850.00

LWRC INTERNATIONAL IC-SPR
Caliber: 5.56 NATO. Capacity: Magpul PMAG 5.56. Barrel: 14.7, 16.1 in.; 1:7 in. RH twist, 1/2x28 muzzle threads. Cold hammer-forged, spiral fluted, NiCorr treated. Stock: LWRC adjustable compact stock. Sights: Low-profile flip-up Skirmish Sights. Weight: 7.0 lbs., 7.3 lbs.
Price: REPR MKII...$2,590.00

LWRC INTERNATIONAL IC-PSD
Caliber: 5.56 NATO. Barrel: 8.5 in. Capacity: Magpul PMAG 30-round magazine. Stock: LWRC adjustable compact stock. Sights: Low-profile, flip-up Skirmish Sights. Weight: 5.9 lbs. Trigger: LWRC Enhanced Fire Control Group. Overall Length: 25-28 in. Features: Part of the Individual Carbine series of rifles. NFA item. LWRCI Monoforge upper receiver with modular 7-in. rail system. Nickel boron-coated bolt carrier, LWRCI High-Efficiency Four-prong Flash Hider.
Price: $2,755.00

LWRC INTERNATIONAL IC-A5
Similar to IC-SPR. Caliber: 5.56 NATO. Barrel: 10.5, 12.7, 14.7, 16.1 in. Features: Has a low-profile two-position adjustable gas block allowing the shooter to compensate for running a suppressor and a longer modular rail system.
Price: $2,865.00

LWRC INTERNATIONAL IC-ENHANCED 5.56
Caliber: 5.56 NATO. Barrel: 12.7, 14.7, 16.1 in. Features: Includes a Picatinny rail at 12 o'clock, a bayonet lug, and is compatible with accessories like the M320 grenade launcher and the M26 shotgun. Add $170 for FDE and OD Green colors
Price: FDE $2,920.00

LWRC INTERNATIONAL SIX8-A5
Caliber: 6.8 SPC II. Capacity: Magpul 20 Round PMAG. Barrel: 14.7, 16.1 in.; 1:10 RH twist, 5/8x24 muzzle threads. Cold hammer-forged, spiral fluted, NiCorr treated. Stock: LWRC adjustable compact stock. Grip: Magpul MOE+. Sights: Low-profile flip-up Skirmish Sights. Weight: 6.5 lbs. Trigger: LWRC Enhanced Fire Control Group. Overall Length: 32-35.25 in. Features: LWRCI proprietary upper and lower receivers optimized for 6.8 SPC II cartridge; adjustable 2-position gas block, Birdcage (A2) Flash Hider; 12-in. user-configurable rail system; ambidextrous charging handle and lower receiver.
Price: FDE $2,870.00

LWRC INTERNATIONAL REPR MKII
Caliber: 6.5 Creedmoor, 7.62 NATO. Rapid Engagement Precision Rifle. Capacity: Magpul 20 Round PMAG. Barrel: 12.7, 16.1, 20, and 22 in. stainless steel. 1:8 RH twist, 5/8x24 muzzle threads. Stock: Magpul PRS. Grip: Magpul MOE+. Sights: Low-profile flip-up Skirmish Sights. Weight: 10.5 lbs. Trigger: Geissele SSA-E 2-Stage Precision. Overall Length: 43.5 in. Non-reciprocating side charging handle, 20-position tunable gas block, short-stroke gas piston system, Monoforge upper receiver with integrated rail base, removable top rail design, removable barrel, fully ambidextrous lower receiver controls including bolt catch and release, magazine release, and safety selector. LWRCI Advanced Triggerguard, Skirmish Back-Up Iron Sights, Enhanced 4-port Ultra Static muzzle brake. Add $560 for Proof carbon-fiber barrel.
Price: REPR MKII...$4,485.00

MIDWEST INDUSTRIES COMBAT RIFLES
Caliber: 5.56 NATO/.223 Rem., .223 Wylde. Barrels: 16, 18, 20 in. Upper receiver: Forged 7075 T6 aluminum, M16/M4 specs, M4 feed ramps,

Prices given are believed to be accurate at time of publication however, many factors affect retail pricing so exact prices are not possible.

78TH EDITION, 2024 ✦ **431**

hardcoat anodized Mil 8625 Type-3 Class-2 Finish, .250 takedown pins. MI M16 bolt carrier group, MI-CRM12.625 Combat series handguard, M-LOK compatible. Criterion barrels, mid-Length hybrid profile, 1:8 twist, .223 Wylde chamber, chrome-lined, .625 diameter. A2 flash hider. Lower receiver: Receiver rear takedown pin detent hole threaded for a 4-40 set screw, Mil-spec-diameter buffer tube. Magpul CTR buttstock, MOE grip, MOE triggerguard. Heavy-duty quick-detach end plate.

Price: 16 in. **$1,400.00**
Price: 18 in. **$1,300.00**
Price: 20 in. **$1,500.00**

MIDWEST INDUSTRIES MI .308 RIFLES
Caliber: .308 Win. Capacity: (1) Magpul 10 round; accepts SR-25 pattern magazines. Barrel: 16, 18 in.; Criterion 1:10 twist, stainless-nitride finish. Upper/Lower Receivers: Forged 7075 aluminum. Stock: Magpul Gen 3 PRS buttstock. Grip: Magpul MOE. Sights: Optics-ready top rail. Weight: 8.2 lbs. for MI-10F-16M. Features: Midwest Industries .308 bolt carrier group, 12-in. M-LOK handguard, two-chamber enhanced muzzle brake, mid-length gas system .750-in. gas block, MI-HDEP heavy-duty quick-detach end plate. Add $50 for 18-in. Criterion barrel. Introduced 2015.

Price: **$1,700**

MIDWEST INDUSTRIES MI TACTICAL RESPONSE RIFLE
Caliber: 5.56 NATO/.223 Rem. Weight: 6.25 lbs. Outfitted with Magpul CTR Stock, MOE grip, MOE triggerguard, heavy duty quick detach end plate MI-HDEP, and has Custom Tactical Response logo laser engraved on receiver. Barrel: 16 in., 1:8 twist. Weight: 6.5 lbs.

Price: **$1,500.00**

NOVESKE RIFLEWORKS GEN 4 N4 PDW
Calibers: 5.56 NATO, 6.5 Grendel, .300 BLK. Barrel: 16 in., stainless steel hammer-forged, muzzle thread pitch 1/2×28. Twist: 1:7. Low-profile adjustable gas block, direct impingement. PDW-style collapsible stock. M-LOK free-float handguard, Magpul MBUS PRO folding sights, and a Geissele Super Badass charging handle. Full-length Picatinny rail, ambidextrous safety selector.

Price: **$3,150.00**

NOVESKE RIFLEWORKS CHAINSAW RIFLE
Caliber: 5.56 NATO/.223 Rem. Noveske's forged product offering based on a hybrid of Gen 1 and Gen 4 designs. Barrel: 16 in. 416R stainless, 1:7 twist. Hand-polished Noveske Match Chamber, mid-length gas tube system. Noveske marked gas block: Low profile, .750 in. journal, pinned to barrel. M4 barrel extension w/extended hand-polished feed ramps, 1/2x28 muzzle threads with an A2 birdcage flash hider. Noveske Chainsaw forged upper receiver w/extended feed ramps. Radian Raptor LT charging handle. Phosphate-coated bolt carrier, full auto compatible, chrome-lined carrier bore and key. Properly staked Grade 8 American-made gas key bolts. Phosphate bolt made from Carpenter 158 heat-treated steel, MPI tested. GEN 4 NSR-15 (M-LOK) free-floating handguard. Flared magazine well. Magpul-enhanced aluminum triggerguard. ALG Defense Advanced Combat Trigger. Stock: Magpul MOE SL. Grip: Magpul MOE K2. Length collapsed: 35 1/4 in. 6.8 lbs. One 30-rd. Gen 3 PMAG. Introduced 2022.

Price: **$2,000.00**

PALMETTO STATE ARMORY AR-15 RIFLE
Chamber: 5.56 NATO. Barrel: 16 in. 4150V Chrome Moly Vanadium Steel, Nitride finish. Barrel Profile: A2 style. Twist Rate: 1:7. M4 extension. Mid-length gas system, Low profile .750-in. gas block. Upper Receiver Style: M4 flat top with feed ramps. Handguard: PSA 13.5 in. Lightweight M-Lok free-float rail. Bolt Steel: Carpenter 158. Bolt Carrier Steel: 8620. Staked gas key. PSA AR-15 Enhanced Polished Trigger (EPT). Mil-spec buffer tube. Magpul MOE Carbine six-position collapsible stock. (1) 30-round magazine (where available by law). Backup Sights: Magpul MBUS. Length: 32 in.

Price: **$1,000.00**

PALMETTO STATE ARMORY GEN 3 PA-10
Caliber: 6.5 Creedmoor, .308 Win. Barrels: 18- or 20-in., stainless-steel heavy barrel, adjustable gas block. Buttstock: PSA Classic M4 Stock, Black 6-position adjustable. Handguards: PSA Classic Polymer Midlength Handguard, Keymod or M-Lok compatible free-floated.

Price: **$1,099.00**

PALMETTO STATE ARMORY H&R M16A1
Caliber: 5.56 NATO. Copy of the gas-operated semi-automatic M16A1 with a 20-in. barrel. Harrington & Richardson was one of only four manufacturers to have made an official M16 variant for the U.S. military. Fixed synthetic stock, A2 carry handle receiver, smooth rifle-length handguard, A2 front sight. Includes sling swivels, 20-round magazine.

Price: **$1,499.00**

PATRIOT ORDNANCE FACTORY MINUTEMAN RIFLE
Caliber: 5.56 NATO, .350 Legend. Direct Impingement. Nitride heat-treated barrel, 16.5 in. Features: Rear QD ambidextrous sling swivel plate, anti-tilt buffer tube, ambidextrous Strike Eagle charging handle. 3.5-lbs. straight match-grade trigger. Mid-length gas system. 6.2 lbs. 34 in. length. Introduced 2022. Add $134 for Patriot Brown or Tungsten finishes.

Price: **$1,613.00**

PATRIOT ORDNANCE FACTORY P415 EDGE
Caliber: 5.56 NATO. Gas-piston operation. Barrel: 16.5 in. Rail length: 14.5 in. Weight: 7 lbs. Collapsed length: 34 in. E2 Extraction Technology, complete ambidextrous fire controls, modular free-floating rail platform, redesigned handguard. Add $134 for Burnt Bronze, Olive Drab, and Tungsten finishes.

Price: **$2,150.00**

PATRIOT ORDNANCE FACTORY PRESCOTT
Caliber: 6mm Creedmoor, 6.5 Creedmoor. Built on Rogue platform. Weight: 7 lbs. Barrel: 20 in. Collapsed length: 41 in. Introduced 2021. Add $134 for Patriot Brown finish. Add $215 for 6mm Creedmoor chambering.

Price: **$2,285.00**

PATRIOT ORDNANCE FACTORY ROGUE

Caliber: 7.62x51mm NATO (.308 Win.) Capacity: One Magpul 20-round magazine. Barrel: 16.5 in., 1:8 twist, 5/8x24 tpi muzzle threads, match-grade stainless steel, Micro-B muzzle brake. Stock: Mission First Tactical. Sights: None, optics-ready with top Picatinny rail. Weight: 5.9 lbs. Trigger: 4.5-lb. POFUSA drop-in trigger system with KNS anti-walk pins. Length: 34 in. Roller cam pin with NP3-coated roller head. Introduced 2020. Add $134 for Patriot Brown or Olive Drab finishes.

Price: **$2,097.00**

PATRIOT ORDNANCE FACTORY REVOLUTION DI

Caliber: 7.62x51mm NATO (.308 Win.) or 6.5 Creedmoor. Introduced 2019. Similar to PD Revolution, but with direct-impingement operation, nine-position adjustable Dictator gas block and Renegade rail. Weight: 6.8 lbs. Barrel: 16.5 in., 18.5 in. for .308 Win.; 20 and 22 in. for 6mm CM and 6.5 CM. Gen 4 ambi lower receiver. Add $134 for Burnt Bronze or Tungsten finishes. Introduced 2019.

Price: **$2,769.00**

PATRIOT ORDNANCE FACTORY WONDER RIFLE

Caliber: 5.56 NATO. Direct impingement. Barrel: 16.5 in. Match-grade Nitride heat-treated Puritan barrel, 1:8 twist, 1/2x28 barrel threads. Lightweight carbine with some upgrades. Ambidextrous rear sling mount, Renegade Rail with heat sink barrel nut, DI bolt carrier group with Roller Cam Pin, single-stage straight match-grade trigger, Strike Eagle Ambi Charging Handle, Micro B single-port muzzle brake. Weight: 6.18 lbs. Length: 3 in. Introduced 2022.

Price: **$1,775.00**

RED ARROW WEAPONS RAW15 .300 BLACKOUT

Caliber: .300 BLK. Barrel: 16 in. free-floated Melonite-coated 4150 chrome-moly barrel, 1:8 twist, DB15 556 muzzle brake, threaded 5/8x24. Red accents on black-anodized hardcoat finish. CMC 2.5-lb single-stage trigger, pistol-length gas system, Magpul CTR stock, Magpul K2+ grip, M-Lok forend. Length: 32.5 to 36.25 in. Weight: 6.9 lbs. Handguard: 15-in. RAW M-LOK Battle Rail. Ambidextrous safety selector, MagPul K2+ Grip, MagPul CTR Stock, Magpul P-Mag 30 rd. Introduced: 2022. 5.56 NATO, 6.5 CM, and .308 Win. chamberings also available. Based in Fork Union, Virginia.

Price: .... **$1,397.00–$1,462.00**

ROCK RIVER ARMS ASCENDANT SERIES

Caliber: .223 Wylde, .350 Legend, .450 Bushmaster. Length: 38.125 in. (collapsed). Weight: 9.4 lbs. Barrel: 18.0-in. 416R fluted stainless steel, media-blasted, cryo-treated. Handguard: RRA 13-in. lightweight, M-LOK, full 12-o'clock Picatinny rail. Trigger: TriggerTech Diamond Single-Stage AR-15 trigger, adjustable from 1.5 to 4 lbs. of pull weight. Magpul PRS Lite stock, Hogue overmolded rubber grip, ambidextrous Radian Raptor charging handle. Also includes Vortex Viper HS 4-16X 44mm riflescope or Vortex Strike Eagle 1-6X 24mm optic. Introduced 2023.

Price: AR1562.A .223 Wylde **$3,235.00**
Price: 350L1562.A .350 Legend **$3,020.00**
Price: 450B1562.A .450 Bushmaster **$3,075.00**

ROCK RIVER ARMS LAR-15 SERIES

Calibers: .223/5.56, .223 Wylde chamber. Rifles and carbines available with a wide range of options, including left-hand versions. Individual nameplates include All Terrain Hunter (ATH), Coyote Carbine, Fred Eichler Series, NM A4, Operator ETR, Predator Pursuit, RRage, X-Series, and others.

Price: .... **$820.00–$2,365.00**

ROCK RIVER ARMS LAR-BT6 .338 LAPUA MAGNUM

Chambering added in 2022. Barrel: 24-in. black nitride stainless steel, 1:10 twist, four-port brake. RRA Ultra Match two-stage trigger. Quick takedown design. Weight: 13.5 lbs. Length: 48 in. Introduced 2020.

Price: **$5,580.00**

ROCK RIVER ARMS LAR-BT3 X-SERIES X-1 RIFLE

Caliber: .308 Win. Barrel: 18 or 20 in. Weight: 8.5-9.7 lbs. Length: 36.5 to 41 in. Introduced 2022.

Price: .... **$2,125.00–$2,460.00**

ROCK RIVER ARMS VARMINT RIFLE LAR-BT3

Caliber: .308 Win. Barrel: 20 in., 1:10 twist, fluted-stainless steel heavy, cryogenically treated. Stock: RRA six-position NSP-2 CAR. Grip: Hogue Rubber. Sights: None, optics-ready full-length top rail. Weight: 9.8 lbs. Trigger: RRA Two Stage. Length: 37 to 39.75 in. Features: RRA lightweight free-float rail, 17 in. extended, M-LOK compatible. Introduced 2020.

Price: **$1,960.00**

ROCK RIVER ARMS OPERATOR ETR CARBINE

Caliber: .308 Win. Barrel: 16-in. chrome lined, 1:10 twist. Weight: 8.2 lbs. Length: 34.5 in. retracted. Stock: RRA six-Position NSP-2 CAR Stock. Hogue Beavertail Grip. Trigger: RRA Two-Stage Ultra Match Trigger. Introduced 2022.

Price: **$1,970.00**

RUGER AR-556 STANDARD

Caliber: 5.56 NATO. Capacity: 30-round magazine. 16.1 in. barrel, 1:8-in. RH twist, 1/2x28 muzzle thread pattern. Features: Basic AR M4-style Modern Sporting Rifle with direct impingement operation, forged aluminum upper and lower receivers, and cold hammer-forged chrome-moly steel barrel with M4 feed ramp cuts. Other features include Ruger Rapid Deploy folding rear sight, milled F-height gas block with post front sight, telescoping six-position stock and one 30-round Magpul magazine. Weight: 6.5 lb. Overall Length: 32.25 to 35.50 in. Introduced 2015. Add $50 for Magpul MOE furniture.

Price: **$1,019.00**

RUGER AR-556 MPR (Multi Purpose Rifle)

Caliber: 5.56 NATO, .350 Legend, .450 Bushmaster. MPR model has 16.1, 18, 18.38, and 18.63 in. barrels with muzzle brake, flat-top upper, 15-in. free-floating handguard with Magpul M-LOK accessory slots, Magpul MOE SL collapsible buttstock and MOE grip. Add $920 for Proof Research Carbon-Fiber Barrel, added December 2022.

Price: 5.56 .... **$1,129.00**
Price: 350 Legend, .450 Bushmaster **$1,309.00**

Prices given are believed to be accurate at time of publication however, many factors affect retail pricing so exact prices are not possible.

78TH EDITION, 2024 ✛ **433**

RUGER AR-556 FREE-FLOAT HANDGUARD

Caliber: 5.56 NATO, .300 BLK. 16.1-in. barrel. Similar to MPR model, with 11-in. aluminum free-floated handguard. Magpul M-LOK accessory attachment slots at the 3, 6, and 9 o'clock positions with additional slots on the angled faces near the muzzle. Introduced 2016. .300 BLK chambering added in 2019.
Price: $1,039.00

RUGER SMALL-FRAME AUTOLOADING RIFLE

Chambering: 7.62 NATO/.308 Win. The SFAR combines the ballistic advantages of .308 Win. in the size of a traditional MSR. Barrel: 16 in., cold hammer-forged, 5R rifling, 5/8x24 muzzle thread, tapered lugs, black-nitride finish. Trigger: Ruger Elite 452. Receivers: CNC-machined from 7075-T6 forgings, oversized magazine well, forward assist, dust cover and brass deflector. Four-position regulated gas block, included 3/16-in. ball-end wrench for regulator adjustment, two-port Boomer muzzle brake. Handguard: Magpul M-LOK accessory attachment slots at the 3:00, 6:00, and 9:00 positions, sockets for QD sling swivels. Model 5610: 16-in. barrel, mid-length gas system, 15-in. Lite free-float handguard. Model 5611: 20-in. barrel, rifle-length gas system, 15-in. handguard with a full Picatinny top rail. Magpul MOE SL stock, MOE grip and one 20-rd. Magpul PMAG magazine. Weight: 6.8 pounds unloaded. Introduced 2022. State-compliant models with 10-rd. magazines added 2023.
Price: $1,329.00

SAVAGE MSR 15 RECON 2.0

Calibers: 5.56 NATO/.223 Rem. Barrel: 16.125 in., 1:8 5R rifling; Melonite QPQ finish. Direct-impingement operation. Nickel-boron coated trigger, free-float handguard, Magpul adjustable buttstock and pistol grip. Recon 1.0 introduced 2017. Recon 2.0 introduced 2021. 7.3 lbs. Length: 33.5 to 36.75 in.
Price: $990.00

SAVAGE MSR 15 RECON LRP

Similar to 2.0 except chambered in 22 Nosler, .224 Valkyrie, 6.8 SPC. 18-in. barrel with 1:7 5R rifling and adjustable gas block. Magpul CTR buttstock and tunable muzzle brake.
Price: $1,249.00

SAVAGE MSR 15 LONG RANGE

Similar to Recon LRP, except chambered only in .224 Valkyrie. 22-in. stainless Savage barrel, custom-length low-profile, gas block, custom free-float handguard.
Price: $2,284.00

SAVAGE MSR 10 HUNTER

Calibers: 6.5 Creedmoor, 308 Win. Barrels: 16 in. 1:10 5R. 7.8 lbs. 35 to 39-in. length. Free-float forend, custom-forged lower receiver and Magpul adjustable buttstock and pistol grip.
Price: $1,480.00

SAVAGE MSR 10 LONG RANGE

Similar to MSR 10 Hunter, but with 20-in. carbon-steel barrel. Built on compact frame with a non-reciprocating side-charging handle.
Price: $2,284.00

SAVAGE MSR 10 PRECISION

Similar to MSR 10 Hunter, but with 22.5-in. stainless-steel heavy barrel. 18-in. Arca handguard, Magpul PRS stock, TangoDown Battlegrip Flip Grip, +2 gas system. 44 in. long, 11.4 lbs.
Price: $2,829.00

SEEKINS PRECISION SP15

Chamber: .223 Wylde/5.56 NATO. The company's entry level-platform. Barrel: 16 in., 1:7 twist 5R chromoly. Muzzle device: Seekins NEST Flash Hider 1/2x28. Receivers: SP15 7075-T6 billet upper/lower receiver set. Handguard: 15 in. SP15 M-LOK. Gas Block: Seekins Low-Profile Adjustable Gas Block. Trigger: Mil-spec. Stock: Six-position adjustable carbine stock. Weight: 7 lbs. Based in Lewiston, Idaho.
Price: $925.00

SEEKINS PRECISION SP15 DMR

Chamber: .223 Wylde/5.56 NATO. Similar to SP15, but with Seekins 10X stock.
Price: $1,795.00

SEEKINS PRECISION NX15

Chamber: .223 Wylde/5.56 NATO. Similar to SP15, but with higher-level components, including an upgraded Timney trigger, NX15 skeletonized upper/lower receiver set and NOX handguard, ambidextrous controls. Barrel: 16 in. 1:8 twist 5R 416 stainless steel. Weight: 7 lbs.
Price: $1,795.00

SIG SAUER 716i TREAD

Caliber: .308 Win. Capacity: one 20-round magazine, compatible with SR-25 magazines. Barrel: 16 in., 1:10 RH twist, stainless steel. Upper/Lower Receivers: Forged aluminum, hardcoat anodized finish. Stock: Magpul SL-K six-position telescoping stock. Sights: None, optics ready. Weight: 8.5 lbs. Trigger: Two-stage match. Overall Length: 33.8 to 37 in. Features: Direct-impingement operating system, integral QD mount, ambi safety selector, charging handle, free-floating 15-in. M-LOK handguard.
Price: $1,650.00

SIG SAUER MCX-SPEAR 277

Caliber: 6.5 Creedmoor, 7.62 NATO, .277 SIG Fury/6.8x51. Special edition commercial variant of the MCX-SPEAR is a gas-piston semi-automatic, some

of which are chambered in .277 SIG Fury, civilian variant of the U.S. Army's 6.8x51 hybrid ammunition. Features a six-position adjustable folding stock, ambidextrous controls, two-stage match-grade trigger and an adjustable gas system. The MCX-Spear will also include a free-float, M-LOK handguard with full-length Picatinny top rail for mounting optics. Barrel: 16 in. long, 1:7 barrel twist, interchangeable. Both non-reciprocating side and rear charging handles, fully ambidextrous controls including bolt release, and two-position adjustable gas piston. Comes with two boxes of .277 SIG Fury ammunition. Length: 34.1 in. Height: 7.97 in. Width: 2.98 in. Weight (w/ magazine): 8.38 lbs. Rifle, SBR, and Pistol variants. Introduced: Feb. 2023. MSRP is for first-run special edition rifle.
Price: **$7,999.00**

SIG SAUER MCX-SPEAR LT
Caliber: 5.56 NATO, 7.62x39mm, .300 Blk. 16-in. carbon-steel barrel on rifle; 11.5-in. and 9-in. for SBRs and pistols. Lightened handguard with attachment screws for additional rigidity and a lightened profile barrel. Ambidextrous bolt catch and release, minimalist, AR-15-style trigger compatibility. Interchangeable barrels, Rocksett SIG QD suppressor-ready flash hider. Barrel twist for 7.62x39 is 1:9.5; for 5.56 NATO, 1:7. Length: 34.5 in. Height: 7.5 in w/o magazine. 5/8x24 muzzle threads on 7.62x39mm barrel, 1/2x28 tpi on 5.56. Weight: 7.6 lbs. Introduced: Sept. 2022.
Price: **$2,799.00**

SIG SAUER M400 TREAD
Caliber: 5.56 NATO/.223 Rem. Capacity: one 30-round magazine, comparable with AR-15 types. Barrel: 16 in., 1:8 RH twist, stainless steel. Upper/Lower Receivers: Forged aluminum, hardcoat anodized finish. Stock: Magpul SL-K six-position telescoping stock. Sights: None, optics-ready. Weight: 7 lbs. Trigger: Single-stage, polished hardcoat trigger. Overall Length: 30.8 in. Features: Direct-impingement operating system, integral QD mount, ambi safety selector, charging handle, free-floating 15-in. M-LOK handguard, mid-length gas system.
Price: **$1,175.00**

SIG SAUER M400 TREAD PREDATOR
Chambering: 5.56 NATO. MSR platform designed for predator hunting. Aluminum frame, Cerakote Elite Jungle finish, lightweight adjustable, 16-in. 1:8-twist stainless threaded barrel with thread protector, lightened free-float M-LOK 15-in. Predator handguard, hardened polished trigger, ambidextrous controls. Ships with five-round magazines. Length: 35.5 in. Height: 7.5 in. Width: 2.5 in. Weight (with magazine): 7.5 lbs. Compatible with a full line of Tread accessories. Introduced March 2021.
Price: **$1,099.00**

SIG SAUER M400-DH3 RIFLE
Caliber: .223 Rem. or 5.56 NATO (.223 Wylde chamber). Specialized version released under world champion 3-Gun competitor and Team SIG Shooter Daniel Horner's DH3 brand. The M400-DH3 Rifle is a SIG Direct Impingement (SDI) aluminum frame rifle with a Cerakote Elite Titanium finish. DH3 fully adjustable competition stock, two-stage adjustable Timney trigger, 16-in. 1:8-twist fluted stainless barrel, three-chamber

compensator, low-profile 3-Gun handguard with M-LOK mounts, ambidextrous controls including bolt catch/release. Ships with one 30-round magazine. Length: 34.5 in. Height: 7.5 in. Width: 2.5 in. Weight (with magazine): 7 lbs. Introduced June 2022.
Price: **$1,699.00**

SIG 516 PATROL
Caliber: 5.56 NATO. Features: AR-style rifle with included 30-round magazine, 16-in. chrome-lined barrel with muzzle brake; free-floating, aluminum quad Picatinny rail, Magpul MOE adjustable stock, black-anodized or Flat Dark Earth finish, various configurations available.
Price: **$2,024.00**

SIG SAUER SIG716 TACTICAL PATROL
Caliber: 7.62 NATO/.308 Win., 6.5 Creedmoor. Features: AR-10-type rifle. Gas-piston operation with three-round position (four-position optional) gas valve; 16-, 18- or 20-in. chrome-lined barrel with threaded muzzle and nitride finish; free-floating aluminum quad rail forend with four M1913 Picatinny rails; telescoping buttstock; lower receiver is machined from a 7075-T6 Aircraft grade aluminum forging; upper receiver, machined from 7075-T6 aircraft grade aluminum with integral M1913 Picatinny rail.
Price: **$2,280.00**

SIG SAUER M400 CLASSIC
Caliber: 5.56 NATO. AR-style rifle with Direct Impingement system, 20-in. chrome-lined barrel with muzzle brake; free-floating M-LOK handguard with lightening cuts, three-chamber compensator, Magpul SLK six-position adjustable stock, various configurations available.
Price: **$1,250.00**

SIG SAUER M400 TREAD COIL
Similar to M400 Tread, but with popular features: Matchlite Duo Trigger, 13-in. lightweight M-LOK handguard, Tread Romeo5 red-dot sight, vertical foregrip.
Price: **$1,329.00**

SIG SAUER MCX VIRTUS PATROL RIFLE
Calibers: 5.56 NATO, 7.62x39mm or .300 Blackout. Features: AR-style rifle. Modular system allows switching between calibers with conversion kit. Features include a 16-in. barrel, aluminum KeyMod handguards, ambi controls and charging handle, choice of side-folding or telescoping stock, auto-regulating gas system to all transition between subsonic and supersonic loads.
Price: **$2,200.00**

SIG SAUER MPX PCC
Caliber: 9mm Luger. Gas-piston operation. Barrel: 16 in., 1:10 twist, carbon steel. M13.5x1mm muzzle threads. Magazine: MPX 30-rd polymer mag. Trigger: Timney Single Stage. Overall Length: 35.25 in. Accessory Rail: M-LOK. Weight: 6.63 lbs.
Price: **$2,180.00**

SMITH & WESSON M&P15
Caliber: 5.56mm NATO/.223. Capacity: 30-shot steel magazine. Barrel: 16 in., 1:9 in. twist. Weight: 6.74 lbs., w/o magazine. Lengths: 32–35 in. overall. Stock: Black synthetic. Sights: Adjustable post front sight, adjustable dual aperture rear sight. Features: 6-position telescopic stock, thermo-set M4 handguard. 14.75 in. sight radius. 7-lbs. (approx.) trigger pull. 7075 T6 aluminum upper, 4140 steel barrel. Chromed barrel bore, gas key, bolt carrier. Hard-coat black-anodized receiver and barrel finish. OR (Optics Ready) model has no sights. TS model has Magpul stock and folding sights. Made in USA by Smith & Wesson.
Price: Sport Model **$739.00**
Price: OR Model **$1,069.00**
Price: TS model **$1,569.00**

SMITH & WESSON M&P15 SPORT II SERIES
Caliber: 5.56mm NATO/.223. Capacity: 30-shot steel magazine. Barrel: 16 in., 1:9-in. twist. Weight: 6.74 lbs., w/o magazine. Lengths: 32 to 35 in. overall. Stock: Black synthetic. Sights: Adjustable post front sight, adjustable dual aperture rear sight. Features: six-position telescopic stock, thermo-set M4 handguard. 14.75 in. sight radius. 7-lb. (approx.) trigger pull. 7075 T6 aluminum upper, 4140 steel barrel. OR (Optics Ready) model has Crimson Trace CTS-103 Red/Green Dot Electronic Sight. Hardcoat black-anodized receiver and barrel finish. Made in USA.
Price: Sport II **$812.00**
Price: Sport II OR **$831.00**

SMITH & WESSON M&P15 VOLUNTEER XV OPTICS READY
Caliber: 5.56mm NATO/.223. Similar to Volunteer XV except has gas block with integral Picatinny-style rail. Weight: 9 lbs. Length: 36.25 in. No. 13510. Introduced 2022.
Price: **$1,049.00**

SMITH & WESSON M&P15 VOLUNTEER XV RED DOT SIGHT
Caliber: 5.56mm NATO/.223. Similar to Volunteer XV except has gas block with integral Picatinny-style rail and includes Crimson Trace red-dot sight. Weight: 9.375 lbs. Length: 36.25 in. No. 13513. Introduced 2022.
Price: **$1,099.00**

SMITH & WESSON M&P15 VOLUNTEER XV SERIES
Caliber: 5.56mm NATO/.223. Capacity: 30-shot steel magazine. Barrel: 16-in. 4140 steel, 1:8 twist. Flat-faced trigger. BCM Gunfighter forend with M-LOK attachments. Gas block with integral Picatinny-style rail. B5 Systems Bravo Stock and P-Grip 23 pistol grip. Chromed firing pin. Forward assist. A2 flash suppressor. Adjustable A2 front sight post. Forged integral triggerguard. Armornite finish on barrel (internal and external). Weight: 8.8 lbs. Length: 36.25 in. No. 13507. Introduced 2022.
Price: **$1,049.00**

SMITH & WESSON M&P15 VOLUNTEER XV DMR
Caliber: 5.56mm NATO/.223. Similar to Volunteer XV Pro except rifle-length gas system and 20-in. barrel (No. 13517). Weight: 8.125 lbs. Length: 40.7 in. Introduced 2022.
Price: **$1,599.00**

SMITH & WESSON M&P15 VOLUNTEER XV PRO
Caliber: 5.56mm NATO/.223. Similar to Volunteer XV except has gas block with integral Picatinny-style rail, B5 SOPMOD stock, and upright B5 grip. Mid-length gas system, 15-in. aluminum S&W M-LOK forend. Primary Weapons Systems muzzle brake, and 5R rifling. Sights: WGS Tactical Folding Sight front and rear. 16-in. target crowned, threaded barrel (No. 13515) or 14.5 in. (No. 13516), the latter with a pinned flash hider. Weight: 6.8 lbs. Length: 36.75 in. Introduced 2022.
Price: **$1,569.00**

SMITH & WESSON M&P10
Caliber: .308 Win., 6.5 Creedmoor. Capacity: 10 rounds. Barrel: 18 to 20 in. Weight: 7.7 pounds. Features: Magpul MOE stock with MOE Plus grip, 15-in. free-float Troy M-LOK handguard, black hard anodized finish. Camo-finish hunting model available w/5-round magazine.
Price: M&P10 OR .308 Win. **$1,679.00**
Price: M&P10 6.5 Creedmoor **$2095.00**

SMITH & WESSON M&P10 SPORT OPTICS READY
Caliber: .308 Win., 6.5 Creedmoor. Capacity: 10 rounds. Barrel: 18 to 20 in. Weight: 7.7 pounds. Features: Magpul MOE stock with MOE Plus grip, 15-in. free-float Troy M-LOK handguard, black hard-anodized finish. Camo-finish hunting model available w/five-round magazine.
Price: M&P10 OR .308 Win. **$1,130.00**
Price: M&P10 6.5 Creedmoor **$2,095.00**

SPRINGFIELD ARMORY HELLION BULLPUP
Caliber: 5.56 NATO. Ambidextrous controls, including the safety, charging handle, magazine, and bolt releases. Reversible case ejection system. Barrel: 16 in., 1:7 rate of twist, Melonite coating. Picatinny top rail, flip-up iron sights. Bravo Company USA BCMGUNFIGHTER Mod 3 grip. Five-position adjustable buttstock. Polymer handguard with nine M-LOK slots, three each at 3, 6 and 9 o'clock positions. Two-position adjustable gas block with "S" suppressed and "N" normal modes. Magazine: 30-round Magpul PMAG. Weight: 8 lbs. Length: 28.25 in. Introduced January 2023.
Price: **$1,999.00**

SPRINGFIELD ARMORY SAINT AR-15 RIFLES
Caliber: 5.56 NATO. Introduced 2016. Springfield Armory's first entry into AR category. Capacity: 30-round magazine. Barrel: 16 in., 1:8 twist. Weight: 6 lbs., 11 oz. Sights: A2-style fixed post front or gas block with Pic rail, flip-up aperture rear. Features: Mid-length gas system, BCM 6-position stock, Mod 3 grip PMT KeyMod handguard 7075 T6 aluminum receivers. In 2020, several models with M-LOK handguards were added. The Bravo Company handguards have an internal aluminum heat shield.
Price: **$1,023.00**

SPRINGFIELD ARMORY SAINT EDGE ATC RIFLE
Chamber: .223 Wylde. Accurized Tactical Chassis rifles comes with guaranteed sub-MOA accuracy for three shots with match-grade ammunition and a skilled shooter. Features: Chassis system of a one-piece monolithic lower machined from 6061 T6 aluminum. Free-floated design keeps the barrel, barrel nut, and gas system from contacting the lower chassis. Also includes Accu-Tite Plus tensioning system, conical set screws in the lower that eliminate play between the upper receiver and lower chassis. Barrel: 18-in. Ballistic Advantage, 1:7-in. rate of twist, Melonite coating. Comes with B5 Systems Enhanced SOPMOD collapsible stock, flat modular match trigger, B5 Systems Type 23 P-Grip, 20-round Magpul PMAG. Weight: 9.5 lbs. Length: 35.5 to 38.25 in. Introduced December 2021.
Price: **$1,379.00**

SPRINGFIELD ARMORY SAINT VICTOR AR-15 RIFLES
Caliber: 5.56 NATO. Capacity: Includes one 30-round Magpul PMAG Gen M3. Barrel: 16-in., CMV, 1:8 twist, Melonite-finished barrels, Springfield

Prices given are believed to be accurate at time of publication however, many factors affect retail pricing so exact prices are not possible.

Armory proprietary muzzle brake. Upper/Lower Receivers: Lowers are Accu-Tite tension-bonded to a flat-top forged upper receiver with Melonite finish. Stock: BCMGUNFIGHTER Mod 0. Pistol Grip: BCMGUNFIGHTER Mod 3. Sights: Spring-loaded, flip-up iron sights adjustable for windage and elevation. Weight: 6.9 lbs. Trigger: Enhanced nickel-boron-coated, single-stage flat trigger. Overall Length: 32.25 to 35.5 in. Features: Direct-impingement mid-length gas system. M16 bolt carrier Melonite finished, HPT/MPI tested, shot peened, and houses a 9310 steel bolt. 15-in. M-LOK free-float handguard, pinned, low-profile gas block. QD mounts built into the end plate and stock. Desert FDE color approx. $60 extra. Introduced 2019. Saint Victor Carbine 9mm (add $150) introduced December 2022.

Price: **$1,150.00**

SPRINGFIELD ARMORY SAINT VICTOR AR-10 RIFLE

Caliber: .308 Win. Capacity: One 20-round Magpul Gen M3. Barrel: 16 in., 1:10 twist, lightweight profile, CMV Melonite finish, SA muzzle brake. Upper/Lower Receivers: Forged Type III hardcoat anodized, 7075 T6 Aluminum. Lower has Accu-Tite Tension System. Stock: Bravo Company six-Position. Pistol Grip: Bravo Company Mod. 3. Sights: Spring-loaded, flip-ups. Weight: 7.8 lbs. Trigger: Enhanced nickel boron-coated, single-stage flat trigger. Overall Length: 34.5 to 37.5 in. Features: Gas system is direct impingement, mid-length, pinned gas block. Bolt carrier group is MPT, Melonite finish with a 9310 steel bolt; handguard is 15-in. M-LOK aluminum free-float with SA locking tabs. Introduced 2019.

Price: **$1,497.00**

STAG ARMS STAG 15 RIFLES

Calibers: 5.56 NATO/.223, 6mm ARC, 6.8 SPC II. Capacities: 20- or 30-round magazine. Features: This manufacturer offers many AR-style rifles or carbines with many optional features including barrel length and configurations, stocks, sights, rail systems and both direct-impingement and gas-piston operating systems. Left-hand models are available on some products. Tactical line added 2022.

Price: Stag 15 Tactical 16 .... **$1,100.00**
Price: Stag 15 M4 .... **$1,100.00**
Price: Stag 15 Retro **$1,400.00**
Price: Stag 15 Super Varminter (6.8) **$1,400.00**
Price: Stag 15 LEO **$1,150.00**
Price: Stag 15 Tactical SBR 10.5 .... **$1,050.00**
Price: Stag 15 3Gun Elite **$1,900.00**

STAG ARMS AR-15 PURSUIT RIFLES

Caliber: .350 Legend. 16-in. stainless-steel nitride-coated barrel, mid-length gas systems, 13.5-in. slim handrails. Weight: 6.2 lbs. Caliber: 6.5 Grendel, 18-in. barrel, rifle-length gas system, 16.5-inch slim handguards. Steel 10-round magazines. 8.2 lbs. Left-hand models available; add $50. Midnight bronze Cerakote. Magpul CTR stock with custom leather stock, ambi safety levers with 60- or 90-degree throw, large charging handle, Magpul K2+ grip, VG6 muzzle brake, Timney two-stage triggers. Lifetime Transferable Warranty and Infinite Shot Barrel Guarantee. Initial rifles are built to order. Made in USA. Introduced 2023.

Price: **$1,600.00**

STAG ARMS AR-10 PURSUIT RIFLES

Similar to AR-15 Pursuit Rifles. Caliber: .308 Win. 16-in. stainless-steel barrel. Caliber: 6.5 Creedmoor, 18-in. barrel. Weight: 7.8 lbs. Magpul magazines.

Price: **$2,200.00**

STAG ARMS AR-10 STYLE RIFLES

Similar to AR-15 models, but chambered in .308 Win. or 6.5 Creedmoor.

Price: Stag 10 Tactical 16 in. **$1,770.00**
Price: Stag 10 Classic 16 in. **$1,650.00**
Price: Stag 10 Classic 18 in. **$1,550.00**
Price: Stag 10 Classic 20 in. **$1,600.00**
Price: Stag 10 Marksman 18 in. LH **$1,850.00**
Price: Stag 10 Long Range 20 in. **$2,120.00**
Price: Stag 10 Long Range 24 in. **$2,300.00**

STONER TACTICAL ORDNANCE SR-15 MOD 2 RIFLE

Caliber: 5.56mm NATO. Capacity: 30-round magazine. Barrel: 16 in. 1:7 twist, free-floated inside M-LOK URX handguard. Weight: 6.3 lbs. Length: 32 to 35 in. overall. Stock: Magpul MOE. Sights: Post front, fully adjustable rear (300m sight). Features: URX-4 upper receiver; two-stage trigger, 30-round magazine. Black finish. Made in USA by Knight's Armament Co.

Price: **$2,900.00**

STONER TACTICAL ORDNANCE SR-15 LPR MOD 2

Caliber: .223. Capacity: 30-round magazine. Barrel: 18 in., free-floated inside M-LOK URSx handguard. Weight: 7.6 lbs. Length: 38 in. overall. Stock: Mag-Pul MOE. Sights: Post front, fully adjustable rear (300m sight). Features: URX-4 upper receiver; two-stage trigger, 30-round magazine. Black finish. Made in USA by Knight's Armament Co.

Price: **$3,200.00**

STONER TACTICAL ORDNANCE SR-25 RIFLE

Caliber: 7.62 NATO. Capacity: 10- or 20-shot steel magazine. Barrel: 16 in. with flash hider. Weight: 8.5 lbs. APC (Carbine) features: Shortened, non-slip handguard; drop-in two-stage match trigger, removable carrying handle, ambidextrous controls, matte-black finish. APR (Rifle) has 20-in. heavy barrel. Made in USA by Knight's Armament Co.

Price: **$5,775.00**

WILSON COMBAT AR-15 RIFLES

Caliber: .204 Ruger, .223 Rem./5.56mm NATO, .223 Wylde, 22 Nosler, .224 Valkyrie, 6mm ARC, 6.5 Grendel, 6.8 SPC, .300 Ham'r, .300 Blackout, .350 Legend, .375 SOCOM, .458 SOCOM, .450 Bushmaster. Capacity: Accepts all M-16/AR-15-style magazines, and includes one 20-round magazine. Barrel: 16.25 in., 1:9-in. twist, match-grade fluted. Weight: 6.9 lbs. Length: 36.25 in. overall. Stock: Fixed or collapsible. Features: Free-float ventilated aluminum quad-rail handguard, mil-spec Parkerized barrel and steel components, anodized receiver, precision CNC-machined upper and lower receivers, 7075 T6 aluminum forgings. Single-stage JP Trigger/Hammer Group, Wilson Combat Tactical muzzle brake, nylon tactical rifle case. Made in USA by Wilson Combat.

Price: Ranger **$2,500.00**
Price: Ultralight Ranger **$2,615.00**
Price: Recon Tactical **$2,450.00**
Price: Protector **$2,100.00**
Price: Super Sniper **$2,525.00**
Price: Urban Super Sniper **$2,450.00**

WILSON COMBAT AR-10 RIFLES

Caliber: .243 Win., .260 Rem., 6.5 Creedmoor, 7mm-08 Rem., .308 Win., .338 Federal, .358 Win. Large-format BILLet-AR rifles with precision-machined match-grade barrels, M-LOK handguard rail, Tactical Trigger Units. Barrels: 14.7-in. barrel with pinned muzzle device on Recon Tactical. Also, 16, 18, and 20 in. fluted or standard Medium Recon-profile barrels. Receivers accept metal or polymer SR-25-pattern magazines.

Price: Recon Tactical **$3,285.00**
Price: Super Sniper **$3,235.00**
Price: Tactical Hunter **$3,335.00**
Price: Ranger **$3,285.00**
Price: Ultralight Ranger **$3,400.00**

WILSON COMBAT AR-9 CARBINE

Caliber: 9mm Luger. AR-9 lower receivers with last-round bolt hold open compatible with 9mm service pistol magazines for Glock, Beretta, and Wilson Combat EDC X9. Accepts standard AR accessories. Integral

Prices given are believed to be accurate at time of publication however, many factors affect retail pricing so exact prices are not possible.

78TH EDITION, 2024 ✦ **437**

triggerguard, flared magwell. Closed-bolt blowback operating system. Match-grade button-rifled 1:10 twist barrels. Introduced 2016.
Price: Recon Tactical..**$2,100.00**

WINDHAM WEAPONRY 20 VARMINT

Caliber: .223 Rem./5.56mm NATO. Capacity: 5+1, ships with one 5-round magazine (accepts all standard AR-15 sizes). Barrel: 20 in., 1:8 RH twist, fluted 416R stainless steel, matte finish. Upper/Lower Receivers: A4-type flattop upper receiver, forged 7075 T6 aircraft aluminum with aluminum triggerguard. Electroless nickel-plated finish. Forend: 15 in. Windham Weaponry aluminum M-LOK free-float. Pistol Grip: Hogue OverMolded rubber pistol grip. Sights: None, optics-ready, Picatinny top rail. Weight: 8.4 lbs. Length: 38.1 in. Features: Gas-impingement system, Carpenter 158 steel bolt. Compass Lake chamber specification with a matched bolt. LUTH MBA-1 stock. Comes with a hard-plastic case and a black web sling.
Price: **$1,560.00**

WINDHAM WEAPONRY A1 GOVERNMENT

Caliber: .223 Rem./5.56mm NATO. Capacity: 30+1, ships with one 30-round magazine (accepts all standard AR-15 sizes). Barrel: 20 in., A2 profile, chrome-lined with A1 flash suppressor, 4150 chrome-moly Vanadium 11595E steel with M4 feed ramps. Rifling: 1:7 RH twist. Receivers: A1 upper with brass deflector and teardrop forward assist. Forend: Rifle-length triangular handguard with A1 Delta Ring. Pistol Grip: A1 Black Plastic Grip. Rear Sight: A1 dual aperture rear sight. Front Sight: Adjustable-height square post in A2 standard base. Trigger: Standard mil-spec trigger. Stock: A2 Solid Stock with Trapdoor Storage Compartment. Weight: 7.45 lbs. Length: 39.5 in.
Price: **$1,345.00**

WINDHAM WEAPONRY DISSIPATOR M4

Caliber: .223 Rem./5.56mm NATO. Similar to Superlight SRC. Barrel: 16 in., M4 profile, chrome-lined with A2 flash suppressor. Flattop-type upper receiver with A4 detachable carry handle. Rifle-length heat-shielded handguards. A2 black plastic grip. Rear Sight: A4 dual-aperture elevation and windage adjustable for 300–600m. Front Sight: adjustable-height square post in A2 standard base. Six-position telescoping buttstock. Weight: 7.2 lbs. Length: 32.375 to 36.125 in.
Price: **$1,275.00**

WINDHAM WEAPONRY SRC-308

Caliber: .308 Win. Capacity: 20+1, ships with one 20-round Magpul PMag magazine. Barrel: 16.5-in., medium-profile, chrome-lined with A2 flash suppressor; 4150M chrome-moly Vanadium 11595E steel; 1:10 right-hand-twist rifling, six lands and grooves. Upper/Lower Receivers: A4-type flattop upper receiver, forged 7075 T6 aircraft aluminum with aluminum triggerguard. Forend: Mid-length tapered shielded handguards. Pistol Grip: Hogue OverMolded rubber pistol grip. Sights: None, optics-ready, Picatinny top rail. Weight: 7.55 lbs. Length: 34.188 to 38 in. Features: Gas-impingement system, Carpenter 158 steel bolt. Compass Lake chamber specification with matched bolt. Six-position telescoping buttstock. Comes with a hard-plastic case and a black web sling. Separate models available in .300 BLK and 7.62x39
Price: **$1,420.00**

WINDHAM WEAPONRY VEX-SS WOOD STOCK SERIES

Caliber: .223 Rem. Capacity: 5+1, ships with one 5-round magazine (accepts all standard AR-15 sizes). Barrel: 20 in., 1:8 RH twist, fluted 416R stainless steel, matte finish. Upper/Lower Receivers: A4-type flat-top upper receiver with optics riser blocks, forged 7075 T6 aircraft aluminum with aluminum triggerguard. Electroless nickel-plated finish. Stock/Forend: laminated wood. Pistol Grip: Hogue OverMolded rubber pistol grip. Sights: None, optics-ready, Picatinny rail partial top rail. Weight: 8.35 lbs. Length: 38.188. Features: Gas-impingement system, Carpenter 158 steel bolt. Compass Lake chamber specification with matched bolt. Wood stock series includes pepper and nutmeg.
Price: **$1,520.00**

BIGHORN ARMORY MODEL 89 BLACK THUNDER
Calibers: .500 S&W Magnum. Capacity: 6-round tubular magazine. Barrel: 16.25 in. steel. Weight: 7 lbs. 6 oz. Length: 36 in. Stock: Black laminate with M-LOK rail on the front of the forend. Sights: Skinner iron sights and factory-installed scout rail. Features: Expansion of the Model 89 lever-action line built as a carbine with a shorter barrel, ideal for hunting, home defense, and survival. Robust stainless steel construction, heat-treated, and coated with a black nitride finish. Bighorn Armory rifles built in Cody, WY.
Price: $1,235.00

BIG HORN ARMORY MODEL 89 RIFLE AND CARBINE
Caliber: .500 S&W Mag. Capacities: 5- or 7-round magazine. Features: Lever-action rifle or carbine chambered for .500 S&W Magnum. 22- or 18-in. barrel; walnut or maple stocks with pistol grip; aperture rear and blade front sights; recoil pad; sling swivels; enlarged lever loop; magazine capacity 5 (rifle) or 7 (carbine) rounds.
Price: $2,424.00

BIG HORN ARMORY MODEL 90 SERIES
Calibers: .460 S&W, .454 Casull. Features similar to Model 89. Several wood and finish upgrades available.
Price: .460 S&W $2,849.00
Price: .454 Casull, .45 Colt....................................$3,049.00
Price: .500 Linebaugh $3,699.00

BROWNING BLR
Features: Lever action with rotating bolt head, multiple-lug breech bolt with recessed bolt face, side ejection. Rack-and-pinion lever. Flush-mounted detachable magazines, with 4+1 capacity for magnum cartridges, 5+1 for standard rounds. Barrel: Button-rifled chrome-moly steel with crowned muzzle. Stock: Buttstocks and fore-ends are American walnut with grip and forend checkering. Recoil pad installed. Trigger: Wide-groove design, trigger travels with lever. Half-cock hammer safety; fold-down hammer. Sights: Gold bead on ramp front; low-profile square-notch adjustable rear. Features: Blued barrel and receiver, high-gloss wood finish. Receivers are drilled and tapped for scope mounts, swivel studs included. Action lock provided. Introduced 1996. Imported from Japan by Browning.

BROWNING BLR GOLD MEDALLION
Calibers: .243 Win., 6.5 Creedmoor, .308 Win., .270 Win., .30-06 Spfld., .300 Win. Mag. Capacity: 3–5 round magazine, depending on caliber. Barrel: 20, 22, or 24 in. Length: 40–45 in. Weight: 6 lbs. 8 oz.–7 lbs. 4 oz. Stock: Grade III/IV Walnut stock with Schnabel forearm and brass spacers and rosewood caps. Features: High Grade lever action centerfire limited edition. Gloss finish engraved receiver built of lightweight aluminum. Gloss blued barrel drilled and tapped for optic mounts. Detachable box magazine. Iron sights. Pachmayr Decelerator recoil pad. Gold-plated trigger and gold inlay receiver branding.
Price: Short actions $1,540.00
Price: Long actions $1,630.00

CHIAPPA MODEL 1892 RIFLE
Calibers: .38 Special/357 Magnum, .38-40, .44-40, .44 Mag., .45 Colt. Barrels: 16 in. (Trapper), 20 in. round and 24 in. octagonal (Takedown). Weight: 7.7 lbs. Stock: Walnut. Sights: Blade front, buckhorn. Trapper model has interchangeable front sight blades. Features: Finishes are blue/case colored. Magazine capacity is 12 rounds with 24 in. bbl.; 10 rounds with 20 in. barrel; 9 rounds in 16 in. barrel. Mare's Leg models have 4-shot magazine, 9- or 12-in. barrel.

Price: $1,329.00
Price: Takedown...$1,435.00
Price: Trapper $1,329.00
Price: Mare's Leg $1,288.00

CHIAPPA MODEL 1886
Caliber: .45-70. Barrels: 16, 18.5, 22, 26 in. Replica of famous Winchester model offered in several variants.
Price: Rifle...$1,709.00
Price: Carbine $1,629.00

CHIAPPA 1892 LEVER-ACTION WILDLANDS
Caliber: .44 Mag. Capacity: 5. Barrel: 16.5 in., stainless steel, Cerakote dark gray or color case finish, heavy. Stock: Wood laminate or hand-oiled walnut. Sights: Fixed fiber-optic front, Skinner peep rear. Weight: 6.3 lbs. Features: Takedown and solid-frame configurations, mag tube fed.
Price: ....$1,434.00-$1,689.00

CIMARRON 1873 SHORT RIFLE
Calibers: .357 Magnum, .38 Special, .32 WCF, .38 WCF, .44 Special, .44 WCF, .45 Colt. Barrel: 20 in. tapered octagon. Weight: 7.5 lbs. Length: 39 in. overall. Stock: Walnut. Sights: Bead front, adjustable semi-buckhorn rear. Features: Has half "button" magazine. Original-type markings, including caliber, on barrel and elevator and "Kings" patent. Trapper Carbine (.357 Mag., .44 WCF, .45 Colt). From Cimarron F.A. Co.
Price: $1,299.00
Price: Trapper Carbine 16-in. bbl. $1,352.00

CIMARRON 1873 DELUXE SPORTING
Similar to the 1873 Short Rifle except has 24-in. barrel with half-magazine.
Price: $1,485.00

CIMARRON 1873 LONG RANGE SPORTING
Calibers: .44 WCF, .45 Colt. Barrel: 30 in., octagonal. Weight: 8.5 lbs. Length: 48 in. overall. Stock: Walnut. Sights: Blade front, semi-buckhorn ramp rear. Tang sight optional. Features: Color casehardened frame; choice of modern blued-black or charcoal blued for other parts. Barrel marked "Kings Improvement." From Cimarron F.A. Co.
Price: $1,385.00

EMF 1866 YELLOWBOY LEVER ACTIONS
Calibers: .38 Special, .44-40, .45 LC. Barrels: 19 in. (carbine), 24 in. (rifle). Weight: 9 lbs. Length: 43 in. overall (rifle). Stock: European walnut. Sights: Bead front, open adjustable rear. Features: Solid brass frame, blued barrel, lever, hammer, buttplate. Imported from Italy by EMF.
Price: Rifle...$1,175.00

EMF MODEL 1873 LEVER-ACTION
Calibers: .32/20, .357 Magnum, .38/40, .44-40, .45 Colt. Barrels: 18 in., 20 in., 24 in., 30 in. Weight: 8 lbs. Length: 43.25 in. overall. Stock: European walnut. Sights: Bead front, rear adjustable for windage and elevation. Features: Color casehardened frame (blued on carbine). Imported by EMF.
Price: $1,250.00

HENRY NEW ORIGINAL RIFLE
Calibers: 360 Buckhammer, .44-40 Win, .45 Colt. Capacity: 13-round tubular magazine. Barrel: 24-in. octagonal blued steel. Weight: 9 lbs. Length: 43 in. Stock: Fancy-grade American Walnut with straight-grip buttstock. Sights: Folding ladder rear with blade front. Features: Hardened brass receiver finished in high polish. Essentially identical to the 1860 original, except for caliber. Serial numbers begin with "BTH" prefix in honor of Benjamin Tyler Henry, inventor of the lever action repeating rifle that went on to become the most legendary firearm in American

Prices given are believed to be accurate at time of publication however, many factors affect retail pricing so exact prices are not possible.

78TH EDITION, 2024 ✦ **439**

CENTERFIRE RIFLES Lever & Slide

history. Made in the USA. Only this standard model New Original is available in the .45 Colt chambering; all other New Original Models below are .44-40 Win. only.

Price: **$2,590.00**
Price: New Original Deluxe Engraved **$3,810.00**
Price: New Original B.T. Henry 200th Anniv. Edition **$4,286.00**
Price: New Original Rare Carbine **$2,590.00**
Price: New Original Iron Framed **$3,023.00**
Price: New Original Silver Deluxe Engraved **$4,078.00**

HENRY SIDE GATE MODELS
Beginning in 2020, Henry began building the centerfire lever actions listed below with a side loading gate in addition to the tubular magazine charging port. These are not to be confused with the specific Henry Side Gate Model H024. NOTE: All previous Henry centerfire models without the side gate are now discontinued and considered "Legacy" models with slightly lower value at time of publication.
Price: Big Boy Color Case Hardened Side Gate **$1,141.00**
Price: Big Boy Steel Side Gate, Carbine or Rifle **$969.00**
Price: Big Boy Steel Side Gate, Large Loop **$986.00**
Price: Color Case Hardened Side Gate .30-30 and .45-70 .... **$1,141.00**
Price: Steel .30-30 Side Gate **$969.00**
Price: Steel .30-30 Side Gate Large Loop **$986.00**
Price: Steel .45-70 Side Gate **$969.00**
Price: Steel Wildlife Edition Side Gate **$1,618.00**

HENRY MODEL H024 SIDE GATE LEVER ACTION
Calibers: .38-55 Win., .30-30 Win., .45-70 Govt, .35 Rem. Capacity: 4 or 5-round tubular magazine. Barrel: 20-in. round blued steel. Weight: 7.5 lbs. Length: 38.3 in. Stock: American Walnut straight style with special deep checkering including floral scroll and Henry logo wood detail not found on any other models. Sights: Fully adjustable semi-buckhorn diamond-insert rear. Front ramp with 0.62-in. ivory bead. Drilled and tapped. Features: This H024 is the debut model using Henry's side loading gate design in addition to the standard tubular loading port. These hardened brass receiver centerfires are instantly recognizable with the special engraved and checkered stocks. Polished brass buttplate, barrel band, and swivel stud. Standard-size lever loop. Transfer bar safety.
Price: **$1,100.00**

HENRY LONG RANGER
Calibers: .223 Rem., .243 Win., 6.5 Creedmoor, .308 Win. Capacity: 4 (.243, 6.5CM, .308) or 5 (.223) box magazine. Barrel: 20 or 22 in. (6.5 Creedmoor) round blued steel. Weight: 7 lbs. Length: 40.5–42.5 in. Stock: Straight-grip, checkered, oil-finished American Walnut. Sights: Two models, one sighted with folding fully adjustable rear and ramp ivory bead front. The other does not have iron sights but includes scope bases and hammer extension instead. Both are drilled and tapped. Features: Geared action with side ejection port. Chromed steel bolt with six lugs. Flush-fit box magazine with side push-button release. Sling studs, rubber recoil pad. Transfer bar safety.
Price: **$1,138.00**
Price: Long Ranger Wildlife Editions **$1,973.00**
Price: Long Ranger Deluxe Engraved **$1,973.00**

HENRY LONG RANGER EXPRESS
Calibers: .223 Rem/5.56 NATO. Capacity: 5-round steel box magazine. Barrel: 16.5-in. threaded round blued steel. Weight: 7 lbs. Length: 37 in. Stock: Birch laminate in black/gray. Sights: Top Picatinny rail. No iron sights. Features: Expansion of the Long Ranger line, this one a more compact platform. Same geared action with side ejection port. Chromed steel bolt

with six lugs. Flush fit dropbox magazine with side push-button release. Sling studs, rubber recoil pad. Transfer bar safety. Hammer extension included. Barrel threaded at 5/8x24.
Price: **$1,235.00**

HENRY X-MODELS
Calibers: .30-30 Win., .45-70 Govt., .45 Colt, .44 Mag., .38 Spl./.357 Mag., 360 Buckhammer. Capacity: 4 (.45-70), 5 (.30-30), or 7 (Big Boys) tubular magazine Barrel: 17.4-, 19.8-, 21.375-in. round blued steel. Weight: 7.3–8.07 lbs. Length: 36.3–40.375 in. Stock: Black synthetic with M-LOK attachment points and lower Picatinny rail. Sights: Fully adjustable fiber-optic front and rear. Also drilled and tapped for Weaver 63B base. Features: Blacked-out lever actions built around several of Henry's existing family lines of long guns. Large loop lever. Barrel threaded at 5/8x24 for easy suppressor or brake attachment. Transfer bar safety. Solid rubber recoil pad. Sling studs. Matte blued steel metalwork.
Price: X-Model **$1,091.00**
Price: Big Boy X-Model **$1,000.00**
Price: X-Model .30-30 .... **$1,019.00**
Price: X-Model .45-70 .... **$1,000.00**

MARLIN MODEL 336
Caliber: .30-30 Win., .35 Rem. Barrel: 20.25-in. round blued. Stock: Walnut pistol grip style with checkering. Features: New 336 model launch under Ruger ownership. Blued metalwork with forward barrel band. Iron sights with hooded front. Crossbolt safety. Gold-plated trigger. Low-profile rubber buttpad. Side loading gate. Sling studs. Red and white bullseye stock insert denotes Ruger production Marlins.
Price: **$1,239.00**

MARLIN 1895 SBL
Calibers: .45-70 Govt. Capacity: 6+1-round tubular magazine. Barrel: 19 in. threaded, cold-hammer-forged stainless steel. Weight: 7.3 lbs. Length: 37.25 in. Stock: Gray laminate with checkering. Sights: Adjustable Ghost ring rear, Tritium fiber-optic front. Picatinny rail. Features: The much-anticipated lever gun launch under Ruger ownership of the Marlin brand. Polished stainless metalwork. Nickel-plated, spiral fluted bolt. Barrel threaded at 11/16x24. Rubber buttpad. Push-button, cross-bolt manual safety and half-cock hammer. Oversized lever loop and slimmed-down forend. Includes swivel studs and offset hammer spur. Marlin horse-and-rider logo laser engraved on the grip. Made in Mayodan, NC. Ruger-made Marlin rifles begin with the serial prefix "RM." Traditional Marlin stock bullseye is now red/white.
Price: **$1,399.00**

MARLIN 1895 GUIDE GUN
Caliber: .45-70 Gov't. Barrel: 24-in. round, cold hammer forged. Weight: 7.4 lbs. Stock: Brown laminate with checkering. Features: Big loop guide gun model variant. Threaded barrel with cap. Semi-buckhorn rear and hooded front sight. Bead blasted satin blued metalwork finish. Nickel-plated bolt. 6+1 capacity. Black rubber recoil pad. Sling studs. Red/White bullseye stock insert denotes Ruger manufacture.
Price: **$1,239.00**

MARLIN 1895 TRAPPER
Calibers: .45-70 Gov't. Capacity: 5+1. Barrel: 16.1 in. stainless round. Weight: 7.1 lbs. Stock: Black laminate with checkering. Features: Short-barreled, large loop model variant. Bead blasted matte stainless metalwork. Threaded barrel with cap. Black rubber recoil pad. Sling studs. It comes standard with Skinner Sights receiver-mounted peep. Red/White bullseye stock insert denotes Ruger manufacture.
Price: **$1,449.00**

NAVY ARMS 1873 RIFLE
Calibers: .357 Magnum, .45 Colt. Capacity: 12-round magazine. Barrels: 20 in., 24.25 in., full octagonal. Stock: Deluxe checkered American walnut. Sights: Gold bead front, semi-buckhorn rear. Features: Turnbull color case-hardened frame, rest blued. Full-octagon barrel. Available exclusively from Navy Arms. Made by Winchester.
Price: **$2,500.00**

NAVY ARMS 1892 SHORT RIFLE
Calibers: .45 Colt, .44 Magnum. Capacity: 10-round magazine. Barrel: 20 in. full octagon. Stock: Checkered Grade 1 American walnut. Sights: Marble's Semi-Buckhorn rear and gold bead front. Finish: Color casehardened.
Price: **$2,300.00**

PEDERSOLI 86/71 BOARBUSTER
Calibers: .45-70 Govt. Capacity: 5-round tubular magazine. Barrel: 19-in. round. Weight: 7.93–8.25 lbs. Length: 37-7/16 in. Stock: Varied by model. Sights: Scout-style Picatinny rail and fiber-optic iron sights. Receiver drilled and tapped for side scope mounts. Features: Big-bore lever action based on the 1886. Several models use two-piece, interchangeable loop loading lever on several models. Pedersoli's Boarbuster line is comprised of five model variants. Mark II wears coated black Walnut with Silicon grip film adjustable cheek piece and Bronze Cerakote metal finish. HV-1 wears orange and black HV-1 camo stocks with Silicon grip film and black Cerakote. Evolution is a classic model with selected Walnut stocks, Silver Cerakote receiver, and blued barrel. Shadow uses gray techno-polymer stock with adjustable cheek riser and ghost ring sights in place of Picatinny rail. Guidemaster wears camo stocks and fully chromed metalwork.
Price: **$1,792.00**

POF-USA TOMBSTONE
Caliber: 9mm Luger. Barrel: 16.5-in. free-floating, fluted steel. Weight: 5.75 lbs. Stock: Black synthetic Magpul SGA. Features: Accepts the same 10- and 20-round magazines as the company's Phoenix pistols. 10.5-in. Modular Receiver Rail (MRR) with M-LOK slots and Pic rails. Ghost ring iron sights. Crossbolt safety. Threaded muzzle with removable dual port brake. Single-stage 3.5-pound nonadjustable trigger.
Price: Black **$1,962.00**
Price: Tan **$2,097.00**

ROSSI R92 LEVER-ACTION CARBINE
Calibers: .38 Special/.357 Magnum, .44 Magnum., .44-40 Win., .45 Colt. Barrels: 16 or 20 in. with round barrel, 20 or 24 in. with octagon barrel. Weight: 4.8–7 lbs. Length: 34–41.5 in. Features: Blued or stainless finish. Various options available in selected chamberings (large lever loop, fiber-optic sights, cheekpiece).
Price: R92 Blued Rifle **$730.00**
Price: R92 Stainless Rifle **$770.00**
Price: R92 Carbine **$725.00**
Price: R92 Stainless Carbine **$770.00**
Price: R92 Octagonal Barrel .... **$830.00–$875.00**
Price: R92 Gold **$810.00**
Price: R92 Triple Black **$925.00**
Price: R92 .454 Casull **$950.00**

UBERTI 1873 SPORTING RIFLE
Calibers: .357 Magnum, .44-40, .45 Colt. Barrels: 16.1 in. round, 19 in. round or 20 in., 24.25 in. octagonal. Weight: Up to 8.2 lbs. Length: Up to 43.3 in. overall. Stock: Walnut, straight grip and pistol grip. Sights: Blade front adjustable for windage, open rear adjustable for elevation. Features: Color casehardened frame, blued barrel, hammer, lever, buttplate, brass elevator. Imported by Stoeger Industries.
Price: Carbine 19-in. bbl. **$1,309.00**
Price: Trapper 16.1-in. bbl. **$1,329.00**
Price: Carbine 18-in. half oct. bbl. **$1,379.00**
Price: Short Rifle 20-in. bbl. **$1,339.00**
Price: Sporting Rifle, 24.25-in. bbl. **$1,339.00**
Price: Special Sporting Rifle, A-grade walnut **$1,449.00**

UBERTI 150TH ANNIVERSARY 1873 RIFLE
Caliber: .45 Colt, .357 Mag. Capacity: 10+1 rounds. Barrel: 20-in. blued octagonal. Weight: 8.2 lbs. Stock: A-Grade Satin Walnut. Iron sights. Blued crescent buttplate. Features: Special anniversary remake of Winchester's Model 1873, "The gun that won the West." Casehardened receiver finish. Sideplate engraving reproduced from an original Winchester by Atelier Giovanelli of Italy.
Price: **$1,799.00**

UBERTI 1860 HENRY
Calibers: .44-40, .45 Colt. Barrel: 24.25 in. half-octagon. Weight: 9.2 lbs. Length: 43.75 in. overall. Stock: American walnut. Sights: Blade front, rear adjustable for elevation. Imported by Stoeger Industries.
Price: 1860 Henry Trapper, 18.5-in. barrel, brass frame **$1,499.00**
Price: 1860 Henry Rifle Iron Frame, 24.25-in. barrel **$1,499.00**

UBERTI 1866 YELLOWBOY DELUXE
Caliber: .45 Colt. Barrel: 20-in. blued octagonal. Weight: 8.2 lbs. Stock: A-Grade Walnut. Brass crescent buttplate. Blued barrel band.

Prices given are believed to be accurate at time of publication however, many factors affect retail pricing so exact prices are not possible.

78TH EDITION, 2024 ◈ 441

Casehardened lever. Iron sights. Features: Remake of Winchester's famed 1866 Yellowboy. Polished brass frame with classically inspired engraving pattern, including a bugling elk. Blank area on right escutcheon intended for the owner's custom engraving.
Price: $1,799.00

WINCHESTER MODEL 94 SHORT RIFLE
Calibers: .30-30, .38-55, .32 Special. Barrel: 20 in. Weight: 6.75 lbs. Sights: Semi-buckhorn rear, gold bead front. Stock: Walnut with straight grip. Fore-end has black grip cap. Also available in Trail's End takedown design in .450 Marlin or .30-30.
Price: $1,230.00
Price: (Takedown) $1,460.00

WINCHESTER MODEL 94 SPORTER
Calibers: .30-30, .38-55. Barrel: 24 in. Weight: 7.5 lbs. Features: Same features of Model 94 Short Rifle except for crescent butt and steel buttplate, 24 in. half-round, half-octagon barrel, checkered stock.
Price: $1,400.00
Price: Deluxe Sporting 24 in. .30-30 Win., .38-55 Win. $2,169.00

WINCHESTER 1873 SHORT RIFLE
Calibers: .357 Magnum, .44-40, .45 Colt. Capacities: Tubular magazine holds 10 rounds (.44-40, .45 Colt), 11 rounds (.38 Special). Barrel: 20 in. Weight: 7.25 lbs. Sights: Marble semi-buckhorn rear, gold bead front. Tang is drilled and tapped for optional peep sight. Stock: Satin finished, straight-grip walnut with steel crescent buttplate and steel fore-end cap. Tang safety. A modern version of the "Gun That Won the West."
Price: $1,300.00
Price: Deluxe Sporting Rifle $1,800.00
Price: Competition Carbine High Grade 20 in..45 Colt or .357 Mag.... $1,839.00
Price: Deluxe Sporting 24 in. .44-40 Win. $2,119.00

WINCHESTER 1873 150TH ANNIVERSARY
Caliber: .44-40 Win. Barrel: 24-in. octagon. Weight: 8.0 lbs. Stock: Grade V/VI Black Walnut straight grip with laser cut 20 LPI checkering. Features: Special anniversary edition of "The gun that won the West." High-gloss blued steel metalwork. Gold-filled 150th-anniversary engraving. Crescent buttplate with engraving detail. Semi buckhorn rear sight with Marble's gold bead front. Receiver drilled and tapped for tang-mounted sight.
Price: $3,659.00

WINCHESTER MODEL 1886 SADDLE RING CARBINE
Calibers: .45-70 Govt, .45-90 Win. Capacity: 7-round tubular magazine. Barrel: 22-in. round polished blued steel. Weight: 8 lbs. Length: 41 in. Stock: Grade I Black Walnut with straight grip and carbine-style forearm, oil finished. Sights: Carbine ladder-style rear and blade front. Features: Full-length magazine tube, steel barrel band. Drilled and tapped for receiver mount sight. Brushed polish receiver finish. Tang safety. Side Saddle Ring.
Price: $1,549.00

WINCHESTER MODEL 1895
Calibers: .30-06 Spfld., .405 Win. Capacity: 4-round internal magazine. Barrel: 24-in. gloss blued steel, button rifled. Weight: 8 lbs. Length: 42 in. Stock: Grade I Black Walnut, straight grip with traditional cut checkering. Sights: Drilled and tapped receiver for side mount sight; Marble Arms gold bead front and Buckhorn rear. Features: Throwback lever gun reminiscent of Teddy Roosevelt's "Big Medicine." Grade I Model 1895 lever action with scalloped receiver, two-piece lever, and Schnabel forend.
Price: ....$1,369.00–$1,439.00
Price: Grade III/IV Black Walnut .30-40 Krag $1,699.00–1,769.00

ARMALITE AR-50A1

Caliber: .50 BMG, .416 Barrett. Capacity: Bolt-action single-shot. Barrel: 30 in. with muzzle brake. National Match model (shown) has 33-in. fluted barrel. Weight: 34.1 lbs. Stock: Three-section. Extruded fore-end, machined vertical grip, forged and machined buttstock that is vertically adjustable. National Match model (.50 BMG only) has V-block patented bedding system, Armalite Skid System to ensure straight-back recoil.

Price: **$3,359.00**

ANSCHUTZ 1782

Calibers: .243 Win., 6.5 Creedmoor, .308 Win., .30-06, 8x57, 9.3x62. Capacity: 3. Barrel: 20.5 to 23.8 in., blued, threaded. Stock: Walnut. Sights: Integrated Picatinny rail. Weight: 8 lbs. Features: Solid-steel milled action, 60-degree bolt lift, sliding safety catch.

Price: **$2,795.00**

BENELLI LUPO

Calibers: .243 Win., 6mm Creedmoor, 6.5 Creedmoor, .308 Win., 6.5 PRC, .30-06 Spfld., .270 Win, 7mm Rem. Mag., .300 Win. Mag. Capacity: 4–5-round box magazine. Barrel: 22 and 24 in. Crio-treated, free-floating, threaded barrel with thread cover. Length: 44.25–46.62 in. Stock: Black Synthetic. Sights: None. Includes two piece Picatinny rail. Weight: 6.9–7.1 lbs. Features: Shims allow stock adjustment. Matte blued metalwork. Progressive comfort recoil reduction system. Sub-MOA guarantee. CombTech cheek pad. Ambidextrous safety. Integral swivel mounts.

Price: **$1,699.00**
Price: B.E.S.T. CAMO, Elevated II or Open Country camo **$1,899.00**
Price: Walnut stock, .308 Win. or .30-06.........................**$2,199.00**

BENELLI LUPO WOOD B.E.S.T.

Calibers: 6.5 Creedmoor, .308 Win., .300 Win. Mag. Capacity: 4–5 round box magazine. Barrel: 22- and 24-in. Crio-treated, free-floating, threaded barrel with thread cover. Length: 44.225–46.625 in. Stock: AA-grade satin Walnut. Sights: Two-piece Picatinny bases. No iron sights. Weight: 7.1 lbs. Features: The new model Lupo replaces synthetic furniture with Walnut but keeps most other features. Also adds B.E.S.T. surface treatment to metal surfaces for added durability. Trigger reach spacers. Ambidextrous safety. Progressive comfort recoil reduction system. Sub-MOA guarantee.

Price: ....**$1,899.00–$2,199.00**

BARRETT FIELDCRAFT HUNTING RIFLE

Calibers: .22-250 Rem., .243 Win., 6mm Creedmoor, .25-06, 6.5 Creedmoor, 6.5x55, 7mm-08 Rem., .308 Win. .270 Win., .30-06. Capacity: 4-round magazine. Barrel: 18 (threaded), 21 or 24 inches. Weight: 5.2-5.6 lbs. Features: Two-position safety, Timney trigger. Receiver, barrels and bolts are scaled for specific calibers. Barrels and action are made from 416 stainless steel and are full-length hand bedded.

Price: ....**$1,879.00-$1,929.00**

BARRETT MRAD

Calibers: .260 Rem., 6.5 Creedmoor, .308 Win., .300 Win. Mag., .338 Lapua Magnum. Capacity: 10-round magazine. Barrels: 20 in., 24 in. or 26 in. fluted or heavy. Features: User-interchangeable barrel system, folding stock, adjustable cheekpiece, 5-position length of pull adjustment button, match-grade trigger, 22-in. optics rail.

Price: ....**$5,850.00–$6,000.00**

BERGARA B-14 SERIES

Calibers: 6.5 Creedmoor, .270 Win., 7mm Rem. Mag., .308 Win., .30-06, .300 Win. Mag. Barrels: 22 or 24 in. Weight: 7 lbs. Features: Synthetic with Soft touch finish, recoil pad, swivel studs, adjustable trigger, choice of detachable mag or hinged floorplate. Made in Spain.

Price: **$825.00**
Price: Walnut Stock (Shown, Top) **$945.00**
Price: Premier Series **$2,190.00**
Price: Hunting and Match Rifle (HMR)(Shown, Bottom).................**$1,150.00**

BERGARA PREMIER CANYON

Calibers: 6.5 Creedmoor, 6.5 PRC, .308 Win., 28 Nosler, .300 Win. Mag., 300 PRC, .375 H&H. Capacity: AICS-style detachable 3-round mag. provided, 5-round long action. 375 uses hinged floorplate with 3-round capacity. Barrel: 20–22 in. No. 4 taper, fluted stainless steel. Weight: 6.2–6.5 lbs. Length: 41–44 in. Stock: AG Composite 100% carbon fiber. Sights: Drilled and tapped for Remington 700 bases with 8-40 screws. Features: Classic style hunting rifle. Bolt uses a non-rotating gas shield, coned bolt nose, and sliding plate extractor. TriggerTech frictionless release trigger with two-position safety. Threaded muzzle with Omni Muzzle Brake. Sniper Grey Cerakote. Guaranteed MOA accuracy.

Price: ....**$2,379.00–$2,429.00**

BERGARA PREMIER DIVIDE

Calibers: 6.5 Creedmoor, 6.5 PRC, .308 Win., .300 Win. Mag. Capacity: AICS-style detachable, 5 standard, 3 magnum. Barrel: 22 in., 24 in. No. 6 CURE carbon fiber. Weight: 7.2–7.4 lbs. Length: 43–46 in. Stock: AG Composite 100% carbon fiber. Sights: Drilled and tapped for Remington 700 bases with 8-40 screws. Features: Built to bridge the divide between tactical and hunting rifles. Bolt uses a non-rotating gas shield, coned bolt nose, and sliding plate extractor. TriggerTech frictionless release trigger with two-position safety. Threaded muzzle with Omni Muzzle Brake. Patriot Brown Cerakote finish. Guaranteed MOA accuracy.

Price: ....**$2,749.00–$2,799.00**

BERGARA PREMIER MG LITE

Calibers: 6.5 Creedmoor, 6.5 PRC, .308 Win., .300 Win Mag. Capacity: 5 standard, 3 magnum. Barrel: 22 in. or 24 in. fully free-floated, proprietary CURE carbon fiber. Weight: 6.7–6.8 lbs. Length: 43–45 in. Stock: Ultra-lightweight XLR Element 4.0 magnesium chassis with folding buttstock. Sights: Drilled and tapped for Remington 700 bases with 8-40 screws. Features: Precision bolt-action hunting rifle with a non-rotating gas shield, coned bolt nose, and sliding plate extractor. TriggerTech frictionless release trigger with two-position safety. Threaded muzzle with Omni Muzzle Brake. Graphite Black Cerakote. Guaranteed MOA accuracy.

Price: ....**$3,229.00–$3,349.00**

BERGARA B-14 SQUARED CREST

Calibers: 6.5 Creedmoor, 6.5 PRC, .308 Win., .300 Win. Mag. Barrel: 20

in., (22 in. .300 WM) round steel. Weights: from 6.8–7.2 lbs. Stock: 100% carbon fiber with carbon spine. Features: Addition to the B-14 bolt action family. Sniper Gray Cerakote metalwork. Sub-MOA guarantee. Threaded muzzle with Omni brake. M5 AICS-style magazine.
Price: **$1,999.00**

BLASER R-8 SERIES
Calibers: Available in virtually all standard and metric calibers from .204 Ruger to .500 Jeffery. Straight-pull bolt action. Barrels: 20.5, 23, or 25.75 in. Weights: 6.375–8.375 lbs. Lengths: 40 in. overall (22 in. barrel). Stocks: Synthetic or Turkish walnut. Sights: None furnished; drilled and tapped for scope mounting. Features: Thumb-activated safety slide/cocking mechanism; interchangeable barrels and bolt heads. Many optional features. Imported from Germany by Blaser USA. *Note, Blaser R8 bolt action series adds a .22 LR rimfire conversion system.*
Price: **$3,787.00**

BLASER R8 ULTIMATE CARBON
Calibers: Available in wide range of calibers from .22 LR to .500 Jeffery, now including 6.5 Creedmoor and 6.5 PRC. Barrel: 20.5, 23, or 25.75 in. Stock: Hand-laid 100% carbon fiber thumbhole stock with Elastomer grip inserts. An Ultimate Carbon Leather variant is available with dark brown weather-proof leather inserts. Sights: Drilled and tapped. Features: Straight-pull bolt-action hunting rifle with interchangeable barrels and bolt heads. Ultimate Carbon variant designed for max performance and minimum weight. Blaser Precision trigger. Thumb-activated safety slide/cocking mechanism. Optional upgrades include an adjustable comb and recoil absorption system or adjustable recoil pad. Imported from Germany by Blaser Group.
Price: **$11,500.00**

BROWNING AB3 COMPOSITE STALKER
Calibers: .243, 6.5 Creedmoor, .270 Win., .270 WSM, 7mm-08, 7mm Rem. Mag., .30-06, .300 Win. Mag., .300 WSM or .308 Win. Barrels: 22 in, 26 in. for magnums. Weights: 6.8–7.4 lbs. Stock: Matte black synthetic. Sights: None. Picatinny rail scope mount included.
Price: **$600.00**
Price: Micro Stalker **$600.00**
Price: Hunter...**$670.00**

BROWNING X-BOLT HUNTER
Calibers: .223, .22-250, .243 Win., 6mm Creedmoor, 6.5 Creedmoor, .25-06 Rem., .270 Win., .270 WSM, .280 Rem., 7mm Rem. Mag., 7mm WSM, 7mm-08 Rem., .308 Win., .30-06, .300 Win. Mag., .300 WSM, .325 WSM, .338 Win. Mag., .375 H&H Mag, 6.8 Western. Barrels: 22 in., 23 in., 24 in., 26 in., varies by model. Matte blued or stainless free-floated barrel, recessed muzzle crown. Weights: 6.3–7 lbs. Stocks: Hunter and Medallion models have black walnut stocks; Composite Stalker and Stainless Stalker models have composite stocks. Inflex Technology recoil pad. Sights: None, drilled and tapped receiver, X-Lock scope mounts. Features: Adjustable three-lever Feather Trigger system, polished hard-chromed steel components, factory pre-set at 3.5 lbs., alloy trigger housing. Bolt unlock button, detachable rotary magazine, 60-degree bolt lift, three locking lugs, top-tang safety, sling swivel studs. Introduced 2008.
Price: Standard calibers **$900.00**

Price: Magnum calibers **$950.00**
Price: Left-hand models..**$940.00–$980.00**

BROWNING X-BOLT WESTERN HUNTER LONG RANGE
Calibers: 6.5 Creedmoor, 6.5 PRC, 7mm Rem. Mag., 28 Nosler, .280 Ackley Improved, .300 Win. Mag., 30 Nosler, .300 Rem. Ultra Mag., .300 PRC, 6.8 Western. Capacity: 3 or 4-round removeable rotary magazine Barrel: 26-in. heavy sporter contour with removeable muzzle brake. Length: 46–46.75 in. Weight: 7 lbs. 7 oz.–7 lbs. 12 oz. Stock: Composite with new adjustable comb system, A-TACS AU camo finish, and textured grip panels. Features: Top tang thumb safety. Extended bolt handle. Feather Trigger, InFlex recoil pad. X-Lock scope mount system. Gold-plated trigger. Sling studs.
Price: ....**$1,099.00–$1,219.00**

BROWNING X-BOLT HUNTER LONG RANGE
Calibers: 6.5 Creedmoor, 6.5 PRC, .308 Win., .270 Win., .30-06, 7MM Rem. Mag., .300 Win. Mag., 6.8 Western. Capacity: 3 to 4. Barrel: 22 to 26 in., blued sporter, heavy. Stock: Satin finish checkered walnut. Sights: None, drilled and tapped. Weight: 7.6 to 8 lbs. Features: Ambidextrous adjustable comb, muzzle brake with suppressor threads.
Price: **$1,300.00**

BROWNING X-BOLT MAX LONG RANGE
Calibers: 6mm Creedmoor, 6.5 Creedmoor, .308 Win., .300 WSM, 7MM Rem. Mag., 28 Nosler, .300 Win.Mag., .300 RUM, 6.5 PRC, 30 Nosler, .300 PRC, 6.8 Western. Capacity: 3 to 4. Barrel: 26 in., satin gray stainless steel sporter, heavy. Stock: Composite black, gray splatter. Sights: None, drilled and tapped. Weight: 8.2 to 8.6 lbs. Features: Adjustable comb, extended bolt handle, three swivel studs for sling and bipod use.
Price: ....**$1,300.00–$1,340.00**
Price: OD Green ....**$1,329.00–$1,379.00**

BROWNING X-BOLT MEDALLION
Calibers: Most popular calibers from .223 Rem. to .375 H&H, 6.8 Western. Barrels: 22, 24 and 26 in. free-floated. Features: Engraved receiver with polished blue finish, gloss finished and checkered walnut stock with rosewood grip and fore-end caps, detachable rotary magazine. Medallion Maple model has AAA-grade maple stock.
Price: **$1,040.00**
Price: Medallion Maple **$1,070.00**

BROWNING X-BOLT HELL'S CANYON
Calibers: .22 Nosler, 6mm Creedmoor, .243 Win., 26 Nosler, 6.5 Creedmoor, .270 Win., .270 WSM, 7mm-08 Rem., 7mm Rem. Mag., .308 Win., .30-06, .300 Win. Mag., .300 WSM, 6.8 Western. Barrels: 22–26-in. fluted and free-floating with muzzle brake or thread protector. Stock: A-TACS AU Camo composite with checkered grip panels. Features: Detachable rotary magazine, adjustable trigger, Cerakote Burnt Bronze finish on receiver and barrel.
Price: ....**$1,260.00–$1,320.00**

BROWNING X-BOLT HELLS CANYON MAX LONG RANGE
Calibers: 6.5 Creed, 6.5 PRC, 7mm Rem. Mag., 28 Nosler, .280 Ackley Improved, .300 Win. Mag., 30 Nosler, .300 Rem. Ultra Mag., .300 PRC, 6.8 Western. Capacity: 3- or 4-round box magazine. Barrel: 26-in. heavy sporter.

Prices given are believed to be accurate at time of publication however, many factors affect retail pricing so exact prices are not possible.

Weight: 8–8 lbs. 7oz. Length: 46-3/4 in. Stock: Composite Max in either A-TACS AU or OVIX camo with adjustable comb, LOP spacers, and vertical pistol grip. Features: Long-range bolt-action platform with steel receiver. Cerakote Burnt Bronze finish. Removeable Browning Recoil Hawg muzzle brake. Top tang thumb safety. Extended bolt handle. Three swivel studs. FeatherTrigger, InFlex recoil pad. Gold-plated trigger and branding detail.
Price: .... **$1,539.00–$1,619.00**

BROWNING X-BOLT MOUNTAIN PRO
Caliber: 6.5 Creedmoor, 6.5 PRC, 6.8 Western, .300 WSM, .30-06 Spfld., 7mm Rem. Mag., 28 Nosler, .300 Win. Mag., 30 Nosler, .300 PRC, .300 Rem. UM. Capacity: 3- or 4-round box magazine. Barrel: 22, 23, 24, or 26 in. sporter weight, threaded, with Recoil Hawg muzzle brake. Length: 42–46.75 in. Weight: 5 lbs. 14 oz.–6 lbs. 6 oz. Stock: Carbon fiber filled with noise-dampening foam and finished with accent graphics. Features: Choice of either Burnt Bronze or Tungsten models. Big game bolt-action semi-custom hunting rifle. New proprietary lapping process for easier bore cleaning and avoiding break-in. Cerakote finish on stainless steel barrel and action. Spiral fluted bolt and barrel. Quarter-pound weight reduction over previous models. Removeable Picatinny accessory rail. Swivel studs. Feather trigger. X-Lock optics mounting system. InFlex recoil pad. Gold-plated trigger and brand detail. Thread protector included. Mountain Pro SPR in either Burnt Bronze or Tungsten w/ 18-, 20-, and 22-in. threaded barrels with Recoil Hawg brake.
Price: .... **$2,479.00–$2,539.00**
Price: MOUNTAIN PRO LR 26 in. heavy contour ....**$2,469.00–$2,579.00**
Price: Mountain Pro SPR .... **$2,659.00–$2,699.00**

BROWNING X-BOLT PRO SERIES
Calibers: 6mm Creedmoor, 6.5 Creedmoor, 26 Nosler, 28 Nosler, .270 Win., 7mm Rem. Mag., .308 Win., .30-06., .300 Win.Mag, 6.8 Western. Detachable rotary magazine. Barrels: 22–26 in. Stainless steel, fluted with threaded/removable muzzle brake. Weights: 6–7.5 lbs. Finish: Cerakote Burnt Bronze. Stock: Second generation carbon fiber with palm swell, textured gripping surfaces. Adjustable trigger, top tang safety, sling swivel studs. Long Range has heavy sporter-contour barrel, proprietary lapping process.
Price: X-Bolt Pro..**$2,070.00–$2,130.00**
Price: X-Bolt Pro Long Range ....**$2,100.00–$2,180.00**
Price: X-Bolt Pro Tungsten ....**$2,070.00–$2,130.00**
Price: PRO LONG RANGE 26-in. heavy barrel,
carbon-fiber stock. ....**$2,239.00–$2,269.00**
Price: Pro McMillian Long Range SPR ....**$2,859.00–$2,899.00**
Price: Pro SPR ....**$2,399.00–$2,429.00**

CADEX DEFENCE CDX-R7 CRBN SERIES
Calibers: 6.5 Creedmoor, 6.5 PRC, .308 Win., .300 WSM, .300 PRC, .338 Lapua Mag. Capacity: Varies by box magazine. Barrel: 24 or 26 in. Proof Research carbon fiber threaded. Weight: 8.2–8.3 lbs. Length: 45.25–48.06 in. Stock: Lightweight Tundra Strike chassis with aluminum bedding blocks available in 14 color combinations. Cadex recoil pad, neoprene cheek pad, and rubberized grip panel. Sights: None. 0 MOA Picatinny rail standard, 20 or 30 MOA rails available. Features: Bolt-action rifle designed with backcountry hunters in mind. Hunting style muzzle brake and bolt knob. Spiral fluted bolt. Cerakote metalwork. DX2 Evo single-/two-stage selectable trigger. Oversized triggerguard and mag release. Hard case included.
Price: **$3,359.00**

CADEX DEFENCE CDX-R7 SPTR SERIES
Calibers: 6.5 Creedmoor, 6.5 PRC, .308 Win., .300 WSM, .300 PRC, 338

Lapua Mag. Capacity: varies by box magazine. Barrel: 24 or 26 in. sporter profile stainless, fluted and threaded. Weight: 8.2–8.5 lbs. Length: 45.25–48.06 in. Stock: Lightweight Tundra Strike chassis with aluminum bedding blocks available in 14 color combinations. Cadex recoil pad, neoprene cheek pad, and rubberized grip panel. Sights: None. 0 MOA Picatinny rail standard, 20 or 30 MOA rails available. Features: Bolt-action rifle similar to the CRBN series, but without the carbon-fiber barrel. Hunting-style muzzle brake and bolt knob. Spiral fluted bolt. DX2 Evo single-/two-stage selectable trigger. Oversized triggerguard and mag release. Hard case included.
Price: **$2,769.00**

CHAPUIS ROLS
Calibers: .30-06 Spfld., .300 Win. Mag., .375 H&H (6.5 Creed & .308 Win. available on Carbon only). Barrel: 24 in., 25.5 in. Weights: 5.3-5.5 lbs. (Carbon); 6.6-7.2 lbs. (Classic & Deluxe) Stock: High-grade Circassian Walnut, pistol grip-style with Schnabel forend on Classic and Deluxe. Carbon-fiber black on Carbon model. Features: Straight-pull bolt action rifle. Sub-MOA accuracy guarantee. Action and locking system tested for up to 123,000 PSI. Manual decocker. Single trigger. Manual safety. Open rifle sights with slots for Recknagel scope mounts. Quick detach rotary magazine. Ready to accept barrels in different calibers. Ships with prestige-grade custom hard case.
Price: Classic w/ bronze receiver, Walnut ....**$5,899.00–$6,299.00**
Price: Deluxe w/ silver engraved receiver, Walnut ....**$6,899.00–$7,399.00**
Price: Carbon w/ carbon-fiber stock, no sights ....**$9,099.00–$9,399.00**

CHEYTAC M-200
Calibers: .357 CheyTac, .408 CheyTac. Capacity: 7-round magazine. Barrel: 30 in. Length: 55 in. stock extended. Weight: 27 lbs. (steel barrel); 24 lbs. (carbon-fiber barrel). Stock: Retractable. Sights: None, scope rail provided. Features: CNC-machined receiver, attachable Picatinny rail M-1913, detachable barrel, integral bipod, 3.5-lb. trigger pull, muzzle brake. Made in USA by CheyTac, LLC.
Price: **$11,700.00**

CHRISTENSEN ARMS RIDGELINE FFT
Calibers: .450 Bushmaster, .22-250 Rem., .243 Rem, 6.5 Creed, 6.5 PRC, 6.5-284, 26 Nosler, .270 Win., 7mm-08, .280 Ackley, 28 Nosler, 7mm Rem. Mag., .308 Win., .30-06, 30 Nosler, .300 WSM, .300 Win. Mag., .300 PRC, .300 RUM. Capacity: FFT hinged floor plate with internal magazine. 4-round standard, 3-round magnum. Barrel: 20 or 22-in. carbon-fiber wrapped stainless, button-rifled, hand-lapped, free-floating. Weight: From 5.3 lbs. Stock: Proprietary Flash Forged Technology (FFT) carbon-fiber sporter style with stainless steel bedding pillars. Choice of black with gray webbing, green with black and tan webbing, Sitka Subalpine camo, or Sitka Elevated II camo. Sights: No iron sights. Drilled and tapped at 6-48 for Remington 700 bases. Features: Upgraded version of the Ridgeline uses the latest in carbon-fiber technology to build the rifle a full pound lighter. New side-baffle brake and stylish paint scheme distinguish the upgraded model. Choice of natural stainless or Burnt Bronze Cerakote metalwork. Enlarged ejection port. Billet aluminum bottom metal. Sub-MOA guarantee, excluding .450 Bushmaster. Multiple calibers available in a left-hand rifle.
Price: **$2,399.00**

CHRISTENSEN ARMS RIDGELINE SCOUT
Calibers: .223 Rem, 6mm ARC, 6.5 Creed, .308 Win., .300 Blackout. Capacity: 10-round AICS box magazine. Barrel: 16-in. carbon-fiber wrapped stainless, button rifled, free-floating. Weight: From 5.9 lbs. Stock: Carbon-fiber composite, sporter style with stainless steel bedding pillars. Tan with black webbing. Sights: No iron sights. 0 MOA rail. Features: Compact, scout-rifle version of the Ridgeline bolt-action hunting rifle. Black nitride-coated action. Flat-shoe TriggerTech trigger. Match chamber. Three-prong flash hider removes for easy suppressor use. Forward mount lower rail with barricade stop. MOA guarantee.
Price: **$2,199.00**

CHRISTENSEN ARMS RIDGELINE TITANIUM EDITION
Calibers: 6.5 Creedmoor, 6.5 PRC, .308 Win., .300 Win. Mag. Capacity: 3 to 4. Barrel: 22 to 24 in., 416R stainless steel, carbon-fiber wrapped. Stock: Carbon-fiber composite, sporter style. Sights: Picatinny rail. Weight: 5.8 lbs. Features: Titanium radial brake, M16-style extractor, LimbSaver recoil pad.
Price: **$2,495.00**

CHRISTENSEN ARMS MODERN HUNTING RIFLE (MHR)
Calibers: 6.5 Creed, 6.5 PRC, 6.8 Western, .308 Win., 7mm PRC, 7mm Rem. Mag., .300 Win. Mag., .300 PRC. Barrel: 22 in., 24 in. carbon-fiber wrapped stainless steel. Weight: 7.4 lbs. Stock: Aluminum mini chassis with FFT carbon-fiber stock. Features: Modular bolt-action design blending chassis rifle design with hunting features. Sub-MOA accuracy guarantee. Removeable side-baffle brake. V-Block bedding. Toolless adjustable comb. Forward Picatinny and M-LOK points. Match chamber. Hand-lapped button-rifled free-floating barrel design. Black nitride action finish. Multiple stock finishes available. TriggerTech trigger. Internal magazine with AICS drop-box compatibility.
Price: **$3,499.00**

COOPER MODEL 21
Calibers: Virtually any factory or wildcat chambering in the .223 Rem. family is available including: .17 Rem., .19-223, Tactical 20, .204 Ruger, .222 Rem., .222 Rem. Mag., .223 Rem, .223 Rem AI, 6x45, 6x47. Single shot. Barrels: 22–24 in. for Classic configurations, 24–26 in. for Varminter configurations. Weights: 6.5–8.0 lbs., depending on type. Stock: AA-AAA select claro walnut, 20 LPI checkering. Sights: None furnished. Features: Three front locking-lug, bolt-action, single-shot. Action: 7.75 in. long, Sako extractor. Button ejector. Fully adjustable single-stage trigger. Options include wood upgrades, case-color metalwork, barrel fluting, custom LOP, and many others.
Price: Classic **$2,495.00**
Price: Custom Classic...**$2,995.00**
Price: Western Classic. **$3,795.00**
Price: Varminter...**$2,495.00**
Price: Mannlicher **$4,395.000**

COOPER MODEL 52
Calibers: .30-06, .270 Win., .280 Rem, .25-06, .284 Win., .257 Weatherby Mag., .264 Win. Mag., .270 Weatherby Mag., 7mm Remington Mag., 7mm Weatherby Mag., 7mm Shooting Times Westerner, .300 Holland & Holland, .300 Win. Mag., .300 Weatherby Mag., .308 Norma Mag., 8mm Rem. Mag., .338 Win. Mag., .340 Weatherby V. Three-shot magazine. Barrels: 22 in. or 24 in. in Classic configurations, 24 in. or 26 in. in Varminter configurations. Weight: 7.75–8 lbs. depending on type. Stock: AA-AAA select claro walnut, 20 LPI checkering. Sights: None furnished. Features: Three front locking-lug bolt-action single shot. Action: 7 in. long, Sako style extractor. Button ejector. Fully adjustable single-stage trigger. Options include wood upgrades, case-color metalwork, barrel fluting, custom LOP, and many others.
Price: Classic. **$2,495.00**
Price: Custom Classic...**$3,335.00**
Price: Western Classic. **$3,995.00**
Price: Jackson Game **$2,595.00**
Price: Jackson Hunter **$2,595.00**
Price: Excalibur...**$2,595.00**
Price: Mannlicher **$4,755.00**
Price: Open Country Long Range **$3,795.00-4,155.00**
Price: Timberline, Synthetic Stock **$2,595.00**
Price: Raptor, Synthetic tactical stock **$2,755.00**

CVA CASCADE
Calibers: .243 Win., 6.5 Creedmoor, 7mm-08 Rem., .308 Win., .350 Legend, .450 Bushmaster, .22-250 Rem., 6.5 PRC, 7mm Rem. Mag., .300 Win. Mag. Capacity: 3 or 4-round flush-fit detachable magazine Barrel: 22-in. 4140 carbon steel in either matte blue or Cerakote FDE. Weight: 6.85–7.25 lbs. Length: 42.5–45.5 in. Stock: Synthetic, fiber-glass reinforced with SoftTouch finish. Available in either charcoal gray or Veil Wideland camo. Sights: Drilled and tapped for Savage 110 mounts; aftermarket CVA 20-MOA one-piece base available. Features: Bolt designed with 70-degree throw. Two-position safety. Threaded muzzle. Dual front swivel studs. Buttstock has adjustable LOP with removeable spacer. MOA guarantee.
Price: ....**$567.00–$658.00**
Price: Cascade SB (Short Barrel) Series...........................**$670.00**

CVA CASCADE XT
Calibers: 6.5 Creedmoor, .308 Win., .450 Bushmaster, .350 Legend, 6.5 PRC, 7mm Rem. Mag., .300 Win. Mag. Barrel: 22, 24, 26 in. #5 Taper fluted, threaded. Stock: Synthetic with Realtree Excape camo and SoftTouch finish. Features: Precision-oriented version of the Cascade bolt action. Heavier barrel with radial muzzle brake. Tactical-style bolt knob. Two-position safety. Dual front swivel studs. Graphite black Cerakote metalwork. MOA guarantee. Flush-fit, dropbox magazine.
Price: **$799.00**

FIERCE FIREARMS RIVAL
Calibers: 6.5 Creedmoor, 6.5 PRC, 7mm Rem., 28 Nosler, .300 Win., .300 PRC, .300 RUM. Capacity: 4 to 5. Barrel: 20 to 26 in., spiral-fluted, match-grade stainless steel or carbon fiber. Stock: Fierce Tech C3 carbon fiber. Sights: None, drilled and tapped. Weight: 6.4 to 7 lbs. Features: Cerakote finish, Trigger Tech trigger, built-in bipod rail.
Price: ....**$2,295.00-$2,795.00**

FIERCE FIREARMS MTN REAPER
Calibers: 6.5 Creed, 6.5 PRC, 7mm PRC, 7mm Rem. Mag., .308 Win., .300 Win. Mag., .300 PRC. Barrel: 18 or 20 in. (short action), 20 or 22 in. (long action) C3 carbon fiber Weight: 5.8-6.6 lbs. Stock: Ultralite magnesium chassis with push button carbon-fiber fold and lock stock. Features: Precision machined two-lug bolt action. 70-degree bolt throw with tactical knob. Bix'nAndy trigger. AccurateMag box magazine. NIX muzzle brake. Limbsaver buttpad. Spiral fluted bolt. 0-MOA scope rail. Guaranteed 1/2 MOA accuracy.
Price: **$3,399.00**

FRANCHI MOMENTUM
Calibers: .243 Win., 6.5 Creedmoor, .270 Win., .308 Win., .30-06, .300 Win. Mag. Barrels: 22 or 24 in. Weights: 6.5–7.5 lbs. Stock: Black

Prices given are believed to be accurate at time of publication however, many factors affect retail pricing so exact prices are not possible.

synthetic with checkered gripping surface, recessed sling swivel studs, TSA recoil pad. Sights: None. Features: Available with Burris Fullfield II 3-9X40mm scope.

Price: Varminter..**$609.00**
Price: With Burris 3-9X scope..**$729.00**

FRANCHI MOMENTUM ELITE

Calibers: .223 Rem., 6.5 Creedmoor, 6.5 PRC, .308 Win., .300 Win. Mag., .350 Legend. Capacity: 3 or 4-round box magazine. Barrel: 22- or 24-in. free floating, cold hammer forged with threaded muzzle brake. Weight: 7.1–7.5 lbs. Stock: Synthetic in True Timber Strata, Realtree Excape, and now also available with Sitka Optifade Elevation II camouflage. Sights: Picatinny rail. Features: TSA recoil pad absorbs up to 50 percent of felt recoil. Sling attachment points recessed into stock. One-piece spiral fluted bolt with three locking lugs and 60-degree throw. Two-position safety. RELIA trigger adjustable from 2 to 4 pounds. Cobalt Cerakote metalwork on the Sitka camo models.

Price: **$899.00**

FRANCHI MOMENTUM ELITE VARMINT

Calibers: .223 Rem., .22-250 Rem., .224 Valkyrie, 6.5 Creedmoor, .308 Win. Capacity: 3–4-round flush magazines or 7–8-round extended magazines. Barrel: 24-in. free-floating, heavy, spiral-fluted, threaded. Weight: 9.0–9.4 lbs. Length: 46.75 in. Stock: Evolved EGONOM-X synthetic with removeable cheek rest and checkered-polymer grip, finished in Sitka OptiFade Subalpine camo. Sights: One-piece Picatinny rail. Features: Varmint addition to the Momentum Elite family gets caliber additions for 2022. Stock designed specifically for varmint hunting. Midnight Bronze Cerakote metalwork. RELIA-Trigger adjustable from 2–4 pounds. MOA accuracy guarantee. DEPENDA bolt with three locking lugs and 60-degree throw.

Price: **$999.00**

FRANCHI MOMENTUM ALL TERRAIN ELITE

Caliber: .223 Rem./5.56 NATO, .308 Win./7.62 NATO. Barrel: 18-in. free-floating, threaded. Weight: 7.5 lbs. Stock: Synthetic in True Timber Strata. Features: Specialized version of the Momentum bolt actions. Optimized for carry. Modular stock with a low-rise comb and M-LOK and QD points. Metalwork in Midnight Bronze Cerakote. Extended Picatinny rail. AICS 10-round magazine. Flip-up adjustable iron sights. Relia adjustable single-stage trigger and MOA guarantee. Threaded barrel with muzzle brake. TSA recoil pad.

Price: **$1,499.00**

GUNWERKS CLYMR

Calibers: 7 LRM, .22-250, 6mm Creed, 6.5 Creed, 6.5-284 Norma, 6.5 PRC, 28 Nosler, 7mm Rem. Mag., 7 SAUM, .300 Win. Mag., 30 Nosler, 300 PRC. Capacity: 3-round capacity in the internal mag. Option to upgrade to dropbox mags. Barrel: Carbon wrapped, threaded, 20- or 22-in. barrel come standard. Upgrade to 18 in. available. Weight: Varies by options selected. Stock: Carbon fiber in choice of ten paint finishes with negative comb and flat toe line. Sights: No sights. Drilled and tapped. Choice of multiple base, scope ring, and scope options direct from the factory. Features: Lightweight, semi-custom, bolt-action hunting rifle built for mountain hunting and available as a user-built rifle system with multiple options. Choice of standard GLR SS action or Titanium action upgrade. Add $150 for Left-hand action. Eleven metal finish colors available, as well as option of directional muzzle brake or thread cap. LOP of 13.5 in. Prices increase significantly as options are added for custom factory builds.

Price: **$5,245.00**

GUNWERKS WERKMAN SYSTEM

Caliber: 6.5 PRC, 7mm PRC, .300 PRC. Barrel: 22-in. stainless steel, cut rifled. Weight: 9.6 lbs. Stock: Gen1 Magnus carbon fiber in tan, gray, or green Fracture paint finish. Features: Bolt-action rifle system with fewer frills. GLR stainless receiver. Threaded barrel with directional brake. TriggerTech trigger. GW floorplate bottom metal. Topped with Revic Werkman RS25 rifle scope. Custom BDC turret matched to Hornady ELD Match ammunition and ballistics data for 1,000 yards. Left-hand action available for +$150.

Price: **$4,950.00**

HEYM EXPRESS BOLT-ACTION RIFLE

Calibers: .375 H&H Mag., .416 Rigby, .404 Jeffery, .458 Lott, .450 Rigby. Capacity: 5. Barrel: 24 in., Krupp steel, hammer-forged. Stock: Custom select European walnut. Sights: Iron, barrel-banded front. Weight: 9 to 10.5 lbs. Features: Caliber-specific action and magazine box, classic English sporting rifle, three-position safety.

Price: **$12,000.00**

HOWA MINI ACTION FULL DIP

Calibers: .223 Rem., 6.5 Grendel, 7.62x39. Capacity: 5. Barrel: 20 in., threaded, heavy. Stock: Hogue pillar-bedded. Sights: 3.5-10x44 scope. Weight: 10 lbs. Features: Full-dipped camo, forged, one-piece bolt with locking lugs.

Price: **$769.00**

HOWA HS CARBON FIBER

Caliber: 6.5 Creedmoor. Capacity: 4. Barrel: 24 in., carbon-fiber wrapped. Stock: Synthetic, CNC-machined aluminum bedding block. Sights: None, drilled and tapped. Weight: 7.8 lbs. Features: Lightweight, hand-finished stock, scope optional.

Price: **$1,819.00**

HOWA CARBON ELEVATE

Calibers: .6.5 Grendel, 6.5 Creedmoor, .308 Win., 6.5 PRC. Capacity: Varies by caliber and depending on flush mount or extended magazine. Barrel: 24-in. heavy threaded barrel. Weight: from 4 lbs. 13 oz. Stock: Stocky's Custom carbon-fiber super lightweight design available in natural carbon fiber or Kryptek Altitude. Sights: No sights. Drilled and tapped. Features: Ultra-lightweight bolt-action hunting rifle with AccuBlock lug bed. Three-position safety. Sub-MOA accuracy assurance. HACT two-stage trigger. LimbSaver buttpad. Suppressor-ready. Sub-MOA guarantee. Manufacturer Lifetime Warranty.

Price: **$1,528.00**

J.P. SAUER & SOHN 404 SYNCHRO XTC

Calibers: .243 Win., .270 Win., 6.5 Creedmoor, 6.5x55, .308 Win., .30-06 Spfld., 7x64, 8x57IS, 9.3x62, 7mm Rem. Mag., .300 Win. Mag., .338 Win. Mag., .404

Prices given are believed to be accurate at time of publication however, many factors affect retail pricing so exact prices are not possible.

78TH EDITION, 2024 ⊕ **447**

Jeffery, 10.3x60R. Barrel: 22-in. fluted, cold-hammer forged. Sights: Integral scope bases. Length: 42 in. Weight: 6.1 lbs. Stock: Carbon-fiber XTC thumbhole style with Green/Black/Grey carbon-fiber camo and adjustable comb. Features: Fully modular concept rifle. Adjustable trigger blade and trigger pull, from 1.2–2.7 lbs. Manual cocking. Threaded muzzle. MagLock magazine safety. Matte black hard anodized aluminum receiver. Engineered for changing bolt heads and barrels. SUS combination tool integrated into front sling swivel. Miniature universal tool integrated into rear sling swivel.
Price: **$8,199.00**

KENNY JARRETT RIFLES
Calibers: Custom built in virtually any chambering including .223 Rem., .243 Improved, .243 Catbird, 7mm-08 Improved, .280 Remington, .280 Ackley Improved, 7mm Rem. Mag., .284 Jarrett, .30-06 Springfield, .300 Win. Mag., .300 Jarrett, .323 Jarrett, .338 Jarrett, .375 H&H, .416 Rem., .450 Rigby, other modern cartridges. Numerous options regarding barrel type and weight, stock styles and material. Features: Tri-Lock receiver. Talley rings and bases. Accuracy guarantees and custom loaded ammunition. Newest series is the Shikar featuring 28-year aged American Black walnut hand-checkered stock with Jarrett-designed stabilizing aluminum chassis. Accuracy guaranteed to be .5 MOA with standard calibers, .75 MOA with magnums.
Price: Shikar Series **$10,320.00**
Price: Signature Series **$8,320.00**
Price: Long Ranger Series **$8,320.00**
Price: Ridge Walker Series **$8,320.00**
Price: Wind Walker **$8,320.00**
Price: Original Beanfield (customer's receiver) **$6,050.00**
Price: Professional Hunter **$11,070.00**
Price: SA/Custom **$7,000.00**

KIMBER HUNTER PRO
Calibers: 6.5 Creedmoor, .308 Win., .280 Ackley Improved. Capacity: 3-round box magazine. Barrel: 22 or 24 in. sporter with satin finish and muzzle brake. Weight: 5 lbs. 7oz.–5 lbs. 12 oz. Length: 41.25 in. Stock: Fiber-reinforced polymer in Desolve Blak pattern with pillar bedding. Sights: No iron sights. Drilled and tapped. Features: Full stainless build based on 84M action with Mauser claw extraction. Three-position wing safety. Sling studs. One-inch rubber recoil pad. Match-grade chamber. Factory adjustable trigger set at 3.5–4 lbs. Sub-MOA guarantee.
Price: **$1,006.00**

MAUSER M-18
Calibers: .223 Rem., .243 Win., 6.5x55, 6.5 PRC, 6.5 Creedmoor, .270 Win., .308 Win., .30-06 Spfld, 8x57IS, 9.3x62, 7mm Rem. Mag., .300 Win. Mag. Capacity: 5-round box magazine. Barrel: 21.75 or 24.5 in. Weight: 6.5–6.8 lbs. Length: 41.7–44.0 in. Stock: Polymer with softgrip inlays. Sights: No iron sights. Drilled and tapped. Features: Adjustable trigger. Three-position safety. Removeable recoil pad section with interior buttstock storage. Budget-priced option tagged "The People's Rifle."
Price: **$699.00**

MAUSER M18 SAVANNA
Calibers: .223 Rem., .243 Win., 6.5 PRC, 6.5 Creedmoor, .270 Win., .308 Win., .30-06 Spfld, 7mm Rem. Mag., .300 Win. Mag. Capacity: 5-round magazine standard; 10-rounders available. Barrel: 21.75 or 24.5-in. cold-hammer forged, German-steel, threaded. Weight: 6.5–6.8 lbs. Length: 41.7–44.0 in. Stock: Savanna Tan Polymer with grip inserts. Sights: No iron sights. Drilled and tapped. Features: Adjustable trigger. Sixty-degree oversized bolt. Three-position safety. Removeable recoil pad section with interior buttstock storage. Sub-MOA guarantee and 10-year warranty.
Price: **$799.00**

MOSSBERG MVP PATROL
.300 AAC Blackout. 16.25-in. barrel. 6.5-lb. weight. 36.5-in. length. 10+1-round capacity
Price: **$638.00**

MOSSBERG MVP SERIES
Caliber: .223/5.56 NATO. Capacity: 10-round AR-style magazines. Barrels: 16.25-in. medium bull, 20-in. fluted sporter. Weight: 6.5–7 lbs. Stock: Classic black textured polymer. Sights: Adjustable folding rear, adjustable blade front. Features: Available with factory mounted 3-9x32 scope, (4-16x50 on Varmint model). FLEX model has 20-in. fluted sporter barrel, FLEX AR-style 6-position adjustable stock. Varmint model has laminated stock, 24-in. barrel. Thunder Ranch model has 18-in. bull barrel, OD Green synthetic stock.
Price: Patrol Model..**$732.00**
Price: Patrol Model w/scope **$863.00**
Price: FLEX Model...**$764.00**
Price: FLEX Model w/scope **$897.00**
Price: Thunder Ranch Model **$755.00**
Price: Predator Model **$732.00**
Price: Predator Model w/scope...**$872.00**
Price: Varmint Model **$753.00**
Price: Varmint Model w/scope **$912.00**
Price: Long Range Rifle (LR)...**$974.00**

MOSSBERG PATRIOT
Calibers: .22-250, .243 Win., .25-06, .270 Win., 7mm-08, .7mm Rem., 7mm PRC., .308 Win., .30-06, .300 Win. Mag., .38 Win. Mag., .375 Ruger, 350 Legend. Capacities: 4- or 5-round magazine. Barrels: 22-in. sporter or fluted, 24 in. Stock: Walnut, laminate, camo or synthetic black. Weights: 7.5–8 lbs. Finish: Matte blued. Sights: Adjustable or none. Some models available with 3-9x40 scope. Other features include Lightning Bolt Action Trigger adjustable from 2 to 7 pounds, spiral-fluted bolt. Not all variants available in all calibers. Introduced in 2015.
Price: Walnut stock **$559.00**
Price: Walnut with premium Vortex Crossfire scope...........**$649.00**
Price: Synthetic stock **$396.00**
Price: Synthetic stock with standard scope.......................**$436.00**
Price: Laminate stock w/iron sights...................................**$584.00**
Price: Deer THUG w/Mossy Oak Infinity Camo stock...........**$500.00**
Price: Bantam **$396.00**
Price: Patriot Predator FDE **$536.00**
Price: Predator Cerakote/Camo **$636.00**

MOSSBERG PATRIOT LR TACTICAL
Caliber: 6.5 Creedmoor, 6.5 PRC, .308 Win. Barrel: 22, 24-in. medium bull threaded. Stock: MDT adjustable for LOP and cheek rest. Features: Latest hunting-meets-long range competition bolt action with the most popular Patriot features plus additional upgrades. M-LOK forend slots. 20 MOA Picatinny rail. Aluminum V-Block bedding. AICS magazine with either a 7- or 10-round capacity.
Price: **$1,085.00**

NEW ULTRA LIGHT ARMS
Calibers: Custom made in virtually every current chambering. Barrel: Douglas, length to order. Weights: 4.75–7.5 lbs. Length: Varies. Stock: Kevlar graphite composite, variety of finishes. Sights: None furnished;

Prices given are believed to be accurate at time of publication however, many factors affect retail pricing so exact prices are not possible.

drilled and tapped for scope mounts. Features: Timney trigger, hand-lapped action, button-rifled barrel, hand-bedded action, recoil pad, sling-swivel studs, optional Jewell trigger. Made in USA by New Ultra Light Arms.

Price: Model 20 Ultimate Mountain Rifle **$3,500.00**
Price: Model 20 Ultimate Varmint Rifle **$3,500.00**
Price: Model 24 Ultimate Plains Rifle **$3,600.00**
Price: Model 28 Ultimate Alaskan Rifle **$3,900.00**
Price: Model 40 Ultimate African Rifle **$3,900.00**

NOSLER M48 MOUNTAIN CARBON

Calibers: 6mm Creedmoor, 6.5 Creedmoor, 6.5 PRC, 26 Nosler, 27 Nosler, .280 Ackley Improved, 28 Nosler, .300 Win. Mag., 30 Nosler, 33 Nosler. Capacity: 3 or 4-round hinged aluminum floorplate. Barrel: 24-in. light Sendero contour, carbon-fiber wrapped with cut rifling. Sights: No iron sights; contoured to accept any standard two-piece scope base that would otherwise fit a Remington 700. Weight: 6.0 lbs. Length: 44.4–45 in. Stock: Carbon-fiber Mountain Hunter stock in either Granite Green or Shale Gray with textured finish. Features: Built around a Model 48 action. Match-grade, cut-rifled, carbon-wrapped, fully free-floating barrel with guaranteed sub-MOA accuracy. Glass and aluminum pillar bedded into ultra-light Mountain Hunter stock. Steel surfaces coated in Tungsten Grey Cerakote for weather resistance. Timney trigger with two-position safety. Threaded muzzle with knurled thread protector. *Note, Nosler has discontinued all rifles except the Mountain Carbon and Long Range Carbon. Liberty and Heritage are no longer in current production.*

Price: **$3,140.00**

NOSLER MODEL 21

Calibers: 22 Nosler, 6.5 Creedmoor, 6.5 PRC, 26 Nosler, 27 Nosler, .280 Ackley Improved, 28 Nosler, .308 Win., .300 Win. Mag., 30 Nosler, 33 Nosler, .375 H&H Magnum. Capacity: 3 or 4 rounds depending on caliber. Barrel: 22- or 24-in. Shilen match-grade stainless Weight: 6.8–7.1 lbs. Length: 41.625–44.5 in. Stock: McMillian Hunters Edge Sporter 100% carbon fiber painted in all-weather epoxy-style finish. Sights: No iron sights; contoured to accept any standard two-piece scope base that would otherwise fit a Remington 700. Features: Nosler's new rifle design for 2022 with a blueprinted action, wire EDM machined receiver, spriral-fluted, one-piece, nitride coated bolt. TriggerTech Frictionless Release trigger. M16-style extractor and fire control group feature tool-less takedown. LOP of 13.5-in. with one-inch recoil pad. Threaded barrel with knurled cover.

Price: **$2,795.00**

NOSLER MODEL 21 CARBON CHASSIS HUNTER

Calibers: 6.5 Creedmoor, 6.5 PRC, 28 Nosler, .300 Win. Mag. Barrel: 24, 26 in. Proof Sendero contour carbon-fiber threaded. Weight: 6.9 lbs. (short actions) 7.1 lbs. (long action) Stock: MDT HNT26 collapsible. Features: Nosler's first chassis rifle on the Model 21 bolt-action family. Blueprinted action with magnesium alloy frame. Fluted bolt with nitride coating. TriggerTech Primary trigger. ARCA rail.

Price: **$5,395.00**

PROOF RESEARCH ASCENSION

Caliber: 6.5 Creed, 6.5 PRC, 7mm Rem. Mag., 7mm PRC, 28 Nosler, .308 Win., .300 Win. Mag., .300 WSM, 300 PRC. Barrel: 20 to 26 in. Proof carbon-fiber wrapped, match-grade Sendero weight. Weight: 5 lbs., 5 oz. to 6 lbs., 4 oz. Stock: PROOF carbon-fiber Monte Carlo-style in multiple colors/patterns. Features: High Country Hunter bolt-action rifle built on a titanium

---

Zermatt Arms receiver. TriggerTech trigger. Threaded barrel with protector; brakes available for an upcharge. Multiple Cerakote action colors. Split rail base. BDL-style magazine. 1/2 MOA accuracy guarantee.

Price: **$7,699.00**

REMARMS MODEL 700 ALPHA 1

Caliber: .223 Rem., .22-250 Rem., .243 Win., 6.5 Creed, 7mm-08 Rem., .270 Win,. .308 Win., .30-06 Spfld., 7mm Rem. Mag., .300 Win. Mag. Barrel: 22, 24 in. fluted 5R w/ Black Cerakote. Stock: AG Composite Gray Speckled Synthetic. Features: First rifle launch from new RemArms. Precision ground recoil lug. Enlarged ejection port. Timney Elite Hunter trigger. Toolless firing pin disassembly. Aluminum Obendorf-style triggerguard. Included Picatinny rail mount. Longer internal magazine for greater case lengths.

Price: **$2,140.00**

RUGER GUIDE GUN

Calibers: .30-06, .300 Win. Mag., .338 Win. Mag., .375 Ruger, .416 Ruger. Capacities: 3 or 4 rounds. Barrel: 20 in. with barrel band sling swivel and removable muzzle brake. Weights: 8–8.12 pounds. Stock: Green Mountain laminate. Finish: Hawkeye matte stainless. Sights: Adjustable rear, bead front. Introduced 2013.

Price: **$1,269.00**

RUGER HAWKEYE

Calibers: .204 Ruger, .223 Rem., .243 Win., .270 Win., 6.5 PRC, 6.5 Creedmoor, 7mm/08, 7mm Rem. Mag., .308 Win., .30-06, .300 Win. Mag., .338 Win. Mag., .375 Ruger, .416 Ruger. Capacities: 4-round magazine, except 3-round magazine for magnums; 5-round magazine for .204 Ruger and .223 Rem. Barrels: 22 in., 24 in. Weight: 6.75–8.25 lbs. Length: 42–44.4 in. overall. Stock: American walnut, laminate or synthetic. FTW has camo stock, muzzle brake. Long Range Target has adjustable target stock, heavy barrel. Sights: None furnished. Receiver has Ruger integral scope mount base, Ruger 1 in. rings. Features: Includes Ruger LC6 trigger, new red rubber recoil pad, Mauser-type controlled feeding, claw extractor, 3-position safety, hammer-forged steel barrels, Ruger scope rings. Walnut stocks have wrap-around cut checkering on the forearm, and more rounded contours on stock and top of pistol grips. Matte stainless all-weather version features synthetic stock. Hawkeye African chambered in .375 Ruger, .416 Ruger and has 23-in. blued barrel, checkered walnut stock, windage-adjustable shallow V-notch rear sight, white bead front sight. Introduced 2007. *(Note: VT Varmint Target and Compact Magnum are no longer currently produced)*

Price: Standard, right- and left-hand.....................................**$939.00**
Price: Compact **$939.00**
Price: Laminate Compact **$999.00**
Price: Compact Magnum **$969.00**
Price: Hawkeye Hunter **$1,099.00**
Price: VT Varmint Target **$1,139.00**
Price: Predator **$1,139.00**
Price: Alaskan...**$1,279.00**
Price: Long Range Hunter **$1,279.00**
Price: African with muzzle brake **$1,279.00**
Price: FTW Hunter **$1,279.00**
Price: Long Range Target **$1,279.00**

SAKO TRG-22 TACTICAL RIFLE

Calibers: 6.5 Creedmoor, .308 Winchester (TRG-22). For TRG-22A1 add .260 Rem. TRG-42 only available in .300 Win. Mag., or .338 Lapua. Features: Target-grade Cr-Mo or stainless barrels with muzzle brake; three locking lugs; 60-degree bolt throw; adjustable two-stage target trigger; adjustable or folding synthetic stock; receiver-mounted integral 17mm axial optics rails with recoil stop-slots; tactical scope mount for modern three-turret tactical scopes (30 and 34 mm tube diameter); optional bipod. 22A1 has folding stock with two-hinge design, M-LOK fore-end, full aluminum middle chassis.

Price: TRG-22	$3,495.00
Price: TRG-22A1	$6,725.00
Price: TRG-42	$4,550.00

SAKO MODEL 85

Calibers: .22-250 Rem., .243 Win., .25-06 Rem., .260 Rem., 6.5x55mm, .270 Win., .270 WSM, 7mm-08 Rem., 7x64, .308 Win., .30-06; 7mm WSM, .300 WSM, .338 Federal, 8x57IS, 9.3x62. Barrels: 22.4 in., 22.9 in., 24.4 in. Weight: 7.75 lbs. Length: NA. Stock: Polymer, laminated or high-grade walnut, straight comb, shadow-line cheekpiece. Sights: None furnished. Features: Controlled-round feeding, adjustable trigger, matte stainless or nonreflective satin blue. Offered in a wide range of variations and models. Introduced 2006. Imported from Finland by Beretta USA.

Price: Grey Wolf	$1,725.00
Price: Black Bear	$1,850.00
Price: Kodiak	$1,950.00
Price: Varmint Laminated	$2,025.00
Price: Classic	$2,275.00
Price: Bavarian	$2,200.00–$2,300.00
Price: Bavarian carbine, Full-length stock	$2,400.00
Price: Brown Bear	$2,175.00

SAKO S20

Calibers: .243 Win., 6.5 Creedmoor, 6.5 PRC, .270 Win., .308 Win., .30-06 Spfld., 7mm Rem. Mag., .300 Win. Mag. Capacity: 5 (3 Magnum), and 10 (7 magnum) double-stacked magazines, glass-reinforced composite. Barrel: 20- to 24-in. cold-hammer forged, fluted, threaded. Weight: 7.3–8.8 lbs. Length: 42.9–46.9 in. Stock: Choice of two interchangeable injection-molded synthetic stock types — tactical precision or ergonomic hunting thumbhole. Sights: Picatinny rail integral to receiver. Features: Designed as a hybrid rifle for both hunters and precision shooters. Full aluminum rifle chassis. Takedown-style stock design allows user configuration. Adjustable recoil pad for LOP and adjustable cheek piece. QD sling attachments. Two-stage multi-adjustable trigger. Five-shot sub MOA guarantee.

Price:	$1,598.00

SAVAGE IMPULSE BIG GAME

Calibers: .243 Win., .308 Win., 6.5 Creedmoor, 7mm PRC, .308 Win., .300 Win. Mag., .300 WSM. Capacity: 2, 3, or 4-round flush-fit detachable box magazine. Barrel: 22- or 24-in. medium contour, carbon steel, fluted, and threaded. Sights: Single piece 20 MOA rail machined into receiver. Length: 43.5–45.5 in. Weight: 8.8–8.9 lbs. Stock: Sporter-style AccuStock with AccuFit user-adjustable system and Kuiu Verde 2.0 camouflage finish. Features: New straight-pull bolt action uses HexLock bolt system. Ambidextrous rotary bolt handle. Tang safety. Free-floating, tool-free, interchangeable bolt head. Four-bolt barrel clamp system. Adjustable

AccuTrigger. Hazel Green Cerakote aluminum receiver. Removeable and user-adjustable round bolt knob handle.

Price:	$1,449.00

SAVAGE IMPULSE HOG HUNTER

Calibers: 6.5 Creedmoor, .308 Win., .30-06 Spfld., .300 Win. Mag. Capacity: 3- or 4-round flush-fit detachable box magazine. Barrel: 18-, 20-, or 24-in. medium contour, carbon steel, threaded. Sights: Single piece 20 MOA rail machined into receiver. Length: 39.25–44.25 in. Weight: 8.41–9.1 lbs. Stock: OD Green Sporter-style AccuStock with AccuFit user-adjustable system. Features: New straight pull bolt action uses HexLock bolt system. Ambidextrous rotary bolt handle. Tang safety. Free-floating, tool-free, interchangeable bolt head. Four-bolt barrel clamp system. Adjustable AccuTrigger. Matte black aluminum receiver. Removeable and user adjustable round bolt knob handle.

Price:	$1,379.00

SAVAGE IMPULSE PREDATOR

Calibers: .22-250 Rem., .243 Win., 6.5 Creedmoor, .308 Win. Capacity: 10-round AICS-style magazine with ambidextrous release. Barrel: 20-in. medium contour, threaded. Sights: Single piece 20 MOA rail machined into receiver. Length: 41.25 in. Weight: 8.75 lbs. Stock: Mossy Oak Terra Gila camouflage AccuStock with AccuFit user-adjustable system. Features: New straight-pull bolt action uses HexLock bolt system. Ambidextrous rotary bolt handle. Tang safety. Free-floating, tool-free, interchangeable bolt head. Four-bolt barrel clamp system. Adjustable AccuTrigger. Matte black aluminum receiver. Removeable and user adjustable round bolt knob handle.

Price:	$1,379.00

SAVAGE IMPULSE MOUNTAIN HUNTER

Caliber: 6.5 Creedmoor, 6.5 PRC, .308 Win., 28 Nosler, 7mm PRC, .300 WSM, .300 Win. mag. Barrel: 22, 24-in. Proof Research carbon-fiber-wrapped stainless steel. Weight: 7.16 to 7.44 lbs. Stock: Synthetic gray with AccuFit system. Features: Latest addition to the straight-pull family. Aluminum receiver with integral 20 MOA rail. Carbon-fiber barrel. Threaded muzzle with included brake. Detachable box magazine. Ambidextrous, removable, multi-position bolt handle.

Price:	$2,437.00

SAVAGE MODEL 110

Caliber: The models below now include 7mm PRC in addition to standard chamberings. Numerous model variants and features.

Price: 110 ULTRALITE	$1,649.00
Price: 110 ULTRALITE HD	$1,649.00
Price: 110 ULTRALITE CAMO	$1,699.00
Price: 110 HIGH COUNTRY	$1,239.00
Price: 110 Timberline LH	$1,239.00
Price: 110 APEX HUNTER XP	$709.00
Price: 110 APEX STORM XP	$819.00
Price: 110 APEX HUNTER XP LH	$709.00

SAVAGE 110 CARBON TACTICAL

Calibers: 6.5 Creedmoor, .308 Win., 6.5 PRC. Capacity: 10-round AICS

Prices given are believed to be accurate at time of publication however, many factors affect retail pricing so exact prices are not possible.

magazine. Barrel: 22-in. Proof Research stainless steel, carbon-fiber wrapped, threaded. Length: 42 in. Weight: 7.65 lbs. Stock: Synthetic AccuFit with included interchangeable LOP spacers and comb risers. Features: Factory blueprinted Model 110 bolt action. User-adjustable AccuTrigger. Tactical knurled bolt handle. One-piece 20MOA rail. Beavertail forend with three sling studs.
Price: $1,789.00

SAVAGE MODEL 110 PRECISION
Calibers: .308 Win., .300 Win. Mag., .338 Lapua, 6.5 Creedmoor. Capacity: 5, 8/10. Barrel: 20 to 24 in., carbon steel, heavy, threaded. Stock: Aluminum chassis. Sights: Picatinny rail. Weight: 8.9 lbs. Features: BA muzzle brake, skeletonized stock with adjustable comb height and LOP.
Price: $1,499.00

SAVAGE MODEL 110 PREDATOR
Calibers: .204 Ruger. .223, .22-250, .243, .260 Rem., 6.5 Creedmoor. Capacity: 4-round magazine. Barrels: 22 or 24 in. threaded heavy contour. Weight: 8.5 lbs. Stock: AccuStock with Mossy Oak Max-1 camo finish, soft grip surfaces, adjustable length of pull.
Price: $899.00

SAVAGE MODEL 110 CARBON PREDATOR
Caliber: .223 Rem., .22-250 Rem., 6mm ARC, 6.5 Creedmoor, .308 Win., .300 Blackout. Barrel: 16, 18, 22-in. Proof Research carbon-fiber-wrapped stainless steel. Weight: 6.5 to 7.2 lbs. Stock: Synthetic gray with AccuFit system. Features: Latest addition to the 110 bolt-action family, now with lighter weight carbon-fiber barrel. AICS detachable box magazine. Spiral-fluted bolt. Threaded barrel. Swivel studs. Two-piece Weaver bases included.
Price: $1,695.00

SAVAGE MODEL 110 TACTICAL
Caliber: .308 Win. Capacity: 10-round magazine. Barrels: 20 or 24 in. threaded and fluted heavy contour. Weight: 8.65 lbs. Stock: AccuStock with soft-grip surfaces, AccuFit system. Features: Top Picatinny rail, right- or left-hand operation.
Price: $784.00
Price: Tactical Desert (6mm, 6.5 Creedmoor, FDE finish $769.00

SAVAGE AXIS II PRECISION
Calibers: .243 Win., .223 Rem, .270 Win., .30-06, .308 Win., 6.5 Creedmoor. Capacity: 5 to 10. Barrel: 22 in., carbon steel, button-rifled heavy, threaded w/cap. Stock: Aluminum MDT chassis. Sights: Picatinny rail. Weight: 9.9 lbs. Features: AccuTrigger, adjustable comb height and LOP spacers, AICS magazine.
Price: $949.00

SAVAGE MODEL 12 VARMINT/TARGET SERIES
Calibers: .204 Ruger, .223 Rem., .22-250 Rem. Capacity: 4-shot magazine. Barrel: 26 in. stainless barreled action, heavy fluted, free-floating and button-rifled barrel. Weight: 10 lbs. Length: 46.25 in. overall. Stock: Dual pillar bedded, low profile, black synthetic or laminated stock with extra-wide beavertail fore-end. Sights: None furnished; drilled and tapped for scope mounting. Features: Recessed target-style muzzle. AccuTrigger, oversized bolt handle, detachable box magazine, swivel studs. Model 112BVSS has heavy target-style prone laminated stock with high comb, Wundhammer palm swell, internal box magazine. Model 12VLP DBM has black synthetic stock, detachable magazine, and additional chamberings in .243, .308 Win., .300 Win. Mag. Model 12FV has blued receiver. Model 12BTCSS has brown laminate vented thumbhole stock. Made in USA by

Savage Arms, Inc.
Price: 12 F Class $1,648.00
Price: 12 Palma $2,147.00

SAVAGE MODEL 12 PRECISION TARGET SERIES BENCHREST
Calibers: .308 Win., 6.5x284 Norma, 6mm Norma BR. Barrel: 29-in. ultra-heavy. Weight: 12.75 lbs. Length: 50 in. overall. Stock: Gray laminate. Features: New Left-Load, Right-Eject target action, Target AccuTrigger adjustable from approx. 6 oz. to 2.5 lbs. oversized bolt handle, stainless extra-heavy free-floating and button-rifled barrel.
Price: $1,629.00

SAVAGE MODEL 12 PRECISION TARGET PALMA
Similar to Model 12 Benchrest but in .308 Win. only, 30-in. barrel, multi-adjustable stock, weighs 13.3 lbs.
Price: $2,147.00

SAVAGE MODEL 12 F/TR TARGET RIFLE
Similar to Model 12 Benchrest but in .308 Win. only, 30-in. barrel, weighs 12.65 lbs.
Price: $1,538.00

SAVAGE MODEL 112 MAGNUM TARGET
Caliber: .338 Lapua Magnum. Single shot. Barrel: 26-in. heavy with muzzle brake. Stock: Wood laminate. Features: AccuTrigger, matte black finish, oversized bolt handle, pillar bedding.
Price: $1,177.00

SEEKINS PRECISION HAVAK ELEMENT
Calibers: 28 Nosler, 6mm Creedmoor, 6.5 Creedmoor, .308 Win., 6.5 PRC, .300 Win. Mag., .300 PRC. Capacity: 3 or 5-round detachable Magpul PMAG or carbon-fiber magazine, depending on caliber. Barrel: 21- or 22-in. Mountain Hunter spiral fluted, built of 5R 416 stainless steel. Sights: 20 MOA rail. Weight: 5.5 lbs. short actions; long actions at 6.0 lbs. Stock: Element camouflage Carbon Composition stock. Features: Drawing on years of precision AR-rifle experience comes the bolt action, hybrid, ultra-lightweight Havak Element. Aerospace-grade 7075 aluminum encases stainless steel on a Mountain Hunter barrel. Four locking lugs on 90-degree bolt with removable head. ATC muzzle brake on long actions. M-16-style extractor. Muzzle threaded at 5/8x24. Integrated recoil lug, and bubble level.
Price: $2,795.00

SEEKINS PRECISION HAVAK PRO HUNTER PH2
Calibers: 6mm Creedmoor, 6.5 Creedmoor, 6.5 PRC, .308 Win., 28 Nosler, 7mm Rem. Mag., .300 Win. Mag., 300 PRC, .338 Win. Mag. Capacity: 5, short action; 3, long action detachable magazine. Barrel: 24 in. short action; 26 in. long action built of 5R 416 stainless steel. Weight: 6.9–7.2 lbs. Stock: Seekins carbon composite in Charcoal Gray. Sights: 20 MOA Picatinny rail with 8-32 screws. Features: Timney Elite Hunter trigger set at 2.5 lbs. Bead-blasted barreled action. Threaded muzzle. Integrated recoil lug and M16-style extractor. Bolt with four locking lugs and 90-degree throw. Removeable bolt head. Extended cartridge overall length with Seekins carbon-fiber magazines.
Price: $1,895.00

SPRINGFIELD ARMORY 2020 WAYPOINT

Calibers: 6mm Creedmoor, 6.5 Creedmoor, .308 Win., 6.5 PRC. Capacity: 3 or 5-round AICS-pattern magazine. Barrel: 20, 22, or 24 in. Option of steel or carbon fiber. Weight: 6 lbs. 10 oz.–7 lbs. 6 oz. Length: 41.5–45.5 in. Stock: Choice of two stock configurations, premium AG Composites carbon fiber with custom camo in Evergreen or Ridgeline. Features: Stainless steel receiver. Dual locking lugs on a fluted bolt. Picatinny rail. 90-degree bolt handle with removeable knob. Enlarged ejection port and sliding extractor. Hybrid dual-plane feed ramp. Adjustable Trigger Tech trigger. Five QD stock mounts. SA Radial muzzle brake. Cerakote metalwork in Desert Verde or Mil-Spec Green. Pachmayr Decelerator recoil pad. Available in two stock configurations, one with three-axis adjustable cheek comb and two barrel choices. Accuracy guarantee of .75 MOA.

Price: Steel barrel, standard stock **$1,699.00**
Price: Steel barrel, adjustable stock.................................. **$1,825.00**
Price: Carbon-fiber barrel, standard stock **$2,275.00**
Price: Carbon-fiber barrel, adjustable stock **$2,399.00**

STEVENS MODEL 334

Calibers: .243 Win., .308 Win., 6.5 Creedmoor. Barrel: 20-in. free-floating button rifled. Stock: Walnut or black synthetic. Features: The first centerfire rifle under the Stevens by Savage name in decades. Budget bolt action built completely in Turkey. Two-stage trigger, 60-degree bolt throw, three-position safety. Three-round box magazine. Drilled and tapped with Savage 110 spacing.

Price: Synthetic **$389.00**
Price: Walnut **$489.00**

STEYR PRO HUNTER II

Calibers: .223 Rem., 7mm-08 Rem., 6.5 Creedmoor, .308 Win. Capacity: 4 to 5. Barrel: 20 in., hammer-forged stainless steel. Stock: Wood laminate, Boyds. Sights: None, drilled and tapped. Weight: 7 lbs. Features: Three-position safety, crisp 3-lb. trigger.

Price: **$1,199.00**

STEYR SSG08

Calibers: .243 Win., 7.62x51 NATO (.308Win), 7.62x63B (.300 Win Mag)., .338 Lapua Mag. Capacity: 10-round magazine. Barrels: 20, 23.6 or 25.6 in. Stock: Dural aluminum folding stock black with .280 mm long UIT-rail and various Picatinny rails. Sights: Front post sight and rear adjustable. Features: High-grade aluminum folding stock, adjustable cheekpiece and buttplate with height marking, and an ergonomical exchangeable pistol grip. Versa-Pod, muzzle brake, Picatinny rail, UIT rail on stock and various Picatinny rails on fore-end, and a 10-round HC-magazine. SBS rotary bolt action with four frontal locking lugs, arranged in pairs. Cold-hammer-forged barrels are available in standard or compact lengths.

Price: **$5,899.00**

STEYR SM 12

Calibers: .243, 6.5x55SE, .270 Win., 7mm-08 Rem., .308 Win., .30-06, .300 Win. Mag., .300 WSM, 9.3x62mm. Barrels: 20-in. blue or 25-in. stainless. Stock: Walnut with checkered grip and fore-end. Available in half or full-length configurations. Sights: Adjustable rear, ramp front with bead. Stainless barrel has no sights. Features: Sling swivels, Bavarian cheekpiece, hand-cocking system operated by thumb manually cocks firing mechanism.

Price: Standard-length stock..**$2,545.00**

Price: Full length (Mannlicher) **$2,750.00**

STRASSER RS 14 EVOLUTION STANDARD

Calibers: .222 Rem., .223 Rem., .300 AAC Blackout, .22-250 Rem., .243 Win., 6 XC, 6.5 Creedmoor, .284 Norma, 6.5x55SE, 6.5x65RWS, .270 Win., 7x64, 7mm-08 Rem, .308 Win., .30-06, 8x57 IS, 8.5x63, 9.3x62, 9.3x57, 7mm Rem. Mag., .300 Win. Mag., .375 Ruger, .338 Win. Mag., .458 Win. Mag., 10.3x68. Capacity: 3 to 7. Barrel: 22 to 24 in., blued. Stock: Grade-1 wood, grade-2 wood, standard or thumbhole. Sights: Integrated Picatinny rail. Weight: 6.75 to 7.725 lbs. Features: Barrel-exchange system, adjustable trigger with trigger set, plasma-hardened bolt.

Price: .... **$3,452.00-$4,033.00**

THOMPSON/CENTER COMPASS II

Calibers: .223 Rem., 5.56 NATO, .243 Win., .270 Win., .300 Win. Mag., .308 Win., .30-06, 6.5 Creedmoor, 7mm Rem. Mag. Capacity: 5 to 6. Barrel: 21.625 to 24 in., blued. Stock: Composite. Sights: Weaver bases or Crimson Trace scope combo. Weight: 8 lbs. Features: Threaded muzzle, three-lug bolt design, three-position safety.

Price: ....**$405.00 to $575.00**

THOMSON/CENTER COMPASS II COMPACT

Calibers: .223 Rem., 5.56 NATO, .243 Win., .308 Win., 6.5 Creedmoor. Capacity: 6. Barrel: 16.5 in., blued. Stock: Composite. Sights: Weaver bases or Crimson Trace scope combo. Weight: 6.5 lbs. Features: 5R rifling, compact size, Generation II trigger.

Price: ....**$405.00 to $575.00**

THOMPSON/CENTER VENTURE MEDIUM ACTION

Calibers: .204, .22-250, .223, .243, 7mm-08, .308 and 30TC. Capacity: 3+1 detachable nylon box magazine. Features: Bolt-action rifle with a 24-in. crowned medium weight barrel, classic-styled composite stock with inlaid traction grip panels, adjustable 3.5- to 5-pound trigger along with a drilled and tapped receiver (bases included). Weight: 7 lbs. Length: 43.5 in.

Price: **$537.00**

THOMPSON/CENTER VENTURE PREDATOR PDX

Calibers: .204, .22-250, .223, .243, .308. Weight: 8 lbs. Length: 41.5 in. Features: Bolt-action rifle similar to Venture medium action but with heavy, deep-fluted 22-in. barrel and Max-1 camo finish overall.

Price: **$638.00**

THOMPSON/CENTER LONG RANGE RIFLE

Calibers: .243 Win., 6.5 Creedmoor, .308 Win. Capacity: 10-round magazine. Barrel: 20 in. (.308), 22 in. (6.5), 24 in. (.243). Fluted and threaded with muzzle brake. Weight: 11-12 lbs. Stock: Composite black with adjustable cheek piece and buttplate, built-in Magpul M-LOK accessory slots. Finish: Black or Flat Dark Earth. Features: Picatinny-style rail, adjustable trigger, Caldwell Pic Rail XLA bipod. From the T/C Performance Center.

Price: **$1,211.00**

THOMPSON/CENTER COMPASS

Calibers: .204 Ruger, .223 Rem, .22-250 Rem., .243 Win., 6.5 Creedmoor, .270 Win., 7mm-08 Rem., 7mm Rem. Mag., .308 Win., .30-06, .300 Win. Mag. Capacity: 4-5-round detachable magazine. Barrel: Match-grade 22 in., (24 in. magnums.) with threaded muzzle. Weight: 7 ¼-7 1/2 lbs. Stock:

Prices given are believed to be accurate at time of publication however, many factors affect retail pricing so exact prices are not possible.

Composite black with textured grip panels.
Price: $399.00

TIKKA T3X SERIES
Calibers: Virtually any popular chambering including .204 Ruger .222 Rem., .223 Rem., .243 Win., .25-06, 6.5x55 SE, .260 Rem, .270 Win., .260 WSM, 7mm-08, 7mm Rem. Mag., .308 Win., .30-06, .300 Win. Mag., .300 WSM. Barrels: 20, 22.4, 24.3 in. Stock: Checkered walnut, laminate or modular synthetic with interchangeable pistol grips. Newly designed recoil pad. Features: Offered in a variety of different models with many options. Left-hand models available. One minute-of-angle accuracy guaranteed. Introduced in 2016. Made in Finland by Sako. Imported by Beretta USA.
Price: Hunter	$875.00
Price: Lite (shown)	$725.00
Price: Varmint	$950.00
Price: Laminate stainless	$1,050.00
Price: Forest	$1,000.00
Price: Tac A1 (shown)	$1,899.00
Price: Compact Tactical Rifle	$1,150.00

WEATHERBY BACKCOUNTRY 2.0
Replaces the original Backcountry family. Upgraded with carbon-fiber Peak44 Blacktooth stock that weights under 20 oz. Other improvements include: second generation 3DHEX recoil pad, the first printed pad made. Deeper spiral fluting on the bolt and threaded bolt handle. Fit with Accubrake ST. Patriot Brown Cerakote finish. Weight from only 5.2 lbs. Carbon models include a carbon-fiber barrel. Ti models are built on a titanium action.
Price: Mark V Backcountry 2.0	$2,699.00–$2,799.00
Price: Mark V Backcountry 2.0 Carbon	$3,299.00–$3,399.00
Price: Mark V Backcountry 2.0 Ti	$3,449.00–$3,599.00
Price: Mark V Backcountry Ti Carbon $	3,849.00–$3,949.00

WEATHERBY MARK V
This classic action goes back more than 60 years to the late '50s. Several significant changes were made to the original design in 2016. Stocks have a slimmer fore-end and smaller grip, which has an added palm swell. The new LXX trigger is adjustable down to 2.5 lbs. and has precision ground and polished surfaces and a wider trigger face. All new Mark V rifles come with sub-MOA guarantee. Range Certified (RC) models are range tested and come with a certified ballistic data sheet and RC engraved floorplate. Calibers: Varies depending on model. Barrels: 22 in., 24 in., 26 in., 28 in. Weight: 5 3/4 to 10 lbs. Stock: Varies depending on model. Sights: None furnished. Features: Deluxe version comes in all Weatherby calibers plus .243 Win., .270 Win., 7mm-08 Rem., .30-06, .308 Win. Lazermark same as Mark V Deluxe except stock has extensive oak leaf pattern laser carving on pistol grip and fore-end; chambered in Wby. Magnums .257, .270 Win., 7mm., .300, .340, with 26 in. barrel. Sporter is same as the Mark V Deluxe without the embellishments. Metal has low-luster blue, stock is Claro walnut with matte finish, Monte Carlo comb, recoil pad. Chambered for these Wby. Mags: .257, .270 Win., 7mm, .300, .340. Other chamberings: 7mm Rem. Mag., .300 Win. Introduced 1993. Six Mark V models come with synthetic stocks. Ultra Lightweight rifles weigh 5.75 to 6.75 lbs.; 24 in., 26 in. fluted stainless barrels with recessed target crown; Bell & Carlson stock with CNC-machined aluminum bedding plate and tan "spider web"

finish, skeletonized handle and sleeve. Available in .243 Win., .25-06 Rem., .270 Win., 7mm-08 Rem., 7mm Rem. Mag., .280 Rem, .308 Win., .30-06, .300 Win. Mag. Wby. Mag chamberings: .240, .257, .270 Win., 7mm, .300. Accumark uses Mark V action with heavy-contour 26 in. and 28 in. stainless barrels with black oxidized flutes, muzzle diameter of .705 in. No sights, drilled and tapped for scope mounting. Stock is composite with matte gel-coat finish, full-length aluminum bedding block. Weighs 8.5 lbs. Chambered for these Wby. Mags: .240, .257, .270, 7mm, .300, .340, .338-378, .30-378. Other chamberings: 6.5 Creedmoor, .270 Win., .308 Win., 7mm Rem. Mag., .300 Win. Mag. Altitude has 22-, 24-, 26-, 28-in. fluted stainless steel barrel, Monte Carlo carbon fiber composite stock with raised comb, Kryptek Altitude camo. Tacmark has 28-in. free floated fluted barrel with Accubrake, fully adjustable stock, black finish. Safari Grade has fancy grade checkered French walnut stock with ebony fore-end and grip cap, adjustable express rear and hooded front sights, from the Weatherby Custom Shop. Camilla series is lightweight model designed to fit a woman's anatomy. Offered in several variations chambered for .240 Wby. Mag., 6.5 Creedmoor, .270 Win., .308 Win., .30-06. Arroyo is available in Weatherby Magnums from .240 to .338-378, plus 6.5 Creedmoor, .300 Win. Mag., and .338 Lapua Mag. Finish is two-tone Cerakote with Brown Sand and FDE added flutes. Carbonmark has 26in. Proof Research carbon fiber threaded barrel and is chambered for .257 and .300 Wby. Mags. Outfitter is chambered for .240-.300 Wby. Magnums plus most popular calibers. Stock has Spiderweb accents. KCR model comes with Krieger Custom Match-grade barrel in .257, 6.5-300, .300 and .30-378 Wby. Magnums. Altitude is lightweight model (5 ¾-6 ¾ lbs.) and comes in Wby. Magnums from .240 to.300, plus 6.5 Creedmoor, .270 Win., .308, .30-06. Dangerous Game Rifle is offered in all Wby. Magnums from .300 to .450, plus .375 H&H. Hand laminated Monte Carlo composite stock. *Note: Most Mark V rifles are available in 6.5 Wby. RPM and 6.5-300 Wby. Mag. chamberings.* All Weatherby Mark V rifles are made in Sheridan, Wyoming.
Price: Mark V Backcountry	$2,499.00
Price: Mark V Backcountry Ti	$3,349.00–$3,449.00
Price: Mark V Deluxe	$2,700.00
Price: Mark V Hunter	$1,499.00
Price: Mark V Lazermark	$2,800.00
Price: Mark V Sporter	$1,800.00
Price: Mark V Ultra Lightweight	$2,300.00
Price: Mark V Accumark	$2,300.00–$2,700.00
Price: Mark V Altitude	$3,000.00–$3,700.00
Price: Mark V Safari Grade Custom	$6,900.00–$7,600.00
Price: Mark V Tacmark	$4,100.00
Price: Mark V Camilla Series	$2,300.00–$2,700.00
Price: Mark V Arroyo	$2,800.00
Price: Mark V Carbonmark	$4,100.00
Price: Mark V Outfitter	$2,600-$2,800.00*
Price: Mark V Krieger Custom Rifle (KCR)	$3,600-$4,100.00*
Price: Mark V Altitude	$2,700.00*
Price: Mark V Dangerous Game Rifle	$3,600.00
Price: Mark V Weathermark	$1,549.00–$1,749.00
Price: Mark V Weathermark Bronze	$1,549.00–$1,749.00
Price: Mark V Carbonmark Pro	$2,999.00–$3,099.00
Price: Mark V Carbonmark Elite	$3,299.00–$3,399.00
Price: MARK V Apex Right Hand	$2,799.00
Price: MARK V Apex Left Hand	$2,899.00

*Add ....$500 for optional Range Certified (RC) model with guaranteed sub-MOA accuracy certificate and target.

WEATHERBY VANGUARD II SERIES
Calibers: Varies depending on model. Most Weatherby Magnums and many standard calibers. Barrels: 20, 24, or 26 in. Weights: 7.5–8.75 lbs. Lengths: 44–46.75 in. overall. Stock: Raised comb, Monte Carlo, injection-molded composite stock. Sights: None furnished. Features: One-piece forged, fluted bolt body with three gas ports, forged and machined receiver, adjustable trigger, factory accuracy guarantee. Vanguard Stainless has 410-Series stainless steel barrel and action, bead blasted matte metal finish. Vanguard Deluxe has raised comb, semi-fancy-grade Monte Carlo walnut stock with maplewood spacers, rosewood fore-end and grip cap, polished action with high-gloss blued metalwork. Sporter has Monte Carlo walnut stock with satin urethane finish, fineline diamond point checkering, contrasting rosewood fore-end tip, matte-blued metalwork. Sporter SS metalwork is 410-Series bead-blasted stainless steel. Vanguard Youth/Compact has 20 in. No. 1 contour barrel, short action, scaled-down nonreflective matte black hardwood stock with 12.5-in. length of pull, and full-size, injection-molded composite stock. Chambered for .223 Rem., .22-250 Rem., .243 Win.,

7mm-08 Rem., .308 Win. Weighs 6.75 lbs.; OAL 38.9 in. Sub-MOA Matte and Sub-MOA Stainless models have pillar-bedded Fiberguard composite stock (Aramid, graphite unidirectional fibers and fiberglass) with 24-in. barreled action; matte black metalwork, Pachmayr Decelerator recoil pad. Sub-MOA Stainless metalwork is 410 Series bead-blasted stainless steel. Sub-MOA Varmint guaranteed to shoot 3-shot group of .00 in. or less when used with specified Weatherby factory or premium (non-Weatherby calibers) ammunition. Hand-laminated, tan Monte Carlo composite stock with black spiderwebbing; CNC-machined aluminum bedding block, 22 in. No. 3 contour barrel, recessed target crown. Varmint Special has tan injection-molded Monte Carlo composite stock, pebble grain finish, black spiderwebbing. 22 in. No. 3 contour barrel (.740-in. muzzle dia.), bead blasted matte black finish, recessed target crown. Back Country has two-stage trigger, pillar-bedded Bell & Carlson stock, 24-in. fluted barrel, three-position safety.

Price: Vanguard Synthetic **$649.00**
Price: Vanguard Stainless **$799.00**
Price: Vanguard Deluxe, 7mm Rem. Mag., .300 Win. Mag..............**$1,149.00**
Price: Vanguard Sporter **$849.00**
Price: Laminate Sporter **$849.00**
Price: Vanguard Youth/Compact **$599.00**
Price: Vanguard S2 Back Country **$1,399.00**
Price: Vanguard RC (Range Certified) **$1,199.00**
Price: Vanguard Varmint Special **$849.00**
Price: Camilla (designed for women shooters) **$849.00**
Price: Camilla Wilderness **$899.00**
Price: Lazerguard (Laser carved AA-grade walnut stock) **$1,199.00**
Price: H-Bar (tactical series) ....**$1,149.00–$1,449.00**
Price: Weatherguard **$749.00**
Price: Modular Chassis **$1,519.00**
Price: Dangerous Game Rifle (DGR) .375 H&H..**$1,299.00**
Price: Safari (.375 or .30-06) **$1,199.00**
Price: First Lite Fusion Camo **$1,099.00**
Price: Badlands Camo **$849.00**
Price: Accuguard **$1,099.00**
Price: Select **$599.00**
Price: Wilderness **$999.00**
Price: High Country **$999.00**

WINCHESTER MODEL 70 SUPER GRADE
Calibers: .270 Win., .270 WSM, 7mm Rem. Mag., .30-06, .300 Win Mag., .300 WSM, .338 Win. Mag. Capacities: 5 rounds (short action) or 3 rounds (long action). Barrels: 24 in. or 26 in. blued. Weights: 8–8.5 lbs. Features: Full fancy Grade IV/V walnut stock with shadow-line cheekpiece, controlled round feed with claw extractor, Pachmayr Decelerator pad. No sights but drilled and tapped for scope mounts.
Price: ....**$1,440.00–$1,480.00**

WINCHESTER MODEL 70 ALASKAN
Calibers: .30-06, .300 Win. Mag., .338 Win. Mag., .375 H&H Magnum. Barrel: 25 in Weight: 8.8 lbs. Sights: Folding adjustable rear, hooded brass bead front. Stock: Satin finished Monte Carlo with cut checkering. Features: Integral recoil lug, Pachmayr Decelerator recoil pad.
Price: **$1,400.00**

WINCHESTER MODEL 70 FEATHERWEIGHT
Calibers: .22-250, .243, 6.5 Creedmoor, 7mm-08, .308, .270 WSM, 7mm WSM, .300 WSM, .325 WSM, .25-06, .270, .30-06, 7mm Rem. Mag., .300 Win. Mag., .338 Win. Mag. Capacities: 5 rounds (short action) or 3 rounds (long action). Barrels: 22-in. blued (24 in. in magnum chamberings). Weights: 6.5–7.25 lbs. Length: NA. Features: Satin-finished checkered Grade I walnut stock, controlled round feeding. Pachmayr Decelerator pad. No sights but drilled and tapped for scope mounts.
Price: **$1,010.00**
Price: Magnum calibers **$1,050.00**
Price: Featherweight Stainless ....**$1,210.00-$1,250.00**

WINCHESTER MODEL 70 SPORTER
Calibers: .270 WSM, 7mm WSM, .300 WSM, .325 WSM, .25-06, .270, .30-06, 7mm Rem. Mag., .300 Win. Mag., .338 Win. Mag., 6.8 Western. Capacities: 5 rounds (short action) or 3 rounds (long action). Barrels: 22 in., 24 in. or 26 in. blued. Weights: 6.5–7.25 lbs. Length: NA. Features: Satin-finished checkered Grade I walnut stock with sculpted cheekpiece, controlled round feeding. Pachmayr Decelerator pad. No sights but drilled and tapped for scope mounts.
Price: **$1,010.00**

WINCHESTER MODEL 70 SAFARI EXPRESS

Calibers: .375 H&H Magnum, .416 Remington, .458 Win. Mag. Barrel: 24 in. Weight: 9 lbs. Sights: Fully adjustable rear, hooded brass bead front. Stock: Satin finished Monte Carlo with cut checkering, deluxe cheekpiece. Features: Forged steel receiver with double integral recoil lugs bedded front and rear, dual steel crossbolts, Pachmayr Decelerator recoil pad.
Price: **$1,560.00**

WINCHESTER MODEL 70 LONG RANGE MB
Calibers: .22-250 Rem., .243 Win., 6.5 Creedmoor, .308 Win., 6.5 PRC, .270 WSM, .300 WSM, 6.8 Western. Capacity: 3, 4, or 5-round internal magazine with hinged floorplate. Barrel: 24-in. matte blued, light varmint contour, fluted with muzzle brake. Weight: 7 lbs. 8oz. Length: 44 in. Stock: Bell & Carlson composite with tan/black spider web and Pachmayr Decelerator recoil pad. Sights: Drilled and tapped. Features: Bolt-action short action designed for long-range hunting and target shooting. Aluminum bedding block. Matte black finish. Controlled round feed with claw extractor. Three-position safety. Flat, bench-rest style fore-end with dual sling studs. Jeweled bolt. Recessed target crown.
Price: **$1,589.00**

WINCHESTER XPR
Calibers: .243, 6.5 Creedmoor, 270 Win., .270 WSM, 7mm-08, 7mm Rem. Mag., .308 Win., .30-06, .300 Win. Mag., .300 WSM, .325 WSM, .338 Win. Mag.,.350 Legend, 6.8 Western. Capacities: Detachable box magazine holds 3 to 5 rounds. Barrels: 24 or 26 in. Stock: Black polymer with Inflex Technology recoil pad. Weight: Approx. 7 lbs. Finish: Matte blue. Features: Bolt unlock button, nickel coated Teflon bolt.
Price: **$549.00**
Price: Mossy Oak Break-Up Country camo stock..**$600.00**
Price: With Vortex II 3-9x40 scope..**$710.00**
Price: XPR Hunter Camo (shown) **$600.00**
Price: XPR Extreme Hunter Midnight MB w/True Timber Midnight camo **$769.00**
Price: XPR Hunter Strata MB w/True Timber Strata camo **$749.00**
Price: XPR Hunter w/ Mossy Oak DNA camo **$649.00**
Price: Sporter w/Grade 1 walnut stock..**$600.00**
Price: True Timber Strata Camo **$600.00**
Price: Thumbhole Varmint Suppressor Ready **$800.00**
Price: Stealth SR..**$669.00**

BALLARD 1875 1 1/2 HUNTER
Caliber: Various calibers. Barrel: 26–30 in. Weight: NA Length: NA. Stock: Hand-selected classic American walnut. Sights: Blade front, Rocky Mountain rear. Features: Color casehardened receiver, breechblock and lever. Many options available. Made in USA by Ballard Rifle & Cartridge Co.
Price: $3,250.00

BALLARD 1875 #3 GALLERY SINGLE SHOT
Caliber: Various calibers. Barrel: 24–28 in. octagonal with tulip. Weight: NA. Length: NA. Stock: Hand-selected classic American walnut. Sights: Blade front, Rocky Mountain rear. Features: Color casehardened receiver, breechblock and lever. Many options available. Made in USA by Ballard Rifle & Cartridge Co.
Price: $3,300.00

BALLARD 1875 #4 PERFECTION
Caliber: Various calibers. Barrels: 30 in. or 32 in. octagon, standard or heavyweight. Weights: 10.5 lbs. (standard) or 11.75 lbs. (heavyweight bbl.) Length: NA. Stock: Smooth walnut. Sights: Blade front, Rocky Mountain rear. Features: Rifle or shotgun-style buttstock, straight grip action, single- or double-set trigger, "S" or right lever, hand polished and lapped Badger barrel. Made in USA by Ballard Rifle & Cartridge Co.
Price: $3,950.00

BALLARD MODEL 1885 LOW WALL SINGLE SHOT RIFLE
Calibers: Various calibers. Barrels: 24–28 in. Weight: NA. Length: NA. Stock: Hand-selected classic American walnut. Sights: Blade front, sporting rear. Features: Color casehardened receiver, breechblock and lever. Many options available. Made in USA by Ballard Rifle & Cartridge Co.
Price: $3,300.00

BALLARD MODEL 1885 HIGH WALL STANDARD SPORTING SINGLE SHOT
Calibers: Various calibers. Barrels: Lengths to 34 in. Weight: NA. Length: NA. Stock: Straight-grain American walnut. Sights: Buckhorn or flattop rear, blade front. Features: Faithful copy of original Model 1885 High Wall; parts interchange with original rifles; variety of options available. Introduced 2000. Made in USA by Ballard Rifle & Cartridge Co.
Price: $3,300.00

BALLARD MODEL 1885 HIGH WALL SPECIAL SPORTING SINGLE SHOT
Calibers: Various calibers. Barrels: 28–30 in. octagonal. Weight: NA. Length: NA. Stock: Hand-selected classic American walnut. Sights: Blade front, sporting rear. Features: Color casehardened receiver, breechblock and lever. Many options available. Made in USA by Ballard Rifle & Cartridge Co.
Price: $3,600.00

BROWN MODEL 97D SINGLE SHOT
Calibers: Available in most factory and wildcat calibers from .17 Ackley Hornet to .375 Winchester. Barrels: Up to 26 in. air-gauged match grade. Weight: About 5 lbs., 11 oz. Stock: Sporter style with pistol grip, cheekpiece and Schnabel fore-end. Sights: None furnished; drilled and tapped for scope mounting. Features: Falling-block action gives rigid barrel-receiver matting; polished blue/black finish. Hand-fitted action. Standard and custom made-to-order rifles with many options. Made in USA by E. Arthur Brown Co., Inc.
Price: Standard model $1,695.00

C. SHARPS ARMS 1874 BRIDGEPORT SPORTING
Calibers: .38-55 to .50-3.25. Barrel: 26 in., 28 in., 30-in. tapered octagon. Weight: 10.5 lbs. Length: 47 in. Stock: American black walnut; shotgun butt with checkered steel buttplate; straight grip, heavy fore-end with Schnabel tip. Sights: Blade front, buckhorn rear. Drilled and tapped for tang sight. Features: Double-set triggers. Made in USA by C. Sharps Arms.
Price: $1,995.00

C. SHARPS ARMS NEW MODEL 1885 HIGHWALL
Calibers: .22 LR, .22 Hornet, .219 Zipper, .25-35 WCF, .32-40 WCF, .38-55 WCF, .40-65, .30-40 Krag, .40-50 ST or BN, .40-70 ST or BN, .40-90 ST or BN, .45-70 Govt. 2-1/10 in. ST, .45-90 2-4/10 in. ST, .45-100 2-6/10 in. ST, .45-110 2-7/8 in. ST, .45-120 3-1/4 in. ST. Barrels: 26 in., 28 in., 30 in., tapered full octagon. Weight: About 9 lbs., 4 oz. Length: 47 in. overall. Stock: Oil-finished American walnut; Schnabel-style fore-end. Sights: Blade front, buckhorn rear. Drilled and tapped for optional tang sight. Features: Single trigger; octagonal receiver top; checkered steel buttplate; color casehardened receiver and buttplate, blued barrel. Many options available. Made in USA by C. Sharps Arms Co.
Price: $1,975.00

C. SHARPS ARMS 1885 HIGHWALL SCHUETZEN RIFLE
Calibers: .30-30, .32-40, .38-55, .40-50. Barrels: 24, 26, 28 or 30 in. Full tapered octagon. Stock: Straight grain American walnut with oil finish, pistol grip, cheek rest. Sights: Globe front with aperture set, long-range fully adjustable tang sight with Hadley eyecup. Finish: Color casehardened receiver group, buttplate and bottom tang, matte blue barrel. Single set trigger.
Price: $2,875.00

CIMARRON BILLY DIXON 1874 SHARPS SPORTING
Calibers: .45-70, .45-90, .50-70. Barrel: 32-in. tapered octagonal. Weight: NA. Length: NA. Stock: European walnut. Sights: Blade front, Creedmoor rear. Features: Color casehardened frame, blued barrel. Hand-checkered grip and fore-end; hand-rubbed oil finish. Made by Pedersoli. Imported by Cimarron F.A. Co.
Price: $2,141.70
Price: Officer's Trapdoor Carbine w/26-in. round barrel.................$2,616.00

CIMARRON ADOBE WALLS ROLLING BLOCK
Caliber: .45-70 Govt. Barrel: 30-in. octagonal. Weight: 10.33 lbs. Length: NA. Stock: Hand-checkered European walnut. Sights: Bead front, semi-buckhorn rear. Features: Color casehardened receiver, blued barrel. Curved buttplate. Double-set triggers. Made by Pedersoli. Imported by Cimarron F.A. Co.
Price: $1,740.00

DAKOTA ARMS SHARPS
Calibers: Virtually any caliber from .17 Ackley Hornet to .30-40 Krag. Features: 26-in. octagon barrel, XX-grade walnut stock with straight grip and tang sight. Many options and upgrades are available.
Price: $4,490.00

EMF PREMIER 1874 SHARPS
Calibers: .45-70, .45-110, .45-120. Barrel: 32 in., 34 in.. Weight: 11–13 lbs. Length: 49 in., 51 in. overall. Stock: Pistol grip, European walnut. Sights: Blade front, adjustable rear. Features: Superb quality reproductions of the 1874 Sharps Sporting Rifles; casehardened locks; double-set triggers; blue barrels. Imported from Pedersoli by EMF.
Price: Business Rifle..$1,585.00
Price: Down Under Sporting Rifle, Patchbox, heavy barrel $2,405.00
Price: Silhouette, pistol-grip............................$1,899.90
Price: Super Deluxe Hand Engraved $3,600.00
Price: Competition Rifle...................................$2,200.00

H&R BUFFALO CLASSIC
Calibers: .45 Colt or .45-70 Govt. Barrel: 32 in. heavy. Weight: 8 lbs. Length: 46 in. overall. Stock: Cut-checkered American black walnut. Sights: Williams receiver sight; Lyman target front sight with 8 aperture inserts. Features: Color casehardened Handi-Rifle action with exposed hammer; color casehardened crescent buttplate; 19th-century checkering pattern. Introduced 1995. Made in USA by H&R 1871, Inc.
Price: Buffalo Classic Rifle..............................$479.00

CENTERFIRE RIFLES Single Shot

HENRY SINGLE SHOT BRASS
Calibers: .44 Mag./.44 Spl., .357 Mag./.38 Spl., .45-70 Govt. Capacity: Single shot. Barrel: 22-in. round blued steel. Weight: 7.01–7.14 lbs. Length: 37.5 in. Stock: American Walnut with English-style straight buttstock. Sights: Fully adjustable folding leaf rear and brass bead front. Also drilled and tapped. Features: Polished brass receiver single-shot break actions built in a limited number of calibers. Sling studs. Brass buttplate. Rebounding hammer safety. Break-action lever can be moved either left or right to open, making it friendly for lefties.
Price: $646.00

HENRY SINGLE SHOT STEEL
Calibers: .223 Rem., .243 Win., .308 Win., .357 Mag./.38 Spl., .44 Mag., .30-30 Win., .45-70 Govt., .350 Legend, 360 Buckhammer, .450 Bushmaster. Capacity: Single-shot. Barrel: 22-in. round blued steel. Weight: 6.73–6.96 lbs. Length: 37.5 in. Stock: Checkered American Walnut, pistol grip style. Sights: Fully adjustable folding leaf rear and brass bead front. Also drilled and tapped. Features: Blued steel receiver single-shot rifles. Solid rubber recoil pad. Rebounding hammer safety. Sling studs. Break-action lever can be moved either left or right to open, making it friendly for lefties. Youth model uses shorter 13-inch LOP, standard model LOP is 14 inches.
Price: $580.00

KRIEGHOFF HUBERTUS SINGLE-SHOT
Calibers: .222, .22-250, .243 Win., .270 Win., .308 Win., .30-06, 5.6x50R Mag., 5.6x52R, 6x62R Freres, 6.5x57R, 6.5x65R, 7x57R, 7x65R, 8x57JRS, 8x75RS, 9.3x74R, 7mm Rem. Mag., .300 Win. Mag. Barrels: 23.5 in. Shorter lengths available. Weight: 6.5 lbs. Length: 40.5 in. Stock: High-grade walnut. Sights: Blade front, open rear. Features: Break-open loading with manual cocking lever on top tang; takedown; extractor; Schnabel forearm; many options. Imported from Germany by Krieghoff International Inc.
Price: Hubertus single shot $7,295.00
Price: Hubertus, magnum calibers $8,295.00

MERKEL K1 MODEL LIGHTWEIGHT STALKING
Calibers: .243 Win., .270 Win., 7x57R, .308 Win., .30-06, 7mm Rem. Mag., .300 Win. Mag., 9.3x74R. Barrel: 23.6 in. Weight: 5.6 lbs. unscoped. Stock: Satin-finished walnut, fluted and checkered; sling-swivel studs. Sights: None (scope base furnished). Features: Franz Jager single-shot break-open action, cocking/uncocking slide-type safety, matte silver receiver, selectable trigger pull weights, integrated, quick detach 1 in. or 30mm optic mounts (optic not included). Extra barrels are an option. Imported from Germany by Merkel USA.
Price: Jagd Stalking Rifle $3,795.00
Price: Jagd Stutzen Carbine $4,195.00
Price: Extra barrels $1,195.00

MILLER ARMS
Calibers: Virtually any caliber from .17 Ackley Hornet to .416 Remington. Falling block design with 24-in. premium match-grade barrel, express sights, XXX-grade walnut stock and fore-end with 24 LPI checkering. Made in several styles including Classic, Target and Varmint. Many options and upgrades are available. From Dakota Arms.
Price: $5,590.00

ROSSI SINGLE-SHOT SERIES
Calibers: .223 Rem., .243 Win., .44 Magnum. Barrel: 22 in. Weight: 6.25 lbs. Stocks: Black Synthetic Synthetic with recoil pad and removable cheek piece. Sights: Adjustable rear, fiber optic front, scope rail. Some models have scope rail only. Features: Single-shot break open, positive ejection, internal transfer bar mechanism, manual external safety, trigger block system, Taurus Security System, Matte blue finish.
Price: $238.00

RUGER NO. 1 SERIES
This model is currently available only in select limited editions and chamberings each year. Features common to most variants of the No. 1 include a falling block mechanism and under lever, sliding tang safety, integral scope mounts machined on the steel quarter rib, sporting-style recoil pad, grip cap and sling swivel studs. Chamberings for 2018 and 2019 were .450 Bushmaster and .450 Marlin. In addition, many calibers are offered by Ruger distributors Lipsey's and Talo, usually limited production runs of approximately 250 rifles, including .204 Ruger, .22 Hornet, 6.5 Creedmoor, .250 Savage, .257 Roberts, .257 Weatherby Mag. and .30-30. For availability of specific variants and calibers contact www.lipseysguns.com or www.taloinc.com.
Price: ....$1,899.00-$2,115.00

SHILOH CO. SHARPS 1874 LONG RANGE EXPRESS
Calibers: .38-55, .40-50 BN, .40-70 BN, .40-90 BN, .40-70 ST, .40-90 ST, .45-70 Govt. ST, .45-90 ST, .45-110 ST, .50-70 ST, .50-90 ST. Barrel: 34-in. tapered octagon. Weight: 10.5 lbs. Length: 51 in. overall. Stock: Oil-finished walnut (upgrades available) with pistol grip, shotgun-style butt, traditional cheek rest, Schnabel fore-end. Sights: Customer's choice. Features: Re-creation of the Model 1874 Sharps rifle. Double-set triggers. Made in USA by Shiloh Rifle Mfg. Co.
Price: $2,059.00
Price: Sporter Rifle No. 1 (similar to above except with 30-in. barrel, blade front, buckhorn rear sight) $2,059.00
Price: Sporter Rifle No. 3 (similar to No. 1 except straight-grip stock, standard wood) $1,949.00

SHILOH CO. SHARPS 1874 QUIGLEY
Calibers: .45-70 Govt., .45-110. Barrel: 34-in. heavy octagon. Stock: Military-style with patch box, standard-grade American walnut. Sights: Semi-buckhorn, interchangeable front and midrange vernier tang sight with windage. Features: Gold inlay initials, pewter tip, Hartford collar, case color or antique finish. Double-set triggers.
Price: $3,533.00

SHILOH CO. SHARPS 1874 SADDLE
Calibers: .38-55, .40-50 BN, .40-65 Win., .40-70 BN, .40-70 ST, .40-90

BN, .40-90 ST, .44-77 BN, .44-90 BN, .45-70 Govt. ST, .45-90 ST, .45-100 ST, .45-110 ST, .45-120 ST, .50-70 ST, .50-90 ST. Barrels: 26 in. full or half octagon. Stock: Semi-fancy American walnut. Shotgun style with cheek rest. Sights: Buckhorn and blade. Features: Double-set trigger, numerous custom features can be added.
Price: $2,044.00

SHILOH CO. SHARPS 1874 MONTANA ROUGHRIDER
Calibers: .38-55, .40-50 BN, .40-65 Win., .40-70 BN, .40-70 ST, .40-90 BN, .40-90 ST, .44-77 BN, .44-90 BN, .45-70 Govt. ST, .45-90 ST, .45-100 ST, .45-110 ST, .45-120 ST, .50-70 ST, .50-90 ST. Barrels: 30 in. full or half octagon. Stock: American walnut in shotgun or military style. Sights: Buckhorn and blade. Features: Double-set triggers, numerous custom features can be added.
Price: $2,059.00

SHILOH CO. SHARPS CREEDMOOR TARGET
Calibers: .38-55, .40-50 BN, .40-65 Win., .40-70 BN, .40-70 ST, .40-90 BN, .40-90 ST, .44-77 BN, .44-90 BN, .45-70 Govt. ST, .45-90 ST, .45-100 ST, .45-110 ST, .45-120 ST, .50-70 ST, .50-90 ST. Barrel: 32 in. half round-half octagon. Stock: Extra fancy American walnut. Shotgun style with pistol grip. Sights: Customer's choice. Features: Single trigger, AA finish on stock, polished barrel and screws, pewter tip.
Price: $3,105.00

THOMPSON/CENTER ENCORE PRO HUNTER PREDATOR RIFLE
Calibers: .204 Ruger, .223 Remington, .22-250 and .308 Winchester. Barrel: 28-in. deep-fluted interchangeable. Length: 42.5 in. Weight: 7.75 lbs. Stock: Composite buttstock and fore-end with non-slip inserts in cheekpiece, pistol grip and fore-end. Realtree Advantage Max-1 camo finish overall. Scope is not included.
Price: $882.00

THOMPSON/CENTER G2 CONTENDER
Calibers: .204 Ruger, .223 Rem., 6.8 Rem. 7-30 Waters, .30-30 Win. Barrel: 23-in. interchangeable with blued finish. Length: 36.75 in. Stock: Walnut. Sights: None. Weight: 5.5 pounds. Reintroduced in 2015. Interchangeable barrels available in several centerfire and rimfire calibers.
Price: $769.00

UBERTI 1874 SHARPS SPORTING
Caliber: .45-70 Govt. Barrels: 30 in., 32 in., 34 in. octagonal. Weight: 10.57 lbs. with 32 in. barrel. Lengths: 48.9 in. with 32 in. barrel. Stock: Walnut. Sights: Dovetail front, Vernier tang rear. Features: Cut checkering, case-colored finish on frame, buttplate, and lever. Imported by Stoeger Industries.

Price: Standard Sharps	$1,919.00
Price: Special Sharps	$2,019.00
Price: Deluxe Sharps	$3,269.00
Price: Down Under Sharps	$2,719.00
Price: Long Range Sharps	$2,719.00
Price: Buffalo Hunter Sharps	$2,620.00
Price: Sharps Cavalry Carbine	$2,020.00
Price: Sharps Extra Deluxe	$5,400.00
Price: Sharps Hunter	$1,699.00

UBERTI 1885 HIGH-WALL SINGLE-SHOT
Calibers: .45-70 Govt., .45-90, .45-120. Barrels: 28–32 in. Weights: 9.3–9.9 lbs. Lengths: 44.5–47 in. overall. Stock: Walnut stock and fore-end. Sights: Blade front, fully adjustable open rear. Features: Based on Winchester High-Wall design by John Browning. Color casehardened frame and lever, blued barrel and buttplate. Imported by Stoeger Industries.
Price: .... $1,079.00–$1,279.00

UBERTI 1885 COURTENEY STALKING RIFLE
Calibers: .303 British, .45-70 Gov't. Capacity: Single shot. Barrel: 24-in. round blued steel. Weight: 7.1 lbs. Length: 37.5 in. Stock: A-Grade Walnut, Prince of Wales buttstock and slim fore-end with African heartwood. Sights: Hooded front and V-style express rear with quarter-rib slot for Weaver rings. Features: Named after English hunter Courteney Selous, this single shot shows traditional British style. Casehardened receiver. Checkered pistol grip. Rubber buttpad. Sling swivels including barrel-mounted front.
Price: $1,689.00

UBERTI SPRINGFIELD TRAPDOOR RIFLE/CARBINE
Caliber: .45-70 Govt., single shot Barrel: 22 or 32.5 in. Features: Blued steel receiver and barrel, casehardened breechblock and buttplate. Sights: Creedmoor style.
Price: Springfield Trapdoor Carbine, 22 in. barrel $1,749.00
Price: Springfield Trapdoor Army, 32.5 in. barrel $2,019.0

CHAPUIS ARMES X4 DOUBLE RIFLE

Caliber: 9.3x74R, .30-06 Spfld. Barrel: 22 in. Weight: 6 lbs. Stock: AAA-grade Circassian Walnut with English-style cheekpiece. Features: The double can be re-regulated for new loads. Built on a Progress 28-gauge scalloped receiver. Intricate engraving. Double triggers and ejectors. Adjustable rear and ramp front sights. Machined for Recknagel scope mounts.

Price: 9.3x74R **$7,299.00**
Price: 30.06 Spfld **$7,599.00**

FAUSTI CLASS EXPRESS

Calibers: .243 Win., 6.5x55, 6.5x57R, 7x57R, .308 Win., .270 Win., .30-06, .30R Blaser, .45-70, .444 Marlin, 9.3x74, 8x57 JRS. Barrel: 24 in. Weight: 7.6 lbs. average. Stock: A-Grade Walnut with oil finish. Pistol grip style. Sights: Fiber-optic sight on ramp, adjustable for elevation. Features: O/U double rifle in a wide range of chamberings. LOP of 14.49 in. Choice of single or double triggers, no selector. Automatic ejectors. Includes VL151 gun case.

Price: **$4,990.00**
Price: CLASS SL EXPRESS **$5,690.00**

FAUSTI DEA EXPRESS

Calibers: .243 Win., 7x57R, .308 Win., .270 Win., .30-06, .30R Blaser, .45-70, .444 Marlin, 9.3x74, 8x57 JRS. Barrel: 24 in. Weight: 7 lbs. average. Stock: A-Grade Walnut with oil finish. Pistol grip style. Sights: Fiber-optic sight on ramp, adjustable for elevation. Features: SxS double rifle in a wide range of chamberings. LOP of 14.49 in. Choice of single or double triggers, no selector. Automatic ejectors. Includes VL151 gun case.

Price: **$6,800.00**

HEYM MODEL 88B SXS DOUBLE RIFLE

Calibers/Gauge: .22 Hornet, .300 Win. Mag., .375 H&H Belted Mag., .375 H&H Flanged Mag., .416 Rigby, .416/500 NE, .450/400 NE 3-in., .450 NE 3.25-in., .470 NE, .500 NE, .577 NE, .600 NE, 20 gauge, and more. Barrel: Up to 26 in., Krupp steel, hammer-forged. Stock: Custom select European walnut. Sights: V rear, bead front. Weight: 9 to 13 lbs. Features: Automatic ejectors, articulated front trigger, stocked-to-fit RH or LH, cocking indicators, engraving available.

Price: **$18,000.00**

HEYM MODEL 89B SXS DOUBLE RIFLE

Calibers/Gauge: .22 Hornet, .300 Win. Mag., .375 H&H Belted Mag., .375 H&H Flanged Mag., .416 Rigby, .416/500 NE, .450/400 NE 3-in., .450 NE 3.25-in., .470 NE, .500 NE, .577 NE, .600 NE, 20 gauge, and more. Barrel: Up to 26 in., Krupp steel, hammer-forged. Stock: Custom select European walnut. Sights: V rear, bead front. Weight: 9-13 lbs. Features: Five frame sizes, automatic ejectors, intercepting sears, stocked-to-fit RH or LH, engraving available.

Price: **$23,000.00**

KRIEGHOFF CLASSIC DOUBLE

Calibers: 7x57R, 7x65R, .308 Win., .30-06, 8x57 JRS, 8x75RS, 9.3x74R, .375NE, .500/.416NE, .470NE, .500NE. Barrel: 23.5 in. Weight: 7.3–11 lbs. Stock: High grade European walnut. Standard model has conventional rounded cheekpiece, Bavaria model has Bavarian-style cheekpiece. Sights: Bead front with removable, adjustable wedge (.375 H&H and below), standing leaf rear on quarter-rib. Features: Boxlock action; double triggers; short opening angle for fast loading; quiet extractors; sliding, self-adjusting wedge for secure bolting; Purdey-style barrel extension; horizontal firing pin placement. Many options available. Introduced 1997. Imported from Germany by Krieghoff International.

Price: **$10,995.00**
Price: Engraved sideplates, add **$4,000.00**
Price: Extra set of rifle barrels, add **$6,300.00**
Price: Extra set of 20-ga. 28 in. shotgun barrels, add **$4,400.00**

KRIEGHOFF CLASSIC BIG FIVE DOUBLE RIFLE

Similar to the standard Classic except available in .375 H&H, .375 Flanged Mag. N.E., .416 Rigby, .458 Win., 500/416 NE, 470 NE, 500 NE. Has hinged front trigger, nonremovable muzzle wedge, Universal Trigger System, Combi Cocking Device, steel trigger guard, specially weighted stock bolt for weight and balance. Many options available. Introduced 1997. Imported from Germany by Krieghoff International.

Price: **$13,995.00**
Price: Engraved sideplates, add **$4,000.00**
Price: Extra set of 20-ga. shotgun barrels, add **$5,000.00**
Price: Extra set of rifle barrels, add **$6,300.00**

MERKEL BOXLOCK DOUBLE

Calibers: 5.6x52R, .243 Winchester, 6.5x55, 6.5x57R, 7x57R, 7x65R, .308 Win., .30-06, 8x57 IRS, 9.3x74R. Barrel: 23.6 in. Weight: 7.7 oz. Length: NA. Stock: Walnut, oil finished, pistol grip. Sights: Fixed 100 meter. Features: Anson & Deeley boxlock action with cocking indicators, double triggers, engraved color casehardened receiver. Introduced 1995. Imported from Germany by Merkel USA.

Price: Model 140-2 .... **$13,255.00**
Price: Model 141 Small Frame SXS Rifle; built on smaller frame, chambered for 7mm Mauser, .30-06, or 9.3x74R **$11,825.00**
Price: Model 141 Engraved; fine hand-engraved hunting scenes on silvered receiver. **$13,500.00**

BROWNING SA-22 SEMI-AUTO 22

Caliber: .22 LR. Capacity: Tubular magazine in buttstock holds 11 rounds. Barrel: 19.375 in. Weight: 5 lbs. 3 oz. Length: 37 in. overall. Stock: Checkered select walnut with pistol grip and semi-beavertail fore-end. Sights: Gold bead front, folding leaf rear. Features: Engraved receiver with polished blue finish; crossbolt safety; easy takedown for carrying or storage. The Grade VI is available with either grayed or blued receiver with extensive engraving with gold-plated animals: right side pictures a fox and squirrel in a woodland scene; left side shows a beagle chasing a rabbit. On top is a portrait of the beagle. Stock and fore-end are of high-grade walnut with a double-bordered cut checkering design. Introduced 1956. Made in Belgium until 1974. Currently made in Japan by Miroku.

Price: Grade I, scroll-engraved blued receiver **$700.00**
Price: Grade II, octagon barrel **$1,000.00**
Price: Grade VI BL, gold-plated engraved blued receiver **$1,640.00**
Price: Challenge w/Grade I Walnut, bull bbl **$959.00**

CZ MODEL 512

Calibers: .22 LR/.22 WMR. Capacity: 5-round magazines. Barrel: 20.5 in. Weight: 5.9 lbs. Length: 39.3 in. Stock: Beech. Sights: Adjustable. Features: The modular design is easily maintained, requiring only a coin as a tool for field stripping. The action of the 512 is composed of an aluminum alloy upper receiver that secures the barrel and bolt assembly and a fiberglass reinforced polymer lower half that houses the trigger mechanism and detachable magazine. The 512 shares the same magazines and scope rings with the CZ 455 bolt-action rifle.

Price: .22 LR **$495.00**
Price: .22 WMR **$526.00**

H&K 416-22

Caliber: .22 LR. Capacity: 10- or 20-round magazine. Features: Blowback semi-auto rifle styled to resemble H&K 416 with metal upper and lower receivers; rail interface system; retractable stock; pistol grip with storage compartment; on-rail sights; rear sight adjustable for wind and elevation; 16.1-in. barrel. Also available in pistol version with 9-in. barrel. Made in Germany by Walther under license from Heckler & Koch and imported by Umarex.

Price: **$599.00**

H&K MP5 A5

Caliber: .22 LR. Capacity: 10- or 25-round magazine Features: Blowback semi-auto rifle styled to resemble H&K MP5 with metal receiver; compensator; bolt catch; NAVY pistol grip; on-rail sights; rear sight adjustable for wind and elevation; 16.1-in. barrel. Also available in pistol version with 9-in. barrel. Also available with SD-type fore-end. Made in Germany by Walther under license from Heckler & Koch. Imported by Umarex.

Price: **$499.00**
Price: MP5 SD....................................**$599.00**

HENRY AR-7 SURVIVAL RIFLE

Caliber: .22 LR. Capacity: 8, detachable steel magazine. Barrel: 16.125-in. steel covered with ABS plastic. Weight: 3.5 lbs. Length: 35 in. Stock: ABS plastic, floating, hollow design allowing rifle to be disassembled and packed inside buttstock. Choice of Black, True Timber Kanati, or Viper Western camo. Sights: Peep rear with blaze orange blade front. Also 3/8-in. grooved receiver. Features: Henry's version of the AR-7 takedown rifle issued to U.S. Air Force pilots. Receiver, barrel, and spare mags stow inside the buttstock.

Rubber buttpad. 14-inch LOP. Two 8-round magazines included. The US Survival Pack includes a black synthetic AR-7 rifle, zippered soft case, and a wide variety of survival gear, including a Henry-branded Buck knife.

Price: AR-7 Black **$319.00**
Price: AR-7 Camo **$388.00**
Price: AR-7 Survival Pack **$577.00**

HOWA M1100

Calibers: .22 LR, .22 WMR, .17 HMR. Capacity: 10. Barrel: 18 in., threaded, blued. Stock: Composite Hogue over-molded. Sights: Picatinny rail. Weight: 9.35 lbs. Features: Guaranteed sub-MOA, two-stage HACT trigger.

Price: **$699.00**

KEL-TEC SU-22CA

Caliber: .22 LR. Capacity: 26-round magazine. Barrel: 16.1 in. Weight: 4 lbs. Length: 34 in. Features: Blowback action, crossbolt safety, adjustable front and rear sights with integral Picatinny rail. Threaded muzzle.

Price: **$547.00**

MAGNUM RESEARCH MAGNUM LITE RIMFIRE

Calibers: .22 LR or .22 WMR Capacity: 10 (.22 LR), 9 (.22 WMR) rotary magazine. Barrel: 17-, 18-, 18.5-, or 19-in. lengths with options of carbon, aluminum-tensioned, threaded, and integrally suppressed TTS-22. Weight: 4 lbs.–4 lbs. 8 oz. Length: 36-5/8–38-5/8 in. Stock: Multiple options including Hogue Overmolded and laminated Barracuda style. Sights: Integral scope base. Features: The Magnum Lite Rimfire (MLR) uses a one-piece forged 6061-T6 receivers that are black hardcoat anodized. Custom barrels. Integral Picatinny rail for easy optics mounting. Upgraded trigger. Multiple stock style and material options, as well as barrel types and lengths. Crossbolt safety and manual bolt hold-open catch. Made in the USA.

Price: Hogue Overmolded **$764.00**
Price: MLR .22 LR w/ aluminum-tensioned barrel **$641.00**
Price: MLR .22 WMR w/ Barracuda stock **$935.00**
Price: MLR .22 LR with Ultra barrel....................................**$596.00**
Price: MLR .22 LR with TTS-22 suppressed barrel **$860.00**

MAGNUM RESEARCH SWITCHBOLT

Caliber: .22 LR. Capacity: 10-round rotary magazine. Barrel: 17-in. carbon. Weight: 4.25 lbs. Length: 35-1/8–35-1/2 in. Stock: Two models, one with Hogue Overmolded Black and the other with colored Ambidextrous Evolution laminate. Sights: Integral scope base. Features: Unique gas-assisted blowback operation. An extension of the lightweight MLR rifles, the Switchbolt was tested and perfected on the professional speed shooting circuit. Built in the USA. Integral Picatinny rail. Machined from 6061-T6, hardcoat anodized. Equipped with a bolt handle on the left side of a right-handed bolt, built for right-handed shooters so the trigger hand never has to leave the stock. Custom-designed Switchbolts are available from the Magnum Research Custom Shop.

Price: Hogue overmolded black stock **$731.00**
Price: Ambidextrous Evolution laminate stock **$893.00**
Price: Blaze 47 wood stock....................................**$420.00**

MOSSBERG MODEL 702 PLINKSTER

Caliber: .22 LR. Capacity: 10-round magazine. Barrel: 18 in. free-floating. Weights: 4.1–4.6 lbs. Sights: Adjustable rifle. Receiver grooved for scope mount. Stock: Wood or black synthetic. Features: Ergonomically placed magazine release and safety buttons, crossbolt safety, free gun lock. Made in USA by O.F. Mossberg & Sons, Inc.

Price: From....................................**$190.00**

MOSSBERG MODEL 715T SERIES

Caliber: .22 LR. Capacity: 10- or 25-round magazine. Barrel: 16.25 or 18 in. with A2-style muzzle brake. Weight: 5.5 lbs. Features: AR style offered in

Prices given are believed to be accurate at time of publication however, many factors affect retail pricing so exact prices are not possible.

78TH EDITION, 2024 ✦ **459**

several models. Flattop or A2 style carry handle.
Price: Black finish $326.00
Price: Black finish, Red Dot sight $375.00
Price: Muddy Girl camo $438.00

ROSSI RS22
Caliber: .22 LR. Capacity: 10-round detachable magazine. Barrel: 18 in. Weight: 4.1 lbs. Length: 36 in. Stock: Black synthetic with impressed checkering. Sights: Adjustable fiber optic rear, hooded fiber optic front. Made in Brazil, imported by Rossi USA.
Price: Standard model, synthetic stock $139.00

RUGER 10/22 AUTOLOADING CARBINE
Caliber: .22 LR. Capacity: 10-round rotary magazine. Barrel: 18.5 in. round tapered (16.12 in. compact model). Weight: 5 lbs. (4.5, compact). Length: 37.25 in., 34 in. (compact) overall. Stock: American hardwood with pistol grip and barrel band, or synthetic. Sights: Brass bead front, folding leaf rear adjustable for elevation. Features: Available with satin black or stainless finish on receiver and barrel. Detachable rotary magazine fits flush into stock, crossbolt safety, receiver tapped and grooved for scope blocks or tip-off mount. Scope base adaptor furnished with each rifle. Made in USA by Sturm, Ruger & Co.
Price: Wood stock... $309.00
Price: Synthetic stock $309.00
Price: Stainless, synthetic stock $339.00
Price: Compact model, fiber-optic front sight $359.00
Price: Go Wild Rockstar Camo...................................... $399.00
Price: Collector's Series Man's Best Friend $399.00
Price: Weaver 3-9x Scope $399.00

RUGER 10/22 TAKEDOWN RIFLE
Caliber: .22 LR. Capacity: 10-round rotary magazine. Barrels: 18.5 in. stainless, or 16.6 in. satin black threaded with suppressor. Easy takedown feature enables quick separation of the barrel from the action by way of a recessed locking lever, for ease of transportation and storage. Stock: Black synthetic. Sights: Adjustable rear, gold bead front. Weight: 4.66 pounds. Comes with backpack carrying bag.
Price: Stainless... $439.00
Price: Satin black w/flash suppressor........................ $459.00
Price: Threaded barrel... $629.00
Price: With Silent-SR suppressor............................. $1,078.00

RUGER 10/22 SPORTER
Same specifications as 10/22 Carbine except has American walnut stock with hand-checkered pistol grip and fore-end, straight buttplate, sling swivels, 18.9-in. barrel, and no barrel band.
Price: $419.00

RUGER 10/22 TARGET LITE
Features a 16 1/8-in. heavy, hammer-forged threaded barrel with tight chamber dimensions, black or red/black laminate stock with thumbhole and adjustable length-of-pull, BX Trigger with 2.5-3 lbs. pull weight, minimal overtravel and positive reset.
Price: $649.00

SAVAGE A17 SERIES
Calibers: .17 HMR, . Capacity: 10-round rotary magazine. Barrel: 22 in. Weight: 5.4–5.6 lbs. Features: Delayed blowback action, Savage AccuTrigger, synthetic or laminated stock. Target model has heavy barrel, sporter or thumbhole stock. Introduced in 2016.
Price: Standard model... $473.00

Price: Sporter (Gray laminate stock) $574.00
Price: Target Sporter... $571.00
Price: Target Thumbhole $631.00
Price: A17 Pro Varmint $739.00
Price: A17 Overwatch camo $599.00
Price: A17 HM2 chambered for 17HM2 with black synthetic stock $409.00

SAVAGE A22 SERIES
Caliber: .22 LR, .22 WMR. Capacity 10-round magazine. Similar to A17 series except for caliber.
Price: $284.00
Price: A22 SS stainless barrel $419.00
Price: Target Thumbhole stock, heavy barrel $449.00
Price: Pro Varmint w/Picatinny rail, heavy bbl., target stock $409.00
Price: 22 WMR $479.00
Price: A22 Pro Varmint $569.00
Price: A22 Pro Varmint Magnum in .22 WMR $739.00
Price: A22 FV-SR Overwatch Camo $429.00
Price: A22 Precision with MDT Chassis $659.00
Price: A22 Precision Lite with carbon-fiber stainless barrel $949.00

SAVAGE A22 BNS-SR
Caliber: .22 LR. Capacity: 10. Barrel: 18 in., carbon steel. Stock: Laminated wood. Sights: Two-piece Weaver bases, no scope included. Weight: 6.6 lbs. Features: Ergonomic stock, AccuTrigger, straight blowback semi-auto.
Price: $479.00

SAVAGE A22 TAKEDOWN
Calibers: .22 LR. Barrel: 18 in. Weight: 6.3 lbs. Stock: Black synthetic adjustable. Features: Latest addition to the semi-auto A22 family now in takedown. Breaks in half with a twist. Threaded barrel with low-profile sights. Crossbolt safety, adjustable AccuTrigger. Storage compartment in pistol grip and magazine compartment in cheek riser. Has 0 MOA rail with a see-through iron sight channel. Includes 10-round rotary magazine.
Price: $479.00

SAVAGE B-SERIES PRECISION
Calibers: .22 LR, .22 WMR, .17 HMR. Capacity: 10-round detachable magazine. Barrel: 18 in heavy carbon steel, threaded. Weight: from 5 lbs. 5 oz. Stock: MDT one-piece billet aluminum chassis with adjustable LOP and comb height. Sights: None. One-piece Picatinny rail. Features: B-Series Precision rifles are built for target performance. They include the B22 in .22 LR, B22 Magnum in .22 WMR, and B17 in .17 HMR. Adjustable AccuTrigger with red trigger detail.
Price: $659.00
Price: B-Series Precision Lite 18 in. carbon fiber bbl. wrap $949.00

SMITH & WESSON M&P15-22 SERIES
Caliber: .22 LR. Capacities: 10- or 25-round magazine. Barrel: 15.5 in., 16 in. or 16.5 in. Stock: 6-position telescoping or fixed. Features: A rimfire version of AR-derived M&P tactical autoloader. Operates with blowback action. Quad-mount Picatinny rails, plain barrel or compensator, alloy upper and lower, matte black metal finish. Kryptek Highlander or Muddy Girl camo finishes available.
Price: Standard $449.00
Price: Kryptek Highlander or Muddy Girl camo $499.00
Price: MOE Model with Magpul sights, stock and grip $609.00
Price: Performance Center upgrades, threaded barrel $789.00
Price: M&P 15 Sport w/Crimson Trace Red Dot sight....................... $759.00

THOMPSON/CENTER T/CR22
Caliber: .22 LR. Capacities: 10-round rotary magazine. Barrel: 20 in.

stainless steel, threaded muzzle. Stock: Hogue overmolded sculpted and ambidextrous thumbhole. Features: Picatinny top rail, sling swivel studs, push-button safety, fully machined aluminum receiver with hole to allow cleaning from rear. From the Smith & Wesson Performance Center.
Price: **$497.00**

VOLQUARTSEN CLASSIC
Calibers: .22 LR, .22 WMR, .17 HMR. Capacity: 10-round rotary magazine. Barrel: .920-in. stainless bull barrel threaded into receiver. Weight: from 5 lbs. 5oz. Stock: Choice of multiple options, including black Hogue or colored laminate wood sporter style. Sights: Integral Picatinny rail Features: Classic semi-automatic is the foundation of all subsequent models. Match bore and chamber tolerances for bolt-action accuracy from a repeater. Stainless steel CNC-machined receiver. TG2000 for crisp 2.25-lb. trigger pull.
Price: **$1,504.00**

VOLQUARTSEN VF-ORYX
Caliber: 22 LR Capacity: 10-round magazine. Barrel: 18.5-in. free-floating, snake-fluted. Weight: 9 lbs. 3 oz. Stock: MDT Oryx one-piece aluminum chassis. Sights: Integral 20 MOA rail. Features: CNC-machined stainless steel receiver. Barrel threaded into receiver for rigidity. CNC'ed bolt with round titanium firing pin and tuned extractor. TG2000 trigger group with crisp 2.25-lb. pull. Stock tailored for bench, bipod, and prone shooting. Adjustable cheek riser, overmolded pistol grip, and LOP spacer.
Price: **$1,944.00**
Price: VF-ORYX-S package with Zeiss Conquest **$3,269.00**

WINCHESTER WILDCAT 22 SR (SUPPRESSOR READY)
Caliber: .22 LR. Capacity: 10-round rotary magazine. Barrel: 16.5-in. precision button-rifled chromoly steel with threaded muzzle, thread protector, and recessed target crown. Weight: 4.0 lbs. Length: 34.75 in. Stock: Black polymer ambidextrous skeletonized buttstock with textured grip panels. Sights: Fully adjustable ghost ring rear and ramped post front. Also, integral Picatinny rail. Features: Suppressor-ready version of the company's lightweight repeating rimfire. Rotary magazine system with last round bolt hold open. Dual ambidextrous magazine releases. Reversible manual safety button. Suppressor not included.
Price: **$299.00**
Price: OD Green (w/ 18-in. barrel) **$269.00**
Price: OD Green SR (w/ threaded 16.5-in barrel) **$289.00**
Price: Forged Carbon Gray (gray carbon-fiber stock) **$309.00**
Price: Combo (black synthetic w/ Reflex Sight) **$319.00**
Price: Forged Carbon Gray SR (threaded 16.5-in. barrel) **$329.00**
Price: VSX Gray SR (w/ True Timber VSX camo) **$329.00**
Price: Wildcat SR True Timber Strata **$329.00**

Prices given are believed to be accurate at time of publication however, many factors affect retail pricing so exact prices are not possible.

78TH EDITION, 2024 ✛ **461**

BERGARA B-14 RIMFIRE
Caliber: .22 LR. Capacity: 10. Barrel: 18 in., 4140 Bergara. Stock: HMR composite. Sights: None. Weight: 9.25 lbs. Features: Threaded muzzle, B-14R action, Remington 700 accessories compatible.
Price: $1,150.00

BROWNING BL-22
Caliber: .22 LR. Capacity: Tubular magazines, 15+1. Action: Short-throw lever action, side ejection. Rack-and-pinion lever. Barrel: Recessed muzzle. Stock: Walnut, two-piece straight-grip Western style. Trigger: Half-cock hammer safety; fold-down hammer. Sights: Bead post front, folding-leaf rear. Steel receiver grooved for scope mount. Weight: 5–5.4 lbs. Length: 36.75–40.75 in. overall. Features: Action lock provided. Introduced 1996. FLD Grade II Octagon has octagonal 24-in. barrel, silver nitride receiver with scroll engraving, gold-colored trigger. FLD Grade I has satin-nickel receiver, blued trigger, no stock checkering. FLD Grade II has satin-nickel receivers with scroll engraving; gold-colored trigger, cut checkering. Both introduced 2005. Grade I has blued receiver and trigger, no stock checkering. Grade II has gold-colored trigger, cut checkering, blued receiver with scroll engraving. Imported from Japan by Browning.
Price: BL-22 Grade I/II, From .... $620.00–$700.00
Price: BL-22 FLD Grade I/II, From .... $660.00–$750.00
Price: BL-22 FLD, Grade II Octagon $980.00

BROWNING T-BOLT RIMFIRE
Calibers: .22 LR, .17 HMR, .22 WMR. Capacity: 10-round rotary box double helix magazine. Barrel: 22-in. free-floating, semi-match chamber, target muzzle crown. Weight: 4.8 lbs. Length: 40.1 in. overall. Stock: Walnut, maple or composite. Sights: None. Features: Straight-pull bolt action, three-lever trigger adjustable for pull weight, dual action screws, sling swivel studs. Crossbolt lockup, enlarged bolt handle, one-piece dual extractor with integral spring and red cocking indicator band, gold-tone trigger. Top-tang, thumb-operated two-position safety, drilled and tapped for scope mounts. Varmint model has raised Monte Carlo comb, heavy barrel, wide forearm. Introduced 2006. Imported from Japan by Browning. Left-hand models added in 2009.
Price: .22 LR, From.. $750.00–$780.00
Price: Composite Target .... $780.00–$800.00
Price: .17 HMR/.22 WMR, From .... $790.00–$830.00

BROWNING T-BOLT TARGET W/ MUZZLE BRAKE
Calibers: .22 LR, .22 WMR, .17 HMR. Capacity: 10-round Double Helix box magazine. Barrel: 16.5-in. heavy bull. Sights: No iron sights. Drilled and tapped. Length: 34.75 in. Weight: 6 lbs. 2 oz. Stock: Black Walnut with satin-finish, checkered, Monte Carlo style. Features: Precision straight-pull bolt-action rimfire. Extra-wide fore-end. Free floating heavy bull target barrel threaded at 1/2x28. Includes removeable muzzle brake. Steel receiver with blued finish. Semi-match chamber and target crown. Top tang safety. Adjustable trigger. Sling studs. Plastic buttplate. Cut checkering at 20 LPI. Gold-plated trigger.
Price: .... $699.00–$739.00

BROWNING T-BOLT MAPLE
Caliber: .22 LR. Barrel: 20-in. threaded (Target SR); 22-in. sporter weight (Sporter). Weight: 4 lbs., 14 oz. (Sporter) 6 lbs., 2 oz. (Target SR). Stock: AAA-Grade Maple with a gloss finish and cut checkering at 20 LPI. Features: Straight-pull bolt action operation in special maple furniture. Double helix 10-round magazine. Adjustable trigger. Polished chamber. Polymer buttplate. Swivel studs. Receiver drilled and tapped.
Price: Maple Sporter $929.00
Price: Maple Target SR $899.00

CHIAPPA LITTLE BADGER
Caliber: .22 LR. Barrel: 16.5-in. blued steel. Weight: 2.9 lbs. Stock: Folding steel rod system. Features: Ultralight, minimalist, folding Take Down Xteme (TDX) version of the skeletonized break-action rimfire. Single shot with shell holder and quad Picatinny forend. OAL of 31 in. Alloy frame. Barrel threaded at 1/2x28. Fixed M1 military-style front sight and adjustable rear. Half cock hammer safety. Picatinny rail behind triggerguard. Ships with polymer tube for storage.
Price: TDX $280.00

CHIPMUNK SINGLE SHOT
Caliber: .22 Short, Long and Long Rifle or .22 WMR. Manually cocked single-shot bolt-action youth gun. Barrel: 16.125 in. blued or stainless. Weight: 2.6 lbs. Length: 30 in., LOP 11.6 in. Stock: Synthetic, American walnut or laminate. Barracuda model has ergonomic thumbhole stock with raised comb, accessory rail. Sights: Adjustable rear peep, fixed front. From Keystone Sporting Arms.
Price: Synthetic .... $163.00-$250.00
Price: Walnut .... $209.00-$270.00
Price: Barracuda .... $258.00-$294.00

COOPER MODEL 57-M REPEATER
Calibers: .22 LR, .22 WMR, .17 HMR, .17 Mach. Barrel: 22 in. or 24 in. Weight: 6.5–7.5 lbs. Stock: Claro walnut, 22 LPI hand checkering. Sights: None furnished. Features: Three rear locking lug, repeating bolt-action with 5-round magazine for .22 LR; 4-round magazine for .22 WMR and 17 HMR. Fully adjustable trigger. Left-hand models add $150 to base rifle price. 0.250-in. group rimfire accuracy guarantee at 50 yards; 0.5-in. group centerfire accuracy guarantee at 100 yards. Options include wood upgrades, case-color metalwork, barrel fluting, custom LOP, and many others.
Price: Classic $2,495.00
Price: Custom Classic..$2,995.00
Price: Western Classic $3,795.00
Price: Schnabel $2,595.00
Price: Jackson Squirrel.......................................$2,595.00
Price: Jackson Hunter $2,455.00
Price: Mannlicher $4,755.00

CZ 457 AMERICAN
Calibers: .17 HMR, .22 LR, .22 WMR. Capacity: 5-round detachable magazine. Barrel: 24.8 in. Weight: 6.2 lbs. Stock: Turkish walnut American style with high flat comb. Sights: None. Integral 11mm dovetail scope base. Features: Adjustable trigger, push-to-fire safety, interchangeable barrel system.

Price:	$476.00
Price: .17 HMR .22 WMR	$496.00
Price: Varmint model	$660.00-$762.00

CRICKETT SINGLE SHOT
Caliber: .22 Short, Long and Long Rifle or .22 WMR. Manually cocked single-shot bolt-action. Similar to Chipmunk but with more options and models. Barrel: 16.125 in. blued or stainless. Weight: 3 lbs. Length: 30 in., LOP 11.6 in. Stock: Synthetic, American walnut or laminate. Available in wide range of popular camo patterns and colors. Sights: Adjustable rear peep, fixed front. Drilled and tapped for scope mounting using special Chipmunk base. Alloy model has AR-style buttstock, XBR has target stock and bull barrel, Precision Rifle has bipod and fully adjustable thumbhole stock.

Price: Alloy	$300.00
Price: XBR	$380.00-$400.00
Price: Precision Rifle	$316.00-$416.00
Price: Adult Rifle	$240.00-$280.00

HENRY LEVER-ACTION RIFLES
Caliber: .22 Long Rifle (15 shot), .22 Magnum (11 shots), .17 HMR (11 shots). Barrel: 18.25 in. round. Weight: 5.5–5.75 lbs. Length: 34 in. overall (.22 LR). Stock: Walnut. Sights: Hooded blade front, open adjustable rear. Features: Polished blue finish; full-length tubular magazine; side ejection; receiver grooved for scope mounting. Introduced 1997. Made in USA by Henry Repeating Arms Co.

Price: H001 Carbine .22 LR	$378.00
Price: H001L Carbine .22 LR, Large Loop Lever	$394.00
Price: H001Y Youth model (33 in. overall, 11-round .22 LR)	$378.00
Price: H001M .22 Magnum, 19.25 in. octagonal barrel, deluxe walnut stock	$525.00
Price: H001V .17 HMR, 20 in. octagonal barrel, Williams Fire Sights	$578.00
Price: Frontier Threaded Barrel, Suppressor-Ready .22 LR	$552.00
Price: Frontier Threaded Barrel, Suppressor-Ready .22 WMR	$656.00

HENRY LEVER-ACTION OCTAGON FRONTIER MODEL
Same as lever rifles except chambered in .17 HMR, .22 Short/Long/LR, .22 Magnum. Barrel: 20 in. octagonal. Sights: Marble's fully adjustable semi-buckhorn rear, brass bead front. Weight: 6.25 lbs. Made in USA by Henry Repeating Arms Co.

Price: H001T Lever Octagon .22 S/L/R	$473.00
Price: H001TM Lever Octagon .22 Magnum, .17 HMR	$578.00

HENRY GOLDEN BOY SERIES
Calibers: .17 HMR, .22 LR (16-shot), .22 Magnum. Barrel: 20 in. octagonal. Weight: 6.25 lbs. Length: 38 in. overall. Stock: American walnut. Sights: Blade front, open rear. Features: Brasslite receiver, brass buttplate, blued barrel and lever. Introduced 1998. Made in USA from Henry Repeating Arms Co.

Price: H004 .22 LR	$578.00
Price: H004M .22 Magnum	$625.00
Price: H004V .17 HMR	$641.00
Price: H004DD .22 LR Deluxe, engraved receiver	$1,575.00-1,654.00

HENRY SILVER BOY
Calibers: 17 HMR, .22 S/L/LR, .22 WMR. Capacities: Tubular magazine. 12 rounds (.17 HMR and .22 WMR), 16 rounds (.22 LR), 21 rounds (.22 Short). Barrel: 20 in. Stock: American walnut with curved buttplate. Finish: Nickel receiver, barrel band and buttplate. Sights: Adjustable buckhorn rear, bead front. Silver Eagle model has engraved scroll pattern from early original Henry rifle. Offered in same calibers as Silver Boy. Made in USA from Henry Repeating Arms Company.

Price: .22 S/L/LR	$630.00
Price: .22 WMR	$682.00
Price: .17 HMR	$709.00
Price: Silver Eagle	$892.00–$945.00

HENRY PUMP ACTION
Caliber: .22 LR. Capacity: 15 rounds. Barrel: 18.25 in. Weight: 5.5 lbs. Length: NA. Stock: American walnut. Sights: Bead on ramp front, open adjustable rear. Features: Polished blue finish; receiver grooved for scope mount; grooved slide handle; two barrel bands. Introduced 1998. Made in USA from Henry Repeating Arms Co.

Price: H003T .22 LR	$578.00
Price: H003TM .22 Magnum	$620.00

MEACHAM LOW-WALL
Calibers: Any rimfire cartridge. Barrels: 26–34 in. Weight: 7-15 lbs. Sights: none. Tang drilled for Win. base, .375 in. dovetail slot front. Stock: Fancy eastern walnut with cheekpiece; ebony insert in forearm tip. Features: Exact copy of 1885 Winchester. With most Winchester factory options available including double-set triggers. Introduced 1994. Made in USA by Meacham T&H Inc.

Price: From	$4,999.00

MOSSBERG MODEL 802
Caliber: .22 LR Capacity: 10-round magazine. Barrel: 18 in. free-floating. Weight: 4.1 lbs. Sights: Adjustable rifle or scope combo variant. Receiver grooved for scope mount. Stock: Black synthetic. Features: Ergonomically placed magazine release and safety buttons, crossbolt safety.

Price: Plinkster	$231.00
Price: Scope combo	$245.00

NEW ULTRA LIGHT ARMS 20RF
Caliber: .22 LR, single-shot or repeater. Barrel: Douglas, length to order. Weight: 5.25 lbs. Length: Varies. Stock: Kevlar/graphite composite, variety of finishes. Sights: None furnished; drilled and tapped for scope mount. Features: Timney trigger, hand-lapped action, button-rifled barrel, hand-bedded action, recoil pad, sling-swivel studs, optional Jewell trigger. Made in USA by New Ultra Light Arms.

Price: 20 RF single shot	$1,800.00
Price: 20 RF repeater	$1,850.00

PEDERSOLI BLACK WIDOW
Calibers: .22 LR. Capacity: Single shot. Barrel: 19-in. round steel. Weight: 3.3 lbs. Stock: Black techno-polymer folder with skeletonized buttstock and removeable forend. Sights: Iron sights. Drilled and tapped for Picatinny rail mounting. Features: Folding-style, single-shot rimfire. Threaded barrel with knurled thread protector cap. Integral ammo storage along buttstock. Forward Picatinny rail at base of forend. Built to fit into medium-sized backpack. European model threaded at ½-20 UNF. American version threaded at ½"-28 TPI.

Price:	$400.00

Prices given are believed to be accurate at time of publication however, many factors affect retail pricing so exact prices are not possible.

78TH EDITION, 2024 ✦ **463**

ROSSI GALLERY

Caliber: 22 LR. Capacity: 15-round tubular magazine. Barrel: 18-in. round. Weight: 5.3 lbs. Length: 36 in. Stock: Choice of either German Beechwood or black synthetic. Sights: Traditional Buckhorn iron sights on wood model; fiber optics on synthetic model. Features: Pump action reminiscent of classic gallery guns of the 1890s. Polished black metalwork. Hammer fired with cross-bolt safety. Sling studs.

Price: German Beechwood..$360.00
Price: Black Polymer $315.00

ROSSI RIO BRAVO

Caliber: 22 LR. Capacity: 15-round tubular magazine. Barrel: 18-in. round. Weight: 5.5 lbs. Length: 36 in. Stock: Choice of either German Beechwood or black synthetic. Sights: Traditional Buckhorn iron sights on wood model; fiber optics on synthetic model. Features: Lever action rimfire based on the company's R92 centerfires. Polished black metal finish. Hammer fired with cross-bolt safety. Sling studs.

Price: German Beechwood.. $370.00
Price: Black Polymer $370.00

ROSSI RIO BRAVO GOLD

Caliber: .22 LR. Capacity: 15-round tubular magazine. Barrel: 18-in. round. Weight: 5.5 lbs. Length: 36 in. Stock: German Beechwood. Sights: Traditional Buckhorn iron sights. Features: New "Gold" version of Rossi's lever-action rimfire based on the R92 centerfire. PVD gold receiver and lever finish with polished black on remaining metalwork. Hammer fired with cross-bolt safety. Sling studs.

Price: $465.00

RUGER AMERICAN RIMFIRE RIFLE

Calibers: .17 HMR, .22 LR,.22 WMR. Capacity: 10-round rotary magazine. Barrels: 22-in., or 18-in. threaded. Sights: Williams fiber optic, adjustable. Stock: Composite with interchangeable comb adjustments, sling swivels. Adjustable trigger.

Price: $359.00

RUGER PRECISION RIMFIRE RIFLE

Calibers: .17 HMR, .22 LR, .22 HMR. Capacity: 9 to 15-round magazine. Barrel: 18 in. threaded. Weight: 6.8 lbs. Stock: Quick-fit adjustable with AR-pattern pistol grip, free-floated handguard with Magpul M-LOK slots. Features: Adjustable trigger, oversized bolt handle, Picatinny scope base.

Price: $529.00

SAVAGE MARK II BOLT-ACTION

Calibers: .22 LR, .17 HMR. Capacity: 10-round magazine. Barrel: 20.5 in. Weight: 5.5 lbs. Length: 39.5 in. overall. Stock: Camo, laminate, thumbhole or OD Green stock available Sights: Bead front, open adjustable rear. Receiver

grooved for scope mounting. Features: Thumb-operated rotating safety. Blue finish. Introduced 1990. Made in Canada, from Savage Arms, Inc.

Price: ....$228.00–$280.00
Price: Varmint w/heavy barrel $242.00
Price: Camo stock $280.00
Price: OD Green stock...$291.00
Price: Multi-colored laminate stock $529.00
Price: Thumbhole laminate stock $469.00

SAVAGE MODEL 93FVSS MAGNUM

Similar to Model 93FSS Magnum except 21-in. heavy barrel with recessed target-style crown, satin-finished stainless barreled action, black graphite/fiberglass stock. Drilled and tapped for scope mounting; comes with Weaver-style bases. Introduced 1998. Imported from Canada by Savage Arms, Inc.

Price: $364.00

SAVAGE B SERIES

Calibers: .17 HMR, .22 LR, 22 WMR. Capacity: 10-round rotary magazine. Barrel: 21 in. (16.25 in. threaded heavy barrel on Magnum FV-SR Model). Stock: Black synthetic with target-style vertical pistol grip. Weight: 6 lbs. Features include top tang safety, Accutrigger. Introduced in 2017.

Price: ....$281.00–$445.00

SAVAGE MARK II MINIMALIST

Choice of Green or Brown Boyd's Minimalist laminate stock design.

Price: $379.00

SAVAGE MODEL 42

Calibers/Gauges: Break-open over/under design with .22 LR or .22 WMR barrel over a .410 shotgun barrel. Under-lever operation. Barrel: 20 in. Stock: Synthetic black matte. Weight: 6.1 lbs. Sights: Adjustable rear, bead front. Updated variation of classic Stevens design from the 1940s.

Price $509.00

SAVAGE RASCAL

Caliber: .22 LR. Capacity: Single shot. Barrel: 16.125-in. carbon steel. Weight: 2.71 lbs. Length: 30.6 in. Stock: Synthetic sporter. Upgraded models available with different stock options. Sights: Adjustable peep sights. Features: Micro-rimfire bolt action with short 11.25-inch length of pull for the smallest framed shooters. Cocks by lifting the bolt and unloads without pulling the trigger. User-adjustable AccuTrigger. Feed ramp. Manual safety.

Price $199.00
Price Rascal FV-SR Left Hand..$249.00
Price Rascal Target..$339.00
Price Rascal Target XP...$429.00

SAVAGE RASCAL MINIMALIST

Caliber: .22 LR. Capacity: single shot. Barrel: 16.125-in. carbon steel, threaded with protector. Length: 30.625 in. Weight: 3.5 lbs. Stock: Minimalist hybrid laminate design in two color options. Features: Addition to the micro-sized Rascal single shot, bolt-action family. Blued carbon steel receiver. Manual safety. Cocks by lifting the bolt. Unloads without pulling

the trigger. 11-degree target crown. Adjustable peep sight. Sling studs. User-adjustable AccuTrigger. Feed ramp. ChevCore Laminate technology with Boyd's stock in two color options: Pink/Purple or Teal/Gray. Short 11.5-in length of pull. Package includes ear plugs and firearms lock.
Price: **$289.00**

STEYR ZEPHYR II
Calibers: .22 LR, .22 WMR, .17 HMR. Capacity: 5-round detachable magazine. Barrel: 19.7 in cold-hammer forged with Mannox finish. Option of standard or threaded. Weight: 5.8 lbs. Length: 39.2 in. Stock: European Walnut with Bavarian cheekpiece and fish scale checkering. Sights: No iron sights. 11mm receiver dovetail. Features: Rebirth of the original Zephyr rifle produced from 1955–1971. Single-stage trigger. Tang safety. Sling swivels. Gold trigger. Pistol grip features inset Steyr logo. Recessed target crown. Dual extractors.
Price **$1,099.00**

TIKKA T1x MTR
Calibers: .22 LR or .17 HMR. Capacity: 10-round polymer magazine. Barrel: 20-in. cold hammer forged, crossover profile. Weight: 5.7 lbs. Length: 39.6 in. Stock: Modular Black synthetic. Sights: No iron sights. Dovetailed and tapped. Features: Stainless steel bolt for smooth movement and weather resistance. Compatible with most T3x accessories. Action shares same bedding surfaces and inlay footprint with the T3x centerfire rifles. Threaded muzzle. Adjustable single-stage trigger.
Price **$529.00**

VOLQUARTSEN SUMMIT
Calibers: .22 LR or .17 Mach2. Capacity: 10-round rotary magazine. Barrel: 16.5-in. lightweight carbon fiber with threaded muzzle. Stainless steel tapered barrel also available. Weight: 4 lbs. 13 oz.–7 lbs. 11 oz. Stock: Available with multiple stock options, including black Hogue, colored Magpul, McMillan Sporter, or Laminated Silhouette Wood sporter. Sights: Integral 20 MOA Picatinny rail. Features: Unique straight-pull bolt-action rimfire inspired by the 10/22 platform. Built for both competition shooting and small game hunting. CNC-machined receiver with integral rail. Suppressor ready. Accepts 10/22-style magazines. Crisp 1.75-lb. trigger pull. Made in the USA.
Price **$1,252.00**

WINCHESTER XPERT
Calibers: .22 LR. Capacity: 10-round rotary detachable magazine, interchangeable with both Wildcat and Ruger 10/22. Barrel: 18-in. precision button rifled with recessed target crown. Weight: 4 lbs. 8 oz. Length: 36.25 in. Stock: Gray Synthetic skeletonized with optional LOP spacers and cheek riser. Sights: Adjustable rear and ramped post front. Drilled and tapped. Features: Bolt-action precision cousin to the Wildcat line of semi-auto rimfires. Xpert uses a rimfire version of the M.O.A. trigger found on Model 70 and XPR rifles. Semi-match Bentz chamber and hemispherical firing pin. Extended bolt handle. Ambidextrous side-mounted mag releases. Plastic butt plate.
Price: **$319.00**
Price: Xpert Suppressor Ready **$349.00**

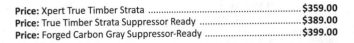

Price: Xpert True Timber Strata **$359.00**
Price: True Timber Strata Suppressor Ready **$389.00**
Price: Forged Carbon Gray Suppressor-Ready **$399.00**

ANSCHUTZ 1903 MATCH
Caliber: .22 LR. Capacity: Single-shot. Barrel: 21.25 in. Weight: 8 lbs. Length: 43.75 in. overall. Stock: Walnut-finished hardwood with adjustable cheekpiece; stippled grip and fore-end. Sights: None furnished. Features: Uses Anschutz Match 64 action. A medium weight rifle for intermediate and advanced Junior Match competition. Available from Champion's Choice.
Price: Right-hand $1,195.00

ANSCHUTZ 1912 SPORT
Caliber: .22 LR. Barrel: 26 in. match. Weight: 11.4 lbs. Length: 41.7 in. overall. Stock: Non-stained thumbhole stock adjustable in length with adjustable buttplate and cheekpiece adjustment. Flat fore-end raiser block 4856 adjustable in height. Hook buttplate. Sights: None furnished. Features: in. Free rifle in. for women. Smallbore model 1907 with 1912 stock: Match 54 action. Delivered with: Hand stop 6226, fore-end raiser block 4856, screwdriver, instruction leaflet with test target. Available from Champion's Choice.
Price: $2,995.00

ANSCHUTZ 1913 SUPER MATCH RIFLE
Same as the Model 1911 except European walnut International-type stock with adjustable cheekpiece, or color laminate, both available with straight or lowered fore-end, adjustable aluminum hook buttplate, adjustable hand stop, weighs 13 lbs., 46 in. overall. Stainless or blued barrel. Available from Champion's Choice.
Price: Right-hand, blued, no sights, walnut stock............................$3,799.00

ANSCHUTZ 1907 STANDARD MATCH RIFLE
Same action as Model 1913 but with 0.875-in. diameter 26-in. barrel (stainless or blues). Length: 44.5 in. overall. Weight: 10.5 lbs. Stock: Choice of stock configurations. Vented fore-end. Designed for prone and position shooting ISU requirements; suitable for NRA matches. Also available with walnut flat-forend stock for benchrest shooting. Available from Champion's Choice.
Price: Right-hand, blued, no sights....................................$2,385.00

BROWNING X-BOLT TARGET MAX COMPETITION
Caliber: 6mm Creed, 6mm GT, 6.5 Creedmoor, .308 Win. Barrel: 26-in. heavy stainless bull (Heavy model), 22-in. fluted sporter weight (Lite model). Weights: 9 to 12 lbs. Stock: Nylon-filled MAX with vertical grip and adjustable comb. Features: Specialized bolt-action target rifles aimed at competitions. Built on stiffer, heavier receivers. Factory ARCA/Swiss rail. Threaded barrel with Recoil Hawg brake. Textured grip panels. Gold-plated trigger. Extra capacity magazine.
Price: Competition Lite $1,779.00
Price: Competition Heavy $1,799.00

CADEX DEFENCE CDX-R7 CPS SERIES
Calibers: 6.5 Creedmoor, .308 Win. Capacity: Multiple magazine sleeves to fit most mags on the market. Barrel: 16.5-in. Bartlein heavy, straight-taper, fluted, threaded. Weight: 10.49 lbs. Length: 33.5 in. Stock: Lightweight with small contour forend tube and rail placement at 3, 6, and 9 o'clock. Takedown QD skeleton buttstock. Available in 14 color combinations. Cadex recoil pad, neoprene cheek pad, and rubberized grip panel. Sights: None. 0 MOA Picatinny rail standard, 20 or 30 MOA rails available. Features: Military-quality bolt-action platform for the civilian market. Spiral fluted bolt. DX2 Evo single-/two-stage selectable trigger. Optional MX2 muzzle brake. Hard case included.
Price: $4,479.00

COLT CBX
Caliber: 6.5 Creedmoor, .308 Win. Barrel: 24 in. (.308), 26 in. (6.5) Weight: 10.75 lbs. Stock: Aluminum chassis with adjustable LOP and cheek riser. Features: Precision bolt-action chassis rifle system. Flat bottom receiver. AICS magazine compatible. User-adjustable trigger. Extended forend with ARCA rail and M-LOK slots. Picatinny rail. 60-degree bolt throw. Black nitride barrel finish. Pistol grip with thumb shelf and ambidextrous magazine latch.
Price: $1,899.00

CZ 457 VARMINT PRECISION CHASSIS
Caliber: .22 LR. Capacity: 5. Barrel: 16.5 or 24 in., suppressor ready, cold hammer-forged, heavy. Stock: Aluminum chassis. Sights: None, integral 11mm dovetail. Weight: 7 lbs. Features: Fully adjustable trigger, receiver mounted push-to-fire safety, swappable barrel system.
Price: $999.00

CZ 457 VARMINT PRECISION TRAINER MTR
Caliber: .22 LR. Capacity: 5-round detachable box magazine. Barrel: 16.2-in. cold hammer forged Varmint weight. Sights: No iron sights, integral 11mm Dovetail. Length: 33.5 in. Weight: 7.1 lbs. Stock: Manners carbon-fiber stock with colored highlights. Forearm is recessed, drilled, and threaded for ARCA rail. Features: The upgraded Varmint Precision Trainer makes use of a barrel borrowed from the Match Target Rifle (MTR). Match chamber. Heavy barrel threaded at 1/2x28. Designed to provide the same look and feel as a full-size tactical rifle but with more economical training. American-style, two position, push-to-fire safety. 60-degree bolt rotation. Fully adjustable trigger. Same swappable barrel system as the Model 455. Competition-grade rimfire rifle.
Price: $1,635.00

GUNWERKS HAMR 2.0
Calibers: .375 CheyTac. Barrel: 30 in. Carbon wrapped, threaded, with aggressive Cadex MX1 muzzle brake. Weight: 21.25 lbs. standard, total package. Stock: Cadex Defence Dual Strike tactical folding chassis-style with adjustable LOP. Sights: Comes standard with user option of scope (Kahles K525i, Leupold Mk 5HD, Revic PMR 428) on a 40 MOA mount. Features: Bolt-action ultra-long-range rifle built as a complete ELR system capable of shooting over two miles. The upgraded 2.0 version includes a carbon-wrapped barrel, new optic choices, and finish options. Included Elite Iron bipod encircles the centerline of the bore. Timney trigger set at 2.5 lbs. Prices increase significantly as options are added for custom factory builds. Long-range data package available.
Price: $9,150.00

HEYM HIGH PERFORMANCE PRECISION RIFLE (HPPR)
Calibers: Standard: .308 Win., 7mm Rem. Mag, .300 Win. Mag. Additional calibers available in 6.5 Creedmoor, 6.5x55, .270 Win., 7x64, .30-06

Spfld., and 8.5x63. Capacity: Detachable box magazine, varies by caliber. Barrel: 26-in. Krupp Steel, hammer forged, threaded, with protector. Sights: Top rail; available paired with Schmidt & Bender Precision Hunter scope. Weight: 8.0 lbs. Stock: PSE Carbon Precision with adjustable comb. Features: Precision shooting bolt actions from Heym built around two models, one SR21 with three-locking-lug turn bolt and the other SR30 straight pull. Single-stage trigger set at 3-lbs. with no creep or overtravel. Guaranteed 5-shot 20mm groups at 100 meters. Sling studs. Rubber recoil pad.
Price: $4,750.00

MASTERPIECE ARMS MPA BA PMR COMPETITION RIFLE
Calibers: .308 Win., 6mm Creedmoor, 6.5 Creedmoor. Capacity: 10. Barrel: 26 in., M24 stainless steel, polished. Stock: Aluminum chassis. Sights: None, optional package with MPA 30mm mount and Bushnell scope. Weight: 11.5 lbs. Features: Built-in inclinometer, MPA/Curtis action, match-grade chamber.
Price: ....$2,999.00-$3,459.00

ROCK RIVER ARMS RBG-1S
Calibers: .308 Win./7.62X51 NATO or 6.5 Creedmoor. Capacity: AICS/ Magpul compatible box magazine. Barrel: 20-, 22-, or 24-in. stainless steel air-gauged, cryo-treated. Weight: 10.2 lbs. Length: 39.5–43.5 in. Stock: KRG adjustable chassis in tan, black or green. Sights: 20 MOA rail. Also has standard scope base holes drilled for use with conventional ring mounts. Features: Rock River's first precision bolt-action rifles series. Precision aluminum bedding. One-piece, interchangeable two-lug bolt. Oversized knurled handle. TriggerTech trigger standard, with option of Timney upgrade. Toolless field adjustability. Guaranteed sub-MOA accuracy.
Price: $4,235.00

SAVAGE 110 ELITE PRECISION *(now adds LH)*
Calibers: .223 Rem., 6mm Creedmoor, 6.5 Creedmoor, .308 Win., .300 Win. Mag., .300 PRC, .338 Lapua. Capacity: 5- or 10-round AICS-pattern detachable box magazine. Barrel: 26 or 30 in stainless steel. Weight: 12.6–14.95 lbs. Stock: Modular Driven Technologies (MDT) Adjustable Core Competition aluminum chassis with Grey Cerakote finish. Sights: 20 MOA rail. Features: Factory blueprinted action. ARCA Rail along entire length of chassis. Titanium Nitride bolt body. User adjustable AccuTrigger. MDT vertical grip. Self-timing taper aligned muzzle brake on short action calibers only.
Price: ....$1,999.00–$2,199.00
Price: Left-hand model $2,199.00

SAVAGE IMPULSE ELITE PRECISION
Calibers: 6mm Creedmoor, 6.5 Creedmoor, .308 Win., 6.5 PRC, .300 Win. Mag., .300 PRC, .338 Lapua. Capacity: 5- or 10-round AICS magazine with ambidextrous release. Barrel: 26 or 30 in. precision button-rifled, stainless steel, modified Palma contour, with muzzle brake. Sights: Integral 20 MOA rail. Weight: 13.7 lbs. Stock: MDT Adjustable Core Competition chassis. Features: The straight-pull bolt action moves to Savage's Precision series rifles for faster split times. Action uses HexLock bolt system. Ambidextrous rotary bolt handle. Adjustable AccuTrigger. Matte black aluminum receiver. Removeable and user-adjustable round bolt knob handle. ARCA rail forend with M-LOK slots.
Price: $2,499.00

SEEKINS PRECISION HAVAK BRAVO
Calibers: 6mm Creedmoor, 6.5 Creedmoor, 6.5 PRC, .308 Win. Capacity: 5-round box magazine. Barrel: 24-in. 5R 416 stainless steel with threaded muzzle. Weight: 9.8 lbs. Stock: KRG Bravo Chassis in Black. OD Green, FDE, or Stealth Gray. Sights: 20 MOA Picatinny rail with five 8-32 screws. Features: Specialty bolt-action rifle built for hard-running, from SWAT to precision shooting. Matte black Cerakoted barreled action. Integrated recoil lug and M16-style extractor. Bolt with four locking lugs and 90-degree throw. Removable bolt head. Extended magazine release.
Price: TRG-22 ....$1,950.00

SEEKINS PRECISION HAVAK ELEMENT
Calibers: .308 Win., 6mm Creedmoor, 6.5 PRC, 6.5 Creedmoor. Capacity: 3 to 5. Barrel: 21 in., Mountain Hunter contour, spiral fluted, threaded. Stock: Carbon composite. Sights: 20 MOA picatinny rail. Weight: 5.5 lbs. Features: Timney Elite Hunter trigger, M16-style extractor, 7075 aerospace aluminum/stainless steel body.
Price: $2,795.00

SEEKINS PRECISION HAVAK HIT
Calibers: 6mm GT, 6mm Creedmoor, 6.5 Creedmoor, .308 Win., 6.5 PRC. Capacity: Varies by chambering, compatible with single- or double-stack AICS magazines. Barrel: 24 in. 416 SS LT Tactical contour, threaded, with 5R rifling. Sights: 20 MOA rail. Length: 43.5 in; 34.5 in. folded. Weight: 11.5 lbs. Stock: Chassis-style, folding, available in black and FDE. Features: Bolt-action chassis rifle. A Pro version for competition is planned to follow. Changeable bolt head, M16-style extractor, integrated recoil lug. Quick-change barrel system. R700 trigger compatibility. Integral 20 MOA Picatinny rail. Carbon-fiber cheek piece, fully adjustable recoil pad, and toolless LOP adjustment.
Price: $2,100.00

SIG SAUER CROSS RIFLE
Calibers: .277 Sig Fury, .308 Win., 6.5 Creedmoor. Capacity: 5. Barrel: 16 to 18 in., stainless steel. Stock: Sig precision, polymer/alloy, folding. Sights: Picatinny rail. Weight: 6.5 to 6.8 lbs. Features: M-LOK rail, two-stage match trigger.
Price: $1,779.00

SAKO TRG-22 BOLT-ACTION
Calibers: .308 Win., .260 Rem, 6.5 Creedmoor, .300 Win Mag, .338 Lapua. Capacity: 5-round magazine. Barrel: 26 in. Weight: 10.25 lbs. Length: 45.25 in. overall. Stock: Reinforced polyurethane with fully adjustable cheekpiece and buttplate. Sights: None furnished. Optional quick-detachable, one-piece scope mount base, 1 in. or 30mm rings. Features: Resistance-free bolt, free-floating heavy stainless barrel, 60-degree bolt lift. Two-stage trigger is adjustable for length, pull, horizontal or vertical pitch. TRG-42 has similar features but has long action and is chambered for .338 Lapua. Imported from Finland by Beretta USA.
Price: TRG-22 ....$3,495.00
Price: TRG-22 with folding stock $6,400.00
Price: TRG-42 ....$4,445.00
Price: TRG-42 with folding stock $7,400.00

SPRINGFIELD ARMORY M1A/M-21 TACTICAL MODEL
Similar to M1A Super Match except special sniper stock with adjustable cheekpiece and rubber recoil pad. Weighs 11.6 lbs. From Springfield Armory.
Price: $3,619.00
Price: Krieger stainless barrel..$4,046.00

Prices given are believed to be accurate at time of publication however, many factors affect retail pricing so exact prices are not possible.

78TH EDITION, 2024 ✦ **467**

ACCU-TEK AT-380 II ACP

Caliber: 380 ACP. Capacity: 6-round magazine. Barrel: 2.8 in. Weight: 23.5 oz. Length: 6.125 in. overall. Grips: Textured black composition. Sights: Blade front, and rear adjustable for windage. Features: Made from 17-4 stainless steel, has an exposed hammer, manual firing-pin safety block and trigger disconnect. Magazine release located on the bottom of the grip. American made, lifetime warranty. Comes with two 6-round stainless steel magazines and a California-approved cable lock. Introduced 2006. Made in USA by Excel Industries.

Price: Satin stainless **$250.00**

ACCU-TEK HC-380

Similar to AT-380 II except has a 13-round magazine.

Price: **$275.00**

ACCU-TEK LT-380

Similar to AT-380 II except has a lightweight aluminum frame. Weight: 15 ounces.

Price: **$275.00**

AMERICAN CLASSIC 1911-A1 II SERIES

Caliber: .45 ACP, 9mm, .38 Super. Capacity: 8+1 magazine Barrel: 5 in. Grips: Checkered walnut. Sights: Novak-style rear, fixed front. Finish: Blue or hard chromed. Other variations include Trophy model with checkered mainspring housing, fiber-optic front sight, hard-chrome finish. Made in the Philippines by Metro Arms, imported by TriStar Arms.

Price: .... **$550.00–$610.00**

AMERICAN CLASSIC COMMANDER

Caliber: 9mm, .45 ACP. Same features as 1911-A1 model except is Commander size with 4.25-in. barrel.

Price: .... **$560.00–$660.00**

AMERICAN CLASSIC TROPHY

Caliber: .45 ACP. Capacity: 8-round magazine. Barrel: 5 in. Grips: Textured hardwood. Sights: Fixed, fiber-optic front/Novak rear. Finish: Hard chrome. Features: Front slide serrations, ambidextrous thumb safety.

Price: **$730.00**

AMERICAN TACTICAL IMPORTS MILITARY 1911

Caliber: .45 ACP. Capacity: 7+1 magazine. Barrel: 5 in. Grips: Textured mahogany. Sights: Fixed military style. Finish: Blue. Also offered in Commander and Officer's sizes and Enhanced model with additional features.

Price: .... **$500.00–$899.00**

AMERICAN TACTICAL IMPORTS HGA FXH-45

Caliber: .45 ACP. Capacity: 7+1 magazine. Barrel: 4.25 or 5 in. Grips: Textured polymer. Sights: Fixed, fiber-optic front. Finish: Black. Hybrid polymer and steel frame with 1911-style action.

Price: .... **$430.00–$520.00**

AMERICAN TACTICAL IMPORTS GSG 1911

Caliber: .22 LR. Capacity: 10+1 magazine. Weight: 34 oz. Other features and dimensions similar to centerfire 1911.

Price: **$299.00**

AMERICAN TACTICAL IMPORTS GSG Firefly HGA

Caliber: .22 LR. Capacity: 10+1 magazine. Weight: 34 oz. Other features and dimensions similar to centerfire SIG P226.

Price: **$299.00**

AMERICAN TACTICAL IMPORTS GSG-MP40P

Caliber: 9mm. Capacity: 30+1 magazine. Barrel: 10.8 in. Weight: 8.3 lbs. Other features and dimensions similar to WWII-era MP-40.

Price: **$580.00**

AMERICAN TACTICAL IMPORTS Omni Hybrid Maxx

Caliber: .5.56 NATO, 300 BLK. Capacity: 30+1 magazine. Barrel: 7.5 or 8.5 in. Weight: 4.8 lbs. AR15 style action.

Price: .... **$345.00-$395.00**

ANDERSON KIGER-9C

Caliber: 9mm. Capacity: 15-round magazine. Barrel: 3.1 in. Weight: 20.6 oz. Length: 7.35 in. overall. Sights: fixed. Features: Polymer frame, striker fire. 9C Pro model has lightweight slide, enhanced controls, and suppressor height sights. Made in USA.

Price: 9C **$439.00**
Price: 9C Pro **$539.00**

AUTO-ORDNANCE 1911A1

Caliber: 45 ACP. Capacity: 7-round magazine. Barrel: 4.25 or 5 in. Weight: 39 oz. Length: 8.5 in. overall. Grips: Brown checkered plastic with medallion. Sights: Blade front, rear drift-adjustable for windage. Features: Same specs as 1911A1 military guns-parts interchangeable. Frame and slide blued; each radius has non-glare finish. Introduced 2002. Made in USA by Kahr Arms.

Price: 1911BKO Parkerized, plastic grips **$673.00**
Price: 1911BKOW Black matte finish, wood grips **$689.00**
Price: Stainless steel finish, G10 grips **$1125.00**

BERETTA MODEL 21A BOBCAT
Calibers: .22 LR. Capacities: 9-round magazine. Barrel: 2.5 in. Weight: 11.8 oz. Sights: Round post front, square notch rear. Grip: G10, wood, or plastic. Finish: Blued, Inox, or FDE. Features: Tip-up barrel, DA/SA trigger, Covert model is suppressor-ready.
Price: .... $255.00–$470.00

BERETTA MODEL 80X CHEETAH
Calibers: .380 Auto. Capacities: 13-round magazine. Barrel: 3.9 in. Weight: 25 oz. Sights: Post front, square notch rear. Grip: Textured plastic. Finish: Blued or two-tone bronze/black. Features: X-treme DA/SA trigger, optic ready.
Price: $799.00

BERETTA 92/96 A1 SERIES
Calibers: 9mm, .40 S&W. Capacities: 15-round magazine; .40 S&W, 12 rounds (M96 A1). Barrel: 4.9 in. Weight: 33-34 oz. Length: 8.5 in. Sights: Fiber-optic front, adjustable rear. Features: Same as other models in 92/96 family except for addition of accessory rail.
Price: $600.00

BERETTA MODEL 92FS
Caliber: 9mm. Capacity: 10-round magazine. Barrels: 4.9 in., 4.25 in. (Compact). Weight: 34 oz. Length: 8.5 in. overall. Grips: Checkered black plastic. Sights: Blade front, rear adjustable for windage. Tritium night sights available. Features: Double action. Extractor acts as chamber loaded indicator, squared triggerguard, grooved front and backstraps, inertia firing pin. Matte or blued finish. Introduced 1977. Made in USA
Price: $600.00
Price: Inox $675.00
Price: Brigadier Inox $760.00

BERETTA MODEL 92G ELITE LTT CENTURION/COMPACT
Calibers: 9mm. Capacities: 15-round magazine. Barrel: 4.7 in. Weight: 33 oz. Length: 8.5 in. Sights: Fiber-optic front, square notch rear. Features: M9A1 frame with M9A3 slide, front and rear serrations, ultra-thin VZ/LTT G10 grips, oversized mag release button, skeletonized trigger, ships with three magazines.
Price: $980.00

BERETTA MODEL 92X FULL SIZE/COMPACT/CENTURION
Calibers: 9mm. Capacities: 15-round magazine. Barrel: 4.3 or 4.7 in. Weight: 33.2 oz. Sights: Fiber-optic front, square notch rear. Features: Vertec style frame, frame-mounted ambi thumb safety, oversized mag release button, Picatinny rail.
Price: $600.00
Price: RDO $620.00
Price: Performance series $1,330.00

BERETTA MODEL 92XI SAO
Caliber: 9mm. Capacities: 15-round magazine. Barrel: 4.7 in. Weight: 33.2 oz. Sights: Fiber-optic front, square notch rear. Features: Vertec-style frame, frame-mounted ambi thumb safety, single action only trigger, Picatinny rail.
Price: $600.00

BERETTA MODEL 3032 TOMCAT
Calibers: .32 Auto. Capacities: 7-round magazine. Barrel: 2.45 in. Weight: 14.8 oz. Sights: Round post front, square notch rear. Grip: G10, wood or plastic. Features: Tip-up barrel, DA/SA trigger.
Price: .... $300.00–$530.00

BERETTA M9 .22 LR
Caliber: .22 LR. Capacity: 10 or 15-round magazine. Features: Black Brunitron finish, interchangeable grip panels. Similar to centerfire 92/M9 with same operating controls, lighter weight (26 oz.).
Price: $390.00

BERETTA MODEL PX4 STORM
Calibers: 9mm, 40 S&W. Capacities: 17 (9mm Para.); 14 (40 S&W). Barrel: 4 in. Weight: 27.5 oz. Grips: Black checkered w/3 interchangeable backstraps. Sights: 3-dot system coated in Superluminova; removable front and rear sights. Features: DA/SA, manual safety/hammer decocking lever (ambi) and automatic firing pin block safety. Picatinny rail. Comes with two magazines (17/10 in 9mm Para. and 14/10 in 40 S&W). Removable hammer unit. American made by Beretta. Introduced 2005.
Price: 9mm or .40 .... $650.00
Price: .45 ACP $700.00
Price: .45 ACP SD (Special Duty) $1,150.00

BERETTA MODEL PX4 STORM SUB-COMPACT
Calibers: 9mm, 40 S&W. Capacities: 13 (9mm); 10 (40 S&W). Barrel: 3, 3.27, or 4 in. Weight: 26.1 oz. Length: 6.2 in. overall. Grips: NA. Sights: 3-dot night sights. Features: Ambidextrous manual safety lever, interchangeable backstraps included, lock breech and tilt barrel system, stainless steel barrel, Picatinny rail.
Price: .... $555.00–$600.00

BERETTA MODEL APX SERIES
Calibers: 9mm, 40 S&W. Capacities: 10, 17 (9mm); 10, 15 (40 S&W). Barrel: 4.25 or 3.7 in. (Centurion). Weight: 28, 29 oz. Length: 7.5 in. Sights: Fixed. Features: Striker fired, 3 interchangeable backstraps included, reversible mag release button, ambidextrous slide stop. Centurion is mid-size with shorter grip and barrel. Magazine capacity is two rounds shorter than standard model.
Price: .... $340.00–$500.00

BERETTA MODEL M9
Caliber: 9mm. Capacity: 15. Barrel: 4.9 in. Weights: 32.2-35.3 oz. Grips: Plastic. Sights: Dot and post, low profile, windage adjustable rear. Features: DA/SA, forged aluminum alloy frame, delayed locking-bolt system, manual

safety doubles as decocking lever, combat-style triggerguard, loaded chamber indicator. Comes with two magazines (15/10). American made by Beretta. Introduced 2005.
Price: $580.00

BERETTA MODEL M9A1

Caliber: 9mm. Capacity: 15. Barrel: 4.9 in. Weights: 32.2-35.3 oz. Grips: Plastic. Sights: Dot and post, low profile, windage adjustable rear. Features: Same as M9, but also includes integral Mil-Std-1913 Picatinny rail, has checkered front and backstrap. Comes with two magazines (15/10). American made by Beretta. Introduced 2005.
Price: $650.00

BERETTA M9A4

Caliber: 9mm. Capacity: 10 or 15. Features: Same general specifications as M9A1 with safety lever able to be converted to decocker configuration. Flat Dark Earth finish. Comes with three magazines, Vertec-style thin grip.
Price: $940.00

BERSA THUNDER 380 SERIES

Caliber: .380 ACP. Barrel: 3.5 in. Weight: 20.5 oz. Length: 6.6 in. overall. Capacity: Thunder 380 8-round, Thunder 380 Plus 15-round. Features: DA/SA trigger, CC model is DAO trigger. X models have threaded muzzles. Imported from Argentina by Eagle Imports, Inc.
Price: .... $275.00–$355.00

BERSA FIRESTORM

Caliber: .380 ACP. Capacity: 7 rounds. Barrel: 3.5 in. Weight: 20.5 oz. Length: 6.6 in. overall. Grip: Rubber wraparound with finger grooves. Features: DA/SA tigger, combat rear sight.
Price: $275.00

BERSA THUNDER 22

Caliber: .22 LR. Capacity: 10-round magazine. Weight: 19 oz. Features: Similar to Thunder .380 Series except for caliber. Alloy frame and slide. Finish: Matte black, satin nickel or duo-tone.
Price: $260.00

BERSA BP SERIES

Caliber: 9mm. Capacity: 8-round magazine. Barrel: 3.3 in. Weight: 21.5 oz. Sights: Fixed or optics-ready. Features: Striker-fire trigger, polymer frame, accessory rail.
Price: $300.00

BERSA TRP SERIES

Caliber: 9mm. Capacity: 13- or 17-round magazine. Barrel: 3.5 or 5 in. Weight: 23-33.9 oz. Grips: Checkered black polymer. Sights: Adjustable or fixed rear, dovetail fiber-optic front. Finish: Matte black or duo-tone. Features: Traditional double/single action trigger.
Price: .... $415.00–$740.00

BRG-USA BRG9 SERIES

Caliber: 9mm. Capacity: 16- or 20-round magazine. Barrel: 4 in. Weight: 30 oz. Sights: Fixed. Finish: Matte black or two-tone. Features: Striker fire. Interchangeable backstraps. Tactical model has threaded barrel and magwell.
Price: BRG9 Elite $249.00
Price: BRG9 Tactical $499.00

BERSA THUNDER PRO XT

Caliber: 9mm. Capacity: 17-round magazine. Barrel: 5 in. Weight: 34 oz. Grips: Checkered black polymer. Sights: Adjustable rear, dovetail fiber optic front. Features: Available with matte or duo-tone finish. Traditional double/single action design developed for competition. Comes with five magazines.
Price: $923.00

BROWNING 1911-22 COMPACT

Caliber: .22 LR Capacity: 10-round magazine. Barrel: 3.625 in. Weight: 15 oz. Length: 6.5 in. overall. Grips: Brown composite. Sights: Fixed. Features: Slide is machined aluminum with alloy frame and matte blue finish. Blowback action and single action trigger with manual thumb and grip safeties. Works, feels and functions just like a full-size 1911. It is simply scaled down and chambered in the best of all practice rounds: .22 LR for focus on the fundamentals.
Price: $500.00

BROWNING 1911-22 A1

Caliber: .22 LR, Capacity: 10-round magazine. Barrel: 4.25 in. Weight: 16 oz. Length: 7.0625 in. overall. Grips: Brown composite. Sights: Fixed. Features: Slide is machined aluminum with alloy frame and matte blue finish. Blowback action and single action trigger with manual thumb and grip safeties. Works, feels and functions just like a full-size 1911. It is simply scaled down and chambered in the best of all practice rounds: .22 LR for focus on the fundamentals.
Price: $500.00

BROWNING 1911-22 BLACK LABEL
Caliber: .22 LR. Capacity: 10-round magazine. Barrels: 4.25 in. or 3.625 in. (Compact model). Weight: 14 oz. overall. Features: Other features are similar to standard 1911-22 except for this model's composite/polymer frame, extended grip safety, stippled black laminated grip, skeleton trigger and hammer. Available with accessory rail (shown). Suppressor Ready model has threaded muzzle protector, 4.875-inch barrel.
Price: **$640.00**
Price: With Rail **$670.00**
Price: Suppressor Ready model.. **$720.00**

BROWNING 1911-380 SERIES
Caliber: .380 Auto. Capacity: 8-round magazine. Barrels: 3.62 or 4.25 in. Weight: 16 oz. Features: Similar to 1911-22 series and variants.
Price: .... **$650.00–$885.00**

BROWNING BUCK MARK CAMPER UFX
Caliber: .22 LR. Capacity: 10-round magazine. Barrel: 5.5-in. tapered bull. Weight: 34 oz. Length: 9.5 in. overall. Grips: Overmolded Ultragrip Ambidextrous. Sights: Pro-Target adjustable rear, ramp front. Features: Matte blue receiver, matte blue or stainless barrel.
Price: Camper UFX... **$400.00–$460.00**

BROWNING BUCK MARK HUNTER
Caliber: .22 LR. Capacity: 10-round magazine. Barrel: 7.25-in. heavy tapered bull. Weight: 38 oz. Length: 11.3 in. overall. Grips: Cocobolo target. Sights: Pro-Target adjustable rear, Tru-Glo/Marble's fiber-optic front. Integral scope base on top rail. Scope in photo not included. Features: Matte blue.
Price: **$500.00**

BROWNING BUCK PRACTICAL URX
Caliber: .22 LR. Capacity: 10-round magazine. Barrels: 5.5-in. tapered bull or 4-in. slab-sided (Micro). Weight: 34 oz. Length: 9.5 in. overall. Grips: Ultragrip RX Ambidextrous. Sights: Pro-Target adjustable rear, Tru-Glo/Marble's fiber-optic front. Features: Matte gray receiver, matte blue barrel.
Price: **$330.00**

BROWNING BUCK MARK MEDALLION ROSEWOOD
Caliber: .22 LR. Capacity: 10-round magazine. Barrel: 5.5-in. Grips: Laminate rosewood colored with gold Buckmark. Sights: Pro-Target adjustable rear, TruGlo/Marble's fiber-optic front. Finish: Matte black receiver, blackened stainless barrel with polished flats. Gold-plated trigger.
Price: **$510.00**

BROWNING BUCK MARK CONTOUR STAINLESS URX
Caliber: .22 LR. Capacity: 10-round magazine. Barrel: 5.5 or 7.25-in. special contour. Grips: Checkered, textured. Sights: Pro-Target adjustable rear, Pro-Target front. Integral scope base on top rail. Finish: Matte black receiver, blackened stainless barrel with polished flats. Gold-plated trigger.
Price: **$550.00**

BROWNING BUCK MARK FIELD TARGET SUPPRESSOR READY
Caliber: .22 LR. Capacity: 10-round magazine. Barrel: 5.5-in. heavy bull, suppressor ready. Grips: Cocobolo target. Sights: Pro-Target adjustable rear, Tru-Glo/Marble's fiber-optic front. Integral scope base on top rail. Scope in photo not included. Features: Matte blue.
Price: **$575.00**

BROWNING BUCK MARK PLUS SERIES
Caliber: .22 LR. Capacity: 10-round magazine. Barrel: 5.5, 5.8, or 6-in. Grips: Polymer. Sights: Pro-Target adjustable rear, Tru-Glo/Marble's fiber-optic front. Integral scope base on top rail. Features: Matte blue. Some suppressor ready. Vision variant has alloy sleeve barrel.
Price: .... **$400.00–$700.00**

CANIK TP9 SERIES
Caliber: 9mm. Capacity: 18-round magazine. Barrel: 4.07-in. Grip: Textured polymer, modular backstraps. Sights: White dot front, u-notch rear. Length: 7.1 in. overall. Weight: 27.8 oz. unloaded. Finish: Matte black, FDE. Features: DA/SA trigger with decocker.

Price: **$404.00**
Price: TP9SA Mod.2.. **$379.00**
Price: TP9SF... **$399.00**
Price: TP9SF Elite **$430.00**
Price: TP9SFx.. **$549.00**
Price: TP9 Elite Combat **$749.00**

CANIK METE SERIES
Caliber: 9mm. Capacity: 18- and 20-round magazine. Barrel: 4.46-in. Grip: Textured polymer, modular backstraps. Sights: White dot 3-dot, optics ready. Length: 7.56 in. overall. Weight: 27.8 oz. unloaded. Finish: Matte black, FDE. Features: Striker fire. MC9 model is compact with 3.1-inch barrel.
Price: Mete SFT **$519.00**
Price: Mete SFX **$574.00**
Price: Mete MC9 .... **$439.00**

CANIK RIVAL SERIES
Caliber: 9mm. Capacity: 18-round magazine. Barrel: 5-in. Grip: Textured polymer, modular backstraps. Sights: Fiber-optic front, adj. rear, optics ready. Length: 8.1 in. overall. Weight: 29.5 oz. unloaded. Finish: Matte black, black with gold accents. Features: Striker fire. Rival-S has an all-metal frame.
Price: Mete SFT **$519.00**
Price: Mete SFX **$574.00**
Price: Mete SFX Rival-S... **$899.00**

CHIAPPA 1911-22
Caliber: .22 LR. Capacity: 10-round magazine. Barrel: 5 in. Weight: 33.5 oz. Length: 8.5 in. Grips: Two-piece wood. Sights: Fixed. Features: A faithful replica of the famous John Browning 1911A1 pistol. Fixed barrel design. Available in black, OD green or tan finish. Target and Tactical models have adjustable sights.
Price: From .... **$230.00–$370.00**

CHIAPPA M9-22 STANDARD
Caliber: .22 LR. Barrel: 5 in. Weight: 2.3 lbs. Length: 8.5 in. Grips: Black molded plastic or walnut. Sights: Fixed front sight and windage adjustable rear sight. Features: The M9 9mm has been a U.S. standard-issue service pistol since 1990. Chiappa's M9-22 is a replica of this pistol in 22 LR. The M9-22 has the same weight and feel as its 9mm counterpart but has an affordable 10-shot magazine for the .22 Long Rifle cartridge, which makes

it a true rimfire reproduction. Comes standard with steel trigger, hammer assembly and a 1/2x28 threaded barrel.
Price: .... **$215.00–$230.00**

CHRISTENSEN ARMS CA9MM
Calibers: 9mm. Barrels: 7.5 or 10 in. Weight: 5.5 lbs. Finish: Black or bronze Cerakote. Features: AR-15 style with blowback system. Threaded muzzle. Brace. Glock magazine compatible.
Price: Aluminum frame **$1,530.00**

CIMARRON MODEL 1911
Caliber: .45 ACP. Barrel: 5 in. Weight: 37.5 oz. Length: 8.5 in. overall. Grips: Checkered walnut. Features: A faithful reproduction of the original pattern of the Model 1911 with Parkerized finish and lanyard ring. Polished or nickel finish available.
Price: .... **$540.00–$850.00**
Price: One Ranger model **$700.00**

CITADEL M-1911
Calibers: .45 ACP, 9mm. Capacity: 7. Barrels: 4.2 or 5 in. Weight: 37.9 oz. Length: 8.5 in. Grips: Cocobolo. Sights: Low-profile combat fixed rear, blade front. Finish: Matte black. Features: Extended grip safety, lowered and flared ejection port, beveled mag well, Series 70 firing system. Built by Armscor (Rock Island Armory) in the Philippines and imported by Legacy Sports.
Price: .... **$510.00–$700.00**
Price: Flag models **$1,030.00**

COBRA ENTERPRISES FS32, FS380
Calibers: .32 ACP or .380 ACP. Capacity: 7 rounds. Barrel: 3.5 in. Weight: 2.1 lbs. Length: 6.375 in. overall. Grips: Black molded synthetic integral with frame. Sights: Fixed. Made in USA by Cobra Enterprises of Utah, Inc.
Price: .... **$138.00–$250.00**

COBRA ENTERPRISES PATRIOT SERIES
Calibers: .380, 9mm or .45 ACP. Capacities: 6-, 7- or 10-round magazine. Barrel: 3.3 in. Weight: 20 oz. Length: 6 in. overall. Grips: Black polymer. Sights: Fixed. Features: Bright chrome, satin nickel or black finish. Made in USA by Cobra Enterprises of Utah, Inc.
Price: .... **$349.00–$395.00**

COBRA DENALI
Caliber: .380 ACP. Capacity: 5 rounds. Barrel: 2.8 in. Weight: 22 oz. Length: 5.4 in. Grips: Black molded synthetic integral with frame. Sights: Fixed. Features: Made in USA by Cobra Enterprises of Utah, Inc.
Price: **$179.00**

COLT MODEL 1991 MODEL O
Caliber: .45 ACP. Capacity: 7-round magazine. Barrel: 5 in. Weight: 38 oz. Length: 8.5 in. overall. Grips: Checkered black composition. Sights: Ramped blade front, fixed square notch rear, high profile. Features: Matte finish. Continuation of serial number range used on original G.I. 1911A1 guns. Comes with one magazine and molded carrying case. Introduced 1991. Series 80 firing system.
Price: Blue **$799.00**
Price: Stainless **$879.00**

COLT COMBAT ELITE SERIES
Caliber: 9mm or .45 ACP. Capacity: 8-round magazine. Barrel: 5 in. Grips: Checkered, G10. Sights: Three white-dot Novak. Features: Brushed stainless receiver with blued slide; adjustable, two-cut aluminum trigger; extended ambidextrous thumb safety; upswept beavertail with palm swell; elongated slot hammer.
Price: .... **$1,230.00–$1,360.00**

COLT COMBAT UNIT SERIES
Caliber: 9mm or .45 ACP. Capacity: 8-round magazine. Barrel: 5 in. Grips: Checkered G10. Sights: Three white-dot Novak. Features: Matte black finish; extended ambidextrous thumb safety; upswept beavertail; Series 80 firing system; National Match Barrel.
Price: .... $1,455.00–$1,555.00

COLT COMMANDER SERIES
Calibers: .45 ACP, 8-shot, 9mm (9 shot). Barrel: 4.25 in. Weight: 26 oz. alloy frame, 33 oz. (steel frame). Length: 7.75 in. overall. Grips: G10 Checkered Black Cherry. Sights: Novak White Dot front, Low Mount Carry rear. Features: Blued slide, black anodized frame. Aluminum alloy frame.
Price: Aluminum frame $999.00
Price: Steel frame $980.00

COLT DEFENDER
Caliber: .45 ACP (7-round magazine), 9mm (8-round). Barrel: 3 in. Weight: 22.5 oz. Length: 6.75 in. overall. Grips: Pebble-finish rubber wraparound with finger grooves. Sights: White dot front, snag-free Colt competition rear. Features: Stainless or blued finish; aluminum frame; combat-style hammer; Hi-Ride grip safety, extended manual safety, disconnect safety. Introduced 1998. Made in USA by Colt's Mfg. Co., Inc.
Price: $980.00

COLT SERIES 70/TRADITIONAL SERIES
Caliber: .45 ACP. Barrel: 5 in. Weight: 37.5 oz. Length: 8.5 in. Grips: Rosewood with double diamond checkering pattern. Sights: Fixed. Features: Custom replica of the Original Series 70 pistol with a Series 70 firing system, original roll marks. Introduced 2002. Made in USA by Colt's Mfg. Co., Inc.
Price: Blued $899.00
Price: Stainless $979.00

COLT 38 SUPER CUSTOM SERIES
Caliber: .38 Super. Barrel: 5 in. Weight: 36.5 oz. Length: 8.5 in. Grips: Wood with double diamond checkering pattern. Finish: Bright stainless. Sights: 3-dot. Features: Beveled magazine well, standard thumb safety and service-style grip safety, flat mainspring housing. Introduced 2003. Made in USA. by Colt's Mfg. Co., Inc.
Price: $1,549.00

COLT M45A1 MARINE PISTOL
Caliber: .45 ACP. Variant of Rail Gun series with features of that model plus Decobond Brown Coating, dual recoil springs system, Novak tritium front and rear 3-dot sights. Selected by U.S. Marine Corps as their Close Quarters Battle Pistol (CQBP).
Price: $1,900.00

COLT DELTA ELITE SERIES
Caliber: 10 mm. Capacity: 8+1. Barrel: 5 in. Grips: Black composite with Delta Medallions. Sights: Novak Low Mount Carry rear, Novak White Dot

front. Finish: Two-tone stainless frame, black matte slide. Features: Up-swept beavertail safety, extended thumb safety, 3-hole aluminum trigger. Accessory rail on some models.
Price: .... $1,180.00–$1,275.00

COLT WILEY CLAPP SERIES
Calibers: 9mm or .45 Auto. Barrel: 4.25 in. Weight: 26 oz. alloy frame. Length: 7.75 in. overall. Grips: Oval grips with fingerprint checkering. Sights: Novak brass bead front, Low Mount Carry rear. Features: Blued slide, black anodized frame. Aluminum alloy frame. Steel slide.
Price: $1,130.00

CZ 75 B
Calibers: 9mm. Capacity: 16-round magazine. Barrel: 4.7 in. Weight: 34.3 oz. Length: 8.1 in. overall. Grips: High impact checkered plastic. Sights: Square post front, rear adjustable for windage; 3-dot system. Features: Single action/double action; firing pin block safety; choice of black polymer, matte or high-polish blue finishes. All-steel frame. B-SA is a single action with a drop-free magazine. Imported from the Czech Republic by CZ-USA.
Price: 75 B $630.00

CZ 75 BD DECOCKER
Similar to the CZ 75B except has a decocking lever in place of the safety lever. All other specifications are the same. Introduced 1999. Imported from the Czech Republic by CZ-USA.
Price: $630.00

CZ 75 B COMPACT
Similar to the CZ 75 B except has 14-round magazine in 9mm, 3.9-in. barrel and weighs 32 oz. Has removable front sight, non-glare ribbed slide top. The triggerguard is squared and serrated; combat hammer. Introduced 1993. Imported from the Czech Republic by CZ-USA. D CPR and P-01 are decocker models.
Price: 9mm, black polymer $665.00
Price: 9mm. D PCR Compact, alloy frame $630.00
Price: 9mm. P-01 Compact, alloy frame $665.00

CZ P-07
Calibers: 9mm. Capacity: 15. Barrel: 3.8 in. Weight: 27.2 oz. Length: 7.3 in. overall. Grips: Polymer black Polycoat. Sights: Blade front, fixed groove rear. Features: The ergonomics and accuracy of the CZ 75 with a totally new trigger system. The new Omega trigger system simplifies the CZ 75

Prices given are believed to be accurate at time of publication however, many factors affect retail pricing so exact prices are not possible.

78TH EDITION, 2024 ✦ 473

trigger system, uses fewer parts and improves the trigger pull. In addition, it allows users to choose between using the handgun with a decocking lever (installed) or a manual safety (included) by a simple parts change. The polymer frame design and a new sleek slide profile (fully machined from bar stock) reduce weight, making the P-07 a great choice for concealed carry.
Price: **$500.00**

CZ P-09 DUTY
Calibers: 9mm. Capacity: 19. Features: High-capacity version of P-07. Accessory rail, interchangeable grip backstraps, ambidextrous decocker can be converted to manual safety.
Price: **$530.00**
Price: Suppressor ready **$629.00**

CZ 75 SP-01
Similar to NATO-approved CZ 75 Compact P-01 model. Features an integral 1913 accessory rail on the dust cover, rubber grip panels, black Polycoat finish, extended beavertail, new grip geometry with checkering on front and back straps, and double or single action operation. Introduced 2005. The Tactical model has an ambidextrous decoker. Imported from the Czech Republic by CZ-USA.
Price: SP-01 .... **$750.00**

CZ P-01
Caliber: 9mm. Capacity: 14-round magazine. Barrel: 3.85 in. Weight: 27 oz. Length: 7.2 in. overall. Grips: Checkered rubber. Sights: Blade front with dot, white outline rear drift adjustable for windage. Features: Based on the CZ 75, except with forged aircraft-grade aluminum alloy frame. Hammer forged barrel, decocker, firing-pin block, M3 rail, dual slide serrations, squared triggerguard, re-contoured trigger, lanyard loop on butt. Serrated front and backstrap. Introduced 2006. Imported from the Czech Republic by CZ-USA.
Price: CZ P-01 .... **$680.00**

CZ P-10 Series
Caliber: 9mm. Capacity: 19- or 21-round magazine. Barrel: 4.5-5.10 in. Weight: 26-29.4 oz. Length: 8 in. overall. Grips: Textured p10 Folymer. Sights: Fixed, 3-dot. Features: Striker fire. Suppressor ready and optic ready on some models.
Price: CZ P-F **$530.00**
Price: CZ P-10 C **$500.00**
Price: CZ P-10 M **$430.00**
Price: CZ P-10 S **$540.00**
Price: CZ P-10 C Suppressor Ready .... **$585.00–$649.00**

CZ BREN 2 MS
Caliber: .223 Rem. or 7.62×39mm. Capacity: 30-round magazine. Barrel: 14.7 in. Features: Pistol version of the 805 Bren rifle.
Price: **$1,780.00**

CZ SCORPION 3+ MICRO
Caliber: 9mm. Capacity: 20-round magazine. Barrel: 4.2 in. Features: Next generation of CZ Scorpion Evo semi-automatic gun. Ambidextrous controls, adjustable sights, accessory rails.
Price: **$1,200.00**

DAN WESSON DWX FULL SIZE
Calibers: 9mm. Capacity: 19-round magazine. Barrel: 5 in. Grips: Checkered red aluminum. Sights: Fixed fiber-optic front/adjustable rear. Length: 8.52 in. overall. Weight: 43 oz. unloaded. Finish: Black Duty Coat. Features: Hybrid pistol built using the single-action fire control group of a Dan Wesson 1911 and frame of a CZ 75 pistol. Compatible with CZ P-09 and CZ P-10 F magazines. Bull barrel and full dust cover with accessory rail. Flat red aluminum trigger. Oversized controls.
Price: **$1,550.00**

DAN WESSON BRUIN
Caliber: 10mm. Capacity: 8-round magazine. Barrel: 6.03 in. Grips: Textured G10. Sights: Fixed, fiber-optic front/adjustable rear. Length: 9.7 in. overall. Weight: 47.1 oz. unloaded. Finish: Black or bronze. Features: 1911 platform with coarse slide serrations, mag well and ambidextrous safety.
Price: **$2,010.00**

DAN WESSON ECP
Calibers: 9mm, .45 ACP. Capacity: 8 (.45) or 9 (9mm). Barrel: 4 in. Features: Forged aluminum frame with flat-top slide, serrated tactical rear and brass bead front sight, checkered frontstrap and backstrap, G10 grips, V-Bob frame, flat trigger.
Price: **$1,455.00**

DAN WESSON GUARDIAN
Calibers: 9mm, .38 Super, .45 ACP. Capacity: 8- or 9-round magazine. Barrel: 5 in. Length: 8.5 in. Grips: Wood. Sights: Fixed night sights. Features: Undercut triggerguard, serrated front strap, V-Bob frame.
Price: **$1,455.00**

DAN WESSON KODIAK
Caliber: 10mm. Capacity: 8-round magazine. Barrel: 6.03 in. Grips: Textured G10. Sights: Fixed, fiber-optic front/adjustable rear. Length: 9.7 in. overall. Weight: 47.1 oz. unloaded. Finish: Black or tri-tone. Features: 1911 platform with coarse slide serrations, mag well and ambidextrous safety. Black version has bronzed controls and barrel, and tri-tone with a matte gray slide.
Price: (tri-tone) **$2,080.00**

DAN WESSON SPECIALIST
Caliber: .45 ACP. Capacity: 8-round magazine. Barrel: 5 in. Grips: G10 VZ Operator II. Sights: Single amber tritium dot rear, green lamp with white target ring front sight. Features: Integral Picatinny rail, 25 LPI frontstrap checkering, undercut triggerguard, ambidextrous thumb safety, extended mag release and detachable two-piece mag well.
Price: **$1,555.00**

Prices given are believed to be accurate at time of publication however, many factors affect retail pricing so exact prices are not possible.

DAN WESSON V-BOB
Caliber: .45 ACP. Capacity: 8-round magazine. Barrel: 4.25 in. Weight: 34 oz. Length: 8 in. Grips: Slim Line G10. Sights: Heinie Ledge Straight-Eight Night Sights. Features: Black matte or stainless finish. Bobtail forged grip frame with 25 LPI checkering front and rear.
Price: $1,655.00

DAN WESSON POINTMAN
Calibers: 9mm, .45 ACP. Capacity: 8 or 9-round magazine. Barrel: 5 in. Length: 8.5 in. Grips: Double-diamond cocobolo. Sights: Adjustable rear and fiber-optic front. Features: Undercut triggerguard, checkered front strap, serrated rib on top of slide.
Price: $1,455.00

DAN WESSON TCP
Calibers: 9mm, .45 ACP. Capacity: 8 (.45) or 9 (9mm). Barrel: 4 in. Features: Forged aluminum frame with flat-top slide, serrated tactical rear and brass bead front sight, checkered frontstrap and backstrap, G10 grips, magwell, flat trigger.
Price: $1,550.00

DAN WESSON VALOR
Caliber: .45 ACP. Capacity: 8-round magazine. Barrel: 5 in. Grips: Textured G10. Sights: Fixed, night-sight front/U-notch rear. Length: 8.75 in. overall. Weight: 39.7 oz. unloaded. Finish: Matte stainless or black Duty Coat. Features: 1911 platform with GI style slide serrations, Stan Chen SI mag well, tapered grip and tactical ambidextrous safety.
Price: (stainless) $1,955.00

DIAMONDBACK DB380
Caliber: .380 ACP. Capacity: 6+1. Barrel: 2.8 in. Weight: 8.8 oz. Features: ZERO-Energy striker firing system with a mechanical firing pin block, steel magazine catch, windage-adjustable sights. Frames available with several color finish options.
Price: .... $290.00–$350.00

DIAMONDBACK DB9
Caliber: 9mm. Capacity: 6+1. Barrel: 3 in. Weight: 11 oz. Length: 5.60 in. Features: Other features similar to DB380 model.
Price: .... $290.00–$350.00

DIAMONDBACK FIREARMS DBX
Caliber: 5.7x28mm. Capacity: 20-round magazine. Barrel: 8 in. Grips: Magpul MOE-K. Sights: Optic-ready, Picatinny rail. Length: 16.9 in. overall, brace folded. Weight: 3 lbs. unloaded. Finish: Black hardcoat-anodized. Features: DBX muzzle brake, compatible with FN Five-seveN, side-folding brace. Uses AR-15 Mil-Spec trigger.
Price: $1,299.00

DIAMONDBACK FIREARMS DBAM29
Caliber: 9mm. Capacity: 12- or 17-round magazine. Barrel: 3.5 in. Grips: Textured grip. Sights: Fixed, 3-dot. Length: 6.6 in. overall. Weight: 21 oz. unloaded. Finish: Black.
Price: $350.00

DOUBLESTAR 1911 SERIES
Caliber: .45 ACP. Capacity: 8-round magazine. Barrels: 3.5 in., 4.25 in., 5 in. Weights: 33–40 oz. Grips: Cocobolo wood. Sights: Novak LoMount 2 white-

Prices given are believed to be accurate at time of publication however, many factors affect retail pricing so exact prices are not possible.

78TH EDITION, 2024 ⊕ 475

dot rear, Novak white-dot front. Features: Single action, M1911-style with forged frame and slide of 4140 steel, stainless steel barrel machined from bar stock by Storm Lake, funneled mag well, accessory rail, black Nitride finish. Optional features include bobtail grip frame, accessory rail.
Price: .... **$1,150.00–$1,840.00**

EAA GIRSAN MC1911 SERIES
Caliber: 9mm, 10mm, .45 ACP. Capacity: 6-, 8- or 9-round magazine. Barrel: 3, 5, or 6 in. Weight: 32-51.2 oz. Length: 8.58-9.63 in. overall. Features: Compact, Full-size, and long barrel 1911-style pistol with steel frame. Manufactured by Girsan and imported by EAA.
Price: .... **$670.00–$1,400.00**

EAA GIRSAN MC28 SA SERIES
Caliber: 9MM. Capacity: 17-round magazine. Barrel: 4.25 in. Weight: 28.8 oz. Length: 7.6 in. overall. Features: Full-size striker-fire pistol with three grip inserts. Some models with red-dot optic. Manufactured by Girsan and imported by EAA.
Price: .... **$400.00–$500.00**

EAA GIRSAN MC P35 SERIES
Caliber: 9MM. Capacity: 15-round magazine. Barrel: 3.8 or 4.8 in. Weight: 25.6-28.8 oz. Length: 8.6 in. overall. Features: Full-size Beretta 92-style pistols. Manufactured by Girsan and imported by EAA.
Price: .... **$600.00–$1,000.00**

EAA GIRSAN REGARD MC SERIES
Caliber: 9MM. Capacity: 18-round magazine. Barrel: 4.9 in. Weight: 34.4 oz. Length: 6.25-7.75 in. overall. Features: Compact and Full-size Browning Hi-Power-style pistols. Manufactured by Girsan and imported by EAA.
Price: .... **$500.00–$900.00**

EAA GIRSAN WITNESS 2311 SERIES
Caliber: 9MM, 10MM, OR .45 ACP. Capacity: 11-, 15- or 17-round magazine. Barrel: 4.2, 5, or 6 in. Weight: 32-51.2 oz. Length: 8.58-9.63 in. overall. Features: 1911-style pistol with polymer double-stack magazine frame. Manufactured by Girsan and imported by EAA.
Price: Steel frame **$999.00**

EAA SAR B6P
Caliber: 9mm. Based on polymer frame variation of CZ 75 design. Manufactured by Sarsilmaz in Turkey. Features similar to Witness series.
Price: .... **$407.00–$453.00**

ED BROWN CLASSIC CUSTOM
Caliber: .45 ACP, 9mm, .38 Super. Capacity: 7-round magazine. Barrel: 5 in. Weight: 40 oz. Grips: Cocobolo wood. Sights: Bo-Mar adjustable rear, dovetail front. Features: Single action, M1911 style, custom made to order, stainless frame and slide available. Special mirror-finished slide.
Price: From **$3,695.00**

ED BROWN FX2
Caliber: 9mm. Capacity: 9-round magazine. Barrels: 4.25 in. Weight: 37 oz. Grips: Textured G10. Sights: Trijicon RMRcc sight 3.25 MOA with Ed Brown designed co-witness rear sight, and Ameri-glo orange front sight. Features: Snakeskin pattern serrations on forestrap and American flag pattern on slide, dehorned edges, beavertail grip safety, Bobtail frame.
Price: .45 ACP From **$4,055.00**

ED BROWN EVO-E9 SERIES
Caliber: 9mm. Capacity: 9-round magazine. Barrels: 4 in. Weight: 35 oz. Grips: Textured G10. Sights: orange front sight, tactical edge U-notch rear. Features: Snakeskin pattern serrations on forestrap and housing, dehorned edges, beavertail grip safety, external extractor, full-size Bobtail frame. Some models equipped with red-dot optic.
Price: .... **$2,520.00–$3,000.00**

ED BROWN EVO-KC9 SERIES
Caliber: 9mm. Capacity: 9-round magazine. Barrels: 4 in. Weight: 34 oz. Grips: Textured G10. Sights: orange front sight, tactical edge U-notch rear. Features: Snakeskin pattern serrations on forestrap and housing, dehorned edges, beavertail grip safety, external extractor, Bobtail frame.
Price: .... **$1,880.00–$2,520.00**

ED BROWN KOBRA CARRY
Caliber: .45 ACP. Capacity: 7-round magazine. Barrels: 4.25 in. Weight: 34 oz. Grips: Hogue exotic wood. Sights: Ramp, front; fixed Novak low-mount night sights, rear. Features: Snakeskin pattern serrations on forestrap and mainspring housing, dehorned edges, beavertail grip safety.
Price: .45 ACP From **$2,995.00**
Price: 9 mm From **$3,095.00**
Price: .38 Super From **$3,095.00**

ED BROWN SPECIAL FORCES
Similar to other Ed Brown products, but with ChainLink treatment on forestrap and mainspring housing. Entire gun coated with Gen III finish. Square cut serrations on rear of slide only. Dehorned. Introduced 2006. Available with various finish, sight and grip options.
Price: From .... **$2,770.00–$4,775.00**

EXCEL ARMS MP-22
Caliber: .22 WMR. Capacity: 9-round magazine. Barrel: 8.5-in. bull barrel. Weight: 54 oz. Length: 12.875 in. overall. Grips: Textured black composition. Sights: Fully adjustable target sights. Features: Made from 17-4 stainless steel, comes with aluminum rib, integral Weaver base, internal hammer, firing pin block. American made, lifetime warranty. Comes with two 9-round stainless steel magazines and a California-approved cable lock. .22 WMR Introduced 2006. Made in USA by Excel Arms.
Price: $525.00

EXCEL ARMS MP-5.7
Caliber: 5.7x28mm. Capacity: 9-round magazine. Features: Blowback action. Other features similar to MP-22. Red-dot optic sights, scope and rings are optional.
Price: $655.00

FMK 9C1 G2
Caliber: 9mm. Capacity: 10+1 or 14+1. Barrel: 4 in. Overall length: 6.85 in. Weight: 23.45 oz. Finish: Black, Flat Dark Earth or pink. Sights: Interchangeable Glock compatible. Features: Available in either single action or double action only. Polymer frame, high-carbon steel slide, stainless steel barrel. Very low bore axis and shock absorbing backstrap are said to result in low felt recoil. DAO model has Fast Action Trigger (FAT) with shorter pull and reset. Made in the USA.
Price: $300.00

FN 502 TACTICAL
Caliber: 22 LR. Capacity: 10- and 15- round magazine. Barrel: 4.6 in. threaded. Grip: Textured polymer. Sights: Suppressor height, fixed front and rear sights. Length: 7.6 in. overall. Weight: 23.7 oz. unloaded. Finish: Matte black or FDE. Features: Hammer-fire, accessory rail.
Price: $470.00

FN 509 SERIES
Caliber: 9mm. Capacity: 10-, 12- or 15-round magazine. Barrel: 3.7 in. Grips: Textured grip, interchangeable backstraps. Sights: Fixed, tall co-witness; FN Low Profile Optics Mounting System. Length: 6.8 in. overall. Weight: 25.5 oz. unloaded. Finish: Black or FDE. Compact, Midsize, and Tactical models sizes.
Price: .... $620.00–$975.00

FN FNX SERIES
Calibers: 9mm, .45 Auto. Capacities: 17-round magazine, .45 ACP (10 or 14 rounds). Barrels: 4 in. (9mm), 4.5 in. .45. Weights: 22–32 oz. (.45). Lengths: 7.4, 7.9 in. (.45). Features: DA/SA operation with decocking/manual safety lever. Has external extractor with loaded-chamber indicator, front and rear cocking serrations, fixed 3-dot combat sights.
Price: 9mm $670.00
Price: .45 ACP $785.00

FN FNX .45 TACTICAL
Similar to standard FNX .45 except with 5.3-in. barrel with threaded muzzle, polished chamber and feed ramp, enhanced high-profile night sights, slide cut and threaded for red-dot sight (not included), MIL-STD 1913 accessory rail, ring-style hammer.
Price: $1,250.00

FN FIVE-SEVEN
Caliber: 5.7x28mm. Capacity: 10- or 20-round magazine. Barrel: 4.8 in. Weight: 23 oz. Length: 8.2 in. Features: Adjustable three-dot system. Single-action polymer frame, chambered for low-recoil 5.7x28mm cartridge.
Price: $1,200.00

FN HIGH POWER
Caliber: 9mm. Capacity: 17-round magazine. Barrel: 4.7 in. Grip: Textured G10. Sights: Steel fixed front and rear. Length: 8 in. overall. Weight: 40 oz. unloaded. Finish: Stainless, Matte black or FDE. Features: Hammer-fire, based on classic High Power pistol.
Price: $1,155.00

GLOCK 17/17C
Caliber: 9mm. Capacities: 17/19/33-round magazines. Barrel: 4.49 in. Weight: 22.04 oz. (without magazine). Length: 7.32 in. overall. Grips: Black polymer. Sights: Dot on front blade, white outline rear adjustable for windage. Features: Polymer frame, steel slide; double-action trigger with Safe Action system; mechanical firing pin safety, drop safety; simple takedown without tools; locked breech, recoil operated action. ILS designation refers to Internal Locking System. Adopted by Austrian armed

Prices given are believed to be accurate at time of publication however, many factors affect retail pricing so exact prices are not possible.

78TH EDITION, 2024 ⊕ 477

forces 1983. NATO approved 1984. Model 17L has 6-inch barrel, ported or non-ported, slotted and relieved slide, checkered grip with finger grooves, no accessory rail. Imported from Austria by Glock, Inc. USA.

Price: 17 Gen 3 .... $500.00
Price: 17L.. $690.00
Price: 17 Gen 4 .... $560.00
Price: 17 Gen 5 .... $650.00

GLOCK GEN4 SERIES
In 2010, a new series of Generation 4 pistols was introduced with several improved features. These included a multiple backstrap system offering three different size options, short, medium or large frame; reversible and enlarged magazine release; dual recoil springs; and RTF (Rough Textured Finish) surface. In Gen4 models, the MOS (Modular Optic System) variant was introduced.

GEN 5 SERIES
A new frame design was introduced in 2017 named Generation 5. The finger grooves were removed for more versatility and the user can customize the grip by using different backstraps, as with the Gen 4 models. A flared mag well and a cutout at the front of the frame give the user more speed during reloading. There is a reversible and enlarged magazine catch, changeable by users, as well as the ambidextrous slide stop lever to accommodate left- and right-handed operators. The rifling and crown of the barrel are slightly modified for increased precision. Gen5 models also include MOS variants.

GLOCK 19/19C
Caliber: 9mm. Capacities: 15/17/19/33-round magazines. Barrel: 4.02 in. Weight: 20.99 oz. (without magazine). Length: 6.85 in. overall. Compact version of Glock 17. 19X model has 17 frame and 19 slide in Coyote Tan finish. Imported from Austria by Glock, Inc.

Price: 19 Gen 3 .... $500.00
Price: 19 Gen 4 .... $560.00
Price: 19 Gen 5 .... $650.00
Price: 19X $680.00

GLOCK 20/20C 10MM
Caliber: 10mm. Capacity: 15-round magazine. Barrel: 4.6 in. Weight: 27.68 oz. (without magazine). Length: 7.59 in. overall. Features: Otherwise similar to Model 17. Gen 3 and Gen 4 SF (Short Frame) model has short frame design. Imported from Austria by Glock, Inc. Introduced 1990.

Price: 20 Gen 3 .... $585.00
Price: 20 Gen 4 .... $630.00
Price: 20 Gen 5 .... $675.00

GLOCK 21/21C
Caliber: .45 ACP. Capacity: 13-round magazine. Barrel: 4.6 in. Weight: 26.28 oz. (without magazine). Length: 7.59 in. overall. Features: Otherwise similar to the Model 17. Imported from Austria by Glock, Inc. Introduced 1991. SF version has tactical rail, smaller diameter grip, 10-round magazine capacity. Introduced 2007.

Price: Gen 3 .... $585.00
Price: 21 Gen 4 .... $630.00
Price: 21 Gen 5 .... $675.00

GLOCK 22/22C
Caliber: .40 S&W. Capacities: 15/17-round magazine. Barrel: 4.49 in. Weight: 22.92 oz. (without magazine). Length: 7.32 in. overall. Features: Otherwise similar to Model 17, including pricing. Imported from Austria by Glock, Inc. Introduced 1990.

Price: Gen 3 .... $555.00
Price: 22C $655.00
Price: 22 Gen 5 .... $590.00

GLOCK 23/23C
Caliber: .40 S&W. Capacities: 13/15/17-round magazine. Barrel: 4.02 in. Weight: 21.16 oz. (without magazine). Length: 6.85 in. overall. Features: Otherwise similar to the Model 22, including pricing. Compact version of Glock 22. Imported from Austria by Glock, Inc. Introduced 1990.

Price: Gen 3 .... $555.00
Price: 23C Compensated $655.00
Price: 23 Gen 5 .... $590.00

GLOCK 24/24C
Caliber: .40 S&W. Capacities: 10/15/17 or 22-round magazine. Features: Similar to Model 22 except with 6.02-inch barrel, ported or non-ported, trigger pull recalibrated to 4.5 lbs.

Price: Gen 3 .... $600.00

GLOCK 26
Caliber: 9mm. Capacities: 10/12/15/17/19/33-round magazine. Barrel: 3.46 in. Weight: 19.75 oz. Length: 6.29 in. overall. Subcompact version of Glock 17. Imported from Austria by Glock, Inc.

Price: 26 Gen 3 .... $555.00
Price: 26 Gen 5 .... $595.00

GLOCK 27
Caliber: .40 S&W. Capacities: 9/11/13/15/17-round magazine. Barrel: 3.46 in. Weight: 19.75 oz. (without magazine). Length: 6.29 overall. Features: Otherwise similar to the Model 22, including pricing. Subcompact version of Glock 22. Imported from Austria by Glock, Inc. Introduced 1996.

Price: 27 Gen 3 .... $550.00
Price: 27 Gen 5 .... $590.00

GLOCK 29
Caliber: 10mm. Capacities: 10/15-round magazine. Barrel: 3.78 in. Weight: 24.69 oz. (without magazine). Length: 6.77 in. overall. Features: Otherwise similar to the Model 20, including pricing. Subcompact version of the Glock 20. SF (Short Frame) model has short frame design. Imported from Austria by Glock, Inc. Introduced 1997.

Price: 29 Gen 3 .... $590.00
Price: 29 Gen 4 .... $630.00

GLOCK 30
Caliber: .45 ACP. Capacities: 9/10/13-round magazines. Barrel: 3.78 in. Weight: 23.99 oz. (without magazine). Length: 6.77 in. overall. Features: Otherwise similar to the Model 21, including pricing. Subcompact version of the Glock 21. Imported from Austria by Glock, Inc. Introduced 1997. SF version has tactical rail, octagonal rifled barrel with a 1:15.75 rate of twist, smaller diameter grip, 10-round magazine capacity. SF (Short Frame) model has short frame design. Introduced 2008.

Price: 30 Gen 3 .... $550.00
Price: 30 Gen 4 .... $630.00

HANDGUNS Autoloaders, Service & Sport

GLOCK 30S
Caliber: .45 ACP. Capacity: 10-round magazine. Barrel: 3.78 in. Weight: 20 oz. Length: 7 in. Features: Variation of Glock 30 with a Model 36 slide on a Model 30SF frame (short frame).
Price: $550.00

GLOCK 31/31C
Caliber: .357 Auto. Capacities: 15/17-round magazine. Barrel: 4.49 in. Weight: 23.28 oz. (without magazine). Length: 7.32 in. overall. Features: Otherwise similar to the Model 17. Imported from Austria by Glock, Inc.
Price: 31 Gen 3 .... $550.00
Price: 31 Gen 4 .... $550.00

GLOCK 32/32C
Caliber: .357 Auto. Capacities: 13/15/17-round magazine. Barrel: 4.02 in. Weight: 21.52 oz. (without magazine). Length: 6.85 in. overall. Features: Otherwise similar to the Model 31. Compact. Imported from Austria by Glock, Inc.
Price: 32 Gen 3 .... $550.00
Price: 32 Gen 4 .... $550.00

GLOCK 33
Caliber: .357 Auto. Capacities: 9/11/13/15/17-round magazine. Barrel: 3.46 in. Weight: 19.75 oz. (without magazine). Length: 6.29 in. overall. Features: Otherwise similar to the Model 31. Subcompact. Imported from Austria by Glock, Inc.
Price: 33 Gen 3 .... $550.00
Price: 33 Gen 4 .... $550.00

GLOCK 34
Caliber: 9mm. Capacities: 17/19/33-round magazine. Barrel: 5.32 in. Weight: 22.9 oz. Length: 8.15 in. overall. Features: Competition version of Glock 17 with extended barrel, slide, and sight radius dimensions. Available with MOS (Modular Optic System).
Price: 34 Gen 3 .... $630.00
Price: 34 Gen 5 .... $700.00

GLOCK 35
Caliber: .40 S&W. Capacities: 15/17-round magazine. Barrel: 5.32 in. Weight: 24.52 oz. (without magazine). Length: 8.15 in. overall. Sights: Adjustable. Features: Otherwise similar to the Model 22. Competition version of the Glock 22 with extended barrel, slide and sight radius dimensions. Available with MOS (Modular Optic System). Introduced 1996.
Price: 35 Gen 3 .... $630.00
Price: 35 Gen 4 .... $729.00

GLOCK 36
Caliber: .45 ACP. Capacity: 6-round magazine. Barrel: 3.78 in. Weight: 20.11 oz. (without magazine). Length: 6.77 overall. Sights: Fixed. Features: Single-stack magazine, slimmer grip than Glock 21/30. Subcompact. Imported from Austria by Glock, Inc. Introduced 1997.
Price: $580.00

GLOCK 37
Caliber: .45 GAP. Capacity: 10-round magazine. Barrel: 4.49 in. Weight: 25.95 oz. (without magazine). Length: 7.32 overall. Features: Otherwise similar to the Model 17. Imported from Austria by Glock, Inc. Introduced 2005.
Price: 37 Gen 3 .... $560.00

GLOCK 38
Caliber: .45 GAP. Capacities: 8/10-round magazine. Barrel: 4.02 in. Weight: 24.16 oz. (without magazine). Length: 6.85 overall. Features: Otherwise similar to the Model 37. Compact. Imported from Austria by Glock, Inc.

Price: 38 Gen 3 .... $560.00

GLOCK 39
Caliber: .45 GAP. Capacities: 6/8/10-round magazine. Barrel: 3.46 in. Weight: 19.33 oz. (without magazine). Length: 6.3 overall. Features: Otherwise similar to the Model 37. Subcompact. Imported from Austria by Glock, Inc.
Price: 39 Gen 3 .... $560.00

GLOCK 40
Caliber: 10mm. Features: Similar features as the Model 41 except for 6.01-in. barrel. Includes MOS optics.
Price: 40 Gen 4 .... $760.00

GLOCK 41 GEN 4
Caliber: .45 ACP. Capacity: 13-round magazine. Barrel: 5.31 in. Weight: 27 oz. Length: 8.9 in. overall. Features: This is a long-slide .45 ACP Gen4 model introduced in 2014. Operating features are the same as other Glock models. Available with MOS (Modular Optic System).
Price: 41 Gen 4 .... $630.00
Price: 41 Gen 4 MOS $760.00

GLOCK 42
Caliber: .380 ACP. Capacity: 6-round magazine. Barrel: 3.25 in. Weight: 13.8 oz. Length: 5.9 in. overall. Features: This single-stack, slimline sub-compact is the smallest pistol Glock has ever made. This is also the first Glock pistol made in the USA.
Price: 42 Gen 4 .... $440.00

GLOCK 43
Caliber: 9mm. Capacity: 6+1. Barrel: 3.39 in. Weight: 17.95 oz. Length: 6.26 in. Height: 4.25 in. Width: 1.02 in. Features: Newest member of Glock's

Slimline series with single-stack magazine.
Price: 42 Gen 4 .... **$500.00**

GLOCK 43X
Caliber: 9mm. Capacity: 17+1. Barrel: 4.02 in. Weight: 24.5 oz. Length: 7.4 in. Height: 5.5 in. Width: 1.3 in. Combines compact slide with full-size frame. MOS variant model available.
Price: 43X Gen 5 .... **$500.00–$685.00**

GLOCK 44
Caliber: .22 LR. Capacity: 10-round magazine. Barrel: 4.02 in. Grips: Textured grip, interchangeable backstraps. Sights: Fixed, dot front/notch rear. Length: 7.28 in. overall. Weight: 14.6 oz. unloaded. Finish: Black. Features: Same size as Glock G19, hybrid slide of polymer and steel.
Price: 44 Gen 5 .... **$390.00**

GLOCK 45
Caliber: 9mm. Capacity: 17+1. Barrel: 3.41 in. Weight: 18.7 oz. Length: 6.5 in. Height: 5.04 in. Width: 1.1 in. Combines Glock 19 slide with G17 frame. MOS variant.
Price: .... **$550.00–$580.00**

GLOCK 47
Caliber: 9mm. Capacity: 17+1. Barrel: 4.49 in. Weight: 25.93 oz. Length: 7.95 in. Height: 5.47 in. Width: 1.34 in. Features MOS.
Price: **$580.00**

GLOCK 48
Caliber: 9mm. Capacity: 10. Barrel: 3.41 in. Weight: 18.7 oz. Length: 6.05 in. Height: 5.04 in. Width: 1.1 in. Features: Silver-colored PVD-coated slide with front serrations. Similar length and height as Model 19 with width reduced to 1.1 inch. MOS variant model available.
Price: 48 Gen 5 .... **$500.00–$540.00**

GRAND POWER P-1 MK7
Caliber: 9mm. Capacity: 15+1 magazine. Barrel: 3.7 in. Weight: 26 oz. Features: Compact DA/SA pistol featuring frame-mounted safety, steel slide and frame and polymer grips. Offered in several variations and sizes. Made in Slovakia
Price: **$449.00**

GUNCRAFTER INDUSTRIES
Calibers: 9mm, .38 Super, .45 ACP or .50 GI. Capacity: 7- or 8-round magazine. Features: 1911-style series of pistols best known for the proprietary .50 GI chambering. Offered in approximately 30 1911 variations. No. 1 has 5-inch heavy match-grade barrel, Parkerized or hard chrome finish, checkered grips and frontstrap, numerous sight options. Other models include Commander-style, Officer's Model, Long Slide w/6-inch barrel and several 9mm and .38 Super versions.

Price: .... **$2,795.00–$5,195.00**

HECKLER & KOCH USP
Calibers: 9mm, .40 S&W, .45 ACP. Capacities: 15-round magazine; .40 S&W, 13-shot magazine; 45 ACP, 12-shot magazine. Barrels: 4.25–4.41 in. Weight: 1.65 lbs. Length: 7.64–7.87 in. overall. Grips: Non-slip stippled black polymer. Sights: Blade front, rear adjustable for windage. Features: New HK design with polymer frame, modified Browning action with recoil reduction system, single control lever. Special "hostile environment" finish on all metal parts. Available in SA/DA, DAO, left- and right-hand versions. Introduced 1993. .45 ACP Introduced 1995. Imported from Germany by Heckler & Koch, Inc.
Price: USP .45 .... **$1,010.00**
Price: USP .40 and USP 9mm **$980.00**

HECKLER & KOCH USP COMPACT
Calibers: 9mm, .357 SIG, .40 S&W, .45 ACP. Capacities: 13-round magazine; .40 S&W and .357 SIG, 12-shot magazine; .45 ACP, 8-shot magazine. Features: Similar to the USP except the 9mm, .357 SIG and .40 S&W have 3.58-in. barrels, measure 6.81 in. overall and weigh 1.47 lbs. (9mm). Introduced 1996. .45 ACP measures 7.09 in. overall. Introduced 1998. Imported from Germany by Heckler & Koch, Inc.
Price: USP Compact .45 .... **$1,100.00**
Price: USP Compact 9mm, .40 S&W **1,000.00**

HECKLER & KOCH USP TACTICAL
Calibers: 9mm, .45 ACP. Capacities: 13-round magazine; .45 ACP, 12-round magazine. Barrels: 4.90-5.09 in. Weight: 1.9 lbs. Length: 8.64 in. overall. Grips: Non-slip stippled polymer. Sights: Blade front, fully adjustable target rear. Features: Has extended threaded barrel with rubber O-ring; adjustable trigger; extended magazine floorplate; adjustable trigger stop; polymer frame. Introduced 1998. Imported from Germany by Heckler & Koch, Inc.
Price: USP Tactical 9mm, .45 .... **$1,410.00**

HECKLER & KOCH HK45

Caliber: .45 ACP. Capacity: 10-round magazine. Barrel: 4.53 in. Weight: 1.73 lbs. Length: 7.52 in. overall. Grips: Ergonomic with adjustable grip panels. Sights: Low profile, drift adjustable. Features: Polygonal rifling, ambidextrous controls, operates on improved Browning linkless recoil system. Available in Tactical and Compact variations. Tactical models come with threaded barrel, adjustable TruGlo high-profile sights, Picatinny rail.

Price: HK45 Compact.. **$710.00**
Price: HK45 Compact Tactical **$830.00**
Price: HK45 Tactical **$830.00**

HECKLER & KOCH MARK 23 SPECIAL OPERATIONS

Caliber: .45 ACP. Capacity: 12-round magazine. Barrel: 5.87 in. Weight: 2.42 lbs. Length: 9.65 in. overall. Grips: Integral with frame; black polymer. Sights: Blade front, rear drift adjustable for windage; 3-dot. Features: Civilian version of the SOCOM pistol. Polymer frame; double action; exposed hammer; short recoil, modified Browning action. Introduced 1996. Imported from Germany by Heckler & Koch, Inc.

Price: **$2,410.00**

HECKLER & KOCH P30 AND P30L

Calibers: 9mm, .40 S&W. Capacities: 13- or 15-round magazines. Barrels: 3.86 in. or 4.45 in. (P30L) Weight: 26–27.5 oz. Length: 6.95, 7.56 in. overall. Grips: Interchangeable panels. Sights: Open rectangular notch rear sight with contrast points. Features: Ergonomic features include a special grip frame with interchangeable backstrap inserts and lateral plates, allowing the pistol to be individually adapted to any user. Browning-type action with modified short recoil operation. Ambidextrous controls include dual slide releases, magazine release levers and a serrated decocking button located on the rear of the frame (for applicable variants). A Picatinny rail molded into the front of the frame. The extractor serves as a loaded-chamber indicator.

Price: P30 .... **$690.00**
Price: P30L... **$690.00**

HECKLER & KOCH P2000

Calibers: 9mm, .40 S&W. Capacities: 13-round magazine; .40 S&W, 12-shot magazine. Barrel: 3.62 in. Weight: 1.5 lbs. Length: 7 in. overall. Grips: Interchangeable panels. Sights: Fixed Patridge style, drift adjustable for windage, standard 3-dot. Features: Incorporates features of HK USP Compact pistol, including Law Enforcement Modification (LEM) trigger, double-action hammer system, ambidextrous magazine release, dual

slide-release levers, accessory mounting rails, recurved, hook trigger guard, fiber-reinforced polymer frame, modular grip with exchangeable backstraps, nitro-carburized finish, lock-out safety device. Introduced 2003. Imported from Germany by Heckler & Koch, Inc.

Price: **$775.00**

HECKLER & KOCH P2000 SK

Calibers: 9mm, .40 S&W. Capacities: 10-round magazine; .40 S&W, 9-round magazine. Barrel: 3.27 in. Weight: 1.3 lbs. Length: 6.42 in. overall. Sights: Fixed Patridge style, drift adjustable. Features: Standard accessory rails, ambidextrous slide release, polymer frame, polygonal bore profile. Smaller version of P2000. Introduced 2005. Imported from Germany by Heckler & Koch, Inc.

Price: **$775.00**

HECKLER & KOCH VP9/VP 40

Calibers: 9mm, .40 S&W. Capacities: 10- or 15-round magazine. .40 S&W (10 or 13). Barrel: 4.09 in. Weight: 25.6 oz. Length: 7.34 in. overall. Sights: Fixed 3-dot, drift adjustable. Features: Striker-fired system with HK enhanced light pull trigger. Ergonomic grip design with interchangeable backstraps and side panels. VP9SK is compact model with 3.4-in. barrel.

Price: VP9/VP40 .... **$690.00**
Price: VP9 Match... **$1,030.00**
Price: VP9L OR.. **$750.00**
Price: VP9SK **$690.00**
Price: VP9SK optic ready **$750.00**
Price: VP9 Tactical OR.. **$900.00**

HI-POINT FIREARMS MODEL 9MM COMPACT

Caliber: 9mm. Capacity: 8-round magazine. Barrel: 3.5 in. Weight: 25 oz. Length: 6.75 in. overall. Grips: Textured plastic. Sights: Combat-style adjustable 3-dot system; low profile. Features: Single-action design; frame-mounted magazine release; polymer frame offered in black or several camo finishes. Scratch-resistant matte finish. Introduced 1993. Comps are similar except they have a 4-in. barrel with muzzle brake/compensator. Compensator is slotted for laser or flashlight mounting. Introduced 1998. Made in USA by MKS Supply, Inc.

Price: C-9 9mm **$180.00**

HI-POINT FIREARMS MODEL 380 POLYMER

Caliber: .380 ACP. Capacities: 10- and 8-round magazine. Weight: 25 oz. Features: Similar to the 9mm Compact model except chambered for adjustable 3-dot sights. Polymer frame with black or camo finish. Action locks open after last shot. Trigger lock.

Price: CF-380 .... **$160.00**

Prices given are believed to be accurate at time of publication however, many factors affect retail pricing so exact prices are not possible.

78TH EDITION, 2024 ✦ **481**

HI-POINT FIREARMS 40 AND 45 SW/POLYMER
Calibers: .40 S&W, .45 ACP. Capacities: .40 S&W, 8-round magazine; .45 ACP, 9 rounds. Barrel: 4.5 in. Weight: 32 oz. Length: 7.72 in. overall. Sights: Adjustable 3-dot. Features: Polymer frames, offered in black or several camo finishes, last round lock-open, grip-mounted magazine release, magazine disconnect safety, integrated accessory rail, trigger lock. Introduced 2002. Made in USA by MKS Supply, Inc.
Price: $180.00

HI-POINT FIREARMS JXP10
Caliber: 10mm. Capacity: 10-round magazine. Similar to .40 S&W and .45 ACP models.
Price: $180.00

ITHACA 1911
Caliber: .45 ACP. Capacity: 7-round capacity. Barrels: 4.25 or 5 in. Weight: 35 or 40 oz. Sights: Fixed combat or fully adjustable target. Grips: Checkered cocobolo with Ithaca logo. Classic 1911A1 style with enhanced features including match-grade barrel, lowered and flared ejection port, extended beavertail grip safety, hand-fitted barrel bushing, two-piece guide rod, checkered front strap.
Price: $1,365.00
Price: Hand fit.. $2,175.00

IVER JOHNSON EAGLE
Calibers: 9mm, .45 ACP, 10mm. Features: Series of 1911-style pistols made in typical variations including full-size (Eagle), Commander (Hawk), Officer's (Thrasher) sizes.
Price: .... $640.00–$1,500.00

KAHR CM SERIES
Calibers: 9mm, .45 ACP. Capacities: 9mm (6+1), .45 ACP (5+1). CM45 Model is shown. Barrels: 3 in., 3.25 in. (45) Weights: 15.9–17.3 oz. Length: 5.42 in. overall. Grips: Textured polymer with integral steel rails molded into frame. Sights: Pinned in polymer sight; drift-adjustable, white bar-dot combat. Features: A conventional rifled barrel instead of the match-grade polygonal barrel on Kahr's PM series; the CM slide stop lever is MIM (metal-injection-molded) instead of machined; the CM series slide has fewer machining operations and uses simple engraved markings instead of roll marking. The CM series are shipped with one magazine instead of two. The slide is machined from solid 416 stainless with a matte finish, each gun is shipped with one 6-round stainless steel magazine with a flush baseplate. Magazines are U.S.-made, plasma welded, tumbled to remove burrs and feature Wolff springs. The magazine catch in the polymer frame is all metal and will not wear out on the stainless steel magazine after extended use.
Price: .... $430.00–$445.00

KAHR CT SERIES
Calibers: 9mm, .45 ACP. Capacities: 9mm (8+1), .45 ACP (7+1). Barrel: 4 in. Weights: 20–25 oz. Length: 5.42 in. overall. Grips: Textured polymer with integral steel rails molded into frame. Sights: Drift adjustable, white bar-dot combat.
Price: $415.00

KAHR CT 380
Caliber: .380 ACP. Capacity: (7+1). Barrel: 3 in. Weight: 14 oz. Other features similar to CT 9/40/45 models.
Price: $390.00

KAHR K SERIES
Calibers: 9mm, 7-shot magazine. Barrel: 3.5 in. Weight: 25 oz. Length: 6 in. overall. Grips: Wraparound textured soft polymer. Sights: Blade front, rear drift adjustable for windage; bar-dot combat style or tritium night sights. Features: Trigger-cocking double-action mechanism with passive firing pin block. Made of 4140 ordnance steel with matte black finish. Introduced 1994. Made in USA by Kahr Arms.
Price: .... $565.00–$665.00

KAHR TP SERIES
Calibers: 9mm. Capacities: TP9 (8-shot magazine). Barrels: 4, 5, or 6 in. Features: Model with 4-inch barrel has features similar to KP GEN 2. The 5-inch model has front and rear slide serrations, white 3-dot sights, mount

for reflex sights. The 6-inch model has the same features plus comes with Leupold Delta Point Reflex sight.

Price: **$610.00**

KAHR MK SERIES MICRO
Similar to the K9 except is 5.35 in. overall, 4 in. high, with a 3.08 in. barrel. Weighs 23.1 oz. Has snag-free bar-dot sights or tritium night sights, polished feed ramp, dual recoil spring system, DAO trigger. Comes with 5-round flush baseplate and 6-shot grip extension magazine. Introduced 1998. Made in USA by Kahr Arms.

Price: .... **$1,000,00–$1,180.00**

KAHR P SERIES
Calibers: .380 ACP, 9mm, .40 S&W, 45 ACP. Capacity: 7-shot magazine. Features: Similar to K9/K40 steel frame pistol except has polymer frame, matte stainless steel slide. Barrel length 3.5 in.; overall length 5.8 in.; weighs 17 oz. Includes two 7-shot magazines, hard polymer case, trigger lock. Introduced 2000. Made in USA by Kahr Arms.

Price: KP9093 9mm **$762.00**
Price: KP4043 .40 S&W **$762.00**
Price: KP4543 .45 ACP **$829.00**
Price: KP3833 .380 ACP (2008)................................. **$667.00**

KAHR PM SERIES
Calibers: 9mm, .40 S&W, .45 ACP. Capacity: 7-round magazine. Features: Similar to P-Series pistols except has smaller polymer frame (Polymer Micro). Barrel length 3.08 in.; overall length 5.35 in.; weighs 17 oz. Includes two 7-shot magazines, hard polymer case, trigger lock. Introduced 2000. Made in USA by Kahr Arms.

Price: **$690.00**

KAHR CW SERIES
Caliber: 9mm or .45 ACP. Capacities: 9mm, 7-round magazine; .45 ACP, 6-round magazine. Barrels: 3.5 and 3.64 in. Weight: 17.7–18.7 oz. Length: 5.9–6.36 in. overall. Grips: Textured polymer. Similar to the P-Series, but CW Series have conventional rifling, metal-injection-molded slide stop lever, no front dovetail cut, one magazine. Made in USA.

Price: **$430.00**

KAHR P380
Caliber: .380 ACP. Capacity: 6+1. Features: Very small DAO semi-auto pistol. Features include 2.5-in. Lothar Walther barrel; black polymer frame with stainless steel slide; drift adjustable white bar/dot combat/sights; optional tritium sights; two 6+1 magazines. Overall length 4.9 in., weight 10 oz. without magazine.

Price: Standard sights **$670.00**
Price: Night sights... **$700.00**

KAHR CW380
Caliber: .380 ACP. Capacity: 6-round magazine. Barrel: 2.58 in. Weight: 11.5 oz. Length: 4.96 in. Grips: Textured integral polymer. Sights: Fixed white-bar combat style. Features: DAO. Black or purple polymer frame, stainless slide.

Price: **$390.00**

KEL-TEC P-11
Caliber: 9mm. Capacity: 10-round magazine. Barrel: 3.1 in. Weight: 14 oz. Length: 5.6 in. overall. Grips: Checkered black polymer. Sights: Blade front, rear adjustable for windage. Features: Ordnance steel slide, aluminum frame. DAO trigger mechanism. Introduced 1995. Made in USA by Kel-Tec CNC Industries, Inc.

Price: From **$285.00**

KEL-TEC PF-9
Caliber: 9mm. Capacity: 7 rounds. Weight: 12.7 oz. Sights: Rear sight adjustable for windage and elevation. Barrel: 3.1 in. Length: 5.85 in. Features: Barrel, locking system, slide stop, assembly pin, front sight, recoil springs and guide rod adapted from P-11. Trigger system with integral hammer block and the extraction system adapted from P-3AT. Mil-Std-1913 Picatinny rail. Made in USA by Kel-Tec CNC Industries, Inc.

Price: From **$290.00**

Prices given are believed to be accurate at time of publication however, many factors affect retail pricing so exact prices are not possible.

78TH EDITION, 2024 ✦ **483**

KELTEC P15
Caliber: 9mm. Capacity: 15-round magazine. Barrel: 4-in. bull. Grip: Textured polymer. Sights: Adjustable tritium and fiber optic. Length: 5.6 in. overall. Weight: 14 ozs. unloaded. Finish: Matte black. Features: Striker-fire, accessory rail, grip safety
Price: $370.00

KEL-TEC P17
Caliber: .22 LR. Capacity: 16-round magazine. Barrel: 3.8 in. Grips: Textured polymer. Sights: Fixed. Length: 6.7 in. overall. Weight: 11.2 oz. unloaded. Finish: Matte black.
Price: $180.00

KEL-TEC P-32
Caliber: .32 ACP. Capacity: 7-round magazine. Barrel: 2.68. Weight: 6.6 oz. Length: 5.07 overall. Grips: Checkered composite. Sights: Fixed. Features: Double-action-only mechanism with 6-lb. pull; internal slide stop. Textured composite grip/frame.
Price: From $330.00

KELTEC P50
Caliber: 5.7 x 28mm. Capacity: 20 round magazine. Barrel: 5-in. bull. Grip: Textured aluminum. Sights: Optic ready. Length: 15 in. overall. Weight: 3.2 lbs. unloaded. Finish: Matte black. Features: Uses FN P90 50-round double stack magazines, QD mount in butt.
Price: $910.00

KEL-TEC P-3AT
Caliber: .380 ACP. Capacity: 7-round magazine Weight: 7.2 oz. Length: 5.2. Features: Lightest .380 ACP made; aluminum frame, steel barrel.
Price: From $280.00

KEL-TEC PLR-16
Caliber: 5.56mm NATO. Capacity: 10-round magazine. Weight: 51 oz. Sights: Rear sight adjustable for windage, front sight is M-16 blade. Barrel: 9.2 in. Length: 18.5 in. Features: Muzzle is threaded 1/2x28 to accept standard

attachments such as a muzzle brake. Except for the barrel, bolt, sights and mechanism, the PLR-16 pistol is made of high-impact glass fiber reinforced polymer. Gas-operated semi-auto. Conventional gas-piston operation with M-16 breech locking system. MIL-STD-1913 Picatinny rail. Made in USA by Kel-Tec CNC Industries, Inc.
Price: Blued $560.00

KEL-TEC PLR-22
Caliber: .22 LR. Capacity: 26-round magazine. Length: 18.5 in. overall. 40 oz. Features: Semi-auto pistol based on centerfire PLR-16 by same maker. Blowback action. Open sights and Picatinny rail for mounting accessories; threaded muzzle.
Price: $400.00

KEL-TEC PMR-30
Caliber: .22 Magnum (.22WMR). Capacity: 30 rounds. Barrel: 4.3 in. Weight: 13.6 oz. Length: 7.9 in. overall. Grips: Glass reinforced Nylon (Zytel). Sights: Dovetailed aluminum with front & rear fiber optics. Features: Operates on a unique hybrid blowback/locked-breech system. It uses a double-stack magazine of a new design that holds 30 rounds and fits completely in the grip of the pistol. Dual opposing extractors for reliability, heel magazine release to aid in magazine retention, Picatinny accessory rail under the barrel, Urethane recoil buffer, captive coaxial recoil springs. The barrel is fluted for light weight and effective heat dissipation. PMR30 disassembles for cleaning by removal of a single pin.
Price: $505.00

KIMBER MICRO DESERT NIGHT
Caliber: .380 ACP. Capacity: 6-round magazine. Barrel: 2.75 in. Weight: 17 oz. Finish: Blued slide, bronze frame. Grips: G10. Mini 1911-style single action with no grip safety.
Price: $610.00

KIMBER MICRO DESERT TAN
Caliber: .380 ACP. Capacity: 6-round magazine. Barrel: 2.75 in. Weight: 17 oz. Finish: Blued slide, tan frame. Grips: G10. Mini 1911-style single action with no grip safety.
Price: $685.00

KIMBER MICRO ECLIPSE
Caliber: .380 ACP. Capacity: 6-round magazine. Barrel: 2.75 in. Weight: 17 oz. Finish: Brush-polished finish. Grips: G10. Mini 1911-style single action with no grip safety.
Price: $710.00

KIMBER MICRO RAPTOR
Caliber: .380 ACP Capacity: 6-round magazine. Sights: Tritium night sights. Finish: Stainless. Features: Variation of Micro Carry with Raptor-style scalloped "feathered" slide serrations and grip panels.
Price: $842.00

KIMBER MICRO STAINLESS
Caliber: .380 ACP. Capacity: 6-round magazine. Barrel: 2.75 in. Weight: 17 oz. Finish: Stainless. Grips: Checkered rosewood. Mini 1911-style single action with no grip safety.
Price: $560.00

KIMBER MICRO TWO TONE
Caliber: .380 ACP. Capacity: 6-round magazine. Barrel: 2.75 in. Weight: 17 oz. Finish: Blued slide, stainless frame. Grips: Checkered rosewood. Mini 1911-style single action with no grip safety.
Price: $560.00

KIMBER COVERT SERIES
Caliber: .45 ACP Capacity: 7-round magazine. Barrels: 3, 4 or 5 in. Weight: 25–31 oz. Grips: Crimson Trace laser with camo finish. Sights: Tactical wedge 3-dot night sights. Features: Made in the Kimber Custom Shop. Finish: Kimber Gray frame, matte black slide, black small parts. Carry Melt treatment. Available in three frame sizes: Custom, Pro and Ultra.
Price: **$1,457.00**

KIMBER CUSTOM II
Caliber: 9mm, .45 ACP. Barrel: 5 in. Weight: 38 oz. Length: 8.7 in. overall. Grips: Checkered black rubber, walnut, rosewood. Sights: Dovetailed front and rear, Kimber low profile adjustable or fixed sights. Features: Slide, frame and barrel machined from steel or stainless steel. Match-grade barrel, chamber and trigger group. Extended thumb safety, beveled magazine well, beveled front and rear slide serrations, high ride beavertail grip safety, checkered flat mainspring housing, kidney cut under trigger guard, high cut grip, match-grade stainless steel barrel bushing, polished breechface, Commander-style hammer, lowered and flared ejection port, Wolff springs, bead blasted black oxide or matte stainless finish. Introduced in 1996. Made in USA by Kimber Mfg., Inc.
Price: Custom II **$871.00**
Price: Two-Tone **$1,136.00**

KIMBER CUSTOM TLE II
Caliber: .45 ACP or 10mm. Features: TLE (Tactical Law Enforcement) version of Custom II model plus night sights, frontstrap checkering, threaded barrel, Picatinny rail.
Price: .45 ACP **$1,007.00**
Price: 10mm **$1,028.00**

KIMBER MICRO 9
Caliber: 9mm. Capacity: 7-round magazine. Barrel: 3.15 in. Weight: 15.6 oz. Features: The easily concealed Micro 9 features mild recoil, smooth trigger pull and the intuitive operation of a 1911 platform. Micro 9 slides are made to the tightest allowable tolerances, with barrels machined from stainless steel for superior resistance to moisture. All Micro 9 frames are shaped from the finest aluminum for integrity and strength. Lowered and flared ejection ports for flawless ejection and a beveled magazine well for fast, positive loading. In 2020, Kimber offered 15 different Micro 9 models with a total of 26 variations.
Prices:.. **$654.00-$1,061.00**

KIMBER STAINLESS II
Same features as Custom II except has stainless steel frame.
Price: Stainless II .45 ACP **$998.00**
Price: Stainless II 9mm **$1,016.00**
Price: Stainless II .45 ACP w/night sights.......................... **$1,141.00**
Price: Stainless II Target .45 ACP (stainless, adj. sight) **$1,108.00**

KIMBER PRO CARRY II
Calibers: 9mm, .45 ACP. Features: Similar to Custom II, has aluminum frame, 4-in. bull barrel fitted directly to the slide without bushing. Introduced 1998. Made in USA by Kimber Mfg., Inc.
Price: Pro Carry II, .45 ACP **$837.00**
Price: Pro Carry II, 9mm **$857.00**
Price: Pro Carry II w/night sights **$977.00**
Price: Two-Tone **$1,136.00**

KIMBER SAPPHIRE PRO II
Caliber: 9mm. Capacity: 9-round magazine. Features: Similar to Pro Carry II, 4-inch match-grade barrel. Striking two-tone appearance with satin silver aluminum frame and high polish bright blued slide. Grips are blue/black G-10 with grooved texture. Fixed Tactical Edge night sights. From the Kimber Custom Shop.
Price: **$1,652.00**

KIMBER RAPTOR II
Caliber: .45 ACP. Capacities: .45 ACP (8-round magazine, 7-round (Ultra and Pro models). Barrels: 3, 4 or 5 in. Weight: 25–31 oz. Grips: Thin milled rosewood. Sights: Tactical wedge 3-dot night sights. Features: Made in the Kimber Custom Shop. Matte black or satin silver finish. Available in three frame sizes: Custom (shown), Pro and Ultra.
Price: .... **$1,192.00–$1,464.00**

KIMBER ULTRA CARRY II
Calibers: 9mm, .45 ACP. Features: Lightweight aluminum frame, 3-in. match-grade bull barrel fitted to slide without bushing. Grips 0.4-in. shorter. Light recoil spring. Weighs 25 oz. Introduced in 1999. Made in USA by Kimber Mfg., Inc.
Price: Stainless Ultra Carry II .45 ACP **$919.00**
Price: Stainless Ultra Carry II 9mm **$1,016.00**
Price: Stainless Ultra Carry II .45 ACP with night sights **$1,039.00**
Price: Two-Tone.. **$1,177.00**

KIMBER CDP II SERIES
Calibers: 9mm, .45 ACP. Features: Similar to Custom II but designed for concealed carry. Aluminum frame. Standard features include stainless steel slide, fixed Meprolight tritium 3-dot (green) dovetail-mounted night sights,

match-grade barrel and chamber, 30 LPI frontstrap checkering, two-tone finish, ambidextrous thumb safety, hand-checkered double diamond rosewood grips. Introduced in 2000. Made in USA by Kimber Mfg., Inc.

Price: Ultra CDP II 9mm (2008) $1,359.00
Price: Ultra CDP II .45 ACP $1,318.00
Price: Compact CDP II .45 ACP $1,318.00
Price: Pro CDP II .45 ACP $1,318.00
Price: Custom CDP II (5-in. barrel, full length grip) $1,318.00

KIMBER CDP

Calibers: 9mm, .45 ACP. Barrel: 3, 4 or 5 in. Weight: 25–31 oz. Features: Aluminum frame, stainless slide, 30 LPI checkering on backstrap and trigger guard, low profile tritium night sights, Carry Melt treatment. Sights: Hand checkered rosewood or Crimson Trace Lasergrips. Introduced in 2017.

Price: $1,173.00
Price: With Crimson Trace Lasergrips.............................. $1,473.00

KIMBER ECLIPSE II SERIES

Calibers: .38 Super, 10 mm, .45 ACP. Features: Similar to Custom II and other stainless Kimber pistols. Stainless slide and frame, black oxide, two-tone finish. Gray/black laminated grips. 30 LPI frontstrap checkering. All models have night sights; Target versions have Meprolight adjustable Bar/Dot version. Made in USA by Kimber Mfg., Inc.

Price: Eclipse Ultra II (3-in. barrel, short grip) $1,350.00
Price: Eclipse Pro II (4-in. barrel, full-length grip) $1,350.00
Price: Eclipse Custom II 10mm $1,350.00
Price: Eclipse Target II (5-in. barrel, full-length grip,
   adjustable sight) $1,393.00

KIMBER ULTRA CDP II

Calibers: 9mm, .45 ACP. Capacities: 7-round magazine (9 in 9mm). Features: Compact 1911-style pistol; ambidextrous thumb safety; carry melt profiling; full-length guide rod; aluminum frame with stainless slide; satin silver finish; checkered frontstrap; 3-inch barrel; rosewood double diamond Crimson Trace laser grips; tritium 3-dot night sights.

Price: $1,603.00

KIMBER STAINLESS ULTRA TLE II

Caliber: .45 ACP. Capacity: 7-round magazine. Features: 1911-style semi-auto pistol. Features include full-length guide rod; aluminum frame with stainless slide; satin silver finish; checkered frontstrap; 3-in. barrel; tactical gray double diamond grips; tritium 3-dot night sights.

Price: $1,136.00

KIMBER SUPER JAGARE

Caliber: 10mm. Capacity: 8+1. Barrel: 6 in, ported. Weight: 42 oz. Finish: Stainless steel KimPro, Charcoal gray frame, diamond-like carbon coated slide. Slide is ported. Sights: Delta Point Pro Optic. Grips: Micarta. Frame has rounded heel, high cut triggerguard. Designed for hunting.

Price: $2,688.00

KIMBER KHX SERIES

Calibers: .45 ACP, 9mm. Capacity: 8+1. Features: This series is offered in Custom, Pro and Ultra sizes. Barrels: 5-, 4- or 3-inch match-grade stainless steel. Weights: 25–38 oz. Finishes: Stainless steel frame and slide with matte black KimPro II finish. Stepped hexagonal slide and top-strap serrations. Sights: Green and red fiber optic and Hogue Laser Enhanced MagGrip G10 grips and matching mainspring housings. Pro and Ultra models have rounded heel frames. Optics Ready (OR) models available in Custom and Pro sizes with milled slide that accepts optics plates for Vortex, Trijicon and Leupold red-dot sights.

Price: Custom OR .45 ACP $1,087.00
Price: Custom OR 9mm $1,108.00
Price: Custom, Pro or Ultra .45...................................... $1,259.00
Price: Custom, Pro or Ultra 9mm $1,279.00

KIMBER AEGIS ELITE SERIES

Calibers: 9mm, .45 ACP. Features: Offered in Custom, Pro and Ultra sizes with 5-, 4.25- or 3-in. barrels. Sights: Green or red fiber optic or Vortex Venom red dot on OI (Optics Installed) models (shown). Grips: G10. Features: Satin finish stainless steel frame, matte black or gray slide, front and rear AEX slide serrations.

Price: .45 ACP $1,021.00
Price: 9mm $1,041.00
Price: .45 OI.. $1,375.00
Price: 9mm OI.. $1,395.00

KIMBER EVO SERIES
Caliber: 9mm. Capacity: 7 rounds. Barrel: 3.16 in. Sights: Tritium night sights. Weight: 19 oz. Grips: G10. Features: Offered in TLE, CDP, Two Tone variants with stainless slide, aluminum frame.
Price: TLE **$925.00**
Price: CDP **$949.00**
Price: Two Tone **$856.00**

LES BAER 1911 ULTIMATE MASTER COMBAT
Calibers: .38 Super, 400 Cor-Bon, .45 ACP (others available). Capacity: 10-shot magazine. Barrels: 5, 6 in. Baer National Match. Weight: 37 oz. Length: 8.5 in. overall. Grips: Checkered cocobolo. Sights: Baer dovetail front, low-mount Bo-Mar rear with hidden leaf. Features: Full-house competition gun. Baer forged NM blued steel frame and double serrated slide; Baer triple port, tapered cone compensator; fitted slide to frame; lowered, flared ejection port; Baer reverse recoil plug; full-length guide rod; recoil buff; beveled magazine well; Baer Commander hammer, sear; Baer extended ambidextrous safety, extended ejector, checkered slide stop, beavertail grip safety with pad, extended magazine release button; Baer speed trigger. Made in USA by Les Baer Custom, Inc.
Price: .45 ACP Compensated **$3,240.00**
Price: .38 Super Compensated **$3,390.00**
Price: 5-in. Standard barrel **$3,040.00**
Price: 5-in. barrel .38 Super or 9mm........................ **$3,140.00**
Price: 6-in. barrel... **$3,234.00**
Price: 6-in. barrel .38 Super or 9mm...................... **$3,316.00**

LES BAER 1911 NATIONAL MATCH HARDBALL
Caliber: .45 ACP. Capacity: 7-round magazine. Barrel: 5 in. Weight: 37 oz. Length: 8.5 in. overall. Grips: Checkered walnut. Sights: Baer dovetail front with under-cut post, low-mount Bo-Mar rear with hidden leaf. Features: Baer NM forged steel frame, double serrated slide and barrel with stainless bushing; slide fitted to frame; Baer match trigger with 4-lb. pull; polished feed ramp, throated barrel; checkered frontstrap, arched mainspring housing; Baer beveled magazine well; lowered, flared ejection port; tuned extractor; Baer extended ejector, checkered slide stop; recoil buff. Made in USA by Les Baer Custom, Inc.
Price: **$2,379.00**

LES BAER 1911 PPC OPEN CLASS
Caliber: .45 ACP, 9mm. Barrel: 6 in, fitted to frame. Sights: Adjustable PPC rear, dovetail front. Grips: Checkered Cocobola. Features: Designed for NRA Police Pistol Combat matches. Lowered and flared ejection port, extended ejector, polished feed ramp, throated barrel, frontstrap checkered at 30 LPI, flat serrated mainspring housing, Commander hammer, front and rear slide serrations. 9mm has supported chamber.
Price: **$2,775.00**
Price: 9mm w/supported chamber **$3,187.00**

LES BAER 1911 BULLSEYE WADCUTTER
Similar to National Match Hardball except designed for wadcutter loads only. Polished feed ramp and barrel throat; Bo-Mar rib on slide; full-length recoil

---

rod; Baer speed trigger with 3.5-lb. pull; Baer deluxe hammer and sear; Baer beavertail grip safety with pad; flat mainspring housing checkered 20 LPI. Blue finish; checkered walnut grips. Made in USA by Les Baer Custom, Inc.
Price: From **$2,461.00**

LES BAER 1911 AMERICAN HANDGUNNER SPECIAL EDITION
Caliber: .45 ACP. Capacity: 8+1 capacity. Barrel: 5 in. Length: 8.5 in. overall. Grips: G10 blue/black. Sights: Low-Mount LBC Adj. Finish: Blued slide, matte stainless frame.
Price: **$2,835.00**

LES BAER 1911 BLACK BEAR
Caliber: 9mm. Capacity: 9+1 capacity. Barrel: 4.25 in. Grips: G10. Sights: Combat night sights.
Price: **$2,900.00**

LES BAER 1911 BOSS .45
Caliber: .45 ACP. Capacity: 8+1 capacity. Barrel: 5 in. Weight: 37 oz. Length: 8.5 in. overall. Grips: Premium Checkered Cocobolo Grips. Sights: Low-Mount LBC Adj. Sight, red fiber-optic front. Features: Speed Trigger, Beveled Mag Well, Rounded for Tactical. Rear cocking serrations on the slide, Baer fiber-optic front sight (red), flat mainspring housing, checkered at 20 LPI, extended combat safety, Special tactical package, chromed complete lower, blued slide, (2) 8-round premium magazines.
Price: **$2,565.00**

LES BAER 1911 CUSTOM CARRY
Caliber: .45 ACP. Capacity: 7- or 10-round magazine. Barrel: 5 in. Weight: 37 oz. Length: 8.5 in. overall. Grips: Checkered walnut. Sights: Baer improved ramp-style dovetailed front, Novak low-mount rear. Features: Baer forged NM frame, slide and barrel with stainless bushing. Baer speed trigger with 4-lb. pull. Partial listing shown. Made in USA by Les Baer Custom, Inc.
Price: Custom Carry 5, blued **$2,190.00**
Price: Custom Carry 5, stainless **$2,290.00**
Price: Custom Carry 5, 9mm or .38 Super **$2,625.00**
Price: Custom Carry 4 Commanche-length, blued **$2,190.00**
Price: Custom Carry 4 Commanche-length, .38 Super ... **$2,550.00**

LES BAER 1911 PREMIER II

Calibers: .38 Super, .45 ACP. Capacity: 7- or 10-round magazine. Barrel: 5 in. Weight: 37 oz. Length: 8.5 in. overall. Grips: Checkered rosewood, double diamond pattern. Sights: Baer dovetailed front, low-mount Bo-Mar rear with hidden leaf. Features: Baer NM forged steel frame and barrel with stainless bushing, deluxe Commander hammer and sear, beavertail grip safety with pad, extended ambidextrous safety; flat mainspring housing; 30 LPI checkered front strap. Made in USA by Les Baer Custom, Inc.

Price: 5 in. .45 ACP **$2,660.00**
Price: 5 in. .38 Super, 9mm.. **$3,250.00**
Price: 6 in. .45 ACP, .38 Super, 9mm.................................... **$3,690.00**
Price: Super-Tac, .45 ACP, .38 Super.................................... **$3,800.00**
Price: 6-in Hunter 10mm.. **$3,799.00**

LES BAER 1911 STINGER

Calibers: .45 ACP or .38 Super. Capacity: 7-round magazine. Barrel: 5 in. Weight: 34 oz. Length: 8.5 in. overall. Grips: Checkered cocobolo. Sights: Baer dovetailed front, low-mount Bo-Mar rear with hidden leaf. Features: Baer NM frame. Baer Commanche slide, Officer's style grip frame, beveled mag well. Made in USA by Les Baer Custom, Inc.

Price: .45 ACP **$2,750.00**
Price: .38 Super **$3,680.00**

LES BAER HEMI 572

Caliber: .45 ACP. Based on Les Baer's 1911 Premier I pistol and inspired by Chrysler 1970 Hemi Cuda muscle car. Features: Double serrated slide, Baer fiber-optic front sight with green insert, VZ black recon grips with hex-head screws, hard chrome finish on all major components, Dupont S coating on barrel, trigger, hammer, ambi safety and other controls.

Price: **$3,430.00**

LES BAER ULTIMATE MASTER COMBAT

Calibers: .45 ACP or .38 Super. A full house competition 1911 offered in 8 variations including 5 or 6-inch barrel, PPC Distinguished or Open class, Bullseye Wadcutter class and others. Features include double serrated slide, fitted slide to frame, checkered front strap and triggerguard, serrated rear of slide, extended ejector, tuned extractor, premium checkered grips, blued finish and two 8-round magazines.

Price: Compensated .45 .... **$3,131.00**
Price: Compensated .38 Super **$3,234.00**

LES BAER 1911 MONOLITH S

Calibers: 10mm, .45 ACP, .38 Super, 9mm, .40 S&W. A full house competition 1911 offered in 14 variations. Unique feature is extra-long dust cover that matches the length of the slide and reduces muzzle flip. Features include flat-bottom double serrated slide, low mount LBC adjustable sight with hidden rear leaf, dovetail front sight, flat serrated mainspring housing, premium checkered grips, blued finish and two 8-round magazines.

Price: .45 ....From **$2,419.00**
Price: .38 Super, .40 S&W ....From **$2,790.00**
Price: 10mm **$3,230.00**

LES BAER KENAI SPECIAL

Caliber: 10mm. Capacity: 9-round magazine. Barrel: 5 in. Features: Hardchrome finish, double serrated slide, Baer fiber-optic front sight with green or red insert, low-mount LBC adjustable rear sight, Baer black recon grips, special bear paw logo, flat serrated mainspring housing, lowered and flared ejection port, extended safety.

Price: **$3,530.00**

LES BAER GUNSITE PISTOL

Calibers: .45 ACP. Capacity: 8-round magazine. Barrel: 5 in. Features: double serrated slide, fitted slide to frame, flat serrated mainspring housing, flared

and lowered ejection port, extended tactical thumb safety, fixed rear sight, dovetail front sight with night sight insert, all corners rounded, extended ejector, tuned extractor, premium checkered grips, blued finish and two 8-round magazines. Gunsite Raven logo on grips and slide.

Price: **$2,750.00**

LIONHEART REGULUS

Caliber: 9mm. Capacities: 10-, 15-, or 18-round magazine. Barrel: 3.7, 4.3 or 4.7 in. Weight: 26.5 oz. Length: 7.5 in Grips: One-piece black polymer with textured design. Sights: Fixed low profile. Novak LoMount sights available. Finish: Cerakote Black, Midnight Bronze, or Concrete Grey. Features: Hammer-forged heat-treated steel slide, hammer-forged aluminum frame. Double-action PLUS action.

Price: **$850.00**

MAGNUM RESEARCH DESERT EAGLE 1911 G

Caliber: .45 ACP. Capacity: 8-round magazine. Barrels: 5 in. or 4.33 in. (DE1911C Commander size), or 3.0 in. (DE1911U Undercover). Grips: Double diamond checkered wood. Features: Extended beavertail grip safety, checkered flat mainspring housing, skeletonized hammer and trigger, extended mag release and thumb safety, stainless full-length guide road, enlarged ejection port, beveled mag well and high-profile sights. Comes with two 8-round magazines.

Price: **$904.00**

MAGNUM RESEARCH DESERT EAGLE MARK XIX

Calibers: .357 Mag., 9 rounds; .44 Mag., 8 rounds; .50 AE, 7 rounds. Barrels: 6 in., 10 in., interchangeable. Weight: 62 oz. (.357 Mag.); 69 oz. (.44 Mag.); 72 oz. (.50 AE) Length: 10.25-in. overall (6-in. bbl.). Grips: Polymer; rubber available. Sights: Blade-on-ramp front, combat-style rear. Adjustable available. Features: Interchangeable barrels; rotating three-lug bolt; ambidextrous safety; adjustable trigger. Military epoxy finish. Satin, bright nickel, chrome, brushed, matte or black-oxide finishes available. 10-in. barrel extra. Imported from Israel by Magnum Research, Inc.

Price: .... **$1,480.00–$2,210.00**

MAGNUM RESEARCH BABY DESERT EAGLE III

Calibers: 9mm, .40 S&W, .45 ACP. Capacities: 10-, 12- or 15-round magazines. Barrels: 3.85 in. or 4.43 in. Weights: 28–37.9 oz. Length: 7.25–8.25 overall. Grips: Ergonomic polymer. Sights: White 3-dot system. Features: Choice of steel or polymer frame with integral rail; slide-mounted decocking safety. Upgraded design of Baby Eagle II series.

Price: .... **$615.00–$700.00**

MAGNUM RESEARCH DESERT EAGLE L5/L6

Caliber: .357 Magnum, .44 Magnum, .50 AE. Capacity: 7, 8 or 9+1. Barrel: 5 in. or 6 in (L6). Weight: 50 to 70 oz. Length: 9.7 in. (L5), 10.8, (L6). Features: Steel barrel, aluminum frame and stainless steel slide with full Weaver-style accessory rail and integral muzzle brake. Gas-operated rotating bolt, single-action trigger, fixed sights.

Price: .... **$1,740.00–$2,010.00**

MOSSBERG MC1SC

Caliber: 9mm Capacity: 6+1 magazine. Barrel: 3.4 in. Sights: Three white-dot, snag-free. TruGlo tritium Pro sights or Viridian E-Series Red Laser available as an option. Weight: 22 oz., loaded. Grips: Integral with aggressive texturing and with palm swell. Features: Glass-reinforced polymer frame, stainless steel slide with multi-angle front and rear serrations, flat-profile trigger with integrated blade safety, ships with one 6-round and one 7-round magazine. Optional cross-bolt safety.

Price: .... **$370.00–$470.00**

Prices given are believed to be accurate at time of publication however, many factors affect retail pricing so exact prices are not possible.

MOSSBERG MC2C
Caliber: 9mm. Capacity: 10, 13- or 15-round magazine. Barrel: 3.9 in. Grips: Textured polymer. Sights: Fixed, 3-dot. Length: 7.1 in. overall. Weight: 21 oz. unloaded. Finish: Matte black. Features: Accessory rail, forward-slide serrations.
Price: .... $430.00–$500.00

MOSSBERG MC2SC
Caliber: 9mm. Capacity: 11- or 14-round magazine. Barrel: 3.4 in. Grips: Textured polymer. Sights: Fixed, 3-dot, optics-ready. Length: 6.2 in. overall. Weight: 19.5 oz. unloaded. Finish: Matte black. Features: Accessory rail, forward-slide serrations.
Price: .... $470.00–$580.00

NIGHTHAWK CUSTOM AGENT2 COMMANDER
Calibers: 9mm, .45 ACP. Capacity: 10-round magazine. Barrel: 4.25 in. Grips: G10 Railscale texture. Sights: Fixed, Heinie Ledge Black rear/gold-bead front. Length: 7.85 in. overall. Weight: 38.6 oz. unloaded. Finish: Smoke Cerakote. Features: Accessory rail, faceted slide with side windows, one-piece mainspring housing/mag well, ultra-high-cut front grip strap.
Price: $4,499.00

NIGHTHAWK CUSTOM BULL OFFICER
Caliber: 9mm. Capacity: 8-round magazine. Barrel: 3.8 in. Grips: Textured carbon fiber. Sights: Fixed, Heinie Ledge Black rear/fiber-optic front. Length: 7.85 in. overall. Weight: 38.2 oz. unloaded. Finish: Black nitride. Features: Bull nose and French border on slide, ultra-high-cut front grip strap, dehorned.
Price: $3,699.00

NIGHTHAWK CUSTOM GRP
Calibers: 9mm, 10mm, .45 ACP. Capacity: 8-round magazine. Features: Global Response Pistol (GRP). Black, Sniper Gray, green, Coyote Tan or Titanium Blue finish. Match-grade barrel and trigger, choice of Heinie or Novak adjustable night sights.
Price: $3,095.00

NIGHTHAWK CUSTOM T4
Calibers: 9mm, .45 ACP Capacities: .45 ACP, 7- or 8-round magazine; 9mm,

9 or 10 rounds; 10mm, 9 or 10 rounds. Barrels: 3.8, 4.25 or 5 in. Weights: 28–41 ounces, depending on model. Features: Manufacturer of a wide range of 1911-style pistols in Government Model (full-size), Commander and Officer's frame sizes. Shown is T4 model, introduced in 2013 and available only in 9mm.
Price: From .... $3,495.00–$3,695.00

NIGHTHAWK CUSTOM THUNDER RANCH
Caliber: 9mm, .45 ACP. Capacity: 8-round (.45 ACP), 10-round (9mm) magazine. Barrel: 5 in. Grips: Textured linen micarta. Sights: Fixed, Heinie Black Ledge rear/gold-bead front. Length: 8.6 in. overall. Weight: 41.3 oz. unloaded. Finish: Smoked nitride. Features: Custom front- and rear-cocking serrations, lanyard-loop mainspring housing, GI-Style nub thumb safety and custom engraving.
Price: $3,399.00

NIGHTHAWK CUSTOM SHADOW HAWK
Caliber: 9mm. Barrels: 5 in. or 4.25 in. Features: Stainless steel frame with black Nitride finish, flat-faced trigger, high beavertail grip safety, checkered frontstrap, Heinie Straight Eight front and rear titanium night sights.
Price: $3,795.00

NIGHTHAWK CUSTOM VICE PRESIDENT
Caliber: 9mm. Capacity: 10-round magazine. Barrel: 4.25 in. Grips: G10 Railscale Ascend texture. Sights: Fixed, Heinie Straight Eight Ledge rear/tritium front. Length: 7.4 in. overall. Weight: 32 oz. unloaded. Finish: Black DLC. Features: Gold titanium nitride barrel, heavy angle slide-lightening cuts, one-piece mainspring housing/mag well, ultra-high-cut front grip strap, dehorned.
Price: $4,199.00

NIGHTHAWK CUSTOM HEINIE LONG SLIDE
Calibers: 10mm, .45 ACP. Barrel: Long slide 6-in. Features: Cocobolo wood grips, black Perma Kote finish, adjustable or fixed sights, frontstrap checkering.
Price: $3,895.00

NIGHTHAWK CUSTOM BORDER SPECIAL
Caliber: .45 ACP Capacity: 8+1 magazine. Barrel: 4.25-in. match grade. Weight: 34 oz. Sights: Heinie Black Slant rear, gold bead front. Grips: Cocobolo double diamond. Finish: Cerakote Elite Midnight black. Features: Commander-size steel frame with bobtail concealed carry grip. Scalloped frontstrap and mainspring housing. Serrated slide top. Rear slide serrations only. Crowned barrel flush with bushing.
Price: $3,699.00

NIGHTHAWK VIP BLACK
Caliber: .45 ACP. Capacity: 8+1 magazine. Hand built with all Nighthawk 1911 features plus deep hand engraving throughout, black DLC finish, custom vertical frontstrap and mainspring serrations, 14k solid gold bead front sight, crowned barrel, giraffe bone grips, custom walnut hardwood presentation case.
Price: $7,999.00

NORTH AMERICAN ARMS GUARDIAN DAO
Calibers: .32 ACP, .380 ACP. Capacity: 6-round magazine. Barrel: 2.49 in. Weight: 20.8 oz. Length: 4.75 in. overall. Grips: Black polymer. Sights: Low-profile fixed. Features: DAO mechanism. All stainless steel construction. Introduced 1998. Made in USA by North American Arms.
Price: .... $400.00–$440.00

Prices given are believed to be accurate at time of publication however, many factors affect retail pricing so exact prices are not possible.

78TH EDITION, 2024 ✛ 489

ORACLE ARMS 2311
Caliber: .9MM. Capacity: 15-, 17- or 21-round magazine. Features: 1911-style platform. Compatible with SIG P320 magazines. Modular grip and magwell. Optics-ready.
Price: With gun lock .... $1,699.00–$2,999.00

PHOENIX ARMS HP22, HP25
Calibers: .22 LR, .25 ACP. Capacities: .22 LR, 10-shot (HP22), .25 ACP, 10-shot (HP25). Barrel: 3 in. Weight: 20 oz. Length: 5.5 in. overall. Grips: Checkered composition. Sights: Blade front, adjustable rear. Features: Single action, exposed hammer; manual hold-open; button magazine release. Available in satin nickel,matte blue finish. Introduced 1993. Made in USA by Phoenix Arms.
Price: With gun lock $162.00
Price: HP Range kit with 5-in. bbl., locking case and
     accessories (1 Mag) $207.00
Price: HP Deluxe Range kit with 3- and 5-in. bbls., 2 mags, case $248.00

REPUBLIC FORGE 1911
Calibers: .45 ACP, 9mm, .38 Super, .40 S&W, 10mm. Features: A manufacturer of custom 1911-style pistols offered in a variety of configurations, finishes and frame sizes, including single- and double-stack models with many options. Made in Texas.
Price: From .... $3,680.00–$4,280.00

ROCK ISLAND ARMORY GI STANDARD SERIES
Calibers: 9mm, .38 Super, .45 ACP. Capacities: 7-, 8-, or 10-round. Grips: Hard rubber or smooth wood. Finish: Parkerized or nickel. Sights: Round post front, fixed rear. Features: 1911 GI-style semi-auto pistol. FS models have 5-in. barrels, MS models have 4.4-in. barrels, CS models have 3.5-in. barrels.
Price: Rock GI Standard FS.................................... $455.00–$510.00
Price: Rock GI Standard MS... $475.00
Price: Rock GI Standard CS $475.00

ROCK ISLAND ARMORY ROCK SERIES
Calibers: 9mm, .38 Super, .45 ACP. Capacities: 7-, 8-, 10-, or 16-round. Grips: Hard rubber or G10 grips. Barrel: 3.6-, 4.25, or 5-inch. Finish: Blued, Duracoat or two-tone finish, matte stainless, or nickel. Sights: Post front, fixed or adjustable rear. Features: 1911-style semi-auto pistol. Rock Ultra has fiber-optic front sight and adjustable rear sight. Some with double-stack magazines.
Price: Rock Standard .... $480.00–$710.00
Price: Rock Ultra.. $610.00–$710.00

ROCK ISLAND ARMORY TCM SERIES
Caliber: .22 TCM. Capacity: 17-round magazine. Barrel: 5 in. Weight: 36 oz. Length: 8.5 in. Grips: Polymer. Sights: Adjustable rear. Features: 1911 platform, chambered for high velocity .22 TCM rimfire cartridge. TAC Ultra

FS comes with interchangeable 9mm barrel.
Price: TCM $640.00
Price: TAC Ultra FS .... $770.00–$830.00

ROCK ISLAND ARMORY PRO MATCH ULTRA SERIES
Caliber: 9mm, .40 S&W, .45 Auto, 10mm. Capacity: 8-, 16-, or 17-round magazine. Barrel: 5 or 6 in. Weight: 40 oz. Length: 8.5 in. Grips: VZ G10. Sights: Fiber-optic front, adjustable rear. Features: Two magazines, upper and lower accessory rails, extended beavertail safety. HC models use double stack magazines.
Price: .... $740.00–$850.00
Price: HC model... $940.00

ROCK ISLAND ARMORY MAPP
Caliber: 9mm. Capacity: 10-round magazine. Barrel: 3.75 or 4.6 in. Browning short recoil action-style pistols with: integrated front sight; snag-free rear sight; DA/SA trigger; thumb safety; polymer frame with accessory rail. FS models has 4.60-inch barrel, MS model has 3.7-inch barrel.
Price: MAPP FS/MS.. $430.00

ROCK ISLAND ARMORY XT22
Calibers: .22 LR, .22 Magnum. Capacities: 10- or 15-round magazine. Barrel: 5 in. Weight: 38 oz. Features: The XT-22 is the only .22 1911 with a forged 4140 steel slide and a one-piece 4140 chrome-moly barrel. Available as a .22/.45 ACP combo.
Price: XT22 Standard $520.00
Price: XT22 Standard Combo.. $770.00
Price: XT22 Magnum $520.00

ROCK ISLAND ARMORY BBR SEIES
Caliber: .380 ACP. Capacity: 7- or 10-round magazine. Barrel: 3.1 or 3.7 inches. Features: Blowback operation. Smaller 1911-A1 design with features identical to full-size model.
Price: .... $345.00–$605.00

ROCK ISLAND ARMORY LI380
Caliber: .380 ACP. Capacity: 8-round magazine. Barrel: 3.5 in. Features: Blowback operation. DA/SA trigger.
Price: $280.00

ROCK ISLAND ARMORY TAC SERIES
Caliber: 9mm, 10mm, or .45 Auto. Capacity: 8-, 14-, 16-, or 17-round magazine. Barrel: 3.62, 4.25, 5, or 5.5 in. Weight: 36-40 oz. Length: 7.1-8.5 in. Grips: VZ G10. Sights: Fiber-optic front, adjustable rear. Features: 1911 platform, two magazines, upper and lower accessory rails, extended beavertail safety, extended dust cover. TAC Ultra models use double-stack magazines.
Price: TAC Standard .... $600.00–$725.00

ROCK ISLAND ARMORY STK100
Caliber: 9mm. Capacity: 17-round magazine. Barrel: 4.5 in. Features: Striker-fire trigger. Metal frame.
Price: $520.00

ROCK ISLAND ARMORY RIA 5.0
Caliber: 9mm. Capacity: 17-round magazine. Barrel: 4.5 inch. Features: Striker-fire trigger. Polymer frame. Patented RVS recoil system that maximizes barrel mass and linear movement for softer felt recoil.
Price: $999.00

ROCK RIVER ARMS LAR-15/LAR-9
Calibers: .223/5.56mm NATO, 9mm. Barrels: 7 in., 10.5 in. Wilson chrome moly, 1:9 twist, A2 flash hider, 1/2x28 thread. Weights: 5.1 lbs. (7-in. barrel), 5.5 lbs. (10.5-in. barrel). Length: 23 in. overall. Stock: Hogue rubber

grip. Sights: A2 front. Features: Forged A2 or A4 upper, single-stage trigger, aluminum free-float tube, one magazine. Similar 9mm Para. LAR-9 also available. From Rock River Arms, Inc.

Price: LAR-15 7 in. A2 AR2115 .... **$1,175.00**
Price: LAR-15 10.5 in. A4 AR2120 .... **$1,055.00**
Price: LAR-9 7 in. A2 9mm2115 .... **$1,320.00**

ROCK RIVER ARMS TACTICAL PISTOL
Caliber: .45 ACP. Features: Standard-size 1911 pistol with rosewood grips, Heinie or Novak sights, Black Cerakote finish.
Price: **$2,200.00**

ROCK RIVER ARMS LIMITED MATCH
Calibers: .45 ACP, 40 S&W, .38 Super, 9mm. Barrel: 5 in. Sights: Adjustable rear, blade front. Finish: Hard chrome. Features: National Match frame with beveled magazine well, front and rear slide serrations, Commander Hammer, G10 grips.
Price: **$3,600.00**

ROCK RIVER ARMS CARRY PISTOL
Caliber: .45 ACP. Barrel: 5 in. Sights: Heinie. Finish: Parkerized. Grips: Rosewood. Weight: 39 oz.
Price: **$1,600.00**

ROCK RIVER ARMS 1911 POLY
Caliber: .45 ACP. Capacity: 7-round magazine. Barrel: 5 in. Weight: 33 oz. Sights: Fixed. Features: Full-size 1911-style model with polymer frame and steel slide.
Price: **$925.00**

RUGER-57
Caliber: 5.7x28mm. Capacity: 20-round magazine. Barrel: 4.94 in. Grips: Textured polymer. Sights: Adjustable rear/fiber-optic front, optic ready. Length: 8.65 in. overall. Weight: 24.5 oz. unloaded. Finish: Black oxide. Features: 1911-style ambidextrous manual safety, Picatinny-style accessory rail, drilled and tapped for optics with adapter plate. Made in the USA.
Price: **$740.00**

RUGER AMERICAN PISTOL
Calibers: 9mm, .45 ACP. Capacities: 10 or 17 (9mm), 10 (.45 ACP). Barrels: 4.2 in. (9), 4.5 in. (.45). Lengths: 7.5 in or 8 in. Weights: 30–31.5 oz. Sights: Novak LoMount Carry 3-Dot. Finish: Stainless steel slide with black Nitride finish. Grip: One-piece ergonomic wrap-around module with adjustable palm swell and trigger reach. Features: Short take-up trigger with positive re-set, ambidextrous mag release and slide stop, integrated trigger safety, automatic sear block system, easy takedown. Introduced in 2016.
Price: **$579.00**

RUGER AMERICAN COMPACT PISTOL
Caliber: 9mm. Barrel: 3.5 in. Features: Compact version of American Pistol with same general specifications.
Price: **$579.00**

RUGER EC9S
Caliber: 9mm. Capacity: 7+1. Barrel: 3.12 in. Grips: Glass-filled nylon. Sights: Fixed. Features: Black glass-filled grip frame. Multiple finishes. Striker-fired operation with smooth trigger pull. Integral safety plus manual safety.
Price: .... **$290.00–$330.00**

RUGER MAX-9
Caliber: 9mm. Capacity: 12+1. Barrel: 3.2 in. Grips: Glass-filled nylon. Sights: Fixed tritium front. Features: Black glass-filled grip frame. Multiple finishes. Striker-fired operation with smooth trigger pull. Integral safety plus manual safety.
Price: .... **$500.00–$520.00**

RUGER SECURITY-9 PRO
Caliber: 9mm. Capacity: 15-round magazine. Barrel: 4 in. Grips: Textured polymer. Sights: Fixed-steel tritium. Length: 7.24 in. overall. Weight: 23.8 oz. unloaded. Finish: Black oxide. Features: Rugged construction with black oxide, through-hardened, alloy-steel slide and barrel and high-performance, glass-filled nylon grip frame. Made in the USA.
Price: **$549.00**

RUGER SECURITY-9 COMPACT PRO
Caliber: 9mm. Capacity: 10-round magazine. Barrel: 3.42 in. Grips: Textured polymer. Sights: Fixed-steel tritium. Length: 6.52 in. overall. Weight: 21.9 oz. unloaded. Finish: Black oxide. Features: Similar to Ruger Security-9 Pro. Precision-machined, hard-coat, anodized aluminum chassis with full-length guide rails. Made in the USA.
Price: **$549.00**

RUGER SECURITY-380
Caliber: .380 Auto. Capacity: 10- or 15-round magazine. Similar to Security-9 but with Lite Rack system, which consists of slide serrations, cocking ears and a lighter recoil spring.
Price: **$369.00**

RUGER SECURITY-9
Caliber: 9mm. Capacity: 10- or 15-round magazine. Barrel: 4 or 3.4 in. Weight: 21 oz. Sights: Drift-adjustable 3-dot. Viridian E-Series Red Laser available. Striker-fired polymer-frame compact model. Uses the same Secure Action as LCP II. Bladed trigger safety plus external manual safety.
Price: **$379.00**
Price: Viridian Laser sight **$439.00**

RUGER LC380
Caliber: .380 ACP. Capacity: 7+1. Barrel: 3.12 in. Grips: Glass-filled nylon. Sights: Adjustable 3-dot. Features: Brushed stainless slide, black glass-filled grip frame, blue alloy barrel finish. Striker-fired operation with smooth trigger pull.
Price: **$560.00**

Prices given are believed to be accurate at time of publication however, many factors affect retail pricing so exact prices are not possible.

78TH EDITION, 2024 ⊕ **491**

RUGER LCP

Caliber: .380. Capacity: 6-round magazine. Barrel: 2.75 in. Weight: 9.4 oz. Length: 5.16 in. Grips: Glass-filled nylon. Sights: Fixed, drift adjustable or integral Crimson Trace Laserguard. MAX model has 10-round magazine.
Price: Blued $280.00
Price: Stainless steel slide... $290.00
Price: Viridian-E Red Laser sight....................................... $350.00
Price: MAX.. $400.00

RUGER LCP II

Caliber: .22 LR. Capacity: 10-round magazine. Barrel: 2.75 in. Weight: 11.2 oz. Length: 5.16 in. Grips: Glass-filled nylon. Sights: Fixed. Features: Lite Rack system. Larger grip frame surface provides better recoil distribution. Finger grip extension included. Improved sights for superior visibility. Sights are integral to the slide, hammer is recessed within slide.
Price: $360.00

RUGER EC9S

Caliber: 9mm. Capacity: 7-shot magazine. Barrel: 3.125 in. Striker-fired polymer frame. Weight: 17.2 oz.
Price: $299.00

RUGER CHARGER

Caliber: .22 LR. Capacity: 15-round BX-15 magazine. Features: Based on famous 10/22 rifle design with pistol grip stock and forend, scope rail, bipod. Black laminate stock. Silent-SR Suppressor available. Add $449. NFA regulations apply. Reintroduced with improvements and enhancements in 2015.
Price: Standard.. $380.00
Price: Takedown $440.00

RUGER MARK IV SERIES

Caliber: .22 LR. Capacity: 10-round magazine. Barrels: 5.5 in, 6.875 in. Target model has 5.5-in. bull barrel, Hunter model 6.88-in. fluted bull, Competition model 6.88-in. slab-sided bull. Weight: 33–46 oz. Grips: Checkered or target laminate. Sights: Adjustable rear, blade or fiber-optic front (Hunter). Features: Updated design of Mark III series with one-button takedown. Introduced 2016. Modern successor of the first Ruger pistol of 1949.
Price: Standard $449.00
Price: Hunter .... $769.00–$799.00
Price: Tactical $600.00

RUGER 22/45 MARK IV PISTOL

Caliber: .22 LR. Features: Similar to other .22 Mark IV autos except has Zytel grip frame that matches angle and magazine latch of Model 1911 .45 ACP pistol. Available in 4.4-, 5.5-in. bull barrels. Comes with extra magazine, plastic case, lock. Molded polymer or replaceable laminate grips. Weight: 25–33 oz. Sights: Adjustable. Updated design of Mark III with one-button takedown. Introduced 2016. LITE models features aluminum barrel sleeve.
Price: Standard... $430.00
Price: Tactical.. $540.00
Price: Lite.. $600.00

RUGER SR22

Caliber: .22 LR. Capacity: 10-round magazine. Barrel: 3.5 or 4.5 in. Weight: 17.5 oz. Length: 6.4 in. Sights: Adjustable 3-dot. Features: Ambidextrous manual safety/decocking lever and mag release. Comes with two interchangeable rubberized grips and two magazines. Black or silver anodized finish. Available with threaded barrel. DA/SA trigger.
Price: Black $439.00
Price: Silver $459.00
Price: Threaded barrel $479.00

RUGER SR1911
Caliber: .45. Capacity: 8-round magazine. Barrel: 5 in. (3.5 in. Officer Model) Weight: 39 oz. Length: 8.6 in., 7.1 in. Grips: Slim checkered hardwood. Sights: Novak LoMount Carry rear, standard front. Features: Based on Series 70 design. Flared and lowered ejection port. Extended mag release, thumb safety and slide-stop lever, oversized grip safety, checkered backstrap on the flat mainspring housing. Comes with one 7-round and one 8-round magazine.
Price: $939.00

RUGER SR1911 OFFICER
Caliber: .45 ACP, 9mm. Capacity: 8-round magazine. Barrel: 3.6 in. Weight: 27 oz. Features: Compact variation of SR1911 Series. Black anodized aluminum frame, stainless slide, skeletonized trigger, Novak 3-dot Night Sights, G10 deluxe checkered G10 grips.
Price: $979.00

SAVAGE 1911
Caliber: .45 ACP, 9mm. Capacity: 8-round magazine. Barrel: 5 in. Weight: 39 oz. Features: 1911 style platform. Multiple finishes. G10 grips.
Price: .... $1,349.00–$1,499.00

SAVAGE STANCE
Calibers: 9mm. Capacity: 7-, 8- or 10-rounds. Barrel: 3-in. Grip: Textured polymer. Sights: 3 white-dot system. Finishes: Cerakote Black, gray or FDE. Features: Polymer frame with chassis system.
Price: $410.00

SCCY CPX
Caliber: 9mm. Capacity: 10-round magazine. Barrel: 3.1 in. Weight: 15 oz. Length: 5.7 in. overall. Grips: Integral with polymer frame. Sights: 3-dot

system, rear adjustable for windage. Features: Zytel polymer frame, steel slide, aluminum alloy receiver machined from bar stock. DAO with consistent 9-pound trigger pull. Concealed hammer. Available with (CPX-1) or without (CPX-2) manual thumb safety. Introduced 2014. CPX-3 is chambered for .380 ACP. Made in USA by SCCY Industries.
Price: CPX-1 .... $284.00
Price: CPX-2 .... $270.00
Price: CPX-3 .... $305.00

SCCY DVG SERIES
Caliber: 9mm. Capacity: 10-round magazine. Barrel: 3.1 in. Weight: 15.5 oz. Length: 6 in. overall. Grips: Integral with polymer frame. Sights: white dot front and optic ready. Features: Zytel polymer frame, steel slide, aluminum alloy receiver machined from bar stock. Striker-fire with 5.5-pound trigger pull. Made in USA.
Price: DVG-1 .... $370.00
Price: DVG-1RDR $399.00
Price: DVG-1RD $470.00

SEECAMP LWS 32/380 STAINLESS DA
Calibers: .32 ACP, .380 ACP. Capacity: 6-round magazine. Barrel: 2 in., integral with frame. Weight: 10.5 oz. Length: 4.125 in. overall. Grips: Glass-filled nylon. Sights: Smooth, no-snag, contoured slide and barrel top. Features: Aircraft quality 17-4 PH stainless steel. Inertia-operated firing pin. Hammer fired DAO. Hammer automatically follows slide down to safety rest position after each shot, no manual safety needed. Magazine safety disconnector. Polished stainless and Cerakote finishes. Introduced 1985.
Price: .32 .... $440.00–$500.00
Price: .380 .... $515.00–$570.00

SIG SAUER 1911
Calibers: .45 ACP. Capacities: 8-round magazine. Barrel: 5 in. Weight: 40.3 oz. Length: 8.65 in. overall. Grips: Checkered wood grips. Sights: Novak night sights. Blade front, drift adjustable rear for windage. Features: Single-action 1911. Hand-fitted dehorned stainless steel frame and slide; match-grade barrel, hammer/sear set and trigger; 25-LPI front strap checkering, 20-LPI mainspring housing checkering. Beavertail grip safety with speed bump, extended thumb safety, firing pin safety and hammer intercept notch. Introduced 2005. XO series has contrast sights, Ergo Grip XT textured polymer grips. STX line available from Sig Sauer Custom Shop; two-tone 1911, non-railed, Nitron slide, stainless frame, burled maple grips. Polished cocking serrations, flat-top slide, mag well. Carry line has Siglite night sights, lanyard attachment point, gray diamondwood or rosewood grips, 8+1 capacity. Compact series has 6+1 capacity, 7.7 OAL, 4.25-in. barrel, slim-profile wood grips, weighs 30.3 oz. Ultra Compact in 9mm or .45 ACP has 3.3-in. barrel, low-profile night sights, slim-profile gray diamondwood or rosewood grips. 6+1 capacity. 1911 C3 is a 6+1 compact .45 ACP, rosewood custom wood grips, two-tone and Nitron finishes. Weighs 30 oz. unloaded, lightweight alloy frame. Length is 7.7 in. Now offered in more than 30 different models with numerous options for frame size, grips, finishes, sight arrangements and other features. From SIG Sauer, Inc.
Price: STX $1,100.00
Price: Fastback Nightmare Carry $1,484.00
Price: Emperor Scorpion Full-Size $1,225.00
Price: Fastback Emperor Scorpion Carry $1,650.00

SIG SAUER P210 CARRY SERIES

Caliber: 9mm. Capacity: 8-round magazine. Barrel: 4.1 or 5 in. Grip: Checkered G10 or wood. Sights: SIGLITE night sights or adjustable. Length: 7.5 in. overall. Weight: 32 ozs. unloaded. Finish: Nitron. Features: Conceal carry version of iconic P210.

Price: Carry.. **$1,299.00**
Price: Target **$1,400.00**

SIG SAUER P220

Caliber: .45 ACP, 10mm. Capacity: 7- or 8-round magazine. Barrel: 4.4 in. Weight: 27.8 oz. Length: 7.8 in. overall. Grips: Checkered black plastic. Sights: Blade front, drift adjustable rear for windage. Optional Siglite night sights. Features: Double action. Stainless steel slide, Nitron finish, alloy frame, M1913 Picatinny rail; safety system of decocking lever, automatic firing pin safety block, safety intercept notch, and trigger bar disconnector. Squared combat-type triggerguard. Slide stays open after last shot. Introduced 1976. P220 SAS Anti-Snag has dehorned stainless steel slide, front Siglite night sight, rounded triggerguard, dust cover, Custom Shop wood grips. Equinox line is Custom Shop product with Nitron stainless slide with a black hard-anodized alloy frame, brush-polished flats and nickel accents. Truglo tritium fiber-optic front sight, rear Siglite night sight, gray laminated wood grips with checkering and stippling. From SIG Sauer, Inc.

Price: Elite **$940.00**
Price: Equinox.. **$1,130.00**
Price: Legion 45 ACP.. **$1,413.00**
Price: Legion 10mm.. **$1,904.00**

SIG SAUER P226

Calibers: 9mm, .40 S&W. Barrel: 4.4 in. Length: 7.7 in. overall. Features: Similar to the P220 pistol except has 4.4-in. barrel, measures 7.7 in. overall, weighs 34 oz. DA/SA or DAO. Many variations available. Snap-on modular grips. Legion series has improved short reset trigger, contoured

and shortened beavertail, relieved triggerguard, higher grip, other improvements. From SIG Sauer, Inc. Five model has SAO trigger. ZEV model comes with red dot optic and threaded barrel.

Price: Nitron **$950.00**
Price: Elite **$1,255.00**
Price: Equinox.. **$1,100.00**
Price: Legion **$1,428.00**
Price: MK25 Navy Version **$1,187.00**
Price: Pro-Cut **$1,330.00**
Price: XFive **$1,430.00**
Price: ZEV **$1,999.00**

SIG SAUER P229

Caliber: Similar to the P220 except chambered for 9mm (10- or 15-round magazines). Barrels: 3.86-in. barrel, 7.1 in. overall length and 3.35 in. height. Weight: 32.4 oz. Features: Introduced 1991. Snap-on modular grips. Frame made in Germany, stainless steel slide assembly made in U.S.; pistol assembled in U.S. Many variations available. Legion series has improved short reset trigger, contoured and shortened beavertail, relieved triggerguard, higher grip, other improvements. Select has Nitron slide, Select G10 grips, Emperor Scorpion has accessory rail, FDE finish, G10 Piranha grips.

Price: Nitron **$870.00**
Price: Elite **$940.00**
Price: Legion **$1,490.00**
Price: M11-A1 .... **$1,030.00**
Price: PRO... **$1,100.00**

SIG SAUER SP2022

Calibers: 9mm. Capacities: 10- or 15-round magazines. Barrel: 3.9 in. Weight: 30.2 oz. Length: 7.4 in. overall. Grips: Composite and rubberized one-piece. Sights: Blade front, rear adjustable for windage. Features: Polymer frame, stainless steel slide; integral frame accessory rail; replaceable steel frame rails; left- or right-handed magazine release, two interchangeable grips.

Price: **$500.00**

SIG SAUER P238

Caliber: .380 ACP. Capacity: 6-round magazine. Barrel: 2.7 in. Weight: 15.4 oz. Length: 5.5 in. overall. Grips: Hogue G-10 and Rosewood grips. Sights: Contrast/Siglite night sights. Features: All-metal beavertail-style frame.

Price: Two Tone **$700.00**

SIG SAUER P320 NITRON

Calibers: 9mm, .45 ACP. Capacities: 15 or 16 rounds. Barrels: 3.6 in. (Subcompact), 3.9 in. (Carry model) or 4.7 in. (Full size). Weights: 26–30 oz. Lengths: 7.2 or 8.0 in overall. Grips: Interchangeable black composite. Sights: Blade front, rear adjustable for windage. Optional Siglite night sights. Features: Striker-fired DAO, Nitron finish slide, black polymer frame. Frame size and calibers are interchangeable. Introduced 2014. Made in USA

Prices given are believed to be accurate at time of publication however, many factors affect retail pricing so exact prices are not possible.

by SIG Sauer, Inc.
Price: Full Size .... $500.00–$585.00
Price: Carry $495.00
Price: Subcompact $600.00

SIG SAUER P320 AXG SERIES
Calibers: 9mm. Capacities: 10 or 17 rounds. Similar to P320 series except with metal frame.
Price: Classic... $1,025.00
Price: Combat $1,035.00

SIG SAUER P320 XCOMPACT SERIES
Calibers: 9mm. Capacities: 10 or 15 rounds. Barrel: 3.6 in. Similar to P320 Compact except with tungsten infused heavy XFULL grip module with a flat skeletonized trigger. Spectre model has a laser-engraved grip module and aggressive slide serrations.
Price: $600.00
Price: Spectre $1,130.00

SIG SAUER MODEL 320 RX SERIES
Caliber: 9mm. Capacity: 17-round magazine. Barrels: 4.7 in. or 3.9 in. Features: Full- and Compact-size models with ROMEO1 Reflex sight, accessory rail, stainless steel frame and slide.
Price: .... $755.00–$830.00

SIG SAUER P365
Caliber: 9mm. Barrel: 3.1 in. Weight: 17.8 oz. Features: Micro-compact striker-fired model with 10-, 12-, or 15-round magazine, stainless steel frame and slide, XRAY-3 day and night sights fully textured polymer grip. ROMEOZero Elite model with red-dot optics. P365X models have XSERIES-style grip module and flat trigger. SAS model has SIG Anti Snag treatment.
Price: P365 NITRON.. $500.00
Price: P365 ROMEOZero Elite $500.00
Price: P365X... $580.00
Price: P365X ROMEOZero Elite $780.00
Price: P365X SAS $585.00

SIG SAUER P365 XL
Caliber: 9mm. Capacity: 12-round magazine. Barrel: 3.7 in. Grips: Textured polymer. Sights: Optic-ready, Day/Night sights. Length: 6.6 in. overall. Weight: 20.7 oz. unloaded. Finish: Nitron. Features: Grip with integrated carry mag well and extended beavertail, flat trigger and optic-ready slide. P365 XL ROMEOZERO model with red-dot optic. X-MACRO model has built-in barrel compensator. Spectre model has a laser engraved grip module and aggressive slide serrations.
Price: P365 XL.. $585.00
Price: P365 XL ROMEOZERO..................................... $785.00
Price: P365 XL X-MACRO $800.00
Price: P365 XL Spectre... $1,030.00

SIG SAUER P365-380
Caliber: .380 Auto. Similar to P365.
Price: P365-380 NITRON $500.00

SIG SAUER M17/M18
Caliber: 9mm. Capacity: 17-round magazine. Barrel: 3.9 in. Grips: Textured polymer. Sights: Siglite front/night rear, optic ready. Length: 7.2 in. overall. Weight: 28.1 oz. unloaded. Finish: Coyote tan. Features: Commercial version of U.S. Military M18, manual thumb safety.
Price: M17 .... $650.00
Price: M18 .... $650.00

SIG SAUER P322
Caliber: .22 LR. Capacity: 10 or 20-round magazine. Barrel: 4 in. Grips: Textured polymer. Sights: Fiber-optic front/adjustable rear or Romeo1Pro red dot. Length: 7 in. Weight: 17.1 oz. unloaded. Finish: Nitron. Ambidextrous controls.
Price: .... $400.00–$550.00

SIG SAUER MPX
Calibers: 9mm. Capacities: 35-round magazine. Barrel: 8 in. Weight: 5 lbs. Features: Semi-auto AR-style gun with closed, fully locked short-stroke pushrod gas system. Copperhead model with 3.5-in. barrel and 20-round magazine.
Price: MPX $1,800.00
Price: MPX Copperhead $1,770.00

SIG SAUER P938
Calibers: 9mm. Capacities: 6-shot mag. Barrel: 3.0 in. Weight: 16 oz. Length: 5.9 in. Grips: Hogue Extreme, Hogue Diamondwood. Sights: Siglite night sights or Siglite rear with Tru-Glo front. Features: Slightly larger version of P238.
Price: BRG.. $600.00
Price: Legion $780.00
Price: SAS... $700.00

SMITH & WESSON CSX SERIES
Calibers: 9mm. Capacities: 10 and 12 rounds. Barrel: 3.1 in. Weights: 19.5 oz. Lengths: 6.1 in. Grips: Polymer. Sights: 3 white-dot system with low-profile rear. Features: Metal alloy frame with stainless steel slide. Ambidextrous controls. Single-action trigger.
Price: $525.00

SMITH & WESSON M&P SHIELD M2.0 SERIES
Calibers: 9mm, .30 Super Carry, .40 S&W, .45 Auto. Capacities: 7- and 8-rounds (9mm), 6- and 7-rounds (.40). Barrel: 3.1-in. Weights: 18.3 oz. Lengths: 6.1 in. Grips: Polymer. Sights: 3 white-dot system with low-profile rear. Finishes: Armornite Black. Features: Polymer frame, micro-compact size. Plus model has .30 Super Carry double stack 12- or 15-round magazine.
Price: .... $505.00–$710.00
Price: Performance Center Edition .... $577.00–$911.00
Price: Plus model.. $515.00

SMITH & WESSON M&P 5.7 SERIES
Calibers: 5.7x28mm. Capacitiy: 22 rounds. Barrels: 5-in. Weights: 26.7 oz. Lengths: 8.5 in. Grips: Polymer. Sights: 3 white-dot system and optic ready. Finish: Armornite Black. Features: Polymer frame with stainless steel slide, barrel and structural components. Flat-face trigger. Picatinny rail.
Price: $680.00

SMITH & WESSON MODEL SD SERIES
Calibers: .40 S&W, 9mm. Capacities: 10+1, 14+1 and 16+1 Barrel: 4 in. Weight: 39 oz. Length: 8.7 in. Grips: Wood or rubber. Sights: Front: Tritium Night Sight, Rear: Steel Fixed 2-Dot. Features: SDT (Self Defense Trigger) for optimal, consistent pull first round to last, standard Picatinny-style rail, slim ergonomic textured grip, textured finger locator and aggressive front and backstrap texturing with front and rear slide serrations.
Price: $380.00

Prices given are believed to be accurate at time of publication however, many factors affect retail pricing so exact prices are not possible.

78TH EDITION, 2024 ✦ 495

SMITH & WESSON SDVE SERIES
Similar to SD Series except with stainless steel slide.
Price: $380.00

SMITH & WESSON MODEL SW1911
Calibers: .45 ACP, 9mm. Capacities: 8 rounds (.45), 7 rounds (subcompact .45), 10 rounds (9mm). Barrels: 3, 4.25, 5 in. Weights: 26.5–41.7 oz. Lengths: 6.9–8.7 in. Grips: Wood, wood laminate or synthetic. Crimson Trace Lasergrips available. Sights: Low-profile white dot, tritium night sights or adjustable. Finish: Black matte, stainless or two-tone. Features: Offered in three different frame sizes. Skeletonized trigger. Accessory rail on some models. Compact models have round-butt frame. Pro Series have 30 LPI checkered frontstrap, oversized external extractor, extended mag well, full-length guide rod, ambidextrous safety.
Price: Standard Model E Series, From $890.00
Price: Pro Series $1,280.00
Price: Scandium Frame E Series $1,290.00

SMITH & WESSON BODYGUARD 380
Caliber: .380 Auto. Capacity: 6+1. Barrel: 2.75 in. Weight: 11.85 oz. Length: 5.25 in. Grips: Polymer. Sights: Integrated laser plus drift-adjustable front and rear. Features: The frame of the Bodyguard is made of reinforced polymer, as is the magazine base plate and follower, magazine catch and trigger. The slide, sights and guide rod are made of stainless steel, with the slide and sights having a Melonite hardcoating.
Price: .... $345.00–$480.00

SMITH & WESSON PERFORMANCE CENTER M&P380 SHIELD EZ
Caliber: .380 ACP. Capacity: 8-round magazine. Barrel: 3.67 in. Grips: Textured polymer. Sights: Fixed, HI-VIZ Litewave H3 Tritium/Litepipe. Length: 6.8 in. overall. Weight: 23 oz. unloaded. Finish: Black Armornite frame and black, silver or gold accents. Features: Easy to rack slide, grip safety, manual thumb safety, accessory rail, reversible magazine release, ported barrel and lightening cuts in slide.
Price: .... $385.00–$560.00

SMITH & WESSON PERFORMANCE CENTER M&P9 AND M&P40 M2.0 C.O.R.E. PRO SERIES
Calibers: 9mm, .40 S&W. Capacity: 17-round (9mm) or 15-round (.40 S&W) magazine. Barrel: 4.25 or 5 in. Grips: Four interchangeable palm-swell inserts. Sights: Fixed, tall 3-dot/C.O.R.E. optics-ready system. Length: 7.5-8.5 in. overall. Weight: 23-27.2 oz. unloaded. Finish: Black Armornite. Features: Accessory rail, reversible magazine release and tuned action with audible trigger reset.
Price: 4.25-in. barrel.. $700.00
Price: 5-in. barrel... $721.00

SMITH & WESSON PERFORMANCE CENTER M&P9 AND M&P40 M2.0 PORTED SERIES
Calibers: 9mm, .40 S&W. Capacity: 17-round (9mm) or 15-round (.40 S&W) magazine. Barrel: 4.25 or 5 in. Grips: Four interchangeable palm-swell inserts. Sights: Fixed, fiber-optic front and rear. Length: 8.5 in. overall. Weight: 23 oz. unloaded. Finish: Black Armornite. Features: Accessory rail, reversible magazine release, ported barrel and slide and tuned action with audible trigger reset.
Price: 4.25-in. barrel.. $700.00
Price: 5-in. barrel... $721.00

SMITH & WESSON PERFORMANCE CENTER M&P9 AND M&P40 M2.0 PORTED C.O.R.E. SERIES
Calibers: 9mm, .40 S&W. Capacity: 17-round (9mm) or 15-round (.40 S&W) magazine. Barrel: 4.25 or 5 in. Grips: Four interchangeable palm-swell inserts. Sights: Fixed, tall 3-dot/C.O.R.E. optics-ready system. Length: 8.5 in. overall. Weight: 23 oz. unloaded. Finish: Black Armornite. Features: Accessory rail, reversible magazine release, oversized slide release, ported barrel and slide, and tuned action with audible trigger reset.
Price: 4.25-in. barrel.. $714.00
Price: 5-in. barrel... $735.00

SMITH & WESSON SHIELD EZ M2.0
Caliber: 9mm or 30 Super Carry. Capacity: 8-round (9mm) 10-round (30 Super Carry) magazine. Barrel: 3.67 in. Grips: Textured polymer. Sights: Fixed, 3-dot. Length: 6.8 in. overall. Weight: 23.2 oz. unloaded. Finish: Black Armornite. Features: Accessory rail and reversible magazine release, with or without manual thumb safety.
Price: $440.00

Prices given are believed to be accurate at time of publication however, many factors affect retail pricing so exact prices are not possible.

SPHINX SDP
Caliber: 9mm. Capacity: 15-shot magazine. Barrel: 3.7 in. Weight: 27.5 oz. Length: 7.4 in. Sights: Defiance Day & Night Green fiber/tritium front, tritium 2-dot red rear. Features: DA/SA with ambidextrous decocker, integrated slide position safety, aluminum MIL-STD 1913 Picatinny rail, Blued alloy/steel or stainless. Aluminum and polymer frame, machined steel slide. Offered in several variations. Made in Switzerland and imported by Kriss USA.
Price: From **$999.00**

SPRINGFIELD ARMORY 1911 GARRISON
Calibers:.45 ACP. Capacity: 7-round magazine. Barrel: 5 in. Grips: Thinline checkered wood. Sights: Low profile, 3-dot. Length: 8.4 in. overall. Weight: 37 oz. unloaded. Finish: Blued or stainless. Features: Heirloom quality 1911.
Price: Blued **$730.00**
Price: Stainless **$760.00**

SPRINGFIELD ARMORY 1911 DS PRODIGY
Caliber: 9mm. Capacity: 17- and 20-round magazine. Barrel: 4.25 or 5 in. Weight: 32.5 or 34 oz. Length: 7.8 or 8.6 in. overall. Double-stack magazine 1911 platform. Sights: Fiber-optic front, black serrated rear, optics-ready. Some models with HEX Dragonfly red dot. Ambidextrous safety. Picatinny rail.
Price: Standard model....................................... **$1,470.00**
Price: HEX optic **$1,700.00**

SPRINGFIELD ARMORY 1911 EMISSARY
Calibers: 9mm or .45 ACP. Capacity: 7-round (.45 ACP) or 9-round (9mm) magazine. Barrel: 4.25- or 5-in. Grips: Textured G10. Sights: Tactical Rack rear/tritium front sights. Length: 8.4 in. overall. Weight: 40 oz. unloaded. Finish: Two-tone, black slide/stainless frame. Features: Square triggerguard, custom milled slide, flat trigger.
Price: .... **.$1,150.00**

SPRINGFIELD ARMORY EMP ENHANCED MICRO
Calibers: 9mm. Capacity: 9-round magazine. Barrel: 3-inch stainless steel match grade, fully supported ramp, bull. Weight: 26 oz. Length: 6.5 in. overall. Grips: Thinline cocobolo hardwood. Sights: Fixed low-profile combat rear, dovetail front, 3-dot tritium. Features: Two 9-round stainless steel magazines with slam pads, long aluminum match-grade trigger adjusted to 5 to 6 lbs., forged aluminum alloy frame, black hardcoat anodized finish; dual spring full-length guide rod, forged satin-finish stainless steel slide. Introduced 2007.
Price: **$1,100.00**

SPRINGFIELD ARMORY HELLCAT 3" MICRO COMPACT
Caliber: 9mm. Capacity: 11- and 13-round magazine. Barrel: 3 in. Grip: Textured polymer. Sights: Fixed, Tritium/Luminescent front, Tactical Rack U-Notch rear. Length: 6 in. overall. Weight: 18.3 oz. unloaded with flush magazine. Finish: Matte black or Desert FDE. Features: Dual captive recoil spring w/ full-length guide rod. With or without manual thumb safety.

Price: **$500.00**
Price: OSP with Optical Sight mount **$520.00**

SPRINGFIELD ARMORY HELLCAT PRO
Caliber: 9mm. Capacity: 15-round magazine. Barrel: 3.7 in. Grip: Textured polymer. Sights: Fixed, Tritium/Luminescent front, Tactical Rack U-Notch rear. Length: 6.6 in. overall. Weight: 21 oz. unloaded. Finish: Matte black or Desert FDE. Features: Dual captive recoil spring w/ full-length guide rod.
Price: **$500.00**
Price: OSP with Optical Sight mount **$630.00**

SPRINGFIELD ARMORY HELLCAT RDP (RAPID DEFENSE PACKAGE)
Caliber: 9mm. Capacity: 11- and 13-round magazine. Barrel: 3.8 in. Grip: Textured polymer. Sights: Fixed, Springfield Armory HEX micro red dot. Length: 7 in. overall. Weight: 19.3 oz. unloaded with flush magazine. Finish: Matte black. Features: Self-indexing single port compensator, with or without manual thumb safety.
Price: **$899.00**

SPRINGFIELD ARMORY XD SERIES
Calibers: 9mm, .40 S&W, .45 ACP. Barrels: 3, 4, 5 in. Weights: 20.5-31 oz. Lengths: 6.26-8 overall. Grips: Textured polymer. Sights: Varies by model; Fixed sights are dovetail front and rear steel 3-dot units. Features: Three sizes in X-Treme Duty (XD) line: Sub-Compact (3-in. barrel), Service (4-in. barrel), Tactical (5-in. barrel). Three ported models available. Ergonomic polymer frame, hammer-forged barrel, no-tool disassembly, ambidextrous magazine release, visual/tactile loaded chamber indicator, visual/tactile striker status indicator, grip safety, XD gear system included. Compact is shipped with one extended magazine (13) and one compact magazine (10). XD Mod.2 Sub-Compact has newly contoured slide and redesigned serrations, stippled grip panels, fiber-optic front sight.
Price: Sub-Compact .... **$380.00–$420.00**
Price: Compact .... **$480.00–$520.00**
Price: Service .... **$480.00–$520.00**
Price: Tactical... **$480.00–$520.00**

SPRINGFIELD ARMORY XD(M) ELITE SERIES
Calibers: 9mm, 10mm, .45 ACP. Barrels: 3.8, 4.5, or 5.2 in. Sights: Fiber-optic front with interchangeable red and green filaments, fixed rear and

Prices given are believed to be accurate at time of publication however, many factors affect retail pricing so exact prices are not possible.

78TH EDITION, 2024 ✦ 497

optic ready or HEX Dragonfly red-dot optic. Grips: Integral polymer with three optional backstrap designs. Removable magwell. Features: Variation of XD design with improved ergonomics, deeper and longer slide serrations, slightly modified grip contours and texturing. Black polymer frame, forged steel slide. Available with compact or full size grip. Precision model with 5.2-in. barrel.

Price: Compact .... **$510.00–$550.00**
Price: Service .... **$600.00–$665.00**
Price: Precision models **$570.00**
Price: Threaded-barrel models **$600.00**

SPRINGFIELD ARMORY MIL-SPEC 1911A1

Caliber: .45 ACP. Capacity: 7-round magazine. Barrel: 5 in. Weights: 35.6–39 oz. Lengths: 8.5–8.625 in. overall. Finish: Stainless steel. Features: Similar to Government Model military .45.

Price: Mil-Spec Parkerized, 7+1, 35.6 oz. **$785.00**
Price: Mil-Spec Stainless Steel, 7+1, 36 oz. **$889.00**

SPRINGFIELD ARMORY 1911 LOADED

Caliber: .45 ACP. Capacity: 7-round magazine. Barrel: 5 in. Weight: 34 oz. Length: 8.6 in. overall. Similar to Mil-Spec 1911A1 with the following additional features: Lightweight Delta hammer, extended and ergonomic beavertail safety, ambidextrous thumb safety, and other features depending on the specific model. MC, Marine, LB and Lightweight models have match-grade barrels, low-profile 3-dot combat sights.

Price: Parkerized **$950.00**
Price: Stainless **$1,004.00**
Price: MC Operator (shown) **$1,308.00**
Price: Marine Operator **$1,308.00**
Price: LB Operator **$1,409.00**
Price: Lightweight Operator **$1,210.00**
Price: 10mm TRP (Trijicon RMR Red Dot Sight) **$2,238.00**

SPRINGFIELD ARMORY TRP

Caliber: .45 ACP. Features: Similar to 1911A1, except checkered frontstrap and mainspring housing, Novak Night Sight combat rear sight and matching dovetailed front sight, tuned, polished extractor, oversize barrel link;

lightweight speed trigger and combat action job, match barrel and bushing, extended ambidextrous thumb safety and fitted beavertail grip safety. Textured G10 grips. Finish: Blued or stainless.

Price: **$1,695.00**
Price: Adjustable rear sight and rail **$1,780.00**

SPRINGFIELD ARMORY RONIN OPERATOR

Calibers: 9mm, 10mm, or .45 ACP. Capacity: 7-round (.45 ACP) or 9-round (9mm) magazine. Barrel: 3-, 4-, 4.25- or 5-in. Grips: Checkered wood. Sights: Fiber-optic front, tactical rack, white-dot rear. Length: 8.6 in. overall. Weight: 40 oz. unloaded. Finish: Two-tone, black slide/stainless frame.

Price: **849.00**
Price: Ronin 4.25 in. **$899.00**
Price: Ronin EMP **$899.00**

SPRINGFIELD ARMORY SA-35

Calibers: 9mm. Capacity: 13-round magazine. Barrel: 4.7 in. Grips: Checkered walnut. Sights: White dot front, tactical-rack rear. Length: 7.8 in. overall. Weight: 31.5 oz. unloaded. Finish: Matte blued. Features: Clone of Iconic Hi-Power pistol.

Price: **$699.00**

STACCATO 2011 SERIES

Calibers: 9mm, .40 S&W, .38 Super. Capacity: 9-, 17- or 21-round magazine. Barrels: 3.9- or 5-in., match-grade. Sights: Optic-ready, Dawson Precision Perfect Impact. Weight: 38–46.5 oz. Finish: Carbon black. Grips: Textured polymer. Features: 4-lb. trigger pull, ambidextrous safety levers, single- or double-stack magazine.

Price: Staccato-C **$1,620.00**
Price: Staccato-C2 .... **$1,955.00**
Price: Staccato-P **$1,790.00**
Price: Staccato-XC **$3,655.00**
Price: Staccato-XL **$2,910.00**

STANDARD MANUFACTURING 1911 SERIES

Caliber: .45 ACP. Capacity: 7-round magazine. Barrel: 5-inch stainless steel match grade. Weight: 38.4 oz. Length: 8.6 in. Grips: Checkered rosewood double diamond. Sights: Fixed, Warren Tactical blade front/U-notch rear. Finish: Blued, case color, or nickel. Features: Forged frame and slide, beavertail grip safety, extended magazine release and thumb safety, checkered mainspring housing and front grip strap.

Price: Blued **$1,295.00**
Price: Blued, Engraved **$1,579.00**
Price: Case Color **$1,599.00**
Price: Case Color, Engraved **$1,899.00**
Price: Nickel **$1,499.00**

STEYR L9-A2 MF
Calibers: 9mm. Capacities: 10 or 17-round. Barrels: 4.5 in. Weight: 27.2 oz. Sights: Trapizoid. Grips: Polymer, textured grip modules. Features: DAO striker-fired operation.
Price: **$655.00**

STOEGER STR-9 COMPACT
Caliber: 9mm. Capacity: 13-round magazine. Barrel: 3.8 in. Grips: Three interchangeable backstraps. Sights: 3-dot sights or tritium night sights. Length: 6.9 in. overall. Weight: 24 oz. unloaded. Finish: Matte black. Features: Compact version of the STR-9 striker-fire pistol. Aggressive forward and rear slide serrations and accessory rail. Made in Turkey.
Price: STR-9 .... **$280.00–$399.00**
Price: STR-9S Combat **$515.00**

TAURUS G2 SERIES
Caliber: 9mm. Capacity: 6+1. Barrel: 3.2 in. Weight: 20 oz. Length: 6.3 in. Sights: Adjustable rear, fixed front. Features: Double/Single Action, polymer frame in blue with matte black or stainless slide, accessory rail, manual and trigger safeties. S models have single-stack magazines, C models have double-stack magazines.
Price: C models................................... **$270.00–$290.00**
Price: S models.................................... **$255.00–$265.00**

TAURUS G3 SERIES
Caliber: 9mm. Capacity: 17-round magazine. Barrel: 4.0-in. Grip: Textured polymer. Sights: White dot front, notch rear. Length: 7.28 in. overall. Weight: 24.8 oz. unloaded. Finish: Matte black, gray, tan. Features: Re-strike trigger, accessory rail.
Price: **$310.00**
Price: T.O.R.O. **$420.00**
Price: G3c compact **$310.00**
Price: G3X **$315.00**

TAURUS GX4 SERIES
Caliber: 9mm. Capacity: 10, 11, and 13-round magazines. Barrel: 3.0-in. Grip: Textured polymer with modular backstrap. Sights: White dot front, notch rear. Length: 7.28 in. overall. Weight: 18.5 oz. unloaded. Finish: Matte black. Striker-fire trigger. T.O.R.O. model comes with red-dot optic. XL models have 3.7-in. barrels.
Price: GX4................................... **$330.00**
Price: GX4 T.O.R.O. **$400.00**
Price: GX4 XL.............................. **$430.00**
Price: GX4 XL T.O.R.O. **$460.00**

TAURUS TH SERIES
Caliber: 9mm or .40 S&W. Capacity: 13 or 17 round (9mm), 11 or 15 round (.40 S&W). Barrel: 3.5 or 4.3 in. Weight: 28 oz. Length: 7.7 in. Sights: Novak drift adjustable. Features: Full-size 9mm double-stack model with SA/DA action. Polymer frame has integral grips with finger grooves and stippling panels. C model has 3.8-in. barrel, 6.8-in. overall length.
Price: **$345.00**

TAURUS TX22
Caliber: .22 LR. Capacity: 10- or 16-round magazine. Barrel: 4.1-in. Grip: Textured polymer, wrap around. Sights: Adjustable rear, white dot front. Length: 7.06 in. overall. Weight: 17.3 oz. unloaded. Finish: Matte black to tan. Compact model has 3.06-in. barrel.
Price: Standard model.............................. **$300.00**
Price: Compact model.............................. **$450.00**

TAURUS MODEL 1911
Calibers: 9mm, .45 ACP. Capacities: .45 ACP 8+1, 9mm 9+1. Barrel: 5 in. Weight: 33 oz. Length: 8.5 in. Grips: Checkered black. Sights: Heinie straight 8. Features: SA. Blued, stainless steel, duotone blue and blue/gray finish. Standard/Picatinny rail, standard frame, alloy frame and alloy/Picatinny rail. Introduced in 2007. Imported from Brazil by Taurus International. Commander model has a 4.25-in. barrel. Officer model has a 3.2-in. barrel.
Price: 1911B, Blue **$580.00**
Price: 1911SS, Stainless Steel **$730.00**
Price: 1911SS-1, Stainless Steel w/rail........ **$750.00**
Price: 1911 Commander **$580.00**
Price: 1911 Officer **$580.00**

TAURUS MODEL 92

Caliber: 9mm. Capacity: 17-round magazine. Barrel: 5 in. Weight: 34 oz. Length: 8.5 in. overall. Grips: Checkered rubber. Sights: Fixed notch rear. 3-dot sight system. Also offered with micrometer-click adjustable night sights. Features: Beretta Model 92 platform. DA, ambidextrous 3-way hammer drop safety, allows cocked and locked carry. Blued, stainless steel, blued with gold highlights, stainless steel with gold highlights, forged aluminum frame, integral key-lock. Imported from Brazil by Taurus International.

Price: 92B **$433.00**
Price: 92SS **$550.00**

TISAS 1911 SERIES

Calibers: 9mm, 10mm, or .45 ACP. Capacity: 7-round (.45 ACP) or 9-round (9mm) magazine. Barrel: 4.25- or 5-in. Grips: Checkered wood, G10. Sights: Ramp front, low-profile rear. Length: 8.5 in. overall. Weight: 39.5 oz. unloaded. Finish: Hard chrome, stainless, parkerized, or blued.

Price: .... **$550.00–$1,000.00**

TRISTAR AMERICAN CLASSIC II 1911

Calibers: 9mm, 10mm, or .45 ACP. Capacity: 7-round (.45 ACP) or 9-round (9mm) magazine. Barrel: 4.25- or 5-in. Grips: Checkered wood. Sights: Ramp front, low-profile rear. Length: 8.5 in. overall. Weight: 39.5 oz. unloaded. Finish: Hard chrome or blued.

Price: **$810.00**
Price: Commander **$730.00**
Price: Trophy **$945.00**

TURNBULL MODEL 1911

Caliber: .45 ACP. Features: An accurate reproduction of 1918-era Model 1911 pistol. Forged slide with appropriate shape and style. Late-style sight with semi-circle notch. Early-style safety lock with knurled undercut thumb piece. Short, wide checkered spur hammer. Hand-checkered double diamond American Black Walnut grips. Hand-polished with period correct Carbonia charcoal bluing. Custom-made to order with many options. Made in the USA by Doug Turnbull Manufacturing Co.

Price: From **$2,625.00**

WALTHER PK380

Caliber: .380 ACP. Capacity: 8-round magazine. Barrel: 3.66 in. Weight: 19.4 oz. Length: 6.5 in. Sights: Three-dot system, drift adjustable rear. Features: DA with external hammer, ambidextrous mag release and manual safety. Picatinny rail. Black frame with black or nickel slide.

Price: **$390.00**
Price: Nickel slide **$440.00**
Price: Laser **$440.00**

WALTHER PDP SERIES

Caliber: 9mm. Capacity: 18-round magazine. Barrel: 4, 4.5 or 5 in. Grip: Textured polymer, modular backstrap. Sights: 3-dot, optics ready. Length: 8 in. overall. Weight: 25.4 ozs. unloaded. Finish: Black. Features: Accessory rail. Compact model has a 15-round magazine, 4-in. barrel.

Price: Full Size... **$595.00**
Price: Compact **$599.00**

WALTHER PDP F-SERIES

Caliber: 9mm. Capacity: 15-round magazine. Barrel: 3.5 or 4 in. Grip: Textured polymer, modular backstrap. Sights: 3-dot, optics ready. Length: 7.25 in. (4-in. barrel) overall. Weight: 24 ozs. (4-in. barrel) unloaded. Finish: Black. Features: Accessory rail. Reduced grip circumference, trigger reach, and slide force.

Price: **$600.00**

WALTHER PPK, PPK/S

Caliber: .380 ACP. Capacities: 6+1 (PPK), 7+1 (PPK/s). Barrel: 3.3 in. Weight: 21-26 oz. Length: 6.1 in. Grips: Checkered plastic. Sights: Fixed. New production in 2019. Made in Fort Smith, AR with German-made slide.

Price: PPK **$570.00**
Price: PPK/S.. **$730.00**

WALTHER PPQ 22 M2

Calibers: .22 LR. Capacities: 10 or 12 rounds. Barrels: 4 or 5 in. Weight: 19 oz. Lengths: 7.1, 8.1 in. Sights: Drift-adjustable. Features: Quick Defense trigger, firing pin block, ambidextrous slidelock and mag release, Picatinny rail. Comes with two interchangeable frame backstraps and hard case.

Price: M2 .22 .... **$385.00**
Price: M2 .22 Tactical **$430.00**

WALTHER CCP M2

Caliber: 9mm. Capacity: 8-round magazine. Barrel: 3.5 in. Weight: 22 oz. Length: 6.4 in. Features: Thumb-operated safety, reversible mag release, loaded chamber indicator. Delayed blowback gas-operated action provides less recoil and muzzle jump, and easier slide operation. Available in all black or black/stainless two-tone finish.

Price: From .... **$470.00–$490.00**

WALTHER PPS M2 SERIES

Caliber: 9mm. Capacity: 6-, 7- or 8-round magazine. Barrel: 3.2 in. Sights: Optic-ready, fixed 3-dot, fixed 3-dot tritium or Crimson Trace Laserguard. Weight: 19.4 oz. Length: 6.3 in. Finish: Carbon black. Grips: Textured polymer. Features: Striker-fire, 6.1-lb. trigger pull.

Price: .... **$450.00–$550.00**

WALTHER P22

Caliber: .22 LR. Barrel: 3.4 in. Weight: 19.6 oz. Length: 6.26 in. Sights: Interchangeable white dot, front, 2-dot adjustable, rear. Features: A rimfire version of the Walther P99 pistol, available in nickel slide with black frame, Desert Camo or Digital Pink Camo frame with black slide.

Price: From **$300.00**
Price: Nickel slide/black frame, or black slide/camo frame **$320.00**
Price: Laser **$320.00**

WALTHER Q4 STEEL FRAME

Caliber: 9mm. Capacity: 15-round magazine. Barrel: 4 in. Grips: Textured polymer, wrap around. Sights: 3-dot night. Length: 7.4 in. overall. Weight: 39.7 oz. unloaded. Finish: Matte black Tenifer. Features: Duty optimized beaver tail, Quick Defense trigger, accessory rail, oversized controls.

Price: **$1,399.00**

WALTHER P99 AS FINAL EDITION

Caliber: 9mm. Capacity: 15-round magazine. Barrel: 3.2 in. Sights: Fixed 3-dot. Weight: 24 oz. Length: 7.1 in. Finish: Two-tone OD green/black. Features: Striker-fire.

Price: **$840.00**

WALTHER Q4 STEEL FRAME

Caliber: 9mm. Capacity: 15-round magazine. Barrel: 4 in. Grips: Textured polymer, wraparound. Sights: 3-dot night and optics-ready. Length: 7.4 in. overall. Weight: 39.7 oz. unloaded. Finish: Matte black Tenifer. Features: Duty-optimized beaver tail, Quick Defense trigger, accessory rail, oversized controls.

Price: **$1,480.00**

WALTHER WMP

Caliber: .22 WMR. Barrel: 4.5 in. Weight: 27.8 oz. Length: 8.2 in. Sights: Fiber-optic front, adjustable, rear and optics-ready.

Price: **$500.00**

WILSON COMBAT ELITE SERIES

Calibers: 9mm, .38 Super, .40 S&W; .45 ACP. Barrel: Compensated 4.1-in. hand-fit, heavy flanged cone match grade. Weight: 36.2 oz. Length: 7.7 in. overall. Grips: Cocobolo. Sights: Combat Tactical yellow rear tritium inserts, brighter green tritium front insert. Features: High-cut frontstrap, 30 LPI checkering on frontstrap and flat mainspring housing, High-Ride Beavertail grip safety. Dehorned, ambidextrous thumb safety, extended ejector, skeletonized ultralight hammer, ultralight trigger, Armor-Tuff finish on frame and slide. Introduced 1997. Made in USA by Wilson Combat. This manufacturer offers more than 100 different 1911 models ranging in price from about $2,800 to $5,000. XTAC and Classic 6-in. models shown. Prices show a small sampling of available models.

Price: Classic, From.. **$3,300.00**
Price: CQB, From **$2,865.00**
Price: Hackathorn Special.. **$3,750.00**
Price: Tactical Carry **$3,750.00**
Price: Tactical Supergrade **$5,045.00**
Price: Bill Wilson Carry Pistol **$3,850.00**
Price: Ms. Sentinel.. **$3,875.00**
Price: Hunter 10mm, .460 Rowland **$4,100.00**
Price: Beretta Brigadier Series, From.................................. **$1,195.00**
Price: X-Tac Series, From **$2,760.00**
Price: Texas BBQ Special, From.. **$4,960.00**

Prices given are believed to be accurate at time of publication however, many factors affect retail pricing so exact prices are not possible.

78TH EDITION, 2024 ✦ 501

BROWNING BUCK MARK PLUS VISION AMERICANA SUPPRESSOR READY

Caliber: .22 LR. Capacity: 10-round magazine. Barrel: 5.875-in. Grip: UFX rubber overmolded grips. Sights: Optics-ready, adjustable Pro-Target with fiber-optic front sight. Length: 9.9 in. overall. Weight: 27 oz. unloaded. Finish: anodized red, white and blue. Features: Blowback operating system, aluminum barrel sleeve with lightening cuts, removable muzzle brake.

Price: **$799.00**

BROWNING BUCK MARK PLUS VISION BLACK/GOLD SUPPRESSOR READY

Caliber: .22 LR. Capacity: 10-round magazine. Barrel: 5.875-in. Grip: UFX rubber overmolded grips. Sights: Optics-ready, adjustable Pro-Target with fiber-optic front sight. Length: 9.9 in. overall. Weight: 27 oz. unloaded. Finish: anodized black and gold. Features: Blowback operating system, aluminum barrel sleeve with lightening cuts, removable muzzle brake.

Price: **$749.00**

CHIAPPA FAS 6007

Caliber: .22 LR. Capacity: 5-round magazine. Barrel: 5.63 in. Weight: 36.8 oz. Length: 13.3 in. Grips: Adjustable right-hand wood. Sights: 2-position front, adjustable target rear. Features: Aluminum receiver. Adjustable trigger.

Price: **$1,600.00**

COLT COMPETITION SERIES

Calibers: .45 ACP, .38 Super or 9mm Para. Full-size Government Model with a 5-in. national match barrel, dual-spring recoil operating system, adjustable rear and fiber-optic front sights, custom G10 Colt logo grips blued or stainless steel finish.

Price: Blued finish.. **$949.00**
Price: Stainless steel **$999.00**
Price: 38 Super **$1,099.00**

COLT SERIES 70 GOLD CUP SERIES

Caliber: .38 Super, 9mm or .45 ACP. Barrel: 5 in. national match. Weight: 37 oz. Length: 8.5 in. Grips: Checkered walnut with gold medallions or blue G10. Sights: Adjustable Bomar rear, target post front. Finish: blued or matte stainless. Features: Flat top slide, flat mainspring housing. Wide three-hole aluminum trigger. Built on the Series 70 firing system.

Price: Trophy model .... **$1,180.00–$1,650.00**
Price: National Match model.. **$1,250.00–$1,300.00**

CZ 75 TS 2 SERIES

Caliber: 9mm or .40 S&W. Capacity: 17- or 20-round magazine. Barrel: 5.28 in. Weight: 48.5 oz. Length: 8.86 in. overall. Features: The handgun is built by CZ's Custom Shop. Ergonomic blue aluminum grip. Adjustable sights. TS 2 Orange is designed for competing in the IPSC Standard division and USPSA Limited division.

Price: **$1,500.00**
Price: TS 2 Orange **$2,100.00**

CZ ACCUSHADOW 2

Calibers: 9mm. Capacities: 17-round magazines. Barrel: 4.89 in. Features: Similar to Shadow 2 except with 1911-style AccuBushing for enhanced accuracy.

Price: **$2,050.00**

CZ P-10 F COMPETITION READY

Caliber: 9mm. Capacity: 19-round magazine. Barrel: 5 in. Sights: Fiber-optic front, fixed rear; optics-ready. Length: 8.5 in. overall. Weight: 30 oz. unloaded. Finish: Nitride black with gold accents. Features: Striker-fire trigger.

Price: **$855.00**

CZ SHADOW 2 SERIES

Caliber: 9mm. Capacity: 17-round magazine. Barrel: 4.89 in. Grips: Textured blue aluminum. Sights: Fiber-optic front, HAJO rear. Length: 8.53 in. overall. Weight: 46.5 oz. unloaded. Finish: Nitride black. Features: Single-action only or DA/SA trigger. Swappable magazine release with adjustable, extended button with three settings. Ambidextrous manual thumb safety.

Price: **$1,235.00**

KIMBER SUPER MATCH II

Caliber: .45 ACP. Capacity: 8-round magazine. Barrel: 5 in. Weight: 38 oz. Length: 8.7 in. overall. Grips: Rosewood double diamond. Sights: Blade front, Kimber fully adjustable rear. Features: Guaranteed to shoot 1-in. groups at 25 yards. Stainless steel frame, black KimPro slide; two-piece magazine well; premium aluminum match-grade trigger; 30 LPI frontstrap checkering; stainless match-grade barrel; ambidextrous safety; special Custom Shop markings. Introduced 1999. Made in USA by Kimber Mfg., Inc.

Price: **$2,313.00**

Prices given are believed to be accurate at time of publication however, many factors affect retail pricing so exact prices are not possible.

RUGER AMERICAN COMPETITION
Caliber: 9mm. Capacity: 17-round magazine. Barrel: 5 in. Grips: Three interchangeable grip inserts. Sights: Adjustable rear, fiber-optic front, optic ready. Length: 8.3 in. overall. Weight: 34.1 oz. unloaded. Finish: Black Nitrite. Features: Slide is drilled and tapped for mounting red-dot reflex optics, ported stainless steel slide. Made in the USA.
Price: $575.00

RUGER MARK IV COMPETITION
Caliber: .22 LR. Capacity: 10-round magazine. Barrel: 6.8-in. slab-side heavy bull. Weight: 45.8 oz. Grips: Checkered laminate. Sights: .125 blade front, micro-click adjustable rear. Features: Loaded Chamber indicator; integral lock, magazine disconnect.
Price: Stainless.. $790.00

RUGER MARK IV TARGET
Caliber: .22 LR. Capacity: 10-round magazine. Barrel: 5.5- or 10-in. heavy bull. Weight: 35.6 oz. Grips: Checkered synthetic or laminate. Sights: .125 blade front, micro-click rear, adjustable for windage and elevation. Features: Loaded Chamber indicator; integral lock, magazine disconnect. Plastic case with lock included.
Price: Blued .... $540.00–$510.00
Price: Stainless .... $680.00–$710.00

RUGER SR1911 TARGET
Calibers: 9mm, 10mm, .45 ACP. Capacities: .45 and 10mm (8-round magazine), 9mm (9 shot). Barrel: 5 in. Weight: 39 oz. Sights: Bomar adjustable. Grips: G10 Deluxe checkered. Features: Skeletonized hammer and trigger, satin stainless finish. Introduced in 2016.
Price: $1,019.00

RUGER SR1911 COMPETITION
Calibers: 9mm. Capacities: .10+1. Barrel: 5 in. Weight: 39 oz. Sights: Fiber-optic front, adjustable target rear. Grips: Hogue Piranha G10 Deluxe checkered. Features: Skeletonized hammer and trigger, satin stainless finish, hand-fitted frame and slide, competition trigger, competition barrel with polished feed ramp. From Ruger Competition Shop. Introduced in 2016.
Price: $2,499.00

SIG SAUER P320 X SERIES
Calibers: 9mm. Capacities: 10 or 17 rounds. Similar to the P320 series except with tungsten-infused heavy XFULL grip module with a flat skeletonized trigger.
Price: MAX $1,490.00
Price: XFull $600.00
Price: X-VTAC $700.00

SIG SAUER P320 X-FIVE SERIES
Calibers: 9mm. Capacities: 10 or 17 rounds. Similar to the P320 series except with a tungsten-infused heavy XFULL grip module with a flat skeletonized trigger. Removable magwell and grip weight, Romeo1PRO optic-ready slide, 5-in. bull barrel, and Dawson Precision fiber-optic adjustable sights.
Price: Legion $940.00

SMITH & WESSON MODEL 41 TARGET
Caliber: .22 LR. Capacity: 10-round magazine. Barrels: 5.5 in., 7 in. Weight: 41 oz. (5.5-in. barrel). Length: 10.5 in. overall (5.5-in. barrel). Grips: Checkered walnut with modified thumb rest, usable with either hand. Sights: .125 in. Patridge on ramp base; micro-click rear-adjustable for windage and elevation. Features: .375 in. wide, grooved trigger; adjustable trigger stop drilled and tapped.
Price: .... $1,220.00–$1,600.00

TRISTAR S.P.S. VISTA
Calibers: 9mm, .38 Super. Capacity: 17-round magazine. Barrels: 5- or 5.5-in., match-grade with compensator. Sights: Optics-ready. Weight: 43 oz. Finish: Black chrome. Grips: Aluminum. Features: Polymer frame, checkered frontstrap serrations, skeletonized trigger and hammer, flared and lowered ejection port, ambidextrous safety, wide mag well. Imported from Spain by TriStar.
Price: $2,450.00

TRISTAR S.P.S. PANTERA
Calibers: 9mm, .40 S&W, .45 ACP. Capacity: 12-, 16- or 18-round magazine. Barrel: 5-in., match-grade. Sights: Bomar-type, fully adjustable rear, fiber-optic front. Weight: 36.6 oz. Finish: Black, black chrome, chrome. Grips: Polymer. Features: Polymer frame, checkered frontstrap serrations, skeletonized trigger and hammer, flared and lowered ejection port, ambidextrous safety, wide mag well, full dust cover. Imported from Spain by TriStar.
Price: $1,680.00

TAURUS TX22 COMPETITION
Caliber: .22 LR. Capacity: 10- or 16-round magazine. Barrel: 5.25 in. Grip: Textured polymer, wrap around. Sights: Adjustable rear, optics-ready. Length: 8.21 in. overall. Weight: 17.3 oz. unloaded. Finish: Matte black. Features: Red-dot optics-ready with mounting plates. The compact model has a 3.06-in. barrel. Steel Challenge Ready (SCR) model has a compensator. Competition models are optics-ready.
Price: Competition model $480.00
Price: SCR model.. $525.00

WALTHER Q5 MATCH STEEL FRAME
Caliber: 9mm. Capacity: 15-round magazine. Barrel: 5 in. Grips: Textured polymer. Sights: LPA fiber-optic front, adj. rear. Length: 8.7 in. overall. Weight: 41.6 oz. unloaded. Finish: Matte black. Features: Metal frame, optic ready, accessory rail.
Price: $1,499.00

Prices given are believed to be accurate at time of publication however, many factors affect retail pricing so exact prices are not possible.

78TH EDITION, 2024 ⬩ 503

CHARTER ARMS BOOMER
Caliber: .44 Special. Capacity: 5-round cylinder. Barrel: 2 in., ported. Weight: 20 oz. Grips: Full rubber combat. Sights: Fixed.
Price: Blued **$443.00**

CHARTER ARMS CHIC LADY & CHIC LADY DAO
Caliber: .38 Special. Capacity: 5-round cylinder. Barrel: 2 in. Weight: 12 oz. Grip: Combat. Sights: Fixed. Features: 2-tone pink or lavender & stainless with aluminum frame. American made by Charter Arms.
Price: Chic Lady **$473.00**
Price: Chic Lady DAO **$483.00**

CHARTER ARMS OFF DUTY
Caliber: .38 Special. Barrel: 2 in. Weight: 12.5 oz. Sights: Blade front, notch rear. Features: 5-round cylinder, aluminum casting, DAO with concealed hammer. Also available with semi-concealed hammer. American made by Charter Arms.
Price: Aluminum **$404.00**
Price: Crimson Trace Laser grip **$657.00**

CHARTER ARMS MAG PUG
Caliber: .357 Mag. Capacity: 5-round cylinder. Barrel: 2.2 in. Weight: 23 oz. Sights: Blade front, notch rear. Features: American made by Charter Arms.
Price: Blued or stainless **$400.00**
Price: 4.4-in. full-lug barrel... **$470.00**
Price: Crimson Trace Laser Grip.. **$609.00**

CHARTER ARMS PITBULL
Calibers: 9mm, 40 S&W, .45 ACP. Capacity: 5-round cylinder. Barrel: 2.2 in. Weights: 20–22 oz. Sights: Fixed rear, ramp front. Grips: Rubber. Features: Matte stainless steel frame or Nitride frame. Moon clips not required for 9mm, .45 ACP.
Price: 9mm **$502.00**
Price: .40 S&W **$489.00**
Price: .45 ACP **$489.00**
Price: 9mm Black Nitride finish **$522.00**
Price: .40, .45 Black Nitride finish.................................... **$509.00**

CHARTER ARMS PATHFINDER
Calibers: .22 LR or .22 Mag. Capacity: 6-round cylinder. Barrel: 2 in., 4 in. Weights: 20 oz. (12 oz. Lite model). Grips: Full. Sights: Fixed or adjustable (Target). Features: Stainless finish and frame.
Price .22 LR **$365.00**
Price .22 Mag **$367.00**
Price: Lite **$379.00**
Price: Target **$409.00**

CHARTER ARMS THE PINK LADY
Caliber: .38 Special. Capacity: 6-round cylinder. Barrel: 2.2 in. Grips: Full. Sights: Fixed rear, LitePipe front. Weight: 12 oz. Features: As the name indicates, the Pink Lady has a pink and stainless steel finish. This is an aluminum-framed revolver from the Undercover Lite series.
Price: **$357.00**

CHARTER ARMS UNDERCOVER
Caliber: .38 Special +P. Capacity: 6-round cylinder. Barrel: 2 in. Weight: 12 oz. Sights: Blade front, notch rear. Features: American made by Charter Arms.
Price: Blued **$346.00**

CHARTER ARMS UNDERCOVER LITE
Caliber: .38 Special. Capacity: 6-round cylinder. Barrel: 2.2 in. Grips: Full. Sights: Fixed rear, LitePipe front. Weight: 12 oz. Features: Aluminum-framed lightweight revolver with anodized finish. Lots of power in a feather-weight package.
Price: **$357.00**

Prices given are believed to be accurate at time of publication however, many factors affect retail pricing so exact prices are not possible.

CHIAPPA RHINO
Calibers: .357 Magnum, 9mm, .40 S&W. Features: 2-, 4-, 5- or 6-inch barrel; fixed or adjustable sights; visible hammer or hammerless design. Weights: 24–33 oz. Walnut or synthetic grips with black frame; hexagonal-shaped cylinder. Unique design fires from bottom chamber of cylinder.
Price: From .... $1,090.00-$1,465.00

CHIAPPA RHINO REVOLVER 30DS NEBULA .357 MAG/3-INCH BBL (30SAR-CALIFORNIA COMPLIANT)
Type of Gun: Revolver, Caliber: .357 Magnum, Action: Single/Double, Barrel Length: 3 in. (76mm) Capacity: 6. Feed In: manual, Trigger System: Single. Grips: Blue laminate medium. Front Sight: Fixed red fiber optic. Rear Sight: Adjustable elevation and windage green fiber optic, Safety: Internal, Weight: 1.7 lbs. Length: 7.5 in. (190 mm) Material: Machined 7075-T6 alloy frame/ steel cylinder and barrel finish: Muti-Color PVD. Extraction: Manual. Notes: Includes three moon clips, removal tool, gun lock and black leather holster.
Price: $1,912.00

COBRA SHADOW
Caliber: .38 Special +P. Capacity: 5 rounds. Barrel: 1.875 in. Weight: 15 oz. Aluminum frame with stainless steel barrel and cylinder. Length: 6.375 in. Grips: Rosewood, black rubber or Crimson Trace Laser. Features: Black anodized, titanium anodized or custom colors including gold, red, pink and blue.
Price: $369.00
Price: Rosewood grips $434.00
Price: Crimson Trace Laser grips........................... $625.00

COLT COBRA
Caliber: .38 Special. Capacity: 6 rounds. Sights: Fixed rear, fiber optic

red front. Grips: Hogue rubbed stippled with finger grooves. Weight: 25 oz. Finish: Matte stainless. Same name as classic Colt model made from 1950–1986 but totally new design. Introduced in 2017. King Cobra has a heavy-duty frame and 3-inch barrel.
Price: $699.00
Price: King Cobra $899.00

COLT NIGHT COBRA
Caliber; .38 Special. Capacity: 6 rounds. Grips: Black synthetic VC G10. Sight: Tritium front night sight. DAO operation with bobbed hammer. Features a linear leaf spring design for smooth DA trigger pull.
Price: $899.00

COLT PYTHON
Caliber: .357 Magnum. Capacity: 6-round cylinder. Barrels: 4.25 and 6 in. Grips: Walnut. Sights: Fully adjustable rear, fixed red ramp interchangeable front. Weights: 42 oz. (4.25 in.), 46 oz. (6 in.). Features: New and improved and available only in stainless steel. Has recessed target crown and user-interchangeable front sight.
Price: $1,499.00

COLT PYTHON 3-INCH BARREL
Caliber: .357 Magnum. Capacity: 6-round cylinder. Barrels: 3, 4.25 and 6 in. Grips: Walnut. Sights: Fully adjustable rear, fixed red ramp interchangeable front. Weight: 42 oz. (4.25 in.), 46 oz. (6 in.). Features: New and improved and available only in stainless steel. Has recessed target crown and user-interchangeable front sight.
Price: $1,499.00

LIPSEY'S EXCLUSIVE COLT PYTHON (TYLER GUN WORKS)
Caliber: .357 Magnum/.38 Special, 3-in. barrel. Tyler Gun Works Premier Grade-Engraved with stag grips.
Price: $2,400.00

Prices given are believed to be accurate at time of publication however, many factors affect retail pricing so exact prices are not possible.

78TH EDITION, 2024 ⊕ **505**

COLT ANACONDA
Caliber: .44 Magnum. Capacity: 6 rounds. Barrel: 6 and 8 in. Grip: Hogue Overmolded. Sights: Fully adjustable rear, fixed red ramp interchangeable front. Weight: 53 oz. (6 in.), 59 oz. (8 in.) Features: New and improved and available in stainless steel only. Has recessed target crown and user-interchangeable front sight.
Price: $1,499.00

COMANCHE II-A
Caliber: .38 Special. Capacity: 6-round cylinder. Barrels: 3 or 4 in. Weights: 33, 35 oz. Lengths: 8, 8.5 in. overall. Grips: Rubber. Sights: Fixed. Features: Blued finish, alloy frame. Distributed by SGS Importers.
Price: $220.00

DAN WESSON 715
Caliber: .357 Magnum. Capacity: 6-round cylinder. Barrel: 6-inch heavy barrel with full lug. Weight: 38 oz. Lengths: 8, 8.5 in. overall. Grips: Hogue rubber with finger grooves. Sights: Adjustable rear, interchangeable front blade. Features: Stainless steel. Interchangeable barrel assembly. Reintroduced in 2014. 715 Pistol Pack comes with 4-, 6- and 8-in. interchangeable barrels.
Price: From $1,558.00
Price: Pistol Pack... $1,999.00

DIAMONDBACK SIDEKICK
Caliber: .22 LR/.22 Mag. Convertible. Action: Single & Double Grips: Checkered glass filled Nylon. Capacity: 9 rounds., Front Sight: Blade., Rear

Sight: Integral., Barrel length: 4.5 inch. Overall Length: 9.875 in. Frame & Handle Material: Zinc., Frame & Handle Finish: Black Cerakote. Weight: 32.5 oz., Twist: 1:16 RH. Grooves: 6. The Sidekick is chambered in both .22 LR and .22 Mag with 9-shot cylinders. It has a 9-round capacity and weighs 32.5 ounces. Swing-out cylinders allow the user to switch between .22 LR and .22 Mag in seconds.
Price: $320.00

EAA WINDICATOR
Calibers: .38 Special, .357 Mag Capacity: 6-round cylinder. Barrels: 2 in., 4 in. Weight: 30 oz. (4 in.). Length: 8.5 in. overall (4 in. bbl.). Grips: Rubber with finger grooves. Sights: Blade front, fixed rear. Features: Swing-out cylinder; hammer block safety; blue or nickel finish. Introduced 1991. Imported from Germany by European American Armory.
Price: .38 Spec. from $354.00
Price: .357 Mag, steel frame from $444.00

KIMBER K6S
Caliber: .357 Magnum. Capacity: 6-round cylinder. Barrel: 2-inch full lug. Grips: Gray rubber. Finish: Satin stainless. Kimber's first revolver, claimed to be world's lightest production 6-shot .357 Magnum. DAO design with non-stacking match-grade trigger. Introduced 2016. CDP model has laminated checkered rosewood grips, Tritium night sights, two-tone black DLC/brushed stainless finish, match grade trigger.
Price: $878.00
Price: 3-in. Barrel... $899.00
Price: Deluxe Carry w/Medallion grips........................... $1,088.00
Price: Custom Defense Package $1,155.00
Price: Crimson Trace Laser Grips $1,177.00
Price: TLE $999.00
Price: DA/SA $949.00

KIMBER K6s DASA TARGET
Caliber: .357 Magnum. Capacity: 6-round cylinder. Barrel: 4 in. Grips: Walnut laminate, oversized. Sights: Fully adjustable rear, fiber-optic front. Features: The DASA is the next evolution of the K6s. The DASA is outfitted

with a double- and single-action trigger mechanism. Kimber's K6s revolvers feature the purportedly smallest cylinder capable of housing 6 rounds of .357 Magnum at 1.39-inch diameter, making for a very slim and streamlined package.

Price: **$989.00**

KIMBER K6s DASA COMBAT

Caliber: .357 Magnum. Capacity: 6-round cylinder. Barrel: 4 in. Grips: Walnut laminate, oversized with finger grooves. Sights: Fixed front and rear with white dots. Features: The DASA Combat is outfitted with a double- and single-action trigger mechanism. Kimber's K6s DASA revolvers have a smooth no-stack double-action trigger and a crisp 3.25- to 4.25-lb. single-action pull. The K6s DASA revolvers are equipped with knurled hammer spur.

Price: **$989.00**

KIMBER K6s DASA TEXAS EDITION

Caliber: .357 Magnum. Capacity: 6-round cylinder. Barrel: 2 in. Grips: Ivory G10. Sights: Fixed front and rear with white dots. Features: The Texas Edition is adorned with ivory G10 grips with the state moto, name and flag on this special edition. The satin finish has American Western cut scroll engraving on the barrel, frame and cylinder. The K6s DASA Texas Edition revolvers are equipped with knurled hammer spur.

Price: **$1,359.00**

KIMBER K6s ROYAL

Caliber: .357 Magnum. Capacity: 6-round cylinder. Barrel: 2 in. Grips: Walnut. Sights: Fixed brass-bead front and rear with white dots. Features: The K6s Royal features a 2-inch barrel for easy concealment. The dovetailed white-dot rear sight complements the brass-bead front sight. The Royal's stainless steel is hand polished to a high shine and a Dark Oil DLC is applied for a unique look.

Price: **$1,699.00**

KORTH USA

Calibers: .22 LR, .22 WMR, .32 S&W Long, .38 Special, .357 Mag., 9mm. Capacity: 6-shot. Barrels: 3, 4, 5.25, 6 in. Weights: 36–52 oz. Grips: Combat, Sport: Walnut, Palisander, Amboina, Ivory. Finish: German Walnut, matte with oil finish, adjustable ergonomic competition style. Sights: Adjustable Patridge (Sport) or Baughman (Combat), interchangeable and adjustable rear w/Patridge front (Target) in blue and matte. Features: DA/SA, 3 models, over 50 configurations, externally adjustable trigger stop and weight, interchangeable cylinder, removable wide-milled trigger shoe on Target model. Deluxe models are highly engraved editions. Available finishes include high polish blued finish, plasma coated in high polish or matte silver, gold, blue or charcoal. Many deluxe options available. From Korth USA.

Price: From **$8,000.00**
Price: Deluxe Editions, from **$12,000.00**

KORTH SKYHAWK

Caliber: 9mm. Barrels: 2 or 3 in. Sights: Adjustable rear with gold bead front. Grips: Hogue with finger grooves. Features: Polished trigger, skeletonized hammer. Imported by Nighthawk Custom.

Price: **$1,699.00**

NIGHTHAWK CUSTOM/KORTH-WAFFEN NXR

Caliber: .44 Magnum. Capacity: 6-round cylinder Barrel: 6 in. Grips: Ivory G10. Sights: Adjustable rear, fast-changeable front. Weight: 3.05 lbs. Features: The NXR is a futuristic looking stainless steel double-action revolver that is black DLC finished. Comes equipped with a removable under-barrel balancing lug/weight. Picatinny rail on top of barrel and underneath for easy accessory mounting.

Price: **$5,299.00**

KORTH-NIGHTHAWK CUSTOM MONGOOSE

Caliber: .357 Mag. Optional 9mm cyl. Barrel lengths: 2.75, 3, 4, 5.25, and 6 in. Full-lug with black DLC finish A silver DLC-finished .357 Magnum Mongoose is available with 4-, 5.25-, or 6-in. barrel configurations.

Price: ....**$3,699.00–$4,999.00**

KORTH-NIGHTHAWK CUSTOM VINTAGE

Caliber: .357 Magnum. Barrel: 4- or 6-in. half-lug. Color-casehardened frame and barrel and charcoal blue cylinder.

Price: **$8,999.00**

Prices given are believed to be accurate at time of publication however, many factors affect retail pricing so exact prices are not possible.

78TH EDITION, 2024 ✦ **507**

ROSSI RM66

Caliber: 357 Magnum. Capacity: 6 rounds. Rear Sight: Adjustable. Front Sight: Removable Serrated Blade. Finish: Stainless Steel. Barrel Length: 6 inches. Grips: wrap-around rubber. Medium-sized frame. Overall Length: 11.14 in. Overall Height: 5.47 in. Overall Width 1.46 in. Overall Weight: 34.40 oz. (unloaded). Safety: Hammer Block.
Price: **$620.00**

ROSSI RP63

Caliber: .357 Magnum. Capacity: 6 rounds. Rear Sight: Fixed. Front Sight: Removable Serrated blade. Finish: Stainless steel. Barrel Length: 3-in. Grips: Rubber. Small-sized frame. Overall Length: 7.95 in. Overall Height: 5.20 in. Overall Width 1.46 in. Overall Weight: 27.30 oz. (unloaded). Safety: Hammer Block.
Price: **$460.00**

RUGER (CUSTOM SHOP) SUPER GP100 COMPETITION REVOLVER

Calibers: .357 Magnum, 9mm. Capacity: 8-round cylinder. Barrels: 5.5 and 6 in. Grips: Hogue hand-finished hardwood. Sights: Adjustable rear, fiber-optic front. Weights: 47 oz., 45.6 oz. Features: Designed for competition, the new Super GP100 is essentially a Super Redhawk with the frame extension removed and replaced by a shrouded, cold hammer-forged barrel. The Super GP utilizes the superior action of the Super Redhawk. The high-strength stainless steel cylinder has a PVD finish and is extensively fluted for weight reduction. Comes with high-quality, impact-resistant case.
Price: **$1,549.00**

RUGER GP-100

Calibers: .357 Mag., .327 Federal Mag., .44 Special Capacities: 6- or 7-round cylinder, .327 Federal Mag (7-shot), .44 Special (5-shot), .22 LR, (10-shot). Barrels: 3-in. full shroud, 4-in. full shroud, 6-in. full shroud. (.44 Special offered only with 3-in. barrel.) Weights: 36–45 oz. Sights: Fixed; adjustable on 4- and 6-in. full shroud barrels. Grips: Ruger Santoprene Cushioned Grip with Goncalo Alves inserts. Features: Uses action, frame features of both the Security-Six and Redhawk revolvers. Full-length, short ejector shroud. Satin blue and stainless steel.
Price: Blued **$769.00**
Price: Satin stainless **$799.00**
Price: .22 LR **$829.00**
Price: .44 Spl. **$829.00**
Price: 7-round cylinder, 327 Fed or .357 Mag **$899.00**

RUGER GP-100 MATCH CHAMPION

Calibers: 10mm Magnum, .357 Mag. Capacity: 6-round cylinder. Barrel: 4.2-in. half shroud, slab-sided. Weight: 38 oz. Sights: Fixed rear, fiber optic front. Grips: Hogue Stippled Hardwood. Features: Satin stainless steel finish.
Price: Blued **$969.00**

RUGER LCR

Calibers: .22 LR (8-round cylinder), .22 WMR, .327 Fed. Mag. .38 Special and .357 Mag., 5-round cylinder. Barrel: 1.875 in. Weights: 13.5–17.10 oz. Length: 6.5 in. overall. Grips: Hogue Tamer or Crimson Trace Lasergrips. Sights: Pinned ramp front, U-notch integral rear. Features: The Ruger Lightweight Compact Revolver (LCR), a 13.5 ounce, small frame revolver with a smooth, easy-to-control trigger and highly manageable recoil.
Price: .22 LR, .22 WMR, .38 Spl., iron sights **$579.00**
Price: 9mm, .327, .357, iron sights...................................**$669.00**
Price: .22 LR, .22WMR, .38 Spl. Crimson Trace Lasergrip **$859.00**
Price: 9mm, .327, .357, Crimson Trace Lasergrip **$949.00**

RUGER LCRX

Calibers: .38 Special +P, 9mm, .327 Fed. Mag., .22 WMR. Barrels: 1.875 in. or 3 in. Features: Similar to LCR except this model has visible hammer, adjustable rear sight. The 3-inch barrel model has longer grip. 9mm comes with three moon clips.
Price: **$579.00**
Price: .327 Mag., .357 Mag., 9mm **$669.00**

RUGER SP-101
Calibers: .22 LR (8 shot); .327 Federal Mag. (6-shot), 9mm, .38 Spl, .357 Mag. (5-shot). Barrels: 2.25, 3 1/16, 4.2 in (.22 LR, .327 Mag., .357 Mag). Weights: 25–30 oz. Sights: Adjustable or fixed, rear; fiber-optic or black ramp front. Grips: Ruger Cushioned Grip with inserts. Features: Compact, small frame, double-action revolver. Full-length ejector shroud. Stainless steel only.

Price: Fixed sights	**$719.00**
Price: Adjustable rear, fiber optic front sights	**$769.00**
Price: .327 Fed Mag 3-in bbl	**$769.00**
Price: .327 Fed Mag	**$749.00**

RUGER REDHAWK
Calibers: .44 Rem. Mag., .45 Colt and .45 ACP/.45 Colt combo. Capacity: 6-round cylinder. Barrels: 2.75, 4.2, 5.5, 7.5 in. (.45 Colt in 4.2 in. only.) Weight: 54 oz. (7.5 bbl.). Length: 13 in. overall (7.5-in. barrel). Grips: Square butt cushioned grip panels. TALO Distributor exclusive 2.75-in. barrel stainless model has round butt, wood grips. Sights: Interchangeable Patridge-type front, rear adjustable for windage and elevation. Features: Stainless steel, brushed satin finish, blued ordnance steel. 9.5 sight radius. Introduced 1979.

Price:	**$1,079.00**
Price: Hunter Model 7.5-in. bbl.	**$1,159.00**
Price: TALO 2.75 in. model	**$1,069.00**

RUGER SUPER REDHAWK
Calibers: 10mm, .44 Rem. Mag., .454 Casull, .480 Ruger. Capacities: 5- or 6-round cylinder. Barrels: 2.5 in. (Alaskan), 5.5 in., 6.5 in. (10mm), 7.5 in. or 9.5 in. Weight: 44–58 oz. Length: 13 in. overall (7.5-in. barrel). Grips: Hogue Tamer Monogrip. Features: Similar to standard Redhawk except has heavy extended frame with Ruger Integral Scope Mounting System on wide topstrap. Wide hammer spur lowered for better scope clearance. Incorporates mechanical design features and improvements of GP-100. Ramp front sight base has Redhawk-style interchangeable insert sight blades, adjustable rear sight. Alaskan model has 2.5-inch barrel. Satin stainless steel and low-glare stainless finishes. Introduced 1987.

Price: .44 Magnum, 10mm	**$1,159.00**

Price: .454 Casull, .480 Ruger	**$1,199.00**
Price: Alaskan, .44 Mag, .454 Casull, .480 Ruger	**$1,189.00**

SMITH & WESSON GOVERNOR
Calibers: .410 Shotshell (2.5 in.), .45 ACP, .45 Colt. Capacity: 6 rounds. Barrel: 2.75 in. Length: 7.5 in., (2.5 in. barrel). Grip: Synthetic. Sights: Front: Dovetailed tritium night sight or black ramp, rear: fixed. Grips: Synthetic. Finish: Matte black or matte silver (Silver Edition). Weight: 29.6 oz. Features: Capable of chambering a mixture of .45 Colt, .45 ACP and .410 gauge 2.5-inch shotshells, the Governor is suited for both close and distant encounters, allowing users to customize the load to their preference. Scandium alloy frame, stainless steel cylinder. Packaged with two full moon clips and three 2-shot clips.

Price:	**$869.00**
Price: w/Crimson Trace Laser Grip	**$1,179.00**

SMITH & WESSON J-FRAME
The J-frames are the smallest Smith & Wesson wheelguns and come in a variety of chamberings, barrel lengths and materials as noted in the individual model listings.

SMITH & WESSON 60LS/642LS LADYSMITH
Calibers: .38 Special +P, .357 Mag. Capacity: 5-round cylinder. Barrels: 1.875 in. (642LS); 2.125 in. (60LS) Weights: 14.5 oz. (642LS); 21.5 oz. (60LS); Length: 6.6 in. overall (60LS). Grips: Wood. Sights: Black blade, serrated ramp front, fixed notch rear. 642 CT has Crimson Trace Laser Grips. Features: 60LS model has a Chiefs Special-style frame. 642LS has Centennial-style frame, frosted matte finish, smooth combat wood grips. Introduced 1996. Comes in a fitted carry/storage case. Introduced 1989. Made in USA by Smith & Wesson.

Price: (642LS)	**$499.00**
Price: (60LS)	**$759.00**
Price: (642 CT)	**$699.00**

SMITH & WESSON MODEL 63
Caliber: .22 LR Capacity: 8-round cylinder. Barrel: 3 in. Weight: 26 oz. Length: 7.25 in. overall. Grips: Black synthetic. Sights: Hi-Viz fiber optic front sight, adjustable black blade rear sight. Features: Stainless steel construction throughout. Made in USA by Smith & Wesson.

Price:	**$769.00**

SMITH & WESSON MODEL 442/637/638/642 AIRWEIGHT
Caliber: .38 Special +P. Capacity: 5-round cylinder. Barrels: 1.875 in., 2.5 in. Weight: 15 oz. Length: 6.375 in. overall. Grips: Soft rubber. Sights: Fixed, serrated ramp front, square notch rear. Features: A family of J-frame .38 Special revolvers with aluminum-alloy frames. Model 637; Chiefs Special-style frame with exposed hammer. Introduced 1996. Models 442, 642; Centennial-style frame, enclosed hammer. Model 638, Bodyguard style, shrouded hammer. Comes in a fitted carry/storage case. Introduced 1989. Made in USA by Smith & Wesson.

Price: From	**$469.00**
Price: Laser Max Frame Mounted Red Laser sight	**$539.00**

Prices given are believed to be accurate at time of publication however, many factors affect retail pricing so exact prices are not possible.

78TH EDITION, 2024 ⬩ **509**

SMITH & WESSON MODELS 637 CT/638 CT

Similar to Models 637, 638 and 642 but with Crimson Trace Laser Grips.
Price: **$699.00**

SMITH & WESSON MODEL 317 AIRLITE

Caliber: .22 LR. Capacity: 8-round cylinder. Barrel: 1.875 in. Weight: 10.5 oz. Length: 6.25 in. overall (1.875-in. barrel). Grips: Rubber. Sights: Serrated ramp front, fixed notch rear. Features: Aluminum alloy, carbon and stainless steels, Chiefs Special-style frame with exposed hammer. Smooth combat trigger. Clear Cote finish. Model 317 Kit Gun has adjustable rear sight, fiber optic front. Introduced 1997.
Price: **$759.00**

SMITH & WESSON MODEL 340/340PD AIRLITE SC CENTENNIAL

Calibers: .357 Mag., 38 Special +P. Capacity: 5-round cylinder. Barrel: 1.875 in. Weight: 12 oz. Length: 6.375 in. overall (1.875-in. barrel). Grips: Rounded butt rubber. Sights: Black blade front, rear notch Features: Centennial-style frame, enclosed hammer. Internal lock. Matte silver finish. Scandium alloy frame, titanium cylinder, stainless steel barrel liner. Made in USA by Smith & Wesson.
Price: **$1,019.00**

SMITH & WESSON MODEL 351PD

Caliber: .22 Mag. Capacity: 5-round cylinder. Barrel: 1.875 in. Weight: 10.6 oz. Length: 6.25 in. overall (1.875-in. barrel). Sights: HiViz front sight, rear notch. Grips: Wood. Features: 7-shot, aluminum-alloy frame. Chiefs Special-style frame with exposed hammer. Nonreflective matte-black finish. Internal lock. Made in USA by Smith & Wesson.
Price: **$759.00**

SMITH & WESSON MODEL 360/360PD AIRLITE CHIEF'S SPECIAL

Calibers: .357 Mag., .38 Special +P. Capacity: 5-round cylinder. Barrel: 1.875 in. Weight: 12 oz. Length: 6.375 in. overall (1.875-in. barrel). Grips: Rounded butt rubber. Sights: Red ramp front, fixed rear notch. Features: Chief's Special-style frame with exposed hammer. Internal lock. Scandium alloy frame, titanium cylinder, stainless steel barrel. Model 360 has unfluted cylinder. Made in USA by Smith & Wesson.
Price: 360 .... **$770.00**
Price: 360PD **$1,019.00**

SMITH & WESSON BODYGUARD 38

Caliber: .38 Special +P. Capacity: 5-round cylinder. Barrel: 1.9 in. Weight: 14.3 oz. Length: 6.6 in. Grip: Synthetic. Sights: Front: Black ramp, Rear: fixed, integral with backstrap. Plus: Integrated laser sight. Finish: Matte black. Features: The first personal protection series that comes with an integrated laser sight.
Price: **$539.00**

SMITH & WESSON MODEL 640 CENTENNIAL DA ONLY

Calibers: .357 Mag., .38 Special +P. Capacity: 5-round cylinder. Barrel: 2.125 in. Weight: 23 oz. Length: 6.75 in. overall. Grips: Uncle Mike's Boot grip. Sights: Tritium Night Sights. Features: Stainless steel. Fully concealed hammer, snag-proof smooth edges. Internal lock.
Price: **$839.00**

SMITH & WESSON MODEL 649 BODYGUARD

Caliber: .357 Mag., .38 Special +P. Capacity: 5-round cylinder. Barrel: 2.125 in. Weight: 23 oz. Length: 6.625 in. overall. Grips: Uncle Mike's Combat. Sights: Black pinned ramp front, fixed notch rear. Features: Stainless steel construction, satin finish. Internal lock. Bodyguard style, shrouded

Prices given are believed to be accurate at time of publication however, many factors affect retail pricing so exact prices are not possible.

hammer. Made in USA by Smith & Wesson.
Price: $729.00

SMITH & WESSON K-FRAME/L-FRAME
The K-frame series are mid-size revolvers and the L-frames are slightly larger.

SMITH & WESSON MODEL 10 CLASSIC
Caliber: .38 Special. Capacity: 6-round cylinder. Features: Bright blued steel frame and cylinder, checkered wood grips, 4-inch barrel and fixed sights. The oldest model in the Smith & Wesson line, its basic design goes back to the original Military & Police Model of 1905.
Price: $739.00

SMITH & WESSON MODEL 17 MASTERPIECE CLASSIC
Caliber: .22 LR. Capacity: 6-round cylinder. Barrel: 6 in. Weight: 40 oz. Grips: Checkered wood. Sights: Pinned Patridge front, micro-adjustable rear. Updated variation of K-22 Masterpiece of the 1930s.
Price: $989.00

SMITH & WESSON MODEL 19 CLASSIC
Caliber: .357 Magnum. Capacity: 6-round cylinder Barrel: 4.25 in. Weight: 37.2 oz. Grips: Walnut. Sights: Adjustable rear, red ramp front. Finish: Polished blue. Classic-style thumbpiece. Reintroduced 2019.
Price: $826.00

SMITH & WESSON MODEL 48 CLASSIC
Same specifications as Model 17 except chambered in .22 Magnum (.22 WMR) and is available with a 4- or 6-inch barrel.
Price: .... $949.00–$989.00

SMITH & WESSON MODEL 64/67
Caliber: .38 Special +P. Capacity: 6-round cylinder Barrel: 3 in. Weight: 33 oz. Length: 8.875 in. overall. Grips: Soft rubber. Sights: Fixed, .125-in. serrated ramp front, square notch rear. Model 67 is similar to Model 64 except for adjustable sights. Features: Satin finished stainless steel, square butt.
Price: From .... $689.00–$749.00

SMITH & WESSON MODEL 66
Caliber: .357 Magnum. Capacity: 6-round cylinder. Barrel: 4.25 in. Weight: 36.6 oz. Grips: Synthetic. Sights: White outline adjustable rear, red ramp front. Features: Return in 2014 of the famous K-frame "Combat Magnum" with stainless finish.
Price: $849.00

SMITH & WESSON MODEL 69
Caliber: .44 Magnum. Capacity: 5-round cylinder. Barrel: 4.25 in. Weight: 37 oz. Grips: Checkered wood. Sights: White outline adjustable rear, red ramp front. Features: L-frame with stainless finish, 5-shot cylinder, introduced in 2014.
Price: $989.00

SMITH & WESSON MODEL 610
Caliber: 10mm. Capacity: 6-round cylinder. Barrels: 4.25 and 6 in. Grips: Walnut. Sights: Fully adjustable rear, fixed red ramp interchangeable front. Weights: 42.6 oz. (4.25 in.), 50.1 oz (6 in.). Features: Built on Smith & Wesson's large N-frame in stainless steel only. Will also fire .40 S&W ammunition. Comes with three moon clips.
Price: $987.00

SMITH & WESSON MODEL 617
Caliber: .22 LR. Capacity: 10-round cylinder. Barrel: 6 in. Weight: 44 oz. Length: 11.125 in. Grips: Soft rubber. Sights: Patridge front, adjustable rear. Drilled and tapped for scope mount. Features: Stainless steel with satin finish. Introduced 1990.
Price: From $829.00

SMITH & WESSON MODEL 648
Caliber: .22 Magnum. Capacity: 8-round cylinder. Barrel: 6 in. Grips: Walnut. Sights: Fully adjustable rear, Patridge front. Weight: 46.2 oz. Features: This reintroduction was originally released in 1989 and produced until 2005. Ideal for target shooting or small-game hunting.
Price: $752.00

Prices given are believed to be accurate at time of publication however, many factors affect retail pricing so exact prices are not possible.

78TH EDITION, 2024 ⬥ **511**

SMITH & WESSON MODEL 686/686 PLUS

Caliber: .357 Mag/.38 Special. Capacity: 6 (686) or 7 (Plus). Barrels: 6 in. (686), 3 or 6 in. (686 Plus), 4 in. (SSR). Weight: 35 oz. (3 in. barrel). Grips: Rubber. Sights: White outline adjustable rear, red ramp front. Features: Satin stainless frame and cylinder. Stock Service Revolver (SSR) has tapered underlug, interchangeable front sight, high-hold ergonomic wood grips, chamfered charge holes, custom barrel w/recessed crown, bossed mainspring.

Price: 686 .... **$829.00**
Price: Plus **$849.00**
Price: SSR **$999.00**

SMITH & WESSON MODEL 986 PRO

Caliber: 9mm. Capacity: 7-round cylinder Barrel: 5-in. tapered underlug. Features: SA/DA L-frame revolver chambered in 9mm. Features similar to 686 PLUS Pro Series with 5-inch tapered underlug barrel, satin stainless finish, synthetic grips, adjustable rear and Patridge blade front sight.

Price: **$1,149.00**

SMITH & WESSON M&P R8

Caliber: .357 Mag. Capacity: 8-round cylinder. Barrel: 5-in. half lug with accessory rail. Weight: 36.3 oz. Length: 10.5 in. Grips: Black synthetic. Sights: Adjustable v-notch rear, interchangeable front. Features: Scandium alloy frame, stainless steel cylinder.

Price: **$1,329.00**

SMITH & WESSON N-FRAME

These large-frame models introduced the .357, .41 and .44 Magnums to the world.

SMITH & WESSON MODEL 25 CLASSIC

Calibers: .45 Colt or .45 ACP. Capacity: 6-round cylinder. Barrel: 6.5 in. Weight: 45 oz. Grips: Checkered wood. Sights: Pinned Patridge front, micro-adjustable rear.

Price: **$1,019.00**

SMITH & WESSON MODEL 27 CLASSIC

Caliber: .357 Magnum. Capacity: 6-round cylinder. Barrels: 4 or 6.5 in. Weight: 41.2 oz. Grips: Checkered wood. Sights: Pinned Patridge front, micro-adjustable rear. Updated variation of the first magnum revolver, the .357 Magnum of 1935.

Price: (4 in.) **$1,019.00**
Price: (6.5 in.) **$1,059.00**

SMITH & WESSON MODEL 29 CLASSIC

Caliber: .44 Magnum Capacity: 6-round cylinder. Barrel: 4 or 6.5 in. Weight: 48.5 oz. Length: 12 in. Grips: Altamont service walnut. Sights: Adjustable white-outline rear, red ramp front. Features: Carbon steel frame, polished-blued or nickel finish. Has integral key lock safety feature to prevent accidental discharges. Original Model 29 made famous by "Dirty Harry" character played in 1971 by Clint Eastwood.

Price: .... **$999.00–$1,169.00**

SMITH & WESSON MODEL 57 CLASSIC

Caliber: .41 Magnum. Capacity: 6-round cylinder. Barrel: 6 in. Weight: 48 oz. Grips: Checkered wood. Sights: Pinned red ramp, micro-adjustable rear.

Price: **$1,009.00**

SMITH & WESSON MODEL 329PD ALASKA BACKPACKER

Caliber: .44 Magnum. Capacity: 6-round cylinder. Barrel: 2.5 in. Weight: 26 oz. Length: 9.5 in. Grips: Synthetic. Sights: Adj. rear, HiViz orange-dot front. Features: Scandium alloy frame, blue/black finish, stainless steel cylinder.

Price: From **$1,159.00**

SMITH & WESSON MODEL 625/625JM

Caliber: .45 ACP. Capacity: 6-round cylinder. Barrels: 4 in., 5 in. Weight: 43 oz. (4-in. barrel). Length: 9.375 in. overall (4-in. barrel). Grips: Soft rubber; wood optional. Sights: Patridge front on ramp, S&W micrometer click rear adjustable for windage and elevation. Features: Stainless steel construction with .400-in. wide semi-target hammer, .312-in. smooth combat trigger; full lug barrel. Glass beaded finish. Introduced 1989. Jerry Miculek Professional (JM) Series has .265-in. wide grooved trigger, special wooden Miculek Grip, five full moon clips, gold bead Patridge front sight on interchangeable front sight base, bead blast finish. Unique serial number run. Mountain Gun has 4-in. tapered barrel, drilled and tapped, Hogue Rubber Monogrip, pinned black ramp front sight, micrometer click-adjustable rear sight, satin stainless frame and barrel weighs 39.5 oz.

Price: 625 or 625JM **$1,074.00**

SMITH & WESSON MODEL 629

Calibers: .44 Magnum, .44 S&W Special. Capacity: 6-round cylinder. Barrels: 4 in., 5 in., 6.5 in. Weight: 41.5 oz. (4-in. bbl.). Length: 9.625 in. overall (4-in. bbl.). Grips: Soft rubber; wood optional. Sights: .125-in. red ramp front, white outline rear, internal lock, adjustable for windage and elevation. Classic similar to standard Model 629, except Classic has full-lug 5-in. barrel, chamfered front of cylinder, interchangeable red ramp front sight with adjustable white outline rear, Hogue grips with S&W monogram, drilled and tapped for scope mounting. Factory accurizing and endurance packages. Introduced 1990. Classic Power Port has Patridge front sight and adjustable rear sight. Model 629CT has 5-in. barrel, Crimson Trace Hoghunter Lasergrips, 10.5 in. OAL, 45.5 oz. weight. Introduced 2006.
Price: From **$949.00**

SMITH & WESSON X-FRAME
These extra-large X-frame S&W revolvers push the limits of big-bore handgunning.

SMITH & WESSON MODEL 500
Caliber: 500 S&W Magnum. Capacity: 5-round cylinder. Barrels: 4 in., 6.5 in., 8.375 in. Weight: 72.5 oz. Length: 15 in. (8.375-in. barrel). Grips: Hogue Sorbothane Rubber. Sights: Interchangeable blade, front, adjustable rear. Features: Recoil compensator, ball detent cylinder latch, internal lock. 6.5-in.-barrel model has orange-ramp dovetail Millett front sight, adjustable black rear sight, Hogue Dual Density Monogrip, .312-in. chrome trigger with overtravel stop, chrome tear-drop hammer, glass bead finish. 10.5-in.-barrel model has red ramp front sight, adjustable rear sight, .312-in. chrome trigger with overtravel stop, chrome teardrop hammer with pinned sear, hunting sling. Compensated Hunter has .400-in. orange ramp dovetail front sight, adjustable black blade rear sight, Hogue Dual Density Monogrip, glass bead finish w/black clear coat. Made in USA by Smith & Wesson.
Price: From **$1,299.00**

SMITH & WESSON MODEL 460V
Caliber: 460 S&W Magnum (Also chambers .454 Casull, .45 Colt). Capacity: 5-round cylinder. Barrels: 7.5 in., 8.375-in. gain-twist rifling. Weight: 62.5 oz. Length: 11.25 in. Grips: Rubber. Sights: Adj. rear, red ramp front. Features: Satin stainless steel frame and cylinder, interchangeable compensator. 460XVR (X-treme Velocity Revolver) has black blade front sight with interchangeable green Hi-Viz tubes, adjustable rear sight. 7.5-in.-barrel version has Lothar-Walther barrel, 360-degree recoil compensator, tuned Performance Center action, pinned sear, integral Weaver base, non-glare surfaces, scope mount accessory kit for mounting full-size scopes, flashed-chromed hammer and trigger, Performance Center gun rug and shoulder sling. Interchangeable Hi-Viz green dot front sight, adjustable black rear sight, Hogue Dual Density Monogrip, matte-black frame and shroud finish with glass-bead cylinder finish, 72 oz. Compensated Hunter has teardrop chrome hammer, .312-in. chrome trigger, Hogue Dual Density Monogrip, satin/matte stainless finish, HiViz interchangeable front sight, adjustable black rear sight. XVR introduced 2006.
Price: 460V **$1,369.00**
Price: 460XVR, fr **$1,369.00**

STANDARD MANUFACTURING S333 THUNDERSTRUCK
Caliber: .22 Magnum. Capacity: 8-round cylinder. Barrel: 1.25 in. Grips: Polymer. Sights: Fixed front and rear. Weight: 18 oz. Features: Designed to be the ultimate in personal protection and featuring two-barrels that fire simultaneously with each trigger pull. The DA revolver has an 8-round, .22 Magnum capacity. Frame is constructed of 7075 aircraft-grade aluminum with anodized finish.
Price: **$429.00**

SUPER SIX CLASSIC BISON BULL
Caliber: .45-70 Government. Capacity: 6-round cylinder. Barrel: 10in. octagonal with 1:14 twist. Weight: 6 lbs. Length: 17.5 in. overall. Grips: NA. Sights: Ramp front sight with dovetailed blade, click-adjustable rear. Features: Manganese bronze frame. Integral scope mount, manual cross-bolt safety.
Price: **$1,500.00**

TAURUS 327
The new Taurus 327 is a double-action/single-action revolver, available with a 2- or 3-inch barrel that is multi-cartridge compatible, can accept .32 H&R Magnum and .32 S&W Long cartridges. The matte black carbon steel or stainless steel barrel, cylinder and frame are backed by a recoil-absorbing rubber grip that is comfortable and provides excellent retention in a compact handgun platform. The Taurus 327's front serrated ramp sight and no-snag rear sight channel provide quick and clear target acquisition.
Price: **$371.00**
Price: **$388.00**

TAURUS 942
Caliber: .22 LR. Capacity: 8-round cylinder. Barrels: 2 and 3 in. Grips: Soft rubber. Sights: Drift-adjustable rear, serrated-ramp front. Weight: 17.8, 25 oz. Features: The 942 is based closely on the Taurus 856 revolver, but chambered in .22 LR with an 8-shot cylinder. Eight models are available: 2- and 3-inch-barrel models with a steel-alloy frame and cylinder in matte-black finish, 2- and 3-inch-barrel models with an ultralight aluminum-alloy frame in hard-coat, black-anodized finish, 2- and 3-inch-barrel models with

a stainless steel frame and cylinder in a matte finish, and 2- and 3-inch-barrel models with an ultralight aluminum-alloy frame in a stainless-matte finish. Imported by Taurus International.
Prce: ....$369.52 - $384.97

TAURUS 605 DEFENDER
Capacity: 5 Rounds, Action Type: Double Action/Single Action, Firing System: Hammer, Front Sight: Night Sight with orange outline, Rear Sight: Fixed, Grip: Hogue Rubber grips, VZ, Altamont. Caliber: .38 Spl. +P, .357 Mag, Frame Size: Small, Barrel Length: 3 in., Overall Length: 7.50 in., Overall Height: 4.80 in., Overall Width: 1.41 in. Weights: 23.52 to 25.52 oz., Features: Extended ejector rod, night sights, Safety: Transfer Bar. Finishes: Matte black oxide, matte stainless steel, tungsten Cerakote.
Price: ....$472.00–$540.00

TAURUS DEFENDER 856
Caliber: .38 Special +P. Capacity: 6-round cylinder. Barrel: 3 in. Grips: Hogue rubber, VZ black/gray, walnut. Sights: Fixed rear, tritium night sight with bright orange outline. Features: The Defender 856 is built on Taurus' small frame, making for a compact defensive revolver. Four standard models are available to include a stainless steel frame with matte finish, an ultralight aluminum-alloy frame with matte finish, stainless steel frame with black Tenifer finish, and an aluminum-alloy frame with hard-coat, black-anodized finish. Two upgrade versions are available with special grips and finish treatments. Imported by Taurus International.
Price: ....$429.00 - $477.00

TAURUS MODEL 17 TRACKER
Caliber: .17 HMR. Capacity: 7-round cylinder. Barrel: 6.5 in. Weight: 45.8 oz. Grips: Rubber. Sights: Adjustable. Features: Double action, matte stainless, integral key-lock.
Price: From **$539.00**

TAURUS MODEL 992 TRACKER
Calibers: .22 LR with interchangeable .22 WMR cylinder. Capacity: 9-round cylinder. Barrel: 4 or 6.5 in with ventilated rib. Features: Adjustable rear sight, blued or stainless finish.
Price: Blue **$640.00**
Price: Stainless **$692.00**

TAURUS MODEL 44SS
Caliber: .44 Magnum. Capacity: 5-round cylinder. Barrel: Ported, 4, 6.5,

8.4 in. Weight: 34 oz. Grips: Rubber. Sights: Adjustable. Features: Double action. Integral key-lock. Introduced 1994. Finish: Matte stainless. Imported from Brazil by Taurus International Manufacturing, Inc.
Price: From .... **$648.00-$664.00**

TAURUS MODEL 65
Caliber: .357 Magnum. Capacity: 6-round cylinder. Barrel: 4-in. full underlug. Weight: 38 oz. Length: 10.5 in. overall. Grips: Soft rubber. Sights: Fixed. Features: Double action, integral key-lock. Matte blued or stainless. Imported by Taurus International.
Price: Blued **$539.00**
Price: Stainless **$591.00**

TAURUS MODEL 66
Similar to Model 65, 4 in. or 6 in. barrel, 7-round cylinder, adjustable rear sight. Integral key-lock action. Imported by Taurus International.
Price: Blue **$599.00**
Price: Stainless **$652.00**

TAURUS MODEL 82 HEAVY BARREL
Caliber: .38 Special. Capacity: 6-round cylinder. Barrel: 4 in., heavy. Weight: 36.5 oz. Length: 9.25 in. overall. Grips: Soft black rubber. Sights: Serrated ramp front, square notch rear. Features: Double action, solid rib, integral key-lock. Imported by Taurus International.
Price: From **$521.00**

TAURUS MODEL 85FS
Caliber: .38 Special. Capacity: 5-round cylinder. Barrel: 2 in. Weights: 17–24.5 oz., titanium 13.5–15.4 oz. Grips: Rubber, rosewood or mother of pearl. Sights: Ramp front, square notch rear. Features: Spurred hammer. Blued, matte stainless, blue with gold accents, stainless with gold accents; rated for +P ammo. Integral keylock. Some models have titanium frame. Introduced 1980. Imported by Taurus International.
Price: From **$379.00**

TAURUS MODEL 856 ULTRALIGHT
Caliber: .38 Special. Capacity: 6-round cylinder. Barrel: 2 in. Matte black or stainless. Weights: 15.7 oz., titanium 13.5–15.4 oz. Grips: Rubber, rosewood or mother of pearl. Sights: Serrated ramp front, square notch rear. Features: Aluminum frame, matte black or stainless cylinder, azure blue, bronze, burnt orange or rouge finish.
Price: .... **$364.00-$461.00**

TAURUS 380 MINI
Caliber: .380 ACP. Capacity: 5-round cylinder w/moon clip. Barrel: 1.75 in. Weight: 15.5 oz. Length: 5.95 in. Grips: Rubber. Sights: Adjustable rear, fixed front. Features: DAO. Available in blued or stainless finish. Five Star (moon) clips included.
Price: Blued **$478.00**
Price: Stainless **$514.00**

Prices given are believed to be accurate at time of publication however, many factors affect retail pricing so exact prices are not possible.

TAURUS MODEL 45-410 JUDGE
Calibers: 2.5-in. .410/.45 Colt, 3-in. .410/.45 Colt. Barrels: 3 in., 6.5 in. (blued finish). Weights: 35.2 oz., 22.4 oz. Length: 7.5 in. Grips: Ribber rubber. Sights: Fiber Optic. Features: DA/SA. Matte stainless and ultra-lite stainless finish. Introduced in 2007. Imported from Brazil by Taurus International.
Price: From **$511.00**

TAURUS JUDGE PUBLIC DEFENDER POLYMER
Caliber: .45 Colt/.410 (2.5 in.). Capacity: 5-round cylinder. Barrel: 2.5-in. Weight: 27 oz. Features: SA/DA revolver with 5-round cylinder; polymer frame; Ribber rubber-feel grips; fiber-optic front sight; adjustable rear sight; blued or stainless cylinder; shrouded hammer with cocking spur; blued finish.
Price: From **$469.00**

TAURUS EXECUTIVE GRADE JUDGE
Caliber: .45 Colt/.410 Capacity: 5 Rounds. Finish: Hand-polished Stainless steel satin. Tuned action. Presentation-grade wood grips and brass bead front sight on a 3-in. barrel. Frame Size: Tracker. Overall Length: 9.50 in. Overall Height: 5.10 in. Overall Width: 1.50 in. Weight: 36 oz. (unloaded). Transfer bar safety.
Prce: **$949.00**

TAURUS DEFENDER 856 T.O.R.O.
Caliber: .38 Special (+P) Capacity: 6 rounds. Barrel length: 3 in. Finish: Stainless steel matte. Optics-ready, accepts compact red-dot sights that fit the Holosun K-footprint. Front Sight: Removable. Rear Sight: Fixed. Small frame. Overall Length 7.50 in. Overall Height: 4.80 in. Overall Width: 1.40 in. Overall Weight: 23.50 oz. (unloaded).
Prce: **$460.00**

TAURUS 605 T.O.R.O.
Caliber: .357 Mag. Capacity: 5 rounds. Otherwise nearly identical to the 856.
Prce: **$470.00**

TAURUS RAGING HUNTER
Calibers: .357 Magnum, .44 Magnum, .454 Casull, .460 Smith & Wesson Magnum. Capacity: 7 (.357), 6 (.44) and 5 (.454) rounds. Barrels: 5.12, 6.75, 8.37 in. Grips: Cushioned rubber. Sights: Adjustable rear, fixed front. Weight: 49 - 59.2 oz. Features: This is a DA/SA big-game-hunting revolver, available in three calibers and three barrel lengths, each featuring a Picatinny rail for easy optic mounting without removing the iron sights. All Raging Hunter models come with factory porting and cushioned rubber grips. Two finishes are available: matte black and two-tone matte stainless. Imported by Taurus International.
Prce: Black **$968.00**
Prce: Two Tone **$983.00**

TAURUS RAGING HUNTER TWO TONE
Caliber: .460 S&W. Barrel: 10.5-in. w/ compensator. Capacity: 5 rounds. Lower Picatinny rail to attach bipods and shooting sticks. A top rail allows for additional sight/scope options. Fixed front sight, fully adjustable rear. Frame Size: Large. Overall length: 16.22 in. Overall height: 6.40 in. Overall width: 1.80 in. Weight: 71.26 oz. (unloaded).
Prce: Black **$1,269.00**

TAURUS RAGING HUNTER 500
Caliber: .500 S&W Magnum. Capacity: 5 rounds. Barrel Length: 5.12, 6.75, and 8.37 in. Finish: Matte black or two-tone. Picatinny rail, ported barrel. Sights: Fixed front. Fully adjustable rear.
Prce: Black .... **$1,069.00–$1,089.00**

TAURUS MODEL 627 TRACKER
Caliber: .357 Magnum. Capacity: 7-round cylinder. Barrels: 4 or 6.5 in. Weights: 28.8, 41 oz. Grips: Rubber. Sights: Fixed front, adjustable rear. Features: Double-action. Stainless steel, Shadow Gray or Total Titanium; vent rib (steel models only); integral key-lock action. Imported by Taurus International.
Price: From **$577.00**

Prices given are believed to be accurate at time of publication however, many factors affect retail pricing so exact prices are not possible.

78TH EDITION, 2024 ✦ 515

TAURUS MODEL 444 ULTRA-LIGHT

Caliber: .44 Magnum. Capacity: 5-round cylinder. Barrels: 2.5 or 4 in. Weight: 28.3 oz. Grips: Cushioned inset rubber. Sights: Fixed red-fiber optic front, adjustable rear. Features: UltraLite titanium blue finish, titanium/alloy frame built on Raging Bull design. Smooth trigger shoe, 1.760-in. wide, 6.280-in. tall. Barrel rate of twist 1:16, 6 grooves. Introduced 2005. Imported by Taurus International.
Price: **$944.00**

TAURUS MODEL 692

Calibers: .38 Special/.357 Magnum or 9mm. **Capacity:** 7-round cylinder. **Barrels:** 3 or 6.5 in, ported. **Sights:** Adjustable rear, fixed front. **Grip:** "Ribber" textured. **Finish:** Matte blued or stainless. **Features:** Caliber can be changed with a swap of the cylinders which are non-fluted.
Price: **$659.00**

TAURUS MODEL 444/454 RAGING BULL SERIES

Calibers: .44 Magnum, .454 Casull. Barrels: 2.25 in., 5 in., 6.5 in., 8.375 in. Weight: 53–63 oz. Length: 12 in. overall (6.5 in. barrel). Grips: Soft black rubber. Sights: Patridge front, adjustable rear. Features: DA, ventilated rib, integral key-lock. Most models have ported barrels. Introduced 1997. Imported by Taurus International.
Price: 444 .... **$900.00**
Price: 454 .... **$1,204.00**

TAURUS MODEL 605 PLY

Caliber: .357 Magnum. **Capacity:** 5-round cylinder. **Barrel:** 2 in. **Weight:** 20 oz. **Grips:** Rubber. **Sights:** Fixed. **Features:** Polymer frame steel cylinder. Blued or stainless. Introduced 1995. Imported by Taurus International.
Price: Blued **$393.00**
Price: Stainless **$410.00**

TAURUS MODEL 905

Caliber: 9mm. **Capacity:** 5-round cylinder. **Barrel:** 2 in. **Features:** Small-frame revolver with rubber boot grips, fixed sights, choice of exposed or concealed hammer. Blued or stainless finish.
Price: Blued **$531.00**
Price: Stainless **$583.00**

Prices given are believed to be accurate at time of publication however, many factors affect retail pricing so exact prices are not possible.

CIMARRON BISLEY MODEL SINGLE-ACTION
Calibers: .357 Magnum, .44 WCF, .44 Special, .45. Features: Similar to Colt Bisley, special grip frame and trigger guard, knurled wide-spur hammer, curved trigger. Introduced 1999. Imported by Cimarron F.A. Co.
Price: From **$636.00**

CIMARRON LIGHTNING SA
Calibers: .22 LR, .32-20/32 H&R dual cyl. combo, .38 Special, .41 Colt. Barrels: 3.5 in., 4.75 in., 5.5 in. Grips: Smooth or checkered walnut. Sights: Blade front. Features: Replica of the Colt 1877 Lightning DA. Similar to Cimarron Thunderer, except smaller grip frame to fit smaller hands. Standard blued, charcoal blued or nickel finish with forged, old model, or color casehardened frame. Dual cylinder model available with .32-30/.32 H&R chambering. Introduced 2001. From Cimarron F.A. Co.
Price: From .... **$503.00–$565.00**
Price: .32-20/.32 H&R dual cylinder **$649.00**

CIMARRON MODEL P SAA
Calibers: .32 WCF, .38 WCF, .357 Magnum, .44 WCF, .44 Special, .45 Colt and .45 ACP. Barrels: 4.75, 5.5, 7.5 in. Weight: 39 oz. Length: 10 in. overall (4.75-in. barrel). Grips: Walnut. Sights: Blade front. Features: Old model black-powder frame with Bullseye ejector, or New Model frame. Imported by Cimarron F.A. Co.
Price: From **$550.00**

CIMARRON MODEL "P" JR.
Calibers: .22 LR, .32-20, .32 H&R, 38 Special Barrels: 3.5, 4.75, 5.5 in. Grips: Checkered walnut. Sights: Blade front. Features: Styled after 1873 Colt Peacemaker, except 20 percent smaller. Blue finish with color case-hardened frame; Cowboy action. Introduced 2001. From Cimarron F.A. Co.
Price: From **$480.00**

CIMARRON U.S.V. ARTILLERY MODEL SINGLE-ACTION
Caliber: .45 Colt. Barrel: 5.5 in. Weight: 39 oz. Length: 11.5 in. overall. Grips: Walnut. Sights: Fixed. Features: U.S. markings and cartouche, casehardened frame and hammer. Imported by Cimarron F.A. Co.
Price: Blued finish... **$594.00**
Price: Original finish **$701.00**

CIMARRON BAD BOY
Calibers: .44 Magnum, 10mm. Capacity: 6-round cylinder. Barrel: 8 in. Grips: Walnut. Sights: Fully adjustable rear, fixed front. Features: Built on a replica Single Action Army Pre-War frame with an 1860 Army-style, one-piece walnut grip. The carbon-alloy steel frame is covered in a classic blue finish and it is fitted with an 8-inch octagon barrel and adjustable sights, and chambered in the popular semi-auto 10mm round in 2020.
Price: **$726.05**

Prices given are believed to be accurate at time of publication however, many factors affect retail pricing so exact prices are not possible.

78TH EDITION, 2024 ✛ **517**

COLT SINGLE ACTION ARMY
Calibers: .357 Magnum, .45 Colt. Capacity: 6-round cylinder. Barrels: 4.75, 5.5, 7.5 in. Weight: 40 oz. (4.75-in. barrel). Length: 10.25 in. overall (4.75-in. barrel). Grips: Black Eagle composite. Sights: Blade front, notch rear. Features: Available in full nickel finish with nickel grip medallions, or Royal Blue with color casehardened frame. Reintroduced 1992. Additional calibers available through Colt Custom Shop.
Price: Blued **$1,599.00**
Price: Nickel.. **$1,799.00**

EAA BOUNTY HUNTER SA
Calibers: .22 LR/.22 WMR, .357 Mag., .44 Mag., .45 Colt. Capacities: 6. 10-round cylinder available for .22LR/.22WMR. Barrels: 4.5 in., 7.5 in. Weight: 2.5 lbs. Length: 11 in. overall (4.625 in. barrel). Grips: Smooth walnut. Sights: Blade front, grooved topstrap rear. Features: Transfer bar safety; 3-position hammer; hammer-forged barrel. Introduced 1992. Imported by European American Armory
Price: Centerfire, blued or case-hardened **$478.00**
Price: Centerfire, nickel **$515.00**
Price: .22 LR/.22 WMR, blued **$343.00**
Price: .22LR/.22WMR, nickel **$380.00**
Price: .22 LR/.22WMR, 10-round cylinder **$465.00**

EMF 1875 OUTLAW
Calibers: .357 Magnum, .44-40, .45 Colt. Barrels: 7.5 in., 9.5 in. Weight: 46 oz. Length: 13.5 in. overall. Grips: Smooth walnut. Sights: Blade front, fixed groove rear. Features: Authentic copy of 1875 Remington with firing pin in hammer; color casehardened frame, blued cylinder, barrel, steel backstrap and trigger guard. Also available in nickel, factory engraved. Imported by E.M.F. Co.
Price: All calibers **$520.00**
Price: Laser Engraved **$800.00**

EMF 1873 GREAT WESTERN II
Calibers: .357 Magnum, .45 Colt, .44/40. Barrels: 3.5 in., 4.75 in., 5.5 in., 7.5 in. Weight: 36 oz. Length: 11 in. (5.5-in. barrel). Grips: Walnut. Sights: Blade front, notch rear. Features: Authentic reproduction of the original 2nd Generation Colt single-action revolver. Standard and bone casehardening. Coil hammer spring. Hammer-forged barrel. Alchimista has case-hardened frame, brass backstrap, longer and wider 1860 grip.
Price: 1873 Californian .... **$545.00–$560.00**
Price: 1873 Custom series, bone or nickel, ivory-like grips **$689.90**
Price: 1873 Stainless steel, ivory-like grips **$589.90**
Price: 1873 Paladin **$560.00**
Price: Deluxe Californian with checkered walnut grips stainless.......... **$780.00**

Price: Buntline **$605.00**
Price: Alchimista.. **$675.00**

EMF 1873 DAKOTA II
Caliber: .357 Magnum, 45 Colt. Barrel: 4.75 in. Grips: Walnut. Finish: black.
Price: **$460.00**

FREEDOM ARMS MODEL 83 PREMIER GRADE
Calibers: .357 Magnum, 41 Magnum, .44 Magnum, .454 Casull, .475 Linebaugh, .500 Wyo. Exp. Capacity: 5-round cylinder. Barrels: 4.75 in., 6 in., 7.5 in., 9 in. (.357 Mag. only), 10 in. (except .357 Mag. and 500 Wyo. Exp.) Weight: 53 oz. (7.5-in. bbl. in .454 Casull). Length: 13 in. (7.5 in. bbl.). Grips: Impregnatedhardwood. Sights: Adjustable rear with replaceable front sight. Fixed rear notch and front blade. Features: Stainless steel construction with brushed finish; manual sliding safety bar. Micarta grips optional. 500 Wyo. Exp. Introduced 2006. Lifetime warranty. Made in USA by Freedom Arms, Inc.
Price: From **$2,738.00**

FREEDOM ARMS MODEL 83 FIELD GRADE
Calibers: .22 LR, .357 Magnum, .41 Magnum, .44 Magnum, .454 Casull, .475 Linebaugh, .500 Wyo. Exp. Capacity: 5-round cylinder. Barrels: 4.75 in., 6 in., 7.5 in., 9 in. (.357 Mag. only), 10 in. (except .357 Mag. and .500 Wyo. Exp.) Weight: 56 oz. (7.5-in. bbl. in .454 Casull). Length: 13.1 in. (7.5 in. bbl.). Grips: Pachmayr standard, impregnated hardwood or Micarta optional. Sights: Adjustable rear with replaceable front sight. Model 83 frame. All stainless steel. Introduced 1988. Made in USA by Freedom Arms Inc.
Price: From **$2,332.00**

FREEDOM ARMS MODEL 97 PREMIER GRADE
Calibers: .17 HMR, .22 LR, .32 H&R, .327 Federal, .357 Magnum, 6 rounds; .41 Magnum, .44 Special, .45 Colt. Capacity: 5-round cylinder. Barrels: 4.25 in., 5.5 in., 7.5 in., 10 in. (.17 HMR, .22 LR, .32 H&R). Weight: 40 oz. (5.5 in. .357 Mag.). Length: 10.75 in. (5.5 in. bbl.). Grips: Impregnated hardwood; Micarta optional. Sights: Adjustable rear, replaceable blade front. Fixed

Prices given are believed to be accurate at time of publication however, many factors affect retail pricing so exact prices are not possible.

rear notch and front blade. Features: Stainless steel construction, brushed finish, automatic transfer bar safety system. Introduced in 1997. Lifetime warranty. Made in USA by Freedom Arms.
Price: From **$2,148.00**

HERITAGE ROUGH RIDER TACTICAL COWBOY
Chambered in .22 LR, is also compatible with the .22 WMR cylinder allowing you to shoot either .22 LR or .22 WMR ammo. The new Heritage Rough Rider Tactical Cowboy features modern day technology into an old classic world. The barrel is threaded for compensators and suppressors. Caliber: .22 LR, Capacity: 6 Rounds, Finish: Black standard. Action Type: Single Action Only. Lands & Grooves: 6. Front Sight: Fiber optic. Rear Sight: Picatinny rail. Safety: Thumb/hammer. Grips: Carbon fiber. Weight: 32.10 oz., Barrel Length: 6.5 in. Overall Length: 11.85 in.
Price: **$212.00**

HERITAGE ROUGH RIDER
Calibers: .22 LR, 22 LR/22 WMR combo, .357 Magnum .44-40, .45 Colt. Capacity: 6-round cylinder. Barrels: 3.5 in., 4.75 in., 5.5 in., 7.5 in. Weights: 31–38 oz. Grips: Exotic cocobolo laminated wood or mother of pearl; bird's head models offered. Sights: Blade front, fixed rear. Adjustable sight on 4.75 in. and 5.5 in. models. Features: Hammer block safety. Transfer bar with Big Bores. High polish blue, black satin, silver satin, casehardened and stainless finish. Introduced 1993. Made in USA by Heritage Mfg., Inc.
Price: Rimfire calibers, From **$200.00**
Price: Centerfire calibers, From... **$450.00**

MAGNUM RESEARCH BFR 20TH ANNIVERSARY
Each hand-crafted 20th Anniversary BFR is part of a limited series, with only 20 pistols to be produced. This custom gun is based on a .45-70 Government long frame model, the first production caliber. A full octagon barrel is added with a custom E-Rod Housing and base pin. Plow-style white polymer grips are hand fit. Exterior surfaces engraved with elegant scrollwork by the artists at Tyler Gun Works. Ships in a beautiful wood case, includes a signed letter of authenticity. Capacity: 5. Caliber: .45/70 Gov't. Barrel: 7.5 in. full octagon. Overall Length: 15-in. Height: 6 in. Cylinder Width: 1.75 in. Finish: Brushed stainless steel. Weight: 4.3 lbs. Sights: Factory black fixed front/rear adjustable. Grip: Plow-style white polymer.
Price: From **$7,000.00**

HERITAGE MANUFACTURING BARKEEP REVOLVER
Caliber: .22 LR. Capacity: 6 rounds. Barrel: 2, 3 in. Grip: Custom scroll wood or gray pearl. Sights: Fixed front and rear. Weight: 2.2 lbs. Features: Heritage Manufacturing's take on the 19th-Century "Storekeeper" single-action revolver. The new Barkeep is chambered in the economical .22 LR but is compatible with an optional interchangeable .22 WMR six-shot cylinder. Available with a black oxide or case-hardened finish. Two grips are also available — custom scroll wood or gray pearl.
Price: Custom wood scroll grips **$180.00**
Price: Gray pearl grips **$189.00**

MAGNUM RESEARCH BFR SINGLE ACTION
Calibers: .44 Magnum, .444 Marlin, .45-70, .45 Colt/.410, .450 Marlin, .454 Casull, .460 S&W Magnum, .480 Ruger/.475 Linebaugh, .500 Linebaugh, .500 JRH, .500 S&W, .30-30. Barrels: 6.5 in., 7.5 in. and 10 in. Weights: 3.6–5.3 lbs. Grips: Black rubber. Sights: Rear sights are the same configuration as the Ruger revolvers. Many aftermarket rear sights will fit the BFR. Front sights are machined by Magnum in four heights and anodized flat black. The four heights accommodate all shooting styles, barrel lengths and calibers. All sights are interchangeable with each BFR's. Features: Crafted in the USA, the BFR single-action 5-shot stainless steel revolver frames are CNC machined inside and out from a pre-heat treated investment casting. This is done to prevent warping and dimensional changes or shifting that occurs during the heat treat process. Magnum Research designed the frame with large calibers and substantial recoil in mind, built to close tolerances to handle the pressure of true big-bore calibers. The BFR is equipped with a transfer bar safety feature that allows the gun to be carried safely with all five chambers loaded.
Price: ....**$1,218.00-$1,302.00**

HERITAGE MANUFACTURING BARKEEP BOOT
Caliber: .22 LR. Capacity: 6 Rounds. Finish: Black standard. Action Type: Single Action Only. Safety: Thumb/Hammer. Grips: Black, gray pearl, custom wood burnt snake. Weight: 25.5 oz. Barrel Length: 1.68 in. Overall Length: 6.38 in.
Price: .... **$196.00–$205.00**

MAGNUM RESEARCH BFR SHORT FRAME
Caliber: .357 Magnum, .44 Magnum. Capacity: 6-round cylinder. Barrels: 5 and 7.5 in. Grips: Standard rubber, Bisley, white polymer or black micarta. Sights: Adjustable rear, fixed front. Weights: 3.5, 3.65 lbs. Features: Made entirely of super tough 17-4PH stainless steel, BFRs are made in the United States and were designed from the outset to handle powerful revolver cartridges. The pre-eminent single-action hunting revolver. Two grip frame options available: a standard plow handle with rubber grip, and Magnum Research iteration of a Bisley with white polymer or black micarta grips.
Price: $1,302.00

MAGNUM RESEARCH BFR LONG FRAME
Caliber: .350 Legend. Capacity: 6-round cylinder. Barrels: 7.5 and 10 in. Grips: Standard rubber, Bisley, white polymer or black micarta. Sights: Adjustable rear, fixed front. Weights: 4.8, 5 lbs. Features: Built on Magnum Research's long frame and made entirely of 17-4PH stainless steel. The first long frame in six-shot configuration. Two grip frame options available: a standard plow handle with rubber grip, and Magnum Research iteration of a Bisley with white polymer or black micarta grips.
Price:... ....$1,302.00

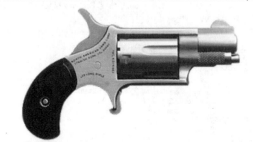

NORTH AMERICAN ARMS MINI
Calibers: .22 Short, 22 LR, 22 WMR. Capacity: 5-round cylinder. Barrels: 1.125 in., 1.625 in. Weight: 4–6.6 oz. Length: 3.625 in., 6.125 in. overall. Grips: Laminated wood. Sights: Blade front, notch fixed rear. Features: All stainless steel construction. Polished satin and matte finish. Engraved models available. From North American Arms.
Price: .22 Short, .22 LR $226.00
Price: .22 WMR $236.00

NORTH AMERICAN ARMS MINI-MASTER
Calibers: .22 LR, .22 WMR. Capacity: 5-round cylinder. Barrel: 4 in. Weight:

10.7 oz. Length: 7.75 in. overall. Grips: Checkered hard black rubber. Sights: Blade front, white outline rear adjustable for elevation, or fixed. Features: Heavy vented barrel; full-size grips. Non-fluted cylinder. Introduced 1989.
Price: .... $284.00–$349.00

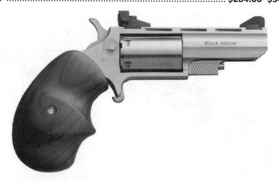

NORTH AMERICAN ARMS BLACK WIDOW
Similar to Mini-Master, 2-in. heavy vent barrel. Built on .22 WMR frame. Non-fluted cylinder, black rubber grips. Available with Millett low-profile fixed sights or Millett sight adjustable for elevation only. Overall length 5.875 in., weighs 8.8 oz. From North American Arms.
Price: Adjustable sight, .22 LR or .22 WMR $352.00
Price: Fixed sight, .22 LR or .22 WMR $288.00

NORTH AMERICAN ARMS "THE EARL" SINGLE-ACTION
Calibers: .22 Magnum with .22 LR accessory cylinder. Capacity: 5-round cylinder. Barrel: 4 in. octagonal. Weight: 6.8 oz. Length: 7.75 in. overall. Grips: Wood. Sights: Barleycorn front and fixed notch rear. Features: Single-action mini-revolver patterned after 1858-style Remington percussion revolver. Includes a spur trigger and a faux loading lever that serves as cylinder pin release.
Price: .... $298.00,$332.00 (convertible)

RUGER NEW MODEL SINGLE-SIX SERIES
Calibers: .22 LR, .17 HMR. Convertible and Hunter models come with extra cylinder for .22 WMR. Capacity: 6. Barrels: 4.62 in., 5.5 in., 6.5 in. or 9.5 in. Weight: 35–42 oz. Finish: Blued or stainless. Grips: Black checkered hard rubber, black laminate or hardwood (stainless model only). Single-Six .17 Model available only with 6.5-in. barrel, blue finish, rubber grips. Hunter Model available only with 7.5-in. barrel, black laminate grips and stainless finish.
Price: (blued) $629.00
Price: (stainless) $699.00

RUGER SINGLE-TEN AND RUGER SINGLE-NINE SERIES
Calibers: .22 LR, .22 WMR. Capacities: 10 (.22 LR Single-Ten), 9 (.22 Mag Single-Nine). Barrels: 5.5 in. (Single-Ten), 6.5 in. (Single-Nine). Weight: 38–39 oz. Grips: Hardwood Gunfighter. Sights: Williams Adjustable Fiber Optic.
Price: $699.00

RUGER NEW MODEL BLACKHAWK/ BLACKHAWK CONVERTIBLE
Calibers: .30 Carbine, .357 Magnum/.38 Special, .41 Magnum, .44 Special, .45 Colt. Capacity: 6-round cylinder. Barrels: 4.625 in., 5.5 in., 6.5 in., 7.5 in. (.30 carbine and .45 Colt). Weights: 36–45 oz. Lengths: 10.375 in. to 13.5 in. Grips: Rosewood or black checkered. Sights: .125-in. ramp front, micro-click rear adjustable for windage and elevation. Features: Rosewood grips, Ruger transfer bar safety system, independent firing pin, hardened chrome-moly steel frame, music wire springs through-out. Case and lock included. Convertibles come with extra cylinder.
Price: Blued $669.00
Price: Convertible, .357/9mm $749.00
Price: Convertible, .45 Colt/.45 ACP.............................. $749.00
Price: Stainless, .357 only.. $799.00

Prices given are believed to be accurate at time of publication however, many factors affect retail pricing so exact prices are not possible.

RUGER BISLEY SINGLE ACTION
Calibers: .44 Magnum. and .45 Colt. Barrel: 7.5-in. barrel. Length: 13.5 in. Weight: 48–51 oz. Similar to standard Blackhawk, hammer is lower with smoothly curved, deeply checkered wide spur. The trigger is strongly curved with wide smooth surface. Longer grip frame. Adjustable rear sight, ramp-style front. Unfluted cylinder and roll engraving, adjustable sights. Plastic lockable case. Orig. fluted cylinder introduced 1985; discontinued 1991. Unfluted cylinder introduced 1986.
Price: **$899.00**

RUGER NEW MODEL SUPER BLACKHAWK
Caliber: .44 Magnum/.44 Special. Capacity: 6-round cylinder. Barrel: 4.625 in., 5.5 in., 7.5 in., 10.5 in. bull. Weight: 45–55 oz. Length: 10.5 in. to 16.5 in. overall. Grips: Rosewood. Sights: .125-in. ramp front, micro-click rear adjustable for windage and elevation. Features: Ruger transfer bar safety system, fluted or unfluted cylinder, steel grip and cylinder frame, round or square back trigger guard, wide serrated trigger, wide spur hammer. With case and lock.
Price: **$829.00**

RUGER NEW MODEL SUPER BLACKHAWK HUNTER
Caliber: .44 Magnum. Capacity: 6-round cylinder. Barrel: 7.5 in., full-length solid rib, unfluted cylinder. Weight: 52 oz. Length: 13.625 in. Grips: Black laminated wood. Sights: Adjustable rear, replaceable front blade. Features: Reintroduced Ultimate SA revolver. Includes instruction manual, high-impact case, set of medium scope rings, gun lock, ejector rod as standard. Bisley-style frame available.
Price: (Hunter, Bisley Hunter) **$959.00**

RUGER NEW VAQUERO SINGLE-ACTION
Calibers: .357 Magnum, .45 Colt. Capacity: 6-round cylinder. Barrel: 4.625 in., 5.5 in., 7.5 in. Weight: 39–45 oz. Length: 10.5 in. overall (4.625 in. barrel). Grips: Rubber with Ruger medallion. Sights: Fixed blade front, fixed notch rear. Features: Transfer bar safety system and loading gate interlock. Blued model color casehardened finish on frame, rest polished and blued. Engraved model available. Gloss stainless. Introduced 2005.
Price: **$829.00**

RUGER NEW MODEL BISLEY VAQUERO
Calibers: .357 Magnum, .45 Colt. Capacity: 6-round cylinder. Barrel: 5.5-in. Length: 11.12 in. Weight: 45 oz. Features: Similar to New Vaquero but with Bisley-style hammer and grip frame. Simulated ivory grips, fixed sights.
Price: **$899.00**

RUGER NEW BEARCAT SINGLE-ACTION
Caliber: .22 LR. Capacity: 6-round cylinder. Barrel: 4 in. Weight: 24 oz. Length: 9 in. overall. Grips: Smooth rosewood with Ruger medallion. Sights: Blade front, fixed notch rear. Distributor special edition available with adjustable sights. Features: Reintroduction of the Ruger Bearcat with slightly lengthened frame, Ruger transfer bar safety system. Available in blued finish only. Rosewood grips. Introduced 1996 (blued), 2003 (stainless). With case and lock.
Price: SBC-4, blued **$639.00**
Price: KSBC-4, satin stainless **$689.00**

RUGER WRANGLER
Caliber: .22 LR. Capacity: 6-round cylinder. Barrel: 3.75, 4.62, 6.5, and 7.5 in. Grips: Checkered synthetic. Sights: Fixed front and rear. Weight: 30 oz. Features: Inexpensive to own and inexpensive to shoot, this SA revolver is built on an aluminum alloy frame and fitted with a cold hammer-forged barrel. Available in three models with three different finishes: Black Cerakote, Silver Cerakote or Burnt Bronze Cerakote. Equipped with a transfer-bar mechanism and a freewheeling pawl, allowing for easy loading and unloading.
Price: **$269.00**

Prices given are believed to be accurate at time of publication however, many factors affect retail pricing so exact prices are not possible.

78TH EDITION, 2024 ✛ **521**

RUGER SUPER WRANGLER
Caliber: .22 LR/.22 WMR. Capacity: 6. Barrel: 5.5-in. Sights: adjustable. New family of single-action revolvers. A steel cylinder frame. The Super Wrangler is a convertible model that ships with two cylinders, one for inexpensive .22 LR and one for powerful .22 WMR ammunition.
Price: **$329.00**

RUGER WRANGLER BIRDSHEAD
Caliber: .22 LR, Grips: Birdshead synthetic. Capacity: 6. Front Sight: Blade. Barrel Length: 3.75 in. Overall Length: 8.62 in. Weight: 28 oz. Finish: Black Cerakote, silver Cerakote, burnt bronze Cerakote, Cylinder Frame Material: Aluminum alloy. Rear Sight: Integral. Twist 1:14 in. RH. Grooves: 6
Price: **$279.00**

STANDARD MANUFACTURING NICKEL SINGLE ACTION
Calibers: .38 Special, .45 Colt. Capacity: 6-round cylinder. Barrels: 4.75, 5.5 and 7.5 in. Grips: Walnut. Sights: Fixed front and rear. Weight: 40 oz. Features: This is one of the finest Single Action Army reproductions ever built, with great attention to detail. Made entirely from 4140 steel, the new nickel-plated revolvers are available in .38 special and the iconic .45 Colt. You can also opt for C-coverage engraving, making for a truly remarkable firearm. One- or two-piece walnut grips available.
Price: .... **$1,995.00 - $3,495.00**

TAYLOR'S CATTLEMAN SERIES
Calibers: .357 Magnum or 45 Colt. Barrels: 4.75 in., 5.5 in., or 7.5 in. Features: Series of Single Action Army-style revolvers made in many variations.
Price: Gunfighter w/blued & color case finish......................................$556.00
Price: Stainless $720.00
Price: Nickel.. $672.00
Price: Charcoal blued $647.00
Price: Bird's Head 3.5- or 4.5-in. bbl., walnut grips $603.00
Price: Engraved (shown)... $925.00

TAYLOR'S & COMPANY TC9 1873 CATTLEMAN
Caliber: 9mm. Barrel: 4.74- and 5.5-in. barrel lengths. The TC9 9mm pistol is offered in two styles; a large army-size, walnut checkered grip and a black checkered standard-size grip. The 9mm revolver clone has a steel frame with a rear frame notch and fixed front blade sight. This iconic 9mm 1873 Cattleman revolver is offered in a black checkered grip, casehardened frame, with a blued steel finish. Add 7% for the color-casehardened version.
Price: Walnut **$546.00**

TAYLOR'S & COMPANY GUNFIGHTER
Caliber: .357 Magnum, .45 Colt. Capacity: 6 rounds. Barrel: 4.75, 5.5 in. Grip: Walnut. Checkered or smooth. Sights: Fixed front and rear. Weight: 2.4 lbs. Features: This 1873 Colt Single Action Army replica features an Army-sized grip for users with large hands. Casehardened finish. Available with Taylor Tuned action for additional cost.
Price: Smooth grip... **$599.00**
Price: Checkered grip **$629.00**

TAYLOR'S & COMPANY GUNFIGHTER DEFENDER
Caliber: .357 Mag., .45 LC Capacity: 6. Weight: 4.75 in. 2.45 lb., 5.5 in. 2.50 lb. Finish: Blue with case hardened frame. Grip/Stock: Checkered walnut. Manufacturer: Uberti. Sights: Fixed front blade. Rear Frame Notch. Overall Length: 4.75 in. (10.35 in.), 5.5 in. (11.10 in.), Action: Taylor tuning available. The Gunfighter Defender with lowered Runnin' Iron hammer, 1860 Army grip is longer and slightly wider than the smaller Navy grip usually found on 1873 single-action models.
Price: .... **$695.00–$847.00**

TAYLOR'S & COMPANY 1860 ARMY SNUB NOSE
Caliber: .36 Caliber, .44 Caliber. Capacity: 6 rounds. Barrel: 3 in. Grip: Checkered flattop birdshead grip. Sights: Fixed front and rear. Weight:

2.3 lbs. Features: 1860 Army Snub Nose blackpowder percussion replica revolver. It features a steel frame, shoulder stock frame cuts and screws, and a round barrel. Barrel and cylinder are blued while the frame is casehardened. A conversion cylinder is available to shoot smokeless ammunition. Manufactured exclusively by Pietta for Taylor's & Company.
Price: **$379.00**

UBERTI 1851–1860 CONVERSION
Calibers: .38 Special, .45 Colt. Capacity: 6-round engraved cylinder. Barrels: 4.75 in., 5.5 in., 7.5 in., 8 in. Weight: 2.6 lbs. (5.5-in. bbl.). Length: 13 in. overall (5.5-in. bbl.). Grips: Walnut. Features: Brass backstrap, trigger guard; color casehardened frame, blued barrel, cylinder. Introduced 2007.
Price: 1851 Navy **$569.00**
Price: 1860 Army **$589.00**

UBERTI 1871–1872 OPEN TOP
Calibers: .38 Special, .45 Colt. Capacity: 6-round engraved cylinder. Barrels: 4.75 in., 5.5 in., 7.5 in. Weight: 2.6 lbs. (5.5-in. bbl.). Length: 13 in. overall (5.5-in. bbl.). Grips: Walnut. Features: Blued backstrap, trigger guard; color casehardened frame, blued barrel, cylinder. Introduced 2007.
Price: .... **$539.00–$569.00**

UBERTI 1873 CATTLEMAN SINGLE-ACTION
Caliber: .45 Colt. Capacity: 6-round cylinder. Barrels: 4.75 in., 5.5 in., 7.5 in. Weight: 2.3 lbs. (5.5-in. bbl.). Length: 11 in. overall (5.5-in. bbl.). Grips: Styles: Frisco (pearl styled); Desperado (buffalo horn styled); Chisholm (checkered walnut); Gunfighter (black checkered), Cody (ivory styled), one-piece walnut. Sights: Blade front, groove rear. Features: Steel or brass backstrap, trigger guard; color casehardened frame, blued barrel, cylinder. NM designates New Model plunger-style frame; OM designates Old Model screw cylinder pin retainer.
Price: 1873 Cattleman Frisco **$869.00**
Price: 1873 Cattleman Desperado (2006) **$889.00**
Price: 1873 Cattleman Chisholm (2006) **$599.00**
Price: 1873 Cattleman NM, blued 4.75 in. barrel **$669.00**
Price: 1873 Cattleman NM, Nickel finish, 7.5 in. barrel **$689.00**
Price: 1873 Cattleman Cody **$899.00**

UBERTI 1873 CATTLEMAN BIRD'S HEAD SINGLE ACTION
Calibers: .357 Magnum, .45 Colt. Capacity: 6-round cylinder. Barrels: 3.5 in., 4 in., 4.75 in., 5.5 in. Weight: 2.3 lbs. (5.5-in. bbl.). Length: 10.9 in. overall (5.5-in. bbl.). Grips: One-piece walnut. Sights: Blade front, groove rear. Features: Steel or brass backstrap, trigger guard; color casehardened frame, blued barrel, fluted cylinder.
Price: **$569.00**

UBERTI CATTLEMAN .22
Caliber: .22 LR. Capacity: 6- or 12-round cylinder. Barrel: 5.5 in. Grips: One-piece walnut. Sights: Fixed. Features: Blued and casehardened finish, steel or brass backstrap/trigger guard.
Price: (brass backstrap, trigger guard) **$539.00**
Price: (steel backstrap, trigger guard) **$559.00**
Price: (12-round model, steel backstrap, trigger guard) **$589.00**

UBERTI 1873 CATTLEMAN BRASS 9MM
Delivering the same performance and standout features as the 1873 Cattleman Brass 9mm, the 1873 Cattleman Brass Dual Cylinder ups the ante with two included cylinders — one chambered in 9mm Luger and the other in .357 Magnum.
Price: **$599.00**

UBERTI 1873 CATTLEMAN BRASS DUAL CYLINDER 9MM/.357 MAGNUM
Delivering the same performance and standout features as the 1873 Cattleman Brass 9mm, the 1873 Cattleman Brass Dual Cylinder ups the ante with two included cylinders — one chambered in 9mm Luger and the other in .357 Magnum.
Price: **$749.00**

UBERTI DALTON REVOLVER
Caliber: .45 Colt. Capacity: 6-round cylinder. Barrel: 5.5 in. Grips: Simulated pearl. Sights: Fixed front and rear. Weight: 2.3 lbs. Features: Uberti USA expands its Outlaws & Lawmen Series of revolvers with the addition of the Dalton Revolver, a faithful reproduction of the Colt Single Action Army revolver used by Dalton Gang leader Bob Dalton. Features hand-chased engraving from famed Italian engraving company, Atelier Giovanelli, on the receiver, grip frame and cylinder.
Price: **$1,109.00**

UBERTI 1873 BISLEY SINGLE-ACTION
Calibers: .357 Magnum, .45 Colt (Bisley); .22 LR and .38 Special. (Stallion), both with 6-round fluted cylinder. Barrels: 4.75 in., 5.5 in., 7.5 in. Weight: 2–2.5 lbs. Length: 12.7 in. overall (7.5-in. barrel). Grips: Two-piece walnut. Sights: Blade front, notch rear. Features: Replica of Colt's Bisley Model. Polished blued finish, color casehardened frame. Introduced 1997.
Price: 1873 Bisley, 7.5-in. barrel **$619.00**

Prices given are believed to be accurate at time of publication however, many factors affect retail pricing so exact prices are not possible.

78TH EDITION, 2024 ✛ **523**

UBERTI 1873 BUNTLINE AND REVOLVER CARBINE SINGLE-ACTION
Caliber: .357 Magnum, .44-40, .45 Colt. Capacity: 6. Barrel: 18 in. Length: 22.9–34 in. Grips: Walnut pistol grip or rifle stock. Sights: Fixed or adjustable.
Price: 1873 Revolver Carbine, 18-in. bbl., 34 in. OAL **$729.00**
Price: 1873 Cattleman Buntline Target, 18-in. bbl. 22.9 in. OAL **$639.00**

UBERTI 1873 EL PATRÓN 9MM
Presented with checkered walnut grips, case-hardened frame, 5.5-inch blued barrel, numbered cylinder, and EasyView sights, the El Patrón has the classic profile of the Old West SAA revolvers.
Price: **$729.00**

UBERTI 1870 SCHOFIELD-STYLE TOP BREAK
Calibers: .38 Special, .44 Russian, .44-40, .45 Colt. Capacity: 6-round cylinder. Barrels: 3.5 in., 5 in., 7 in. Weight: 2.4 lbs. (5-in. barrel) Length: 10.8 in. overall (5-in. barrel). Grips: Two-piece smooth walnut or pearl. Sights: Blade front, notch rear. Features: Replica of Smith & Wesson Model 3 Schofield. Single-action, top break with automatic ejection. Polished blued finish (first model). Introduced 1994.
Price: .... **$1,189.00-$1,599.00**

UBERTI STAINLESS STEEL SHORT STROKE CMS PRO
Caliber: .45 Colt. Capacity: 6-round cylinder. Barrel: 3.5 in. Grips: Synthetic traditional. Sights: Fixed front and rear. Weight: 2.1 lbs. Features: Made specifically for the rigors of Cowboy Mounted Shooting competition, and built entirely of stainless steel. Good for quick, one-handed shooting while riding a horse. Features low-profile, short-stroke hammer with 20-percent less travel. Extra-wide, deeply grooved hammer, and chambered in the classic .45 Colt.
Price: **$909.00**

UBERTI STAINLESS STEEL SHORT STROKE CMS KL PRO
Caliber: .45 Colt. Capacity: 6-round cylinder. Barrel: 3.5 in. Grips: Synthetic bird's head. Sights: Fixed front and rear. Weight: 2.1 lbs. Features: Made specifically for the rigors of Cowboy Mounted Shooting competition, and built entirely of stainless steel. This model is the result of the partnership between Uberti USA and legendary Cowboy Mounted Shooter competitor Kenda Lenseigne, winner of multiple world and national mounted shooting championships. It features a modified bird's-head grip with Lenseigne's brand on the grip and her signature engraved on the barrel. Features low-profile, short-stroke hammer with 20-percent less travel. Extra-wide, deeply grooved hammer, and chambered in the classic .45 Colt.
Price: **$909.00**

UBERTI USA DALTON
Caliber: .357 Magnum. Capacity: 6 rounds. Barrel: 5.5 in. Grip: Simulated pearl. Sights: Fixed front and rear. Weight: 2.3 lbs. Features: Uberti USA Outlaw & Lawmen Series of revolvers adds the Dalton — a faithful reproduction of the Colt Single Action Army revolver used by Dalton Gang leader Bob Dalton. Features hand-chased engraving from famed Italian engraving company, Atelier Giovanelli on the receiver, grip frame, and cylinder. This new version is chambered in .357 Magnum.
Price: **$1,109.00**

UBERTI USA FRANK
Caliber: .357 Magnum. Capacity: 6 rounds. Barrel: 7.5 in. Grip: Simulated ivory. Sights: Fixed front and rear. Weight: 2.3 lbs. Features: Uberti USA Outlaw & Lawmen Series of revolvers adds a .357 Magnum version of the Frank revolver, a faithful reproduction of the outlaw Frank James' 1875 Remington. Finished in nickel plating, the grip is simulated ivory with a lanyard loop.
Price: **$949.00**

UBERTI USA HARDIN
Caliber: .45 Colt. Capacity: 6 rounds. Barrel: 7 in. Grip: Simulated bison horn. Sights: Fixed front and rear. Weight: 2.6 lbs. Features: Uberti USA Outlaw & Lawmen Series adds the Hardin, a faithful reproduction of the Smith & Wesson Top-break revolver used by John Wesley Hardin. Features a case-colored frame and charcoal blue barrel and cylinder along with simulated bison-horn grip, chambered in .45 Colt.
Price: **$1,479.00**

UBERTI USA TEDDY
Caliber: .45 Colt. Capacity: 6 rounds. Barrel: 5.5 in. Grip: Simulated ivory. Sights: Fixed front and rear. Weight: 2.3 lbs. Features: Replica of the revolver Theodore Roosevelt carried on many of his adventures. A replica 1873 Colt, this one is chambered in .45 Colt, and features a nickel finish, full laser engraving along the frame, cylinder, and barrel, and simulated ivory grips.
Price: **$1,249.00**

AMERICAN DERRINGER MODEL 1
Calibers: All popular handgun calibers plus .45 Colt/.410 Shotshell. Capacity: 2, (.45-70 model is single shot). Barrel: 3 in. Overall length: 4.82 in. Weight: 15 oz. Features: Manually operated hammer-block safety automatically disengages when hammer is cocked. Texas Commemorative has brass frame and is available in .38 Special, .44-40. or .45 Colt.
Price: .... **$635.00–$735.00**
Price: Texas Commemorative **$835.00**

AMERICAN DERRINGER MODEL 8
Calibers: .45 Colt/.410 shotshell. Capacity: 2. Barrel: 8 in. Weight: 24 oz.
Price: **$915.00**
Price: High polish finish **$1,070.00**

AMERICAN DERRINGER DA38
Calibers: .38 Special, .357 Magnum, 9mm Luger. Barrel: 3.3 in. Weight: 14.5 oz. Features: DA operation with hammer-block thumb safety. Barrel, receiver and all internal parts are made from stainless steel.
Price: .... **$690.00–$740.00**

BOND ARMS TEXAS DEFENDER DERRINGER
Calibers: Available in more than 10 calibers, from .22 LR to .45 LC/.410 shotshells. Barrel: 3 in. Weight: 20 oz. Length: 5 in. Grips: Rosewood. Sights: Blade front, fixed rear. Features: Interchangeable barrels, stainless steel firing pins, cross-bolt safety, automatic extractor for rimmed calibers. Stainless steel construction, brushed finish. Right or left hand.
Price: **$543.00**
Price: Interchangeable barrels, .22 LR thru .45 LC, 3 in. **$139.00**
Price: Interchangeable barrels, .45 LC, 3.5 in. .... **$159.00–$189.00**

BOND ARMS RANGER II
Caliber: .45 LC/.410 shotshells or .357 Magnum/.38 Special. Barrel: 4.25 in. Weight: 23.5 oz. Length: 6.25 in. Features: This model has a trigger guard. Intr. 2011. From Bond Arms.
Price: **$673.00**

BOND ARMS CENTURY 2000 DEFENDER
Calibers: .45 LC/.410 shotshells. or .357 Magnum/.38 Special. Barrel: 3.5 in. Weight: 21 oz. Length: 5.5 in. Features: Similar to Defender series.
Price: **$517.00**

BOND ARMS COWBOY DEFENDER
Calibers: From .22 LR to .45 LC/.410 shotshells. Barrel: 3 in. Weight: 19 oz. Length: 5.5 in. Features: Similar to Defender series. No trigger guard.
Price: **$493.00**

BOND ARMS GRIZZLY
Calibers: .45 Colt/.410 bore. Capacity: 2 rounds. Barrel: 3 in. Grips: Rosewood. Sights: Fixed front and rear. Features: Similar to other Bond Arms derringers, this model is chambered in .45 Colt and 2.5-inch, .410-bore shotshells. Vibrant rosewood grips with grizzly-bear artwork adorn the Grizzly. It includes a matching leather holster embossed with a grizzly bear.
Price: **$377.00**

BOND ARMS SNAKE SLAYER
Calibers: .45 LC/.410 shotshell (2.5 in. or 3 in.). Barrel: 3.5 in. Weight: 21 oz. Length: 5.5 in. Grips: Extended rosewood. Sights: Blade front, fixed rear. Features: Single-action; interchangeable barrels; stainless steel firing pin. Introduced 2005.
Price: **$603.00**

BOND ARMS ROUGHNECK
Calibers: 9mm, .357 Magnum, .45 ACP. Capacity: 2 rounds. Barrel: 2.5 in. Grips: Textured rubber. Sights: Fixed front and rear. Weight: 22 oz. Features: A member of the new Bond Arms Rough series of derringers that includes the premium features found in all Bond guns, including stainless steel barrel, cross-bolt safety, retracting firing pin, spring-loaded, cam-lock lever and rebounding hammer. Each gun of the new series undergoes a quick clean up and deburring and then is bead-blasted, giving it a rough finish. This lightweight tips the scales at 22 ounces.
Price: **$269.00**

BOND ARMS ROWDY XL
Caliber: .45 Colt/.410. Barrel: 3.5 in. Extended grip size. Length: 5.75 in. Weight 22 oz. Grip: B6 Resin.
Price: **$349.00**

BOND ARMS CYCLOPS
Caliber: .45-70 Govt. Barrel: 4.25 in. Length: 6.75 in. Grip: B6 Nylon. Weight: 28 oz. Extended grip. Trigger pull: 7 lbs.
Price: **$699.00**

BOND ARMS SNAKE SLAYER IV
Calibers: .45 LC/.410 shotshell (2.5 in. or 3 in.). Barrel: 4.25 in. Weight: 22 oz. Length: 6.25 in. Grips: Extended rosewood. Sights: Blade front, fixed rear. Features: Single-action; interchangeable barrels; stainless steel firing pin. Introduced 2006.
Price: **$648.00**

Prices given are believed to be accurate at time of publication however, many factors affect retail pricing so exact prices are not possible.

78TH EDITION, 2024 ✦ **525**

BOND ARMS STINGER

Calibers: 9mm, .380 ACP. The All-New Stinger has the same quality as Bond Arms' regular models but has half the weight and a slimmer profile. Features: Stainless steel matte barrel, 7075 anodized aluminum frame. Total weight: 12 oz. Rebounding hammer, retracting firing pins, cross-bolt safety. Comes with standard rubber grips and a slimmer set of polymer grips.
Price: **$379.00**

BOND ARMS STUBBY

Caliber: .22 LR, .380 ACP, 9mm. Barrel: 2.2 in. Thin nylon grip. Fixed sight. Length: 4.5 in. Height: 3.75 in. Weight: 13.3 oz. Trigger pull: 7 lbs. Width: 5/16 in.
Price: **$297.00**

COBRA STANDARD SERIES DERRINGERS

Calibers: .22 LR, .22 WMR, .25 ACP, .32 ACP. Barrel: 2.4 in. Weight: 9.5 oz. Length: 4 in. overall. Grips: Laminated wood or pearl. Sights: Blade front, fixed notch rear. Features: Choice of black powder coat, satin nickel or chrome finish. Introduced 2002. Made in USA by Cobra Enterprises of Utah, Inc.
Price: **$169.00**

COBRA LONG-BORE DERRINGERS

Calibers: .22 WMR, .38 Special, 9mm. Barrel: 3.5 in. Weight: 16 oz. Length: 5.4 in. overall. Grips: Black or white synthetic or rosewood. Sights: Fixed. Features: Chrome, satin nickel, or black Teflon finish. Introduced 2002. Made in USA by Cobra Enterprises of Utah, Inc.
Price: **$187.00**

COBRA TITAN .45 LC/.410 DERRINGER

Calibers: .45 LC, .410 or 9mm, 2-round capacity. Barrel: 3.5 in. Weight: 16.4 oz. Grip: Rosewood. Features: Standard finishes include: satin stainless,

black stainless and brushed stainless. Made in USA by Cobra Enterprises of Utah, Inc.
Price: **$399.00**

DOUBLETAP DERRINGER

Calibers: .45 Colt or 9mm Barrel: 3 in. Weight: 12 oz. Length: 5.5 in. Sights: Adjustable. Features: Over/under, two-barrel design. Rounds are fired individually with two separate trigger pulls. Tip-up design, aluminum frame.
Price: **$499.00**

HEIZER PAK1

Caliber: 7.2x39. Similar to Pocket AR but chambered for 7.62x39mm. Single shot. Barrel: 3.75 in., ported or unported. Length: 6.375 in. Weight: 23 oz.
Price: **$339.00**

HEIZER PS1 POCKET SHOTGUN

Calibers: .45 Colt or .410 shotshell. Single-shot. Barrel: Tip-up, 3.25 in. Weight: 22 oz. Length: 5.6 in. Width: .742 in Height: 3.81 in. Features: Available in several finishes. Standard model is matte stainless or black. Also offered in Hedy Jane series for the women in pink or in two-tone combinations of stainless and pink, blue, green, purple. Includes interchangeable AR .223 barrel. Made in the USA by Heizer Industries.
Price: **$499.00**

HEIZER POCKET AR

Caliber: .223 Rem./5.56 NATO. Single shot. Barrel: 3.75 in., ported or non-ported. Length: 6.375 in. Weight: 23 oz. Features: Similar to PS1 pocket shotgun but chambered for .223/5.56 rifle cartridge.
Price: **$339.00**

Prices given are believed to be accurate at time of publication however, many factors affect retail pricing so exact prices are not possible.

HENRY MARE'S LEG

Calibers: .22 LR, .22 WMR, .357 Magnum, .44 Magnum, .45 Colt.
Capacities: 10 rounds (.22 LR), 8 rounds (.22 WMR), 5 rounds (others).
Barrel: 12.9 in. Length: 25 in. Weight: 4.5 lbs. (rimfire) to 5.8 lbs. (centerfire calibers). Features: Lever-action operation based on Henry rifle series and patterned after gun made famous in Steve McQueen's 1950s TV show, "Wanted: Dead or Alive." Made in the USA.

Price: .22 LR...**$462.00**
Price: .22 WMR **$473.00**
Price: Centerfire calibers **$1,024.00**

MAXIMUM SINGLE-SHOT

Calibers: .22 LR, .22 Hornet, .22 BR, .22 PPC, 223 Rem., .22-250, 6mm BR, 6mm PPC, .243, .250 Savage, 6.5mm-35M, .270 MAX, .270 Win., 7mm TCU, 7mm BR, 7mm-35, 7mm INT-R, 7mm-08, 7mm Rocket, 7mm Super-Mag., .30 Herrett, .30 Carbine, .30-30, .308 Win., 30x39, .32-20, .350 Rem. Mag., .357 Mag., .357 Maximum, .358 Win., .375 H&H, .44 Mag., .454 Casull. Barrel: 8.75 in., 10.5 in., 14 in. Weight: 61 oz. (10.5-in. bbl.); 78 oz. (14-in. bbl.). Length: 15 in., 18.5 in. overall (with 10.5- and 14-in. bbl., respectively). Grips: Smooth walnut stocks and fore-end. Also available with 17-finger-groove grip. Sights: Ramp front, fully adjustable open rear. Features: Falling block action; drilled and tapped for M.O.A. scope mounts; integral grip frame/receiver; adjustable trigger; Douglas barrel (interchangeable). Introduced 1983. Made in USA by M.O.A. Corp.

Price: **$1,062.00**

NOSLER MODEL 48 CUSTOM HANDGUN (NCH)

Calibers: 22 Nosler, 7mm-08, 6mm Creedmoor, 6.5 Creedmoor, .308 Winchester. Standard barrel length 15 in. 12- to 18-inch barrels available upon request. Stock: CNC machined 6061-T6 aircraft-grade aluminum. Bedded action. Free-floated barrel. Finish: Variety of Cerakote colors and combinations. Action: single-shot, solid bottom receiver. Brake: Harrell's Precision Tactical 4-Port is available. Grip: Accepts standard AR-15 grips. Ships with Hogue OverMolded rubber grip with finger grooves. Barrel: Shilen 416R stainless heavy contour. Threaded at the muzzle, supplied with thread protector. Barrel fluting is available for an additional charge.

Price: **$2,495.00**

SAVAGE ARMS 110 PCS (PISTOL CHASSIS SYSTEM)

Calibers: 6.5 Creedmoor, .308 Win., .350 Legend, .300 AAC BLK., .223 Rem. Features: Carbon steel, matte black, barrel and receiver. Medium-contour 10.5-in. barrel, with threaded muzzle (5/8x24). Machined aluminum, 1-piece chassis with 7-in. free-floating modular forend with M-LOK slots and Cerakote finish. 1-Piece 0 MOA rail. Left-hand bolt, right-side eject. Spiral fluted bolt body. 2.5 to 6-lb. user-adjustable AccuTrigger, Picatinny rail at rear of chassis. Accepts most AR-15 pistol grips. Barricade grooves milled into the front of the magazine well, ambidextrous magazine release and AICS magazine.

Price: From **$999.00**

THOMPSON/CENTER ENCORE PRO HUNTER

Calibers: .223, .308. Single shot, break-open design. Barrel: 15 in. Weight: 4.25–4.5 lbs. Grip: Walnut on blued models, rubber on stainless. Matching fore-end. Sights: Adjustable rear, ramp front. Features: Interchangeable barrels, adjustable trigger. Pro Hunter has "Swing Hammer" to allow reaching the hammer when the gun is scoped. Other Pro Hunter features include fluted barrel.

Price: From **$779.00**

THOMPSON/CENTER G2 CONTENDER

Calibers: .22 LR or .357 Magnum. A second generation Contender pistol maintaining the same barrel interchangeability with older Contender barrels and their corresponding forends (except Herrett fore-end). The G2 frame will not accept old-style grips due to the change in grip angle. Incorporates an automatic hammer block safety with built-in interlock. Features include trigger adjustable for overtravel, adjustable rear sight; ramp front sight blade, blued steel finish.

Price: From **$729.00**

Prices given are believed to be accurate at time of publication however, many factors affect retail pricing so exact prices are not possible.

78TH EDITION, 2024 ⊕ 527

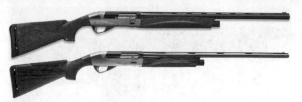

BENELLI ETHOS
Gauges: 12 ga., 20 ga., 28 ga. 3 in. Capacity: 4+1. Barrel: 26 in. or 28 in. (Full, Mod., Imp. Cyl., Imp. Mod., Cylinder choke tubes). Weights: 6.5 lbs. (12 ga.), 5.3–5.7 (20 & 28 ga.). Length: 49.5 in. overall (28 in. barrel). Stock: Select AA European walnut with satin finish. Sights: Red bar fiber optic front, with three interchangeable inserts, metal middle bead. Features: Utilizes Benelli's Inertia Driven system. Recoil is reduced by Progressive Comfort recoil reduction system within the buttstock. Twelve and 20-gauge models cycle all 3-inch loads from light 7/8 oz. up to 3-inch magnums. Also available with nickel-plated engraved receiver. Imported from Italy by Benelli USA, Corp.
Price: **$1,999.00**
Price: Engraved nickel-plated (shown)............................**$2,149.00**
Price: 20 or 28 ga. (engraved, nickel plated only)............**$2,149.00**

BENELLI ETHOS BE.S.T.
Benelli expands its Ethos line with the new BE.S.T. model, so named for the Benelli Surface Treatment, a proprietary coating that protects steel from rust and corrosion and was tested over several months in saltwater with no signs of corrosion. Parts treated with BE.S.T. are backed with a 25-year warranty against rust and corrosion.
Price: $2,199.00

BENELLI ETHOS CORDOBA BE.S.T.
Gauge: 12 ga. 3in., 20ga. 3in, 28ga. 3in. Barrel: 28 in. or 30 in. ventilated wide rib. Length: 49.5 –51.5 in. Weight: 5.4–7.0 lbs. Stock: Black Synthetic. Features: Benelli expands their Ethos line of Inertia-Driven semi-autos with the new BE.S.T. (Benelli Surface Treatment). This Cordoba version is designed for high-volume shooting like that of dove hunting in Argentina — the gun's namesake location. Specialty features include ported barrels, ComforTech recoil-reducing system, and lighter weight. Fiber optic front sight with mid-rib bead on a wide broadway sight channel. Shell View system places small windows in the magazine tube for quickly visualizing remaining shell count. Advertised to handle 3-inch magnum rounds down to the lightest 7/8-ounce loads. Ships with five extended Crio chokes (C, IC, M, IM, F).
Price: $2,349.00

BENELLI ETHOS SPORT
Gauges: 12 ga., 20 ga., 28 ga. 3 in. Capacity: 4+1. Barrel: Ported, 28 in. or 30 in. (12 ga. only). Full, Mod., Imp. Cyl., Imp. Mod., Cylinder extended choke tubes. Wide rib. Other features similar to Ethos model.
Price: **$2,269.00**

BENELLI ETHOS SUPER SPORT
Gauge: 12 ga. 3in., 20ga. 3in. Barrel: 26 in. or 28 in. ventilated wide rib. Length: 49.5–51.5 in. Weight: 5.4–7.0 lbs. Stock: Carbon-fiber finish composite stock and fore-end. Features: Benelli expands their Ethos semi-automatic line with the Super Sport competition-ready model. Lightweight, weather-resistant carbon-fiber finish furniture. Inertia-Driven semi-automatic with ComforTech recoil-reducing system. Ported Crio barrel. Fiber optic front sight and mid-barrel bead. Nickel-plated receiver. Capacity of 4+1 rounds. Ships with five extended Crio chokes (C, IC, M, IM, F).
Price: **$2,299.00**

BENELLI M2 FIELD
Gauges: 12 ga., 20 ga. Barrel: 24, 26, and 28 in. Crio treated. Stock: Black synthetic, Mossy Oak Bottomland, Gore Optifade, Realtree Max-7. Features:

The workhorse Field line gets a full redesign for 2023, including sleeker stock dimensions, a longer forend grip surface, an oversized bolt release button, and a new MicroCell recoil unit. A revised bolt touts improved smoothness of cycling with Benelli's Inertia Drive system. Ships with Crio chokes. Available in both standard and compact models.
Price: Black **$1,399.00**
Price: Camo **$1,499.00**

BENELLI M2 TURKEY EDITION
Gauges: 12 ga. and 20 ga., Full, Imp. Mod, Mod., Imp. Cyl., Cyl. choke tubes. Barrel: 24 in. Weight: 6-7 lbs. Stock: 12 ga. model has ComfortTech with pistol grip, Bottomland/Cerakote finish. 20 ga. has standard stock with Realtree APG finish. Features: From the Benelli Performance Shop.
Price: 20 ga. standard stock **$3,199.00**
Price: 12 ga. pistol grip stock **$3,399.00**

BENELLI MONTEFELTRO
Now updated with Benelli's Inertia-Drive bolt system. 12 and 20 ga. 24, 26, 28in barrels. Three Crio chokes. Satin Walnut stocks. Red fiber optic front sight. Standard and compact versions available.
Price: **$1,499.00**

BENELLI SUPER BLACK EAGLE III (SBE3)
Gauge: 12 ga. 3 in., 20 ga. 3 in., 28 ga. 3 in. Barrel: 26, 28 or 30-in. ventilated rib. Length: 47.5–49.5 in. Weight: 5.8–6.9 lbs. Stock: Synthetic with multiple finish choices. Features: Benelli expands their inertia-driven semi-automatic SBE III line by adding a 3-inch chambered 28-gauge model for 2022, which will have slimmer lines. Models available in Black synthetic, Realtree MAX-5, Gore OptiFade Timber, and Mossy Oak Bottomland. ComforTech stock for recoil reduction, Easy Locking bolt, and beveled loading port. Realtree Max-7 camo available across the line on both right- and left-hand models. 28-Gauge additions: 3-in. chambers now available in variants with black synthetic and all camos. 26- or 28-in. barrels.
Price: **$1,999.00–2,199.00**
Price: 28 ga. Black **$1,899.00**
Price: 28 ga. Camo **$1,999.00**

BENELLI SUPER BLACK EAGLE III BE.S.T.
Benelli expands its SBE III line with the new BE.S.T. model, so named for the Benelli Surface Treatment, a proprietary coating that protects steel from rust and corrosion and was tested over several months in saltwater with no signs of corrosion. Parts treated with BE.S.T. are backed with a 25-year warranty against rust and corrosion. The BE.S.T. package will be available on select SBE III models.
Price: $2,199.00

BENELLI SUPERSPORT & SPORT II
Gauges: 20 ga., 12 ga., 3-in. chamber. Capacity: 4+1. Barrels: 28 in., 30 in., ported, 10mm sporting rib. Weight: 7.2–7.3 lbs. Lengths: 49.6–51.6 in. Stock: Carbon fiber, ComforTech (Supersport) or walnut (Sport II). Sights: Red bar front, metal midbead. Sport II is similar to the Legacy model except has nonengraved dual tone blued/silver receiver, ported wide-rib barrel, adjustable buttstock, and functions with all loads. Walnut stock with satin finish. Introduced 1997. Features: Designed for high-volume sporting clays. Inertia-driven action, Extended CrioChokes. Ported. Imported from Italy by Benelli USA.
Price: SuperSport **$2,199.00**
Price: Sport II **$1,899.00**

Prices given are believed to be accurate at time of publication however, many factors affect retail pricing so exact prices are not possible.

BENELLI SUPER VINCI
Gauge: 12 ga.. 2 3/4 in., 3 in. and 3 1/2 in. Capacity: 3+1. Barrels: 26 in., 28 in. Weights: 6.9–7 lbs. Lengths: 48.5–50.5 in. Stock: Black synthetic, Realtree Max4 and Realtree APG. Features: Crio Chokes: C,IC,M,IM,F. Length of Pull: 14.375 in. Drop at Heel: 2 in. Drop at Comb: 1.375 in. Sights: Red bar front sight and metal bead mid-sight. Minimum recommended load: 3-dram, 1 1/8 oz. loads (12 ga.). Receiver drilled and tapped for scope mounting. Imported from Italy by Benelli USA., Corp.
Price: Black Synthetic Comfortech **$1,799.00**
Price: Camo **$1,899.00**

BERETTA A300 ULTIMA TURKEY
Gauges: 12 ga., 20 ga. Barrels: 24 in. Stock: Synthetic in Realtree Edge or Mossy Oak DNA. Features: New turkey hunting-specific addition to A300 Ultima family of semi-autos. Low-profile receiver with oversized loading port. Enlarged controls. Picatinny top rail. Mid bead and fiber optic front sight. KickOff recoil system comes standard. Extended Mobil choke.
Price: Black Synthetic Comfortech **$999.00**

BERETTA A400 UPLAND 28
Gauges: 28 ga. Barrels: 28 in. with 5x5 top rib. Stock: Wood, pistol grip style. Features: Latest addition to the A400 Upland family of gas-operated semi-autos. Nickel-plated receiver with unique "28" gauge-specific receiver engraving. Magnum, 3-in. chamber. Field strip without tools. Extralight recoil pad. Ships with three OPHC flush chokes.
Price: Black Synthetic Comfortech **$1,829.00**

BROWNING A5
Gauges: 12 ga, 3 or 3.5 in.; 16 ga., 2.75 in. Barrel: 26, 28, or 30 in. Weight: 5.95–7.0 lbs. Stock: Dependent on model, but current listings include high-gloss Walnut, black synthetic, or camouflage variants. Features: Operates on Kinematic short-recoil system, different from the classic Auto-5 long-recoil action built since 1903 and discontinued in the 1990's. New model features lengthened forcing cone, interchangeable choke tubes, and ventilated rib with multiple front sight options depending on model. A5 Full Camo: Composite stock models with complete camo coverage.
Price: .... **$2,049.00–$2,129.00**
Price: A5 Wicked Wing with Vintage Tan camo .... **$2,279.00–$2,379.00**
Price: A5 in Vintage Tan camo **$1,939.00**
Price: A5 Lightning Sweet 16 w/lightweight black anodized receiver ..**$1,819.00**
Price: A5 Sweet 16 w/ brushed nickel receiver & oil finish Walnut.**$2,029.00**
Price: A5 Sweet 16 with Mossy Oak Shadow Grass Habitat camo ..**$1,999.00**

BROWNING MAXUS II
Gauge: 12 ga. With models in both 3 or 3.5 in. Barrel: 26, 28, or 30 in. Weight: 7.0–7.3 lbs. Stock: Dependent on model, but current listings include black synthetic and camouflaged variants. Features: Builds on Browning's Power Drive gas-operated Maxus autoloader in a II version with enhancements. Chrome chamber and bore. Ramped triggerguard for easier loading. Composite stock can be trimmed and is shim adjustable for cast, drop, and LOP. Rubber overmolding on the stock, including SoftFlex cheek pad and Inflex recoil pad. Oversized controls. New screw-on magazine cap design. Includes Invector-Plus choke tubes, extended on most models, as well as an ABS hard case.
Price: Maxus II Ultimate with nickel receiver & Grade III Walnut ...**$2,059.00**
Price: Maxus II Wicked Wing in Vintage Tan Camo.......................**$2,159.00**
Price: Maxus II Camo in Vintage Tan **$1,979.00**
Price: Maxus II Hunter in matte black/ Satin finish Walnut............**$1,669.00**

BROWNING GOLD LIGHT 10 GAUGE
Gauge: 10 ga. 3 1/2 in. Capacity: 4 rounds. Barrels: 24 (NWTF), 26 or 28 in. Stock: Composite with Dura-Cote Armor coating. Mossy Oak camo (Break-Up Country or Shadow Grass Blades). Weight: Approx. 9.5 pounds. Gas operated action, aluminum receiver, three standard Invector choke tubes. Receiver is drilled and tapped for scope mount. National Wild Turkey Foundation model has Hi-Viz 4-in-1 fiber optic sight, NWTF logo on buttstock.
Price: Mossy Oak Camo finishes..**$1,780.00**
Price: NWTF Model..**$1,900.00**

BROWNING GOLD 10 GAUGE FIELD
Gauge: 10 ga. 3.5 in. Barrel: 26 in. or 28 in. with ventilated rib. Weight: 9 lbs. 9 oz.–9 lbs. 10 oz. Length: 48.0–50.0 in. Stock: Composite with camouflage coverage in either Mossy Oak Shadow Grass Habitat or Mossy Oak Break-Up Country. Features: Browning's autoloading Gold Light 10-gauge shotgun is redesigned as the Gold 10 Gauge Field. The new style composite stock and forearm wear textured gripping surfaces with the buttstock able to be trimmed up to ¾-inch to shorten LOP. Added Inflex recoil pad. Silver bead front sight. Integral sling swivel studs. Capacity of 4+1 magnum shells. Standard Invector-style flush-mount interchangeable choke tubes with three included (F, M, IC).
Price: **$1,859.00**

BROWNING SILVER
Gauges: 12 ga., 3 in. or 3 1/2 in.; 20 ga., 3 in. chamber. Barrels: 26 in., 28 in., 30 in. Invector Plus choke tubes. Weights: 7 lbs., 9 oz. (12 ga.), 6 lbs., 7 oz. (20 ga.). Stock: Satin finish walnut or composite. Features: Active Valve gas system, semi-humpback receiver. Invector Plus choke system, three choke tubes. Imported by Browning.
Price: Silver Field, 12 ga..**$1,070.00**
Price: Silver Field, 20 ga..**$1,140.00**
Price: Black Lightning, 12 ga...**$1,140.00**
Price: Silver Field Composite, 12 ga., 3 in. **$1,000.00**
Price: Silver Field Composite, 12 ga., 3 1/2 in..................**$1,070.00**
Price: Silver Field Rifled Deer Matte, 20 ga.....................**$1,200.00**
Price: Cerakote/Camo.. ....**$1,399.00**

CHARLES DALY MODEL 600
Gauges: 12 ga. or 20 ga. (3 in.) or 28 ga. (2 3/4 in.). Capacity: 5+1. Barrels: 26 in., 28 in. (20 and 28 ga.), 26 in., 28 in. or 30 in. (12 ga.). Three choke tubes provided (Rem-Choke pattern). Stock: Synthetic, wood or camo. Features: Comes in several variants including Field, Sporting Clays, Tactical and Trap. Left-hand models available. Uses gas-assisted recoil operation. Imported from Turkey.
Price: Field 12, 20 ga...**$480.00**
Price: Field 28 ga. **$531.00**
Price: Sporting **$858.00**
Price: Tactical **$685.00**

CZ-USA 712 G3
Gauges: 12 ga. Barrels: 20, 26, 28 in. with 7mm flat-vent rib. Stock: Turkish Walnut, synthetic camo Terra. Features: Redesign third-generation gas-operated gun chambering 2.75- or 3-in. shells. Two interchangeable pistons are included for light and heavy loads. Chrome-lined barrel. Ships with five extra-long Active-Choke tubes.
Price: G3 Standard or Utility (20 in.) **$579.00**
Price: G3 Camo **$679.00**

Prices given are believed to be accurate at time of publication however, many factors affect retail pricing so exact prices are not possible.

78TH EDITION, 2024 ⊕ 529

CZ 1012
Gauge: 12 ga., 3 in. Capacity: 4+1. Barrel: 28 in., 8mm flat ventilated rib. Weight: 6.5-6.9 lbs. Length: 47 in. Stock: Options in either Turkish walnut or black synthetic. Features: The company's first gas-less, inertia-driven semi-automatic wears a gloss-black chrome barrel finish along with a choice of three receiver finishes: standard blued, bronze or gray. Oversized controls ideal for use when wearing gloves. Cross-bolt safety located at front of trigger guard. Addition of 26-inch barreled models to the existing 1012 inertia-driven repeater lineup. Includes two camouflaged synthetic stock options as well as checkered Walnut, consistent with the existing 1012 family. Includes five chokes (F, IM, M, IC, C).
Price: $645.00

EUROPEAN AMERICAN ARMORY (EAA) MC312 GOBBLER
Gauge: 12 ga., 3.5 in. Barrel: 24 in., with ventilated turkey rib. Length: 50 in. Stock: Synthetic camouflage with either straight or pistol-grip options. Features: The MC312 inertia-driven semi-auto produced by Girsan gets a turkey upgrade with a shorter barrel, mid-bead, Picatinny rail cut into the receiver, Cerakote finish receiver and barrel, cross-bolt safety, sling studs, rubber buttpad, fiber-optic front sight, and field-tested reflex optic. Includes flush mount choke tubes.
Price: $600.00

EUROPEAN AMERICAN ARMORY (EAA) AKKAR CHURCHILL 220
Gauge: 20 ga. Barrel: 18.5 in. Length: 37.5 in. Weight: 5.0 lbs. Stock: Black synthetic pistol grip style. Features: This Turkish-made semi-automatic springs from the Churchill 220 series of gas-driven repeaters is now re-vamped for home defense and tactical use. Optics rail machined into receiver for easy target acquisition with included red-dot optic on quick-release mount. Semi-enhanced loading port. Accessible controls. 5+1 round capacity. Checkered pistol grip stock. Black rubber recoil pad, sling swivels. Door-breaching choke tube and shrouded red fiber-optic front sight.
Price: $561.00

EAA/GIRSAN MC312
Gauge: 12 ga. Barrel: 28 in. vent rib. Length: 50 in. Weight: 6.95 lbs. Stock: Polymer in choice of either black or camo. Features: Inertia-driven single-action hunting autoloader. Lightweight aircraft aluminum receiver 5+1 round capacity. Fiber-optic front sight. Passed EAA's 5,000-round test with no cleaning and 10,000-round test with no parts replacement.
Price: .... $431.00–$499.00

EAA/GIRSAN MC312 GOOSE
Gauge: 12 ga. Barrel: 30-in. vent rib. Length: 52 in. Weight: 6.75 lbs. Stock: Black polymer. Features: Goose variant of the inertia-driven MC312 line. Lightweight aircraft aluminum receiver with machined integral accessory rail for the included red-dot optic. Fiber-optic front sight. Ships with five extended choke tubes. Same 5+1 capacity as the standard MC312.
Price: $627.00

FRANCHI AFFINITY
Gauges: 12 ga., 20 ga. Three-inch chamber also handles 2 3/4-inch shells. Barrels: 26 in., 28 in., 30 in. (12 ga.), 26 in. (20 ga.). 30-in. barrel available only on 12-ga. Sporting model. Weights: 5.6–6.8 pounds. Stocks: Black synthetic or Realtree Camo. Left-hand versions available. Catalyst model has stock designed for women.
Price: Synthetic $789.00
Price: Synthetic left-hand action $899.00

Price: Camo $949.00
Price: Compact $849.00
Price: Catalyst $969.00
Price: Sporting $1,149.00
Price: Companion $1,599.00

FRANCHI AFFINITY 3
Price: Camo and Cerakote 12-ga. models $1,099.00
Price: Left-Hand Models in 12 or 20 Ga $899.00

FRANCHI AFFINITY ELITE
Gauges: 12ga. 3 in., 12ga. 3.5in., 20ga. 3 in. Barrel: 26 or 28 in. ventilated rib. Length: 48.5–50.75 in. Weight: 6.0–7.1 lbs. Stock: Synthetic with OptiFade Marsh or OptiFade Timber camo. Features: The Affinity Elite lineup offers semi-customized features building on the Affinity Italian-made family of Inertia-Drive semi-autos. Cerakote and OptiFade camo finishes. Oversized controls, lengthened forcing cone, TruGlo front sight. Oversized loading port, ambidextrous safety, chrome lined barrel. Drilled and tapped for optics mounting. Twin Shock Absorber (TSA) recoil pad allows for LOP adjustments. Capacity of 4+1 rounds. Includes shims for fitting drop and cast. Ships with three extended waterfowl chokes (Close, Mid, Long-Range).
Price: Synthetic $1,249.00

J.P. SAUER & SOHN SL5 TURKEY
Gauge: 12 ga. 3 in. Barrel: 18.5-in. deep-drilled, chrome-lined, with stepped rib. Weight: 7 lbs. Stock: Fixed synthetic pistol-grip style in choice of three Mossy Oak camo patterns: Obsession, Bottomland, or New Bottomland. Features: Durable inertia-driven semi-automatic with black anodized receiver. Oversized bolt handle and release button. Removeable Picatinny rail. Cervellati recoil pad and sling attachments. Red single-bead LPA front fiber-optic sight. Made in Italy and backed by 10-year warranty. Ships with three chokes: flush Cylinder, extender CRIO Plus Modified, and Carlson extended Turkey choke.
Price: $1,199.00

J.P. SAUER & SOHN SL-5 WATERFOWL
Gauges: 12 ga. Barrels: 26, 28, 30-in. chrome-lined with stepped rib. Stock: Synthetic with choice of black or Fred Bear Old School camouflage. Features: Latest addition to the inertia-driven semi-automatic line. Steel upper receiver and aluminum lower. Magnum 3.5-in. chamber. Extended bolt handle and release button. Cervellati recoil pad. Rubberized comb. Ships with five Crio Plus extended chokes.
Price: Black Synthetic $1,579.00
Price: Fred Bear Old School Camo $1,679.00
Price: Fred Bear Camo/Cerakote $1,779.00

MOSSBERG MODEL 935 MAGNUM
Gauge: 12 ga. 3 in. and 3 1/2-in., interchangeable. Barrels: 22 in., 24 in., 26 in., 28in. Weights: 7.25–7.75 lbs. Lengths: 45–49 in. overall. Stock: Synthetic. Features: Gas-operated semi-auto models in blued or camo finish. Fiber-optics sights, drilled and tapped receiver, interchangeable Accu-Mag choke tubes.
Price: 935 Magnum Turkey Pistol grip; full pistol grip stock $924.00
Price: 935 Magnum Grand Slam: 22 in. barrel $756.00
Price: 935 Magnum Waterfowl: 26 in. or 28 in. barrel .... $660.00–$735.00
Price: 935 Pro Series Waterfowl $875.00

MOSSBERG 940 JM PRO
Gauge: 12 ga., 3 in. Capacity: 9+1. Barrel: 24 in., ventilated rib. Weight: 7.75 lbs. Length: 44.75 in. Stock: Choice of either black synthetic or Black Multicam. Features: Created in conjunction with speed shooter Jerry Miculek, the new 940 JM Pro uses a redesigned gas system built for fast-

Prices given are believed to be accurate at time of publication however, many factors affect retail pricing so exact prices are not possible.

cycling competition. Adjustable for length of pull, cast and drop. Hi-Viz green front fiber-optic sight, oversized controls. Nickel-boron coated internal parts and anodized receivers in either tungsten gray or black. Competition-level loading port allows for quad loading, elongated pinch-free elevator, and anodized bright orange follower. Black synthetic model uses gold finish appointments and a tungsten-gray receiver. Multicam model wears black-anodized receiver. Ships with Briley Extended choke tube set.
Price: **$1,015.00**

MOSSBERG 940 PRO FIELD
Gauge: 12 ga. 3 in. Barrel: 28-in. vent rib. Length: 47.5 in. Weight: 7.75 lbs. Stock: Black synthetic, adjustable for LOP, cast and drop. Features: Field hunting variant of the 940 Pro lineup. Includes an Accu-Set of choke tubes. Fiber-optic front sight, matte blue metalwork finish. Oversized controls. Sling studs. LOP adjustable from 13–14.25 inches. 4+1-round capacity.
Price: **$903.00**

MOSSBERG 940 PRO FIELD WALNUT
Gauges: 12 ga. Barrel: 28in. Stock: Walnut with LOP spacers.
Price: **$1,061.00**

MOSSBERG 940 PRO SNOW GOOSE
Gauge: 12 ga. 3 in. Barrel: 28-in. vent rib. Length: 50.75 in. Weight: 8.25 lbs. Stock: True Timber Viper Snow camo synthetic, adjustable for LOP, cast and drop. Features: High-capacity 12+1 in the extended magazine tube, unique to the Snow Goose model. LOP adjustable from 13–14.25 in. TriComp fiber-optic front sight. X-Factor extended choke tube. Metalwork finished in Battleship Gray Cerakote.
Price: **$1,165.00**

MOSSBERG 940 PRO TURKEY
Gauge: 12 ga. 3 in. Barrel: 18 or 24-in. vent rib. Length: 39.25–44.75 in. Weight: 7.25–7.5 lbs. Stock: Synthetic in Mossy Oak Greenleaf camo, adjustable for LOP, cast and drop. Features: Turkey-specific variants of the 940 Pro lineup, these with shorter barrels, Greenleaf camo, and fitted with X-Factor XX-Full Turkey choke tubes. Optics-ready cutout. Compsight fiber optics. LOP adjustable from 13–14.25 in. Both models carry 4+1-round capacity.
Price: **$1,120.00**

MOSSBERG 940 PRO WATERFOWL
Gauge: 12 ga. 3 in. Barrel: 28-in. vent rib. Length: 48.75 in. Weight: 7.75 lbs. Stock: Synthetic in True Timber Prairie camo, adjustable for LOP, cast and drop. Features: Waterfowl-specific variant of the 940 Pro lineup. Includes a set of X-Factor extended choke tubes, TriComp fiber-optic front sight. Oversized controls. LOP adjustable from 13–14.25 inches. 4+1-round capacity.
Price: **$1,092.00**

MOSSBERG SA-20
Gauge: 20 or 28 ga. Barrels: 20 in. (Tactical), 26 in. or 28 in. Weight: 5.5–6 lbs. Stock: Black synthetic. Gas operated action, matte blue finish. Tactical model has ghost-ring sight, accessory rail.

Price: 20 ga. .... **$592.00–$664.00**
Price: 28 ga. .... **$588.00–$675.00**

MOSSBERG SA-410 FIELD
Gauge: .410 bore, 3 in. Capacity: 4+1. Barrel: 26 in., ventilated rib. Weight: 6.5 lbs. Length: 46 in. Stock: Black synthetic. Features: Mossberg offers the baby bore for small-game and field hunters as well as light recoiling plinking with this lightweight gas-driven autoloader. Metalwork is finished in matte blue. Brass front bead, fixed 13.75 in. length of pull, ventilated rubber buttpad. Cross-bolt safety, easy-load elevator. Includes Sport Set flush fit chokes (F, IM, M, IC, C).
Price: **$616.00**

MOSSBERG SA-410 TURKEY
Gauge: .410 bore, 3 in. Capacity: 4+1. Barrel: 26 in., ventilated rib. Weight: 6.5 lbs. Length: 46 in. Stock: Synthetic stock with Mossy Oak Bottomland camouflage. Features: Mossberg expands its baby-bore turkey lineup with this gas-driven semi-automatic. Both the stocks and metalwork wear full camouflage coverage. Rear fiber-optic ghost-ring sight and front green fiber-optic. Top Picatinny rail for easy optics mounting. Cross-bolt safety, easy-load elevator. Ships with an XX-Full Extended Turkey choke.
Price: **$735.00**

RETAY GORDION
Gauge: 12 ga., 3 in. Barrels: 26 in., 28 in., ventilated rib. Weight: 6.5-6.75 lbs. Stock: Choice of black synthetic, several Realtree camo patterns, or Turkish walnut. Features: The Turkish-made Gordion line of semi-automatics uses an inertia-plus action and bolt system. Oversized SP controls, quick unload system, TruGlo red front sight. Choice of matte or polished black receiver and barrel, or full camouflage coverage. Easy-Load port as well as Easy Unload system that allows the magazine tube to be emptied without racking the action. Includes a stock adjustment ship kit, TSA airline-approved hard case, and five flush choke tubes (F, IM, M, IC, S).
Price: .... **$799.00–$899.00**
Price: Gordion Turkey 24-in. barrel, Realtree or Mossy Oak camo ... **$925.00**

RETAY MASAI MARA
Gauges: 12 ga., 3.5 in., 20 ga., 3 in. Barrels: 26 in., 28 in., ventilated rib. Weight: 6.5-6.75 lbs. Stock: Choice of synthetic in black or numerous camouflage patterns or two grades of Turkish walnut. Features: The Turkish-made Masai Mara line of semi-automatics uses an inertia-plus action and bolt system. Oversized controls, Easy Unload system, TruGlo red fiber-optic front sight. Options in Cerakote metalwork or anodized finishes. Push-button removeable trigger group for both safety and easy field cleaning. Microcell rubber recoil pad. Includes a TSA airline-approved hard case and ships with five flush choke tubes (F, IM, M, IC, S).
Price: **$1,099.00**
Price: Upland Grade 2 .... **$1,399.00**
Price: Upland Grade 3 .... **$1,900.00**
Price: Comfort Grade 2 .... **$1,399.00**
Price: Comfort Grade 4 .... **$1,999.00**
Price: SP Air King Waterfowl Camo/Cerakote **$1,600.00**
Price: SP Air King Waterfowl Cerakote **$1,600.00**

SAVAGE RENEGAUGE FIELD
Gauges: 12 ga. 3 in. Barrel: 26 or 28 in. fluted carbon steel with ventilated rib. Weight: 7.9–8.0 lbs. Length: 47.5–49.5 in. Stock: Grey synthetic stock with Monte Carlo-style cheekpiece. Adjustable for length of pull, comb height, drop and cast with included inserts. Features: American-made D.R.I.V. (Dual Regulating Inline Valve) gas system. Single-piece, chrome-plated action bar assembly and chrome-plated reciprocating components. Melonite-finished external metalwork. Stock rod buffer to reduce felt recoil. Red fiber-optic sight, competition-ready easy-loading port, oversized controls. 4+1 round capacity. Includes three Beretta/Benelli style chokes (IC, M, F) and hard case.
Price: **$1,489.00**

SAVAGE RENEGAUGE TURKEY
Gauge: 12 ga. 3 in. Barrel: 24-in. fluted carbon steel with ventilated rib. Weight: 7.8 lbs. Length: 49.5 in. Stock: Camo synthetic stock with Monte Carlo-style cheekpiece, adjustable for length of pull, comb height, drop and cast with included inserts. Choice of Mossy Oak Bottomland or Mossy Oak Obsession camouflage finishes. Features: American-made D.R.I.V. (Dual Regulating

Prices given are believed to be accurate at time of publication however, many factors affect retail pricing so exact prices are not possible.

78TH EDITION, 2024 ✦ 531

Inline Valve) gas system. Single-piece, chrome-plated action bar assembly and chrome-plated reciprocating components. Stock rod buffer to reduce felt recoil. Red fiber-optic front sight, competition-ready loading port, oversized controls. 4+1 round capacity. Includes four Beretta/Benelli style chokes (EF, F, IC, M) and hard case.

Price: **$1,599.00**

SAVAGE RENEGAUGE WATERFOWL

Gauge: 12 ga. 3 in. Barrel: 26- or 28-in. fluted carbon steel with ventilated rib. Weight: 7.8 lbs. Lengths: 47.5–49.5 in. Stock: Camouflage synthetic stock with Monte Carlo-style cheekpiece, adjustable for length of pull, comb height, drop and cast with included inserts. Mossy Oak Shadow Grass Blades camouflage. Features: American-made D.R.I.V. (Dual Regulating Inline Valve) gas system. Single-piece, chrome-plated action bar assembly and chrome-plated reciprocating components. Stock rod buffer to reduce felt recoil. Red fiber-optic sight, competition-ready easy loading port, oversized controls. 4+1 round capacity. Includes three Beretta/Benelli style chokes (IC, M, F) and hard case.

Price: **$1,959.00**

SAVAGE RENEGAUGE COMPETITION

Gauge: 12 ga. 3in. Barrel: 24-in. fluted carbon steel with ventilated rib. Weight: 8.2 lbs. Length: 46.2 in. Stock: Black synthetic Monte Carlo style, adjustable for length of pull, comb height, drop and cast. Features: American-made D.R.I.V. (Dual Regulating Inline Valve) gas system. Single-piece, chrome-plated action bar assembly and chrome-plated reciprocating components. Stock rod buffer to reduce felt recoil. Extended magazine tube with 9+1 capacity. Melonite finished barrel and Red Cerakote receiver. Hi-Viz Tri-Comp front sight. Competition-ready loading port, oversized controls. Extended Skeet2 Light Mod (.015-in.) choke tube of Beretta/Benelli-style.

Price: **$1,959.00**

SAVAGE RENEGAUGE PRAIRIE

Gauge: 12 ga. 3 in. Barrel: 28 in. fluted carbon steel with ventilated rib. Weight: 7.9 lbs. Length: 49.5 in. Stock: Camo synthetic sporter style, adjustable for length of pull, comb height, drop and cast with included inserts. Features: American-made D.R.I.V. (Dual Regulating Inline Valve) gas system. Single-piece, chrome plated action bar assembly and chrome-plated reciprocating components. True Timber Prairie camouflage stock finish with Brown Sand Cerakote metalwork. Stock rod buffer to reduce felt recoil. Red fiber-optic sight, competition-ready easy-loading port, oversized controls. 4+1 round capacity. Includes three Beretta/Benelli style chokes (IC, M, F) and hard case.

Price: **$1,599.00**

STANDARD MANUFACTURING SKO-12

Gauge: 12 ga., 3 in. Capacity: 5-round magazine. Barrel: 18-7/8-in. Weight: 7 lbs., 10 oz. Length: 38 in. Stock: Synthetic with six-position buttstock and will accept any Mil-Spec buttstock. Features: Gas-operated semi-automatic. Receivers machined from aircraft-grade aluminum and Mil-Spec hard anodized. Extended 22-inch Picatinny rail. Ambidextrous safety, AR-style mag and bolt release. MOE slots on fore-end. Tru-Choke thread pattern.

Price: **$1,100.00**

STANDARD MANUFACTURING SKO SHORTY

Gauge: 12 ga., 3 in. Capacity: 5-round magazine. Barrel: 18-7/8-in. Weight: 7.14 lbs. Length: 28.75 in. Stock: Black synthetic with forward vertical grip, but without a buttstock. Features: Gas-operated semi-automatic. Receivers machined from aircraft-grade aluminum and Mil-Spec hard anodized. Ambidextrous safety, AR-style mag and bolt release. MOE slots on fore-end. No sights or top rail. Tru-Choke thread pattern. Buttstock conversion kit available from manufacturer.

Price: **$599.00**

STEVENS MODEL 560

Gauges: 12 ga. Barrels: 28 in black matte. Stock: Turkish Walnut, checkered with a satin finish. Features: New budget autoloader built in Turkey for Stevens by Savage. Gas operated with 3-inch chamber and aluminum alloy receiver. Hard chrome-lined barrel. Oversized controls. Fiber-optic front sight. Available in both standard and compact variants at the same price. Ships with three flush choke tubes.

Price: **$499.00**

STOEGER M3K

Gauges: 12 ga. Barrels: 24 in. Stock: Black synthetic. Features: Race-ready factory semi-automatic build for 3-Gun competitors. Oversized controls with contrasting blue anodizing. Enlarged loading port and elongated carrier. A 3-inch chamber and 4+1-round capacity. Uses the Inertia-Drive system. Upgraded recoil pad and integrated cheek pad. Ships with three choke tubes.

Price: **$669.00**

STOEGER M3020

Gauges: 20 ga. Barrels: 18.5, 24, 26, 28 in. Stock: Black synthetic, Gloss Walnut, Camo. Features: Inertia-driven semi-automatic 20-gauge family chambered for 2.75- and 3-in. shells. Fiber-optic front sight. Includes numerous model variants and styles. A shim kit comes standard.

Price: Standard or Compact Black..**$559.00**
Price: Defense ghost ring sights 20 in. **$619.00**
Price: Upland Walnut/Cerakote **$669.00**
Price: Turkey w/Camo 24 in. **$619.00**
Price: Hunter w/Camo/Cerakote **$669.00**

STOEGER M3000

Gauges: 12 ga. Barrels: 24, 26, 28 in. Stock: Black synthetic, Camo, Walnut. Features: Redesigned in 2023 as a 3-inch chambered 12-gauge semi-auto. New recoil pad and removable cheek pieces on all except satin walnut models. Stock grip areas are trimmer with an overall less boxy look. Oversized controls, slimmer magazine cap, and beveled loading port. Red fiber-optic front sight. Ships with three choke tubes.

Price: Black Synthetic **$559.00**
Price: Satin Walnut **$619.00**
Price: Camo..**$619.00**
Price: Camo/Cerakote...**$669.00**
Price: Walnut/Cerakote...**$669.00**

STOEGER M3500

Redesigned for 2023 with slimmer stock dimensions, oversized controls, and an easy-grip magazine cap. View from receiver to rib is lower. Upgraded recoil pad. Addition of cheek pad on all but walnut models.

Price: Black..**$669.00**
Price: Camo...**$769.00**
Price: Camo/Cerakote **$799.00**
Price: Waterfowl Special **$849.00**
Price: Snow Goose **$929.00**

STOEGER M3500 PREDATOR/TURKEY

Gauge: 12 ga., 3.5 in. Capacity: 4+1. Barrel: 24 in., ventilated rib. Length: 46 in. Weight: 7.5 lbs. Stock: Synthetic Mossy Oak Overwatch. Features: Stoeger expands its M3500 line of inertia-driven autoloaders with a predator- and turkey-specific model with a shorter barrel and rubber pistol grip. Red bar fiber-optic front sight. Receiver drilled and tapped for optics mounting. Ships with a paracord sling and five extended chokes, including MOJO Predator and MOJO Turkey tubes.
Price: $929.00

STOEGER M3500 WATERFOWL
Gauge: 12 ga. 3.5 in. Barrel: 28 in. ventilated rib. Length: 50 in. Weight: 8.2 lbs. Stock: Synthetic with distressed white Cerakote finish. Features: Stoeger combines the M3500 Waterfowl semi-auto with the 922R-compliant extended magazine Freedom Series to create the higher-capacity M3500 Snow Goose. Full 10+1 capacity. Inertia-driven autoloader with oversized controls. Beveled loading port. Distressed white Cerakote finish on stock, fore-end, receiver, and barrel act as winter camo. Red bar front sight. Includes paracord sling and shim kit for adjusting drop and cast. Ships with five extended choke tubes (IC, M, XFT, Close Range, Mid Range).
Price: $899.00

TRISTAR VIPER G2
Gauges: 12 ga., 20 ga. 2 3/4 in. or 3 in. interchangeably. Capacity: 5-round magazine. Barrels: 26 in., 28 in. (carbon fiber only offered in 12-ga. 28 in. and 20-ga. 26 in.). Stock: Wood, black synthetic, Mossy Oak Duck Blind camouflage, faux carbon fiber finish (2008) with the new Comfort Touch technology. Features: Magazine cutoff, vent rib with matted sight plane, brass front bead (camo models have fiber-optic front sight), shot plug included, and 3 Beretta-style choke tubes (IC, M, F). Viper synthetic, Viper camo have swivel studs. Five-year warranty. Viper Youth models have shortened length of pull and 24 in. barrel. Sporting model has ported barrel, checkered walnut stock with adjustable comb. Imported by Tristar Sporting Arms Ltd.

Price:	$549.00
Price: Camo models	$640.00
Price: Silver Model	$670.00–$715.00
Price: Youth Model	$565.00
Price: Sporting Model	$825.00

TRISTAR VIPER G2
Gauges: 12 ga., 20ga. 28 ga., .410 bore Barrels: 26, 28, (30-in. Snow Camo only). Stock: Depending on model, premium-select walnut (Pro Bronze), select walnut (Silver), synthetic (Camo). Features: Gas-operated autoloader with 3-inch chambers. Last shot bolt hold open. Rubber recoil pad. Chrome-lined chamber. Shim kits included. Fiber-optic front sight. Manual E-Z load magazine cutoff. Oversized controls. Triangular safety. Enlarged mag well. Ships with three Beretta/Benelli Mobil choke tubes.

Price: G2 Pro Camo (12, 20)	$855.00
Price: G2 Pro Silver (12, 20, 28, .410)	$870.00–$900.00
Price: G2 Pro Bronze (12, 20, 16 28, .410)	$990.00–$1,050.00

TRISTAR VIPER MAX
Gauge: 12. 3 1/2 in. Barrel: 24–30 in., threaded to accept Benelli choke tubes. Gas-operated action. Offered in several model variants. Introduced in 2017.
Price: .... $630.00–$730.00

WEATHERBY SA-SERIES
Gauges: 12 ga., 20 ga., 3 in. Barrels: 26 in., 28 in. flat ventilated rib. Weight: 6.5 lbs. Stock: Wood and synthetic. Features: The SA-08 is a reliable workhorse that lets you move from early season dove loads to late fall's heaviest waterfowl loads in no time. Available with wood and synthetic stock options in 12- and 20-gauge models, including a scaled-down youth model to fit 28 ga. Comes with 3 application-specific choke tubes (SK/IC/M). Made in Turkey.

Price: SA-08 Synthetic	$649.00
Price: SA-08 Synthetic Youth	$649.00
Price: SA-08 Deluxe	$849.00

WEATHERBY 18I WATERFOWLER
Gauges: 12 ga. Barrels: 28 in. Stock: Synthetic camo. Features: 3.5 inch "Super Magnum" chamber.
Price: .... $1,239.00–$1,249.00

WINCHESTER SUPER X3
Gauge: 12 ga., 3 in. and 3 1/2 in. Barrels: 26 in., 28 in., .742-in. back-bored; Invector Plus choke tubes. Weights: 7–7.25 lbs. Stock: Composite, 14.25 in. x 1.75 in. x 2 in. Mossy Oak New Break-Up camo with Dura-Touch Armor Coating. Pachmayr Decelerator buttpad with hard heel insert, customizable length of pull. Features: Alloy magazine tube, gunmetal grey Perma-Cote UT finish, self-adjusting Active Valve gas action, lightweight recoil spring system. Electroless nickel-plated bolt, three choke tubes, two length-of-pull stock spacers, drop and cast adjustment spacers, sling swivel studs. Introduced 2006. Made in Belgium, assembled in Portugal.

Price: Field	$1,140.00
Price: Sporting, adj. comb	$1,700.00
Price: Long Beard, pistol grip camo stock	$1,270.00
Price: Composite Sporting	$1,740.00

WINCHESTER SX-4
Gauge: 12 ga., 3 in. and 3 1/2 in. Capacity: 4-round magazine. Barrels: 22 in., 24 in., 26 in. or 28 in. Invector Plus Flush choke tubes. Weight: 6 lbs. 10 oz. Stock: Synthetic with rounded pistol grip and textured gripping surfaces, or satin finished checkered grade II/III Turkish walnut. Length-of-pull spacers. Several camo finishes available. Features: TruGlo fiber optic front sight, Inflex Technology recoil pad, active valve system, matte blue barrel, matte black receiver. Offered in Standard, Field, Compact, Waterfowl, Cantilever Buck, Cantilever Turkey models.

Price: Synthetic	$940.00
Price: Field	$940.00–$1,070.00
Price: Upland Field	$1,100.00
Price: Waterfowl Hunter	$940.00–$1,070.00
Price: Waterfowl Hunter in Mossy Oak Shadow Grass Habitat	$1,099.00
Price: Waterfowl Hunter Compact in Mossy Oak Shadow Grass Habitat	$959.00
Price: Hybrid Hunter	$1,040.00
Price: Hybrid Hunter in Mossy Oak Shadow Grass Habitat	$1,079.00
Price: NWTF Cantilever Turkey, Mossy Oak Obsession	$1,070.00
Price: 20-gauge, 3-inch models	$939.00
Price: Universal Hunter in MOBU camo	$1,069.00
Price: Universal Hunter 12 and 20 ga. in Mossy Oak DNA camo	$1,149.00
Price: SX4 Left Hand 12 ga. in multiple variants	$1,129.00

ARMSCOR/ROCK ISLAND ARMORY ALL GENERATION SERIES
Gauge: 12 ga. 3 in., 20 ga. 3 in., .410 bore 3 in. **Barrel:** 18.5, 26, 28 in. smoothbore contoured. **Length:** 41.0–48.2 in. **Weight:** 7.10–8.82 lbs. **Stock:** Black polymer with LOP spacers and adjustable cheek rest for customized fit. **Features:** Pump-action shotgun designed to accommodate a wide range of ages and physical sizes of shooters. The All Generation Series includes multiple models designed to customize the fit. Comes packaged with multiple stock spacers and an adjustable comb and ergonomic forend. Lightweight aluminum receiver with anodized finish. Magazine tube capacity 5+1 rounds in all chamberings. Bead front sight. Black rubber recoil pad. Interchangeable chokes (F, M, IM) except 18.5-inch barreled option, which has a Slug Choke.
Price: **$299.00**

BENELLI SUPERNOVA
Gauge: 12 ga. 3 1/2 in. **Capacity:** 4-round magazine. **Barrels:** 24 in., 26 in., 28 in. **Lengths:** 45.5–49.5 in. **Stock:** Synthetic; Max-4, Timber, APG HD (2007). **Sights:** Red bar front, metal midbead. **Features:** 2 3/4 in., 3 in. chamber (3 1/2 in. 12 ga. only). Montefeltro rotating bolt design with dual action bars, magazine cutoff, synthetic trigger assembly, adjustable combs, shim kit, choice of buttstocks. Introduced 2006. Imported from Italy by Benelli USA.
Price: **$549.00**
Price: Camo stock **$669.00**
Price: Rifle slug model ....**$829.00–$929.00**
Price: Tactical model ....**$519.00–$549.00**

BENELLI NOVA
Gauges: 12 ga., 20 ga. **Capacity:** 4-round magazine. **Barrels:** 24 in., 26 in., 28 in. **Stock:** Black synthetic, Max-4, Timber and APG HD. **Sights:** Red bar. **Features:** 2 3/4 in., 3 in. (3 1/2 in. 12 ga. only). Montefeltro rotating bolt design with dual action bars, magazine cut-off, synthetic trigger assembly. Introduced 1999. Field & Slug Combo has 24 in. barrel and rifled bore; open rifle sights; synthetic stock; weighs 8.1 lbs. Imported from Italy by Benelli USA.
Price: Field Model **$449.00**
Price: Max-5 camo stock **$559.00**
Price: H20 model, black synthetic, matte nickel finish **$669.00**
Price: Tactical, 18.5-in. barrel, Ghost Ring sight **$459.00**
Price: Black synthetic youth stock, 20 ga. **$469.00**

BENELLI NOVA TURKEY
Gauge: 20 ga. 3 in. **Barrel:** 24 in. with ventilated rib. **Length:** 45.5 in. **Weight:** 6.5 lbs. **Stock:** Synthetic with full Mossy Oak Bottomland camouflage. **Features:** Benelli's new addition to the Nova family targets run-and-gun hunters seeking a lighter-built and -recoiling turkey gun. Ergonomic forend. Red bar fiber-optic front sight. Magazine cutoff button. Ships with three chokes (IC, M, F).
Price: **$559.00**

BROWNING BPS
Gauges: 10 ga., 12 ga., 3 1/2 in.; 12 ga., 16 ga., or 20 ga., 3 in. (2 3/4 in. in target guns), 28 ga., 2 3/4 in., 5-shot magazine, .410, 3 in. chamber. **Barrels:** 10 ga. 24 in. Buck Special, 28 in., 30 in., 32 in. Invector; 12 ga., 20 ga. 22 in., 24 in., 26 in., 30 in., 32 in. (Imp. Cyl., Mod. or Full), .410 26 in. (Imp. Cyl., Mod. and Full choke tubes.) Also available with Invector choke tubes,

12 or 20 ga. Upland Special has 22-in. barrel with Invector tubes. BPS 3 in. and 3 1/2 in. have back-bored barrel. **Weight:** 7 lbs., 8 oz. (28 in. barrel). **Length:** 48.75 in. overall (28 in. barrel). **Stock:** 14.25 in. x 1.5 in. x 2.5 in. Select walnut, semi-beavertail fore-end, full pistol grip stock. **Features:** All 12 ga. 3 in. guns except Buck Special and game guns have back-bored barrels with Invector Plus choke tubes. Bottom feeding and ejection, receiver top safety, high post vent rib. Double action bars eliminate binding. Vent rib barrels only. All 12 and 20 ga. guns with 3 in. chamber available with fully engraved receiver flats at no extra cost. Each gauge has its own unique game scene. Introduced 1977. Stalker is same gun as the standard BPS except all exposed metal parts have a matte blued finish and the stock has a black finish with a black recoil pad. Available in 10 ga. (3 1/2 in.) and 12 ga. with 3 in. or 3 1/2 in. chamber, 22 in., 28 in., 30 in. barrel with Invector choke system. Introduced 1987. Rifled Deer Hunter is similar to the standard BPS except has newly designed receiver/magazine tube/barrel mounting system to eliminate play, heavy 20.5-in. barrel with rifle-type sights with adjustable rear, solid receiver scope mount, "rifle" stock dimensions for scope or open sights, sling swivel studs. Gloss or matte finished wood with checkering, polished blue metal. Medallion model has additional engraving on receiver, polished blue finish, AA/AAA grade walnut stock with checkering. All-Purpose model has Realtree AP camo on stock and fore-end, HiVis fiber optic sights. Introduced 2013. Imported from Japan by Browning.
Price: Field, Stalker models ....**$600.00–$700.00**
Price: Camo coverage..**$820.00**
Price: Deer Hunter..**$830.00**
Price: Deer Hunter Camo..**$870.00**
Price: Field Composite Field Composite in Mossy Oak Shadow
         Grass Habitat **$799.00**
Price: Field Composite in Mossy Oak Shadow Grass Habitat 10 ga. ..**$899.00**
Price: Field Composite in Mossy Oak Break-Up Country 10 ga. **$899.00**
Price: Field Composite Camo **$779.00**
Price: Magnum Hunter (3 1/2 in.) ....**$800.00–$1,030.00**
Price: Medallion **$830.00**
Price: Trap **$840.00**

BROWNING BPS 10 GAUGE SERIES
Similar to the standard BPS except completely covered with Mossy Oak Shadow Grass camouflage. Available with 26- and 28-in. barrel. Introduced 1999. Imported by Browning
Price: Mossy Oak camo **$950.00**
Price: Synthetic stock, Stalker **$800.00**

BROWNING BPS MICRO MIDAS
Gauges: 12 ga, 20 ga., 28 ga. or .410 bore. **Barrels:** 24 or 26 in. Three Invector choke tubes for 12 and 20 ga., standard tubes for 28 ga. and .410. **Stock:** Walnut with pistol grip and recoil pad. Satin finished and scaled down to fit smaller statured shooters. Length of pull is 13.25 in. Two spacers included for stock length adjustments. **Weights:** 7–7.8 lbs.
Price: ....**$700.00–$740.00**

CZ 612
Gauge: 12 ga. Chambered for all shells up to 3 1/2 in. **Capacity:** 5+1, magazine plug included with Wildfowl Magnum. **Barrels:** 18.5 in. (Home Defense), 20 in. (HC-P), 26 in. (Wildfowl Mag.) **Weights:** 6–6.8 pounds. **Stock:** Polymer. **Finish:** Matte black or full camo (Wildfowl Mag.) HC-P model has pistol grip stock, fiber optic front sight and ghost-ring rear. Home Defense Combo comes with extra 26-in. barrel.
Price: Wildfowl Magnum **$428.00**
Price: Home Defense ....**$304.00–$409.00**
Price: Target..**$549.00**

CZ MODEL 620/628 Field Select
Gauges: 20 ga. or 28 ga. **Barrel:** 28 inches. **Weight:** 5.4 lbs. **Features:** Similar to Model 612 except for chambering. Introduced in 2017.
Price: **$429.00**

ESCORT FIELDHUNTER TURKEY
Gauges: 12 ga., 3 in., 20 ga., 3 in, .410 bore, 3 in. **Capacity:** 4+1. **Barrels:** 22 in., 24 in., 26 in., ventilated rib. **Length:** 42-46 in. **Weight:** 6.0-6.9 lbs. **Stock:** Synthetic with camo finish. **Features:** The pump-action Turkey model addition to the FieldHunter family is built of aircraft alloy with a black chrome-finished steel barrel that is camo coated. Cantilever Weaver optics rail, fully adjustable green rear fiber-optic sight with windage-adjustable front red fiber-optic sight. Cross-bolt safety, rubber butt pad, sling studs. Includes three chokes (Ext Turkey, F, IM).
Price: **$399.00**

EUROPEAN AMERICAN ARMORY (EAA) AKKAR CHURCHILL 620
Gauge: 20 ga. Barrel: 18.5 in. Length: 37.5 in. Weight: 5.0 lbs. Stock: Black Synthetic pistol grip style. Features: This Turkish-made pump builds on the Churchill 620 series of slide actions now re-vamped for home defense and tactical use. Optics rail machined into receiver for easy target acquisition with included red-dot optic on quick-release mount. Semi-enhanced loading port. Accessible controls. Checkered pistol grip stock. Black rubber recoil pad, sling swivels. Door-breaching choke tube and shrouded red fiber-optic front sight.
Price: $427.00

HARRINGTON & RICHARDSON (H&R) PARDNER PUMP
Gauges: 12 ga., 20 ga. 3 in. Barrels: 21–28 in. Weight: 6.5–7.5 lbs. Stock: Synthetic or hardwood. Ventilated recoil pad and grooved fore-end. Features: Steel receiver, double action bars, cross-bolt safety, easy takedown, ventilated rib, screw-in choke tubes.
Price: .... $231.00–$259.00

IAC MODEL 97T TRENCH GUN
Gauge: 12 ga., 2 3/4 in. Barrel: 20 in. with cylinder choke. Stock: Hand rubbed American walnut. Features: Replica of Winchester Model 1897 Trench Gun. Metal handguard, bayonet lug. Imported from China by Interstate Arms Corp.
Price: $465.00

IAC HAWK SERIES
Gauge: 12, 2 3/4 in. Barrel: 18.5 in. with cylinder choke. Stock: Synthetic. Features: This series of tactical/home defense shotguns is based on the Remington 870 design. 981 model has top Picatinny rail and bead front sight. 982 has adjustable ghost ring sight with post front. 982T has same sights as 982 plus a pistol grip stock. Imported from China by Interstate Arms Corporation.
Price: 981 .... $275.00
Price: 982 .... $285.00
Price: 982T $300.00

ITHACA MODEL 37 FEATHERLIGHT
Gauges: 12 ga., 20 ga., 16 ga., 28 ga. Capacity: 4+1. Barrels: 26 in., 28 in. or 30 in. with 3-in. chambers (12 and 20 ga.), plain or ventilated rib. Weights: 6.1–7.6 lbs. Stock: Fancy-grade black walnut with Pachmayr Decelerator recoil pad. Checkered fore-end made of matching walnut. Features: Receiver machined from a single block of steel or aluminum. Barrel is steel shot compatible. Three Briley choke tubes provided. Available in several variations including turkey, home defense, tactical and high-grade.
Price: 12 ga., 16 ga. or 20 ga. From $895.00
Price: 28 ga. $1,149.00
Price: Turkey Slayer w/synthetic stock $925.00
Price: Trap Series 12 ga... $1,020.00
Price: Waterfowl.. $885.00
Price: Home Defense 18- or 20-in. bbl............................... $784.00

ITHACA DEERSLAYER III SLUG
Gauges: 12 ga., 20 ga. 3 in. Barrel: 26 in. fully rifled, heavy fluted with 1:28 twist for 12 ga. 1:24 for 20 ga. Weights: 8.14–9.5 lbs. with scope mounted. Length: 45.625 in. overall. Stock: Fancy black walnut stock and fore-end. Sights: NA. Features: Updated, slug-only version of the classic Model 37. Bottom ejection, blued barrel and receiver.
Price: $1,350.00

KEYSTONE SPORTING ARMS 4200 MY FIRST SHOTGUN
Gauges: .410 bore. 3 in. Barrel: 18.5 in. Length: 37 in. Stock: Turkish Walnut. Features: Marketed as a Crickett "My First Shotgun," this pump-action baby bore holds 5+1 rounds of 2.75-inch shells or 4+1 rounds of 3 inch. Aluminum receiver with matte blue metalwork. MC-1 choke. Blade-style front sight. Checkered stocks with rubber recoil pad. Length of pull built for small-frame shooters at only 12 in.
Price: $399.00

MAVERICK 88 FIELD
Gauges: 12ga., 20 ga. Barrels: 22, 26, 28-in. ventilated rib. Stock: Synthetic Mossy Oak Bottomland camo. Features: Three new All-Purpose Field camo variants. A 3-inch chamber, 5+1-round capacity. Dual extractors, twin action bars, steel-to-steel lockup, and anti-jam elevator for reliable operation. The 22-in. Bantam model shortens LOP to 12 in. Modified choke tube included, but Maverick 88 accessories interchangeable with Mossberg 500.
Price: $293.00

MOSSBERG MODEL 835 ULTI-MAG
Gauge: 12 ga., 3 1/2 in. Barrels: Ported 24 in. rifled bore, 24 in., 28 in., Accu-Mag choke tubes for steel or lead shot. Combo models come with interchangeable second barrel. Weight: 7.75 lbs. Length: 48.5 in. overall. Stock: 14 in. x 1.5 in. x 2.5 in. Dual Comb. Cut-checkered hardwood or camo synthetic; both have recoil pad. Sights: White bead front, brass mid-bead; fiber-optic rear. Features: Shoots 2 3/4-, 3- or 3 1/2-in. shells. Back-bored and ported barrel to reduce recoil, improve patterns. Ambidextrous thumb safety, twin extractors, dual slide bars. Mossberg Cablelock included. Introduced 1988.
Price: Turkey .... $601.00–$617.00
Price: Waterfowl .... $518.00–$603.00
Price: Turkey/Deer combo............................ $661.00–$701.00
Price: Turkey/Waterfowl combo $661.00
Price: Tactical Turkey... $652.00

MOSSBERG 835 ULTI-MAG TURKEY
Gauges: 12 ga. Barrels: 24 in. Stock: Synthetic in Mossy Oak Greenleaf camo. Features: Turkey-specific, optics-ready. Receiver machined for direct mounting of RMSc-pattern optics. A 5+1-round capacity. Magnum 3.5-inch chamber. Full Mossy Oak Greenleaf coverage.
Price: $693.00

MOSSBERG MODEL 500 SPORTING SERIES
Gauges: 12 ga., 20 ga., .410 bore, 3 in. Barrels: 18.5 in. to 28 in. with fixed or Accu-Choke, plain or vent rib. Combo models come with interchangeable second barrel. Weight: 6.25 lbs. (.410), 7.25 lbs. (12). Length: 48 in. overall (28-in. barrel). Stock: 14 in. x 1.5 in. x 2.5 in. Walnut-stained hardwood, black synthetic, Mossy Oak Advantage camouflage. Cut-checkered grip and fore-end. Sights: White bead front, brass mid-bead; fiber-optic. Features: Ambidextrous thumb safety, twin extractors, disconnecting safety, dual action bars. Quiet Carry fore-end. Many barrels are ported. FLEX series has many modular options and accessories including barrels and stocks. From Mossberg. Left-hand versions (L-series) available in most models.
Price: Turkey $486.00
Price: Waterfowl $537.00
Price: Combo $593.00
Price: FLEX Hunting.. $702.00
Price: FLEX All Purpose $561.00

Prices given are believed to be accurate at time of publication however, many factors affect retail pricing so exact prices are not possible.

78TH EDITION, 2024 ⊕ 535

SHOTGUNS Pumps

Price: Field **$419.00**
Price: Slugster **$447.00**
Price: FLEX Deer/Security combo.................... **$787.00**
Price: Home Security 410 .... **$477.00**
Price: Tactical.................................**$486.00–$602.00**

MOSSBERG 500 TURKEY
Gauges: 20 ga., .410 bore. Barrels: 22 to 24 in. Stock: Synthetic Mossy Oak Greenleaf camo. Features: Two new optics-ready turkey hunting variants. Receiver machined for direct mounting of RMSc-pattern optics. 5+1-round capacity. Fiber-optic front sight. Has a 3-inch chamber. X-Factor ported choke tube.
Price: **$644.00**

MOSSBERG 590S
Gauge: 12 ga. 3 in. with 1.75-in. short shell and 2.75 in. capability. Barrel: 18.5 or 20 in., matte blued. Length: 39.5–41 in. Weight: 6.75–7.25 lbs. Stock: Black Synthetic with fixed LOP; Model with Ghost ring sights uses tactical stock with M-LOK attachment points. Features: Standard model with 18.5-in. barrel allows capacities of 9+1, 6+1, or 5+1. Model with 20-in. barrel and ghost ring sights has capacities of 13+1, 8+1, or 7+1. The former uses a fixed cylinder bore. The latter features the Accu-Choke system with cylinder bore choke included. Both models cycle all length of shells without adapters or adjustment.
Price: Standard 18.5 in. **$623.00**
Price: Ghost Ring 20 in. **$731.00**

MOSSBERG SHOCKWAVE SERIES
Gauges: 12, 20 ga. or .410 cylinder bore, 3-inch chamber. Barrel: 14 3/8, 18.5 in. Weight: 5 – 5.5 lbs. Length: 26.4 - 30.75 in. Stock: Synthetic or wood. Raptor bird's-head type pistol grip. Nightstick has wood stock and fore-end.
Price: **$455.00**
Price: CTC Laser Saddle Model.................... **$613.00**
Price: Ceracote finish **$504.00**
Price: Nightstick (shown)........................... **$539.00**
Price: Mag-Fed **$721.00**
Price: SPX w/heatshield ....**$560.00–$710.00**

REMARMS FIELDMASTER
Gauges: 12 ga., 20 ga. Barrels: 26, 28 in. (21-in. Compact 20-ga. model available). Stock: Standard-grade American Walnut. Features: New RemArms pump action in the old Express style, now called Fieldmaster. Milled steel receiver. Twin action bars. Matte black metalwork. Ventilated rib barrel with single front bead. Drilled and tapped receiver. Left-hand 12-gauge model available. Includes three flush Rem chokes.
Price: **$609.00**

REMARMS FIELDMASTER SYNTHETIC
Gauges: 12 ga. (20 ga. Compact only). Barrels: 26, 28 (12 ga.), 21 in. (20 ga.) Stock: Black synthetic. Features: New RemArms pump action in the old Express style, now called Fieldmaster Synthetic. Milled steel receiver. Twin action bars. Matte black metalwork. Adjustable comb insert available. Drilled and tapped receiver. Includes three flush Rem chokes.
Price: **$559.00**

RETAY GPS
Gauges: 12 ga. 3 in. Barrel: 18.5 in. Weight: 6 lbs. 9 oz. Stock: Black ABS synthetic. Features: Retay's first pump-action shotgun is the GPS, short for Geometric Pump System. Extra-short travel pump action. Anodized aluminum receiver. 5+1-round capacity. Chrome-lined barrel with elongated, back-bored forcing cones. Crossbolt safety. Milled aluminum trigger housing and guard. Integral sling swivel mounts. Beavertail adapter for optics mounting. High visibility front blade sight. Comfort rubber recoil pad. Ships with removeable MaraPro chokes (S, M, F).
Price: **$349.00**

RETAY GPS XL
Gauge: 12 ga. 3.5 in. Barrel: 28 in. Weight: oz. Stock: Black or camo ABS synthetic. Features: Retay's pump-action GPS expands to the XL, chambering magnum rounds. GPS, short for Geometric Pump System, uses a short-travel pump action with a frictionless forend design. Anodized aluminum receiver, chrome-lined barrel with elongated, back-bored forcing cones. Crossbolt safety. Milled aluminum trigger housing and guard. Integral sling swivel mounts. Red fiber-optic front sight. Rubber recoil pad. Ships with MaraPro chokes.
Price: **$419.00**

STEVENS MODEL 320
Gauges: 12 ga., or 20 ga. with 3-in. chamber. Capacity: 5+1. Barrels: 18.25 in., 20 in., 22 in., 26 in. or 28 in. with interchangeable choke tubes. Features include all-steel barrel and receiver; bottom-load and ejection design; black synthetic stock.
Price: Security Model **$276.00**
Price: Field Model 320 with 28-inch barrel........................ **$251.00**
Price: Combo Model with Field and Security barrels **$307.00**

STEVENS 320 SECURITY THUMBHOLE
Gauges: 12 ga. 3 in., or 20 ga. 3in. Barrel: 18.5-in. chrome alloy steel matte black. Weight: 7.0–7.3 lbs. Length: 39.1 in. Stock: Black matte synthetic with thumbhole cutout. Features: Pump action with dual slide bars and rotary bolt. Thumbhole stock design with ambidextrous cheek riser and grip texture. Swivel studs. Bottom-loading tubular magazine with 5+1-round capacity. Black rubber recoil pad. Ghost Ring Sight or Front Bead Sight models available in both chamberings.
Price: 12-ga. Front Bead Sight Model **$275.00**
Price: 12-ga. Ghost Ring Sight Model **$305.00**
Price: 20-ga. Front Bead Sight Model **$275.00**
Price: 20-ga. Ghost Ring Sight Model **$305.00**

STEVENS 320 TURKEY THUMBHOLE
Gauges: 12 ga. 3 in., or 20 ga. 3 in. Barrel: 22-in. chrome alloy steel matte black with ventilated rib. Weight: 7.6 lbs. Length: 43.4 in. Stock: Olive drab green matte synthetic with thumbhole cutout. Features: Pump action with dual slide bars and rotary bolt. Thumbhole stock design with ambidextrous cheek riser and grip texture. Swivel studs. Bottom-loading tubular magazine with 5+1-round capacity. Black rubber recoil pad. Adjustable fiber-optic turkey sights. Extended Win-Choke-style Extra Full choke tube.
Price: 12-ga. Front Bead Sight Model **$323.00**

Prices given are believed to be accurate at time of publication however, many factors affect retail pricing so exact prices are not possible.

STOEGER P3000
Gauges: 12 ga. Barrels: 28 in. Stock: Synthetic in Realtree Max-7 camo
Features: Redesigned in 2023 as a 3-inch chambered 12-gauge pump
action. Improved ergonomics. Barrel extension reaches deeper into the
receiver for greater longevity of the action. Pistol grip inset with Stoeger
logo cap. Integrated swivel studs.
Price: $389.00

STOEGER P3500
Gauges: 12 ga. Barrels: 26, 28 in. Stock: Synthetic in Realtree Max-7 camo.
Features: Redesigned in 2023 as a hunting gun with checkered synthetic
stocks, integrated swivel studs, and slimmer stock lines. Twin steel action
bars, no-stick pump action, and rotating bolt head. Cycles 2.75-, 3-, and 3.5-
inch shells.
Price: $439.00

TRISTAR COBRA III FIELD
Gauges: 12 ga., 3 in., 20 ga., 3 in. Barrels: 26 in., 28 in., ventilated rib. Weight:
6.7-7.0 lbs. Length: 46.5-48.5 in. Stock: Field models available with either
Turkish walnut or black synthetic furniture. Features: Third model upgrade to
the Cobra pump-action line with extended fore-end. Rubber buttpad, cross-
bolt safety, chrome-lined barrel, high-polish blue metalwork, sling studs.
Includes three Beretta Mobil-style choke tubes (IC, M, F).

Price: .... $305.00—$335.00

TRISTAR COBRA III YOUTH
Gauge: 20 ga., 3 in. Barrel: 24 in., ventilated rib. Weight: 5.4-6.5 lbs.
Length: 37.7 in. Stock: Version III youth models available with black
synthetic, Realtree Max-5 camo or Turkish-walnut furniture. Features: Third
iteration of the Cobra pump-action with extended fore-end. Ventilated
rubber buttpad, cross-bolt safety, chrome-lined barrel, sling studs. Shorter
length of pull on Youth model. Includes three Beretta Mobil-style choke
tubes (IC, M, F).

Price: .... $305.00—$365.00

WINCHESTER SUPER X (SXP)
Gauges: 12 ga., 3 in. or 3 1/2 in. chambers; 20 ga., 3 in. Barrels: 18 in.,
26 in., 28 in. Barrels .742-in. back-bored, chrome plated; Invector Plus
choke tubes. Weights: 6.5–7 lbs. Stocks: Walnut or composite. Features:
Rotary bolt, four lugs, dual steel action bars. Walnut Field has gloss-
finished walnut stock and forearm, cut checkering. Black Shadow Field has
composite stock and forearm, non-glare matte finish barrel and receiver.
SXP Defender has composite stock and forearm, chromed plated, 18-in.
cylinder choked barrel, non-glare metal surfaces, five-shot magazine,
grooved forearm. Some models offered in left-hand versions. Reintroduced
2009. Made in USA by Winchester Repeating Arms Co.
Price: Black Shadow Field, 3 in. $380.00
Price: Black Shadow Field, 3 1/2 in. $430.00
Price: SXP Defender...$350.00—$400.00
Price: SXP Universal Hunter 12 and 20 ga. Mossy Oak DNA camo.....$509.00
Price: Hybrid Hunter in Mossy Oak Shadow Grass Habitat $449.00
Price: Waterfowl Hunter 3 in. $460.00
Price: Waterfowl Hunter 3 1/2 in. $500.00
Price: Waterfowl Hunter in Mossy Oak Shadow Grass Habitat $499.00
Price: Turkey Hunter 3 1/2 in. $520.00
Price: Black Shadow Deer $520.00
Price: Trap $480.00
Price: Field, walnut stock..$400.00—$430.00
Price: 20-ga., 3-in. models...$379.00
Price: Extreme Defender FDE $549.00

Prices given are believed to be accurate at time of publication however, many factors affect retail pricing so exact prices are not possible.

78TH EDITION, 2024 ⊕ **537**

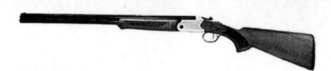

AMERICAN TACTICAL INC (ATI) CRUSADER

Gauges: 12 ga., 3 in. 20 ga., 3 in., 28 ga., 2.75 in, .410 bore, 3 in. Barrels: 26 in., 28 in., 30 in., ventilated rib. Weight: 6.0-6.5 lbs. Stock: Turkish walnut with oil finish. Features: ATI's new O/U line has both Field and Sport models. Made from 7075 aluminum with laser engraving on the receiver. Single selective trigger, fiber-optic front sight, extractors, chrome-moly steel barrel. Ships with five chokes: flush on the Field, extended on the Sport.
Price: Crusader Field **$499.00**
Price: Crusader Sport **$549.00**

BENELLI 828U

Gauges: 12 ga. 3 in. Barrels: 26 in., 28 in. Weights: 6.5–7 lbs. Stock: AA-grade satin walnut, fully adjustable for both drop and cast. Features: New patented locking system allows use of aluminum frame. Features include carbon fiber rib, fiber-optic sight, removable trigger group, and Benelli's Progressive Comfort recoil reduction system.
Price: Matte black..**$2,699.00**
Price: Nickel **$3,199.00**
Price: 20-gauge Nickel **$3,199.00**

BENELLI 828U STEEL BE.S.T.

Gauges: 12 ga., 20 ga. Barrels: 26, 28, 30 in. Stock: AA-grade satin walnut with Progressive Comfort system. Features: Sleek steel receiver that is slightly heavier yet balanced for a smooth swing. Red fiber-optic front sight. Progressive comfort stock system. Gloss-blued barrel finish with satin BE.S.T steel corrosion-resistant treatment. Dual ejectors. Has 3-in. chambers. Ships with five Crio chokes. 6.85-7.65 pounds.
Price: **$3,399.00**

BENELLI 828U LIMITED EDITION

With nickel-plated steel frame, elegant engraved and gold inlayed game scene, and AA-grade Walnut. This 12 ga. with 28-in. barrel shows metalwork finished in B.E.S.T. coating. Limited to 200 units.
Price: **$6,499.00**

BERETTA 686/687 SILVER PIGEON SERIES

Gauges: 12 ga., 20 ga., 28 ga., 3 in. (2 3/4 in. 28 ga.). .410 bore, 3 in. Barrels: 26 in., 28 in. Weight: 6.8 lbs. Stock: Checkered walnut. Features: Inter-changeable barrels (20 ga. and 28 ga.), single selective gold-plated trigger, boxlock action, auto safety, Schnabel fore-end.
Price: 686 Silver Pigeon Grade I $2,350.00
Price: 686 Silver Pigeon Grade I, Sporting $2,400.00
Price: 687 Silver Pigeon Grade III $3,430.00
Price: 687 Silver Pigeon Grade V $4,075.00

BERETTA 687 SILVER PIGEON III

Gauges: 12 ga. 3 in., 20 ga. 3 in., 28 ga. 2.75 in., .410 bore, 3 in. Barrels: 26, 28, 30 in. with 6x6 windowed rib. Stock: Class 2.5 Walnut with gloss finish. Features: The 687 Silver Pigeon III stems from the 680 series design. Trapezoid shoulders and dual conical locking lugs. Fine engraving with game scenes and floral motif done with 5-axis laser. MicroCore 20mm buttpad. The 28-gauge and .410-bore doubles are built on a smaller frame. Gold-colored single selective trigger. Tang safety selector. Steelium barrels. The 12, 20, and 28 gauges use 70mm Optima HP choke tubes while the .410 is equipped with 50mm Mobil Chokes.
Price: **$2,699.00**

BERETTA MODEL 687 EELL

Gauges: 12 ga., 20 ga., 28 ga., 410 bore. Features: Premium-grade model with decorative sideplates featuring lavish hand-chased engraving with a classic game scene enhanced by detailed leaves and flowers that also cover the trigger guard, trigger plate and fore-end lever. Stock has high-grade, specially selected European walnut with fine-line checkering. Offered in three action sizes with scaled-down 28 ga. and .410 receivers. Combo models are available with extra barrel sets in 20/28 or 28/.410.
Price: **$7,995.00**
Price: Combo model **$9,695.00**

BERETTA 687 EELL DIAMOND PIGEON

Gauges: 12, 20 ga. , 28 ga., .410 bore. Barrels: 26, 28, 30 in. cold hammer-forged with top rib. Stock: Select Grade 3 Walnut with choice of English or pistol grip stock. Features: Low-profile box lock O/U action with full side plates hand-engraved with wild game scenes and floral motifs, signed by the engraver. Handfit wood buttpads. Schnabel forend on sporting model; semi-beavertail on field model. MGS trigger. Fixed or interchangeable chokes available. Ships with Beretta hard case.
Price: **$7,549.00**

BERETTA MODEL 690

Gauge: 12 ga. 3 in. Barrels: 26 in., 28 in., 30 in. with OptimaChoke HP system. Features: Similar to the 686/687 series with minor improvements. Stock has higher grade oil-finished walnut. Re-designed barrel/fore-end attachment reduces weight.
Price: ....**$2,650.00–$3,100.00**

BERETTA MODEL 692 SPORTING

Gauge: 12 ga., 3 in. Barrels: 30 in. with long forcing cones of approximately 14 in.. Skeet model available with 28- or 30-in. barrel, Trap model with 30 in or 32 in. Receiver is .50-in. wider than 682 model for improved handling. Stock: Hand rubbed oil finished select walnut with Schnabel fore-end. Features include selective single adjustable trigger, manual safety, tapered 8mm to 10mm rib.
Price: **$4,800.00**
Price: Skeet **$5,275.00**
Price: Trap **$5,600.00**

BERETTA DT11

Gauge: 12 ga. 3 in. Barrels: 30 in., 32 in., 34 in. Top rib has hollowed bridges. Stock: Hand-checkered buttstock and fore-end. Hand-rubbed oil, Tru-Oil or wax finish. Adjustable comb on skeet and trap models. Features: Competition model offered in Sporting, Skeet and Trap models. Newly designed receiver, top lever, safety/selector button.
Price: Sporting **$8,650.00**
Price: Skeet **$8,650.00**
Price: Trap **$8,999.00**

BERETTA ULTRALEGGERO

Gauges: 12 ga. Barrels: 26, 28 in. Steelium Optima-Bore HP with 6x6 rib. Weight: 6.4-6.6 pounds. Stock: Wood with Schnabel forend. Features: Built to be the lightest steel receiver shotgun on the market, using techno-polymer receiver inserts. Extralight recoil pad. Single mechanical trigger. Includes ABS hard case and OCHP choke tubes.

Price: **$2,999.00**

BLASER F3 SUPERSPORT

Gauge: 12 ga., 3 in. Barrel: 32 in. Weight: 9 lbs. Stock: Adjustable semi-custom, Turkish walnut wood grade: 4. Features: The latest addition to the F3 family is the F3 SuperSport. The perfect blend of overall weight, balance and weight distribution make the F3 SuperSport the ideal competitor. Briley Spectrum-5 chokes, free-floating barrels, adjustable barrel hanger system on o/u, chrome plated barrels full length, revolutionary ejector ball system, barrels finished in a powder coated nitride, selectable competition trigger.

Price: SuperSport..**$9,076.00**
Price: Competition Sporting..............................**$7,951.00**
Price: Superskeet...**$9,076.00**
Price: American Super Trap................................**$9,530.00**

BROWNING CYNERGY

Gauges: .410 bore, 12 ga., 20 ga., 28 ga. Barrels: 26 in., 28 in., 30 in., 32 in. Stocks: Walnut or composite. Sights: White bead front most models; HiViz Pro-Comp sight on some models; mid bead. Features: Mono-Lock hinge, recoil-reducing interchangeable Inflex recoil pad, silver nitride receiver; striker-based trigger, ported barrel option. Imported from Japan by Browning.

Price: Field Grade Model, 12 ga. **$1,910.00**
Price: CX composite **$1,710.00**
Price: CX walnut stock **$1,780.00**
Price: Field, small gauges..................................**$1,940.00**
Price: Ultimate Turkey, Mossy Oak Breakup camo..........................**$2,390.00**
Price: Ultimate Turkey in Mossy Oak Bottomland camo **$2,549.00**
Price: Micro Midas **$1,979.00**
Price: Feather **$2,269.00**
Price: Wicked Wing **$2,339.00**
Price: Wicked Wing in Vintage Tan camo w/ Cerakote barrels **$2,499.00**

BROWNING CITORI SERIES

Gauges: 12 ga., 20 ga., 28 ga., .410 bore. Barrels: 26 in., 28 in. in 28 ga. and .410 bore. Offered with Invector choke tubes. All 12- and 20-ga. models have back-bored barrels and Invector Plus choke system. Weights: 6 lbs., 8 oz. (26 in. .410) to 7 lbs., 13 oz. (30 in. 12 ga.). Length: 43 in. overall (26-in. bbl.). Stock: Dense walnut, hand checkered, full pistol grip, beavertail fore-end. Field-type recoil pad on 12 ga. field guns and trap and skeet models. Sights: Medium-raised beads, German nickel silver. Features: Barrel selector integral with safety, automatic ejectors, three-piece takedown. Imported from Japan by Browning.

Price: White Lightning **$2,670.00**
Price: Feather Lightning......................................**$2,870.00**
Price: Gran Lightning..**$3,300.00**
Price: Crossover (CX) **$2,140.00**
Price: Crossover (CX) w/adjustable comb **$2,560.00**
Price: Crossover (CXS).......................................**$2,140.00**
Price: Crossover Target (CXT) **$2,260.00**
Price: Crossover Target (CXT) w/adjustable comb..........**$2,660.00**
Price: Crossover (CXS).......................................**$2,190.00**
Price: Crossover (CXS) w/adjustable comb **$2,590.00**
Price: Crossover (CXS Micro) **$2,140.00**
Price: White Lightning .410 bore and 28 ga. ....**$2,669.00–$2,739.00**
Price: CX White..**$2,379.00**
Price: CX White Adjustable..................................**$2,939.00**
Price: CX Micro **$2,469.00**
Price: CXS 20/28 Ga. Combo **$3,939.00**

Price: CXS White..**$2,439.00**
Price: CXT White..**$2,499.00**

BROWNING CITORI TRAP MAX

Gauge: 12 ga., 2.75 in. Barrels: 30 in., 32 in., ported with 5/16 to 7/16 adjustable ventilated rib. Weight: 9.0-9.2 lbs. Length: 47.75-49.75 in. Stock: Grade V/VI black walnut with gloss-oil finish. Features: Graco adjustable Monte Carlo comb. Buttplate adjusts for location and angle. GraCoil recoil reduction system increases comfort and offers length-of-pull adjustment. Adjustable rib allows for 50/50 or 90/10 POI. Semi-beavertail forearm with finger grooves, Pachmayr Decelerator XLT recoil pad. Close radius grip and palm swell. Triple Trigger System with three trigger shoes, gold-plated trigger, Hi-Viz Pro Comp sight, ivory mid-bead, polished blue barrels, Silver-Nitride receiver, chrome-plated chamber. Five Invector DS Extended choke tubes ideal for trap (F, LF, M, IM, IM).

Price: **$5,859.00**

BROWNING 725 CITORI

Gauges: 12 ga., 20 ga., 28 ga. or .410 bore. Barrels: 26 in., 28 in., 30 in. Weights: 5.7–7.6 lbs. Length: 43.75–50 in. Stock: Gloss oil finish, grade II/III walnut. Features: New receiver that is significantly lower in profile than other 12-gauge Citori models. Mechanical trigger, Vector Pro lengthened forcing cones, three Invector-DS choke tubes, silver nitride finish with high relief engraving.

Price: 725 Field (12 ga. or 20 ga.) **$2,560.00**
Price: 725 Field (28 ga. or .410 bore) **$2,590.00**
Price: 725 Field Grade VI **$6,000.00**
Price: 725 Feather (12 ga. or 20 ga.).................**$2,670.00**
Price: 725 Sporting **$3,270.00**
Price: 725 Sporting w/adjustable comb................**$3,600.00**
Price: 725 Sporting Golden Clays **$5,440.00**
Price: 725 Trap **$3,400.00**

BROWNING CITORI 725 SPORTING MEDALLION HIGH GRADE

Gauge: 12 ga. 3 in. Barrels: 30 or 32 in., steel with floating 5/16 to 7/16-in. rib. Weight: 7 lbs. 8 oz.–7 lbs. 10 oz. Length: 48–50 in. Stock: Grade IV Turkish Walnut with gloss oil finish. Features: Browning expands the higher end of the Citori family. Extensive receiver engraving with gold enhancement. Cut checkering at 20 LPI and right-hand palm swell. HiViz Pro-Comp front sight. Chrome-plated chamber. Tapered locking bolt and full-width hinge pin. Triple trigger system with three included shoes. Blued receiver finish and polished blued barrels. Inflex recoil pad. Gold-plated trigger. Name plate inlay for owner's initials. Includes five Invector DS extended choke tubes (F, IM, M, IC, SK) and Negrini locking hard case.

Price: **$7,069.00**

BROWNING CITORI HIGH GRADE 50TH ANNIVERSARY

Gauges: 12 ga. Barrels: 30, 32 in. Stock: Grade IV Turkish Walnut with premium gloss oil finish. Features: Limited edition O/U commemorating the 50th anniversary. Built for hunting and target shooting. Silver nitride receiver extensive engraving with gold accents. HiViz Pro-Comp front sight. Checkering cut at 20 LPI. Ships with five Midas choke tubes.

Price: **$8,399.00**

BROWNING CITORI COMPOSITE

Gauges: 12 ga. Barrels: 26, 28, 30 in. Stock: Black composite with adjustable comb. Features: Synthetic stocked addition to the Citori O/U family. Has 3-inch chambers. Polished blue metalwork with non-glare stock finish.

Prices given are believed to be accurate at time of publication however, many factors affect retail pricing so exact prices are not possible.

78TH EDITION, 2024 ✦ **539**

Ivory front bead. Inflex 2 recoil pad. Overmolded grip panels. Gold-plated trigger. Ships with three InvectorPlus flush choke tubes.

Price: $2,199.00

CAESAR GUERINI

Gauges: 12 ga., 20 ga., 28 ga., also 20/28 gauge combo. Some models are available in .410 bore. Barrels: All standard lengths from 26–32 inches. Weights: 5.5–8.8 lbs. Stock: High-grade walnut with hand-rubbed oil finish. Features: A wide range of over/under models designed for the field, sporting clays, skeet and trap shooting. The models listed below are representative of some of the different models and variants. Many optional features are offered including high-grade wood and engraving, and extra sets of barrels. Made it Italy and imported by Caesar Guerini USA.

Price: Summit Sporting....................................$3,995.00
Price: Summit Limited $4,895.00
Price: Summit Ascent $5,135.00
Price: Tempio $4,325.00
Price: Ellipse $4,650.00
Price: Ellipse Curve $7,500.00
Price: Ellipse Curve Gold....................................$8,900.00
Price: Ellipse EVO Sporting $6,950.00
Price: Magnus $5,075.00
Price: Maxum $6,825.00
Price: Forum $11,500.00
Price: Woodlander $3,795.00
Price: Invictus Sporting $7,400.00
Price: Maxum Trap...$9,295.00
Price: Maxum Sporting......................................$7,150.00

CAESAR GUERINI REVENANT

Addition of a new combo set to the high-grade 2019 Revenant O/U with a tapered, solid rib and highly engraved maple leaf and branch design receiver. Now with a 20/28-gauge combo barrel set.

Price: $13,495.00

CAESAR GUERINI REVENANT SPORTING

Gauge: 20 ga. 3 in., 28 ga. 2.75 in. Barrels: 28 or 30 in. with non-ventilated center rib, tapered from 8–6mm. Weight: 6 lbs. 6 oz.–6 lbs. 11 oz. Stock: Extra-deluxe wood grade with hand-rubbed oil finish. Left-hand stock option available by special order. Features: Fine-grade over-under Sporting version of the Revenant. Hand-polished coin finish with Invisalloy protective finish. Long-tang triggerguard. Anson rod fore-end escutcheon. Intricate engraving and gold inlay that takes over 40-hours to produce each Revenant action. Wood butt plate. Silver front bead. Checkered at 26 LPI. Premium Revenant gun case included. Ships with five nickel-plated flush-fitting chokes.

Price: $14,750.00

CAESAR GUERINI SYREN JULIA SPORTING

Gauges: 12 ga. 2.75 in. Barrels: 30 in. ventilated rib tapered from 10–8mm. Weight: 7 lbs. 15 oz. Stock: Deluxe Turkish Walnut with hand-rubbed, semi-gloss oil finish. Left-hand stock option and adjustable comb (RH) available by special order Features: Named after Julia, daughter of Julius Caesar, as a top-tier, competition-grade target gun in the Syren line of shotguns for women. Fantasy-style receiver engraving depicting a woman's face evolving from floral scrollwork. Rich case color hardened finish. Checking cut at 26 LPI. Black rubber recoil pad. DuoCon forcing cones. White Bradley style front sight and silver center bead. DTS trigger system with take-up, over-travel, and LOP adjustments. Manual safety. Includes six MAXIS competition chokes as well as plastic hard case, combination locks, and velvet sleeves.

Price: $6,050.00

CHAPUIS FAISAN

Gauges: 12 ga., 20 ga., 28 ga., (.410 bore on Classic only). Barrels: 28 in. with ventilated rib. Weight: 5.5 to 6.2 pounds. Stock: Grade-3 Walnut (Classic), Grade-5 Circassian Walnut (Artisan). Features: Fine over-under line built on an all-steel action. "Faisan" French for "pheasant." Receivers scaled to gauges. Low profile keeps barrels closer to the supporting hand to make pointing intuitive. Round action. Single trigger. Automatic safety and auto ejectors. Brass front bead. Pistol grip-style buttstock. Classic receiver is laser engraved; Artisan is hand-engraved, both with coin finish and game scenes. Ships with five choke tubes and custom hard case.

Price: Classic 12-ga. $5,299.00
Price: Classic 20-ga. $5,599.00
Price: Classic 28-ga. $6,699.00
Price: Classic .410...$6,199.00
Price: Artisan 12-ga. $10,899.00
Price: Artisan 20-ga. $11,099.00
Price: Artisan 28-ga. $12,229.00

CHARLES DALY 202

Gauges: 12 ga., 3 in., 20 ga., 3 in., .410 bore, 3 in. Barrels: 26 in., 28 in., ventilated rib. Length: 43-45 in. Weight: 6.2-7.3 lbs. Stock: Checkered walnut. Features: The new Charles Daly 202 line of O/U shotguns are built of aluminum alloy. Silver receivers are engraved with a dog scene. Single selective mechanical reset trigger, fixed fiber-optic front sight, extractors, rubber buttpad. Includes five extended Mobil style chokes (SK, IC, M, IM, F).

Price: $499.00

CHARLES DALY TRIPLE MAGNUM

Gauges: 12 ga. Barrels: 28 in. Stock: Addition of True Timber DRT or Prairie camouflage synthetic. Features: Triple-barreled break-action shotgun with full camo coverage of barrels and stocks. Set of five Interchangeable MC-5 Rem chokes. Distributed by Chiappa Firearms. Magnum 3.5-inch chambers. Single non-selective mechanical trigger with right, left, top firing sequence.

Price: $2,073.00–2,159.00

CONNECTICUT SHOTGUN A10 AMERICAN

Gauges: 12 ga., 20 ga., 28 ga., .410 bore. 2 3/4, 3 in. Sidelock design. Barrels: 26 in., 28 in., 30 in. or 32 in. with choice of fixed or interchangeable chokes. Weight: 6.3 lbs. Stock: Hand rubbed oil finish, hand checkered at 24 LPI. Black, English or Turkish walnut offered in numerous grades. Pistol or Prince of Wales grip, short or long tang. Features: Low-profile, shallow frame full sidelock. Single-selective trigger, automatic ejectors. Engraved models available. Made in the USA by Connecticut Shotgun Mfg. Co.

Price: 12 ga. $9,999.00
Price: Smaller ga. $11,900.00
Price: Sporting Clays.......................................$14,950.00

CONNECTICUT SHOTGUN MODEL 21 O/U

Gauge: 20 ga. 3 in. Barrels: 26–32 in. chrome-lined, back-bored with extended forcing cones. Weight: 6.3 lbs. Stock: A Fancy (2X) American walnut, standard point checkering, choice of straight or pistol grip. Higher grade walnut is optional. Features: The over/under version of Conn. Shotgun's replica of the Winchester Model 21 side-by-side, built using the same machining, tooling, techniques and finishes. Low-profile shallow frame with blued receiver. Pigeon and Grand American grades are available. Made in the USA by Connecticut Shotgun Mfg. Co.

Price: $4,545.00

CZ ALL TERRAIN SERIES

Gauges: 12 ga., 3 in., 20 ga., 3 in. Barrels: 28 in., 30 in. Stock: Walnut, various styles. Features: CZ's new All-Terrain series encompasses five existing

shotgun models. The new package includes upgraded wood, OD Green Cerakote finish on all metalwork, as well as a set of rare earth magnets added to the extractor/ejectors of the SxS and O/U models to keep shells from dropping out while handling a dog or working in the blind.
Price: Upland Ultralight All-Terrain 12 ga. or 20 ga. $890.00
Price: Redhead Premier All-Terrain 12 ga. or 20 ga. $1,123.00
Price: Drake All-Terrain 12 ga. or 20 ga. $791.00

CZ REDHEAD PREMIER
Gauges: 12 ga., 20 ga., (3 in. chambers), 28 ga. (2 3/4 in.). Barrel: 28 in. Weight: 7.4 lbs. Length: NA. Stock: Round-knob pistol grip, Schnabel fore-end, Turkish walnut. Features: Single selective triggers and extractors (12 & 20 ga.), screw-in chokes (12 ga., 20 ga., 28 ga.) choked IC and Mod (.410), coin-finished receiver, multi chokes. From CZ-USA.
Price: Deluxe $953.00
Price: Mini (28 ga., .410 bore) $1,057.00
Price: Target $1,389.00
Price: 16 ga., 28 in. barrel...$988.00

CZ REDHEAD PREMIER PROJECT UPLAND
Gauge: 12, 20, 28 ga. Barrel: 28 in. with 8mm flat vent rib. Length: 43.75 in. Weight: 6.9–7.7 lbs. Stock: Grade III Turkish Walnut. Features: Project Upland hunting O/U with silver satin chrome receiver finish. One piece CNC'd action, 3-in. chamber. Gloss black chrome barrel finish. Brass front bead. Single mechanical trigger selectable for barrels. Manual tang safety. Patent pending magnetic chambers. Includes five chokes (F, IM, M, IC, C).
Price: 12 & 20 ga. $1,509.00
Price: 28 ga. $1,609.00

FABARM ELOS 2 ELITE
Gauge: 12 ga. 3 in., 20 ga. 3 in. Barrels: 28 in. ventilated rib. Stock: Deluxe-grade European Walnut with matte oil finish and pistol grip design. Features: Left-handed stock option available by special order. Rich case-colored action with gold inlay of sporting birds. Hand-cut checkering. Brass front bead. Single gold-plated trigger. TriBore HP barrel and Inner HP flush-fitting chokes. Ships with Integrale case.
Price: $3,325.00

FABARM ELOS N2 ALLSPORT COMBO
Gauge: 12 ga. Barrels: 30 in. O/U with 34 in. Unsingle combo; 32 in. O/U with 34 in. Unsingle combo. Stock: Turkish Walnut with TriWood enhanced finish. Available with left-hand stock option or Modified Compact Stock with shorter LOP. Features: The Elos N2 Allsport Type T Combo is built for competition shooting. Microcell 22mm recoil pad. Quick Release Rib (QRR) rib on O/U barrels. Adjustable competition trigger. Adjustable comb. TriBore HP barrel. Hand-cut checkering. Single trigger. Includes five EXIS HP Competition extended choke tubes. Ships with hard case.
Price: $3,325.00

F.A.I.R. CARRERA ONE
Gauge: 12 ga. 3 in. Barrels: 30 in. chrome-lined with flat 11mm vent rib. Optional 28, 30 in. Weight: 7 lbs. Stock: Selected European Walnut with ergonomic sporting design and XR-Stock adjustment system (comb/heel) in bright oil finish. Features: FAIR's latest sporting O/U with oversize cross-locking bolt on double lugs. Black bright action with golden clay pigeon and model names. Triple-depth laser engraving, black selective single trigger, top tang manual safety. Long-stroke automatic ejectors. Oil-resistant ventilated rubber recoil pad. Fine-pitch laser checkering. Red fiber-optic front sight. Technichoke XP70 system with 5 tubes. Packed in V500SP case.

Price: $1,988.00

F.A.I.R. CARRERA ONE HR
Gauge: 12 ga. 3 in. Barrels: 30 in. chrome-lined with 15mm wide high vent rib. Optional 28, 30 in. Weight: 7.5 lbs. with mounted chokes. Stock: Selected European Walnut with ergonomic sporting design and XR-Stock adjustment system (comb/heel) Monte Carlo style, in bright oil finish. Features: FAIR's latest sporting O/U with oversize cross-locking bolt on double lugs, this HR variant with a high rib. Black bright action with golden clay pigeon and model names. Triple-depth laser engraving, black selective single trigger, top tang manual safety, long-stroke automatic ejectors. Oil-resistant ventilated rubber recoil pad. Fine-pitch laser checkering. Fiber-optic front sight. Technichoke XP70 system with 5 tubes (F, IM, M, IC, C). Packed in V500SP case.
Price: $2,198.00

FAUSTI CLASS ROUND BODY
Gauges: 16 ga., 20 ga., 28 ga.. Barrels: 28 or 30 in. Weights: 5.8–6.3 lbs. Lengths: 45.5–47.5 in. Stock: Turkish walnut Prince of Wales style with oil finish. Features include automatic ejectors, single selective trigger, laser-engraved receiver.
Price: $4,199.00

FAUSTI CALEDON
Gauges: 12 ga., 16 ga., 20 ga., 28 ga. and .410 bore. Barrels: 26 in., 28 in., 30 in. Weights: 5.8–7.3 lbs. Stock: Turkish walnut with oil finish, round pistol grip. Features: Automatic ejectors, single selective trigger, laser-engraved receiver. Coin finish receiver with gold inlays.
Price: 12 ga. or 20 ga. $1,999.00
Price: 16 ga., 28 ga., .410 bore $2,569.00

FRANCHI INSTINCT SERIES
Gauges: 12 ga., 16 ga., 20 ga., 28 ga., .410 bore, 2 1/5 in. 2 3/4 in., 3 in." Barrels: 26 in., 28 in. Weight: 5.3–6.4 lbs. Lengths: 42.5–44.5 in. Stock: AA-grade satin walnut (LS), A-grade (L) with rounded pistol grip and recoil pad. Single trigger, automatic ejectors, tang safety, choke tubes. L model has steel receiver, SL has aluminum alloy receiver. Sporting model has higher grade wood, extended choke tubes. Catalyst model is designed for women, including stock dimensions for cast, drop, pitch, grip and length of pull.
Price: L $1,299.00
Price: SL $1,599.00
Price: Sporting..$1,999.00
Price: Catalyst...$1,469.00
Price: SL 28 ga. and .410 bore $1,699.00

FRANCHI INSTICT SIDEPLATE
Gauges: 16 ga., 28 ga Barrels: 28 in. Stock: AA-Grade Walnut with Prince of Wales grip and Schnabel forend. Features: Addition of two gauges to the upland O/U family. Three-inch chambers. Gold-inlaid game scenes and blued barrels. Auto ejectors and auto safety. Ships with five extended choke tubes and a custom-fitted hard case.
Price: $2,399.00

KOLAR SPORTING CLAYS
Gauge: 12 ga., 2 3/4 in. Barrels: 30 in., 32 in., 34 in.; extended choke tubes. Stock: 14.625 in. x 2.5 in. x 1.875 in. x 1.375 in. French walnut. Four stock versions available. Features: Single selective trigger, detachable, adjustable for length; overbored barrels with long forcing cones; flat tramline rib; matte blue finish.

Made in U.S. by Kolar.
Price: Standard **$11,995.00**
Price: Prestige.. **$14,190.00**
Price: Elite Gold **$16,590.00**
Price: Legend **$17,090.00**
Price: Select **$22,590.00**
Price: Custom .... **Price on request**

KOLAR AAA COMPETITION TRAP

Gauge: 12 ga. Similar to the Sporting Clays gun except has 32 in. O/U 34 in. Unsingle or 30 in. O/U 34 in. Unsingle barrels as an over/under, unsingle, or combination set. Stock dimensions are 14.5 in. x 2.5 in. x 1.5 in.; American or French walnut; step parallel rib standard. Contact maker for full listings. Made in USA by Kolar.
Price: Single bbl. **$8,495.00**
Price: O/U **$11,695.00**

KOLAR AAA COMPETITION SKEET

Similar to the Sporting Clays gun except has 28 in. or 30 in. barrels with Kolarite AAA sub-gauge tubes; stock of American or French walnut with matte finish; flat tramline rib; under barrel adjustable for point of impact. Many options available. Contact maker for complete listing. Made in USA by Kolar.
Price: Max Lite **$13,995.00**

KRIEGHOFF K-80 SPORTING CLAYS

Gauge: 12 ga. Barrels: 28 in., 30 in., 32 in., 34 in. with choke tubes. Weight: About 8 lbs. Stock: #3 Sporting stock designed for gun-down shooting. Features: Standard receiver with satin nickel finish and classic scroll engraving. Selective mechanical trigger adjustable for position. Choice of tapered flat or 8mm parallel flat barrel rib. Free-floating barrels. Aluminum case. Imported from Germany by Krieghoff International, Inc.
Price: Standard grade with five choke tubes **$12,395.00**

KRIEGHOFF K-80 SKEET

Gauge: 12 ga., 2 3/4 in. Barrels: 28 in., 30 in., 32 in., (skeet & skeet), optional choke tubes. Weight: About 7.75 lbs. Stock: American skeet or straight skeet stocks, with palm-swell grips. Walnut. Features: Satin gray receiver finish. Selective mechanical trigger adjustable for position. Choice of ventilated 8mm parallel flat rib or ventilated 8–12mm tapered flat rib. Introduced 1980. Imported from Germany by Krieghoff International, Inc.
Price: Standard, skeet chokes **$11,795.00**

KRIEGHOFF K-80 TRAP

Gauge: 12 ga., 2 3/4 in. Barrels: 30 in., 32 in. (Imp. Mod. & Full or choke tubes). Weight: About 8.5 lbs. Stock: Four stock dimensions or adjustable stock available; all have palm-swell grips. Checkered European walnut. Features: Satin nickel finish. Selective mechanical trigger, adjustable for position. Ventilated step rib. Introduced 1980. Imported from Germany by Krieghoff International, Inc.
Price: K-80 O/U (30 in., 32 in., Imp. Mod. & Full **$11,795.00**
Price: K-80 Unsingle (32 in., 34 in., Full), standard **$13,995.00**
Price: K-80 Combo (two-barrel set), standard **$17,995.00**

KRIEGHOFF K-20

Similar to the K-80 except built on a 20-ga. frame. Designed for skeet, sporting clays and field use. Offered in 20 ga., 28 ga. and .410; Barrels: 28 in., 30 in. and 32 in. Imported from Germany by Krieghoff International Inc.
Price: K-20, 20 ga. **$11,695.00**
Price: K-20, 28 ga. **$12,395.00**
Price: K-20, .410 .... **$12,395.00**
Price: K-20 Sporting or Parcours.. **$12,395.00**
Price: K-20 Victoria **$12,395.00**

MERKEL MODEL 2001EL O/U

Gauges: 12 ga., 20 ga., 3 in., 28 ga. 2-3/4 in. chambers. Barrels: 12 ga. 28 in.; 20 ga., 28 ga. 26.75 in. Weight: About 7 lbs. (12 ga.). Stock: Oil-finished walnut; English or pistol grip. Features: Self-cocking Blitz boxlock action with cocking indicators; Kersten double cross-bolt lock; silver-grayed

receiver with engraved hunting scenes; coil spring ejectors; single selective or double triggers. Imported from Germany by Merkel USA.
Price: **$13,255.00**

MERKEL MODEL 2000CL

Similar to Model 2001EL except scroll-engraved casehardened receiver; 12 ga., 20 ga., 28 ga. Imported from Germany by Merkel USA.
Price: **$12,235.00**

MOSSBERG SILVER RESERVE II

Gauge: 12 ga., 3 in. Barrels: 28 in. with ventilated rib, choke tubes. Stock: Select black walnut with satin finish. Sights: Metal bead. Available with extractors or automatic ejectors. Also offered in Sport model with ported barrels with wide rib, fiber optic front and middle bead sights. Super Sport has extra wide high rib, optional adjustable comb.
Price: Field **$773.00**
Price: Sport **$950.00**
Price: Sport w/ejectors... **$1,070.00**
Price: Super Sport w/ejectors **$1,163.00**
Price: Super Sport w/ejectors, adj. comb **$1,273.00**

MOSSBERG INTERNATIONAL SILVER RESERVE FIELD SERIES

Gauge: Options depend on model, but include 12 ga. 3 in., 20 ga. 3 in., 28 ga. 2.75 in., and .410 bore 3 in., as well as a 20-ga. Youth. Barrels: 26- or 28-in. ventilated rib. Weight: 6.5–7.5 lbs. Length: 42.25–45 in. Stock: Choice of black synthetic or satin Black Walnut, depending upon model, as well as a Youth-sized model with shorter LOP. Features: Matte blue barrel finish. Satin silver receiver on all except the synthetic model with a matte blue receiver. Dual shell extractors. Tang-mounted safety/barrel selector. Includes flush-mount Field set of five chokes (Cyl, IC, M, IM, F).
Price: Eventide Black Synthetic 12-ga. **$636.00**
Price: Black Walnut Price 12, 20, 28 ga., .410 and 20-ga. Youth **$692.00**

MOSSBERG INTERNATIONAL GOLD RESERVE

Gauge: 12 ga. 3 in., 20 ga. 3 in., and .410 bore 3 in. Barrels: 28 or 30 in. ventilated rib. Weight: 6.5–7.5 lbs. Length: 45.0–48.0 in. Stock: Grade-A Satin Black Walnut. Adjustable stock on Super Sport model. Features: Dual locking lugs and Jeweled action. Chrome-lined bores and chambers. Competition-ready dual shell ejectors. Tang-mounted safety/barrel selector with scroll engraving. Polished silver receiver with scroll-engraved receiver with 24-Karat gold inlay on the underside receiver. Black Label variants wear polished black receiver with same embellishments. Includes set of five Extended Sport chokes (SK, IC, M, IM, F).
Price: Black Walnut 12 or 20 ga., .410 .... **$983.00**
Price: Black Label 12 & 20 ga. **$1,135.00**
Price: Super Sport in 12 ga with fully adjustable stock **$1,221.00**

PERAZZI HIGH TECH 2020

Gauge: 12 ga., 3 in. Barrels: 27-9/16 in., 28-3/8 in., 29-1/2 in., 30-3/4 in., 31-1/2 in., flat ramped stepped 9/32 x 3/8 in. rib. Weight: 8 lbs.-8 lbs., 8 oz. Stock: Oil-finish, high-grade walnut, HT design standard or custom adjustable. Features: The competition grade High Tech 2020 is made in Italy. Logo engraving across silver-finish receiver. Hand-cut checkering, blued-steel barrels. Removeable trigger group with coil or flat springs and selector. Ventilated mid-rib. Interchangeable chokes available on demand.
Price: **$21,075.00**

PERAZZI MX8/MX8 TRAP/SKEET

Gauge: 12 ga., 20 ga. 2 3/4 in. Barrels: Trap: 29.5 in. (Imp. Mod. & Extra Full), 31.5 in. (Full & Extra Full). Choke tubes optional. Skeet: 27.625 in. (skeet & skeet). Weights: About 8.5 lbs. (trap); 7 lbs., 15 oz. (skeet). Stock:

Prices given are believed to be accurate at time of publication however, many factors affect retail pricing so exact prices are not possible.

Interchangeable and custom made to customer specs. Features: Has detachable and interchangeable trigger group with flat V springs. Flat .4375 in. vent rib. Many options available. Imported from Italy by Perazzi USA, Inc.

Price: Trap **$11,760.00**
Price: Skeet **$11,760.00**

PERAZZI MX8

Gauge: 12 ga., 20 ga. 2 3/4 in. Barrels: 28.375 in. (Imp. Mod. & Extra Full), 29.50 in. (choke tubes). Weight: 7 lbs., 12 oz. Stock: Special specifications. Features: Has single selective trigger; flat .4375 in. x .3125 in. vent rib. Many options available. Imported from Italy by Perazzi USA, Inc.

Price: Standard **$11,760.00**
Price: Sporting **$11,760.00**
Price: SC3 Grade (variety of engraving patterns) **$21,000.00**
Price: SCO Grade (more intricate engraving/inlays) **$36,000.00**

PIOTTI BOSS

Gauges: 12 ga., 16 ga., 20 ga., 28 ga., .410 bore. Barrels: 26–32 in., chokes as specified. Weight: 6.5–8 lbs. Stock: Dimensions to customer specs. Best quality figured walnut. Features: Essentially a custom-made gun with many options. Introduced 1993. SportingModel is production model with many features of custom series Imported from Italy by Wm. Larkin Moore.

Price: **$78,000.00**
Price: Sporting Model.................................... **$27,200.00**

RIZZINI AURUM

Gauges: 12 ga., 16 ga., 20 ga., 28 ga., .410 bore. Barrels: 26, 28, 29 and 30, set of five choke tubes. Weight: 6.25 to 6.75 lbs. (Aurum Light 5.5 to 6.5 lbs.) Stock: Select Turkish walnut with Prince of Wales grip, rounded fore-end. Hand checkered with polished oil finish. Features: Boxlock low-profile action, single selective trigger, automatic ejectors, engraved game scenes in relief, light coin finish with gold inlay. Aurum Light has alloy receiver.

Price: 12, 16, 20 ga.. **$3,425.00**
Price: 28, .410 bore.. **$3,625.00**
Price: Aurum Light 12, 16, 20 ga............................... **$3,700.00**
Price: Aurum Light 28, .410 bore.............................. **$3,900.00**

RIZZINI ARTEMIS

Gauges: 12 ga., 16 ga., 20 ga., 28 ga., .410 bore. Same as Upland EL model except dummy sideplates with extensive game scene engraving. Fancy European walnut stock. Fitted case. Introduced 1996. Imported from Italy by Fierce Products and by Wm. Larkin Moore & Co.

Price: **$3,975.00**
Price: Artemis Light **$4,395.00**

RIZZINI BR 460

Gauge: 12 ga., 3 in. Barrels: 30 in., 32 in., with 10mm x 6mm ventilated rib. Length: 43-45 in. Weight: 8.3 lbs. Stock: Walnut with hand-rubbed oil finish and adjustable comb. Features: These Rizzini O/U Competition guns are produced in Skeet, Sporting, Trap, and Double Trap, each with different characteristics. Choice of fixed or interchangeable chokes and fixed, adjustable or ramped rib. Stock checkered at 28 LPI. White rounded style front sight with silver mid-bead. Rubber buttpad. Either standard or long forcing cones depending on model. Ships with hard case and velvet stock sleeve.

Price: **$7,045.00**

RIZZINI FIERCE 1 COMPETITION

Gauges: 12 ga., 20 ga., 28 ga. Barrels: 28, 30 and 32 in. Five extended completion choke tubes. Weight: 6.6 to 8.1 lbs. Stock: Select Turkish walnut, hand checkered with polished oil finish. Features: Available in trap, skeet

or sporting models. Adjustable stock and rib available. Boxlock low-profile action, single selective trigger, automatic ejectors, engraved game scenes in relief, light coin finish with gold inlay. Aurum Light has alloy receiver.

Price: **$4,260.00**

SKB 90TSS

Gauges: 12 ga., 20 ga., 2 3/4 in. Barrels: 28 in., 30 in., 32 in. Three SKB Competition choke tubes (SK, IC, M for Skeet and Sporting Models; IM, M, F for Trap). Lengthened forcing cones. Stock: Oil finished walnut with Pachmayr recoil pad. Weight: 7.1–7.9 lbs. Sights: Ventilated rib with target sights. Features: Boxlock action, bright blue finish with laser engraved receiver. Automatic ejectors, single trigger with selector switch incorporated in thumb-operated tang safety. Sporting and Trap models have adjustable comb and buttpad system. Imported from Turkey by GU, Inc.

Price: Skeet **$1,470.00**
Price: Sporting Clays, Trap.................................**$1,800.00**

SKB MODEL 690 FIELD

Gauge: 12, 20, 28 ga., .410 bore. Barrel: 26, 28 in. Weight: 6 lbs. 10 oz. –7 lbs. 14 oz. Stock: Grade II Turkish Walnut with pistol grip butt and Schnabel forend with high-gloss poly finish. Features: The 690 Field is built on a box lock receiver, cut with CNC machines from a solid billet of chrome-moly steel. White chrome receiver finish. Chrome lined barrels with 3-in. chambers and lengthened forcing cones and automatic ejectors. Also available as a 28-ga./.410 bore multi-gauge set. Youth model available in 12 and 20 ga. with 26-in. barrels and 13-in. LOP. Includes chokes in F, IM, M, IC, S.

Price: **$1,369.00**
Price: Multi-Gauge Set **$2,169.00**
Price: Youth Model **$1,369.00**

SKB MODEL 720 FIELD

Gauge: 12, 20, 28 ga., .410 bore. Barrel: 26, 28, 30 in. Weight: 6 lbs. 10 oz. –7 lbs. 14 oz. Stock: Select Grade II Turkish Walnut. Features: The 720 Field is built on a boxlock receiver, cut with CNC machines from a solid billet of chrome-moly steel. Brushed white chrome receiver is laser engraved with upland and waterfowl scenes and gold scroll. Chrome-lined barrels with 3-in. chambers (except 28 ga.) and lengthened forcing cones and automatic ejectors. Mechanical trigger. Also available as a 28-ga./.410-bore multi-gauge set with 28-in. barrels. Youth model available in 20 ga. with 26-in. barrels and 13-in. LOP. Includes top-thread internal chokes in F, IM, M, IC, S.

Price: **$1,569.00**
Price: Multi-Gauge Set **$2,369.00**
Price: Youth Model **$1,569.00**

STEVENS MODEL 555

Gauges: 12 ga., 20 ga., 28 ga., .410; 2 3/4 and 3 in. Barrels: 26 in., 28 in. Weights: 5.5–6 lbs. Features: Five screw-in choke tubes with 12 ga., 20 ga., and 28 ga.; .410 has fixed M/IC chokes. Turkish walnut stock and Schnabel fore-end. Single selective mechanical trigger with extractors.

Price: **$705.00**
Price: Enhanced Model...**$879.00**

STOEGER CONDOR

Gauge: 12 ga., 20 ga., 2 3/4 in., 3 in.; 16 ga., .410. Barrels: 22 in., 24 in., 26 in., 28 in., 30 in. Weights: 5.5–7.8 lbs. Sights: Brass bead. Features: IC, M, or F screw-in choke tubes with each gun. Oil finished hardwood with pistol grip and fore-end. Auto safety, single trigger, automatic extractors.

Price: .... **$449.00–$669.00**
Price: Combo with 12 and 20 ga. barrel sets **$899.00**
Price: Competition.. **$669.00**

SYREN JULIA FIELD
Gauges: 20 ga., 28 ga. Barrels: 28 in. Stock: Deluxe-grade Turkish Walnut with semi-gloss oil finish. Features: Designed specifically for women as part of Caesar Guerini's Syren division is built as a field gun. Side plate action with fantasy-style engraving depicting a woman's face evolving from a floral scroll. Color-casehardened finish. Single selective trigger, silver front bead, and manual safety. Left-hand stock option and 20/28 combo sets available by special order. Ships with a hard case, velvet sleeves, and five flush choke tubes.

Price: **$6,250.00**

TRISTAR HUNTER MAG CAMO
Gauge: 12 ga., 3.5 in. Barrels: 26 in., 28 in., 30 in., ventilated rib. Length: 44-48 in. Weight: 7.3-7.9 lbs. Stock: Synthetic, with choice of black or numerous Mossy Oak patterns. Features: The 3.5-inch magnum chambered Hunter Mag O/U expands with the addition of Cerakote/Mossy Oak combination models. Steel mono-block construction, extractors, rubber recoil pad, fiber-optic front sight, single selective trigger, chrome-lined barrel, swivel studs. Includes five Mobil-style choke tubes (SK, IC, M, IM, F).

Price: .... **$655.00–$760.00**

TRISTAR SETTER
Gauge: 12 ga., 20 ga., 3-in. Barrels: 28 in. (12 ga.), 26 in. (20 ga.) with ventilated rib, three Beretta-style choke tubes. Weights: 6.3–7.2 pounds. Stock: High gloss wood. Single selective trigger, extractors.

Price: .... **$535.00–$565.00**
Price: Sporting Model... **$824.00–$915.00**

TRISTAR TT-15 FIELD
Gauges: 12 ga., 3 in., 20 ga., 3 in., 28 ga., 2.75 in., .410 bore, 3 in. Barrel: 28 in., ventilated rib. Length: 45 in. Weight: 5.7-7.0 lbs. Stock: Turkish walnut. Features: Field hunting O/U model with steel mono-block construction, mid-rib, top-tang barrel selector and safety. Chrome-lined barrel and chamber, engraved silver receiver, single selective trigger, fiber-optic front sight, auto ejectors. Includes five Mobil-style extended, color-coded chokes (SK, IC, M, IM, F).

Price: **$855.00**

TRISTAR TRINITY
Gauges: 12 ga., 3 in., 16 ga., 2.75 in., 20 ga., 3 in. Barrels: 26 in., 28 in., steel ventilated rib. Weight: 6.3-6.9 lbs. Length: 43.5-45.5 in. Stock: Oil-finished Turkish walnut with checkering. Features: The CNC-machined all-steel receiver Trinity wears 24-karat gold inlay on the silver-finish engraved receiver. Barrels are blued steel. Single selective trigger, red fiber-optic front sight, rubber buttpad, dual extractors. Includes five Beretta Mobil-style chokes (SK, IC, M, IM, F).

Price: **$685.00**

TRISTAR TRINITY LT
Gauges: 12 ga., 3 in., 20 ga., 3 in., 28 ga., 2.75 in., .410 bore, 3 in. Barrels: 26 in., 28 in, ventilated rib. Weight: 5.3-6.3 lbs. Length: 43.5-45.5 in. Stock: Oil-finished Turkish walnut with checkering. Features: The CNC-machined lightweight aluminum-alloy receiver Trinity LT is engraved and wears a silver finish. Barrels are blued steel. Single selective trigger, red fiber-optic front sight, rubber buttpad, dual extractors. Includes five Beretta Mobil-style chokes (SK, IC, M, IM, F).

Price: ....**$685.00–$700.00**

WEATHERBY ORION
Gauge: 12, 20 ga. Barrel: 26, 28 in. ventilated rib. Weight: 6.2–7.0 lbs. Stock: Gloss-finished A-Grade Turkish Walnut. Features: The new line of Orion O/U shotguns are built at the new factory in Sheridan, WY. Ambidextrous top tang safety. Low-profile receiver, chrome-lined bores with automatic

ejectors. Each ships with three interchangeable chokes (F, M, IC). 20-ga. versions introduced to each line in 2022. Sporting variant uses 30-in. barrels, adjustable comb, ported barrels, and five extended choke tubes.

Price: Orion I.. **$1,049.00**
Price: Orion Matte Blue...................................... **$1,049.00**
Price: Orion Sporting... **$1,149.00**

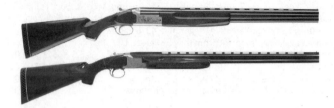

WINCHESTER MODEL 101
Gauge: 12 ga., 2 3/4 in., 3 in. Barrels: 28 in., 30 in., 32 in., ported, Invector Plus choke system. Weights: 7 lbs. 6 oz.–7 lbs. 12. oz. Stock: Checkered high-gloss grade II/III walnut stock, Pachmayr Decelerator sporting pad. Features: Chrome-plated chambers; back-bored barrels; tang barrel selector/safety; Signature extended choke tubes. Model 101 Field comes with solid brass bead front sight, three tubes, engraved receiver. Model 101 Sporting has adjustable trigger, 10mm runway rib, white mid-bead, Tru-Glo front sight, 30 in. and 32 in. barrels. Model 101 Pigeon Grade Trap has 10mm steel runway rib, mid-bead sight, interchangeable fiber-optic front sight, porting and vented side ribs, adjustable trigger shoe, fixed raised comb or adjustable comb, Grade III/IV walnut, 30 in. or 32 in. barrels, molded ABS hard case. Reintroduced 2008. Made in Belgium by FN. Winchester 150th Anniversary Commemorative model has grade IV/V stock, deep relief scrolling on a silver nitride finish receiver.

Price: Field **$1,900.00**
Price: Sporting **$2,380.00**
Price: Pigeon Grade Trap **$2,520.00**
Price: Pigeon Grade Trap w/adj. comb................ **$2,680.00**

ARRIETA SIDELOCK DOUBLE

Gauges: 12 ga., 16 ga., 20 ga., 28 ga., .410 bore. Barrels: Length and chokes to customer specs. Weight: To customer specs. Stock: To customer specs. Straight English with checkered butt (standard), or pistol grip. Select European walnut with oil finish. Features: Essentially custom gun with myriad options. H&H pattern hand-detachable sidelocks, selective automatic ejectors, double triggers (hinged front) standard. Some have self-opening action. Finish and engraving to customer specs. Imported from Spain by Quality Arms, Wm. Larking Moore and others.

Price: Model 557 ....**$6,970.00**
Price: Model 570 ....**$7,350.00**
Price: Model 578 ....**$12,200.00**
Price: Model 600 Imperial **$14,125.00**
Price: Model 803 ....**$17,000.00**
Price: Model 931 ....**$40,000.00**

BERETTA 486 PARALELLO

Gauges: 12 ga., 20 ga., 3 in., or 28 ga. 2 3/4 in. Barrels: 26 in., 28 in., 30 in. Weight: 7.1 lbs. Stock: English-style straight grip, splinter fore-end. Select European walnut, checkered, oil finish. Features: Round action, Optima-Choke Tubes. Automatic ejection or mechanical extraction. Firing-pin block safety, manual or automatic, open top-lever safety. Imported from Italy by Beretta USA

Price: **$5,350.00**

CHAPUIS CHASSEUR

Gauges: 12 ga., 20 ga., 28 ga. Barrels: 28 in. with wide solid rib. Weight: 5.5 to 6.2 pounds. Stock: AAA-Grade Walnut (Classic), Grade-5 Circassian Walnut (Artisan). Features: Fine side-by-side built on a scalloped boxlock action. Extensive receiver engraving of game scenes and acanthus scrolls. Laser engraving on Classic; hand engraving on Artisan. Classic straight grip stock style. Automatic safety. Double triggers. Auto ejectors. Brass front bead. Snag-free checkered wood buttplate. Ships with five choke tubes and a custom hard case.

Price: Classic 12-ga. **$5,449.00**
Price: Classic 20-ga. **$5,699.00**
Price: Classic 28-ga. **$6,899.00**
Price: Artisan 12-ga. **$10,899.00**
Price: Artisan 20-ga. **$11,199.00**
Price: Artisan 28-ga. **$12,499.00**

CHARLES DALY 500

Gauge: .410 bore, 3 in. Barrel: 28 in. Length: 43.25 in. Weight: 4.4 lbs. Stock: Checkered walnut English-style buttstock. Features: Charles Daly's new pair of baby-bore SxS Model 500 includes two versions, both steel, one with a black engraved receiver and the other black engraved with gold accents. Double triggers, extractors, manual safety, brass front bead. Includes five Mobil-style chokes (SK, IC, M, IM, F).

Price: ....**$725.00–$875.00**

CIMARRON 1878 COACH GUN

Gauge: 12 ga. 3 in. Barrels: 20 in., 26 in. Weights: 8–9 lbs. Stock: Hardwood. External hammers, double triggers. Finish: Blue, Cimarron "USA", Cimarron "Original."

Price: Blue ....**$597.00 (20 in.)–$623.00 (26 in.)**

CIMARRON DOC HOLLIDAY MODEL

Gauge: 12 ga. Barrels: 20 in., cylinder bore. Stock: Hardwood with rounded pistol grip. Features: Double triggers, hammers, false sideplates.

Price: **$1,581.00**

CONNECTICUT SHOTGUN MANUFACTURING CO. RBL

Gauges: 12 ga., 16 ga., 20 ga.. Barrels: 26 in., 28 in., 30 in., 32 in. Weight: NA. Length: NA. Stock: NA. Features: Round-action SxS shotguns made in the USA. Scaled frames, five TruLock choke tubes. Deluxe fancy grade walnut buttstock and fore-end. Quick Change recoil pad in two lengths. Various dimensions and options available depending on gauge.

Price: 12 ga. **$3,795.00**
Price: 16 ga. **$3,795.00**
Price: 20 ga. Special Custom Model **$7,995.00**

CONNECTICUT SHOTGUN MANUFACTURING CO. MODEL 21

Gauges: 12 ga., 16 ga., 20 ga., 28 ga., .410 bore. Features: A faithful re-creation of the famous Winchester Model 21. Many options and upgrades are available. Each frame is machined from specially produced proof steel. The 28 ga. and .410 guns are available on the standard frame or on a newly engineered small frame. These are custom guns and are made to order to the buyer's individual specifications, wood, stock dimensions, barrel lengths, chokes, finishes and engraving.

Price: 12 ga., 16 ga. or 20 ga **$15,000.00**
Price: 28 ga. or .410 ....**$18,000.00**

CZ ALL TERRAIN SERIES

Gauges: 12 ga., 3 in., 20 ga., 3 in. Barrels: 28 in., 30 in. Stock: Walnut, various styles. Features: CZ's new All-Terrain series encompasses five existing shotgun models. The new package includes upgraded wood, OD Green Cerakote finish on all metalwork, as well as a set of rare earth magnets added to the extractor/ejectors of the SxS and O/U models to keep shells from dropping out while handling a dog or working in the blind.

Price: Bobwhite G2 All-Terrain 12 ga. or 20 ga. **$828.00**

CZ BOBWHITE G2 INTERMEDIATE

Built on the Bobwhite G2 but with more compact dimensions for smaller-framed shooters.

The 26-in. barrel is 2 in. shorter than standard. Length of pull is also shorter at 14 in. even. Available only in 20 ga. Built for teens/smaller-stature shooters, as well as handling in tight spaces. All other features remain the same.

Price: **$709.00**

CZ BOBWHITE G2 PROJECT UPLAND

Gauge: 12, 20, 28 ga. Barrel: 28 in. with 8mm flat rib.Weight: 6.25–7.15 lbs. Stock: English-style straight grip with Grade III Turkish Walnut. Features: Project Upland hunting SxS designed with crowd-sourced input. Lovely color casehardened receiver finish, dual extractors, and gloss black chrome barrel finish. Splinter forend. Dual triggers and manual tang safety. Hand-engraving borrowed from Sharp Tail model. Includes five chokes (F, IM, M, IC, C).

Price: 12 & 20 ga. **$1,429.00**
Price: 28 ga. **$1,529.00**

CZ BOWWHITE G2 SOUTHPAW

Built on the Bobwhite G2 but the stock is "cast-on," or built in the opposite direction so it properly fits when brought up to the left shoulder. All other features remain, with the Southpaw using 28-in. barrels and available in 12 or 20 ga.

Price: **$709.00**

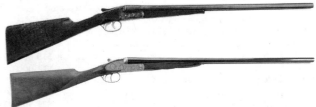

CZ SHARP-TAIL

Gauges: 12 ga., 20 ga., 28 ga., .410. (5 screw-in chokes in 12 and 20 ga. and fixed

Prices given are believed to be accurate at time of publication however, many factors affect retail pricing so exact prices are not possible.

78TH EDITION, 2024 ⊕ **545**

chokes in IC and Mod in .410). Barrels: 26 in. or 28 in. Weight: 6.5 lbs. Stock: Hand-checkered Turkish walnut with straight English-style grip and single selective trigger.

Price: Sharp-Tail **$1,022.00**
Price: Sharp-Tail Target................................. **$1,298.00**

CZ HAMMER COACH
Gauge: 12 ga., 3 in. Barrel: 20 in. Weight: 6.7 lbs. Features: Following in the tradition of the guns used by the stagecoach guards of the 1880s, this cowboy gun features double triggers, 19th-century color casehardening and fully functional external hammers.

Price: **$922.00**
Price: Classic model w/30-in. bbls. **$963.00**

EMF MODEL 1878 WYATT EARP
Gauge: 12. Barrel: 20 in.. Weight: 8 lbs. Length: 37 in. overall. Stock: Smooth walnut with steel butt place. Sights: Large brass bead. Features: Colt-style exposed hammers rebounding type; blued receiver and barrels; cylinder bore. Based on design of Colt Model 1878 shotgun. Made in Italy by Pedersoli.

Price: **$1,590.00**
Price: Hartford Coach Model........................... **$1,150.00**

EUROPEAN AMERICAN ARMORY (EAA) CHURCHILL 512
Gauges: 12 ga., 3in., 20 ga., 3 in., 28 ga., 3 in., .410 bore. Barrels: 26 in., 28 in. Length: 45-47 in. Stock: Standard Turkish walnut. Features: These Turkish made Akkar side-by-sides have a Nitride-silver receiver, rubber buttpad, checkered stock, single selective gold-plated trigger, front bead, manual safety, chrome-lined barrels, extractors. Ships with three choke tubes.

Price: **$1,355.00**

FABARM AUTUMN
Gauges: 20 ga. 3 in. Barrels: 28 or 30 in. with textured top rib. Weight: 5 lbs. 9 oz.–6 lbs. 2 oz. Stock: Deluxe Turkish Walnut with hand-oiled matte finish. Available in either English-style straight stock or standard pistol grip style. Left-hand option available by special order. Features: Fine grade side-by-side built in Italy. Color casehardened receiver finish with ornamental scroll engraving. Four lug locking system. Monolithic action design machined from steel forging. Splinter fore-end with English stock or Semi-beavertail with pistol-grip stock. Hand-fit walnut buttplate. Single trigger, tang-mounted safety/selector, auto-ejectors. Ships with Integrale case. Includes five INNER HP long choke tubes.

Price: **$4,095.00**

FAUSTI DEA SERIES
Gauges: 12 ga., 16 ga., 20 ga., 28 ga., .410. Barrels: 26 in., 28 in., 30 in. Weight: 6–6.8 lbs. Stock: AAA walnut, oil finished. Straight grip, checkered butt, classic fore-end. Features: Automatic ejectors, single non-selective trigger. Duetto model is in 28 ga. with extra set of .410 barrels. Made in Italy and imported by Fausti, USA.

Price: 12 ga. or 20 ga. **$5,590.00**
Price: 16 ga., 28 ga., .410 ....**$6,260.00**
Price: Duetto...**$5,790.00**

FOX, A.H.
Gauges: 16 ga., 20 ga., 28 ga., .410. Barrels: Length and chokes to customer specifications. Rust-blued Chromox or Krupp steel. Weight: 5.5–6.75 lbs. Stock: Dimensions to customer specifications. Hand-checkered Turkish Circassian walnut with hand-rubbed oil finish. Straight, semi or full pistol grip; splinter, Schnabel or beavertail fore-end; traditional pad, hard rubber buttplate or skeleton butt. Features: Boxlock action with automatic ejectors; double or Fox single selective trigger. Scalloped, rebated and color case-hardened receiver; hand finished and hand-engraved. Grades differ in engraving, inlays, grade of wood, amount of hand finishing. Introduced 1993. Made in U.S. by Connecticut Shotgun Mfg.

Price: CE Grade **$19,500.00**
Price: XE Grade **$22,000.00**
Price: DE Grade **$25,000.00**
Price: FE Grade..................................... **$30,000.00**
Price: 28 ga./.410 CE Grade **$21,500.00**
Price: 28 ga./.410 XE Grade **$24,000.00**
Price: 28 ga./.410 DE Grade **$27,000.00**
Price: 28 ga./.410 FE Grade...................... **$32,000.00**

MERKEL MODEL 147SL
H&H style sidelock action with cocking indicators, ejectors. Silver-grayed receiver and sideplates have arabesque engraving, fine hunting scene engraving. Limited edition. Imported from Germany by Merkel USA.

Price: Model 147SL **$13,255.00**

MERKEL MODEL 280EL, 360EL
Similar to Model 47E except smaller frame. Greener crossbolt with double under-barrel locking lugs, fine engraved hunting scenes on silver-grayed receiver, luxury-grade wood, Anson and Deeley boxlock action. H&H ejectors, single-selective or double triggers. Introduced 2000. Imported from Germany by Merkel USA.

Price: Model 280EL (28 ga., 28 in. barrel, Imp. Cyl. and Mod. chokes) **$8,870.00**
Price: Model 360EL (.410, 28 in. barrel, Mod. and Full chokes).......**$8,870.00**

MERKEL MODEL 280SL AND 360SL
Similar to Model 280EL and 360EL except has sidelock action, double triggers, English-style arabesque engraving. Introduced 2000. Imported from Germany by Merkel USA.

Price: Model 280SL (28 ga., 28 in. barrel, Imp. Cyl. and Mod. chokes) **$13,255.00**
Price: Model 360SL (.410, 28 in. barrel, Mod. and Full chokes) **$13,255.00**

MERKEL MODEL 1620
Gauge: 16 ga. Features: Greener crossbolt with double under-barrel locking lugs, scroll-engraved casehardened receiver, Anson and Deeley boxlock action, Holland & Holland ejectors, English-style stock, single selective or double triggers, or pistol grip stock with single selective trigger. Imported from Germany by Merkel USA.

Price: Model 1620EL............................... **$8,870.00**
Price: Model 1620EL Combo; 16- and 20-ga. two-barrel set **$13,255.00**

MERKEL MODEL 40E
Gauges: 12 ga., 20 ga. Barrels: 28 in. (12 ga.), 26.75 in. (20 ga.). Weight: 6.2 lbs. Features: Anson & Deeley locks, Greener-style crossbolt, automatic ejectors, choice of double or single trigger, blue finish, checkered walnut stock with cheekpiece.

Price: **$4,795.00**

PIOTTI KING NO. 1
Gauges: 12 ga., 16 ga., 20 ga., 28 ga., .410. Barrels: 25–30 in. (12 ga.), 25–28 in. (16 ga., 20 ga., 28 ga., .410). To customer specs. Chokes as specified. Weight: 6.5–8 lbs. (12 ga. to customer specs.). Stock: Dimensions to customer specs. Finely figured walnut; straight grip with checkered butt with classic splinter fore-end and hand-rubbed oil finish standard. Pistol grip, beavertail fore-end. Features: Holland & Holland pattern sidelock action, automatic ejectors. Double trigger; non-selective single trigger optional. Coin finish standard; color case-hardened optional. Top rib; level, file-cut; concave, ventilated optional. Very fine, full coverage scroll engraving with small floral bouquets. Imported from Italy by Wm. Larkin Moore.

Price: **$42,800.00**

PIOTTI LUNIK SIDE-BY-SIDE SHOTGUN
Similar to the Piotti King No. 1 in overall quality. Has Renaissance-style large scroll engraving in relief. Best quality Holland & Holland-pattern sidelock ejector double with chopper lump (demi-bloc) barrels. Other mechanical specifications remain the same. Imported from Italy by Wm. Larkin Moore.

Price: **$46,000.00**

PIOTTI PIUMA
Gauges: 12 ga., 16 ga., 20 ga., 28 ga., .410. Barrels: 25–30 in. (12 ga.), 25–28 in. (16 ga., 20 ga., 28 ga., .410). Weights: 5.5–6.25 lbs. (20 ga.). Stock: Dimensions to customer specs. Straight grip stock with walnut checkered butt, classic splinter fore-end, hand-rubbed oil finish are standard; pistol grip, beavertail fore-end, satin luster finish optional. Features: Anson & Deeley boxlock ejector double with chopper lump barrels. Level, file-cut rib, light scroll and rosette engraving, scalloped frame. Double triggers; single non-selective optional. Coin finish standard, color case-hardened optional. Imported from Italy by Wm. Larkin Moore.

Price: **$25,000.00**

SAVAGE FOX A-GRADE
Gauge: 12 or 20. Barrels: 26 or 28 in. with solid rib and IC, M, and F choke tubes. Features: Straight-grip American walnut stock with splinter fore-end, oil finish and cut checkering. Anson & Deeley-style boxlock action, Holland & Holland-style ejectors, double triggers and brass bead sight. A re-creation of the famous Fox double gun, presented by Savage and made at the Connecticut Shotgun Manufacturing Co. plant.
Price: **$5,375.00**

SKB 200 SERIES
Gauges: 12 ga., 20 ga., .410, 3 in.; 28 ga., 2 3/4 in. Barrels: 26 in., 28 in. Five choke tubes provided (F, IM, M, IC, SK). Stock: Hand checkered and oil finished Turkish walnut. Prince of Wales grip and beavertail fore-end. Weight: 6–7 lbs. Sights: Brass bead. Features: Boxlock with platform lump barrel design. Polished bright blue finish with charcoal color case hardening on receiver. Manual safety, automatic ejectors, single selective trigger. 200 HR target model has high ventilated rib, full pistol grip. 250 model has decorative color casehardened sideplates. Imported from Turkey by GU, Inc.
Price: 12 ga., 20 ga..**$2,100.00**
Price: 28 ga., .410..**$2,250.00**
Price: 200 28 ga./.410 Combo **$3,300.00**
Price: 200 HR 12 ga., 20 ga. **$2,500.00**
Price: 200 HR 28 ga., .410 ....**$2,625.00**
Price: 200 HR 28 ga./.410 combo **$3,600.00**
Price: 250 12 ga., 20 ga. **$2,600.00**
Price: 250 28 ga., .410..**$2,725.00**
Price: 250 28 ga./.410 Combo..............................**$3,700.00**

SKB 7000SL SIDELOCK
Gauges: 12 ga., 20 ga. Barrels: 28 in., 30 in. Five choke tubes provided (F, IM, M, IC, SK). Stock: Premium Turkish walnut with hand-rubbed oil finish, fine-line hand checkering, Prince of Wales grip and beavertail fore-end. Weights: 6–7 lbs. Sights: Brass bead. Features: Sidelock design with Holland & Holland style seven-pin removable locks with safety sears. Bison Bone Charcoal casehardening, hand engraved sculpted sidelock receiver. Manual safety, automatic ejectors, single selective trigger. Available by special order only. Imported from Turkey by GU, Inc.
Price: **$6,500.00**

STOEGER UPLANDER
Gauges: 12 ga., 20 ga., .410, 3 in.; 28 ga., 2 3/4. Barrels: 22 in., 24 in., 26 in., 28 in. Weights: 6.5–7.3 lbs. Sights: Brass bead. Features: Double trigger, IC & M choke tubes included with gun. Other choke tubes available. Tang auto safety, extractors, black plastic buttplate. Imported by Benelli USA.
Price: Standard **$449.00**
Price: Supreme (single trigger, AA-grade wood) **$549.00**
Price: Longfowler (12 ga., 30-in. bbl.) **$449.00**
Price: Home Defense (20 or 12 ga., 20-in. bbl., tactical sights) **$499.00**
Price: Double Defense (20 ga.) fiber-optic sight, accessory rail **$499.00**

STOEGER COACH GUN
Gauges: 12 ga., 20 ga., 2 3/4 in., 3 in., .410 bore, Barrel: 20 in. Weight: 6.5 lbs. Stock: Brown hardwood, classic beavertail fore-end. Sights: Brass bead. Features: Double or single trigger, IC & M choke tubes included, others available. Tang auto safety, extractors, black plastic buttplate. Imported by Benelli USA.
Price: **$549.00**

Price: **$449.00**
Price: .410 bore, 3-inch, 20-in. barrel...............**$449.00**
Price: Black-finished hardwood/polished-nickel model **$549.00**

TRISTAR BRISTOL
Gauges: 12 ga. 3 in., 20 ga. 3 in., 28 ga. 2.75 in., .410 bore 3 in. Barrels: 28 in. Weight: 5.08–6.74 lbs. Stock: Select Turkish Walnut with oil finish, English style. Features: Side-by-side double available in four gauges, each built on a true steel frame. Laser-engraved detail. Features an English-style straight stock paired with case colored receiver. Dual-purpose tang safety/barrel selector. Auto-ejectors, brass front sight, single selective trigger. Chrome-lined chamber and barrel. Includes five Beretta-style choke tubes (SK, IC, M, IM, F).
Price: ....$1,065.00–$1,100.00

TRISTAR BRISTOL
Gauge: 12 ga. 3 in., 16 ga., 20 ga. 3 in., 28 ga. 2.75 in., .410 bore 3 in. Barrels: 28 in. Weight: 5.08–6.74 lbs. Stock: Select Turkish Walnut with oil finish, English style. Features: Side-by-side double available in four gauges, each built on a true steel frame. Laser engraved detail. Features an English-style straight stock paired with case colored receiver. Dual purpose tang safety/barrel selector. Auto-ejectors, brass front sight, single selective trigger. Chrome-lined chamber and barrel. Includes five Beretta-style choke tubes (SK, IC, M, IM, F).
Price: 12 and 20 ga. **$1,160.00**
Price: 16, 28 ga., and .410 bore **$1,190.00**

TRISTAR BRISTOL SILVER
Gauge: 12 ga. 3 in., 16 ga., 20 ga. 3 in., 28 ga. 2.75 in., .410 bore 3 in. Barrels: 28 in. Weight: 5.08–6.74 lbs. Stock: Select Turkish Walnut with oil finish, pistol grip style. Features: Side-by-side double available in four gauges, each built on a true steel frame. Laser engraved detail. Features a nickel-finished receiver with 24-Karat gold inlay on the bottom of the receiver, as well as semi-pistol grip-style stock. Dual-purpose tang safety/barrel selector. Auto-ejectors, brass front sight, single selective trigger. Chrome-lined chamber and barrel. Includes five Beretta-style choke tubes (SK, IC, M, IM, F).
Price: 12 and 20 ga. **$1,100.00**
Price: 16, 28 ga., and .410 bore **$1,130.00**

YILDIZ ELEGANT
Gauge: .410 bore, 3 in. Barrels: 26 in., 28 in., 30 in., with 7mm or 8mm rib. Weight: 4.8-6.0 lbs. Stock: Oil-finish selected walnut from standard through Grades 3 and 5, some pistol grip and others straight English-style. Features: Built of 4140 Steel, with varying degrees of receiver engraving. Manual or automatic safety, extractors or ejectors, depending on model. Single selective trigger, front bead, full black rubber recoil pad. Models include: A1, A3, A4, A5, and Special Lux. Includes five Mobil chokes. Manufactured in Turkey and imported/sold through Academy.
Price: **$479.00**

Prices given are believed to be accurate at time of publication however, many factors affect retail pricing so exact prices are not possible.

78TH EDITION, 2024 ⬥ **547**

BROWNING BT-99 TRAP
Gauge: 12 ga. Barrels: 30 in., 32 in., 34 in. Stock: Walnut; standard or adjustable. Weights: 7 lbs. 11 oz.–9 lbs. Features: Back-bored single barrel; interchangeable chokes; beavertail forearm; extractor only; high rib.
Price: BT-99 w/conventional comb, 32- or 34-in. barrel..................**$1,470.00**
Price: BT-99 w/adjustable comb, 32- or 34-in. barrel.....................**$1,840.00**
Price: BT-99 Max High Grade w/adjustable comb, 32- or
     34-in. barrel..**$5,340.00**
Price: Micro Adjustable LOP Model....................................... **$1,669.00**

CHARLES DALY 101
Gauges: 12 ga., 3 in., 20 ga., 3in., .410 bore. Barrels: 26 in., 28 in. Weight: 5.0-8.1 lbs. Length: 41.75-43.75 in. Stock: Choice of either checkered walnut or black synthetic stocks. Features: These updated break-action single shots have become more affordable than ever. Though built of steel, they're still quite light. Brass front bead, manual safety, single trigger, extractor, rubber butt pad. Includes a Modified Beretta/Benelli Mobil choke tube.
Price: ....**$119.00-$129.00**

HENRY .410 LEVER-ACTION SHOTGUN
Gauge: .410, 2 1/2 in. Capacity: 5. Barrels: 20 or 24 in. with either no choke (20 in.) or full choke (24 in.). Stock: American walnut. Sights: Gold bead front only. Finish: Blued. Introduced in 2017. Features: Design is based on the Henry .45-70 rifle.
Price: 20-in. bbl...**$893.00**
Price: 24-in. bbl... **$947.00**

HENRY SIDE GATE LEVER ACTION 410 MODEL H018G-410R
Gauge: .410 bore 2.5in. Barrel: 19.75 in. smoothbore, round blued steel. Weight: 7.09 lbs. Length: 38.1 in. Stock: American Walnut with checkering. Features: This model launches as a blued steel companion to Henry's polished brass version last year. This is the more compact of the pair of lever action 410's. Has Henry's new side-loading gate in addition to the tubular loading port and magazine capacity of six rounds. Adjustable semi-buckhorn rear sight with diamond insert and brass bead front post sight. Black ventilated rubber recoil pad, transfer bar safety, sling swivel studs. Fixed cylinder bore choke.
Price: **$969.00**

HENRY X-MODEL 410
Gauges: .410 bore 2.5 in. Barrel: 19.8 in. smoothbore, round blued steel. Weight: 7.5 lbs. Length: 38.6 in. Stock: Black synthetic with textured panels. Features: Henry's first blacked-out model with matte blued steel receiver. Side loading gate in addition to tubular port with magazine capacity of 6+1 rounds. Black solid rubber recoil pad. Green fiber-optic front sight, transfer bar safety, swivel studs, large loop lever. Tactical features include lower Picatinny rail and M-LOK attachment points at fore-end. Drilled and tapped for a Weaver 63B optics mount. Includes Invector choke.
Price: **$1,000.00**

HENRY SINGLE-SHOT SHOTGUN
Gauges: 12 ga., 20 ga. or .410 bore, 3 1/2 in. (12 ga.), 3 in. (20 ga. and 410). Barrels: 26 or 28 in. with either modified choke tube (12 ga., 20 ga., compatible with Rem-Choke tubes) or fixed full choke (.410). Stock: American walnut, straight or pistol grip. Sights: Gold bead front only. Weight: 6.33 lbs. Finish: Blued or brass receiver. Features: Break-open single-shot design. Introduced in 2017.
Price: **$448.00**
Price: Brass receiver, straight grip....................................**$576.00**

HENRY SINGLE SHOT SLUG
Gauges: 12 ga. 3 in. Barrel: 24-in. round blued steel. Weight: 6.88 lbs. Length: 39.5 in. Stock: American Walnut. Features: The company's first slug-hunting shotgun, with a fully-rifled 1:35 twist barrel. This single shot is finished in traditional blued steel and checkered walnut with a black rubber recoil pad. Buttstock has a 14-inch LOP. Sling studs. Rebounding hammer safety. Fiber optic sights. Drilled and tapped for a Weaver 82 base.
Price: **$560.00**

HENRY AXE
Gauge: .410 bore 2.5 in. Barrel: 15.14 in. smoothbore, round blued steel. Weight: 5.75 lbs. Length: 26.4 in. Stock: American Walnut with unique axe-handle-style rear grip. Features: Henry's Axe is most closely related to the handgun-chambered Mare's Leg platform, but this time with a slightly different design and firing .410 shotshells. Both the standard Steel and Brass Axe have a 5-round capacity with the addition of a loading gate. Short barrel takes interchangeable Invector-style chokes and ships with a full tube. Brass front bead, swivel studs, transfer bar safety. Drilled and tapped for optics mounting.
Price: **$1,049.00**
Price: Brass Axe **$1,132.00**

HENRY SINGLE SHOT TURKEY
Gauges: 12 ga. 3.5 in. Barrel: 24-in. round. Weight: 6.78 lbs. Length: 39.5 in. Stock: American Walnut covered in Mossy Oak Obsession camo. Features: The company's first dedicated turkey-hunting shotgun wears full-coverage Mossy Oak Obsession, the official camouflage pattern of the National Wild Turkey Federation. Fiber-optic front and rear sights. Drilled and tapped for a Weaver 82 base. Black solid rubber recoil pad creates a 14-inch LOP. Swivel studs. Rebounding hammer safety. Includes an extended Turkey choke.
Price: **$687.00**

KEYSTONE SPORTING ARMS 4100 My First Shotgun
Gauges: .410 bore 3 in. Barrel: 18.5 in. Length: 32 in. Weight: 4.2 lbs. Stock: Turkish Walnut. Features: Marketed as a Crickett "My First Shotgun," this single-shot baby bore uses a folding design. Recoil reducing chamber and soft rubber recoil pad. Aluminum receiver with matte blue metalwork. Blade-style front sight. Checkered stock. Length of pull built for small-frame shooters at 11 inches. Fixed modified choke.
Price: **$179.00**

KRIEGHOFF K-80 SINGLE BARREL TRAP GUN
Gauge: 12 ga., 2 3/4 in. Barrel: 32 in., 34 in. Unsingle. Fixed Full or choke tubes. Weight: About 8.75 lbs. Stock: Four stock dimensions or adjustable stock available. All hand-checkered European walnut. Features: Satin nickel finish. Selective mechanical trigger adjustable for finger position. Tapered step vent rib. Adjustable point of impact.
Price: Standard Grade Full Unsingle...............................**$12,995.00**

KRIEGHOFF KX-6 SPECIAL TRAP GUN
Gauge: 12 ga., 2 3/4 in. Barrel: 32 in., 34 in.; choke tubes. Weight: About 8.5 lbs. Stock: Factory adjustable stock. European walnut. Features: Ventilated tapered step rib. Adjustable position trigger, optional release trigger. Fully adjustable rib. Satin gray electroless nickel receiver. Fitted aluminum case. Imported from Germany by Krieghoff International, Inc.
Price: **$5,995.00**

Prices given are believed to be accurate at time of publication however, many factors affect retail pricing so exact prices are not possible.

LJUTIC MONO GUN SINGLE BARREL
Gauge: 12 ga. Barrel: 34 in., choked to customer specs; hollow-milled rib, 35.5-in. sight plane. Weight: Approx. 9 lbs. Stock: To customer specs. Oil finish, hand checkered. Features: Custom gun. Pull or release trigger; removable trigger guard contains trigger and hammer mechanism; Ljutic pushbutton opener on front of trigger guard. From Ljutic Industries.
Price: Std., med. or Olympic rib, custom bbls., fixed choke. **$7,495.00**
Price: Stainless steel mono gun.. **$8,495.00**

LJUTIC LTX PRO 3 DELUXE MONO GUN
Deluxe, lightweight version of the Mono gun with high-quality wood, upgrade checkering, special rib height, screw-in chokes, ported and cased.
Price: **$8,995.00**
Price: Stainless steel model... **$9,995.00**

ROSSI CIRCUIT JUDGE
Revolving shotgun chambered in .410 (2 1/2- or 3-in./.45 Colt. Based on Taurus Judge handgun. Features include 18.5-in. barrel; fiber-optic front sight; 5-round cylinder; hardwood Monte Carlo stock.
Price: **$689.00**

ROSSI TUFFY SINGLE SHOT 410 TURKEY
Gauge: .410 bore 3 in. Barrel: 26 in. Length: 41 in. Weight: 58.80 oz. Stock: Olive drab green polymer thumbhole-style with integral buttstock shell holders. Features: Part of Rossi's single-shot, break-action Tuffy family, the new 410 Turkey has an extended barrel length and gobbler-specific choke. Polymer receiver with steel frame structure. Matte black finish metalwork. Bead front sight. Picatinny top rail for easy optics mounting. Sling swivels. Black rubber buttpad. Transfer bar safety. Extended Extra Full Turkey choke.
Price: Standard Grade Full Unsingle **$220.00**

SAVAGE 212/220
Gauges: 12 ga., 3 in., 20 ga., 3 in. Barrel: 22 in., carbon steel. Weight: 7.34-7.75 lbs. Length: 43 in. Stock: Synthetic AccuFit stock with included LOP and comb inserts. Thumbhole model uses gray wood laminate. Features: The bolt-action Savage models 212 and 220, so named for their chamberings, are available in Slug, Slug Camo, Thumbhole, Left-Handed and Turkey models. Choice of button-rifled slug barrels or smoothbore. Detachable box magazine, thread-in barrel headspacing. User adjustable AccuTrigger and AccuStock internal chassis. Oversized bolt handle, Picatinny optics rail, sling studs, rubber buttpad.
Price: .... **$629.00–$799.00**
Price: 212 Turkey w/extended X-Full choke........................ **$779.00**
Price: 220 Turkey w/extended X-Full choke........................ **$695.00**

STEVENS 301 TURKEY XP
Gauges: 20 ga., 3 in., .410 bore, 3 in. Barrel: 26 in., black matte. Weight: 5.07 lbs. Length: 41.5 in. Stock: Camouflage synthetic stock and fore-end with either Mossy Oak Obsession or Mossy Oak Bottomland pattern. Features: Single-shot break action with removable one-piece rail. XP variant includes mounted and bore-sighted 1x30 red-dot optic. Barrel optimized for Federal Premium TSS Heavyweight turkey loads. Swivel studs, front bead, manual hammer block safety, rubber recoil pad. Includes Winchoke pattern Extra Full turkey choke.
Price: **$239.00**

STEVENS 301 TURKEY THUMBHOLE
Gauges: .410 bore 3 in. Barrel: 26 in. chrome alloy steel black matte. Weight: 5.07 lbs. Length: 41.5 in. Stock: Olive drab green matte synthetic thumbhole style. Features: Continuation of the 301 single-shot break-action line with a removeable one-piece rail and gobbler-specific features. Ambidextrous cheek riser. Barrel optimized for Federal Premium Heavyweight TSS turkey loads. Swivel studs, front bead sight, manual hammer block safety, rubber recoil pad. Includes Win-Choke pattern Extra Full turkey choke.
Price: **$229.00**

STEVENS 555 TRAP
Gauges: 12 ga., 3 in., 20 ga., 3 in. Barrel: 30 in., raised ventilated rib. Weight: 6.6-6.8 lbs. Length: 47.5 in. Stock: Turkish walnut stock and fore-end with adjustable comb and oil finish. Features: Lightweight silver aluminum receiver scaled to gauge with steel breech reinforcement. Top single barrel with shell extractor. Manual tang safety, front bead, chrome-lined barrel, semi-gloss metalwork finish. Includes three chokes.
Price: **$689.00**

STEVENS 555 TRAP COMPACT
Gauges: 12 ga., 3 in., 20 ga., 3 in. Barrel: 26 in., raised ventilated rib. Weight: 7.3-7.5 lbs. Length: 42.5 in. Stock: Turkish walnut stock and fore-end with adjustable comb and oil finish. Features: Lightweight silver aluminum receiver scaled to gauge with steel breech reinforcement. Top single barrel with shell extractor. Manual tang safety, front bead, chrome-lined barrel, semi-gloss metalwork finish. Compact 13.5 in. length of pull. Includes three chokes.
Price: **$689.00**

TAR-HUNT RSG-12 PROFESSIONAL RIFLED SLUG GUN
Gauge: 12 ga., 2 3/4 in., 3 in., Capacity: 1-round magazine. Barrel: 23 in., fully rifled with muzzle brake. Weight: 7.75 lbs. Length: 41.5 in. overall. Stock: Matte black McMillan fiberglass with Pachmayr Decelerator pad. Sights: None furnished; comes with Leupold windage or Weaver bases. Features: Uses rifle-style action with two locking lugs; two-position safety; Shaw barrel; single-stage, trigger; muzzle brake. Many options available. All models have area-controlled feed action. Introduced 1991. Made in U.S. by Tar-Hunt Custom Rifles, Inc.
Price: 12 ga. Professional model **$3,495.00**
Price: Left-hand model **$3,625.00**

TAR-HUNT RSG-20 MOUNTAINEER SLUG GUN
Similar to the RSG-12 Professional except chambered for 20 ga. (2 3/4 in. and 3 in. shells); 23 in. Shaw rifled barrel, with muzzle brake; two-lug bolt; one-shot blind magazine; matte black finish; McMillan fiberglass stock with Pachmayr Decelerator pad; receiver drilled and tapped for Rem. 700 bases. Right- or left-hand versions. Weighs 6.5 lbs. Introduced 1997. Made in USA by Tar-Hunt Custom Rifles, Inc.
Price: **$3,495.00**

TRISTAR LR94
Gauges: .410 bore. Barrels: 22, 24 in. Stock: Turkish Walnut, checkered and oil finished. Features: The company's first lever-action firearm. Top safety, blade/bead front sight and rifle-style rear sight. 2.5-inch chamber. Side-loading gate and tubular magazine. Leather-wrapped lever. Accepts CT-1 interchangeable choke tubes. Choice of three finish options.
Price: Matte walnut **$990.00**
Price: Case Color/walnut **$1,100.00**
Price: Nickel/walnut **$1,070.00**

AMERICAN TACTICAL BULLDOG
Gauge: 12 ga. 3 in., 20 ga. 3 in. Barrel: 16 and 18.5 in. with ported shroud. Length: 23.5–26 in. Weight: 4.5 lbs. Stock: Black synthetic with fixed bullpup style with adjustable cheek riser. Features: Gas-operated tactical bullpup shotgun with AR-style charging handle, adjustable cheek rest, and both Picatinny and M-LOK rails. Housing for spare five-round magazine. Extra magazine can also be attached to the bottom rail and used as a fore grip. Includes quick acquisition flip-up sights and three choke tubes.
Price: $359.00

ARMSCOR VRF-14
Gauge: 12 ga. Barrel: 14 in. Length: 26 in. Weight: 6.6 lbs. Stock: Black polymer with full-top forend and sling adapter rear. Features: Semi-automatic short-barreled firearm in 12-ga. Pistol-grip style designed to be fired from the hip. Built with a 7075 aluminum receiver, Bufferbolt system, and full-length top Picatinny rail. Flip-up front and rear sights. Five-round magazine included, but also compatible with VR-Series 9 and 19-round mags.
Price: $599.00

BENELLI M2 TACTICAL
Gauge: 12 ga., 2 3/4 in., 3 in. Capacity: 5-round magazine. Barrel: 18.5 in. IC, M, F choke tubes. Weight: 6.7 lbs. Length: 39.75 in. overall. Stock: Black polymer. Standard or pistol grip. Sights: Rifle type ghost ring system, tritium night sights optional. Features: Semi-auto inertia recoil action. Cross-bolt safety; bolt release button; matte-finish metal. Introduced 1993. Imported from Italy by Benelli USA.
Price: ....$1,239.00–$1,359.00

BENELLI M3 TACTICAL
Gauge: 12 ga., 3 in. Barrel: 20 in. Stock: Black synthetic w/pistol grip. Sights: Ghost ring rear, ramp front. Convertible dual-action operation (semi-auto or pump).
Price: $1,599.00

BENELLI M4 TACTICAL
Gauge: 12 ga., 3 in. Barrel: 18.5 in. Weight: 7.8 lbs. Length: 40 in. overall. Stock: Synthetic. Sights: Ghost Ring rear, fixed blade front. Features: Auto-regulating gas-operated (ARGO) action, choke tube, Picatinny rail, standard and collapsible stocks available, optional LE tactical gun case. Introduced 2006.
Price: $1,999.00
Price: M4 H20 Cerakote Finish $2,269.00

BENELLI NOVA TACTICAL
Gauge: 12 ga., 3 in. Barrel: 18.5 in. Stock: Black synthetic standard or pistol grip. Sights: Ghost ring rear, ramp front. Pump action.
Price: $439.00

BENELLI VINCI TACTICAL
Gauge: 12 ga., 3 in. Barrel: 18.5 in. Semi-auto operation. Stock: Black synthetic. Sights: Ghost ring rear, ramp front.
Price: $1,349.00
Price: ComforTech stock..$1,469.00

BERETTA A300 ULTIMA PATROL
Gauges: 12 ga., 20 ga. Barrel: 19.1 in. Stock: Synthetic. Features: New defense-style addition to A300 Ultima family of semi-autos. Low profile receiver with oversized loading port. Enlarged controls. Wide 7x7 stepped

---

rib with mid bead. KickOff recoil system included as standard configuration on most models. Tactical sights with fiber optic front. Thinner forend with M-LOK and QD points. 7+1 round extended magazine tube secured with barrel clamp.
Price: Black or Gray $1,099.00
Price: Tiger Stripe..$1,199.00

CHARLES DALY AR 410 UPPER
Gauge: .410 bore 2.5 in. Barrel: 19 in. Length: 26.75 in. Weight: 4.9 lbs. Stock: Upper only with quad Picatinny rail fore-end. Features: Charles Daly enters the AR market with a .410 bore shotgun upper. Built of black anodized aluminum. Auto-ejection, gas-operated system. Windage-adjustable rear sight and elevation adjustable rear flip-up sights. Ships with a five-round magazine but compatible with 10 and 15 rounders. This upper must be used with a Mil-Spec lower and carbine-length buffer tube.
Price: $415.00

GARAYSAR FEAR 116
Gauge: 12 ga. 3 in. Barrel: 20 in. 4140 steel. Length: 39 in. Weight: 8.8 lbs. Stock: Synthetic available in a variety of colors and finishes. Features: Gas-operated semi-automatic with an aluminum receiver. Adjustable cheek rest. Front and rear flip-up sights. Ships with two five-round magazines, but also accepts 10-round mags. Includes five choke tubes (F, IM, M, IC, C), choke tube case, and hard case.
Price: $589.00

GARAYSAR FEAR BULLPUP
Gauge: 12 ga. 3 in. Barrel: 18.5 in. Length: 28.34 in. Stock: Black synthetic, with both green and FDE to follow. Features: Gas-regulated, semi-automatic bullpup-style shotgun. Built on an aluminum receiver with 4140 steel barrel. Bullpup family available in multiple model variants including 104, 105, 106, and 109, each with different options on a similar build. Ships with two five-round magazines, but also accepts 10- and 15-round mags. Adjustable cheek riser. Multiple choke options dependent on model; some fixed, others interchangeable.
Price: $489.00

IVER JOHNSON STRYKER-12
Gauge: 12 ga., 3 in. Barrel: 20 in., smoothbore with muzzle brake. Length: 43 in. Stock: Black synthetic two-piece, pistol-grip stock. Features: This AR15-style semi-auto shotgun uses a standard AR15 bolt and mag release. A2-style detachable carry handle with adjustable sight, fiber-optic front sight. Light rails on both sides and bottom of fore-end. Push button releases the stock and leaves the pistol grip for a modular platform. Cross-bolt safety, thick rubber buttpad. Ships with two MKA 1919 5-round box magazines.
Price: $495.00

IWI TAVOR TS-12
Gauge: 12 ga. 3 in. Barrel: 18.5 in. Length: 28.34 in. Weight: 8.9 lbs. Stock: Synthetic fixed bullpup style, with Black, OD green and FDE color options. Features: Gas-driven semi-automatic bullpup design that feeds from one of three magazine tubes. Each tube holds four 3-in. shells or five 2.75-in. rounds. Max capacity 15 rounds. Includes four sling attachment points, M-LOK rails, and extended Picatinny top rail. Crossbolt safety. Bullhead bolt system. Uses Benelli/Beretta-style Mobil choke tubes.
Price: $1,399.00

Prices given are believed to be accurate at time of publication however, many factors affect retail pricing so exact prices are not possible.

KALASHNIKOV KOMP12

Gauge: 12 ga. 3 in. Barrel: 18.25 in. with external threading. Weight: 17 lbs. Stock: Synthetic skeleton-style, collapsible. Features: The Kalashnikov USA x Dissident Arms KOMP12 is an American-made semi-automatic based on the Russian Saiga series. Adjustable gas system. Extended charging handle, aluminum handguard rail, enhanced safety lever. Flared magazine well, tuned trigger. Top Picatinny rail for optics. Threaded flash suppressor. Magpul AK pistol grip. Zinc phosphate parkerized undercoat with Dissident Arms Black, Red, and Sniper Grey color scheme. Ships with Dissident SGM 12-round magazine.
Price: **$1,499.00**

KEL-TEC KSG BULL-PUP TWIN-TUBE

Gauge: 12 ga. Capacity: 13+1. Barrel: 18.5 in. Overall Length: 26.1 in. Weight: 8.5 lbs. (loaded). Features: Pump-action shotgun with two magazine tubes. The shotgun bears a resemblance to the South African designed Neostead pump-action gun. The operator is able to move a switch located near the top of the grip to select the right or left tube, or move the switch to the center to eject a shell without chambering another round. Optional accessories include a factory installed Picatinny rail with flip-up sights and a pistol grip. KSG-25 has 30-in. barrel and 20-round capacity magazine tubes.
Price: **$990.00**
Price: KSG-25 .... **$1400.00**

KELTEC KSG410

Gauge: .410 bore. Barrel: 18.5 in. Stock: Synthetic bullpup style in Black or FDE. Features: Baby bore bullpup touted as "sidekick with no kick." Only 1.7 inches wide with two magazine tubes. Capacity of 5+5+1 rounds. Fiber-optic sights, top carry handle/sight rail. Overall length of 26.1 in. keeps it legal as a shotgun. Three-inch chamber.
Price: **$495.00**

KEL-TEC KS7 BULLPUP

Gauge: 12 ga., 3 in. Capacity: 6+1. Barrel: 18.5 in. Length: 26.1 in. Weight: 5.9 lbs. Stock: Black synthetic bullpup. Features: The pump-action KS7 Bullpup is a compact self-defense shotgun. Carry handle, Picatinny rail, M-LOK mounting points. Rear loading, downward ejection, ambidextrous controls. Cylinder choke.
Price: **$495.00**

MOSSBERG MAVERICK 88 CRUISER

Gauges: 12 ga., 3 in., 20 ga., 3in. Capacity: 5+1 or 7+1 capacity. Barrels: 18.5 in., 20 in. Length: 28.125-30.375 in. Weight: 5.5-6.0 lbs. Stock: Black synthetic pistol grip. Features: Fixed cylinder bore choke, blued metalwork, bead front sight, cross-bolt safety.
Price: **$231.00**

MOSSBERG MODEL 500 SPECIAL PURPOSE

Gauges: 12 ga., 20 ga., .410, 3 in. Barrels: 18.5 in., 20 in. (Cyl.). Weight: 7 lbs. Stock: Walnut-finished hardwood or black synthetic. Sights: Metal bead front. Features: Slide-action operation. Available in 6- or 8-round models. Top-mounted safety, double action slide bars, swivel studs, rubber recoil pad. Blue, Parkerized, Marinecote finishes. Mossberg Cablelock included. The HS410 Home Security model chambered for .410 with 3 in. chamber; has pistol grip fore-end, thick recoil pad, muzzle brake and has special spreader choke on the 18.5-in. barrel. Overall length is 37.5 in. Blued finish; synthetic field stock. Mossberg Cablelock and video included. Mariner model has Marinecote metal finish to resist rust and corrosion. Synthetic field stock; pistol grip kit included. 500 Tactical 6-shot has black synthetic tactical stock. Introduced 1990.
Price: 500 Mariner.. **$636.00**
Price: HS410 Home Security.. **$477.00**
Price: Home Security 20 ga. **$631.00**
Price: FLEX Tactical.. **$672.00**
Price: 500 Chainsaw pistol grip only; removable top handle **$547.00**
Price: JIC (Just In Case).. **$500.00**
Price: Thunder Ranch **$553.00**

MOSSBERG 590S SHOCKWAVE

Gauge: 12 ga. 1.7–3 in. Barrel: 14.375 and 18.5 in. Length: 26.37–30.75 in. Weight: 5.3–5.5 lbs. Stock: Black synthetic with Raptor grip and corn-cob forend with strap. Features: The upgraded 590S version of the pistol grip Shockwave is built to cycle any length shells without adapter or adjustment, from 1.75 to 3-in. Bead front sight, matte blued metalwork, shorter-barreled model uses heavy-walled barrel. Both feature fixed cylinder bore choke.
Price: **$623.00**

MOSSBERG MODEL 590 SPECIAL PURPOSE

Gauges: 12 ga., 20 ga., .410 3 in. Capacity: 9-round magazine. Barrel: 20 in. (Cyl.). Weight: 7.25 lbs. Stock: Synthetic field or Speedfeed. Sights: Metal bead front or Ghost Ring. Features: Slide action. Top-mounted safety, double slide action bars. Comes with heat shield, bayonet lug, swivel studs, rubber recoil pad. Blue, Parkerized or Marinecote finish. Shockwave has 14-inch heavy walled barrel, Raptor pistol grip, wrapped fore-end and is fully BATFE compliant. Magpul model has Magpul SGA stock with adjustable comb and length of pull. Mossberg Cablelock included. From Mossberg.
Price: **$559.00**
Price: Flex Tactical **$672.00**
Price: Tactical Tri-Rail Adjustable.. **$879.00**
Price: Mariner **$756.00**
Price: Shockwave.. **$455.00–$721.00**
Price: MagPul 9-shot **$836.00**

MOSSBERG 930 SPECIAL PURPOSE SERIES

Gauge: 12 ga., 3 in. Barrel: 18.5-28 in. flat ventilated rib. Weight: 7.3 lbs. Length: 49 in.. Stock: Composite stock with close radius pistol grip; Speed Lock forearm; textured gripping surfaces; shim adjustable for length of pull, cast and drop; Mossy Oak Bottomland camo finish; Dura-Touch Armor Coating. Features: 930 Special Purpose shotguns feature a self-regulating gas system that vents excess gas to aid in recoil reduction and eliminate stress on critical components. All 930 autoloaders chamber both 2 3/4 inch and 3-in. 12-ga. shotshells with ease — from target loads, to non-toxic magnum loads, to the latest sabot slug ammo. Magazine capacity is 7+1 on models with extended magazine tube, 4+1 on models without. To complete the

Prices given are believed to be accurate at time of publication however, many factors affect retail pricing so exact prices are not possible.

78TH EDITION, 2024 ✛ **551**

package, each Mossberg 930 includes a set of specially designed spacers for quick adjustment of the horizontal and vertical angle of the stock, bringing a custom-feel fit to every shooter. All 930 Special Purpose models feature a drilled and tapped receiver, factory-ready for Picatinny rail, scope base or optics installation. 930 SPX models conveniently come with a factory-mounted Picatinny rail and LPA/M16-Style Ghost Ring combination sight right out of the box. Other sighting options include a basic front bead, or white-dot front sights. Mossberg 930 Special Purpose shotguns are available in a variety of configurations; 5-round tactical barrel, 5-round with muzzle brake, 8-round pistol-grip, and even a 5-round security/field combo.

Price: Tactical 5-Round **$612.00**
Price: Home Security...**$662.00**
Price: Standard Stock **$787.00**
Price: Pistol Grip 8-Round **$1,046.00**
Price: 5-Round Combo w/extra 18.5-in. barrel **$693.00**
Price: Chainsaw **$564.00**

MOSSBERG 940 PRO TACTICAL-HOLOSUN COMBO
Gauges: 12 ga. Barrels: 18.5 in. Stock: Black synthetic. Features: Same system as 940 Pro family with the receiver machined for direct micro-dot optics mounting and a Holosun HS407K along with a fiber-optic front.
Price: **$1,333.00**

RETAY MASAI MARA WARDEN
Gauge: 12 ga., 3 in. Barrel: 18.5 in. Weight: 6.6 lbs. Stock: Black Synthetic. Features: The Turkish-made Masai Mara line of semi-automatics uses an inertia-plus action and bolt system. Oversized controls, quick unload system, Picatinny rail, extended charging handle, ghost-ring sights. Push-button removeable trigger group. Microcell rubber recoil pad. Includes a hard case and ships with five MaraPro choke tubes.
Price: **$1,099.00**

ROCK ISLAND ARMORY/ARMSCOR VRBP-100
Gauge: 12 ga., 3 in. Capacity: 5+1. Barrel: 20 in. contoured. Length: 32 in. Weight: 7.94 lbs. Stock: Black polymer bullpup design with pistol grip. Features: Semi-automatic bullpup design. Compatible with all VR Series magazines. Matte-black anodized finish. Includes rubber spacers to adjust length of pull. Full length top rail with flip-up sights, right-sided Picatinny accessory rail. Ships with three interchangeable chokes.
Price: **$774.00**

ROCK ISLAND ARMORY/ARMSCOR VRPA-40
Gauge: 12 ga., 3 in. Capacity: 5+1. Barrel: 20 in., contoured. Length: 55.11 in. Weight: 6.9 lbs. Stock: Black synthetic. Features: The VRPA40 marks the more affordable pump action addition to the VR family of shotguns. Magazine fed, aluminum heat shield, fiber-optic front sight, adjustable rear sight, Picatinny rail. Marine black anodized, compatible with VR series 9-round magazines. Mobil chokes.
Price: **$399.00**

ROCK ISLAND ARMORY/ARMSCOR VR82
Gauge: 20 ga. 3 in. Barrel: 18 in. contoured. Length: 38 in. Weight: 7.5 lbs. Stock: Black polymer thumbhole style. Features: The semi-automatic VR82 is the little brother of the VR80. Built of 7075 T6 aluminum for lighter weight. Magazine fed with 5+1 capacity but also accepts VR-series 10- and 20-round mags. Ambidextrous controls, flip-up sights, barrel shroud. Fore-end accepts most aftermarket accessories. Compatible with most buffer tube stocks and pistol grips. Black anodized finish. Mobil choke.
Price: **$729.00**

ROCK ISLAND PF14
Gauges: 12 ga. Barrel: 14.1 in. Stock: Black synthetic with F-Grip. Features: Handheld pump-action defense shotgun with five-round capacity. Bead front sight. Overall length of 26.1 inches. Includes sling adapter and forend strap. Chambered for 2.75- or 3-inch loads.
Price: **$369.00**

ROCK ISLAND VRPF14
Gauges: 12 ga. Barrel: 14.1 in. Stock: Black synthetic with F-Grip. Features: Handheld pump-action defense shotgun. Like other VR series, is magazine-fed, and mags are interchangeable. Bead front sight. Overall length of 26.1 inches. Includes sling adapter and forend strap. Chambered for 2.75- or 3-inch loads.
Price: **$449.00**

SAVAGE RENEGAUGE SECURITY
Gauge: 12 ga. 3 in. Barrel: 18.5 in. Melonite-treated, fluted, with ventilated rib. Length: 40 in. Weight: 7.3 lbs. Stock: Matte gray synthetic with adjustable LOP, comb height, and drop/cast. Features: Savage's self-regulating DRIV gas system. One-piece chrome-plated action bar and reciprocating components. Stock rod buffer to reduce recoil. Adjustable ghost ring sights and one-piece rail. Oversized controls. Includes three flush choke tubes (IC, M, F) and hard case.
Price: **$1,499.00**

SMITH & WESSON M&P-12
Gauge: 12 ga. 3 in. Barrel: 19 in. Length: 27.8 in. Weight: 8.3 lbs. Stock: Black synthetic with fixed stock. Features: Single barrel pump-action shotgun with two independent magazine tubes. Capacity of seven rounds of 2-3/4-in. shells or six rounds of 3-in. shells per tube. Vertical foregrip, action lock lever button, and push button mag tube selector. Ships with four interchangeable pistol grip palm swell inserts. Picatinny top rail, M-LOK barrel slots. Includes Rem-Choke-style choke tubes (M, C), choke wrench, and foam-lined hard case.
Price: **$1,185.00**

STANDARD MANUFACTURING DP-12 PROFESSIONAL
Gauge: 12 ga. 3 in. Barrels: 18-7/8 in. Length: 29.5 in. Weight: 9 lb. 12 oz. Stock: Synthetic with anodized aluminum. Features: Upgraded Professional version of the pump-action DP-12 high-capacity defense shotgun. Additions include an aluminum rail with front grip, which wears an integral laser and flashlight. Precision-honed bores and chambers finished with hand-lapping. PVD coating on all critical wear areas. Mil-spec hard anodized finish with accents in either Blue or OD Green. Includes Reflex Sight with multiple brightness levels. Ships with both soft and hard cases
Price: **$3,250.00**

WINCHESTER SXP EXTREME DEFENDER
Gauge: 12 ga., 3 in. Barrel: 18 in., with Heat Shield. Length: 38.5 in. Weight: 7.0 lbs. Stock: Flat Dark Earth composite with textured grip panels and pistol grip. Features: Aluminum-alloy receiver, hard-chrome chamber and bore, Picatinny rail with ghost-ring sight, blade front sight. Two interchangeable comb pieces and two quarter-inch length-of-pull spacers for custom fit. Side-mounted Picatinny accessory rails, sling studs, Inflex recoil pad. Includes one Invector Plus cylinder choke and one Door Breacher choke.
Price: **$529.00**

CHIAPPA LE PAGE PERCUSSION DUELING PISTOL
Caliber: .45. Barrel: 10 in. browned octagon, rifled. Weight: 2.5 lbs. Length: 16.6 in. overall. Stock: Walnut, rounded, fluted butt. Sights: Blade front, open-style rear. Features: Double set trigger. Bright barrel, silver-plated brass furniture. External ramrod. Made by Chiappa.
Price: Chiappa 940.001 ....$779.00

CVA OPTIMA PISTOL
Caliber: .50. Barrel: 14 in., 1:28-in. twist, Cerakote finish. Weight: 3.7 lbs. Length: 19 in. Stock: Black synthetic, Realtree Xtra Green. Sights: Scope base mounted. Features: Break-open action, all stainless construction, aluminum ramrod, quick-removal breech plug for 209 primer. From CVA.
Price: PP222SM Stainless/Realtree Xtra, rail mount $354.00
Price: PP221SM Stainless/black, rail mount...$307.00

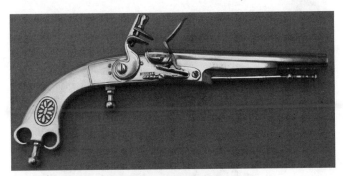

DIXIE MURDOCK SCOTTISH HIGHLANDER'S PISTOL
Caliber: .352. Barrel: 7.5 in., blued steel finish, round. Weight: 3.75 lbs. Length: 18.25 in. overall. Stock: Steel frame. Sights: None. Features: Flintlock, steel ramrod. An exact copy of an Alexander Murdock Scottish pistol of the 1770s. Made in India. Imported by Dixie Gun Works.
Price: Dixie Gun Works FH1040................................$425.00

DIXIE MODEL 1855 U.S. DRAGOON PISTOL
Caliber: .58. Barrel: 12 in., bright finish, round. Weight: 2.25 lbs. Length: 16.75 in. overall. Stock: Walnut. Sights: Fixed rear and front sights. Features: Percussion, swivel-style, steel ramrod. Made by Palmetto Arms. Imported by Dixie Gun Works.
Price: Dixie Gun Works PH1000 ....$650.00

LYMAN PLAINS PISTOL
Caliber: .50 or .54. Barrel: 8 in.; 1:30-in. twist, both calibers. Weight: 3.1 lb. Length: 15 in. overall. Stock: Walnut. Sights: Blade front, square-notch rear adjustable for windage. Features: Polished brass triggerguard and ramrod tip, color case-hardened coil spring lock, spring-loaded trigger, stainless steel nipple, blackened iron furniture. Hooked patent breech, detachable belt hook. Introduced 1981. From Lyman Products.
Price: 6010608 .50-cal. $426.00
Price: 6010609 .54-cal. $426.00
Price: 6010610 .50-cal Kit $349.00
Price: 6010611 .54-cal. Kit......................................$349.00

PEDERSOLI CARLETON UNDERHAMMER MATCH PERCUSSION PISTOL
Caliber: .36. Barrel: 9.5 in., browned octagonal, rifled. Weight: 2.25 lbs. Length: 16.75 in. overall. Stock: Walnut. Sights: Blade front, open rear, adjustable for elevation. Features: Percussion, under-hammer ignition, adjustable trigger, no half cock. No ramrod. Made by Pedersoli. Imported by Dixie Gun Works.
Price: Dixie Gun Works FH0332..$925.00

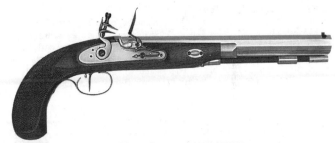

PEDERSOLI CHARLES MOORE ENGLISH DUELING PISTOL
Caliber: .45. Barrel: 11 in., 1:18 twist Weight: 2.5 lbs. Length: 16.5 in. overall. Stock: Walnut. Sights: Fixed. Features: Flintlock or percussion. Single set, adjustable trigger. Blued barrel and lock, steel furniture left in the white. Wooden ramrod. Replica of a fine British dueling pistol made by Charles Moore in London. Made by Pedersoli. Imported by Dixie Gun Works.
Price: Dixie Gun Works Flintlock FH0237 ....$795.00
Price: Dixie Gun Works Percussion PH0501 ....$610.00

PEDERSOLI FRENCH AN IX NAPOLEONIC PISTOL
Caliber: .69. Barrel: 8.25 in. Weight: 3 lbs. Length: 14 in. overall. Stock: Walnut. Sights: None. Features: Flintlock, case-hardened lock, brass furniture, buttcap, lock marked "Imperiale de S. Etienne." Steel ramrod. Made by Pedersoli. Imported by Dixie Gun Works.
Price: Dixie Gun Works FH0890...$740.00

PEDERSOLI FRENCH AN IX GENDARMERIE NAPOLEONIC PISTOL
Caliber: .69. Barrel: 5.25 in. Weight: 3 lbs. Length: 14 in. overall. Stock: Walnut. Sights: None. Features: Flintlock, case-hardened lock, brass furniture, buttcap, lock marked "Imperiale de S. Etienne." Steel ramrod. Imported by Dixie Gun Works.
Price: Dixie Gun Works Gendarmerie FHO954 ....$725.00

Prices given are believed to be accurate at time of publication however, many factors affect retail pricing so exact prices are not possible.

78TH EDITION, 2024 ⬥ 553

PEDERSOLI FRENCH AN XIII NAPOLEONIC PISTOL
Caliber: .69. Barrel: 8.25 in. Weight: 3 lbs. Length: 14 in. overall. Stock: Walnut half-stock. Sights: None. Features: Flintlock, case-hardened lock, brass furniture, butt cap, lock marked "Imperiale de S. Etienne." Steel ramrod. Made by Pedersoli. Imported by Dixie Gun Works.
Price: Dixie Gun Works AN XIII FHO895 .... **$725.00**

PEDERSOLI HARPER'S FERRY 1805 PISTOL
Caliber: .58. Barrel: 10 in. Weight: 2.5 lbs. Length: 16 in. overall. Stock: Walnut. Sights: Fixed. Features: Flintlock or percussion. Case-hardened lock, brass-mounted German silver-colored barrel. Wooden ramrod. Replica of the first U.S. government made flintlock pistol. Made by Pedersoli. Imported by Dixie Gun Works.
Price: Dixie Gun Works Flint RH0225 .... **$565.00**
Price: Dixie Gun Works Flint Kit RH0411 .... **$450.00**
Price: Dixie Gun Works Percussion RH0951 .... **$565.00**
Price: Dixie Gun Works Percussion Kit RH0937 .... **$395.00**

PEDERSOLI HOWDAH HUNTER PISTOLS
Caliber: .50, 20 gauge, .58. Barrels: 11.25 in., blued, rifled in .50 and .58 calibers. Weight: 4.25 to 5 lbs. Length: 17.25 in. Stock: American walnut with checkered grip. Sights: Brass bead front sight. Features: Blued barrels, swamped barrel rib, engraved, color case-hardened locks and hammers, captive steel ramrod. Available with detachable shoulder stock, case, holster and mold. Made by Pedersoli. Imported by Dixie Gun Works, Cabela's, Taylor's and others.
Price: Dixie Gun Works, 50X50, PH0572 .... **$895.00**
Price: Dixie Gun Works, 58XD58, PH09024 .... **$895.00**
Price: Dixie Gun Works, 20X20 gauge, PH0581 .... **$850.00**
Price: Dixie Gun Works, 50X20 gauge, PH0581 .... **$850.00**
Price: Dixie Gun Works, 50X50, Kit, PK0952 .... **$640.00**
Price: Dixie Gun Works, 50X20, Kit, PK1410 .... **$675.00**
Price: Dixie Gun Works, 20X20, Kit, PK0954 .... **$640.00**

PEDERSOLI KENTUCKY PISTOL
Caliber: .45, .50, .54. Barrel: 10.33 in. Weight: 2.5 lbs. Length: 15.4 in. overall. Stock: Walnut with smooth rounded birds-head grip. Sights: Fixed. Features: Available in flint or percussion ignition in various calibers. Case-hardened lock, blued barrel, drift-adjustable rear sights, blade front. Wooden ramrod. Kit guns of all models available from Dixie Gun Works. Made by Pedersoli. Imported by Dixie Gun Works, EMF and others.
Price: Dixie Gun Works .45 Percussion, PH0440 .... **$395.00**
Price: Dixie Gun Works .45 Flint, PH0430 .... **$437.00**
Price: Dixie Gun Works .45 Flint, Kit FH0320 .... **$325.00**

Price: Dixie Gun Works .50 Flint, PH0935 .... **$495.00**
Price: Dixie Gun Works .50 Percussion, PH0930 .... **$450.00**
Price: Dixie Gun Works .54 Flint, PH0080 .... **$495.00**
Price: Dixie Gun Works .54 Percussion, PH0330 .... **$450.00**
Price: Dixie Gun Works .54 Percussion, Kit PK0436 .... **$325.00**
Price: Dixie Gun Works .45, Navy Moll, brass buttcap, Flint PK0436 ...... **$650.00**
Price: .45, Navy Moll, brass buttcap, Percussion PK0903 ....**$595.00**

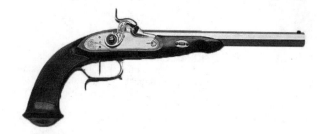

PEDERSOLI LE PAGE PERCUSSION DUELING PISTOL
Caliber: .44. Barrel: 10 inches, browned octagon, rifled. Weight: 2.5 lbs. Length: 16.75 inches overall. Stock: Walnut, rounded checkered butt. Sights: Blade front, open-style rear. Features: Single set trigger, external ramrod. Made by Pedersoli. Imported by Dixie Gun Works.
Price: Dixie, Pedersoli, PH0431 ....**$950.00**
Price: Dixie, International, Pedersoli, PH0231..................................**$1,250.00**

PEDERSOLI MAMELOUK
Caliber: .57. Barrel: 7-5/8 in., bright. Weight: 1.61 lbs. Length: 13 in. overall. Stock: Walnut, with brass end cap and medallion. Sights: Blade front. Features: Flint, lanyard ring, wooden ramrod. Made by Pedersoli. Available on special order from IFG (Italian Firearms Group)
Price: .... **TBD at time of order**

PEDERSOLI MANG TARGET PISTOL
Caliber: .38. Barrel: 11.5 in., octagonal, browned; 1:15-in. twist. Weight: 2.5 lbs. Length: 17. in. overall. Stock: Walnut with fluted grip. Sights: Blade front, open rear adjustable for windage. Features: Browned barrel, polished breech plug, remainder color case-hardened. Made by Pedersoli. Imported by Dixie Gun Works.
Price: PH0503 .... **$1,795.00**

Prices given are believed to be accurate at time of publication however, many factors affect retail pricing so exact prices are not possible.

PEDERSOLI MORTIMER TARGET PISTOL

Caliber: .44. Barrel: 10 in., bright octagonal on Standard, browned on Deluxe, rifled. Weight: 2.55 lbs. Length: 15.75 in. overall. Stock: Walnut, checkered saw-handle grip on Deluxe. Sights: Blade front, open-style rear. Features: Percussion or flint, single set trigger, sliding hammer safety, engraved lock on Deluxe. Wooden ramrod. Made by Pedersoli. Imported by Dixie Gun Works.
Price: Dixie, Flint, FH0316 ....$1,175.00
Price: Dixie, Percussion, PH0231 ....$1,095.00
Price: Dixie, Deluxe, FH0950 ....$2,220.00

TRADITIONS KENTUCKY PISTOL

Caliber: .50. Barrel: 10 in., 1:20 in. twist. Weight: 2.75 lbs. Length: 15 in. Stock: Hardwood full stock. Sights: Brass blade front, square notch rear adjustable for windage. Features: Polished brass finger spur-style trigger guard, stock cap and ramrod tip, color case-hardened leaf spring lock, spring-loaded trigger, No. 11 percussion nipple, brass furniture. From Traditions, and as kit from Bass Pro and others.
Price: P1060 Finished $244.00
Price: KPC50602 Kit $209.00

PEDERSOLI PHILADELPHIA DERRINGER

Caliber: .45. Barrel: 3.1 in., browned, rifled. Weight: 0.5 lbs. Length: 6.215 in. Stock: European walnut checkered. Sights: V-notch rear, blade front. Features: Back-hammer percussion lock with engraving, single trigger. Made by Pedersoli. Imported by Dixie Gun Works.
Price: Dixie, PH0913 . ... $550.00
Price: Dixie, Kit PK0863 . ... $385.00

PEDERSOLI QUEEN ANNE FLINTLOCK PISTOL

Caliber: .50. Barrel: 7.5 in., smoothbore. Stock: Walnut. Sights: None. Features: Flintlock, German silver-colored steel barrel, fluted brass triggerguard, brass mask on butt. Lockplate left in the white. No ramrod. Introduced 1983. Made by Pedersoli. Imported by Dixie Gun Works.
Price: Dixie, RH0211 .... $495.00
Price: Dixie, Kit, FH0421 .... $375.00

PEDERSOLI REMINGTON RIDER DERRINGER

Caliber: 4.3 mm (BB lead balls only). Barrel: 2.1 in., blued, rifled. Weight: 0.25 lbs. Length: 4.75 in. Grips: All-steel construction. Sights: V-notch rear, bead front. Features: Fires percussion cap only – no powder. Available as case-hardened frame or polished white. Made by Pedersoli. Imported by Dixie Gun Works.
Price: Dixie, Case-hardened PH0923. .... $210.00

PEDERSOLI SCREW BARREL PISTOL

Caliber: .44. Barrel: 2.35 in., blued, rifled. Weight: 0.5 lbs. Length: 6.5 in. Grips: European walnut. Sights: None. Features: Percussion, boxlock with center hammer, barrel unscrews for loading from rear, folding trigger, external hammer, combination barrel and nipple wrench furnished. Made by Pedersoli. Imported by Dixie Gun Works.
Price: Dixie, PH0530. .... $225.00
Price: Dixie, PH0545. .... $175.00

TRADITIONS TRAPPER PISTOL

Caliber: .50. Barrel: 9.75 in., octagonal, blued, hooked patent breech, 1:20 in. twist. Weight: 2.75 lbs. Length: 15.5 in. Stock: Hardwood, modified saw-handle style grip, halfstock. Sights: Brass blade front, rear sight adjustable for windage and elevation. Features: Percussion or flint, double set triggers, polished brass triggerguard, stock cap and ramrod tip, color case-hardened leaf spring lock, spring-loaded trigger, No. 11 percussion nipple, brass furniture. From Traditions and as a kit from Bass Pro and others.
Price: P1100 Finished, percussion.. $329.00
Price: P1090 Finished, flint $369.00
Price: KPC51002 Kit, percussion $299.00
Price: KPC50902 Kit, flint $359.00

TRADITIONS VEST POCKET DERRINGER

Caliber: .31. Barrel: 2.35 in., round brass, smoothbore. Weight: .75 lbs. Length: 4.75 in. Grips: Simulated ivory. Sights: Front bead. Features: Replica of riverboat gambler's derringer. No. 11 percussion cap nipple, brass frame and barrel, spur trigger, external hammer. From Traditions.
Price: P1381, Brass $194.00
Price: Dixie, White, PH0920. .... $175.00

DANCE AND BROTHERS PERCUSSION REVOLVER

Caliber: .44. Barrel: 7.4 in., round. Weight: 2.5 lbs. Length: 13 in. overall. Grips: One-piece walnut. Sights: Brass blade front, hammer notch rear. Features: Reproduction of the C.S.A. revolver. Brass trigger guard. Color case-hardened frame Made by Pietta. Imported by Dixie Gun Works and others.
Price: Dixie Gun Works RH0344 .... **$350.00**

GRISWOLD AND GUNNISON PERCUSSION REVOLVER

Caliber: .36. Barrel: 7.5 in., round. Weight: 2.5 lbs. Length: 13.25 in. Grips: One-piece walnut. Sights: Fixed. Features: Reproduction of the C.S.A. revolver. Brass frame and triggerguard. Made by Pietta. Imported by EMF, Cabela's and others.
Price: EMF PF51BRGG36712 .... **$235.00**

NORTH AMERICAN COMPANION PERCUSSION REVOLVER

Caliber: .22. Barrel: 1-1/8 in. Weight: 5.1 oz. Length: 4 in. overall. Grips: Laminated wood. Sights: Blade front, notch rear. Features: All stainless steel construction. Uses No. 11 percussion caps. Comes with bullets, powder measure, bullet seater, leather clip holster, gun rag. Long Rifle frame. Introduced 1996. Made in U.S. by North American Arms.
Price: NAA-22LR-CB Long Rifle frame **$251.00**

NORTH AMERICAN SUPER COMPANION PERCUSSION REVOLVER

Caliber: .22. Barrel: 1-5/8 in. Weight: 7.2 oz. Length: 5-1/8 in. Grips: Laminated wood. Sights: Blade font, notched rear. Features: All stainless steel construction. No. 11 percussion caps. Comes with bullets, powder measure, bullet seater, leather clip holster, gun rag. Introduced 1996. Larger "Magnum" frame. Made in U.S. by North American Arms.
Price: NAA-Mag-CB Magnum frame **$296.00**

PEDERSOLI REMINGTON PATTERN TARGET REVOLVER

Caliber: .44. Barrel: 8 in., tapered octagon progressive twist. Weight: 2.75 lbs. Length: 13-3/4 in. overall. Grips: One-piece hardwood. Sights: V-notch on top strap, blued steel blade front. Features: Brass trigger guard, Non-reflective coating on the barrel and a wear resistant coating on the cylinder, blued steel frame, case-hardened hammer, trigger and loading lever. Made by Pedersoli. Imported by EMF, Dixie Gun Works, Cabela's and others.
Price: EMF Steel Frame PF58ST448 .... **$1,010.00**

PIETTA TEXAS PATTERSON PERCUSSION REVOLVER

Caliber: .36. Barrel: 9 in. tapered octagon. Weight: 2.75 lbs. Length: 13.75 in. Grips: One-piece walnut. Sights: Brass pin front, hammer notch rear. Features: Folding trigger, blued steel furniture, frame and barrel; engraved scene on cylinder. Ramrod: Loading tool provided. Made by Pietta. Imported by E.M.F, Dixie Gun Works.
Price: EMF PF36ST36712 .... **$610.00**

PIETTA 1851 NAVY MODEL PERCUSSION REVOLVER

Caliber: .36, .44, 6-shot. Barrel: 7.5 in. Weight: 44 oz. Length: 13 in. overall. Grips: Walnut. Sights: Post front, hammer notch rear. Features: Available in brass-framed and steel-framed models. Made by Pietta. Imported by EMF, Dixie Gun Works, Cabela's, Cimarron, Taylor's, Traditions and others.
Price: Brass frame EMF PF51BR36712 .... **$230.00**
Price: Steel frame EMF PF51CH36712 .... **$275.00**

PIETTA 1851 NAVY LONDON MODEL PERCUSSION REVOLVER

Caliber: .36, 6-shot. Barrel: 7.5 in. Weight: 44 oz. Length: 13 in. overall. Grips: Walnut. Sights: Post front, hammer notch rear. Features: steel frame and steel trigger guard and back strap. Available with oval trigger guard or squared back trigger guard. Made by Pietta. Imported by EMF, Dixie, Gun Works, Cabela's, Cimarron, Taylor's, Traditions and others.
Price: EMF PF51CHS36712 .... **$275.00**

PIETTA 1851 NAVY SHERIFF'S MODEL PERCUSSION REVOLVER

Caliber: .44, 6-shot. Barrel: 5.5 in. Weight: 40 oz. Length: 11 in. overall. Grips: Walnut. Sights: Post front, hammer notch rear. Features: Available in brass-framed and steel-framed models. Made by Pietta. Imported by EMF, Dixie, Gun Works, Cabela's.
Price: Brass frame EMF PF51BR44512 .... **$235.00**
Price: Steel frame EMF PF51CH44512 .... **$275.00**

PIETTA 1851 NAVY CAPTAIN SCHAEFFER MODEL PERCUSSION REVOLVER

Caliber: .36, 6-shot. Barrel: 4 in. Weight: 40 oz. Length: 9.5 in. overall. Grips: Grips Ultra-ivory (polymer). Sights: Post front, hammer notch rear. Features: Polished steel finish, completely laser engraved. Made by Pietta. Imported by EMF
Price: EMF PF51LESS36312UI **$395.00**

Prices given are believed to be accurate at time of publication however, many factors affect retail pricing so exact prices are not possible.

PIETTA 1851 NAVY YANK PEPPERBOX MODEL PERCUSSION REVOLVER
Caliber: .36, 6-shot. Barrel: No Barrel. Weight: 36 oz. Length: 7 in. overall. Grips: One-piece walnut. Sights: Post front, hammer notch rear. Features: There is no barrel. Rounds fire directly out of the chambers of the elongated cylinder. Made by Pietta. Imported by EMF, Dixie Gun Works and Taylor's & Co.
Price: EMF PF51PEPPER36 .... **$235.00**

PIETTA 1851 NAVY BUNTLINE MODEL PERCUSSION REVOLVER
Caliber: .44, 6-shot. Barrel: 12 in. Weight: 36 oz. Length: 18.25 in. overall. Grips: Walnut. Sights: Post front, hammer notch rear. Features: Available in brass-framed and steel-framed models. Made by Pietta. Imported by EMF, Dixie Gun Works (Brass only).
Price: Brass frame EMF PF51BR4412 .... **$245.00**
Price: Steel frame EMF PF51CH4412 .... **$295.00**

PIETTA 1851 NAVY SNUBNOSE MODEL PERCUSSION REVOLVER
Caliber: .44, 6-shot. Barrel: 3 in. Weight: 36 oz. Length: 8.25 in. overall. Grips: Birds-head grip frame, one-piece checkered walnut. Sights: Post front, hammer notch rear. Features: Color case-hardened, steel-frame. Made by Pietta. Imported by Dixie Gun Works.
Price: Dixie SS1249 .... **$395.00**

PIETTA 1858 GENERAL CUSTER
Caliber: .44, 6-shot. Barrel: 8 in., blued. Grips: Two-piece wood. Sights: Open. Weight: 2.7 lbs. Features: Nickel-plated trigger guard, color case-hardened hammer, laser engraving.
Price: **$360.00**

PIETTA 1860 ARMY MODEL PERCUSSION REVOLVER
Caliber: .44. Barrel: 8 in. Weight: 2.75 lbs. Length: 13.25 in. overall. Grips: One-piece walnut. Sights: Brass blade front, hammer notch rear. Features: Models available with either case-hardened, steel frame, brass trigger guard, or brass frame, trigger guard and backstrap. EMF also offers a model with a silver finish on all the metal. Made by Pietta. Imported by EMF, Cabela's, Dixie Gun Works, Taylor's and others.
Price: EMF Brass Frame PF60BR448 .... **$260.00**
Price: EMF Steel Frame PF60CH448 .... **$295.00**
Price: EMF Steel Frame Old Silver finish PF60OS448 .... **$325.00**
Price: EMF Steel Frame Old Silver finish Deluxe Engraved PF60CHES448 ....**$350.00**

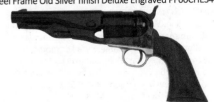

PIETTA 1860 ARMY SHERIFF'S MODEL PERCUSSION REVOLVER
Caliber: .44. Barrel: 5.5in. Weight: 40 oz. Length: 11.5 in. overall. Grips: One-piece walnut. Sights: Brass blade front, hammer notch rear. Features: Case-hardened, steel frame, brass trigger guard. Made by Pietta. Imported by EMF, Cabela's, Dixie Gun Works and others.
Price: EMF PF60CH44512 .... **$295.00**

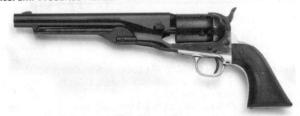

PIETTA 1860 ARMY SNUBNOSE MODEL PERCUSSION REVOLVER
Caliber: .44. Barrel: 3 in. Weight: 36 oz. Length: 8.25 in. overall. Grips: Birds-head grip frame, one-piece, checkered walnut. Sights: Brass blade front, hammer notch rear. Features: Fluted cylinder, case-hardened, steel frame, brass trigger guard, Made by Pietta. Imported by EMF.
Price: EMF PF51CHLG44212CW **$385.00**

PIETTA NAVY 1861 PERCUSSION REVOLVER
Caliber: .36. Barrel: 8 in. Weight: 2.75 lbs. Length: 13.25 in. overall. Grips: One-piece walnut. Sights: Brass blade front, hammer notch rear. Features: Steel, case-hardened frame, brass-grip frame, or steel-grip frame (London Model), case-hardened creeping loading lever. Made by Pietta. Imported by EMF, Dixie Gun Works, Cabela's and others.
Price: EMF with brass triggerguard PF61CH368CIV **$300.00**
Price: EMF with steel triggerguard PF61CH368................................. **$300.00**

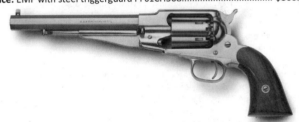

PIETTA 1858 REMINGTON ARMY REVOLVER
Caliber: .44. Barrel: 8 in., tapered octagon. Weight: 2.75 lbs. Length: 13.5 in. overall. Grips: Two-piece walnut. Sights: V-notch on top strap, blued steel blade front. Features: Brass triggerguard, blued steel backstrap and frame, case-hardened hammer and trigger. Also available, a brass-framed model, and an all stainless steel model. Made by Pietta. Imported by EMF, Dixie Gun Works, Cabela's and others.
Price: EMF Steel Frame PF58ST448... **$290.00**
Price: EMF Brass Frame PF58BR448... **$250.00**
Price: EMF Stainless Steel PF58SS448... **$430.00**

PIETTA 1858 REMINGTON TARGET REVOLVER
Caliber: .44. Barrel: 8 in., tapered octagon. Weight: 2.75 lbs. Length: 13.5 in. overall. Grips: Two-piece walnut. Sights: Adjustable rear, ramped blade front. Features: Brass triggerguard, blued steel frame, case-hardened hammer, and trigger. Also available, a brass-framed model. Made by Pietta. Imported by EMF, Dixie Gun Works, Cabela's and others.
Price: EMF PF58STT448... **$350.00**

PIETTA 1858 REMINGTON SHIRIFF'S MODEL REVOLVER
Caliber: .36 and .44. Barrel: 5.5in., tapered octagon. Weight: 2.75 lbs. Length: 11.5 in. overall. Grips: Two-piece checkered walnut. Sights: V-notch on top strap, blued steel blade front. Features: Brass triggerguard, blued steel backstrap and frame, case-hardened hammer and trigger. Also available in a

Prices given are believed to be accurate at time of publication however, many factors affect retail pricing so exact prices are not possible.

78TH EDITION, 2024 ✦ **557**

color case-hardened-framed model, and in an all stainless steel model. Made by Pietta. Imported by EMF, and others.
Price: EMF Blued Steel Frame PF58ST36612.................................... **$290.00**
Price: EMF Color Case-Hardened frame PF58CH44512CW................. **$395.00**
Price: EMF Stainless Steel PF58SS44512CW **$490.00**

PIETTA 1858 REMINGTON BUFFALO BILL COMMEMORATIVE REVOLVER
Caliber: .44. Barrel: 8 in., tapered octagon. Weight: 2.75 lbs. Length: 13-3/4 in. overall. Grips: Two-piece walnut. Sights: V-notch on top strap, blued steel blade front. Features: Gold-filled engraving over dark blue steel. A higher-grade gun commemorating the life of Buffalo Bill Cody. Made by Pietta. Imported by EMF.
Price: EMF PF58BB448 .... **$695.00**

PIETTA REMINGTON BELT MODEL REVOLVER
Caliber: .36. Barrel: 6.5 in., octagon. Weight: 44 oz. Length: 12.5 in. overall. Grips: Two-piece walnut. Sights: V-notch on top strap, blued steel blade front. Features: Brass triggerguard, blued steel backstrap and frame, case-hardened hammer and trigger. Made by Pietta. Imported by Dixie Gun Works.
Price: Dixie RH0214 .... **$295.00**

PIETTA 1863 REMINGTON POCKET MODEL REVOLVER
Caliber: .31, 5-shot. Barrel: 3.5 in. Weight: 1 lb. Length: 7.6 in. Grips: Two-piece walnut. Sights: Pin front, groove-in-frame rear. Features: Spur trigger, iron-, brass- or nickel-plated frame. Made by Pietta. Imported by EMF (Steel Frame), Dixie Gun Works, Taylor's and others.
Price: Brass frame, Dixie PH0407 .... **$260.00**
Price: Steel frame, Dixie PH0370... **$295.00**
Price: Nickel-plated, Dixie PH0409 .... **$315.00**

PIETTA LEMATT REVOLVER
Caliber: .44/20 Ga. Barrel: 6.75 in. (revolver); 4-7/8 in. (single shot). Weight: 3 lbs., 7 oz. Length: 14 in. overall. Grips: Hand-checkered walnut. Sights: Post front, hammer notch rear. Features: Exact reproduction with all-steel construction; 44-cal., 9-shot cylinder, 20-gauge single barrel; color case-hardened hammer with selector; spur triggerguard; ring at butt; lever-type barrel release. Made by Pietta. Imported by EMF, Dixie Gun Works and others.
Price: EMF Navy PFLMSTN44634 .... **$1,075.00**
Price: EMF Cavalry PFLMST44712 .... **$1,100.00**
Price: EMF Army PFLMSTA44634 .... **$1,100.00**

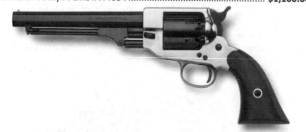

PIETTA SPILLER & BURR PERCUSSION REVOLVER
Caliber: .36. Barrel: 7 in., octagon. Weight: 2.5 lbs. Length: 12.5 in. overall. Grips: Two-piece walnut. Sights: V-notch on top strap, blued steel blade front. Features: Reproduction of the C.S.A. revolver. Brass frame and trigger guard. Also available as a kit. Made by Pietta. Imported by Dixie Gun Works, Traditions, Midway USA and others.
Price: Dixie RH0120... **$275.00**
Price: Dixie kit RH0300 .... **$235.00**

PIETTA STARR DOUBLE-ACTION ARMY REVOLVER
Caliber: .44. Barrel: 6 in. tapered round. Weight: 3 lbs. Length: 11.75 in. Grips: One-piece walnut. Sights: Hammer notch rear, dovetailed front. Features: Double-action mechanism, round tapered barrel, all blued frame

and barrel. Made by Pietta. Imported by Dixie Gun Works and others.
Price: Dixie RH460... **$565.00**

PIETTA STARR SINGLE-ACTION ARMY REVOLVER
Caliber: .44. Barrel: 8 in. tapered round. Weight: 3 lbs. Length: 13.5 in. Grips: One-piece walnut. Sights: Hammer notch rear, dovetailed front. Features: Single-action mechanism, round tapered barrel, all blued frame and barrel. Made by Pietta. Imported by Cabela's, Dixie Gun Works and others.
Price: Dixie RH460...**$550.00**

PIETTA 1873 PERCUSSION REVOLVER
Caliber: .44. Barrel: 5.5 in. Weight: 40 oz. Length: 11.25 in. overall. Grips: One-piece walnut. Sights: V-notch on top strap, blued steel blade front. Features: A cap-and-ball version of the Colt Single Action Army revolver. Made by Pietta. Imported by EMF, Cabela's, Dixie Gun Works and others.
Price: EMF PF73CHS434NM **$360.00**

TRADITIONS U.S. MARSHAL
Caliber: .36, 6-shot. Barrel: 8 in., blued. Grips: One-piece walnut. Sights: Open, hammer/blade. Weight: 2.61 lbs. Features: Case-hardened frame, single action, U.S. Marshal logo on grips.
Price: **$351.00**

TRADITIONS WILDCARD
Caliber: .36, 6-shot. Barrel: 7.375 in., blued octagon. Grips: Simulated stag. Sights: Open, hammer/blade. Weight: 2.5 lbs. Features: 1851 "Gunfighter," 13.5-in. overall length, case-hardened frame.
Price: **$409.00**

UBERTI 1847 WALKER PERCUSSION REVOLVER
Caliber: .44. Barrel: 9 in. Weight: 4.5 lbs. Length: 15.7 in. overall. Grips: One-piece hardwood. Sights: Brass blade front, hammer notch rear. Features: Copy of Sam Colt's first U.S. contract revolver. Engraved cylinder, case-hardened hammer and loading lever. Blued finish. Made by Uberti. Imported by Cabela's, Cimarron, Dixie Gun Works, EMF, Taylor's, Uberti U.S.A. and others.
Price: Uberti USA, standard model, blued steel 340200 .... **$429.00**

UBERTI DRAGOON PERCUSSION REVOLVERS
Caliber: .44. Barrel: 7.5 in. Weight: 4.1 lbs. Grips: One-piece walnut. Sights: Brass blade front, hammer notch rear. Features: Four models of the big .44 caliber revolvers that followed the massive Walker model and pre-dated the sleek 1860 Army model. Blued barrel, backstrap and trigger guard. Made by Uberti. Imported by Uberti USA, Dixie Gun Works, Taylor's and others.
Price: Uberti USA, Whitneyville Dragoon 340830 .... **$429.00**
Price: Uberti USA, First Model Dragoon 340800 .... **$429.00**
Price: Uberti USA, Second Model Dragoon 340810 .... **$429.00**
Price: Uberti USA, Third Model Dragoon 340860.............................. **$429.00**

    Prices given are believed to be accurate at time of publication however, many factors affect retail pricing so exact prices are not possible.

UBERTI 1849 POCKET MODEL WELLS FARGO PERCUSSION REVOLVER
Caliber: .31. Barrel: 4 in., seven-groove, RH twist. Weight: About 24 oz. Grips: One-piece walnut. Sights: Brass pin front, hammer notch rear. Features: Unfluted cylinder with stagecoach holdup scene, cupped cylinder pin, no grease grooves, one safety pin on cylinder and slot in hammer face. Made by Uberti. Imported by Uberti USA, Cimarron, Dixie Gun Works and others.
Price: Uberti USA 340350 .... **$349.00**

UBERTI 1849 WELLS FARGO PERCUSSION REVOLVER
Caliber: .31. Barrel: 4 in.; seven-groove; RH twist. Weight: About 24 oz. Grips: One-piece walnut. Sights: Brass pin front, hammer notch rear. Features: No loading lever, Unfluted cylinder with stagecoach holdup scene, cupped cylinder pin, no grease grooves, one safety pin on cylinder and slot in hammer face. Made by Uberti. Imported by Uberti USA, Cimarron, Dixie Gun Works and others.
Price: Uberti USA 340380 .... **$349.00**

UBERTI NAVY MODEL 1851 PERCUSSION REVOLVER
Caliber: .36, 6-shot. Barrel: 7.5 in. Weight: 44 oz. Length: 13 in. overall. Grips: One-piece walnut. Sights: Post front, hammer notch rear. Features: Brass backstrap and trigger guard, or steel backstrap and trigger guard (London Model), engraved cylinder with navy battle scene; case-hardened hammer, loading lever. Made by Uberti and Pietta. Imported by Uberti USA, Cabela's, Cimarron, and others.
Price: Uberti USA Brass grip assembly 340000 .... **$329.00**
Price: Uberti USA London Model 340050 .... **$369.00**

UBERTI 1860 ARMY REVOLVER
Caliber: .44. Barrel: 8 in. Weight: 44 oz. Length: 13.25 in. overall. Grips: One-piece walnut. Sights: Brass blade front, hammer notch rear. Features: Steel or case-hardened frame, brass triggerguard, case-hardened creeping loading lever. Many models and finishes are available for this pistol. Made by Uberti. Imported by Cabela's, Cimarron, Dixie Gun Works, EMF, Taylor's, Uberti U.S.A. and others.
Price: Uberti USA, roll engraved cylinder 340400 .... **$349.00**
Price: Uberti USA, full fluted cylinder 340410 .... **$369.00**

UBERTI 1861 NAVY PERCUSSION REVOLVER
Caliber: .36 Barrel: 7.5 in. Weight: 44 oz. Length: 13.25 in. overall. Grips: One-piece walnut. Sights: Brass blade front, hammer notch rear. Features: Brass backstrap and trigger guard, or steel backstrap and trigger guard (London Model), engraved cylinder with navy battle scene; case-hardened hammer, loading lever. Made by Uberti. Imported by Uberti USA, Cabela's, Cimarron, Dixie Gun Works, Taylor's and others.
Price: Uberti USA Brass grip assembly 340630 .... **$349.00**
Price: Uberti USA London Model 340500 .... **$349.00**

UBERTI 1862 POLICE PERCUSSION REVOLVER
Caliber: .36, 5-shot. Barrel: 5.5 in., 6.5 in., 7.5 in. Weight: 26 oz. Length: 12 in. overall (6.5 in. bbl.). Grips: One-piece walnut. Sights: Fixed. Features: Round tapered barrel; half-fluted and rebated cylinder; case-hardened frame, loading lever and hammer; brass trigger guard and backstrap. Made by Uberti. Imported by Cimarron, Dixie Gun Works, Taylor's, Uberti U.S.A. and others.
Price: Uberti USA 340700 .... **$369.00**

UBERTI 1862 POCKET NAVY PERCUSSION REVOLVER
Caliber: .36, 5-shot. Barrel: 5.5 in., 6.5 in. Weight: 26 oz. Length: 12 in. overall (6.5 in. bbl.). Grips: One-piece walnut. Sights: Fixed. Features: Octagon barrel; case-hardened frame, loading lever and hammer; silver or brass trigger guard and backstrap; also available in an all stainless steel version. Made by Uberti. Imported by Uberti USA, Cimarron, Dixie Gun Works, Taylor's and others.
Price: Uberti USA 340750 .... **$369.00**

UBERTI LEACH AND RIGDON PERCUSSION REVOLVER
Caliber: .36. Barrel: 7.5 in., octagon to round. Weight: 2.75 lbs. Length: 13 in. Grips: One-piece walnut. Sights: Hammer notch and pin front. Features: Steel frame. Reproduction of the C.S.A. revolver. Brass backstrap and trigger guard. Made by Uberti. Imported by Uberti USA, Dixie Gun Works and others.
Price: Uberti USA 340030 .... **$349.00**

UBERTI NEW ARMY REMINGTON PERCUSSION REVOLVER
Caliber: .44, 6-shot. Barrel: Tapered octagon 8 in. Weight: 32 oz. Length: Standard 13.5 in. Grips: Two-piece walnut. Sights: Standard blade front, groove-in-frame rear; adjustable on some models. Features: Many variations of this gun are available. Target Model (Uberti U.S.A.) has fully adjustable target rear sight, target front, .36 or .44. Made by Uberti. Imported by Uberti USA, Cimarron F.A. Co., Taylor's and others.
Price: Uberti USA Steel frame, 341000 .... **$369.00**
Price: Uberti USA Stainless, 341020 .... **$449.00**

Prices given are believed to be accurate at time of publication however, many factors affect retail pricing so exact prices are not possible.

78TH EDITION, 2024 ✛ **559**

ARMI SPORT ENFIELD THREE-BAND P1853 RIFLE

Caliber: .58. Barrel: 39 in. Weight: 10.25 lbs. Length: 52 in. overall. Stock: European walnut. Sights: Blade front, flip-up rear with elevator marked to 800 yards. Features: Reproduction of the original three-band rifle. Percussion musket-cap ignition. Blued barrel with steel barrelbands, brass furniture. Case-hardened lock. Lockplate marked "London Armory Co. and Crown." Made by Euro Arms, Armi Sport (Chiappa). Imported by Dixie Gun Works and others.
Price: Dixie Gun Works rifled bore PR1130 ....**$895.00**
Price: Dixie Gun Work smooth bore PR1052.......................**$750.00**

CVA ACCURA IN-LINE BREAK-ACTION RIFLE

Caliber: .50. Barrel: 28 in. fluted. Weight: 7.5 lbs. Length: Standard 45 in. Stock: Ambidextrous solid composite in standard or thumbhole. Sights: Adj. fiber-optic. Features: Break-action, quick-release breech plug, aluminum loading rod, cocking spur, lifetime warranty. By CVA.
Price: CVA PR3120NM (Accura MR Nitride with Black Stocks
 and Scope Mount)...**$493.00**

CVA ACCURA V2 LR NITRIDE "SPECIAL EDITION" IN-LINE BREAK-ACTION RIFLE

Caliber: .50. Barrel: 30 in. fluted. Weight: 7.5 lbs. Length: Standard 45 in. Stock: Ambidextrous solid composite. Sights: Adj. fiber-optic. Features: Break-action, quick-release breech plug, aluminum loading rod, cocking spur, equipped with a genuine, Nitride treated, 30-inch Bergara Barrel, and a deep pistol grip stock decorated in APG camo. Lifetime warranty. By CVA.
Price: CVA PR6124NM **$449.00**

CVA ACCURA LR

Caliber: .45, .50. Barrel: 30 in., Nitride-treated, 416 stainless steel Bergara. Stock: Ambidextrous thumbhole camo. Sights: DuraSight Dead-On one-piece scope mount, scope not included. Weight: 6.75 lbs. Features: Reversible hammer spur, CrushZone recoil pad, quick-release breech plug.
Price: **$605.00**

CVA ACCURA MR (MOUNTAIN RIFLE) IN-LINE BREAK-ACTION RIFLE

Caliber: .50. Barrel: 25 in. Weight: 6.35 lbs. Length: Standard 45 in. Stock: Ambidextrous solid composite. Sights: DuraSight DEAD-ON One-Piece Scope Mount. Features: Break-action, quick-release breech plug, aluminum loading rod, cocking spur, and a deep pistol grip stock decorated in Realtree APG camo. Lifetime warranty. By CVA.
Price: CVA PR3121SNM **$546.00**

CVA ACCURA MR-X

Caliber: .50. Barrel: 26 in., 1:28 in. twist, Nitride-treated stainless steel. Drilled and tapped for a scope and sights. Weight: 8.75 lbs. Features: 3/4x24 threaded barrel, adjustable comb, carbon-fiber collapsable loading rod, Quake sling, free-floating barrel, True Timber Strata camo.
Price: CVA PR3121SNM **$730**

CVA ACCURA LRX

Caliber: .45 and .50. Barrel: 30 in. Nitride-treated stainless steel Bergara barrel. Comes with a carbon-fiber collapsible field rod, which you carry on your hip, a configuration that allows the barrel to be completely free-floated. The stock also wears a height-adjustable comb. Utilizes CVA's screw-in/out breech plug system.
Price: **$675.00**

CVA PLAINS RIFLE

Caliber: .50. Barrel: 28 in., Nitride, fluted, stainless steel Bergara. Stock:

Ambidextrous composite Realtree MAX-1 XT. Sights: DuraSight Dead-On one-piece scope mount, scope not included. Weight: 7.2 lbs. Features: Solid aluminum PalmSaver ramrod, reversible cocking spur, Quake Claw sling.
Price: **$593.00**

CVA OPTIMA V2

Caliber: .50. Barrel: 26 in., 1:28 in. twist, Nitride-treated stainless steel. Free-floating barrel, drilled and tapped for a scope and sights. Weight: 8.75 lbs. Features: Triggerguard actuated breeching lever, ambidextrous stock, Crush Zone recoil pad, DuraSight DEAD-ON one-piece scope mount or DuraSight fiber-optic sight, aluminum PalmSaver ramrod, Realtree Escape or True Timber Strata camo.
Price: PR2037NM LR TH Cerakote Burnt Bronze/Nitride/
 Realtree Escape 28-in. Barrel..................................... **$520.00**
Price: PR2038SM LR TH Stainless Steel/Realtree
 Escape 28-in. Barrel. **$435.00**
Price: PR2039N Nitride/Realtree Escape 26-in. Barrel. **$455.00**
Price: PR2039NM Nitride/Realtree Escape 26-in. Barrel.................. **$450.00**
Price: PR2040S Stainless Steel/Realtree Escape 26-in. Barrel. **$415.00**
Price: PR2040SM Stainless Steel/Realtree Escape 26-in. Barrel.......... **$405.00**
Price: PR2041NW NORTHWEST Nitride/Realtree
 Escape 26-in. Barrel. **$455.00**
Price: PR6022SM Stainless Steel/True Timber Strata 26-in. Barrel. **$405.00**

CVA Wolf V2

Caliber: .50. Barrel: 26 in., 1:28 in. twist, Nitride-treated stainless steel. Free-floating barrel, drilled and tapped for a scope and sights. Weight: 8.75 lbs. Features: breeching button, ambidextrous LOP adjustable stock, Quick-Release Breech Plug, aluminum PalmSaver ramrod, True Timber Strata camo.
Price: **$340.00**

DIXIE DELUXE CUB RIFLE

Caliber: .32, .36. Barrel: 28 in. octagonal. Weight: 6.5 lbs. Length: 44 in. overall. Stock: Walnut. Sights: Fixed. Features: Each gun available in either flint or percussion ignition. Short rifle for small game and beginning shooters. Brass patchbox and furniture. Made by Pedersoli for Dixie Gun Works.
Price: Dixie Gun Works (.32-cal. flint) PR3130....................................**$890.00**
Price: Dixie Gun Works (.36-cal. flint) FR3135.............................**$890.00**
Price: Dixie Gun Works (.32-cal. Percussion kit) PK3360....................**$690.00**
Price: Dixie Gun Works (.36-cal. Percussion kit) PK3365....................**$690.00**
Price: Dixie Gun Works (.32-cal. Flint kit) PK3350.......................**$710.00**
Price: Dixie Gun Works (.36-cal. Flint kit) PK335 ....**$710.00**
Price: Dixie Gun Works (.32-cal. percussion) PR3140........................**$850.00**
Price: Dixie Gun Works (.36-cal. percussion) PR3145........................**$850.00**

DIXIE PENNSYLVANIA RIFLE

Caliber: .45 and .50. Barrel: 41.5 in. octagonal, .45/1:48, .50/1:56 in. twist. Weight: 8.5, 8.75 lbs. Length: 56 in. overall. Stock: European walnut, full-length stock. Sights: Notch rear, blade front. Features: Flintlock or percussion, brass patchbox, double-set triggers. Also available as kit guns for both calibers and ignition systems. Made by Pedersoli for Dixie Gun Works.
Price: Dixie Gun Works (.45-cal. flint) FR1060..................................**$1,100.00**
Price: Dixie Gun Works (.50-cal. flint) FR3200........................... **$1,100.00**
Price: Dixie Gun Works (.45-cal. Percussion kit) PR1075.................... **$910.00**
Price: Dixie Gun Works (.50-cal. Percussion kit) PK3365.................... **$910.00**
Price: Dixie Gun Works (.45-cal. Flint kit) FR1065 .... **$910.00**
Price: Dixie Gun Works (.50-cal. Flint kit) FK3420 .... **$910.00**
Price: Dixie Gun Works (.45-cal. percussion) FR1070..................... **$1,050.00**
Price: Dixie Gun Works (.50-cal. percussion) PR3205..................... **$1,050.00**

EUROARMS 1803 HARPER'S FERRY FLINTLOCK RIFLE

Caliber: .54. Barrel: 35.5 in., smoothbore. Weight: 9.5 lbs. Length: 50.5 in. overall. Stock: Half-stock, walnut w/oil finish. Sights: Blade front, notched rear. Features: Color case-hardened lock, browned barrel, with barrel key. Made by Euroarms. Imported by Dixie Gun Works.
Price: Dixie Gun Works FR0171 ....**$795.00**

EUROARMS J.P. MURRAY ARTILLERY CARBINE

Caliber: .58. Barrel: 23.5 in. Weight: 8 lbs. Length: 39.5 in. Stock: European walnut. Sights: Blade front, fixed notch rear. Features: Percussion musket-cap ignition. Reproduction of the original Confederate carbine. Lock marked "J.P.

BLACKPOWDER Muskets & Rifles

Murray, Columbus, Georgia." Blued barrel. Made by Euroarms. Imported by Dixie Gun Works and others.
Price: Dixie, Gun Works PR0173 ....**$1,100.00**

EUROARMS ENFIELD MUSKETOON P1861
Caliber: .58. Barrel: 24 in. Weight: 9 lbs. Length: 40 in. overall. Stock: European walnut. Sights: Blade front, flip-up rear with elevator marked to 700 yards. Features: Reproduction of the original cavalry version of the Enfield rifle. Percussion musket-cap ignition. Blued barrel with steel barrelbands, brass furniture. Case-hardened lock. Euroarms version marked London Armory with crown. Pedersoli version has Birmingham stamp on stock and Enfield and Crown on lockplate. Made by Euroarms. Imported by Dixie Gun Works and others.
Price: Dixie Gun Works PR0343 ....**$1,050.00**

KNIGHT DISC EXTREME
Caliber: .52. Barrel: 26 in., fluted stainless, 1:28 in. twist. Weight: 7 lbs. 14 oz. to 8 lbs. Length: 45 in. overall. Stock: Carbon Knight straight or thumbhole with blued or SS; G2 thumbhole; left-handed Nutmeg thumbhole. Ramrod: Solid brass extendable jag. Sights: Fully adjustable metallic fiber optics. Features: Bolt-action rifle, full plastic jacket ignition system, #11 nipple, musket nipple, bare 208 shotgun primer. With recommended loads, guaranteed to have 4-inch, three-shot groups at 200 yards. Also available as a Western gun with exposed ignition. Made in the U.S. by Knight Rifles.
Price: **$591.00**

KNIGHT LITTLEHORN IN-LINE RIFLE
Caliber: .50. Barrel: 22 in., 1:28 in. twist. Weight: 6.7 lbs. Length: 39 in. overall. Stock: 12.5-in. length of pull, G2 straight or pink Realtree AP HD. Ramrod: Carbon core with solid brass extendable jag. Sights: Fully adjustable Williams fiber optic. Features: Uses four different ignition systems (included): Full Plastic Jacket, #11 nipple, musket nipple or bare 208 shotgun primer; vented breech plug, striker-fired with one-piece removable hammer assembly. Finish: Stainless steel. With recommended loads, guaranteed to have 4-inch, three-shot groups at 200 yards. Also available as Western gun with exposed ignition. Made in U.S. by Knight Rifles.
Price: Muzzleloaders.com MLHW702C ....**Starting at $390.00**

KNIGHT MOUNTAINEER IN-LINE RIFLE
Caliber: .45, .50, .52. Barrel: 27 in. fluted stainless steel, free floated. Weight: 8 lbs. (thumbhole stock), 8.3 lbs. (straight stock). Length: 45.5 inches. Sights: Fully adjustable metallic fiber optic. Features: Bolt-action rifle, adjustable match-grade trigger, aluminum ramrod with carbon core, solid brass extendable jag, vented breech plug. Ignition: Full plastic jacket, #11 nipple, musket nipple, bare 208 shotgun primer. With recommended loads, guaranteed to have 4-inch, three-shot groups at 200 yards. Also available as Western gun with exposed ignition. Made in U.S. by Knight Rifles.
Price: Muzzleloaders.com MMT707SNMNT ....**Starting at $1,016.00**

KNIGHT ULTRA-LITE IN-LINE RIFLE
Caliber: .45 or .50. Barrel: 24 in. Stock: Black, tan or olive-green Kevlar spider web. Weight: 6 lbs. Features: Bolt-action rifle. Ramrod: Carbon core with solid brass extendable jag. Sights: With or without Williams fiber-optic sights, drilled and tapped for scope mounts. Finish: Stainless steel. Ignition: 209 Primer with Full Plastic Jacket, musket cap or #11 nipple, bare 208 shotgun primer; vented breech plug. With recommended loads, guaranteed to have 4-inch, three-shot groups at 200 yards. Also available as Western version with exposed ignition. Made in U.S. by Knight Rifles.
Price: Muzzleloaders.com MULE704TNT ....**Starting at $1,217.00**

KNIGHT PEREGRINE
Caliber:.40, Barrel: 28 in. Green Mountain stainless helical-fluted barrel, 1:16 in. twist. Weight 7.4 lbs. Overall Length 46.25 in. Designed and built for increased velocities and accuracy at greater distances. Features: solid carbon fiber w/aluminum bed block for free-floating barrel design, Sage Brush Camo, Bare Primer Tungsten Carbide Inserted Breech Plug, Timney Match-Grade Trigger. Included is a Lee Hand Press with adjustable sizing die for bullets.
Price: **$1,569.00**

LYMAN DEERSTALKER RIFLE
Caliber: .50, .54. Barrel: 28 in. octagon, 1:48 in. twist. Weight: 10.8 lbs. Length: 45 in. overall. Stock: European walnut with black rubber recoil pad. Sights: Lyman's high visibility, fiber-optic sights. Features: Fast-twist rifling for conical bullets. Blackened metal parts to eliminate glare, stainless steel nipple. Hook breech, single trigger, coil spring lock. Steel barrel rib and ramrod ferrules. From Lyman.
Price: Muzzleloaders.com 6033146/7. 50-cal /.54-cal. flint **$448.00**
Price: Muzzleloaders.com 6033140/7 .50-cal /.54-cal. percussion **$398.00**

LYMAN GREAT PLAINS RIFLE
Caliber: .50, .54. Barrel: 32 in., 1:60 in. twist. Weight: 11.6 lbs. Stock: Walnut. Sights: Steel blade front, buckhorn rear adjustable for windage and elevation, and fixed notch primitive sight included. Features: Percussion or flint ignition. Blued steel furniture. Stainless steel nipple. Coil spring lock, Hawken-style triggerguard and double-set triggers. Round thimbles recessed and sweated into rib. Steel wedge plates and toe plate. Introduced 1979. From Lyman.
Price: 6031102/3 .50-cal./.54-cal percussion **$784.00**
Price: 6031105/6 .50-cal./.54-cal flintlock **$839.00**
Price: 6031125/6 .50-ca./.54-cal left-hand percussion **$824.00**
Price: 6031137 .50-cal. left-hand flintlock **$859.00**
Price: 6031111/2 .50/.54-cal. percussion kit.......................................**$639.00**
Price: 6031114/5 .50/.54-cal. flintlock kit..**$689.00**

LYMAN GREAT PLAINS HUNTER MODEL
Similar to Great Plains model except 1:32 in. twist, shallow-groove barrel for conicals or sabots, and comes drilled and tapped for Lyman 57GPR peep sight.
Price: 6031120/1 .50-cal./.54-cal percussion....................................**$791.00**
Price: 6031148/9 .50-cal./.54-cal flintlock **$839.00**
Price: 6031112 .50-cal./.54-cal percussion kit **$669.00**
Price: 6031115 .50-cal/.54-cal flintlock kit...**$729.00**

LYMAN TRADE RIFLE
Caliber: .50, .54. Barrel: 28 in. octagon, 1:48 in. twist. Weight: 10.8 lbs. Length: 45 in. overall. Stock: European walnut. Sights: Blade front, open rear adjustable for windage, or optional fixed sights. Features: Fast-twist rifling for conical bullets. Polished brass furniture with blue steel parts, stainless steel nipple. Hook breech, single trigger, coil spring percussion lock. Steel barrel rib and ramrod ferrules. Introduced 1980. From Lyman.
Price: 6032125/6 .50-cal./.54-cal. percussion....................................**$565.00**
Price: 6032129/30 .50-cal./.54-cal. flintlock **$583.00**

PEDERSOLI 1777 CHARLEVILLE MUSKET
Caliber: .69. Barrel: 44.75 in. round, smoothbore. Weight: 10.5 lbs. Length: 57 in. Stock: European walnut, fullstock. Sights: Steel stud on upper barrelband. Features: Flintlock using one-inch flint. Steel parts all polished armory bright, brass furniture. Lock marked Charleville. Made by Pedersoli. Imported by Cabela's, Dixie Gun Works, others.
Price: Dixie Gun Works FR0930 .... **$1,450.00**

PEDERSOLI 1795 SPRINGFIELD MUSKET
Caliber: .69. Barrel: 44.75 in., round, smoothbore. Weight: 10.5 lbs. Length: 57.25 in. Stock: European walnut, fullstock. Sights: Brass stud on upper barrelband. Features: Flintlock using one-inch flint. Steel parts all polished armory bright, brass furniture. Lock marked US Springfield. Made by Pedersoli. Imported by Cabela's, Dixie Gun Works, others.
Price: Dixie Gun Works FR3210 .... **$1,495.00**

PEDERSOLI POTSDAM 1809 PRUSSIAN MUSKET
Caliber: .75. Barrel: 41.2 in. round, smoothbore. Weight: 9 lbs. Length: 56 in. Stock: European walnut, fullstock. Sights: Brass lug on upper barrelband. Features: Flintlock using one-inch flint. Steel parts all polished armory bright, brass furniture. Lock marked "Potsdam over G.S." Made by Pedersoli.

BLACKPOWDER Muskets & Rifles

Imported by Dixie Gun Works.
Price: Dixie Gun Works FR3175 .... $1,575.00

PEDERSOLI 1816 FLINTLOCK MUSKET
Caliber: .69. Barrel: 42 in., smoothbore. Weight: 9.75 lbs. Length: 56-7/8 in. overall. Stock: Walnut w/oil finish. Sights: Blade front. Features: All metal finished in "National Armory Bright," three barrel bands w/springs, steel ramrod w/ button-shaped head. Made by Pedersoli. Imported by Dixie Gun Works.
Price: Dixie Gun Works PR3180, Percussion conversion $1,495.00

PEDERSOLI 1841 MISSISSIPPI RIFLE
Caliber: .54, .58. Barrel: 33 inches. Weight: 9.5 lbs. Length: 48.75 in. overall. Stock: European walnut. Sights: Blade front, notched rear. Features: Percussion musket-cap ignition. Reproduction of the original one-band rifle with large brass patchbox. Color case-hardened lockplate with browned barrel. Made by Pedersoli. Imported by Dixie Gun Works, Cabela's and others.
Price: Dixie Gun Works PR0870 (.54 caliber).........:...................$1,200.00
Price: Dixie Gun Works PR3470 (.58 caliber).....................................$1,100.00

PEDERSOLI 1854 LORENZ RIFLE
Caliber: .54. Barrel: 37 in. Weight: 9 lbs. Length: 49 in. overall. Stock: European walnut. Sights: Blade front, rear steel open, flip-up style. Features: Percussion musket-cap ignition. Armory bright lockplate marked "Konigi. Wurt Fabrik." Armory bright steel barrel. Made by Pedersoli. Imported by Dixie Gun Works.
Price: Dixie Gun Works PR3156...$1,500.00

PEDERSOLI 1857 MAUSER RIFLE
Caliber: .54. Barrel: 39.75 in. Weight: 9.5 lbs. Length: 52 in. overall. Stock: European walnut. Sights: Blade front, rear steel adjustable for windage and elevation. Features: Percussion musket-cap ignition. Color case-hardened lockplate marked "Konigi. Wurt Fabrik." Armory bright steel barrel. Made by Pedersoli. Imported by Dixie Gun Works.
Price: Dixie Gun Works PR1330...$1,695.00

PEDERSOLI 1861 RICHMOND MUSKET
Caliber: .58. Barrel: 40 inches. Weight: 9.5 lbs. Length: 55.5 in. overall. Stock: European walnut. Sights: Blade front, three-leaf military rear. Features: Reproduction of the original three-band rifle. Percussion musket-cap ignition. Lock marked C. S. Richmond, Virginia. Armory bright. Made by Pedersoli. Imported by Dixie Gun Works and others.
Price: Dixie Gun Works PR4095...$1,150.00

PEDERSOLI 1861 SPRINGFIELD RIFLE
Caliber: .58. Barrel: 40 inches. Weight: 10 lbs. Length: 55.5 in. overall. Stock: European walnut. Sights: Blade front, three-leaf military rear. Features: Reproduction of the original three-band rifle. Percussion musket-cap ignition. Lockplate marked 1861 with eagle and U.S. Springfield. Armory bright steel. Made by Armi Sport/Chiappa, Pedersoli. Imported by Cabela's, Dixie Gun Works, others.
Price: Cabela's $1,199.00

PEDERSOLI BAKER CAVALRY SHOTGUN
Gauge: 20. Barrels: 11.25 inches. Weight: 5.75 pounds. Length: 27.5 in. overall. Stock: American walnut. Sights: Bead front. Features: Reproduction of shotguns carried by Confederate cavalry. Single non-selective trigger, back-action locks. No. 11 percussion musket-cap ignition. Blued barrel with steel furniture. Case-hardened lock. Pedersoli also makes a 12-gauge coach-length version of this back-action-lock shotgun with 20-inch barrels, and a full-length version in 10, 12 and 20 gauge. Made by Pedersoli. Imported by Cabela's and others.
Price: Cabela's $1,099.00

PEDERSOLI BRISTLEN MORGES AND WAADTLANDER TARGET RIFLES
Caliber: .44, .45. Barrel: 29.5 in. tapered octagonal, hooked breech. Weight: 15.5 lbs. Length: 48.5 in. overall. Stock: European walnut, halfstock with hooked buttplate and detachable palm rest. Sights: Creedmoor rear on Morges, Swiss Diopter on Waadtlander, hooded front sight notch. Features: Percussion back-action lock, double set, double-phase triggers, one barrel key, muzzle protector. Specialized bullet molds for each gun. Made by Pedersoli. Imported by Dixie Gun Works and others.
Price: Dixie Gun Works, .44 Bristlen Morges PR0165 ....$2,995.00
Price: Dixie Gun Works, .45 Waadtlander PR0183 ....$2,995.00

PEDERSOLI BROWN BESS
Caliber: .75. Barrel: 42 in., round, smoothbore. Weight: 9 lbs. Length: 57.75 in. Stock: European walnut, fullstock. Sights: Steel stud on front serves as bayonet lug. Features: Flintlock using one-inch flint with optional brass flash guard (SCO203), steel parts all polished armory bright, brass furniture. Lock marked Grice, 1762 with crown and GR. Made by Pedersoli. Imported by Cabela's, Dixie Gun Works, others.
Price: Dixie Gun Works Complete Gun FR0810............................. $1,350.00
Price: Dixie Gun Works Kit Gun FR0825 .... $1,050.00
Price: Dixie Gun Works Trade Gun, 30.5-in. barrel FR0665 .... $1,495.00
Price: Dixie Gun Works Trade Gun Kit FR0600 .... $975.00

PEDERSOLI COOK & BROTHER CONFEDERATE CARBINE/ARTILLERY/RIFLE
Caliber: .58 Barrel: 24/33/39 inches. Weight: 7.5/8.4/8.6 lbs. Length: 40.5/48/54.5 in. Stock: Select oil-finished walnut. Features: Percussion musket-cap ignition. Color case-hardened lock, browned barrel. Buttplate, triggerguard, barrelbands, sling swivels and nose cap of polished brass. Lock marked with stars and bars flag on tail and Athens, Georgia. Made by Pedersoli. Imported by Dixie Gun Works, others.
Price: Dixie Gun Works Carbine PR0830 ....$995.00
Price: Dixie Gun Works Artillery/Rifle PR32165 .... $995.00

PEDERSOLI COUNTRY HUNTER
Caliber: .50. Barrel: 26 in. octagonal. Weight: 6 lbs. Length: 41.75 in. overall. Stock: European walnut, halfstock. Sights: Rear notch, blade front. Features: Percussion, one barrel key. Made by Pedersoli. Imported by Dixie Gun Works.
Price: Cherry's Fine Guns Percussion, .50 .... $675.00
Price: Cherry's Fine Guns Flint, .50..$688.00

PEDERSOLI ENFIELD MUSKETOON P1861
Caliber: .58. Barrel: 33 in. Weight: 9 lbs. Length: 35 in. overall. Stock: European walnut. Sights: Blade front, flip-up rear with elevator marked to 700 yards. Features: Reproduction of the original cavalry version of the Enfield rifle. Percussion musket-cap ignition. Blued barrel with steel barrelbands, brass furniture. Case-hardened lock. Euroarms version marked London Armory with crown. Pedersoli version has Birmingham stamp on stock and Enfield and Crown on lockplate. Made by Euroarms, Pedersoli. Imported by Cabela's and others.
Price: Cabela's $1,099.00

PEDERSOLI FRONTIER RIFLE
Caliber: .32, .36, .45, .50, .54. Barrel: 39 in., octagon, 1:48 twist. Weight: 7.75 lbs. Length: 54.5 in. Stock: American black walnut. Sights: Blade front, rear drift adjustable for windage. Features: Color case-hardened lockplate and cock/hammer, brass triggerguard and buttplate; double set, double-phased triggers. Made by Pedersoli. Imported by Dixie Gun Works, and by Cabela's (as the Blue Ridge Rifle).
Price: Cabela's Percussion $599.00
Price: Cabela's Flintlock $649.00

PEDERSOLI ENFIELD THREE-BAND P1853 RIFLE
Caliber: .58. Barrel: 39 in. Weight: 10.25 lbs. Length: 52 in. overall. Stock: European walnut. Sights: Blade front, flip-up rear with elevator marked to 800 yards. Features: Reproduction of the original three-band rifle. Percussion musket-cap ignition. Blued barrel with steel barrelbands, brass furniture. Case-hardened lock. Lockplate marked "London Armory Co. and Crown." Made by Pedersoli. Imported by Cabela's.
Price: Cabela's $1,149.00

PEDERSOLI INDIAN TRADE MUSKET
Gauge: 20. Barrel: 36 in., octagon to round, smoothbore. Weight: 7.25 lbs. Length: 52 in. overall. Stock: American walnut. Sights: Blade front sight, no rear sight. Features: Flintlock. Kits version available. Made by Pedersoli. Imported by Dixie Gun Works.
Price: Dixie Gun Works, FR3170.. $1,095.00
Price: Dixie Gun Works Kit, FK3370... $995.00

PEDERRSOLI JAEGER RIFLE
Caliber: .54. Barrel: 27.5 in. octagon, 1:24 in. twist. Weight: 8.25 lbs. Length:

Prices given are believed to be accurate at time of publication however, many factors affect retail pricing so exact prices are not possible.

BLACKPOWDER Muskets & Rifles

43.5 in. overall. Stock: American walnut; sliding wooden patchbox on butt. Sights: Notch rear, blade front. Features: Flintlock or percussion. Conversion kits available, and recommended converting percussion guns to flintlocks using kit LO1102 at $209.00. Browned steel furniture. Made by Pedersoli. Imported by Dixie Gun Works.

Price: Dixie Gun Works Percussion, PR0835......................**$1,350.00**
Price: Dixie Gun Works Flint, PR0835.............................**$1,450.00**
Price: Dixie Gun Works Percussion, kit gun, PK0146.........................**$1,075.00**
Price: Dixie Gun Works Flint, kit gun, PKO143................................**$1,100.00**

PEDERSOLI KENTUCKY RIFLE
Caliber: .32, .45 and .50. Barrel: 35.5 in. octagonal. Weight: 7.5 (.50 cal.) to 7.75 lbs. (.32 cal.) Length: 51 in. overall. Stock: European walnut, full-length stock. Sights: Notch rear, blade front. Features: Flintlock or percussion, brass patchbox, double-set triggers. Also available as kit guns for all calibers and ignition systems. Made by Pedersoli. Imported by Dixie Gun Works.

Price: Dixie Gun Works Percussion, .32, PR3115...................**$750.00**
Price: Dixie Gun Works Flint, .32, FR3100...........................**$775.00**
Price: Dixie Gun Works Percussion, .45, FR3120...................**$750.00**
Price: Dixie Gun Works Flint, .45, FR3105 ....**$775.00**
Price: Dixie Gun Works Percussion, .50, FR3125...................**$750.00**
Price: Dixie Gun Works Flint, .50, FR3110 ....**$775.00**

PEDERSOLI KODIAK DOUBLE RIFLES AND COMBINATION GUN.
Caliber: .50, .54 and .58. Barrel: 28.5 in.; 1:24/1:24/1:48 in. twist. Weight: 11.25/10.75/10 lbs. Stock: Straight grip European walnut. Sights: Two adjustable rear, steel ramp with brass bead front. Features: Percussion ignition, double triggers, sling swivels. A .72-caliber express rifle and a .50-caliber/12-gauge shotgun combination gun are also available. Blued steel furniture. Stainless steel nipple. Made by Pedersoli. Imported by Dixie Gun Works and some models by Cabela's and others.

Price: Dixie Gun Works Rifle 50X50 PR0970.....................**$1,525.00**
Price: Dixie Gun Works Rifle 54X54 PR0975.....................**$1,525.00**
Price: Dixie Gun Works Rifle 58X58 PR0980.....................**$1,525.00**
Price: Dixie Gun Works Combo 50X12 gauge PR0990 ....**$1,350.00**
Price: Dixie Gun Works Express Rifle .72 caliber PR0916 ....**$1,550.00**

PEDERSOLI MAGNUM PERCUSSION SHOTGUN & COACH GUN
Gauge: 10, 12, 20 Barrel: Chrome-lined blued barrels, 25.5 in. Imp. Cyl. and Mod. Weight: 7.25, 7, 6.75 lbs. Length: 45 in. overall. Stock: Hand-checkered walnut, 14-in. pull. Features: Double triggers, light hand engraving, case-hardened locks, sling swivels. Made by Pedersoli. From Dixie Gun Works, others.

Price: Dixie Gun Works 10-ga. PS1030 ....**$1,250.00**
Price: Dixie Gun Works 10-ga. kit PS1040 ....**$975.00**
Price: Dixie Gun Works 12-ga. PS0930 ....**$1,175.00**
Price: Dixie Gun Works 12-ga. Kit PS0940 ....**$875.00**
Price: Dixie Gun Works 12-ga. Coach gun, CylXCyl, PS0914 ....**$1,150.00**
Price: Dixie Gun Works 20-ga. PS0334 ....**$1,175.00**

PEDERSOLI MORTIMER RIFLE & SHOTGUN
Caliber: .54, 12 gauge. Barrel: 36 in., 1:66 in. twist, and cylinder bore. Weight: 10 lbs. rifle, 9 lbs. shotgun. Length: 52.25 in. Stock: Halfstock walnut. Sights: Blued steel rear with flip-up leaf, blade front. Features: Percussion and flint ignition. Blued steel furniture. Single trigger. Lock with hammer safety and "waterproof pan" marked Mortimer. A percussion .45-caliber target version of this gun is available with a peep sight on the wrist, and a percussion shotgun version is also offered. Made by Pedersoli. Imported by Dixie Gun Works.

Price: Dixie Gun Works Flint Rifle, FR0151 ....**$1,575.00**

Price: Dixie Gun Works Flint Shotgun FS0155 ....**$1,525.00**

PEDERSOLI OLD ENGLISH SHOTGUN
Gauge: 12 Barrels: Browned, 28.5 in. Cyl. and Mod. Weight: 7.5 lbs. Length: 45 in. overall. Stock: Hand-checkered American maple, cap box, 14-in. pull. Features: Double triggers, light hand engraving on lock, cap box and tang, swivel studs for sling attachment. Made by Pedersoli. From Dixie Gun Works, others.

Price: Dixie Gun Works PR4090 ....**$1,750.00**

PEDERSOLI ROCKY MOUNTAIN & MISSOURI RIVER HAWKEN RIFLES
Caliber: .54 Rocky Mountain, .45 and .50 in Missouri River. Barrel: 34.75 in. octagonal with hooked breech; Rocky Mountain 1:65 in. twist; Missouri River 1:47 twist in .45 cal., and 1:24 twist in .50 cal. Weight: 10 lbs. Length: 52 in. overall. Stock: Maple or walnut, halfstock. Sights: Rear buckhorn with push elevator, silver blade front. Features: Available in Percussion, with brass furniture and double triggers. Made by Pedersoli. Imported by Dixie Gun Works and others.

Price: Dixie Gun Works Rocky Mountain, Maple PR3430 ....**$1,395.00**
Price: Dixie Gun Works Rocky Mountain, Walnut PR3435 ....**$1,195.00**
Price: Dixie Gun Works Missouri River, .50 Walnut PR3415 ....**$1,275.00**
Price: Dixie Gun Works Missouri River, .45 Walnut PR3405 ....**$1,275.00**

PEDERSOLI PENNSYLVANIA RIFLE
Caliber: .32, .45 and .50. Barrel: 41.5 in. browned, octagonal, 1:48 in. twist. Weight: 8.25 lbs. Length: 56 in. overall. Stock: American walnut. Sights: Rear semi-buckhorn with push elevator, steel blade front. Features: Available in flint or percussion, with brass furniture, and double triggers. Also available as a kit. Made by Pedersoli. Imported by Dixie Gun Works and others.

Price: Dixie Gun Works Flint .32 FR3040 ....**$950.00**
Price: Dixie Gun Works Percussion .32 PR3055.........................**$900.00**
Price: Dixie Gun Works Flint .45 PR3045.............................**$950.00**
Price: Dixie Gun Works Percussion .45 PR3060.........................**$900.00**
Price: Dixie Gun Works Flint .50 PR3050.............................**$950.00**
Price: Dixie Gun Works Percussion .50 PR3065.........................**$900.00**
Price: Dixie Gun Works Flint Kit .32 FK3260 ....**$750.00**
Price: Dixie Gun Works Percussion kit .32 PK3275.....................**$695.00**
Price: Dixie Gun Works Flint kit .45 FK3265 ....**$750.00**
Price: Dixie Gun Works Percussion kit .45 PR3280.....................**$695.00**
Price: Dixie Gun Works Flint kit .50 FK3270 ....**$750.00**
Price: Dixie Gun Works Percussion kit .50 PK3285.....................**$695.00**

PEDERSOLI SHARPS NEW MODEL 1859 MILITARY RIFLE AND CARBINE
Caliber: .54. Barrel: 30 in., 6-groove, 1:48 in. twist. Weight: 9 lbs. Length: 45.5 in. overall. Stock: Oiled walnut. Sights: Blade front, ladder-style rear. Features: Blued barrel, color case-hardened barrelbands, receiver, hammer, nose cap, lever, patchbox cover and buttplate. Introduced in 1995. Rifle made by Pedersoli. Rifle imported from Italy by Dixie Gun Works and others.

Price: Dixie Gun Work Rifle PR0862 ....**$1,650.00**
Price: Dixie Gun Work Carbine (22-in. barrel) PR0982 ....**$1,400.00**

PEDERSOLI SHARPS MODEL 1863 SPORTING RIFLE
Caliber: .45. Barrel: 32 in., octagon, 6-groove, 1:18 in. twist. Weight: 10.75 lbs. Length: 49 in. overall. Stock: Oiled walnut. Sights: Silver blade front, flip-up rear. Features: Browned octagon barrel, color case-hardened receiver, hammer and buttplate. Rifle made by Pedersoli. Imported by Dixie Gun Works and others.

Price: Dixie Gun Work Rifle PR5001 ....**$1,500.00**

PEDERSOLI SHARPS CONFEDERATE CARBINE
Caliber: .54. Barrel: 22 in., 6-groove, 1:48 in. twist. Weight: 8 lbs. Length: 39 in. overall. Stock: Oiled walnut. Sights: Blade front, dovetailed rear. Features: Browned barrel, color case-hardened receiver, hammer, and lever. Brass buttplate and barrel bands. Rifle made by Pedersoli. Imported by Dixie Gun Works and others.

Price: Dixie Gun Work Carbine PR3380..**$1,395.00**

PEDERSOLI TRADITIONAL HAWKEN TARGET RIFLE
Caliber: .50 and .54. Barrel: 29.5 in. octagonal, 1:48 in. twist. Weight: 9 or 8.5

Prices given are believed to be accurate at time of publication however, many factors affect retail pricing so exact prices are not possible.

lbs. Length: 45.5 in. overall. Stock: European walnut, halfstock. Sights: Rear click adjustable for windage and elevation, blade front. Features: Percussion and flintlock, brass patchbox, double-set triggers, one barrel key. Flint gun available for left-handed shooters. Both flint and percussion guns available as kit guns. Made by Pedersoli. Imported by Dixie Gun Works.
Price: Dixie Gun Works Percussion, .50 PR0502....................$650.00
Price: Dixie Gun Works Percussion, .54 PR0507....................$650.00
Price: Dixie Gun Works Flint, .50 FR1332 ....$725.00
Price: Dixie Gun Works Flint, .54 FR3515 ....$725.00

PEDERSOLI TRYON RIFLE
Caliber: .50. Barrel: 32 in. octagonal, 1:48 in. twist. Weight: 9.5 lbs. Length: 49 in. overall. Stock: European walnut, halfstock. Sights: Elevation-adjustable rear with stair-step notches, blade front. Features: Percussion, brass patchbox, double-set triggers, two barrel keys. Made by Pedersoli. Imported by Dixie Gun Works.
Price: Percussion, PR0860 .... $1,100.00

PEDERSOLI VOLUNTEER RIFLE
Caliber: .451. Barrel: 33 in., round interior bore 1:21 in. twist. Weight: 9.5 lbs. Length: 49 in. Stock: Oiled Grade 1 American walnut. Sights: Blade front, ladder-style rear. Features: Checkered stock wrist and fore-end. Blued barrel, steel ramrod, bone charcoal case-hardened receiver and hammer. Designed for .451 conical bullets. Compare to hexagonal-bored Whitworth Rifle below. Hand-fitted and finished.
Price: Dixie Gun Works PR3150...... .... $1,295.00

PEDERSOLI WHITWORTH RIFLE
Caliber: .451. Barrel: 36 in., hexagonal interior bore 1:20 in. twist. Weight: 9.6 lbs. Length: 52.5 in. Stock: Oiled Grade 1 American walnut. Sights: Blade front, ladder-style rear. Features: Checkered stock wrist and fore-end. Blued barrel, steel ramrod, bone charcoal case-hardened receiver and hammer. Designed for .451 conical hexagonal bullet. Compare to round-bored Volunteer Rifle above. Hand-fitted to original specifications using original Enfield arsenal gauges.
Price: Dixie Gun Works PR3256...... .... $1,750.00

PEDERSOLI ZOUAVE RIFLE
Caliber: .58 percussion. Barrel: 33 inches. Weight: 9.5 lbs. Length: 49 inches. Stock: European walnut. Sights: Blade front, three-leaf military rear. Features: Percussion musket-cap ignition. One-piece solid barrel and bolster. Brass-plated patchbox. Made in Italy by Pedersoli. Imported by Dixie Gun Works, others.
Price: Dixie Gun Works PF0340. ....$975.00

REMINGTON MODEL 700 ULTIMATE MUZZLELOADER
Caliber: .50 percussion. Barrel: 26 in., 1:26 in. twist, satin stainless steel, fluted. Length: 47 in. Stock: Bell & Carlson black synthetic. Sights: None on synthetic-stocked model. Ramrod: Stainless steel. Weight: 8.5 lbs. Features: Remington single shot Model 700 bolt action, re-primable cartridge-case ignition using Remington Magnum Large Rifle Primer, sling studs.
Price: 86960 Starting at $1,015.00

THOMPSON/CENTER IMPACT MUZZLELOADING RIFLE
Caliber: .50. Barrel: 26 in., 1:28 twist, Weather Shield finish. Weight: 6.5 lbs. Length: 41.5 in. Stock: Straight Realtree Hardwoods HD or black composite. Features: Sliding-hood, break-open action, #209 primer ignition, removable breech plug, synthetic stock adjustable from 12.5 to 13.5 in., adjustable fiber-optic sights, aluminum ramrod, camo, QLA relieved muzzle system.
Price: .50-cal Stainless/Realtree Hardwoods, Weather Shield $324.00
Price: .50-cal Blued/Black/scope, case............................ ....$263.00

THOMPSON/CENTER PRO HUNTER FX
Caliber: .50 as muzzleloading barrel. Barrel: 26 in., Weather Shield with relieved muzzle on muzzleloader; interchangeable with 14 centerfire calibers. Weight: 7 lbs. Length: 40.5 in. overall. Stock: Interchangeable American

walnut butt and fore-end, black composite, FlexTech recoil-reducing camo stock as thumbhole or straight, rubber over-molded stock and fore-end. Ramrod: Solid aluminum. Sights: Tru-Glo fiber-optic front and rear. Features: Blue or stainless steel. Uses the frame of the Encore centerfire pistol; break-open design using triggerguard spur; stainless steel universal breech plug; uses #209 shotshell primers. Made in U.S. by Thompson/Center Arms.
Price: .50-cal Stainless/Black FlexTech Stock Model 5800.................. $649.00
Price: .50-cal Stainless/Engraved frame FlexTech RT-AP camo............$709.00

THOMPSON/CENTER TRIUMPH BONE COLLECTOR
Caliber: .50. Barrel: 28 in., Weather Shield coated. Weight: 6.5 lbs. Overall: 42 in. Stock: FlexTech recoil-reducing. Black composite or Realtree AP HD camo straight, rubber over-molded stock and fore-end. Sights: Fiber optic. Ramrod: Solid aluminum. Features: Break-open action. Quick Detachable Speed Breech XT plug, #209 shotshell primer ignition, easy loading QLA relieved muzzle. Made in U.S. by Thompson/Center Arms. Available from Cabela's, Bass Pro.
Price: .50-cal Synthetic Realtree AP, fiber optics.... .... $720.00
Price: .50-cal Synthetic/Weather Shield Black..................................... $638.00
Price: .50-cal. Weather Shield/AP Camo..$679.00
Price: .50 cal. Silver Weather Shield/AP Camo......................................$689.00

THOMPSON/CENTER STRIKE
Caliber: .50. Barrel: 24 or 20 in., nitride finished, tapered barrel. Weight: 6.75 or 6.25 lbs. Length: 44 in. or 40 in. Stock: Walnut, black synthetic, G2-Vista Camo. Finish: Armornite nitride. Features: Break-open action, sliding hammerless cocking mechanism, optional pellet or loose powder primer holders, easily removable breech plugs retained by external collar, aluminum frame with steel mono-block to retain barrel, recoil pad. Sights: Williams fiber-optic sights furnished, drilled and tapped for scope. Made in the U.S. by Thompson/Center.
Price: .50 cal. 24-in. barrel, black synthetic stock $499.00
Price: .50 cal. 24-in. barrel, walnut stock $599.00
Price: .50 cal. 24-in. barrel, G2 camo stock $549.00

TRADITIONS BUCKSTALKER IN-LINE RIFLE
Caliber: .50. Barrel: 24 in., Cerakote finished, Accelerator Breech Plug. Weight: 6 lbs. Length: 40 in. Stock: Synthetic, G2 Vista camo or black. Sights: Fiber-optic rear. Features: Break-open action, matte-finished action and barrel. Ramrod: Solid aluminum. Imported by Traditions.
Price: R72003540 .50-cal. Youth Synthetic stock/blued........................$219.00
Price: R72103540 .50-cal. Synthetic stock/Cerakote $329.00
Price: R5-72003540 .50-cal. Synthetic stock/blued, scope.................. $294.00
Price: R5-72103547 .50-cal. Synthetic stock/Cerakote, scope $369.00

TRADITIONS BUCKSTALKER XT
Caliber: .50. Barrel: 24 in. Twist rate: 1:28. Ignition: 209 primer. Features: Upgraded premium-grade Chromoly steel barrel, Elite XT trigger system upgrade. Uses the Dual Safety System, Accelerator Breech Plug (the plug is removable by hand and allows the use of loose or pelletized powder), and what Traditions calls its Speed Load System. Variants include a G2 Vista camo or black stock, various finish options, and scoped and non-scoped versions. For Idaho and Oregon, the Buckstalker XT Northwest Magnum features the musket ignition, open breech, and open-sights.
Price: ....$253–$461

TRADITIONS BUCKSTALKER XT NORTHWEST MAGNUM
Caliber: 50. Barrel: 24 in. 1:28 in. twist, CeraKote finish barrel and action.

Prices given are believed to be accurate at time of publication however, many factors affect retail pricing so exact prices are not possible.

Overall length: 40 in. Drilled and tapped for a scope. Weight: 6 lbs. Features: Chromoly tapered, fluted barrel, Musket cap ignition, Elite XT Trigger System, Accelerator breech plug, Speed Load System, Dual Safety System, Quick-T Ramrod Handle, sling swivel studs, solid aluminum ramrod. Comes with sight. Available in Black/SS Cerakote.
Price: **$329.00**

TRADITIONS CROCKETT RIFLE
Caliber: .32. Barrel: 32 in., 1:48 in. twist. Weight: 6.75 lbs. Length: 49 in. overall. Stock: Beech, inletted toe plate. Sights: Blade front, fixed rear. Features: Set triggers, hardwood halfstock, brass furniture, color case-hardened lock. Percussion. Imported by Traditions.
Price: R26128101 .32-cal. Percussion, finished **$543.00**
Price: RK52628100 .32-cal. Percussion, kit......................... **$479.00**

TRADITIONS EVOLUTION BOLT-ACTION BLACKPOWDER RIFLE
Caliber: .50 percussion. Barrel: 26 in., 1:28 in. twist. Cerakote finished barrel and action. Length: 39 in. Sights: Steel Williams fiber-optic sights. Weight: 7 to 7.25 lbs. Length: 45 in. overall. Features: Bolt action, cocking indicator, thumb safety, shipped with adaptors for No. 11 caps, musket caps and 209 shotgun-primer ignition, sling swivels. Ramrod: Aluminum, sling studs. Available with exposed ignition as a Northwest gun. Imported by Traditions.
Price: R67113350 .50-cal. synthetic black, Cerakote........................... **$250.00**
Price: R67113353 .50-cal. synthetic Realtree AP camo...... ....**$299.00**

TRADITIONS HAWKEN WOODSMAN RIFLE
Caliber: .50. Barrel: 28 in., blued, 15/16 in. flats. Weight: 7 lbs., 11 oz. Length: 44.5 in. overall. Stock: Walnut stained hardwood. Sights: Beaded blade front hunting-style open rear adjustable for windage and elevation. Features: Brass patchbox and furniture. Double-set triggers. Flint or percussion. Imported by Traditions.
Price: R2390801 .50-cal. Flintlock **$544.00**
Price: R24008 .50-cal. Percussion **$499.00**

TRADITIONS KENTUCKY DELUXE
Caliber: .50. Barrel: 33.5 in., blued octagon. Stock: Walnut-finished select hardwood. Sights: Fixed blade. Weight: 7 lbs. Features: Double set trigger, brass patch box, available as a kit, authentic wooden ramrod.
Price: .... **$379.00-$485.00**

TRADITIONS KENTUCKY RIFLE
Caliber: .50. Barrel: 33.5 in., 7/8 in. flats, 1:66 in. twist. Weight: 7 lbs. Length: 49 in. overall. Stock: Beech, inletted toe plate. Sights: Blade front, fixed rear. Features: Full-length, two-piece stock; brass furniture; color case-hardened lock. Flint or percussion. Imported by Traditions.
Price: R2010 .50-cal. Flintlock,1:66 twist **$509.00**
Price: R2020 .50-cal. Percussion, 1:66 twist...................... **$449.00**
Price: KRC52206 .50-cal. Percussion, kit.............................. **$343.00**

TRADITIONS MOUNTAIN RIFLE
Caliber: .50. Barrel: 32 in., octagon with brown Cerakote finish. Stock: Select hardwoods. Sights: Primitive, adjustable rear. Weight: 8.25 lbs. Features: Available in percussion or flintlock, case-hardened lock, wooden ramrod, available as a kit.
Price: .... **$494.00-$649.00**

TRADITIONS NITROFIRE
Caliber: .50. Barrel: 26 in., 1:24 in. VAPR twist, CeraKote finish barrel and action. Overall length: 42 in. Drilled and taped for scope and for sights. Weight: 6.6 lbs. (rifle only). Features: 26 in. Chromoly steel-fluted barrel, 209 ignition, Elite XT Trigger System, Fast Action Release Button, Speed Load System, solid aluminum ramrod with Quick-T Ramrod Handle, available scoped or non-scoped, various camo patterns and finishes.
Price: ....**$570.00–$731.00**

TRADITIONS PA PELLET FLINTLOCK
Caliber: .50. Barrel: 26 in., blued, 1:28 in. twist., Cerakote. Weight: 7 lbs. Length: 45 in. Stock: Hardwood, synthetic and synthetic break-up, sling swivels. Fiber-optic sights. Features: New flintlock action, removable breech plug, available as left-hand model with hardwood stock. Imported by Traditions.
Price: .... **$505–$683**

TRADITIONS PENNSYLVANIA RIFLE
Caliber: .50. Barrel: 40.25 in., 7/8 in. flats, 1:66 in. twist, octagon. Weight: 9 lbs. Length: 57.5 in. overall. Stock: Walnut. Sights: Blade front, adjustable rear. Features: Single-piece walnut stock, brass patchbox and ornamentation. Double-set triggers. Flint or percussion. Imported by Traditions.
Price: R2090 .50-cal. Flintlock **$865.00**
Price: R2100 .50-cal. Percussion... **$834.00**

TRADITIONS SHEDHORN SIDELOCK MUZZLELOADERS
Caliber: .50. Barrel: 26 in. 1:28 in. twist, CeraKote finish barrel and action. Overall length: 45 in. Drilled and tapped for a scope. Weight: 6 lbs. Features: Chromoly tapered, fluted barrel, Musket cap ignition, fires loose blackpowder or Pyrodex, double set trigger system, Accelerator breech plug, sling swivel studs, solid aluminum ramrod. Drilled and tapped for scope. Available in camo, wood or black and various color finishes.
Price: .... **$468–$559**

TRADITIONS PURSUIT ULTRALIGHT MUZZLELOADER
Caliber: .50. Barrel: 26 in., chromoly tapered, fluted barrel with premium Cerakote finish, Accelerator Breech Plug. Weight: 5.5 lbs. Length: 42 in. Stock: Rubber over-molded Soft Touch camouflage, straight and thumbhole stock options. Sights: Optional 3-9x40 scope with medium rings and bases, mounted and bore-sighted by a factory-trained technician. Features: Break-open action, Williams fiber-optic sights. Imported by Traditions.
Price: Pursuit G4 Ultralight .50 Cal. Select Hardwoods/
    Cerakote R741101NS.....................................**$469.00**
Price: Pursuit G4 Ultralight .50 Cal. Mossy Oak Break Up Country Camo/
    Cerakote R7411416 ....**$404.00**
Price: Pursuit G4 Ultralight .50 Cal. Mossy Oak Break Up Country/Cerakote/
    Scope/Carrying Case.... .... **$479.00**

TRADITIONS PURSUIT XT .45 CALIBER
Caliber: 45. Barrel: 26 in. 1:20 in. twist, CeraKote finish barrel and action. Overall length: 42 in. Drilled and tapped for a scope. Weight: 5.75 lbs (rifle only). Features: Chromoly tapered, fluted barrel, extended ambidextrous hammer extension, TAC2 Trigger System, Accelerator Breech Plug, recoil-reducing buttstock & buttpad, LT-1 alloy frame, Hogue Comfort-Grip Overmolding, Speed Load System, Dual Safety System, Quick-T Ramrod Handle, sling swivel studs, 209 shotgun primer ignition, solid aluminum ramrod—available scoped or non-scoped, various camo patterns and finishes.
Price: ....**$448.00–$636.00**

TRADITIONS PURSUIT XT .50 CALIBER
Caliber: 50. Barrel: 26 in. 1:20 in. twist, CeraKote finish barrel and action. Overall length: 42 in. Drilled and tapped for a scope. Weight: 5.75 lbs (rifle only). Features: Chromoly tapered, fluted barrel, extended ambidextrous hammer extension, TAC2 Trigger System, Accelerator Breech Plug, recoil-reducing buttstock & buttpad, LT-1 alloy frame, Hogue Comfort-Grip Overmolding, Speed Load System, Dual Safety System, Quick-T Ramrod Handle, sling swivel studs, 209 shotgun primer ignition, solid aluminum ramrod—available scoped or non-scoped, various camo patterns and finishes.
Price: ....**$448.00–$636.00**

TRADITIONS PURSUIT XT NORTHWEST MAGNUM
Caliber: 50. Barrel: 26 or 30 in. 1:24 in. VAPR twist, CeraKote finish barrel and action. Overall length: 42 or 46 in. Drilled and tapped for a scope. Weight: 5.75 lbs (rifle only). Features: Chromoly tapered, fluted barrel, Musket cap ignition, TAC2 Trigger System, Accelerator Breech Plug, recoil-reducing buttstock & buttpad, LT-1 alloy frame, Hogue Comfort-Grip Overmolding, Speed Load System, Dual Safety System, Quick-T Ramrod Handle, sling swivel studs, 209 shotgun primer ignition, solid aluminum ramrod. Comes with sights — available scoped or non-scoped, various camo patterns and finishes.
Price: ....**$419.00–$472.00**

TRADITIONS TRACKER IN-LINE RIFLE
Caliber: .50. Barrel: 24 in., blued or Cerakote, 1:28 in. twist. Weight: 6 lbs., 4 oz. Length: 43 in. Stock: Black synthetic. Ramrod: Synthetic, high-impact polymer. Sights: Lite Optic blade front, adjustable rear. Features: Striker-fired action, thumb safety, adjustable trigger, rubber buttpad, sling swivel studs. Takes 150 grains of Pyrodex pellets, one-piece musket cap and 209 ignition systems. Drilled and tapped for scope. Legal for use in Northwest. Imported by Traditions.
Price: R44003470 .50-cal. Synthetic/blued **$184.00**

TRADITIONS VORTEK STRIKERFIRE .50 CALIBER
Caliber: 50. Barrel: 28 or 30 in. VAPR 1:24 in. VAPR twist, CeraKote finish barrel and action. Overall length: 44 or 46 in. Drilled and tapped for a scope. Weight: 6-6.25 lbs (rifle only). Features: Chromoly tapered, fluted barrel, Strikerfire System and button, recessed De-Cocking button, TAC2 Trigger System, Accelerator Breech Plug, recoil-reducing buttstock and buttpad, LT-1 alloy frame, Hogue Comfort-Grip Overmolding, Speed Load System, Dual Safety System, Quick-T Ramrod Handle, sling swivel studs, 209 shotgun primer ignition, solid aluminum ramrod. Available scoped or non-scoped, various camo patterns and finishes.
Price: ....**$461.00–$642.00**

TRADITIONS VORTEK STRIKERFIRE .45 CALIBER
Caliber: 45. Barrel: 28 or 30 in. 1:20 in. twist, CeraKote finish barrel, and action. Overall length: 44 or 46 in. Drilled and tapped for a scope. Weight: 6-6.25 lbs (rifle only). Features: Chromoly tapered, fluted barrel, Strikerfire System and button, recessed De-Cocking button, TAC2 Trigger System, Accelerator Breech Plug, recoil-reducing buttstock and buttpad, LT-1 alloy frame,   Hogue Comfort-Grip Overmolding, Speed Load System, Dual Safety System, Quick-T Ramrod Handle, sling swivel studs, 209 shotgun primer ignition, solid aluminum ramrod. Available scoped or non-scoped, various camo patterns and finishes.
Price: ....**$461.00–$642.00**

TRADITIONS VORTEK STRIKERFIRE LDR
Caliber: .50. Barrel: 30 in., chromoly, tapered, fluted barrel. Weight: 6.8

lbs. Length: 46 in. Stock: Over-molded soft-touch straight stock, removable buttplate for in-stock storage. Finish: Premium Cerakote and Realtree Xtra. Features: Break-open action, sliding hammerless cocking mechanism, drop-out trigger assembly, speed load system, Accelerator Breech Plug, recoil pad. Sights: Optional 3-9x40 muzzleloader scope. Imported by Traditions.
Price: R491140WA Synthetic/black Hogue Over-mold,
Cerakote barrel, no sights..**$499.00**

WOODMAN ARMS PATRIOT
Caliber: .45, .50. Barrel: 24 in., nitride-coated, 416 stainless, 1:24 twist in .45, 1:28 twist in .50. Weight: 5.75 lbs. Length: 43-in. Stocks: Laminated, walnut or hydrographic dipped, synthetic black, over-molded soft-touch straight stock. Finish: Nitride black and black anodized. Features: Break-open action, hammerless cocking mechanism, match-grade patented trigger assembly, speed load system, recoil pad. Sights: Picatinny rail with built-in rear and 1-inch or 30 mm scope mounts, red fiber-optic front bead.
Price: Patriot .45 or .50-cal...**$899.00**

UBERTI 1858 NEW ARMY REMINGTON TARGET CARBINE REVOLVER
Caliber: .44, 6-shot. Barrel: Tapered octagon, 18 in. Weight: 70.4 oz. Length: Standard 35.3 in. Stock: Walnut. Sights: Standard blade front, adjustable rear. Features: Replica of Remington's revolving rifle of 1866. Made by Uberti. Imported by Uberti USA, Cimarron F.A. Co., Taylor's and others.
Price: Uberti USA, 341200...**$559.00**

Prices given are believed to be accurate at time of publication however, many factors affect retail pricing so exact prices are not possible.

AIR ARMS ALFA SPORT COMPETITION PCP PISTOL
Caliber: .177 pellets. Barrel: Rifled, 9.6 in. Weight: 2 lbs. Length: 16.9 inches. Power: Precharged pneumatic. Sights: Front adjustable width post, fully adjustable rear blade. Features: Single shot, 10m competition class pistol, highly adjustable trigger, internal power regulator for consistent velocity, factory trigger pull set to 8 oz., ambidextrous stippled walnut grip, anti-flip muzzle brake, can be dry fired, 80 shots per fill. Velocity: 500 fps.
Price: **$1,094.00**

AIRFORCE TALON P PCP AIR PISTOL
Caliber: .25. Barrel: Rifled 12.0 in. Weight: 4.3 lbs. Length: 27.75–32.25 in. Sights: None, grooved for scope. Features: Quick-detachable air tank with adjustable power. Match-grade Lothar Walther barrel, massive power output in a highly compact size, two-stage trigger, single shot, open sights optional. Velocity: 500–900 fps.
Price: **$570.00**

AIR VENTURI V10 MATCH AIR PISTOL
Caliber: .177 pellets. Barrel: Rifled. Weight: 1.95 lbs. Length: 12.6 in. Power: Single-stroke pneumatic. Sights: Front post, fully adjustable rear blade. Features: 10m competition class pistol, fully adjustable trigger, 1.5-lb. trigger pull. Velocity: 400 fps.
Price: **$300.00**

AIR VENTURI AV-46M MATCH AIR PISTOL
Caliber: .177 pellets. Barrel: Rifled. Weight: 2.6 lbs. Length: 16.5 in. Power: Single-stroke pneumatic. Sights: Front post, fully adjustable rear blade. Features: Bolt action, 18 lb. cocking effort, red and black laminate grip, two-stage adjustable trigger, adjustable/removable palm shelf, made by Alpha Precision, entry-level 10m competition pistol, can be dry fired. Velocity: 480 fps.
Price: **$700.00**

ASG STI DUTY ONE CO2 BB PISTOL
Caliber: .177 steel BBs. Barrel: Smoothbore Weight: 1.82 lbs. Length: 8.66 in. Power: CO2. Sights: Fixed. Features: Blowback, accessory rail, and metal slide. Velocity: 383 fps.
Price: **$120.00**

ATAMAN AP16 REGULATED COMPACT AIR PISTOL
Caliber: .22 pellets. Barrel: Rifled match. Weight: 1.76 lbs. Length: 12.0 in. Power: Precharged pneumatic. Sights: Fixed front ramp, Adjustable rear notch. Features: 7-round rotary magazine, adjustable trigger, 300 Bar max fill, regulated for hunting power, exceptional build quality, available in satin

and blued finishes Velocity: 590 fps.
Price: **$1,249.00**

ATAMAN AP16 REGULATED STANDARD AIR PISTOL
Caliber: .22 pellets. Barrel: Rifled match. Weight: 2.2 lbs. Length: 14.37 in. Power: Precharged pneumatic. Sights: Fixed front ramp, adjustable rear notch. Features: 7-round rotary magazine, adjustable trigger, 300 Bar max fill, regulated for hunting power, exceptional build quality, Velocity: 656 fps.
Price: **$1,249.00**

BARRA BLACK OPS CO2 REVOLVER
Caliber: .177 BBs. Barrel: Smoothbore, 2.5 in. Weight: 1.92 lbs. Length: 7.25 in. Power: CO2. Sights: Fixed front, adjustable rear. Features: 6-round cylinder with realistic shells, Weaver-style scope rail, operates either double or single action, working ejector rod, black metal frame with black plastic grips, available with 2.5-in. barrel and chrome finish. Velocity: 435 fps.
Price: **$80.00**

BEEMAN 2004 (P17) PISTOL
Caliber: .177 pellet. Barrel: Rifled. Weight: 1.7 lbs. Length: 9.25 in. Power: Single-stroke pneumatic. Sights: Adjustable fiber-optic. Features: Polymer frame, recoilless. Velocity: 410 fps.
Price: **$65.00**

BEEMAN 2027 PCP PISTOL
Caliber: .177 Barrel: Rifled. Weight: 1.7 lbs. Length: 9.25 in. Power: Precharged pneumatic. Sights: Adjustable open sights. Features: Textured grip, 12-round magazine, adjustable velocity, 60 shots per fill (at 600 fps), adjustable trigger. Velocity: 600 fps.
Price: **$190.00**

BENJAMIN MARAUDER PCP PISTOL
Caliber: .22 Barrel: Rifled. Weight: 2.7-3 lbs. Length: Pistol length 18 in./ Carbine length 29.75 in. Power: Precharged pneumatic Sights: None. Grooved for optics. Features: Multi-shot (eight-round rotary magazine), bolt action, shrouded steel barrel, two-stage adjustable trigger, includes both pistol grips and a carbine stock and is built in America. Velocity: 700 fps.
Price: **$420.00**

BENJAMIN MARAUDER WOODS WALKER PCP PISTOL
Caliber: .22 Barrel: Rifled. Weight: 2.7 lbs. Length: Pistol length 18 in./ Carbine length 29.75 in. Power: Precharged pneumatic Sights: Includes

Prices given are believed to be accurate at time of publication however, many factors affect retail pricing so exact prices are not possible.

78TH EDITION, 2024 ✦ **567**

CenterPoint Multi-TAC Quick Aim Sight. Features: Multi-shot (8-round rotary magazine) bolt action, shrouded steel barrel, two-stage adjustable trigger, includes both pistol grips and a carbine stock and is built in America. Velocity: 700 fps.
Price: **$510.00**

BENJAMIN TRAIL MARK II NP AIR PISTOL
Caliber: .177 pellets. Barrel: Rifled. Weight: 3.43 lbs. Length: 16 in. Power: Single cock, nitro piston. Sights: Fiber-optic front, fully adjustable rear. Features: Grooved for scope, Velocity: To 625 fps.
Price: **$124.00**

BERETTA APX BLOWBACK AIR PISTOL
Caliber: .177 steel BBs. Barrel: Smoothbore. Weight: 1.47 lbs. Length: 7.48 in. Power: CO2. Sights: Fixed. Features: Highly accurate replica action pistol, 19-shot capacity, front accessory rail, metal and ABS plastic construction. Velocity: 400 fps.
Price: **$75.00**

BERETTA M84FS AIR PISTOL
Caliber: .177 steel BBs. Barrel: Smoothbore Weight: 1.4 lbs. Length: 7 in. Power: CO2. Sights: Fixed. Features: Highly realistic replica action pistol, blowback operation, full metal construction. Velocity: To 360 fps.
Price: **$105.00**

BERETTA PX4 STORM CO₂ PISTOL
Caliber: .177 pellet /.177 steel BBs. Barrel: Rifled Weight: 1.6 lbs. Length: 7.6 in. Power: CO2. Sights: Blade front sight and fixed rear sight. Features: Semi-automatic, 16-shot capacity with a maximum of 40 shots per fill, dual ammo capable. Velocity: To 380 fps.
Price: **$110.00**

BERETTA ELITE II CO₂ PISTOL
Caliber: .177 steel BBs. Barrel: Smoothbore Weight: 1.5 lbs. Length: 8.5 in. Power: CO2. Sights: Blade front sight and fixed rear sight. Features: Semi-automatic, 19-shot capacity. Velocity: Up to 410 fps.
Price: **$58.00**

BERETTA M9A3 FULL AUTO BB PISTOL
Caliber: .177 steel BBs. Barrel: Smoothbore Weight: NA. Length: NA. Power: CO2. Sights: Blade front sight and fixed rear sight. Features: Can operate as semi-automatic or fully automatic, full size 18-shot magazine, blowback slide, single/double action, ambidextrous safety. Velocity: To 380 fps.
Price: **$170.00**

BERETTA 92A1 CO2 FULL AUTO BB PISTOL
Caliber: .177 steel BBs. Barrel: Smoothbore Weight: 2.4 lbs. Length: 8.5 in. Power: CO2. Sights: Fixed. Features: Highly realistic replica action pistol, 18-shot semi-automatic, full metal construction, selectable fire semi-automatic and full-automatic. Velocity: To 330 fps.
Price: **$150.00**

BERETTA 92FS CO₂ PELLET GUN
Caliber: .177 pellets. Barrel: Rifled Weight: 2.75 lbs. Length: 8.0 in. Power: CO2. Sights: Fixed front sight, rear adjustable for windage. Features: Highly realistic replica-action pistol, eight-shot semi-automatic, full metal construction, available in various finishes and grips. Velocity: To 425 fps.
Price: ....**$240.00–$320.00**

BERSA THUNDER 9 PRO BB PISTOL
Caliber: .177 steel BBs. Barrel: Smoothbore Weight: 1.17 lbs. Length: 7.56 in. Power: CO2. Sights: Fixed, 3 white dot system. Features: Highly realistic replica action pistol, 19-shot semi-automatic, composite/synthetic construction Velocity: To 400 fps.
Price: $55.00v

BERSA BP9CC BLOWBACK AIR PISTOL
Caliber: .177 steel BBs. Barrel: Smoothbore. Weight: 1.35 lbs. Length: 6.61 in. Power: CO2. Sights: Fixed 3-dot system. Features: Blowback, metal slide, weaver accessory rail, is also available in a nonblowback version. Velocity: 350 fps.
Price: $100.00

BROCOCK ATOMIC XR PCP PISTOL
Calibers: .177, .22, .25. Barrel: Rifled, match grade. Weight: 4 lbs. Length: 14 in. Power: Precharged pneumatic. Sights: None, 11mm rail. Features: Optional Picatinny top and side rail, side lever action, single-shot tray or 11-shot magazine, weight and position adjustable trigger, shrouded barrel with adaptor for second-stage silencer, side power adjustor. Up to 30–33 shots and 16–18 ft-lbs of energy at full power depending on caliber. Velocities: Adjustable.
Price: $1,599.00

BROWNING BUCK MARK URX

BROWNING BUCK MARK AIR PISTOL
Caliber: .177 pellets. Barrel: Rifled Weight: 1.5 lbs. Length: 12.0 in. Power: Single cock, spring-piston. Sights: Front ramp sight, fully adjustable rear notch sight. Features: Weaver rail for scope mounting, light cocking force. Velocity: 360 fps.
Price: $50.00

CHIAPPA AG92 CO₂ PISTOL
Caliber: .177 pellets. Barrel: Rifled, 4.8 in. Weight: 1.3 lbs. Length: 8.6 in. Power: CO2. Sights: Adjustable rear. Features: Powered by two 12-gram CO2 cylinders, holds two seven-round pellet cylinders, single/double action, polymer frame reinforced with fiberglass. Velocity: 330 fps.
Price: $139.00

CHIAPPA FAS 6004 PNEUMATIC PISTOL
Caliber: .177 pellets. Barrel: Rifled. Weight: 2 lbs. Length: 11.0 in. Power: Single stroke pneumatic. Sights: Fully adjustable target rear sight. Features: Walnut ambidextrous grip, fully adjustable trigger. Also available with an adjustable target grip. Velocity: 330 fps.
Price: ....$443.00–$569.00

CHIAPPA RHINO 50DS CO₂ REVOLVER
Caliber: .177 BBs. Barrel: Smoothbore, 5 in. Weight: 2.5 lbs. Length: 9.5 in. Power: CO2. Sights: Adjustable rear sight. Features: Single/double action, six-shot capacity, black or silver frame, under-barrel accessory rail. Velocity: 330 fps.
Price: ....$150.00–$180.00

COBRAY INGRAM M11 CO₂ BB SUBMACHINE GUN
Caliber: .177 BBs. Barrel: Smoothbore. Weight: 1.2 lbs. Length: 10.0 in. Power: CO2. Sights: Fixed sights. Features: Semi-automatic, 39-shot capacity, folding metal stock. Velocity: 394 fps.
Price: $90.00

COLT DEFENDER BB PISTOL
Caliber: .177 steel BBs. Barrel: Smoothbore Weight: 1.6 lbs. Length: 6.75 in. Power: CO2. Sights: Fixed with blade ramp front sight. Features: Semi-

Prices given are believed to be accurate at time of publication however, many factors affect retail pricing so exact prices are not possible.

78TH EDITION, 2024 ✦ 569

automatic, 16-shot capacity, all metal construction, realistic weight and feel. Velocity: 410 fps.
Price: $43.00

COLT 1911 A1 CO₂ PELLET PISTOL
Caliber: .177 pellets. Barrel: Rifled Weight: 2.4 lbs. Length: 9.0 in. Power: CO2. Sights: Blade ramp front sight and adjustable rear sight. Features: Semi-automatic, 8-shot capacity, all metal construction, realistic weight and feel. Velocity: 425 fps.
Price: $260.00

COLT COMMANDER CO₂ PISTOL
Caliber: .177 steel BBs. Barrel: Smoothbore. Weight: 2.1 lbs. Length: 8.5 in. Power: CO2. Sights: Blade front sight and fixed rear sight. Features: Semi-automatic, blowback action, 18-shot capacity, highly realistic replica pistol. Velocity: 325 fps.
Price: $96.00

CROSMAN MK45 BB PISTOL
Caliber: .177 steel BBs. Barrel: Smoothbore. Weight: 1.1 lbs. Length: 7.5 in. Power: CO2. Sights: Fixed. Features: 20-round drop-out magazine, accessory rail. Velocity: 480 fps.
Price: $49.00

COLT M45 QCBP CO₂ PISTOL
Caliber: .177 steel BBs. Barrel: Smoothbore. Weight: 1.75 lbs. Length: 8.75 in. Power: CO2. Sights: Fixed three-dot sights, rear sight adjustable for windage. Features: Blowback action, 19-round drop-free magazine, desert tan steel slide, polymer frame, under-barrel Picatinny rail. Velocity: 400 fps.
Price: $59.00

COLT PYTHON CO₂ PISTOL
Caliber: .177 steel BBs. Barrel: Smoothbore Weight: 1.1 lbs. Length: 11.5 in. Power: CO2. Sights: Fixed front, adjustable rear. Features: Includes three 10-round removable clips, double/single action. Velocity: 410 fps.
Price: $35.00

COLT SAA CO₂ PELLET REVOLVER
Caliber: .177 pellets. Barrel: Rifled. Weight: 2.1 lbs. Length: 11 in. Power: CO2. Sights: Blade front sight and fixed rear sight. Features: Full metal revolver with manual safety, realistic loading, six individual shells, highly accurate, full metal replica pistol, multiple finishes and grips available. Velocity: 380 fps.
Price: $101.00

JOHN WAYNE "DUKE" COLT SINGLE ACTION ARMY CO₂ PELLET REVOLVER
Caliber: .177 steel BBs. Barrel: Smoothbore. Weight: 2.1 lbs. Length: 11 in. Power: CO2. Sights: Blade front sight and fixed rear sight. Features: Officially licensed "John Wayne Duke" imagery and signature, full metal revolver with manual safety, realistic loading, six individual shells, highly accurate, full metal replica pistol, multiple finishes and grips available. Velocity: 380 fps.
Price: $135.00

COMETA INDIAN AIR PISTOL
Caliber: .177 pellets. Barrel: Rifled. Weight: 2.43 lbs. Length: 10.43 in. Power: Spring Powered. Sights: Blade front sight and adjustable rear sight. Features: Single shot, cold hammer-forged barrel, textured grips. Velocity: 492 fps.
Price: ....$199.00–$219.00

CROSMAN 2240 CO₂ PISTOL
Caliber: .22. Barrel: Rifled. Weight: 1.8 lbs. Length: 11.13 in. Power: CO2. Sights: Blade front, rear adjustable. Features: Single-shot bolt action, ambidextrous grip, all metal construction. Velocity: 460 fps.
Price: $84.00

CROSMAN 2300S TARGET PISTOL
Caliber: .177 pellets. Barrel: Rifled. Weight: 2.66 lbs. Length: 16 in. Power: CO2. Sights: Front fixed sight and Williams notched rear sight. Features: Meets IHMSA rules for Production Class Silhouette Competitions. Lothar

Walter match-grade barrel, adjustable trigger, adjustable hammer, stainless steel bolt, 60 shots per CO2 cartridge. Velocity: 520 fps.
Price: **$350.00**

CROSMAN 2300T CO2 PISTOL
Caliber: .177 pellets. Barrel: Rifled. Weight: 2.66 lbs. Length: 13.25 in. Power: CO2. Sights: fixed front sight and LPA rear sight. Features: Single-shot, bolt action, adjustable trigger, designed for shooting clubs and organizations that teach pistol shooting and capable of firing 40 shots per CO2 cartridge. Velocity: 420 fps.
Price: **$230.00**

CROSMAN 1701P SILHOUETTE PCP AIR PISTOL
Caliber: .177 pellets. Barrel: Rifled Lothar Walther Match. Weight: 2.5 lbs. Length: 14.75 in. Power: precharged pneumatic. Sights: fixed front sight rear sight not included. Features: Adjustable trigger, designed for shooting silhouette competition, 50 shots per fill. Velocity: 450 fps.
Price: **$500.00**

CROSMAN 1720T PCP TARGET PISTOL
Caliber: .177 pellets. Barrel: Rifled Lothar Walther Match. Weight: 2.96 lbs. Length: 18.00 in. Power: Precharged Pneumatic. Sights: Not included. Features: Adjustable trigger, designed for shooting silhouettes, fully shrouded barrel, 50 shots per fill. Velocity: 750 fps.
Price: **$522.00**

CROSMAN SNR357 BB CO₂ REVOLVER
Caliber: .177 steel BBs/.177 pellets. Barrel: Smoothbore, 2.5 in. Weight: 1.9 lbs. Length: 6.75 in. Power: CO2. Sights: Fixed front, adjustable rear sight. Features: six-shot capacity, full metal construction, swing-out cylinder, double or single action, comes with reusable shells. Velocity: Up to 500 fps with alloy pellets.
Price: **$99.00**

CROSMAN SR357 BB CO₂ REVOLVER
Caliber: .177 steel BBs. Barrel: Smoothbore Weight: 2.00 lbs. Length: 11.73 in. Power: CO2. Sights: Adjustable rear sight, fixed front blade. Features: Full metal revolver in "stainless steel" finish. Swing-out cylinder. Double or single action. Comes with shells for BBs. Velocity: Up to 450 fps.
Price: **$156.00**

CROSMAN FULL AUTO A4P PISTOL
Caliber: .177 steel BBs. Barrel: Smoothbore. Weight: 6 lbs. Length: 21.2 in. Power: CO2. Sights: None, comes with red-dot sight. Features: Tactical-style AR full-/semi-auto pistol, blowback action, AR-compatible pistol grip, quad rail forearm for accessory mounting, 25-round removable magazine, uses two 12-gram CO2 cylinders. Velocity: Up to 400 fps.
Price: **$231.00**

CROSMAN FULL AUTO P1 PISTOL
Caliber: .177 steel BBs. Barrel: Smoothbore Weight: 2.5 lbs. Length: 8.5 in. Power: CO2. Sights: Fixed, rail-mounted laser included. Features: Full-/semi-auto pistol, blowback action, metal frame and slide, single/double action, 20-round removable magazine, Picatinny rail. Velocity: 400 fps.
Price: **$207.00**

CROSMAN TRIPLE THREAT CO₂ REVOLVER
Caliber: .177 steel BBs/.177 pellets. Barrel: Rifled. Weight: Variable. Length: Variable. Power: CO2. Sights: Adjustable rear sight. Features: Comes with three barrels (3, 6, and 8 in.) and six-shot BB clip and 10-shot .177 lead pellet clip, single/double action, diecast full metal frame. Velocity: Up to 425 fps. with steel BBs.
Price: **$120.00**

CROSMAN C11 CO₂ BB GUN
Caliber: .177 steel BBs. Barrel: Smoothbore Weight: 1.4 lbs. Length: 7.0 in. Power: CO2. Sights: Fixed. Features: Compact semi-automatic BB pistol,

Prices given are believed to be accurate at time of publication however, many factors affect retail pricing so exact prices are not possible.

78TH EDITION, 2024 ⊕ **571**

front accessory rail. Velocity: 480 fps.
Price: **$60.00**

CROSMAN CM9B MAKO BB PISTOL
Caliber: .177 BBs. Barrel: Smoothbore. Weight: 1.7 lbs. Length: 8.6 in. Power: CO_2. Sights: Fiber optic. Blowback action, tricolor, accessory rail. Velocity: 425 fps.
Price: **$72.00**

CROSMAN PFM16 FULL METAL CO₂ BB PISTOL
Caliber: .177 steel BBs. Barrel: Smoothbore Weight: 1.6 lbs. Length: 6.5 in. Power: CO_2. Sights: Fixed. Features: Compact semi-automatic BB pistol, full metal construction, 20-shot capacity, kit includes: CO_2, BBs, and holster. Velocity: 400 fps.
Price: **$60.00**

CROSMAN PFAM9B FULL AUTO PISTOL
Caliber: .177 steel BBs. Barrel: Smoothbore Weight: 1.6 lbs. Length: 6.5 in. Power: CO_2. Sights: Fixed. Features: Full metal construction, full-auto, blowback slide, 20-shot capacity. Velocity: 400 fps.
Price: **$156.00**

CROSMAN AMERICAN CLASSIC P1377/1322 AIR PISTOL
Caliber: .177 or .22. Barrel: Rifled Weight: 2 lbs. Length: 13.63 in. Power: Multi-pump pneumatic. Sights: front blade and ramp, adjustable rear. Features: Single shot, bolt action, available with brown (.177 only) or black grips, pistol grip shoulder stock available separately. Velocities: To 695 fps (.177); to 460 fps (.22).
Price: .... **$72.00–$88.00**

CROSMAN VIGILANTE CO₂ REVOLVER
Caliber: .177 steel BBs/.177 pellets. Barrel: Rifled. Weight: 2 lbs. Length: 11.38 in. Power: CO_2. Sights: Blade front, rear adjustable. Features: Single- and double-action revolver (10-shot pellet/six-shot BBs) synthetic frame and finger-molded grip design. Velocity: 465 fps.
Price: **$73.00**

CROSMAN 1911 CO₂ BB PISTOL
Caliber: .177 steel BBs. Barrel: Smoothbore. Weight: 0.88 lbs. Length: 7.9 in. Power: CO_2. Sights: Fixed. Features: 20-round capacity, double-action-only, Picatinny under-rail. Velocity: 480 fps.
Price: **$60.00**

CZ P-09 DUTY CO₂ PISTOL
Caliber: .177 BBs/.177 flat-head pellets. Barrel: Rifled. Weight: 1.6 lbs. Length: 8.2 in. Power: CO_2. Sights: Three-dot fixed sights. Features: Blowback action, manual safety, double-action-only trigger, 16-round capacity in a 2x8 shot stick magazine, Weaver-style accessory rail, threaded muzzle, blue or two-tone finish, ambidextrous safety with decocker. Velocity: 492 fps.
Price: **$123.00**

CZ-75 CO₂ PISTOL
Caliber: .177 BBs. Barrel: Smooth. Weight: 2.1 lbs. Length: 8.2 in. Power: CO_2. Sights: Fixed sights. Features: Blowback action, manual safety, full metal construction, single-action trigger, removable 17-round BB magazine, Weaver-style accessory rail, also available as a non-blowback compact version. Velocity: 312 fps.
Price: **$220.00**

CZ 75 SP-01 SHADOW CO₂ BB PISTOL
Caliber: .177 steel BBs. Barrel: Smoothbore threaded for barrel extension. Power: CO_2. Weight: 1.3 lbs. Length: 8.4 in. Sights: Fiber optics front and rear. Features: Non-blowback, double action, accessory rail, 21-round capacity, also available in a heavier-weight, blowback version. Velocity: 380 fps.
Price: **$65.00**

CZ SHADOW 2 CO₂ BB PISTOL
Caliber: .177 steel BBs. Barrel: Smoothbore. Weight: 2.7 lbs. Length: 8.5 in. Power: CO_2. Sights: Fiber optic, adjustable rear. Features: Full metal construction, adjustable travel trigger, adjustable hop up, double action, checkered grip, individual serial number, blowback, 18-round dropout magazine, uses one 12-gram CO_2 cylinder, under-barrel accessory rail, adjustable magazine release. Velocity: 285 fps.
Price: **$300.00**

CZ 75 P-07 DUTY PISTOL
Caliber: .177 steel BBs. Barrel: Smoothbore. Weight: 1.81 lbs. Length: 7.5 in. Power: CO2. Sights: Fixed. Features: Full metal construction, accessory rail, blowback, 20-round dropout magazine, threaded barrel, blue or two-tone finish. Also available in a non-blowback, lower-priced version. Velocity: 342 fps.
Price: **$120.00**

CZ 75D COMPACT CO_2 BB PISTOL
Caliber: .177 steel BBs. Barrel: Smoothbore. Weight: 1.5 lbs. Length: 7.4 in. Power: CO2. Sights: Adjustable rear sight and blade front sight. Features: Compact design, non-blowback action, blue or two-tone finish, accessory rail. Velocity: 380 fps.
Price: **$63.00**

DAISY POWERLINE 340 AIR PISTOL
Caliber: .177 steel BBs. Barrel: Smoothbore. Weight: 1.0 lbs. Length: 8.5 in. Power: Single cock, spring-piston. Sights: Rear sight fixed, front blade. Features: Spring-air action, 200-shot BB reservoir with a 13-shot Speed-load Clip located in the grip. Velocity: 240 fps.
Price: **$30.00**

DAISY POWERLINE 415 CO_2 BB PISTOL
Caliber: .177 steel BBs. Barrel: Smoothbore. Weight: 1.0 lbs. Length: 8.6 in. Power: CO2. Sights: Front blade, Rear fixed open rear. Features: Semi-automatic 21-shot BB pistol. Velocity: 500 fps.
Price: **$39.00**

DAISY 426 PISTOL
Caliber: .177 steel BBs. Barrel: Smoothbore. Weight: 1 lbs. Length: 6.8 in. Power: CO2. Sights: Front blade, rear fixed open. Features: Semi-automatic, eight-shot removable clip, lower accessory rail Velocity: 430 fps.
Price: **$33.00**

DAISY POWERLINE 5501 CO_2 PISTOL
Caliber: .177 steel BBs. Barrel: Smoothbore. Weight: 1.0 lbs. Length: 6.8 in. Power: CO2. Sights: Blade and ramp front, fixed rear. Features: CO2 semi-automatic blowback action. 15-shot clip. Velocity: 430 fps.
Price: **$77.00**

DAN WESSON 2.5/4/6/8 IN. REVOLVER
Caliber: .177 BBs or .177 pellets. Barrel: Smoothbore (BB version) or Rifled (Pellet version). Weights: 1.65–2.29 lbs. Lengths: 8.3–13.3 in. Power: CO2. Sights: Blade front and adjustable rear. Features: Highly realistic replica revolver with swing-out six-shot cylinder, Weaver-style scope rail, multiple finishes and grip configurations, six realistic cartridges, includes a speedloader. Velocities: 318–426 fps.
Price: .... **$150.00–$210.00**

DAN WESSON 715 2.5/4 /6 IN. REVOLVER
Caliber: .177 BBs or .177 pellets. Barrel: Smoothbore (BB version) or Rifled (pellet version). Weights: 2.2–2.7 lbs. Lengths: 8.3–11.7 in. Power: CO2. Sights: Blade front and adjustable rear. Features: Highly realistic replica revolver, accessory rail, multiple finishes and grip configurations, six realistic cartridges, includes a speedloader. Velocities: 318–426 fps.
Price: **$160.00**

DAN WESSON VALOR 1911 PISTOL
Caliber: .177 pellets. Barrel: Rifled. Weight: 2.2 lbs. Length: 8.7 in. Power: CO2. Sights: Non-adjustable. Features: Non-blowback, full metal construction, 12-round capacity in two six-round drum magazines. Velocities: 332 fps.
Price: **$140.00**

DIANA AIRBUG CO_2 PISTOL
Caliber: .177, .22 pellets. Barrel: Rifled, 8.3 in. Weight: 2 lbs. Length: 14 in. Power: CO2. Sights: Front post, adjustable rear. Features: Hardwood, ambidextrous grip, bolt action, nine-shot (.117), seven-shot (.22), or single shot, comes with a soft-sided case. Velocities: 525 fps (.177), 460 fps (.22).
Price: **$180.00**

DIANA BANDIT PCP PISTOL
Caliber: .177, .22 pellets. Barrel: Rifled, 9.5 in. Weight: 2.2 lbs. Length: 20.1 in. Power: Precharged pneumatic. Sights: Front post, adjustable rear, 11mm dovetail under rear sight. Features: Hardwood, ambidextrous grip,

bolt action, nine-shot (.117), seven-shot (.22), or single shot, two-stage adjustable Diana Improved Trigger (DIT), comes with a soft-sided case. Velocities: 725 fps (.177), 630 fps (.22).
Price: **$250.00**

DIANA LP 8 PISTOL
Caliber: .177 pellets. Barrel: Rifled. Weight: 3.20 lbs. Length: 7.00 in. Power: Spring powered. Sights: Fixed front sight with fully adjustable rear sight. Features: Powerful spring-powered air pistol, single cock delivers full power, exceptional design and build quality. Velocity: 700 fps.
Price: **$350.00**

EVANIX AR6-P PCP PISTOL
Caliber: .22 pellets. Barrel: Rifled, 10 in. Weight: 3.1 lbs. Length: 17.3 in. Power: Precharged pneumatic. Sights: None, 11mm dovetail rail. Features: Ambidextrous walnut target-style grips, six-shot magazine, spare mag included. Velocity: Up to 900 fps.
Price: **$660.00**

FEINWERKBAU P11 PICCOLO AIR PISTOL
Caliber: .177 pellets. Barrel: Rifled. Weight: 1.6 lbs. Length: 13.58 in. Power: Precharged pneumatic. Sights: Front post, fully adjustable rear blade, Features: 10m competition class pistol, meets ISSF requirements, highly adjustable match trigger, Velocity: 492 fps.
Price: **$1,600.00**

FEINWERKBAU P8X PCP 10-METER AIR PISTOL
Caliber: .177 pellets. Barrel: Rifled, 8.6 in. Weight: 2.09 lbs. Length: 16.33 in. Power: Precharged pneumatic. Sights: Front post, fully adjustable rear blade. Features: 10m competition class pistol with highly customizable grip system, meets ISSF requirements, highly adjustable match trigger. Also available with a shorter barrel. Velocity: 508 fps.
Price: **$2,100.00**

GAMO C-15 BONE COLLECTOR CO2 PISTOL
Caliber: .177 BB/.177 pellets. Barrel: Smooth. Weight: 1.5 lbs. Length: 10 in. Power: CO2. Sights: Fixed. Features: Blowback action, approx. 80 shots per CO2 cylinder, single/double action, manual safety, has two side-by-side eight-shot magazines Velocity: 450 fps with PBA pellets.
Price: **$94.00**

GAMO GP-20 COMBAT CO₂ BB PISTOL
Caliber: .177 BBs. Barrel: Smooth. Weight: 1 lb. Length: 10 in. Power: CO2. Sights: Fixed with fiber-optic rear. Features: Single/double action, manual safety, 20 BB magazine. Velocity: 400 fps.
Price: **$40.00**

GAMO P-900 IGT AIR PISTOL
Caliber: .177 pellets. Barrel: Rifled. Weight: 1.3 lbs. Length: 12.6 in. Power: Single cock, gas pistol. Sights: Fiber-optic front and fully adjustable fiber-optic rear. Features: Break-barrel single-shot, ergonomic design, rubberized grip. Velocity: 508 fps.
Price: **$84.00**

GAMO P-25 AIR PISTOL
Caliber: .177 pellets. Barrel: Rifled. Weight: 1.5 lbs. Length: 7.75 in. Power: CO2. Sights: Fixed. Features: Semi-automatic, 16-shot capacity, realistic blowback action. Velocity: 450 fps.
Price: **$84.00**

GAMO P-27 AIR PISTOL
Caliber: .177 BB/.177 pellets. Barrel: Smooth. Weight: 1.5 lbs. Length: 7 in. Power: CO2. Sights: Fixed with white dots. Features: Single/double action, semi-automatic, 16-shot capacity in two eight-round clips, non-blowback action, rail under barrel. Velocity: 400 fps.
Price: **$63.00**

GAMO PR-776 CO₂ REVOLVER
Caliber: .177 pellets. Barrel: Rifled. Weight: 2.29 lbs. Length: 11.5 in. Power: CO2. Sights: Fixed front sight with fully adjustable rear sight. Features: All metal frame, comes with two eight-shot clips, double- and single-action. Velocity: 438 fps.
Price: **$110.00**

GAMO PT-85 CO₂ PISTOL
Caliber: .177 pellets. Barrel: Rifled. Weight: 1.5 lbs. Length: 7.8 in. Power: CO2. Sights: Fixed. Features: Semi-automatic, 16-shot capacity, realistic blowback action. Velocity: 450 fps.
Price: **$95.00**

GLETCHER NGT F CO₂ BB REVOLVER
Caliber: .177 steel BBs. Barrel: Smoothbore. Weight: 1.54 lbs. Length: 9.00 in. Power: CO2. Sights: Fixed. Features: Full metal frame, highly realistic replica, seven-shot cylinder with realistic "shells," double action and single action, available in blued and polished silver finishes, also available in a

pellet version with a rifled barrel ($170–$200). Velocity: 403 fps.
Price: .... **$170.00–$190.00**

GLOCK 17 GEN 3/GEN 4/GEN 5 CO₂ PISTOL
Caliber: .177 BBs. Barrel: Smoothbore. Weight: 1.6 lbs. Length: 7.75 in. Power: CO2. Sights: Fixed. Features: Blowback action, metal slide and magazine, 18-BB capacity, manual safety, double-action trigger, replica of the Glock 17 firearm. Velocity: 365 fps.
Price: .... **$74.00–$140.00**

GLOCK 19 GEN3 CO₂ PISTOL
Caliber: .177 BBs. Barrel: Smoothbore. Weight: 1.6 lbs. Length: 7.25 in. Power: CO2. Sights: Fixed Features: Non-blowback action, manual safety, 16-BB capacity, integrated Weaver-style accessory rail, double-action trigger, replica of the Glock 19 firearm. Velocity: 410 fps.
Price: **$54.00**

GLOCK 19 X CO₂ PISTOL
Caliber: .177 BBs. Barrel: Smoothbore. Weight: 1.6 lbs. Length: 7.5 in. Power: CO2. Sights: Fixed. Features: Blowback action, desert tan, metal slide, manual safety, 18-BB magazine, integrated Weaver-style accessory rail, double-action trigger, replica of the Glock 19 firearm. Velocity: 377 fps.
Price: **$75.00**

HAMMERLI AP-20 AIR PISTOL
Caliber: .177 pellets. Barrel: Rifled, match. Weight: 2.2 lbs. Length: 16.34 in. Power: Precharged pneumatic. Sights: Fully adjustable micrometer. Features: Two-stage adjustable trigger factory set to 500-gram pull weight, single shot, bolt action, up to 180 shots per fill, walnut grip with 3D adjustment, tunable front sight with three widths, adjustable width rear sight, comes with six barrel jackets in different colors. Velocity: 492 fps.
Price: **$900.00**

HATSAN USA JET II PCP PISTOL/CARBINE COMBO
Calibers: .177, .22, .25. Barrel: Rifled, 7.9 in. Weight: 2 lbs. without buttstock. Length: 15 in. without buttstock. Power: Precharged pneumatic. Stock: Ambidextrous synthetic. Sights: Three integrated flip-up sights, Picatinny rail for scope mounting. Features: Easily converts from pistol to

carbine with a removable and adjustable buttstock, 22.8 – 24.6 in. with buttstock, side lever cocking, removable dual black air cylinders with built-in pressure gauge, replacement air cylinders also available in red, blue, or green, two Picatinny side rails, shrouded barrel, two 6-8 shot magazines (depending on caliber) included, 30-48 shots per fill depending on caliber. Velocities: .177/788 fps, .22/700 fps, .25/600 fps with lead pellets.
Price: **$350.00**

HATSAN MODEL 25 SUPERCHARGER QE AIR PISTOL
Caliber: .177 or .22 pellets. Barrel: Rifled. Weight: 3.9 lbs. Length: 20 in. Power: Single cock, air piston. Sights: Fiber-optic front and fully adjustable fiber-optic rear. Features: Molded right-handed grips, fully adjustable "Quattro" two-stage trigger, Quiet Energy-integrated sound moderator, 11mm dovetail grooves, XRS recoil reduction system. Velocity: 800 fps.
Price: **$120.00**

H&K VP9 BB CO₂ PISTOL
Caliber: .177 steel BBs. Barrel: Smoothbore. Weight: 1.42 lbs. Length: 7.2 in. Power: CO2. Sights: Fixed. Features: Highly realistic replica, blowback action, integrated front weaver accessory rail, 18-round magazine. Velocity: 350 fps.
Price: **$95.00**

H&K HK45 CO₂ BB PISTOL
Caliber: .177 steel BBs. Barrel: Smoothbore. Weight: 1.4 lbs. Length: 8.0 in. Power: CO2. Sights: Fixed. Features: Highly realistic replica, integrated front weaver accessory rail, 20-shot capacity, double-action-only. Velocity: 400 fps.
Price: **$38.00**

H&K USP CO₂ BB PISTOL
Caliber: .177 BBs. Barrel: Smoothbore. Weight: 2.15 lbs. Length: 7.75 in. Power: CO2. Sights: Fixed white dot. Features: Highly realistic replica, blowback, integrated front weaver accessory rail, single action/double action, realistic hammer movement, 16-shot drop-free magazine, metal barrel and slide. Also available in a less expensive non-blowback version. Velocity: 325 fps.
Price: **$88.00**

Prices given are believed to be accurate at time of publication however, many factors affect retail pricing so exact prices are not possible.

78TH EDITION, 2024 ◈ 575

MORINI MOR-162EL AIR PISTOL

Caliber: .177 pellets. Barrel: Rifled. Weight: 2.25 lbs. Length: 16.14 in. Power: Precharged pneumatic. Sights: Front post, rear adjustable for windage. Features: Adjustable electronic trigger, single-shot bolt action, extreme match-grade accuracy, over 200 regulated shots per 200 bar fill, available with different grip sizes. Velocity: 500 fps.
Price: $2,250.00

MORINI CM 200EI AIR PISTOL

Caliber: .177 pellets. Barrel: Lothar Walther rifled. Weight: 2.17 lbs. Length: 15.75 in. Power: Precharged pneumatic. Sights: Front post, rear diopter/micrometer adjustable. Features: Adjustable electronic trigger, single-shot bolt action, digital manometer, battery life of 15,000 shots, match-grade accuracy, available with medium or large grip size, muzzle compensator, 150 regulated shots per 200 bar fill, comes with two air cylinders. Velocity: 492 fps.
Price: $2,600

RUGER MARK IV PELLET PISTOL

Caliber: .177 pellets. Barrel: Rifled. Weight: 2.15 lbs. Length: 11 in. Power: Spring piston. Sights: Fiber-optic fixed front, adjustable rear. Features: Single shot, single-stage trigger, single stroke cocking. Velocity: 369 fps.
Price: $55.00

SCHOFIELD NO. 3 REVOLVER, FULL METAL

Caliber: .177 steel BBs or .177 pellets. Barrel: Smoothbore. Weight: 2.4 lbs. Length: 12.5 in. Power: CO2. Sights: Fixed. Features: Highly detailed replica top-break revolver, six-shot capacity, realistic reusable cartridges, available in distressed black with imitation wood grips and plated steel with imitation ivory grips. Velocity: Up to 430 fps.
Price: $110.00

SIG SAUER X-FIVE ASP .177 CO₂ PISTOL

Caliber: .177 pellets. Barrel: Smoothbore. Weight: 2.75 lbs. Length: 8.7 in. Power: CO2. Sights: Adjustable. Features: Realistic replica action pistol, 20-shot capacity, front accessory rail, black or silver finish, full metal construction, metal slide with blowback action. Velocity: 430 fps.
Price: $160.00

SIG SAUER 1911 METAL BLOWBACK CO₂ BB PISTOL

Caliber: .177 steel BBs. Barrel: Smoothbore. Weight: 2.0 lbs. Length: 8.75 in. Power: CO2. Sights: Fixed. Features: Extremely Realistic replica action pistol, 18-shot capacity, front accessory rail, full metal construction, metal slide with blowback action. Velocity: 330 fps.
Price: $140.00

SIG SAUER P226 CO₂ PELLET PISTOL

Caliber: .177 pellets. Barrel: Rifled. Weight: 2.35 lbs. Length: 8.25 in. Power: CO2. Sights: Fixed. Features: Highly detailed replica action pistol, 16-shot capacity, front accessory rail, full metal construction, metal slide with blowback action, available in dark earth and black. Velocity: 450 fps.
Price: $130.00

SIG SAUER P320 CO₂ PISTOL

Caliber: .177 BBs/.177 pellets. Barrel: Rifled. Weight: 2.2 lbs. Length: 9.6 in. Power: CO2. Sights: Fixed, white dot. Features: 30-round belt-fed magazine, front accessory rail, polymer frame, metal slide with blowback action, black or coyote tan finish. Velocity: 430 fps.
Price: $140.00

SIG SAUER P365 CO₂ PISTOL
Caliber: .177 BBs. Barrel: Smoothbore. Weight: .8 lbs. Length: 5.75 in. Power: CO2. Sights: Fixed, white dot. Features: 12-round magazine, metal slide with blowback action, black finish, slide locks back after last shot. Velocity: 295 fps.
Price: **$130.00**

SMITH & WESSON MODEL 29 CO₂ REVOLVER
Caliber: .177 BBs. Barrel: Smoothbore, 8.375 in. Weight: 2.65 lbs. with cartridges. Length: 12.14 in. Power: CO2. Sights: Fixed front, adjustable rear. Features: Brown faux wood grip, single/double action, approximately 60 shots per 12-gram cartridge, removable bullet casings. Velocity: 425 fps.
Price: **$150.00**

SMITH & WESSON M&P CO₂ PISTOL
Caliber: .177 steel BBs. Barrel: Smoothbore. Weight: 1.5 lbs. Lengths: 7.5 in. Power: CO2. Sights: Blade front and ramp rear fiber optic. Features: Integrated accessory rail, removable 19-shot BB magazine, double-action-only, synthetic frame available in dark earth brown or black color. Velocity: 300–480 fps.
Price: **$50.00**

SMITH & WESSON M&P 9 M2.0 CO₂ PISTOL
Caliber: .177 steel BBs. Barrel: Smoothbore. Weight: 1.45 lbs. Length: 7.5 in. Power: CO2. Sights: Fixed front sight, fully adjustable rear sight. Features: Blowback action, full-size drop-free magazine with 18-round capacity, comes with three interchangeable backstraps, double- and single-action trigger, Picatinny accessory rail, last-round hold open, ambidextrous slide release. Velocity: 400 fps.
Price: **$110.00**

SMITH & WESSON 327 TRR8 CO₂ BB PISTOL
Caliber: .177 steel BBs. Barrel: Smoothbore. Weight: 2.0 lbs. Length: 12 in. Power: CO2. Sights: Fiber-optic front sight, fully adjustable fiber-optic rear sight. Features: High-quality replica, top-mounted weaver scope rail, weaver accessory rail under the barrel, swing-out cylinder, removable casings and functioning ejector. Velocity: 400 fps.

Price: **$110.00**

SPRINGFIELD ARMORY 1911 MIL-SPEC CO₂ BB PISTOL
Caliber: .177 BBs. Barrel: Smoothbore, 4.1 in. Weight: 2.0 lbs. Length: 8.6 in. Power: CO2. Sights: Fixed 3-dot. Features: Full metal construction, blowback slide, 18-round magazine, single action, checkered grips, approximately 65 shots per fill, slide locks back after last shot, functioning grip safety. Velocity: 320 fps.
Price: **$130.00**

SPRINGFIELD ARMORY XDE CO₂ BB PISTOL
Caliber: .177 BBs. Barrel: Smoothbore, 4.3 in. Weight: 1.95 lbs. Length: 7.75 in. Power: CO2. Sights: Fixed fiber optic. Features: Full metal construction, blowback slide, 18-round drop-free magazine, double/single action, functional takedown lever, ambidextrous safety and magazine release, checkered grips, single slot Picatinny rail, front and rear slide serrations. Velocity: 380 fps.
Price: **$120.00**

SPRINGFIELD ARMORY XDM CO₂ BB PISTOL
Caliber: .177 BBs. Barrel: Smoothbore. Weight: 1.9 lbs. Length: 8 in. Power: CO2. Sights: Fixed fiber optic. Features: Blowback metal slide, polymer frame, interchangeable backstraps, grip safety and trigger safety, functional striker status indicator, 20-round drop-free magazine, functional slide stop lever, field strips like real XDM, Picatinny accessory rail, functional takedown lever, ambidextrous magazine release, slide locks back after last shot, available with 3.8- or 4.5-in. barrel, blue or two tone. Velocity: 325 fps.
Price: .... **$140.00–$170.00**

STEYR M9-A1 PISTOL
Caliber: .177 BBs. Barrel: Smoothbore Weight: 1.2 lbs. Length: 7.5 in. Power: CO2. Sights: Fixed. Features: Non-blowback, accessory rail, metal slide, two-tone or blue finish, 19-round capacity. Velocity: 449 fps.
Price: Blue **$55.00**

Price: Two-tone **$110.00**

STI DUTY ONE CO₂ BB PISTOL
Caliber: .177 steel BBs. Barrel: Smoothbore. Weight: 1.2 lbs. Length: 8.8 in. Power: CO2. Sights: Fixed. Features: Blowback, accessory rail, metal slide,

---

Prices given are believed to be accurate at time of publication however, many factors affect retail pricing so exact prices are not possible.

78TH EDITION, 2024 ✛ **577**

threaded barrel, 20-round magazine. Velocity: 397 fps.
Price: **$110.00**

SWISS ARMS SA92 BB PISTOL
Caliber: .177 BBs. Barrel: Smoothbore. Weight: 2.5 lbs. Length: 8.5 in. Power: CO2. Sights: Fixed. Features: Blowback, accessory rail, full metal construction, stainless finish with brown grips, 20-round magazine. Velocity: 312 fps.
Price: .... **$120.00–$140.00**

SWISS ARMS SA 1911 BB PISTOL
Caliber: .177 BBs. Barrel: Smoothbore. Weight: 2 lbs. Length: 8.6 in. Power: CO2. Sights: Fixed. Features: Blowback, slide locks back when empty, metal construction, single-action-only, desert tan, checkered grips, functional grip safety, accessory rail on some models, 18-round magazine. Velocity: 320 fps.
Price: **$120.00**

TANFOGLIO WITNESS 1911 CO₂ BB PISTOL, BROWN GRIPS
Caliber: .177 steel BBs. Barrel: Smoothbore. Weight: 1.98 lbs. Length: 8.6 in. Power: CO2. Sights: Fixed. Features: Often recognized as the "standard" for 1911 replica action pistols, 18-shot capacity, full metal construction with metal slide with blowback action. Velocity: 320 fps.
Price: **$160.00**

UMAREX LEGENDS MAKAROV ULTRA BLOWBACK CO₂ BB PISTOL
Caliber: .177 steel BBs. Barrel: Smoothbore. Weight: 1.40 lbs. Length: 6.38 in. Power: CO2. Sights: Fixed. Features: Highly realistic replica, all-metal construction with blowback action, semi-automatic and full-auto capable, 16-round capacity. Velocity: 350 fps.
Price: **$70.00**

UMAREX LEGENDS M712 BROOM HANDLE FULL-AUTO CO₂ BB PISTOL
Caliber: .177 steel BBs. Barrel: Smoothbore. Weight: 3.10 lbs. Length: 12.00 in. Power: CO2. Sights: Fixed front sight with rear sight adjustable for elevation. Features: Highly realistic replica that functions as the original, all-metal construction with blowback action, semi- and full-auto capable, 18-round capacity. Velocity: 360 fps.
Price: **$140.00**

UMAREX LEGENDS P08 BLOWBACK CO₂ BB PISTOL
Caliber: .177 steel BBs. Barrel: Smoothbore. Weight: 1.90 lbs. Length: 8.75 in. Power: CO2. Sights: Fixed. Features: Highly realistic replica that functions as the original, all-metal construction with blowback action, 21-round capacity. Also available in a less expensive, non-blowback version. Velocity: 300 fps.
Price: **$133.00**

UMAREX BRODAX BB REVOLVER
Caliber: .177 steel BBs. Barrel: Smoothbore. Weight: 1.52 lbs. Length: 10.0 in. Power: CO2. Sights: Fixed. Features: Aggressively styled BB revolver, 10-shot capacity, top accessory rail, front accessory rail, synthetic construction. Velocity: 375 fps.
Price: **$44.00**

UMAREX D17 BB PISTOL
Caliber: .177 BBs. Barrel: Smoothbore. Weight: 1.6 lbs. Length: 9.5 in. Power: Spring piston. Sights: Fixed fiber optic. Features: Integrated accessory rail, 15-shot capacity. Velocity: 200 fps.
Price: **$22.00**

UMAREX SA10 CO₂ PISTOL
Caliber: .177 pellet or steel BBs. Barrel: 5.0 in. rifled. Weight: 2.05 lbs. Length: 9.25 in. Power: CO2. Sights: Fixed. Features: Full metal slide with polymer grips, blowback action, ported slide with gold-look barrel and breech block, threaded muzzle, magazine holds the CO2 cylinder, an eight-shot rotary clip, and three additional clips, under-barrel accessory rail. Velocity: 420 fps.
Price: **$99.00**

Prices given are believed to be accurate at time of publication however, many factors affect retail pricing so exact prices are not possible.

UMAREX STEEL STORM CO₂ PISTOL
Caliber: .177 steel BBs. Barrel: Smooth, 7.5 in. Weight: 2.7 lbs. Length: 15 in. Power: CO2. Sights: Fixed, Picatinny accessory rail. Features: Submachine gun styling, blowback action, uses two 12-gram CO2 cylinders, 30-round nonremovable magazine, 300-round reservoir, full or semi-automatic modes, six-shot bursts in full-auto mode, up to 300 shots per fill, CO2 housed in a drop-out magazine, can be bulk filled with an adapter (not included). Velocity: 430 fps.
Price: $122.00

UMAREX STRIKE POINT PELLET MULTI-PUMP AIR PISTOL
Caliber: .177 pellets. Barrel: Rifled. Weight: 2.6 lbs. Length: 14.00 in. Power: Multi-pump pneumatic. Sights: Adjustable rear sight, fixed fiber-optic front sight. Features: Variable power based on the number of pumps, bolt action, includes integrated "Silenceair" moderator for quiet shooting. Velocity: Up to 650 fps.
Price: $55.00

UMAREX TAC BB PISTOL WITH FOLDING STOCK
Caliber: .177 BB. Barrel: Smooth bore. Weight: 1.85 lbs. Length: 22.5 in. Power: CO2. Sights: Rear adjustable for windage, blade front. Features: Four Picatinny rails, foldable shoulder stock, semi-automatic. Velocity: 410 fps.
Price: $66.00

UMAREX TDP 45 BB PISTOL
Caliber: .177 BB. Barrel: Smoothbore. Weight: 1 lb. Length: 6.5 in. Power: CO2. Sights: Fixed. Features: 19-round drop-free magazine, double-action-only, under-barrel accessory rail, semi-automatic. Velocity: 410 fps.
Price: $40.00

UMAREX TREVOX AIR PISTOL
Caliber: .177 pellets. Barrel: Rifled. Weight: 3.5 lbs. Length: 18.25 in. Power: Gas piston. Sights: Adjustable rear sight, fixed fiber-optic front sight. Features: Full power from a single cock, suitable for target practice and plinking, includes integrated "Silenceair" moderator for quiet shooting. Velocity: 540 fps.
Price: $90.00

UMAREX XBG CO₂ PISTOL
Caliber: .177 steel BBs. Barrel: Smoothbore. Weight: 0.7 lbs. Length: 6.75 in. Power: CO2. Sights: Fixed. Features: 19-shot capacity, under-barrel accessory rail, double-action-only. Velocity: 410 fps.

Price: $34.00

UZI (KWC) MINI CARBINE
Caliber: .177 steel BBs. Barrel: Smoothbore. Weight: 4.8 lbs. Length: 24/25 in. Power: CO2. Sights: Adjustable. Features: Realistic replica airgun, 25-shot capacity, foldable stock, semi-automatic with realistic blowback system, heavy bolt provides realistic "kick" when firing. Velocity: 344 fps.
Price: $185.00

WALTHER LP500 COMPETITION PCP AIR PISTOL
Caliber: .177 pellets. Barrel: Rifled, match grade. Weight: 2 lbs. Length: 16.5 in. Power: Precharged pneumatic. Sights: Adjustable for windage and elevation. Features: Mechanical trigger, carbon-fiber air cylinder, up to 150 shots per fill, adjustable sight radius, walnut grip with adjustable palm shelf, single shot, five-way adjustable match trigger. Velocity: 500 fps.
Price: $1,890.00

WALTHER CP88 CO₂ PISTOL
Caliber: .177 pellets. Barrel: Rifled. Weight: 2.3-2.5 lbs. Length: 7-9 in. Power: CO2. Sights: Blade ramp front sight and adjustable rear sight. Features: Manual safety, semi-auto repeater, single or double action, available with 4- or 6-in. barrel, available in multiple finishes and grip materials, eight-shot capacity. Velocity: 450 fps.
Price: $180.00

WALTHER CP99 CO₂ PISTOL
Caliber: .177 pellets. Barrel: Rifled Weight: 1.6 lbs. Length: 7.1 in. Power: CO2. Sights: Fixed front and fully adjustable rear sight. Features: Extremely realistic replica pistol, single and double action, eight-shot rotary magazine. Velocity: 360 fps.
Price: $220.00

Prices given are believed to be accurate at time of publication however, many factors affect retail pricing so exact prices are not possible.

78TH EDITION, 2024 ✦ 579

WALTHER CP99 COMPACT PISTOL
Caliber: .177 steel BBs. Barrel: Smoothbore. Weight: 1.7 lbs. Length: 6.6 in. Power: CO_2. Sights: Fixed front and rear. Features: Extremely realistic replica pistol, semi-automatic 18-shot capacity, available in various configurations, including a nickel slide. Velocity: 345 fps.
Price: $62.00

WALTHER PPQ M2 CO_2 PISTOL
Caliber: .177 pellets. Barrel: Rifled. Weight: 1.4 lbs. Length: 7.0 in. Power: CO_2. Sights: Fixed front and rear sight adjustable for elevation. Features: Extremely realistic replica pistol, blowback action, 20-shot drop-free magazine, metal slide, polymer frame. Velocity: 380 fps.
Price: $90.00

WALTHER P38 CO_2 BB PISTOL
Caliber: .177 steel BBs. Barrel: Smoothbore. Weight: 1.9 lbs. Length: 8.5 in. Power: CO_2. Sights: Fixed. Features: Authentic replica action pistol, blowback action, semi-automatic 20-shot magazine. Velocity: 400 fps.
Price: $75.00

WALTHER PPK/S CO_2 PISTOL
Caliber: .177 steel BBs. Barrel: Smoothbore. Weight: 3.7 lbs. Length: 6.1 in. Power: CO_2. Sights: Fixed. Features: Authentic replica action pistol, blowback slide locks back after last shot, stick-style magazine with 15-shot capacity. Velocity: 295 fps.
Price: ....$57.00–$86.00

WALTHER PPS M2 BLOWBACK COMPACT CO_2 PISTOL
Caliber: .177 steel BBs. Barrel: Smoothbore. Weight: 1.2 lbs. Length: 6.38 in. Power: CO_2. Sights: Fixed. Features: Authentic replica action pistol, blowback action, semi-automatic 18-shot capacity. Velocity: 390 fps.
Price: $54.00

WEBLEY AND SCOTT MKVI REVOLVER
Caliber: .177 pellets. Barrel: Rifled, 6 in. Weight: 2.4 lbs. Length: 11.25 in. Power: CO_2. Sights: Fixed. Features: Authentic replica pistol, single/double action, can be field stripped, full metal construction, six-shot capacity,

available in silver or distressed finish. Also available with a 2.5- or 4-in. barrel. Velocity: 430 fps.
Price: $166.00

WEBLEY AND SCOTT NEMESIS CO_2 PISTOL
Caliber: .177 OR .22 pellets. Barrel: Rifled. Weight: 2 lbs. Length: 10.25 in. Power: CO_2. Sights: Fiber-optic fixed. Features: Bolt action, the bolt can be swapped from right to left, tandem self-indexing magazine system (2x7 in .177 or 2x6 in .22), single-shot tray included, storage for magazine in grip, Picatinny rail for accessories, 3/8-in. dovetail for optics mounting, ambidextrous grip, 1/2-inch UNF threaded barrel, approximately 40 shots per CO_2 cylinder, two-stage adjustable trigger. Velocities: 450 fps (.177), 370 fps (.22).
Price: .... $112.00–$123.00

WEIHRAUCH HW 40 PCA AIR PISTOL
Caliber: .177, .20, .22. Barrel: Rifled. Weight: 1.7 lbs. Length: 9.5 in. Power: Single-stroke spring piston. Sights: Fiber optic, fully adjustable. Features: Automatic safety, two-stage trigger, single shot. Velocity: 400 fps.
Price: $324.00

WEIHRAUCH HW 44 AIR PISTOL, FAC VERSION
Caliber: .177, .22. Barrel: Rifled. Weight: 2.9 lbs. Length: 19 in. Power: Precharged pneumatic. Sights: None. Features: Ambidextrous safety, two-stage adjustable match trigger, built-in suppressor, Weaver-style scope rail, 10-shot magazine, built-in air cartridge with quick fill, internal pressure gauge. Velocity: 750 (.177), 570 (.22) fps.
Price: $1,100.00

WEIHRAUCH HW 45 AIR PISTOL
Caliber: .177, .20, .22. Barrel: Rifled. Weight: 2.5 lbs. Length: 10.9 in. Power: Single-stroke spring piston. Sights: Fiber optic, fully adjustable. Features: Automatic safety, two-stage trigger, single shot, two power levels, blued or two tone. Velocity: 410/558 (.177), 394/492 (.20), 345/427 (.22) fps.
Price: $578.00

WEIHRAUCH HW 75 AIR PISTOL
Caliber: .177. Barrel: Rifled. Weight: 2.3 lbs. Length: 11 in. Power: Single-stroke spring piston. Sights: Micrometer adjustable rear. Features: Ambidextrous, adjustable match-type trigger, single shot. Velocity: 410 fps.
Price: $555.00

WINCHESTER MODEL 11 BB PISTOL
Caliber: .177 steel BBs. Barrel: Smoothbore. Weight: 1.9 lbs. Length: 8.5 in. Power: CO_2. Sights: Fixed. Features: All-metal replica action pistol, blowback action, 4-lb. two-stage trigger, semi-automatic 15-shot capacity. Velocity: 410 fps.
Price: $100.00

AIR ARMS TX200 MKIII AIR RIFLE

Calibers: .177, .22. Barrel: Rifled, Lothar Walter match-grade, 13.19 in. Weight: 9.3 lbs. Length: 41.34 in. Power: Single cock, spring-piston. Stock: Various; right- and left-handed versions, multiple wood options. Sights: 11mm dovetail. Features: Fixed barrel, heirloom-quality craftsmanship, holds the record for the most winning spring-powered airgun in international field target competitions. Velocities: .177, 930 fps/.22, 755 fps.
Price: .... **$860.00–$997.00**

AIR ARMS PRO-SPORT RIFLE

Calibers: .177, .22. Barrel: Rifled, Lothar Walter match-grade, 9.5 in. Weight: 9.03 lbs. Length: 40.5 in. Power: Single cock, spring-piston. Stock: Various; right- and left-handed versions, multiple wood options. Sights: 11mm dovetail. Features: Fixed barrel, heirloom-quality craftsmanship, unique inset cocking arm. Velocities: .177, 950 fps/.22, 750 fps.
Price: .... **$1,033.00–$1,230.00**

AIR ARMS S510 XTRA PCP AIR RIFLE

Calibers: .177, .22, .25. Barrel: Rifled, Lothar Walter match-grade, 19.45 in. Weight: 7.55 lbs. Length: 43.75 in. Power: Precharged pneumatic. Stock: Right-handed, multiple wood options. Sights: 11mm dovetail. Features: Side-lever action, 10-round magazine, shrouded barrel, variable power, heirloom-quality craftsmanship. Velocities: .177, 1,050 fps/.22, 920 fps/.25, 850 fps.
Price: .... **$1,328.00–$1,588.00**

AIR ARMS ULTIMATE SPORTER XS XTRA PCP RIFLE

Calibers: .177, .22, .25. Barrel: Rifled, Lothar Walter match-grade, 19.4 in. Weight: 8.2 lbs. Length: 43.7 in. Power: Precharged pneumatic. Stock: Fully adjustable, ambidextrous black Soft-Touch, walnut, or laminated wood. Sights: None, 11mm dovetail. Features: Side-lever action, sling mounts, accessory rail, two 10-shot magazines included, two-stage adjustable trigger, integrated suppressor, variable power, up to 35-60 shots per fill depending on caliber, also available in a lower power version. Velocities: .177, 1,035 fps/.22, 950 fps/.25, 815 fps.
Price: **$1,635.00–1,700.00**

AIR ARMS S510 XS TDR RIFLE

Calibers: .177, .22. Barrel: Rifled, Lothar Walter match-grade, 15.55 in. Weight: 6.2 lbs. Length: 40.5 in. Power: Precharged pneumatic. Stock: Fully adjustable, ambidextrous black Soft-Touch or walnut. Sights: 11mm dovetail. Features: Takedown rifle breaks down in seconds, comes with a hard case with custom cut foam, side-lever action, 10-shot magazine, integrated suppressor, variable power, built-in manometer, adjustable two-stage trigger. Velocities: .177, 1,035 fps/.22, 950 fps.
Price: **$1,365.00–1,575.00**

AIR ARMS S510 TC XTRA PCP AIR RIFLE

Calibers: .177, .22, .25. Barrel: Rifled, Lothar Walter match-grade, 15.55 in. (carbine) or 19.75 in. (rifle version). Weight: 7.3 lbs (carbine) or 7.5 lbs (rifle). Length: 37.8 in (carbine) or 43.7 in. (rifle). Power: Precharged pneumatic. Stock: Right-handed, multiple wood options. Sights: 11mm dovetail. Features: Available in carbine and rifle configurations, side-lever action, 10-round magazine, shrouded barrel, variable power, heirloom-quality craftsmanship. Velocities: .177, 1,050 fps/.22, 920 fps/.25, 850 fps.
Price: **$1,550.00**

AIR ARMS S510 TACTICAL RIFLE

Calibers: .177, .22 pellets, also in .25-caliber high-power version. Barrel: Rifled, Lothar Walter match-grade, 15.55 in. Weight: 6.2 lbs. Length: 35.4-38.8 in. Power: Precharged pneumatic. Stock: Fully adjustable, ambidextrous black. Sights: None, Picatinny rail. Features: Available in standard and high-power versions, forend Picatinny rail, adjustable CTR stock, M-LOK slots on three sides, drop-down cocking lever, two 10-shot magazines included, adjustable two-stage trigger, moderator, integrated suppressor, variable power in high-power version, built-in manometer. Velocities: .177, 1,035 fps/.22, 950 fps.
Price: .... **$1,822.00–$1,946.00**

AIR ARMS GALAHAD RIFLE REG FAC

Calibers: .22, .25. Barrel: Rifled, Lothar Walter match-grade, 19.4 in. Weight: 8.6 lbs. Length: 35.5 in. Power: Precharged pneumatic. Stock: Ambidextrous bullpup stock available in "soft touch" synthetic over beech or walnut. Sights: 11mm dovetail. Features: Moveable side-lever action, 10-shot magazine, available with an integrated moderator, variable power with an integrated regulator, heirloom-quality craftsmanship. Velocity: .22, 900 fps/.25, 800 fps.
Price: .... **$1,798.00–$1,921.00**

AIRFORCE CONDOR SS RIFLE

Calibers: .177, .20, .22, .25. Barrel: Rifled, Lothar Walther match-grade, 18 or 24 in. Weight: 6.1 lbs. Length: 38.1-38.75 in. Power: Precharged pneumatic. Stock: Synthetic pistol grip, tank acts as the buttstock. Sights: Grooved for scope mounting. Features: Single shot, adjustable power, automatic safety, large 490cc tank volume, extended scope rail allows easy mounting of the largest airgun scopes, optional CO2 power system available, manufactured in the USA. Velocities: .177, 1,450 fps/.20, 1,150 fps/.22, 1,250 fps/.25, 1,100 fps.
Price: **$814.00**

AIRFORCE EDGE 10-METER AIR RIFLE

Caliber: .177. Barrel: Rifled, Lothar Walther match-grade, 12 in. Weight: 6.1 lbs. Length: 40.00 in. Power: Precharged pneumatic. Stock: Synthetic pistol grip, tank acts as the buttstock. Sights: Front sight only or match front globe and rear micrometer adjustable diopter sight. Features: Single shot, automatic safety, two-stage adjustable trigger, accepted by CMP for completive shooting, available in multiple colors and configurations, manufactured in the USA. Velocity: 530 fps.
Price: .... **$640.00–$800.00**

AIRFORCE ESCAPE/SS/UL AIR RIFLE

Calibers: .22, .25. Barrel: Rifled, Lothar Walther match-grade, 12, 18, or 24 in. Weight: 4.3-5.3 lbs. Length: 32.3-39.00 in. Power: Precharged pneumatic. Stock: Synthetic pistol grip, tank acts as the buttstock. Sights: Grooved for scope mounting. Features: Single shot, adjustable power, automatic safety, extended scope rail allows easy mounting of the largest airgun scopes, manufactured in the USA. Velocities: .22, 1,300 fps/.25, 1,145 fps.
Price: .... **$750.00–$830.00**

Prices given are believed to be accurate at time of publication however, many factors affect retail pricing so exact prices are not possible.

78TH EDITION, 2024 ✦ **581**

AIRFORCE TALON SS PCP RIFLE
Calibers: .177, .20, .22, 25. Barrel: Rifled, Lothar Walther match-grade, 12 in. Weight: 5.25 lbs. Length: 32.75in. Power: Precharged pneumatic, Stock: Synthetic pistol grip. Sights: None, grooved for scope mounting. Features: Single shot, removable moderator to reduce noise, adjustable power, can be easily broken down for compact transport, red or blue anodized frame, automatic safety, two-stage nonadjustable trigger, 490cc air tank, up to 50 ft-lbs of energy, manufactured in the USA. Velocities: 1,000 fps (.177), 800 fps (.20), 800 fps (.22), 665 fps (.25).
Price: **$750.00**

AIRFORCE TEXAN, LSS, CF, SS, CARBINE PCP RIFLE
Calibers: .257, .308, .357, .457, .510. Barrel: Rifled, Lothar Walther, 34.00 in. Weight: 7.65 lbs. Length: 48.00 in. Power: Precharged pneumatic. Stock: Synthetic pistol grip, tank acts as the buttstock. Sights: Open sights, also grooved for scope mounting. Features: Single shot, capable of producing over 700 ft-lbs in .510 caliber, adjustable power, easy side lever cocking, two-stage adjustable for position trigger, automatic safety, open receiver accepts a vast selection of off-the-shelf or custom cast ammunition, manufactured in the USA. Available with a carbon-fiber tank (CF model), sound-reducing technology (LSS model), sound-suppressed (SS model), and a shortened 24.5-inch barrel (Carbine model). Velocities: Up to 1,100 fps, depending on caliber.
Price: **$1,200.00**

AIRFORCE INTERNATIONAL LYNX V10 AIR RIFLE
Calibers: .177, .22. Barrel: Rifled, hammer-forged barrel, 18.5 in. Weight: 7.25 lbs. Length: 41.30 in. Power: Precharged pneumatic. Stock: Natural or black hardwood stock. Sights: 11mm dovetail for scope mounting. Features: Multi-shot magazine varies by caliber, side-lever action, adjustable power and adjustable trigger, Spanish-made. Velocities: .177, 1,000 fps/.22, 700 fps.
Price: **$700.00**

AIRFORCE INTERNATIONAL MODEL 94 SPRING AIR RIFLE
Calibers: .177, .22, 25. Barrel: Rifled, hammer forged, 18.75 in. Weight: 7.5 lbs. Length: 44.9 in. Power: Spring piston. Stock: Synthetic with textured grip and forearm. Sights: Fixed fiber-optic front and adjustable fiber-optic rear. Features: Single shot, adjustable two-stage trigger, 32-lb. cocking effort, integral muzzle brake. Velocities: 1,100 fps (.177)/900 fps (.22)/700 fps (.25).
Price: **$190.00**

AIRFORCE INTERNATIONAL MODEL 95 SPRING AIR RIFLE
Calibers: .177, .22. Barrel: Rifled, hammer forged. Weight: 7.25 lbs. Length: 44.9 in. Power: Spring piston. Stock: Hardwood stock with checkering on grip and forearm. Sights: None, 11mm dovetail for scope mounting. Features: Single shot, adjustable trigger, 32-lb. cocking effort. Velocities: .177, 980 fps/.22, 835 fps.
Price: **$230.00**

AIRFORCE INTERNATIONAL ORION PCP RIFLE
Calibers: .177, .22, .25. Barrel: Rifled, hammer-forged barrel, 18.5 in. Weight: 8 lbs. Length: 41 in. Power: Precharged pneumatic. Stock: Checkered wood. Sights: None, 11mm dovetail for scope mounting. Features: Bolt action, high-efficiency sound reduction system, sling swivel studs, 11-17 shot magazine dependent on caliber, adjustable power, and adjustable trigger. Velocities: .177, 1,000 fps/.22, 700 fps/.25, 700 fps.
Price: **$700.00**

AIRGUN TECHNOLOGY URAGAN 2 KING RIFLE
Calibers: .177, .22, .25 or .30. Barrel: Hammer-forged, 23.6 or 27.6 in. Weight: 9.6 lbs. Length: 35.4 – 39.4 in. Power: Precharged pneumatic. Stock: Ambidextrous walnut, synthetic, or laminate bullpup stock. Sights: None, 20 MOA Picatinny rail for scope mounting. Features: Reversible biathlon side lever, under-barrel Picatinny accessory rail, 1060cc composite dual air cylinders, 9 to 15-shot magazine depending on caliber, and sound moderator.
Price: ....**$1,995.00–$2,195.00**

AIRGUN TECHNOLOGY VULCAN 3 - 500 BULLPUP RIFLE
Calibers: .177, .22, .25 or .30. Barrel: 19.7. Weight: 7.5 lbs. Length: 31.4. Power: Precharged pneumatic. Stock: Ambidextrous walnut bullpup stock with polymer cheekpiece. Sights: None, 20 MOA sloped Weaver-style rail for scope mounting. Features: Ambidextrous biathlon-style side lever, Picatinny under-rail, improved trigger and safety system, modified sound moderator, adjustable power, two 9 to 15-shot magazines depending on caliber, 480cc carbon-fiber air bottle, soft case. Also available with a 27.6-in. barrel with a 580cc air bottle (Vulcan 3 - 700 model).
Price: **$1,800.00**

AIR VENTURI AVENGER RIFLE
Caliber: .177, .22, .25. Barrel: Rifled, 22.75 in. Weight: 6.0 lbs. Length: 42.75 in. Power: Precharged pneumatic. Stock: Ambidextrous synthetic or wood stock. Sights: None, Picatinny rail. Features: Side-lever cocking, externally adjustable regulator, hammer spring adjustment screw, two-stage adjustable trigger, shrouded barrel, easy access degassing screw, includes two magazines and a single-shot loading tray, 8 (.25) or 10 shot (.177 and .22) capacity. Velocities: .177, 1,000 fps; .22, 930 fps; .25, 900 fps.
Price: ....**$400.00–$480.00**

AIR VENTURI SENECA DOUBLE SHOT .50 CAL DOUBLE BARREL AIR SHOTGUN
Caliber: No. 8 shot or .50 slug. Barrel: Smooth, double barrel, 20.9 in. Weight: 8.55 Length: 43.5 in. Power: Precharged pneumatic. Stock: Ambidextrous wood stock. Sights: Front bead with no rear sight. Features: Up to five shots per fill, shoots shotshells, airbolts, or round balls. Thread on chokes, optional dovetail rail, two-stage non-adjustable trigger. Velocity: Up to 1,130 fps with shotshells.
Price: **$950.00**

AIR VENTURI SENECA DRAGON CLAW PCP AIR RIFLE
Caliber: .50-cal. pellet or airbolt. Barrel: Rifled 21.65 in. Weight: 8.5 Length: 42.1 in. Power: Precharged pneumatic. Stock: Right-handed wood stock.

Sights: Fixed front sight with fully adjustable rear sight. Features: Massive 500cc reservoir delivers several powerful shots, 230 ft-lbs of energy at the muzzle on high setting, two power levels, dual air chambers, build-in manometer, 11mm scope rail. Velocity: 639 fps.
Price: $800.00

AIR VENTURI SENECA DRAGONFLY MK2 MULTI-PUMP AIR RIFLE
Calibers: .177, .22. Barrel: Rifled 22.75 in. Weight: 6.5 lbs. Length: 40 in. Power: Multi-pump pneumatic. Stock: Ambidextrous wood. Sights: Fixed front sight with fully adjustable rear. Features: Butterfly High-Efficiency Pump System, threaded muzzle adapter, 11mm dovetail optics rail, variable power based on the number of pumps. Bolt action, single shot, and multi-shot capability. Velocities: 850 fps (.177), 730 fps (.22).
Price: $230.00

AIR VENTURI SENECA WING SHOT II SHOTGUN
Caliber: .50. Barrel: Smoothbore 22.5 in. Weight: 7.4 lbs. Length: 43.0 in. Power: Precharged pneumatic. Stock: Ambidextrous wood. Sights: Fixed bead shotgun-style. Features: 244cc reservoir delivers several powerful shots, shoots shot cartridges and round ball, exceptionally reliable. Use as a shotgun to hunt birds or small game or as a slug gun to hunt larger game. Velocity: 760 fps (with slug), 1,130 fps.
Price: $925.00

AMERICAN AIR ARMS EVOL CLASSIC CARBINE
Calibers: .22, .25, or .30. Barrel: Hammer forged, rifled, threaded, 15 in. (.22), 18 in (.25 or .30). Weight: 7-7.2 lbs. Length: 36-39 in. with moderator. Power: Precharged pneumatic. Stock: Walnut. Sights: None, Picatinny rail. Features: Upper and lower chassis made from aluminum, titanium air cylinder, Picatinny underside accessory rail, adjustable two-stage trigger set to 10 ounces, 9-13 shot rotary magazine, Magpul stock and grip, manufactured in the USA in very limited quantities. Also available in a tactical version. Velocity: Adjustable.
Price: $2,895.00

AMERICAN AIR ARMS SLAYER HI-POWER BULLPUP RIFLE
Calibers: .308 or .357. Barrel: Rifled, threaded, 24 in (.357) or 26 in. (.308). Weight: 7.2 lbs. Length: 36-40 in with moderator. Power: Precharged pneumatic. Stock: Synthetic adjustable length stock. Sights: None, Picatinny rail. Features: Titanium reservoir, 3-lb. cocking effort, six- (.357 caliber) or seven- (.308 caliber) round rotary magazine, adjustable two-stage trigger, underside accessory rail, rear velocity adjuster, available in right or left hand, manufactured in the USA in very limited quantities. Velocity: 950 fps.
Price: $2,795.00

ANSCHUTZ 9015 AIR RIFLE
Caliber: .177. Barrel: Rifled, 16.5 in. Weight: Variable from 8.1 to 11 pounds. Length: Variable from 39.0 to 47 in. Power: Precharged pneumatic. Stock: Fully adjustable variable composition. Sights: Fully adjustable target sights with interchangeable inserts. Features: Single shot, ambidextrous grip, adjustable match trigger, exchangeable air cylinder with integrated manometer, approximately 200 shots per fill, available with a bewildering array of options. Also available in lower-priced Club and Junior versions. Velocity: 560 fps.
Price: ....$3,095.00–$4,795.00

ASELKON M-10 PCP RIFLE
Caliber: .177, .22, .25. Barrel: Rifled, 21.7 in. Weight: 6.3 lbs. Length: 33.5 in. Power: Precharged pneumatic. Stock: Camo, wood, or black synthetic. Sights: None, Picatinny rail. Features: 10- (.25), 12- (.22) or 14- (.177) shot magazine, 275cc fill volume, adjustable trigger, side lever cocking, approximately 55-70 shots per fill depending on caliber, and comes with a plastic hard case. Velocities: Up to 950 fps (.177 or .22), 850 fps (.25).
Price: $440.00

ASG TAC-4.5 CO₂ BB RIFLE
Caliber: .177 steel BBs. Barrel: Smoothbore. Weight: 3.5 lbs. Length: 36.0 in. Power: CO2 Stock: Synthetic thumbhole stock. Sights: Fixed fiber-optic front sight and fully adjustable fiber-optic rear sight/weaver rail for optics. Features: Semi-automatic action, includes bipod, 21-shot capacity. Velocity: 417 fps.
Price: $120.00

ATAMAN BULLPUP MR2 PCP RIFLE
Calibers: .25, .357. Barrel: Lothar Walther rifled match-grade free-floating, 20.5 in. Weight: 7.7-8.4 lbs. Length: 32.3 in. Power: Precharged pneumatic. Stock: Ambidextrous bullpup stock available in walnut or "soft touch" synthetic. Sights: Integrated Picatinny rails for scope mounting. Features: Multi-shot side-level action, shot capacity varies on caliber, adjustable match trigger, finely tuned regulator matched to optimal velocity in each caliber for maximum accuracy. Velocities: .25, 985 fps/.35, 900 fps.
Price: ....$1,700.00–$2,000.00

ATAMAN M2R ULTRA-C CARBINE
Calibers: .177, .22, .25. Barrel: Lothar Walther rifled match-grade, 11.2 in. Weight: 6.2 lbs. Length: 32.3 in. Power: Precharged pneumatic. Stock: Ambidextrous folding stock available in various configurations and finishes. Sights: None, Picatinny rail for scope mounting. Features: Also available in bullpup and tactical configurations, shrouded, 8- to 12-shot magazine dependent on caliber, adjustable match trigger. Velocities: .177, 850 fps/.22, 850 fps/.25, 900 fps.
Price: ....$1,490.00–$1,600.00

BARRA 400 E ELECTRIC RIFLE
Caliber: .177 BB. Barrel: Smoothbore, 19 in. Weight: 7.5 lbs. Length: 42.25 in. Power: AEG (electric). Stock: Black synthetic tactical style. Sights: Removable flip-up front and rear peep, Picatinny rail. Features: Ambidextrous elect fire semi- or full-automatic, lithium battery gives over 1,000 shots per charge, 50-round BB repeater, CNC-machined aluminum handguard and receiver, six-position adjustable buttstock, AR-style pistol grip, QD sling mount, speedloader, M-LOK slots on forearm sides. Velocity: 410 fps.
Price: $400.00

BARRA SPORTSMAN 900 RIFLE
Calibers: .177 BB or pellet. Barrel: Rifled, 20.1 in. Weight: 4.4 lbs. Length: 39.4 in. Power: Multi-pump. Stock: Black synthetic. Sights: Fixed fiber-optic front, fully adjustable rear. Features: 50 round BB repeater or single shot pellet, 3/8-in. rail for mounting optics, Picatinny accessory rails on forearm sides, 6.25-lb. trigger pull, 4x15 scope included. Velocity: 670 fps.
Price: **$70.00**

BEEMAN R9 AIR RIFLE
Calibers: .177, .20, .22. Barrel: Rifled 16.33 in. Weight: 7.3 lbs. Length: 43 in. Power: Break-barrel, spring-piston. Stock: Ambidextrous walnut-stained beech, cut-checkered pistol grip, Monte Carlo comb and rubber buttpad. Sights: None, grooved for scope. Features: German quality, limited lifetime warranty, highly adjustable match-grade trigger, extremely accurate. Velocities: .177, 935 fps/.20, 800 fps/.22, 740 fps.
Price: **$625.00**

BEEMAN AR2078A CO$_2$ RIFLE
Calibers: .177, .22 pellets. Barrel: Rifled, 21.50 in. Weight: 7.5 lbs. Length: 38 in. Power: CO2. Stock: Beech. Sights: Competition diopter peep sight, 11mm dovetail. Features: Bolt action, single shot, operates on two standard 12-gram CO2 cylinders or with tank adapter and connector, adjustable trigger, approximately 60 shots per fill. Velocities: .177, 650/.22, 500 fps.
Price: **$260.00**

BEEMAN COMMANDER PCP RIFLE
Calibers: .177, .22 pellets. Barrel: Rifled. Weight: 8 lbs. Length: 43 in. Power: Precharged pneumatic. Stock: Hardwood thumbhole. Sights: Adjustable fiber optic, comes with a 4x32 scope. Features: Up to 100 shots per fill, 10-shot magazine, built-in noise suppressor. Velocities: .177, 1,100/.22, 1,000 fps.
Price: **$270.00**

BEEMAN COMPETITION PCP RIFLE
Caliber: .177 pellets. Barrel: Rifled. Weight: 8.8 lbs. Length: 41.7 in. Power: Precharged pneumatic. Stock: Adjustable hardwood. Sights: None, dovetail grooves. Features: Side lever cocking, up to 200 shots per fill, single shot, built-in noise suppressor, 10m competition, adjustable trigger, adjustable pistol grip, comb, and buttplate. Velocity: 550 fps.
Price: **$1,059.00**

BEEMAN GAS RAM DUAL CALIBER AIR RIFLE COMBO
Calibers: .177, .22. Barrel: Rifled. Weight: 8.5 lbs. Length: 45.5 in. Power: Break-barrel, gas-piston. Stock: Ambidextrous hardwood stock. Sights: Fiber optic with adjustable rear, includes 4x32 scope with mount. Features: Single-shot, adjustable two-stage trigger, 35 to 40-lb. cocking effort, comes with both .177- and .22-caliber barrels. Velocities: .177, 1,000 fps/.22, 850 fps.
Price: **$190.00**

BEEMAN NEW CHIEF II PCP RIFLE
Calibers: .177, .22 pellets. Barrel: Rifled. Weight: 6.8 lbs. Length: 39 in. Power: Precharged pneumatic. Stock: Synthetic. Sights: Adjustable fiber optic. Features: Up to 100 shots per fill, 10-shot magazine, built-in noise suppressor. Velocities: .177, 1,000/.22, 830 fps.
Price: **$260.00**

BEEMAN PCP UNDER LEVER RIFLE
Calibers: .177, .22 pellets. Barrel: Rifled. Weight: 7.3 lbs. Length: 32 in. Power: Precharged pneumatic. Stock: Bullpup-style wood. Sights: Adjustable fiber optic. Features: 10-shot magazine, unique front under-level cocking system, built-in noise suppressor. Velocity: .177, 1,000/.22, 830 fps.
Price: **$300.00**

BEEMAN QB II MODEL 1085 CO$_2$ RIFLE
Calibers: .177, .22 pellets. Barrel: Rifled. Weight: 6.5 lbs. Length: 38.6 in. Power: CO2. Stock: Synthetic thumbhole. Sights: Fiber optic, 11mm dovetail. Features: Uses two 12-gram CO2 cartridges, a 10-shot magazine, and an accessory rail under the forend. Velocities: .177, 650/.22, 500 fps.
Price: **$160.00**

BEEMAN SILVER KODIAK X2 COMBO AIR RIFLE
Calibers: .177, .22. Barrel: Rifled. Weight: 9 lbs. Length: 45.5 in. Power: Break-barrel, gas ram piston. Stock: Ambidextrous hardwood stock. Sights: Open includes 4x32 scope and rings. Features: Satin finish nickel-plated receiver and barrels, single-shot, easily exchangeable .177- and .22-cal. barrels, two-stage trigger. Velocities: .177, 1,200 fps/.22, 830 fps.
Price: **$180.00**

BENJAMIN 392 / 397 AIR RIFLE
Calibers: .177, .22. Barrel: Rifled 19.25 in. Weight: 5.5 lbs. Length: 36.25 in. Power: Multi-pump pneumatic. Stock: Ambidextrous wood or synthetic stock. Sights: Front ramp and adjustable rear sight. Features: Multi-pump system provides variable power, single-shot bolt action. Velocities: .177, 800 fps/.22, 685 fps.
Price: **$237.00**

BENJAMIN ARMADA PCP RIFLE
Calibers: .177, .22, .25. Barrel: Rifled, 20 in. Weight: 7.3 lbs. (10.3 lbs. with scope and bipod). Length: 42.8 in. Power: Precharged pneumatic. Stock: Adjustable mil-spec AR-15-style buttstock, all metal M-LOK-compatible handguard with 15 in. of Picatinny rail space. Sights: None, Weaver/Picatinny rail for scope mounting. Features: Fully shrouded barrel with integrated suppressor, dampener device, bolt action, multi-shot, choked barrel for maximum accuracy. Velocities: .177, 1,100 fps/.22, 1,000 fps/.25, 900 fps.
Price: **$693.00**

BENJAMIN AKELA PCP AIR RIFLE
Calibers: .22. Barrel: Rifled. Weight: 7.7 lbs. Length: 32.9 in. Power: Precharged pneumatic. Stock: Bullpup-style Turkish walnut stock. Sights: None, Picatinny rail for scope mounting. Features: Side cocking lever, adjustable trigger shoe, 3,000 psi pressure, up to 60 shots per fill, 12-shot rotary magazine. Velocity: 1,000 fps.
Price: .... **$556.00–$632.00**

BENJAMIN BULLDOG .357 BULLPUP
Caliber: .357. Barrel: Rifled 28 in. Weight: 7.7 lbs. Length: 36 in. Power: Precharged pneumatic. Stock: Synthetic bullpup stock with pistol grip, black or Realtree camo. Sights: Full top Picatinny rail. Features: Innovative bullpup design, massive power output of up to 180 ft-lbs, five-shot magazine, shrouded barrel for noise reduction, large cylinder delivers up to 10 usable shots, available in multiple bundled configurations and stock finishes. Velocity: Up to 900 fps based on projectile weight.
Price: .... **$903.00–$1,102.00**

BENJAMIN CAYDEN PCP AIR RIFLE
Calibers: .22. Barrel: Rifled. Weight: 7.95 lbs. Length: 40.8 in. Power: Precharged Pneumatic. Stock: Turkish walnut stock with adjustable cheekpiece. Sights: None, grooved 11mm dovetail for scope mounting. Features: Side cocking lever, adjustable trigger shoe, 3,000 psi pressure, up to 60 shots per fill, 12-shot rotary magazine. Velocity: 1,000 fps.
Price: **$632.00**

BENJAMIN GUNNAR AIR RIFLE
Calibers: .22 or .25. Barrel: Rifled. Weight: 9.8 lbs. Length: Adjustable. Power: Precharged pneumatic. Stock: Synthetic, ambidextrous. Sights: None, Picatinny rail for scope mounting. Features: Bolt action, side lever cocking, adjustable AR-style stock, shrouded barrel with integrated suppressor, 500cc reservoir, adjustable regulator and five-position external power adjuster, Picatinny rail for monopod, multi-shot. Velocity: 1,000 fps (.22), 900 fps (.25).
Price: **$999.00**

BENJAMIN KRATOS PCP AIR RIFLE
Calibers: .22, .25. Barrel: Rifled. Weight: 8.26 lbs. Length: 43.35 in. Power: Precharged pneumatic. Stock: Turkish walnut stock with adjustable cheekpiece. Sights: None, Picatinny rail for scope mounting. Features: Side cocking lever, adjustable trigger shoe, 3,000 psi pressure, up to 60 shots per fill, 12-shot rotary magazine in .22, 10-shot rotary magazine in .25. Velocities: 1,000 fps (.22), 900 fps (.25).
Price: **$664.00**

BENJAMIN MARAUDER PCP AIR RIFLE
Caliber: .177, .22, .25. Barrel: Rifled 20 in. Weight: Synthetic 7.3 lbs/Hardwood 8.2 lbs. Length: 42.8 in. Power: Precharged pneumatic. Stock: Ambidextrous stock available in hardwood or synthetic, adjustable cheek riser. Sights: None, grooved for scope mounting. Features: Multi-shot bolt action, 10-shot in .177 and .22, eight-shot in .25, user-adjustable performance settings for power and shot count, reversible bolt handle. Also available with options such as an integrated regulator for shot-to-shot consistency, a Pictatinny rail, and Lothar Walther barrel. Velocities: .177, 1,100 fps/.22, 1,000 fps/.25, 900 fps.
Price: .... **$556.00–$630.00**

BENJAMIN MARAUDER SEMI-AUTOMATIC PCP AIR RIFLE
Caliber: .22. Barrel: Rifled 20 in. Weight: Hardwood 8.2 lbs. Length: 42.8 in. Power: Precharged pneumatic. Stock: Hardwood ambidextrous with adjustable cheek riser. Sights: None, grooved for scope mounting. Features: Multi-shot semi-automatic action, 10-shot, regulated, up to 60 shots per fill, ambidextrous charging handle, shrouded barrel with integrated resonance dampener. Velocity: 950 fps.
Price: .... **$736.00–$766.00**

BENJAMIN PROWLER NITRO PISTON BREAK-BARREL RIFLE
Calibers: .177, .22. Barrel: Rifled. Weight: 6.4 lbs. Length: 45 in. Power: Break-barrel, Nitro-piston. Stock: Ambidextrous synthetic. Sights: None, comes with a CenterPoint 4x32 scope. Features: Reduced recoil, 35-lb. cocking effort, single-shot, adjustable two-stage trigger. Velocities: 1,200 fps (.177), 950 fps (.22).
Price: **$143.00**

BENJAMIN TRAIL STEALTH NITRO PISTON 2 (NP2) BREAK-BARREL AIR RIFLE
Calibers: .177, .22. Barrel: Rifled 15.75 in. Weight: 8.3 lbs. Length: 46.25 in. Power: Break-barrel, 2nd generation gas-piston. Stock: Ambidextrous thumbhole stock available in wood and synthetic, with multiple finishes and patterns. Sights: None, Picatinny rail for scope mounting, multiple CenterPoint scope options available as factory bundles. Features: Very quiet due to the shrouded barrel with an integrated suppressor, extremely easy cocking, single-shot, advanced adjustable two-stage trigger, and innovative sling mounts for optional Benjamin break-barrel rifle sling. Velocities: .177, 1,400 fps/.22, 1,100 fps.
Price: **$290.00**

BENJAMIN VAPORIZER NITRO PISTON RIFLE
Calibers: .22. Barrel: Rifled 15 in. Weight: 8.5 lbs. Length: 46.5 in. Power: Break-barrel, Nitro Piston. Stock: Ambidextrous synthetic. Sights: Adjustable, Picatinny rail for scope mounting. Features: SBD sound suppression, shrouded barrel with integrated suppressor, single-shot, adjustable two-stage trigger. Velocity: 950 fps.
Price: .... **$230.00–$241.00**

BLACK OPS TACTICAL SNIPER GAS-PISTON AIR RIFLE
Calibers: .22. Barrel: Rifled. Weight: 9.6 lbs. Length: 44.0 in. Power: Break-barrel, gas-piston. Stock: Ambidextrous pistol grip synthetic stock. Sights: none, Weaver rail for scope mounting, includes a 4x32 scope. Features: Muzzle brake helps with cocking force, single-shot, single cock delivers

maximum power, adjustable single-stage trigger. Velocities: .177, 1,250 fps/.22, 1,000 fps.

Price: $250.00

BROCOCK GHOST HP PCP RIFLE

Calibers: .177, .22, .25, .30. Barrel: Rifled, 23 in. Weight: 7.5 lbs. Length: 33.7 in. Power: Precharged pneumatic. Stock: Ambidextrous polymer. Sights: None, adjustable Picatinny rail. Features: Titanium chassis to maximize rigidity, quick and easy interchangeable barrel system, finger-adjustable power settings, swappable side lever, adjustable check and buttpad, left- or right-hand magazine feed, comes with a hard case, fully adjustable match trigger, shrouded barrel with 1/2-inch UNF threads, three accessory rails. Up to 21 (.30) to 190 (.177) shots and 26 (.177) to 95 ft-lbs (.30) of energy at full power, depending on caliber. Also available in lower-powered Carbine and Plus versions. Velocities: Adjustable.

Price: $2,095.00

BROCOCK SNIPER XR MAGNUM PCP RIFLE

Calibers: .22, .25. Barrel: Rifled, Lothar Walther, 22 in. Weight: 7.3 lbs. Length: 39 in. Power: Precharged pneumatic. Stock: Black or sand-colored ballistic nylon thumbhole. Sights: None, 11mm rail. Features: Hi-Lo power adjuster, breech block made of aircraft-grade alloy, Huma regulator for shot-to-shot consistency, side lever, adjustable cheek and buttpad, 10-shot rotary magazine or single-shot tray, match-grade trigger, full-length built-in baffled silencer with adaptor for second-stage silencer, two pressure gauges, three-position power adjustor. Up to 45-50 shots and 46-55 ft-lbs of energy at full power, depending on caliber. Velocities: Adjustable.

Price: $1,854.00

BSA R-10 SE PCP RIFLE

Calibers: .177, .22, .25. Barrel: Rifled, BSA-made cold hammer-forged precision barrel, 15 in. Weight: 7.4 lbs. Length: 40 in. Power: Precharged pneumatic. Stock: Available right- or left-hand, walnut, laminate, camo or black synthetic. Sights: None, grooved for scope mounting. Features: Adjustable buttpad, customer configurable shroud, up to 52-63 shots per fill depending on caliber, adjustable two-stage trigger, comes with two 10-shot magazines (eight-shot for .25 caliber), with last-shot indicator, fully regulated valve for maximum accuracy and shot consistency, also available with lower power/velocity and as a shorter carbine. Velocities: 950 fps (.177)/800 fps (.22)/665 fps (.25).

Price: ....$1,300.00–$1,496.00

BSA DEFIANT BULLPUP AIR RIFLE

Calibers: .177, .22. Barrel: Rifled, cold hammer-forged precision barrel, 18.5 in. Weight: 9 lbs. Length: 31 in. Power: Precharged pneumatic. Stock: Ambidextrous Walnut, black soft-touch or black pepper laminate with adjustable buttpad. Sights: None, grooved for scope mounting. Features: Multi-shot bolt action, two 10-shot magazines, enhanced valve system for maximum shot count and consistency, integrated suppressor, adjustable two-stage trigger. Velocities: 825 fps (.177)/570 fps (.22).

Price: ....$1,599.00–$1,699.00

BSA GOLD STAR SE PCP AIR RIFLE

Caliber: .177. Barrel: Rifled, BSA-made enhanced cold hammer-forged precision barrel, 15.2 in. Weight: 7 lbs. Length: 35.8 in. Power: Precharged pneumatic. Stock: Highly adjustable gray laminate field target competition stock. Sights: None, grooved for scope mounting. Features: Multi-shot bolt action, 10-shot magazine, fully regulated valve for maximum accuracy and shot consistency, 70 consistent shots per charge, free-floating barrel with 1/2 UNF threaded muzzle, includes adjustable air stripper, adjustable match-grade trigger. Velocity: 800 fps.

Price: $1,500.00

BSA METEOR SUPER BREAK-BARREL RIFLE

Caliber: .177 or .22 pellets. Barrel: Rifled, cold hammer-forged, 18.5 in. Weight: 6.6 lbs. Length: 43.5 in. Power: Gas piston. Stock: Ambidextrous Minelli beech stock. Sights: Adjustable open, grooved for scope mounting. Features: Single shot, two-stage adjustable trigger, checkered forend and grip, threaded muzzle. Velocities: 807 (.177)/571 (.22) fps.

Price: $500.00

BSA SCORPION SE PCP AIR RIFLE

Calibers: .177, .22, .25. Barrel: Rifled, 15.2 in. Weight: 6.8 lbs. Length: 35 in. Power: Precharged pneumatic. Stock: Ambidextrous Monte Carlo stock in wood, camo or black. Sights: None, 11mm scope rail. Features: 10-shot (.177 and .22) or eight-shot (.25) magazines with last shot indicator, approximately 30-45 shots per fill depending on caliber, two-stage adjustable trigger. Velocity: 930 fps (.177), 770 fps (.22), 680 fps (.25).

Price: $1,100.00

BSA ULTRA CLX PCP RIFLE

Calibers: .177, .22. Barrel: Rifled, BSA-made cold hammer-forged precision barrel, 12.5 in. Weight: 5.6 lbs. Length: 32 in. Power: Precharged pneumatic. Stock: Ambidextrous beech. Sights: None, grooved for scope mounting. Features: 12-shot magazine with shot countdown indicator, fully adjustable trigger, 60-72 shots per fill. Also available with a limited edition walnut stock. Velocities: 700 fps (.177)/570 fps (.22).

Price: $1,080.00

BSA ULTRA JSR AIR RIFLE

Calibers: .177, .22. Barrel: Rifled, BSA-made cold hammer-forged precision barrel, 12 in. Weight: 4.95 lbs. Length: 27 in. Power: Precharged pneumatic. Stock: Beech. Sights: None, grooved for scope mounting. Features: Built for younger or smaller framed shooters, 10-shot magazine, fully regulated valve for maximum accuracy and shot consistency, free-floating, shrouded barrel, two-stage adjustable trigger, threaded muzzle, .177 available in two power configurations. Velocities: 560 or 800 fps (.177)/600 fps (.22).

Price: $700.00

Prices given are believed to be accurate at time of publication however, many factors affect retail pricing so exact prices are not possible.

BUSHMASTER MPW FULL-AUTO BB RIFLE
Caliber: .177 BB. Barrel: Smoothbore. Weight: 6.5 lbs. Length: 21 in. Power: CO2. Stock: six-position adjustable nylon stock with AR-compatible pistol grip. Sights: None, comes with a red dot and Picatinny rail. Features: AR platform with mock suppressor, accepts AR stocks, AR-compatible buffer tube and pistol grip, full- or semi-auto modes, two-tone black/flat dark earth, blowback action, quad rail forearm for accessory mounting, 25-round drop-out magazine, uses two 12-gram CO2 cylinders, fully auto with up to 1,400 rounds per minute. Also comes in a dual-action semi-/full-auto version. Velocity: 430 fps.
Price: **$246.00**

COMETA FENIX 400 PREMIER STAR AIR RIFLE
Calibers: .177, .22, .25. Barrel: Rifled. Weight: 7.5 lbs. Length: 39.4 in. Power: Gas power piston. Stock: Walnut. Sights: Adjustable, grooved for scope mounting. Features: Single shot. Velocities: 1,080 fps (.177)/900 fps (.22)/700 fps (.25).
Price: **$330.00**

COMETA FUSION PREMIER STAR AIR RIFLE
Calibers: .177, .22. Barrel: Cold hammer-forged, rifled. Weight: 7.5 lbs. Length: 44.9 in. Power: Gas power piston. Stock: Walnut. Sights: None, grooved for scope mounting. Features: Single shot, bull barrel, checkered stock, adjustable riser, adjustable trigger. Velocities: 1,080 fps (.177)/900 fps (.22).
Price: **$265**

CROSMAN CHALLENGER PCP COMPETITION AIR RIFLE
Caliber: .177. Barrel: Match-grade Lothar Walther rifled barrel. Weight: 7 lbs. Length: 41.75 in. Power: Precharged pneumatic. Stock: Highly adjustable ambidextrous synthetic competition stock. Sights: Globe front sight and Precision Diopter rear sight. Features: Redesigned in 2022, built-in regulator for shot-to-shot consistency, 3,000 psi reservoir to give more shots per fill, single-shot, adjustable two-stage match-grade trigger with an adjustable shoe, approved by the Civilian Marksmanship Program (CMP) for 3-position air rifle Sporter Class competition, swappable side-lever cocking handle. Velocity: 580 fps.
Price: **$1,145.00**

CROSMAN FULL-AUTO AK1 RIFLE
Caliber: .177 BBs. Barrel: Smooth. Weight: 8 lbs. Length: 34.5 in. Power: CO2. Stock: Synthetic adjustable/folding five-position buttstock. Sights: Open, Picatinny rail. Features: Releasable magazine holds two CO2 cartridges and spring feeds 28 BBs, shoots full or semiauto with blowback, AK-compatible pistol grip, quad-rail forearm for accessory mounting. Velocity: 430 fps.
Price: **$240.00**

CROSMAN FULL AUTO R1 CO2 RIFLE
Caliber: .177 BBs. Barrel: Smooth, 10 in. Weight: 6 lbs. Length: 26.25-29.5

in. Power: CO2. Stock: Synthetic six-position adjustable buttstock. Sights: None, Picatinny rail, comes with a red-dot sight. Features: 25-round drop-free magazine, full- or semi-auto with blowback, powered by two CO2 cartridges, AR-compatible buffer tube and pistol grip, quad-rail forearm for accessory mounting, speedloader included, also available as a semi-automatic version. Velocity: 430 fps.
Price: **$204.00**

CROSMAN M4-177 RIFLE
Caliber: .177 steel BBs, .177 pellets. Barrel: Rifled 17.25 in. Weight: 3.75 lbs. Length: 33.75 in. Power: Multi-pump pneumatic. Stock: M4-style adjustable plastic stock. Sights: Weaver/Picatinny rail for scope mounting and flip-up sights. Bundled packages include various included sighting options. Features: Single-shot bolt action, lightweight and very accurate, multiple colors available. "Ready to go" kits are available complete with ammo, safety glasses, targets, and extra five-shot pellet magazines. Velocity: 660 fps.
Price: .... **$72.00–$89.00**

CROSMAN 362 MULTIPUMP AIR RIFLE
Caliber: .22 pellets. Barrel: Rifled. Power: Multi-pump pneumatic. Stock: Synthetic stock. Sights: Adjustable rear sight. Features: Single-shot, bolt action. Velocity: Up to 850 fps.
Price: **$110.00**

CROSMAN 760 PUMPMASTER AIR RIFLE
Caliber: .177 steel BBs, .177 pellets. Barrel: Rifled 16.75 in. Weight: 2.75 lbs. Length: 33.5 in. Power: Multi-pump pneumatic. Stock: Ambidextrous plastic stock. Sights: Blade and ramp, rear sight adjustable for elevation, grooved for scope mounting. Features: Single-shot pellet, BB repeater, bolt action, lightweight, accurate and easy to shoot. Multiple colors available and configurations are available. "Ready to go" kits are available complete with ammo, safety glasses, targets and extra five-shot pellet magazines. Velocity: 625 fps.
Price: .... **$50.00–$78.00**

CROSMAN DIAMONDBACK SBD AIR RIFLE
Caliber: .22. Barrel: Rifled. Weight: 8.5 lbs. Length: 46.5 in. Power: Break-barrel, Nitro-piston. Stock: Synthetic with pistol grip. Sights: Open sights, dovetail for scope mounting, includes CenterPoint 4x32 scope and rings. Features: SBD sound suppression system, sling mounts, single-shot, adjustable two-stage trigger. Velocities: 1,100 fps.
Price: **$177.00**

CROSMAN DRIFTER PISTOL/RIFLE KIT
Caliber: 22. Barrel: Rifled, 14.6 in. Weight: 1.9 lbs. Power: Multi-pump pneumatic. Sights: Front fiber optic, adjustable open/peep rear. Features:

Single shot, bolt action, carbon-fiber hydro dip, kit comes with removable shoulder stock, pistol grip, carry pouch, pellets. Velocity: 550 fps.
Price: **$170.00**

CROSMAN F4 NITRO PISTON AIR RIFLE

Caliber: .177. Barrel: Rifled. Weight: 6.0 lbs. Length: 43.5 in. Power: Break-barrel, Nitro Piston. Stock: Synthetic thumbhole style. Sights: None, dovetail for scope mounting, includes CenterPoint 4x32 scope and rings. Features: QuietFire sound suppression for reduced recoil and noise, single-shot, adjustable two-stage trigger. Velocities: Up to 1,200 fps.
Price: **$150.00**

CROSMAN FIRE NITRO PISTON AIR RIFLE

Caliber: .177. Barrel: Rifled. Weight: 6.0 lbs. Length: 43.5 in. Power: Break-barrel, Nitro-piston. Stock: Synthetic thumbhole style. Sights: None, dovetail for scope mounting, includes CenterPoint 4x32 scope and rings. Features: Integrated muzzle brake for reduced recoil and noise, single-shot, adjustable two-stage trigger. Velocities: 1,200 fps.
Price: **$154.00**

CROSMAN ICON PCP RIFLE

Caliber: .177 or .22 pellets. Barrel: Rifled, 21 in. Weight: 7 lbs. Length: 38.5 in. Power: Precharged pneumatic. Stock: Ambidextrous tactical all-weather synthetic. Sights: Fiber-optic front and fully adjustable rear with 11mm dovetail optics rail. Features: Bolt action, threaded muzzle, 2,000 psi pressure gauge with up to 30 effective shots per fill, 12-shot (.177) or 10-shot (.22) auto-indexing magazine, textured pistol grip and forearm, raised cheekpiece, rear sling loop, 1/2x20 UNF muzzle threads for moderator, two-stage adjustable trigger. Velocity: Up to 1,000 fps (.177) or 900 fps (.22).
Price: **$300**

CROSMAN MAG-FIRE EXTREME/ULTRA/MISSION BREAK-BARREL AIR RIFLES

Caliber: .177, .22. Barrel: Rifled. Weight: 6.5 lbs. Length: 43 in. Power: Break-barrel. Stock: Ambidextrous synthetic. Sights: Adjustable rear sight, Picatinny rail for scope mounting, includes 3-9x40 scope and rings. Features: Extreme has a tactical-style stock with adjustable cheekpiece and pistol grip, Ultra has an all-weather stock with soft-touch inserts, Mission has a thumbhole-style stock, 12-shot magazine, QuietFire sound suppression, adjustable two-stage trigger, sling mount. Velocities: 1,300 fps (.177)/975 fps (.22).
Price: .... **$205.00–$252.00**

CROSMAN OPTIMUS AIR RIFLE COMBO

Caliber: .177, .22. Barrel: Rifled. Weight: 6.5 lbs. Length: 43 in. Power: Break-barrel. Stock: Ambidextrous wood. Sights: Fiber optic with adjustable

rear sight, dovetail for scope mounting, includes CenterPoint 4x32 scope and rings. Features: Single-shot, adjustable two-stage trigger. Velocities: 1,200 fps (.177)/950 fps (.22).
Price: **$165.00**

CROSMAN REPEATAIR 1077/1077 FREESTYLE CO₂ RIFLE

Caliber: .177 pellets. Barrel: Rifled 20.38 in. Weight: 3.75 lbs. Length: 36.88 in. Power: CO2. Stock: Wood or ambidextrous plastic stock. Sights: Blade and ramp, rear sight adjustable for windage and elevation, grooved for scope mounting. Features: Multi-shot, semi-automatic, 12-shot magazine, lightweight, fun and easy to shoot. Freestyle has three-tone color, and modernized buttpad and magazine design. "Ready to go" kits are available complete with ammo, CO2, targets, target trap, etc. Velocity: 625 fps.
Price: .... **$79.00–$136.00**

CROSMAN 2100B CLASSIC AIR RIFLE

Caliber: .177 steel BBs, .177 pellets. Barrel: Rifled 20.84 in. Weight: 4.81 lbs. Length: 39.75 in. Power: Multi-pump pneumatic. Stock: Ambidextrous plastic stock with simulated wood grain. Sights: Blade and ramp, rear sight adjustable for windage and elevation, grooved for scope mounting. Features: Adult-size inexpensive airgun, single-shot, bolt action, lightweight, accurate and easy to shoot. Velocity: 755 fps.
Price: .... **$83.00–$90.00**

CROSMAN SHOCKWAVE NP AIR RIFLE

Calibers: .177, .22. Barrel: Rifled 15 in. Weight: 6.0 lbs. Length: 43.5 in. Power: Break-barrel, gas-piston. Stock: Ambidextrous synthetic with dual raised cheekpieces. Sights: Front fiber-optic sight and fully adjustable fiber-optic rear, Weaver/Picatinny rail for scope mounting, includes 4x32 scope and rings. Features: Single-shot, includes bipod, adjustable two-stage trigger. Velocities: .177, 1,200 fps/.22, 950 fps.
Price: ....**$145.00–$177.00**

CROSMAN ST-1 FULL-AUTO CO₂ RIFLE/PISTOL

Caliber: .177 BBs. Barrel: Smooth, 6.125-15.5 in. Weight: 6.3 lbs. Length: 17.75-33 in. Power: CO2. Stock: Removable two-position adjustable nylon fiber tactical buttstock. Sights: None, comes with a red-dot sight, Picatinny rail. Features: Removable barrel extender, scannable QR code for VIP access, quad-rail forearm, textured nonslip grips, 25-round quick reload reservoir, 400 BB reservoir, adjustable removable stock, convertible from rifle to pistol, and can be configured as a rifle, carbine, or pistol, blowback action, powered by two CO2 cartridges. Velocity: 430 fps.
Price: **$300.00**

CROSMAN TYRO AIR RIFLE

Calibers: .177. Barrel: Rifled. Weight: 4.9 lbs. Length: 37.5 in. Power: Break-barrel, spring-piston. Stock: Synthetic thumbhole with spacers to adjust the length of pull. Sights: Front fiber optic and adjustable rear. Features: Single-shot, sized for smaller shooters. Velocities: 720 fps with alloy pellets.
Price: **$83.00**

Prices given are believed to be accurate at time of publication however, many factors affect retail pricing so exact prices are not possible.

CROSMAN VALIANT SBD NP AIR RIFLE
Calibers: .177, .22. Barrel: Rifled, 15.75 in. Weight: 7.95 lbs. Length: 46 in. Power: Break-barrel, nitro-piston. Stock: Hardwood thumbhole. Sights: Adjustable rear, fixed front. Features: Adjustable two-stage trigger, 11mm optics rail, comes with a CenterPoint 4X32 scope. Velocities: .177, 1,400 fps/.22, 1,100 fps. with alloy pellets.
Price: ....$177.00–$189.00

DAISY 1938 RED RYDER AIR RIFLE
Caliber: .177 steel BBs. Barrel: Smoothbore 10.85 in. Weight: 2.2 lbs. Length: 35.4 in. Power: Single-cock, lever action, spring-piston. Stock: Solid wood stock and forend. Sights: Blade front sight, adjustable rear sight. Features: 650 BB reservoir, single-stage trigger. Velocity: 350 fps.
Price: $45.00

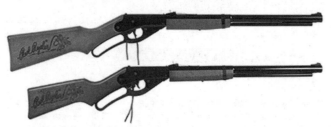

DAISY ADULT RED RYDER BB RIFLE
Caliber: .177 steel BBs. Barrel: Smoothbore 10.85 in. Weight: 2.95 lbs. Length: 36.75 in. Power: Single-cock, lever action, spring-piston. Stock: Solid wood stock and forend. Sights: Blade front sight, adjustable rear sight. Features: A larger, adult-size version of the classic youth Red Ryder with 650 shot reservoir, 18-lb. cocking effort. Velocity: 350 fps.
Price: $55.00

DAISY MODEL 499B CHAMPION COMPETITION RIFLE
Caliber: .177 BBs. Barrel: Smoothbore, 20.88 in. Weight: 3.1 lbs. Length: 36.25. Power: Lever-action spring piston. Stock: Hardwood. Sights: Hooded front with aperture inserts and adjustable rear peep sight. Features: Single shot, 5m competition rifle. Velocity: 240 fps.
Price: $176.00

DAISY MODEL 599 COMPETITION AIR RIFLE
Caliber: .177 pellets. Barrel: Rifled, cold hammer-forged BSA barrel, 20.88 in. Weight: 7.1 lbs. Length: 34.35–37.25 in. Power: Precharged pneumatic. Stock: Ambidextrous beech wood stock with vertical and length of pull adjustment, adjustable comb. Sights: Hooded front and diopter rear sight. Features: Trigger weight adjustable down to 1.5 lbs, rotating trigger adjustment for positioning right or left, straight-pull T-bolt handle, removable power cylinder. Velocity: 520 fps.
Price: $595.00

DAISY MODEL 25 PUMP GUN
Caliber: .177 steel BBs. Barrel: Smoothbore. Weight: 3 lbs. Length: 37 in. Power: pump action, spring-air. Stock: Solid wood buttstock. Sights: Fixed front and rear sights. Features: 50-shot BB reservoir, removable screw-out shot tube, decorative engraving on receiver, rear sight can be flipped over to change from open to peep sight. Velocity: 350 fps.
Price: $44.00

DAISY MODEL 105 BUCK AIR RIFLE
Caliber: .177 steel BBs. Barrel: Smoothbore 7.97 in. Weight: 1.6 lbs. Length: 29.8 in. Power: Single-cock, lever action, spring-piston. Stock: Solid wood buttstock. Sights: Fixed front and rear sights. Features: 400-BB reservoir, single-stage trigger. Velocity: 275 fps.
Price: $36.00

DAISY AVANTI MODEL 753S MATCH GRADE AVANTI
Caliber: .177 pellets. Barrel: Rifled, Lothar Walther, 19.5 in. Weight: 7.3 lbs. Length: 38.5 in. Power: Single-stroke pneumatic. Stock: Ambidextrous wood or synthetic. Sights: Globe front sight and Precision Diopter rear sight. Features: Full-size wood stock, additional inserts available for the front sight, fully self-contained power system, excellent "first" rifle for all 10m shooting disciplines. Velocity: 495 fps.
Price: $275.00

DAISY POWERLINE MODEL 35 AIR RIFLE
Caliber: .177 steel BBs, .177 pellets. Barrel: Smoothbore. Weight: 2.25 lbs. Length: 34.5 in. Power: Multi-pump pneumatic. Stock: Ambidextrous plastic stock, available in black and pink camo. Sights: Blade and ramp, rear sight adjustable for elevation, grooved for scope mounting. Features: Single-shot pellet, BB repeater, lightweight, accurate, and easy to shoot. Velocity: 625 fps.
Price: ....$44.00–$60.00

DAISY POWERLINE MODEL 880 AIR RIFLE
Caliber: .177 steel BBs, .177 pellets. Barrel: Rifled, 21 in. Weight: 3.1 lbs. Length: 37.6 in. Power: Multi-pump pneumatic. Stock: Synthetic. Sights: Fiber-optic front sight, rear sight adjustable for elevation, grooved for scope mounting. Features: Single-shot pellet, 50-shot BB, lightweight, accurate, and easy to shoot. Velocity: 800 fps (BBs), 665 fps (pellets).
Price: $55.00

DAISY POWERLINE 901 AIR RIFLE
Caliber: .177 steel BBs, .177 pellets. Barrel: Rifled 20.8 in. Weight: 3.2 lbs. Length: 37.75 in. Power: Multi-pump pneumatic. Stock: Ambidextrous black wood grain plastic. Sights: Front fiber-optic sight, rear blade sight adjustable for elevation, grooved for scope mounting. Features: Full-size adult airgun, single-shot pellet, BB repeater, bolt action. "Ready to go" kit available complete with ammo, safety glasses, Shatterblast targets, 4x15 scope, and mounts. Velocity: 750 fps.
Price: $71.00

DAISY CAMO OR PINK LEVER ACTION MODEL 1999 RIFLE
Caliber: .177 steel BBs. Barrel: Smoothbore. Weight: 2.2 lbs. Length: 35.4 in. Power: Single-cock, lever action, spring-piston. Stock: Synthetic camo or pink. Sights: Fixed front and rear fiber-optic sights. Features: Oversized loop lever, designed for ages 10 and above. Velocity: 350 fps.
Price: $44.00

Prices given are believed to be accurate at time of publication however, many factors affect retail pricing so exact prices are not possible.

78TH EDITION, 2024 ⟡ 589

DAYSTATE DELTA WOLF RIFLE

Calibers: .177, .22, .25, .30. Barrel: Rifled, 17 in. (.177 or .22) or 23 in. (.177, .22, .25, .30). Weight: 7.4–7.8 lbs. Length: 28.4–33.1 in. Power: Precharged pneumatic. Stock: AR style. Sights: None, 22mm Picatinny rail. Features: Advanced Velocity Technology with display touchscreen, multi-caliber with fast-change barrel system, factory set power profiles for each caliber, built-in chronograph that allows the shooter to dial in their preferred velocity, OEM Huma-Air regulated, large-capacity (8- to 13-shot) magazine, Bluetooth connectivity, switchable side lever action, carbon-fiber shroud and optional silencer, removable air tank. Velocity: Adjustable.
Price: ....$2,695.00–$2,895.00

DAYSTATE HUNTSMAN REVERE AIR RIFLE

Calibers: .177, .22, .25. Barrel: Match grade, rifled, 17 in. Weight: 6.4 lbs. Length: 36.5 in. Power: Precharged pneumatic. Stock: Right-handed Monte Carlo walnut. Sights: None, 11mm grooved dovetail for scope mounting. Features: Side-lever action, HUMA air regulator, 13- (.177), 11- (.22) or 10- (.25) shot rotary magazine, single-shot loading tray, 20–46 shots per fill depending on caliber, adjustable two-stage trigger, shrouded barrel, available in a left-handed version. Velocity: Adjustable.
Price: $1,500.00

DAYSTATE RED WOLF HILITE HP RIFLE

Calibers: .177, .22, .25, .30. Barrel: Fully shrouded carbon fiber, 23 in. Weight: 8.5 lbs. Length: 45 in. Power: Precharged pneumatic. Stock: Ambidextrous walnut, red laminate, or blue laminate. Sights: None, 11mm grooved dovetail for scope mounting. Features: Three individual programmed energy and velocity settings, computer-controlled MCT firing system, LCD screen displays air pressure, battery state, number of shots fired, 13- (.177), 11- (.22), 10- (.25) or eight- (.30) shot magazine or single-shot tray for .177, .22, or .25, 30–150 shots per fill depending on caliber, fully adjustable electronic release trigger from ounces to pounds, right- or left-hand reversible side cocking. Velocity: Adjustable.
Price: $3,000.00

DAYSTATE WOLVERINE 2 HP HILITE HUMA RIFLE

Calibers: .22, .25, or .30. Barrel: Match-grade shrouded rifled, 23 in.

Weight: 8.4 lbs. Length: 44 in. Power: Precharged pneumatic. Stock: Ambidextrous thumbhole walnut or laminate. Sights: None, 11mm grooved dovetail for scope mounting. Features: Right- or left-hand reversible side-lever cocking, HUMA air regulator, adjustable buttpad, 10-shot magazine, 120–140 shots per charge, two-stage adjustable trigger. Velocity: Adjustable.
Price: $2,500.00

DIANA CHASER CO₂ AIR RIFLE/PISTOL KIT

Caliber: .177, .22. Barrel: Rifled, 17.7 in. Weight: 3.1 lbs. Length: 38.4 in. Power: CO2. Stock: Ambidextrous synthetic. Sights: Front fiber-optic and adjustable rear, 11mm dovetail for scope mounting. Features: Shrouded barrel, two-stage adjustable trigger, single-shot (can use indexing 7–9 shot magazines from the Stormrider), approximately 50 shots per CO2 cylinder, kit includes a soft case, Chaser pistol, buttstock, and rifle barrel. Velocities: 642 fps (.177 rifle), 500 fps (.22 rifle).
Price: $200.00

DIANA 34 EMS BREAK-BARREL AIR RIFLE

Caliber: .177, .22. Barrel: Rifled, 19.5 in. Weight: 7.85 lbs. Length: 46.3 in. Power: Break-barrel, spring-piston, convertible to N-TEC gas piston. Stock: Ambidextrous wood or thumbhole synthetic. Sights: Front fiber-optic and micrometer adjustable rear, 11 mm dovetail. Features: Two-stage adjustable trigger, single-shot, removable 1/2 in UNF threaded barrel, EMS (easy modular system) allows for easy changing of barrels, adjustable barrel alignment, two-piece cocking lever. Velocities: 890 fps (.177), 740 fps (.22).
Price: ....$450.00–$500.00

DIANA 54 AIRKING PRO LAMINATE AIR RIFLE

Caliber: .177, .22. Barrel: Rifled, 17.3 in. Weight: 10.25 lbs. Length: 44in. Power: Spring piston side lever. Stock: Red and black laminated or beechwood. Sights: Adjustable rear, 11 mm dovetail. Features: Two-stage adjustable trigger, single-shot, forearm swivel stud to attach a bipod, adjustable barrel weight, checkered grip and forearm. Velocities: 1,100 fps (.177), 990 fps (.22).
Price: ....$800.00–$850.00

DIANA MAUSER K98 AIR RIFLE

Calibers: .177, .22. Barrel: Rifled 18.0 in. Weight: 9.5 lbs. Length: 44 in. Power: Break-barrel, spring-piston. Stock: Authentic Mauser K98 hardwood stock. Sights: Front post and fully adjustable rear, 11mm dovetail grooved for scope mounting. Features: European quality, fixed barrel with under-lever cocking, exceptional two-stage adjustable match trigger, single-shot, German manufactured to stringent quality control and testing, limited lifetime warranty. Velocities: .177, 1,150 fps/.22, 850 fps.
Price: $450.00

DIANA OCTOBERFEST AIR RIFLE

Calibers: .177 BB. Barrel: Rifled, 21.5 in. Weight: 7.2 lbs. Length: 44 in. Power: Spring-piston. Stock: Hardwood. Sights: Tapered front post, adjustable rear. Features: 100-round under-barrel tube magazine, top-cocking lever, fixed barrel, single-shot, designed after Diana's Gallery Guns of the Past. Velocity: 400 fps.
Price: **$200.00**

DIANA 350 N-TEC MAGNUM PREMIUM AIR RIFLE
Calibers: .177, .22. Barrel: Rifled 19.5 in. Weight: 6.7 lbs. Length: 48.5 in. Power: Break-barrel, German gas piston. Stock: Ambidextrous, available in beech and synthetic. Sights: Front post and fully adjustable rear, grooved for scope mounting. Features: European quality, exceptional two-stage adjustable match trigger, single-shot, German manufactured to stringent quality control and testing, limited lifetime warranty. Velocities: .177, 1,250 fps/.22, 1,000 fps.
Price: **$500.00**

DIANA MODEL RWS 48 AIR RIFLE, T06 TRIGGER
Calibers: .177, .22. Barrel: Rifled 17 in. Weight: 8.5 lbs. Length: 42.13 in. Power: Single-cock, side lever, spring piston. Stock: Ambidextrous beech thumbhole stock. Sights: Blade front, fully adjustable rear, grooved for scope mounting. Features: European quality, exceptional two-stage match trigger, single-shot, German manufactured to stringent quality control and testing, limited lifetime warranty. Velocities: .177, 1,100 fps/.22, 900 fps.
Price: **$550.00**

DIANA RWS 460 MAGNUM AIR RIFLE
Calibers: .177, .22. Barrel: Rifled 18.44 in. Weight: 8.3 lbs. Length: 45 in. Power: Under-lever, spring piston. Stock: Right-hand hardwood with grip and forend checkering. Sights: Post front and fully adjustable rear, grooved for scope mounting. Features: European quality, exceptional two-stage adjustable match trigger, single-shot, German manufactured to stringent quality control and testing, limited lifetime warranty. Various bundled configurations are available. Velocity: .177, 1,200 fps/.22, 1,000 fps.
Price: **$500.00**

DIANA STORMRIDER GEN 2 PCP RIFLE
Calibers: .177, .22. Barrel: Rifled 19 in. Weight: 5.0 lbs. Length: 40.5 in. Power: Precharged pneumatic. Stock: Checkered beech. Sights: Blade front, fully adjustable rear, 11 mm dovetail grove. Features: Entry-level PCP rifle, nine-shot (.177) or seven-shot (.22) capacity, adjustable two-stage trigger, built-in muzzle brake, integrated pressure gauge. Velocities: 1,050 fps (.177)/900 fps (.22).
Price: **$300.00**

DIANA TRAILSCOUT CO₂ RIFLE
Caliber: .177, .22 pellet. Barrel: Rifled, 19 in. Weight: 4.6 lbs. Length: 38.9 in. Power: CO2. Stock: Synthetic. Sights: Adjustable rear. Features: Uses three 12g CO2 cylinders, can be used single shot or with a seven- (.22) or nine- (.177) shot magazine, bolt action, adjustable trigger, approximately 100 shots per fill. Velocities: 660 fps (.177), 560 fps (.22).
Price: **$180.00**

DIANA XR200 PREMIUM PCP RIFLE
Calibers: .177, .22, .25, .30 pellet. Barrel: Rifled, Lothar Walther, 21.6 in. Weight: 6.5 lbs. Length: 42.9 in. Power: Precharged pneumatic. Stock: Green synthetic or beech wood, ambidextrous with adjustable cheekpiece. Sights: None, 11mm dovetail grove. Features: Optional slug barrel, rotatable manometer for easy reading, 8-14 shot magazine depending on caliber, includes two-shot adapter, adjustable two-stage trigger, ALTAROS regulator for shot-to-shot consistency, built-in compensator, under-rail for bipod, case included. Velocities: Adjustable.
Price: ....**$1231.00–$1,338.00**

DPMS SBR FULL-AUTO BB RIFLE
Caliber: .177 BB. Barrel: Smoothbore. Weight: 6.2 lbs. Length: 26.5 in. Power: CO2. Stock: Adjustable six-position buttstock with AR-compatible pistol grip. Sights: Folding BUIS front and rear with Picatinny rail. Features: Blowback action, quad-rail forearm for accessory mounting, 25-round drop-out magazine, fully auto with up to 1,400 rounds per minute. Also comes in a dual-action semi-/full-auto version. Velocity: 430 fps.
Price: ....**$214.00–$246.00**

EDGUN LELYA 2.0 PCP RIFLE
Calibers: .177, .22, or .25 pellet. Barrel: Rifled, Alfa Precision, 15.4 in. Weight: 6.4 lbs. Length: 23.5 in. Power: Precharged pneumatic. Stock: Walnut ambidextrous bullpup style. Sights: None, Weaver-style rail for scope mounting. Features: Dual side-lever cocking for ambidextrous cocking, adjustable hammer spring tension, two-stage adjustable trigger, 35–50 shots per fill depending on caliber, 10-round (in .177 or .22) or nine-round magazine (.25), sling loop in the rear of the stock, fully shrouded barrel. Velocities: Approximately 920 fps (.177), 900 fps (.22), 880 fps (.25).
Price: **$1,949.00**

EDGUN LESHIY 2 STANDARD PCP AIR RIFLE
Calibers: .177, .22, .25, or .30 pellets. Barrel: Rifled, 9.85 in. Weight: 5 lbs. Length: 25.5 in. overall. Power: Precharged pneumatic. Stock: Ambidextrous adjustable. Sights: None, Weaver-style rail for scope mounting. Features: Semi-automatic, folding stock that is compact to carry (13.5 inches when folded), red and grey laminate AR pistol grip, includes two eight-round magazines, single-stage trigger, Picatinny forearm accessory rail, unique hammerless design, 18–36 shots per fill depending on caliber. Velocities: 900 fps (.177), 870 fps (.22), 800 fps (.25), 740 fps (.30).
Price: **$2,700.00**

EDGUN MATADOR R5M STANDARD PCP RIFLE
Calibers: .177, .22, or .25. Barrel: Rifled, Lothar Walther, 18.75 in. Weight: 6.75 lbs. Length: 27.5 in. Power: Precharged pneumatic. Stock: Ambidextrous walnut thumbhole or synthetic. Sights: None, Weaver rail for scope mounting. Features: Adjustable trigger, adjustable hammer spring tension, designed and manufactured in Russia, 40–60 shots per fill depending on caliber, also available with a longer barrel, ambidextrous safety. Velocities: 950 fps (.177), 920 fps (.22 and .25).
Price: $2,200.00

EVANIX RAPTOR PCP AIR RIFLE
Calibers: .177, .22, .25, .30. Barrel: Rifled, 18.9 in. or 23.6 in. (.30 cal.). Weight: 7.2 lbs. Length: 31.5 in. or 33.9 in. (.30) overall. Power: Precharged pneumatic. Stock: Ambidextrous wood thumbhole. Sights: None, grooved 11mm dovetail for scope mounting. Features: Multi-shot side-lever action, shot count varies based on caliber. Velocities: Variable.
Price: $1,170.00

EVANIX REX AIR RIFLE
Calibers: .22, .25, .35 (9mm), .45. Barrel: Rifled, 19.68 in. Weight: 5.51 lbs. Length: 35.82 in. overall. Power: Precharged pneumatic. Sights: Weaver rail for scope mounting Features: Lightweight, compact and massively powerful, single shot, capable of over 200 ft-lbs at the muzzle in .45 caliber. Velocities: .22, 1,080 fps/.25, 970 fps/.35, 860 fps/.45, 700 fps.
Price: .... $799.00–$1,149.00

FEINWERKBAU 500 AIR RIFLE
Caliber: .177. Barrel: Rifled 13.8 in. Weight: 7.05 lbs. Length: 43.7 in. Power: Precharged pneumatic. Stock: Ambidextrous beech with adjustable cheekpiece and buttstock. Sights: Globe front sight and diopter rear. Features: Meets requirements for ISSF competition, trigger pull weight adjusts from 3.9 to 7.8 ounces, bolt action, competition-grade airgun. Velocity: 574 fps.
Price: $1,400.00

FEINWERKBAU 800X FIELD TARGET AIR RIFLE
Caliber: .177. Barrel: Rifled 16.73 in. Weight: 11.7–15.05 lbs. Length: 49.76 in. Power: Precharged pneumatic. Stock: Highly adaptable field target competition stock. Sights: None, 11mm grooved for scope mounting. Features: Approximately 100+ shots per fill, adjustable trigger shoe, adjustable hand rest, vertically adjustable butt pad, adjustable butt hook, vertically and laterally adjustable comb, five-way adjustable match trigger, bolt action, competition-grade airgun. Also available in a smaller, lower-priced model for Junior competition. Velocity: 825 fps.
Price: $3,400.00

FEINWERKBAU 900 ALU RIFLE
Caliber: .177. Barrel: Rifled. Power: Precharged pneumatic. Stock: Highly adjustable silver or black field target competition stock. Sights: Adjustable Vario, 11mm grooved for scope mounting. Features: Adjustable absorber, maintenance-free pressure reducer, 13 different color options available, Centra sights optional, mesh pro grips, right- or left-hand grips in S, M, or L, adjustable trigger shoe, adjustable hand rest, vertically adjustable butt pad, adjustable butt hook, vertically and laterally adjustable comb, five-way adjustable match trigger, competition-grade airgun.
Price: $4,280.00

FEINWERKBAU P75 BIATHLON AIR RIFLE
Caliber: .177. Barrel: Rifled 16.73 in. Weight: 9.26 lbs. Length: 42.91 in. Power: Precharged pneumatic. Stock: Highly adaptable laminate wood competition. Sights: Front globe with aperture inserts and diopter micrometer rear. Features: Bolt action, competition-grade airgun, five-way adjustable match trigger. Velocity: 564 fps.
Price: $3,700.00

FX IMPACT AIR RIFLE
Calibers: .25, .30. Barrel: Rifled 24.4 in. Weight: 7.0 lbs. Length: 34.0 in. Power: Pre-charged pneumatic. Stock: Compact bullpup stock in various materials and finishes Sights: None, 11mm grooved for scope mounting. Features: Premium airgun brand known for exceptional build quality and accuracy, regulated for consistent shots, adjustable two-stage trigger, FX smooth twist barrel, multi-shot side lever action, fully moderated barrel, highly adjustable and adaptable air rifle system. Velocities: .25, 900 fps/.30, 870 fps.
Price: ....$2,099.00–$2,349.00

FX CROWN MK II PCP RIFLE
Calibers: .177, .22, .25, .30. Barrel: Rifled, 15, 19.7, 23.6, or 27.6 in. Weight: 6.2–6.8 lbs. Length: 38.5–43 in. Power: Precharged pneumatic. Stock: Ambidextrous stock in walnut, laminate, or synthetic. Sights: None, 20-MOA Picatinny rail. Features: Optional adjustable laminated GRS stock, Smooth Twist X barrels that can be swapped to change caliber and twist rate, adjustable 15-oz. two-stage trigger, externally adjustable regulator, adjustable power wheel and hammer spring, side-lever cocking, removable carbon-fiber tank, 45–200 shots per fill depending on caliber, dual manometers, built-in muzzle shroud, multiple-shot magazine (13–22 shots depending on caliber), 28–70 ft-lbs of energy depending on caliber. Velocities: .177, 1,000 fps/.22, 920 fps/.25, 900 fps/.30, 870 fps.
Price: ....$2,050.00–$2,100.00

FX DREAMLINE CLASSIC PCP RIFLE
Calibers: .177, .22, .25, .30. Barrel: Rifled, match grade, 19.7 or 23.6 in. Weight: 5.7–6.4 lbs. Length: 38.4–42.9 in. Power: Precharged pneumatic. Stock: Ambidextrous in walnut, laminate, or synthetic. Sights: None, 11 mm dovetail. Features: Optional adjustable laminated GRS stock, Smooth Twist X barrels that can be swapped to change caliber and twist rate, free-floating barrel, 1/2-inch UNF threaded, adjustable match trigger, AMP externally adjustable regulator, adjustable power wheel and hammer spring, side-lever cocking, dual manometers, removable multiple-shot magazine (13–22 shots depending on caliber), 18–45 ft-lbs of energy depending on caliber (.30 TBA). Can be converted to bullpup or tactical models by changing barrels and stocks. Velocities: .177, 940 fps/.22, 920 fps/.25, 890 fps/.30, TBA.
Price: ....$1,000.00–$1,330.00

Prices given are believed to be accurate at time of publication however, many factors affect retail pricing so exact prices are not possible.

FX IMPACT MK III PCP RIFLE

Calibers: .177, .22, .25, .30, .35. Barrel: Rifled, 19.7–31.5 in. Weight: 6.1–7.35 lbs. Length: 25–44 in. Power: Precharged pneumatic. Stock: Compact synthetic bullpup stock. Sights: None, 20-MOA Picatinny rail. Features: Dual regulated for consistent shots, tool-free Quick Tune adjustment system, 16-step power wheel, ambidextrous short-throw cocking lever, dual manometers, 18- to 34-shot magazine depending on caliber, AR-style grip, built-in shroud, match trigger, carbon-fiber-wrapped air tank, Smooth Twist X barrels that can be swapped to change caliber and twist rate, highly adjustable and adaptable air rifle system. Velocities: Adjustable.
Price: .... **$2,200.00–$2,300.00**

FX MAVERICK SNIPER PCP AIR RIFLE

Calibers: .22, .25, .30. Barrel: Rifled 27.6 in. Weight: 7.2 lbs. Length: 36 in. Power: Precharged pneumatic. Stock: Tactical style with AR-style grip. Sights: None, 20-MOA Picatinny rail for scope mounting. Features: Three Picatinny rails for accessories, adjustable match trigger, threaded barrel shroud, side lever action, dual AMP regulators, 580cc carbon-fiber air cylinder, dual manometers, 90 (.30), 170 (.25), 270 (.22) maximum shots per fill, 18- (.22), 16- (.25), 13- (.30) shot magazine, includes one magazine and a hard case, also available in a compact version. Velocities: .22, 1,000 fps/.25, 1,000 fps/.30, 900 fps.
Price: **$2,000.00**

FX WILDCAT MKIII SNIPER AIR RIFLE

Calibers: .22, .25, .30. Barrel: Rifled 23.6 in. Length: 37.75 in. Power: Precharged pneumatic. Stock: Compact bullpup synthetic stock. Sights: None, Picatinny rail for scope mounting. Features: Externally adjustable regulator, adjustable two-stage trigger, FX Smooth Twist X barrel, multi-shot side lever action, 300cc aluminum air cylinder, adjustable hammer spring tension, comes standard with the Superior STX liner to swap calibers, threaded muzzle, up to 35–90 shots per fill depending on caliber, 18- (.22), 16- (.25) or 13-round (.30) capacity magazine. Velocity: .22, 950 fps/.25, 970 fps/.30, 930 fps.
Price: **$1,700.00**

FX .30 BOSS AIR RIFLE

Caliber: .30. Barrel: Rifled 24.4 in. Weight: 7.0 lbs. Length: 47.5 in. Power: Precharged pneumatic. Stock: Thumbhole, synthetic. Sights: None. 11mm grooved for scope mounting. Features: Regulated for consistent shots, adjustable two-stage trigger, FX smooth twist barrel, multi-shot side lever action, fully moderated barrel. Velocities: .22, 1,200 fps/.25, 900 fps.
Price: .... **$1,700.00–$2,000.00**

FX ROYALE 400 AIR RIFLE

Caliber: .177, .22. Barrel: Rifled 19.5 in. Weight: 7.5 lbs. Length: 40.25 in. Power: Precharged pneumatic. Stock: Thumbhole, synthetic. Sights: None. 11mm dovetailed for scope mounting. Features: FX smooth twist barrel, removable carbon-fiber air cylinder, fully shrouded barrel, adjustable power, up to 100 shots per fill, side lever action, two-stage adjustable trigger, adjustable buttplate, 12-shot rotary magazine. Velocities: .177, 950 fps/.22, 950 fps.
Price: **$1,600.00**

*scope not included

GAMO COYOTE WHISPER FUSION PCP AIR RIFLE

Calibers: .177, .22. Barrel: Cold hammer-forged match-grade rifled barrel, 24.5 in. Weight: 6.6 lbs. Length: 42.9 in. Power: Precharged pneumatic. Stock: Ambidextrous hardwood stock. Sights: None, grooved for scope mounting. Features: European class airgun, highly accurate and powerful, adjustable two-stage trigger, integrated moderator, 10-shot bolt action. Velocities: .177, 1,200 fps/.22, 1,000 fps.
Price: **$574.00**

GAMO DELTA FOX JUNIOR RIFLE KIT

Calibers: .177 pellet. Barrel: Rifled. Weight: 4.6 lbs. Length: 39.7 in. Power: Single-stroke spring piston. Stock: Synthetic. Sights: Adjustable fiber optic. Features: 19-lb. cocking effort, comes with pellets and targets, single shot, designed as an introductory pellet rifle. Velocity: 750 fps with alloy pellets.
Price: **$120.00**

GAMO WILDCAT WHISPER BREAK-BARREL AIR RIFLE

Calibers: .177, .22. Barrel: Rifled, 19.1 in. Weight: 5.6 lbs. Length: 44.5 in. Power: Gas piston, break barrel. Stock: Ambidextrous synthetic stock. Sights: Fixed, grooved for scope mounting, includes a 4x32 scope. Features: Single shot, Inert Gas Technology (IGS), 30-lb. cocking effort, Whisper noise suppression. Velocities: .177, 1,350 fps/.22, 975 fps.
Price: **$136.00**

GAMO SWARM MAXXIM 10X GEN2 MULTI-SHOT AIR RIFLE

Calibers: .177, .22. Barrel: Rifled 19.9 in. Weight: 5.64 lbs. Length: 45.3 in. Power: Break-barrel, gas-piston. Stock: Ambidextrous glass-filled nylon stock. Sights: None, grooved for scope mounting, includes recoil-reducing rail, 3-9x32 scope and mounts. Features: 10-shot multi-shot system allows for automatic loading with each cock of the barrel, easy cocking, adjustable two-stage trigger, all-weather fluted barrel with an integrated suppressor. Velocities: .177, 1,300 fps/.22, 1,000 fps.
Price: **$210.00**

GAMO SWARM MAGNUM 10X GEN 3I MULTI-SHOT AIR RIFLE

Caliber: .177, .22 pellet. Barrel: Rifled 21.3 in. Weight: 6.88 lbs. Length: 49.2 in. Power: Break-barrel, gas-piston. Stock: Ambidextrous lightweight nylon thumbhole. Sights: None, grooved for scope mounting, includes recoil-reducing rail, 3-9x40 scope and mounts. Features: 10-shot multi-shot system allows for inertia-feed automatic loading with each cock of the barrel, checkering on grip and forearm, adjustable two-stage trigger, features Whisper Fusion integrated suppressor technology, Shock Wave Absorber recoil pad. Velocity: 1,300 fps with alloy pellets.
Price: **$320.00**

GAMO URBAN PCP AIR RIFLE

Caliber: .22. Barrel: Cold hammer-forged match-grade rifled barrel. Weight: 6.7 lbs. Length: 42.0 in. Power: Precharged pneumatic. Stock: Ambidextrous composite thumbhole stock. Sights: None, grooved for scope mounting, Features: European-class airgun, highly accurate and powerful, adjustable two-stage trigger, integrated moderator, 10-shot bolt action. Velocity: 800 fps.
Price: **$380.00**

GAMO BIG BORE TC35 AIR RIFLE
Caliber: .35. Barrel: rifled, 14.96 in. Weight: 6.0 lbs. Length: 35.88 in. Power: Precharged pneumatic. Stock: Ambidextrous. Sights: None, Weaver rail for scope mounting, Features: Produces up to 170 ft-lbs of muzzle energy, adjustable trigger, two power settings, shrouded barrel, single-shot action allows for an extremely wide range of ammo choices.
Price: $1,150.00

GAMO BIG BORE TC45 AIR RIFLE
Caliber: .45. Barrel: rifled, 24.24 in. Weight: 8.0 lbs. Length: 47.13 in. Power: Precharged pneumatic. Stock: Ambidextrous. Sights: None, Weaver rail for scope mounting. Features: Produces over 400 ft-lbs of muzzle energy shooting 350-grain cast slugs, adjustable trigger, two power settings, shrouded barrel, single shot action allows for an extremely wide range of ammo choices.
Price: $1,500.00

GAMO VARMINT AIR RIFLE
Caliber: .177 pellets. Barrel: Rifled, 18 in. Weight: 5.5 lbs. Length: 43.3 in. Power: Break-barrel, spring piston. Stock: Ambidextrous lightweight composite with dual raised cheekpieces. Sights: None, grooved for scope mounting, includes 4x32 scope and mounts. Features: Lightweight, single-shot, 30-lb. cocking effort, adjustable trigger, steel barrel with an all-weather fluted polymer jacket. Velocity: 1,250 fps with alloy pellets.
Price: $105.00

GAMO WHISPER FUSION MACH 1 AIR RIFLE, IGT
Calibers: .177, .22. Barrel: Rifled 20.5 in. Weight: 6.6 lbs. Length: 46 in. Power: Break-barrel, Inert Gas Technology gas piston. Stock: Lightweight composite stock with ambidextrous cheekpiece. Sights: Globe fiber-optic front and fully adjustable fiber-optic rear, grooved for scope mounting, includes Shock Wave Absorber recoil-reducing pad, 3-9x40 scope and heavy-duty mount. Features: Integrated Gamo "Whisper" noise dampening system and bull barrel noise suppression system for maximum stealth, single-shot, 32-lb. cocking effort, adjustable two-stage trigger. Velocities: .177, 1,420 fps/.22, 1,020 fps.
Price: $290.00

GLETCHER M1891 CO₂ BB RIFLE
Caliber: .177 BBs. Barrel: Smooth, 16 in. Weight: 5.6 lbs. Length: 22.44 in. Power: CO2. Stock: Imitation wood. Sights: Adjustable rear with a removable front globe. Features: Reproduction of the Mosin-Nagant sawed-off rifle, working sliding metal bolt action, built-in hex wrench for changing CO2 cylinders, 16-BB capacity, approximately 120 shots per fill. Velocity: 427 fps.
Price: $280.00

GLETCHER M1944 CO₂ BB RIFLE
Caliber: .177 BBs. Barrel: Smooth, 16 in. Weight: 8.21 lbs. Length: 40.5 in with bayonet folded. Power: CO2. Stock: Imitation wood. Sights: Adjustable rear with a removable front globe. Features: Reproduction of the Russian Mosin-Nagant rifle, working sliding metal bolt action, built-in hex wrench for changing CO2 cylinders, 16-BB capacity, approximately 120 shots per fill, integral folding bayonet, reproduction sling included. Velocity: 427 fps.
Price: $360.00

HAMMERLI AR20 SILVER AIR RIFLE
Calibers: .177. Barrel: Rifled Lothar Walther 19.7 in. Weight: 8.75 lbs. Length: 41.65–43.66 in. Power: Precharged pneumatic. Stock: Ambidextrous aluminum stock with vertically adjustable buttpad and spacers for adjusting the length. Sights: Globe front and fully adjustable diopter rear, grooved for scope mounting. Features: Single shot, ambidextrous cocking piece, removable aluminum air cylinder, meets ISSF requirements. The stock is available in several colors. Velocity: 557 fps.
Price: $1,100.00

H&K HK416 CO₂ BB RIFLE
Caliber: .177 BBs. Barrel: Smoothbore, 14 in. Weight: 5.3 lbs. Length: 28.5 in. Power: CO2. Sights: Flip-up front and rear. Stock: Polymer. Features: 500-round BB reservoir with 36 BBs in the feeding portion, semi-automatic, uses two 12-gram CO2 cylinders, six-shot burst mode, Picatinny accessory rails on all sides, collapsible stock, AR-style grip. Velocity: 450 fps.
Price: $115.00

H&K MP5 K-PCW CO₂ BB COMPACT SUBMACHINE GUN
Caliber: .177 BBs. Barrel: Smoothbore. Weight: 2.4 lbs. Length: 24.5 in. Power: CO2. Sights: Post globe front, adjustable rear. Features: 40-round removable banana-style magazine, semi-automatic, recoils like a firearm, folding stock, forward grip. Velocity: 400 fps.
Price: $89.00

H&K MP7 BREAK-BARREL PELLET GUN
Caliber: .177 pellets. Barrel: Rifled. Weight: 6.0 lbs. Length: 23.0–31.5 in. Power: Spring piston. Stock: Collapsible wire. Sights: None, Axeon Optics 1xRDS red dot. Features: Single shot, adjustable length of pull, Picatinny rails on top and sides, faux suppressor. Velocity: 490 fps.
Price: $106.00

HATSAN USA EDGE CLASS AIRGUNS
Calibers: .177, .22, .25. Barrel: Rifled 17.7 in. Weight: 6.4–6.6 lbs. Length: 43 in. Power: Break-barrel, spring-piston and gas-spring variations. Stock: Multiple synthetic and synthetic skeleton stock options. Available in different colors such as black, muddy girl camo, moon camo, etc. Sights: Fiber-optic front and fully adjustable fiber-optic rear, grooved for scope mounting, includes 3-9x32 scope and mounts. Features: European manufacturing with German steel, single-shot, adjustable two-stage trigger, performance tested at the factory with lead pellets for accurate velocity specifications. Velocities: .177, 1,000 fps/.22, 800 fps/.25, 650 fps.
Price: ....$140.00–$180.00

Prices given are believed to be accurate at time of publication however, many factors affect retail pricing so exact prices are not possible.

HATSAN USA AIRMAX PCP AIR RIFLE

Calibers: .177, .22, .25. Barrel: Rifled 23.0 in. Weight: 10.8 lbs. Length: 37 in. Power: Precharged pneumatic. Stock: Ambidextrous wood bullpup. Sights: None, combination Picatinny rail and 11mm dovetail for scope mounting. Features: Multi-shot side-lever action, 10-shot .177 and .22 magazines/nine-shot .25 magazine, "Quiet Energy" barrel shroud with an integrated suppressor, removable air cylinder, fully adjustable two-stage "Quattro" trigger, "EasyAdjust" elevation comb, sling swivels, includes two magazines. Velocities: .177, 1,170 fps/.22, 1,070 fps/.25, 970 fps.
Price: $630.00

HATSAN USA BULLBOSS QE AIR RIFLE

Calibers: .177, .22, .25. Barrel: Rifled 23.0 in. Weight: 8.6 lbs. Length: 36.8 in. Power: Precharged pneumatic. Stock: Ambidextrous synthetic or hardwood bullpup. Sights: None, innovative dual-rail 11mm dovetail and Weaver compatible for scope mounting. Features: Multi-shot side-lever action, 10-shot .177 and .22 magazines/nine-shot .25 magazine, "Quiet Energy" barrel shroud with an integrated suppressor, European manufacturing with German steel, removable air cylinder, fully adjustable two-stage "Quattro" trigger, performance tested at the factory with lead pellets for accurate velocity specifications. Velocities: .177, 1,170 fps/.22, 1,070 fps/.25, 970 fps.
Price: .... $510.00–$560.00

HATSAN USA BARRAGE SEMI-AUTOMATIC PCP AIR RIFLE

Calibers: .177, .22, .25. Barrel: Rifled, 19.7 in. Weight: 10.1 lbs. Length: 40.9 in. Power: Precharged pneumatic. Stock: Ambidextrous adjustable synthetic thumbhole stock with integrated magazine storage. Sights: None, innovative dual-rail 11mm dovetail and Weaver compatible for scope mounting. Features: Air-driven true semi-automatic action, 14 shots in .177 and 12 shots in .22, "Quiet Energy" barrel shroud with an integrated suppressor, 500cc cylinder with 250-BAR capacity, European manufacturing with German steel, performance tested at the factory with lead pellets for accurate velocity specifications. Velocities: .177, 1,100 fps/.22, 1,000 fps/.25, 900 fps.
Price: $1800.00

HATSAN BLITZ FULL AUTO PCP AIR RIFLE

Calibers: .22, .25, .30. Barrel: Rifled 23 in. Weight: 8.8 lbs. Length: 45.2 in. Power: Precharged pneumatic. Stock: Synthetic. Sights: Adjustable, innovative dual-rail 11mm dovetail and Weaver compatible for scope mounting. Features: Full/semi-automatic selector switch, 1,000 rounds per minute cyclic rate, includes two 21- (.22), 19- (.25), or 16-round (.30) SwingLoad magazines, 100–130 shots per fill depending on the rate of fire and caliber, gas-operating cycling mechanism does not require batteries, "Quiet Energy" barrel shroud, adjustable cheekpiece and buttpad, carry handle, three Picatinny forearm accessory rails. Velocities: 1,050 fps (.22), 970 fps (.25), 730 fps (.30).
Price: $1,000.00

HATSAN USA BULLMASTER SEMI-AUTOMATIC PCP AIR RIFLE

Calibers: .177, .22, .25. Barrel: Rifled, 19.7 in. Weight: 10.3 lbs. Length: 30.9 in. Power: Precharged pneumatic. Stock: Ambidextrous adjustable synthetic bullpup stock with integrated magazine storage. Sights: None, innovative dual-rail 11mm dovetail and Weaver compatible for scope mounting. Features: Air-driven true semi-automatic action, 14 shots in .177 and 12 shots in .22, "Quiet Energy" barrel shroud with an integrated suppressor, 500cc cylinder with 250-BAR capacity, European manufacturing with German steel, performance tested at the factory with lead pellets for accurate velocity specifications. Velocities: .177, 1,100 fps/.22, 1,000 fps/.25 900 fps.
Price: $800.00

HATSAN USA FACTOR RC PCP RIFLE

Calibers: .177, .22, .25. Barrel: Rifled, 23 in. Weight: 7.9 lbs. Length: 40.3–42.9 in. Power: Precharged pneumatic. Stock: Ambidextrous adjustable synthetic tactical stock. Sights: None, innovative dual-rail 11mm dovetail and Weaver-compatible for scope mounting. Features: Removable 580cc carbon-fiber air tank, two-stage adjustable trigger, right/left reversible side lever, threaded muzzle, externally adjustable regulator, up to 120–140 shots per fill depending on caliber, includes two 24- (.177), 21- (.22) or 19-round (.25) magazines, "Quiet Energy" barrel shroud with an integrated suppressor. Also available in .30 and .35 calibers (BP version). Velocities: .177, 1,010 fps/.22, 950 fps/.25 870 fps with lead pellets.
Price: $1,050.00

HATSAN USA HERCULES BULLY PCP AIR RIFLE

Calibers: .177, .22, .25, .30, .35, .45. Barrel: Rifled 23 in. Weight: 13 lbs. Length: 48.4 in. Power: Precharged pneumatic. Stock: Adjustable synthetic all-weather bullpup stock with sling mounts. Sights: None, innovative dual-rail 11mm dovetail and Weaver compatible for scope mounting. Features: Available in 6 calibers, 500cc of air via carbon-fiber reservoir, multi-shot side-lever action, 17-shot .177 magazine, 14-shot .22 magazine, 13-shot .25 magazine, 10-shot .30 magazine, nine-shot .35 magazine, seven-shot .45 magazine. "Quiet Energy" barrel shroud with an integrated suppressor, European manufacturing with German steel, fully adjustable two-stage "Quattro" trigger, performance is tested at the factory with lead pellets for accurate velocity specifications. Velocities: .177, 1,450 fps/.22, 1,300 fps/.25, 1,200 fps/.30, 1,070 fps/.35, 910 fps/.45, 850 fps.
Price: $900.00

HATSAN USA FLASH QE PCP RIFLE

Calibers: .177, .22, .25. Barrel: Rifled, 17.7 in. Weight: 5.9 lbs. Length: 42.3 in. Power: Precharged pneumatic. Stock: Ambidextrous synthetic or hardwood thumbhole. Sights: None, innovative dual-rail 11mm dovetail and Weaver-compatible for scope mounting. Features: Very lightweight, multi-shot side-lever action, multi-shot magazine (shot count varies by caliber). "Quiet Energy" barrel shroud with an integrated suppressor, European manufacturing with German steel, fully adjustable two-stage "Quattro" trigger, performance tested at the factory with lead pellets for accurate velocity specifications. Velocities: .177, 1,250 fps/.22, 1,100 fps/.25, 900 fps.
Price: .... $310.00–$390.00

HATSAN USA FLASHPUP QE PCP RIFLE

Calibers: .177, .22, .25. Barrel: Rifled, 19.4 in. Weight: 6.1 lbs. Length: 32.0 in. Power: Precharged pneumatic. Stock: Ambidextrous hardwood bullpup. Sights: None, dual-rail 11mm dovetail and Weaver-compatible for scope mounting. Features: Very lightweight, multi-shot side-lever action, multi-shot magazine (shot count varies by caliber). "Quiet Energy" barrel shroud with an integrated suppressor, European manufacturing with German steel, fully adjustable two-stage "Quattro" trigger, performance tested at the factory

Prices given are believed to be accurate at time of publication however, many factors affect retail pricing so exact prices are not possible.

78TH EDITION, 2024 ✦ 595

with lead pellets for accurate velocity specifications. Velocity: .177, 1,250 fps/.22, 1,100 fps/.25, 900 fps.

Price: **$360.00**

HATSAN USA GLADIUS AIRGUN

Calibers: .177, .22, .25. Barrel: Rifled, 23 in. Weight: 10.6 lbs. Length: 38 in. Power: Precharged pneumatic. Stock: Ambidextrous adjustable synthetic bullpup stock with integrated magazine storage Sights: None, dual-rail 11mm dovetail and Weaver-compatible for scope mounting. Features: Six-way variable power, multi-shot side-lever action, 10-shot .177 and .22 magazines/nine-shot .25 magazine, "Quiet Energy" barrel shroud with an integrated suppressor, European manufacturing with German steel, removable air cylinder, fully adjustable two-stage "Quattro" trigger, performance tested at the factory with lead pellets for accurate velocity specifications. Velocities: .177, 1,070 fps/.22, 970 fps/.25, 870 fps.

Price: ....**$730.00–$750.00**

HATSAN USA MOD 87 QE VORTEX AIR RIFLE

Calibers: .22. Barrel: Rifled 10.6 in. Weight: 7.4 lbs. Length: 44.5 in. Power: Break-barrel, gas-spring. Stock: Synthetic all-weather stock with adjustable cheekpiece. Sights: Fiber-optic front sight and fully adjustable fiber-optic rear sight, grooved for scope mounting, includes 3-9x32 scope and mounts. Features: "Quiet Energy" barrel shroud with an integrated suppressor, European manufacturing with German steel, single-shot, fully adjustable two-stage "Quattro" trigger, performance tested at the factory with lead pellets for accurate velocity specifications. Velocities: .177, 1,000 fps/.22, 800 fps/.25, 650 fps.

Price: **$215.00**

HATSAN USA MOD 125 SNIPER VORTEX AIR RIFLE

Calibers: .177, .22, .25. Barrel: Rifled 19.6 in. Weight: 9 lbs. Length: 48.8 in. Power: Break-barrel, gas-spring. Stock: Synthetic all-weather stock with adjustable cheekpiece, available in black or camo options. Sights: Fiber-optic front and fully adjustable fiber-optic rear, grooved for scope mounting, includes 3-9x32 scope and mounts. Features: Integrated suppressor, European manufacturing with German steel, single-shot, fully adjustable two-stage "Quattro" trigger, performance tested at the factory with lead pellets for accurate velocity specifications. Velocities: .177, 1,250 fps/.22, 1,000 fps/.25, 750 fps.

Price: ....**$350.00–$380.00**

HATSAN USA MOD 135 QE VORTEX AIR RIFLE

Calibers: .177, .22, .25, .30. Barrel: Rifled 10 in. Weight: 9.9 lbs. Length: 47.2 in. Power: Break-barrel, gas-spring. Stock: Turkish walnut stock with grip and forend checkering, adjustable buttplate and cheekpiece. Sights: Fiber-optic front and fully adjustable fiber-optic rear, dual-rail 11mm dovetail and Weaver-compatible for scope mounting. Features: "Big-bore" break-barrel airgun, "Quiet Energy" barrel shroud with integrated suppressor, European manufacturing with German steel, single-shot, fully adjustable two-stage "Quattro" trigger, performance tested at the factory with lead pellets for accurate velocity specifications. Velocities: .177, 1,250 fps/.22, 1,000 fps/.25, 750 fps/.30, 550 fps.

Price: **$300.00**

HATSAN USA AT44S-10 QE PCP AIRGUN

Calibers: .177, .22, .25. Barrel: Rifled 19.5 in. Weight: 8 lbs. Length: 45.4 in. Power: Precharged pneumatic. Stock: Various configurations, synthetic all-

weather stock with front accessory rail and sling mounts. Turkish hardwood with sling mounts, full tactical stock with soft rubber grip inserts, adjustable buttstock and cheek riser. Sights: None, dual-rail 11mm dovetail and Weaver-compatible for scope mounting. Features: Multi-shot side-lever action, 10-shot .177 and .22 magazines/nine-shot .25 magazine. "Quiet Energy" barrel shroud with an integrated suppressor, European manufacturing with German steel, removable air cylinder, fully adjustable two-stage "Quattro" trigger, performance tested at the factory with lead pellets for accurate velocity specifications. Velocities: .177, 1,070 fps/.22, 970 fps/.25, 870 fps.

Price: ....**$460.00–$500.00**

HATSAN USA ALPHA YOUTH QE AIR RIFLE

Calibers: .177. Barrel: Rifled 15.4 in. Weight: 5.3 lbs. Length: 37.8 in. Power: Spring piston. Stock: Synthetic ambidextrous. Sights: Fiber-optic front and fully adjustable fiber-optic rear, dual-rail 11mm dovetail and Weaver-compatible for scope mounting. Features: Easy cocking, designed for smaller, younger shooters, single-shot, integrated Quiet Energy sound reducing moderator, adjustable trigger. Velocity: 600 fps with lead-free pellets.

Price: **$110.00**

HATSAN USA BT BIG BORE CARNIVORE QE AIR RIFLE

Calibers: .30, .35. Barrel: Rifled 23 in. Weight: 9.3 lbs. Length: 48.9 in. Power: Precharged pneumatic. Stock: Synthetic all-weather stock with sling mounts, front accessory rail, adjustable cheekpiece and buttpad. Sights: None, dual-rail 11mm dovetail and Weaver-compatible for scope mounting. Features: Multi-shot bolt action, six-shot .35 magazine/seven-shot .30 magazine. "Quiet Energy" barrel shroud with an integrated suppressor, European manufacturing with German steel, removable air cylinder, fully adjustable two-stage "Quattro" trigger, performance tested at the factory with lead pellets for accurate velocity specifications. Velocities: .30, 860 fps/.35, 730 fps.

Price: **$500.00**

HATSAN USA HYDRA QE AIR RIFLE

Calibers: .177, .22, .25. Barrel: Rifled 17.7 in. Weight: 6.8 lbs. Length: 42.7 in. Power: Precharged pneumatic. Stock: Turkish walnut. Sights: None, dual-rail 11mm dovetail and Weaver-compatible for scope mounting. Features: Multi-caliber platform with Versi-Cal technology, swap calibers with a single thumb screw, extra barreled receivers sold separately, Quiet Energy fully shrouded barrel, fully adjustable two-stage "Quattro" trigger, multi-shot (14 rounds, .177; 12 rounds, .22; 10 rounds, .25). Velocities: .177, 1,250 fps/.22, 1,120 fps/.25, 900 fps (with lead-free pellets).

Price: **$400.00**

HATSAN USA INVADER AUTO AIR RIFLE

Calibers: .22, .25. Barrel: Rifled 19.7 in. Weight: 8.2 lbs. Length: 40.5 in. Power: Precharged pneumatic. Stock: Black ambidextrous thumbhole tactical style. Sights: Adjustable on removable carry handle, Picatinny rail for scope mounting. Features: Approximately 50 shots per fill, adjustable cheekpiece, built in magazine storage, three Picatinny rails for accessories, Quiet Energy fully shrouded barrel, multi-shot (12 rounds, .22; 10 rounds, .25). Velocities: .22, 1,100 fps/.25, 900 fps.

Price: **$610.00**

HATSAN USA NEUTRONSTAR PCP AIR RIFLE

Calibers: .177, .22, .25. Barrel: Rifled, 23 in. Weight: 8.4 lbs. Length: 43.5 in. Power: Precharged pneumatic. Stock: Turkish walnut. Sights: None, dual-rail 11mm dovetail and Weaver-compatible for scope mounting. Features: Adjustable cheekpiece and buttpad, shrouded barrel with threaded muzzle

Prices given are believed to be accurate at time of publication however, many factors affect retail pricing so exact prices are not possible.

cap, fully adjustable two-stage "Quattro" trigger, arm accessory rail, lever action, single-shot tray and multi-shot (14 rounds, .177; 12 rounds, .22; 10 rounds, .25). Velocities: .177, 1,400 fps/.22, 1,250 fps/.25, 1,050 fps (with lead-free pellets).

Price: **$850.00**

HATSAN USA PILEDRIVER BIG BORE PCP AIR RIFLE
Calibers: .45, .50. Barrel: Rifled 33 in. Weight: 10 lbs. Length: 46.5 in. Power: Precharged pneumatic. Stock: Bullpup-style synthetic thumbhole stock with adjustable cheekpiece. Sights: None, dual-rail 11mm dovetail and Weaver-compatible for scope mounting. Features: 480cc carbon-fiber tank, long side lever for easy cocking, three Picatinny accessory rails, 4–6 shots in .45 caliber, 3–5 shots in .50 caliber, fully adjustable two-stage "Quattro" trigger. Velocities: .45, 900 fps/.50, 850 fps.

Price: **$1,180.00**

HATSAN USA VECTIS LEVER ACTION PCP AIR RIFLE
Calibers: .177, .22, .25. Barrel: Rifled 17.7 in. Weight: 7.1 lbs. Length: 41.3 in. Power: Precharged pneumatic. Stock: Synthetic all-weather stock. Sights: Fiber-optic front and rear, combination dual 11mm dovetail and Weaver-compatible for scope mounting. Features: Multi-shot lever action, 14-shot .177 magazine, 12-shot .22 magazine, 10-shot .25 magazine. "Quiet Energy" barrel shroud with integrated suppressor, fully adjustable two-stage "Quattro" trigger, Picatinny under-barrel accessory rail. Velocities: .177, 1,150 fps/.22, 1,000 fps/.25, 900 fps.

Price: **$370.00**

HATSAN ZADA BREAK-ACTION RIFLE
Calibers: .177, .22, .25. Barrel: Rifled, 14.5 in. Weight: 6.2 lbs. Length: 45 in. Power: Spring piston. Stock: Synthetic tactical style. Sights: Fiber-optic front and adjustable rear, 4x32 scope included. Features: Single shot, "Quiet Energy" barrel shroud with an integrated suppressor, fully adjustable trigger, checkered grip and forearm. Velocities: .177, 1,100 fps/.22, 800 fps/.25, 700 fps with lead pellets.

Price: **$130.00**

HELLRAISER HELLBOY RIFLE
Caliber: .177 BB. Barrel: 14.5 in. Weight: 5.2 lbs. Length: 30–33.5 in. Power: CO2 cartridge. Stock: Synthetic, tactical style. Sights: Open sights adjustable for windage and elevation, Picatinny rail for scope mounting. Features: Based on the M4 carbine, full-metal construction of barrel, magazine, and receiver, stock adjustable for length of pull, semi-automatic, 18-round magazine, removable carry handle, integrated sling swivels. Velocity: 495 fps.

Price: **$180.00**

JEFFERSON STATE ROGUE RAPTOR AIR RIFLE
Calibers: .177, .22, .25, .30. Barrel: TJ Hammer forged, 22 in. Weight: 8 lbs. Length: 43 in. Power: Precharged pneumatic. Stock: Highly adjustable. Sights: None, with Picatinny rail for scope mounting. Features: Side lever cocking, interchangeable barrel and probe for quick caliber changes, high-capacity magazine, externally adjustable regulator, 500cc carbon-fiber bottle, two-stage four-way adjustable trigger, shrouded barrel, built-in power adjuster, compatible with AR-15 stocks and grips, spare magazines store in Picatinny rail, 26-in. barrel available as an option. Also available in a Mini Raptor version (34 in. OAL, 7 lbs.) Velocities: Adjustable.

Price: **$1,600.00**

KALIBRGUN CRICKET 2 BULLPUP PCP AIR RIFLE
Caliber: .177 .22, .25, .30. Barrel: Rifled, Lothar Walther or CZ barrel (depending on caliber), 23.6 in. Weight: 7.5 lbs. Length: 33.1 in. Power: Precharged pneumatic. Stock: Ambidextrous wood or synthetic bullpup with synthetic cheek piece. Sights: None, Weaver rail for scope mounting. Features: Switchable (left/right) side lever cocking system, adjustable power, 14-shot (.177 or .22), 12-shot (.25) or 10-shot magazine (.30), 35–75 shots per fill depending on caliber, stock has integral magazine holder, adjustable two-stage trigger, also available in a tactical version. Velocity: Up to 915–970 fps depending on caliber.

Price: **$1,895.00**

KRAL ARMS PUNCHER MEGA PCP AIR RIFLE
Calibers: .177, .22, .25. Barrel: Rifled 21.0 in. Weight: 8.35 lbs. Length: 42.0 in. Power: Precharged pneumatic. Stock: Ambidextrous stock available in synthetic with adjustable cheek piece, and Turkish walnut. Sights: None, 11mm grooved dovetail for scope mounting. Features: Multi-shot side-lever action, 14-shot .177 magazine, 12-shot .22 magazine, 10-shot .25 magazine, half-shrouded barrel with integrated suppression, available in blue and satin marine finish, adjustable two-stage trigger. Velocities: .177, 1,070 fps/.22, 975 fps/.25, 825 fps.

Price: **$600.00**

KRAL ARMS PUNCHER PRO 500 PCP AIR RIFLE
Calibers: .177, .22, .25. Barrel: Rifled, 20.9 in. Weight: 8.5 lbs. Length: 41.3 in. Power: Precharged pneumatic. Stock: Monte Carlo hardwood right-handed. Sights: None, 11mm grooved dovetail for scope mounting. Features: Multi-shot rear bolt action, 14-shot .177 magazine, 12-shot .22 magazine, 10-shot .25 magazine, fully shrouded barrel with integrated suppression, two-stage adjustable trigger, 70–80 shots per fill depending on caliber. Velocities: .177, 1,100 fps/.22, 900 fps/.25, 850 fps.

Price: **$725.00**

KRAL ARMS PUNCHER BREAKER PCP AIR RIFLE
Calibers: .177, .22, .25. Barrel: Rifled 21 in. Weight: 7.4 lbs. Length: 29 in. Power: Precharged pneumatic. Stock: Ambidextrous bullpup available in synthetic and Turkish walnut. Sights: None, 11mm grooved dovetail for scope mounting. Features: Multi-shot side-lever action, 14-shot .177 magazine, 12-shot .22 magazine, 10-shot .25 magazine, half-shrouded barrel with integrated suppression, available in blue and satin marine finish, adjustable two-stage trigger. Velocities: .177, 1,100 fps/.22, 975 fps/.25, 825 fps.
Price: $600.00

KRAL ARMS PUNCHER BIG MAX PCP RIFLE
Calibers: .177, .22, .25. Barrel: Rifled 22 in. Weight: 9.5 lbs. Length: 42.1 in. Power: Precharged pneumatic. Stock: Ambidextrous Turkish walnut pistol grip. Sights: None, 11mm grooved dovetail for scope mounting. Features: Multi-shot side-lever action, 14-shot .177 magazine, 12-shot .22 magazine, 10-shot .25 magazine, shrouded barrel, adjustable two-stage trigger, massive dual air reservoirs with total of 850cc. Velocities: .177, 1,070 fps/.22, 975 fps/.25, 825 fps.
Price: $690.00

LCS AIR ARMS SK19 FULL-AUTO AIRGUN
Calibers: .22, .25. Barrel: Lothar Walther match grade, 23 in. Weight: 7.75 lbs. Length: 35.0 in. Power: Precharged pneumatic. Stock: Laminate with adjustable cheek piece. Sights: None, Picatinny rail for scope mounting. Features: Made in USA, selector for semi- or full-auto fire, tunable regulated action, carbon-fiber barrel shroud, 480cc or 580cc removable tank, optional 580cc tank available, hard case, 19-shot magazine. Velocity: 890–910 fps.
Price: $2,300.00

MARKSMAN 2066 BREAK-BARREL RIFLE
Caliber: .177 or .22 pellet. Barrel: Rifled. Weight: 6.3 lbs. Length: 43.25 in. Power: Spring piston, 11mm rail. Stock: Wood. Sights: Fiber optic. Features: Built-in noise suppressor, single shot, comes with a 4x32 scope. Velocities: 800 (.177)/600 (.22) fps.
Price: $110.00

PBBA PRO 20-GAUGE AIR SHOTGUN
Calibers: 20 gauge. Barrel: 32 in. Weight: 9.5. Length: 53.5 in. Power: Precharged pneumatic. Stock: Laminate with adjustable cheek piece. Sights: None, rail for scope mounting. Features: Tip-up barrel for loading or barrel swap, pattern mimics a 20-gauge shotgun, separate cocking knob, sling studs, made in USA, 20-in. .457-caliber barrel available as an accessory.
Price: $1,750.00

RAPID AIR WEAPONS RAW HM1000X LRT RIFLE
Calibers: .22, .25, .30, .357. Barrel: Lothar Walther match grade with

polygonal rifling, 24 in. Weight: 7 lbs., 13 oz. Length: 45.4 in. Power: Precharged pneumatic. Stock: Laminate with adjustable cheek piece. Sights: Grooved for scope mounting. Features: Picatinny rail and M-LOK mounting slots, match-grade trigger, multi-shot rotary magazine, adjustable power, side-lever cocking, regulated, quick-fill system, available with right- or left-hand actions. Velocities: .22, 950 fps/.25, 900 fps/.30, NA/.357, NA.
Price: $2,200.00

RAPID AIR WEAPONS RAW HM1000X CHASSIS RIFLE
Calibers: .22, .25. Barrel: Lothar Walther match grade with polygonal rifling, 24 in. Weight: 7 lbs., 13 oz. Length: 43–47 in. Power: Precharged pneumatic. Stock: Synthetic AR-15 style. Sights: Grooved for scope mounting. Features: Chassis constructed from aluminum, designed to accept all AR-15 buttstocks, buffer tubes, and pistol grips, Picatinny rail and M-LOK mounting slots, match-grade trigger, 12-shot rotary magazine, adjustable power, side-lever cocking, regulated, quick-fill system. Velocities: .22, 950 fps/.25, 920 fps.
Price: $2,000.00

RAPID AIR WEAPONS RAW TM1000 BENCHREST RIFLE
Calibers: .177, .22. Barrel: Lothar Walther match grade with polygonal rifling, 24 in. Weight: 9.2–10.5 lbs. Length: 44 in. Power: Precharged pneumatic. Stock: Walnut or black laminate. Sights: Grooved for scope mounting. Features: Built to specifications, target model, internally fitted regulator, fixed bottle, quick fill coupling, approximately 80 shots depending on settings and caliber, Picatinny rail and M-LOK mounting slots, stainless steel ported shroud, adjustable cheek piece and buttpad, match-grade trigger, single shot, 10-in. long accessory rail under barrel, side-lever cocking, right- or left-handed action. Velocities: Dependent on settings and caliber.
Price: $2,200.00

RUGER 10/22 CO_2 RIFLE
Calibers: .177 pellets. Barrel: Rifled 18 in. Weight: 4.5 lbs. Length: 37.1 in. Power: Two 12-gram CO2 cylinders. Stock: Synthetic stock. Sights: Rear sight adjustable for elevation, accepts aftermarket rail. Features: 10-shot Ruger-style rotary magazine, bolt cocks rifle, 3-lb. single-action trigger pull, sling attachments. Velocity: 650 fps.
Price: $150.00

RUGER AIR MAGNUM COMBO
Calibers: .177, .22. Barrel: Rifled 19.5 in. Weight: 9.5 lbs. Length: 48.5 in. Power: Break-barrel, spring piston. Stock: Ambidextrous Monte Carlo synthetic stock with textured grip and forend. Sights: Fiber-optic front and fully adjustable fiber-optic rear, Weaver scope rail, includes 4x32 scope and mounts. Features: Single-shot, two-stage trigger. Velocities: .177, 1,400 fps/.22, 1,200 fps.
Price: $170.00

RUGER EXPLORER RIFLE
Caliber: .177 pellets. Barrel: Rifled 15 in. Weight: 4.45 lbs. Length: 37.12 in. Power: Break-barrel, spring piston. Stock: Ambidextrous synthetic skeleton stock. Sights: Fiber-optic front and fully adjustable fiber-optic rear, grooved for

scope mounting. Features: Designed as an entry-level youth break-barrel rifle, easy to shoot and accurate, single-shot, two-stage trigger. Velocity: 495 fps.
Price: **$69.00**

RUGER IMPACT MAX ELITE RIFLE
Caliber: .22. Barrel: Rifled 15 in. Weight: 7.5 lbs. Length: 44.75 in. Power: Break-barrel, TNT gas-piston. Stock: Ambidextrous wood, includes rifle sling. Sights: Fiber-optic front and fully adjustable fiber-optic rear, Picatinny optics rail, includes scope and mounts. Features: Integrated "SilencAIR" suppressor. Velocity: 800 fps with lead pellets.
Price: **$150.00**

RUGER TARGIS HUNTER MAX AIR RIFLE COMBO
Caliber: .22. Barrel: Rifled 18.7 in. Weight: 9.85 lbs. Length: 44.85 in. Power: Break-barrel, spring piston. Stock: Ambidextrous synthetic stock with texture grip and forend, includes rifle sling. Sights: Fiber-optic front and fully adjustable fiber-optic rear, Picatinny optics rail, includes scope and mounts. Features: Integrated "SilencAIR" suppressor, single shot, two-stage trigger. Velocity: 1,000 fps.
Price: **$159.00**

SIG SAUER MCX CO₂ RIFLE & SCOPE, BLACK
Caliber: .177. Barrel: Rifled 17.7 in. Weight: 7.9 pounds. Length: 34.7 in. Power: CO2. Stock: Synthetic stock, various color options. Sights: Varies with model, Weaver rail system for iron sight systems, red-dot systems, and traditional scope mounting. Features: 30-round semi-auto, reliable belt-fed magazine system, very realistic replica. Velocity: 700 fps.
Price: **$310.00**

SIG SAUER MPX GEN 2 CO2 RIFLE
Caliber: .177 pellet. Barrel: Rifled, 8 in. Weight: 6.2 pounds. Length: 25.8 in. Power: CO2. Stock: Synthetic stock. Sights: Adjustable folding dual-aperture open sights. Features: Picatinny accessory rail, M-LOK system handguard, flat-blade trigger, 30-round semi-automatic, Roto Belt magazine, ambidextrous safety levers, very realistic replica. Velocity: 450 fps.
Price: **$230.00**

SPRINGFIELD ARMORY M1A UNDER-LEVER RIFLE
Caliber: .177 or .22. Barrel: Rifled 18.9 in. Weight: 9.9 pounds. Length: 45.6 in. Power: Spring piston under-lever. Stock: Ambidextrous wood. Sights: Fixed front, rear peep adjustable for windage and elevation. Features: Fixed barrel, single shot, realistic replica of the National Match firearm, 35-lb. cocking effort, two-stage non-adjustable trigger. Velocity: 1,000 fps (.177), 750 fps (.22).
Price: **$246.00**

SPRINGFIELD ARMORY M1A CO2 BB CARBINE
Caliber: .177 BBs. Barrel: Smoothbore, 17.25 in. Weight: 5.7 lbs. Length:

35.8 in. Power: CO2. Stock: Ambidextrous synthetic wood. Sights: Fixed front, rear peep adjustable for windage. Features: 15-round drop-free magazine, blowback action, approximately 40 shots per CO2 cylinder, semi-automatic, realistic replica of the M1 carbine, two-stage non-adjustable trigger. Velocity: 425 fps.
Price: **$250.00**

STOEGER S4000-E SUPPRESSED PCP RIFLE COMBO
Caliber: .177 or .22 pellets. Barrel: Rifled, 18.5 in. Weight: 7.65 lbs. Length: 44.25 in. Power: Break-action gas ram. Stock: Black or camo synthetic or hardwood. Sights: Adjustable fiber optic, 11mm dovetail. Features: Automatic ambidextrous safety, interchangeable blue and orange embossed grips, includes a 4X32 scope, fully shrouded suppressed barrel, adjustable two-stage trigger, single shot. Velocities: 1,000 fps (.177), 800 fps (.22).
Price: .... **$180.00–$200.00**

STOEGER XM1 PCP RIFLE
Caliber: .177 or .22 pellets. Barrel: Rifled, 22 in. Weight: 5.7 lbs. Length: 39 in. Power: Precharged pneumatic. Stock: Black or camo thumbhole synthetic. Sights: Adjustable fiber optic, 11 mm dovetail. Features: Approximately 50 shots per charge, nine-shot (.177) or seven-shot (.22) removable rotary magazine, available as a kit with a 4x32 scope, checkered stock, interchangeable cheekpiece, pistol grip, and buttpad, adjustable trigger, available as a suppressed model, Picatinny rails on each side, bolt action. Velocities: 1,200 fps (.177), 1,000 fps (.22).
Price: .... **$250.00–$300.00**

SWISS ARMS TAC1 AIR RIFLE COMBO
Caliber: .177 pellet. Barrel: Rifled 18.4 in. Weight: 7.8 lbs. (with scope and mount). Length: 43.75 in. Power: Spring piston. Stock: Ambidextrous tan thumbhole synthetic. Sights: None, grooved 11mm dovetail for scope mounting. Features: Comes with 4x32 scope and mount, single shot. Velocity: 1,200 fps.
Price: **$150.00**

UMAREX EMBARK AIR RIFLE
Caliber: .177. Barrel: Rifled 15 in. Weight: 4.45 lbs. Length: 37.25 in. Power: Spring piston. Stock: Ambidextrous neon green thumbhole synthetic. Sights: Fully adjustable micrometer rear, grooved 11mm dovetail for scope mounting. Features: Official air rifle for the Student Air Rifle program, 12-in. length of pull, muzzle brake, 16.5-lb. cocking effort, 4.25-lb. trigger pull, automatic safety. Velocity: 510 fps.
Price: **$125.00**

UMAREX EMERGE AIR RIFLE
Caliber: .177 or .22. Barrel: Rifled, 21 in. Weight: 9 lbs. Length: 47 in. Power: Break barrel, gas piston. Stock: Synthetic. Sights: Fiber-optic front and rear, Picatinny rail, comes with a 4x32 scope. Features: 12-shot auto-advancing rotary magazine, integrated SilencAir technology, textured grip and forearm. Velocities: 1,000 (.177)/800 (.22) fps.
Price: **$190.00**

UMAREX FUSION 2 CO₂ RIFLE
Calibers: .177 pellets. Barrel: Rifled, 18.5 in. Weight: 5.95 lbs. Length: 40.55 in. Power: CO2. Stock: Ambidextrous, synthetic, thumbhole. Sights: None, Picatinny rail for scope mounting. Features: SilencAir noise dampening, uses two 12-gram cylinders or one 88-gram cylinder, nine-shot rotary magazine, bolt action, M-LOK slots on both sides, single-stage trigger. Velocity: 700 fps.
Price: **$160.00**

UMAREX GAUNTLET 2 PCP AIR RIFLE
Caliber: .22, .25, .30. Barrel: Rifled 28.25 in. Weight: 8.5 lbs. Length: 47 in. Power: Precharged pneumatic. Stock: Ambidextrous synthetic. Sights: None, grooved 11mm dovetail for scope mounting. Features: 10-shot (.177), eight-shot (.25) or seven-shot (.30) magazine, 25 (.30), 50 (.25), or 70 (.22) shots per fill, removable aluminum air cylinder, multi-shot bolt action, four baffle sound reduction, height-adjustable cheek comb, M-LOK accessory slots on sides and bottom or forearm, adjustable single-stage trigger. Available in a lower-powered version for the Canadian market. Velocities: 1,075 fps (.177), 985 fps (.25), 950 fps (.30).
Price: **$450.00**

UMAREX HAMMER AIR RIFLE
Caliber: .50. Barrel: Rifled 29.5 in. Weight: 8.5 Length: 43.75 in. Power: Precharged pneumatic. Stock: Nymax synthetic. Sights: None, Picatinny rail for scope mounting. Features: Fires three full-power shots, 2-lb. straight-pull bolt cocks the rifle and advances the magazine, 4,500 psi built-in carbon-fiber tank with quick disconnect Foster fitting, trigger-block safety, will not fire without magazine, Magpul AR grip, full-length composite barrel shroud, comes with two double chamber magazines. Also available in a shorter, lighter carbine version and lower-powered version for the Canadian market. Velocities: 1,130 fps (180-grain non-lead bullet), 760 fps (550-grain lead slug).
Price: **$1,000.00**

UMAREX LEGENDS COWBOY LEVER ACTION RIFLE
Calibers: .177 BBs. Barrel: 19.25 in smoothbore. Weight: 7.75 lbs. Length: 38.0 in. Power: CO2. Stock: Faux wood polymer. Sights: Blade front sight with rear sight adjustable for elevation. Features: Lever action, 10-shot capacity, ejectable cartridges, full metal frame, powered by two CO2 capsules, saddle ring. Velocity: 600 fps.
Price: **$225.00**

UMAREX LEGENDS M1A1 FULL AUTO BB GUN
Calibers: .177 BBs. Barrel: Smoothbore, 12.0 in. Weight: 7.75 lbs. Length: 31.75 in. Power: CO2. Stock: Synthetic faux-wood polymer. Sights: Fixed. Features: Semi-auto and full-auto fire capability, a 30-round drop-free magazine with two CO2 cartridges, full metal frame, blowback action, sling mounts. Velocity: 435 fps.
Price: **$300.00**

UMAREX LEGENDS M3 GREASE GUN
Calibers: .177 BBs. Barrel: Smoothbore. Power: CO2. Stock: Synthetic with collapsible wire butt. Sights: Fixed. Features: Semi-auto and full-auto fire capability, operates on two 12-gram CO2 cylinders, a 30-round drop-free magazine with two CO2 cartridges, full metal frame, blowback action, and sling mounts . Velocity: 435 fps.
Price: **$250.00**

UMAREX NOTOS CRK PCP CARBINE
Caliber: .22. Barrel: Rifled, 11.75 in. Weight: 4 lbs. Power: Precharged pneumatic. Stock: Synthetic. Sights: None, Picatinny rail for scope mounting. Features: Adjustable length buttstock, shrouded barrel, up to 40 shots per fill, 21 regulated shots per fill, seven-shot rotary-indexing magazine, single-shot tray, side lever charging system. Optional grips and sights available to convert to a pistol. Velocity: 700 fps.
Price: **$280.00**

UMAREX NXG APX MULTIPUMP RIFLE
Calibers: .177 BB or pellet. Barrel: Rifled, 20 in. Weight: 3.4 lbs. Length: 39 in. Power: Multipump. Stock: Ambidextrous synthetic. Sights: Adjustable, 3/8-in. dovetail, 4x15 scope and rings. Features: Single-shot pellet or 75-round BB repeater, automatic safety, multipump, 2–10 pumps, bolt action, 3.5-lb. trigger pull, 14.25-in. length of pull. Velocity: Up to 800 fps.
Price: **$75.00**

UMAREX ORIGIN PCP RIFLE
Caliber: .22 or .25 Barrel: Rifled, 22.9 in. Weight: 6.8 lbs. Length: 43.1 in. Power: Precharged pneumatic. Stock: Synthetic. Sights: None, Picatinny rail for scope mounting. Features: Hand-pump friendly Ever-Pressure pre-pressurized tank system, shoots at full power with approximately 100 pumps, up to 40 shots (.22) or 20 shots (.25) per fill, eight-shot (.25) or 10-shot (.22) rotary-indexing magazine, side lever charging system, two-stage adjustable trigger, automatic overpressure air release, integrated sound suppressor. Velocity: 1,100 fps (.22), 950 fps (.25).
Price: **$400.00**

Prices given are believed to be accurate at time of publication however, many factors affect retail pricing so exact prices are not possible.

UMAREX PRIMAL 20 PCP SLUG GUN
Caliber: 20-ga. slugs. Barrel: Smoothbore with rifled choke tube. Weight: 11 lbs. Power: Precharged pneumatic. Stock: Ambidextrous synthetic thumbhole. Sights: None, Picatinny rail for scope mounting. Features: Ambidextrous reversible bolt action, two-round sliding magazine, cocked bolt indicator, textured forearm and pistol grip, includes two magazines, sling stud hole in stock. Velocity: 700 fps with a 395-grain slug.
Price: $650.00

UMAREX STEEL STRIKE CO_2 GUN
Calibers: .177 BB. Barrel: Smoothbore, 9 in. Weight: 3.7 lbs. Length: 27.75 in. Power: CO2. Stock: Ambidextrous collapsible synthetic. Sights: Flip-up open, Picatinny rail. Features: Uses two 12-gram CO2 cylinders, 900-round BB reservoir that feeds a 30-round magazine, fires semi-automatic or six-shot burst, Picatinny accessory rails on sides and under-barrel. Velocity: 400 fps.
Price: $115.00

UMAREX SURGEMAX ELITE AIR RIFLE COMBO, GAS PISTON
Calibers: .177, .22. Barrel: Rifled 15.9 in. Weight: 7 lbs. Length: 45.3 in. Power: Break-barrel, gas-piston. Stock: Ambidextrous synthetic thumbhole. Sights: Adjustable, Weaver rail for scope mounting, includes 4X32 scope and mounts. Features: Single shot, two-stage adjustable trigger, sound suppression system. Velocities: .177, 1,050 fps/.22, 900 fps.
Price: $150.00

UMAREX SYNERGIS UNDER LEVER AIR RIFLE, COMBO
Calibers: .177, .22 pellets. Barrel: 18.5 in rifled. Weight: 8.3 lbs. Length: 45.3 in. Power: Gas piston under lever. Stock: Synthetic. Sights: None, Picatinny rail for scope mounting. Features: 3-9x32 scope, two magazines, 10-shot (.22) or 12-shot (.177) repeater, fixed barrel, removable magazine, integrated suppressor, two-stage nonadjustable trigger. Velocities: 1,000 fps (.177), 900 fps (.22).
Price: $200.00

WALTHER LG400 UNIVERSAL AIR RIFLE, AMBI GRIP
Caliber: .177. Barrel: Advanced match-grade rifled barrel 16.53 in. Weight: 8.6 lbs. Length: 43.7 in. Power: Precharged pneumatic. Stock: Ambidextrous competition, highly adjustable wood stock. Sights: Olympic-grade, match Diopter/Micrometer adjustable. Features: Professional-class 10m target rifle, meets ISSF requirements. Velocity: 557 fps.
Price: $2,000.00

WALTHER MAXIMATHOR AIR RIFLE
Calibers: .22, .25. Barrel: Advanced match-grade rifled barrel, 23.5 in. Weight: 9.6 lbs. Length: 41.75 in. Power: Precharged pneumatic. Stock: Ambidextrous wood stock. Sights: None, grooved 11mm dovetail for scope mounting. Features: Bolt-action eight-shot magazine. Velocities: .22, 1,260 fps/.25, 1,000 fps.
Price: $630.00

WALTHER LEVER-ACTION CO_2 RIFLE, BLACK
Caliber: .177. Barrel: Rifled 18.9 in. Weight: 6.2 lbs. Length: 39.2 in. Power: CO2 Stock: Ambidextrous wood stock. Sights: Blade front, adjustable rear. Features: Lever-action repeater, eight-shot rotary magazine, Wild West replica airgun. Velocity: 600 fps.
Price: $500.00

WALTHER LG400 JUNIOR AIR RIFLE
Caliber: .177. Barrel: Advanced match-grade rifled barrel, 16.53 in. Weight: 7.7 lbs. Length: 39.8 in. Power: Precharged pneumatic. Stock: Ambidextrous highly adjustable competition laminate wood stock. Sights: Olympic-grade, match Diopter/Micrometer adjustable. Features: Designed for young shooters and clubs, 10m competition target rifle, meets ISSF requirements, removable air cylinder delivers up to 400 shots per fill. Velocity: 570 fps.
Price: $2,444.00

WALTHER REIGN UXT PCP BULLPUP RIFLE
Caliber: .22, .25. Barrel: Rifled, 23.6 in. Weight: 5.5 lbs. Length: 34 in. Power: Precharged pneumatic. Stock: Ambidextrous bullpup synthetic. Sights: None, Picatinny rail. Features: 10-shot (.22) or nine-shot (.25) auto-indexing magazine, 40–60 shots per fill, adjustable trigger, ambidextrous cocking level, quick-detach sling mount, muzzle shroud. Velocities: 975 fps (.22), 840 fps (.25).
Price: ....$480.00–$600.00

WEIHRAUCH HW50S SPRING PISTON RIFLE
Caliber: .177, .22. Barrel: Rifled, 15.5 in. Weight: 6.8 lbs. Length: 40.5 in. Power: Spring piston. Stock: Checkered beech wood. Sights: Front globe and adjustable rear. Features: Single shot, 24-lb. cocking effort, two-stage adjustable Rekord trigger. Velocity: 820 fps (.177), 574 fps (.22).
Price: $470.00

WEIHRAUCH HW90 SPRING PISTON RIFLE
Caliber: .177, .22, .25. Barrel: Rifled, 19.7 in. Weight: 6.8 lbs. Length: 45.3 in. Power: Spring piston. Stock: Checkered beech wood. Sights: Front globe and

Prices given are believed to be accurate at time of publication however, many factors affect retail pricing so exact prices are not possible.

78TH EDITION, 2024 ✦ 601

adjustable rear, 11 mm dovetail for scope mounting. Features: Single shot, 46-lb. cocking effort, two-stage adjustable Rekord trigger. Velocity: 1,050 fps (.177), 853 fps (.22), 625 fps (.25).
Price: **$835.00**

WEIHRAUCH HW97K/KT AIR RIFLE
Caliber: .177, .20, .22. Barrel: Rifled, 11.81 in. Weight: 8.8 lbs. Length: 40.1 in. Power: Under-lever, spring-piston. Stock: Various, beech wood, blue-grey laminated, or synthetic, with or without thumbhole. Sights: None, grooved for scope. Features: Silver or blue finish, highly adjustable match-grade trigger. Extremely accurate fixed barrel design. Velocity: 820 fps (.177), 755 fps (.22).
Price: **$710.00**

WEIHRAUCH HW100 SK PCP RIFLE
Caliber: .177, .22. Barrel: Rifled, 15.7 in. Weight: 8.6 lbs. Length: 38.4 in. Power: Precharged pneumatic. Stock: Monte Carlo walnut stock with a raised cheekpiece. Sights: Grooved for scope mounting. Features: Multi-shot side lever, includes two 14-round magazines, shrouded barrel, two-stage adjustable match trigger. Also available in a longer barrel (S) and a thumbhole stock (T) version. Velocity: 1,135 fps (.177), 870 fps (.22).
Price: **$1,645.00**

WEIHRAUCH HW110 ST PCP RIFLE, FAC VERSION
Caliber: .177, .20, .22. Barrel: Rifled 30.5 in. Weight: 7.5 lbs. Length: 46 in. Power: Precharged pneumatic. Stock: Black Soft Touch coated wood. Sights: None, Picatinny rail grooved for scope mounting. Features: Includes two 10-shot magazines, side lever action, fully regulated, internal pressure gauge, two-stage adjustable match trigger, available in a shorter carbine version. Velocities: 1,050 fps (.177), 965 fps (.20), 1,025 fps (.22).
Price: **$1,225.00**

WESTERN BIG BORE BUSHBUCK 45 PCP RIFLE
Caliber: .45. Barrel: Rifled, 30 in. Weight: 10.25 lbs. Length: 49.5 in. Power: Precharged pneumatic. Stock: Walnut or laminate. Sights: None, Picatinny rail for scope mounting. Features: One-piece aluminum receiver and Picatinny rail, all-steel air cylinder, accuracy tested to 250 yards, two 600 ft-lb or four 400 ft-lb shots per fill, accommodates extra-long bullets, approximately 3-lb. trigger pull, sling studs, single shot, also available in a shorter carbine version, made in USA.
Price: **$1,895.00**

WESTERN BIG BORE RATTLER .357 PCP RIFLE
Caliber: .357. Barrel: Rifled, TJ hammer-forged, 28 in. Weight: 9.2 lbs. Length: 40 in. Power: Precharged pneumatic. Stock: Synthetic, tactical style. Sights: None, Picatinny rail for scope mounting. Features: 15 full-power shots, up to 270 ft-lbs of energy, semi-automatic, hammerless firing system, 580cc removable air bottle for quick changes in the field, adjustable regulator, quick and easy power adjustments, accommodates from 81-grain pellets to 174-grain slugs, three Picatinny accessory rails, solid aluminum shroud silencing system, made in USA. Velocity: Adjustable.
Price: **$2,695.00**

WESTERN BIG BORE SIDEWINDER PCP RIFLE
Caliber: .22, .25, .30. Barrel: Rifled, TJ hammer-forged, 23 in. Weight: 8 lbs. Length: 35 in. Power: Precharged pneumatic. Stock: Synthetic, tactical style. Sights: None, Picatinny rail for scope mounting. Features: Select-fire semi- or full-auto, removable magazine, 15 (.22 or .25) or 12 (.30) shots, Picatinny under-rail for accessory mounting, accepts additional side rails, 580cc removable air bottle for quick changes in the field, adjustable regulator, quick and easy power adjustments, AR-compatible grip, 50–75 shots per fill, 50–90 ft-lbs of energy depending on caliber, made in USA. Velocity: Adjustable.
Price: **$2,000.00**

WESTERN JUSTICE ANNIE OAKLEY LIL SURE SHOT/JOHN WAYNE LIL DUKE BB RIFLE
Caliber: .177 steel BBs. Barrel: Smooth. Weight: 2.6 lbs. Length: 34 in. Power: Spring piston, lever action. Stock: Hardwood. Sights: Adjustable for elevation, 11mm dovetail mount. Features: 550-round BB reservoir, single-stage trigger, 16-lb. cocking effort, manual safety, available embossed with either Annie Oakley or John Wayne likeness. Velocity: 350 fps.
Price: .... **$55.00–$70.00**

WINCHESTER MODEL 12 YOUTH PUMP ACTION BB GUN
Caliber: .177 steel BBs. Barrel: Smooth. Weight: 3.2 lbs. Length: 34.25 in. Power: Spring piston, pump action. Stock: Synthetic brown faux wood. Sights: Modeled after the famous Winchester Model 12 shotgun, adjustable for windage and elevation. Features: Single pump per shot, 250-round BB reservoir, 14-in. length of pull. Velocity: 350 fps.
Price: **$55.00**

WINCHESTER 77XS MULTI-PUMP AIR RIFLE
Caliber: .177 steel BBs, .177 pellet. Barrel: Rifled 20.8 in. Weight: 3.1 lbs. Length: 37.6 in. Power: Multi-pump pneumatic. Stock: Ambidextrous synthetic thumbhole stock. Sights: Blade front, adjustable rear, grooved for scope mounting, includes 4x32 scope and mounts. Features: Single-shot pellet, 50-round BB repeater, bolt action, lightweight, accurate and easy to shoot. Velocity: 800 fps.
Price: **$119.00**

WINCHESTER BIG BORE MODEL 70 PCP RIFLE
Calibers: .35, .45. Barrel: Rifled, 20.87 in. Weight: 9 lbs. Length: 41.75 in. Power: Precharged pneumatic. Stock: Right-handed hardwood. Sights: None, grooved for scope mounting. Features: Multi-Shot big bore (six shots .35/ five shots .45), highly stable shot strings for maximum accuracy, traditional Winchester styling, .35 produces up to 134 ft-lbs of energy, .45 produces

over 200 ft-lbs of energy. Velocities: .35, 865 fps/.45, 803 fps.

Price: $840.00

ZBROIA HORTIZIA PCP RIFLE

Calibers: .177, .22. Barrel: Rifled, 13, 17.7, or 21.7 in. Weight: 6.8, 7.1, or 7.5 lbs. Length: 28, 31.7, or 43.7 in. Power: Precharged pneumatic. Stock: Black-stained ash Monte Carlo-style wood stock. Sights: None, grooved for scope mounting. Features: Up to 100 shots per fill in .177 caliber or 60 shots in .22 caliber, free-floated barrel with 12 grooves, two-stage adjustable trigger that is detachable, side-lever cocking, 10- or 12-shot repeater, built-in manometer with 4,351 psi fill, available in three barrel lengths, made in Ukraine. Velocities: .177, 1,000 fps/.22, 980 fps.

Price: $850.00

ZBROIA KOZAK TACTICAL PCP RIFLE

Calibers: .177, .22. Barrel: Rifled, 13, 17.7, or 21.7 in. Weight: 6.6 lbs. Length: 30, 32.7, or 36.6 in. Power: Precharged pneumatic. Stock: Black-stained ash wood semi-bullpup design with adjustable cheekpiece. Sights: None, grooved for scope mounting. Features: Up to 100 shots per fill (.22 caliber), free-floated barrel with 12 grooves, two-stage adjustable trigger, side-lever cocking, 10- or 12-shot repeater, built-in manometer with 4,351 psi fill, available in three barrel lengths, made in Ukraine. Velocities: .177, 1,000 fps/.22, 980 fps.

Price: $870.00

Prices given are believed to be accurate at time of publication however, many factors affect retail pricing so exact prices are not possible.

78TH EDITION, 2024 ✦ **603**

An * after the cartridge means these loads are available with Nosler Partition or Swift A-Frame bullets.
Wea. Mag.= Weatherby Magnum. Spfd. = Springfield. A-Sq. = A-Square. N.E.=Nitro Express.

Cartridge	Bullet Wgt. Grs.	VELOCITY (fps)					ENERGY (ft. lbs.)					TRAJ. (in.)			
		Muzzle	100 yds.	200 yds.	300 yds.	400 yds.	Muzzle	100 yds.	200 yds.	300 yds.	400 yds.	100 yds.	200 yds.	300 yds.	400 yds.
17, 22															
17 Hornet	15.5	3860	2924	2159	1531	1108	513	294	160	81	42	1.4	0	-9.1	-33.7
17 Hornet	20	3650	3078	2574	2122	1721	592	421	294	200	131	1.1	0	-6.4	-20.6
17 Hornet	25	3375	2842	2367	1940	1567	632	448	311	209	136	1.4	0	24.8	56.3
17 Remington Fireball	20	4000	3380	2840	2360	1930	710	507	358	247	165	1.6	1.5	-2.8	-13.5
17 Remington Fireball	25	3850	3280	2780	2330	1925	823	597	429	301	206	0.9	0	-5.4	NA
17 Remington	20	4200	3544	2978	2477	2029	783	558	394	272	183	0	-1.3	-6.6	-17.6
17 Remington	25	4040	3284	2644	2086	1606	906	599	388	242	143	2	1.7	-4	-17
4.6x30 H&K	30	2025	1662	1358	1135	1002	273	184	122	85	66	0	-12.7	-44.5	—
4.6x30 H&K	40	1900	1569	1297	1104	988	320	218	149	108	86	0	-14.3	-39.3	—
204 Ruger (Hor)	24	4400	3667	3046	2504	2023	1032	717	494	334	218	0.6	0	-4.3	-14.3
204 Ruger (Fed)	32 Green	4030	3320	2710	2170	1710	1155	780	520	335	205	0.9	0	-5.7	-19.1
204 Ruger	32	4125	3559	3061	2616	2212	1209	900	666	486	348	0	-1.3	-6.3	—
204 Ruger	32	4225	3632	3114	2652	2234	1268	937	689	500	355	0.6	0	-4.2	-13.4
204 Ruger	40	3900	3451	3046	2677	2336	1351	1058	824	636	485	0.7	0	-4.5	-13.9
204 Ruger	45	3625	3188	2792	2428	2093	1313	1015	778	589	438	1	0	-5.5	-16.9
5.45x39mm	60	2810	2495	2201	1927	1677	1052	829	645	445	374	1	0	-9.2	-27.7
221 Fireball	40	3100	2510	1991	1547	1209	853	559	352	212	129	0	-4.1	-17.3	-45.1
221 Fireball	50	2800	2137	1580	1180	988	870	507	277	155	109	0	-7	-28	0
22 Hornet (Fed)	30 Green	3150	2150	1390	990	830	660	310	130	65	45	0	-6.6	-32.7	NA
22 Hornet	34	3050	2132	1415	1017	852	700	343	151	78	55	0	-6.6	-15.5	-29.9
22 Hornet	35	3100	2278	1601	1135	929	747	403	199	100	67	2.75	0	-16.9	-60.4
22 Hornet	40	2800	2397	2029	1698	1413	696	510	366	256	177	0	-4.6	-17.8	-43.1
22 Hornet	45	2690	2042	1502	1128	948	723	417	225	127	90	0	-7.7	-31	0
218 Bee	46	2760	2102	1550	1155	961	788	451	245	136	94	0	-7.2	-29	0
222 Rem.	35	3760	3125	2574	2085	1656	1099	759	515	338	213	1	0	-6.3	-20.8
222 Rem.	50	3345	2930	2553	2205	1886	1242	953	723	540	395	1.3	0	-6.7	-20.6
222 Remington	40	3600	3117	2673	2269	1911	1151	863	634	457	324	1.07	0	-6.13	-18.9
222 Remington	50	3140	2602	2123	1700	1350	1094	752	500	321	202	2	-0.4	-11	-33
222 Remington	55	3020	2562	2147	1773	1451	1114	801	563	384	257	2	-0.4	-11	-33
222 Rem. Mag.	40	3600	3140	2726	2347	2000	1150	876	660	489	355	1	0	-5.7	-17.8
222 Rem. Mag.	50	3340	2917	2533	2179	1855	1238	945	712	527	382	1.3	0	-6.8	-20.9
222 Rem. Mag.	55	3240	2748	2305	1906	1556	1282	922	649	444	296	2	-0.2	-9	-27
22 PPC	52	3400	2930	2510	2130	NA	1335	990	730	525	NA	2	1.4	-5	0
223 Rem.	35	3750	3206	2725	2291	1899	1092	799	577	408	280	1	0	-5.7	-18.1
223 Rem.	35	4000	3353	2796	2302	1861	1243	874	607	412	269	0.8	0	-5.3	-17.3
223 Rem.	64	2750	2368	2018	1701	1427	1074	796	578	411	289	2.4	0	-11	-34.1
223 Rem.	75	2790	2562	2345	2139	1943	1296	1093	916	762	629	1.5	0	-8.2	-24.1
223 Remington	40	3650	3010	2450	1950	1530	1185	805	535	340	265	2	1	-6	-22
223 Remington	40	3800	3305	2845	2424	2044	1282	970	719	522	371	0.84	0	-5.34	-16.6
223 Remington (Rem)	45 Green	3550	2911	2355	1865	1451	1259	847	554	347	210	2.5	2.3	-4.3	-21.1
223 Remington	50	3300	2874	2484	2130	1809	1209	917	685	504	363	1.37	0	-7.05	-21.8
223 Remington	52/53	3330	2882	2477	2106	1770	1305	978	722	522	369	2	0.6	-6.5	-21.5
223 Remington (Win)	55 Green	3240	2747	2304	1905	1554	1282	921	648	443	295	1.9	0	-8.5	-26.7
223 Remington	55	3240	2748	2305	1906	1556	1282	922	649	444	296	2	-0.2	-9	-27
223 Remington	60	3100	2712	2355	2026	1726	1280	979	739	547	397	2	0.2	-8	-24.7
223 Remington	62	3000	2700	2410	2150	1900	1240	1000	800	635	495	1.6	0	-7.7	-22.8
223 Remington	64	3020	2621	2256	1920	1619	1296	977	723	524	373	2	-0.2	-9.3	-23
223 Remington	69	3000	2720	2460	2210	1980	1380	1135	925	750	600	2	0.8	-5.8	-17.5
223 Remington	75	2790	2554	2330	2119	1926	1296	1086	904	747	617	2.37	0	-8.75	-25.1
223 Rem. Super Match	75	2930	2694	2470	2257	2055	1429	1209	1016	848	703	1.2	0	-6.9	-20.7
223 Remington	77	2750	2584	2354	2169	1992	1293	1110	948	804	679	1.93	0	-8.2	-23.8
223 WSSM	55	3850	3438	3064	2721	2402	1810	1444	1147	904	704	0.7	0	-4.4	-13.6
223 WSSM	64	3600	3144	2732	2356	2011	1841	1404	1061	789	574	1	0	-5.7	-17.7
5.56 NATO	55	3130	2740	2382	2051	1750	1196	917	693	514	372	1.1	0	-7.3	-23
5.56 NATO	75	2910	2676	2543	2242	2041	1410	1192	1002	837	693	1.2	0	-7	-21
224 Wea. Mag.	55	3650	3192	2780	2403	2057	1627	1244	943	705	516	2	1.2	-4	-17
22 Nosler	55	3350	2965	2615	2286	1984	1370	1074	833	638	480	0	-2.5	-10.1	-24.4
22 Nosler	77	2950	2672	2410	2163	1931	1488	1220	993	800	637	0	-3.4	-12.8	-29.7
224 Valkyrie	90	2700	2542	2388	2241	2098	1457	1291	1140	1003	880	1.9	0	-8.1	-23.2
224 Valkyrie	75	3000	2731	2477	2237	2010	1499	1242	1022	833	673	1.6	0	-7.3	-21.5

Cartridge	Bullet Wgt. Grs.	VELOCITY (fps)					ENERGY (ft. lbs.)					TRAJ. (in.)			
		Muzzle	100 yds.	200 yds.	300 yds.	400 yds.	Muzzle	100 yds.	200 yds.	300 yds.	400 yds.	100 yds.	200 yds.	300 yds.	400 yds.
224 Valkyrie	60	3300	2930	2589	2273	1797	1451	1144	893	688	522	1.3	0	-6.5	-19.8
225 Winchester	55	3570	3066	2616	2208	1838	1556	1148	836	595	412	2	1	-5	-20
22-250 Rem.	35	4450	3736	3128	2598	2125	1539	1085	761	524	351	6.5	0	-4.1	-13.4
22-250 Rem.	40	4000	3320	2720	2200	1740	1420	980	660	430	265	2	1.8	-3	-16
22-250 Rem.	40	4150	3553	3033	2570	2151	1530	1121	817	587	411	0.6	0	-4.4	-14.2
22-250 Rem.	45 Green	4000	3293	2690	2159	1696	1598	1084	723	466	287	1.7	1.7	-3.2	-15.7
22-250 Rem.	50	3725	3264	2641	2455	2103	1540	1183	896	669	491	0.89	0	-5.23	-16.3
22-250 Rem.	52/55	3680	3137	2656	2222	1832	1654	1201	861	603	410	2	1.3	-4	-17
22-250 Rem.	60	3600	3195	2826	2485	2169	1727	1360	1064	823	627	2	2	-2.4	-12.3
22-250 Rem.	64	3425	2988	2591	2228	1897	1667	1269	954	705	511	1.2	0	-6.4	-20
220 Swift	40	4200	3678	3190	2739	2329	1566	1201	904	666	482	0.51	0	-4	-12.9
220 Swift	50	3780	3158	2617	2135	1710	1586	1107	760	506	325	2	1.4	-4.4	-17.9
220 Swift	50	3850	3396	2970	2576	2215	1645	1280	979	736	545	0.74	0	-4.84	-15.1
220 Swift	50	3900	3420	2990	2599	2240	1688	1298	992	750	557	0.7	0	-4.7	-14.5
220 Swift	55	3800	3370	2990	2630	2310	1765	1390	1090	850	650	0.8	0	-4.7	-14.4
220 Swift	55	3650	3194	2772	2384	2035	1627	1246	939	694	506	2	2	-2.6	-13.4
220 Swift	60	3600	3199	2824	2475	2156	1727	1364	1063	816	619	2	1.6	-4.1	-13.1
22 Savage H.P.	70	2868	2510	2179	1874	1600	1279	980	738	546	398	0	-4.1	-15.6	-37.1
22 Savage H.P.	71	2790	2340	1930	1570	1280	1225	860	585	390	190	2	-1	-10.4	-35.7
6mm (24)															
6mm BR Rem.	100	2550	2310	2083	1870	1671	1444	1185	963	776	620	2.5	-0.6	-11.8	0
6mm Norma BR	107	2822	2667	2517	2372	2229	1893	1690	1506	1337	1181	1.73	0	-7.24	-20.6
6mm Creedmoor	108	2786	2618	2456	2299	2149	1861	1643	1446	1267	1106	1.5	0	-6.6	-18.9
6mm PPC	70	3140	2750	2400	2070	NA	1535	1175	895	665	NA	2	1.4	-5	0
6mm ARC	103	2800	2623	2452	2288	2130	1793	1573	1375	1197	1038	1.8	0	-7.6	-21.8
6mm ARC	105	2750	2580	2417	2260	2108	1763	1552	1362	1190	1036	1.9	0	-7.8	-22.4
6mm ARC	108	2750	2582	2421	2265	2115	1813	1599	1405	1230	1072	1.9	0	-7.8	-22.4
243 Winchester	55	4025	3597	3209	2853	2525	1978	1579	1257	994	779	0.6	0	-4	-12.2
243 Win.	58	3925	3465	3052	2676	2330	1984	1546	1200	922	699	0.7	0	-4.4	-13.8
243 Winchester	60	3600	3110	2660	2260	1890	1725	1285	945	680	475	2	1.8	-3.3	-15.5
243 Win.	70	3400	3020	2672	2350	2050	1797	1418	1110	858	653	0	-2.5	-9.7	—
243 Winchester	70	3400	3040	2700	2390	2100	1795	1435	1135	890	685	1.1	0	-5.9	-18
243 Winchester	75/80	3350	2955	2593	2259	1951	1993	1551	1194	906	676	2	0.9	-5	-19
243 Win.	80	3425	3081	2763	2468	2190	2984	1686	1357	1082	852	1.1	0	-5.7	-17.1
243 Win.	87	2800	2574	2359	2155	1961	1514	1280	1075	897	743	1.9	0	-8.1	-23.8
243 Win.	95	3185	2908	2649	2404	2172	2140	1784	1480	1219	995	1.3	0	-6.3	-18.6
243 W. Superformance	80	3425	3080	2760	2463	2184	2083	1684	1353	1077	847	1.1	0	-5.7	-17.1
243 Winchester	85	3320	3070	2830	2600	2380	2080	1770	1510	1280	1070	2	1.2	-4	-14
243 Winchester	90	3120	2871	2635	2411	2199	1946	1647	1388	1162	966	1.4	0	-6.4	-18.8
243 Winchester*	100	2960	2697	2449	2215	1993	1945	1615	1332	1089	882	2.5	1.2	-6	-20
243 Winchester	105	2920	2689	2470	2261	2062	1988	1686	1422	1192	992	2.5	1.6	-5	-18.4
243 Light Mag.	100	3100	2839	2592	2358	2138	2133	1790	1491	1235	1014	1.5	0	-6.8	-19.8
243 WSSM	55	4060	3628	3237	2880	2550	2013	1607	1280	1013	794	0.6	0	-3.9	-12
243 WSSM	95	3250	3000	2763	2538	2325	2258	1898	1610	1359	1140	1.2	0	-5.7	-16.9
243 WSSM	100	3110	2838	2583	2341	2112	2147	1789	1481	1217	991	1.4	0	-6.6	-19.7
6mm Remington	80	3470	3064	2694	2352	2036	2139	1667	1289	982	736	2	1.1	-5	-17
6mm R. Superformance	95	3235	2955	2692	2443	3309	2207	1841	1528	1259	1028	1.2	0	-6.1	-18
6mm Remington	100	3100	2829	2573	2332	2104	2133	1777	1470	1207	983	2.5	1.6	-5	-17
6mm Remington	105	3060	2822	2596	2381	2177	2105	1788	1512	1270	1059	2.5	1.1	-3.3	-15
240 Wea. Mag.	87	3500	3202	2924	2663	2416	2366	1980	1651	1370	1127	2	2	-2	-12
240 Wea. Mag.	100	3150	2894	2653	2425	2207	2202	1860	1563	1395	1082	1.3	0	-6.3	-18.5
240 Wea. Mag.	100	3395	3106	2835	2581	2339	2559	2142	1785	1478	1215	2.5	2.8	-2	-11
25-20 Win.	86	1460	1194	1030	931	858	407	272	203	165	141	0	-23.5	0	0
25-45 Sharps	87	3000	2677	2385	2112	1859	1739	1384	1099	862	668	1.1	0	-7.4	-22.6
25-35 Win.	117	2230	1866	1545	1282	1097	1292	904	620	427	313	2.5	-4.2	-26	0
250 Savage	100	2820	2504	2210	1936	1684	1765	1392	1084	832	630	2.5	0.4	-9	-28
257 Roberts	100	2980	2661	2363	2085	1827	1972	1572	1240	965	741	2.5	-0.8	-5.2	-21.6
257 Roberts	122	2600	2331	2078	1842	1625	1831	1472	1169	919	715	2.5	0	-10.6	-31.4
257 Roberts+P	100	3000	2758	2529	2312	2105	1998	1689	1421	1187	984	1.5	0	-7	-20.5
257 Roberts+P	117	2780	2411	2071	1761	1488	2009	1511	1115	806	576	2.5	-0.2	-10.2	-32.6
257 Roberts+P	120	2780	2560	2360	2160	1970	2060	1750	1480	1240	1030	2.5	1.2	-6.4	-23.6
257 R. Superformance	117	2946	2705	2478	2265	2057	2253	1901	1595	1329	1099	1.1	0	-5.7	-17.1
25-06 Rem.	87	3440	2995	2591	2222	1884	2286	1733	1297	954	686	2	1.1	-2.5	-14.4

Cartridge	Bullet Wgt. Grs.	VELOCITY (fps)					ENERGY (ft. lbs.)					TRAJ. (in.)			
		Muzzle	100 yds.	200 yds.	300 yds.	400 yds.	Muzzle	100 yds.	200 yds.	300 yds.	400 yds.	100 yds.	200 yds.	300 yds.	400 yds.
25-06 Rem.	90	3350	3001	2679	2378	2098	2243	1790	1434	1130	879	1.2	0	-6	-18.3
25-06 Rem.	90	3440	3043	2680	2344	2034	2364	1850	1435	1098	827	2	1.8	-3.3	-15.6
25-06 Rem.	100	3230	2893	2580	2287	2014	2316	1858	1478	1161	901	2	0.8	-5.7	-18.9
25-06 Rem.	117	2990	2770	2570	2370	2190	2320	2000	1715	1465	1246	2.5	1	-7.9	-26.6
25-06 Rem.*	120	2990	2730	2484	2252	2032	2382	1985	1644	1351	1100	2.5	1.2	-5.3	-19.6
25-06 Rem.	122	2930	2706	2492	2289	2095	2325	1983	1683	1419	1189	2.5	1.8	-4.5	-17.5
25-06 R. Superformance	117	3110	2861	2626	2403	2191	2512	2127	1792	1500	1246	1.4	0	-6.4	-18.9
25 WSSM	85	3470	3156	2863	2589	2331	2273	1880	1548	1266	1026	1	0	-5.2	-15.7
25 WSSM	115	3060	2844	2639	2442	2254	2392	2066	1778	1523	1398	1.4	0	-6.4	-18.6
25 WSSM	120	2990	2717	2459	2216	1987	2383	1967	1612	1309	1053	1.6	0	-7.4	-21.8
257 Wea. Mag.	87	3825	3456	3118	2805	2513	2826	2308	1870	1520	1220	2	2.7	-0.3	-7.6
257 Wea. Mag.	90	3550	3184	2848	2537	2246	2518	2026	1621	1286	1008	1	0	-5.3	-16
257 Wea. Mag.	100	3555	3237	2941	2665	2404	2806	2326	1920	1576	1283	2.5	3.2	0	-8
257 Wea. Mag.	110	3330	3069	2823	2591	2370	2708	2300	1947	1639	1372	1.1	0	-5.5	-16.1
257 Scramjet	100	3745	3450	3173	2912	2666	3114	2643	2235	1883	1578	2.1	2.77	0	-6.93
6.5															
6.5 Grendel	123	2590	2420	2256	2099	1948	1832	1599	1390	1203	1037	1.8	0	-8.6	-25.1
6.5x47 Lapua	123	2887	NA	2554	NA	2244	2285	NA	1788	NA	1380	NA	4.53	0	-10.7
6.5x50mm Jap.	139	2360	2160	1970	1790	1620	1720	1440	1195	985	810	2.5	-1	-13.5	0
6.5x50mm Jap.	156	2070	1830	1610	1430	1260	1475	1155	900	695	550	2.5	-4	-23.8	0
6.5x52mm Car.	139	2580	2360	2160	1970	1790	2045	1725	1440	1195	985	2.5	0	-9.9	-29
6.5x52mm Car.	156	2430	2170	1930	1700	1500	2045	1630	1285	1005	780	2.5	-1	-13.9	0
6.5x52mm Carcano	160	2250	1963	1700	1467	1271	1798	1369	1027	764	574	3.8	0	-15.9	-48.1
6.5x55mm Swe.	93	2625	2350	2090	1850	1630	1425	1140	905	705	550	2.4	0	-10.3	-31.1
6.5x55 Swe.	93	3281	2952	2796	2359	-	2223	1799	1614	1149	-	1.2	0	-6.2	-
6.5x55mm Swe.	123	2750	2570	2400	2240	2080	2065	1810	1580	1370	1185	1.9	0	-7.9	-22.9
6.5x55mm Swe.	139/140	2850	2640	2440	2250	2070	2525	2170	1855	1575	1330	2.5	1.6	-5.4	-18.9
6.5x55mm Swe.	140	2550	NA	NA	NA	NA	2020	NA	NA	NA	NA	0	0	0	0
6.5x55mm Swe.	140	2735	2563	2397	2237	2084	2325	2041	1786	1556	1350	1.9	0	-8	-22.9
6.5x55mm Swe.	156	2650	2370	2110	1870	1650	2425	1950	1550	1215	945	2.5	0	-10.3	-30.6
260 Rem.	100	3200	2917	2652	2402	2165	2273	1889	1561	1281	1041	1.3	0	-6.3	-18.6
260 Rem.	130	2800	2613	2433	2261	2096	2262	1970	1709	1476	1268	1.8	0	-7.7	-22.2
260 Remington	125	2875	2669	2473	2285	2105	2294	1977	1697	1449	1230	1.71	0	-7.4	-21.4
260 Remington	140	2750	2544	2347	2158	1979	2351	2011	1712	1448	1217	2.2	0	-8.6	-24.6
6.5 Creedmoor	93	3314	2990	2689	2407	-	2267	1846	1493	1196	-	1.1	0	-5.9	-
6.5 Creedmoor	120	3020	2815	2619	2430	2251	2430	2111	1827	1574	1350	1.4	0	-6.5	-18.9
6.5 Creedmoor	120	3050	2850	2659	2476	2300	2479	2164	1884	1634	1310	1.4	0	-6.3	-18.3
6.5 Creedmoor	130	2875	2709	2550	2396	2247	2386	2119	1877	1657	1457	1.6	0	-6.9	-20
6.5 Creedmoor	140	2550	2380	2217	2060	1910	2021	1761	1527	1319	1134	2.3	0	-9.4	-27
6.5 Creedmoor	140	2710	2557	2410	2267	2129	2283	2033	1805	1598	1410	1.9	0	-7.9	-22.6
6.5 Creedmoor	140	2820	2654	2494	2339	2190	2472	2179	1915	1679	1467	1.7	0	-7.2	-20.6
6.5 C. Superformance	129	2950	2756	2570	2392	2221	2492	2175	1892	1639	1417	1.5	0	-6.8	-19.7
6.5x52R	117	2208	1856	1544	1287	1104	1267	895	620	431	317	0	-8.7	-32.2	—
6.5x57	131	2543	2295	2060	1841	1638	1882	1532	1235	986	780	0	-5.1	-18.5	-42.1
6.5 PRC	143	2960	2808	2661	2519	2381	2782	2503	2248	2014	1800	1.5	0	-6.4	-18.2
6.5 PRC	147	2910	2775	2645	2518	2395	2764	2514	2283	2069	1871	1.5	0	-6.5	-18.4
6.5-284 Norma	142	3025	2890	2758	2631	2507	2886	2634	2400	2183	1982	1.13	0	-5.7	-16.4
6.5-284 Norma	156	2790	2531	2287	2056	-	2697	2220	1812	1465	-	1.9	0	-8.6	-
6.5 Weatherby RPM	127	3225	3011	2809	2615	2429	2933	2554	2224	1928	1664	3	3.7	0	-8.8
6.5 Weatherby RPM	140	2975	2772	2579	2393	2215	2751	2389	2067	1780	1525	3.8	4.5	0	-10.6
6.5 Weatherby RPM	140	3075	2885	2703	2529	2361	2939	2587	2272	1988	1766	3.4	4.1	0	-9.5
6.71 (264) Phantom	120	3150	2929	2718	2517	2325	2645	2286	1969	1698	1440	1.3	0	-6	-17.5
6.5 Rem. Mag.	120	3210	2905	2621	2353	2102	2745	2248	1830	1475	1177	2.5	1.7	-4.1	-16.3
264 Win. Mag.	100	3400	3104	2828	2568	2322	2566	2139	1775	1464	1197	1.1	0	-5.4	-16.1
264 Win. Mag.	125	3200	2978	2767	2566	2373	2841	2461	2125	1827	1563	1.2	0	-5.8	-16.8
264 Win. Mag.	130	3100	2900	2709	2526	2350	2773	2427	2118	1841	1594	1.3	0	-6.1	-17.6
264 Win. Mag.	140	3030	2782	2548	2326	2114	2854	2406	2018	1682	1389	2.5	1.4	-5.1	-18
6.5 Nosler	129	3400	3213	3035	2863	2698	3310	2957	2638	2348	2085	0.9	0	-4.7	-13.6
6.5 Nosler	140	3300	3118	2943	2775	2613	3119	2784	2481	2205	1955	1	0	-5	-14.6
6.71 (264) Blackbird	140	3480	3261	3053	2855	2665	3766	3307	2899	2534	2208	2.4	3.1	0	-7.4
6.8 REM SPC	90	2840	2444	2083	1756	1469	1611	1194	867	616	431	2.2	0	-3.9	-32
6.8 REM SPC	110	2570	2338	2118	1910	1716	1613	1335	1095	891	719	2.4	0	-6.3	-20.8
6.8 REM SPC	120	2460	2250	2051	1863	1687	1612	1349	1121	925	758	2.3	0	-10.5	-31.1

Cartridge	Bullet Wgt. Grs.	VELOCITY (fps)					ENERGY (ft. lbs.)					TRAJ. (in.)			
		Muzzle	100 yds.	200 yds.	300 yds.	400 yds.	Muzzle	100 yds.	200 yds.	300 yds.	400 yds.	100 yds.	200 yds.	300 yds.	400 yds.
6.8mm Rem.	115	2775	2472	2190	1926	1683	1966	1561	1224	947	723	2.1	0	-3.7	-9.4
27															
270 Win.	96	3543	3173	2834	2519	-	2676	2146	1712	1352	-	0.9	0	-5.3	-
270 Win. (Rem.)	115	2710	2482	2265	2059	NA	1875	1485	1161	896	NA	0	4.8	-17.3	0
270 Win.	120	2675	2288	1935	1619	1351	1907	1395	998	699	486	2.6	0	-12	-37.4
270 Win.	140	2940	2747	2563	2386	2216	2687	2346	2042	1770	1526	1.8	0	-6.8	-19.8
270 Win. Supreme	130	3150	2881	2628	2388	2161	2865	2396	1993	1646	1348	1.3	0	-6.4	-18.9
270 Win. Supreme	150	2930	2693	2468	2254	2051	2860	2416	2030	1693	1402	1.7	0	-7.4	-21.6
270 W. Superformance	130	3200	2984	2788	2582	2393	2955	2570	2228	1924	1653	1.2	0	-5.7	-16.7
270 Winchester	100	3430	3021	2649	2305	1988	2612	2027	1557	1179	877	2	1	-4.9	-17.5
270 Winchester	130	3060	2776	2510	2259	2022	2702	2225	1818	1472	1180	2.5	1.4	-5.3	-18.2
270 Winchester	135	3000	2780	2570	2369	2178	2697	2315	1979	1682	1421	2.5	1.4	-6	-17.6
270 Winchester*	140	2940	2700	2480	2260	2060	2685	2270	1905	1590	1315	2.5	1.8	-4.6	-17.9
270 Winchester*	150	2850	2585	2336	2100	1879	2705	2226	1817	1468	1175	2.5	1.2	-6.5	-22
277 Fury	140	3000													
270 WSM	130	3275	3041	2820	2609	2408	3096	2669	2295	1564	1673	1.1	0	-5.5	-16.1
270 WSM	140	3125	2865	2619	2386	2165	3035	2559	2132	1769	1457	1.4	0	-6.5	-19
270 WSM	150	3000	2795	2599	2412	2232	2997	2601	2250	1937	1659	1.5	0	-6.6	-19.2
270 WSM	150	3120	2923	2734	2554	2380	3242	2845	2490	2172	1886	1.3	0	-5.9	-17.2
6.8 Western	162	2875	2711	2552	2399	2251	2973	2642	2342	2070	1823	1.6	0	-7	-20
6.8 Western	165	2970	2815	2667	2524	2385	3226	2902	2605	2333	2084	1.2	0	-6.3	-18.1
6.8 Western	170	2920	2754	2593	2439	2289	3218	2862	2538	2244	1978	1.3	0	-6.7	-19.3
6.8 Western	175	2835	2686	2541	2402	2266	3123	2803	2509	2241	1995	1.7	0	-7	-20.1
270 Wea. Mag.	100	3760	3380	3033	2712	2412	3139	2537	2042	1633	1292	2	2.4	-1.2	-10.1
270 Wea. Mag.	130	3375	3119	2878	2649	2432	3287	2808	2390	2026	1707	2.5	-2.9	-0.9	-9.9
270 Wea. Mag.	130	3450	3194	2958	2732	2517	3435	2949	2525	2143	1828	1	0	-4.9	-14.5
270 Wea. Mag.*	150	3245	3036	2837	2647	2465	3507	3070	2681	2334	2023	2.5	2.6	-1.8	-11.4
27 Nosler	150	3300	3143	2983	2828	2676	3638	3289	2964	2663	2385	1	0	-4.9	-14.2
7mm															
7mm BR	140	2216	2012	1821	1643	1481	1525	1259	1031	839	681	2	-3.7	-20	0
275 Rigby	140	2680	2455	2242	2040	1848	2233	1874	1563	1292	1062	2.2	0	-9.1	-26.5
7mm Mauser*	139/140	2660	2435	2221	2018	1827	2199	1843	1533	1266	1037	2.5	0	-9.6	-27.7
7mm Mauser	139	2740	2556	2379	2209	2046	2317	2016	1747	1506	1292	1.9	0	-8.1	-23.3
7mm Mauser	154	2690	2490	2300	2120	1940	2475	2120	1810	1530	1285	2.5	0.8	-7.5	-23.5
7mm Mauser	175	2440	2137	1857	1603	1382	2313	1774	1340	998	742	2.5	-1.7	-16.1	0
7x30 Waters	120	2700	2300	1930	1600	1330	1940	1405	990	685	470	2.5	-0.2	-12.3	0
7x30 Waters	120	2700	2425	2167	1926	1702	1942	1567	1251	988	772	2.2	0	-9.7	-28.8
7mm-08 Rem.	120	2675	2435	2207	1992	1790	1907	1579	1298	1057	854	2.2	0	-9.4	-27.5
7mm-08 Rem.	120	3000	2725	2467	2223	1992	2398	1979	1621	1316	1058	2	0	-7.6	-22.3
7mm-08 Rem.	139	2840	2608	2387	2177	1978	2489	2098	1758	1463	1207	1.8	0	-7.9	-23.2
7mm-08 Rem.*	140	2860	2625	2402	2189	1988	2542	2142	1793	1490	1228	2.5	0.8	-6.9	-21.9
7mm-08 Rem.	154	2715	2510	2315	2128	1950	2520	2155	1832	1548	1300	2.5	1	-7	-22.7
7-08 R. Superformance	139	2950	2857	2571	2393	2222	2686	2345	2040	1768	1524	1.5	0	-6.8	-19.7
7x64mm	173	2526	2260	2010	1777	1565	2452	1962	1552	1214	941	0	-5.3	-19.3	-44.4
7x64mm Bren.	140	2950	2710	2483	2266	2061	2705	2283	1910	1597	1320	1.5	0	-2.9	-7.3
7x64mm Bren.	154	2820	2610	2420	2230	2050	2720	2335	1995	1695	1430	2.5	1.4	-5.7	-19.9
7x64mm Bren.*	160	2850	2669	2495	2327	2166	2885	2530	2211	1924	1667	2.5	1.6	-4.8	-17.8
7x64mm Bren.	175	2650	2445	2248	2061	1883	2728	2322	1964	1650	1378	2.2	0	-9.1	-26.4
7x65mmR	173	2608	2337	2082	1844	1626	2613	2098	1666	1307	1015	0	-4.9	-17.9	-41.9
275 Rigby	139	2680	2456	2242	2040	1848	2217	1861	1552	1284	1054	2.2	0	-9.1	-26.5
284 Winchester	150	2860	2595	2344	2108	1886	2724	2243	1830	1480	1185	2.5	0.8	-7.3	-23.2
280 R. Superformance	139	3090	2890	2699	2516	2341	2946	2578	2249	1954	1691	1.3	0	-6.1	-17.7
280 Rem.	139	3090	2891	2700	2518	2343	2947	2579	2250	1957	1694	1.3	0	-6.1	-17.7
280 Remington	140	3000	2758	2528	2309	2102	2797	2363	1986	1657	1373	2.5	1.4	-5.2	-18.3
280 Remington*	150	2890	2624	2373	2135	1912	2781	2293	1875	1518	1217	2.5	0.8	-7.1	-22.6
280 Remington	160	2840	2637	2442	2556	2078	2866	2471	2120	1809	1535	2.5	0.8	-6.7	-21
280 Remington	165	2820	2510	2220	1950	1701	2913	2308	1805	1393	1060	2.5	0.4	-8.8	-26.5
280 Ack. Imp.	140	3150	2946	2752	2566	2387	3084	2698	2354	2047	1772	1.3	0	-5.8	-17
280 Ack. Imp.	150	2900	2712	2533	2360	2194	2800	2450	2136	1855	1603	1.6	0	-7	-20.3
280 Ack. Imp.	160	2950	2751	2561	2379	2205	3091	2686	2331	2011	1727	1.5	0	-6.9	-19.9
7x61mm S&H Sup.	154	3060	2720	2400	2100	1820	3200	2520	1965	1505	1135	2.5	1.8	-5	-19.8
7mm Dakota	160	3200	3001	2811	2630	2455	3637	3200	2808	2456	2140	2.1	1.9	-2.8	-12.5
7mm Rem. Mag.	127	3314	3050	2802	2567	-	3096	2623	2214	1858	-	1.1	0	-5.5	-
7mm Rem. Mag.	139	3190	2986	2791	2605	2427	3141	2752	2405	2095	1817	1.2	0	-5.7	-16.5
7mm Rem. Mag. (Rem.)	140	2710	2482	2265	2059	NA	2283	1915	1595	1318	NA	0	-4.5	-1.57	0
7mm Rem. Mag.*	139/140	3150	2930	2710	2510	2320	3085	2660	2290	1960	1670	2.5	2.4	-2.4	-12.7
7mm Rem. Mag.	150/154	3110	2830	2568	2320	2085	3221	2667	2196	1792	1448	2.5	1.6	-4.6	-16.5

Cartridge	Bullet Wgt. Grs.	VELOCITY (fps)					ENERGY (ft. lbs.)					TRAJ. (in.)			
		Muzzle	100 yds.	200 yds.	300 yds.	400 yds.	Muzzle	100 yds.	200 yds.	300 yds.	400 yds.	100 yds.	200 yds.	300 yds.	400 yds.
7mm Rem. Mag.*	160/162	2950	2730	2520	2320	2120	3090	2650	2250	1910	1600	2.5	1.8	-4.4	-17.8
7mm Rem. Mag.	165	2900	2699	2507	2324	2147	3081	2669	2303	1978	1689	2.5	1.2	-5.9	-19
7mm Rem Mag.	175	2860	2645	2440	2244	2057	3178	2718	2313	1956	1644	2.5	1	-6.5	-20.7
7 R.M. Superformance	139	3240	3033	2836	2648	2467	3239	2839	2482	2163	1877	1.1	0	-5.5	-15.9
7 R.M. Superformance	154	3100	2914	2736	2565	2401	3286	2904	2560	2250	1970	1.3	0	-5.9	-17.2
7mm Rem. SA ULTRA MAG	140	3175	2934	2707	2490	2283	3033	2676	2277	1927	1620	1.3	0	-6	-17.7
7mm Rem. SA ULTRA MAG	150	3110	2828	2563	2313	2077	3221	2663	2188	1782	1437	2.5	2.1	-3.6	-15.8
7mm Rem. SA ULTRA MAG	160	2850	2676	2508	2347	2192	2885	2543	2235	1957	1706	1.7	0	-7.2	-20.7
7mm Rem. SA ULTRA MAG	160	2960	2762	2572	2390	2215	3112	2709	2350	2029	1743	2.6	2.2	-3.6	-15.4
7mm Rem. WSM	140	3225	3008	2801	2603	2414	3233	2812	2438	2106	1812	1.2	0	-5.6	-16.4
7mm Rem. WSM	160	2990	2744	2512	2081	1883	3176	2675	2241	1864	1538	1.6	0	-7.1	-20.8
7mm Wea. Mag.	139	3300	3091	2891	2701	2519	3361	2948	2580	2252	1958	1.1	0	-5.2	-15.2
7mm Wea. Mag.	140	3225	2970	2729	2501	2283	3233	2741	2315	1943	1621	2.5	2	-3.2	-14
7mm Wea. Mag.	140	3340	3127	2925	2732	2546	3467	3040	2659	2320	2016	0	-2.1	-8.2	-19
7mm Wea. Mag.	150	3175	2957	2751	2553	2364	3357	2913	2520	2171	1861	0	-2.5	-9.6	-22
7mm Wea. Mag.	154	3260	3023	2799	2586	2382	3539	3044	2609	2227	1890	2.5	2.8	-1.5	-10.8
7mm Wea. Mag.*	160	3200	3004	2816	2637	2464	3637	3205	2817	2469	2156	2.5	2.7	-1.5	-10.6
7mm Wea. Mag.	165	2950	2747	2553	2367	2189	3188	2765	2388	2053	1756	2.5	1.8	-4.2	-16.4
7mm Wea. Mag.	175	2910	2693	2486	2288	2098	3293	2818	2401	2033	1711	2.5	1.2	-5.9	-19.4
7mm PRC	160	3000	2840	2686	2537	2393	3197	2865	2563	2287	2035	1.4	0	-6.2	-17.9
7mm PRC	175	3000	2861	2727	2597	2470	3497	3181	2890	2620	2371	1.4	0	-6	-17.2
7mm PRC	180	2975	2855	2739	2626	2516	3439	3168	2915	2679	2459	1.4	0	-6	-17.1
7.21(.284) Tomahawk	140	3300	3118	2943	2774	2612	3386	3022	2693	2393	2122	2.3	3.2	0	-7.7
7mm STW	140	3300	3086	2889	2697	2513	3384	2966	2594	2261	1963	0	-2.1	-8.5	-19.6
7mm STW	140	3325	3064	2818	2585	2364	3436	2918	2468	2077	1737	2.3	1.8	-3	-13.1
7mm STW	150	3175	2957	2751	2553	2364	3357	2913	2520	2171	1861	0	-2.5	-9.6	-22
7mm STW	175	2900	2760	2625	2493	2366	3267	2960	2677	2416	2175	0	-3.1	-11.2	-24.9
7mm STW Supreme	160	3150	2894	2652	2422	2204	3526	2976	2499	2085	1727	1.3	0	-6.3	-18.5
7mm Rem. Ultra Mag.	140	3425	3184	2956	2740	2534	3646	3151	2715	2333	1995	1.7	1.6	-2.6	-11.4
7mm Rem. Ultra Mag.	160	3225	3035	2854	2680	2512	3694	3273	2894	2551	2242	0	-2.3	-8.8	-20.2
7mm Rem. Ultra Mag.	174	3040	2896	2756	2621	2490	3590	3258	2952	2669	2409	0	-2.6	-9.9	-22.2
7mm Firehawk	140	3625	3373	3135	2909	2695	4084	3536	3054	2631	2258	2.2	2.9	0	-7.03
7.21 (.284) Firebird	140	3750	3522	3306	3101	2905	4372	3857	3399	2990	2625	1.6	2.4	0	-6
.28 Nosler	160	3300	3114	2930	2753	2583	3883	3444	3049	2693	2371	1.1	0	-5.1	-14.9
30															
300 ACC Blackout	110	2150	1886	1646	1432	1254	1128	869	661	501	384	0	-8.3	-29.6	-67.8
300 AAC Blackout	125	2250	2031	1826	1636	1464	1404	1145	926	743	595	0	-7	-24.4	-54.8
300 AAC Blackout	220	1000	968	-	-	-	488	457	-	-	-	0	-	-	-
30 Carbine	110	1990	1567	1236	1035	923	977	600	373	262	208	0	-13.5	0	0
30 Carbine	110	2000	1601	1279	1067	—	977	626	399	278	—	0	-12.9	-47.2	—
300 Whisper	110	2375	2094	1834	1597	NA	1378	1071	822	623	NA	3.2	0	-13.6	NA
300 Whisper	208	1020	988	959	NA	NA	480	451	422	NA	NA	0	-34.1	NA	NA
303 Savage	190	1890	1612	1327	1183	1055	1507	1096	794	591	469	2.5	-7.6	0	0
30 Remington	170	2120	1822	1555	1328	1153	1696	1253	913	666	502	2.5	-4.7	-26.3	0
7.62x39mm Rus.	123	2360	2049	1764	1511	1296	1521	1147	850	623	459	3.4	0	-14.7	-44.7
7.62x39mm Rus.	123/125	2300	2030	1780	1550	1350	1445	1125	860	655	500	2.5	-2	-17.5	0
30-30 Win.	55	3400	2693	2085	1570	1187	1412	886	521	301	172	2	0	-10.2	-35
30-30 Win.	125	2570	2090	1660	1320	1080	1830	1210	770	480	320	-2	-2.6	-19.9	0
30-30 Win.	140	2500	2198	1918	1662	—	1943	1501	1143	858	—	2.9	0	-12.4	—
30-30 Win.	150	2390	2040	1723	1447	1225	1902	1386	989	697	499	0	-7.5	-27	-63
30-30 Win. Supreme	150	2480	2095	1747	1446	1209	2049	1462	1017	697	487	0	-6.5	-24.5	0
30-30 Win.	160	2300	1997	1719	1473	1268	1879	1416	1050	771	571	2.5	-2.9	-20.2	0
30-30 Win. Lever Evolution	160	2400	2150	1916	1699	NA	2046	1643	1304	1025	NA	3	0.2	-12.1	NA
30-30 PMC Cowboy	170	1300	1198	1121	—	—	638	474	—	—	—	0	-27	0	0
30-30 Win.*	170	2200	1895	1619	1381	1191	1827	1355	989	720	535	2.5	-5.8	-23.6	0
300 Savage	150	2630	2354	2094	1853	1631	2303	1845	1462	1143	886	2.5	-0.4	-10.1	-30.7
300 Savage	150	2740	2499	2272	2056	1852	2500	2081	1718	1407	1143	2.1	0	-8.8	-25.8
300 Savage	180	2350	2137	1935	1754	1570	2207	1825	1496	1217	985	2.5	-1.6	-15.2	0
30-40 Krag	180	2430	2213	2007	1813	1632	2360	1957	1610	1314	1064	2.5	-1.4	-13.8	0
7.65x53mm Arg.	180	2590	2390	2200	2010	1830	2685	2280	1925	1615	1345	2.5	0	-27.6	0
7.5x53mm Argentine	150	2785	2519	2269	2032	1814	2583	2113	1714	1376	1096	2	0	-8.8	-25.5
308 Marlin Express	140	2800	2532	2279	2040	1818	2437	1992	1614	1294	1207	2	0	-8.7	-25.8
308 Marlin Express	160	2660	2430	2226	2026	1836	2513	2111	1761	1457	1197	3	1.7	-6.7	-23.5
307 Winchester	150	2760	2321	1924	1575	1289	2530	1795	1233	826	554	2.5	-1.5	-13.6	0
307 Winchester	160	2650	2386	2137	1904	1688	2494	2022	1622	1287	1688	2.3	0	-10	-29.6
7.5x55 Swiss	180	2650	2450	2250	2060	1880	2805	2390	2020	1700	1415	2.5	0.6	-8.1	-24.9

Cartridge	Bullet Wgt. Grs.	VELOCITY (fps)					ENERGY (ft. lbs.)					TRAJ. (in.)			
		Muzzle	100 yds.	200 yds.	300 yds.	400 yds.	Muzzle	100 yds.	200 yds.	300 yds.	400 yds.	100 yds.	200 yds.	300 yds.	400 yds.
7.5x55mm Swiss	165	2720	2515	2319	2132	1954	2710	2317	1970	1665	1398	2	0	-8.5	-24.6
30 Remington AR	123/125	2800	2465	2154	1867	1606	2176	1686	1288	967	716	2.1	0	-9.7	-29.4
308 Winchester	55	3770	3215	2726	2286	1888	1735	1262	907	638	435	-2	1.4	-3.8	-15.8
308 Win.	110	3165	2830	2520	2230	1960	2447	1956	1551	1215	938	1.4	0	-6.9	-20.9
308 Win. PDX1	120	2850	2497	2171	NA	NA	2164	1662	1256	NA	NA	0	-2.8	NA	NA
308 Win.	139	2904	2609	2333	2074	-	2602	2101	1680	1327	-	1.7	0	-8.1	-
308 Winchester	150	2820	2533	2263	2009	1774	2648	2137	1705	1344	1048	2.5	0.4	-8.5	-26.1
308 W. Superformance	150	3000	2772	2555	2348	1962	2997	2558	2173	1836	1540	1.5	0	-6.9	-20
308 Win.	155	2775	2553	2342	2141	1950	2650	2243	1887	1577	1308	1.9	0	-8.3	-24.2
308 Win.	155	2850	2640	2438	2247	2064	2795	2398	2047	1737	1466	1.8	0	-7.5	-22.1
308 Winchester	165	2700	2440	2194	1963	1748	2670	2180	1763	1411	1199	2.5	0	-9.7	-28.5
308 Winchester	168	2680	2493	2314	2143	1979	2678	2318	1998	1713	1460	2.5	0	-8.9	-25.3
308 Win. Super Match	168	2870	2647	2462	2284	2114	3008	2613	2261	1946	1667	1.7	0	-7.5	-21.6
308 Win. (Fed.)	170	2000	1740	1510	NA	NA	1510	1145	860	NA	NA	0	0	0	0
308 Winchester	178	2620	2415	2220	2034	1857	2713	2306	1948	1635	1363	2.5	0	-9.6	-27.6
308 Win. Super Match	178	2780	2609	2444	2285	2132	3054	2690	2361	2064	1797	1.8	0	-7.6	-21.9
308 Winchester*	180	2620	2393	2178	1974	1782	2743	2288	1896	1557	1269	2.5	-0.2	-10.2	-28.5
30-06 Spfd.	55	4080	3485	2965	2502	2083	2033	1483	1074	764	530	2	1.9	-2.1	-11.7
30-06 Spfd. (Rem.)	125	2660	2335	2034	1757	NA	1964	1513	1148	856	NA	0	-5.2	-18.9	0
30-06 Spfd.	125	2700	2412	2143	1891	1660	2023	1615	1274	993	765	2.3	0	-9.9	-29.5
30-06 Spfd.	125	3140	2780	2447	2138	1853	2736	2145	1662	1279	953	2	1	-6.2	-21
30-06 Spfd.	139	2986	2686	2405	2142	-	2751	2227	1785	1416	-	1.6	0	-7.6	-
30-06 Spfd.	150	2910	2617	2342	2083	1853	2820	2281	1827	1445	1135	2.5	0.8	-7.2	-23.4
30-06 Superformance	150	3080	2848	2617	2417	2216	3159	2700	2298	1945	1636	1.4	0	-6.4	-18.9
30-06 Spfd.	152	2910	2654	2413	2184	1968	2858	2378	1965	1610	1307	2.5	1	-6.6	-21.3
30-06 Spfd.*	165	2800	2534	2283	2047	1825	2872	2352	1909	1534	1220	2.5	0.4	-8.4	-25.5
30-06 Spfd.	168	2710	2522	2346	2169	2003	2739	2372	2045	1754	1497	2.5	0.4	-8	-23.5
30-06 M1 Garand	168	2710	2523	2343	2171	2006	2739	2374	2048	1758	1501	2.3	0	-8.6	-24.6
30-06 Spfd. (Fed.)	170	2000	1740	1510	NA	NA	1510	1145	860	NA	NA	0	0	0	0
30-06 Spfd.	178	2720	2511	2311	2121	1939	2924	2491	2111	1777	1486	2.5	0.4	-8.2	-24.6
30-06 Spfd.*	180	2700	2469	2250	2042	1846	2913	2436	2023	1666	1362	-2.5	0	-9.3	-27
30-06 Superformance	180	2820	2630	2447	2272	2104	3178	2764	2393	2063	1769	1.8	0	-7.6	-21.9
30-06 Spfd.	220	2410	2130	1870	1632	1422	2837	2216	1708	1301	988	2.5	-1.7	-18	0
30-06 High Energy	180	2880	2690	2500	2320	2150	3315	2880	2495	2150	1845	1.7	0	-7.2	-21
30 T/C	150	2920	2696	2483	2280	2087	2849	2421	2054	1732	1450	1.7	0	-7.3	-21.3
30 T/C Superformance	150	3000	2772	2555	2348	2151	2997	2558	2173	1836	1540	1.5	0	-6.9	-20
30 T/C Superformance	165	2850	2644	2447	2258	2078	2975	2560	2193	1868	1582	1.7	0	-7.6	-22
300 Rem SA Ultra Mag	150	3200	2901	2622	2359	2112	3410	2803	2290	1854	1485	1.3	0	-6.4	-19.1
300 Rem SA Ultra Mag	165	3075	2792	2527	2276	2040	3464	2856	2339	1898	1525	1.2	0	-7	-20.7
300 Rem SA Ultra Mag	180	2960	2761	2571	2389	2214	3501	3047	2642	2280	1959	2.6	2.2	-3.6	-15.4
300 Rem. SA Ultra Mag	200	2800	2644	2494	2348	2208	3841	3104	2761	2449	2164	0	-3.5	-12.5	-27.9
7.82 (308) Patriot	150	3250	2999	2762	2537	2323	3519	2997	2542	2145	1798	1.2	0	-5.8	-16.9
300 RCM	150	3265	3023	2794	2577	2369	3550	3043	2600	2211	1870	1.2	0	-5.6	-16.5
300 RCM Superformance	150	3310	3065	2833	2613	2404	3648	3128	2673	2274	1924	1.1	0	-5.4	-16
300 RCM Superformance	165	3185	2964	2753	2552	2360	3716	3217	2776	2386	2040	1.2	0	-5.8	-17
300 RCM Superformance	180	3040	2840	2649	2466	2290	3693	3223	2804	2430	2096	1.4	0	-6.4	-18.5
300 WSM	150	3300	3061	2834	2619	2414	3628	3121	2676	2285	1941	1.1	0	-5.4	-15.9
300 WSM	180	2970	2741	2524	2317	2120	3526	3005	2547	2147	1797	1.6	0	-7	-20.5
300 WSM	180	3010	2923	2734	2554	2380	3242	2845	2490	2172	1886	1.3	0	-5.9	-17.2
300 WSM	190	2875	2729	2588	2451	2319	3486	3142	2826	2535	2269	0	3.2	-11.5	-25.7
308 Norma Mag.	180	2975	2787	2608	2435	2269	3536	3105	2718	2371	2058	0	-3	-11.1	-25
308 Norma Mag.	180	3020	2820	2630	2440	2270	3645	3175	2755	2385	2050	2.5	2	-3.5	-14.8
300 Dakota	200	3000	2824	2656	2493	2336	3996	3542	3131	2760	2423	2.2	1.5	-4	-15.2
300 H&H Mag.	180	2870	2678	2494	2318	2148	3292	2866	2486	2147	1844	1.7	0	-7.3	-21.6
300 H&H Magnum*	180	2880	2640	2412	2196	1990	3315	2785	2325	1927	1583	2.5	0.8	-6.8	-21.7
300 H&H Mag.	200	2750	2596	2447	2303	2164	3357	2992	2659	2355	2079	1.8	0	-7.6	-21.8
300 H&H Magnum	220	2550	2267	2002	1757	NA	3167	2510	1958	1508	NA	-2.5	-0.4	-12	0
300 Win. Mag.	139	3363	3036	2733	2449	-	3490	2845	2305	1851	-	1.1	0	-5.7	-
300 Win. Mag.	150	3290	2951	2636	2342	2068	3605	2900	2314	1827	1424	2.5	1.9	-3.8	-15.8
300 WM Superformance	150	3400	3150	2914	2690	2477	3850	3304	2817	2409	2043	1	0	-5.1	-15
300 Win. Mag.	165	3100	2877	2665	2462	2269	3522	3033	2603	2221	1897	2.5	2.4	-3	-16.9
300 Win. Mag.	178	2900	2760	2568	2375	2191	3509	3030	2606	2230	1897	2.5	1.4	-5	-17.6
300 Win. Mag.	178	2960	2770	2588	2413	2245	3463	3032	2647	2301	1992	1.5	0	-6.7	-19.4
300 WM Super Match	178	2960	2770	2587	2412	2243	3462	3031	2645	2298	1988	1.5	0	-6.7	-19.4
300 Win. Mag.*	180	2960	2745	2540	2344	2157	3501	3011	2578	2196	1859	2.5	1.2	-5.5	-18.5
300 WM Superformance	180	3130	2927	2732	2546	2366	3917	3424	2983	2589	2238	1.3	0	-5.9	-17.3
300 Win. Mag.	190	2885	1691	2506	2327	2156	3511	3055	2648	2285	1961	2.5	1.2	-5.7	-19

Cartridge	Bullet Wgt. Grs.	VELOCITY (fps)					ENERGY (ft. lbs.)					TRAJ. (in.)			
		Muzzle	100 yds.	200 yds.	300 yds.	400 yds.	Muzzle	100 yds.	200 yds.	300 yds.	400 yds.	100 yds.	200 yds.	300 yds.	400 yds.
300 Win. Mag.	195	2930	2760	2596	2438	2286	3717	3297	2918	2574	2262	1.5	0	-6.7	-19.4
300 Win. Mag.*	200	2825	2595	2376	2167	1970	3545	2991	2508	2086	1742	-2.5	1.6	-4.7	-17.2
300 Win. Mag.	220	2680	2448	2228	2020	1823	3508	2927	2424	1993	1623	2.5	0	-9.5	-27.5
300 Rem. Ultra Mag.	150	3450	3208	2980	2762	2556	3964	3427	2956	2541	2175	1.7	1.5	-2.6	-11.2
300 Rem. Ultra Mag.	150	2910	2686	2473	2279	2077	2820	2403	2037	1716	1436	1.7	0	-7.4	-21.5
300 Rem. Ultra Mag.	165	3350	3099	2862	2938	2424	4110	3518	3001	2549	2152	1.1	0	-5.3	-15.6
300 Rem. Ultra Mag.	180	3250	3037	2834	2640	2454	4221	3686	3201	2786	2407	2.4	0	-3	-12.7
300 Rem. Ultra Mag.	180	2960	2774	2505	2294	2093	3501	2971	2508	2103	1751	2.7	2.2	-3.8	-16.4
300 Rem. Ultra Mag.	200	3032	2791	2562	2345	2138	4083	3459	2916	2442	2030	1.5	0	-6.8	-19.9
300 Rem. Ultra Mag.	210	2920	2790	2665	2543	2424	3975	3631	3311	3015	2740	1.5	0	-6.4	-18.1
30 Nosler	180	3200	3004	2815	2635	2462	4092	3606	3168	2774	2422	0	-2.4	-9.1	-20.9
30 Nosler	210	3000	2868	2741	2617	2497	4196	3836	3502	3193	2906	0	-2.7	-10.1	-22.5
300 Wea. Mag.	100	3900	3441	3038	2652	2305	3714	2891	2239	1717	1297	2	2.6	-0.6	-8.7
300 Wea. Mag.	150	3375	3126	2892	2670	2459	3794	3255	2786	2374	2013	1	0	-5.2	-15.3
300 Wea. Mag.	150	3600	3307	3033	2776	2533	4316	3642	3064	2566	2137	2.5	3.2	0	-8.1
300 Wea. Mag.	165	3140	2921	2713	2515	2325	3612	3126	2697	2317	1980	1.3	0	-6	-17.5
300 Wea. Mag.	165	3450	3210	3000	2792	2593	4360	3796	3297	2855	2464	2.5	3.2	0	-7.8
300 Wea. Mag.	178	3120	2902	2695	2497	2308	3847	3329	2870	2464	2104	2.5	-1.7	-3.6	-14.7
300 Wea. Mag.	180	3330	3110	2910	2710	2520	4430	3875	3375	2935	2540	1	0	-5.2	-15.1
300 Wea. Mag.	190	3030	2830	2638	2455	2279	3873	3378	2936	2542	2190	2.5	1.6	-4.3	-16
300 Wea. Mag.	220	2850	2541	2283	1964	1736	3967	3155	2480	1922	1471	2.5	0.4	-8.5	-26.4
300 Pegasus	180	3500	3319	3145	2978	2817	4896	4401	3953	3544	3172	2.28	2.89	0	-6.79
300 Norma Magnum	215	3017	2881	2748	2618	2491	4346	3963	3605	3272	2963	NA	NA	NA	NA
300 Norma Magnum	230	2934	2805	2678	2555	2435	4397	4018	3664	3334	3028	NA	NA	NA	NA
300 Norma Magnum	225	2850	2731	2615	2502	2392	4058	3726	3417	3128	2859	1.6	0	-6.7	-18.9
300 PRC	212	2860	2723	2589	2849	2565	3850	3489	3156	2849	2565	1.6	0	-6.8	-19.3
300 PRC	225	2810	2692	2577	2465	2356	3945	3620	3318	3036	2773	1.7	0	-6.9	-19.5
31															
32-20 Win.	100	1210	1021	913	834	769	325	231	185	154	131	0	-32.3	0	0
303 British	150	2685	2441	2211	1993	1789	2401	1985	1628	1323	1066	2.2	0	-9.3	-27.4
303 British	180	2460	2124	1817	1542	1311	2418	1803	1319	950	687	2.5	-1.8	-16.8	0
303 Light Mag.	150	2830	2570	2325	2094	1884	2667	2199	1800	1461	1185	2	0	-8.4	-24.6
7.62x54mm Rus.	146	2950	2730	2520	2320	NA	2820	2415	2055	1740	NA	2.5	2	-4.4	-17.7
7.62x54mm Rus.	174	2800	2607	2422	2245	2075	3029	2626	2267	1947	1664	1.8	0	-7.8	-22.4
7.62x54mm Rus.	180	2580	2370	2180	2000	1820	2650	2250	1900	1590	1100	2.5	0	-9.8	-28.5
7.7x58mm Jap.	150	2640	2399	2170	1954	1752	2321	1916	1568	1271	1022	2.3	0	-9.7	-28.5
7.7x58mm Jap.	180	2500	2300	2100	1920	1750	2490	2105	1770	1475	1225	2.5	0	-10.4	-30.2
8mm															
8x56 R	205	2400	2188	1987	1797	1621	2621	2178	1796	1470	1196	2.9	0	-11.7	-34.3
8x57mm JS Mau.	139	3018	2724	2448	2189	-	2812	2290	1849	1479	-	1.5	0	-7.3	-
8x57mm JS Mau.	165	2850	2520	2210	1930	1670	2965	2330	1795	1360	1015	2.5	1	-7.7	0
32 Win. Special	165	2410	2145	1897	1669	NA	2128	1685	1318	1020	NA	2	0	-13	-19.9
32 Win. Special	170	2250	1921	1626	1372	1175	1911	1393	998	710	521	2.5	-3.5	-22.9	0
8mm Mauser	170	2360	1969	1622	1333	1123	2102	1464	993	671	476	2.5	-3.1	-22.2	0
8mm Mauser	196	2500	2338	2182	2032	1888	2720	2379	2072	1797	1552	2.4	0	-9.8	-27.9
325 WSM	180	3060	2841	2632	2432	2242	3743	3226	2769	2365	2009	1.4	0	-6.4	-18.7
325 WSM	200	2950	2753	2565	2384	2210	3866	3367	2922	2524	2170	1.5	0	-6.8	-19.8
325 WSM	220	2840	2605	2382	2169	1968	3941	3316	2772	2300	1893	1.8	0	-8	-23.3
8mm Rem. Mag.	185	3080	2761	2464	2186	1927	3896	3131	2494	1963	1525	2.5	1.4	-5.5	-19.7
8mm Rem. Mag.	220	2830	2581	2346	2123	1913	3912	3254	2688	2201	1787	2.5	0.6	-7.6	-23.5
33															
338 Federal	180	2830	2590	2350	2130	1930	3200	2670	2215	1820	1480	1.8	0	-8.2	-23.9
338 Marlin Express	200	2565	2365	2174	1992	1820	2922	2484	2099	1762	1471	3	1.2	-7.9	-25.9
338 Federal	185	2750	2550	2350	2160	1980	3105	2660	2265	1920	1615	1.9	0	-8.3	-24.1
338 Federal	210	2630	2410	2200	2010	1820	3225	2710	2265	1880	1545	2.3	0	-9.4	-27.3
338 Federal MSR	185	2680	2459	2230	2020	1820	2950	2460	2035	1670	1360	2.2	0	-9.2	-26.8
338-06	200	2750	2553	2364	2184	2011	3358	2894	2482	2118	1796	1.9	0	-8.22	-23.6
330 Dakota	250	2900	2719	2545	2378	2217	4668	4103	3595	3138	2727	2.3	1.3	-5	-17.5
338 Lapua	250	2900	2685	2481	2285	2098	4668	4002	2416	2899	2444	1.7	0	-7.3	-21.3
338 Lapua	250	2963	2795	2640	2493	NA	4842	4341	3881	3458	NA	1.9	0	-7.9	0
338 Lapua	285	2745	2616	2491	2369	2251	4768	4331	3926	3552	3206	1.8	0	-7.4	-21
338 Lapua	300	2660	2544	2432	2322	-	4715	4313	3940	3592	-	1.9	0	-7.8	-
338 RCM Superformance	185	2980	2755	2542	2338	2143	3647	3118	2653	2242	1887	1.5	0	-6.9	-20.3
338 RCM Superformance	200	2950	2744	2547	2358	2177	3846	3342	2879	2468	2104	1.6	0	-6.9	-20.1
338 RCM Superformance	225	2750	2575	2407	2245	2089	3778	3313	2894	2518	2180	1.9	0	-7.9	-22.7
338 WM Superformance	185	3080	2850	2632	2424	2226	3896	3337	2845	2413	2034	1.4	0	-6.4	-18.8

Cartridge	Bullet Wgt. Grs.	VELOCITY (fps)					ENERGY (ft. lbs.)					TRAJ. (in.)			
		Muzzle	100 yds.	200 yds.	300 yds.	400 yds.	Muzzle	100 yds.	200 yds.	300 yds.	400 yds.	100 yds.	200 yds.	300 yds.	400 yds.
338 Win. Mag.	200	3030	2820	2620	2429	2246	4077	3532	3049	2621	2240	1.4	0	-6.5	-18.9
338 Win. Mag.*	210	2830	2590	2370	2150	1940	3735	3130	2610	2155	1760	2.5	1.4	-6	-20.9
338 Win. Mag.*	225	2785	2517	2266	2029	1808	3871	3165	2565	2057	1633	2.5	0.4	-8.5	-25.9
338 WM Superformance	225	2840	2758	2582	2414	2252	4318	3798	3331	2911	2533	1.5	0	-6.8	-19.5
338 Win. Mag.	230	2780	2573	2375	2186	2005	3948	3382	2881	2441	2054	2.5	1.2	-6.3	-21
338 Win. Mag.*	250	2660	2456	2261	2075	1898	3927	3348	2837	2389	1999	2.5	0.2	-9	-26.2
338 Ultra Mag.	250	2860	2645	2440	2244	2057	4540	3882	3303	2794	2347	1.7	0	-7.6	-22.1
338 Lapua Match	250	2900	2760	2625	2494	2366	4668	4229	3825	3452	3108	1.5	0	-6.6	-18.8
338 Lapua Match	285	2745	2623	2504	2388	2275	4768	4352	3966	3608	3275	1.8	0	-7.3	-20.8
33 Nosler	225	3025	2856	2687	2525	2369	4589	4074	3608	3185	2803	0	-2.8	-10.4	-23.4
33 Nosler	265	2775	2661	2547	2435	2326	4543	4167	3816	3488	3183	0	-3.4	-12.2	-26.8
33 Nosler	300	2550	2445	2339	2235	2134	4343	3981	3643	3327	3033	0	-4.3	-15	-32.6
8.59(.338) Galaxy	200	3100	2899	2707	2524	2347	4269	3734	3256	2829	2446	3	3.8	0	-9.3
340 Wea. Mag.*	210	3250	2991	2746	2515	2295	4924	4170	3516	2948	2455	2.5	1.9	-1.8	-11.8
340 Wea. Mag.*	250	3000	2806	2621	2443	2272	4995	4371	3812	3311	2864	2.5	2	-3.5	-14.8
338 A-Square	250	3120	2799	2500	2220	1958	5403	4348	3469	2736	2128	2.5	2.7	-1.5	-10.5
338-378 Wea. Mag.	225	3180	2974	2778	2591	2410	5052	4420	3856	3353	2902	3.1	3.8	0	-8.9
338 Titan	225	3230	3010	2800	2600	2409	5211	4524	3916	3377	2898	3.07	3.8	0	-8.95
338 Excalibur	200	3600	3361	3134	2920	2715	5755	5015	4363	3785	3274	2.23	2.87	0	-6.99
338 Excalibur	250	3250	2922	2618	2333	2066	5863	4740	3804	3021	2370	1.3	0	-6.35	-19.2
34, 35															
348 Winchester	200	2520	2215	1931	1672	1443	2820	2178	1656	1241	925	2.5	-1.4	-14.7	0
348 Winchester LeveRevolution	200	2560	2294	2044	1811	1597	2910	2336	1855	1456	1133	2.6	0	-10.9	-32.6
357 Magnum	158	1830	1427	1138	980	883	1175	715	454	337	274	0		-33.1	0
350 Legend	145	2350	1916	1539	1241	n/a	1778	1182	763	496	n/a	0	-8.1	-31.2	NA
350 Legend	150	2325	1968	1647	1373	na	4800	1289	903	628	na	0	-7.6	-28.1	na
350 Legend	160	2225	1843	1509	1243	na	1759	1206	809	548	na	0	-8.9	-33.2	na
350 Legend	180	2100	1762	1466	1230	na	1762	1240	859	604	na	0	-9.8	-36	na
350 Legend	265	1060	990	936	890	na	661	577	515	466	na	0	-34.1	-107.4	na
35 Remington	150	2300	1874	1506	1218	1039	1762	1169	755	494	359	2.5	-4.1	-26.3	0
35 Remington	200	2080	1698	1376	1140	1001	1921	1280	841	577	445	2.5	-6.3	-17.1	-33.6
35 Remington	200	2225	1963	1722	1505	—	2198	1711	1317	1006	—	3.8	0	-15.6	—
35 Rem. Lever Evolution	200	2225	1963	1721	1503	NA	2198	1711	1315	1003	NA	3	-1.3	-17.5	NA
360 Buckhammer	180	2399	1948	1557	1247	1051	2300	1517	969	621	441	-3.4	-16.3	-43.7	NA
360 Buckhammer	200	2217	1794	1434	1166	1008	2183	1429	914	604	452	-4.1	-19.1	-51.3	NA
356 Winchester	200	2460	2114	1797	1517	1284	2688	1985	1434	1022	732	2.5	-1.8	-15.1	0
356 Winchester	250	2160	1911	1682	1476	1299	2591	2028	1571	1210	937	2.5	-3.7	-22.2	0
358 Winchester	200	2475	2180	1906	1655	1434	2720	2110	1612	1217	913	2.9	0	-12.6	-37.9
358 Winchester	200	2490	2171	1876	1619	1379	2753	2093	1563	1151	844	2.5	-1.6	-15.6	0
358 STA	275	2850	2562	2292	2039	NA	4958	4009	3208	2539	NA	1.9	0	-8.6	0
350 Rem. Mag.	200	2710	2410	2130	1870	1631	3261	2579	2014	1553	1181	2.5	-0.2	-10	-30.1
35 Whelen	200	2675	2378	2100	1842	1606	3177	2510	1958	1506	1145	2.5	-0.2	-10.3	-31.1
35 Whelen	200	2910	2585	2283	2001	1742	3760	2968	2314	1778	1347	1.9	0	-8.6	-25.9
35 Whelen	225	2500	2300	2110	1930	1770	3120	2650	2235	1870	1560	2.6	0	-10.2	-29.9
35 Whelen	250	2400	2197	2005	1823	1652	3197	2680	2230	1844	1515	2.5	-1.2	-13.7	0
358 Norma Mag.	250	2800	2510	2230	1970	1730	4350	3480	2750	2145	1655	2.5	1	-7.6	-25.2
358 STA	275	2850	2562	2292	2039	1764	4959	4009	3208	2539	1899	1.9	0	-8.58	-26.1
9.3mm															
9.3x57mm Mau.	232	2362	2058	1778	1528	NA	2875	2182	1630	1203	NA	0	-6.8	-24.6	NA
9.3x57mm Mau.	286	2070	1810	1590	1390	1110	2710	2090	1600	1220	955	2.5	-2.6	-22.5	0
370 Sako Mag.	286	3550	2370	2200	2040	2880	4130	3570	3075	2630	2240	2.4	0	-9.5	-27.2
9.3x62mm	184	2953	2650	2366	2100	-	3562	2869	2287	1802	-	1.7	0	-7.9	-
9.3x62mm	232	2625	2302	2002	1728	-	2551	2731	2066	1539	-	2.6	0	-11.3	-
9.3x62mm	250	2550	2376	2208	2048	—	3609	3133	2707	2328	—	0	-5.4	-17.9	—
9.3x62mm	286	2360	2155	1961	1778	1608	3537	2949	2442	2008	1642	0	-6	-21.1	-47.2
9.3x62mm	286	2400	2163	1941	1733	—	3657	2972	2392	1908	—	0	-6.7	-22.6	—
9.3x64mm	286	2700	2505	2318	2139	1968	4629	3984	3411	2906	2460	2.5	2.7	-4.5	-19.2
9.3x72mmR	193	1952	1610	1326	1120	996	1633	1112	754	538	425	0	-12.1	-44.1	—
9.3x74mmR	250	2550	2376	2208	2048	—	3609	3133	2707	2328	—	0	-5.4	-17.9	—
9.3x74Rmm	286	2360	2136	1924	1727	1545	3536	2896	2351	1893	1516	0	-6.1	-21.7	-49
375															
375 Winchester	200	2200	1841	1526	1268	1089	2150	1506	1034	714	527	2.5	-4	-26.2	0
375 Winchester	250	1900	1647	1424	1239	1103	2005	1506	1126	852	676	2.5	-6.9	-33.3	0
376 Steyr	225	2600	2331	2078	1842	1625	3377	2714	2157	1694	1319	2.5	0	-10.6	-31.4
376 Steyr	270	2600	2372	2156	1951	1759	4052	3373	2787	2283	1855	2.3	0	-9.9	-28.9
375 Dakota	300	2600	2316	2051	1804	1579	4502	3573	2800	2167	1661	2.4	0	-11	-32.7

Cartridge	Bullet Wgt. Grs.	VELOCITY (fps)					ENERGY (ft. lbs.)					TRAJ. (in.)			
		Muzzle	100 yds.	200 yds.	300 yds.	400 yds.	Muzzle	100 yds.	200 yds.	300 yds.	400 yds.	100 yds.	200 yds.	300 yds.	400 yds.
375 N.E. 2-1/2"	270	2000	1740	1507	1310	NA	2398	1815	1362	1026	NA	2.5	-6	-30	0
375 Flanged	300	2450	2150	1886	1640	NA	3998	3102	2369	1790	NA	2.5	-2.4	-17	0
375 Ruger	250	2890	2675	2471	2275	2088	4636	3973	3388	2873	2421	1.7	0	-7.4	-21.5
375 Ruger	260	2900	2703	2514	2333	—	4854	4217	3649	3143	—	0	-4	-13.4	—
375 Ruger	270	2840	2600	2372	2156	1951	4835	4052	3373	2786	2283	1.8	0	-8	-23.6
375 Ruger	300	2660	2344	2050	1780	1536	4713	3660	2800	2110	1572	2.4	0	-10.8	-32.6
375 H&H Magnum	250	2890	2675	2471	2275	2088	4636	3973	3388	2873	2421	1.7	0	-7.4	-21.5
375 H&H Magnum	250	2670	2450	2240	2040	1850	3955	3335	2790	2315	1905	2.5	-0.4	-10.2	-28.4
375 H&H Magnum	270	2690	2420	2166	1928	1707	4337	3510	2812	2228	1747	2.5	0	-10	-29.4
375 H&H Mag.	270	2800	2562	2337	2123	1921	4700	3936	3275	2703	2213	1.9	0	-8.3	-24.3
375 H&H Magnum*	300	2530	2245	1979	1733	1512	4263	3357	2608	2001	1523	2.5	-1	-10.5	-33.6
375 H&H Mag.	300	2660	2345	2052	1782	1539	4713	3662	2804	2114	1577	2.4	0	-10.8	-32.6
375 H&H Hvy. Mag.	270	2870	2628	2399	2182	1976	4937	4141	3451	2150	1845	1.7	0	-7.2	-21
375 H&H Hvy. Mag.	300	2705	2386	2090	1816	1568	4873	3793	2908	2195	1637	2.3	0	-10.4	-31.4
375 H&H Mag	350	2300	2052	1821	-	-	4112	3273	2578	-	-	0	-6.7	-	-
375 Rem. Ultra Mag.	270	2900	2558	2241	1947	1678	5041	3922	3010	2272	1689	1.9	2.7	-8.9	-27
375 Rem. Ultra Mag.	260	2950	2750	2560	2377	—	5023	4367	3783	3262	—	0	-3.8	-12.9	—
375 Rem. Ultra Mag.	300	2760	2505	2263	2035	1822	5073	4178	3412	2759	2210	2	0	-8.8	-26.1
375 Wea. Mag.	260	3000	2798	2606	2421	—	5195	4520	3920	3384	—	0	-3.6	-12.4	—
375 Wea. Mag.	300	2700	2420	2157	1911	1685	4856	3901	3100	2432	1891	2.5	-0.04	-10.7	0
378 Wea. Mag.	260	3100	2894	2697	2509	—	5547	4834	4199	3633	—	0	-4.2	-14.6	—
378 Wea. Mag.	270	3180	2976	2781	2594	2415	6062	5308	4635	4034	3495	2.5	2.6	-1.8	-11.3
378 Wea. Mag.	300	2929	2576	2252	1952	1680	5698	4419	3379	2538	1881	2.5	1.2	-7	-24.5
375 A-Square	300	2920	2626	2351	2093	1850	5679	4594	3681	2917	2281	2.5	1.4	-6	-21
38-40 Win.	180	1160	999	901	827	764	538	399	324	273	233	0	-33.9	0	0
40, 41															
400 Legend	215	2250	1872	1540	1270	NA	2416	1673	1132	770	NA	1.8	-4.9	-26.4	NA
400 A-Square DPM	400	2400	2146	1909	1689	NA	5116	2092	3236	2533	NA	2.98	0	-10	NA
400 A-Square DPM	170	2980	2463	2001	1598	NA	3352	2289	1512	964	NA	2.16	0	-11.1	NA
408 CheyTac	419	2850	2752	2657	2562	2470	7551	7048	6565	6108	5675	-1.02	0	1.9	4.2
405 Win.	300	2200	1851	1545	1296		3224	2282	1589	1119		4.6	0	-19.5	0
450/400-3"	400	2050	1815	1595	1402	NA	3732	2924	2259	1746	NA	0	NA	-33.4	NA
416 Ruger	400	2400	2151	1917	1700	NA	5116	4109	3264	2568	NA	0	-6	-21.6	0
416 Dakota	400	2450	2294	2143	1998	1859	5330	4671	4077	3544	3068	2.5	-0.2	-10.5	-29.4
416 Taylor	375	2350	2021	1722	na	na	4600	3403	2470	NA	NA	0	-7	NA	NA
416 Taylor	400	2350	2117	1896	1693	NA	4905	3980	3194	2547	NA	2.5	-1.2	15	0
416 Hoffman	400	2380	2145	1923	1718	1529	5031	4087	3285	2620	2077	2.5	-1	-14.1	0
416 Rigby	350	2600	2449	2303	2162	2026	5253	4661	4122	3632	3189	2.5	-1.8	-10.2	-26
416 Rigby	400	2370	2210	2050	1900	NA	4990	4315	3720	3185	NA	2.5	-0.7	-12.1	0
416 Rigby	400	2400	2115	1851	1611	—	5115	3973	3043	2305	—	0	-6.5	-21.8	—
416 Rigby	400	2415	2156	1915	1691	—	5180	4130	3256	2540	—	0	-6	-21.6	—
416 Rigby	410	2370	2110	1870	1640	NA	5115	4050	3165	2455	NA	2.5	-2.4	-17.3	0
416 Rigby No. 2	400	2400	2115	1851	1611	—	5115	3973	3043	2305	—	0	-6.5	-21.8	—
416 Rem. Mag.*	350	2520	2270	2034	1814	1611	4935	4004	3216	2557	2017	2.5	-0.8	-12.6	-35
416 Rem. Mag.	400	2400	2142	1901	1679	—	5116	4076	3211	2504	—	3.1	0	-12.7	—
416 Rem. Mag	450	2150	1925	1716	-	-	4620	3702	2942	-	-	0	-7.8	-	-
416 Wea. Mag.*	400	2700	2397	2115	1852	1613	6474	5104	3971	3047	2310	2.5	0	-10.1	-30.4
10.57 (416) Meteor	400	2730	2532	2342	2161	1987	6621	5695	4874	4147	3508	1.9	0	-8.3	-24
500/416 N.E.	400	2300	2092	1895	1712	—	4697	3887	3191	2602	—	0	-7.2	-24	—
404 Jeffrey	400	2150	1924	1716	1525	NA	4105	3289	2614	2064	NA	2.5	-4	-22.1	0
404 Jeffrey	400	2300	2053	1823	1611	—	4698	3743	2950	2306	—	0	-6.8	-24.1	—
404 Jeffery	400	2350	2020	1720	1458	—	4904	3625	2629	1887	—	0	-6.5	-21.8	—
404 Jeffery	450	2150	1946	1755	-	-	4620	3784	3078	-	-	0	-7.6	-	-
425, 44															
425 Express	400	2400	2160	1934	1725	NA	5115	4145	3322	2641	NA	2.5	-1	-14	0
44-40 Win.	200	1190	1006	900	822	756	629	449	360	300	254	0	-33.3	0	0
44 Rem. Mag.	210	1920	1477	1155	982	880	1719	1017	622	450	361	0	-17.6	0	0
44 Rem. Mag.	240	1760	1380	1114	970	878	1650	1015	661	501	411	0	-17.6	0	0
444 Marlin	240	2350	1815	1377	1087	941	2942	1753	1001	630	472	2.5	-15.1	-31	0
444 Marlin	265	2120	1733	1405	1160	1012	2644	1768	1162	791	603	2.5	-6	-32.2	0
444 Mar. Lever Evolution	265	2325	1971	1652	1380	NA	3180	2285	1606	1120	NA	3	-1.4	-18.6	NA
444 Mar. Superformance	265	2400	1976	1603	1298	NA	3389	2298	1512	991	NA	4.1	0	-17.8	NA
45															
45-70 Govt.	250	2025	1616	1285	1068	—	2276	1449	917	634	—	6.1	0	-27.2	—
45-70 Govt.	300	1810	1497	1244	1073	969	2182	1492	1031	767	625	0	-14.8	0	0

Cartridge	Bullet Wgt. Grs.	VELOCITY (fps)					ENERGY (ft. lbs.)					TRAJ. (in.)			
		Muzzle	100 yds.	200 yds.	300 yds.	400 yds.	Muzzle	100 yds.	200 yds.	300 yds.	400 yds.	100 yds.	200 yds.	300 yds.	400 yds.
45-70 Govt. Supreme	300	1880	1558	1292	1103	988	2355	1616	1112	811	651	0	-12.9	-46	-105
45-70 Govt.	325	2000	1685	1413	1197	—	2886	2049	1441	1035	—	5.5	0	-23	—
45-70 Lever Evolution	325	2050	1729	1450	1225	NA	3032	2158	1516	1083	NA	3	-4.1	-27.8	NA
45-70 Govt. CorBon	350	1800	1526	1296			2519	1810	1307			0	-14.6	0	0
45-70 Govt.	405	1330	1168	1055	977	918	1590	1227	1001	858	758	0	-24.6	0	0
45-70 Govt. PMC Cowboy	405	1550	1193	—	—	—	1639	1280	—	—	—	0	-23.9	0	0
45-70 Govt. Garrett	415	1850	—	—	—	—	3150	—	—	—	—	3	-7	0	0
45-70 Govt. Garrett	530	1550	1343	1178	1062	982	2828	2123	1633	1327	1135	0	-17.8	0	0
450 Bushmaster	250	2200	1831	1508	1480	1073	2686	1860	1262	864	639	0	-9	-33.5	0
450 Dakota	500	2,450	2219	2000	1796	1607	6663	5466	4440	3581	2867	0	-5.6	-20	-45.1
450 Dakota	600	2,350	2169	1997	1833	1679	7356	6267	5312	4476	3755	0	-5.9	-20.6	-45.6
450 Marlin	325	2225	1887	1587	1332	—	3572	2570	1816	1280	—	4.2	0	-18.1	—
450 Marlin	350	2100	1774	1488	1254	1089	3427	2446	1720	1222	922	0	-9.7	-35.2	0
450 Mar. Lever Evolution	325	2225	1887	1585	1331	NA	3572	2569	1813	1278	NA	3	-2.2	-21.3	NA
457 Wild West Magnum	350	2150	1718	1348	NA	NA	3645	2293	1413	NA	NA	0	-10.5	NA	NA
450/500 N.E.	400	2050	1820	1609	1420	—	3732	2940	2298	1791	—	0	-9.7	-32.8	—
450 N.E. 3-1/4"	465	2190	1970	1765	1577	NA	4952	4009	3216	2567	NA	2.5	-3	-20	0
450 N.E.	480	2150	1881	1635	1418	—	4927	3769	2850	2144	—	0	-8.4	-29.8	—
450 N.E. 3-1/4"	500	2150	1920	1708	1514	NA	5132	4093	3238	2544	NA	2.5	-4	-22.9	0
450 No. 2	465	2190	1970	1765	1577	NA	4952	4009	3216	2567	NA	2.5	-3	-20	0
450 No. 2	500	2150	1920	1708	1514	NA	5132	4093	3238	2544	NA	2.5	-4	-22.9	0
450 Ackley Mag.	465	2400	2169	1950	1747	NA	5947	4857	3927	3150	NA	2.5	-1	-13.7	0
450 Ackley Mag.	500	2320	2081	1855	1649	NA	5975	4085	3820	3018	NA	2.5	-1.2	-15	0
450 Rigby	500	2350	2139	1939	1752	—	6130	5079	4176	3408	—	0	-6.8	-22.9	—
450 Rigby	550	2100	1866	1651	·	·	5387	4256	3330	·	·	·	·	·	·
458 Win. Magnum	400	2380	2170	1960	1770	NA	5030	4165	3415	2785	NA	2.5	-0.4	-13.4	0
458 Win. Magnum	465	2220	1999	1791	1601	NA	5088	4127	3312	2646	NA	2.5	-2	-17.7	0
458 Win. Magnum	500	2040	1823	1623	1442	1237	4620	3689	2924	2308	1839	2.5	-3.5	-22	0
458 Win. Mag.	500	2140	1880	1643	1432	—	5084	3294	2996	2276	—	0	-8.4	-29.8	—
458 Win. Magnum	510	2040	1770	1527	1319	1157	4712	3547	2640	1970	1516	2.5	-4.1	-25	0
458 Lott	465	2380	2150	1932	1730	NA	5848	4773	3855	3091	NA	2.5	-1	-14	0
458 Lott	500	2300	2029	1778	1551	—	5873	4569	3509	2671	—	0	-7	-25.1	—
458 Lott	500	2300	2062	1838	1633	NA	5873	4719	3748	2960	NA	2.5	-1.6	-16.4	0
460 Short A-Sq.	500	2420	2175	1943	1729	NA	6501	5250	4193	3319	NA	2.5	-0.8	-12.8	0
460 Wea. Mag.	500	2700	2404	2128	1869	1635	8092	6416	5026	3878	2969	2.5	0.6	-8.9	-28
475															
500/465 N.E.	480	2150	1917	1703	1507	NA	4926	3917	3089	2419	NA	2.5	-4	-22.2	0
470 Rigby	500	2150	1940	1740	1560	NA	5130	4170	3360	2695	NA	2.5	-2.8	-19.4	0
470 Nitro Ex.	480	2190	1954	1735	1536	NA	5111	4070	3210	2515	NA	2.5	-3.5	-20.8	0
470 N.E.	500	2150	1885	1643	1429	—	5132	3945	2998	2267	—	0	-8.9	-30.8	—
470 Nitro Ex.	500	2150	1890	1650	1440	1270	5130	3965	3040	2310	1790	2.5	-4.3	-24	0
475 No. 2	500	2200	1955	1728	1522	NA	5375	4243	3316	2573	NA	2.5	-3.2	-20.9	0
50, 58															
50 Alaskan	450	2000	1729	1492	NA	NA	3997	2987	2224	NA	NA	0	-11.25	NA	NA
500 Jeffery	570	2300	1979	1688	1434	—	6694	4958	3608	2604	—	0	-8.2	-28.6	—
505 Gibbs	525	2300	2063	1840	1637	NA	6166	4922	3948	3122	NA	2.5	-3	-18	0
505 Gibbs	570	2100	1893	1701	·	·	5583	4538	3664	·	·	0	-8.1	·	·
505 Gibbs	600	2100	1899	1711	·	·	5877	4805	3904	·	·	0	-8.1	·	·
500 N.E.	570	2150	1889	1651	1439	—	5850	4518	3450	2621	—	0	-8.9	-30.6	—
500 N.E.-3"	570	2150	1928	1722	1533	NA	5850	4703	3752	2975	NA	2.5	-3.7	-22	0
500 N.E.-3"	600	2150	1927	1721	1531	NA	6158	4947	3944	3124	NA	2.5	-4	-22	0
495 A-Square	570	2350	2117	1896	1693	NA	5850	4703	3752	2975	NA	2.5	-1	-14.5	0
495 A-Square	600	2280	2050	1833	1635	NA	6925	5598	4478	3562	NA	2.5	-2	-17	0
500 A-Square	600	2380	2144	1922	1766	NA	7546	6126	4920	3922	NA	2.5	-3	-17	0
500 A-Square	707	2250	2040	1841	1567	NA	7947	6530	5318	4311	NA	2.5	-2	-17	0
500 BMG PMC	660	3080	2854	2639	2444	2248	13688	500 yd. zero	3.1	3.9	4.7	2.8	NA		
577 Nitro Ex.	750	2050	1793	1562	1360	NA	6990	5356	4065	3079	NA	2.5	-5	-26	0
577 Tyrannosaur	750	2400	2141	1898	1675	NA	9591	7633	5996	4671	NA	3	0	-12.9	0
600, 700															
600 N.E.	900	1950	1680	1452	NA	NA	7596	5634	4212	NA	NA	5.6	0	0	0
700 N.E.	1200	1900	1676	1472	NA	NA	9618	7480	5774	NA	NA	5.7	0	0	0
50 BMG															
50 BMG	624	2952	2820	2691	2566	2444	12077	11028	10036	9125	8281	0	-2.9	-10.6	-23.5
50 BMG Match	750	2820	2728	2637	2549	2462	13241	12388	11580	10815	10090	1.5	0	-6.5	-18.3

Notes: Blanks are available in 32 S&W, 38 S&W and 38 Special. "V" after barrel length indicates test barrel was vented to produce ballistics similar to a revolver with a normal barrel-to-cylinder gap. Not all loads are available from all ammo manufacturers. Listed loads are those made by Remington, Winchester, Federal, and others. DISC. is a discontinued load.

Cartridge	Bullet Wgt. Grs.	VELOCITY (fps)			ENERGY (ft. lbs.)			Mid-Range Traj. (in.)		Bbl. Lgth. (in).
		Muzzle	50 yds.	100 yds.	Muzzle	50 yds.	100 yds.	50 yds.	100 yds.	
22, 25										
221 Rem. Fireball	50	2650	2380	2130	780	630	505	0.2	0.8	10.5"
25 Automatic	35	900	813	742	63	51	43	NA	NA	2"
25 Automatic	45	815	730	655	65	55	40	1.8	7.7	2"
25 Automatic	50	760	705	660	65	55	50	2	8.7	2"
30										
7.5mm Swiss	107	1010	NA	NA	240	NA	NA	NA	NA	NA
7.62x25 Tokarev	85	1647	1458	1295	512	401	317	0	-3.2	4.75
7.62mmTokarev	87	1390	NA	NA	365	NA	NA	0.6	NA	4.5"
7.62 Nagant	97	790	NA	NA	134	NA	NA	NA	NA	NA
7.63 Mauser	88	1440	NA	NA	405	NA	NA	NA	NA	NA
30 Luger	93	1220	1110	1040	305	255	225	0.9	3.5	4.5"
30 Carbine	110	1790	1600	1430	785	625	500	0.4	1.7	10"
30 Super Carry	100	1250	1129	1041	347	283	241	-0.6	-7.2	NA
30 Super Carry	115	1150	1044	970	338	278	240	-0.9	-8.9	4"
30-357 AeT	123	1992	NA	NA	1084	NA	NA	NA	NA	10"
32										
32 NAA	80	1000	933	880	178	155	137	NA	NA	4"
32 S&W	88	680	645	610	90	80	75	2.5	10.5	3"
32 S&W Long	98	705	670	635	115	100	90	2.3	10.5	4"
32 Short Colt	80	745	665	590	100	80	60	2.2	9.9	4"
32 H&R	80	1150	1039	963	235	192	165	NA	NA	4"
32 H&R Magnum	85	1100	1020	930	230	195	165	1	4.3	4.5"
32 H&R Magnum	95	1030	940	900	225	190	170	1.1	4.7	4.5"
327 Federal Magnum	85	1400	1220	1090	370	280	225	NA	NA	4-V
327 Federal Magnum	100	1500	1320	1180	500	390	310	-0.2	-4.5	4-V
32 Automatic	60	970	895	835	125	105	95	1.3	5.4	4"
32 Automatic	60	1000	917	849	133	112	96			4"
32 Automatic	65	950	890	830	130	115	100	1.3	5.6	NA
32 Automatic	71	905	855	810	130	115	95	1.4	5.8	4"
8mm Lebel Pistol	111	850	NA	NA	180	NA	NA	NA	NA	NA
8mm Steyr	112	1080	NA	NA	290	NA	NA	NA	NA	NA
8mm Gasser	126	850	NA	NA	200	NA	NA	NA	NA	NA
9mm, 38										
380 Automatic	60	1130	960	NA	170	120	NA	1	NA	NA
380 Automatic	75	950	NA	NA	183	NA	NA	NA	NA	3"
380 Automatic	85/88	990	920	870	190	165	145	1.2	5.1	4"
380 Automatic	90	1000	890	800	200	160	130	1.2	5.5	3.75"
380 Automatic	95/100	955	865	785	190	160	130	1.4	5.9	4"
38 Super Auto +P	115	1300	1145	1040	430	335	275	0.7	3.3	5"
38 Super Auto +P	125/130	1215	1100	1015	425	350	300	0.8	3.6	5"
38 Super Auto +P	147	1100	1050	1000	395	355	325	0.9	4	5"
38 Super Auto +P	115	1130	1016	938	326	264	225	1	-9.5	-
9x18mm Makarov	95	1000	930	874	211	182	161	NA	NA	4"
9x18mm Ultra	100	1050	NA	NA	240	NA	NA	NA	NA	NA
9x21	124	1150	1050	980	365	305	265	NA	NA	4"
9x21 IMI	123	1220	1095	1010	409	330	281	-3.15	—	5
9x23mm Largo	124	1190	1055	966	390	306	257	0.7	3.7	4"
9x23mm Win.	125	1450	1249	1103	583	433	338	0.6	2.8	NA
9mm Steyr	115	1180	NA	NA	350	NA	NA	NA	NA	NA
9mm Luger	88	1500	1190	1010	440	275	200	0.6	3.1	4"
9mm Luger	90	1360	1112	978	370	247	191	NA	NA	4"
9mm Luger	92	1325	1117	991	359	255	201	-3.2	—	4
9mm Luger	95	1300	1140	1010	350	275	215	0.8	3.4	4"
9mm Luger	100	1180	1080	NA	305	255	NA	0.9	NA	4"
9mm Luger Guard Dog	105	1230	1070	970	355	265	220	NA	NA	4"

Cartridge	Bullet Wgt. Grs.	VELOCITY (fps)			ENERGY (ft. lbs.)			Mid-Range Traj. (in.)		Bbl. Lgth. (in.)
		Muzzle	50 yds.	100 yds.	Muzzle	50 yds.	100 yds.	50 yds.	100 yds.	
9mm Luger	115	1155	1045	970	340	280	240	0.9	3.9	4"
9mm Luger	123/125	1110	1030	970	340	290	260	1	4	4"
9mm Luger	124	1150	1040	965	364	298	256	-4.5	—	4
9mm Luger	135	1010	960	918	306	276	253	—	—	4
9mm Luger	140	935	890	850	270	245	225	1.3	5.5	4"
9mm Luger	147	990	940	900	320	290	265	1.1	4.9	4"
9mm Luger +P	90	1475	NA	NA	437	NA	NA	NA	NA	NA
9mm Luger +P	115	1250	1113	1019	399	316	265	0.8	3.5	4"
9mm Federal	115	1280	1130	1040	420	330	280	0.7	3.3	4"V
9mm Luger Vector	115	1155	1047	971	341	280	241	NA	NA	4"
9mm Luger +P	124	1180	1089	1021	384	327	287	0.8	3.8	4"
38										
38 S&W	146	685	650	620	150	135	125	2.4	10	4"
38 S&W Short	145	720	689	660	167	153	140	-8.5	—	5
38 Short Colt	125	730	685	645	150	130	115	2.2	9.4	6"
39 Special	100	950	900	NA	200	180	NA	1.3	NA	4"V
38 Special	110	945	895	850	220	195	175	1.3	5.4	4"V
38 Special	110	945	895	850	220	195	175	1.3	5.4	4"V
38 Special	130	775	745	710	175	160	120	1.9	7.9	4"V
38 Special Cowboy	140	800	767	735	199	183	168			7.5" V
38 (Multi-Ball)	140	830	730	505	215	130	80	2	10.6	4"V
38 Special	148	710	635	565	165	130	105	2.4	10.6	4"V
38 Special	158	755	725	690	200	185	170	2	8.3	4"V
38 Special +P	95	1175	1045	960	290	230	195	0.9	3.9	4"V
38 Special +P	110	995	925	870	240	210	185	1.2	5.1	4"V
38 Special +P	125	975	929	885	264	238	218	1	5.2	4"
38 Special +P	125	945	900	860	250	225	205	1.3	5.4	4"V
38 Special +P	129	945	910	870	255	235	215	1.3	5.3	4"V
38 Special +P	130	925	887	852	247	227	210	1.3	5.5	4"V
38 Special +P	147/150	884	NA	NA	264	NA	NA	NA	NA	4"V
38 Special +P	158	890	855	825	280	255	240	1.4	6	4"V
357										
357 SIG	115	1520	NA	NA	593	NA	NA	NA	NA	NA
357 SIG	124	1450	NA	NA	578	NA	NA	NA	NA	NA
357 SIG	125	1350	1190	1080	510	395	325	0.7	3.1	4"
357 SIG	135	1225	1112	1031	450	371	319	—	—	4
357 SIG	147	1225	1132	1060	490	418	367	—	—	4
357 SIG	150	1130	1030	970	420	355	310	0.9	4	NA
356 TSW	115	1520	NA	NA	593	NA	NA	NA	NA	NA
356 TSW	124	1450	NA	NA	578	NA	NA	NA	NA	NA
356 TSW	135	1280	1120	1010	490	375	310	0.8	3.5	NA
356 TSW	147	1220	1120	1040	485	410	355	0.8	3.5	5"
357 Mag., Super Clean	105	1650								
357 Magnum	110	1295	1095	975	410	290	230	0.8	3.5	4"V
357 (Med.Vel.)	125	1220	1075	985	415	315	270	0.8	3.7	4"V
357 Magnum	125	1450	1240	1090	585	425	330	0.6	2.8	4"V
357 Magnum	125	1500	1312	1163	624	478	376	—	—	8
357 (Multi-Ball)	140	1155	830	665	420	215	135	1.2	6.4	4"V
357 Magnum	140	1360	1195	1075	575	445	360	0.7	3	4"V
357 Magnum FlexTip	140	1440	1274	1143	644	504	406	NA	NA	NA
357 Magnum	145	1290	1155	1060	535	430	360	0.8	3.5	4"V
357 Magnum	150/158	1235	1105	1015	535	430	360	0.8	3.5	4"V
357 Mag. Cowboy	158	800	761	725	225	203	185			
357 Magnum	165	1290	1189	1108	610	518	450	0.7	3.1	8-3/8"
357 Magnum	180	1145	1055	985	525	445	390	0.9	3.9	4"V
357 Magnum	180	1180	1088	1020	557	473	416	0.8	3.6	8"V
357 Mag. CorBon F.A.	180	1650	1512	1386	1088	913	767	1.66	0	
357 Mag. CorBon	200	1200	1123	1061	640	560	500	3.19	0	
357 Rem. Maximum	158	1825	1590	1380	1170	885	670	0.4	1.7	10.5"
40, 10mm										
40 S&W	120	1150	-	-	352	-	-	-	-	-

Cartridge	Bullet Wgt. Grs.	VELOCITY (fps)			ENERGY (ft. lbs.)			Mid-Range Traj. (in.)		Bbl. Lgth. (in).
		Muzzle	50 yds.	100 yds.	Muzzle	50 yds.	100 yds.	50 yds.	100 yds.	
40 S&W	125	1265	1102	998	444	337	276	-3	—	4
40 S&W	135	1140	1070	NA	390	345	NA	0.9	NA	4"
40 S&W Guard Dog	135	1200	1040	940	430	325	265	NA	NA	4"
40 S&W	155	1140	1026	958	447	362	309	0.9	4.1	4"
40 S&W	165	1150	NA	NA	485	NA	NA	NA	NA	4"
40 S&W	175	1010	948	899	396	350	314	—	—	4
40 S&W	180	985	936	893	388	350	319	1.4	5	4"
40 S&W	180	1000	943	896	400	355	321	4.52	—	4
40 S&W	180	1015	960	914	412	368	334	1.3	4.5	4"
400 Cor-Bon	135	1450	NA	NA	630	NA	NA	NA	NA	5"
10mm Automatic	155	1125	1046	986	436	377	335	0.9	3.9	5"
10mm Automatic	155	1265	1118	1018	551	430	357	—	—	5
10mm Automatic	170	1340	1165	1145	680	510	415	0.7	3.2	5"
10mm Automatic	175	1290	1140	1035	650	505	420	0.7	3.3	5.5"
10mm Auto. (FBI)	180	950	905	865	361	327	299	1.5	5.4	4"
10mm Automatic	180	1030	970	920	425	375	340	1.1	4.7	5"
10mm Auto H.V.	180	1240	1124	1037	618	504	430	0.8	3.4	5"
10mm Auto	200	1100	1015	951	537	457	402	-1.1	-9.6	NA
10mm Automatic	200	1160	1070	1010	495	510	430	0.9	3.8	5"
10.4mm Italian	177	950	NA	NA	360	NA	NA	NA	NA	NA
41 Action Exp.	180	1000	947	903	400	359	326	0.5	4.2	5"
41 Rem. Magnum	170	1420	1165	1015	760	515	390	0.7	3.2	4"V
41 Rem. Magnum	175	1250	1120	1030	605	490	410	0.8	3.4	4"V
41 (Med. Vel.)	210	965	900	840	435	375	330	1.3	5.4	4"V
41 Rem. Magnum	210	1300	1160	1060	790	630	535	0.7	3.2	4"V
41 Rem. Magnum	240	1250	1151	1075	833	706	616	0.8	3.3	6.5V
44										
44 S&W Russian	247	780	NA	NA	335	NA	NA	NA	NA	NA
44 Special	210	900	861	825	360	329	302	5.57	—	6
44 Special FTX	165	900	848	802	297	263	235	NA	NA	2.5"
44 S&W Special	180	980	NA	NA	383	NA	NA	NA	NA	6.5"
44 S&W Special	180	1000	935	882	400	350	311	NA	NA	7.5"V
44 S&W Special	200	875	825	780	340	302	270	1.2	6	6"
44 S&W Special	200	1035	940	865	475	390	335	1.1	4.9	6.5"
44 S&W Special	240/246	755	725	695	310	285	265	2	8.3	6.5"
44-40 Win.	200	722	698	676	232	217	203	-3.4	-23.7	4
44-40 Win.	205	725	689	655	239	216	195	—	—	7.5
44-40 Win.	210	725	698	672	245	227	210	-11.6	—	5.5
44-40 Win.	225	725	697	670	263	243	225	-3.4	-23.8	4
44-40 Win. Cowboy	225	750	723	695	281	261	242			
44 Rem. Magnum	180	1610	1365	1175	1035	745	550	0.5	2.3	4"V
44 Rem. Magnum	200	1296	1193	1110	747	632	548	-0.5	-6.2	6
44 Rem. Magnum	200	1400	1192	1053	870	630	492	0.6	NA	6.5"
44 Rem. Magnum	200	1500	1332	1194	999	788	633	—	—	7.5
44 Rem. Magnum	210	1495	1310	1165	1040	805	635	0.6	2.5	6.5"
44 Rem. Mag. FlexTip	225	1410	1240	1111	993	768	617	NA	NA	NA
44 (Med. Vel.)	240	1000	945	900	535	475	435	1.1	4.8	6.5"
44 R.M. (Jacketed)	240	1180	1080	1010	740	625	545	0.9	3.7	4"V
44 R.M. (Lead)	240	1350	1185	1070	970	750	610	0.7	3.1	4"V
44 Rem. Magnum	250	1180	1100	1040	775	670	600	0.8	3.6	6.5"V
44 Rem. Magnum	250	1250	1148	1070	867	732	635	0.8	3.3	6.5"V
44 Rem. Magnum	275	1235	1142	1070	931	797	699	0.8	3.3	6.5"
44 Rem. Magnum	300	1150	1083	1030	881	781	706	—	—	7.5
44 Rem. Magnum	300	1200	1100	1026	959	806	702	NA	NA	7.5"
44 Rem. Magnum	330	1385	1297	1220	1406	1234	1090	1.83	0	NA
44 Webley	262	850	—	—	—	—	—	—	—	—
440 CorBon	260	1700	1544	1403	1669	1377	1136	1.58	NA	10"
45, 50										
450 Short Colt/450 Revolver	226	830	NA	NA	350	NA	NA	NA	NA	NA
45 S&W Schofield	180	730	NA	NA	213	NA	NA	NA	NA	NA
45 S&W Schofield	230	730	NA	NA	272	NA	NA	NA	NA	NA

Cartridge	Bullet Wgt. Grs.	VELOCITY (fps)			ENERGY (ft. lbs.)			Mid-Range Traj. (in.)		Bbl. Lgth. (in).
		Muzzle	50 yds.	100 yds.	Muzzle	50 yds.	100 yds.	50 yds.	100 yds.	
45 G.A.P.	165	1007	936	879	372	321	283	-1.4	-11.8	5
45 G.A.P.	185	1090	970	890	490	385	320	1	4.7	5"
45 G.A.P.	230	880	842	NA	396	363	NA	NA	NA	NA
45 Automatic	150	1050	NA	NA	403	NA	NA	NA	NA	NA
45 Automatic	165	1030	930	NA	385	315	NA	1.2	NA	5"
45 Automatic Guard Dog	165	1140	1030	950	475	390	335	NA	NA	5"
45 Automatic	185	1000	940	890	410	360	325	1.1	4.9	5"
45 Auto. (Match)	185	770	705	650	245	204	175	2	8.7	5"
45 Auto. (Match)	200	940	890	840	392	352	312	2	8.6	5"
45 Automatic	200	975	917	860	421	372	328	1.4	5	5"
45 Automatic	230	830	800	675	355	325	300	1.6	6.8	5"
45 Automatic	230	880	846	816	396	366	340	1.5	6.1	5"
45 Automatic +P	165	1250	NA	NA	573	NA	NA	NA	NA	NA
45 Automatic +P	185	1140	1040	970	535	445	385	0.9	4	5"
45 Automatic +P	200	1055	982	925	494	428	380	NA	NA	5"
45 Super	185	1300	1190	1108	694	582	504	NA	NA	5"
45 Win. Magnum	230	1400	1230	1105	1000	775	635	0.6	2.8	5"
45 Win. Magnum	260	1250	1137	1053	902	746	640	0.8	3.3	5"
45 Win. Mag. CorBon	320	1150	1080	1025	940	830	747	3.47		
455 Webley MKII	262	850	NA	NA	420	NA	NA	NA	NA	NA
45 Colt FTX	185	920	870	826	348	311	280	NA	NA	3"V
45 Colt	200	1000	938	889	444	391	351	1.3	4.8	5.5"
45 Colt	225	960	890	830	460	395	345	1.3	5.5	5.5"
45 Colt + P CorBon	265	1350	1225	1126	1073	884	746	2.65	0	
45 Colt + P CorBon	300	1300	1197	1114	1126	956	827	2.78	0	
45 Colt	250/255	860	820	780	410	375	340	1.6	6.6	5.5"
454 Casull	250	1300	1151	1047	938	735	608	0.7	3.2	7.5"V
454 Casull	260	1800	1577	1381	1871	1436	1101	0.4	1.8	7.5"V
454 Casull	300	1625	1451	1308	1759	1413	1141	0.5	2	7.5"V
454 Casull CorBon	360	1500	1387	1286	1800	1640	1323	2.01	0	
460 S&W	200	2300	2042	1801	2350	1851	1441	0	-1.6	NA
460 S&W	260	2000	1788	1592	2309	1845	1464	NA	NA	7.5"V
460 S&W	250	1450	1267	1127	1167	891	705	NA	NA	8.375-V
460 S&W	250	1900	1640	1412	2004	1494	1106	0	-2.75	NA
460 S&W	300	1750	1510	1300	2040	1510	1125	NA	NA	8.4-V
460 S&W	395	1550	1389	1249	2108	1691	1369	0	-4	NA
475 Linebaugh	400	1350	1217	1119	1618	1315	1112	NA	NA	NA
480 Ruger	325	1350	1191	1076	1315	1023	835	2.6	0	7.5"
50 Action Exp.	300	1475	1251	1092	1449	1043	795	-	-	6"
50 Action Exp.	325	1400	1209	1075	1414	1055	835	0.2	2.3	6"
500 S&W	275	1665	1392	1183	1693	1184	854	1.5	NA	8.375
500 S&W	300	1950	1653	1396	2533	1819	1298	—	—	8.5
500 S&W	325	1800	1560	1350	2340	1755	1315	NA	NA	8.4-V
500 S&W	350	1400	1231	1106	1523	1178	951	NA	NA	10"
500 S&W	400	1675	1472	1299	2493	1926	1499	1.3	NA	8.375
500 S&W	440	1625	1367	1169	2581	1825	1337	1.6	NA	8.375
500 S&W	500	1300	1178	1085	1876	1541	1308	—	—	8.5
500 S&W	500	1425	1281	1164	2254	1823	1505	NA	NA	10"

Note: The actual ballistics obtained with your firearm can vary considerably from the advertised ballistics.
Also, ballistics can vary from lot to lot with the same brand and type load.

| Cartridge | Bullet Wt. Grs. | Velocity (fps) 22-1/2" Bbl. | | Energy (ft. lbs.) 22-1/2" Bbl. | | Mid-Range Traj. (in.) | Muzzle Velocity |
		Muzzle	100 yds.	Muzzle	100 yds.	100 yds.	6" Bbl.
17 Aguila	20	1850	1267	NA	NA	NA	NA
17 Hornady Mach 2	15.5	2050	1450	149	75	NA	NA
17 Hornady Mach 2	17	2100	1530	166	88	0.7	NA
17 HMR Lead Free	15.5	2550	1901	NA	NA	0.9	NA
17 HMR TNT Green	16	2500	1642	222	96	NA	NA
17 HMR	17	2550	1902	245	136	NA	NA
17 HMR	17	2650	na	na	na	na	NA
17 HMR	20	2375	1776	250	140	NA	NA
17 Win. Super Mag.	15	3300	2496	363	207	0	NA
17 Win. Super Mag.	20 Tipped	3000	2504	400	278	0	NA
17 Win. Super Mag.	20 JHP	3000	2309	400	237	0	NA
17 Win. Super Mag.	25 Tipped	2600	2230	375	276	0	NA
5mm Rem. Rimfire Mag.	30	2300	1669	352	188	NA	24
22 Short Blank	—	—	—	—	—	—	—
22 Short CB	29	727	610	33	24	NA	706
22 Short Target	29	830	695	44	31	6.8	786
22 Short HP	27	1164	920	81	50	4.3	1077
22 Colibri	20	375	183	6	1	NA	NA
22 Super Colibri	20	500	441	11	9	NA	NA
22 Long CB	29	727	610	33	24	NA	706
22 Long HV	29	1180	946	90	57	4.1	1031
22 LR Pistol Match	40	1070	890	100	70	4.6	940
22 LR Shrt. Range Green	21	1650	912	127	NA	NA	NA
CCI Quiet 22 LR	40	710	640	45	36	NA	NA
22 LR Sub Sonic HP	38	1050	901	93	69	4.7	NA
22 LR Segmented HP	40	1050	897	98	72	NA	NA
22 LR Standard Velocity	40	1070	890	100	70	4.6	940
22 LR AutoMatch	40	1200	990	130	85	NA	NA
22 LR HV	40	1255	1016	140	92	3.6	1060
22 LR Silhoutte	42	1220	1003	139	94	3.6	1025
22 SSS	60	950	802	120	86	NA	NA
22 LR HV HP	40	1280	1001	146	89	3.5	1085
22 Velocitor GDHP	40	1435	0	0	0	NA	NA
22 LR Segmented HP	37	1435	1080	169	96	2.9	NA
22 LR Hyper HP	32/33/34	1500	1075	165	85	2.8	NA
22 LR Expediter	32	1640	NA	191	NA	NA	NA
22 LR Stinger HP	32	1640	1132	191	91	2.6	1395
22 LR Lead Free	30	1650	NA	181	NA	NA	NA
22 LR Hyper Vel	30	1750	1191	204	93	NA	NA
22 LR Shot #12	31	950	NA	NA	NA	NA	NA
22 WRF LFN	45	1300	1015	169	103	3	NA
22 Win. Mag. Lead Free	28	2200	NA	301	NA	NA	NA
22 Win. Mag.	30	2200	1373	322	127	1.4	1610
22 Win. Mag. V-Max BT	33	2000	1495	293	164	0.6	NA
22 Win. Mag. JHP	34	2120	1435	338	155	1.4	NA
22 Win. Mag. JHP	40	1910	1326	324	156	1.7	1480
22 Win. Mag. FMJ	40	1910	1326	324	156	1.7	1480
22 Win. Mag. Dyna Point	45	1550	1147	240	131	2.6	NA
22 Win. Mag. JHP	50	1650	1280	300	180	1.3	NA
22 Win. Mag. Shot #11	52	1000	—	NA	—	—	NA

Dram Equiv.	Shot Ozs.	Load Style	Shot Sizes	Brands	Velocity (fps)
10 Gauge 3-1/2" Magnum					
Max	2-3/8	magnum blend	5, 6, 7	Hevi-shot	1200
4-1/2	2-1/4	premium	BB, 2, 4, 5, 6	Win., Fed., Rem.	1205
Max	2	premium	4, 5, 6	Fed., Win.	1300
4-1/4	2	high velocity	BB, 2, 4	Rem.	1210
Max	18 pellets	premium	00 buck	Fed., Win.	1100
Max	1-7/8	Bismuth	BB, 2, 4	Bis.	1225
Max	1-3/4	high density	BB, 2	Rem.	1300
4-1/4	1-3/4	steel	TT, T, BBB, BB, 1, 2, 3	Win., Rem.	1260
Mag	1-5/8	steel	T, BBB, BB, 2	Win.	1285
Max	1-5/8	Bismuth	BB, 2, 4	Bismuth	1375
Max	1-1/2	hypersonic	BBB, BB, 2	Rem.	1700
Max	1-1/2	heavy metal	BB, 2, 3, 4	Hevi-Shot	1500
Max	1-1/2	steel	T, BBB, BB, 1, 2, 3	Fed.	1450
Max	1-3/8	steel	T, BBB, BB, 1, 2, 3	Fed., Rem.	1500
Max	1-3/8	steel	T, BBB, BB, 2	Fed., Win.	1450
Max	1-3/4	slug, rifled	slug	Fed.	1280
Max	24 pellets	Buckshot	1 Buck	Fed.	1100
Max	54 pellets	Super-X	4 Buck	Win.	1150
12 Gauge 3-1/2" Magnum					
Max	2-1/4	premium	4, 5, 6	Fed., Rem., Win.	1150
	2 1/4	TSS	7	Fed	1200
	2 1/4	TSS	9	Fed	1200
Max	2	Lead	4, 5, 6	Fed.	1300
Max	2	Copper plated turkey	4, 5	Rem.	1300
Max	18 pellets	premium	00 buck	Fed., Win., Rem.	1100
Max	1-7/8	Wingmaster HD	4, 6	Rem.	1225
Max	1-7/8	heavyweight	5, 6	Fed.	1300
Max	1-3/4	high density	BB, 2, 4, 6	Rem.	1300
Max	1-7/8	Bismuth	BB, 2, 4	Bis.	1225
Max	1-5/8	blind side	Hex, 1, 3	Win.	1400
Max	1-5/8	Hevi-shot	T	Hevi-shot	1350
Max	1-5/8	Wingmaster HD	T	Rem.	1350
Max	1-5/8	high density	BB, 2	Fed.	1450

Dram Equiv.	Shot Ozs.	Load Style	Shot Sizes	Brands	Velocity (fps)
12 Gauge 3-1/2" Magnum (cont.)					
Max	1-5/8	Blind side	Hex, BB, 2	Win.	1400
Max	1-3/8	Heavyweight	2, 4, 6	Fed.	1450
Max	1-3/8	steel	T, BBB, BB, 2, 4	Fed., Win., Rem.	1450
Max	1-1/2	FS steel	BBB, BB, 2	Fed.	1500
Max	1-1/2	Supreme H-V	BBB, BB, 2, 3	Win.	1475
Max	1-3/8	H-speed steel	BB, 2	Rem.	1550
Max	1-1/4	Steel	BB, 2	Win.	1625
Max	24 pellets	Premium	1 Buck	Fed.	1100
Max	54 pellets	Super-X	4 Buck	Win.	1050
12 Gauge 3" Magnum					
4	2	premium	BB, 2, 4, 5, 6	Win., Fed., Rem.	1175
	2	TSS	7 & 9	Fed	1150
4	1-7/8	premium	BB, 2, 4, 6	Win., Fed., Rem.	1210
4	1-7/8	duplex	4x6	Rem.	1210
Max	1-3/4	turkey	4, 5, 6	Fed., Flo.,	1227
Win., Rem.	NA	1300	BB, 2, 4	Rem.	1450
Max	1-3/4	high density	BB, 2, 4	Rem.	1450
Max	1-5/8	high density	BB, 2	Fed.	1450
	1 3/4	TSS	7	Fed	1200
	1 3/4	TSS	9	Fed	1200
Max	1-5/8	Wingmaster HD	4, 6	Rem.	1227
Max	1-5/8	high velocity	4, 5, 6	Fed.	1350
4	1-5/8	premium	2, 4, 5, 6	Win., Fed., Rem.	1290
Max	1-1/2	Wingmaster HD	T	Rem.	1300
Max	1-1/2	Hevi-shot	T	Hevi-shot	1300
Max	1-1/2	high density	BB, 2, 4	Rem.	1300
Max	1-1/2	slug	slug	Bren.	1604
Max	1-5/8	Bismuth	BB, 2, 4, 5, 6	Bis.	1250
4	24 pellets	buffered	1 buck	Win., Fed., Rem.	1040
4	15 pellets	buffered	00 buck	Win., Fed., Rem.	1210
4	10 pellets	buffered	000 buck	Win., Fed., Rem.	1225
4	41 pellets	buffered	4 buck	Win., Fed., Rem.	1210
Max	1-3/8	heavyweight	5, 6	Fed.	1300

Dram Equiv.	Shot Ozs.	Load Style	Shot Sizes	Brands	Velocity (fps)
12 Gauge 3" Magnum (cont.)					
Max	1-3/8	high density	B, 2, 4, 6	Rem. Win.	1450
Max	1-3/8	slug	slug	Bren.	1476
Max	1-3/8	blind side	Hex, 1, 3, 5	Win.	1400
Max	1-1/4	slug, rifled	slug	Fed.	1600
Max	1-3/16	saboted	slug	Rem.	1500
slug	copper slug	Rem.	NA	1500	1700
Max	7/8	slug, rifled	slug	Rem.	1875
Max	1-1/8	low recoil	BB	Fed.	850
Max	1-1/8	steel	BB, 2, 3, 4	Fed., Win., Rem.	1550
Max	1-1/16	high density	2, 4	Win.	1400
Max	1	steel	4, 6	Fed.	1330
Max	1-3/8	buckhammer	slug	Rem.	1500
Max	1	TruBall slug	slug	Fed.	1700
Max	1	slug, rifled	slug, magnum	Win., Rem.	1760
Max	1	saboted	T, BBB, BB, 2, 4, 5, 6	Fed., Win.	1450
slug	slug	Rem., Win., Fed.	$10**	1550	1400
Max	385 grs.	partition	3, 4	Fed.	1600
gold	slug	Win.	NA	2000	1400
Max	1-1/8	Rackmaster	slug	Win.	1700
Max	300 grs.	XP3	slug	Win.	2100
3-5/8	1-3/8	steel	BBB, BB, 1, 2, 3, 4	Win., Fed., Rem.	1275
Max	1-1/8	snow goose FS	BB, 2, 3, 4	Fed.	1635
Max	1-1/8	steel	BB, 2, 4	Rem.	1500
Max	1-1/8	steel	T, BBB, BB, 2, 4, 5, 6	Fed., Win.	1450
Max	1-1/8	steel	BB, 2	Fed.	1400
Max	1-1/8	FS lead	3, 4	Fed.	1600
Max	1-3/8	Blind side	Hex, BB, 2	Win.	1400
4	1-1/4	steel	T, BBB, BB, 1, 2, 3, 4, 6	Win., Fed., Rem.	1400
Max	1-1/4	FS steel	BBB, BB, 2	Fed.	1450
12 Gauge 2-3/4"					
Max	1-5/8	magnum	4, 5, 6	Win., Fed.	1250
Max	1-3/8	lead	4, 5, 6	Fiocchi	1485
Max	1-3/8	turkey	4, 5, 6	Fio.	1250
Max	1-3/8	steel	4, 5, 6	Fed.	1400
Max	1-3/8	Bismuth	BB, 2, 4, 5, 6	Bis.	1300

Dram Equiv.	Shot Ozs.	Load Style	Shot Sizes	Brands	Velocity (fps)
12 Gauge 2-3/4" (cont.)					
3-3/4	1-1/2	magnum	BB, 2, 4, 5, 6	Win., Fed., Rem.	1260
Max	1-1/4	blind side	Hex, 2, 5	Win.	1400
Max	1-1/4	Supreme H-V	4, 5, 6, 7-1/2	Win. Rem.	1400
3-3/4	1-1/4	high velocity	BB, 2, 4, 5, 6, 7-1/2, 8, 9	Win., Fed., Rem., Fio.	1330
Max	1-1/4	high density	B, 2, 4	Win.	1450
Max	1-1/4	high density	4, 6	Rem.	1325
3-1/4	1-1/4	Standard velocity	6, 7-1/2, 8, 9	Win., Fed., Rem., Fio.	1220
Max	1-1/8	Hevi-shot	5	Hevi-shot	1350
3-1/4	1-1/8	Standard velocity	4, 6, 7-1/2, 8, 9	Win., Fed., Rem., Fio.	1255
Max	1-1/8	steel	2, 4	Rem.	1390
Max	1	steel	BB, 2	Fed.	1450
3-1/4	1	standard velocity	6, 7-1/2, 8	Rem., Fed., Fio., Win.	1290
3-1/4	1-1/4	target	7-1/2, 8, 9	Win., Fed., Rem.	1220
3	1-1/8	spreader	7-1/2, 8, 8-1/2, 9	Fio.	1200
3	1-1/8	target	7-1/2, 8, 9, 7-1/2x8	Win., Fed., Rem., Fio.	1200
2-3/4	1-1/8	target	7-1/2, 8, 8-1/2, 9, 7-1/2x8	Win., Fed., Rem., Fio.	1145
2-3/4	1-1/8	low recoil	7-1/2, 8	Rem.	1145
2-1/2	26 grams	low recoil	8	Win.	980
2-1/4	1-1/8	target	7-1/2, 8, 8-1/2, 9	Rem., Fed.	1080
Max	1	spreader	7-1/2, 8, 8-1/2, 9	Fio.	1300
3-1/4	28 grams (1 oz)	target	7-1/2, 8, 9	Win., Fed., Rem., Fio.	1290
3	1	target	7-1/2, 8, 8-1/2, 9	Win., Fio.	1235
2-3/4	1	target	7-1/2, 8, 8-1/2, 9	Fed., Rem., Fio.	1180
3-1/4	24 grams	target	7-1/2, 8, 9	Fed., Win., Fio.	1325
3	7/8	light	8	Fio.	1200
3-3/4	8 pellets	buffered	000 buck	Win., Fed., Rem.	1325
4	12 pellets	premium	00 buck	Win., Fed., Rem.	1290
3-3/4	9 pellets	buffered	00 buck	Win., Fed., Rem., Fio.	1325
3-3/4	12 pellets	buffered	0 buck	Win., Fed., Rem.	1275
4	20 pellets	buffered	1 buck	Win., Fed., Rem.	1075
3-3/4	16 pellets	buffered	1 buck	Win., Fed., Rem.	1250
4	34 pellets	premium	4 buck	Fed., Rem.	1250
3-3/4	27 pellets	buffered	4 buck	Win., Fed., Rem., Fio.	1325
		PDX1	1 oz. slug, 3-00 buck	Win.	1150
Max	1 oz	segmenting, slug	slug	Win.	1600

Dram Equiv.	Shot Ozs.	Load Style	Shot Sizes	Brands	Velocity (fps)
12 Gauge 2-3/4" (cont.)					
Max	1	Saboted slug	slug	Win., Fed., Rem.	1450
Max	1-1/4	slug, rifled	slug	Fed.	1520
Max	1-1/4	slug	slug	Lightfield	1440
Max	1-1/4	Saboted slug	attached sabot	Rem.	1550
Max	1	slug, rifled	slug, magnum	Rem., Fio.	1680
Max	1	slug, rifled	slug	Win., Fed., Rem.	1610
Max	1	Sabot slug	slug	Sauvestre	1640
Max	7/8	slug, rifled	slug	Rem.	1800
Max	400	plat. tip	sabot slug	Win.	1700
Max	385 grains	Partition Gold Slug	slug	Win.	1900
Max	385 grains	Core-Lokt bonded	sabot slug	Rem.	1900
Max	325 grains	Barnes Sabot	slug	Fed.	1900
Max	300 grains	SST Slug	sabot slug	Hornady	2050
Max	3/4	Tracer	#8 + tracer	Fio.	1150
Max	130 grains	Less Lethal	.73 rubber slug	Lightfield	600
Max	3/4	non-toxic	zinc slug	Win.	NA
3	1-1/8	steel target	6-1/2, 7	Rem.	1200
2-3/4	1-1/8	steel target	7	Rem.	1145
3	1#	steel	7	Win.	1235
3-1/2	1-1/4	steel	T, BBB, BB, 1, 2, 3, 4, 5, 6	Win., Fed., Rem.	1275
3-3/4	1-1/8	steel	BB, 1, 2, 3, 4, 5, 6	Win., Fed., Rem., Fio.	1365
3-3/4	1	steel	2, 3, 4, 5, 6, 7	Win., Fed., Rem., Fio.	1390
Max	7/8	steel	7	Fio.	1440
16 Gauge 2-3/4"					
3-1/4	1-1/4	magnum	2, 4, 6	Fed., Rem.	1260
3-1/4	1-1/8	High velocity	4, 6, 7-1/2	Win., Fed., Rem., Fio.	1295
Max	1-1/8	Bismuth	4, 5	Bis.	1200
2-3/4	1-1/8	Standard velocity	6, 7-1/2, 8	Fed., Rem., Fio.	1185
2-1/2	1	dove	6, 7-1/2, 8, 9	Fio., Win.	1165
2-3/4	1		6, 7-1/2, 8	Fio.	1200
Max	15/16	steel	2, 4	Fed., Rem.	1300
Max	7/8	steel	2, 4	Win.	1300
3	12 pellets	buffered	1 buck	Win., Fed., Rem.	1225
Max	4/5	slug, rifled	slug	Win., Fed., Rem.	1570
Max	.92	Sabot slug	slug	Sauvestre	1560

Dram Equiv.	Shot Ozs.	Load Style	Shot Sizes	Brands	Velocity (fps)
20 Gauge 3" Magnum					
	1 5/8	TSS	7 & 9	Fed	1000
	1 5/8	TSS	8 & 10	Fed	1000
	1 1/2	TSS	7	Fed	1100
	1 1/2	TSS	9	Fed	1100
3	1-1/4	premium	2, 4, 5, 6, 7-1/2	Win., Fed., Rem.	1185
Max	1-1/4	Wingmaster HD	4, 6	Rem.	1185
3	1-1/4	turkey	4, 6	Fio.	1200
Max	1-1/4	Hevi-shot	2, 4, 6	Hevi-shot	1250
Max	1-1/8	high density	4, 6	Rem.	1300
Max	18 pellets	buck shot	2 buck	Fed.	1200
Max	24 pellets	buffered	3 buck	Win.	1150
2-3/4	20 pellets	buck	3 buck	Rem.	1200
Max	1	hypersonic	2, 3, 4	Rem.	Rem.
3-1/4	1	steel	1, 2, 3, 4, 5, 6	Win., Fed., Rem.	1330
Max	1	blind side	Hex, 2, 5	Win.	1300
Max	7/8	steel	2, 4	Win.	1300
Max	7/8	FS lead	3, 4	Fed.	1500
Max	1-1/16	high density	2, 4	Win.	1400
Max	1-1/16	Bismuth	2, 4, 5, 6	Bismuth	1250
Mag	5/8	saboted slug	275 gr.	Fed.	1900
Max	3/4	TruBall slug	slug	Fed.	1700
20 Gauge 2-3/4"					
2-3/4	1-1/8	magnum	4, 6, 7-1/2	Win., Fed., Rem.	1175
2-3/4	1	high velocity	4, 5, 6, 7-1/2, 8, 9	Win., Fed., Rem., Fio.	1220
Max	1	Bismuth	4, 6	Bis.	1200
Max	1	Hevi-shot	5	Hevi-shot	1250
Max	1	Supreme H-V	4, 6, 7-1/2	Win. Rem.	1300
Max	1	FS lead	4, 5, 6	Fed.	1350
Max	7/8	Steel	2, 3, 4	Fio.	1500
2-1/2	1	standard velocity	6, 7-1/2, 8	Win., Rem., Fed., Fio.	1165
2-1/2	7/8	clays	8	Rem.	1200
2-1/2	7/8	promotional	6, 7-1/2, 8	Win., Rem., Fio.	1210
2-1/2	1	target	8, 9	Win., Rem.	1165
Max	7/8	clays	7-1/2, 8	Win.	1275
2-1/2	7/8	target	8, 9	Win., Fed., Rem.	1200

Dram Equiv.	Shot Ozs.	Load Style	Shot Sizes	Brands	Velocity (fps)
20 Gauge 2-3/4" (cont.)					
Max	3/4	steel	2, 4	Rem.	1425
2-1/2	7/8	steel - target	7	Rem.	1200
1-1/2	7/8	low recoil	8	Win.	980
Max	1	buckhammer	slug	Rem.	1500
Max	5/8	Saboted Slug	Copper Slug	Rem.	1500
Max	20 pellets	buffered	3 buck	Win., Fed.	1200
Max	5/8	slug, saboted	slug	Win.,	1400
2-3/4	5/8	slug, rifled	slug	Rem.	1580
Max	3/4	saboted slug	copper slug	Fed., Rem.	1450
Max	3/4	slug, rifled	slug	Win., Fed., Rem., Fio.	1570
Max	.9	sabot slug	slug	Sauvestre	1480
Max	260 grains	Partition Gold Slug	slug	Win.	1900
Max	260 grains	Core-Lokt Ultra	slug	Rem.	1900
Max	260 grains	saboted slug	platinum tip	Win.	1700
Max	3/4	steel	2, 3, 4, 6	Win., Fed., Rem.	1425
Max	250 grains	SST slug	slug	Hornady	1800
Max	1/2	rifled, slug	slug	Rem.	1800
Max	67 grains	Less lethal	2/.60 rubber balls	Lightfield	900
28 Gauge 3"					
Max	7/8	tundra tungsten	4, 5, 6	Flocchi	TBD

Dram Equiv.	Shot Ozs.	Load Style	Shot Sizes	Brands	Velocity (fps)
28 Gauge 2-3/4"					
2	1	high velocity	6, 7-1/2, 8	Win.	1125
2-1/4	3/4	high velocity	6, 7-1/2, 8, 9	Win., Fed., Rem., Fio.	1295
2	3/4	target	8, 9	Win., Fed., Rem.	1200
Max	3/4	sporting clays	7-1/2, 8-1/2	Win.	1300
Max	5/8	Bismuth	4, 6	Bis.	1250
Max	5/8	steel	6, 7	NA	1300
Max	5/8	slug		Bren.	1450
410 Bore 3"					
	13/16	TSS	9	Fed	1100
Max	11/16	high velocity	4, 5, 6, 7-1/2, 8, 9	Win., Fed.,	1175
Rem., Fio.	$10	1135	6	NA	1400
Max	9/16	Bismuth	4	Bis.	1175
Max	3/8	steel	6	NA	1400
2410 Bore 3" (cont.)					
		judge	9 pellets #4 Buck	Fed.	1100
Max	Mixed	Per. Defense	3DD/12BB	Win.	750
410 Bore 2-1/2"					
Max	1/2	high velocity	4, 6, 7-1/2	Win., Fed., Rem.	1245
Max	1/5	slug, rifled	slug	Win., Fed., Rem.	1815
1-1/2	1/2	target	8, 8-1/2, 9	Win., Fed., Rem., Fio.	1200
Max	1/2	sporting clays	7-1/2, 8, 8-1/2	Win.	1300
Max		Buckshot	5-000 Buck	Win.	1135
		judge	12-bb's, 3 disks	Win.	TBD
Max	Mixed	Per. Defense	4DD/16BB	Win.	750
Max	42 grains	Less lethal	4/.41 rubber balls	Lightfield	1150

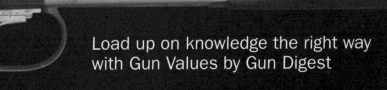

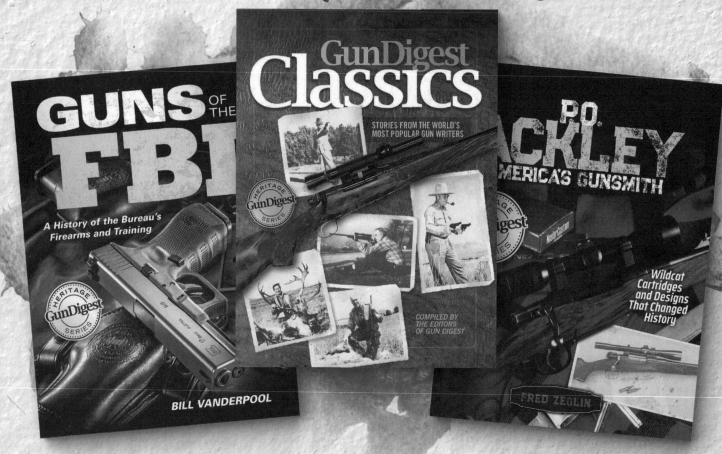